The Handbook of Global Shadow Banking, Volume I

Luc Nijs

The Handbook of Global Shadow Banking, Volume I

From Policy to Regulation

palgrave
macmillan

Luc Nijs

ISBN 978-3-030-34742-0 ISBN 978-3-030-34743-7 (eBook)
https://doi.org/10.1007/978-3-030-34743-7

This Palgrave Macmillan imprint is published by the registered company Springer Nature Switzerland AG.
The registered company address is: Gewerbestrasse 11, 6330 Cham, Switzerland

Preface

Writing a book is often a challenge, yes even a struggle from time to time. Writing a book on shadow banking goes quite a bit beyond that struggle. It's like shooting a moving target. Worse, it's like a Tour de France but then only with climbs 'hors catégorie'. But when persisting, it yields its benefits. If you can navigate, possibly over time, beyond the window dressing language of regulators, supervisors, lobbyists and the likes and can lift the fog on the paradigm and the schism that financial regulation has created between the regulated and less or otherwise regulated part of the financial industry, you're ultimately in a much better position to focus on what really matters. It also allows you to see much clearly the relative safety that was created in recent years through all the different layers of incoming regulation which was built on the existing and largely outdated regulatory infrastructure.

For those reasons only, I considered that I didn't want to write a book that had the 'look and feel' of an ordinary textbook. Not that there is something wrong with that but I felt that incremental value over and beyond existing literature could only come from a book that would allow to move across the different components of the shadow banking segment and allow for a deeper understanding of the different shadow banking facilities and their functionalities in the different countries and regions of the world. It would further cater to the interactions and cross-dynamics between regulation, macroeconomics, risk management, supervision, macroprudential oversight and aligned domains as monetary and fiscal policies.[1] I realized quickly in the process that meeting that objective wasn't possible if I would stick to a traditional textbook setting where individual topics would be digested separately and isolated from the other topics at hand.

[1] In particular fiscal policies are extremely relevant as they are directly linked, instrumental and very effective in triggering and fostering economic growth; see e.g., IMF, (2015), Fiscal Policy and Long-Term Growth, IMF Policy Paper, Washington DC, June. Much more than, for example, public investments, see: A. Berg et al., (2015), Some Misconceptions about Public Investment Efficiency and Growth, IMF Working Paper, WP/15/272, December 23.

So I had to come up with a different strategy, one that would cater to the objectives of a book that is called 'the global handbook on shadow banking' and therefore needs to aim for a certain level of completeness, realizing that a 100% completeness is a theoretical and unachievable goal within the context of one book and a broad topic like 'shadow banking'. But I thought I needed to give it a try. It would also need to demonstrate the complexity and the interwoven dimensions of the different shadow banking segments.[2] And I would have to do that by respecting and honoring the different aspects indicated in the previous paragraph. A normal textbook setting would have not been able to cater properly to that objective. I therefore decided that creating a book that would live up to all of this would look quite different and would have a structure that would foremost facilitate the above-mentioned objectives.

In this first volume, the shadow banking sector will be explored, segment by segment: from their historical emergence all the way through to how they have been regulated in recent years. The survey isn't limited to the regulatory and oversight choices effectively made, but also other options that (could) have been on the table, but were denied or neglected. Did all those incoming regulations and policies have made the sector safer?

The first six chapters of the book (Chaps. 2, 3, 4, 5, 6 and 7), after the initial introduction, are spent on an analysis of why there is a shadow banking market, and why we are so concerned about financial intermediation outside the regulated banking sector. I therefore don't shy away from 'old' and 'new' topics and those topics that will stick with us for years to come. I gently touch upon policy responses around the world, and the impact they had or are expected to have. I could have limited myself to an analysis of the nature of credit, maturity and liquidity transformation. But that would have yielded an informative brochure at best, but not the type of cross-dimensional analysis I was looking for.

So starting in Chap. 8, I wonder at length about the relationship between policy dimensions and regulation, regulation that was built above and beyond existing financial regulation. It will be demonstrated that building and executing proper financial regulation is a lot harder when built on the ruins of a system that just failed than if you have to build it from scratch. The overall conclusion is that regulation creates 'marginal improvements' at best, but that it has stayed too much within the traditional paradigm to make a real difference. To what degree that is due to enhanced lobbying efforts I leave up to you to decide. The sheer complexity of the regulation in place feels a lot like a 'negotiated solution' rather than one with tight objectives that were pre-defined. I also take the opportunity in that part of the book to start bringing in macroeconomics, macro/micro-prudential dimensions[3] as well as their direct and adjacent domains as monetary and fiscal policy, without losing track of an ongoing analysis of incoming regulation and policy

---

[2] And the fact that they are embedded in large global, multijurisdictional conglomerates whereby credit chains have become long-winded and spanning multiple jurisdictions. See for a review of the supervisory challenges in such an environment: T. Eisenbach et al., (2017), Supervising Large, Complex Financial Institutions: What Do Supervisors Do?, FRBNY Economic Policy Review, February, pp. 57–77.

[3] See for an overview: S. Claessens, (2015), An Overview of Macroprudential Policy Tools, Annual Review of Financial Economics, Vol. 7, pp. 397–422; L. D. Wall, (2015), Stricter Microprudential Supervision Versus Macroprudential Supervision, Journal of Financial Regulation and Compliance, Vol. 23, Issue 4, pp. 354–368.

responses.[4] Doing that forced me to retake some earlier, already discussed topics. But I realized as well that the time that people read books, with titles like these, from cover to cover is long behind us, and so rebuilding part of the topics in a different context was an honorable and justified objective, or at least I thought and think it is. Some that feel differently will potentially experience the setup and structure of the text as somewhat confusing or maybe even wildly chaotic. That was a risk I was willing to take. But to compensate for that, I ensured an extensive and well-documented index where the focused or specialist reader can quickly identify the areas in the book that cater to his or her needs so that they can avoid having to work through topics and thoughts that are of lesser interest.

The last chapter is somewhat different and more philosophical in nature. Chapter 11 asks the question to what degree the tax system is embedded and instrumental to creating the shadow banking market and the externalities it has and will cause. In particular given their inexplicable willingness to favor debt over equity (debt bias). We will review the status quo and I will suggest a Pigovian tax model that would, as by the nature of a Pigovian levy, focus on reducing or neutralizing the externalities caused by the (shadow) banking system, a model I first suggested in 2015. We have seen, only recently, the Pigovian instrument occur in the financial sector despite the fact that Pigovian instruments belong in the wisdom toolbox of every regulators.[5]

A root-cause analysis of complex problems takes time. However, it is more the first-line nature of the regulator to regulate in white heat the symptoms of the previous crisis than to create a well-balanced framework (possible on a regional or global level although all that seems very difficult if not impossible) that can resist time. It (such a root-cause analysis) will undeniably force the parties involved to rethink the economy[6] and its process which the (shadow) banking market ultimately feeds into or drops its Cuckoo's eggs. Besides the fact that a lot of regulatory context is still designed on expert fora which traditionally have been very influenced by the players of the financial industry, the one thing that is still lacking most is a clear vision how the (shadow) banking sector can contribute to the real economy, productivity and growth.[7] Without such a clear vision, everything else doesn't really matter, because if you don't know where you're going it doesn't really matter how you get there.

Whether you call it 'shadow banking', 'market-based finance' or 'parallel banking' matters less. The Financial Stability Board, the supervisory guardian of shadow banking around the world, has made a significant U-turn in this respect in recent years regarding a segment that requires meaningful regulation and oversight. In all honesty, I have to admit that one gets intellectually bruised pretty badly if one listens and accepts the

[4] See C. Lopez et al., (2015), Macroprudential Policy: What Does it Really Mean, Working Paper, mimeo.

[5] T. Hartford, (2015), The Pillars of Tax Wisdom, Financial Times, November 20.

[6] T. Mitchell, (2008), Rethinking Economy, Geoforum, Vol. 39, pp. 1116–1121.

[7] B. Stellinga, (2015), Europese Financiële Regulering Voor en Na De Crisis, WRR Working Paper Nr. 15, p. 83. There is loosely a limited to modest positive relationship between credit supply and productivity growth, but a material negative impact on productivity of credit supply contractions. See F. Manaresi and N. Pierri, (2019), Credit Supply and Productivity Growth, IMF Working Paper Nr. WP/19/107, May.

arguments given at face value. I'm surprised to see and hear the constant rehashing of invalid arguments favoring, for instance, market-based finance as an attractive channel to promote SME funding.

The regulatory channels seem somewhat in lockdown not to say outright ignorance, and questions are being asked about the need for (a better balance between) ex ante versus ex post regulation,[8] realizing that the natural instability of a free market mechanism cannot be avoided at any time, whatever the legislation one puts in place. A holistic and systematic design of regulation is needed rather than the transaction-based one.[9] And so (complementary) suggestions were made to, for instance, limit the limited liability concept of legal entities, something our current business environment is built on but which has not been with us all that long.[10] 'Piercing the corporate veil' could put a halt to the eternality producing dynamics of the (shadow) banking sphere as it even under current regulatory dynamics can be used 'in order to bring corporate actors' behavior into conformity with a particular statutory scheme',[11] prioritizing shareholder welfare, or better stakeholder value, not shareholder value.[12] A more principle-based regulatory model rather than an endless codex might do the trick. Often it is anyway forgotten that regulation comes at a cost, a significant cost, so significant that it does not only warrant better and more focused attention but also that the legal principle of 'proportionality' might be at risk here.[13] The cost of financial regulation, in contrast to other laws, focuses on the behavioral, market, general equilibrium and political reactions.[14] A better and more trans-

---

[8] Ex ante is necessary but inherently insufficient; ex post deals with the aftermath, the clean-up and who picks up what part of the damage. The mechanical relation between those two segments prevents the creation of a true holistic regulatory model and avoids painful discussion about hidden topics like regulatory arbitrage and corporate governance, and abuse of corporate structures and corporate law at large. See regarding the emergence of the corporate form as we know it, for instance, G. Dari-Mattiacci et al., (2017), The Emergence of the Corporate Form, The Journal of law, Economic and Organization, Vol. 33., Nr. 2, pp. 193–236.

[9] If you do this, then… 'or' to counter this, 'the regulation responds with'. The regulator, policy design segment and the law profession are still pondering about how such regulation should be designed. Holistic and systematic regulation that deals with the unexpected, the unknown unknows, is regulation that meets qualities and properties our current legislative infrastructure cannot cater to. It's like building a Spanish hacienda on top of a drained swamp. It only works for a little while.

[10] A.G. Haldane, (2015), Who Owns a Company, Speech given by Andrew G Haldane, Chief Economist, Bank of England, University of Edinburgh Corporate Finance Conference, May 22.

[11] J. R. Macey, (2014), The Three Justifications for Piercing the Corporate Veil, Harvard Law School Forum on Corporate Governance and Financial Regulation, March 27.

[12] Based on the idea that everybody is willing to sacrifice some money for our beliefs. Why not the companies we own? See: L. Zingales, (2018), Public Companies Should Prioritise Shareholder Welfare, Not Value, FT, December 11. Decent governance also reduces financial intermediation costs for banks, sovereign and non-bank corporations, see: M. Jarmuzek and T. Lybek, (2018), Can Good Governance Lower Financial Intermediation Costs?, IMF Working Paper Nr. WP/18/279, December.

[13] Also recently: F. Restoy, (2019), Proportionality in Financial Regulation: Where Do we go from Here?, Speech by Mr Fernando Restoy, Chairman, Financial Stability Institute, Bank for International Settlements, at the BIS/IMF policy implementation meeting on proportionality in financial regulation and supervision, Basel, Switzerland, 8 May, via bis.org

[14] J.H. Cochrane, (2014), Challenges for Cost-Benefit Analysis of Financial Regulation, The Journal of Legal Studies, Vol. 43, Issue S2, pp. S63–S105.

parent process is an often cited objective. That is because currently the previous crisis drives the response, not the objective and the way it is translated in the process followed by the regulator. There is also no real tradition of monitoring or communicating the cost and benefits of regulation in a quantitative way. That is because the regulators understand very little about the causality between benefits and incurred costs in (financial) regulation. Or worse, they think they do without proper justification. And so, ineffective regulation stays in place long after its ineffectiveness has become clear and more new regulation is built on the carcass of old, ineffective regulation impacted optimal functioning of markets, competition and the relation with adjacent policy spheres such as monetary and fiscal policy. The solution comes from within the regulators' process and is not endogenous as some claim,[15] but is immanent to the process. Financial regulation should be welfare optimizing and welfare inducing and that can only happen when the process takes into account how all parties involved represent their interest and weigh in on the writing process, impact assessment and so on and ultimately co-determine the shaping of the final texts. Because make no mistake, vulnerabilities are still in the market and in fact they are bigger and brighter than at the time of the 2008 crisis,[16] and many of the umbrella objectives like growth, price and financial stability and so on are often intrinsically conflicting in nature.[17]

Both financial regulation and vulnerabilities stifle productivity, and productivity expansion is needed for economic growth.[18] But there is no silver bullet or well-defined list of factors that lead to productivity growth. We know however that reliable institutions, fully operating markets and competition may provide incentives for investment, human capital accumulation and productivity growth, but other factors do too. But even if we could agree on their absolute performance, we would fall over each other debating the relative importance or ranking of these elements in the mix.[19]

---

[15] J.C. Coates IV, (2014), Cost-Benefit Analysis of Financial Regulation: Case Studies and Implications, Harvard John. M. Olin Center for Law, Economics and Business, Discussion Paper Nr. 757.

[16] See the annual BIS reporting on the matter; see for the recent report: BIS, (2015), 85th Annual Report, Basel June 28.

[17] See e.g. S. Kim and A. Mehrotra, (2015), Managing Price and Financial Stability Objectives-What Can We Learn From The Asia-Pacific Region?, BIS Working Paper Nr. 533, Basel, December.

[18] Which determinants are constitutive for growth is still largely up for discussion and matrixes and tools are designed and (re)shaped. One of the factors that are always tabled is 'financial development and institutional robustness'. See e.g. R. Cherif et al., (2018), Sharp Instrument: A Stab at Identifying the Causes of Economic Growth, IMF Working Paper Nr. WP/18/117, May. Financial development is mostly beneficial for emerging economies, but largely detrimental for advanced economies. Financial innovations trigger financial instability with a 1- to 2-year delay. See in detail: S.B. Naceur et al., (2019), Taming Financial Development to Reduce Crises, IMF Working Paper Nr. WP/19/94, April.

[19] M. Sánchez, (2015), Productivity, Growth, and the Law, Remarks by Mr Manuel Sánchez, Deputy Governor of the Bank of Mexico, at the Annual Bank Conference on Development Economics, organized jointly by the World Bank and the Bank of Mexico, Mexico City, June 16, p. 3.

Toward the end, I have argued that the factor that is most missing is capital or equity if you want, in contrast to debt. Both are needed to create a resilient and robust financial infrastructure.[20] Thinking there is as such competition or a stifling effect between bank-based and market-based financial models is essentially a misnomer.[21] They can perfectly live together and each in their own way contribute to economic growth. Bank-based models have, for example, a pedigree of being better equipped to deal with the asymmetry in the SME sector than a market-based model.[22] Market-based models tend to facilitate better larger deals and are better at bringing down the cost of funding under constant risk terms. But they are more procyclical and recover better after recessions. Ying and Yang and all is just fine. But not when we treat them like they are identical. Being equal doesn't mean being identical and so they shouldn't be treated that way. A market-based system is inherently unstable and requires an exogenous backstop in order to rebalance. The question that we can ask is whether the Treasury Department should function as a final backstop to make this happen over and over again, realizing the private money creating features of the shadow banking segment, or whether only equity should make that happen. Underwriting unlimited private money creation is like underwriting a house that is already on fire: you can only lose and will have to fight moral hazard[23] left, right and center. Just like piercing the corporate veil will equity bring responsibility and accountability back to the center of the business models in the financial sector. So equity might be a better disinfectant for many of the problems experienced in the 2008 crisis. However, more equity will create some sort of ex ante identical position for (shadow) banks, but the development and end position will be different and raising equity post-crash delivers crowded trades and misallocations.[24]

It therefore would have been way too easy to limit a shadow banking analysis to the analysis of leverage, maturity and liquidity transformation and regulatory arbitrage. Of course, these are key ingredients and have shaped the dynamics largely so far. But also data availability and how the supervisory model has been developed are essential too. Supervision is never a pure objective and biases are undeniable.[25] That counts if your object of 'affection' is a shadow banking market that is agile, driven by financial innovation[26] and co-shaped by

[20] An infrastructure that is characterized by rising levels of market concentration and consequently market power. In its most recent World Economic Outlook the IMF indicates that, besides a number of other conclusions, further market concentration and corporate market power will make it for difficult for monetary policy to stabilize output. See in detail: IMF, (2019), The Rise of Corporate Market Power and its Macro-Economic Effects, April, Chapter 2, pp. 55–76.

[21] J. Weidmann, (2015), Of Credit and Capital – What is needed for an Efficient and Resilient Financial System? Speech by Dr Jens Weidmann, President of the Deutsche Bundesbank, at the IIF (Institute of International Finance) Europe Summit, Frankfurt am Main, June 25, pp. 2–3.

[22] See extensively: S. Aiyar et al., (2015), Revitalizing Securitization for Small and Medium-Sized Enterprises in Europe, IMF Staff Discussion Note Nr. SDN/15/07, May.

[23] S. L. Schwarcz, (2016), Misalignment: Corporate Risk-Taking and Public Duty, Notre Dame Law Review Vol. 92, pp. 1–50.

[24] C. Bertsch and M. Mariathasan, (2015), Fire Sale Bank Recapitalizations, Sveriges Riksbank Working Paper Series Nr. 312, September, Stockholm.

[25] R. Jansen and M. Aelen, (2015), Biases in Supervision: What Are They and How Can We Deal With Them?, DNB Occasional Studies Nr. 13-6.

[26] S. Rossi, (2018), Which New Frontiers in Banking? Speaking Notes by Salvatore Rossi, Senior Deputy Governor of the Bank of Italy and President of IVASS, 2018 Conference on "New Frontiers

regulatory interventions. And those datasets are used for regulatory design as well. Admati has already indicated a while ago that 'flawed and ineffective financial regulation fails to counter, and may exacerbate, distorted incentives within the financial system. The forces that lead to excessive fragility through unnecessary and dangerous levels of leverage, opacity, complexity and interconnectedness also distort credit markets and create other inefficiencies'...'confusions about the sources of the problems and about the tradeoffs associated with specific tools have muddled the policy debate and have allowed narrow interests and political forces to derail progress towards a safer and healthier financial system.'[27] In fact, the regulator has often been an initiator of regulatory arbitrage, the contributor to systemic risk and used econometric model-based regulation to solve issues.[28] Even more regulation has become tainted as it has been blamed for 'coding' selectively 'certain assets, endowing them with the capacity to protect and produce private wealth. With the right legal coding, any object, claim, or idea can be turned into capital'.[29]

And then there is the demand side of the shadow banking market. The demand for safe assets has been outstripping the supply in recent years and for almost two decades. The welfare economics we created triggers a demand that couldn't be met in the Treasuries market only, and so artificial solutions were created that over-lubricated the economic machine and ultimately derailed it. If market-based finance cannot live without an external backstop,[30] it will never have the feature of 'stability' the way we want it to see. In fact, asking implicitly for the sovereign to underwrite the 'free' markets sounds like a horrible and equally unrealistic idea. Shadow banking or market-based finance implies that a lot of it is conducted not in a firm but facilitated by markets. A sovereign that is not involved in the money creation process is in no position to facilitate a backstop. That would be like underwriting insurance that provides coverage under all conditions and situations imaginable and unimaginable.

If that is near impossible under normal circumstances it is totally impossible under the constrained condition the supervisors and regulators are operating at present. Many critical concepts are still under development and embryonically understood (vulnerability, contagion, interconnectedness etc.), and although I'm not prepared to go as far as saying that 'we don't know anything' about the intrinsic and hidden risks in shadow banking,[31] I'm prepared to proclaim that knowledge and granularity of data is indeed thin, very thin about what constitutes often large parts of shadow banking segments in some countries.

---

in Banking: from Corporate Governance to Risk Management", Rome, Faculty of Economics, Sapienza University 16 March.

[27] A.R. Admati, (2015), Rethinking Financial Regulation: How Confusions Have Prevented Progress, Stanford University, Rock Center for Corporate Governance, Working Paper Series Nr. 207, June 25, p. 1.

[28] S. Kleimeier, et al., (2015), Deposit Insurance in Times of Crises: Safe Haven or Regulatory Arbitrage?, University of Maastricht Working Paper Nr. RM/15/026.

[29] Stocks, bonds, ideas and even expectations – assets that exist only in law – are coded to give financial advantage to their holders, thereby allowing wealth creation and production of inequality. Regulation is tainted as 'pervasive', including the people who shape it, and the governments that enforce it, documents Pistor. See in detail: K. Pistor, (2019), The Code of Capital: How the Law Creates Wealth and Inequality, Princeton University Press, May 28, Princeton, New Jersey.

[30] See for an extensive overview: I. Hardie and D. Howarth (eds.), (2013), Market-Based Banking and the International Financial Crisis, Oxford University Press, Oxford.

[31] R. Lenser, (2015), Hidden Dangers that Banking Regulators Fail to Chart, Financial Times, April 20.

And then we're not even talking about the interconnectedness, contagion effects and so on . Mapping it doesn't equal understanding it, regulating it, sustaining it or stabilizing it after it has destabilized. Some aspects can't even be regulated (e.g. moral hazard) might be the conclusion, and peer disciplining through market-based forces and mutualization post-crisis might not function effectively or not at all.[32] In other cases, we might not be willing to live with the consequences of such interventions[33] or need to realize that the use of market-based probabilities in policy and regulatory decision making has severe limits.[34]

Just like the regulator co-shaped the shadow banking market through its incoming regulation, so do monetary policies. It creates inefficient allocations and might trigger or at least enhance the probability of a financial crisis.[35] In such an environment a new reassessment of the economic role of the state might be warranted.[36] Mandating private rent-seeking economic agents to guard a public interest of this size might not be such a great idea to begin with as profit-seeking and risk-taking go hand in hand (and reinforce each other), even for the best and brightest financial institutions out there: '[a] more profitable core business allows a bank to borrow more and take side risks on a larger scale, offsetting lower incentives to take risk of given size. Consequently, more profitable banks may have higher risk-taking incentives.'[37] And that poses 'a direct risk for real assets and the real economy overall.'[38] Having these financial institutions listed makes them prone to 'short-termism' mainstream in public markets. Also that is a characteristic of market-based finance and which doesn't bode well with the real economy whose objectives tend to be, in general, of a longer duration.[39] A full re-engineering of our financial and capitalist system might well be a necessity in this context.[40] Financial stability monitoring,[41] even

[32] F. Palazzo, (2015), Peer Discipline via Loss Mutualization, Working Paper, November 2, mimeo.

[33] A. Uluc and T. Wieladek, (2015), Capital Requirements, Risk Shifting and the Mortgage Market, Bank of England Working paper Nr. 572, December, London and M. Croisignani, (2015), Why Are Banks Not Recapitalized During Crises, Oesterreichische Nationalbank Working Paper Nr. 203, June, Vienna.

[34] R. Armenter, (2015), On the Use of Market-Based Probabilities for Policy Decisions, Federal Reserve Bank of Philadelphia Working Paper Nr. 15-44, December.

[35] A. Cesa-Bianchi and A. Rebucci, (2015), Does Easing Monetary Policy Increase Financial Instability?, Bank of England Staff Working Paper Nr. 570, December, London also published in Journal of Financial Stability Vol. 30, June, pp. 111–125.

[36] G. Mastromatteo and L. Esposito, (2015), The Two Approaches to Money: Debt, Central banks and Functional Finance, Levy Economics Institute, Working Paper Nr. 855, November.

[37] N. Martynova et al., (2015), Bank Profitability and Risk-Taking, IMF Working Paper Nr. WP/15/249, November.

[38] L. Mutkin, (2015), Mispricing Derivatives a Danger for Real Assets, Financial Times, December 16.

[39] J. Plender, (2015), Shareholder Short-Termism is Damaging the Economy, Financial Times, November 8.

[40] A. Nesvetailova, (2015), A Crisis of the Overcrowded Future: Shadow Banking and the Political Economy of Financial Innovation, New Political Economy, Vol. 20, Issue 3, pp. 431–453; M. Wolf, (2014), The Shifts and the Shocks. What we've Learned- and Have Still to Learn From the Financial Crisis, Penguin Press, New York.

[41] Rather than monitor we should rethink financial stability at its core. Haldane provides some reflections given the experiences in previous years and points some areas of contention, and thus

when it is forward looking, needs to be met with a healthy dose of skepticism.[42] I therefore can only disagree with Jeffrey M. Lancker, the president of the Federal Reserve Bank of Richmond, when he states that 'the intent is not for regulators to decide how much maturity transformation is too much – that is ultimately a question for markets to decide. Instead, our goal should be to make credible changes in policy that properly align the incentives of financial market participants to monitor and control risk.'[43] It ignores the fact that direct interventions are a real and effective policy option, even when carefully observing the proportionality of any given intervention. If society doesn't want to pick up the pieces and act as a lender of last resort after the next wave of financial innovation and creative destruction it often goes hand in hand with, the regulator will have to step in and rewrite the rules of the game. That is unlikely to happen as long as they are very dependent on the banking system to hold their paper and facilitate fund raising at very, very mild conditions in recent years.

Regardless of how you feel about any of these matters, I have tried to allow for as many viewpoints to be represented (even when they contradict and trust me they do), without shying away from giving mine from time to time and as always accompanied by extensive research, analysis and context from various parts of the world. The book therefore has stayed adequate and attractive for both industry professionals and academics and their students who are eager to delve a little deeper. It will also prove to be instrumental for policy makers, serious enthusiasts and everybody who is interested in issues that are centered on a multidisciplinary paradigm. The extensive footnote apparatus will help the focused and analytical research-driven reader. For the industry professional and those that scan the text in search for answers, the index will facilitate locating the part and areas in the book that are most of interest to them and will cover the different functional domains already indicated. I have tried to make the content of the book as time resistant as possible and therefore only as little as possible and 'as actual as possible' datasets have been used as

---

some room for academic improvement of our understanding. On that list are some usual suspects such as optimal capital levels, multi-polar regulation, stress-testing and financial stability model improvements and so on but also issues such as the political economy of financial regulation, and an assessment of the contribution of the financial system to the economy and society at large. See in detail: A.G. Haldane, (2017), Rethinking Financial Stability, Speech given by Andrew G Haldane, Chief Economist, Bank of England, at the 'Rethinking Macroeconomic Policy IV' Conference, Washington, DC, Peterson Institute for International Economics 12 October. Also as an extensive working paper: D. Aikman et al., (2018), Rethinking Financial Stability, Bank of England Working Paper Nr. 712, February 23. Regarding the contribution of financial development see, for example, the positive relation between credit and industrial pollution (negative indirect externality): R. de Haas and A. Popov, (2018), Financial Development and Industrial Pollution, ECB Discussion Paper Nr. Nr. 1, July 16.

[42] T. Adrian et al., (2015), Financial Stability Monitoring, Annual Review of Financial Economics, Vol. 7, pp. 357–395.

[43] J.M. Lancker, (2014), Maturity Mismatch and Financial Stability, President's Message. Nobody can disagree with the latter aspect but the former triggers some serious questions as to whether the regulators should not directly intervene in what is considered a serious source of externalities. Also in environmental aspects has the regulator used both instruments: (1) discourage such externality-inducing behavior, mainly (indirectly) through taxes and (2) effectively reduce the amount of externality-inducing output (e.g. direct reduction of CO_2 emissions), Econ Focus, 2014 Q1, p. 1.

they will most likely be outdated by the time the book hits the (electronic) shelves. But they are part of the context and deserve some space in a book that carries 'global handbook' in its title. When I started writing the volumes in early 2013, I was under the impression that the pace and magnitude of attention for shadow banking were waning; now being halfway through 2019, I can say out loud that that was a major misperception back then. Recent years brought many new evolutions and dynamics in many spheres, often more in niche areas and refinements across the board, but nevertheless very relevant for the financial industry and the shadow banking market as such. It has set a tone that will continue in the years to come. A consolidating work that tries to bring together what has been done (thereby drawing extensively on existing research, and without which the writing of these handbooks clearly would not have been possible), what has been learned and what already has been forgotten, as well as those things that we anticipate will happen in this 52+ trillion USD market,[44] and also zooms in on all those things that are left open or have been dealt with in an unsatisfying way deserve equal attention and the book in front of you does exactly that. Happy reading!

P.S. The content of both volumes is updated up till and including June 30, 2019. I produced an extensive non-layered, non-staggered index to facilitate easy identification of possible areas of interest. Non-published articles or papers can be accessed through srn.com and/or the relevant webpage of the university or institution. Updates, most likely in e-format, will be made available between editions of the book. Please visit the book website for further information.

June 2019 Luc Nijs

[44] Reports Monitor, (2019), Global Shadow Banking Market Size, Status and Forecast 2019-2025, January 16, via reportsmonitor.com

Contents

List of Tables

List of Boxes

1

Introduction

1.1 Introduction: The Concept of Shadow Banking

If we want to be successful in analyzing what has become a global phenomenon, we need to jump through the complex and difficult hoop(s) of trying to define the concept of shadow banking (SB). That is likely to pose significant problems, at least if we try to be fully comprehensive and as accurate as we possibly can be. We will most likely end up with a cascade of different components of different (existing) definitions and partial descriptions of what altogether might turn out to be a reflection of the shadow banking world. In that sense, shadow banking is effectively somewhat of a parallel universe.

1.2 An Industry with Many Faces

We are therefore at risk of defining 'shadow banking' as everything that happens behind the curtain, while everything that happens on the podium, in the limelight and therefore subject to regulation, would then become the officially regulated (and therefore licensed) banking sector. The tone is set: we're on a mission but unsure yet where we want to end. If we can agree on the fact that the shadow banking industry historically has grown driven by innovation, it will be no surprise to experience that the shadow banking industry is not an accurately defined industry where regulation built a nice framework around and which is now for everybody consistently observable. It has multiple layers, looks and feels different in different parts of the world as it is continuously co-shaped by (different) regulation trying to work its way into the caves and dens of that part of the financial industry happening behind the curtain. Just like water flows to its lowest point regardless of the many hurdles it may face, capital will always flow to that part of the spectrum where it can operate freely (i.e. as unregulated as possible) and generate the returns it is looking for undone of restrictions

L. Nijs, *The Handbook of Global Shadow Banking, Volume I*,
https://doi.org/10.1007/978-3-030-34743-7_1

that the formal banking sector imposes. Not surprisingly that shadow banking therefore is characterized by moving paradigms (or is 'one' moving paradigm) with many different layers that requires puzzling together. That way it has become a house with many rooms, each with its own particularities, shenanigans and intricacies.

But let's not be mistaken: the shadow banking industry is considered a USD 60–75 trillion + industry (depending on how you measure it; on more of that later). To compare: the global economy is valued at around USD 100 trillion. It is therefore not something we can sweep under the carpet, in particular because it is linked to 'Main Street' and the 'regulated part of the global financial infrastructure'. It has generated the attention of policy makers and regulators globally. They are trying each from their perspective, to channel the operations and intrinsic risks of the system via regulation, with a minimum objective of sheltering the official part of the industry and protect the real economy from a potential fallout.

That makes sense as long as we could possibly stick to a reasonable way of regulating industries. For over 100 years now, regulators try to find that equilibrium where regulation can play its role without disproportionately hampering economic activity. We have, during that period, explored every corner of that equation: from communism to socialism to the other extreme opposite which society has come to qualify as neoliberalism. We learned that centralizing policy leads to an implosion of the system and it literally faints under its own weight, caused by the fact that the market dynamics couldn't play properly and therefore resources were not optimally allocated. It leads many to believe that Western capitalism (and aligned market liberalism) was the only valid model left.[1] Recent times have learned us otherwise. The aforementioned 'neoliberalism' has been claimed as the major cause underlying the market meltdown in 2008 and everything that followed from there. I beg to disagree. Neoliberalism and its most recent advocates like F. von Hayek, L. von Mises, M. Friedman and the likes indeed have been using varying strategies to submit society to market imperatives assuming that would optimize resource allocation and maximize prosperity for all or at least those that meaningfully used the opportunities a free market provides. Regulatory impact needs to be limited as much as possible as it would unbalance the natural equilibrium the market always will move toward. However, during the last 2–3 decades, the regulatory impact in many countries around the world, including those in many Western capitalist nations, has only increased and in a very significant way. A quick check taught me that in many countries the volume of the 'official journal' where legislation is published after it successfully went through the national parliamentary process often quadrupled during the last 2–3 decades. For example, in my own country Belgium, the 'official gazette' in 1991, when I started Law School, counted a 'miserable' 25,000 pages. That has, in 2018, crept up to well over 100,000 pages. So, there is apparently no lack of regulation but a lack of proper, effective and adequate regulation.

To prove my point, I will go back for a second to the very early days of neoliberalism, that is, right after the crash of 1929. In the early '30s of the last century, the mood was understandably anti-liberal. Those remaining liberals joined forces and created the Walter

[1] F. Fukuyama, (1992), *The End of History and the Last Man*, Free Press, NY.

Lippman Colloquium that had its first session in Paris in 1938. During that session where people like Hayek, von Mises and Rüstow were present, they discussed the recent book of W. Lippman called *The Good Society*. In short: their conclusion was that the 'old' or 'laissez faire' liberalism had failed and that the world was in need for a new sort of liberalism which was coined by Rüstow 'neoliberalism'. Already during the first meeting, it was clear that there was a schism in the group: on the one hand von Hayek and Von Mises and the others represented by Rüstow. Von Hayek and von Mises were not prepared to let go of the old 'laissez faire' capitalism. Rüstow c.s. took a different approach and wanted neoliberalism to create an alternative for the failed classical liberalism while at the same time provide an adequate alternative to the rising communist threat coming from the East. Their proposition, which is the original neoliberal axiom, is that the effective functioning is subject to a strong rule of law (that could avoid concentration in industries as was the case in the last two decades of the nineteenth century in Germany). The rule of law would have to be a partner of the free market to ensure it effective and optimally functioning. To that end the regulator was best placed to provide a regulatory framework within which the free market adequately functions. The regulator was not best placed to do enhanced handholding for the free market as it had proven in previous decades that it could not adequately replace the free market. The free market and the regulator were partners, yin and yang; they were communicating vessels through which society could indicate which values they prioritized at any given point in time and which mechanism re-established the equality of society versus economy. Only 50 years later, J. Habermas, 'avant la lettre', concluded that the economy was colonizing other spheres of private and social life. These were the first steps of the submission of society and political life to the imperatives of what was then the beginning of a (globalizing) free market.[2] It does not only demonstrate how neoliberalism got adrift already in the early days (it got so bad that Hayek and von Mises called Rüstow c.s. 'socialists of the worst kind' at later gatherings of the group especially after the group restarted the meetings in Europe after the end of the Second World War), but also that anno 2019 we are still not in a position (by far not) to get that equilibrium right. The regulator, as always, in white heat enacts legislation that tries to micro-manage the industries it tries to regulate rather than provide a framework for effective performance. The regulator wants the market to contribute to its wider objectives and the market needs the 'rule of law' in order to not get out of whack and not become subject to the Schumpeterian 'creative destruction' competitive markets are continuously exposed to. I'm afraid the shadow banking sphere will undergo the same faith as the rest of the regulated financial sector.

But first we need to go back to our (attempt) of a definition. While the name 'shadow banking' seems to conjure an image of a strange, mysterious and parallel universe, the term itself is commonly used, and this despite its pejorative connotation,[3] to refer to

[2] J. Habermas, (1981), *Theorie des Kommunikativen Handelns*, (Bd. 1: Handlungsrationalität und gesellschaftliche Rationalisierung, Bd. 2: Zur Kritik der funktionalistischen Vernunft), Suhrkamp.
[3] Federal Reserve Bank of Minneapolis, (2010) *The Region Magazine*, Interview with Gary Gorton, December 1, 2010.

market-funded (i.e. in contrast to bank funding) credit intermediation techniques. Although the term 'shadow banking' is recent, most of its components are not[4]: repurchase agreements have been in use since 1917, the first securitization transaction was executed in 1970 and the first MMMF ('Money Market Mutual Funds') was established in 1971. The obscurity of the shadow banking sector is undeniably linked to their alleged involvement in the 2008–2009 financial crisis. Starting in 2007, the liquidity in the US repurchase agreement market contracted already significantly. In 2008, a MMMF could not obtain financial support.[5] It might be useful to keep in mind that MMMFs account for a significant amount of the short-term wholesale funding market (infra) and that way can and did unbalance the regulated financial sector. The regulated and unregulated banking sectors are ultimately communicating vessels.

The contemporary definition(s) of shadow banking in vogue piles together divergent institutions, instruments as well as markets. That makes the analysis more complicated and un-transparent.[6] If one tries to assess the level of systemic risk a vehicle, institution or sector provides, it often helps being as specific as possible in defining its role in the wider global financial radar.[7]

A second problem is that the shadow banking sector in recent years has been expanding to include new types of activities driven by (the need for) financial innovation. It caught the attention of the regulators, market observers and others already in the early 2000s when it was coined to describe how the growth of financial market disintermediation outside the regulators' purview contributes to liquidity shocks.[8] That was followed in 2012 by Treasury Secretary T. Geithner saying that '[a] large shadow banking system had developed without meaningful regulation, using trillions of dollars in short-term debt to fund inherently risky financial activity'[9] as well as B. Bernanke saying '[a]s became apparent during the crisis, a key vulnerability of the system was the heavy reliance of the shadow banking sector'.[10]

The growth of shadow banking can be traced to multiple developments. Deregulation and competition encouraged commercial banks to enter higher-risk businesses. Financial innovations such as securitization contributed to an 'originate-to-distribute' model, where loans were transformed into securities for sale, funded by financial markets rather than deposits. Other products, such as MMMFs, substituted for traditional deposits but

---

[4] G. Gorton and A. Metrick, (2010), Regulating the Shadow Banking System, Brookings Working Paper on Economic Activity, Fall.

[5] F. Norris, (2008), Pride Goeth Before a Fall, *NY Times*, September 16.

[6] S. L. Schwarcz, (2012), Regulating Shadow Banking, *Review of Banking and Financial Law*, Vol. 31, Nr. 1, pp. 619–642.

[7] A. Turner, (2012), Shadow Banking and Financial Stability, Lecture at the Cass Business School, March 14.

[8] P. McCulley, (2009), The Shadow Banking System and Hyman Minsky's Economic Journey, Global Central Bank Focus, PIMCO.

[9] Timothy Geithner, (2012), Financial Crisis Amnesia, *Wall Street Journal*, Op-Ed, March 2.

[10] Ben Bernanke, Russell Sage Foundation and the Century Foundation Conference on 'Rethinking Finance', New York, April 13, 2012.

generally were not insured or backed by a central bank. Some contend growth was fueled by regulatory arbitrage,[11] demand from institutional cash pools,[12] financial engineering and growth in financial market intermediation.[13]

That confusion shows as we line up the different (non-exhaustive) attempts of a possible definition,[14] all of which hover between an entity-, a functional or an activity-based approach[15]:

1. 'A system of credit intermediation that involves entities and activities outside the regular banking system, and raises i) systemic risk concerns, in particular by maturity/liquidity transformation, leverage and flawed credit risk transfer, and/or ii) regulatory arbitrage concerns.'[16]
2. 'Shadow banks are financial intermediaries that conduct maturity, credit, and liquidity transformation without access to central bank liquidity or public sector credit guarantees. Examples of shadow banks include finance companies, asset-backed commercial paper conduits, limited-purpose finance companies, structured investment vehicles, credit hedge funds, money market mutual funds, securities lenders, and government-sponsored enterprises.'[17]
3. 'Shadow banking, as usually defined, comprises a diverse set of institutions and markets that, collectively, carry out traditional banking functions – but do so outside, or in ways only loosely linked to, the traditional system of regulated depository institutions. Examples of important components of the shadow

---

[11] S. L. Schwarcz, (2012), Regulating Shadow Banking, *Review of Banking and Financial Law*, Vol. 31, Nr. 1, pp. 619–642.

[12] Z. Pozsar, (2011), Institutional Cash Pools and the Triffin Dilemma of the U.S. Banking System, International Monetary Fund.

[13] S. L. Schwarcz, (2012), Regulating Shadow Banking, *Review of Banking and Financial Law*, Vol. 31, Nr. 1, pp. 619–642.

[14] See for a historical analysis: I. D. Lazcano, (2013), The Historical Role of the European Shadow Banking System in the Development and Evolution of Our Monetary Institutions, CITYPERC Working Paper Nr. 2013/05, London.

[15] See for an alternative write-up of the garden variety of definition and conceptualizations of shadow banking and its subcultures: E. Agirman et al., (2014), Shadow Banking: an Overview, Working Paper, pp. 5–6, mimeo and a comparison with the traditional banking system (pp. 7–9); J. Poshmann, (2014), The Shadow Banking System – Survey and Typological Framework, Working Papers on Global Financial Markets Nr. 27, University of Jena/Halle, March; and IMF, (2014), Global Financial Stability Report, chapter two: Shadow Banking around the Globe: how Large, and How Risky?, October, pp. 65–104.

[16] FSB, (2011), Shadow Banking: Strengthening Oversight and Regulation, Recommendations of the Financial Stability Board, Basel, October 27.

[17] Z. Pozsar, et al., (2012), Shadow Banking, Staff Report Nr. 458 (original July 2010), Federal Reserve Bank of New York, NY NY, February.

banking system include securitization vehicles, asset-backed commercial paper (ABCP) conduits, money market mutual funds, markets for repurchase agreements (repos), investment banks, and mortgage companies.'[18]

4. 'Shadow banking refers to bank-like financial activities that are conducted outside the traditional commercial banking system, many of which are unregulated or lightly regulated. Many of the activities performed within the shadow banking system take funds from savers and investors and ultimately provide them to borrowers. Within this broad definition are investment banks, finance companies, money market funds, hedge funds, special purpose entities, and other vehicles that aggregate and hold financial assets.'[19]
5. 'In its broadest definition, shadow banking includes familiar institutions as investment banks, money-market mutual funds, and mortgage brokers; rather old contracts, such as sale and repurchase agreements ("repo"); and more esoteric instruments such as asset-backed securities (ABS), collateralized-debt obligations (CDO), and asset-backed commercial paper (ABCP).'[20]
6. 'Shadow banking refers simply to maturity transformation – the funding of pools of longer-term financial assets with short-term (that is, money-market) liabilities – that takes place outside the terms of the banking social contract. A non-exhaustive list of shadow banking institutions would include: repo-financed dealer firms; securities lenders; structured investment vehicles (SIVs); asset-backed commercial paper conduits; some varieties of credit-oriented hedge funds; and, most importantly, money market mutual funds, which absorb other forms of short-term credit and transform them into true demand obligations.'[21]
7. 'The shadow banking system describes a web of financial instruments (asset-backed securities, credit derivatives, money market mutual funds, repurchase agreements) that connected commercial and household borrowers to investors in capital markets.'[22]
8. 'Shadow banking is the whole alphabet soup of levered up nonbank investment conduits, vehicles, and structures.'[23]

[18] Ben Bernanke, (2012), Russell Sage Foundation and the Century Foundation Conference on "Rethinking Finance," New York, April 13, 2012.

[19] Financial Crisis Inquiry Commission, (2010), Shadow Banking and the Financial Crisis, Washington, DC.

[20] G. Gorton and A. Metrick, (2010), Regulating the Shadow Banking System, Brookings Working Paper on Economic Activity, Fall.

[21] M. Ricks, (2010), Shadow Banking and Financial Regulation, Harvard Law School, blog September 18.

[22] E. F. Gerding, (2011), The Shadow Banking System and its Legal Origins, University of Colorado Law School; S.L. Schwarcz, (2015), The Governance Structure of Shadow Banking: rethinking Assumptions about Limited Liability, *The Journal of Financial Perspectives*, Vol. 3, Issue 1, pp. 101–140.

[23] P. McCulley, (2007), Teton Reflections, PIMCO Global Central Bank Focus, September.

9. 'Shadow banks are financial intermediaries that conduct maturity, credit, and liquidity transformation without explicit access to central bank liquidity or public sector credit guarantees.'[24]
10. 'A Shadow bank is a non-bank financial institution that behaves like a bank, borrows short-term in rollover debt markets, leverages itself significantly, and lend and invests in longer-term illiquid assets. Unlike banks however, the shadow banks are much less regulated.'[25]
11. 'Shadow banking comprises a set of activities, markets, contracts, and institutions that operate partially (or fully) outside the traditional commercial banking sector, and, as such, are either lightly regulated or not regulated at all. The distinguished feature of shadow banking is that it decomposes the process of credit intermediation into a sequence of discrete operations. A shadow banking system can be composed of a single entity that intermediates between end-suppliers and end-borrowers of funds, or it could involve multiple entities forming a chain.'[26]
12. 'All types of financial activity outside the regulated banking sector that rely on some sort of external (private or public) backstop.'[27]
13. 'Shadow banks are "cream skimmers" i.e. they only provide actuarially-based financing either to seasoned borrowers or to borrowers with easy-to-value collateral.'[28]
14. 'A shadow bank is an institution or bank-sponsored special purpose vehicle that has persuaded its customers that its liabilities can be redeemed de facto at par without delay even though they are not formally protected by government guarantees.'[29]
15. '"[S]hadow banking" is the set of "activities related to credit intermediation, liquidity and maturity transformation that take place outside the regulated banking system."'[30]

[24] Z. Pozsar et al., (2012), Shadow Banking, Federal Reserve of NY, Staff Report Nr. 458, February 2012 (revised, original July 2010) and N. Cetorelli, and S. Peristiani, (2012), The Role of Banks in Asset Securitization, Federal Reserve Bank of New York Economic Policy Review, Vol. 18, Nr. 2, pp. 47–64.

[25] V.V. Acharya, and T. S. Öncü, (2010), The Repurchase Agreement (Repo) Market, In Regulating Wall Street, The Dodd-Frank Act and the New Architecture of Global Finance, ed. V. V. Acharya, T. F. Cooley, M. Richardson, and I. Walter, chapter 11. New York University Stern School of Business and John Wiley & Sons, Hoboken.

[26] S. Gosh et al., (2012), Chasing the Shadows: How Significant is Shadow banking in Emerging Markets, Economic premise, World Bank, September 2012, Nr. 88.

[27] S. Claessens and L. Ratnovski, (2014), What is Shadow Banking, IMF Working Paper Nr. WP/14/25, p. 4.

[28] D. Hancock and W. Passmore, (2015), Shadow Banks as "Cream Skimmers", Board of Governors of the Federal Reserve System, Working Paper, Washington, January 14, mimeo.

[29] E.J. Kane, (2012), The Inevitability of Shadow Banking, Presentation for the 2012 Financial Markets Conference at the Federal Reserve Bank of Atlanta. Atlanta, April 10, p. 2.

[30] K. Bakk-Simon, et al., (2012), Shadow Banking in the Euro Area, ECB Occasional Paper Series Nr. 133, Frankfurt, p. 8.

16. 'The "shadow banking system" can broadly be described as credit intermediation involving entities and activities outside the regular banking system.'[31]
17. 'Shadow banks are institutions or chains of institutions that get involved in two particularly bank-like activities; either, they create credit, such as by using the same assets multiple times, or they engage in maturity transformation.'[32]

As time goes by, alternative viewpoints were and are developed and measurement models identified (flow of funds, noncore liabilities, etc.) which in turn will lead to new or adjusted definitions and combined supervisory techniques and models,[33] which will self-evidently trigger new critiques.[34] Throughout the book, these alternative and novel models and definitions will be discussed in their appropriate context.

1.3 Demarcation Lines and Characteristics

A word of caution is warranted before digging into this paragraph. Many words, concepts and abbreviations are being used without being explained. Don't worry at this stage. Each of them will receive their proper amount of attention at the right place in this work. For those that continue to feel materially uncomfortable with such a massive set of undefined concepts and abbreviations, I can refer to the abbreviation list and glossary which can be found at the very beginning of this work. So here we go.

Despite the myriad of definitions and viewpoints, there are a number of common characteristics that can help as cornerstones when trying to define and draw lines around the concept. There are three obvious criteria that can be found back invariable across the definitions: (1) all players in the field are involved in credit intermediation, raising short-term funds from financial markets to deploy elsewhere, including maturity and/or liquidity transformation. Shadow banking relies on financial markets,

---

[31] Financial Stability Board (FSB), (2011), Shadow Banking: Strengthening Oversight and Regulation, Recommendations of the Financial Stability Board, Basel, p. 1. They indicate that clear common agreed definition, and that all is about measurement. So then the question is what one wants to measure, which will require scoping and thus a definition. Definition or from the Latin 'dēfīniō' means setting boundaries, setting something apart from the other, by making it explicit (infra). See for a nice review of the possible approaches: J. Gallin, (2013), Shadow Banking and the Funding of the Nonfinancial Sector, Finance and Economics Discussion Series Divisions of Research & Statistics and Monetary Affairs Federal Reserve Board, Washington, DC, Nr. 2013-50, May 16, pp. 1–17.

[32] P. Tucker, (2012), Shadow Banking: thoughts for a Possible Policy Agenda, Speech given at the European Commission High Level Conference, Brussels, April 27.

[33] FSB, (2013), Global Shadow banking Monitoring Report, Annex 2: Monitoring Shadow Banking in Canada – A Case for Combining Activities with Entities, November 14, Basel, pp. 26–29.

[34] See for a write-up: IMF, (2014), Global Financial Stability Report, chapter two: Shadow Banking around the Globe: how Large, and How Risky?, October, pp. 66–74; T. Adrian and A.B. Ashcraft, (2012), Shadow Banking: A Review of the Literature, Federal Reserve Bank of NY Staff Papers, Nr. 580, October, pp. 1–4; T. Adrian and A.B. Ashcraft, (2012), Shadow Banking Regulation, Federal Reserve Bank of NY Staff Papers, Nr. 559, April, pp. 5–8. See, for example, EC, (2014), Financial Stability Report, November, pp. 95–97.

not bank deposits, as the source of funds; (2) the funds raised and deployed in the shadow banking sector are not guaranteed, in that there is no explicit government insurance for their safe return to investors in the event of an organizational/asset value/entity failure; (3) the players and institutions in the shadow banking sector have no access to a central bank in the event of a liquidity/funding problem.

Regarding a number of characteristics, there are little consensuses. Leverage is regularly highlighted as a noted shadow banking characteristic. While some activities in shadow banking rely on leverage to increase returns, this is not a unique characteristic. Hedge funds, private equity (PE) firms and banks use leverage as a normal tool in their business. Some therefore consider hedge funds, particularly credit hedge funds, to be part of shadow banking, others don't. However, a report by the Alternative Investment Management Association notes, hedge funds 'do not engage in any significant sense in credit, liquidity or maturity transformation, so their activity is not "bank-like".[35] A hedge fund's source of funds, investor capital, generally matches liquidity and maturity constraints of the underlying investments. This is not a banking surrogate.' That is true but also irrelevant. If one considers the total credit hedge fund market and the liquidity they provide in the leveraged loan and high-yield market, they can be considered of systemic relevance especially since the refinancing of those loans is based upon discretionary judgment by the hedge fund manager and will be driven by market conditions and potential redemptions by investors the hedge fund itself experiences. The same argument can be applied mutatis mutandis for private equity funds especially since many of these funds have been putting sizeable amounts to work this way during certain periods of time. Off-balance sheet treatment was also a noted characteristic of the special-purpose entities (SPEs) that played a role in the growth of the sector before 2008. With new accounting treatments issued in 2009, many such entities are now consolidated. As a result, off-balance sheet treatment by itself is not/no longer a necessary feature of a shadow banking component.[36]

Given that the regular banking system is (carefully) regulated to reduce risks to depositors and to financial markets, critics of shadow banking argue it has the potential to create risks in the broader financial system (infra). This view has been exacerbated by the perceived role of shadow banking in the 2007–2009 financial crisis. The risks are thought to include[37]:

- Opportunities for regulatory arbitrage.
- Build-up of leverage outside the regulated banking system.
- Uncertainty and stress, for direct surrogates of regular bank deposits, which may lead to 'runs' on those institutions. This needs to be offset by the tremendous benefits they bring, that is, by broadening the availability of investment options and, as a result, channels credit more efficiently, enabling risk diversification and financial innovation.

---

[35] Alternative Investment Management Association (AIMA), (2012), The Role of Credit Hedge Funds in the Financial System: Asset Managers, Not Shadow Banks, March, London.

[36] Financial Accounting Standards Board, Financial Accounting Statements Nr. 166, Accounting for Transfers of Financial Assets, and No. 167, Amendments to FASB Interpretation Nr. 46(R).

[37] Ibid. endnote 6.

Consequently Deloitte has come to define shadow banking as: '[s]hadow banking is a market-funded, credit intermediation system involving maturity and/or liquidity transformation through securitization and secured-funding mechanisms. It exists at least partly outside of the traditional banking system and does not have government guarantees in the form of insurance or access to the central bank.'[38] They created a shadow banking index based around these criteria. Those criteria included (1) credit intermediation, (2) maturity/liquidity transformation, (3) outside the regulated banking system, (4) lacks government guarantee/access to central bank liquidity and (5) credit risk transfer.

The entities that fall beyond the scope of their definition include money market mutual funds (MMMF), asset-backed commercial paper (ABCP) conduits, asset-backed securities (ABS), non-agency mortgage-backed securities (MBS), collateralized debt obligations (CDOs), repurchase agreements (repos), securities lending and agency mortgage-backed securities.[39] In light of the criteria mentioned above, they have excluded hedge funds, non-money market mutual funds, financial companies, insurance firms and activities such as swaps/derivatives and clearing. Auction rate securities are not included in the Deloitte Shadow Banking Index due to lack of data even though they conform to the Deloitte Shadow Banking Index's definition of the shadow banking system. The Deloitte Shadow Banking Index is designed to track the size and changes in shadow banking. They particularly highlight the problem that the sector is subject to change and as such reflects a continuously changing paradigm. They indicate: '[s]hadow banking is not a constant, and is considered to be immune to the effects of global economic forces and regulations. Instead it is directly affected by regulations and actions of the financial services industry.'[40]

They go on to describe the components and changes over time. Although that is something that will be covered extensively in a later chapter, we will here focus on the major categories and their relevance in the SB industry. When analyzed over the last decade, the major components in order of relevance are: until their exclusion from the shadow banking sector (supra), agency MBS were the largest component, followed by repos, MMMFs and securitization vehicles (ABS, non-agency MBS and CDOs) of which the largest component is the non-agency MBS. The Deloitte Shadow Banking Index has been updated while staying faithful to the key SB characteristics including credit and maturity transformation, no backstop or central bank (CB) window and which might involve leverage and off-balance sheet treatment.[41]

It is fair to say that the development and understanding of shadow banking and its activities have been largely occurring post-2008 crisis and therefore have been determined by our understanding of what happened during that crisis and the many parties, entities, activities and capital flows and money creation concepts involved. A traditional

[38] Deloitte, (2012), The Shadow Banking Index: Shedding Light on Banking's Shadows, Center for Financial Services, June.

[39] Agency MBS includes MBS and CMOs (collateralized mortgage obligations).

[40] Deloitte, (2012), Ibid. p. 6. The methodology of the index is described on p. 7.

[41] A. Schneider, (2013), Growth and Evolution of the U.S. Shadow Banking System, Deloitte, Presentation, April.

segmentation of the shadow banking industry would include the analysis of money market funds, securitization, securities lending and repos. At the margin, although that qualification is subject to constant change, activities as PE and hedge funds and more recently asset managers, blockchain applications and crowdfunding platforms have been included in the scoping of shadow banking activities, often referring to the material use of leverage or the absence of a true backstop in their business model that would absorb losses when things go wrong and therefore might have macroprudential implications.

Going forward and regardless of the somewhat unclear demarcation lines, a central focus on three criteria is essential to determine the gravity of activities around its shadow banking core: (1) credit transformation and transfer, (2) maturity transformation and (3) liquidity transformation. They will be discussed extensively in terms of their definition and how they show up in shadow banking activities. There are obviously other criteria thinkable but they are often secondary to any of those listed. When the activities demonstrating characteristics as indicated are then funded with funding showing deposit-like characteristics, the intensity of possible concern should rise.

Not surprising is the fact that our understanding of shadow banking has predominantly been modeled along the lines of the activities and entities involved in shadow banking activities during the 2008 crisis.[42] Also the suggested regulations to deal with the shadow banking segment and activities have largely been centered and structured along the lines of our 2008 crisis experiences.[43] Not good or bad in itself, it makes sense to anticipate on future changes in the definition, scoping and activities of shadow banks and the potential economic damage (and benefits) they might cause or bring. These changes are caused by 'natural market effects and adjustments as well as changes triggered by changing regulation and macro-prudential oversight'. Up till today, many see the revival of certain areas of the shadow banking market as key to any meaningful recovery, although we have witnessed different types of recoveries around the world since 2008 demonstrating different intensities and characteristics. Their understanding is that shadow banking is an essential part of the financial infrastructure and therefore a well-functioning shadow banking market is key to a recovery of the real economy and in particular certain segments.[44] Any of the envisaged shadow banking entities and transactions are engaged in one or multiple key risk transformations: (1) risk diversification, (2) leverage, (3) maturity mismatch and (4) liquidity mismatch.

For most part of the last decade, the shadow banking industry has been larger in size relative to the traditional banking sector. Even in 2008, when the traditional banking sector was firing from all cylinders, the US shadow banking industry was with its USD 21 trillion considerably larger than the USD 15 trillion of the traditional banking sector, although the asset base of both sectors is not mutually exclusive. It should also be noted that a large

---

[42] See for a well-designed write-up: Financial Crisis Inquiry Commission, (2010), Shadow Banking and the Financial Crisis, Final Staff Report, June.

[43] See, for example, G. Gorton and A. Metrick, (2010), Regulating the Shadow Banking System, Brookings Papers on Economic Activity, Fall.

[44] An often heard example is the recovery in the housing and real estate market who seems to be dependent on securitized products. See, for example, Christopher Whalen, (2013) Why Fixing the Shadow Banking Sector is Essential for the U.S. Housing market, NFI Working Paper.

portion of shadow banking exists (even anno 2019) within the bank holding companies[45] and banking institutions that are regulated by the Federal Reserve (and other central banks around the world). This has implications on the relative safety of components sponsored by 'banks' that may be forced to support shadow banking activities in the event of a liquidity or funding issue. An example would be the structured investment vehicles (SIVs), many of which were absorbed on the balance sheets of their parent banks during the financial crisis.

The most important game changer post-crisis was, besides the monetary policy of central banks in general, the impact of newly arrived legislation that has (or had) the potential to become a straightjacket for the industry. Given the link with the regulated banking sector, it undeniably has an impact on that part of the financial spectrum. Later on, we will dedicate a full chapter to the ongoing regulatory tsunamis across the world in this space, but it makes sense for the sake of completeness and coloring the full picture to at least provide a snapshot of what the existing and upcoming regulation is all about. The underlying driver is that the shadow banking industry can potentially be the source of systemic risk and propagate shocks through the financial system and the economy and therefore a threat to overall financial stability.

So as said, in the last few years, there has been a barrage of new legislation coming in that tackles the many different components of the industry. A non-exhaustive and limited overview would invariably include[46]:

a. Money market mutual funds

- Adoption of new SEC rules amending rule 2a-7 in 2010 (and later on in 2014 as well as 2016[47]). These rules require MMMFs to improve liquidity, invest in higher credit quality securities, maintain portfolios with shorter maturity limits, prepare for and anticipate large redemptions, engage in periodic stress tests, conduct greater due diligence ('look through') on repo counterparties, use only cash or government securities as collateral and to conduct independent credit analysis of each security purchased and so on.
- Proposed new regulations requiring money market funds to adopt a floating net asset value (NAV), impose capital requirements and restrict redemptions.

[45] R. Raykov and C. Silva-Buston, (2018), Multi-Bank Holding Companies and Bank Stability, Bank of Canada Staff Working Paper Nr. 51, October. This paper studies the relationship between bank holding company affiliation and the individual and systemic risk of banks. They show that banks that are part of a holding parent company are more resilient than independent banks. Examining the impact of the liquidity of the holding on resiliency shows that banks are more fragile when the liquidity of the holding is lower, consistent with internal capital markets playing a role in stabilizing banks. They also show that banks whose holdings display low liquidity levels rebalance their portfolios towards riskier activities, such as non-traditional banking activities.

[46] See in detail: T. Adrian and A. B. Ashcraft, (2012), Shadow Banking Regulation, Staff Report Nr. 559, April, Federal Reserve Bank of New York, NY NY. For an assessment of the regulatory impact, Ibid. pp. 38 ff. Also: Securities and Exchange Commission (SEC), (2010), SEC Approves Money Market Fund Reforms to Better Protect Investors, Press Release, January 27. Similar efforts have been made in Europe and will be discussed in the relevant chapters.

[47] See for details the money market-specific chapter.

b. Asset-backed commercial paper conduits

- New (ASC 810) rules related to accounting consolidation
- Basel III increased capital and liquidity requirements for ABCP conduits sponsored by banks[48]
- Various impact (transparency, risk retention, registration, etc.) following the introduction of the Dodd-Frank Act

c. Private-label securitization (ABS, MBS and CDOs)

- ASC 810 rules related to accounting consolidation
- New disclosure requirements in securitization transactions
- Basel II/III: Increased capital and liquidity requirements, including securitization exposures in the trading book
- Risk retention rules, removing rating references and so on following the introduction of the Dodd-Frank Act

d. Repos and securities financing/lending

Regulatory intervention included dealing with 'reducing demand and supply for intra-day credit, shortening the window for the daily unwind, increasing transparency and speeding settlement finality'.

The FSB has established a task force to examine the regulation of repos and securities lending from a financial stability perspective. Their findings and suggest will be 'in extenso' discussed in the regulatory chapters.

e. Agency MBS (government-sponsored enterprises [GSEs])

It is still somewhat unclear at this time what role the GSEs will play in the future or whether they will stay under government control. The Treasury released a paper in February 2011 saying, '[t]he Administration will work with the Federal Housing Finance Agency ("FHFA") to develop a plan to responsibly reduce the role of the Federal National Mortgage Association ("Fannie Mae") and the Federal Home Loan Mortgage Corporation ("Freddie Mac") in the mortgage market and, ultimately, wind down both institutions.' Anno November 2013 and onward however, a number of hedge fund managers are trying to force a breakthrough in this matter. A privatization is still in the works, despite being around since 2014 (see Box 1.1).

f. Securitization

Multiple changes have been made to the risk retention, structuring, disclosure and due diligence rules.

g. Hedge fund and private equity regulation. Occurred mainly in Europe through the AIFM (Alternative Investment Fund Managers) legislation.

h. Protocols for the use of non-cash collateral between market participants and between market participants and the respective central banks.

[48] Although the new European securitization framework lowers once again the capital requirements for qualifying simple transparent and standardized (STS) securitized products (infra).

Box 1.1 The Battle for Fannie Mae and Freddy Mac

Let's go back for a second. When mortgage giants Fannie Mae and Freddie Mac were taken over by the Bush Administration in 2008, the nearly $200 billion bailout was the largest in history. Since that time however, and aided by the rapid recovery of the housing market, the two housing giants have once again become profitable, and they have paid the government in dividends an amount equal to the original bailout.

However, the federal government still owns the 80% stake in the companies it bought in 2008. Like any investor it is looking for more than just getting their money back. In November 2013, a group of private investors were preparing to put forward a proposal which would privatize and ultimately end a dispute over the remaining privately held Fannie and Freddie stock which was not eliminated during the original bailout.[49] The action is caused by an old pain: back in 2008, when the federal government put Fannie and Freddie into conservatorship, it provided backstop financing and in return required the companies to pay the government a 10% dividend before any money went to private stakeholders. What the federal government did not do was fully nationalize these companies—as this would have required it to put Fannie and Freddie's debt on its own books.

But this decision came back to bite the government when the firms' fortunes turned around in 2012 and the return for the government was limited by the 10% dividend agreement. The remaining profits would go to the remaining shareholders. Trying to deal with the situation, the Treasury Department and the Fannie and Freddie's conservator—the FHFA—decided to change the terms of the bailout and force the housing giants to send all of their profits back to the feds. This action seems fair on its face. After all, there wouldn't be any Fannie Mae and Freddie Mac profits had the government not bailed them out. But to others, this action is an example of changing the rules in the middle of the game. One example is Perry Capital, a hedge fund that began purchasing shares in Fannie and Freddie on the open market in 2010 under the expectation that it could share in the companies' good fortune once the housing market recovered.

Over the summer of 2013, several hedge funds, including Perry Capital, Fairholme Capital, Pershing Capital and many more, filed a suit against the government in federal court seeking to overturn Treasury's decision to take Fannie and Freddie's profits. Their proposal was that the owners of preferred stock—which would have been receiving of dividends if the Treasury hadn't changed the terms of the agreement—would become the new owners of Fannie and Freddie. Reporting at that time stated: '[t]he deal would see the investor group take control of Fannie and Freddie's core businesses of guaranteeing mortgage-backed securities, in two newly-capitalized insurance companies. Fannie and Freddie's portfolio of previously-written guarantees and mortgage holdings would stay in government hands to be wound down, potentially at considerable profit to taxpayers. A common securitization platform, used to standardize mortgage-backed securities, would also stay in public hands.'[50] The bottom line would be that Fannie and Freddie go back into private hands and the Treasury would be left with the 10% dividend.

(continued)

[49] H. Sender and S. Foley, (2013), Investors Pitch to Take over Fannie May and Freddy Mac, *Financial Times*, November 13.

[50] H. Sender and S. Foley, (2013), Ibid.

Box 1.1 (continued)

In late November 2013, the Obama administration responded by indicating: 'the Obama administration believes the risks are too great that this model would recreate the risks of the past'. It clarified that their size and infrastructure would enable the two GSEs to stifle competition and raise entry barriers within the securitization market. 'All of us should fear that we could re-create a duopoly that the market would perceive as too-big-to-fail market entities with an implicit government guarantee, the core of the failed GSE business model we are trying to replace.'[51] Nevertheless, things are powering on in silence and the push toward re-privatization of both institutions might be in the making.[52] During late 2015 both institutions were still around and in full swing.[53] That is all the more surprising as they were at the center of the US real estate meltdown in 2007 and onward.[54] They were still in some sort of 'conservatorship' by the US Treasury and the profits flow entirely back to the Treasury[55] (effective nationalization) although some shares of both companies are floating. So although full privatization had been on the table somewhat for a while, it seemed that we were moving away from that momentum late 2015 and the right conclusion was that for quite some time to come nothing much will change or happen with Fannie and Freddy. Most likely not until a new president is installed early 2017. That might sound and is highly unsatisfying for all parties involved, but the heavy lifting needed for this file to fall in place properly requires a momentum that was not there at the moment.[56] The collateral damage was uncertain and the political courage absent especially since a full recapitalization would require a new Congressional spending authorization. A natural recap based on retained earnings would take forever.[57]

The following years we became only a bit wiser. First of all, it was only in February 2018 that the US Supreme Court put the litigation to bed that some

(continued)

---

[51] C. Benson, (2013), Obama Opposes Plans for Privatization of Fannie May Economic Director says, *Chicago Tribune*, November 20.

[52] Knowledge@wharton, (2015), Gaining Traction: Fannie and Freddie Flirt with Re-privatization, April 17; A contrario: M. Frankel, (2015), The Government Might Leave Fannie Mae and Freddie Mac Alone, April 17, fool.com

[53] B. McLean, (2015), Fannie and Freddy are Back, Bigger and Badder then Ever, *NY Times*, July 20. See also her newest on the matter: Shaky Ground, (2015), The Strange Saga of the U.S. Mortgage Giants, Columbia Global Reports, Columbia University, NY.

[54] See for a nice and extensive write-up of the shaky history of both institutions since 2007: W. Scott Frame et al., (2015), The Rescue of Fannie Mae and Freddie Mac, Federal Reserve Bank of New York Staff Reports, Nr. 719, March.

[55] Which has led to many debates and court cases for that matter: see T. Braithwaite, (2015), Funds Appeal over Fannie and Freddy, *Financial Times*, June 29 (the original judgment indicated that the private ownership rights of shareholders are 'extinguished' while the companies were under government conservatorship).

[56] J. Carney, (2015), Why Nothing Much Will Change For Fannie and Freddy Anytime Soon, *Wall Street Journal*, October 6.

[57] Or 18 years to be precise as calculated by J. Parrott and M. Zandi, (2015), Privatizing Fannie and Freddy: Be Careful What You Ask For, Moody's Analytics, May 15.

Box 1.1 (continued)

investor group has started in 2015. It left unchanged a 2017 lower court ruling that the investor group could not pursue legal claims accusing the government of unlawfully channeling profits from the two lenders to the US Treasury as well as overstepping its authority.[58] That ruling was based on a 2008 law that laid the groundwork for the seizure of the two companies by the US government. And so the two companies remained under the conservatorship of the Federal Housing Finance Agency (FHFA).

But since January 2017, the Trump administration is in place and they had already indicated before that the idea was to indeed put the two companies back in private hands ('it was a top 10 priority'). It took until June 2018 before the Trump administration proposed a privatization of the two lenders.[59] But the plan was, according to some, half-baked and didn't remove the government from the housing sector. The subsidies would only shift away from the two biggest lenders, as other firms could apply for the same charter as the two mortgage firms. The proposal stays silent on housing policies and lending standards. We know that lending standards and housing policies (and boosting mortgage lending) set determine and inflate housing prices and lead to deteriorating lending standards. The two biggest lenders buy these loans or loan portfolios from banks and resell them as MBS. As the credit line of the two lenders comes from the US government, leaving the system in place essentially guarantees future taxpayers' bailouts when the next crisis comes along.[60] Only eliminating (and not restructuring) the GSE model would take that risk away.[61] The public-private partnership underlying the GSE model leads only to crony capitalism, higher mortgage debt, higher home prices, taxpayer bailouts and no appreciable expansion of homeownership, Michel correctly argues.

Early 2019 US Senate Banking Committee Chairman Mike Crapo released an outline to overhaul the nation's housing finance system, which would see Fannie Mae and Freddie Mac privatized after years of government control. Lawmakers have been trying and failing to overhaul Fannie and Freddy for over a decade. The outline should kickstart a housing finance reform debate in Congress.[62] The plan, although lacking details so far, would not only privatize

(continued)

[58] L. Hurley, (2018), U.S. Top Court Rejects Investor Appeals over Fannie Mae, Freddy Mac, Reuters, February 20 (reuters.com).

[59] B. Lane, (2018), End of Conservatorship? Trump Administration proposes privatizing Fannie Mae, Freddy Mac. Government Reveals Plan to Reshape Country's Housing Finance System, *Housingwire*, June 21.

[60] N. Sridhar, (2018), Trump's Plan To Privatize Fannie Mae and Freddy Mac Leaves Taxpayers on the Hook for Future Bailouts, Hit and Run blog, reason.com, June 29.

[61] N. Michel, (2018), Is Mel Watt Setting Up Another Bailout, May 22, Forbes.com

[62] P. Schroeder, (2019), Senate Housing Finance Reform Outline Would Privatize Fannie, Freddie, Reuters.com, February 1. During the years up till 2019, both GSE entities have generated USD 292 billion in dividends for the government based on an initial bailout investment of USD 191 billion (research from investment bank Keefe, Bruyette & Woods). In the aftermath of launching the proposal, the Trump administration indicated they are willing to bypass Congress for getting the privatization deal done: Trump admin considers sidestepping Congress to overhaul Fannie and Freddie, *The Real Deal*, February 14, 2019, therealdeal.com

Box 1.1 (continued)

Fannie Mae and Freddie Mac but would also invite private competition into the mortgage guarantor market by placing limits on how many mortgage each of the two entities can guarantee. No banks would be allowed in that space. The ensure transparency and oversight eligible mortgages would have to meet certain standards (to improve the likelihood of payment) including capital, leverage and risk requirements. Fannie and Freddie however would continue subject to oversight by the FHFA.[63]

The holistic housing reform plan (THoR) developed by the Treasury Department is expected toward mid-2019.[64] Given the amount of items it has to cover, a privatization of Fannie and Freddie will not be accomplished before the closing date of this manuscript.[65] One of the most visible elements is how to disentangle Fannie and Freddie from government control. At this stage and although both companies are publicly listed, the stock is worth close to nothing given the government control and the net sweep in place in favor of the government which makes that all cash flows generated automatically is transferred to the Treasury. Although investors in both companies have been hung up in court for years now on the matter, a new era will arise in case the government control aspect is removed and the value of the shares will skyrocket. Who will be entitled to those gains and how will it fit into the larger reform of the housing (mortgage) market announced. And what are the long-term effects of such a move? Expectations are that a privatization of both entities as well as more comprehensive reform will benefit bank but negatively impact non-banks.[66] How the 'going private' process will exactly look like is still somewhat unclear at this stage but will undeniably include raising capital (or ordinary and/or preferred securities) to exit the conservatorship. In each scenario, the Treasury will observe that it will not have to backchannel liquidity back to the two companies that it earlier has drained under the cash sweep. Whatever the scenario it is clear that future shareholders will not have direct and full access to the earnings of the existing capital structure. Leaving existing shareholders with nothing while raising over USD 100 billion from what is likely the same pool of investors seems like an impossible task.[67]

---

[63] On April 4, 2019, Mark Calabria was confirmed as the new director of the FHFA.

[64] It was requested by President Trump by memorandum on March 27, 2019.

[65] E. Small, (2019), Don't Expect a Deal on Fannie and Freddie Anytime Soon, April 1, via therealdeal.com. The main reform options are a light version (recapitalization and out the government control), or a thorough more encompassing reform of the housing (mortgage) industry, the administration and Congress, and there was an effort by the incumbent administration and Congress to align views; the water is still very deep and cold. A lot of noise and threatening both ways is expected, in particular the threat of the President to take unilateral action. See, for example, A. Back, (2019), Sound and Fury over Fannie Mae and Freddie Mac, WSJ, June 12, via wj.com

[66] B. Sinnock, (2019), Downsizing Fannie, Freddie Could Help Banks, Hurt Nonbanks, National Mortgage News, via nationalmortgagenews.com, April 4; G. Bradford, (2019), Fannie and Freddie: October Named For Taking Capital Raise Steps, via seekingalpha.com, April 27.

[67] For a comprehensive review of the (what could be) appropriate role of government in US mortgage markets: Special Issue of the Economic Policy Review 2018, Vol. 24, Nr. 3, December.

i. Registration of the use of certain products and the volume of leverage and notification in trade registers.
j. Many aligned and adjacent pieces of (existing) legislation have been adjusted to better reflect and fit in the new legislative infrastructure being designed.
k. Basel III and IV (or Basel III bis if you want) have impacted not only the banking landscape but also the operational scope of those bank holding companies including the shadow banking sphere.

Given the multitude of regulatory restrictions, we speculate that shadow banking in the US will likely remain stagnant for the near-to-midterm. The evolution since the 2007–2009 crises will be analyzed at a later stage. However, what we do know already at this stage is that financial innovation continues and it is possible new shadow markets will emerge both in the US and elsewhere around the world.

It is clear that shadow banking cannot be eliminated completely because many of its components, including repurchase agreements and securities lending, are vital to the functioning of the financial system. The challenge to regulators is to ensure that the positive contributions of shadow banking are cultivated while its potentially negative attributes are minimized through appropriate regulation, monitoring and/or management (infra). It is unlikely that the debate about the shadow banking system will subside anytime soon, but how the system will evolve remains a highly pertinent question.

The recent Basel III/IV rules impose additional pressure on banks through higher capital buffers and more stringent liquidity requirements. In total, these global regulatory developments add to the uncertainty in areas like securitization, which may impact its future role in shadow banking. But the aforementioned innovations in regulatory arbitrage may once again result in some explosive growth, possibly posing increased systemic risk to the financial system. It is precisely for this reason that the evolution of shadow banking deserves continued vigilance.[68] It is to be understood that this effort should form an intrinsic part of any effort to redesign the banking sector as such. In 2019 there is very little convincing evidence left that we are looking at any sort of major redesign of our global financial infrastructure. Even more, some of the key reform tasks that regulators around the world set for themselves after the 2008 crisis are now at risk of not being implemented, or only in a skewed way and possibly some reforms that have been implemented over the last couple of years are at risk of being reversed.[69]

[68] ECB, (2013), Enhancing the Monitoring of Shadow Banking, ECB Monthly Bulletin, Frankfurt, February, pp. 89–99.

[69] See regarding separation of banking units and adequate ring fencing rules: E. Dunkley, (2015), Banks Score Victory on Ringfencing Rules, Financial Times, October 15. But there were pockets of hope at the same time that some regulators will push through: J. Brunsden, (2015), Banks Fume at EU Move to Strengthen Break-Up Powers, *Financial Times*, October 29, and J. Brunsden, (2015), Europe to Press Ahead with Bank Depositor Bailout Scheme, *Financial Times*, October 21. Some ended in vain, for example, the rollback of some of the Dodd-Frank Act (2018) and the removal of the EU proposal to split up banks or split up their trading units: S. Brush and J. Glover, (2017), Banks Win as EU Scraps Proposal to Split Off Trading Units, Bloomberg, October 24, Bloomberg.com

The Capital Markets Union proposal in the EU came at a point in time that there was (and is) a material underinvestment[70] from both the sovereign (due to austerity) and the corporate sector (due to financialization), and the European Banking Union manufactured in recent years still needs to evidence its adequate functioning under distress. A banking Union would also help to break the detrimental link between banks and sovereigns. As banks are deleveraging (somewhat), non-banks are substituting for part of the reduced bank lending, but to do so would need regulatory support—while the shadow banking sector more generally will come under closer regulatory and supervisory scrutiny.[71] Although there is consensus about the need to supervise, monitor and direct the shadow banking sector[72] as such, different countries and regions have been dealing with in separate shapes and forms, but very few common denominators.

And admittedly, it is a fine line to walk. Fueling economic growth while deleveraging, ensuring credit availability without blowing one bubble after the other, while ensuring macroprudential oversight in a private sector with an overwhelmingly important public mandate is truly a challenge. And throwing regulation at it will not do the trick in itself, especially not the overly complex financial regulation as we know it, to a large degree the result of enhanced lobbying from the financial sector. Bringing finance closer back to its real economic counterpart will undeniably include that financial innovation truly reflects and preferably solves real economic dynamics, risks and challenges. The other issue is that the system needs to become more long-term oriented, but that poses in itself distinct challenges. Landau, within the context of a G20, indicated about this some time ago: 'first, the natural reluctance of investors to irrevocably commit resources over the long run and their subsequent preference for liquid financial instruments; and, second, the intrinsic difficulty of assessing (and pricing) risk over very long horizons. Obviously those two problems are related: the higher the future uncertainty, the greater the preference for short-term (liquid) investments.'[73] Indeed, long-term investments trigger a cascade of legal, geopolitical, technological and economic challenges and then trickle down in the complexity of pricing risks which all can act as significant impediments to long-term finance. Financial innovation therefore has a role to play in solving some of the issues in long-term (LT)-Financing in often more illiquid markets and not in enhancing returns in short-term liquid markets. The consequences of the short-termism have been that 'risk could be constantly assessed, priced and, if necessary, adjusted. Therefore, risk had to be

---

[70] J. Brunsden, (2015), Capital Markets Union Push Comes Amid European Investment Crunch, *Financial Times*, September 30.

[71] See G. Wehinger, (2013), Banking in a Challenging Environment: Business Models, Ethics and Approaches Towards Risks, *OECD Journal Financial Market Trends*, Vol. 2012/2, pp. 1–10.

[72] B.S. Bernanke, (2013), The Crisis as a Classic Financial Panic, Remarks by Ben S. Bernanke Chairman Board of Governors of the Federal Reserve System at Fourteenth Jacques Polak Annual Research Conference Sponsored by the International Monetary Fund Washington, DC, November 8.

[73] J. P. Landau, (2013), Deleveraging Long-Term Finance and the G20 Agenda, Remarks at the BIS-Bank of Russia Seminar Moscow, July, p. 9.

traded, and traded safely. Liquidity and risk became closely entangled.'[74] Landau therefore argues that financial innovation might be instrumental when it facilitates greater distinction between managing risk on one hand and doing maturity transformation on the other, assuming not a single instrument will perform all functions at the same time. Therefore, he argues 'rather than holding a portfolio of complex assets (equities or securitized products), investors would decide on a (variable) mix of two specialised instruments: one providing safe maturity transformation over very long horizons, the other providing exposure to specific risks on projects, sectors or whole economies. Making long-term maturity transformation absolutely safe should therefore become one aim of financial innovation.'[75] That requires a full integrity of the process, of which we know it has been badly distorted by bad and misaligned incentives left, right and center. It further will need larger amounts of collateral that are available for longer periods that they now typically are.

1.4 Even If We Do Everything Right, There Is Still a Lot We have to Live With

Despite all the lessons we learned over the last decade and the realities we accepted (or had to accept), there is still a lot on the table we have to (learn to) live with. Those harsh realities include that people are in most instances irrational[76] (rational calculation is severely

[74] Ibid. p. 10. That has quite some implications, argues Landau: (1) liquidity and fundamental performance risks cannot be distinguished on the basis of market prices, since both are closely mingled in a single instrument. So, if the total amount of risk per unit of capital is capped by risk management practices (VaR for instance) and if liquidity risk increases (or is expected to potentially increase), very little is left to cover fundamental risk; (2) expertise for dealing with non-liquid assets may have shrunk among asset managers, as a premium is set on the ability to trade profitably and efficiently; and (3) the coexistence of deep market liquidity and ultra-efficient trading technology changes the incentives and horizons. Significant resources are invested in improving the performance of (very) short-term arbitrage rather than assessing the probability distribution of cash flows over very long-term horizons for complex projects. It has created a system prone to fragility and sudden stops as the liquidity of assets depends on information sensitivity. Debt markets, as discussed elsewhere in the book, have become information insensitive as a default model, become sensitive to information under distress especially now that financial products are all built around maturity transformation and risk sharing. Landau argues '[i]ndeed, one can think of a sort of trilemma between some main characteristics of financial instruments: the ability to do maturity transformation (provide liquidity); the capacity for transferring risk; and utility as a reliable store of value (meaning the absence or virtual absence of valuation risk). No existing instruments can simultaneously fulfil those three functions. As an attempt to solve that trilemma, recent (structured) securitization techniques ended up by failing on every front' (p. 11).

[75] Ibid. p. 11.

[76] A. Dombret, (2015), Shaken But Not Stirred? The Banking System Seven Years After the Crisis, Speech by Dr. Andreas Dombret, Member of the Executive Board of the Deutsche Bundesbank, at the Financial Markets Group Research Centre of the London School of Economics and Political Science, London, October 29, 2015, p. 2. See also on irrational exuberance: R. Schiller, (2015), Irrational Exuberance, Princeton University Press, Princeton.

limited—internally, by our limited neurological capacities, and externally, by uncertainty in a complex world). These human limitations are not mitigated by market structures. Regulation cannot assume rational behavior but has to live with interconnection and herding behavior and the negative externalities it might cause. Unregulated markets have made herding behavior worse. Markets are no natural phenomenon but artificial non-self-regulating entities and constructs. Despite the fact that another major revamp of the banking sector has occurred through Basel III, there are still a number of challenges out there. Dombret qualifies them as being: (1) even if we manage and supervise (shadow) bank properly we will have to do so in a multi-polar regulatory framework.[77] Multi-polarity refers to the now multiple regulatory requirements that banks have to meet. Rather than having to meet just one capital ratio, they now will have to surpass several minimum requirements. The same holds true for liquidity and leverage standards and all sorts of macroprudential buffers. Multi-polar regulation is a 'third way' between overly complex measures on the one hand and very simple measures on the other. Both alternatives have failed in the past argues Dombret and advocates this third way when highlighting 'I believe it to be a reasonable approach, because it keeps in check the complexity that is inherent in today's risk-based regulations. Each of the new instruments will capture and limit the risks from banks with differing business models and risk profiles.'[78] (2) It is not only capital requirements that make banks stable and safer. Bank resolution and recovery contributes its fair share also in reducing the moral hazard implicit in our contemporary banking sector and models. The total loss-absorbing capacity of systemically important banks will ensure that the market for loss-absorbing debt can and will mature and can lead to attractive investment opportunities when aligned with proper disclosure requirements; and (3) we need to adapt to new market structures. They are going to be less liquid and that will require banks and shadow banks to revisit their business models and transactions. It puts upfront the focus on the fact that regulation for shadow banks needs to be both ex-ante (open structured regulation to capture future evolutions) and ex-post (as market instability will also happen in the future regardless of what regulation we put in place and therefore ring fencing and contagion mitigating measures are utmost needed).

Dombret is positive about that happening 'markets are going to be less conducive for the generation of quick profits, but that was what was intended by the reforms – what we very much need are informed and committed investors, not short-termism. This will strengthen stability.' As will become clear throughout the book, I can only partially concur with that and will reveal, cruising through the different shadow banking domains, that most incoming legislation is prone to intrinsic weaknesses and defaults. The fact that most banking institutions have weathered the (regulatory) storm without a true overhaul of their business models evidences that intrinsically.[79] Dombret believes market forces will go the extra mile that regulation can't go (or doesn't want to go as regulation doesn't need to intervene in the strategic orientation of banks). The question is whether that is justified given the intensely

[77] See on the concept of multi-polar regulation: A.G. Haldane, (2015), Multi-Polar Regulation, International Journal of Central Banking, Vol. 11, Nr. 3, pp. 385–400.

[78] Dombret, (2015), Ibid. p. 4.

[79] The bank business models have been 'stirred' but not 'shaken' to stay with Dombret's terminology.

important public mandate these private institutions have. The negative externalities they can cause and have caused have led me to put my head around a different tax system for financial institutions (see the relevant chapter on Pigovian taxes for the FI sector).

That seems all the more relevant now that ring fencing of deposits is no longer required under contemporary regulation as was the plan during the aftermath of the financial crisis. Even more, the implicitly existing safe harbor which shadow banking entities need to replicate banking allow them access to directly sellable assets at any point in time.[80] The safe harbor rules have forced unsecured lenders to act and request more collateral thereby squeezing bank funding capacity. The same safe harbor rule exists in the repo and derivative regulation and activates in case of insolvency or bankruptcy and has been, as will be discussed later, considered excessive by any standard by scholars. Duffie and Skeel comment on this situation 'safe harbours could potentially raise social costs through five channels: (1) lowering the incentives of counterparties to monitor the firm; (2) increasing the ability of, or incentive for, the firm to become too big to fail; (3) inefficient substitution away from more traditional forms of financing; (4) increasing the market impact of collateral fire sales; and (5) lowering the incentives of a distressed firm to file for bankruptcy in a timely manner.'[81] Despite the fact that regulation aims to restrict eligibility, many exposures seem to be under-highlighted.[82] And so do many other features that are of macroprudential relevance but seem to miss the mark in microprudentially focused legislation.[83]

---

[80] For example, see the Directive 2009/44/EC: Directive 2009/44/EC of the European Parliament and of the Council of May 6, 2009, amending Directive 98/26/EC on settlement finality in payment and securities settlement systems and Directive 2002/47/EC on financial collateral arrangements as regards linked systems and credit claims, L/146 of June 10, 2009, pp. 37–43 which grants eligibility to all credit claims 'in the form of a loan'. That safe harbor rules also exist in the relevant Directives regarding central Securities Depositories.

[81] D. Duffie, and D. Skeel, (2012), A Dialogue on the Costs and Benefits of Automatic Stays for Derivatives and Repurchase Agreements, Rock Center for Corporate Governance Working Paper Nr. 108, Stanford University, March, mimeo. See for Duffie's argumentation when repos should be exempt from bankruptcy and failure Resolutions, D. Duffie, (2014), When Should Repos Be Exempt from Bankruptcy and Failure Resolution processes?, Presentation FRBB/FRBNY Conference on Risks of Wholesale Funding August. See in further detail: (1) E.R. Morrison et al., (2014), Rolling Back the Repo Safe Harbors, Harvard Law School Center of Law, Economics and Business, Discussion paper Nr. 793; (2) D. A. Skeel Jr. and T. H. Jackson, (2012), Transaction Consistency and the New Finance in Bankruptcy, Columbia Law Review, Vol. 112, pp. 152–202, (3) V. Acharya and S. Öncü, (2013), A Proposal for the Resolution of Systemically Important Assets and Liabilities: The Case of the Repo Market, International Journal of Central Banking, January, pp. 291–349 and (4) S. Infante, (2013), Repo Collateral Fire Sales: The Effects of Exemption from Automatic Stay, Finance and Economics Discussion Series Nr. 2013-83, Board of Governors of the Federal Reserve System (U.S.).

[82] E. Perotti, (2012), The Roots of Shadow Banking, DSF Policy Paper Series, June, pp. 6–7.

[83] See, for example, C. Calmès and R. Théoret, (2009), Off-Balance-Sheet Activities and the Shadow Banking System. An Application of the Hausman Test with Higher Moments Instruments, ESG Cahiers de Recherche Nr. 09-2009 regarding the volatility enhancing dynamic of shadow banking generated non-interest income for banking groups and the implications for risk management protocols and so on.

1.5 Unintentional Ignorance or Worse When Defining Demarcation Lines?

The regulators and supervisors have, after the crisis, been focusing on what they knew was lying in front of them. Their focus has been intentionally or not on those entities and transactions that engage in credit intermediation and while doing so also engage in credit, liquidity and maturity transformations, and this all happens outside the traditional regulatory banking framework. Many other spheres, however, could also have been included, was it not that they were apparently out of scope when focusing on those entities that triggered one way or the other the 2007–2009 financial crisis.

One such area has been dark pools. Dark pool operators are regulated in a variety of ways across jurisdictions. Some are operated and regulated as exchanges, while some have the option of operating and being regulated as a facility of an exchange, in which case the requirements applicable to exchanges apply. Dark pools are essentially a private forum on which securities, often in bulk or as block trades, can be traded often by institutional investors. The liquidity in those dark pools is called dark liquidity. From a regulatory point of view, there are essentially three major concerns[84]:

(1) Price Discovery[85]: There is the potential that the development of dark pools and use of dark orders could inhibit price discovery if orders that otherwise might have been publicly displayed become dark.
(2) Fragmentation of Information and Liquidity: The growing number of separately organized dark pools poses liquidity search challenges for market participants. In addition to the basic logistical task and cost of establishing connectivity or access to many different venues, multiple dark pools may pose specific information fragmentation problems due to their lack of pre-trade transparency, and the possibility that post-trade information may not, in some jurisdictions, be consolidated with post-trade information from other venues.
(3) Fairness and Market Integrity: Fairness includes access to markets, access to information and disclosure rules and rules of conduct. Despite the fact that there have been meaningful policy concerns[86] regarding these dark pools, and the fact that they have been linked to increased volatility in markets and so on, it has received very little attention by regulators and supervisors.[87] It might well be the next sweet spot for causing

[84] See in detail: IOSCO, (2011), Principles for Dark Liquidity, Final Report, FR 06/11, pp. 20–24.

[85] See in detail: H. Zhu, (2013), Do Dark Pools Harm Price Discovery, MIT Working Paper, mimeo; M. Fleming and G. Nguyen, (2013), Order Flow Segmentation and the Role of Dark Pool Trading in the Price Discovery of U.S. Treasury Securities, FED NY Staff Reports, Nr. 624, revised edition August 2015.

[86] G. Shorter and R.S. Miller, (2014), Dark Pools in Equity Trading: Policy Concerns and Recent Developments, Congressional Research Service, Report 7-5700, September 26.

[87] There are always exceptions to the general rule, see, for example, IISD, (2012), Financial Stability and Systemic Risk, June, pp. 20–23.

turbulence or worse systemic risk and appropriate contagion effects. However, given the not-so-direct link with the entities and activities that caused the 2008 financial meltdown,[88] it has not been received, unjustifiably so, the proper attention it clearly deserves. That can be said about many areas that possibly contain elements that can trigger a systemic crisis but are all characterized as having no direct relationship with the areas that posed systemic risk during the 2008 financial crisis. Although their regulators and supervisory bodies try to encapsulate 'alien areas' of potential systemic risk, the underlying theory and conceptual understanding is not in place (yet). Maybe a holistic approach to systemic will turn out to be merely a theoretical approximation rather than to be achieved in practice. Probability ultimately is an 'odd' phenomenon and a holistic approach would require combining dimensions that always creates loopholes through which new ways of systemic risk might materialize. But as far as our understanding allows us to run, we will delve into the trenches of possible systemic risk and causes of financial instability.

1.6 Demarcation Lines of Shadow Banking Revisited

There are many opinions as to what exactly defines shadow banking. Some refer to it as securitization activities, others equate it with non-traditional bank activities and yet others refer to it as a potpourri of all sort of non-bank lending. Sensu lato, it can be concurred with the fact that shadow banking can be described as 'all financial activities, except traditional banking, which require a private or public backstop to operate'.[89] Those backstops can come from the private sector in the form of franchise value of a bank or insurance company, or from the public sector in the form of a government guarantee. The need for a backstop is a crucial feature of shadow banking, which distinguishes it from the 'usual' intermediated capital market activities, such as custodians, hedge funds, leasing companies and so on.[90] It has been proven during the 2008 financial crisis that the private backstop is unreliable and that the public backstop is the only hardcore backstop there is to the system. That in itself triggers multiple policy questions (infra). The positive definition stands opposite the FSB's already mentioned negative definition as shadow banking being 'credit intermediation involving entities and activities (fully or partially) outside the regular banking system'.[91] Besides the fact that the demarcation lines are fairly

[88] See for an explicit example of ignoring dark pools because it doesn't fit the 2008 crisis-induced definition of shadow banking: EC, (2012), Green Paper Shadow Banking, COM(2012), 102 final, Brussels.

[89] S. Claessens and L. Ratnovski, (2014), What is Shadow Banking?, IMF Working Paper Nr. WP/14/25, Washington, DC, p. 3.

[90] S. Claessens and L. Ratnovski, (2014), Ibid. p. 3.

[91] FSB (Financial Stability Board), (2013), Strengthening Oversight and Regulation of Shadow Banking. An Overview of Policy Recommendations, August 29, London.

wide and therefore might include companies and activities which are not necessarily seen a shadow banking activities (financing companies, leasing companies, credit hedge funds, etc.), the bigger issue is the fact that it offsets shadow banking as something that happens outside the 'traditional banking sector'. That is conflicting with reality as much of the shadow banking tends to happen within the larger cocoon of the traditional banking sector, and more particularly within those traditional banks that are of systemic relevance. Included are activities such as liquidity puts to securitization SIVs, collateral operations of dealer banks, repos and so on (infra).[92] A breakdown is needed of what is included in the shadow banking system and judges it on its own merits. That, in particular, involves an analysis of the demand/supply side of each of those intermediation activities and to what they respond, for example, demand for safe assets in securitization, the need to efficiently use scarce collateral to support a large volume of secured transactions, including repos and so on.[93]

As will be evidenced later on, the shadow banking activities are not purely a supply-side story but that there is effective genuine demand to which those intermediation parties respond and therefore cannot be purely limited to regulatory arbitrage. A functional analysis and a deep understanding of the demand side of things combined with how the services are provided are critical for a comprehensive understanding of the shadow banking market.[94] A problem that we will face if we use a functional approach, and which is typical and occurs frequently, is that it doesn't provide us with a (comprehensive list) of activities or characteristics that embodies the shadow banking industry. The direct consequence is that we might get a decent picture of how things are today, but are failing to come up with a mechanism that will help us to see where future shadow banking activities and risks might emerge. That is problematic if one is to reflect on the shadow banking activities and definitely if the reflection is geared toward making policy recommendations. Although that in itself is not the purpose of this book, any comprehensive work on any topic including shadow banking requires to go 'the extra mile' in figuring out how an industries' future can help us understand (or maybe even predict) where the shadow banking industry will be going. In fact, and we will cover that topic extensively later on, the shadow banking market in 2008 when we went in the crisis is by far not the shadow banking market as we know it today.[95] That statement is most likely going to be true years down the road as well. A deeper analysis is not only

---

[92] N. Cetorelli, and S. Peristiani, (2012), The Role of Banks in Asset Securitization, Federal Reserve Bank of New York Economic Policy Review, Vol. 18, Nr. 2, pp. 47–64; Z. Pozsar, and M. Singh, (2011), The Nonbank-bank Nexus and the Shadow Banking System, IMF Working Paper Nr. 11/289, Washington, DC.

[93] S. Claessens and L. Ratnovski, (2014), Ibid. intro, p. 3.

[94] N. Cetorelli et al. (2012), Ibid.; S. Claessens, et al., (2012), Shadow Banking: Economics and Policy, IMF Staff Discussion Note Nr. SDN/12/12, Washington, DC.; Z. Pozsar, et al. (2010), Shadow Banking, New York Fed Staff Report Nr. 458, NY NY (revised 2012).

[95] See infra and, for example, T. Adrian, et al., (2013), Shadow Bank Monitoring, New York Fed Staff Report Nr. 638, NY NY.

needed to better understand the different characteristics of the activities included in our definition but even more importantly the different risk profiles of each of those activities and what that means for the systemic risk[96] they might add (or not) to the industry and the banking sector as such. What has been proven problematic in the financial crisis was our ability to see high concentrations of risks in the financial infrastructure as such which requires a breakdown of individual activities and how they interact and behave interdependently. And now we don't even mention the differences that might exist in the nature of shadow banking activities in different countries and parts of the world. Claessens et al. comment: '[r]elated, most studies focus on the U.S. and say little about shadow banking in other countries where what it can take on very different forms. In Europe, lending by insurance companies is sometimes called shadow banking. "Wealth management products" offered by banks in China and lending by bank affiliated finance companies in India are also called shadow banking. It is unclear though how much do these activities have in common with U.S. shadow banking.'[97]

The spectrum of financial activities can be constructed in such a way that on both sides of the equation there are the traditional banking, insurance and capital market activities.

That would include on the one hand the (1) traditional banking (deposit taking and lending) and insurance activities and on the other side of the spectrum the typical intermediation activities in the (non)-banking sector. Those entities would include for the capital markets sphere 'hedge funds, underwriters, investment companies, market makers, custodians and brokers. On the non-banking side that would be leasing and finance companies as well as dedicated corporate tax vehicles.'

Within that bipolar space the middle ground is taken by the shadow banking market. Claessens et al. distinguish in that context four categories of activities in that space[98]:

1. Securitization which includes tranching of claims, maturity transformation, liquidity 'puts' from banks to SIVs and support to par value money funds.
2. Collateral services, primarily through dealer banks, including supporting the efficient re-use of collateral in repo transactions, for over-the-counter (OTC) derivatives and in prime brokerage; securities lending.
3. Bank wholesale funding arrangement, including the use of collateral in repos and the operations of the tri-party repo market.
4. Deposit taking and/or lending by non-banks, including that by insurance companies (e.g. France) and bank-affiliated companies (e.g. India and China).

They conclude that a good definition for shadow banking would therefore be and as highlighted above: 'all financial activities, except traditional banking, which require a private or public backstop to operate'. The benefit is that it does not only describe and

---

[96] S. Claessens and L. Ratnovski, (2014), Ibid. p. 3 ('e.g. a commitment by a bank to provide credit to a single firm vs. liquidity support to SIVs').

[97] S. Claessens and L. Ratnovski, (2014), Ibid. p. 3 in fine.

[98] S. Claessens and L. Ratnovski, (2014), Ibid. p. 4.

include all current activities but very likely all future branching out in terms of shadow banking activities. Also newcomers to the space as 'agency real estate investment trusts (REITs), leveraged finance, and reinsurance in the U.S.'[99] are properly included with this definition. The constant evolution of activities and how the financial infrastructure changes its own paradigm poses an interesting but to a large degree also a material problem for the regulator and the real economy. The constant monitoring that most regulatory advisory committees advocate with respect to the shadow banking industry reveals the Achilles heel in the whole story, that is, we seem 'still' to be backward looking and analyze things through the rear window in the hope we can learn something from it that is going to be useful going forward. To paraphrase, there will be a next financial crisis, we just know where it will show up. That capitalism is inherently unstable needs no further proof or evidence.

What is problematic however is the fact that shadow banking, just like the traditional banking sector, needs a permanent (financial) backstop. In the traditional banking sector, that backstop is provided through the deposit insurance mechanisms in place in many countries of the world, and under extreme pressure governments have been found willing to shelter the total financial infrastructure rather than the savings itself (often up to a certain level). Just like traditional banking, shadow banking is prone to a set of risks. The most common and most visible in both sectors are credit, liquidity and maturity risk. In the traditional sector, they are often well known and observable. In the shadow banking sector however, part of the credit intermediation activities are geared toward risk transformation and often includes risk stripping (infra).

The purpose of risk transformation is to strip assets of 'undesirable' risks that certain investors do not wish to bear. That can be the case for a variety of reasons, for example, as they do not have the competitive advantage, or as regulations inhibits the type of risks they can take on and so on.[100] As will be discussed extensively later on, the demand side of the securitization market was in search for cheap, safe and liquid private assets. Those were sheltered and the remaining risk (tranches) was either kept by the banks itself or by institutional investors for them those riskier assets were part of their investment strategy. Another problem that makes the need for a backstop extra problematic is the fact that, in contrast to traditional banking where the credit transformation happens on one balance sheet and is therefore better observable, in the shadow banking and particularly securitization sphere, the risk transformation happens over the multiple balance sheets which makes the observability more difficult but also the concentration and aggregate volumes of risks more difficult to assess. Claessens and Ratnovski comment: '[i]t uses the law of large numbers, monitoring, and capital cushions to "convert" risky loans into safe assets – bank deposits. Shadow banking transforms risks using different mechanisms, many more akin to those used in capital markets. It aims to distribute the undesirable risks across the financial system ("sell them off" in a diversified way).'[101] The different tranches of a securitized instrument pose different types of credit and liquidity risks or it facilitates the use of collateral to reduce

[99] T. Adrian, et al., (2013), Shadow Bank Monitoring, New York Fed Staff Report Nr. 638, NY.

[100] S. Claessens and L. Ratnovski, (2014), Ibid. p. 5.

[101] Ibid. p. 5.

counterparty exposures in repo markets and for OTC derivatives.[102] It therefore uses many different tools of the traditional banking sector. In that lies the need for a permanent backstop.

Despite the fact that the activities are built around the idea of migration, stripping and repackaging, certain types of fairly synchronic risks can be distributed and diversified away, certain types of risks cannot be stripped away which stay behind in the system ('tail risks'), risks that are often rare and mostly systemic. Those tail risks can include 'systemic liquidity risk in securitization, risks associated with large borrowers' bankruptcy in repos and securities lending and the systematic component of credit risk in non-bank lending (e.g. for leveraged buyouts)'.[103] For the model to be sustainable over time, the shadow banking intermediation parties need to have a balance sheet with sufficient equity (or to be precise 'loss-absorbing capital') to ensure that others don't have to pick up the tag if those tail risks emerge.

Claessens and Ratnovski continue their analysis and argue that generating sufficient loss-absorbing capacity is impossible to do so internally for shadow banking entities as the margins for their services are too low to act as a backstop. Those services are low margin in nature (low value added as well for that matter) and can never generate a sufficient internal backstop for those tail risks.[104] Therefore a, not only permanent, but also external backstop is needed to cover those residual tail risks that stay behind in the system after all the synchronic risks have been redistributed to other parties in the market. That backstop needs to be material as the volumes in the system are significant, margins or low and global infrastructure development is high and competitive in nature. But more importantly, the tail risks in the shadow banking system are systemic in nature and therefore, given their often high concentration, occur en masse and can be very disruptive.

Although debatable, two distinct ways (one private and one public model) of creating an external backstop have been identified[105]:

- The first is private—by using the franchise value of existing financial institutions. As indicated above many shadow banking activities operate within large existing traditional banks or transfer risks to them (as with liquidity puts in securitization or with backstops for REITs).
- The second is public—by using explicit or implicit government guarantees.

Examples[106] of the latter include, besides the general implicit guarantee provided to the 'too-big-to-fail', large banks active in shadow banking, the Federal Reserve securities lending facility (TSLF) that backstops the collateral intermediation processes.

---

[102] V. Acharya, & T. Öncü, (2013), A Proposal for the Resolution of Systemically Important Assets and Liabilities: The Case of the Repo Market, *International Journal of Central Banking*, Vol. 9 (January), pp. 291–349; G. Gorton, and A. Metrick, (2012), Securitized Banking and the Run on Repo, *Journal of Financial Economics*, Vol. 104, Nr. 3, pp. 425–451.

[103] S. Claessens and L; Ratnovski, (2014), Ibid. p. 5.

[104] Besides the fact that most SB services use external data to measure and are therefore contestable.

[105] S. Claessens and L. Ratnovski, (2014), Ibid. p. 5 in fine.

[106] Referred to by Claessens and Ratnovski, Ibid. pp. 5–6.

But also the implicit too-big-to-fail guarantees for tri-party repo clearing banks and other dealer banks[107] and the bankruptcy stay exemptions for repos which in effect guarantee the exposure of lenders[108] or the implicit, reputational and other guarantees on bank-affiliated products (the so-called wealth management products in China)[109] or on liabilities of non-bank finance companies are all considered examples.[110]

It could therefore be claimed that a distinct characterization of shadow banking activities is the fact that they need a permanent external financial backstop. Correctly so, the normal capital market players typically don't require such a backstop. That is because some, like custodian or market-making services, involve no risk transformation, while others, like hedge funds, have high margins and investors that do not seek to avoid specific risks.[111] As argued above, also the traditional banking sector requires a backstop although there are differences between those two positions. The most important being that the shadow banking sector combines risk transformation, low margins and high scale with residual 'tail' risks and therefore can be considered are systemically important. Although conceptually attractive, I wonder about the long-term validity of the framework. It is perfectly imaginable that, beyond the securitization and collateralization activities, there will be activities emerging that do not necessarily fit within the backstop framework. The shape and activities of the shadow banking sector will ultimately always be a function of the type of demand they experience from the market as well as the type and sort of regulation the traditional banking sector will be exposed going forward.

The good (or bad) news is that, under the Basel III rules as enacted, securitized products qualify under the liquidity rules as set out by BIS (Bank for International Settlements), given a haircut of 25% and after discretionary approval of the national regulator and/or supervisor.[112]

Indeed, securitized products and in particular residential mortgage-backed securities (RMBS) can be eligible for level 2B (which allows them access to the liquidity framework, but as said with a 25% haircut) qualification. To be precise:

---

[107] M. Singh, (2012), Puts in the Shadow, IMF Working Paper Nr. WP/12/229, Washington, DC.

[108] E. Perotti, (2013), The Roots of Shadow Banking, CEPR Policy Insight 69, cepr.org

[109] N. Lardy, (2013), Shadow Banking in China, Presentation at the Chicago Fed's Sixteenth Annual International Banking Conference or E. Avgouleas and D. Xu, (2017), Overhauling China's Financial Stability Regulation: Policy Riddles and Regulatory Dilemmas, *Asian Journal of Law and Society*, Vol. 4, Issue 4, May, pp. 1–57.

[110] V. Acharya, et al., (2013), The Growth of a Shadow Banking System in Emerging Markets: Evidence from India, Volume 39, December, pp. 207–230.

[111] S. Claessens and L. Ratnovski, (2014), Ibid. p. 6.

[112] I deny here for a second the exemptions securitized products can get if they meet the STS criteria under European regulation where they can benefit from lower capital requirements than the standard Basel III standards.

'Residential mortgage backed securities (RMBS) that satisfy all of the following conditions may be included in Level 2B, subject to a 25% haircut:

- not issued by, and the underlying assets have not been originated by the bank itself or any of its affiliated entities;
- have a long-term credit rating from a recognized ECAI ("External Credit Assessment Institution") of AA or higher, or in the absence of a long term rating, a short-term rating equivalent in quality to the long-term rating;
- traded in large, deep and active repo or cash markets characterized by a low level of concentration;
- have a proven record as a reliable source of liquidity in the markets (repo or sale) even during stressed market conditions, i.e. a maximum decline of price not exceeding 20% or increase in haircut over a 30-day period not exceeding 20 percentage points during a relevant period of significant liquidity stress;
- the underlying asset pool is restricted to residential mortgages and cannot contain structured products; the underlying mortgages are "full recourse" loans (i.e. in the case of foreclosure the mortgage owner remains liable for any shortfall in sales proceeds from the property) and have a maximum loan-to-value ratio (LTV) of 80% on average at issuance; and
- the securitizations are subject to "risk retention" regulations which require issuers to retain an interest in the assets they securitize.'[113]

Given the nexus between the shadow and traditional banking sector, the focus should predominantly go toward the concentration of risks and the exposure within the balance sheet of the traditional banking sector or in the portfolio of large institutional investors (especially those that manage public or pension funds). Admitted, that is more pragmatically oriented but allows to focus on where the issues might show up (also in the future). The tail risk in the shadow banking sector only requires policy attention to the degree that the real economy or investors are directly (as investors in the shadow banking market) or directly (as investor in the traditional banking sector or as institutional investors in fixed income products) exposed to asymmetric risk, absorbing part of the pain of the emergence of that tail risk at the level of the credit intermediation vehicle. As I will advocate later, it is not unimaginable that dark pools will play a more material role in the future where the argument of backstop might be less transparent to argue or to observe to begin with.

Nevertheless, the backstop argument provided by Claessens and Ratnovski can and will be materially useful and instrumental in future policy design. In particular:

[113] BIS, (2013), Basel III: The Liquidity Coverage Ratio and Liquidity Risk Monitoring Tools, Basel, pp. 14–15.

- First, it 'gives direction on where to look for new shadow banking risks': among financial activities that need franchise value or government guarantees to operate as well as non-traditional activities that fall outside the traditional banks or insurance companies. Claessens and Ratnovski refer to, for example, liquidity services provided by sponsor banks to exchange traded funds (ETFs), or large-scale commercial bank backstops for leveraged financing and buyouts.[114]
- Second, the model can be used to explain 'why shadow banking poses significant macro-prudential and other regulatory challenges as the shadow banking actors use backstops to execute their business model'. Backstops, of whatever sort of type, reduce market discipline and thus can enable shadow banking to accumulate (systemic) risks on a large scale given the volumes processed. Regulation and supervision should play its role. However, the effects of accumulated tail risk will always show up in a delayed fashion through the balance sheets of traditional banks and other instructional investors. Meaningful supervisory steering become very difficult and yes problematic for that matter.
- Third, Claessens and Ratnovski suggest that shadow banking is nevertheless almost always within regulatory reach, directly or indirectly. Regulators can, as they claim, 'control shadow banking by affecting the ability of regulated entities to use their franchise value to support shadow banking activities (e.g. limiting the ability of banks to offer liquidity support to SIVs). Or by managing the (implicit) government guarantees (e.g. by limiting the ability to extend the safety net to non-bank activities and entities).'[115] Although correct, I cannot imagine that a structural meaningful approach can be built around what are largely post-event or 'ad hoc' measures of a nature indicated. In order to shelter traditional banking balance sheets (and ultimately the taxpayer) that also enjoy a traditional backstop from government, the accumulation of tail risk that will trickle down from the shadow banking balance sheets involved to the traditional banking balance sheet needs to be pre-emptively discouraged. The accumulation of tail risk can meaningfully be defined as a negative externality in a Pigovian way. I argued elsewhere[116] that the shadow banking systemic exposure toward risk needs to be massaged by a form of Pigovian tax that, in contrast to a corporate income tax driven model as we know it, directly targets the (detrimental) intermediation activity that creates the negative externality and taxes those activity in line with expected exposures (with post-adjustment).
- Finally, they suggest that the migration of risks from the regulated sector to shadow banking—often suggested as a possible unintended consequence of tighter bank regulation—is a lesser problem than some fear. Shadow banking activities, they claim,[117]

---

[114] S. Claessens and L. Ratnovski, (2014), Ibid. p. 6.

[115] S. Claessens and L. Ratnovski, (2014), Ibid. p. 6.

[116] L. Nijs, (2016), Neoliberalism 2.0. Regulating and Financing Globalizing Markets. A Pigovian Approach to 21st Century markets, Palgrave Macmillan, London, in particular chapter 6. A fully reworked and updated chapter on the Pigovian dimension of (shadow) banking can be found in this book.

[117] S. Claessens and L. Ratnovski, (2014), Ibid. p. 7.

cannot migrate on a large scale to areas of the financial system that do not have access to franchise values or government guarantees. I concur with the fact that this by itself does not make spotting the activity occurring within the reach of the regulator necessarily easier, but at least it narrows the task. And it provides for a starting point when it comes to measuring the shadow banking system: activities within banks.[118] I do wonder why they conclude so. The credit intermediation process often happens offshore and/or outside the direct remit of parent traditional bank 'balance sheet' due to consolidation rules. It can therefore be perfectly contractually structured in such a way that the shadow banking activities do not fall under the direct parent banking regulatory supervision. However, this does not imply that at the end of the road the potential exposure, which is tail risk, and therefore 'by definition' characterized by low frequency, will trigger parent bank balance sheet coverage. I see no evidence why a large amount of shadow banking activity can't move away from the traditional banking franchise coverage, while keeping contractual coverage of risk (and therefore will not show up on bank balance sheets). This is ultimately not so much different than the capital relief transactions (CRTs-infra) that banks engaged in after the financial crisis to offload risk from their loan books and comply with incoming Basel III rules, that is, either you reduce the size of your loan book or you shift (only) the risk off-balance. Just like with the CRTs, the shadow banking activities, the traditional banks move away part of the risk but not everything (as there are no buyers for tail risk in the market). What stays behind in terms of risk therefore is in a natural way systemically relevant. That besides the fact that the non-synchronic risk distribution in (some) securitized products stays either on the balance sheet of the offshore vehicle or on the balance sheet of the banking franchise (mezzanine and equity tranches), which constitutes as a material exposure in itself.

[118] Claessens et al. (2014), Ibid. p. 7.

2

The Typology of Shadow Banking

2.1 Introduction

Shadow banking (SB) activities consist of credit, maturity and liquidity transformation that take place without direct and explicit access to public sources of liquidity or credit backstops.[1] The specialized financial intermediaries that engage in those activities are bound together along an intermediation chain called the shadow banking system (SBS).[2] The term shadow banking emerged in 2007 for the first time.[3] Prior to the 2007–2009 financial crisis, the shadow banking system provided credit by 'issuing liquid, short-term liabilities against risky, long-term, and often opaque assets'. The large amounts of credit intermediation provided by the shadow banking system 'contributed to asset price appreciation in residential and commercial real estate markets prior to the financial crisis and to the expansion of credit more generally'.[4] The funding of credit through the shadow banking system significantly reduced the cost of borrowing during the run-up to the financial crisis, at the expense of increasing the volatility of the cost of credit through the cycle.

During the financial crisis, the system came under severe strain, and many parts of it collapsed. The emergence of shadow banking thus shifted the systemic risk-return trade-off toward cheaper credit intermediation during booms, at the cost of more severe crises and more expensive intermediation during downturns.[5]

In those shadow banking systems, credit is 'intermediated' through, for example, a wide range of securitization and secured funding techniques, including asset-backed

---

[1] Z. Pozsar et al., (2013), Shadow banking, NY FED FRBNY Policy Review, December 2013, p. 1.

[2] See for a map of the shadow banking system: http://www.newyorkfed.org/research/economists/adrian/1306adri_map.pdf

[3] P. McCulley, (2007), Teton Reflections, PIMCO Global Central Bank Focus, September.

[4] Z. Pozsar et al. (2013), Ibid. p. 1.

[5] Z. Pozsar et al. (2013), Ibid. p. 2.

L. Nijs, *The Handbook of Global Shadow Banking, Volume I*,
https://doi.org/10.1007/978-3-030-34743-7_2

commercial paper (ABCP), asset-backed securities (ABS), collateralized debt obligations (CDOs) and repurchase agreements (repos).[6]

Credit intermediaries' reliance on short-term liabilities to fund illiquid long-term assets is an inherently fragile activity that can make the shadow banking system prone to runs. Shadow banks conduct credit, maturity and liquidity transformation much like traditional banks do. However, what distinguishes shadow banks is their lack of access to public sources of liquidity, such as the Federal Reserve's discount window.[7]

Governments have decided to shield the traditional banking system from the risks inherent in maturity transformation by granting them access to backstop liquidity in the form of discount window lending. A failure of the system can obviously have adverse effects on the real economy.[8] The shadow banking system was presumed to be safe owing to these liquidity backstops in the form of contingent lines of credit and tail-risk insurance in the form of wraps and guarantees.[9] The credit lines and tail-risk insurance filled a backstop role for shadow banks. These forms of liquidity and credit insurance provided by the private sector allowed shadow banks to perform credit, liquidity and maturity transformation by issuing highly rated and liquid short-term liabilities.[10] However, these guarantees also acted to transfer systemic risk between the core financial institutions and the shadow banks.[11] During the financial crisis, the solvency of those providers was put in question as well as the confidence in the system deteriorated.

It took a series of official liquidity facilities and credit guarantees to stabilize the system. Nevertheless, a large portion of the shadow banking system collapsed during the interim, and several shadow intermediation activities disappeared completely.[12] The financial system is prone to excessive lowering of underwriting standards and to overly aggressive structuring of securities due to a number of agency problems.[13]

---

[6] Z. Pozsar et al. (2013), Ibid. p. 1.

[7] Z. Pozsar et al. (2013), Ibid. p. 2; D. Diamond, and P. Dybvig, (1983), Bank Runs, Deposit Insurance, and Liquidity, *Journal of Political Economy* 91, Nr. 3 (June), pp. 401–419; S. Morris, and H. S. Shin, (2004), Coordination Risk and the Price of Debt, European Economic Review 48, Nr. 1 (February), pp. 133–153.

[8] Z. Pozsar et al. (2013), Ibid. p. 2; A. B. Ashcraft, (2005), Are Banks Really Special? New Evidence from the FDIC-Induced Failure of Healthy Banks, American Economic Review 95, Nr. 5 (December), pp. 1712–1730; B. S. Bernanke, (1983), Non-monetary Effects of the Financial Crisis in the Propagation of the Great Depression, American Economic Review Vol. 73, Nr. 3 (June), pp. 257–276.

[9] Z. Pozsar et al. (2013), Ibid. p. 2.

[10] Z. Pozsar et al. (2013), Ibid. p. 2.

[11] Z. Pozsar et al. (2013), Ibid. p. 2.

[12] Z. Pozsar et al., (2013), Ibid. p. 3.

[13] See for a list of them: A. B. Ashcraft, and T. Schuermann, (2008), Understanding the Securitization of Subprime Mortgage Credit, Foundations and Trends in Finance Vol. 2, Nr. 3 (July), pp. 191–309.

An underestimation of the aggregate risk and asset price correlations were the main drivers behind the failure of private sector guarantees to keep the shadow banking sector stable.[14,15] The underestimation of correlations enabled financial institutions to hold insufficient amounts of capital against the puts that underpinned the stability of the shadow banking system, which made these puts unduly cheap to sell.[16]

To make the list of elements complete that contributed to the dynamics of the shadow banking system in the midst of the 2008 financial crisis was that investors also overestimated the value of private credit and liquidity enhancement mechanisms. In addition, the likely underpricing of public sector liquidity and credit puts would have provided further incentives for risk-taking behavior.[17]

The emergency liquidity facilities launched by the Federal Reserve and the guarantee schemes created by other government agencies during the financial crisis were direct responses to the liquidity and capital shortfalls of shadow banks.[18]

Pozsar et al. catalog different types of shadow banks and describe the asset and funding flows within the shadow banking system. Adrian and Shin on the other hand focus on the role of security brokers and dealers in the shadow banking system and discuss implications for financial regulation.[19]

2.2 The Institutional Dynamics of Shadow Banking

2.2.1 The Funding Flows or the Dynamics of Shadow Credit Intermediation

In the traditional regulated banking system, credit intermediation between economic agents (savers and borrowers) occurs in a single entity (and thus one balance sheet). Savers entrust their money to banks in the form of deposits, which the institutions use to fund the extension of loans to borrowers. Banks issue debt and equity to finance their interme-

[14] J. Coval, J. Jurek, and E. Stafford, (2009), The Economics of Structured Finance, *Journal of Economic Perspectives* Vol. 23, Nr. 1 (winter), pp. 3–25.

[15] Z. Pozsar et al., (2013), Ibid. p. 3; T. Adrian, and H. S. Shin, (2010), Liquidity and Leverage, *Journal of Financial Intermediation* Vol. 19, Nr. 3 (July), pp. 418–437; J. Geanakoplos, (2010), The Leverage Cycle, in Daron Acemoglu, Kenneth Rogoff, and Michael Woodford, (eds.), NBER Macroeconomics Annual 2009 University of Chicago Press, Chicago.

[16] N. Gennaioli, A. Shleifer, and R. Vishny, (2013), A Model of Shadow Banking, Journal of Finance, *The Journal of Finance* Volume Vol. 68, Issue 4 (August), pp. 1331–1363, demonstrating the link between shadow banking and neglected risk; Z. Pozsar et al., (2013), Ibid. p. 3.

[17] Z. Pozsar et al. (2013), Ibid. p. 3.

[18] Z. Pozsar et al. (2013), Ibid. p. 3.

[19] See for both: T. Adrian, and H. S. Shin, (2009), The Shadow Banking System: Implications for Financial Regulation, Banque de France Financial Stability Review, Nr. 13 (September), pp. 1–10; Z. Pozsar, (2008), The Rise and Fall of the Shadow Banking System, Moody's economy.com

diation activities. Relative to direct lending (i.e. savers lending directly to borrowers), banks issue safe, demandable deposits, thus removing the need for savers to monitor the risk-taking behavior of these institutions. That is our traditional view on banking as described by Pozsar et al.[20] Pozsar et al. advance to define three core elements of shadow banking, that is,

> credit intermediation, the subset of financial intermediation that involves borrowing and lending through credit instruments, consists of credit, maturity, and liquidity transformation. Credit transformation refers to the enhancement of the credit quality of debt issued by the intermediary through the use of priority of claims. For example, the credit quality of senior deposits is better than the credit quality of the underlying loan portfolio, owing to the presence of more junior claims. Maturity transformation refers to the use of short-term deposits to fund long-term loans, which creates liquidity for the saver but exposes the intermediary to rollover and duration-mismatch risks. Liquidity transformation refers to the use of liquid instruments to fund illiquid assets. For example, a pool of illiquid whole loans might trade at a lower price than a liquid rated security secured by the same loan pool, as certification by a credible rating agency would reduce information asymmetries between borrowers and savers.[21]

Pozsar et al. add to that that '[c]redit intermediation is frequently enhanced through the use of third-party liquidity and credit guarantees, generally in the form of liquidity or credit put options'.[22] They lay out the framework by which official enhancements are analyzed.[23] Official enhancements to credit intermediation can be classified into four categories, depending on whether they are direct or indirect and explicit or implicit[24]:

1. Liabilities with 'direct' official enhancement. These stay on the balance sheet of the financial institution. Off-balance-sheet liabilities are obviously only indirectly enhanced by the public sector/taxpayer. Similar institutions are available in Europe and elsewhere around the world, although often using different mechanisms and embedded into different policy objectives.
2. Activities with a 'direct' by 'implicit' official enhancement including debt issued or guaranteed by government-sponsored enterprises. They benefit from an implicit credit put by the taxpayer.
3. Liabilities with indirect official enhancement generally include the off-balance-sheet activities of depository institutions, such as unfunded credit card loan commitments and lines of credits to conduits.

[20] Z. Pozsar et al. (2013), Ibid. pp. 3–4.

[21] Z. Pozsar et al. (2013), Ibid. pp. 3–4.

[22] For further details: Z. Pozsar et al. (2013), Ibid. p. 4.

[23] See also: R. C. Merton, (1977) An Analytical Derivation of the Cost of Deposit Insurance and Loan Guarantees: An Application of Modern Option Pricing Theory, *Journal of Banking and Finance* Vol.1, Nr. 1 (June), pp. 3–11; R. C. Merton, and Z. Bodie, (1993) Deposit Insurance Reform: A Functional Approach, Carnegie-Rochester Conference Series on Public Policy 38, June, pp. 1–34.

[24] See for an extensive write-up of the categories: Z. Pozsar et al. (2013), Ibid. p. 4.

4. Activities with indirect and implicit official enhancement include asset management activities such as bank-affiliated hedge funds and money market mutual funds as well as the securities lending of custodian banks.

Finally, some activities do not benefit from any form of official enhancement and are said to be unenhanced, for example, guarantees made by monoline insurance companies. Further, the securities lending activities of insurance companies, pension funds and certain asset managers do not benefit from access to official liquidity either. Therefore shadow credit intermediation can be defined to include all credit intermediation activities that are implicitly enhanced, indirectly enhanced or unenhanced by official guarantees.[25]

The Topology of Pre-Crisis Shadow Banking Activities and Liabilities can therefore be constructed as a construction of direct and indirect public enhancements which are either explicit or implicit in nature.[26]

2.2.2 Historical Evolution and Categorization of Shadow Banking Activities

In this subsection, I will review the historical evolution of the shadow banking market which will also explain to a large degree the categorization of the shadow banking market as we know it (or at least knew it). As Pozsar[27] argues, the rise of the CDO market and the fact that these tools changed in nature from being initially used to manage and mitigate tools to sources of credit risk itself happened in tandem with the increasing use of special-purpose vehicles (SPVs). That evolution went hand-in-hand with another very crucial dynamic, that is, the credit business model at financial institutions changed from 'originate-to-maturity' to 'originate-to-distribute'.

2.2.2.1 Changing Business Models in the Financial Sector

Regulation, innovation and competition reshaped the standard business model in the financial industry since the late 1980s. That old model consisted of borrowing short, lending long and then holding the loan to maturity as an investment (the 'originate-to-hold' or the 'originate-to-maturity' model).[28] That has migrated to an 'originate-to-distribute model'. The direct implication was that the way risk was managed and mitigated and the credit intermediation process functioned totally changed in dynamics including how and who absorbed the ultimate credit risk of these products. The credit risk more and more was absorbed by the capital markets and less by the balance sheets of the banks.

The implication is that, now that the capital markets absorb the ultimate credit risk due to the new originate-to-distribute model, the business requires (or actually 'implies')

---

[25] Z. Pozsar et al. (2013), Ibid. p. 4.

[26] See table 1 at Z. Pozsar et al. (2013), Ibid. pp. 5–6 for a full overview of the different categories.

[27] Z. Pozsar, (2008), The Rise and Fall of the Shadow Banking System, Moody's Regional Financial Review, July, pp. 13–25.

[28] Pozsar (2008), Ibid. p. 13.

continuously liquid money and securities markets to run through the typical supply chain of asset originators, asset packagers and asset managers.

Although the first MBS ('mortgage-backed securities') were issued in the late 1970s, it has grown increasingly more complex in the following two decades to a large degree caused by securitization of increasingly more risky loans and whereby the system became more opaque and less transparent that in the initial period. This process was fueled by loose monetary policy and low interest rates.[29]

The initial CDOs were created by pooling corporate loans. These loans were pooled in the balance sheet of the bank (i.e. the assets of the CDO) and then sliced the asset pool by on the intrinsic riskiness of the underlying loans. That created A, B, C, ... tranches with increasing intrinsic riskiness. From senior tranches (least risky) to the mezzanine tranches (increased risky) to the equity riskiness (most risky).[30]

The rationale on behalf of the banks is clear. Following the introduction of the Basel accord,[31] the banks had to hold more capital against their risk-weighted assets. Either they reduced the amount of risky assets, that is, their loan book to corporate and individuals thereby reducing their market share and profitability, or one reduced the intrinsic riskiness of the assets one has on its balance sheet. This pooling and tranching of loans allowed banks to sell credit risk in concentrated forms using equity tranches and to hold on to credit risk in diluted form through senior tranches, allowing them to set aside a much smaller amount of capital than for whole loans.

2.2.2.2 Ex Cathedra: Capital Relief Transactions[32]

In fact, there is quite a parallel with the capital relief transactions (CRTs) which have become popular in the years after the financial crisis and which have caused concerns by regulators and academics that they have the potential, in a similar way as the structured products, to undermine the robustness of the financial system.

Under a CRT, a bank pays a third party, such as a hedge fund or pension fund, to take on some of the risk associated with its loans. That makes it easier for the bank to meet regulators' capital-to-risk requirements. CRTs often involve complex structures in which special-purpose companies are set up to provide protection to the bank through a credit default swap (CDS), a derivatives contract that pays the buyer if a designated bond or loan portfolio defaults, and are in turn funded through the sale of notes to investors. As

[29] Pozsar (2008), Ibid. p. 13.

[30] Pozsar (2008), Ibid. p. 13.

[31] Basel II requires a 35% risk weight on residential mortgages, a 20% risk weight on AAA-rated residential MBSs and a mere 7% risk weight on AAA-rated tranches of ABS CDOs that invest in residential MBSs. The sizes of these risk weights are logical, as individual mortgages are riskier than an MBS that invests in a pool of thousands of individual mortgages. Furthermore, the AAA-rated tranches are protected by overcollateralization and subordination. Similarly, CDOs investing in a diversified pool of MBS tranches have more credit enhancement built in through an extra layer of overcollateralization and subordination.

[32] See J. Kahn and L. Vaughan, (2013), Banks Allying With Hedge Funds as Capital Rules Bite, September 13, via Bloomberg.com

in the run-up to the financial crisis, today's widespread use of CRTs could mask banks' true financial condition and make it difficult to spot systemic risks.[33]

Under Basel III, a set of rules that started to come into effect in 2014, banks are required to have enough capital to cover 8% of their risk-weighted assets, with an increasing share consisting of equity and retained earnings. Before Basel III, banks had to hold only 2% in this so-called core tier 1 capital; by 2019, that has risen to 4.5% and total capital ratios will have to be as high as 13%.

Basel III requires banks to raise the ratio of their capital to their assets, which are weighted according to their risk. The rules reduce the types of capital that banks can count toward the ratio while increasing the amount of assets they must offset. CRTs help banks by lowering the risk weight assigned to their assets, allowing the institutions to reach the capital target without raising additional funds. For example, a portfolio of loans to small and medium-sized companies might have a risk weight of 6%, based on historical losses. That means the bank would have to hold in reserve capital equal to 6% of the portfolio to cover potential losses.

By transferring the risk of default to a hedge fund through a CRT, the bank can reduce the risk weight of the portfolio to well below 1%. In the past, during the CDO era, parties could sell uncollateralized credit-default protection. Under Basel III regulations adopted so far, US and European regulators will no longer grant banks significant capital relief for a CRT unless the CRT investor posts enough collateral, in the form of cash or low-risk securities such as US Treasuries, to cover all possible defaults in the slice of the portfolio they're insuring.

Most CRTs reduce the capital a bank has to hold against a particular pool of loans by 65–85%. The instruments in its basic format can be used to hedge the credit risk is in the loan portfolios but the reduced capital needs can take over as a document argument for a bank to enter into those arrangements.

That was how things went 'in the beginning', but over time the balance sheet CDOs that were essentially there to fine-tune risk on balance sheet coming from loan portfolios of banks and to manage capital requirements changed in nature and were increasingly used 'to pool traded wholesale loans and corporate bonds, earning a spread between the yield offered on these assets and the payment made to various tranches (arbitrage CDOs)'.[34] The originate-to-mature model changed into an originate-to-distribute and

[33] At the end of 2012, Citigroup completed a CRT with New York-based private-equity firm Blackstone Group LP (BX). The deal enabled Citigroup to reduce by as much as 90% the amount of capital it had to hold against a USD 1 billion portfolio of shipping loans. In return for insuring the bank against some potential losses on the loans, Blackstone is earning returns of about 15% annually. Citi indicated the purpose of the deal was to mitigate credit risk in the bank's loan book and increase its ability to lend to the shipping sector. The evolution and consequences of this deal are in my understanding very similar to the CDO evolution during the last decade. The sequence of creating instruments to shift risk off-balance, freedom up balance sheet space in order to provide even more funding on the same small capital base, assuming we can all agree that Basel III has not 'materially' increased the regulatory capital needs for banks but only marginally. The CRTs are, just like CDO, financed in the capital markets. Getting closer to systemic risk is hardly impossible.

[34] Z. Pozsar, (2008), Ibid. p. 14.

accordingly the role of CDOs changed from one of repackaging existing loans and bonds to one of facilitating the creation of new loans.[35]

Not only had the nature of the CDOs and the reason for using and creating them changed but also the underlying assets that were repackaged. From 2006 onward the CDO market grew considerably, to a very large degree driven by the attractive yields, which were considerably larger than the yields on comparably rated corporate or sovereign instruments. That was an attractive play for those institutions that were struggling to earn sufficient yield on their fixed income investment.

Securitization as a technique has been around for decades now and as such there is nothing that morally nor technically can be argued against using it. In the wake of the financial crisis, securitization took a nosedive but from 2012 onward, the technique re-emerged. Ultimately, what was toxic was the content of the CDO, not the CDO itself.

The comeback of securitization is related to the growth in economic activity: in order for car loans to be securitized, say, consumers have to be buying cars. Investors desperate for yield are also stimulating supply: securitized paper can offer decent returns, particularly at the riskier end of the spectrum. Support comes out of remarkable corner: policy makers want to get more credit flowing to the economy and are happy to rehabilitate once-suspect financial practices to get there.

In Europe, where there is more reliance on bank funding than in the US (where the capital markets take a larger stake in financing companies), its banks need more capital, and absent that are the weak link in the nascent recovery because they fail to meet demand for credit from consumers and small businesses. This is in large part because regulators want banks to be less risky, by increasing the ratio of equity to loans. As banks are reluctant to raise capital, they need to shed assets. This is where securitization helps: by bundling up the loans on their books (which form part of their assets) and selling them to outside investors, such as asset managers or insurance firms, banks can both slim their balance sheet and improve capital ratios. Securitization airlifts assets off the balance sheets of banks, freeing up capital, and drops them onto the balance sheets of real-money investors.

That may not seem urgent now, as Europe's banks are flooded with cheap money from the European Central Bank (ECB) and have years before stricter capital ratios officially kick in. But at some point, markets will have to take over financing banks. Such airlifts would neatly transform Europe's inflexible bank-led system into something more akin to America's.[36] The good news is that, in contrast to prior to the 2008 crisis, and in order to avoid deteriorating underwriting conditions, those involved in creating securitized products will have to retain some of the risk linked to the original loan, thus keeping skin in the game.

---

[35] Z. Pozsar, (2008), Ibid. p. 14.

[36] See in detail: The Economist, (2014), Back from the Dead: The Return of Securitization, January 11.

2.3 The Investors in the Shadow Banking Market Before the Crisis

In its original format, the tranching of different levels of risk is honest and genuine. Different investors with different risk appetite and different types of balance sheets could shop for the product that provided them with the most adequate risk-return profile they could justify.[37] In effect, the losses associated with mezzanine and equity tranches did end up being well diversified. So, the whole rationale made sense. Those who ended up with the most risky parts of the CDO capital structure often hedged their positions avoiding material impact on their balance sheet when losses had to be taken. But that is not where the problem was. In contrast, however, senior exposures did not end up dispersed at all, as they stayed with a small group of banks and monoline insurers.[38]

2.4 The Emerging Structure of the Shadow Banking Market

The accumulation of massive amounts of senior and super-senior CDO tranches in SIVs and the build-up of enormous securitization pipelines through conduits formed a network of highly levered off-balance-sheet vehicles that constituted a shadow banking system.[39]

Comparing the traditional model what was called originate-to-distribute model, we get the following picture: under the traditional model, short-term funding and long-term lending occurred on banks' singular balance sheets—and loans were held on to as investments. Loan portfolios were kept diversified and those systemic risks that were impossible to diversify away were hedged by building up reserves of liquid and safe assets to be used as cushions during bad times. Contrast this to the new model where loans are sold after they are originated, and then are securitized into ABSs. ABS tranches are re-securitized into CDOs, which might even be re-securitized further into other CDOs. The senior tranches of CDOs (themselves long-term credit instruments) are held by banks as investments in off-balance-sheet SIVs, which rely on short-term funding in the ABCP market, where the bulk of funds were provided by money market funds (MMFs)—the modern-day equivalents of bank deposits. Thus, credit intermediation still means borrowing short and lending long, even in the originate-to-distribute model.[40] But, while the originate-to-distribute model allowed for credit risk to be sliced, diced and dispersed, it did not eliminate credit risk itself, Pozsar comments.[41]

---

[37] Z. Pozsar, (2008), Ibid. p. 16.

[38] See for details Z. Pozsar, (2008), Ibid. p. 16.

[39] See for a visualization: Z. Pozsar, (2008), Ibid. p. 18. The appendix to the article provides a roadmap and guidance to the visualization (pp. 22–25).

[40] Z. Pozsar, (2008), Ibid. p. 17.

[41] Z. Pozsar, (2008), Ibid. p. 19.

Three takeaways from the emerging shadow banking structure can be reported: (1) through the originate-to-distribute model, the regulated banking system created far more credit and offered far more liquidity guarantees than what their capital bases were able to support, (2) the originate-to-distribute model and the strong demand for and from CDOs also enabled and encouraged the underwriting of some loans (subprime mortgages and leveraged loans) that would never have been made if banks had to hold on to them as whole loans, (3) the originate-to-distribute model empowered credit markets to grow very large in size and significance relative to regulated banks in the credit intermediation process, but without access to a safety net that was available for regulated banks in times of stress.[42]

2.5 The Size and Design of the Shadow Banking Market

2.5.1 The Credit Intermediation Process

The shadow banking industry is built around two essential components, that is, securitization and wholesale funding. Also, the shadow banking industry is built, like traditional banking, around intermediation. The difference in that intermediation process between shadow and traditional banking is that in contrast to traditional banking, where credit intermediation is performed 'under one roof'—that of a bank—in the shadow banking system it is performed through a chain of non-bank financial intermediaries in a multi-step process. These steps entail the 'vertical slicing' of traditional banks' credit intermediation process and include (1) loan origination, (2) loan warehousing, (3) ABS issuance, (4) ABS warehousing, (5) ABS CDO issuance, (6) ABS 'intermediation' and (7) wholesale funding.[43] The shadow banking system performs these steps of intermediation in a strict, sequential order. Each step is handled by a specific type of shadow bank and through a specific funding technique. Each of those seven steps takes place in the shadow banking system itself, often executed by different parties in the process, some being specialized shadow banking institutions and some by traditional banking intermediaries like commercial banks and insurance companies.

Those seven steps can be described as follows[44]:

1. Loan origination of car loans, leases and (non-conforming) mortgages is performed by traditional finance companies who itself are funded by commercial paper and medium-term notes (MTNs).
2. The leading forward of those loans ('loan warehousing') happens through multi- and single seller conduits and is often funded through asset-backed commercial paper (ABCP).

[42] Z. Pozsar, (2008), Ibid. pp. 19–20.
[43] Z. Pozsar et al. (2013), Ibid. pp. 6–7.
[44] Z. Pozsar et al. (2013), Ibid. pp. 6–7.

3. The pooling and structuring of loans into asset-backed securities happens through broker-dealers' ABS syndicate desk.
4. ABS warehousing is then facilitated through trading books and is funded through repurchase agreements, total return swaps or hybrid and repo conduits.
5. The pooling and structuring of ABS into CDOs are also conducted by broker-dealers' ABS syndicate desks.
6. The ABS intermediation is performed by limited-purpose finance companies, structured investment vehicles (SIVs), securities arbitrage conduits and credit hedge funds, which are funded in a variety of ways including, for example, repos, ABCP, MTNs, bonds and capital notes.
7. The funding of all-of-the-above activities and entities is conducted in wholesale funding markets by funding providers such as regulated and unregulated money market intermediaries and direct money market investors (such as securities lenders).[45]

Now, the seven-step process indicated is a blueprint model. In reality, processes can be shorter or longer. Pozsar et al. illustrate that, for example, an intermediation chain might stop at step two if a pool of prime auto loans is sold by a captive finance company to a bank-sponsored multi-seller conduit for term warehousing purposes.

Typically, the poorer an underlying loan pool's quality at the beginning of the chain, the longer the credit intermediation chain will be to allow shadow credit intermediation to transform long-term, risky, opaque assets into short-term and less risky highly rated assets that can be used as collateral in short-term money markets.[46]

In conclusion, the intermediation chain always starts with origination and ends with wholesale funding, and each shadow bank appears only once in the process. The lower the quality of the underlying long-term loans, the longer the process will take. The shorter-term and higher quality the underlying loans (e.g. car loans), the shorter the transformation process will be.

2.5.2 The Shadow Banking System Dissected

Traditionally three subgroups of the shadow banking system are distinguished: (1) the government-sponsored shadow banking subsystem, (2) the 'internal' shadow banking subsystem and (3) the 'external' shadow banking subsystem.[47]

1. The Government-Sponsored Shadow Banking System

Historically, this was the first leg of the shadow banking system to emerge. With the creation of the Federal Home Loan Banks (FHLB) system in 1932, the Federal National Mortgage Association (Fannie Mae) in 1938, the Government National Mortgage

[45] For a visual see Z. Pozsar et al. (2013), Ibid. p. 8.

[46] Z. Pozsar et al. (2013), Ibid. p. 7.

[47] See extensively: Z. Pozsar et al. (2013), Ibid. pp. 8–12.

Association (Ginnie Mae) in 1968 and the Federal Home Loan Mortgage Corporation (Freddie Mac) in 1970, the government created shadow banking institutions that implicitly were enjoying backstops on their liabilities provided by the, in this case, US taxpayer. Over time, they developed five distinct intermediation techniques[48]:

1. Term loan warehousing provided to banks by the FHLB (Federal Home Loan Banks)
2. Credit risk transfer and transformation through credit insurance provided by the shadow banking institutions
3. Originate-to-distribute securitization functions provided for banks by the shadow banking institutions
4. Maturity transformation conducted through the shadow banking institutions' retained portfolios
5. Pass-through MBS funding of mortgage credit

In those techniques, these government-backed shadow banks did not originate loans themselves but also processed them and funding them. They are prohibited from loan origination. They create a secondary market for mortgages to facilitate their funding.

2. The Internal Shadow Banking System

In parallel to the government-backed shadow banking system, a fully-fledged shadow banking system emerged. Starting in the 1980s, commercial banks re-invented themselves from low performing and low return utility companies who originated loans and held them until maturity into high performance and high return on equity (ROE) that developed shadow banking activities that increased profitability. The sector changed from being a credit-risk-sensitive, deposit-funded, spread-based business to a less/limited credit-risk-sensitive wholesale-funded process.[49] Indeed, the typical shadow banking activities were executed off balance sheet through various subsidiaries.

BHCs typically engage in the following activities: (1) originate loans in their bank or finance company subsidiaries; (2) warehouse and accumulate loans in off-balance-sheet conduits that are managed by their broker-dealer subsidiaries, with funding through wholesale funding markets and liquidity enhancements by bank subsidiaries; (3) securitize loans through their broker-dealer subsidiaries by transferring them from the conduit into bankruptcy-remote special-purpose vehicles and (4) fund the safest tranches of structured credit assets in off-balance-sheet ABS intermediaries (such as SIVs) that are managed from the asset management subsidiary of the holding company and are funded through wholesale funding markets with backstops by the bank subsidiaries.[50]

[48] Z. Pozsar et al. (2013), Ibid. p. 8.

[49] Z. Pozsar et al. (2013), Ibid. p. 9.

[50] Z. Pozsar et al. (2013), Ibid. pp. 9–10. See for a visual overview: http://www.newyorkfed.org/research/economists/adrian/1306adri_A2.pdf

According to Pozsar et al., three key elements are relevant in this respect:

To begin with, the process of lending and the uninterrupted flow of credit to the real economy no longer rely only on banks, but on a process that spans a network of banks, broker-dealers, asset managers and shadow banks funded through wholesale funding and capital markets globally.

Second, bank subsidiaries' only direct involvement in the shadow credit intermediation process is at the loan origination level. The indirect involvement of commercial bank subsidiaries is broader.

Third, securitization techniques have increased the implicit leverage of bank holding companies, sometimes called 'capital efficiency'.[51]

3. The External Shadow Banking System

The external layer of the shadow banking system consists of a global network of balance sheets. The origination, warehousing and securitization of loans are conducted mainly from the US, but the funding and maturity transformation of structured credit assets are conducted from the US, Europe and offshore financial centers.[52] The external shadow banking system is characterized[53] by (1) the credit intermediation of the broker-dealers; (2) the credit intermediation process of independent, non-bank specialist intermediaries and (3) the credit puts provided by private credit-risk repositories.

1. Diversified Broker-Dealers

These include the stand-alone investment banks as they existed prior to 2008 as diversified broker-dealers (DBDs).

2. The Independent-Specialists-Based Credit Intermediation Process

The credit intermediation process that runs through a network of independent specialists is the same as those of FHCs (Federal Housing Company) and DBDs (diversified broker-dealers) and results in the same credit intermediation functions as those performed by traditional banks. The independent-specialists-based intermediation process includes the following types of entities: stand-alone and captive finance companies on the loan origination side, independent multi-seller conduits on the loan warehousing side[54] and limited-purpose finance companies, independent SIVs and credit hedge funds on the ABS intermediation side.

---

[51] Z. Pozsar et al. (2013), Ibid. p. 10.

[52] Z. Pozsar et al. (2013), Ibid. p. 10.

[53] Pozsar et al. (2013), Ibid. pp. 10–13.

[54] Captive finance companies are finance companies that are owned by non-financial corporations, typically manufacturing firms or homebuilders. They are used to provide vendor financing to the clients of their parents and benefit from cross-guarantees. Stand-alone finance companies, as the name suggests, stand on their own and are not subsidiaries of any corporate entity. See Pozsar et al. (2013), Ibid. footnote 8 p. 11.

3. Private Credit-Risk Repositories

The shadow credit intermediation processes of independent specialists, BHCs and DBDs rely heavily on private credit-risk repositories.[55] Private risk repositories specialize in providing credit transformation services in the shadow banking system and include mortgage insurers, monoline insurers, diversified insurance companies and credit hedge funds. These entities facilitate the securitization process by providing tail-risk insurance for structured credit products in various forms. Different credit-risk repositories correspond to specific stages of the shadow credit intermediation process.[56]

Effectively, the various forms of credit put options provided by private risk repositories absorb tail risk from loan pools, turning the enhanced securities into less risky ones (at least from the perspective of investors prior to the crisis).[57]

In conclusion, the shadow banking system has three subsystems that intermediate different types of credit in fundamentally different ways. The shadow banking system was shaped to a large degree by the unique mix of economic and regulatory conditions that came together during the period 2005–2008. Nevertheless, those institutions that were able to develop a competitive edge, by not being driven by regulatory arbitrage, have built a parallel banking system the economy benefited from.

It is fair to say that over the last couple of decades, many traditional banking activities have been pushed out into the shadow banking system. The jury is still out to what the shadow banking system can remain stable or autonomously stabilize over the different credit cycles without the help of official credit and liquidity puts. The answer to that question has significant policy implications. Either the backstops that are available to the traditional banking sector should be extended to the shadow banking sector or alternatively the shadow banking sector needs to be severely constrained and regulated.[58]

What we do know is that the emergency lending facilities made available by governments after the fall of Lehman Brothers qualified as a backstop to all seven steps in the process discussed.[59]

While much of the current and future reform efforts are focused on remediating the excesses of the recent credit bubble, it can be observed that increased capital and liquidity standards for depository institutions and insurance companies are likely to increase the returns to shadow banking activity.

---

[55] See further: http://www.newyorkfed.org/research/economists/adrian/1306adri_A5.pdf

[56] CDS was also used for hedging warehouse and counterparty exposures. For example, a broker-dealer with a large exposure to subprime MBS that it warehoused for an ABS CDO deal in the making could purchase CDS protection on its MBS warehouse. In turn, the broker-dealer could also purchase protection (a counterparty hedge) from a credit hedge fund or credit derivative product company on the counterparty providing the CDS protection on subprime MBS. See further Z. Pozsar et al. (2013), Ibid. p. 12.

[57] Z. Pozsar et al. (2013), Ibid. p. 12.

[58] See also: http://www.newyorkfed.org/research/economists/adrian/1306adri_A6.pdf

[59] http://www.newyorkfed.org/research/economists/adrian/1306adri_A7.pdf and http://www.newyorkfed.org/research/economists/adrian/1306adri_A8.pdf

2.6 Temporary Conclusions

Beyond the fact that we now understand the drivers behind the emergence of the shadow banking industry and its role in the recent financial crisis, we have come to understand that the increasingly important nexus between the banking sector and the capital markets overall, something that was not or at least less the case prior to the emergence of the shadow banking system. That has distinct policy implications, that is, the success of macroprudential regulation will depend on being able to internalize the externalities that are generated in the shadow banking system. Before the current financial crisis, the global economy was often described as being 'awash with liquidity', meaning that the supply of credit was plentiful. The financial crisis has led to a drying up of this particular metaphor. Understanding the nature of liquidity in this sense leads us to the importance of financial intermediaries in a financial system built around capital markets, and the critical role played by monetary policy in regulating credit supply.[60] The supply of credit (or at least the credit risk) is increasingly born by capital markets rather than the banking sector. Traditionally, banks were the dominant suppliers of credit, but their role has increasingly been supplanted by market-based institutions—especially those involved in the securitization process. Across the world, with a few notable exceptions, 'market-based assets' (i.e. broker-dealers assets) are considerably larger than the bank assets, non-financial corporate assets and household assets.[61]

The role of securitization in the process has been largely discussed above. There was a reason for that: the fluctuations of market funding conditions have important implications for financial stability and international capital flows. Indeed, there is an intimate connection between the emergence of subprime mortgages and the large US external deficits in the period 2005–2007. The chain that ties the two is securitization. It was discussed how securitization works and how it was supposed to distribute risk among those investors that can tolerate specific types of risk and also how in reality it has led to a concentration of risk. And there was a reason for that. As Adrian and Song (2009) explain: Banks and other intermediaries wanted to increase their leverage—to become more indebted—so as to spice up their short-term profit. So, rather than dispersing risks evenly throughout the economy, banks and other intermediaries bought each other's securities with borrowed money. As a result, far from dispersing risks, securitization had the perverse effect of concentrating all the risks in the banking system itself.[62] Increased leverage leads to global imbalances.

In a traditional banking system that intermediates between retail depositors and ultimate borrowers, the total quantity of deposits represents the obligation of the banking system to creditors outside the banking system.

However, securitization opens up potentially new sources of funding for the banking system by tapping new creditors. The new creditors who buy the securitized claims include pension funds, mutual funds and insurance companies, as well as foreign investors such as foreign central banks. Foreign central banks have been a particularly important funding source for residential mortgage lending in the US. When the claims and obligations between

[60] T. Adrian and H. S. Shin, (2009), The Shadow Banking System: Implications for Financial Regulation, Federal Reserve Bank of New York Staff Reports, Nr. 382, July 2009.

[61] See for datasets and visuals Adrian and Shin, Ibid. (2009), pp. 1–6.

[62] Adrian and Shin (2009), Ibid. p. 11.

leveraged entities have been netted out, the lending to ultimate borrowers must be funded either from the equity of the intermediary sector or by borrowing from creditors outside the intermediary sector. When balance sheets are aggregated across banks, all the claims and obligations between banks cancel out. So, the aggregate balance sheet for the banking sector as a whole could then be constructed as follows: **Total lending to firms and households (Assets) = Total equity + Liabilities to non-bank (Deposits + securitized debt).**[63] Consequently, aggregate lending to end-user borrowers by the banking system must be financed either by the equity in the banking system or by borrowing from creditors outside the banking system.

When the financial crisis hit, obviously the investors in prioritized products took a hit, but the banks took a larger hit, that is, the large financial intermediaries are more exposed in the sense that they face the danger of seeing their capital wiped out. The severity of the credit crisis lies precisely in the fact that the bad loans were not all passed on to final investors. The increased supply of credit caused the need for new assets to finance a process that took longer than the expansion process of bank's balance sheets being financing by the capital markets directly. The slack in balance sheet capacity needed to be used up.[64]

2.7 The Implications of a Market-Based Financial System

In a market-based financial system, banking and capital market developments are inseparable, and funding conditions are closely tied to fluctuations in the leverage of market-based financial intermediaries. Offering a window on liquidity, the balance sheet growth of broker-dealers provides a sense of the availability of credit. Contractions of broker-dealer balance sheets have tended to precede declines in real economic growth, even before the 2008–2009 turmoil. Market-based credit has seen the most dramatic contraction in the current financial crisis. The most dramatic fall is in the subprime category, but credit supply of all categories has collapsed, ranging from auto loans, credit card loans and student loans.[65] However, the drying up of credit in the capital markets would have been missed if one paid attention to bank-based lending only. Commercial bank lending has picked up pace after the start of the financial crisis, even as market-based providers of credit have contracted rapidly. Banks have traditionally played the role of a buffer for their borrowers in the face of deteriorating market conditions (as during the 1998 crisis) and appear to be playing a similar role in the current crisis. Referring back to the leverage example above and bringing in the haircuts (Table 2.1) on the repo agreements during the initial part of the financial crisis, the following conclusions can be drawn.

[63] Adrian and Shin (2009), Ibid. p. 12.

[64] For more details, see D. Greenlaw, J. Hatzius, A. Kashyap and H.S. Shin, (2008), Leveraged Losses: Lessons from the Mortgage Market Meltdown, US Monetary Policy Forum Report, Nr. 2. FSF-CGFS Working Group, (2009), The Role of Valuation and Leverage in Procyclicality, CGFS Papers Nr. 34: T. Adrian and H. S. Shin (2009), Money, Liquidity and Monetary Policy, NY FED Staff Report Nr. 360.

[65] T. Adrian and H. S. Shin, (2009), Money, Liquidity and Monetary Policy, Federal Bank of New York Staff Report, Nr. 390, January 2009, p. 3.

Table 2.1 Haircuts on repo agreements (%)

Securities	April 2009	August 2009
US treasuries	0.25	3
Investment grade bonds	0–3	8–12
High-yield bonds	10–15	25–40
Equities	15	20
Senior leveraged loans	10–12	15
Mezzanine leveraged loans	18–25	35+
Prime MBS	2–4	10–20
ABS	3–5	50–60

Source: IMF, (2008), Global Financial Stability Report, April, Washington

The fluctuations in leverage resulting from shifts in funding conditions are closely associated with epochs of financial booms and busts. Fluctuations in funding conditions have an impact on macroeconomic variables. Adrian and Shin[66] provide more detail and also show that commercial bank assets have no such predictive feature as consistent with the earlier literature which found little relationship between commercial bank asset growth and macroeconomic variables. They show that monetary policy has a direct impact on broker-dealer asset growth via short-term interest rates, yield spread and risk measures.

Adrian and Shin conclude that in a hypothetical world where deposit-taking banks are the only financial intermediaries, their liabilities as measured by traditional monetary aggregates—such as M2—would be good indicators of the aggregate size of the balance sheets of leveraged institutions. Instead, they have emphasized market-based liabilities such as repos and commercial paper as better indicators of credit conditions that influence the economy. Their results highlight the ways that monetary policy and policies toward financial stability are linked. When the financial system as a whole holds long-term, illiquid assets financed by short-term liabilities, any tensions resulting from a sharp pullback in leverage will show up somewhere in the system.[67] In a financial system in which balance sheets are continuously marked to market, asset price changes appear immediately as changes in net worth, eliciting responses from financial intermediaries who adjust the size of their balance sheets. Adrian and Shin[68] evidence that marked-to-market leverage is strongly procyclical. Such behavior has aggregate consequences.

---

[66] T. Adrian, and H. S. Shin (2008), Financial Intermediaries, Financial Stability, and Monetary Policy, Federal Reserve Bank of Kansas City 2008 Jackson Hole Economic Symposium Proceedings.

[67] Adrian and Shin (2009), Ibid. p. 11. See also T. Adrian, et al., (2009), Global Liquidity and Exchange Rates, Federal Reserve Bank of New York, Harvard University, and Princeton University, Federal Reserve Bank of New York Staff paper, Nr. 361; T. Adrian, et al., (2010), Asset Prices, Macroeconomic Dynamics, and Financial Intermediation, Federal Reserve Bank of New York and Princeton University, Federal Reserve Bank of New York Staff paper, Nr. 422. T. Adrian and H. S. Shin, (2008), Financial Intermediary Leverage and Value at Risk, Federal Reserve Bank of New York Staff Reports, Nr. 338; B. Holmström and J. Tirole, (1997), Financial Intermediation, Loanable Funds, and the Real Sector, *Quarterly Journal of Economics* Vol. 112, pp. 663–692; N. Kiyotaki, and J. Moore, (1997), Credit Cycles, *Journal of Political Economy* Vol. 105, pp. 211–248.

[68] T. Adrian and H. S. Shin, (2010), Liquidity and Leverage, Federal Reserve Bank of New York, Staff Paper, Nr. 328.

2.8 The Linkage of the Different National Shadow Banking Systems Based on Fund Flows[69]

The financial system channels savings from savers to those who draw on the savers' funds—from ultimate lenders to ultimate borrowers. Some credit will be directly provided from the lender to the borrower, as is the case with Treasury securities, municipal bonds and corporate bonds. A large part of the financing in today's economy is intermediated in wholesale money markets through banks and other financial intermediaries and lent in the capital markets. This is nowadays considered as shadow banking.

The idea is to get an understanding of the shadow banking system[70] in the broader context of the operation of the international capital markets, leveraging on the work by the IMF's Statistics Department (STA) on global flow of funds (GFF).

The new GFF conceptual framework[71] is aimed at constructing a GFF matrix, mapping domestic and external financial stocks which can be then broken down bilaterally (potentially) by the 30 or so jurisdictions identified by the IMF as hosting systemically important financial sectors. They account for about 90% of the cross-border claims. The methodology is particularly important as it is expected that the shadow banking system is expected to grow in the years to come.

Adrian et al. (2013)[72] list several reasons for why the shadow banking system may arise, such as specialization and regulatory arbitrage, and they also list the potential costs of the shadow banking system, such as the leverage cycle, funding fragilities and neglected risks. A broader question is what role the international context plays in the fluctuations in the size of the shadow banking system. A useful distinction in this regard is that between core and noncore liabilities of the banking and intermediation sector more generally.[73]

Core liabilities can be defined as the funding that the intermediaries draw on during normal times and is sourced (in the main) domestically. The constituents of core funding will depend on the context and the economy in question, but retail deposits of the domestic household sector would be a good first conjecture in defining core liabilities. When banking sector assets are growing strongly during a lending boom, the core funding avail-

---

[69] See in detail: L. Errico, et al., (2014), Mapping the Shadow Banking System through a Global Flow of Funds Analysis, IMF Working Paper, WP/14/10.

[70] Shadow banking for this purpose can be defined as a global space concept (matrix), which reaches outside traditional borders of banks and non-banks, and is quantified using a survey of financial liabilities covering institutions, markets and financial instruments. Therefore, the shadow banking defined in this paper combines non-core liabilities of other depository corporations (ODCs), also more commonly referred to as banks, and other financial corporations (OFCs).

[71] See Errico et al., (2014), annex 1 and 2 provide details on the Balance Sheet Approach Matrix Methodology, External Funds of Flow Matrix Methodology, pp. 41–47.

[72] T. Adrian, et al., (2013), Shadow Bank Monitoring, Federal Reserve Bank of New York Staff Report Nr. 638.

[73] H. S. Shin, and K. Shin, (2010), Procyclicality and Monetary Aggregates, NBER working Paper Nr. 16836.

able to the intermediary sector is likely to be insufficient to finance the rapid growth in new lending. That is, the pool of retail deposits is not likely to be sufficient to fund the increase in bank credit.[74] Such procyclical behavior of the banking sector has consequences for capital flows. When credit is expanding rapidly, outstripping the pool of available retail deposits, the bank will turn to other sources of funding to support its credit growth, typically from other banks operating as wholesale lenders in the capital market.[75]

As traditional deposit funding does not keep up with the credit growth, the banking sector's expansion is funded by noncore liabilities (in this example, from foreign creditors), building up vulnerabilities to deleveraging by foreign creditors. Noncore liabilities then equate the funding flows associated with the shadow banking system. The incidence of noncore liabilities of the banking system has value in signaling the onset of financial crises.[76] Whereas current account gaps have traditionally been considered as the determinant of capital flows, many recent research have drawn attention to the dramatic increase in gross capital flows, especially through the banking sector.[77] It was concluded that 'large gross financial flows entail potential stability risks that may be only distantly related, if related at all, to the global configuration of saving-investment discrepancies'.[78] The growth in capital flows was associated with increased leverage and the size of the banking sector as a whole. Within that space the interaction of global and local banks as the driver of fluctuations in financial conditions is of key importance[79] (infra).

The global Funds of Flow analysis has two dimensions[80]: One dimension is the mapping of the balance sheet of each sector to other sectors in the domestic economy and the rest of the world. The second dimension is the mapping of the external sector to all the jurisdictions globally.

---

[74] Errico et al. (2014), Ibid. p. 5.

[75] J.-H. Hahm, et al., (2013), Noncore Bank Liabilities and Financial Vulnerability, *Journal of Money, Credit and Banking* Vol. 45, Issue 1, August, pp. 3–36. (op. cit. Errico et al. (2014) Ibid. p. 6).

[76] Hahm et al. (2013), Ibid. (op. cit. Errico et al. (2014) Ibid. p. 6).

[77] Errico et al. (2014), Ibid. pp. 7–8; C. Borio, and P. Disyatat, (2011), Global Imbalances and the Financial Crisis: Link or no link?, BIS Working Papers Nr. 346; K. J. Forbes, and F. E. Warnock, (2012), Capital Flow Waves: Surges, Stops, Flight and Retrenchment, *Journal of International Economics*, Vol. 88, Issue 2, pp. 235–251; P. Lane, and B. Pels, (2011), Current Account Balances in Europe, Working Paper, Trinity College Dublin; M. Obstfeld, (2012), Does the Current Account Still Matter?, *American Economic Review*, Vol. 102, Issue 3, pp. 1–23; H. Rey, (2013), Dilemma not Trilemma: The Global Financial Cycle and Monetary Policy Independence, proceedings of the Federal Reserve Bank of Kansas City Economic Symposium at Jackson Hole.

[78] Obstfeld, (2012), Ibid. p. 3. (op. cit. Errico et al. (2014) Ibid. p. 6).

[79] M. Schularick, and M. Taylor, (2012), Credit Booms Gone Bust: Monetary Policy, Leverage Cycles, and Financial Crises, 1870–2008, *American Economic Review* Vol. 102, pp. 1029–1061; P.-O. Gourinchas, and M. Obstfeld, (2012), Stories of the Twentieth Century for the Twenty-First, *American Economic Journal: Macroeconomics*, Vol. 4, Issue 1, pp. 226–265. (op. cit. Errico et al. (2014) Ibid. p. 6).

[80] L. Errico, et al., (2013), Global Flow of Funds: Mapping Bilateral Geographic Flows, 59th International Statistical Institute (ISI) World Statistics Congress, Statistics Department, International Monetary Fund.

Errico et al.[81] illustrate the potential usefulness of GFF analysis in the context of identifying both the directions and the magnitudes of the capital flows associated with the shadow banking system in the US. Although retrospective the exercise provides many useful lessons on what types of data would have been informative during the boom phase and directs the policy makers to ask the right questions. Going forward, it holds out hopes that a more systematic application of the methods described in their paper may illuminate the nature of the link between capital flows between sectors.

Errico et al. use the balance sheet approach.[82] The matrix identifies nine sectors: eight domestic sectors and the non-residents sector. That allows to conclude the implication of foreign countries (and through which instruments) they participated in the credit intermediation between US savers and US borrowers. Earlier Shin[83] already provided additional evidence that some of the funding that was taken out of the US by the European banks were recycled back into the US for the purchase of non-Treasury securities and shares, so that the European banks became part of the overall intermediation system linking US savers and US borrowers.

The findings of the GFF matrix about the direction of flow and quantities behind those flows include[84]:

- First, the shadow banking system is intimately tied to the workings of the formal banking system—the ODCs sector, and so tracking the ODCs sector gives information on the composition of the flows in the shadow banking system.
- Second, in spite of the categorization of non-banks as 'Other Financial Corporations' (OFCs), the legal form of the claim can give estimates of the counterparty in the capital inflows through the purchase of securitized claims.
- The fact that deposits form the main part of the external claims and liabilities suggests that interbank claims form the bulk of the cross-border linkages for the US banking sector. Banks located in the UK play an important role in the US banking system.
- Around 50% of the assets of the prime MMFs are the obligations of European banks. Many European banks use a centralized funding model in which available funds are deployed globally through a centralized portfolio allocation decision.[85]

[81] Errico et al. (2014), Ibid. p. 9.

[82] More details see Errico et al. (2014), Ibid. pp. 9–13.

[83] H. S. Shin, (2012), Global Banking Glut and Loan Risk Premium, Mundell-Fleming Lecture, IMF Economic Review Vol. 60, Issue 2, pp. 155–192.

[84] Errico et al. (2014), Ibid. pp. 15–16. Bank for International Settlements, 2010, Funding Patterns and Liquidity Management of Internationally Active Banks, CGFS Paper Nr. 39, May 2010, Bank for International Settlements (BIS), (2011), Global Liquidity: Concept, Measurement and Policy Implications, CGFS Papers Nr. 45, Committee on the Global Financial System.

[85] Bank for International Settlements (BIS), (2010), Funding Patterns and Liquidity Management of Internationally Active Banks, CGFS Paper Nr. 39, May; C. Borio, and P. Disyatat, (2011), Global Imbalances and the Financial Crisis: Link or no link?, BIS Working Papers Nr. 346; V. Bruno, and H. S. Shin, (2012), Capital Flows, Cross-Border Banking and Global Liquidity, NBER Working Paper Nr. 19038.

- An important component of the capital outflows from the US through the banking sector is accounted for by the activity of foreign banks. Shin (2012) points to further evidence from the money market funds (MMFs) sector that the foreign banks engaged in sending funds to their headquarters were the European banks.

Measuring the broad categories of credit and funding involved in the US shadow banking (financial intermediary sector) system provided the following results. There are five subsectors in the US that are associated with financial intermediation—the US-chartered banking, credit unions, finance companies, security broker-dealers and the asset-backed securities (ABS) issuers. The two sectors that saw the greatest fluctuations (during 1995–2012) were the ABS-issuer sector and the security broker-dealer sector, both associated with the market-based intermediation sector where credit intermediation takes place through the securitization of financial claims.[86] Comparing these intermediation data with the expansion of the intermediary sector during and upward phase of the credit boom (supra), the ABS-issuer sector and broker-dealer sector could be seen as an approximation to the noncore liabilities of the intermediation system.[87]

Adrian and Ashcraft demonstrated the time path of relative sizes of funding sources of the US intermediation sector. It shows the gradual decline of the traditional funding sources of the banking sector in the form of deposits, and the relative increase in market-based funding sources.[88]

To confirm the significance of the capital flows associated with the shadow banking system for credit availability in the US and more generally, they run panel regressions with various loan categories within the financial system as being the dependent variable. With the exception of large corporates, most domestic firms and households engage with the international credit system only indirectly, with most positions intermediated by the domestic banking system. The capital flows associated with the shadow banking system, as it was shown in detail using the US as an example, affect the funding environment faced by domestic banks.[89]

Errico et al. conclude that the noncore liabilities of the intermediary sector are closely associated with the growth of lending which gives support to their initial premise on the role of noncore liabilities financing the marginal increase in lending during a boom. When intermediary assets are growing strongly during a lending boom, the pool of domestic retail deposits is not likely to be sufficient to fund the increase in

---

[86] T. Adrian, and H. S. Shin, (2010), The Changing Nature of Financial Intermediation and the Financial Crisis of 2007–09, *Annual Review of Economics*, Vol. 2, pp. 603–618. Errivo et al. (2014), Ibid. p. 25.

[87] Errico et al., (2014), Ibid. p. 25.

[88] T. Adrian, and A. B. Ashcraft, (2012), Shadow Banking: A Review of the Literature, Federal Reserve Bank of New York Staff Report Nr. 580.

[89] Errico et al., (2014), Ibid. p. 28. See also: V. Bruno, and H. S. Shin, (2012), Capital Flows, Cross-Border Banking and Global Liquidity, NBER Working Paper Nr. 19038; V. Bruno, and H. S. Shin, (2012), Capital Flows and the Risk-Taking Channel of Monetary Policy, NBER Working Paper Nr. 18942.

lending. Other sources of funding must then be tapped to fund rapidly increasing lending, and the state of the financial cycle is thus often reflected in the composition of intermediary liabilities.[90]

Their results on the information value of noncore liabilities are obtained even when controlling for global factors of credit availability, domestic demand and risk-on sentiment. In the absence of a cross-country consistent domestic credit rates, they have used a deposit rate as a proxy of domestic credit rates or a proxy for the domestic costs of borrowing.[91]

One piece in the puzzle may be the role of non-financial corporations as surrogate financial intermediaries that operate across borders. When corporate activity straddles the border, measuring exposures at the border itself may not capture the strains on corporate balance sheets.[92] A further insight would be to trace and quantify how much repos of shadow banks fund credit to the real economy and how much support risk taking and how much support inter-system liquidity redistribution by market participants.[93]

The benefits of the GFF approach are that it has the potential to deliver input in the following fields: (i) providing a consistent and comparable official global estimate of the shadow banking sector to assess what the estimate tells us about repo concentration risks; maturity and liquidity transformation; leverage and credit-risk transfer and the quality of collateral, to facilitate the monitoring of regulatory boundaries, (ii) measuring the impact of unconventional monetary policy through core (monetary aggregates) and noncore (shadow banking) liabilities, (iii) developing and quantifying global liquidity funding aggregates and (iv) measuring noncore liabilities as an indicator of financial crisis vulnerability.[94]

---

[90] Errico et al., (2014), Ibid. p. 29.

[91] Errico et al., (2014), Ibid. p. 30; M. Chamon, and C. Crowe, (2012), Evidence on Financial Globalization and Crisis: Predictive Indicators of Crises – Macroprudential Indicators, Institutional Environment, Micro, Working Paper, International Monetary Fund, Washington DC; N. Cetorelli and L. S. Goldberg, (2012), Banking Globalization and Monetary Transmission, *Journal of Finance* Vol. 67, Issue 5, pp. 1811–1843.

[92] Errico et al., (2014), Ibid. p. 38.

[93] Errico et al., (2014), Ibid. p. 38.

[94] Errico et al., (2014), Ibid. p. 38. J.-H. Hahm, et al., (2013), Non-Core Bank Liabilities and Financial Vulnerability, *Journal of Money, Credit and Banking*, Vol. 45, pp. 3–36, investigates the role of non-core liabilities in signaling financial vulnerability; K. J. Forbes, and F. E. Warnock, (2012), Capital Flow Waves: Surges, Stops, Flight and Retrenchment, *Journal of International Economics*, Vol. 88, Issue 2, pp. 235–251; H. Satoru, and L. Cavieres, (2012), OECD Financial Statistics for Measuring the Structure and Size of the Shadow Banking System, IFC Bulletin Nr. 36; M. Schularick, and A. M. Taylor, (2012), Credit Booms Gone Bust: Monetary Policy, Leverage Cycles, and Financial Crises, 1870–2008, *American Economic Review* Vol. 102, pp. 1029–1061; H. S. Shin, (2012), Global Banking Glut and Loan Risk Premium, Mundell-Fleming Lecture, IMF Economic Review Vol. 60, Issue 2, pp. 155–192; H. S. Shin, and Y. Zhao, (2013), Monetary Aggregates and Global Liquidity: Evidence from Individual Firm Data from Asia, Working Paper for ADB interim conference, Hong Kong, January; M. Singh, and J. Aitken, (2010), The (Sizable) Role of Rehypothecation in the Shadow Banking System, International Monetary Fund, Working Paper Nr. WP/10/172.

2.9 An Alternative Model to Defining the Shadow Banking Industry

2.9.1 Introduction

The Financial Stability Board (FSB) uses a certain and specific methodology for measuring the size and intensity of the shadow banking market. The parameters make sense but are not 'exclusive' in nature. Scholars have been developing an alternative approach[95] to estimate the size of the shadow banking system, using official data reported to the IMF complemented by other data sources. They base their alternative approach on the expansion of the noncore liabilities concept developed in recent literature to encompass all noncore liabilities of both bank and non-bank financial institutions. As opposed to existing measures of shadow banking, their newly developed measures capture nontraditional funding raised by traditional banks.

The conclusion of their 26-country (and growing) analysis as described below is that noncore liabilities are procyclical and display more volatility than core liabilities for most jurisdictions in the sample. They also compare our measures to existing measures, such as the measure developed by the Financial Stability Board ('FSB'). A central aspect of these efforts has been a closer examination of the less traditional financial intermediation activities, with a focus on the funding sources of financial intermediaries. In that analysis they focused also on the relation between the shadow banking sector and the regulated banking sector and preferably throughout the economic cycle. That makes sense as traditionally banks raise funds by accepting deposits from households and non-financial corporations and then use the deposits to finance their lending activities. These deposits can be viewed as the 'core' funding of the financial system. During periods of rapid economic growth, core funding is likely to be insufficient to finance the growth in credit demand. As a result, nontraditional ('noncore') sources are tapped by banks and non-bank financial institutions alike. Consequently, the state of the business cycle is often reflected in the composition of financial sector funding sources (i.e. noncore liabilities correlate positively with the business cycle).[96]

Recent literature[97] suggests that the size, source and composition of noncore liabilities provide useful insights into the financial system's health and the potential for spillovers to the real economy. As the findings of the FSB already highlighted the lack of true harmonization of data and reporting in this matter limit and constrain further analysis and understanding. Additionally, most of the analysis of nontraditional funding sources has so far focused on non-bank financial institutions, associating these with the shadow bank-

[95] A. Harutyunyan et al., (2015), Shedding Light on Shadow Banking, IMF Working paper, Nr. WP/15/1.

[96] See for an illustration: H. S. Shin, and K. Shin, (2010), Procyclicality and Monetary Aggregates, NBER Working Paper, Nr. 16836, Figure 11.

[97] S. Chen et al., (2012), Exploring the Dynamics of Global Liquidity, IMF Working Paper, Nr. WP/12/246.

ing system. Attempts have been made at measuring the SBS as non-bank financial intermediation and while doing so they used various SBS definitions.[98] Most if not all of these approaches miss however significant nontraditional banking activities carried out by the banks themselves, thus leading to an incomplete picture of the SB system and of the potential vulnerabilities associated with it. Against this background Harutyunyan et al. propose an alternative approach to estimate the size of the SB system, based on the expansion of the noncore liabilities concept developed by Shin and Shin[99] in 2010. That model encompasses 'all noncore liabilities of both banks and nonbank financial institutions'. The more comprehensive concept of noncore liabilities produces a more analytically relevant measure of those financial (credit) intermediation activities comprising the SBS, both across countries and over time. The demarcation line of their model is as such that credit intermediation is viewed as a chain of activities between financial institutions and the other institutional sectors using a variety of financial instruments, consisting of both traditional and shadow banking activities. They consider shadow banking to be all intermediation that can be characterized as nontraditional from the point of view of the funding source. To this end, they subdivide the non-equity funding of financial intermediation into core (traditional) and noncore (nontraditional) liabilities. In this framework, core liabilities include bank deposits mainly from non-financial corporations and households, while noncore liabilities include all the remaining funding sources, particularly market funding.[100] Their findings are in line with Shin and Shin to the effect that compared to core liabilities, average growth rates for both noncore liabilities measures had greater variation during the period 2001–2013 and that in many of the jurisdictions considered (including the US, euro area and Japan) noncore liabilities are procyclical.

In Shin and Shin's model, they lay out the conceptual distinction between core and noncore liabilities of the banking sector as different means of funding. Their paper discusses how these two types of liabilities relate to monetary and credit aggregates and, using monetary data for the Republic of Korea, finds that noncore liabilities increase the vulnerability of the banking sector to sharp exchange rate depreciation and to increases in borrowing spreads. Their model has triggered a widespread release of models and assessments that have all sought to apply the core-noncore framework to construct indicators of credit cycles and to derive macroprudential policy conclusions. The already highlighted

[98] See for an overview Harutyunyan et al., Ibid. Appendix 1, pp. 29–31. See also in detail: FSB, (2013), Strengthening Oversight and Regulation of Shadow Banking: An Overview of Policy Recommendations; Bakk-Simon et al., (2012), Shadow Banking in the Euro Area: An Overview, European Central Bank, Occasional Paper Series, Nr. 133; Z. Pozsar, et al., (2010), Shadow Banking, FRBNY Staff Report Nr. 458 (New York: Federal Reserve Bank of New York); S. Claessens et al., (2012), Shadow Banking: Economics and Policy, IMF Staff Discussion Note 12/12; H. Satoru, L. Cavieres, (2012), OECD Financial Statistics for Measuring the Structure and Size of the Shadow Banking System, IFC Bulletin, Nr. 36.

[99] H. S. Shin, and K. Shin, (2010), Procyclicality and Monetary Aggregates, NBER Working Paper, Nr. 16836. They however were not the first as Schularick and Taylor (2009) already discussed the link between credit dynamics and liability composition; see in detail: M. Schularick and A.M. Taylor, (2009), Credit Booms Gone Bust: Monetary Policy, Leverage Cycles and Financial Crises, 1870–2008, *American Economic Review*, American Economic Association, Vol. 102, Issue 2, pp. 1029–1061.

[100] Harutyunyan et al., Ibid. p. 5.

Chen et al.[101] suggest that monitoring developments in noncore (or shadow banking) funding can provide useful insights on financial sector developments and their implications for the real economy while Hahm et al.[102] explain how lending booms coincide with shifts from core to noncore liabilities. In 2012 and building on their earlier model, Hahm et al.[103] built a model of credit supply and show that banks turn to noncore liabilities when they need to finance a rapid expansion of credit. The main intuition of Harutyunyan et al.'s paper is that core liabilities (traditional bank deposits) are 'sticky' and do not move as procyclically and, for this reason, do not keep up with the expansion of the balance sheet during a credit boom. In that spirit Errico et al.[104] created the global flow of funds framework and map the shadow banking system in the US. The Shin and Shin model has also been extensively tested[105] on a variety of credit booms, financial instability and financial crisis. The key concept to study these scenarios is procyclical balance sheet leverage of the banking system. The approach taken by Harutyunyan et al. focuses on noncore liabilities in measuring and analyzing shadow banking. However, it relates to the stream of literature interpreting shadow banking from the perspective of nontraditional credit intermediation. That body of research came to emerge based on the initial findings of Pozsar[106] and Adrian and Shin[107] who focused on the role of the SB system in undermining financial stability in light of the global financial crisis. They take an institutional approach toward the shadow banking industry as they identify a shadow bank as an institution outside the banking system's regulatory framework (i.e. for most countries all banks are excluded, regardless of their funding structure) which nonetheless provides financial intermediation services similar to those of banks.[108] This is the framework that is also followed by the FSB when performing their analysis of about the size and shape of the shadow banking market.

---

[101] S. Chen et al., (2012), Exploring the Dynamics of Global Liquidity, IMF Working Paper, Nr. WP/12/246.

[102] J. H. Hahm, et al., (2011), Noncore Bank Liabilities and Financial Vulnerability, NBER Working Paper, Nr. 18428, later on published as J. H. Hahm et al., (2013), Noncore Bank Liabilities and Financial Vulnerability, *Journal of Money, Credit and Banking*, Vol. 45, issue 1, pp. 3–36.

[103] J. H. Hahm et al., (2012), Macroprudential Policies in Open Emerging Economies, R. Reuven (ed.), Asia's Role in the Post-Crisis Global Economy, Asia Economic Policy Conference Volume, San Francisco, CA, chapter 2.

[104] L. Errico et al., (2014), Mapping the Shadow Banking System through a Global Flow of Funds Analysis, IMF Working Paper, Nr. WP/14/10.

[105] See, for example, H. S. Shin et al., (2012), Global Banking Glut and Loan Risk Premium, Mundell-Fleming Lecture, *IMF Economic Review*, Vol. 60, Issue 2, pp. 155–192; T. Adrian et al., (2009), The Shadow Banking System: Implications for Financial Regulation, *Banque de France Financial Stability Review*, Vol. 13, pp. 1–10; T. Adrian, (2012), Which Financial Frictions? Parsing the Evidence from the Financial Crisis of 2007–9, NBER Working Papers, Nr. 18335.

[106] Z. Pozsar, (2008), The Rise and Fall of the Shadow Banking System, Moody's Economy.com – Regional Financial Review, July.

[107] T. Adrian et al., (2009), The Shadow Banking System: Implications for Financial Regulation, *Banque de France Financial Stability Review*, Vol. 13, pp. 1–10.

[108] See for a comprehensive overview: Z. Pozsar et al., (2010), Shadow Banking, FRBNY Staff Report Nr. 458 (New York: Federal Reserve Bank of New York) and T. Adrian and A.B. Ashcraft, (2012), Shadow Banking: A Review of the Literature, Federal Reserve Bank of New York Staff Report Nr. 580 (New York: Federal Reserve Bank October 2012.

Harutyunyan et al. take a somewhat different approach. They identify shadow banking as nontraditional financial intermediation, which is determined by the funding source used by financial intermediaries to finance a portion of their assets. Before elaborating on their model, they make explicit that the regulatory aspect is not an explicit defining characteristic of shadow banking in their methodology. This is due to the fact that both banks and non-banks may be involved in the shadow banking market, irrespective of the regulatory regime. However, given that core funding of the financial system consists of (insured) bank deposits, the regulatory aspect at the activity level applies implicitly. Nontraditional funding sources (noncore liabilities) in their approach are thus defined based on the following three dimensions: (i) the types of financial institutions that are issuers of noncore liabilities, (ii) the holders of noncore liabilities (counterparts) and (iii) the financial instruments that are the components of noncore liabilities.[109]

2.9.2 Shadow Banking as Nontraditional Intermediation

The analysis encompasses three levels: (1) institutional, (2) counterparties and (3) the type of financial instruments.

From an institutional point of view, they consider that all financial institutions involved in the credit intermediation chain may potentially issue SB-like liabilities. That makes sense as at the level of individual institutions, banks' involvement in SB activities can be significant. Harutyunyan et al. illustrate and defend their position to include banks in their analysis as follows:

> [c]onsider the case of a bank that securitizes a portion of its balance sheet. If the transaction is carried out by establishing a special purpose vehicle (i.e., the transaction is mediated by a nonbank financial institution), the resulting securities would be captured by existing methodologies attempting to measure the SBS. If, on the other hand, the bank were to securitize directly (on-balance sheet securitization), the resulting securities (including covered bonds) would not be captured by those same methodologies, but would be captured in our measure.

Obviously, this is a very straightforward position on a conceptual level, its application is less so because of the very heterogeneous nature (across countries and sectors) of some non-bank financial intermediaries. Therefore they include as providers of financial intermediation services, institutions that belong to both the other depository corporations (ODCs) and other financial corporations (OFCs) sectors. Three major groups of OFCs can be identified: insurance corporations and pension funds, other financial intermediaries (OFIs) and financial auxiliaries. In particular, they include as issuers of SBS-like liabilities: (i) banks; (ii) money market funds (MMFs) and (iii) all non-bank financial institutions, except non-MMF investment funds (IFs), insurance corporations and pension funds (ICPFs) and financial auxiliaries. Those financial auxiliaries are jointly referred to as the other financial intermediaries (OFIs). The OFI category consists of specific institutions for some countries (e.g. financial vehicle corporations), while for others, it is

[109] Harutyunyan et al., Ibid. p. 7.

calculated as a residual once IF and ICPF liabilities are excluded from total assets of non-bank financial institutions. The rationale for excluding IFs and ICPFs from their shadow banking measure lies in the very specific nature of the financial services they provide, which generally does not involve credit intermediation. The exclusion of ICPF liabilities from shadow banking is widely accepted[110] although the FSB in their 2014 monitoring report argues in favor of including of them as issuers of SB-like liabilities.[111] At the end of the day, this can be argued both ways. Harutyunyan et al. take the valid position 'that the business model of most IFs consists of investing assets on behalf of their clients, who bear the risk of loss. In other words, IFs generally do not participate directly in credit provision and maturity transformation. Finally, while the IF subsector may include some types of institutions that are potential issuers of SBS-like liabilities, the lack of data granularity (e.g., detailed balance sheets by type of fund) prevents a more in-depth assessment and their inclusion in our SBS measure'.[112]

After they defined the issuers of SB-like liabilities, they introduce the notion of 'ultimate domestic creditors' (i.e. being the holders of those SB-like liabilities). These are basically the domestic fund providers to financial intermediaries and include (i) IFs, ICPFs and financial auxiliaries, (ii) non-financial corporations, (iii) households including non-profit institutions serving households (NPISH) and (iv) state and local government. Liabilities to the central government and the central bank are not part of either core or noncore liabilities. This is due to the special nature of their deposits and loans within the financial system, which are intended for policy purposes. This excludes the central government and the central bank from being part of the "ultimate domestic creditors".

The counterparts of the funding raised through the issuance of core or noncore liabilities may thus be divided into three main categories: (i) ultimate domestic creditors, (ii) other resident creditors that issue SBS-like liabilities (banks, MMFs and OFIs) and (iii) non-resident creditors.[113]

At the level of the financial instruments, they divide the non-equity funding sources used by the issuers of SB-like liabilities into core and noncore liabilities. They exclude the liabilities in the form of derivatives and other unclassified liabilities as they are not considered to be core or noncore sources of funding. That holds true for own funding which are excluded in the analysis.[114]

Summarized they argue,[115] the components of a broad and narrow definition of noncore liabilities can be categorized as such that the broad measure of noncore liabilities, which includes intra-SB positions, is most useful for financial stability assessment purposes, as it reflects all exposures of the SB market, including its level of interconnectedness within the SBS. The narrow measure of noncore liabilities reflects the net exposure of the SB market to macroeconomic sectors outside the SB market. The broad and narrow measures complement each other and can be interpreted as the upper and lower bounds, respectively, of the estimated size and interconnectedness of the SB market in a given

[110] Harutyunyan et al., Ibid. p. 8.

[111] FSB, (2014), Global Shadow Banking Monitoring Report 2014.

[112] Harutyunyan et al., Ibid. p. 8.

[113] Harutyunyan et al., Ibid. p. 9.

[114] See in detail: Harutyunyan et al., Ibid. pp. 10–12.

[115] See in detail: Harutyuntan et al., Ibid. pp. 10–12.

country or country grouping. That re-iterates what was already said about the demarcation lines and the different categorizations of noncore liabilities. The distinction between the broad and narrow measures of noncore liabilities lies in the counterparts. The narrow measure includes ultimate domestic creditors and non-residents as counterparts. The broad measure includes all liabilities included in the narrow measures plus intra-SB positions, that is, those held by banks, MMFs and OFIs.

The issuers and instruments are similar in both categories and include (1) restricted deposits, (2) debt securities, (3) loans and (4) MMF shares or units. Those instruments are issued by banks, MMFs and OFIs. The distinction in the different categories comes down to the different group of counterparties. The narrow measure includes ultimate domestic creditors and non-residents as counterparts. The broad measure includes all liabilities included in the narrow measures plus intra-SB market positions, that is, those held by banks, MMFs and OFIs. Both measures include ultimate creditors and non-residents as counterparts. The narrow measure includes only a subset of the OFC sector, while the broad measure includes all OFCs and all ODCs. Or to spell the categories out:

- the narrow category includes households, non-financial corporations, state and local governments, non-residents, insurance corporations, pension funds and non-MMF investment funds
- the broad category includes households, non-financial corporations, state and local governments, non-residents, banks, MMFs and OFCs.

The credit intermediation network and the activities of the SB market within the network are complex and subject to continuous change.[116] The initial funding sources of core and noncore liabilities issued by financial intermediaries are the ultimate domestic creditors and non-residents.

Reminding of the bigger picture, the alternative model of Harutyunyan et al. is special in the sense that unlike other measures of shadow banking, their approach shows how nontraditional financial intermediation is conducted by both ODCs (banks and MMFs) and OFIs.

2.9.3 The Findings of the Alternative Model

In this subsection, I will discuss their findings and contrast them with other models used.[117] The analysis includes a review of the (1) core and noncore liabilities, (2) the growth rates and variability of those liabilities and (3) a comparison with the FSB estimates. The conclusions will follow from that analysis.

---

[116] See for a visualization Harutyunyan et al., Ibid. p. 13. Their visualization shows that banks issue both core and noncore liabilities, while MMFs and OFIs issue only noncore liabilities. The funding is used to support lending directed both among financial intermediaries and outside the system. The narrow noncore liabilities measure excludes intra-SB market positions, so that the (re)investment of funds within the SBS does not affect the narrow measure. The sum of the intra-SB and narrow noncore liabilities denotes the broad noncore liabilities measure.

[117] See for an overview of the assumptions, scoping and country selection: Harutyunyan et al., Ibid. p. 14.

2.9.3.1 Size of the Core and Noncore Liabilities[118]

The measurement is expressed as broad noncore liabilities in percentage of gross domestic product (GDP). For example, in the euro area and the US, broad noncore liabilities as a share of GDP swelled between end-2002 and end-2008. However, by Q3 of 2013 noncore liabilities had fallen close to their end-2002 levels.[119]

An interesting observation is the difference between the broad and the narrow noncore liabilities measures. This difference can be interpreted as the size of intra-SB balance sheet positions (e.g. an SB institution financing another SB institution using an SB-like instrument).

2.9.3.2 Growth Rates and Variability of Those Liabilities[120]

The core liabilities follow a more stable pattern relative to the two categories of noncore liabilities at least in terms of growth rates. They demonstrate a rather steady growth rate over the time period considered in the study and this for most of the countries involved in the analysis.

2.9.3.3 Comparison with the FSB Analysis and Methodology[121]

As indicated, also the FSB estimates on an annual basis. These estimates refer to the size of the OFI sector which they define as 'all financial institutions that are not classified as banks, insurance companies, pension funds, public financial institutions, central banks, or financial auxiliaries'. For the years 2002–2013, Harutyunyan et al. compare and contrast their findings of noncore liabilities measures to those of the FSB. The set of countries include the G7 and a number of emerging economies. The two main differences between their measure and the FSB estimate are that (i) the FSB includes shares issued by IFs, which we exclude from noncore liabilities; and (ii) the FSB excludes bank liabilities that in our approach belong to the noncore liabilities measures. The comparison between the two models is quite troublesome as banks have a very large share in Harutyunyan's measure of noncore liabilities, while they are excluded by the FSB. Secondly, Harutyunyan's noncore liabilities measure for the euro area only includes securitization vehicles among OFI liabilities, while the FSB measure's institutional coverage is wider.

A general comment, and which Harutyunyan et al. also highlight,[122] is that the differences between the two outcomes need to be interpreted with caution given the data gaps

[118] See in extenso: Harutyunyan et al., Ibid. pp. 15–20.

[119] The full set of findings can be found in Appendix 3, pp. 35–40.

[120] See in extenso: Harutyunyan et al., Ibid. pp. 21–22.

[121] See in detail: Harutyunyan et al., Ibid. pp. 22–23.

[122] Harutyunyan et al., Ibid. p. 24.

that exist. Not all countries report to the IMFs Supplemental Reserve Facility (SRF) and therefore datasets are complemented. However, those alternative sources are not reported by countries at the level of granularity needed for the methodologies used.[123] As Harutyunyan et al. indicate 'insufficient granularity with regards to different types of OFCs and subcategories of some instruments (particularly debt securities) prevent the full application of our methodology'.[124] That implies that this, like most methodologies capturing the shadow banking system, work still needs to be done, for example, with respect to the refinement of the boundary between core and noncore liabilities for certain borderline instrument subcategories (e.g. debt securities).

Nevertheless, their methodology and their measurements with respect to core and noncore liabilities contain useful dynamics vis-à-vis the wider economic cycle. An important lesson from their assessment is the demonstration and quantification of how the funding structure of the financial system changes with the business cycle to assess whether noncore liability growth outpaces growth in core liabilities during economic booms. With respect to the largest jurisdictions, they find evidence of procyclicality for the noncore ratio indicator in both the US and the euro area. In the case of the US, they find that GDP growth leads the rebalancing of the funding structure by about two quarters, whereas for the euro area we find that the two growth rates correlate with no lag. Both for the US and the euro area, the growth rate of the share of noncore liabilities follows closely the GDP growth. One way to interpret this is that (i) balance sheet expansions during the pre-crisis credit boom were largely funded through noncore liabilities and, likewise, (ii) the significant deleveraging of the post-crisis periods has affected mostly noncore liabilities. This result is also consistent with that of Shin and Shin, who find that noncore liabilities are procyclical.[125] Regarding the remaining countries, they find that there is inconclusive evidence of noncore liabilities being procyclical. That results in the fact that GDP, core liabilities and noncore liabilities all grow over the horizon considered, but noncore liabilities grow faster than core liabilities.[126]

---

[123] Harutyunyan et al., Ibid. pp. 32–34 (Appendix 2) provide an overview of the data sources used per country.

[124] They specify: '[f]or example, certain debt securities, such as certificates of deposit and long-term bonds, represent more traditional, stable financing sources. However, given that the SRFs and most other data sources provide no additional breakdown of debt securities, we included all debt securities into noncore liabilities. Similarly, the majority of our data sources did not provide granular balance sheet data for the OFC subsectors. To overcome these data gaps we made some estimations, especially when deriving the narrow noncore liabilities measure to exclude intra-SBS positions. Additionally, in some cases, data were available for a more limited set of periods. A further complication for this exercise stemmed from differences in terminology across countries. For example, the equivalents of MMFs use different names across countries. Similarly, instruments such as debt securities spanned a wide range of terminologies depending on the data source. Finally, while the SRFs contain a standardized set of metadata, the metadata accompanying alternate data sources used in our analysis were scarce and not focused on essential aspects, such as the types and definitions of institutions, instruments and counterparts covered' (p. 24).

[125] Harutyunyan et al., Ibid. pp. 25–26.

[126] Harutyunyan et al., Ibid. p. 27.

2.9.3.4 Conclusions

As detailed Harutyunyan et al.'s methodology is based on the expansion of noncore liabilities concept as developed by Shin and Shin to encompass all noncore liabilities of both banks and non-bank financial institutions. Their position is that all financial institutions involved in the credit intermediation chain may potentially issue SB-like liabilities. They show that banks issue a large portion of noncore liabilities relative to the total, particularly in the euro area. As Shiller[127] already pointed out in 2012 the involvement of banks in shadow banking activities can be very material. One of their key findings is that average growth rates for both noncore liabilities measures had greater variation during the observed period than core liabilities and that in many of the jurisdictions considered, noncore liabilities are procyclical.

A second novel observation is that their methodology generates data on intra-SB activities, derived as difference between the estimation of broad and narrow SB measures.[128]

No doubt that their methodology and findings will become an additional analytical and macroprudential tool in the hands of national and international regulators and supervisors. Also here the Achilles heel however is the data availability and granularity of the datasets in particular with respect to subcategories of financial instruments issued by both banks and OFIs. Better datasets would allow a better categorization of instruments into core and noncore categories. Furthermore, improving the availability of separate balance sheet data for different types of OFCs would permit a more accurate identification of issuers of SB-like liabilities.

Many different measurement systems have been discussed that capture the large or narrow, activity- or entity-based shadow banking model and its size. The FSB has been evolving in the way they measure the SB market just like other public interest organizations have been making suggestions along the line. What has become clear is that the (more granular) data gathering has posed some serious challenges. Not only in the way how to collect them but also how to use them. Agresti[129] provides an overview of important aspects that need to be taken into account in addressing measurement issues for the shadow banking focusing on the use of aggregate data. First, there are the natural limitations in aggregate macroeconomic data for shadow banking purposes. And second, she points at how the determination of a perimeter of the shadow banking is strongly related from a micro prospective to a better understanding of the regulatory and the accounting framework.

---

[127] R. J. Shiller, (2012), Finance and the Good Society, Princeton University Press, Princeton NJ.

[128] Harutyunyan et al., Ibid. p. 28.

[129] A.M. Agresti, (2016), Shadow Banking: Some Considerations for Measurements Purposes, contribution to the IFC workshop on "Combining Micro and Macro Statistical Data for Financial Stability Analysis. Experiences, Opportunities and Challenges", Warsaw, December 14–15.

2.10 More Variation of Shadow Banking Definitions Under Way

The many complications in defining shadow banking and the blurred boundaries have caused many attempts to (re)define the shadow banking segment. That in itself is a noble exercise, but the real added value lies in the nexus with the government policies and the implications a redefinition might have.

One of those attempts[130] defines shadow banking as 'cream skimmers' who only provide actuarially-based financing either to seasoned borrowers or to borrowers with easy-to-value collateral. The implication of the presence of shadow banks is that fewer loans are originated and social welfare declines. When considering the newer definitions of shadow banking, we keep the 2013 FSB definition in mind which is somewhat of a benchmark and which reads as 'credit intermediation involving entities and activities outside of the regular banking system'. The definition is broad and narrow at the same time. It is broad because it includes many definitions and entities, but narrow as it excludes banking conglomerates who engage in these activities. Hard demarcation lines were never given, as the FSB understands that these are moving paradigms and a static definition would make authorities end up behind the curve at some point when understanding the shadow banking market reality as it unfolds.

Other definitions of the early generation were 'short-term market-based financing of longer-term loans, usually through collateral-based lending or securitization'...' 'financial intermediaries that conduct maturity, credit, and liquidity transformation without access to central bank liquidity, or public sector guarantees'.[131] The pain in those early definitions, according to Hancock and Passmore, is that they ignore 'the possibility that financial institutions may engage in the same transformations with implicit access to central bank liquidity and/or implicit government backing. Moreover, some nonbank financial institutions (e.g., insurance companies) may have access to other government-backed liquidity programs'.[132] These definitions aren't 'based on more fundamental descriptions of the preferences of economic agents and of the technologies used by such agents when optimizing their utility'.[133] The two lending technologies they focus on are (1) relationship-based lending ('finding credible borrowers and providing a management input that creates wealth for the borrower') and (2) actuarially-based lending. The former refers to the traditional lending concept where the latter refers to 'funding where the interest rate offered on a new loan is equal to the risk-free rate plus a mark-up that covers the probability of default multiplied by the (expected) losses given default'.[134] Their model has been

---

[130] D. Hancock and W. Passmore, (2015), Shadow Banks as 'Cream Skimmers', Board of Governors of the Federal Reserve System, Working Paper, draft.

[131] Z. Pozsar, et al. (2012), Shadow Banking, Federal Reserve Bank of New York Staff Report, Nr. 458, February, p. i.

[132] Hancock & Passmore, (2015), Ibid. p. 3.

[133] Hancock & Passmore, (2015), Ibid. p. 4.

[134] Hancock & Passmore, (2015), Ibid. p. 4.

developed to assess those lending techniques and conclude that the shadow bank lending technology is actuarial in nature and 'can effectively "cream skim" particular types of loans from the banking system, which employs relationship-based technologies'.

Their concern goes beyond the identification itself but includes the regulatory implication. When the regulator and supervisor continue to be focused on the 'activity and entity' combined approach, the regulator will miss, by and far, the shadow banking component embedded in the traditional banking sector. Similar concerns were ventilated when discussing Cetorellis' concept of 'hybrid intermediaries'.[135] But Hancock and Passmore don't stop when concluding that traditional banking is relationship-based lending and shadow banking is actuarially-based lending, but further lament that that distinction has important implications for loan origination, loan maturity and ultimately social welfare in general. That in itself raises questions regarding the implicit subsidies that the banking sector receives from their governments. But they don't want to go as far as recommending that this demarcation line should determine what should fall within the government safety net or not. They refer to Duffie who already in 2012 correctly indicated that '[n]othing about the boundaries of the regulated banking system should be taken on principle. Which activities are allowed within this specially protected regulatory environment is a cost-benefit decision that should be based on how dangerous it would be for these activities to be interrupted, what sorts of collateral damage might be caused by their failure, and what risks these activities would pose to financial stability if conducted outside the regulated banking system'.[136]

Under relationship banking, the bank invests time upfront to understand the borrower's default probability. If later on the borrower is in no further need for a bank relationship, it can turn to actuarially-based financing. The implications are that the bank seems no longer an interesting party and the bank 'can no longer price the second period of the loan contract using a loan payment that averages over possible default risks'. The reason for that is that the bank needs to be concerned of 'cream skimming' of low-risk borrowers. The only thing the bank can do is reduce the interest (relative to the fault potential). The learning curve of the bank will imply that banks going forward, will invest in loan origination as the profit potential over the course of the full relationship has dropped and borrowers are less likely to accept pre-payment penalties and so on. They indicate 'without the ability to "lock-in" borrowers for two periods, the bank scales back its relationship investments and social welfare declines'.[137] The aggregate implication is reduced wealth accumulation.[138]

Shadow banks 'cream skim' the traditional banks, that is, 'a shadow bank cannot provide the borrower with an investment, but can provide financing for the loan in the second period once the default probability type for the project is known'...and 'the borrower will

[135] See infra; N. Cetorelli, (2014), Hybrid Intermediaries, Federal Reserve Bank of NY Staff Report Nr. 705, December.

[136] D. Duffie, (2012), Drawing Boundaries Around and Through the Banking System, World Economic Forum: Financial Development Report, Chapter 1.2, October 31.

[137] See for a quantification of the social cost: Hancock and Passmore, (2015), Ibid. p. 16. op. cit. Hancock & Passmore, (2015), Ibid. p. 5.

[138] Hancock and Passmore, (2015), Ibid. pp. 6–7.

switch the source of financing if the utility from staying with the bank is less than the utility from switching to a shadow bank'.[139] The shadow bank will refinance the loan after the traditional bank invested in understanding the actual default risk. The only alternative is to reduce loan origination as reducing the interest rate on the loan by the traditional bank upfront is no viable alternative, when competing with shadow banks managing an unregulated balance sheet. It all comes close to Cetorelli's analysis that in order to stay competitive, banks must diversify and be active in a wide credit intermediation chain, creating those 'hybrid intermediaries'.[140]

The analysis of Hancocks and Passmore contribute in a number of ways to our understanding of the shadow banking market, without violating any of the other shadow banking explanations,[141] but in three ways that require and desire further attention: (1) there are clear limitations to model-based regulation,[142] (2) the demarcation line between traditional banks and shadow banks equals a competition between 'relationship-based lending' and 'actuarially-based lending' and that shadow banks cream skim the most profitable banks from the traditional banking sector and (3) regulation in this field is inadequate to limit the social cost. Although there are government support models (e.g. Fannie Mae and Freddie Mac), the banks are able, when providing mortgages, to access market-based cost of funding and capture some of the interest component the bank would lose toward the later part of the banking relationship with any given customer (but with low-risk borrowers in particular). They indicate that '[h]owever, government actions that allow the bank to capture some of the marginal costs associated with lending to the borrowers who can switch to actuarially-based financing in the second period do not resolve the problem that the banking system must carry the costs associated with relationship banking'.[143]

They suggest that government action should focus on lowering the cost of funding to banks, subsidize the bank's upfront investment in new loans and insure banks against the risk of borrower default once the banking relationship is established. That however doesn't take away some of the key characteristics of shadow banks, that is, actuarially-based bank-

[139] Hancock and Passmore, (2015), Ibid. p. 11.

[140] See also N. Cetorelli, (2014), Surviving Credit Market Competition, Economic Inquiry, Vol. 52, Issue 1, pp. 320–340.

[141] The four mainstream explanations of shadow banking are as discussed: (1) shadow banking is the pooling and tranching of cash flows from loans to create safe assets for investors worldwide (G. Gorton, and G. Pennacchi, (1990), Financial Intermediation and Liquidity Creation, *Journal of Finance*, Vol. 45, Nr. 1, pp. 49–72), (2) shadow banking is regulatory arbitrage (V. V. Acharya, et al., (2010), Securitization without Risk Transfer, National Bureau of Economic Research, Working Paper Nr. 15730), (3) shadow banking is maturity transformation (G. Gorton, and A. Metrick, (2012), Securitized Banking and the Run on Repo, *Journal of Financial Economics*, Vol. 104, Nr. 3, pp. 425–461) and (4) shadow banking is the exploitation of short-sighted investors by the banking industry (N. Gennaioli, et al., (2013), A Model of Shadow Banking, Journal of Finance, Vol. 68, Nr.4, pp. 1331–1363).

[142] See also and more articulated: M. Behn, et al., (2015), The Limits of Model-Based Regulation, SAFE Working Paper Nr. 75. They indicate that 'model-based regulation was meant to enhance the stability of the financial sector by making capital charges more sensitive to risk'...and that 'the introduction of complex regulation adversely affected the credit risk of financial institutions'.

[143] See for more details: Hancock and Passmore, (2015), Ibid. pp. 21–22.

ing is intrinsically more fragile than traditional banking. Two reasons emerge to explain that position: (1) actuarially-based lending lack uniqueness as this type of lending is based on expectations of credit loss for large classes of similar loans which do not account for potential externalities that degrade collateral values (correlation), and (2) there is no competitive advantage in actuarially-based financing and so narrow margins require persistent high levels of leverage (even if equity would be only slightly more expensive).[144] Government support should then be limited to fostering relationship-lending and not pushing around financial claims.

[144] Hancock and Passmore, (2015), Ibid. pp. 22–23. See in detail: (1) S. G. Hanson, et al., (2011), A Macroprudential Approach to Financial Regulation, *Journal of Economic Perspectives*, Vol. 25, Nr. 1, pp. 3–28, and (2) J. C. Stein, (2011), Monetary Policy as Financial-Stability Regulation, National Bureau of Economic Research Working Paper, Nr. 16883.

3

Financial Intermediation: A Further Analysis

3.1 Introduction

Since shadow banking has only in recent decades become a large segment of financial services provision, its economic role is not yet well understood although we have been making progress since the 2007 financial crisis. The term 'shadow banking' was coined by McCulley[1] at the 2007 Jackson Hole Symposium, but Rajan (2005),[2] without actually using the term, had identified some of the vulnerabilities of what constituted shadow banking at the same symposium two years earlier.

The various definitions of shadow banking were reviewed in Chap. 1. Although they were all comprehensive, they often varied in nature. However, the two shadow banking activities that are most important economically and therefore justify receiving more and separate attention and in terms of financial stability at present are 'securitization' and 'collateral intermediation'. Shadow banking is often seen as a form of regulatory arbitrage, but this is an incomplete view. Being a heavily regulated industry, the operations of the financial sector certainly involve various forms of arbitrage. Hence much analysis of financial services—including that of shadow banking—comes with the caveat that one cannot tell whether a particular service serves a genuine economic function or is a consequence of regulatory arbitrage. However, shadow banking, at least in part, also responds to genuine economic demand (although assessing its overall economic value is a topic that

[1] P. McCulley, (2007), Teton Reflections, PIMCO Global Central Bank Focus, 2007; and later on P. McCulley, (2009), The Shadow Banking System and Hyman Minsky's Economic Journey, PIMCO Global Central Bank Focus, May.

[2] R. Rajan, (2005), Has Financial Development Made the World Riskier?, In Proceedings of the 2005 Jackson Hole Economic Policy Symposium, Federal Reserve Bank of Kansas City, pp. 313–369.

L. Nijs, *The Handbook of Global Shadow Banking, Volume I*,
https://doi.org/10.1007/978-3-030-34743-7_3

requires additional analysis). Understanding these demand factors, and how they affect the system's operations and risks, is essential for formulating policy responses.[3]

Similar to traditional banks, which issue 'safe' liabilities to fund risky projects, shadow banking focuses on intermediating credit from savers to borrowers and managing counterparty risks. However, its activities occur outside traditional banks, albeit with their support. A number of features fostered its development[4]:

1. The demand for 'private money': investments perceived as highly safe, liquid and redeemable at par. The demand for private money is linked to the investment needs of institutional cash investors, whose total balances significantly exceed the (inelastic) supply of short-term government debt and insured deposits[5] although the demand for safe assets as a ratio to GDP appears historically remarkably stable and has always been met by a combination of public and private instruments.[6]
2. Risks arising from private money creation: banks respond to a demand for private safe assets[7] by producing them through tranching of cash flows, portfolio diversification and residual risk retention, in the process becoming exposed to extreme adverse events (i.e. 'tail risks')[8], that is, unstable expansions of leverage,[9] the possibility of runs on private money supplied in the form of repurchase agreements[10] and the amount of private money creation may be excessive because agents do not internalize the costs of crises.[11]

---

[3] S. Claessens et al. (2012), Shadow Banking: Economics and Policy, IMF Staff Discussion Note, SDN 12/12, December 2012, p. 4.

[4] S. Claessens et al. (2012), Shadow Banking: Economics and Policy, IMF Staff Discussion Note, SDN 12/12, December 2012, p. 5.

[5] R. Greenwood, et al. (2012), A Comparative-Advantage Approach to Government Debt Maturity, Harvard Business School Working Paper Nr. 11–035; A. Turner, (2012), Shadow Banking and Financial Instability, speech at Cass Business School, March 14.

[6] G. Gorton, et al. (2012), The Safe-Asset Share, American Economic Review: Papers & Proceedings, Vol. 102, Nr. 3, May, pp. 101–06; G. Gorton, and A. Metrick, (2012), Securitized Banking and the Run on Repo, *Journal of Financial Economics*, Vol. 104, Nr. 3, pp. 425–51.

[7] See, for example, for a very good study on the rise and fall of the demand for securitized products: S. Chernenko et al., (2014), The Rise and Fall of Demand for Securitizations, NBER Working Paper Series, Nr. 20,777. They find considerable heterogeneity in investor demand for securitizations in the pre-crisis period. Both investor beliefs and incentives (and inexperience of fund managers) help to explain this variation in demand. A more uniform picture was observed of investor behavior in the crisis. Consistent with theories of optimal liquidation, investors largely traded in more liquid securities.

[8] N. Gennaioli, et al., (2012), Neglected Risks, Financial Innovation, and Financial Fragility, *Journal of Financial Economics*, Vol. 104, pp. 452–468; and Gennaioli et al., (2013), A Model of Shadow Banking, *The Journal of Finance*, Volume 68, Issue 4 (August), pp. 1331–1363.

[9] J. Geanakoplos, (2010), The Leverage Cycle, in NBER Macroeconomic Annual 2009, (ed. by D. Acemoglu, K. Rogoff, and M. Woodford), Cambridge, Massachusetts, National Bureau of Economic Research Vol. 24, pp. 1–65).

[10] G. Gorton, and A. Metrick, (2012), Securitized Banking and the Run on Repo, *Journal of Financial Economics*, Vol. 104, Nr. 3, pp. 425–451; A. Martin, et al., (2011), Repo Runs, Federal Reserve Bank of NY, Staff Report Nr. 444.

[11] M. Ricks, (2012), Reforming the Short-Term Funding Markets, John M. Olin Center for Law, Economics and Business Discussion Paper Nr. 713, Harvard University Cambridge, Massachusetts; J.C. Stein, (2012), Monetary Policy as Financial Stability Regulation, *Quarterly Journal of Economics*, Vol. 127, pp. 57–95.

3. Market failures in the securitization process; that includes (i) the fragility of the short-term funding[12] that supports securitization, (ii) that securitization allows financial institution to lever up more by using repo funding that supports securitization[13], (iii) regulatory arbitrage and imperfect risk transfers and (iv) highlight problems of regulatory arbitrage and imperfect risk transfers from banks.[14]
4. The support of collateral-based operations in the financial system. Such financial innovations can arise from structural changes and policy reforms, and how financial sector and (unconventional) monetary policies need to adapt to the challenges innovations pose.[15] Related are prevailing legal rules, which can effectively subsidize the use of some derivatives and repo contracts, with negative implications for financial stability.[16]

Any policy response as Claessens et al. indicate should be centered around four major themes: (1) dealing with regulatory arbitrage, the focus of much recent regulatory actions; (2) addressing systemic risks within the shadow banking system (including the regulation of dealer banks and money market funds, and dealing with innovation and complexity); (3) addressing demand-side pressures, including possibly accommodating a shortage of safe and liquid assets with government (or publicly guaranteed) short-term debt issuance and (4) importantly, considering its macroeconomic and monetary implications.[17]

3.2 Risk-Stripping Through Securitization and the Need for 'Safe' Assets

Securitization can be defined as the process, whereby through tranching repackages cash flows from underlying loans and other debt securities thereby creating assets that often were perceived as safe or at least safer than the intrinsic counterparty risk embedded in the

[12] G. Gorton, and A. Metrick, (2012), Securitized Banking and the Run on Repo, *Journal of Financial Economics*, Vol. 104, Nr. 3, pp. 425–51.

[13] T. Adrian, and H. Song S, (2009), Money, Liquidity and Monetary Policy, Federal Reserve Bank of New York Staff Report Nr. 360. H.S. Shin, (2009), Securitization and Financial Stability, *The Economic Journal*, Vol. 119, pp. 309–332.

[14] V.V. Acharya, et al., (2013), Securitization without Risk Transfer, NBER Working Paper Nr. 15,730, National Bureau of Economic Research, Cambridge, Massachusetts and *Journal of Financial Economics*, Vol. 107, pp. 515–536.

[15] P. Mehrling, (2010), The New Lombard Street: How the Fed Became the Dealer of Last Resort Princeton University Press, Princeton, New Jersey; M. Singh, and J. Aitken, (2010), The (Sizable) Role of Rehypothecation in the Shadow Banking System, IMF Working Paper Nr. WP/10/172, Washington M. Singh, and P. Stella, (2012), Money and Collateral, IMF Working Paper Nr. WP/12/95, Washington; M. Singh, (2011), Velocity of Pledged Collateral: Analysis and Implications, IMF Working Paper NR. WP/11/256, Washington.

[16] B. Tuckman, (2010), Amending Safe Harbors to Reduce Systemic Risk in OTC Derivatives Market, Centre for Financial Stability, New York; E. Perotti, (2012), The Roots of Shadow Banking, Bank of England, Mimeo; K. Summe, (2011), An Examination of Lehman Brothers' Derivatives Portfolio Post-Bankruptcy: Would Dodd-Frank Would Have Made any Difference, Working Paper Hoover Institution, Stanford University.

[17] Claessens et al. (2012), Ibid. p. 7.

underlying portfolio of loans. As illustrated before, there was significant demand from institutional investors for those products, and were a direct alternative for deposit-like investments. They were also enthusiastically received by banks itself who used the products for repo funding and to enhance leverage.

Claessens et al. comment: '[t]he risks and market failures in the securitization process include regulatory arbitrage by banks, extensive use through various "puts" of (implicit) public safety net subsidies, a disregard of tail risks, and a possibility of runs on money market funds. While securitization has declined since the crisis in response to realized risks and tighter regulation, many of these market failures remain and risks could reemerge'.[18]

3.2.1 The Securitization Machine

The classic banking function is traditionally a string of credit, maturity and liquidity transformation. Securitization resembles the process for safe, liquid short-term investments. It was already demonstrated that the securitization process is a string of steps involving different parties and a variety of balance sheets. A further distinction is the fact that in the process there is the unique characteristic of 'risk-stripping' that occurs, that is, the stripping of credit risk (into tranches often referred to senior, mezzanine and equity portions of tranches). This (stripping, or better, transfer of credit risk) happens in the first step in the process. In the second step is for the long-term security to be sold to, often an offshore special-purpose vehicle (SPV), that, also often, is being financed in the short-term money market. What comes out on the other side is a safe 'short-term' asset. A further stripping occurred in the process, that is, the stripping of the maturity dynamic of the security. The long-term security became a short-term security.

The asset created is often referred to as a structured money market instrument of which the most well known are the asset-backed commercial paper (ABCP). The third step in the process intends to liquefy the safe short-term asset (so that it c.q. they become tradable). That process is conducted using 'puts'. The puts are essentially commitments of banks to provide liquidity support to the SPV. That was often combined with money market funds holding the created assets so that stable liquid assets can be transferred to investors. Stable in the sense that their NAV ('net asset value') stays constant. Stable NAV claims are claims that have an explicit or implicit commitment to return[19] at least a principal of investment on demand. That way the third level of risk-stripping is completed, that is, the transfer of liquidity risk.

---

[18] Claessens et al. (2012), Ibid. p. 7.

[19] The credit transformation special-purpose vehicles (SPVs) have matched maturity funding and issue asset-backed securities (ABS) or collateralized debt obligations (not shown). The maturity transformation SPVs are funded short term (are maturity mismatched) and issue asset-backed commercial paper (ABCP) or other structured money market instruments, such as auction rate securities (not shown). Private collateral (PC) includes ABS, corporate bonds and equities. $1 NAV is the stable net asset value (a promise to repay at least USD $1 on USD $1 invested). R = repo; RR = reverse repo: see Claessens et al. (2012), Ibid. p. 8 footnote.

If we bring the comparison with the traditional banking model (i.e. the allocation of savings by backs to government securities) back on the table, we can assess the situation as such that bank-based intermediation tends to happen on and out of a single balance sheet, whereas in the securitization process the risks are carried throughout a chain of balance sheets including various capital sources and the aforementioned puts. Additionally, the key difference between securitization and the allocation of cash pool savings to government debt is that the latter does not involve credit-risk transformation (although it still involves some maturity and liquidity risk transformation, since cash pools can prefer assets with shorter maturity and higher liquidity than that of long-term government debt).[20]

Securitization solves a number of problems. To begin with there is constantly a high demand by the investment community worldwide for safe, liquid and short-term investments ('money-like claims') that allows them to manage their day-to-day cash balances. The second element is built around the need for banks to use those securitized assets ('AAA') to attract repo funding and increase leverage (supra). That can happen directly via institutional investor and their cash pools or indirectly through the aforementioned money market funds.[21]

The 'safe portion ('AAA') accounted often for about a third of the total issuance[22] while the remainder was held by specialty investors, hedge funds and long-term investors like hedge funds and insurers. Remarkably enough, the securitization circus was to a large degree a demand-driven phenomenon. The excess liquidity that is available in the global financial infrastructure needs to find a home, but at a rate above the short-term deposit or interbanking rate.

Also corporations account these days for a sizeable amount of liquidity that requirements manage on a day-to-day basis.[23]

Corporations and the asset management industry were and are on the outlook for higher returns but with similar safety levels, maturity and liquidity as a traditional bank deposit. It can be notified that the final holders of these corporate and asset management allocations are often also individuals.

The reason why that historically emerged, that is, the fact that corporations and large asset managers allocate the short-term liquidity to parties outside the traditional banking sector, lies in the fact that the traditional banking sector is not particularly well equipped to intermediate large cash balances as those coming from corporations and so on. The reason for that is related to the deposit insurance mechanism that historically insured deposits up to 100,000 USD and then after the 2008 crisis started that has been drummed up to 250,000 USD, which for institutional cash pools is still a trivial amount. Every

---

[20] Claessens et al. (2012), Ibid. p. 8.

[21] For a visualization of the different processes, see Claessens et al. (2012), pp. 8–9.

[22] D. Greenlaw, et al., (2008), Leveraged Losses: Lessons from the Mortgage Market Meltdown, U.S. Monetary Policy Forum Report, Nr. 2, February.

[23] See for details Claessens et al. (2012), Ibid. p. 10 and in extenso Z. Pozsar, (2011), Institutional Cash Pools and the Triffin Dilemma of the U.S. Banking System, IMF Working Paper Nr. 11/190, Washington.

amount higher than the 250,000 USD therefore indirectly qualifies as junior unsecured debt (e.g. to some of the other outstanding debt, e.g. repos the bank has outstanding). Even spreading tens of billions of USD over reliable banks in smaller (insured) tranches work proves to be ineffective and most likely unworkable. Due to certain peculiarities in the US tax code, large amounts of cash are not repatriated by US corporations (as they would then become taxable) and they stay offshore where they don't benefit from the deposit insurance mechanism.

Therefore the safe tranches of the securitized products became the next-best alternative to insured deposits available. Supply of the securitized products happens broadly through two channels: (1) government-only funds investing in short-term government debt, or other government-guaranteed short-term claims and repos backed by it, (2) and prime funds investing in commercial paper, uninsured bank deposits and repos often backed by private collateral.[24] Where invested, private and public debt was relatively evenly split before the crisis, which change dramatically in the run-up to the crisis when confidence in private debt deteriorated rapidly and the invested amounts in T-bonds and insured deposits rose.[25]

The other argument on the emergence of the securitization machine was the fact that banks had high demand for securitized debt which was used as collateral to attract repos and by doing so increased their leverage and ultimately returns. Banks traditionally held the most risky parts of the securitized products themselves[26] (the mezzanine and equity portion) as investors were looking for 'safe' liquid short-term assets. By pledging high-quality securitized debt, banks could raise wholesale funds (and increase leverage) more cheaply and in larger volumes than if they relied on traditional liabilities, such as deposits and unsecured funding.[27]

The safer tranches were also held for 'regulatory arbitrage'. Securitization as was conducted offered two ways to reduce such capital charges. One way was to hold securitized debt through affiliated investment vehicles (e.g. SIVs) that were funded in short-term money markets and relied on both implicit (thus not requiring capital charges) and explicit credit and liquidity support from banks.

Apart from regulatory arbitrage, holding securitized assets on bank books can destabilize the financial system. The tradable debt on the books allows banks to leverage its books in boom times beyond what the balance sheet can normally justify and therefore can lead

[24] For details and datasets: G. Gorton, et al. (2012), The Safe-Asset Share, American Economic Review: Papers & Proceedings, Vol. 102, Nr. 3, May, pp. 101–106.

[25] Short-term public debt is the sum of treasury securities and agency- and GSE-backed securities. Short-term bank debt is the sum of checkable deposits and currency and time and savings deposits. Short-term private debt is the sum of open market paper, federal funds and security repurchase agreements: Claessens et al. (2012), Ibid. p. 13 note.

[26] V. Acharya, et al., (2009), Manufacturing Tail Risk: A Perspective on the Financial Crisis of 2007–2009, Foundations and Trends in Finance, Vol. 4, Nr. 4, pp. 247–325. N. Gennaioli, et al., (2013), A Model of Shadow Banking, *Journal of Finance*, Volume 68, Issue 4, pp. 1331–1363.

[27] Claessens et al. (2012), Ibid. p. 12.

to procyclicality, exuberance or the opposite depending on the phase of the economic cycle the economy is in.[28] Shin[29] further points at the fact that holdings of securitized debt by banks represent a lack of risk transfer from banks to the rest of the financial system, negating a potential benefit of securitization.[30]

3.2.2 Risk Dynamics in the Securitization Process and Regulatory Oversight

Besides the un-transparency caused by the fact that the risk-stripping of the different risks involved (see supra) happened over a variety of balance sheets, therefore aggregate views were not available displaying the total risk distribution and volumes of the different risks. That showed up (un)intentionally in the ratings that were given by the rating agencies. Even more, the correlation among risks was ignored, the tranching process led to a buildup of 'tail risks', the occurrence of rare negative events. The consequence was a total ignorance of the aggregate, undiversified exposures to low-probability risks (e.g. a significant structural drop in the housing prices as we have witnessed in the US). That led to credit and liquidity risk. That caused two problems on banks' balance sheets: (1) the credit risk on those balance sheets via their loan/investment portfolio was higher than initially anticipated. This problem has stayed to a large degree unsolved under Basel III as the regulator has a questionable way of interpreting the intrinsic risk in assets across the different categories. A significant part of the sovereign bond issues by governments are still considered risk-free and therefore no capital has to be held against those assets, and (2) when the capital market funding dried up in the run-up to the financial crisis, and given the fact that the banks committed to providing liquidity to the SPVs (supra) offering those securitized products, they now had to take the liquidity risk (of the SPVs) on their own balance sheets. That on top of the fact that the banks, as indicated, often kept the most risky tranches on their books anyway.

The consequence was that risk exposure blew up on the banks' balance sheets; SPVs failed which reneged on (implicit) liquidity puts. Not only the banks but also the institutional investors had to face the music as their safe ('AAA') tranches turned out to be more risky than anticipated. The most impacted were those that invested in securitized products using significant amounts of leverage, that is, levered holders of securitized claims (such as hedge funds). Their very thin capital base evaporated quickly, in particular when their money market funding dried up. While many of these levered investors went overboard, this had little systemic implications, that is, shadow banking does not always involve puts to the safety mechanism.

---

[28] J. Geanakoplos, (2010), The Leverage Cycle, in NBER Macroeconomic Annual 2009, (ed. by D. Acemoglu, K. Rogoff, and M. Woodford), Vol. 24, pp. 1–65, National Bureau of Economic Research, Cambridge, Massachusetts; A. Shleifer, and R. W. Vishny, (2010), Unstable Banking, Journal of Financial Economics, Vol. 97, pp. 306–318; A. Boot, and L. Ratnovski, (2012), Banking and Trading, IMF Working Paper Nr. WP/12/238, Washington.

[29] H.S. Shin, (2009), Securitization and Financial Stability, The Economic Journal, Vol. 119, pp. 309–332.

[30] Claessens et al. (2012), Ibid. p. 13.

In the initial years of the crisis, private-label securitization (i.e. not guaranteed by the government one way or the other) was also, to a large degree, caused by very low demand, as the perception or qualification of 'safe' or 'low risk' was no longer associated with these assets. Also, the supply of instruments (loans and loan portfolios) dried up or at least are at much lower levels than before the crisis, and so there is less inventory that can be turned into securitized products. It was observed that from 2011 to 2012 onward, the securitization process started in many economies, including the US and Europe (supra).

Claessens et al. commented in 2012: '[o]nce economic activity and private credit demand recover, securitization may resume in advanced countries. It will, however, likely more resemble how it was in the 1980s; that is, used as a technology to diversify idiosyncratic risk and funded by unlevered, real money accounts'.[31] Judging back from 2019, I'm not so sure that that has become a distinct reality. In the aftermath of the 2007 crisis, the attention of the securitization machine initially shifted from real estate loan portfolios to personal loans, car loans credit card debt and student loans and infrastructure debt (CLOs). Even new niche areas are created as the VC debt ABS market which bundle loans provided to early or seed capital stage biotech or healthcare firms.[32] The securitization pie has been shrinking but became more esoteric. But the intention stayed the same, that is, to shift credit, maturity and liquidity risk of the banks' balance sheets in order to allow more leverage and more investments on a low equity base. Also, there is a variety among different countries: 2013 was tough on many counts. In contrast, in 2014, the RMBS market revived and so did the securitized SME loan market.[33]

The road the securitization machine traveled post-crisis has not been a walk in the park.[34] But with some regulatory help, the industry regained its ground although not with volumes as was the case before the crisis, definitely not in Europe.

3.2.3 The Long-Term Financing Needs of the EU

The EU, as highlighted before, issued in March 2014 a communication[35] on the future of finance, that is, on the future of long-term financing in the EU. The idea was to stimulate new and different ways of unlocking long-term financing and support Europe's return to

[31] Claessens et al. (2012), Ibid. p. 14.

[32] T. Alloway, (2014), Yield hunters Soak Up Venture Capital Debt, *Financial Times*, February 3, 2014. Other new areas of ABS are music portfolio's and airline leases, solar panel leases, peer-to-peer loans and income portfolio of single-family rental properties.

[33] C. Thompson, (2014), UK Commercial Mortgage-Backed Securities enjoy revival, *Financial Times*, January 28.

[34] A. Barker and C. Binham, (2015), EU Seeks to Relax Securitization Rules, *Financial Times*, February 17. The regulator however angered the securitization industry mid 2015 with new and additional disclosure rules for a wide variety of securitized products: T. Hale, (2015), New Regulatory Measures Anger European Securitization Industry, *Financial Times*, May 17.

[35] Communication of the Commission to the Council and the European parliament on Long-Term Financing of the European Economy, SWD(2014)105. That was following a public consultation based on the green book published in 2013 titled: Green Paper on the Long Term Financing of the European Economy, (March 25, 2013).

sustainable economic growth. Significant long-term investment will be needed under the Europe 2020 (actually 2050) strategy and the 2030 climate and energy package, in infrastructure, new technologies and innovation, R&D and human capital. The economic and financial crisis had affected the ability of the financial sector to channel funds to the real economy, in particular to long-term investment. Europe has always relied heavily on banks financing the real economy (two-thirds of funding comes from banks, compared to one-third in the US). The package of measures adopted included a communication on the long-term financing of the economy, a legislative proposal for new rules for occupational pension funds[36] and a communication on crowdfunding.[37] The actions that were suggested can be categorized as follows:

1. Mobilizing private sources of long-term financing: the actions include finalizing the details of the prudential framework for banks and insurance companies in a way that supports long-term investments in the real economy, mobilizing more personal pension savings and exploring ways to foster more cross-border flows of savings and the merits of a possible EU savings account.

   In that context, the legislative proposal indicated for new rules on occupational pension funds (IORP 2) should contribute to more long-term investment. The proposal has three main objectives:

   - to ensure that pension scheme members are properly protected against risks;
   - to fully reap the benefits of the single market for occupational pensions by removing obstacles to cross-border provision of services;
   - to reinforce the capacity of occupational pension funds to invest in financial assets with a long-term economic profile and thereby support the financing of growth in the real economy.

2. Making better use of public funding: fostering the activity of national promotional banks (financial institutions, created by governments, that provide financing for the purposes of economic development) and promoting better cooperation among existing national export credit schemes (institutions that act as an intermediary between national governments and exporters to issue export financing). Both of these play an important role in long-term financing.
3. Developing European capital markets: facilitating SMEs' access to capital markets and to larger investment pools by creating a liquid and transparent secondary market for corporate bonds, reviving securitization markets with due consideration to the risks as well as to the differentiated nature of such products and improving the EU environment for covered bonds and private placement.

---

[36] Proposal for a Directive of the European Parliament and of the Council, on the activities and supervision of institutions for occupational retirement provision, COM(2014) 167 final, 2014/0091 (COD).

[37] Communication: Unleashing the potential of Crowdfunding in the European Union, COM(2014) 172 final.

4. Improving SMEs' access to financing: the actions set out in the communication on long-term financing include improving credit information on SMEs, reviving the dialogue between banks and SMEs and assessing best practices on helping SMEs access capital markets. Raising awareness and providing information on projects are also among the key elements of the actions put forward in the communication on crowdfunding adopted, in which the Commission proposed to:

   - promote industry best practices, raise awareness and facilitate the development of a quality label
   - closely monitor the development of crowdfunding markets and national legal frameworks
   - regularly assess whether any form of further EU action—including legislative action—is necessary. The goal is to identify the issues that may need to be addressed in order to support the growth of crowdfunding.

5. Attracting private finance to infrastructure to deliver on Europe 2020: increasing availability of information on infrastructure investment plans and improving the credit statistics on infrastructure loans.
6. Enhancing the wider framework for sustainable finance: improving the corporate governance regime for long-term financing, for example, regarding shareholder engagement (by revising the Shareholders' Rights Directive—proposal due to be adopted shortly), employee ownership, corporate governance reporting and environmental, social and governance (ESG) issues.

That initiative has been absorbed by the wider 2015 Capital Markets Union as was launched in February 2015 (infra).

With respect to securitization in particular, the initial communication commented specifically. Securitization transactions enable banks to refinance loans by pooling assets and converting them into securities that are attractive to institutional investors. From a bank's perspective, such transactions unlock capital resources, increasing the ability of banks to expand their lending and finance economic growth. For institutional investors, such securities, if of sufficient size, offer liquid investment opportunities in asset classes in which they do not invest directly, for example, SMEs or mortgages.

Some securitization models were inadequately regulated in the past. The weaknesses of these models have been identified early on and addressed in the subsequent EU financial reform. Risk retention ('skin-in-the-game') requirements have been in place in the EU banking sector since 2011 and have been widened to all financial sectors. In addition, disclosure obligations have been reinforced to allow investors to develop a thorough understanding of the instruments in which they invest. Many concrete actions are being taken by the authorities to make securitization transactions more standardized and transparent, thereby enhancing investors' confidence. EU institutions and agencies need to increase their cooperation and develop synergies, for instance, in terms of the standardization of reporting templates. In addition, initiatives led by industry such as the implementation of labeling contribute also to these objectives.

Despite these measures, only moderate recovery of this market has been observed so far. This is in large part due to the stigma still attached to these transactions and to their regulatory treatment. Many stakeholders have called for a differentiation of securitization products for prudential purposes in order to foster the development of sustainable securitization markets. EIOPA's technical report for Solvency II and the Commission proposal on banking structural reform introduce a differentiation for 'high'-quality securitization products.

Further in this chapter, we will look closer at the EU securitization regulation and its evolution in recent years.

3.2.4 Regulatory Dynamics Regarding Securitization

In light of the above and given the experience during the financial crisis, the IOSCO (International Organization of Securities Commissions) issued its recommendations in November 2012.[38] The IOSCO believes that securitization markets can play a role in supporting economic growth.

The Bank for International Settlements (BIS) by then already issued their view in their '[r]evision to the Basel securitization framework-consultation document',[39] within which the Basel Committee concluded that both external ratings for, and bank assessments of, securitization exposures often did not accurately reflect the risks of securitization. It further proposed substantial changes in how banks calculate their risk-based capital requirements related to securitization exposures. The proposed revisions are intended to, among other things, make capital requirements for securitizations more prudent and risk sensitive and to mitigate mechanistic reliance on external credit ratings. It provides an overview of the two proposed alternatives for calculating the capital for securitization exposures, specifically discussing the major components of each alternative and how both alternatives work.

3.2.4.1 The 2012–2013 Proposal of the Basel Committee

The BCBS concluded that the weaknesses of securitizations include (i) an overly mechanistic reliance on external credit ratings, (ii) risk weights for highly rated senior securitization exposures that are too low and (iii) risk weights for low-rated senior exposures that are too high. To address these concerns, the Basel Committee proposed two alternative approaches ('Alternative A' and 'Alternative B') for determining risk weights of securitization exposures. Both alternatives include a Revised Ratings-Based Approach (the 'RRBA'), a Simplified Supervisory Formula Approach (the 'SSFA') and a Modified Supervisory Formula Approach (the 'MSFA'). The SSFA is similar to the simplified

---

[38] IOSCO, (2012), Global Developments in Securitisation Regulation, Final Report (November 2012).

[39] BIS, (2012), Revisions to the Basel Securitisation Framework Consultative Document, Basel, December.

supervisory formula that the US federal banking agencies adopted in their final market risk capital rules, which took effect January 1, 2013[40], and included as part of the proposed risk-based capital rules (June 2012).

The up till then applied securitization framework included two approaches to quantify required capital for credit risk, a Standardized Approach (the 'SA') and an internal ratings-based approach (the 'IRBA'). Under the SA, the more basic of the two approaches, banks use ratings from external credit rating agencies to quantify required capital for credit risk. Under the IRBA, the more complex approach, banks can use their own internal estimated risk parameters for calculating credit risk when there is no external rating. Only banks meeting certain conditions and disclosure requirements may use the IRBA.

Under both the SA and the IRBA, a bank incorporates a Ratings-Based Approach (the 'RBA') into its analysis. The existing RBA consists of risk-weight tables, which are different for each approach. The Basel Committee proposed to revise the RBA by, among other things, replacing the dual tables with one revised table to be used for both approaches. According to the Proposed Revisions, by using a single RBA, the Basel Committee 'seeks to reduce arbitrage opportunities across banks that use different regulatory capital regimes for securitization exposures and to make the overall capital framework more consistent'.[41] Other revisions in the RRBA included a proposal to give national regulators the discretion to increase risk weights for high-risk pool assets. The RRBA also included revised parameters for senior and non-senior tranches, where both tranches would be adjusted by tranche maturity and non-senior tranches would also be adjusted based on their thickness within the structure of a securitization.

In order to apply the RRBA, there must be at least two eligible credit ratings for a securitization exposure, and a bank must use the lower of the two ratings (or the second best in the case of more than two available ratings). According to the Basel Committee, requiring at least two ratings and using the lower of the two 'mitigates the risk of relying on a potentially flawed methodology or isolated errors embedded in the ratings of a single rating agency'.[42]

Industry, despite overall significant concern with the proposed models, seems to favor model A as Alternative A would permit the use of the MSFA, RRBA or SSFA for all exposures (other than re-securitizations), which, among other things, would avoid 'significant differences in risk weights between senior and subordinate tranches in securitization tranches'.[43] By contrast, Alternative B is too restricted and that its 'resulting contrasts in risk weights between senior and subordinated securitization exposures and between securitizations of high quality senior exposures and relatively lower quality exposures is not warranted in many transactions'.[44]

[40] See Risk-Based Capital Guidelines: Market Risk, 77 Fed. Reg. 53,060 (Aug. 30, 2012), accessible: http://www.gpo.gov/fdsys/pkg/FR-2012-08-30/pdf/2012-16759.pdf

[41] BIS (2012), Ibid. Consultative document.

[42] BIS (2012), Ibid. Consultative document.

[43] http://www.americansecuritization.com/content.aspx?id=9178#.UvDTEz1dW8A

[44] http://www.americansecuritization.com/content.aspx?id=9178#.UvDTEz1dW8A

In December 2013, that was followed by a second consultative BIS document.[45] Relative to the first consultation, the major changes in this consultative document apply to the hierarchy of approaches and the calibration of capital requirements.

For the hierarchy, the Committee has proposed a simple framework akin to that used for credit risk:

- Where banks have the capacity and supervisory approval to do so, they may use an internal ratings-based approach to determine the capital requirement based on the risk of the underlying pool of exposures, including expected losses.
- If this internal ratings-based approach cannot be used for a particular securitization exposure, an external ratings-based approach may be used (assuming that the use of ratings is permitted within the relevant jurisdiction).
- Finally, if neither of these approaches can be used, a Standardized Approach would be applied. This is based on the underlying capital requirement that would apply under the Standardized Approach for credit risk, and other risk drivers.

In reviewing the calibration of the approaches, the Committee has revised some of the modeling assumptions behind the original calibration proposed in the first consultative document. These changes result in greater consistency with the underlying credit-risk framework. The result is to significantly reduce capital requirements vis-à-vis the initial proposals, although capital requirements remain more stringent than under the existing framework. The Committee also proposes to set a 15% risk-weight floor for all approaches, instead of the 20% floor originally proposed. It was waiting until the end of 2014 before the final rules arrived (see infra).

3.2.5 The 2014 (Final) Revisions to the Securitization Framework

The Basel Committee published mid-December 2014 the revised securitization framework,[46] which aims to address a number of shortcomings in the Basel II securitization framework and to strengthen the capital standards for securitization exposures held in the banking book. The new framework has come into effect January 2018. This excludes securitization exposures held in the trading book will be subject to the revised framework for the trading book and which will be dealt with separately (infra).

---

[45] BIS, (2013), Revisions to the Securitisation Framework, Basel, December.

[46] BIS, (2014), Revisions to the Securitization Framework, Basel III Document, December 11, on which the review in this book is materially based.

This release has been front run by two consultation rounds[47] and a quantitative impact study.[48] The release forms part of the Committee's broader Basel III agenda to reform regulatory standards for banks in response to the global financial crisis and thus contributes to a more resilient banking sector.

The Committee in developing these new standards has been working together intensively with the International Organization of Securities Commissions (IOSCO) to review securitization markets and to identify factors that may be hindering the development of sustainable securitization markets. The parameters as set out by IOSCO have the intention to help build simple, transparent and sustainable securitization.

3.2.5.1 Shortcomings in the Basel II Framework

The crisis highlighted several weaknesses in the Basel II securitization framework, including concerns that it could generate insufficient capital for certain exposures. This led the Committee to decide that the securitization framework needed to be reviewed. Under the current Basel II securitization framework, banks are required to hold regulatory capital against all their securitization exposures. The Committee identified a number of shortcomings relating to the calibration of risk weights and a lack of incentives for good risk management, namely:

a. Mechanistic reliance on external ratings;
b. Excessively low-risk weights for highly rated securitization exposures;
c. Excessively high-risk weights for low-rated senior securitization exposures;

[47] The final rules demonstrate large similarities with the initial 2012/2013 and 2014 proposals, but there are also some material differences. The Original Proposals contained a number of significant changes to the Basel II securitization framework, including two alternative hierarchies of approaches for determining the regulatory capital requirements for securitization exposures, enhancements to the existing ratings-based and supervisory formula approaches, the introduction of a simplified supervisory formula approach, certain concentration ratio based approaches and a 20% risk-weight floor. But concerns were raised during the consultative process with respect to the calibration, the usability and the lack of risk sensitivity and capital neutrality (market participants argued that a bank should not be required to hold substantially more capital in relation to a securitization exposure than if it held the underlying exposures directly) of the proposed approaches, and concerns were expressed that the resulting increases in capital requirements would be unduly conservative.

[48] Discussed and referred to supra. The revised 2013 proposals contained a number of key changes from the original proposals, including a simplified hierarchy of approaches, starting with an internal ratings-based approach, followed by an external ratings-based approach and then a Standardized Approach (If none of the approaches could be used, a 1250% risk weight would be applied). The approaches themselves were revised and in some respects were simplified; the calibration of the approaches was adjusted, resulting in reductions in risk weights compared with the original proposals; and the Revised Proposals also contained a number of changes and clarifications to the original proposals, including a 15% risk-weight floor. See for a full review of the changes that occurred moving from the proposals to the final rules: K. Hawken et al., (2014), Revisions To Basel Securitisation Framework—Final Rules, December 31, via mondaq.com

d. Cliff effects[49] and
e. Insufficient risk sensitivity of the framework.

The above shortcomings translate into specific objectives that the revisions to the framework seek to achieve: reduce mechanistic reliance on external ratings, increase risk weights for highly rated securitization exposures, reduce risk weights for low-rated senior securitization exposures, reduce cliff effects and enhance the risk sensitivity of the framework.

The intention of the revised securitization framework is to be more risk sensitive; be more prudent in terms of its calibration, broadly consistent with the underlying framework for credit risk, and be as simple as possible. In addition, it should give incentives to improve risk management by assigning capital charges using the best and most diverse information available to banks. Finally, it should be transparent and enable comparability across banks and jurisdictions. This framework aims to achieve the right balance between these objectives.

3.2.5.2 Key Areas of Adjustment

The key areas of adjustment can be highlighted as being:

The Basel II framework consists of two hierarchies, depending on the approach to credit risk used for the type of underlying exposures securitized: one for the Standardized Approach (SA), used by banks that apply the SA credit-risk framework for the asset class which comprises the underlying pool of securitized exposures, and one for the internal ratings-based (IRB) approach, used by banks that apply an IRB approach to credit risk for the asset class which comprises the underlying pool of securitized exposures.

The SA securitization framework is aimed at less sophisticated banks. The treatment of the exposure depends upon whether the bank is acting as investor, originator or providing a third-party facility (e.g. a liquidity facility to guarantee timely payments of principal and interest to investors where there might be timing differences in the receipt of principal and interest amounts from the pool of assets that was securitized).

The IRB approach is aimed at more sophisticated banks and allows for a more granular assessment of the relevant risks associated with the securitization exposures concerned.

Overall, the Basel II framework includes four Ratings-Based Approach (RBA) look-up tables (two under the IRB securitization framework and two others under the SA securitization framework), two internal approaches for non-rated exposures (supervisory formula approach [SFA] and internal assessment approach [IAA]) and several exceptional treatments. In Basel III securitization framework, the Committee has revised the hierarchy to reduce the reliance on external ratings as well as to simplify it and limit the number of approaches. The revised hierarchy of approaches in the revised framework for securitization exposures is[50] as follows:

---

[49] Cliff effects were observed during the financial crisis where small changes in the quality of the underlying pool of securitized exposures quickly led to significant increases in capital requirements.

[50] See for a detailed review and applications of the different approaches BIS, (2014), Ibid. pp. 15–27 and the caps and maximum capital requirements pp. 27–29.

1. Securitization Internal Ratings-Based Approach (SEC-IRBA)
2. Securitization External Ratings-Based Approach (SEC-ERBA)
3. Securitization Standardized Approach (SEC-SA)

The SEC-IRBA is at the top of the revised hierarchy. The underlying model is the Simplified Supervisory Formula Approach (SSFA) and it uses K_{IRB} information as a key input. KIRB is the capital charge for the underlying exposures using the IRB framework (either the advanced or foundation approaches). In order to use the SEC-IRBA, the bank should have the same information as under the Basel II SFA: (i) a supervisory-approved IRB model for the type of underlying exposures in the securitization pool and (ii) sufficient information to estimate K_{IRB}. There is, however, a change with respect to the application of IRB methods to reduce arbitrage opportunities. Under the Basel II securitization framework, if the bank is using the IRB approach for some exposures and the SA for other exposures in the underlying pool, it should generally use the approach corresponding to the predominant share of exposures within the pool. The Basel II framework provides no guidance about determining predominance for so-called mixed pools. In the revised framework, if the bank can calculate K_{IRB} for at least 95% but less than 100% of the underlying exposure amounts of a securitization, it must use a pro-rata approach, applying SA risk weights for exposures for which it cannot calculate K_{IRB} and IRB risk weights for exposures for which it can calculate K_{IRB}.

A bank that cannot calculate K_{IRB} for a given securitization exposure would have to use the SEC-ERBA, provided that this method is implemented by the national regulator. A bank that cannot use the SEC-IRBA or the SEC-ERBA (either because the tranche is unrated or because its jurisdiction does not permit the use of ratings for regulatory purposes) would use the SEC-SA, with a generally more conservative calibration and using K_{SA} as input. To limit the number of options available to banks, if a bank did not apply SEC-IRBA or SEC-ERBA, it would have to apply the SEC-SA with KSA input for all the underlying exposures (even for those for which the bank could calculate K_{IRB}). K_{SA} is the capital charge for the underlying exposures using the Standardized Approach for credit risk. A slightly modified (and more conservative) version of the SEC-SA would be the only approach available for re-securitization exposures. In general, a bank that cannot use SEC-IRBA, SEC-ERBA or SEC-SA for a given securitization exposure would assign the exposure a risk weight of 1250%.

3.2.5.3 Hierarchy and Different Approaches

The Basel II securitization framework does not include an explicit maturity adjustment in either the SFA or the RBA. The Committee has identified this as a flaw of the Basel II approaches. In terms of risk drivers used, the SEC-IRBA and SEC-ERBA can be compared, respectively, to the Basel II SFA and RBA as follows.

a. SEC-IRBA

One of the major shortcomings of the SFA identified by the Committee is the sharp cliff effects in marginal capital charges. This is driven in part due to the lack of an adequate incorporation of maturity.

Under the SFA, the maturity of assets in the underlying pool is only partially considered—through K_{IRB} when calculating capital requirements.

The SFA looks only at the risk of default over a one-year horizon, ignoring the risk of a potential deterioration afterward; it implicitly assumes that a given tranche will not incur any market value loss until the values for all more-junior tranches have been reduced to zero. Reasonable economic risk models would be unlikely to make this assumption when tranche maturity is greater than one year. As the relevant effects of maturity are, however, not fully captured through K_{IRB} alone, the SEC-IRBA incorporates tranche maturity as an additional risk driver. All other inputs (i.e. K_{IRB}, attachment and detachment points, number of exposures in the pool and the pool loss-given default) are used under the SFA.

b. SEC-ERBA

The Basel II RBA assigns risk weights according to the external rating of the exposure, the seniority and the granularity of the underlying pool. The Committee has revised the extent to which external ratings reflect some other relevant risk characteristics and has determined that it is necessary to consider additional risk drivers relative to the Basel II RBA, namely:

- Tranche thickness of non-senior tranches (i.e. the size of the tranche relative to the entire securitization transaction). Under the Basel II RBA, tranche thickness is not fully taken into account. While credit rating agencies consider tranche thickness, analysis performed by the Committee suggests that capital requirements for a given rating of a mezzanine tranche should differ significantly based on tranche thickness.
- Tranche maturity: A rating agency typically targets a given level of expected loss per rating, while the capital charge reflects its expected loss rate conditional on the assumed stress event occurring (unexpected loss). As such, a tranche's unstressed expected loss rate (as reflected in the credit rating) is not a sufficient statistic for determining its stressed expected loss rate (i.e. its unexpected loss rate). The mapping between expected and unexpected loss rates depends in part on tranche maturity.

Notwithstanding, to address concerns about potentially overstating maturity effects, the Committee has reduced the risk weights for longer-maturity tranches assigned under the SEC-ERBA relative to those proposed in the second consultative document. Finally, the Committee has found that credit rating agencies already take granularity into account when assigning a rating to a tranche. In particular, in order to achieve a certain rating, credit rating agencies require different levels of credit enhancement depending on the pool's granularity (the less granular is the pool, the more credit enhancement is required).

3.2.5.4 Improvements to the Securitization Framework

The revised Basel III securitization framework represents a significant improvement to the Basel II framework in terms of reducing complexity of the hierarchy and the number of approaches. Under the revisions there would be only three primary approaches, as opposed to the multiple approaches and exceptional treatments allowed in the Basel II framework.

Further, the application of the hierarchy no longer depends on the role that the bank plays in the securitization—investor or originator or on the credit-risk approach that the bank applies to the type of underlying exposures. Rather, the revised hierarchy of approaches relies on the information that is available to the bank and on the type of analysis and estimations that it can perform on a specific transaction.

The mechanistic reliance on external ratings has been reduced; not only because the RBA is no longer at the top of the hierarchy, but also because other relevant risk drivers have been incorporated into the SEC-ERBA (i.e. maturity and tranche thickness for non-senior exposures).

3.2.5.5 Extensive Review of the 2014 Changes[51]

The review will fall apart in a section regarding credit risk and a section regarding revisions. The latter includes those changes to other items than the securitization framework itself and can be considered less relevant within this context. The intention is not to provide a fully comprehensive review of the changes but to focus on those changes that help to improve our understanding of the impact of the changes in terms of capital adequacy and risk management that shape the context for our shadow banking analysis.

1. Coverage under the new framework

Banks must apply the securitization framework for determining regulatory capital requirements on exposures arising from traditional and synthetic securitizations or similar structures that contain features common to both. Since securitizations may be structured in many different ways, the capital treatment of a securitization exposure must be determined on the basis of its economic substance rather than its legal form.

A traditional securitization is a structure where the cash flow from an underlying pool of exposures is used to service at least two different stratified risk positions or tranches reflecting different degrees of credit risk. Payments to the investors depend upon the performance of the specified underlying exposures, as opposed to being derived from an obligation of the entity originating those exposures. The stratified/

[51] The 2014 changes replace the 2006 Basel II Securitization Framework (paragraphs 538–643) 'Basel II—International Convergence of Capital Measurement and Capital Standards: A Revised Framework—Comprehensive Version and certain items related to Basel 2.5; Basel 2.5—Enhancements to the Basel II framework (2009).

tranched structures that characterize securitizations differ from ordinary senior/subordinated debt instruments in that junior securitization tranches can absorb losses without interrupting contractual payments to more senior tranches, whereas subordination in a senior/subordinated debt structure is a matter of priority of rights to the proceeds of liquidation.

A synthetic securitization is a structure with at least two different stratified risk positions or tranches that reflect different degrees of credit risk where credit risk of an underlying pool of exposures is transferred, in whole or in part, through the use of funded (e.g. credit-linked notes) or unfunded (e.g. credit default swaps) credit derivatives or guarantees that serve to hedge the credit risk of the portfolio. Accordingly, the investors' potential risk is dependent upon the performance of the underlying pool. Banks' exposures to a securitization are hereafter referred to as 'securitization exposures'.

A re-securitization exposure is a securitization exposure in which the risk associated with an underlying pool of exposures is tranched and at least one of the underlying exposures is a securitization exposure. In addition, an exposure to one or more re-securitization exposures is a re-securitization exposure. An exposure resulting from retranching of a securitization exposure is not a re-securitization exposure if the bank is able to demonstrate that the cash flows to and from the bank could be replicated in all circumstances and conditions by an exposure to the securitization of a pool of assets that contains no securitization exposures. Underlying instruments in the pool being securitized may include but are not restricted to the following: loans, commitments, asset-backed and mortgage-backed securities (MBSs), corporate bonds, equity securities and private equity investments. The underlying pool may include one or more exposures.

2. Operational Requirements for the Recognition of Risk Transference

2.1. Traditional Securitizations

When measuring the risk-weighting assets, the originating bank[52] may exclude only if all of the following conditions have been met. Banks meeting these conditions must still hold regulatory capital against any securitization exposures they retain.

- Significant credit risk associated with the underlying exposures has been transferred to third parties.
- The transferor does not maintain effective or indirect control over the transferred exposures. The exposures are legally isolated from the transferor in such a way (e.g. through the sale of assets or through subparticipation) that the exposures are put beyond the reach of the transferor and its creditors, even in bankruptcy or receivership. Banks should obtain legal opinion that confirms true sale. The transferor is deemed to have maintained effective control over the transferred credit-risk exposures

[52] See for a review of the definitions used: BIS, (2014), Revisions to the Securitization Framework, Basel III Document, December 11, pp. 7 ff.

if it (i) is able to repurchase from the transferee the previously transferred exposures in order to realize their benefits or (ii) is obligated to retain the risk of the transferred exposures. The transferor's retention of servicing rights to the exposures will not necessarily constitute indirect control of the exposures.
- The securities issued are not obligations of the transferor. Thus, investors who purchase the securities only have claim to the underlying exposures.
- The transferee is an SPE and the holders of the beneficial interests in that entity have the right to pledge or exchange them without restriction.
- Clean-up calls[53] must satisfy the conditions set out in the securitization framework.
- The securitization does not contain clauses that (i) require the originating bank to alter the underlying exposures such that the pool's credit quality is improved unless this is achieved by selling exposures to independent and unaffiliated third parties at market prices, (ii) allow for increases in a retained first-loss position or credit enhancement provided by the originating bank after the transaction's inception or (iii) increase the yield payable to parties other than the originating bank, such as investors and third-party providers of credit enhancements, in response to a deterioration in the credit quality of the underlying pool.
- There must be no termination options/triggers except eligible clean-up calls, termination for specific changes in tax and regulation or early amortization provisions which result in the securitization transaction failing the operational requirements as set out by the securitization framework.

2.2. Synthetic Securitizations

For synthetic securitizations, the use of credit-risk mitigation (CRM) techniques (i.e. collateral, guarantees and credit derivatives) for hedging the underlying exposure may be recognized for risk-based capital purposes only if the conditions outlined below are satisfied:

- Credit-risk mitigants must comply with the requirements in the Basel II framework.
- Eligible collateral is limited to that specified in the Basel II framework. Eligible collateral pledged by SPEs may be recognized. Eligible guarantors are defined in paragraph 195 of the Basel II framework. Banks may not recognize SPEs as eligible guarantors in the securitization framework.
- Banks must transfer significant credit risk associated with the underlying exposures to third parties.
- The instruments used to transfer credit risk may not contain terms or conditions that limit the amount of credit risk transferred, such as those provided below:

[53] A clean-up call is an option that permits the securitization exposures (e.g. asset-backed securities) to be called before all of the underlying exposures or securitization exposures have been repaid. In the case of traditional securitizations, this is generally accomplished by repurchasing the remaining securitization exposures once the pool balance or outstanding securities have fallen below some specified level. In the case of a synthetic transaction, the clean-up call may take the form of a clause that extinguishes the credit protection (BIS, Ibid. p. 7)

- clauses that materially limit the credit protection or credit-risk transference (e.g. an early amortization provision in a securitization of revolving credit facilities that effectively subordinates the bank's interest; significant materiality thresholds below which credit protection is deemed not to be triggered even if a credit event occurs; or clauses that allow for the termination of the protection due to deterioration in the credit quality of the underlying exposures);
- clauses that require the originating bank to alter the underlying exposures to improve the pool's average credit quality;
- clauses that increase the banks' cost of credit protection in response to deterioration in the pool's quality;
- clauses that increase the yield payable to parties other than the originating bank, such as investors and third-party providers of credit enhancements, in response to a deterioration in the credit quality of the reference pool and
- clauses that provide for increases in a retained first-loss position or credit enhancement provided by the originating bank after the transaction's inception.

• A bank should obtain a legal opinion that confirms the enforceability of the contract.
• Clean-up calls must satisfy the conditions as set out by the securitization framework.

2.3. Securitizations Containing Early Amortization Provisions[54]

A securitization transaction is deemed to fail the operational requirements if the bank (i) originates/sponsors a securitization transaction that includes one or more revolving credit facilities, and (ii) the securitization transaction incorporates an early amortization or similar provision that, if triggered, would (a) subordinate the bank's senior or pari passu interest in the underlying revolving credit facilities to the interest of other investors, (b) subordinate the bank's subordinated interest to an even greater degree relative to the interests of other parties or (c) in other ways increase the bank's exposure to losses associated with the underlying revolving credit facilities.

If a securitization transaction contains a number of specific cases of an early amortization provision and meets the operational requirements, an originating bank may exclude the underlying exposures associated with such a transaction from the calculation of risk-weighted assets, but must still hold regulatory capital against any securitization exposures they retain in connection with the transaction.

---

[54] An early amortization provision is a mechanism that, once triggered, accelerates the reduction of the investor's interest in underlying exposures of a securitization of revolving credit facilities and allows investors to be paid out prior to the originally stated maturity of the securities issued. A securitization of revolving credit facilities is a securitization in which one or more underlying exposures represent, directly or indirectly, current or future draws on a revolving credit facility. Examples of revolving credit facilities include but are not limited to credit card exposures, home equity lines of credit, commercial lines of credit and other lines of credit (BIS, Ibid. p. 8).

2.4. Operational Requirements and Treatment of Clean-Up Calls

For securitization transactions that include a clean-up call, no capital will be required due to the[55]presence of a clean-up call if the following conditions are met: (i) the exercise of the clean-up call must not be mandatory, in form or in substance, but rather must be at the discretion of the originating bank; (ii) the clean-up call must not be structured to avoid allocating losses to credit enhancements or positions held by investors or otherwise structured to provide credit enhancement; and (iii) the clean-up call must only be exercisable when 10% or less of the original underlying portfolio or securities issued remains, or, for synthetic securitizations, when 10% or less of the original reference portfolio value remains.

Securitization transactions that include a clean-up call that does not meet all of the criteria result in a capital requirement for the originating bank. For a traditional securitization, the underlying exposures must be treated as if they were not securitized. Additionally, banks must not recognize in regulatory capital any gain on sale. For synthetic securitizations, the bank purchasing protection must hold capital against the entire amount of the securitized exposures as if they did not benefit from any credit protection. If a clean-up call, when exercised, is found to serve as a credit enhancement, the exercise of the clean-up call must be considered a form of implicit support provided by the bank and must be treated in accordance with the supervisory guidance pertaining to securitization transactions.

In order to be eligible for this treatment, a certain level of due diligence needs to be adhered to.[56]

2.5. Treatment of the Securitization Exposures

Regulatory capital is required for banks' securitization exposures, including those arising from the provision of credit-risk mitigants to a securitization transaction, investments in asset-backed securities, retention of a subordinated tranche and extension of a liquidity facility or credit enhancement, as set forth in the following sections. Repurchased securitization exposures must be treated as retained securitization exposures. Banks must deduct from Common Equity Tier 1 any increase in equity capital resulting from a securitization transaction, such as that associated with expected future margin income resulting in a gain on sale that is recognized in regulatory capital.[57]

The risk-weighted asset amount of a securitization exposure is computed by multiplying the exposure amount, as defined at the beginning of this subsection, by the appropriate risk weight determined in accordance with the hierarchy of approaches. That hierarchy was indicated above.[58]

---

[55] Under the clause, the issuer may reduce its own administrative expenses by buying back the remaining issue when the principal has been reduced to an insignificant amount, usually to less than 10% of the original issue.

[56] See for details: BIS, Ibid. p. 13.

[57] Par. 74 of BIS, (2011), Basel III: A Global Regulatory Framework for more Resilient Banks and Banking Systems—revised version June 2011.

[58] And is further detailed in BIS, (2014), Ibid. par. 42–47.

2.6. Treatment of Overlapping Exposures

For the purposes of calculating capital requirements, a bank's exposure A overlaps another exposure B if in all circumstances the bank will preclude any loss for the bank on exposure B by fulfilling its obligations with respect to exposure A. For example, if a bank provides full credit support to some notes and holds a portion of these notes, its full credit support obligation precludes any loss from its exposure to the notes. If a bank can verify that fulfilling its obligations with respect to exposure A will preclude a loss from its exposure to B under any circumstance, the bank does not need to calculate risk-weighted assets for its exposure to B. To arrive at an overlap, a bank may, for the purposes of calculating capital requirements, split or expand its exposures. That is, splitting exposures into portions that overlap with another exposure held by the bank and other portions that do not overlap and expanding exposures by assuming for capital purposes that obligations with respect to one of the overlapping exposures are larger than those established contractually. The latter could be done, for instance, by expanding either the trigger events to exercise the facility and/or the extent of the obligation.[59] Overlap could also be recognized between relevant capital charges for exposures in the trading book and capital charges for exposures in the banking book, provided that the bank is able to calculate and compare the capital charges for the relevant exposures.

2.7. Treatment of Credit-Risk Mitigation for Securitization Exposures

2.7.1. Eligible Credit-Risk Mitigation Techniques for Protection Buyers

A bank may recognize credit protection purchased on a securitization exposure when calculating capital requirements subject to the following:

- Collateral recognition is limited to that permitted under the credit-risk mitigation framework of the Basel II framework; collateral pledged by SPEs may be recognized.
- Credit protection provided by the entities listed in the Basel II framework may be recognized. SPEs cannot be recognized as eligible guarantors.
- Where guarantees or credit derivatives fulfill the minimum operational conditions as specified in the Basel II framework, banks can take account of such credit protection in calculating capital requirements for securitization exposures.

---

[59] For example, a liquidity facility may not be contractually required to cover defaulted assets or may not fund an ABCP program in certain circumstances. For capital purposes, such a situation would not be regarded as an overlap to the notes issued by that ABCP conduit. However, the bank may calculate risk-weighted assets for the liquidity facility as if it were expanded (either in order to cover defaulted assets or in terms of trigger events) to preclude all losses on the notes. In such a case, the bank would only need to calculate capital requirements on the liquidity facility (BIS, (2014), Ibid. p. 14.

2.7.2. Full or Proportional Cover

When a bank provides full (or pro rata) credit protection to a securitization exposure, the bank must calculate its capital requirements as if it directly holds the portion of the securitization exposure on which it has provided credit protection.

2.7.3. Tranched Protection

In the case of tranched credit protection, the original securitization tranche will be decomposed into protected and unprotected sub-tranches:

The protection provider must calculate its capital requirement as if directly exposed to the particular sub-tranche of the securitization exposure on which it is providing protection, and as determined by the hierarchy of approaches for securitization exposures. Provided that the conditions set out are met, the protection buyer may recognize tranched protection on the securitization exposure. In doing so, it must calculate capital requirements for each sub-tranche separately and as follows: For the resulting unprotected exposure(s), capital requirements will be calculated as determined by the hierarchy of approaches for securitization exposures. For the guaranteed/protected portion, capital requirements will be calculated according to the applicable CRM framework.

If, according to the hierarchy of approaches, the bank must use the SEC-IRBA or SEC-SA, the parameters should be calculated separately for each of the sub-tranches as if the latter would have been directly issued as separate tranches at the inception of the transaction. The value for KIRB (respectively KSA) will be computed on the underlying portfolio of the original transaction.

If, according to the hierarchy of approaches, the bank must use the SEC-ERBA for the original securitization exposure, the relevant risk weights for the different sub-tranches will be calculated subject to the following:

- For the sub-tranche of highest priority, the bank will use the risk weight of the original securitization exposure.
- For a sub-tranche of lower priority:
  - Banks must infer a rating from one of the subordinated tranches in the original transaction. The risk weight of the sub-tranche of lower priority will be then determined by applying the inferred rating to the SEC-ERBA. The thickness input will be computed for the sub-tranche of lower priority only.
  - Should it not be possible to infer a rating, the risk weight for the sub-tranche of lower priority will be computed using the SEC-SA applying the adjustments to the determination of A and D of the methodology. The risk weight for this sub-tranche will be obtained as the greater of a) the risk weight determined through the application of the SEC-SA with the adjusted A and D points and b) the SEC-ERBA risk weight of the original securitization exposure prior to recognition of protection.

Under all approaches, a lower priority sub-tranche must be treated as a non-senior securitization exposure even if the original securitization exposure prior to protection qualifies as senior.

2.8. Maturity Mismatches

A maturity mismatch exists when the residual maturity of a hedge is less than that of the underlying exposure. When protection is bought on a securitization exposure(s), for the purpose of setting regulatory capital against a maturity mismatch, the capital requirement will be determined in accordance with the Basel II framework. When the exposures being hedged have different maturities, the longest maturity must be used. When protection is bought on the securitized assets, maturity mismatches may arise in the context of synthetic securitizations (when, e.g. a bank uses credit derivatives to transfer part or all of the credit risk of a specific pool of assets to third parties). When the credit derivatives unwind, the transaction will terminate. This implies that the effective maturity of all the tranches of the synthetic securitization may differ from that of the underlying exposures. Banks that synthetically securitize exposures held on their balance sheet by purchasing tranched credit protection must treat such maturity mismatches in the following manner: For securitization exposures that are assigned a risk weight of 1250%, maturity mismatches are not taken into account. For all other securitization exposures, the bank must apply the maturity mismatch treatment set forth in the Basel II framework. When the exposures being hedged have different maturities, the longest maturity must be used.

3.2.5.6 Summarized: The New BCBS Securitization Rules

In Table 3.1 the new December 2014 securitization rules are summarized.[60] Note that these rules cannot be read and applied independently, but should be read in conjunction with jurisdiction-specific implementation rules (IOSCO-based) and special regimes (e.g. the STS securitization proposal in the EU).

3.2.6 Recent Securitization Policy Revisions and Regulation

Banks are, or at least were, the electric fuse box of the economic and business systems in countries and the world. Based on their extensive knowledge, they were typically better informed on the loans they originate than other financial intermediaries. The question arises whether securitized loans are of lower credit quality than otherwise similar non-securitized loans. The question then arises if one can assess the effect of securitization

[60] Further details can be found in the December 2014 BCBS final report on securitization as already highlighted (note that the 2016 update will be discussed a little further in this chapter and that ideally both should be read together); further reference can also be made to: S. Bell et al., (2015), Revisions to the Securitization Framework: Final Rules published by the Basel Committee, May 15, dsupra Business Advisors, via jdsupra.com; K. Hawken et al., (2014), Revisions to Basel Securitization Framework- Final Rules, December 22, via mayorbrown.com

Table 3.1 The new BCBS 2014 securitization rules

The final December 2014 rules focus on (1) increased risk sensitivity; (2) being more prudent in terms of calibration, broadly consistent with the underlying framework for credit risk; (3) simplicity; (4) assigning capital charges based on the best and most diverse information available to banks; (5) transparency; and (6) comparability across banks and jurisdictions.
The revised securitization framework is broadly similar to the revised proposals. In particular, the basic hierarchy of approaches is unchanged, as are the 15% risk-weight floor and the availability of certain caps. However, there are some changes, particularly with respect to maturity, and some further clarifications.
Banks will be required to apply the revised securitization framework to their exposures to traditional and synthetic securitizations held in their banking book.
A synthetic securitization is defined as a structure with at least two different stratified risk positions or tranches that reflect different degrees of credit risk where the credit risk of an underlying pool of exposures is transferred, in whole or in part, through the use of funded or unfunded credit derivatives or guarantees that serve to hedge the credit risk of the portfolio and where the investors' potential risk is dependent on the performance of the underlying pool.
Securitization exposures may include investments in asset-backed securities, retention of subordinated tranches, credit enhancement, liquidity facilities, interest rate and currency swaps and credit derivatives.
The risk-weighted amount of a securitization exposure will, as a general principle, be calculated by multiplying the amount of the securitization exposure by the risk weight determined under the applicable approach under the revised securitization framework.

The hierarchy of approaches under the revised securitization framework is as follows: **Securitization Internal Ratings-Based Approach (SEC-IRBA)** **Securitization External Ratings-Based Approach (SEC-ERBA) (if permitted by local regulator)** **Securitization Standardized Approach (SEC-SA)** **1250% risk weight** Additional features: The risk weights calculated under the SEC-IRBA, the SEC-ERBA and the SEC-SA will be subject to a floor risk weight of 15%. A number of risk weight caps are used: (1) a risk-weight cap for senior securitization exposures, using a 'look-through' approach, (2) a maximum capital requirement for banks acting as originators, sponsors or investors using the SEC-IRBA and (3) a maximum capital requirement for banks acting as originators or sponsors (but not banks acting as investors) using the SEC-ERBA or the SEC-SA. Banks that want to use any of the methods indicated above will have to comply with due diligence rules: (1) a comprehensive understanding of the risk characteristics of the securitization exposures, (2) a comprehensive understanding of the risk characteristics of the underlying pools and the ability to access performance information on an ongoing basis and (3) a thorough understanding of all structural features of a securitization that would materially impact the performance of the bank's exposures to the transaction. Non-compliance will lead to a 1250% risk weighting. There are relief rules: a bank has more than one exposure to a securitization. They will not be required to calculate risk-weighted assets for one of those exposures to the extent that it meets the conditions to show that they overlap. In the case of currency and interest rate swaps, under each of the SEC-IRBA, the SEC-ERBA and the SEC-SA, the risk weight will be inferred from a securitization exposure that ranks pari passu, or failing that, from the next subordinated tranche.	The securitization internal ratings-based approach (the 'SEC-IRBA') is at the top of the hierarchy of approaches.[a] This is based on the capital charge for the underlying pool of exposures calculated under the IRB approach. An IRB pool is a securitization pool for which the bank is able to use an IRB approach to calculate capital requirements for all underlying exposures because firstly it has supervisory approval to use an IRB approach and secondly it has sufficient information to calculate the IRB capital requirements for the applicable type of exposures. Under the revised securitization framework, it has now been established that the SEC-IRBA can only be used in the case of a mixed pool where the bank can calculate KIRB for at least 95% of the underlying exposure amounts. If this is not the case, the bank will need to use the next available approach in the hierarchy. If it is not possible to use the SEC-IRBA (e.g. if the bank does not have sufficient information on the underlying assets), it will then need to use the securitization external ratings-based approach (the 'SEC-ERBA'), which is based on external (or inferred) credit ratings, provided the use of this approach is permitted in the applicable jurisdiction. For example, it will not be available in the US since references to credit ratings in regulations are not permitted under Dodd-Frank. In the case of unrated exposures to asset-backed commercial paper programs, the bank may be able to use an internal assessment approach ('IAA').[b] The SEC-ERBA is based on the credit rating (from an external rating agency or where a rating can be inferred) of the exposure. For securitization exposures with long-term ratings, the risk weights will depend on the following factors: (a) external or inferred rating; (b) seniority of the tranche; (c) maturity of the tranche and (d) for non-senior tranches, tranche thickness. If neither the SEC-IRBA nor the SEC-ERBA may be used, the securitization standardized approach (the 'SEC-SA') will be applicable. Under the SEC-SA, the calculation of the applicable risk weight will be based on the capital charges for the underlying exposures using the Standardized Approach. In the event that none of the above approaches are available, a 1250% risk weight will need to be applied.

(continued)

Table 3.1 (continued)

[a]In order to calculate the capital requirements for a securitization exposure under the SEC-IRBA, the following bank-supplied inputs will be required to be used: (a) the capital charge for the underlying exposures under the IRB approach had such exposures not been securitized ('K_{IRB}'), (b) the tranche attachment point ('A') (representing the threshold at which losses in the underlying pool would first be allocated to the securitization exposure), (c) the tranche detachment point ('D') (representing the threshold at which losses in the underlying pool would result in a total loss of principal for the relevant tranche) and (d) a supervisory parameter, 'p'. The formula for the supervisory parameter, 'p', includes an adjustment for the maturity of the particular tranche. The maturity adjustment concept was the subject of considerable discussion during the consultation process. The maturity of the tranche can be calculated for the purposes of the SEC-IRBA using either of the following methods: (a) on the basis of the weighted average maturity of the contractual cash flows of the relevant tranche, but only if such contractual payments are unconditional and not dependent on the actual performance of the securitized assets, or (b) on the basis of final legal maturity, subject to a haircut. Maturity is subject to a floor of one year and a cap of five years

[b]The IAA contains information regarding the credit quality of unrated securitization exposures to asset-backed commercial paper programs such as liquidity facilities and credit enhancement, provided that the bank has supervisory approval and an approved IRB model and certain operational requirements are met in relation to the bank's internal assessment process

activity on loans' relative credit quality. Marques-Ibanez[61] went through this exercise based on a detailed dataset from the euro-denominated syndicated loan market. They find that 'at issuance, banks do not seem to select and securitize loans of lower credit quality.[62] Following securitization, however, the credit quality of borrowers whose loans are securitized deteriorates by more than those in the control group.'[63] This seems to point at the fact that 'poorer performance by securitized loans might be linked to banks' reduced monitoring incentives'.[64]

This obviously needs to be judged against weaknesses as identified by the BCBS in 2014.[65] They identified two material weaknesses to the framework being (1) mechanic reliance on external ratings and (2) insufficient risk sensitivity. Under the Basel II framework, there was quite some risk-weight arbitrage going on.[66] Buchanan point out however that the pre-crisis story on securitization is not a simple matter of moral

---

[61] D. Marques-Ibanez, (2016), Securitization and Credit Quality, IMF Working Paper Series Nr. WP/16/221, November (later on also in European Financial Management, Vol. 25, Issue 2, pp. 407–434).

[62] That seems to be in line with the 'signaling hypothesis', that is, 'that based on observables at the time of issuance, originating banks would be securitizing those loans with lower credit risk' (Ibid., p. 9). He further details that 'the signaling argument relies on the fact that outsiders could only roughly assess the credit quality of the borrower through observable indicators such as credit ratings or accounting statements. In contrast banks may possess a more accurate view on the future performance on the loans they originated due to their access to proprietary information on the borrower. Hence, banks would have an incentive to use this information and securitize apparently good loans' (Ibid. p. 10).

[63] See also: U. Albertazzi et al., (2015), Asymmetric Information in Securitization: An Empirical Assessment, *Journal of Monetary Economics*, Vol. 71, pp. 33–49; V. Bord et al., (2015), Does Securitization of Corporate Loans Lead to Riskier Lending?, *Journal of Money, Credit and Banking* Vol. 47, pp. 415–444; G. Cerqueiro et al., (2016), Collateralization, Bank Loan Rates and Monitoring: Evidence from a Natural Experiment. *Journal of Finance*, Vol. 71, pp. 1295–1322; R. Elul, (2015), Securitization and Mortgage Default, *Journal of Financial Services Research* Vol. 49, pp. 281–309; C. Jessen and D. Lando, (2015) Robustness of Distance-to-Default, *Journal of Banking and Finance*, Vol. 50, pp. 493–505; Y. Wang, and H. Xia, (2015), Do Lenders Still Monitor When They Can Securitize Loans? *Review of Financial Studies*, Vol. 28, pp. 2354–2391.

[64] Banks tend to, when they securitize, retain them for collateral purposes. Changes in the risk-based capital ratios (increase due to transfer of risky assets), risk-weighted solvency ratios (improved) and in the leverage ratios (no reduction) of securitizer banks have been observed mainly due to the issuances of ABSs eligible as collateral. See in detail: A.D. Scopelliti, (2017), Securitisation, Bank Capital and Financial Regulation:Evidence from European Banks, Warwick Working Paper, June, mimeo.

[65] BCBS, (2014), Revisions to the Securitization Framework, July. Please observe that the securitization framework was impacted by both BCBS, (2016), Revisions to the Securitization Framework, July, and the December 2017 overall Basel III reform package. See Ibid. pp. 3–52; BCBS, (2017), Basel III: Finalising Post-Crisis Reforms, December. In particular the Standardized Approach to credit risk plays a role here. See BCBS, (2017), High-Level Summary of Basel III Reforms, pp. 2–4.

[66] Regarding size and scope of the regulatory arbitrage, see in extenso M. Effing, (2016), Arbitraging theBasel Securitization Framework: Evidence from German ABS Investment, ESRB Working Paper Nr. 22, September. Three findings in particular were of interest: (1) banks arbitrage Basel II risk weights for ABS. Banks tend to buy the securities with the highest yields and the worst collateral in a group of ABS with the same risk weight (and, therefore, the same capital charge), (2) banks operating with low capital adequacy ratios close to the regulatory minimum requirement are found to arbitrage risk weights most aggressively and (3) banks with tight regulatory constraints buy riskier ABS with lower capital requirements than other banks.

failures but that it rather lies in the more subtle elements of the financial system. It might be a matter of flawed incentives and the shifting of responsibility for handling risk. The shifting of risk and ethics is a difficult story[67] and one that isn't often told.

3.2.6.1 The 2016 Update to the Securitization Framework

Following the 2014 new securitization framework, which was introduced after the financial crisis showed a number of material weaknesses being embedded in the Basel II standards, the 2016 update was largely due to the Basel Committee and the International Organization of Securities Commissions (IOSCO) jointly conducting work to review securitization markets and to identify factors that may be hindering the development of sustainable securitization markets. The Committee and IOSCO issued in July 2015 criteria that could help—and to assist the financial industry's development of—simple, transparent and comparable securitization. The 2016 update[68] now reflects all the STC (simple, transparent and comparable) criteria. The STC criteria[69] developed explicitly excluded short-term securitizations (and more specifically, ABCP conduits/programs) from the scope of the criteria. However, short-term securitization instruments other than ABCP should not be prevented from qualifying for STC status simply because their maturity is shorter than one year, provided that they qualify under the existing STC criteria.

During the same period, the EBA released their securitization report[70] with focus on risk retention and due diligence. Since the introduction of the risk retention, due diligence and disclosure rules in the EU through CRD II in 2011, a very limited number of breaches of the requirements have been reported. Only in one case it led to sanctions in the form of additional risk weights as per Article 407 of the CRR.[71]

[67] B.G. Buchanan, (2016), Securitization: A Financing Vehicle for All Season?, *Journal of Business Ethics*, October, Vol. 138, Issue 3, pp. 559–577.

[68] BCBS, (2016), Revisions to the Securitization Framework, July, p. 1. The changes are based on the sound practices as detailed on in the BCBS report (2015) regarding '[c]riteria for identifying simple, transparent and comparable securitisations', July 23.

[69] Ibid. pp. 5 ff.

[70] As warranted under Article 410(1) of Regulation (EU) No 575/2013 (the Capital Requirements Regulation, or CRR).

[71] See EBA, (2016), EBA Report on Securitization, Risk Retention, Due diligence and Disclosure, Report EBA-Op-2016–06, April 12. It needs to be observed at this stage that Mirza and Stevens conclude that forcing originators to hold additional skin-in-the-game reduces welfare. The question remains to what degree skin-in-the-game retention rules do effectively benefit markets, and whether the risk retention rule has improved the performance of the underlying loans. The initial evidence seems to be positive. So far after introduction of the rule we have observed issuances that are up. But issuers do not always use the horizontal risk retention, which from a regulatory point of view is the optimal structure (G. Chemla, and C. Hennessy, (2014), Skin in the Game and Moral Hazard, *Journal of Finance*, Vol. 69, Issue 4, pp. 1597–1641; T. Begley, and A. Purnanandam,

Before looking at the European STS regulation, it might be good to shortly detail the concept of the STS criteria[72]:

- Simplicity refers to the 'homogeneity of underlying assets with simple characteristics, and a transaction structure that is not overly complex'.
- Transparency is put in place to provide 'investors with sufficient information on the underlying assets, the structure of the transaction and the parties involved in the transaction, thereby promoting a more thorough understanding of the risks involved'. The form in which the information is available should not hinder transparency, but instead it should support investors in their assessment.
- Comparability should assist investors in 'their understanding of such investments and enable more straightforward comparison between securitization products within an asset class'.

(2017), Design of Financial Securities: Empirical Evidence from Private-label RMBS Deals, *Review of Financial Studies*, Vol. 30, Issue 1, pp. 120–161). Also other changes have been observed post-introduction of the retention rule: 'issuances that previously would have contained an entire large loan are being replaced by multiple, smaller issuances that each contain only a portion of a larger loan, with each small deal having a different issuer. This allows issuers to limit their potential losses, since the amount an issuer is required to retain for a small security is less than it would be on a large security'. See J. Disalvo and R. Johnston, (2018), Skin in the Game in the CMBS Market, FRB of Philadelphia, Q1 Report, pp. 11–17. J. Yang concludes that asset securitization plays a role in supplying alternative liquid assets (fiat money). As the economy can invest its resources more efficiently in high-yielding illiquid assets (capital) due to securitization, both consumption and welfare increase overall. See in detail: J. Yang, (2019), Alchemy of Financial Innovation: Securitization, Liquidity and Optimal Monetary Policy, Bank of Korea Working Paper Nr. 10, February. See a contrario: J.I. Peña, (2019), Credit Cycles, Securitization, and Credit Default Swaps, Universidad Carlos III de Madrid – Department of Business Administration Working Paper, January 6, mimeo. Also E. Elul, (2015), Securitization and Mortgage Default, Working Paper FRB of Philadelphia, February; A. Bisbey, (2017), Large CMBS Loans Are Being Carved Up to Spread Risk, but…, American Banker, May. The implication of this phenomenon is that spreading a loan across multiple CMBS deals in this way means more claimants if the loan defaults, which could complicate the resolution effort. In recent times Furfine concluded that that risk retention implementation is associated with mortgages being issued with markedly higher interest rates, yet notably lower loan-to-value ratios and higher income to debt-service ratios. These findings suggest that the risk retention rules have made securitized loans safer, yet at a significant cost to borrowers. Roughly three times the amount of risk is retained compared to the situation prior to the introduction of the rule. See in detail: C. Furfine, (2019), The Impact of Risk Retention Regulation on the Underwriting of Securitized Mortgages, *Journal of Financial Services Research*, March, pp. 1–24. Bayeh et al. demonstrate that higher bank competition reduces efficiency. More importantly, their findings suggest that banks securitizing their loans are more cost efficient than other banks. A. Bayeh et al., (2018), Competition, Securitization, and Efficiency in US Banks, Working Paper Nr. September 27., mimeo.

[72] BCBS, (2015), Criteria for Identifying Simple, Transparent and Comparable Securitisations, July 23 (bis.org)

Those three criteria will be judged along the lines of 14 different markers[73] positioned across 3 different types of risk.[74] The three risks are (1) asset risk, risk related to the underlying asset pool; (2) structural risk, relates to transparency risk surrounding the securitization process, and (3) fiduciary and services risk, relates to the governance of all parties involved in the securitization process.

The markers are as follows:

Asset risk	Nature of the assets
	Asset performance history
	Payment status
	Consistency of underwriting
	Asset selection and transfer
	Initial and ongoing data
Structural risk	Redemption cash flow
	Currency and interest rate asset and liability mismatches
	Payment priorities and observability
	Voting and enforcement rights
	Documentation disclosure and legal review
	Alignment of interest
Fiduciary and services risk	Fiduciary and contractual responsibilities
	Transparency to investors

3.2.6.2 The European STS Regulation

After a very short legislative process, the STS regulation was adopted and published with a view toward full implementation by January 1, 2019. Two pieces of regulation were enacted simultaneously: regulation (EU) 2017/2402 (the securitization regulation itself) and regulation (EU) 2017/2401 (the securitization prudential regulation, or SPR, regarding capital reduction for certain securitized products).[75] Before we dive into the analysis, let's first have a look at the content of the STS regulation.

---

[73] That is a minimum. Other markets might be included to reflect specific needs and applications related to collateral affairs, regulatory issues or investor mandates. Tightening skin-in-the-game also directly reduces theresources available to those who most need them. See A. Mirza and E. Stephens, (2016), Securitization and Aggregate Investment Efficiency, Working Paper, May 10, mimeo. They refer to incomplete markets to explain that effect which they describe as follows: '[w]hen intermediaries are forced to hold some of the idiosyncratic risk associated with their investments however, a pecuniary externality can generate inefficient investment ex-ante and excessive fire-sales ex-post (due to higher valuations ed.)' (p. 29).

[74] BCBS, (2015), Criteria for Identifying Simple, Transparent and Comparable Securitisations, July 23, pp. 5 ff. including the annex for a further elaboration of these markers.

[75] Regulation (EU) 2017/2401 of the European Parliament and of the Council of 12 December 2017 amending Regulation (EU) No 575/2013 on prudential requirements for credit institutions and investment firms, OJ L 347, 28.12.2017, pp. 1–34 and Regulation (EU) 2017/2402 of the European Parliament and of the Council of 12 December 2017 laying down a general framework for securitization and creating a specific framework for simple transparent and standardized securitization, and amending Directives 2009/65/EC, 2009/138/EC and 2011/61/EU and Regulations (EC) No 1060/2009 and (EU) No 648/2012, OJ L 347, 28.12.2017, pp. 35–80. The Regulation came into force in January 2018 and will be applicable as of January 1, 2019.

Some of the more general features include the following:

- The new framework replaces the existing EU securitization framework. Previously, different rules applied to different investors. At that time, securitization provisions were embedded in different pieces of EU financial regulation, for example, Solvency II, CRR and AIFM Regulation. When insurance firms and (alternative) investment firms are involved, different rules applied. Outside those categories there was no regulation in place. The new rules apply to all European securitizations.
- Some STS securitizations will benefit from favorable capital treatment (and some will not). We have discussed that the STS stamp is linked to eligibility criteria. Examples include homogeneous assets (i.e. where the contractual and credit risks as well as prepayment and cash flow-related characteristics are sufficiently similar). It can also involve the maturity of the assets involved. For example, in the case of an ABCP product that is looking for an STS approval, the pool of assets where the remaining weighted average life can be no more than one year, and no such transactions may have a residual maturity of longer than three years.[76] CMBS are excluded from that favorable capital treatment mainly due to perceived vulnerabilities. Overall we can say that traditional ABS and ABCP are looking at beneficial capital treatment while synthetic or more actively managed structures are looking at a less favorable treatment, although the door is kept open for future changes to the regulation in this respect.[77] It should be noted that the preferential capital treatment from a regulatory point of view changes the CRR regulation which is applicable to credit institutions and investment firms but not pension and (re)-insurance firms who are, for now, excluded.
- Further general elements in the regulation include a definition of securitization whereby it refers to non-recourse credit risk associated with underlying exposure(s) upon whose performance the payments in the transaction or scheme exclusively depend.[78] That credit risk is divided in different tranches with subordination that determines the distribution of losses during the ongoing life of the transaction. Re-securitization and ABS backed by unverified loans are excluded as well as specialized lending formats of physical assets.

---

[76] Following a lobby by the car industry, one of the largest users of ABCP, their ABCP products backed by car or equipment loans or leases can have a remaining exposure weighted average life of up to three and a half years, provided that none of the underlying assets has a residual maturity of longer than six years.

[77] This sounds like a compromise in the legislative process. The EBA flagged already in its 2015 report on synthetic securitization that these products that are used by credit institutions to move credit-risk off-balance sheet have done fairly well in the past. See EBA, (2015), The EBA Report on Synthetic Securitization, EBA/Op/2015/26. The EBA felt it could be justified extending the preferential capital treatment to the senior tranches of the synthetic product (under conditions including a full cash-funded credit protection for investors).

[78] Most ABS transactions are structured to achieve a true ale of the underlying assets. Otherwise, how else would be diversification and appropriate risk allocation in the market as an objective be achieved. Contractually, these structures are executed on a non-resource basis. At least, that is what you would expect. However, many securitization transactions show signs of implicit recourse, that is, the granting of non- contractual stipulated support activities of a transaction provided by the originator. Sidki argues that the motivation for this lies in the originator's moral hazard to retain his

- The Regulation applies to institutional investors and to originators, sponsors, original lenders and securitization special-purpose entities ('SSPEs'). The concept of institutional investors includes (re)insurance firms, institutions for occupational retirement provision, alternative investment fund managers (AIFM), undertakings for the collective investment in transferable securities (UCITS) if internally managed or otherwise its management company and credit institutions and investment firms. The role of sponsors is limited to credit institutions and investment firms, whereas any entity that pursues the defined activities can act as originator or original lender.
- The general framework requires institutional investors to verify or due diligence certain aspect of the transaction. Those elements include the credit-granting process of the originator (unless that is a EU credit institution or investment firm), the compliance of the originator, sponsor or original lender with the risk retention rules, the articles regarding the provision of required information by the originator or sponsor and certain risk characteristics which need to be monitored on an ongoing basis.
- The transparency dimension implies that the originator or sponsor have to provide potential investors on a regular basis with sufficient relevant information in particular on the underlying exposure. They have to involve third parties in case they are required to provide the necessary information. The information flow is channeled through a single and supervised source of data (securitization repository).
- In terms of risk retention, the following aspects were agreed: the originator, sponsor or original lender retains a material net economic interest in the securitization and this on an ongoing basis. The material net economic interest shall be not less than 5%, based on notional value at origination and not subject to any credit-risk mitigation, selling or hedging; only one of the parties shall retain the material net economic interest (i.e. no split) and, if no agreement reached between the parties, the originator shall fulfill the risk retention obligation. There are five different risk retention approved.[79] It will all be about the technical details as the chosen risk retention model makes explicit

reputation and capital market access. At the same time, implicit recourse in securitization transactions might also help to better allocate risk among capital market investors. See in detail: M. Sidki, (2014), Securitization with Implicit Recourse: Some Thoughts on the Economic Rationale, *The Journal of Structured Finance*, Vol. 19, Nr. 4, pp. 35–44. It is correctly pointed out that '[s]tructural support of a securitization transaction prior to its closing has to be differentiated from implicit support activities. While the former are performed as credit enhancements in the form of contractual credit support, which is adequately assessed by regulators and accountants in the process of structuring, the latter are non-stipulated. Hence, implicit recourse can be narrowed down as the granting of non-contractual (in the sense of exceeding the contractual) stipulated support activities of a transaction provided by the originator's implicit recourse runs contrary to the original asset sale including its underlying risks and negates or at least distorts any balance sheet removal or regulatory relief' (p. 2). See also in a wider context on the matter: S.C. Wenz, (2017), The Yield of Asset-Backed Securities After the Financial Crisis: An Empirical Approach, dissertation, TU Darmstadt, mimeo.

[79] There are many more risk retention methods available. See the extensive 2014 SEC report 'Risk Retention Methods' detailing the different methods available (via sec.gov). On December 15, 2017, the EBA released draft technical standards detailing on the different methods approved (EBA/CP/2017/22); final draft on July 31, 2018 (EBA/RTS/2018/01). The five methods approved by the EBA are (1) the retention of not less than 5% of the nominal value of each of the tranches sold or transferred to investors; (2) the retention of the originator's interest of not less than 5% of the

the risk actually transferred and the alignment in terms of risk sharing between the parties involved and the ultimate end-investor in the product. An entity shall not, for the purposes of risk retention, be considered to be an originator where it has been established or operates for the 'sole purpose' of securitizing exposures. This is to avoid that an empty shell will qualify as an originator. The EBA produced criteria to define what constitutes 'sole purpose' and on risk retention in general.[80]

- Also the 'selection of assets be securitized' required attention. To avoid that (intentionally or due to negligence) assets with a higher than general credit-risk profile are being transferred, the regulation makes explicit that originators will not be permitted to select assets to be transferred to a securitization special-purpose entity ('SSPE') with the aim of rendering losses on such assets, measured over the life of the transaction (or a maximum of four years where the life of the transaction is longer than four years), higher than the losses over the same period on 'comparable' assets[81] held on the balance sheet of the originator. It is a complicated way to avoid that the originator might exploit informational benefits it might have over investors. Higher than comparable risk assets (that remain on the balance sheet of the originator) can only be securitized when being clearly communicated to (potential) investors ('clearly and conspicuously communicated'). The communication requirements address both the relationship with investor and national authorities.[82]
- There is a specific provision (article 6) on 'cherry picking' that prohibits originators from intentionally securitizing assets which are more likely to suffer losses than comparable assets kept on the originator's balance sheet. However, as discussed, higher credit risk than average assets can be securitized under circumstances.

nominal value of each of the securitized exposures; (3) the retention of randomly selected exposures equivalent to not less than 5% of the nominal value of the securitized exposures; (4) the retention of the first-loss tranche; and (5) the retention of a first-loss exposure of not less than 5% of every securitized exposure (articles 5–9).

[80] Initially the consultation papers: EBA, (2017), Draft Regulatory Technical Standards Specifying the Requirements for Originators, Sponsors and Original Lenders Relating to Risk Retention, EBA/CP/2017/22, December 15; final draft on July 31, 2018 (EBA/RTS/2018/01).

[81] Comparable is defined as those assets which share similar characteristics in terms of the most relevant factors determining their expected performance. The performance of the selected assets should reasonably be expected not to be significantly different from that of the non-securitized assets over the life of the transaction based on indications such as past performance of applicable assets.

[82] Still there is a major concern here. The EBA technical standards allow for a different route through which higher credit-risk assets can be securitized. It indicates that even where no such communication has been made, an originator will not be considered to have intentionally breached the selection of assets provision (in the absence of evidence to the contrary), if it proves that it has established and applied policies and procedures to ensure that the securitized assets would reasonably be expected not to lead to higher losses than those on comparable assets held on its balance sheet. The policies of the originator need to be appropriate. The layering of possibilities that are linked to subjective qualitative and quantitative assessments has a tendency of not working properly in practice, often due to its sheer complexity, the multi-causality when things go wrong and the inability to allocate responsibility to a party in what by any standard is a complex, slightly opaque and known for its overlapping set of responsibilities among the parties involved.

- Specific conditions will have to be met before a 'seller' of a securitization position can sell that position to a retail client.
- The STS criteria itself are set out only in general terms, and not on an asset-class-specific basis. There are further specific provisions for ABCP products. More details on the STS standards can be found in the STS standards produced by the EBA/ESMA.[83] In terms of 'simplicity', the conditions are all about portfolio construction and cash flows. That implies that only true sales transactions are eligible, no active management is possible, no defaulted exposures, no assets that require a sale to feed the cash flow of the product and most importantly the assets included should be homogeneous in nature. One can imagine that the status of the homogeneous nature of the underlying exposure can lead to quite some debate and the technical issue was delegated to the EBA.[84] The EBA is favoring an approach that would specify a list of asset categories as well as list of 'risk factors' to be considered when determining whether an asset pool is sufficiently homogeneous. Each category of securitized securities would then get their own set of risk factors. Risk factors include type of obligor, type of credit facility and collateral, repayment mechanics and industrial sector. 'Transparency' relates obviously to the data availability for investors which include historical default and loss performance data (> five years), an independently verified ample of exposure, a cash flow waterfall model based on existing liabilities and the underlying exposure, ongoing notification of investors by originator and sponsor in case of material changes. The 'standardization' of the product is built around the discussed risk retention standards, mitigation of interest and currency risks, write-up of the responsibilities of all parties involved and actions and remediation in case of breach of criteria, delinquency or conflicts of interest. The originator, sponsor or SSPE can use third-party certification agent to assess the compliance of a securitization with the STS criteria. Incorrect notification will however continue to be their liability.
- Any securitization which involves a non-EU originator, sponsor or SSPE will not be able to qualify as STS. All securities will have to be notified to the ASMA. Existing products that meet the STS standards will benefit from the reduced capital charge starting January 1, 2019.
- Securitizations of non-performing loans, managed CLOs and CMBS are unlikely to qualify for STS status. The same holds true for synthetic securitizations. Although the technical standards seem to work out negative for synthetic securitizations, it should

[83] The STS regulation itself has been criticized for being very vague regarding the STS criteria. The concern has been how granular the homogeneity requirement will be and how asset pools need to be grouped (class or common characteristics). The EBA put out a consultation in April 2018 regarding STS standards for both (non)-ABCP products: EBA/CP/2018/05 and EBA/CP/2018/04, April 20, followed by a public hearing in June 2018; ESMA, (2017), Draft technical standards on content and format of the STS notification under the Securitisation Regulation, ESMA33-128-33, December 19. That was followed by a public hearing on February 19, 2018. See the clarifying presentation released following that hearing: EBA, (2018), Homogeneity of Underlying Exposures in Securitisation, Consultation on Regulatory Technical Standards, (via eba.europe.org). See infra this chapter on final RTS on the matter.

[84] The EBA released consultation papers on the homogeneity of the underlying exposures: EBA/CP/2017/21 (December 15, 2017) and final draft EBA/RTS/2018/02 (July 31, 2018).

not be forgotten that the EBA in its 2015 report on synthetic securitizations was bold enough to recommend lower capital requirements for (the senior tranches) of those products.[85]

- National competent authorities will supervise compliance. Sanctions are foreseen, including large fines. However, the competent authorities must take into account, when determining the applicable sanction, the extent to which the infringement is intentional or results from negligence, as well as other factors including the materiality, gravity and duration of any infringement and the level of cooperation by the responsible party with the competent authority.

3.2.6.3 STS Regulation Analysis

Much has been said regarding the STS-securitization regulation enacted. Not only the content of the regulation but also how it fits into the wider CMU project[86] the EU has embarked on. The dynamic is for the EU to move away from banking finance into market-based finance. Securitization is a relevant instrument to achieve that objective. But since we know that it has the potential to destabilize markets easily, the idea was developed to create a market for securitized products that is STS (simple transparent and standardized) so that it reduced the ability to destabilize markets through contagion spreading markets due to uncertainty about intrinsic value of underlying assets and/or the ability to create systemic risk.

Hereafter, I provide an overview of the most consistent (and persistent) arguments raising doubt about both the objective and the effectiveness of the STS regulation[87]:

- It has been highlighted that the STS instrument has been put in place not so much to move toward a market-based finance but merely as a funding tool for banks.[88] Arguments that it creates a deeper monetary union, supports job creation and contrib-

[85] See EBA, (2015), The EBA Report on Synthetic Securitization, EBA/Op/2015/26.

[86] The CMU project is obviously much wider in terms of its objective. As a vehicle to accelerate sustainable growth, it includes measures to (1) finance innovation, start-ups and non-listed companies, (2) make it easier for companies to enter and raise capital on public markets, (3) invest for long-term infrastructure and sustainable investment, (4) foster retail investing, (5) strengthen the banking capacity to support the wider capacity, (6) strengthen the capacity of EU capital markets and (7) facilitate cross-border investments in the EU. See in detail: EC, (2016), Communication from the Commission to the European Parliament, the Council, the European Central Bank, The European Economic and Social Committee and the Committee of the Regions, Capital Markets Union, Accelerating Reform, COM(2016)601final, September 14.

[87] I recommend reading this part in parallel to the relevant parts of the 'where to go from here' chapter on securitization and the dedicated chapter on securitizations.

[88] M. Aalbers and E. Engelen, (2015), Guest Editorial: The Political Economy of the Rise, Fall and Rise again of Securitization, Environment & Planning A, Vol. 47, Issue 8, pp. 1597–1605; E. Engelen, (2015), Don't Mind the Funding Gap: What Dutch Post-Crisis Storytelling Tells Us about Elite Politics in Financialized Capitalism, Environment and Planning A, Vol. 47, Issue 8, pp. 1606–1623; E. Engelen, (2017), Shadow Banking after the Crisis: The Dutch Case, Theory, Culture and Society, Vol. 34, Issue 5–6, pp. 53–75. A large-scale study supports the

utes to sustainable (real economic) growth[89] seem more like storytelling than rather based on empirical evidence.[90]

- The idea that securitization provides banks with a tool for transferring risk off their balance sheets and free up more capital can then be used to grant new credit including SMEs.[91] That sounds more like a tool for banks to raise cheaper funding, knowing that the EC, in parallel with the STS regulation, enacted a regulation to change the Capital Requirements Directive including a capital relief for banks that comply with the STS standards.[92] The post-crisis securitization market apparently was too expensive under Basel III norms both for structurers and end-investors. The regulation foresees in a material reduction of capital charges for the senior tranches of securitized products.[93] The technique of tranching has been accepted throughout the STS proposal. Tranching as a technique was discussed before as well as the fact that this practice allowed banks in particular to originate and securitize loans of poorer quality, and which received a rating designation higher than deserved. That was possible for two reasons: the formulas that underscored the way in which assets were bundled and the credit enhancement

view that securitizations have been used mainly by large and profitable banks, with the objective of improving their capital ratios and reducing the cost of funding. With few exceptions, the banks that did securitize their assets reduced their credit and liquidity risks. See in detail: F. Panetta and A.F. Pozozolo, (2018), Why do Banks Securitize their Assets? Bank-Level Evidence from over One Hundred Countries in the Pre-Crisis Period, Bank of Italy Working Paper Nr. 1183, July 20.

[89] D. Pesendorfer, (2015), Capital Markets Union and Ending Short-Termism; Lessons from the European Commission' Public Consultation, Law and Financial Markets Review, Vol. 9, Issue 3, pp. 202–209.

[90] See the massive evidence contradicting these statements or claims in the chapter 'Future Directions' (chapter 7 Volume II). Including SME financing and securitizations. See also: E. Engelen and A. Glasmacher, (2016), 'Simple, Transparent and Standardized'. Narratives, Law and the Interest Coalitions behind the European Commission's Capital Markets Union, Feps Studies, September, pp. 5 ff.

[91] See in detail: H. Kramer-Eis et al., (2015), SME Securitization- At a Crossroads, EIF Working Paper Nr. 2015/31, December, Luxembourg. It is extensively discussed why the securitization of SME loans is so problematic relative to, for example, mortgage loans. See the chapter 'where to go from here'. In short, it all comes down to asymmetric risk and information that makes SME loan pools heterogeneous and therefore unprofitable to securitize. Unprofitable because the spread on the securitized product (as a whole) is as large (approx.) as the aggregate spread of the initial aggregate SME loan pool. Therefore it doesn't happen. It still is problematic transferring asymmetric risk to a third party and reduce overall risk exposure across the securitized product. See also: U. Albertazzi et al., (2016), Information Asymmetry and the Securitization of SME loans, Bank of Italy Working Paper Nr. 1091, December.

[92] Regulation (EU) 2017/2401 of the European Parliament and of the Council of 12 December 2017 amending Regulation (EU) No 575/2013 on prudential requirements for credit institutions and investment firms, OJ L 347, 28.12.2017, pp. 1–34.

[93] This is probably the right time to remind the reader of the elsewhere discussed feature that tranching (in itself) concentrates uncertainty and thus that even a simple securitization model enhances rather than reduces overall risk concentration (rather than distribution). See in detail: A. Antionades and N. Tarashev, (2014), Securitisations: Tranching Concentrates Uncertainty, BIS Quarterly Review, December, pp. 37–53.

mechanisms.[94] Tranching also exacerbates possible conflicts of interest between the different tranche-holders since the different tranches attract different attitudes to risk taking. Allowing tranching as a technique therefore raises the question regarding a possible resurgence of all sorts of business and market practices that are still possible without violating the regulation as it stands.

- The reliance on external ratings is confirmed in the regulation despite its troublesome past.[95]
- The understanding that an STS label will take away the stigma securitization has to live with since the financial crisis. European securitizations have shown to be more stable and less default-prone than their US counterparts (EU: full-recourse loans vs. US: largely non-recourse loans).[96] A differently structured bankruptcy law[97] in Europe might explain that difference away rather than the superiority of European securitization standards or superior risk management strategies applied by European banks.[98]
- There is, besides the issue of which attributes can be designated to securitization products, the issue of collateral damage to different asset classes in particular real estate and the bubbles it produced.[99]

---

[94] See also on this particular issue: V. Bavoso, (2016), Simple, Transparent and Standardized Securitisation. Business as Usual, Feps Working Paper, September, pp. 9 ff.

[95] Ibid. pp. 13 ff.

[96] See in detail: R. Harris and A. Meir, (2015), Recourse Structure of Mortgages: A Comparison between the US and Europe, CESinfo DICE Report 4/2015 December, pp. 15–22.

[97] McGowan and Nguyen evaluate whether US foreclosure law causes lenders to securitize mortgage loans. Lenders are more likely to securitize GSE-eligible mortgage loans when subject to borrower-friendly foreclosure law. The effects are present before and after the financial crisis and imply that borrower-friendly foreclosure law increases taxpayers' holdings of mortgage debt by $140bn per annum. This highlights how lenders use securitization to exploit the GSEs' guarantees and transfer credit default risk. In detail: D. McGowan and H. Nguyen, (2018), Risk Transfer and Foreclosure Law: Evidence from the Securitization Market, Working Paper, August 29, mimeo.

[98] E. Engelen and A. Glasmacher, (2016), 'Simple, Transparent and Standardized'. Narratives, Law and the Interest Coalitions behind the European Commission's Capital Markets Union, Feps Studies, September, pp. 7–8; J.W. Singer, (2015), No Freedom Without Regulation: The Hidden Lesson of the Subprime Crisis, Yale University Press, New Haven, Connecticut; T. Bayoumi, (2017), Unfinished Business. The Unexplored Causes of the Financial Crisis and the Lessons Yet to be Learned, Yale University Press, New Haven, Connecticut. In fact there is proof that default rates different materially between non-recourse and full-recourse states in the US: See in detail: A.C. Ghent and M. Kudlyak, (2011), Recourse and Residential Mortgage Default: Evidence from US States, Review of Financial Studies, Vol. 24, Issue 9, pp. 3139–3186.

[99] See extensively in the chapters 'Pigovian tax' (vol. I) and the 'where to go from here' (Vol. II). Negative equity holds back consumer spending. Combined with austerity it has been the main driver behind a below-standard economic performance during almost a decade in Europe. One can qualify these side effects as negative externalities and therefore I qualify them as Pigovian targets. See also: M. Aalbers, (2017), The Variegated Financialization of Housing. IJURR, Vol. 41, Issue 4, pp. 542–554; G. Wijburg, and M. Aalbers, (2017), The Alternative Financialization of the German Housing Market, Housing Studies, Vol. 32, Issue 7, pp. 301–320; S. Quinn, (2010), Government Policy, Housing, and the Origins of Securitization, 1780–1968. University of California, Berkeley, CA.

- The STS standard is to incentivize end-investors and structurers to buy and produce STS-comply securitization products rather than non-complying ones.[100] It should be observed that the STS criteria used only partly comply with the STS criteria expressed by IOSCO/BCBS in their 2015 criteria overview.[101] In 2018, this framework was complemented with a framework for STS criteria for short-term securitizations/ABCP products.[102]
- Regarding the STS criteria itself, it can be observed that only the quality of the securitization process is observed (structuring, tranching, rating and distribution) and not the quality of the input (raw material or mortgage contracts).[103] Strangely enough, as it was the input asymmetry in quality between reality and perception was underlying

---

[100] See the introductory comments in the EC Proposal for STS securitizations (Proposal for a REGULATION OF THE EUROPEAN PARLIAMENT AND OF THE COUNCIL amending Regulation (EU) No 575/2013 on prudential requirements for credit institutions and investment firms COM/2015/0473 final – 2015/0225 (COD)), in particular pp. 7–11. See also: European Parliament, Committee on Economic and Monetary Affairs, DRAFT REPORT on the proposal for a regulation of the European Parliament and of the Council laying down common rules on securitisation and creating a European framework for simple, transparent and standardised securitisation and amending Directives 2009/65/EC, 2009/138/EC, 2011/61/EU and Regulations (EC) No 1060/2009 and (EU) No 648/2012 (COM(2015)0472 – C8-0288/2015 – 2015/0226(COD))2015/0226(COD), June 2016.

[101] IOSCO/BCBS, (2015), Criteria for Identifying Simple, Transparent and Comparable Securitisations, July.

[102] IOSCO/BCBS, (2018), Criteria for Identifying Simple, Transparent and Comparable Short-Term Securitisations, May 14. The criteria published take account of the characteristics of asset-backed commercial paper (ABCP) conduits, such as (1) the short maturity of the commercial paper issued, (3) the different forms of program structures and (3) the existence of multiple forms of liquidity and credit support facilities. Changes made include clarifying that the criteria do not automatically exclude equipment leases and auto loan and lease securitizations from the short-term STC framework. Similar to the STC criteria for term securitizations, the short-term STC criteria are non-exhaustive and non-binding. Just like was the case for the 2015 STS criteria, standards were designed for a reduction of capital weighting (preferential capital treatment) for these short-term products: BCBS, (2018), Capital Treatment for Simple, Transparent and Comparable Short-Term Securitisations, May 14. They take into account the changes to the overall securitization framework as agreed in 2016: BCBS, (2016), Revisions to the Securitisation Framework, July 11 as impacted by the BCBS, (2017), Basel III: Finalising Post-Crisis Reforms, December 7 conditions. Provided that the expanded set of STC short-term criteria are met, STC short-term securitizations will receive the same modest reduction in capital requirements as other STC term securitizations. Changes made include setting the minimum performance history for non-retail and retail exposures at five years and three years, respectively, and clarifying that the provision of credit and liquidity support to the ABCP structure can be performed by more than one entity, subject to certain conditions.

[103] Cullen laments in the same direction when arguing: 'that current analyses of the likely effects of securitisation on asset markets, particularly housing markets, are deficient. Instead of highlighting flaws in the securitisation process through improved incentives—which I term "process-focused" regulation—analysis of incentives ought to concentrate on the excessive credit-origination which techniques such as securitisation facilitates. This is particularly relevant to housing bubbles, the greatest threat to financial stability.' See J. Cullen, (2017), Securitization, Ring-Fencing and Housing Bubbles: Financial Stability Implications of UL and EU Bank Reforms, University of Oslo Faculty of Law Legal Studies Research Paper Series Nr. 2017-13.

the securitization issues during the financial crisis. The quality of the securitizing products highly depends on the input material.[104]

- The notion of simple transparent and standardized criteria is often misleading. Only professional investors are allowed in. And the information duty on originators is massive (article 5 and onward of the regulation). Also the use of hedging for interest rate and FX purposes is framed as being almost inevitable.
- Engelen concludes that the criteria used predominantly mirror existing industry practices often referred to as 'common standards in international finance' so as to include even synthetic products[105] (using CDS) known as CDO-squared can fall within scope (often referred to as re-securitizations).[106] Some of these concerns have been mitigated or even neutralized in the final regulation. But the problem has to a certain degree only shifted. The regulation allows the EBA to create technical standards (RTS) and some of the initial concerns raised by Engelen might appear again through the backdoor of these standards. That leads to the following more overall concern.
- A lot of critical components are delegated away from the regulator, for example, information obligation and so on. These however are critical components to assess STS as a cornerstone of a market-based financial system. The process of delegating individual items has only just begun and will take its time and given the number of institutions involved will enhance complexity and opacity at the same time.[107] Also the guide-

[104] There is also no limit to, for example, loan-to-value or loan-to-income ratios of mortgages eligible: see E. Engelen and A. Glasmacher, (2016), 'Simple, Transparent and Standardized'. Narratives, Law and the Interest Coalitions behind the European Commission's Capital Markets Union, Feps Studies, September, pp. 9 ff. There are also many exemptions listed in the memorandum of the EC: loans that have gone into arrears but with a new debt plan agreed upon, often by extending the maturity of the debt instrument. So even 'subprime mortgages' by any standard can be included without violating TS criteria.

[105] Synthetic Securitization is making a comeback. See in detail: O. Kaya, (2017), Synthetic Securitization. Making a Silent Comeback, Deutsche Bank Research, February 21.

[106] Ibid. pp. 10–11. Also: S.L. Schwarcz, (2016), Securitization and Post-Crisis Financial Regulation, Cornell Law Review, Vol. 102, pp. 115–139. He addresses two market-failure causes (complexity and change). He seems mildly positive regarding the European STS model (from that perspective) and recommends the US adopts a similar approach. Also: P. de Goia Carabellese, (2018), Securitization and Structured Finance: From Shadow Banking to Legal Harmonization, in Research Handbook on Shadow Banking, Legal and Regulatory Aspects (eds. I. H.-Y. Chiu and I.G. MacNeil), Edward Elgar Publishing, Cheltenham, UK, pp. 117–160.

[107] The process of delegating technical aspects started after the STS regulation came into force in January 2018. See, for example, the following features one is currently looking into: ESMA, (2017), ESMA Consult on Securitization requirements, ESMA Brief ESMA71-99-916. Included are the features: The contents and format of underlying exposures and investor report templates, the operational standards for providing these reports to securitization repositories and the operational standards for accessing this information from securitization repositories as well as the contents and format of the notification to ESMA of a securitization's STS status. Also: ESMA, (2018), ESMA Consult on Requirements for Securitization, ESMA Brief ESMA33-128-109, March 23.

lines[108] interpreting the STS criteria have been in the making[109] (and some still are) following the entering into force of the regulation.[110] For now, what we have is a piece of regulation that provides a broad legal framework and their regulatory treatment.

- The calibrations for senior tranches will be improved which provides for a serious incentive for institutional cash pools, with often narrow investment guideline, to buy into the product group.
- Holding mortgage pools in a securitized format becomes considerably cheaper capital-wise than as a diversified traditional loan book. To get there, the EC was even willing to tweak the post-crisis capital arrangements as foreseen under Basel III/CRR.[111] The political objective apparently justifies the container model of securitization as was

[108] The arsenal of guidelines has been developed based on the following criteria: it constitutes a single point of interpretation and is cross-sectoral applicable. There will be separate guidelines for non-ABCP and ABCP instruments. There are layers of interpretation: green implies that the concept is self-explanatory and the interpretation merely serves the correct interpretation of the STS criteria; yellow implies that there is a substantial element of uncertainty and interpretation is necessary and required; red implies that interpretation is crucial and even then consistency might be difficult to achieve. See in detail and for applications of each of the categories: EBA, (2018), EBA Consultation Paper on the Guidelines on Interpretation of STS Criteria, Public Hearing, June 11, via eba.europe.org

[109] Based on articles 19(2) and 23(3) of the Securitization Regulation.

[110] The EBA is responsible and the EBA Guidelines will play a crucial role in the new EU securitization framework, by providing a single point of consistent interpretation of the STS criteria to originators, sponsors, investors and competent authorities throughout the Union. Draft Guidelines have been released for both ABCP and non-ABCP securitization products. See EBA, (2018), Draft Guidelines on the STS criteria for (Non)-ABCP Securitizations, EBA/CP/2018/04, EBA/CP/2018/05, April 20. Earlier on, they released similar consultations regarding risk retention (December 2017, EBA/CP/2017/22), the homogeneity of the underlying exposures in securitization (December 2017, EBA/CP/2017/21) and significant risk transfers (September 2017, EBA-DP-2017-03). The memorandum to the regulation seems rather relaxed with respect to risk retention, a critical component of post-crisis regulation. The Memorandum makes explicit that (1) the risk can be retained by either the sponsor/originator or original lender, (2) bank can decide which part of the securitized instrument to retain (equity or mezzanine tranches) and (3) there is no risk retention if the assets are fully, unconditionally and irrevocably guaranteed by public bodies. The latter in particular is deeply concerning as it deals with a major agency conflict that stays largely unresolved. See regarding agency conflicts in securitization: W.S. Frame, (2017), Agency Conflicts in Residential Mortgage Securitization: What Does the Empirical Literature Tell Us?, Federal Reserve bank of Atlanta Working Paper Nr. 1, March. It was commented that '[s]ecuritization itself may not have been a problem, but rather the origination and distribution of observably riskier loans. Low-documentation mortgages, for which asymmetric information problems are acute, performed especially poorly during the crisis. Securitized low-documentation mortgages performed better when included in deals where security issuers were affiliated with lenders or had significant reputational capital at stake....'

[111] There is an exception foreseen (article 248 of Regulation (EU) No 575/2013 (CRR) for institutions that provide excessive implicit support for securitizations. Originator institutions and sponsor institutions that have failed to comply with the relevant requirements shall at a minimum hold own funds against all of the securitized exposures as if they had not been securitized. The concept of 'implicit support' allows diverging interpretations and therefore the EBA was mandated to issue guidelines on what constitutes arm's length conditions and when a transaction is not structured to

developed in the STS directive. Input legitimacy and output legitimacy are clearly not in sync here. One can only wonder to what degree also here there is an unfortunate collusion between governing through financial markets by the European regulator[112] and this beyond their institutional capacity[113] and the unholy dynamics of public/private co-regulation.[114] The material gap between 'narratives and content'[115] and the hastiness with which this piece of legislation has been rushed through the regulatory channels raises questions on what the prime argument was for this to happen: creating a European market-based financial system (in line with the US) or whether it was primarily designed to create a market for securitizations which are a source of funding for predominantly large (mortgage) banks.[116]

- Another point of concern regarding the STS regulation is that there is very little room for the bigger picture issues. For example, not a single word is said about the impact of securitized products on the (de)stabilizing question in markets. Post-financial crisis it was argued that securitization improves financial stability if the securitized assets are

provide support. See for those guidelines: EBA, (2016), Final Report: Guidelines on Implicit Support for Securitization Transactions, EBA/GL/2016/08, October 3.

[112] B. Braun et al., (2018), Governing through Financial Markets: Towards a Critical Political Economy of Capital Markets Union, Vol. 22, Issue 2, pp. 101–116; B. Braun, (2018), Central Banking and the Infrastructural Power of Finance: The Case of ECB Support for Repo and Securitisation Markets, Socio-Economic Review, DOI: https://doi.org/10.1093/ser/mwy008. Also earlier on Hübner wondered why securitization now has become such a prime pillar of the CMU, a project with a string political commitment to market-based finance. She wonders if the whole idea is not based on a monetary objective of stabilizing the eurozone. See in detail: M. Hübner, (2016), Securitisation to the Rescue: The European Capital Markets Union Project, the Euro Crisis and the ECB as 'Macro-economic Stabilizer of Last Resort', Febs Report, September.

[113] See also C. Ban, (2016), Grey Matter on Shadow Banking: International Organizations and Expert Strategies in Global Financial Governance, GEGI Working Paper, Boston University. He concludes that '[t]he evidence suggests that their experts ((ed.) of the IMF, BIS and FSB) embedded a bland reformism opposed to both strong and "light touch" regulation at the core of the emerging regulatory regime. In so doing, these technocrats reinforced each other's expertise, excluded some potential competitors (legal scholars), coopted others (select Fed and elite academic economists) and deployed measurement, mandate, and status strategies to assert issue control. Finally, rather than derive authority from high-status publications on shadow banking, academic economists' most effective source of influence was their credibility as arbitrageurs between several professional fields.'

[114] N. Dorn, (2015), Capital Cohabitation: EU Capital Markets Union as Public and Private Co-regulation, *Capital Markets Law Journal*, Vol. 11, Issue 1, pp. 84–102; EBF, (2016), EBF Asks EU Policy Makers to Bring Forward Adoption of STS Proposal. Brussels, April 27.

[115] And that includes the EC commissioned Impact Assessment that goes with the proposal (SWD(2015) 185 final) of September 30, 2015 which includes a highly unconvincing, paper-thin, slightly over half a page literature overview (p. 130). The exact same thing could be said about the reference document on securitizations used by the European Parliament: A. Delivioras (EP), (2016), Understanding Securitization: Background-Benefits-Risks, p. 22, January, revised version.

[116] E. Engelen and A. Glasmacher, (2018), The Waiting Game: How Securitization Became the Solution for the Growth Problem of the EU, Competition and Change, Vol. 22, Issue 2, pp. 165–183.

held by capital market participants, rather than financial intermediaries.[117] But as more and more research emerged, that statement is not unconditionally true. More precise would be to say that the existence of the securitization market stabilizes the economy under the condition that financial intermediaries do not engage in the acquisition of securitized assets.[118] It could therefore be argued that the regulation as it stands is not sufficiently emerged in the macroeconomic nature of the financial activity that is being regulated.[119] That is unfortunately an often recurring problem in financial law. Gerding makes explicit that regulation was at the heart of the problem causing bank investments into MBS and thus creating the transmission line between the bank and real estate crisis the US witnessed. After he demonstrated how loosening legal restrictions on bank participation in MBS markets contributed to fueling the transmission line between banks and the real estate sector, he goes on to detail which inadequacies exist in the financial diversification theory (or asset pricing theory if you want) and how only restrictions for bank to invest in certain real estate products can counterbalance the impact of cyclicality and the concentration of investment in some of these segments.[120]

- The EC sees a mitigation of contagion in markets due to asymmetry following the STS-label introduction. The consistency and homogeneity of the assets used combined with the transparency enforced should undeniably lead to a neutralization of contagion. It is unclear if they believe it will be reduced rather than neutralized. That sounds trivial but it is not. A model with even a minimum of information friction embedded will demonstrate that 'in boom periods or mild recessions, the degree of adverse selection in resale markets for securitized assets is limited because of the reputation-based guarantees by asset originators.[121] This supports investment and output. However, in a deep recession,

[117] In any case, higher securitization propensities weaken the financial stability of banks with relevant effects on different sectors of the economy. In detail: A. Mazzochetti et al., (2018), Systemic Financial Risk Indicators and Securitized Assets: an Agent-Based Framework, MPRA Working Paper Nr. 89,779, October 24.

[118] A. Grodecka, (2016), Subprime Borrowers, Securitization and the Transmission of Business Cycles, Sveriges Riksbank Working Paper Series Nr. 317, March.

[119] Interest rate hikes slow down growth but lead intermediation to migrate from banks' balance sheets to non-banks via increased securitization activity. Systemic risk increases when intermediation is pushed outside the regulatory framework. See in detail: A. Pescatori and J. Solé, (2016), Credit, Securitization and Monetary Policy: Watch Out for Unintended Consequences, IMF Working Paper Series Nr. WP/16/76, March. As such, higher interest rates have the potential for unintended consequences.

[120] E.F. Gerding, (2015), Bank Regulation and Securitization: How the Law Improved Transmission Lines between Real Estate and Banking Crisis, Georgia Law Review, Vol. 50, pp. 1–42.

[121] The link between reputation of issuers and performance has been examined. Deku et al. examine the link between issuer reputation and mortgage-backed security (MBS) performance. They find that, overall, MBS sold by reputable issuers are collateralized by higher quality asset pools which have lower delinquency rates and are less likely to be downgraded. However, as credit standards declined during the boom period of 2005–2007, asset pools securitized by reputable issuers were of worse quality compared to those securitized by less reputable issuers. Therefore, reputation as a self-disciplining mechanism failed to incentivize the production of high-quality securities during the credit boom. See in detail: S.L. Deku et al., (2019), Do Reputable Issuers Provide Better Quality Securitizations, ECB Working Paper Nr. 2236, February 7.

characterized by high dispersion of asset qualities, there is a sudden surge in adverse selection due to an economy-wide default on reputation-based guarantees, which persistently depresses the output in the economy.' The negative moral hazard caused by exploiting information asymmetry isn't gone under this regulation, it has become more opaque and its size might have become somewhat smaller, but when reputation contamination[122] is at the heart of market contagion, the opaqueness makes things worse, as now institutional agents will scrutinize securitized products less because of the regulatory STS stamp it carries. In a market-based model however, regulatory stamps do not replace reputation and questions regarding the valuation of the underlying assets. It is remarkable however to see that even the impact assessment ordered by the EC is silent on the matter.[123]

Finally, the issue regarding 'informational advantage' has not been properly addressed in the regulation. Informational advantage tends to show up in two different ways: One way is to adopt lax screening standards, and simply pass off the risks to potential buyers. The other way is to make securities intentionally opaque and difficult to evaluate their risks and values through repackaging, and thereby amplifying informational advantage.[124] Securitization facilitates private liquidity provision and relaxes financial constraints. Li[125] wondered why mortgages relatively illiquid while MBSs were already trading prior to 2008 and came up with that answer. By optimally engineering the cash flow of asset into tranches, impatient agents can create large chunks of information-insensitive securities, which improves overall market liquidity. Or put differently in case of asymmetric information (i.e. when asset owner possesses private information) 'impatient market parties post asset-backed security contracts after they privately observe signals of the quality of their own assets, while patient agents direct their search towards different contracts'. The consequence is that the ABS market is incomplete and that only certain sub-segments of the ABS market trade in equilibrium.[126] This has policy implications as both in the US and European securitization regulation a risk retention of 5% is foreseen.[127] Li's study

---

[122] S. Deku et al., (2019), Trustee Reputation in Securitization: When Does it Matter?, Financial Markets, Institutions & Instruments, Vol. 28, Issue 2, pp. 61–84. Engaging reputable trustees benefit from lower spreads on their MBSs.

[123] See regarding the notion of the fragility of resale markets in securitized products: M. Kuncl, (2016), Fragility of Resale Markets for Securitized Assets and Policy of Asset Purchases, Bank of Canada Working Paper Nr. 46, October.

[124] See extensively: T. Sogo and K. Kawai, (2016), Planned Opaqueness in Securitization, Working Paper, mimeo, September 22.

[125] Q. Li, (2017), Securitization and Liquidity when Asset Owners Possess Private Information, Working Paper, February 17, mimeo.

[126] Question then is 'what is the optimal security design for banks who have private information and issue ABS instruments' since securitization creates value for the society only 'by mitigating informational frictions in the financial markets'. Li comments '[a]n asset-backed security can be 'good' because it is backed by an asset that is more likely to pay out a high dividend, or it can be 'good' because its holder has the priority to receive payments when a bad state occurs' (p. 25).

[127] Either vertically through retaining a slice of each tranche or horizontally through retaining the first-loss tranche.

demonstrates that complying with the risk retention regulation horizontally is less costly to the sponsor, since it's difficult to sell the first-loss tranche anyway.

Throughout 2018 and into 2019, the EBA and ESMA have been churning out technical standards on a variety of issues including transparency requirements, risk retention rules, the homogeneity requirement for asset pools backing STS securitizations, significant risk transfer (SRT) rules[128] and a number of pure procedural issues.

3.2.6.4 SME Securitization and Financing

It is discussed throughout different chapters in both volumes why securitization as a tool is largely non-instrumental to deepen the liquidity of the capital pool available for SMEs.[129] Part has to do with the nature of the securitization product, part has to do with the fact contemporary business practices in the securitization distribution model and part has to do with the nature of a typical SME loan book[130] and the presence of asymmetric information in the securitization of SME loans.[131] The originate-to-distrib-

[128] See, for example, the EBA, (2017), On the Significant Risk Transfer in Securitization, Discussion Paper EBA-DP-2017-03, September 19.

[129] See the recently announced FSB project dealing with evaluation on the effects of financial reforms on small- and medium-sized enterprise (SME) financing on August 13, 2018. The project is part of a broader mandate to evaluate the effect of enacted regulation and policies in a variety of domains: FSB, (2017), Framework for Post-Implementation Evaluation of the Effects of the G20 Financial Regulatory Reforms, July 3. The real question should be about the link between SME finance and entrepreneurialism: M. Ayyagari et al., (2017), What Determines Entrepreneurial Outcomes Across the World? Role of Initial Conditions, Review of Financial Studies, Vol. 30, Issue 7, pp. 2478–2522; R. Gopalan et al., (2016), Do Debt Contract Enforcement Costs Affect Financing and Asset Structure? Review of Financial Studies, Vol. 29, Issue 10, pp. 2773–2813. Here and there support emerges for securitization as a vehicle to remove financing hurdles for MEs and decrease the cost of bank financing. O. Kaya and O. Masetti, (2019), Small- and Medium-Sized Enterprise Financing and Securitization: Firm-Level Evidence from the Euro Area Economic Inquiry, Vol. 57, Issue 1, pp. 391–409. They (supporting studies) however stay far and few between.

[130] See also: EIF, (2017), European Small Business Finance Outlook, Working Paper Nr. 43, June; C. Masiak, (2017), Financing of European SMEs: Patterns, Determinants and Dynamics over Time, Presentation 5th Annual Meeting of the Knowledge Programme—European Investment Bank, March 7, eib.org; A. Rahman et al., (2017), Determinants of SME Financing: Evidence from Three Central European Countries, Review of Economic Perspectives, Vol. 17, Issue 3, pp. 263–285, September; S. Roux and F. Savignac, (2017), SMEs' Financing: Divergence Across Euro Area Countries?, Banque de France Working Paper Nr. 654, December; IOSCO, (2015), SME Financing Through Capital Markets, Final Report, FR11/2015, July.

[131] Interesting as a parallel thought process is the fact that volumes of securitization in catastrophe risk are low. Relative to securitization, reinsurance features lower adverse selection costs because reinsurers possess superior underwriting resources than ordinary capital market investors. Insurers' risk transfer choices trade off the costs and benefits of reinsurance relative to securitization. Low risks are transferred via reinsurance, while intermediate and high risks are transferred via partial and full securitization, respectively. An increase in the loss size increases the trigger risk level above which securitization is chosen. Hence, catastrophe exposures, which are characterized by lower probabilities and higher severities, are more

ute model[132] has been at the center of the post-crisis discussion and blamed for igniting the crisis due to the presence of asymmetric information.[133] The claim was that banks possess soft information on the lenders of the repackaged loans. They would use that information to select which instruments to securitize and offload it. The availability of the securitization instrument therefore allowed banks to be more relaxed in loan origination standards and screening post-closing of the deal.[134] To what extent that has been the case in practice is however largely undetermined, although the moral hazard argu-

---

likely to be retained or reinsured rather than securitized, Subramanian and Wang conclude. Lower probabilities and higher severities are criteria one can apply directly to SME loan books, with factual modifications obviously. A. Subramanian and J. Wang, (2018), Reinsurance Versus Securitization of Catastrophe Risk Insurance: Mathematics and Economics, Vol. 82C, Elsevier, pp. 55–72. In the same direction: J.D. Cummins and P. Trainar, (2009), Securitization, Insurance, and Reinsurance, *Journal of Risk & Insurance*, Vol. 76, Issue 3, pp. 463–492. They go directly to the point this belief is essential: [t]raditional reinsurance operates efficiently in managing relatively small, uncorrelated risks and in facilitating efficient information sharing between cedants and reinsurers. However, when the magnitude of potential losses and the correlation of risks increase, the efficiency of the reinsurance model breaks down, and the cost of capital may become uneconomical. At this juncture, securitization has a role to play by passing the risks along to broader capital markets. Securitization also serves as a complement for reinsurance in other ways such as facilitating regulatory arbitrage and collateralizing low-frequency risks.

[132] In fact it was deregulation that helped create the originate-to-distribute model. That has a number of implications. See D. McGowan and H. Nguyen, (2019), Deregulation and the Securitization Boom, Working Paper, June, mimeo.

[133] Schwarcz has been arguing that financial regulation in originate-to-distribute models face often on asymmetric information. However, he argues, the real challenge is that the relevant market failure is less likely to be asymmetric information than mutual misinformation—neither the originator (i.e. seller) of the loans nor the buyer may fully understand the risks. Complex markets and segments tend to have that effect (securitization, structured finance, collateralization and re-use of collateral, etc.). The regulation of collateralization levels and interconnectedness faces fundamentally different challenges than those underlying the (technically) analogous post-Depression regulation of 'margin' lending to acquire publicly traded stock, he argues. See in detail: S.L. Schwarcz, (2018), Secured Transactions and Financial Stability: Regulatory Challenges, Law & Contemporary Problems, Vol. 81, Issue 1, pp. 45–62. He identifies a number of problematic areas that requires a 'different' type of regulation: (1) moral hazard in the secured loan origination markets, (2) levels of collateralization and re-use, (3) collateralization as a source of interconnectedness, (4) access of SIFIs to reorganization financing, (5) remedies against collateral, (6) non-traditional secured transactions and (7) de facto collateral rights. Also: S. Flynn et al., (2018), Informational Efficiency in Securitization after Dodd-Frank, Sixth Annual Conference on Financial Market Regulation, Conference Paper, November 5. Echeverry identifies two information frictions between issuers and investors: (1) incomplete information on the underlying loans. Prices of junior tranches appear no more informative than those of AAA tranches within 'low-doc' deals, while the latter are no less informative within 'full-doc' deals. Only secondary is the lack of investor sophistication. See in detail: D. Echeverry, (2019), Information Frictions in Securitization Markets: Unsophisticated Investors or Opaque Assets? University of Notre Dame—Mendoza College of Business Working Paper, February 28, mimeo.

[134] Daley et al. studied the effect of credit ratings on loan origination and securitization. That turned out to be a two-step process: (1) banks decide whether to originate a given loan pool or not, and obtain private information about the pools originated, and (2) each bank chooses what portion of the pool's cash own rights to retain and what portion to securitize. Their study highlights how 'credit ratings affect the trade-off between productive efficiency (i.e. efficiency of the origination process) and allocative efficiency (i.e. efficiency of the securitization process)'. Credit ratings increase

ment is obvious.[135] Albertazzi et al.[136] have been assessing the role of asymmetric information in that segment of the securitization market where it is likely to be most pervasive, that is, securities backed by loans to SMEs.[137] A typical SME loan book is more opaque than other loan books due to the different idiosyncratic risks embedded in the different loan securities. They also broadened the scope of the analysis to include both securitized and non-securitized loans originated. To that effect they observed the performance in terms of default status. They conclude, within the context of their stylized mode, that 'adverse selection is widespread but that moral hazard is confined to weak relationships, indicating that a strong relationship is a credible enough commitment to monitor after securitization. Importantly, the selection of which loans to securitize based on observables is such that it largely offsets the (negative) effects of asymmetric information, rendering the overall unconditional quality of securitized loans significantly better than that of non-securitized ones.'[138] In short they conclude that despite the presence of asymmetric information, no argument could be withheld that credit-risk transfers lead to lax credit standards.

It is clear that because of all these reasons, SMEs have not able to benefit from lowering market interest rates in recent years, or at least not to the same extent as other market agents. And a wider securitization industry within the context of the CMU isn't going to help make this problem go away any time soon. What is said however is that banks who are less-deposit-funded, less profitable and less capitalized are more inclined to securitize and will do so in larger volumes.[139] Although the fact that securitization has not directly

allocative efficiency by reducing costly retention and increase the supply of credit, but reduce average quality of loans originated and can lead to an oversupply of credit relative to first best. Credit shopping and manipulation were not used as variables, but ceteris paribus these variables have the same overall effect as reducing the informativeness of ratings. See in detail: B. Delay et al., (2017), Securitization, Ratings and Credit Supply, Working Paper, September mimeo.

[135] See, for example, U. Albertazzi et al., (2015), Asymmetric Information in Securitization: An Empirical Assessment, *Journal of Monetary Economics* Vol. 71, pp. 33–49; B.J. Keys et al., (2010), Did Securitization Lead to Lax Screening? Evidence from Subprime Loans 2001–2006, Quarterly Journal of Economics Vol. 125, pp. 307–362.

[136] U. Albertazzi et al., (2017), Asymmetric Information and the Securitization of SME Loans, BIS Working Paper Nr. 601, January.

[137] A securitization is affected by asymmetric information if 'conditional on the characteristics of the securitized loans which are observable to the investors—there is a positive correlation between the errors of the model for the probability of a loan being securitized, and those for the probability that the loan goes into default (or deteriorates)'; Ibid. p. 3. The information asymmetry takes one of two forms: frictions due to adverse selection and those stemming from moral hazard.

[138] Ibid. pp. 3–4, 23 ff.

[139] O. Abdesalam et al., (2017), Asset Securitization and Bank Risk: Do Religiosity or Ownership Structure Matter, Working Paper, mimeo. They 'find that banks with higher securitization activity have consistently shown a riskier profile by being significantly less adequately capitalized and offering higher ratio of net loans to total assets.' That is even true within the Islamic bank sphere which are relative to their Western peers less risk inclined. There is evidence that bank risk declines in the year of the securitization and increases in the following year. They also show that this effect is driven by low-risk securitization deals. They also show that the risk reduction effect is weaker in crisis

affected the supply of new SME loans, it did contribute to risk-rebalancing effects of securitization on the balance sheet of those banks.[140]

More positive we can be about the EC's proposal to give small- and medium-sized enterprises (SMEs) better access to financing through public markets. Despite the benefits of stock exchange listings, EU public markets for SMEs can struggle to attract new issuers. Already in the Mid-Term Review of the CMU Action Plan in June 2017, the EC announced a proposal to adapt the rules to broaden access to capital markets for SMEs.[141] Overall the aim is to cut red tape for small and medium companies trying to list and issue securities on 'SME Growth Markets', a new category of trading venue dedicated to small issuers, and to foster the liquidity of publicly listed SME shares. The proposed rules can be summarized as follows[142]:

- Adapt current obligations to keep registers of persons that have access to price-sensitive information (insider lists) so as to avoid excessive administrative burden for SMEs, while ensuring that competent authorities can still investigate cases of insider dealing. Rules will also ensure that manager's transactions will be timely disclosed to the markets.
- Allow issuers with at least three years of listing on SME Growth Markets (a new category of trading venue)[143] to produce a lighter prospectus when transferring to a regulated market.[144]

periods relative to normal times. F. Battaglia et al., (2018), Securitization and Crash Risk: Evidence from Large European Banks, Bank of Finland Research Discussion Papers Nr. 26, December 11. Their paper provides evidence that bank risk declines in the year of the securitization and increases in the following year. They also show that this effect is driven by low-risk securitization deals. Risk reduction effect is weaker in crisis periods relative to normal times.

[140] D. Castellani, (2017), Mortgage-backed Securitization and SME Lending During the Financial and Economic Crisis: Evidence from the Italian Cooperative Banking System, Review of Banking, Finance and Monetary Economics, Vol. 47, Issue 1, pp. 187–222.

[141] EC, (2018), Proposal for a REGULATION OF THE EUROPEAN PARLIAMENT AND OF THE COUNCIL amending Regulations (EU) No 596/2014 and (EU) 2017/1129 as regards the promotion of the use of SME growth markets, COM(2018) 331 final/2018/0165 (COD), May 24; EC, (2018), COMMISSION DELEGATED REGULATION (EU) .../...of XXX amending Commission Delegated Regulation (EU) 2017/565 as regards certain registration conditions to promote the use of SME growth markets for the purposes of Directive 2014/65/EU of the European Parliament and of the Council, May 24.

[142] EC, (2018), Capital Markets Union: Making it Easier for Smaller Businesses to Get Financing through Capital Markets, Press Release IP/18/3727, May 24; EC, Frequently Asked Questions: Easier Access to Financing for Smaller Businesses through Capital Markets, Fact Sheet Memo/18/3728, May 24.

[143] They are defined as Multilateral Trading Facilities (a type of trading venue) where at least 50% of issuers are SMEs.

[144] These proposed alleviations will be limited to SME Growth Markets and will not be extended to SMEs listed on regulated markets. Otherwise, investors will be faced with a complex situation whereby companies listed on the same stock exchange are subject to two different sets of rules (alleviated requirements for SMEs, and normal requirements for all other companies), Ibid. factsheet EC.

- Make it easier for trading venues specialized in bond issuance to register as SME Growth Markets. This will be done by setting a new definition of debt-only issuers. Those would be companies that issue less than EUR 50 million of bonds over a 12-month period.
- It will become easier for growth market operators to alleviate from the rule that half-year reports need to be produced.
- Create a common set of rules on liquidity contracts for SME Growth Markets in all member states, in parallel to national rules. This refers to agreements between issuers and financial intermediaries (a bank or an investment firm) for buying and selling shares of and on behalf of the issuer. By so doing, the financial intermediary enhances the liquidity of the shares.

The proposal will be embedded in regulation through changes to the Market Abuse Regulation and the Prospectus Regulation and further technical amendments to delegated acts under the Markets in Financial Instruments Directive (MiFID II). Whether or not the proposal will be a success will depend on the appetite investors will develop for investing in debt instruments of SME organizations. The main problem that still stands is that debt markets are information-insensitive and given its size debt market investors tend to allocate in large chunks based on summarized quality criteria developed by others. It remains largely unclear how that modus operandi will fit with the objective of the proposal. Also an unknown factor is the question regarding the cross-border appetite to invest in SME type of risks. Reducing the red tape is one thing but making capital flows run through the model a totally different thing. There seems to be no real mechanics in place within the context of the proposal to remedy these issues.

3.2.6.5 So Now What: Securitization, Global Regulatory Reform and Attempted Revival in Europe

It's time to recap. We worked through a material amount of recent changes, regulatory adjustments and conceptual redesign and some redesign of the securitization framework. But where do we stand now? Securitization got tainted during the 2007 financial crisis but beyond has been a long-standing strategy to fund illiquid assets. The basic idea still stands: the ability to acquire a broad range of financial assets and to create tranches with specific seniority, maturity and return characteristic, and accompanying credit ratings means that securitized products can be tailored to the specific needs of various investor classes. Securitization had to live with changing Basel capital rules and the Basel rules evolved to reflect experiences without damaging the benefits of securitizations. Particularly the recent redesign (Basel III securitization framework) balances the need to properly reflect identified risks without holding back a further evolution of the industry. No wonder that recent capital and other regulatory requirements have led to withdrawals by FIs from certain parts of the market. And so the question raises to what degree securitization can still play the role of efficient management of banks' balance sheets.

Although it could come in handy, I will not review or summarize the Basel III and specific securitization rules.[145] I pondered for a long time if I would develop a comparative analysis of the US and European Securitization rules. Although an attractive idea, I stayed short of doing so, simply because it would be either too simple or too burdensome for the kind of work this book tries to be.[146] What is clear however is the fact that both Basel III and the securitization framework redesign are complex and interact on various levels. Bjerke sums up a few:

> [f]or example, a bank outside the United States may be subject to improved capital charges if a borrower has a rating whereas in the United States, such ratings will not determine the applicable risk weight. An institution that is limited by the leverage ratio may determine that it will look to riskier credits to clear its hurdle rates, whereas a firm that is more constrained by its risk-weighted capital requirements may determine that it is economically more feasible to take a higher-rated exposure. The liquidity ratio will impact funding commitments, and effectively increase a bank's cost of making undrawn revolver commitments, delayed draw term loans and letter of credit commitments. Similarly, the way in which banks will value certain collateral and guarantees will differ based on their other exposures and applicable manner in which they calculate their capital requirements.[147]

From the early start, the securitization product has been a capital maximizing relief tool for banks.[148] Retaining ownership while transferring risk and thereby reducing capital is essential and will continue to play a role for banks. Securitization ultimately formalizes funding for underlying bank obligations that 'meet or exceed the duration requirements of such underlying obligations' taking into account the NSFR. It will also play a role to get relief of the LCR[149] by selling or receiving a payment for a revolver or delayed funding obligation. Also risk weighting can be optimized by transferring exposures with certain

[145] For those looking for a quick refresher, see B. Bjerke, (2017), Securitization in Light of the New Regulatory Landscape, in the International Comparative Legal Guide to Securitization 2017, pp. 24–27.

[146] I got convinced there are sufficient excellent alternatives. See, for example, the excellent annualized overview that Hogan Lovells produces regarding the comparative dynamics regarding securitization on both sides of the pond called 'Summary of key EU and U.S. Regulatory Developments Relating to Securitization Transactions'. Country-specific analysis can be found in the International Comparative Legal Guide on Securitizations released annually.

[147] B. Bjerke, (2017), Securitization in Light of the New Regulatory Landscape, in International Comparative Legal Guide to Securitization 2017, p. 27. Also: B. Bjerke, (2018), Regulatory Drivers of Securitizations, in International Comparative Legal Guide to Securitization 2018, online via iclg.com

[148] For some that's enough to ban the product altogether as capital relief with high leverage ratios is a recipe for disaster over and over again. Although I'm not totally opposing that line of thinking, it is a symptomatic approach. The constant and growing demand for 'safe assets' underlying the securitization market for beyond what the sovereign bond market can yield embeds much more complexity than capital charges for banks. Banning securitization for the capital relief argument is an honest argument but the wrong fight ultimately.

[149] See also in the recent Basel III monitoring review: EBA, (2018), Basel III Monitoring Exercise. Results based on Data of 31 December 2017, October 4.

characteristics off balance at least when meeting the Basel III operational requirements.[150] Indeed, the choice for which product to push out is for a bank a trade-off between what type of capital or ratio constrained they face and the operational requirements for each sub-product group in the securitization space. A bank that is constrained by the risk-weighting capital ratios might decide that synthetic securitization is the best balance and optimization between capital relief and control over the underlying assets. To get it right 'collateral, guarantees, credit derivatives and other credit risk mitigation techniques for hedging the underlying exposure', the Basel operational criteria need to be met to be recognized for securitization purposes.[151] And they need to be executed in such a way that they meet the accounting rules for taking the assets off balance. In short, the Basel III ratios and in particular the risk-weighting and leverage ratios will drive the future of securitization in the context of balance sheet optimization. The discussed STS criteria are a necessary step to build a sustainable industry. However, it was pointed out before that concentrating risk through tranching increases tail risk in a way we didn't understand before the crisis, came to learn after the crisis but then later on decided to forget. That could cost us dearly over time as it injects a boom and bust model into the industry that at some point will lead to a regulatory insight which will demonstrate characteristics no longer willing to altogether accept the risks.

Given the closing date for the manuscript of this book, it wasn't witnessed whether the STS securitization introduction in Europe, which came full force in 2019, will live up to its promise. A slight uptick in early 2019 isn't sufficient to conclude so and might not even be the result of the STS regulation.[152] Given the dismal state of securitization in Europe in prior years, I guess a minimal uptick can be expected anyway, a trend that also in 2018 could be witnessed. Whether it will really go strong and become a planning technique for banks remains to be seen. Many items and considerations have the potential to materially poop the party. And that besides the fact that in the run-up to the new securitization legislation and coming into force we have witnessed a material level of lobbying to that effect.[153] Throughout the book I have tried to give an honest account about everything including securitization. That is harder than it sounds: the avalanche of opinions on each and every single item, the massive amount of research, the outcomes that often point in all directions, the question about the usefulness of outcomes when being the product of stylized facts and so on lobbyists can do better and can definitely do better than the impact assessment the EC commissioned prior to throwing in the STS proposal. The defense that securitization is still 'badly understood' and that bad vibes keep circling the

---

[150] For those not willing to dig into phone books of guidelines, see for the list: B. Bjerke, (2017), Securitization in Light of the New Regulatory Landscape, in the International Comparative Legal Guide to Securitization 2017, p. 28.

[151] And that is a lot, see B. Bjerke, (2017), ibid. p. 28.

[152] The EBA will assess the impact of the STS regulation starting 2019 but the first results will likely only be compiled after the close of the manuscript.

[153] That was often accompanied by a level of arrogance unnecessary, unconvincing, un-preferred and edging counterproductive. See, for example, R. Hopkin, (2016), Now is Not the Time to Delay Securitisation's Revival, June 13, via afme.eu; R. Hopkin, (2017), Reviving Securitization in Europe: Is the End in Sight at Last, ICLG to Securitization 2017, pp. 30–33.

battered product group kills it all. Let's face it the way it is: securitization has always been a capital relief tool for banks, and therefore a tool to maximize profits on as little as equity possible. That's ok, as long as you're willing to clean up your own mess when things go wrong. Reality tells us differently. Second, STS criteria will only be convincing if they prove their robustness over time. There are some really painful open wounds in those criteria, which cosmetically have been shifted toward delegated regulation and technical bulletins. So for all we know it could be a 'jack in the box'. What we do know is that the tranching exercise is not neutral and in fact elevates credit risk above and beyond the aggregate risk attached to the underlying assets. That is anyway the case when concentrating risks which enhance tail risk. That securitization adds to economic growth is largely untested and evidence so far has been unconvincing, if not because of the methodology used to test it. And lastly, that it would be a tool to provide more and deeper liquidity to SMEs. Let's be fair here as well. Arranging data in such a way that one indirectly could assume it has a positive effect doesn't outweigh the direct evidence that it does not. And it does not for reasons we know already years on end. The risks in an SME loan book are too idiosyncratic and not aligned for the system of tranching to work effectively. The cost that the ultimate investor would require for taking that pool of undefined risk that typically embodies MSE loan books would leave no margin for the offering bank relative to the underlying payout of the assets.[154] So not viable product for the bank, unless you sell it ignoring that specific fact. Ultimately, the buyers of securitized products buy in their understanding a debt product, with a (often external if not self-produced internal) credit rating. They are in what we called the informative-insensitive debt markets, and so they don't effectively analyze the intrinsic risk of the securitized product they are about to buy. And so we come full circle.

Doesn't STS matter at all then? It does, but not in a way that matters at a time when it really needs to work its magic and protect investor and public interest. So there you have it. And I forgot, banks tend to get very sloppy when they source (mortgage) loans when they know already that the loan book will be offloaded later on. The proprietary nature of a loan book that stays on the balance sheet works self-disciplining and so it should. It brings banking I guess much closer to its original commitment and the gentlemen's agreement with society underlying their business model.[155] Ultimately, an industry that long term cannot survive without the backstop of a lender-of-last resort and the ultimate backstop it provides doesn't operate in the full free market, but in a sort of encapsulated regulatory Disneyland. That backstop means the Treasury absorbs risks on behalf of certified banks and should be adequately rewarded. But apparently nobody ever told them, even not our democratic representatives.

---

[154] The uniformity of risk in a pool of mortgage loans is higher making it a much more attractive product group.

[155] Rather than maximize profits on an ever narrowing string of equity, bulking volumes of leverage, the feasible alternative is to expand their balance sheet in an orderly fashion and still generate attractive risk-adjusted returns based on enhanced allocation efficiencies. But then again, they gave that skillset away when they, starting in the late 1970s, loaded up their balance sheets with mortgage loans rather than business loans.

Now as already indicated above, the volume of new issuances continues to disappoint. It seems there was a bottom building in 2013–2014 where, respectively, 75.9 and 78.2 billion Euro was issued. Although that has grown to 111.7 billion Euro, it stays wildly short of the approx. 500 billion Euro in 2007. There is a lot of hope that the STS regulation will change the outlook of the European securitization industry. But the primary regulation is just the anchor and secondary regulation and guidelines will have to work their magic to solve any remaining issues. And there are a few. Disappointing it was that the following features did not make it in the final primary regulation: (1) restriction on permitted market participants, (2) public disclosure of information listing the names of investors and (3) an increase in the risk retention rate. And only the issues related to self-certified residential loan securitizations and acquired portfolios have been partly settled. Unresolved stayed the issues related to provisions for third-country-originated transactions, adjusted standards for existing and legacy transactions and a suboptimal grandfathering provision for legacy transactions.[156]

3.2.6.6 Secondary EU Regulation Regarding Securitization

The primary regulation leaves many features undefined. It's up to the regulator and aligned bodies to fill in the gaps. The EBA and ESMA received 30 mandates to develop criteria and so on following the primary securitization regulation. I will not review all of them, insofar as they have been developed yet, but have picked out the most important ones.

Homogeneity of Underlying Exposures

The STS regulation requires 'that the STS securitization shall be backed by a pool of underlying exposures that are homogeneous in terms of asset type' (art. 20, the homogeneity criterion). But it doesn't spell out what 'homogeneity' exactly means. Throughout late 2017 and the first half of 2018, consultations have been released by the EBA. This resulted in a final RTS (regulatory technical standards) released on July 31, 2018.[157] The RTS specifies which underlying exposures are deemed homogeneous. It establishes four conditions for the underlying exposures to be considered homogeneous: (1) they have been underwritten according to similar underwriting standards; (2) they are serviced according to similar servicing procedures; (3) they fall within the same asset category; (4) and, for a majority of asset categories, they need to be homogeneous with reference to at least one homogeneity factor. The final RTS will clearly have to indicate

---

[156] See for an analysis of the outstanding issues: R. Jones and L. Cohen, (2017), Securitization Reform Analysis, the International Comparative Legal Guide to: Securitization 2017, Macmillan, pp. 34–39.

[157] EBA, (2018), Final Draft Regulatory Technical Standards On the Homogeneity of the Underlying Exposures in Securitization under Articles 20(14) and 24(21) of Regulation (EU) No 2017/2402 laying down a general framework for securitization and creating a specific framework for simple transparent and standardized securitization, EBA/RTS/2018/02, July 31.

that the criteria and risk factors can be applied and analyzed in a flexible manner to fit a particular transaction. These RTSs will ultimately be applicable to STS ABCP and to STS term securitizations.[158]

The RTS further specifies a list of asset categories as well as lists of the homogeneity factors available for the majority of the asset categories, a list reflecting the most common types of underlying exposures securitized in market practice: residential mortgages; commercial mortgages; credit facilities to individuals for personal, family and household consumption purposes; credit facilities to enterprises and corporates including SMEs; auto loans and leases; credit card receivables; and trade receivables. The EBA is further developing guidelines for other STS criteria, beyond homogeneity.

Risk Retention and Related Matters

These draft technical standards set the requirements for originator, sponsors and original lenders related to risk retention, in particular with regard to: (1) the modalities for retaining risk, including fulfillment through a synthetic or contingent form of retention; (2) the measurement of the level of retention; (3) the prohibition of hedging or selling the retained interest; (4) the condition for retention on a consolidated basis; and (5) the conditions for exempting transactions based on a clear, transparent and accessible index.[159]

The final draft on this matter was released on July 31, 2018.[160] The RTS specifies in greater detail the risk retention requirement and, in particular, the matters listed in Article 6(7) of the Securitisation Regulation (including the modalities of retaining risk, the measurement of the level of retention, the prohibition of hedging or selling the retained interest and the conditions for retention on a consolidated basis).[161] The finalized RTS will replace the Commission Delegated Regulation on risk retention.[162]

---

[158] There was a separate draft consultation issued in 2018 to specifically focus on adapted interpretations for STS ABCP: EBA, (2018), Draft Guidelines on the STS Criteria for ABCP Securitisation, EBA/CP/2018/04, April 20. Final Guidelines: EBA, (2018), Final Report on Guidelines on the STS Criteria for ABCP Securitisation, EBA/CP/2018/08, December 12. They provide answer to questions such as 'What is "active portfolio management"? When should exposures be considered "similar"? What information on underlying exposures is relevant? The required expertise of originators, original lenders and servicers. Exposures in default and to credit-impaired obligors. What constitutes "predominant dependence" on asset sales? What is "appropriate" hedging? What interest rates may be referenced? What exposures can be treated as "substantially similar" for the purpose of comparable data on historical default and loss performance?' M. Daley. (2019), EBA STS Guidelines now in Force, May 17, dlapiperblog.org

[159] See A. Bak, (2018), Reviving Securitisation in Europe, ICLG Securitisation, 2018, via iclg.com

[160] See initial draft released in December 2017. See high up in this chapter for full reference.

[161] EBA, (2018), Final Draft Regulatory Technical Standards, Specifying the Requirements for Originators, Sponsors and Original Lenders Relating to Risk Retention pursuant to Article 6(7) of Regulation (EU) 2017/2402, EBA/RTS/2018/01, July 31.

[162] Commission Delegated Regulation (EU) No 625/2014 of 13 March 2014 supplementing Regulation (EU) No 575/2013 of the European Parliament and of the Council by way of regulatory technical standards specifying the requirements for investor, sponsor, original lenders and originator institutions relating to exposures to transferred credit risk. Text with EEA relevance OJ L 174, June 13, 2014, pp. 16–25.

Continuation of the existing approach toward risk retention should be warranted as a breach in methodology will create material compliance hurdles and outright confusion. Open-ended issues are still jurisdictional scope, consolidated application and grandfathering.[163]

Disclosure Requirements, Operational Standards and Access Conditions for All Securitizations

This involves particularly paper pushing and will deal with the details of what data must be provided as well as the reporting templates. As far as we can oversee based on the draft guidelines, the EBA/ESMA will start from the existing reporting templates and adjust them to reflect the STS criteria. Private transactions will be exempted from these reporting standards. That seems to be broadly in line with the content of the main regulation on private securitizations. It is somewhat unclear what the position will be of ABCP transactions and ABCP programs (which are typically private deals). It is pointed out that they are out of scope for these RTS but yet are specifically contemplated. In the slipstream of this RTS, there are two that deal respectively with fees for securitization repositories and the registration as a securitization repository.[164]

Content and Format of the STS Notification

The RTS/ITS provide details and specify the information that the originator, sponsor and SSPE (securitization special-purpose entity) are required to provide in order to comply with their STS notification requirements. Most of it is bureaucracy. It is required that the identity of the originator of ABCP transactions. That seems somewhat inconsistent with the disclosure requirements as it applies to ABCP securitizations. For private securitizations the identification should be limited to the unique reference number assigned by ESMA to the STS notification document. Investors can then cross-check for that number on ESMAs' website before engaging in a private securitization deal.[165]

[163] A. Bak, (2018), Reviving Securitisation in Europe, ICLG Securitisation, 2018, via iclg.com

[164] See ESMA, (2017), Draft Technical Standards on Disclosure Requirements, Operational Standards, and Access Conditions under the Securitisation Regulation, Consultation Paper, ESMA33-128-107, December 19. The final report: ESMA, (2018), Technical Standards on Disclosure Requirements under the Securitisation Regulation, ESMA33-128-474, August 22. Regarding the securitization repositories: ESMA, (2018), Draft Technical Standards on the Application for Registration as a Securitisation Repository under the Securitisation Regulation, ESMA33-128-109, March 23. For non-ABCPs: EBA, (2018), Draft Guidelines on the STS criteria for Non-ABCP Securitisation, EBA/CP/2018/05, April 20. Final guidelines on the STS criteria for Non-ABCP Securitisation: EBA, (2018), Guidelines on STS criteria for non-ABCP Securitization, EBA?GL/2018/09, December 12, via eba.europe.eu

[165] ESMA, (2018), Draft RTS and ITS on STS Notification under Regulation (EU) N° 2017/2402, Final report, ESMA33-128-477, July 16.

Third-Party Firms Providing STS Verification Services

Third parties can be used by originators, sponsors or SSPEs for services that relate to validating compliance with STS criteria. ESMA can specify the conditions under which a firm can become an authorized STS verifier. One of the RTS provides further details which information need to be provided in order to be authorized for such authorization.[166]

Adjustments Related to Lower Capital Requirements

It was highlighted before that when meeting the STS criteria, FIs could benefit from lower capital requirements[167] relative to what would be the case for the underlying loan book or securities when an—on average—similar risk profile was present. Therefore that parallel to the new securitization regulation, the CRR regulation has been undergoing adjustments to reflect those principles. But also in this case the devil in somewhat in the detail, as they are key to the functioning of the new CRR regime for both STS and non-STS securitizations. Fleshing them all out here would be impossible given the context of this book and would deserve a significant major reference work on its own. I will limit myself here to shedding some light on where we are, as the story is still written, why it is relevant and what ratios will be impacted.

- The EBA consulted[168] on the RTS for conditions for the use of K_{IRB} (capital requirement calculation) which is relevant for banks when applying the SEC-IRBA methodology to calculate capital requirements for STS qualifying products.[169]
- Guidelines have been provided[170] with respect to the 'hierarchy of approaches' for calculating capital requirements of securitization positions of which the SEC-IRBA is the most preferred, all other criteria allowing.

---

166 ESMA, (2018), Draft RTS on Authorisation of Firms Providing STS Verification Services, Final Report, ESMA33-128-473, July 16.

167 Securitization tends to structurally have a positive effect on bank profitability. Bank risk, cost of funding, liquidity and regulatory capital individually and jointly mediate the securitization-profitability relationship. In detail: M. Bakoush, (2014), Securitization and Bank Profitability, Working Paper, September 12, mimeo.

168 EBA, (2018), Draft Regulatory Technical Standards on the Conditions to Allow Institutions to Calculate KIRB in Accordance with the Purchased Receivables Approach under Article 255 of [Regulation (EU) 2017/2401 amending Regulation (EU) No 575/2013], EBA/CP/2018/10, June 19. Final draft issued April 4, 2019.

169 See higher up in the securitization chapter for details on the method. The method should be used by banks when information is available to calculate the capital charge on the underlying securitized pool (K_{IRB}) and the position is backed by a pool of qualifying exposures (an IRB pool). The bank then has the permission to use the IRB approach given the quality of the IRB pool. Risk-weighted exposures are then calculated using the IRB method, which typically has a floor of 15% (and a ceiling of 1250%) based on rating, seniority and maturity unless they constitute an STS exposure.

170 When it is indicated that guidelines were released or issued, it is often referred to the guidelines prior to the STS securitization regulation as they were developed based on the CRR legislation

- Specific guidelines were issued related to the computation of K_{IRB} for dilution risk.
- Guidelines were developed regarding the determination of tranche maturity and weighted average life (WAL).
- Details were released regarding the estimates of probability of default and loss-given default using incremental risk capital.
- Guidelines in the making[171] relate to issues as 'implicit support',[172] 'STS eligibility of synthetic securitization'[173] and 'significant risk transfers'.[174] Regarding synthetic securitizations, two items are relevant to follow up on: (1) time calls and (2) pro-rata amortizations.[175] Let's deal with number two first. In capital requirement deals, a most relevant question is that of placing risk and more specifically junior or first-loss risk. If a capital deal amortizes sequentially, that is, senior notes pay down first, the deal becomes increasingly less and less efficient over time. The portfolio shrinks in size but the tranches stay the same size and so does the coupon which can be pricey. It seems that the EBA will allow pro-rata amortization meaning that the protection will shrink over time (in line with the portfolio). Also our first feature 'time calls' are relevant in this respect. It refers to the fact that if a deal has a replenishment period, allowing new exposures to be added over time and thus keeping the portfolio the same size, and once that period is over, the issuer can call the deal or re-issue as it see fit. Under the ECBs Single Supervisory Mechanism seems to be approved, but the EBA has echoed ideas not to ban time calls but to limit the replenishment period to the remaining weighted average life of the assets. That implies that the assets in the portfolio will carry a pay down pretty much until the issuer can call (or calls) the deal. The trade-off for policy makers goes like this: for capital relief to be justified, risk effectively needs to leave the balance sheet. What that exactly means can be nightmare to figure out. But underlying that is the concern that risk transfer markets are used to flatten bank capital ratios,

---

which goes obviously further back in time than the STS securitization regulation. Adjustments to those guidelines are still to be expected for many of these items unless specifically indicated.

[171] A number of these developments will go on beyond the cut-off date of this manuscript.

[172] Initial Guidelines: EBA, (2016), Guidelines on Implicit Support for Securitisation Transactions, EBA/GL/2016/08, October 3.

[173] This one is particularly relevant and equally debated. Underlying discussion is whether synthetic securitizations can meet STS standards altogether. The primary STS securitization regulation left the door open to answer that question with a yes. However, during the consulting phase, it became clear that the EBA, through their guidelines could poop the party, forcing banks to look for capital relief elsewhere. A possible way would be to not provide capital relief or only under harsh conditions. Another way would be to provide no capital relief deal ex ante, but only possible ex post. FIs would then never know for sure whether a risk transfer would provide capital relief. That opaqueness could deter many in practice from engaging in those deals altogether. What adds to the complexity is that the regulator has never formally indicated the list of requirements for recognizing risk transfer deals in regulatory capital, but has always engaged in a 'case by case' scenario.

[174] See already in 2017: EBA, (2017), On the Significant Risk Transfer in Securitisation, Discussion Paper, EBA-DP-2017-03, September 19.

[175] See in detail: O. Sanderson, (2018), EBA Plan Could Cut Benefits of Synthetic Securitization, February 1, via globalcapital.com. See A. Delivorias, (2016), Synthetic Securitization, A Closer Look, EP Briefing June 2016, via europarl.europa.eu

without a commensurate transfer of risk. Transfer of risk[176] can be by taking contractually the risk of the balance sheet, but it doesn't end there. Transactions which pay out so much in coupon that the counterparty (the buyer of securitized products) was never at risk don't seem to fit those criteria. Capital relief seems unwarranted in those cases and lead to discussions between parties involved.[177]

3.2.6.7 Liquidity Coverage Ratio and Solvency II

The securitization package requires adjustments to the LCR and the Solvency II legislation (dealing with the capital requirements for insurance investors). Although an alignment was created between the LCR eligibility criteria and the STS criteria, the STS products were not promoted up which implies that they didn't generate a more beneficial treatment from a LCR point of view. That is even the case for senior tranches for both term and ABCP. On July 13, 2018, the Commission adopted the LCR Delegated Regulation without material change regarding that specific point. That could very well have material implications on the willingness of banks to engage in the European securitizations.[178] The EC seems to have scored own goals in this matter.[179] Although the technicalities differ, the same situation occurred with respect to the integration of the STS products in the Solvency II legislation. For senior STS products, the position taken seems defendable, but the risk factor attached to mezzanine and junior products remain very high. For non-STS products, there is no relief foreseen whatsoever.[180] I invite the reader

[176] Credit-risk transfers (CRTs) can help to price credit risk, because they are transparent, open priced in liquid markets and there is no counterparty risk. See in detail: S.M. Wachter, (2018), Credit Risk Transfer, Informed Markets, and Securitization, Economic Policy Review Vol. 24, Nr. 3, pp. 117–131; P. Morganti, (2018), A Securitization-based Model of Shadow Banking with Surplus Extraction and Credit Rik Transfer, in Shadow Banking: Financial Intermediation beyond Banks (Ed. Esa Jokivuolle), SUERF Conference Proceedings 2018/1, Larcier, pp. 98–107.

[177] For example, deals between Barclays and Unicredit in 2008 ended up in UK Court in 2012 because of this issue. See Barclays bank Plc vs. Unicredit bank Ag & Anor, via Casemine.com

[178] A. Ali, (2018), European ABS LCR Rules Disappoint, Could Drive bank Exodus, July 24, via globalcapital.com

[179] M. Daley, (2018), LCR vs. CMU: EC Scores an Own Goal, July 28, via lexicology.com

[180] The final regulation came through on June 1, 2018: Commission Delegated Regulation (EU) 2018/1221 of 1 June 2018 amending Delegated Regulation (EU) 2015/35 as regards the calculation of regulatory capital requirements for securitizations and simple transparent and standardized securitizations held by insurance and reinsurance undertakings (Text with EEA relevance), C/2018/3302, OJ L 227, 10.9.2018, pp. 1–6. In the final regulation, the Commission has developed a new calibration for non-senior tranches of STS securitizations, which should also benefit from an adapted capital charge under Solvency II with improved risk sensitivity. I personally see that as a good thing, at least from the perspective of the CMU development. Insurance companies and related investors have a role to play in the distribution of risk across the different market players based on their risk appetite and longevity. Those investors are better placed to absorb mezzanine and junior tranches and have the potential to provide risk-return levels these investors are looking for. BUT where I see the pain is that the capital that is freed up will not necessarily flow back into the economy. And if it does it will most likely go back into the system as new mortgages, which

to benchmark those findings against the principles and objectives as set out by the IOSCO with respect to securities regulation. That will be an interesting puzzle and will require to stagger the analysis based on the structure of the principled framework: (1) principles relating to the regulator, (2) principles for self-regulation, (3) principles for the enforcement of securities regulation, (4) principles for cooperation in regulation, (5) principles for issuers and principles related to clearing and settlement.[181]

Turk reminds us, despite the avalanche of securitization regulation that has been issued in recent years, that 'for practical purposes, little of that reform has been imposed by the statutory rulemaking process established under the Dodd-Frank Act. Instead, the bulk of actual policymaking has occurred much more informally, through enforcement actions against large financial institutions that have resulted in a series of multi-billion dollar settlements. By pursuing a strategy of "regulation by settlement," regulators have implicitly promulgated a novel legal prohibition on misconduct in securitization markets, roughly equivalent to a negligence standard.'[182]

---

ultimately is a low value-adding industry. The justification of the lower capital charge is not only in its input legitimacy, but also in its output legitimacy, that is, what value does the freed-up capital bring to the economy. If that question cannot be answered, or only in a negative way, and so the value is limited to enhancing returns on a string of equity for banks, we might have no capital relief or securitization model altogether, as it will concentrate risks and create systemic risk at the level of the interconnected banking system without any proper benefits. Legislators will then have to do soul-searching and conclude this was another self-orchestrated corporate governance failure drama. It would have been better to analyze deeper the alternative of covered bonds that have repeatedly been presented as a direct alternative for securitization techniques. See S. Cabó-Valverde et al., (2011), Are Covered Bonds a Substitute for Mortgage-Backed Securities, Federal Reserve Bank of Chicago Working Paper Nr. 2011-14, Chicago; S.E. Dincă, (2014), Covered Bonds v. Asset Securitization, Theoretical and Applied Economic, Vol. 21, Nr. 11, pp. 71–84; N. Boesel et al., (2016), Do European Banks with a Covered Bond Program Still Issue Asset-Backed Securities for Funding, Utrecht University, School of Economics Discussion Paper Nr. 16-03 (the answer is by the way yes); A. Arif, (2017), Deciphering Securitisation and Covered Bonds: Economic Analysis and Regulations, PhD thesis, December 11; T. Ahnert, (2018), Covered Bonds as a Source of Funding for Banks' Mortgage Portfolios, Bank of Canada Financial System Review, June, pp. 37–49. See for a variety of alternatives to securitization: S.L. Schwarcz, (2013), Securitization, Structured Finance and Covered Bonds, *The Journal of Corporation Law*, Vol. 39, issue 1, pp. 129–154. See also the EC impact assessment underlying the introduction of the covered bond legislation: EC, (2018), Impact Assessment, Accompanying the document Proposal for a Directive of the European Parliament and the Council on the issue of covered bonds and covered bond public supervision and amending Directive 2009/65/EC and Directive 2014/59/EU And Proposal for a Regulation of the European Parliament and the Council on amending Regulation(EU) No 575/2013 as regards exposures in the form of covered bonds (SWD 2018-50 final- 2018/042 (COD)). The EBA produced an analysis to what degree European secured notes (ESNs), which are covered-bond-like dual recourse instruments, may provide a useful funding alternative to banks engaged in lending to SMEs and lending to infrastructure projects. See in detail: EBA, (2018), EBA Report on the European Secured Notes (ESNs), July 24.

[181] There are more principles and layers; see IOSCO, (2017), Objectives and Principles of Securities Regulation, May, via iosco.org

[182] M.C. Turk, (2018), Securitization Reform after the Crisis: Regulation by Rulemaking or Regulation by Settlement? Review of Banking and Financial Law, Vol. 37, pp. 757–769. The more elaborated conference contribution is also very recommendable (accessible through SSRN).

3.2.6.8 Multijurisdictional Securitization in the New Era

Given the complexity of dealing with one securitization platform or set of regulation, it needs not a whole lot of convincing that dealing with multijurisdictional (e.g. mostly between the EU and the USA)[183] is a complex environment full of intricacies. Not only because of the complex set of rules and how they interact but also these rules and technical support policy documents are only gradually introduced and only much later on adopted, and so overlap reality when instruments are securitized on an ongoing basis. And even if the rules look the same, the often aren't. An example: both United States and European Union laws require 5% credit-risk retention[184] for securitization transactions. While the jurisdictional scope of the US rules and EU rules overlaps, their requirements vary significantly, so it has always been a challenge to structure a transaction that is economically efficient and where retention of the same 5% interest complies with both regimes. A variety of new EU securitization rules that came into force on January 1, 2019, make this challenge even more difficult, claim Sweet et al.[185] So there I am always a bit of old and a bit of new in terms of regulations that apply.

Then there is also the jurisdictional overlap. The US risk retention rules apply to sponsors of 'securitization transactions' within the jurisdictional scope of the US, but the scope of that jurisdiction is unclear. The EU securitization rules, including their risk retention components, apply to any transaction that constitutes a 'securitization' for the purposes of the EU rules. They apply indirectly via various types of EU-regulated investors. The EU rules currently do not explicitly address the jurisdictional scope of their direct obligations, so that scope remains unclear. Therefore, it may be necessary to structure a securitization transaction to comply with both sets of rules. For example, a securitization transaction issued by a US issuer will be required to comply with the EU rules in addition to the US rules if any purchaser is to be an EU Institutional Investor, Sweet et al. highlight.

Similar asymmetries are identified between EU and US rules when it comes to (1) which types of transactions are covered, (2) tranching rules, (3) who (which entity) should hold the risk (in risk retention rules which can be the sponsor, the originator or the original lender or a combination of both), (4) different methods for holding risks (the US

---

[183] The differences in securitization markets are discussed elsewhere, but different policies are accountable for the large differences in size and scope between the US and EU securitization markets. The early support to use external credit scores/FICO scores in the US helped to overcome the asymmetric nature, and FICO scores actually enable risk transfer by reducing information asymmetry problems. Moreover, while limiting screening reduces the upfront costs of lending, it also increases loans made to uncreditworthy borrowers. And because increasing loans made to bad borrowers raises the rates good borrowers have to pay (to compensate investors for higher defaults), US rules that sacrifice information for more 'complete' markets may be a bad bargain, Bhide explains. A. Bhide, (2017), Formulaic Transparency: The Hidden Enabler of Exceptional U.S. Securitization *Journal of Applied Corporate Finance*, Vol. 29, Issue 4, pp. 96–111.

[184] There are some accounting issues here, see Q. Zhao, (2019), Interaction Between Securitization Gains and Abnormal Loan Loss Provisions: Credit Risk Retention and Fair Value Accounting, Journal of Business Finance and Accounting, Vol. 46, Issue 7–8, pp. 813–842.

[185] C.A. Sweet et al., (2019), Multijurisdictional Securitization in the Age of the New EU Securitization Rules, February 20, via lexicology.com

works with one method 'the eligible vertical interest' whereas the EU accepts five methods including something that looks like a eligible vertical interest, but not quite as the 'nominal rule' only requires retention of tranches sold or transferred to investors, whereas the US option requires retention of the required percentage of each class of ABS interests issued). Only one of the EU options can be applied to a transaction, (5) the EU and US rules exempt different types of transactions. In the US products that consist of only 'qualified residential mortgages' are exempt, or when asset pool benefit from government guarantees and some re-securitizations. The EU rules contain a different, and much narrower, list of exemptions, generally limited to securitized exposures on, or that are fully, unconditionally and irrevocably guaranteed by a number of predetermined governments, (6) under EU rules requirements may be satisfied on a synthetic or contingent basis, while that might not be sufficient for US rules, (7) transfer and hedging of positions, and (8) both sets of rules cover different time periods.

3.3 Does Securitization Concentrate Uncertainty?

3.3.1 Introduction

Even when securitized assets are simple, transparent and of high quality, risk assessments will be uncertain. This will call for safeguards against potential undercapitalization. Since the uncertainty concentrates mainly in securitization tranches of intermediate seniority, the safeguards applied to these tranches should be substantial, proportionately much larger than those for the underlying pool of assets. That is what Antoniades and Tarashev concluded.

The past decade has witnessed the spectacular rise of the securitization market, its dramatic fall and, recently, its timid revival. Much of this evolution reflected the changing fortunes of securitizations that were split into tranches of different seniority. Initially, such securitizations appealed strongly to investors searching for yield, as well as to banks seeking to reduce regulatory capital through the sale of judiciously selected tranches.[186] The financial crisis has exposed the widespread underestimation of tranche riskiness and illustrated that even sound risk assessments were not immune to substantial uncertainty. They further argue that 'constructing simple and transparent asset pools would be a step towards reducing some of this uncertainty. That said, substantial uncertainty would remain and would concentrate in particular securitization tranches. Despite the simplicity and transparency of the underlying assets, these tranches would not be simple'.[187]

[186] J. Hull and A. White, (2012), Ratings, Mortgage Securitizations, and the Apparent Creation of Value, in A. Blinder, A. Lo and B. Solow (eds.), Rethinking the Financial System, Chapter 7, Russell Sage Foundation.

[187] A. Antoniades and N. Tarashev, (2014), Securitizations Concentrate Uncertainty, BIS Quarterly Review December 2014, pp. 37–53.

They focus on the uncertainty inherent in estimating the risk parameters of a securitized pool and study how it translates into uncertainty about the distribution of losses across tranches of different seniority. The uncertainty could be small for junior tranches, which are the first to be wiped out following even small adverse shocks, or for tranches that are senior enough to enjoy substantial credit protection. In the middle of a securitization's capital structure, however, mezzanine tranches would be subject to considerable uncertainty because of the so-called cliff effect: a small estimation error could mean that the risk of such a tranche is as low as that of a senior tranche or as high as that of a junior tranche.

Pool-wide uncertainty concentrates in tranches in the vicinity of the cliff and, if ignored, raises the possibility of severe undercapitalization for these tranches. Based on a stylized example, their analysis reveals that this possibility is substantial even for extremely simple and transparent underlying assets. And while regulatory capital tends to increase with assets' riskiness, ignoring uncertainty results in a similarly elevated degree of undercapitalization throughout. Safeguards are thus needed to address this issue head on. Since the issue pertains mainly to mezzanine tranches, the safeguards applied to them should be proportionately much larger than those for the underlying asset pool.

They demonstrate, using an extremely simple and transparent securitization, the potential undercapitalization of tranches when model parameters are uncertain but treated as known, that is, when no allowance is made for estimation error. They do so after having reviewed the issuance and rating performance of securitization tranches and abstracted from uncertainty and adopted the benchmark credit-risk model that underlies the Basel capital framework, they compare capital requirements across different types of securitization exposures. The December 2014 revised securitization framework as discussed above can be seen as a good step in the direction of solving some of the problems as the 2014 redress addresses various types of uncertainty, including model uncertainty, while our analysis focuses exclusively on estimation uncertainty.

Their study implies to demonstrate the sensitivity of exposure-level regulatory capital to risk parameters. The regulatory (capital) model for portfolio credit risk is a stylized description of a bank's future losses. It aims to specify the average level of losses—which can be determined in advance—as well as possible deviations from the average. These unknown, random deviations are the credit risk against which the bank builds a capital cushion. The regulatory model's distinguishing feature—a single source of risk for the aggregate portfolio—stems from two assumptions.

The first assumption is that the portfolio comprises a very large number of small assets, that is, the portfolio is asymptotic. An adverse negative shock somewhere in the book will be compensated by a positive impact elsewhere. And when the assets are of comparably small size, such idiosyncratic shocks balance each other: asset-specific risks are diversified away at the portfolio level. If the portfolio were subject only to such idiosyncratic risk, actual losses would be known for sure, that is, there would be losses but no credit risk at the level of the portfolio as a whole.

The second modeling assumption is that there is a single additional source of risk and it cannot be diversified away. This common risk factor is interpreted as relating to general economic conditions. For example, it may capture unexpected swings in energy prices or natural catastrophes that affect all assets in the portfolio. It thus generates correlation of losses and maintains portfolio credit risk.[188]

---

[188] Antoniades and Tarashev, (2014), Ibid. pp. 39–40.

The two assumptions are the reasons why the regulatory model is referred to as the asymptotic single risk factor (ASRF) model. The parameters of this model—such as individual probabilities of default (PD), loss-given default (LGD) and dependence on the common factor—shape the mapping from the common factor to portfolio losses. Provided that these parameters are known with certainty, the mapping is one-to-one: if the trajectory of the common factor were known, so would be aggregate portfolio losses. The regulatory target is to limit the one-year likelihood of bank failure to 0.1%. This requires setting regulatory capital to a critical level of one-year portfolio losses that can be exceeded only with 0.1% probability. Thus, the bank's regulatory capital is equal to the portfolio losses that would materialize if the common factor were at its critical level.[189]

If we then turn our attention to the allocation of regulatory capital, the following analysis can be shared. The capital allocated to a particular exposure is equal to the exposure's contribution to the critical level of portfolio losses. Namely, it is equal to the expected losses on the exposure—roughly, the product of its PD and LGD—conditional on the common factor being at the chosen critical level (henceforth, 'conditional expected losses'). This holds irrespective of the exposure type, for example, a loan, a securitization of loans or a securitization tranche. Even though exposure-level capital is always based on the same risk metric—conditional expected losses—its actual value would depend on the exposure type and the risk characteristics of the underlying assets.

Hull and White focus on homogeneous loans—which have the same size and risk parameters—and on only one risk parameter, the unconditional PD, keeping LGD and common factor dependence in the background at benchmark levels, they treat these loans as underpinning exposures that are infinitesimally small parts of the bank's overall portfolio. Exposures underpinned by a simple aggregation of homogeneous loans would face proportionately the same regulatory capital. Let's take an example: if the PD of a loan is 3%, the capital allocated to this loan would be $0.10 per $1 of exposure. Pooling many such loans in a securitization would then call for summing up the individual requirements, resulting again in regulatory capital of $0.10 per $1 of exposure.[190]

Likewise, the same regulatory capital would apply to a composite exposure that consists of an equal fraction of each underlying loan, often referred to as a vertical tranche. Across all these exposure types, the structure of the underlying risks does not change from the point of view of the metric used for regulatory capital, that is, they all feature the same conditional expected losses per unit of exposure.

The picture changes dramatically when the securitization is sliced into tranches of different seniority, which absorb pool losses sequentially. In this case, conditional expected losses are no longer distributed uniformly across tranches but are mostly concentrated in only some of them. And so is regulatory capital. Hull and White then demonstrate[191] that the high concentration makes the regulatory capital for tranches of intermediate seniority substantially more sensitive to risk parameter values than the capital for a vertical tranche.

---

[189] See for a quantification of this Hull and White, (2014), Ibid. Annex 1, pp. 52–53.

[190] Antoniades and Tarashev, (2014), Ibid. pp. 40–41.

[191] Antoniades and Tarashev, (2014), Ibid. pp. 41–46.

3.3.2 Regulatory Capital in Case of Different Tranches of Seniority

Unlike vertical tranches, tranches that absorb losses sequentially offer a spectrum of risk characteristics and, thus, appeal to a broader investor base. Such tranches are defined by an attachment and a detachment point. The riskiness of a tranche decreases with the tranche's seniority in the securitization's capital structure. A junior tranche, for example, could have attachment and detachment points equal to 0% and 10%, respectively, of the pool exposure. Such a tranche would be intact if there are no losses but would be partly eroded with the first losses. The erosion will be complete when losses reach 10% of the pool exposure. By contrast, a mezzanine tranche with attachment and detachment points of 10% and 20%, respectively, is initially protected but would be affected as soon as losses exceed 10% of the pool size. Finally, a senior tranche with attachment and detachment points of 20% and 100%, respectively, will be the most protected, starting to incur losses only when both the junior and mezzanine tranches are wiped out.[192]

Such securitized tranches are defined by an attachment and a detachment point. The attachment point indicates the minimum of pool-level losses at which a given tranche begins to suffer losses. In turn, the detachment point corresponds to the amount of pool losses that completely wipe out the tranche.

For given attachment and detachment points, the risk of a tranche would depend on the risk characteristics of the underlying pool. Our main focus is on the underlying assets' PD. The 2014 revisions discussed to the regulatory framework for securitizations take explicit account of several additional risk characteristics, such as the number of assets in the pool (i.e. the pool's granularity) and the correlation of associated losses.

In order to measure the sensitivities mentioned, Hull and White focus on the presence of idiosyncratic risk and, to a second, pool-specific risk factor. They calculate the 'regulatory' capital as the expected loss on a tranche, conditional on the critical level of the global common factor.

Then two hypotheses[193] can be distinguished: (1) perfectly diversified pool with single common risk factor and an (2) imperfectly diversified pool or second common factor.

1. Perfectly Diversified Pool with Single Common Risk Factor

They study a securitized pool, which possesses the two key properties of the bank's overall portfolio: full diversification of idiosyncratic risk and exposure to a single common risk factor. Paralleling the bank's portfolio, knowledge of the critical level of the common factor implies knowledge of the critical level of pool-wide losses. Given a loan PD of 3%, this level—and, thus, pool-wide capital—is equal to $0.10 per $1 of exposure.

Knowledge of the conditional pool losses translates into knowledge of the conditional losses on each tranche. By construction, a tranche with a detachment point below 10% of the pool size is sure to be fully wiped out when the common risk factor is at its critical

---

[192] Antoniades and Tarashev, (2014), Ibid.

[193] Antoniades and Tarashev, (2014), Ibid. pp. 42–46.

level. Thus, the regulatory capital for such a tranche is $1 per $1 of exposure. By contrast, a tranche with an attachment point above 10% is fully shielded from losses when the common factor is at its critical level. The regulatory capital for this tranche is thus $0. As the pool's conditional losses are entirely concentrated in the most junior 10% of the tranches, so is the pool's capital, that is, the so-called cliff effect.

The cliff effect is less dramatic for a thick tranche. The regulatory capital for such a tranche, which has different attachment and detachment points, is equal to the aggregate capital for the thin tranches between these points. Aggregating across thin tranches on the two sides of the cliff dampens the effect of thick tranche seniority on regulatory capital. The cliff effect shapes the sensitivity of a tranche's regulatory capital to risk parameters. To see this, suppose that an increase in the PD of the underlying assets raises the securitized pool's regulatory capital from $0.10 to $0.12 per $1 of exposure.

Being subject to the extreme version of the cliff effect, a thin tranche with attachment/detachment points at 11% would see its regulatory capital rise by the maximum possible amount: from $0 to $1 per $1 of exposure. Given the less pronounced version of the cliff effect in the context of thick tranches, the corresponding rise for a 7%–15% tranche would be lower, albeit still substantial: from $0.38 to $0.63. By comparison, a vertical tranche, which is not subject to the cliff effect, would see its regulatory capital rise only as much as that for the overall pool: from $0.10 to $0.12 per $1 of exposure.

2. Imperfectly Diversified Pool or Second Common Factor

The two assumptions that give rise to the extreme version of the cliff effect—full diversification of idiosyncratic risk and a single common risk factor—may be too strong. If either of these assumptions is violated within a securitized pool, knowledge of the global common factor would no longer imply knowledge of pool-wide losses. Conditional on the critical level of the global factor, there would be residual risk, which we study in the context of two different pools.

They observe two elements:

- In the first pool, there is residual idiosyncratic risk.[194] This arises when there is a small number of underlying assets and, thus, idiosyncratic risk cannot be diversified at the level of the pool. In line with standardized and liquid credit default swap indices,[195] they assume that the pool comprises 125 assets.
- In the other pool, the source of residual risk is a second, pool-specific factor. This second factor could arise when the loans in the pool are to obligors in the same industry and are thus more strongly correlated with each other than with loans in the overall bank portfolio.[196] In line with Duponcheele et al.,[197] they assume that, conditional on

[194] See in detail: I. Fender, N. Tarashev and H. Zhu, (2008), Credit Fundamentals, Ratings and Value-at-Risk: CDOs Versus Corporate Exposures, BIS Quarterly Review, March, pp. 87–101.

[195] Such as Dow Jones CDX North America and Markit iTraxx® Europe.

[196] See in detail: M. Pykhtin, and A. Dev, (2002), Credit Risk in Asset Securitisations: Analytical Model, Risk, Vol. 15, Issue 5, May, pp. 16–20.

[197] G. Duponcheele, et al., (2013), A Principles-Based Approach to Regulatory Capital for Securitisations, Risk Control Working Paper.

the global risk factor, the intra-pool asset correlation is equal to 10%. Conditional on the critical level of the global factor, residual risk maintains the randomness of pool losses and it is now their expected—or average—level that delivers pool-wide regulatory capital. Continuing with a loan PD of 3%, this capital is again $0.10 per $1 of exposure.

Residual risk has a direct bearing on the allocation of regulatory capital across tranches. Take, for instance, a thin tranche with an attachment/detachment point to the left of 10% of the pool size. There would be cases when conditional pool-wide losses are below this level, implying the tranche is unaffected, and other cases in which they are above, implying that the tranche is wiped out. Aggregation across all alternative outcomes results in regulatory capital below $1 per $1 of exposure to this tranche.

The residual risk affects the sensitivity of tranches to risk parameters. In their study, Antoniades and Tarashev conclude based on their securitized pool of assets that 'an increase in the PD of the underlying assets raises regulatory capital from $0.10 to $0.12 per $1 of exposure to either of the two pools studied. A thin tranche with attachment/detachment points at 11% would see its regulatory capital rise from $0.37 to $0.55 per $1 of exposure (for the pool with a second risk factor) or from $0.27 to $0.72 (for the pool with a small number of assets). The corresponding changes for a 7%–15% tranche would be from $0.39 to $0.55 and from $0.37 to $0.62, respectively'.[198] The conclusions further reveal that residual risk reduces substantially the sensitivity of thin tranches to the asset PD but only marginally the sensitivity of thick tranches.

3.3.3 The Illusion of Risk-Free in (Re)-securitizations

Instead of comprising individual bonds or loans, the pool underlying a securitization may itself comprise other securitizations or tranches of securitizations. For instance, the run-up to the global financial crisis witnessed the rise of securitizations of mezzanine tranches, or mezzanine re-securitizations. From 2005 to 2007, the senior tranches of mezzanine re-securitizations could rely on a wide investor base thanks to perceptions that they were virtually risk-free. Such perceptions turned out to be wrong.

Antoniades and Tarashev argue that the poor performance of senior tranches of mezzanine re-securitizations during the crisis can be explained with an overlooked inherent feature of these re-securitizations: high correlation of the underlying assets. They illustrate their position with a two-stage securitization. In the first stage, 1 million homogeneous loans are split equally into 1000 pools and then each pool is securitized. All first-stage securitizations are divided in the same way into junior, mezzanine and senior tranches. In the second stage, the 1000 first-stage mezzanine tranches are all pooled together and securitized.

The goal of the second-stage securitization is to create a senior tranche that is subject to so little risk that it merits an AAA rating. The risk characteristics of a first-stage mezzanine tranche would differ from those of an individual loan. Such a tranche is shielded by the corresponding junior tranche from the first losses on the underlying pool, that is,

[198] Antoniades and Tarashev, (2014), Ibid. p. 46.

from the losses triggered mainly by loan-specific, idiosyncratic shocks. Nevertheless, the mezzanine tranche is exposed to widespread, systematic shocks that are strong enough to completely wipe out the junior tranche. And the same systematic shocks would also dominate in mezzanine tranches from other first-stage securitizations. In turn, the greater relative role of systematic shocks in the mezzanine tranches than in the individual underlying loans implies that the losses on these tranches would be more strongly correlated than loan losses.

Over a range of PDs from 0.3% to 2%, losses on first-stage mezzanine tranches are substantially more correlated than loan defaults. For any pair of loans, if there is at least one default, the likelihood of two defaults is lower than 3%. In the context of mezzanine tranches, the corresponding likelihood is 20 times larger. Namely, if at least one of two first-stage mezzanine tranches is subject to default losses, the other is as well with likelihood greater than 60%.

The strong correlation of losses on first-stage mezzanine tranches undermines the benefits of pooling these tranches together at the second-stage securitization. The higher this correlation, the smaller is the scope for diversification and the higher is the probability of large losses on the mezzanine re-securitization. In fact, for the mezzanine re-securitizations implied by their stylized example, the highest rating of a senior tranche with a realistic attachment point is A, several notches below the desired AAA rating. This is true even if the risk of the re-securitization's junior tranche is quite low, corresponding to a BBB rating.

This can explain why senior tranches of mezzanine re-securitizations did not live up to their AAA ratings during the crisis. The admittedly stylized example above brings to the fore a key feature of first-stage mezzanine tranches that rating agencies underappreciated prior to the crisis: since these tranches are largely protected from idiosyncratic shocks, their losses are highly correlated. And it is thus unrealistic to expect that securitizing such tranches could generate diversification benefits that give rise to low-risk securities.[199]

3.3.4 Tranching Riskiness, Uncertainty and Its Implications

As discussed above, the regulatory capital for mezzanine tranches of these securitizations can be quite sensitive to risk parameters. This sensitivity implies that ignoring potential errors in risk parameter estimates can lead to large errors in regulatory capital calculations.[200]

---

[199] See further for the parameters of the study and the calculus involved: Antoniades and Tarashev, (2014), Ibid. pp. 44–45. See for a similar study with similar results: J. Hull, and A. White, (2010), The Risk of Tranches created from Mortgages, *Financial Analysts Journal*, Vol. 66, Nr. 5, pp. 54–67.

[200] See for a variation on this view: I. Fender, and J. Mitchell, (2009), The Future of Securitisation: How to Align Incentives, BIS Quarterly Review, September, pp. 27–43. They argue that, when a securitization originator's uncertainty about tranche riskiness differs from that of an investor, the credibility of the securitization process is at stake. To support this credibility, it is thus necessary to impose specific retention requirements on originators.

In the final part of their study, Antoniades and Tarashev quantify the impact of estimation errors on the calculation of regulatory capital in a stylized setting.[201] As in the rest of their study, they consider a pool of homogeneous assets. For simplicity, they assume that the model used to measure credit risk is correct and that all but one of its parameters are known.

To quantify the severity and probability of potential capital shortfalls, they calculate the 'expected undercapitalization' of a securitization tranche. This statistic reflects two pieces of information: first, the extent of the shortfall for each value of PD above the estimated level of PD and, second, the probability of each PD, given the estimated PD.[202] That implies that expected undercapitalization is equal to the weighted sum of potential capital shortfalls, using the corresponding probabilities as weights.

Their results quantify the expected undercapitalization of tranches from the three underlying pools discussed above. These pools are simple and transparent,[203] as they comprise homogeneous assets with a single uncertain risk parameter, that is, the PD. Their findings are as follows, given that if regulatory capital treats a PD estimate as error-free, the expected undercapitalization would reflect the seniority of the tranche, as well as the type and riskiness of the underlying pool. The two assumptions, as discussed above, are the reasons why the regulatory model is referred to as the Asymptotic Single Risk Factor (ASRF) model. In accordance with the ASRF model, one subject to a second risk factor and one comprising 125 assets and thus featuring incomplete diversification of idiosyncratic risk. In each case, they derive the expected undercapitalization of various tranches for different PD estimates.

In the absence of regulatory safeguards for estimation error, there is a high likelihood of severe undercapitalization of mezzanine tranches.

The results are that:

- ASRF pool-wide regulatory capital of \$0.1.
- Tranches with detachment points below the pool-wide regulatory capital are fully capitalized, at \$1 per \$1 of exposure, and thus can never experience a capital shortfall.
- For tranches most vulnerable to the cliff effect—that is, with attachment points slightly above the pool-wide regulatory capital—expected undercapitalization is extremely high: \$0.60 per \$1 of exposure. Of course, expected undercapitalization declines with the seniority of the thin tranche, that is, as it becomes less likely that the true PD is sufficiently high to matter.

---

[201] Antoniades and Tarashev, (2014), Ibid. pp. 46–50.

[202] That is based on Tarashev's earlier work; see N. Tarashev, (2010): Measuring Portfolio Credit Risk Correctly: Why Parameter Uncertainty Matters, *Journal of Banking and Finance*, Nr. 34, September, pp. 2065–2076.

[203] A discussion paper, EBA (2014), has published a list of proposed criteria that simple and transparent securitizations should satisfy. These criteria include homogeneous underlying assets, well-defined capital structures, enforceable repayment schedules and long performance history of the underlying assets. See in detail: European Banking Authority, (2014), EBA Discussion Paper on Simple Standard and Transparent Securitizations, EBA/DP/2014/02, October. See earlier in this chapter for a discussion and full update on the issue.

- In the other pools: residual risk in these pools' conditional losses weakens the cliff effect and results in regulatory capital being more evenly spread across tranches than in the ASRF pool.
- As a result capital shortfalls are also more evenly spread out. This is why expected undercapitalization has a lower peak but affects a wider range of thin tranches.
- In practice, attachment and detachment points differ, that is, tranches are thick.
- Taking the PD estimate at face value leads to quite similar capital requirements for thick tranches across the three pool types.
- Expected undercapitalizations are thus also similar: between $0.06 and $0.10 per $1 of exposure to mezzanine tranches with a thickness of 8 percentage points.

To underscore the large magnitude of expected undercapitalization for mezzanine tranches, they refer to vertical tranches from the same underlying asset pools. As such tranches are not subject to the cliff effect, the impact of estimation error on their regulatory capital is much smaller. Namely, the expected undercapitalization is roughly $0.01 per $1 of exposure to a vertical tranche. If the pool were sliced into tranches of different seniority, this undercapitalization would be concentrated in mezzanine tranches ($0.01). These results are robust to changes in the riskiness of the underlying portfolio.[204]

Their overall conclusion is that 'risk models to assess potential losses and set capital and simplifications of reality, but they also take as inputs parameters that are themselves estimated with uncertainty. The true value of a parameter can differ from the one that the bank or regulators based capital calculations on. This opens the door to uncertainty-driven undercapitalization. The uncertainty inherent in estimating asset level PDs will concentrate in mezzanine tranches and, if ignored, can lead to substantial undercapitalization of these tranches'.[205]

To put things in context: Antoniades and Tarashev use extremely simple and transparent asset pools, which should bring to a minimum the scope for estimation uncertainty. Their results show that the simplicity and transparency of the asset pool would not translate into simple-to-assess mezzanine tranches. It is thus important to prevent the uncertainty inherent in risk assessments from raising the specter of undercapitalization and ultimately impairing the functioning of the securitization market. The changes

[204] An increase in the asset-level PD sets three forces in motion. First, all else the same, a higher asset-level PD is estimated with more noise, implying higher likelihood and severity of undercapitalization. Second, in line with the regulatory model, Antoniades and Tarashev's setting accounts for an empirical regularity that a higher PD goes hand in hand with a lower default correlation. See Antoniades and Tarashev, (2014), Ibid. p. 49. And the lower the default correlation, the lower the noise in PD estimates, all else the same. A higher default correlation implies that observed default rates are more likely to be either very large or very small, irrespective of the true underlying PD. Thus, the higher the default correlation, the less informative are the default rates and, ultimately, the noisier is the PD estimate. Third, regulatory capital is less sensitive to noise around high PD estimates than around low PD estimates. The second and third forces reduce the likelihood and severity of undercapitalization and, in their stylized setting, roughly balance the effect of the first force.

[205] See Antoniades and Tarashev, (2014), Ibid. p. 50.

to the regulatory framework for securitizations as discussed earlier in this chapter, which impose substantial capital safeguards on mezzanine tranches, would help avoid such an outcome.

3.4 Comparative Securitization Regulation Post-2008 Crisis

Both in the US and Europe regulatory, initiatives were taken with respect to the securitization industry. In the US most of it was embedded in the 2010 enacted legislation but which requires up till today substantial ongoing rulemaking in order to implement its specific provisions. In the European Union, the impact on securitization transactions has come from various regulatory reforms such as the Basel II and III accords, various capital requirements including the latest Capital Requirements Directive and Capital Requirements Regulation (together the 'CRD/CRR'), the Credit Agency Regulation (the 'CRA Regulation'), the Alternative Investment Fund Managers Directive (the 'AIFMD') and the Solvency II Directive. Recently the Securitization proposal can be added to that list (the EU regulatory development is discussed in the European chapter).[206]

As a kind of opening position, I have summarized in Table 3.2 the regulatory individual initiatives (which are also political reactions to the 2008 crisis) on both sides of the Atlantic.[207]

The overall critique on the enacted regulation is that it, just like is the case for other SB segments, a potpourri of things that go in the toolbox but lack the intrinsic consistency to really combat market failures. Most macroprudential initiatives are theory-less and monetary policy often ineffective. A more systemic approach is therefore needed. The five most frequent market failures (or features that cause them) are (1) complexity,[208] (2) conflicts,[209] (3) complacency,[210] (4) change[211] and a type of (5) tragedy of the com-

[206] See for a full and twice per year updated comparison between the US and European regulatory initiatives in the securitization field: Hogan Lovells, (2015 and following years), Summary of Key EU and US Regulatory Developments Relating to Securitization Transactions, most recent edition: June. The analysis is developed across the following areas: risk retention, due diligence, disclosure and the role of credit rating agencies and analyzes the differences in the US and the European reforms in these individual areas.

[207] See also in detail: J.H.P. Kravitt et al., (2015), Implementation of Securitization Regulatory Reform, *The Journal of Structured Finance*, Spring, Vol. 21, Nr. 1, pp. 83–91.

[208] It can make disclosure insufficient to eliminate information asymmetry; complexity makes understanding harder, which increases the chance of panics; complexity heightens the risk of 'mutual misinformation'.

[209] Refers to classical principal-agent conflicts or intra-firm between higher- and lower-ranked managers.

[210] Includes human irrationality, including the tendencies to over-rely on heuristics, such as credit ratings, in order to try to simplify complexity; to see what we want to see in the face of uncertainty; failing to perform sufficient due diligence (tendency to discount actual risk), and is largely inevitable.

[211] The difficulty of regulating a constantly changing financial system.

Table 3.2 Regulatory initiatives in the US and Europe post-2008 crisis in the field of securitization

	Europe	US	Comments
General comments		Through Dodd-Frank Act and Basel III implementation	
Disclosure	Incentivizing STS (simple transparent and standardized) securitizations implies enhanced disclosure. Disclosure is much more likely to be effective for securitizations that are simple transparent and standardized than for more complex securitization transactions. These STS requirements include meeting the following concepts or standards: true sale or similar transfer of the underlying financial assets, being homogenous, creditworthy and not constituting already securitized financial assets. Further: interest-rate risk and exchange-rate risk must be hedged; the underlying financial assets cannot include or be buttressed by derivatives (synthetic). The originator or sponsor must provide investors a cash flow model and also provide them access to information on historical default, delinquency and loss performance for substantially similar financial assets to those being securitized (and samples of the securities need to be audited)	For each ABS, the disclosure of information regarding the financial assets backing each class (sometimes called 'tranche') of those securities. The US only contemplates limited standardization. For registered ABS only, issuers are required: to perform a review of assets underlying an ABS which is designed and effected to provide reasonable assurance that the disclosure regarding the pool assets in the prospectus is accurate in all material respects to disclose the nature and the findings and conclusions of such review	Disclosure in itself is meaningless, especially for highly complex transactions (too burdensome). Disclosure combined with STS makes therefore sense

Risk retention	Must retain an unhedged material net economic interest in the securitization of at least 5%. Different methods are available, but cannot be mixed.	To retain a portion of the credit risk (so-called skin in the game) for any financial asset (including mortgage loans, other than qualified residential mortgages) that the securitizer, through the issuance of an asset-backed security, transfers, sells or conveys to a third party. Different methods are available and can be combined.	The purpose of risk retention is to reduce moral hazard resulting from the originate-to-distribute model of loan origination, thereby improving the quality of the financial assets underlying securitization transactions. Risk retention has always been part of market functioning also pre-crisis. The real problem was the overvaluation of assets. OTC (originate-to-distribute models caused banks to lower screening efforts)
Rating sagency reform	They require rating agencies to disclose the fees charged to their clients. Sunshine is the best disinfectant, but doesn't take out the conflict of interest	To include in any report accompanying a credit rating a description of the representations, warranties and enforcement mechanisms available to investors and how these differ from the representations, warranties and enforcement mechanisms in issuances of similar securities	Not a lot has happened and practice is still heavily reliant on ratings. Conflict of interest is still an issue
Capital requirements	Basel III aligned initiatives. 25% reduction in capital surcharge when meeting STS standards	To protect firms against economic shocks. To hold more capital than they would be required to hold for investments in other types of securities (in line with Basel III)	Heavily criticized as being 'punitive' and 'capital neutrality' is advocated in case of similar assets

(continued)

Table 3.2 (continued)

	Europe	US	Comments
Due diligence requirements	Standard pre-closing due diligence but also post-closing due diligence, including requiring investors to perform regular stress tests on the cash flows and financial asset values supporting the underlying securitization exposures	Third parties may be engaged to conduct portions of the due diligence[a]: If the issuer attributes findings to the third party, the third party must consent to being named as an 'expert' in the prospectus the issuer may rely on a review by an affiliated (but not an unaffiliated) originator. If assets in the pool deviate from disclosed underwriting criteria, the issuer must disclose: how the assets deviate, and the amount and characteristics of non-conforming assets which entity determined that the non-conforming assets should be included in the pool if compensating or other factors were used to determine that assets should be included	Seems to confirm existing practice rather than adding anything material

[a]SEC, (2014), Asset-Backed Securities Disclosure and Registration, RIN 3235-AK37, Nr. 2014-177, via sec.gov

mons.[212,213] The first two can have distinct securitization-specific dimensions: (1) STS products have performed better under distress than complex products, but self-designation or self-certification[214] under the EU proposal might trigger moral hazard, (2) securitization proposals are tied to the past and current financial infrastructure and therefore not equipped to deal with change. Change[215] can create failures that cannot be fully predicted and are therefore to a certain degree evitable. In short, the focus is too much on objectives, the parties involved and the regulator to the degree that the 'big picture' is being missed. It can be therefore concluded that from a market failure and structural point of view (too ad hoc), regulatory initiatives on both sides of the Atlantic can be considered insufficient. Since some of the exposure left is to a certain inevitable ex ante regulation should be largely complemented with ex post regulation which will mitigate unavoidable consequences.[216]

3.5 Securitization Regulation in the US

3.5.1 Capital Charges and Basel III Implementation

Following the Dodd-Frank introduction in 2010, many implementation regulations followed. The three federal banking agencies[217] adopted, for example, a final rule (the 'Rule') that implements the Basel III regulatory capital framework and comprehensively revises the regulatory capital requirements for all US banking organizations. Among other things, the Rule broadens the definition of a securitization exposure to encompass a wider range of investments and imposes new due diligence requirements for banking organizations that invest in securitization exposures. On June 12, 2012, the Agencies approved a joint notice of proposed rulemaking (the 'NPR') which proposed revisions to the capital adequacy guidelines and prompt corrective action rules then in effect to incorporate the

[212] As market participants suffer from the actions of other market participants, that is, the benefits of exploiting finite capital resources accrue to individual participants, the costs are distributed among many (externality concept).

[213] Discussed in: S. L. Schwarcz, (2012), Controlling Financial Chaos: The Power and Limits of Law, Wisconsin Law Review, pp. 815–840.

[214] K. Mullin, (2015), STS Self-Certification? Barking Up the Wrong Tree, International Financing Review, August 27, via ifre.com

[215] See in detail: S.L. Schwarcz, (2016), Regulating Financial Change: A Functional Approach, Minnesota Law Review, Vol. 100, Issue 4, pp. 1441–1494.

[216] Discussed later but see also: S.L. Schwarcz, (2015), Securitization and Post-Crisis Financial Regulation, Working Paper, December 9 and I. Anatawi and S.L. Schwacz, (2013), Regulating Ex-Post: How Law Can Address the Inevitability of Financial Failure, Texas Law Review, Vol. 92, pp. 75–131.

[217] The three Agencies are the Board of Governors of the Federal Reserve System ('FRB'), the Office of the Comptroller of the Currency ('OCC') and the Federal Deposit Insurance Corporation ('FDIC').

standards of the Basel III accord, as modified consistent with the Dodd-Frank Wall Street Reform and Consumer Protection Act (the 'Dodd-Frank Act').

With regard to the treatment of securitization exposures, it includes both a Standardized Approach that generally applies to all banking organizations, and an advanced approach for the largest and most internationally active institutions. Consistent with the NPR, the Rule defines a securitization exposure as 'an on- or off-balance sheet credit exposure (including credit-enhancing representations and warranties) that arises from a traditional or synthetic securitization (including a re-securitization), or an exposure that directly or indirectly references a securitization exposure'.[218] According to the agencies, both the designation of an investment as a securitization exposure and the calculation of the risk-based capital requirements for a securitization exposure are to be guided by the economic substance of a transaction rather than its legal form. As stated in the preamble to the Rule, provided there is a tranching of the underlying credit risk, a securitization exposure could include, among other things, loans, asset-backed securities, mortgage-backed securities, re-securitizations, lines of credit and other liquidity facilities, guarantees and other types of credit derivatives, loan servicing assets and servicer cash advance facilities and credit-enhancing representations and warranties. Interest-only strips and retained tranches may also cause an investment to be a securitization exposure. If there is no tranching of the underlying credit risk, the preamble to the Rule indicates that the obligation would not be treated as a securitization exposure.

Overall, coverage has been broadened from the prior US capital requirements under Basel II. In addition, a 20% floor has been established as the minimum risk weight for any securitization exposure, regardless of the underlying credit risk.

The agencies have stated that all or substantially all of the underlying exposures of a securitization must be financial exposures, that is, loans, commitments, credit derivatives, guarantees, asset-backed securities, mortgage-backed securities, other debt securities or equity securities. According to the Agencies, the securitization framework is designed to address the tranching of the credit risk of financial exposures and is not designed to apply, for example, to credit exposures to commercial or industrial companies or non-financial assets. Therefore, as stated in the preamble to the Rule, a specialized loan to finance the construction or acquisition of large-scale projects (e.g. airports or power plants), objects (e.g. ships or satellites) or commodities (e.g. reserves, precious metals or oil) would not be a securitization exposure because the assets backing the loan (e.g. the facility, object or commodity) are non-financial assets. An issuance, whether tranched or untranched, backed by a lien on assets generally is not a securitization exposure, but an issuance backed by a financial instrument that is in turn backed by a lien on assets may be. Further, a loan to finance the construction or acquisition of commercial real estate that is not 'specialized' should be treated the same as a project finance loan or other 'specialized' loan.

---

[218] See Regulatory Capital Rules: Regulatory Capital, Implementation of Basel III, Capital Adequacy, Transition Provisions, Prompt Corrective Action, Standardized Approach for Risk-weighted Assets, Market Discipline and Disclosure Requirements, Advanced Approaches Risk-Based Capital Rule, and Market Risk Capital Rule, 78 Fed. Reg. 55,340, 55,482 (Sept. 10, 2013).

The Rule provides some exemptions from the definition of a securitization exposure. For instance, an operating company does not fall within the scope of a securitization exposure, even if substantially all of its assets are financial exposures, since operating companies are generally established to conduct business with clients with the goal of earning a profit in their own right and generally produce goods or provide services beyond the business of investing, reinvesting, holding or trading in financial assets. As a result, an equity investment in an operating company would generally not be treated as a securitization exposure.[219]

In addition, the Rule exempts exposures to investment funds and pension funds. Investment funds registered with the SEC under the Investment Company Act of 1940 and pension funds regulated under ERISA[220] are exempt because such entities are intensively regulated and are subject to strict leverage requirements.[221] For investment funds that are not specifically excluded from the securitization framework, the Rule provides discretion to the primary federal supervisor of a banking organization 'to exclude from the definition ... those transactions in which the underlying exposures are owned by an investment firm that exercises substantially unfettered control over the size and composition of its assets, liabilities, and off-balance sheet exposures'.[222]

The Rule acknowledges that '[t]he line between securitization exposures and non-securitization exposures may be difficult to identify in some circumstances'.[223] The Rule states that the Agencies may expand the scope of the securitization framework to include other transactions if doing so is justified by the economics of the transaction, and that the Agencies will consider the economic substance, leverage and risk profile of a transaction to ensure that an appropriate risk-based capital treatment is applied.[224] A number of factors will be considered when assessing the economic substance of a transaction (e.g. the amount of equity in the structure, overall leverage, redemption rights and the ability of the junior tranches to absorb losses without interrupting the flow of contractual payments to more senior tranches). Even so, the distinction between a financial asset and a non-financial asset may be blurry at times, and the factors that the Agencies are required to consider when making this determination may present significant implementation burdens.

---

219 Ibid. 55,430.

220 Employee Retirement Income Security Act of 1974 (ERISA) is a federal law that sets minimum standards for pension plans in private industry. ERISA does not require any employer to establish a pension plan. It only requires that those who establish plans must meet certain minimum standards. The law generally does not specify how much money a participant must be paid as a benefit. ERISA requires plans to regularly provide participants with information about the plan including information about plan features and funding; sets minimum standards for participation, vesting, benefit accrual and funding; requires accountability of plan fiduciaries; and gives participants the right to sue for benefits and breaches of fiduciary duty. ERISA also guarantees payment of certain benefits through the Pension Benefit Guaranty Corporation, a federally chartered corporation, if a defined plan is terminated.

221 Ibid. 55,430–55,431.

222 Ibid. 55,431.

223 Ibid. 55,431.

224 Ibid. 55,431.

The Agencies rejected concerns that the scope of the securitization framework was overly broad and the suggestion that the definition of 'securitization exposure' be narrowed to exposures to the tranched credit risk associated with an identifiable pool of assets. According to the Agencies, narrowing the definition in this manner would exclude certain credit-risk exposures that are appropriately captured, such as certain first-loss or other tranched guarantees provided to a single underlying exposure.[225]

As in the NPR, the Rule defines a synthetic securitization as a transaction in which the following occurs:

> (1) all or a portion of the credit risk of one or more underlying exposures is transferred to one or more third parties through the use of one or more credit derivatives or guarantees (other than a guarantee that transfers only the credit risk of an individual retail exposure); (2) the credit risk associated with the underlying exposures has been separated into at least two tranches reflecting different levels of seniority; (3) performance of the securitization exposures depends upon the performance of the underlying exposures; and (4) all or substantially all of the underlying exposures are financial exposures (such as loans, commitments, credit derivatives, guarantees, receivables, asset-backed securities, mortgage-backed securities, other debt securities, or equity securities).[226]

This definition has been adopted largely as proposed, except that the Rule clarifies that, in addition to transactions in which a portion of the credit risk is transferred, transactions in which such risk is retained through the use of credit derivatives are subject to the securitization framework.[227]

The Agencies rejected requests that re-securitizations that include a minimal amount (e.g. less than 5%) of securitization exposures among the underlying assets be exempted from the definition of re-securitization, or that a pro-rata treatment be applied so that only that portion of a securitization backed by underlying securitization exposures be subject to a higher capital surcharge. Instead, the Rule retains the proposed definition of a re-securitization exposure as 'an on- or off-balance sheet exposure to a re-securitization; or an exposure that directly or indirectly references a re-securitization exposure'.[228] However, pass-through securities that are pooled together to back newly issued tranched securities are not treated as re-securitizations because the underlying pass-through securities do not provide tranched credit protection and for that reason are not considered to be securitizations.[229]

225 Ibid. 55,430.
226 Ibid. 55,431.
227 Ibid. 55,431
228 Ibid. 55,431.
229 Ibid. 55,432.

The Rule eliminates the use of a ratings-based approach for assigning risk-based capital requirements to securitization exposures[230] and replaces it with the SSFA. With the elimination of the ratings-based approach, banking organizations are required to calculate risk weights internally. The SSFA, which is a simplified version of the supervisory formula approach used in Basel II, may be applied for this purpose. Adopted in the Rule largely as proposed, the SSFA starts with a baseline capital requirement derived from the risk weights that apply to the exposures underlying a securitization, and then adjusts those risk weights based on the level of subordination of a banking organization's investment within the structure of a securitization. Thus, the SSFA applies relatively higher capital requirements to more risky junior tranches of a securitization, which are the first to absorb losses, and relatively lower requirements to more senior tranches.

The SSFA raised several concerns on the NPR. In particular, implementation of the SSFA would generally restrict credit growth and create competitive inequities with other jurisdictions implementing ratings-based approaches.[231] Although the Agencies acknowledged that there may be differences in capital requirements under the SSFA and a ratings-based approach, they noted that the Dodd-Frank Act prohibited them from referring to or relying on credit ratings in their regulations. However, the Agencies indicated that they would monitor the SSFA and consider modifications, if any, based on its performance. Concern was also raised about the 20% floor level for all securitization exposures and requested that it be lowered for certain low-risk exposures. In response, the Agencies justified the floor level by stating that a 20% floor 'is prudent given the performance of many securitization exposures during the recent crisis'.[232]

As an alternative to the SSFA, a banking organization may choose to apply a 1250% risk weight to any securitization exposure (e.g. apply a 100% capital charge). Commenters criticized this provision on the grounds that it would penalize banks in certain circumstances and could require them to hold more capital against a securitization exposure than the actual exposure amount at risk. They requested that the amount of risk-based capital required to be held against an institution's exposure be capped at the exposure amount.[233] However, the Agencies retained this provision as proposed in the NPR, based on their stated desire to provide simplicity and comparability in risk-weighted asset amounts for the same securitization exposure across banking institutions.

As an alternative to the SSFA, banking organizations may continue to apply the gross-up approach, which was available under the Agencies' capital requirements under Basel II. In this approach, an asset's percentage risk weight is based on the amount of credit-enhanced assets (i.e. the tranches of a securitization that are senior to an organization's exposure) for which the bank directly or indirectly assumes the credit risk. To calculate the risk weight of a securitization exposure under the gross-up approach, a banking organization must provide four inputs: (i) the dollar amount of the exposure; (ii) the pro-rata share (i.e. the par value of the organization's exposure as a percentage of the par value of

[230] As required by Section 939A of the Dodd-Frank Act.

[231] Ibid. 55,437.

[232] Ibid. 55,437.

[233] Ibid. 55,435.

the entire tranche of which the exposure is a part); (iii) the enhanced amount (i.e. the par value of all the tranches that are more senior to the tranche of which the exposure is a part); and (iv) the applicable risk weight (i.e. the weighted average of the risk weights of the assets underlying the securitization as calculated under the Standardized Approach). A banking organization calculates the credit equivalent amount of its exposure by adding the amount of its direct exposure to the product of the enhanced amount, the pro-rata share and the applicable risk weight, provided, as noted above, that the risk weight may not be less than 20%.

Concern was expressed regarding the potential differences in risk weights for similar exposures when using the gross-up approach as compared to the SSFA and the resulting potential for capital arbitrage.[234] In response, the agencies stated that arbitrage opportunities were significantly reduced by the requirement in the Rule that banking organizations apply either approach consistently across all of its securitization exposures. Further, according to the Agencies, frequent changes in the approach used should be unnecessary absent significant changes in the nature of a banking organization's securitization activities, and they expected banking organizations to provide upon request a rationale for any change they may make.

The Rule provides a different treatment of securitization exposures for asset-backed commercial paper ('ABCP') programs. An ABCP program is defined as 'a program established primarily for the purpose of issuing commercial paper that is investment grade and backed by underlying exposures held in a securitization SPE ("Special Purpose Entity")'.[235] Under the Rule, when calculating the amount of a banking organization's off-balance-sheet exposure to an ABCP program, such as through a liquidity facility provided to support such a program, the notional amount of its exposure may be reduced to the maximum potential amount that the banking organization could be required to fund given the ABCP program's current underlying assets. Thus, as the Rule illustrates in an example, if the maximum amount that could be drawn due to the current volume and credit quality of the program's assets is $100, but the maximum amount that could be drawn against the same assets could increase to as much as $200 based on a change in credit quality, then the exposure amount is $200.[236]

3.5.2 Due Diligence Requirements

Regulators have argued that, during the financial crisis, many banks relied excessively on ratings issued by rating agencies and did not perform adequate internal credit analysis of their securitization exposures. As a result, the Rule requires banks to satisfy specific due diligence requirements for securitization exposures. Consistent with the NPR, a banking organization

234 Ibid. 55,434.

235 Ibid. 55,435.

236 Ibid. 55,435.

must demonstrate, to the satisfaction of its federal supervisor, a comprehensive understanding of the features of a securitization exposure that would materially affect its performance.

In performing its due diligence review of a securitization exposure, a banking organization must consider the following: (i) structural features of the securitization that materially impact the performance of the exposure (e.g. cash-flow waterfalls, waterfall-related triggers and deal-specific definitions of default); (ii) information regarding the performance of the underlying credit exposures; (iii) relevant market data for the securitization (e.g. sales price and volatility, trading volume, market rating and size, depth and concentration level of the market for securitization); and (iv) for re-securitization exposures, performance information on the underlying securitization exposures (e.g. issuer name and credit quality and the characteristics of the securitization exposure). If an organization fails to satisfy these requirements for a securitization exposure, the Rule imposes a 1250% risk weight on the exposure by default. An organization may review ratings issued by ratings agencies, but may not rely on them to satisfy its due diligence requirements.

Concern was expressed that a banking organization may be unable to meet the due diligence requirements due to a lack of available data and proposed that the risk weight be increased progressively based on the severity and duration of an organization's failure to perform due diligence. Concerns were also raised that supervisors may apply the due diligence requirements unevenly. The Agencies, however, determined that the data requirements and the 1250% risk-weight requirement were appropriate 'given that such information is required to monitor appropriately the risk of the underlying assets'.[237] The compliance deadline was January 1, 2014 for advanced approach banking organizations (unless the organization is a savings and loan holding company) and January 1, 2015 for all other covered banking organizations.

Meanwhile, certain exemptions trickle down eroding some of the initial goal setting, for example, on trust preferred securities (TruPS CDOs).[238]

As a final point on the topic, an overview of the securitization volumes (primary issuance) is provided (Table 3.3) for both Europe and the US. Both markets have always been very different in size and depth, but that distinction is increasing in recent years, with the ECB policies in the center of the argument. In 2013, more than half the asset-backed deals created in Europe this year have been retained by banks—that is, held as collateral for cheap ECB loans. The benefits of securitization, when properly used, are in shifting risk to enable banks to lend more. Shuffling loans between banks and the ECB do not achieve this.[239]

---

[237] Ibid. 55,433.

[238] G. Chon, (2014), US Community Banks Win Reprieve on Volcker, *Financial Times*, January 15. Lobbying is ongoing for a similar exemption for CLO's bundling loans to companies.

[239] *Financial Times*, (2014), Securitization: Regulatory Insecurity. Regulators Can Do More to Fix the Damage They Caused This market, January 1.

Table 3.3 Securitization (primary issuance, US: mortgage-only) volumes in the US and Europe

Year/region	Europe (in Bn. Euro)	US (in Bn. USD)
2006	481.0	2691.1
2007	593.6	2434.2
2008	819.2	934.9
2009	423.9	2172.1
2010	378	2012.6
2011	376.8	1724.8
2012	257.8	2195.1
2013	180.8	2120.2
2014	217.1	1439.6
2015	216.6	1800.7
2016	239.6	2044.2
2017	236.5	1934.8
2018	269.4	1898.6
2019	32.4 (Q1)	318.4 (Q1)

AFME securitization dataset; via afme.eu. Datasets between the AFME (EU) and Sifma (US- sifma.org) differ (somewhat) which stays largely unexplained as methodologies and data gathering are not (fully) disclosed. See also AFME/SIFA websites for non-mortgage-related issuance volumes

3.6 Collateral Intermediation

Collateral intermediation or collateral-based support is one of the other key functions of the shadow banking system. The model revolves around the re-use of scarce collateral in such a way that it can support a wide variety and large volume of transactions in the financial space (much larger than the value of the collateral obviously). The dealer banks, which are central in this business model and considered to be part of the shadow banking system (in the sense that they are not subject to the regulation as the traditional banking sector).

3.6.1 How Does It Work?

Collateral intermediation works underpin a large number of financial transactions. Nevertheless, it also serves the real economy as well to a large degree, although that function often stays under-highlighted. The transactions vary from secured funding (mostly vis-à-vis non-banking institutions), securities lending and hedging (often including OTC derivatives). In contrast to the securitization process, which focuses on safe assets only, the collateral intermediation focuses on all type of assets including those with varying, volatile or pure investment-grade assets. This can therefore include AAA-rated T-bonds all the down to C-rated corporate bonds. The only condition often is that the asset(s) needs to have a market-cleared price. The number of dealer banks that are involved in these types of transactions is limited and their exact position is often elusive vis-à-vis other financial agents. Claessens et al. indicated that their comparative advantage includes 'having incurred the fixed costs of entry, and benefitting from economies of scale and network centrality effects (compared to other traditional banks)'.[240] They further indicate that a major concern is that their advantages also derive from the fact that they are perceived to have very low counterparty risks.

The function of these dealers' banks is that they are essentially 'source collateral'. They obtain it from parties that require funding, or from agents that want to enhance their return by 'renting out' their assets as collateral.[241] Then, collateral is pledged to other parties to obtain funding or support other contracts. This put in motion a full cycle of transaction where the (single unit of a) collateral is re-used across a wide set of transactions. The initial collateral often comes from hedge funds and other market agents that need to borrow cash or other securities.

Table 3.4 illustrates how a piece of collateral (e.g. a US treasury bond) may be used by a hedge fund to get financing ('cash') from a prime broker (in the table Party A). The same collateral may then be used by as margin for party B on, for example, an 'out-of-the-money' OTC derivative position. Party B may then pass the bond to a money market fund (Party C) that will hold it for a short tenor (or until maturity). In this example the same treasury bond has been used three times as collateral, from the original hedge fund owner to the money market fund.

The over-the-counter (OTC) positions are off-balance-sheet items, hence the parenthesis.

Between (1) the hedge fund and Party A, (2) Party A and Party B and (3) Party B and Party C, the collateral (US T-bond) is exchanged for cash.

There are other providers of collateral which include insurers, pension funds and sovereign wealth funds and others, which hold some of their assets with custodians. Often, these owners 'rent out' or 'lent out' their securities through repo and securities lending arrangements to augment overall returns (earning them a 'convenience fee'). Especially if you are a long(er) term holder of securities, there is the ability to earn an extra income while holding those securities for the longer term. Users of rented collateral primarily include hedge funds and mutual funds, which need specific types of collateral to support their operations. Claessens et al. argue that 'by facilitating financial transactions, offering higher returns to savers, and offering lower funding costs to borrowers (e.g., when a hedge fund can, because of its use of collateral, leverage its net worth and take a long position in a corporate bond), collateral intermediation benefits the real economy'.[242] I'm not particularly charmed (nor convinced) by the argument that this would benefit the real economy, unless the hedge fund world would be considered part of the real economy. Besides the fact that there are intrinsic risks in securities lending transactions, the lower cost of funding argument is doubtful. In the post-crisis 2008 world, it can be observed that lower

[240] Claessens et al., (2012), Shadow Banking: Economics and Policy, IMF Staff Discussion Note SDN 12/12, p. 14.

[241] See in detail for this: M. Singh, and J. Aitken, (2010), The (Sizable) Role of Re-hypothecation in the Shadow Banking System, IMF Working Paper Nr. WP/10/172, Washington.

[242] Claessens et al., (2012), Ibid. pp. 14–15.

Table 3.4 Collateral intermediation or re-hypothecation

Hedge fund		Party A		Party B		Party C (MMF)	
Assets	Liabilities	Assets	Liabilities	Assets	Liabilities	Assets	Liabilities
US T-bond			Party B (OTC position)	Party A (OTC position)		US T-bond	

leveraged institutions carry a higher valuation multiple (and thus a lower cost of funding) than those institutions with higher leverage.

The new paradigm therefore is in contrast to the old one where higher leverage leads to lower cost of funding, but lower leverage (which leads to lower return on equity) is gratified with a higher valuation multiple and higher leverage carries a lower valuation multiple. That observation triggers a rethink of the whole systematic approach of the banking model. A full shock-absorbing banking balance should then theoretically be compensated for its ultimately robustness, and the only intrinsic risk in that banking model would be the credit risk of the loan portfolio. Robustness carries a higher valuation multiple as it provides investors with the visibility that is apparently valued. Also systemic risk would disappear (or at least to a large degree) as banks would reduce their interdependence significantly. Both the observation and my conclusion don't seem to be far off from the conceptual proposition and analysis of Admati and Hellwig[243] in 2013.

Re-hypothecation is the re-use of collateral that involves an explicit title transfer and is generally used in prime brokerage activities. It is standard to use title transfer in repo, securities lending and OTC derivative contracts. The acquirer has full title to the collateral received and, as the new owner, is completely free to deal with the collateral as she sees fit. In return, the parties agree that once the collateral provider has discharged his financial obligation to the collateral taker, the collateral taker will return equivalent collateral to the collateral provider. OTC derivative contracts under the International Swaps and Derivatives Association's English Law agreements also use title transfer in collateral support agreements. In a repo there is an outright sale of the security and a specific price and date at which the security will be bought back. Securities lending transactions generally have no set end date and no set price. A 30-year US treasury bond could earn more than its coupon over its tenor by being 'rented out'. The rent on this loan is determined by the demand for the security being rented out, the counterparty risk of the intermediary and the tenor of the loan. Even if the underlying instrument is of long maturity, loans are of short tenor, so the instrument returns to the original owner generally within a year.

There is significant and increasing demand for those collateral intermediation services, although it has reduced somewhat in recent years. A reduction in those transactions is often caused by increasing concern of providers about counterparty risk (which then forego the extra income and leave the securities sit idle) and, for example, the central banks purchase of high-quality asset purchases from the market (large asset purchase programs) as we have witnessed in Europe and the US in recent years. It can also be due to the widening of the pool of collateral-eligible assets (which increases the pledge ability of these assets as collateral.[244] Not only the value of the collateral available but also the collateral velocity[245] is determined by arguments as counterparty risk or general risk aversion or a temporary 'risk-off' mentality in the market.

---

[243] A. Admati and M. Hellwig, (2013), The Bankers New Clothes: What's wrong with Banking and What to Do about It, Princeton University Press, Princeton NJ.

[244] M. Singh, and P. Stella, (2012), Money and Collateral, IMF Working Paper Nr. WP/12/95, Washington.

[245] Defined as the volume of secured transactions divided by the stock of source collateral.

Singh[246] argues that collateral intermediation, to the extent that it supports credit, implicitly supports the real economy—albeit he immediately indicates that the quantification of the economic value creation is complex. In this context that is an understatement. When collateral use drops, financial intermediation slows, with effects similar to the drying up of interbank markets. Nevertheless, it is expected that, in the long run, demand for these services is about to increase. Especially since market participants are increasingly seeking the security of collateral to underpin a wider range of claims, and new regulations, such as increased requirements for collateral in derivatives, including in central clearing, are also likely to increase the demand for collateral-based operations.[247] The OTC market, valued consistently above 600 trillion USD[248] globally and which has continued to increase after 2008 is thoroughly under-collateralized. Additionally, some counterparties (e.g. sovereigns, quasi-sovereigns, large pension funds and insurers and AAA corporations) are often not required to post collateral. The remaining exposures will have to be collateralized when moved to CCP (Central Clearing Party Clearing House[249]) to avoid creating puts to the safety net. As such, there is likely to an increased demand for collateral worldwide.

[246] M. Singh, (2012), The Other Deleveraging, IMF Working Paper Nr. WP/12/178, Washington.

[247] See for quantification: Claessens et al. (2012), p. 16; M. Singh, (2011), Velocity of Pledged Collateral: Analysis and Implications, IMF Working Paper No. 11/256 (Washington: International Monetary Fund) and M. Singh, (2012), The Other Deleveraging, IMF Working Paper Nr. WP/12/178, Washington.

[248] There is much debate about the size of the OTC market. It is argued that a better estimate may be based on adding 'in-the-money' (or gross positive value) and 'out-of-the-money' (or gross negative value) derivative positions (to obtain total exposures), further reduced by the 'netting' of related positions. Once these are taken into account, the resulting exposures are currently about $3 trillion, down from $5 trillion. See in detail: BIS (Bank for International Settlements), 2012, Uncovered Counterparty Exposures in Global OTC Derivatives Markets, BIS Quarterly Review, June and M. Singh, (2010), Collateral, Netting and Systemic Risk in OTC Derivatives Markets, IMF Working Paper Nr. WP/10/99, Washington. The under-collateralization is estimated (by BIS) at 1.5 trillion USD or about half of the exposure. See for a recent overview of the OTC interest derivative market, by far the largest OTC market: J. Gyntelberg and C. Upper, (2013), The OTC derivatives Market in 2013, BIS Quarterly review December 2013 and the bi-annual BIS release on the matter: BIS, (2015), Statistical release OTC derivatives statistics at end-December 2014 Monetary and Economic Department, April 2015. Regular updates regarding OTC statistics can be found through bis.org.

[249] Recent regulatory efforts focus on moving OTC derivatives contracts to central counterparties (CCPs). A CCP will be collecting collateral and netting bilateral positions. While CCPs do not have explicit taxpayer backing, they may be supported in times of stress. For example, the U.S. Dodd-Frank Act allows the Federal Reserve to lend to key financial market infrastructures during times of crises. Incentives to move OTC contracts could come from increasing bank capital charges on OTC positions that are not moved to CCP. See in detail: BCBS (Basel Committee on Banking Supervision), 2012, Capital Requirements for Bank Exposures to Central Counterparties, Bank for International Settlements, July. See for the technical aspects: BIS, (2013), Capital Treatment of Bank Exposures to Central Counterparties, (July).

3.6.2 Risk Analysis for Collateral Intermediation Activities[250]

By far the largest risk exposure in the collateral chain of the intermediation process is the liquidity exposure the dealer bank is exposed to. This is in particular the case when dealer banks, on a regular basis, use the collateral from clients for its funding purposes. A sudden customer withdrawal can then have severe liquidity implication which will have to find new sources of collateral. Prime brokerage clients like hedge funds wanted their collateral back in 2008 creating instability for the larger dealer banks.[251] When the dealer bank is also a depository bank (so not a stand-alone financial institution), the safety put by the government is seriously large. The implication is not only that the collateral risk is moved to the depository part of the business but also that the collateral intermediation activities are enjoying an artificially low cost of funding.[252] The good old 1933 Steagall Glass Act and its attempted re-introduction in the aftermath of the financial 2008 crisis were driven, to a large degree, by the risk centered around those activities (as part of the wider trading activities).

Another public put the activity is benefiting from is the 'financial contract status' of derivatives and repos'. In legal terms some derivatives and repo contracts enjoy beneficial treatment in bankruptcy situations (i.e. automatic stay—they are prioritized in reorganization because they are deemed to be too interconnected with financial markets and thus too disruptive to adjust or play around with). The immediate consequence is a reduced market discipline and implicitly subsidizes the contracts' counterparty (i.e. the dealer bank as part of the shadow banking system). There seems to be no immediate economic justification available but no legal changes are on the horizon.[253]

Other risks mainly occur in specific transactions which include the tri-party repo transactions and which have become a major source of funding for (dealer)-bank in recent years (see Box 3.1). In a typical tri-party repo, an intermediary (one of two clearing banks) facilitates a repo operation between counterparties. This market has specific institutional arrangements and risks and is subject to an increasing amount of regulation to reduce (systemic) risks.

---

[250] Claessens et al., (2012), Ibid. pp. 16–17.

[251] D. Duffie, (2010), The Failure Mechanics of Dealer Banks, Journal of Economic Perspectives, Vol. 24, No. 1, pp. 51–72 and Squam Lake, (2010), Prime Brokers and Derivatives Dealers, in The Squam Lake Report: Fixing the Financial System, ed. by Kenneth R. French, Martin N. Baily, John Y. Campbell, John H. Cochrane, Douglas W. Diamond, Darrell Duffie, Anil K. Kashyap, Frederic S. Mishkin, Raghuram G. Rajan, David S. Scharfstein, Robert J. Shiller, Hyun Song Shin, Matthew J. Slaughter, Jeremy C. Stein, and René M. Stulz (Princeton and Oxford: Princeton University Press).

[252] A. W.A. Boot, Arnoud, and L. Ratnovski, (2012), Banking and Trading, IMF Working Paper 12/238 (Washington: International Monetary Fund) and M. Singh, (2012), Puts in the Shadows, IMF Working Paper No. 12/229 (Washington: International Monetary Fund).

[253] K. Summe, (2011), An Examination of Lehman Brothers' Derivatives Portfolio Post- Bankruptcy: Would Dodd-Frank Would Have Made Any Difference? Hoover Institution, Stanford University; P. Bolton, and M. Oehmke, (2011), Credit Default Swaps and the Empty Creditor Problem, Review of Financial Studies, Vol. 24, Nr. 8, pp. 2617–2655; D. Duffie, and D. A. Skeel, (2012), A Dialogue on the Costs and Benefits of Automatic Stays for Derivatives and Repurchase Agreements, Institute for Law & Economic Research Paper Nr. 12-02, Philadelphia, University of Pennsylvania) and Rock Center for Corporate Governance at Stanford University Working Paper Nr. 108;

Box 3.1 The Tri-Party Repo Market[254]

A tri-party repo (TPR) facility is an arrangement whereby a clearing bank acts as an intermediary for two repo counterparties. According to Singh[255] around 50 to 70% of repo operations in the US are cleared using TPR, with recent volumes approaching $1.8 trillion, much below the $3 trillion in 2008. The size of the TPR can be compared to the bilateral pledged collateral market used by hedge funds and others. The non-TPR repo market is estimated at about $750 billion, of which about $500 billion is in the US. Securities lending is valued to be about $800 billion in the US and about $200 billion in Europe. Hence, the non-TPR market could be about 40 to 50% of overall repo activities.

The TPR market has become a major source of wholesale funding for banks and dealer banks. The US market in particular is serviced by two clearing banks, Bank of New York and JP Morgan. The pledged collateral is held with custodians and can therefore not be repledged. The TPR arrangement has, according to Claessens et al.,[256] several advantages: 'outsourcing collateral management to the TPR clearer, saving back office costs for counterparties, and creating economies of scale, as securities are simply moved from one account to another within the clearer's books. It also allows market participants to exchange collateral baskets, outsource risk management (haircut calculation, margin calls, and substitution), pricing, and other ancillary tasks'.

A distinguishing and characterizing feature of the US TPR market is the 'daily unwind process'. Borrowers typically require access to their pledged securities for routine daily trading purposes. The daily unwind facilitates that requirement. At the start of each trading day, the collateral is returned to borrowers and cash to lenders, even if these were pledged under term transactions. Collateral and cash are then returned back to the clearing bank before close of

(continued)

R.R. Bliss, and G. Kaufman, (2005), Derivatives and Systemic Risk: Netting, Collateral and Closeout, Federal Reserve Bank of Chicago Working Paper Nr. 2005-03.

[254] For more context see L. Brickler et al., (2011), Everything You Wanted to Know about the Tri-Party Repo Market, but Didn't Know to Ask, Liberty Street Economics, April 11, via http://libertystreeteconomics.newyorkfed.org/; A. Martin, (2011), Stabilizing the Tri-Party Repo Market by Eliminating the Unwind, July 20, via http://libertystreeteconomics.newyorkfed.org/; A. Martin, (2011), Remaining Risks in the Tri-Party Repo Market, November 7, via http://libertystreeteconomics.newyorkfed.org/; A. Copeland and I. Selig, (2014), Don't Be Late! The Importance of Timely Settlement of Tri-Party Repo Contracts, Liberty Street Economics, October 20, via http://libertystreeteconomics.newyorkfed.org/; A. Martin and S. McLaughlin, (2015), Financial Innovation: The Origins of the Tri-Party Repo Market, Part I & II, Liberty Street Economics, May 11–12, via http://libertystreeteconomics.newyorkfed.org/; J. Adenbaum et al., (2015), The Tri-Party Repo Market Like You Have Never Seen It Before, Liberty Street Economics, October 19, via http://libertystreeteconomics.newyorkfed.org/; A. Copeland et al., (2012), Key Mechanics of the U.S. Tri-Repo Market, FRBNY Economic Policy Review, Vol. 18, pp. 1–12; A. Copeland, et al., (2014), Repo Runs: Evidence from The Tri-Party Repo Market, *Journal of Finance* Vol. 69, pp. 2343–2380; A. Copeland, et al., (2012), Mapping and Sizing the U.S. Repo Market, Federal Reserve Bank of New York Liberty Street Economics Blog, via http://libertystreeteconomics.newyorkfed.org/. On the EU side: L. Mancini et al., (2015), The Euro Interbank Repo Market, Working Paper, May 19.

[255] M. Singh, (2012), Puts in the Shadows, IMF Working Paper Nr. WP/12/229, Washington.

[256] See further Claessens et al. (2012), Annex 2, p. 30.

Box 3.1 continued

business. Effectively, it is an intra-day operation. Borrowers that have financing needs during the day can be served through a clearing bank that can extend them overdrafts as unsecured exposures. More and more however, regulators are starting to require collaterals for those overdrafts. The implication of the transactions is that risks associated with lending are 'fully' transferred twice during a business day timeline: overnight they are secured with the ultimate lenders, and with the clearing bank and unsecured during the day.

There are a number of integrated risks in the unwinding process. Clearing banks tend to carry large volumes of unsecured exposures relative to their capital base. Since capital is returned to them on a daily basis, the lenders appreciate their arrangement as short-term and money-like contracts. However, given the counterparty risk, the arrangement can be seen as inherently vulnerable and unstable of which proof can be found in the 2008 crisis where there was need for other private safe asset arrangements and official sector support through the primary dealer credit facility was needed to stabilize these facilities. These arrangements are inherently unstable in a similar way as prime money market funds as discussed.

Not surprisingly that in the unwind process, one of the focal point is in the regulatory overhaul. Current regulatory efforts primarily focus on limiting the duration of intra-day credit by pushing the unwind to later in the day and improving intra-day collateral management.[257] Nevertheless the intra-day exposures remain sizeable and operationally difficult to reduce and the systemic importance of this market may preclude an unwinding of the Bank of New York and JP Morgan. In continental Europe and the UK, TPR activity has increased in recent years to roughly €1.1 trillion due to multinational/corporate treasuries keeping money overseas and counterparty risk concerns regarding large banks, with the key agents Euroclear and Clearstream—which do not provide intra-day financing.[258]

In 2012 the Tri-party Repo Infrastructure Reform Task Force released its seven-point roadmap for reforms needed to (1) sharply reduce the market's reliance on discretionary extensions of intra-day credit by the clearing banks and (2) foster improvements in market participants' liquidity and credit-risk management practices and a big chunk of that reform process is now in place or being implemented.[259]

[257] See in detail: A. Copeland, A. Marin, and M. Walker, (2010), The Tri-Party Repo Market before the 2010 Reforms, FRBNY Staff Report Nr. 477, New York, Federal Reserve Bank of New York and D. Tarullo, (2012), Shadow Banking after the Financial Crisis, speech at the Federal Reserve Bank of San Francisco Conference on 'Challenges in Global Finance: The Role of Asia,' June 12, San Francisco.

[258] Claessens et al. (2012), Ibid. Annex 2, p. 30.

[259] See also: NY FED, (2015), Update on Tri-Party Repo Infrastructure Reform, Liberty Street Economics, June 24, via http://libertystreeteconomics.newyorkfed.org/. For many in the field the reform insofar implemented haven't taken out the risk identified. See, for example, F. MCKenna, (2018), Reforms Haven't Eliminated Risk of Another Lehman-Type Failure, September 14, via marketwatch.com

3.7 What Policy Direction to Take?

Given the size of the shadow banking industry,[260] further thinking is needed how we want to manage an increasing size of the global financial infrastructure. Estimates about the size vary and exact numbers are not what is essential in the debate. Claessens et al. indicate however some essential aspects when it comes to data about the shadow banking industry, in particular about the quality of the datasets and the consistency and uniformity of measuring capital flows in the shadow banking industry. They indicate that better measurement starts with consensus about whether to cover net or gross activities and stock or flows. Some studies use a gross measure, including all US dollar-denominated securitized assets (private and government sponsored), all non-deposit money market liabilities (including assets of banks, dealer banks, finance companies, government-sponsored enterprises and a wide range of (now non-existent) maturity transformation vehicles funded in asset-backed commercial paper markets) as well as money market mutual funds. Such gross measures (can) include significant double counting. They conclude that while useful for financial stability purposes (to capture total exposures of a system), they can overestimate the importance of shadow banking. For collateral, it may be valid to count collateral as many times as it is used. If the objective were to measure the value of assets currently in use as collateral, however, it would be necessary to adjust for double counting. In other parts of the world, granularity is often needed to get a better understanding. As the Financial Stability Board[261] in 2012 already concluded: [t]here is a great need to collect better data on various types of activities: (1) the demand of non-bank institutional cash investors for safe, short-term and liquid assets; (2) collateral intermediation, specifically the ultimate sources and volume of source collateral, and its velocity and the length of collateral chains; and (3) the degree of (under) collateralization of OTC derivative exposures.

Just like in the traditional banking sector where 'too big to fail' should actually read 'too complex to govern', also with respect to shadow banking, the question is all about risk management. More in particular, the notion of systemic risk reveals the fact that risk management at the level of a particular private party can be considered ok or even for a large size of private agents in a particular field doesn't necessarily imply that this also results to macro-stability of the system. Macroprudential overview is absolutely required and an essential role for a state or supranational level that wants to ensure the 'going concern' and 'effective functioning' of the global financial infrastructure.

---

[260] Indications can be found at Claessens et al. Ibid. (2012), p. 18.

[261] FSB (Financial Stability Board) 2012, Global Shadow Banking Monitoring Report 2012, 18 November, Basel, Bank for International Settlements.

Financial intermediation is the driving force in the complex ecosystem of shadow banking.[262] It links traditional banks, dealer banks and non-banks together. Two processes are key however[263]:

- Securitization chains, which transform risky assets into safe and liquid claims through the tranching of claims and the use of puts from the main banking system
- Collateral chains, which re-use collateral to reduce counterparty risk between borrowers and lenders

These transactions create important links with regulated (bank) and semi-regulated (broker-dealer) entities, which commonly (for broker-dealers, always) are SIFIs and which include (1) commercial banks, which are active in securitization chains. They offer explicit and implicit support to SPVs, and also directly invest in safe tranches of securitized debt, and (2) dealer banks, which play a central role in intermediating collateral.

Ultimately the systems link savers and borrowers together. The ultimate savers, which include short-term household and corporate savings and long-term household savings. The shadow banking system liaises with savers through the asset management complex, which includes money funds and real investors (insurance, pension funds). The ultimate borrowers, which include corporations and households, and associated investors, which include lenders wishing to securitize assets and leveraged investors (primarily hedge funds) that seek to borrow against collateral.[264]

Understanding the complexities of the different processes and activities in the shadow banking system is a good starting point on how to regulate (where needed) the integrated activities. It can be agreed upon that to the degree that shadow banking activities have economic and financial market gravitas, regulation should be aware of the implication on the efficiency of the markets and the impact on the traditional banking sector and its functions given the connection between the two systems. Regulation should therefore focus on systemic risks, that is, risk exposures that are on aggregate endangering the stability of the financial system without the micro-risk at the level of the individual market participants being a problem—even when they have a valid economic and financial markets rational.

The policy chapter will provide further details on, for example, the FSB and EU proposals in this respect. The lack of regulation before and during the financial crisis has been obvious and has been well documented.[265] Examples of shadow banking based on regula-

---

[262] For a visualization see Claessens et al. (2012), p. 20.

[263] Claessens et al. (2012), Ibid. p. 19.

[264] Claessens et al. (2012), Ibid. p. 19.

[265] T. Adrian, and B. Ashcraft, (2012), Shadow Banking Regulation, FRBNY Staff Report Nr. 559, New York, Federal Reserve Bank of New York; E. Kane, (2012), The Inevitability of Shadowy Banking, presentation at the Federal Reserve Bank of Atlanta, March 19; I. Ötker-Robe, et al., (2011), The Too-Important-to-Fail Conundrum: Impossible to Ignore and Difficult to Resolve, Staff Discussion Note Nr. SDN/11/12, Washington; G. Gorton, and A. Metrick, (2010), Regulating the Shadow Banking System, Brookings Papers on Economic Activity, Fall, pp. 261–297;

tory weaknesses before the crisis include the use by banks of affiliated investment vehicles to offload credit risks (and economize on capital charges), credit and liquidity guarantees with too little provisioning and investments in structured products where capital charges did not reflect underlying risks. What ultimately is key is the fact that regulation can act as a backstop, that is, reduce the risk of spillovers from the shadow banking system to the main banking system and through it to the public safety net.

Reducing systemic risk in shadow banking activities with effective economic and financial validity requires, as indicated, a macroprudential approach of some sort, that is, adopting policy measures that try to correct market failures and externalities arising from shadow banking that can lead to systemic risk. The right mix of tools and method of management and oversight includes regulation, supervision and monitoring the demand-supply relationship for certain types of assets as well as the monitoring of the concentration of risks and in particular the aforementioned credit, liquidity and maturity risks in the system. Finally, there is the macroeconomic implications of the system. Monetary transactions in the system are impacted by the shadow banking industry, even in normal economic and financial times. The behavior of and the nexus with the traditional banking sector requires a permanent supervision of potential spillover of systemic risk and the danger of high concentration of risks or liquidity.

It should be noted that there is quite some disagreement about the right policy approach for the shadow banking system. That can go from as extreme as the requirement for shadow banks to become or merge with traditional banks. That should provide supervisory coverage and will (most likely) avoid regulatory arbitrage. However this ignores certain key characteristics typical to the shadow banking industry. Claessens et al. indicate '[s]hadow banking is more procyclical (e.g., due to varying margin requirements), risky (because of scalability, low margins, and the ability to take large undiversified exposures), and harder to regulate (because risk profiles of market-based operations can change very rapidly) than traditional banks. Merging can then compromise commercial banks' stability, including their retail operations'.[266] Reality doesn't seem to follow that path, at least judging the financial regulation (being) put in place, that is, Volcker rule and EU regulation with respect to the banning or limiting commercial banks from (certain) trading activities.

The other extreme proposes to build firewalls around the shadow banking industry and reduce the ties between shadow banking and traditional banking but leave the shadow banking part unregulated. This is in order to reduce the risks of spillovers and limit the moral hazard arising from misuse of the public safety net. The question is, however, if it is realistic to reduce the ties between the two parts and if so at what cost? Commercial banks require tradable assets, access to hedging options, diversification and the likes. Further and given the size of the shadow banking operations versus the

V. Acharya, et al., 2009, Manufacturing Tail Risk: A Perspective on the Financial Crisis of 2007–09, Foundations and Trends in Finance, Vol. 4, Nr. 4, pp. 247–325; C. Pazarbasioglu, et al., (2011), Contingent Capital: Economic Rationale and Design Features, Staff Discussion Note Nr. SDN/11/01, Washington; J. Zhou, et al., (2012), From Bail-out to Bail-in: Mandatory Debt Restructuring of Systemic Financial Institutions, IMF Staff Discussion Note Nr. SDN/12/03, Washington.

[266] Claessens et al., (2012), Ibid. p. 23.

global financial infrastructure, it is realistic to assume that even on a stand-alone basis they could be a threat to macroeconomic stability and pose a systemic risk to the system creating all sort of negative externalities for the real economy. Data availability, which is already a problem, would become even more problematic.

The middle ground supports the view to reduce the reduction of private safe assets. That equals a mild separation for specific types of banks[267] (with e.g. limited funding). Others would supervise and regulate the level of financial innovation[268] coming from the industry, which is considered unrealistic and its usefulness it doubted.

3.8 Regulating Risk as the Central Policy Objective

Dealer banks are the central concept in the shadow banking system and is considered inherently fragile and unstable[269] and are therefore considered systemically important (SIFIs). That is the consequence of a combination of the use of high leverage, a procyclical business model and uninsured and therefore unstable wholesale funding. Therefore that most of the SIFIs now have access to central bank liquidity facilities either through commercial banks or directly through their converted bank-holding companies. The question is if that is preferable as they often hold very little effective deposits (which was what the liquidity facility initially wanted to ensure).[270] The bank can therefore shift risky assets to the shadow banking part which now enjoys the same stability, that is, which in a way poses a moral hazard.[271] This is particularly true as dealer banks have an inclination (and ability) to take more (tail i.e. extreme) risk with tradable assets that have a highly skewed payout model. In the US, the Dodd-Frank Act provides authorities with powers to move a systemically important broker-dealer under the supervision and regulation of the Federal Reserve. This seems preferred from a supervisory point of view, but it does not address how to effectively regulate dealer banks, that is, a broker-dealer that is an integrated part of a banking group. The public safety net can extend to the whole SIFI, the broker-dealer operations can dwarf its banking part, especially since deposits of US and

---

[267] M. Ricks, (2012), Reforming the Short-Term Funding Markets, John M. Olin Center for Law, Economics and Business Discussion Paper Nr. 713, Cambridge, Massachusetts, Harvard University; G. Gorto, and A. Metrick, (2010), Regulating the Shadow Banking System, Brookings Papers on Economic Activity, Fall, pp. 261–297.

[268] E. Fielding, et al., (2010), The National Transportation Safety Board: A Model for Systemic Risk Management.

[269] D. Duffie, (2010), The Failure Mechanics of Dealer Banks, *Journal of Economic Perspectives*, Vol. 24, Nr. 1, pp. 51–72.

[270] M. Singh, (2012), Puts in the Shadows, IMF Working Paper Nr. WP/12/229, Washington.

[271] A.W.A. Boot, (2011), Banking at the Cross Roads: How to Deal with Marketability and Complexity, presentation to the Federal Reserve Bank of Atlanta's Conference on Navigating the New Financial Landscape, March 31; A.W.A. Boot, and L. Ratnovski, (2012), Banking and Trading, IMF Working Paper Nr. WP/12/238, Washington.

EU SIFIs—that is, the bank part—are often less than a third of the overall assets of the SIFI in the bank-holding company.[272]

As, for example, the EU regulatory initiative (see relevant MMF chapter) in 2013–2014 has proven, the regulation of MMMFs is another key area of concern from a policy point of view. The size of the industry combined with the fact that it offers on par guarantees that cannot be supported in times of stress when asset values drop makes it very vulnerable and systemic. A myriad of solutions[273] has been suggested which include lowering the average asset maturity of MMFs, introducing capital requirements, requiring a floating NAV and using two-class claims on assets (one redeemable at par and the other contingent on the NAV). However it is clear that a full removal of risk from the MMMF area will impact its functioning and role toward the economy and its customers.[274]

As already hinted at above, the tri-party repo transactions need further attention from a regulatory point of view. Those should include (1) initiatives limiting the duration of intra-day exposures and improving collateral management and (2) the reduction of systemic risk caused by the fact that these transactions run through two private clearing banks (Bank of New York and JP Morgan). In some countries that process is handled by 'market structures or utilities which reduces the risk in those 2 institutions and reduce the net for a public safety net under stress'. Also here the question arises, partly due to a lack of focused research, how the system can be made more robust without affecting their intermediary role between banks and broker-dealers.[275]

Nevertheless, important issues have stayed unsolved until now. Most importantly, financial innovation as such and the macro-stability of the system are two areas of ongoing policy concern. The shadow banking system has many links, both nationally and internationally, between banks and SIFIs and banks and non-banks, and they often

---

[272] B. Tuckman, (2012), Federal Liquidity Options: Containing Runs on Deposit-Like Assets without Bailouts or Moral Hazard, Center for Financial Stability Policy Paper, January 24. Similarly, while Dodd-Frank enables an orderly liquidation of a dealer bank by the Federal Deposit Insurance Corporation, the precise processes have neither been fully articulated in theory nor tried in practice. At the same time, Dodd-Frank has tightened the rules of lender-of-last-resort support to non-banks.

[273] P. McCabe, (2011), An A-/B-share Capital Buffer Proposal for Money Market Funds, Board of Governors of the Federal Reserve. Mimeo; E. Rosengren, (2012), Our Financial Structures–Are They Prepared for Financial Instability? Keynote remarks at the Conference on Post-Crisis Banking, Amsterdam, The Netherlands, June 29 (Federal Reserve Bank of Boston); SEC (Securities and Exchange Commission), (2012), Testimony on Perspectives on Money Market Mutual Fund Reforms by Chairman Mary L. Schapiro before the Committee on Banking, Housing, and Urban Affairs of the United States Senate, June 21; Squam Lake (Working Group on Financial Regulation), (2010), Reforming Money Market Funds, Working Paper, University of Chicago; R. Wermers, (2012), Runs on Money Market Mutual Funds, Working Paper, University of Maryland.

[274] Claessens et al., (2012), Ibid. p. 24, refer to examples such as imposing capital requirements may open the door to (1) relaxing investment standards, (2) make MMFs quasi-banks, (3) necessitate the need for detailed bank-type regulations and (4) removing the par guarantees (i.e. MMFs becoming a version of mutual funds) may dramatically shrink the system as investors shift funds to bank deposits and elsewhere. That besides the fact that attempts to remove the par guarantees may be ineffective because some of the guarantees are implicit.

[275] Claessens et al., (2012), Ibid. p. 25.

involve very complex contractual arrangements and prone to implicit commitments. The role of financial innovation and the design of new financial instruments happen at an ever increasing rate, and the content of these products is often not fully understood by all investors. The true robustness of some of these products was only tested and demonstrated under stress in the 2008 crisis. The fact that many of these transactions is between multiple agents, often located in different jurisdictions, makes the environment very complex. As indicated above, reducing financial innovation is difficult, the question whether regulation or whatever method would be the best way to do and the policy options are very unclear also with respect to the explicit and implicit cost it would carry. A macroprudential approach, that is, to identify market failures and externalities that can lead to systemic risk, and to adopt policy measures that try to correct them seems to be a more practical and realistic way forward. However, timeliness and enforceability and a permanent need to adapt the supervision and regulation will be required to make it a meaningful exercise.

3.9 Policy Implications and Demand-Supply Dynamics

As already referred to in the introductory chapters, the shadow banking industry emerged historically as a consequence of the need of cash pools to gain access to safe liquid short-term assets in volumes larger than what the short-term government bond market (could) provide. Such demand was a major force before the crisis behind the expansion of prime money funds and the assets they invested in as well as the emergence of the tri-party repo market. The adjustments in relative prices—the rates of return on various types of assets[276]—that occurred has not fully removed the demand-supply mismatch. As Claessens et al. indicate,[277] the reason is that the demand for safe assets (volume of cash pools) and the supply of truly safe assets (short-term government debt) are relatively price-inelastic, which can make the equilibrium price of government-guaranteed safe assets very high (and their yields very low or negative), creating incentives for the system to create private safe assets.

The mismatch between demand and supply creates an incentive to create private 'safe' assets which potentially can pose a systemic risk as those private assets do not benefit from a natural backstop as government bonds. As Claessens et al. demonstrate with adequate numbers, the growth in the volume of secured wholesale funding (used against private safe assets) and the mismatch between the demand and supply of privately provided 'safe' assets had an almost one-to-one relationship prior to the crisis. The mismatch peaked at roughly USD 2.5 trillion just before the crisis—after it had surged by $1.5 trillion in the three preceding years—and has fallen since on the back of increased issuance of short-

[276] G.R. Duffee, (1996), Idiosyncratic Variation of Treasury Bill Yields, *Journal of Finance*, Vol. 51, No. 2, pp. 527–552. R. Greenwood S. Hanson, and J. Stein, (2012), A Comparative-Advantage Approach to Government Debt Maturity, Harvard Business School Working Paper Nr. 11-035.

[277] Claessens et al., (2012), Ibid. p. 25.

term government-guaranteed debt.[278] Continued excess demand will stay a driver behind the creation of private 'safe and liquid' assets and require continuous monitoring.

There have been scholars[279] who have advocated that, in order to match demand-supply, governments need to expand the supply of short-term safe and liquid assets and crowd out the assets created by the private shadow banking market. That would imply that the governments would issue more short-term bonds (T-bills) and would reduce as such demand for securitized assets. Central banks could also play a role in expanding the supply of safe assets by, for example, issuing central bank bills or extending the right to maintain deposit accounts with the central bank to non-banks. That, however, comes with some key debt management issues. Issuing more (short-term) debt than needed for operational and monetary or budgetary purposes, it implicitly absorbs a certain interest rate and operational risks from the private sector which it now caters to. This is not a problem when the private sector is more likely to create risky money-type claims when the yield curve is steeper, precisely the case when the issuance of short-term government paper is cheap (i.e. in non-distress situations).[280] The question is really if this is something we really want, that is, the government engaging in creating financial market assets with the sole purpose of catering to a particular investment clientele. Do we want the government to cater to the demand of certain private sector agents and if so, can we properly define 'safe liquid assets' as that notion is vague, changes constantly and might have different definitions in other parts of the world, fostering a carry trade. And what about the demand that is not driven by large cash pools? It is unjustifiable that the government would put in place demand-side policies that would implicitly subsidize banks' investments in market-based debt instruments.[281]

Other macro-implications of shadow banking and potential regulation are the procyclicality which is common to finance but in particular visual in the shadow banking scene. The real risk is the impact that might have on the real economy. As Brunnemeyer and Pedersen highlight, 'secured lending and repos rely on mark-to-market prices and margins/haircuts that adjust over the financial cycle. In the extreme, some collateral may become unacceptable during periods of turmoil. More generally, investments by financial intermediaries in tradable, mark-to-market assets or the use of such assets as collateral

---

[278] Claessens et al., (2012), Ibid. p. 26.

[279] R. Greenwood, S. Hanson, and J. Stein, (2012), A Comparative-Advantage Approach to Government Debt Maturity, Harvard Business School Working Paper Nr. 11-035; Z. Pozsar, (2011), Institutional Cash Pools and the Triffin Dilemma of the U.S. Banking System, IMF Working Paper Nr. WP/11/190, Washington and, (2012), A Macro View of Shadow Banking: Do T-Bill Shortages Pose a New Triffin Dilemma, in Is U.S. Government Debt Different?, (ed.) Franklin Allen, Wharton Financial Institutions Center; G. Gorton, et al., (2012), The Safe-Asset Share, American Economic Review: Papers & Proceedings, Vol. 102, Nr. 3, May, pp. 101–106; T. Adrian, and H. S. Shin, (2010), Liquidity and Leverage, *Journal of Financial Intermediation*, Vol. 19, Nr. 3, pp. 418–437; A. Turner, (2012), Shadow Banking and Financial Instability, speech at Cass Business School, March 14.

[280] T. Adrian, and H. S. Shin, (2010), Liquidity and leverage, *Journal of Financial Intermediation*, Vol. 19, Nr. 3, pp. 418–437.

[281] Claessens et al., (2012), Ibid. p. 27.

encourage procyclicality in the form of more lax lending in upturns and a risk of fire sales in downturns'.[282] Securitization creates claims that are safe in most states of the world but become risky in others, contributing to tail risks.[283] In general the shadow banking services and industry enable or even foster greater financial system interconnectedness, which in turn reduces idiosyncratic risk through diversification but on the down side exposes the system to spillovers in the event of large shocks.[284]

Procyclicality can have many sources which include:

- Mark-to-market rules
- Evolution of margin requirements relative to collateral values
- Lending standards relative to collateral values
- Design of compensation packages

Academia hasn't really figured out yet which ones contribute most to the emergence of the phenomenon. Procyclicality could potentially be mitigated by margin requirements or haircuts for certain classes of assets to have minimums or to be calibrated through the cycle.[285] In certain situations that seems rather easy to implement (tri-party agreements) but will be more difficult in OTC markets due to bilateral collateral agreements and can distort the price setting of pledged collateral.

Monetary transmission (e.g. interest rate transmission) requires a well-functioning capital market infrastructure including the shadow banking scene. The volume and velocity of collateral and the quality of private safe and liquid assets can therefore have an impact of monetary policy transmissions and ultimately can lead macroeconomic implications. The 'well-being' of the shadow banking system needs to be accounted for in taking monetary policy decisions. And monetary policy can affect risk taking in shadow banking. When, for example, the interest rate is low, a steeper yield curve that increases the payoff to maturity transformation and risk taking can lead shadow banking to expand rapidly, potentially leading to financial fragility.[286]

---

[282] M. Brunnermeier, and L. H. Pedersen, (2009), Market Liquidity and Funding Liquidity, Review of Financial Studies, Vol. 22, Nr. 6, pp. 2201–2238.

[283] N. Gennaioli, et al. (2012), Neglected Risks, Financial Innovation, and Financial Fragility, *Journal of Financial Economics*, Vol. 104, pp. 452–468.

[284] D. Acemoglu, et al., (2012), Systemic Risk and Stability in Financial Networks, Working Paper, MIT Cambridge, Massachusetts.

[285] P. Fegatelli, (2010), The Role of Collateral Requirements in the Crisis: One Tool for Two Objectives, Working Paper Nr. 44, Banque Central du Luxembourg, Luxembourg; L. Valderrama, (2010), Countercyclical Regulation under Collateralized Lending, IMF Working Paper Nr. WP/10/220, Washington; BCBS (Basel Committee on Banking Supervision), (2012), Capital Requirements for Bank Exposures to Central Counterparties, Bank for International Settlements, July.

[286] T. Adrian, and H. S. Shin, (2010), Liquidity and leverage, *Journal of Financial Intermediation*, Vol. 19, Nr. 3, pp. 418–437. G. De Nicolò, et al., (2012), Externalities and Macro-Prudential Policy, IMF Staff Discussion Note Nr. SDN12/05, Washington; G. De Nicolò, et al., (2010), Monetary Policy and Bank Risk Taking, IMF Staff Position Note Nr. SPN/10/09, Washington; M. Singh, and P. Stella, (2012), Money and Collateral, IMF Working Paper Nr. WP/12/95, Washington. op. cit. Claessens et al., Ibid. p. 28.

Without engaging in populist rhetoric, it can be stated that shadow banking produces and supports a number of economically useful activities and transactions. Claessens et al. remind that 'research has not been able to differentiate the economic drivers of shadow banking from regulatory arbitrage, making policy recommendations more difficult'.[287] Given the wide variety of activities, transactions and functions, a multifaceted response is required, which is what we see unfurling both in Europe and the US. In other parts of the world, we see a more fragmented response, often due to incomplete or immature shadow banking infrastructures.

3.10 The Way Forward for Securitization

In the wake of the financial crisis,[288] new securitization activity came to a halt in all asset classes that did not have an implicit or explicit government guarantee. Though securitization has since resumed in most asset classes, including automobiles, credit cards, collateralized loan obligations (CLOs) and commercial mortgage-backed securities (CMBSs), the private-label residential mortgage-backed securities market remains stagnant with only modest upswings in the period 2016–2019. That is at least for the US.[289] Europe is still largely 'dead in the water' even halfway 2019. Not that we haven't bottomed in Europe in terms of volume years ago, but a really convincing recovery is not in the cards at the moment. The EU puts its hope on the effect of the STS regulation coming in.[290] The future behind the close of the manuscript holds that answer. Both the US and Europe have taken measures to contain risk while at the same time, stimulating the revival of the segment with a view toward increasing lending patterns by banks, who can 'free up their balance sheet'[291] this way. RMBS have seen the largest change (decline), but not surpris-

[287] Claessens et al., (2012), Ibid. p. 28.

[288] See for a general but complete overview on the matter: R. Saleuddin, (2015), Regulating Securitized Products. A Post-Crisis Guide, Palgrave, Basingstoke, July; M. Choudhry, (2013), The Mechanics of Securitization: A Practical Guide to Structuring and Closing Asset-Backed Security Transactions, Wiley, Basingstoke.

[289] See L. Goodman, (2015), The Rebirth of Securitization. Where is the Private-Label Mortgage Market?, Housing Finance Policy Center, Urban Institute, mimeo, pp. 1–3.

[290] Regulation effective as of January 1, 2019.

[291] There has been evidence of that both ways, but most point in the direction that there is no clear positive correlation between enhanced liquidity, due to the sell-off of assets, and credit supply. Most of the evidence points out that a long-term banking relationship is the best way to relax credit constraints rather than anything else. However, to the extent that ABS activity by banks lowers lending standards in normal times, banks with more ABS activity may reduce their lending more in crisis times as an ex post effect of a previously higher risk adoption. On the other hand, a relationship with a bank that is more involved in securitization activities relaxes credit constraints in normal periods. In contrast, while a relationship with a firm's main bank that issues covered bonds reduces credit rationing during crisis periods, the issuance of asset-backed securities by a firm's main bank aggravates these firm's credit rationing in crisis periods; see S. Carbó-Valverde et al., (2012), Lending Relationships and Credit Rationing: the Impact of Securitization, Department of Accountancy, Finance and Insurance (AFI), KU Leuven Working Paper Nr. 1272.

ingly, mortgages exhibited the most severe dislocations of any asset class and were also the only asset class to experience significant policy changes affecting already-outstanding securities in the wake of the crisis. That had to do with pre-crisis weaknesses in the cash flow waterfall, weaknesses in loan underwriting, its bankruptcy remoteness[292] and the lack of consistency in loan-level information.[293] The revival of the asset securitization segments can also be explained by the fact that issuer and investor interests were better aligned in other segments compared to the mortgage segment.[294] That aspects, called 'ambiguity' by Anderson[295] is what caused the 2008 market freeze. She demonstrates and investigates how ambiguity affects origination and securitization decisions. Her model captures many features of the crisis, including market freezes and fire sales (i.e. ambiguity aversion), as well as the timing and duration of the freeze and the decision-making and participative process of economic agents. The presence of ambiguity also reduces real economic activity, which stresses the role for policymaking in this respect.

Part of the ambiguity and the misalignment has been pushed out of the securitization model. The misalignment has been somewhat corrected through the risk retention regulation for asset securitization (often a net economic interest of not less than 5%),[296] that is, the issuer has to retain a certain proportion of securitized assets and further information disclosure regarding the product.[297] But there are some limitation to what they can solve:

[292] G. Chiesa, (2015), Bankruptcy Remoteness and Incentive-compatible Securitization, Financial Markets, Institutions & Instruments, Vol. 24, Issue 2–3, pp. 241–265, May/August.

[293] See L. Goodman, (2015), The Rebirth of Securitization. Where is the Private-Label Mortgage Market?, Housing Finance Policy Center, Urban Institute, mimeo, pp. 5–10.

[294] See L. Goodman, (2015), Ibid. pp. 11–15.

[295] A.G. Anderson, (2015), Ambiguity in Securitization Markets, Finance and Economics Discussion Series 2015-033. Washington, Board of Governors of the Federal Reserve System, May, pp. 2–6.

[296] Observe that this is the case for sponsors and originators but also AIFM denominated funds that are looking to invest in securitized products (art. 17 of the AIFM Directive): see in detail AIMA (Alternative Investment Management Association), (2013), Article 17 of AIFMD—A Barrier to Investment in Securitisation Positions, September.

[297] Hidden and/or asymmetric information in securitized products contributing to 'hidden information frameworks' can encompass asymmetric information: (1) between insiders and outside investors as to the value of non-securitized assets; (2) between classes of outside investors as to the value of securitized assets; or (3) between insiders and outsiders as to the value of securitized assets. Asset securitization is driven by the tendency of the market to match claims with investors who are best informed about asset values; see in detail: E.M. Iacobuci and R.A. Winter, (2001), Asset Securitization and Asymmetric Information, *Journal of Legal Studies*, Vol. 34, Nr. 1, pp. 161–206. They conclude '[w]here an informational asymmetry is different between two classes of assets owned by a corporation, as in the three theories, the market can achieve this efficient matching only by splitting the ownership of the two classes. Asset securitization is thus a response to the asymmetry across assets in the informational asymmetry across investors as to the asset returns.' See also: D.O. Beltran and C.P. Thomas, (2010), Could Asymmetric Information Alone Have Caused the Collapse of Private-Label Securitization?, Board of Governors of the Federal Reserve System, International Finance Discussion Papers, Nr. 1010, October; U. Albertazzi, et al., (2015), Asymmetric Information in Securitization: An Empirical Assessment, *Journal of Monetary Economics*, Vol. 71, April, pp. 33–49.

a flat-rate retention requirement can't be optimal for all asset types and although both risk retention and information disclosure regulations are effective in reducing investors' informational loss, neither can unconditionally enhance social welfare compared to an unregulated scenario.[298] The simple, standardized and transparent (STS) model as approached by in the EU securitization regulation[299] and as discussed in the EU chapter can avoid confusion or ambiguity, but also that system is not default-free as discussed in the EU chapter. There are many technical challenges, and a number of broader policy issues. Thiemann wraps them together for us: (1) securitization activities are prone to legal engineering. The CMU only contains limited proposals of how to contain the ingenuity of private actors to circumvent regulation, (2) who are potential buyers for mezzanine securitization tranches in order to achieve risk transfer and diversification. Institutional cash pools are looking for the senior tranches; (3) overcoming information asymmetry in SME securitization are not really addressed in the proposals.[300]

And, not to forget, there are associated regulatory cost: risk retention regulation aggravates adverse selection problem because it undermines the channel of informational revelation by the choice of securitization intensity, and information disclosure requirement incurs a signaling cost by distorting banks' securitization intensity in sending signals. One could say that in an optimal scenario, information disclosure requirement complement risk retention regulation but only when investors are sufficiently risk averse.[301] But there is a wider macro- and public interest dynamics to securitization. We are becoming aware that there is a link between securitization and asset prices that increases in the growth rate of the volume of ABS issuance lead to a sizable decline in bond and equity premia. Further it has been observed that where banks select their portfolio of assets and create synthetic securities, the compensation for undertaking risk decreases as securitization increases. The pooling and tranching of credit assets relaxes both the funding and the risk constraints banks face allowing them to increase balance sheet holdings.[302] Accordingly, Akosy and Basso conclude 'the drop in risk premium may be unrelated to a decline in actual risk'.

But the problem goes way deeper. Kuncl[303] in his turn argues that when retaining part of the risk, the issuer of securitized assets may credibly signal its quality (or put differently he suggests that risk retention contributes to a reduction in the asymmetry of information). However, in the boom stage of the business cycle, this practice is inefficient, information on asset quality remains private and lower quality assets accumulate on balance sheets of

---

[298] See also: F. Cortes and A. Thokar, (2015), Does Securitization Increase Risk?: a Theory of Loan Securitization, Reputation, and Credit Screening, Working Paper, mimeo, December 5.

[299] And based on the BCBS criteria for STS securitizations: BCBS, (2015), Criteria for Identifying Simple, Transparent and Comparable Securitisations, Basel, July.

[300] M. Thiemann, (2015), Capital Markets Union. How to Achieve Risk Diversification Through Standardized Securitization, FEPS Policy Brief, April.

[301] See in extenso: G. Guo and H.-M. Wu, (2014), A Study on Risk Retention Regulation in Asset Securitization Process, *Journal of Banking & Finance*, Vol. 45(C), pp. 61–71.

[302] Y. Aksoy and H.S. Basso, (2015), Securitization and Asset prices, Banco de España, Documentos de Trabajo Nr. 1526. Spain is one of the largest securitizing countries in Europe especially relative to its economy but also in absolute terms.

[303] M. Kuncl, (2015), Securitization under Asymmetric Information over the Business Cycle, Bank of Canada/Banque de Canada Working Paper Nr. 2015-9.

financial intermediaries. This prolongs and deepens a subsequent recession with an intensity proportional to the length of the preceding boom. In recessions, he further argues, amplification of adverse selection problems on resale markets for securitized assets might occur. These are especially severe after a prolonged boom period and when securitized high-quality assets are no longer traded. He concludes therefore that improperly designed regulation requiring higher explicit risk retention may even become counterproductive due to a negative general equilibrium effect, that is, it may adversely affect both the quantity and the quality of investment in the economy. Since self-regulation by risk retention[304] (Box 3.2) is not sufficient, more standardization and transparency is necessary, especially in boom stages of the business cycle, to address the problem of asymmetry of information.

Box 3.2 Risk Retention in Europe Versus the US[305]

Risk retention in Europe is settled through the CRR[306] and has opted in for the indirect approach. The current European risk retention framework requires investors to satisfy themselves that the risk retention rules have been complied with and imposes regulatory capital penalties on investors' holding of assets which fail to comply (the 'indirect approach').[307]

(*continued*)

[304] The EBA feels different about that and endorsed the existing risk retention rules included in article 405 of the CRR; EBA, (2015), EBA Report on Securitisation Risk Retention, Due Diligence and Disclosure, December 22, London.

[305] For the US portion based on A.M. Faulkner, (2015), Regulators Adopt Final Risk Retention Rules for Asset-Backed Securities, Skadden's 2015 Insights—Financial Regulation, January, via skadden.com. For the official SEC documents: SEC, (2014), Credit Risk Retention, via sec.gov. See for a broader comparison between the US and the EU in terms of securitization: T.C. Fuhriman, (2013), The Global Financial Crisis & Asset-Backed Securitization Regulatory Responses Thereto in the EU and the United States, Kyungpook National University Law Journal, Vol. 43, Issue 8 (August), pp. 29–36.

[306] The risk retention part is in force since mid-2014 and absorbed by the STS regulation in 2017.

[307] EBA, (2015), EBA Report on Securitisation Risk Retention, Due Diligence and Disclosure, December 22, London, pp. 15–25. Despite the many advantages of the 'direct approach', the EBA sticks with the 'indirect' approach. CRR Article 405 places the onus on the investor institutions (so-called 'indirect' approach) to ensure that the multiple components of the risk retention requirements are satisfied: type of retainer (originator, original lender or sponsor), forms of retention used (five possible forms), level of net economic interest retained and assessment of the consolidated situation of the retainer. Conversely, a 'direct' approach would put the obligations on the originator, original lender or sponsor to comply with the retention requirements. The 'indirect' approach adopted in the CRR ensures that investor institutions buy only securitizations subject to the retention requirement. This approach addresses the misalignment of incentives (in particular with the 'originate-to-distribute' business model used in the US) between the originator, sponsor and original lenders and investors and ensures that EU investor institutions conduct proper due diligence before investing in securitization positions. Imposing the requirement on the investor also has the benefit of making the rules enforceable, unlike imposing a requirement on the originator (so-called direct approach) which would raise legal issues when the originator/sponsor/original lender is located outside the EU/EEA or are non-regulated entities. On the other hand, the 'indirect' approach appears on some occasions to act as a disincentive to investors in Europe. Submissions to the EBA's questionnaire on securitization risk retention, due diligence and transparency require-

Box 3.2 continued

In short, the EU risk retention rules prohibit affected investors from becoming exposed to the credit risk of a securitization unless any of the sponsor, the originator or the original lender in the transaction discloses that it will retain an interest of not less than 5% of the securitized exposures. Should an affected CRR investor invest in a securitization transaction that does not meet the risk retention, due diligence and disclosure requirements of the EU risk retention rules in any material respect by reason of such investor's negligence or omission, the competent authorities must impose a proportionate additional risk weight against the relevant securitization position equal to no less than 250% (capped at 1250%) of the original risk weight of that position. Securitization transactions that do not comply with the EU risk retention rules may be marketed and sold to investors other than affected investors; however, the extent of the reduction in liquidity and its effect on pricing for a transaction held only by non-affected investors is unclear.[308]

This differs from the US risk retention framework which requires the originator or sponsor to satisfy itself that the US equivalent of the risk retention rules have been complied with (the 'direct approach').[309] The final rules generally (there are quite some exemptions,[310] both in Europe and the US[311]) require a

(continued)

ments from industry stakeholders suggested that the indirect regime (i.e. where the investor bears the onus of monitoring compliance) sometimes causes legal uncertainty for investors, because it is difficult for investors to ascertain whether the original lender, originator or sponsor is complying with the risk retention requirement on an ongoing basis. Furthermore, the indirect approach does not require EU originators to retain any economic interest in transactions sold to non-EU investors. Indeed, the burden is on the investors which means that if the securitization transaction does not have any EU/EEA investors, the originator, sponsor or original lender does not need to comply with the retention requirement. In contrast to an 'indirect' approach, a 'direct' approach puts a direct legal obligation on the originator, original lender or sponsor to retain a meaningful exposure to credit risk. Placing the obligation directly on the originator, original lender and sponsor instead of the investors reduces the legal uncertainty of non-compliance on investors and has the potential to improve investor certainty and to encourage new investors to invest in securitizations.

[308] Latham & Watkins, (2014), EU Risk Retention Rules and CLOs—the Journey's End?, Structured Finance and Securitization Commentary Nr. 1704, June 26.

[309] See for a comparison of both approaches: EBA, (2015), EBA Report on Securitisation Risk Retention, Due Diligence and Disclosure, December 22, London, pp. 15–17.

[310] Exemptions also exist for certain types of assets and transactions, the most significant of which is the US exemption for qualified residential mortgages (QRMs). A pool comprised entirely of QRMs has no retention requirement. The exclusion for QRMs means that risk retention will not be required for most RMBS transactions. In the EU proposal, an exemption from the 5% requirement in case the securitization is guaranteed by a financial institution whose risk weight is equal or below 50% under CRD IV. While in theory it sounds alright as the guarantee protects investors, in reality this is a problem because it creates counterparty risk in case the guarantor cannot deliver on its commitments; Finance Watch, (2015), STS Securitization Q&A, p.3.

[311] It was only in October 2014 that the relevant regulators in the US adopted a final set of rules implementing the credit-risk retention requirements of the Dodd-Frank Act. Relevant documents

Box 3.2 continued

sponsor of an ABS transaction or its majority-owned affiliate to retain an economic interest equal to at least 5%[312] of the aggregate credit risk of the assets collateralizing an issuance. In some circumstances a portion of the risk retention may be retained by the originator of the assets that collateralize the ABS.

The standard forms of risk retention in the US[313] are an 'eligible horizontal residual interest' and an 'eligible vertical interest'. An 'eligible horizontal residual interest' must have the most subordinate claim to payments of both principal and interest by the issuing entity and, if an issuing entity has insufficient funds to satisfy its obligation to pay interest and principal due, requires the holder to absorb any shortfalls prior to any reduction in the amounts payable to any other ABS interest.

An 'eligible vertical interest' is an interest in each class of ABS interests in the transaction that constitutes the same portion of each class or a single vertical security entitling the holder to a specified percentage of the amounts paid on each class of ABS interests in the issuing entity.

A sponsor may satisfy the risk retention requirements by retaining a combination of eligible horizontal residual interests and eligible vertical interests so long as the combined percentages equal at least 5% (i.e. L-shaped risk retention method combining horizontal and vertical risk retention is not possible under the European CRR).[314]

A sponsor also may, under US protocol, fund an eligible horizontal cash reserve account held by a trustee in cash or cash equivalents. An eligible horizontal residual interest (or the amount held in an eligible horizontal cash reserve account) is subject to a 'fair value' valuation in accordance with generally accepted accounting principles, and the sponsor's valuation methodology must be disclosed.

Special US risk retention alternatives are available for revolving-pool securitizations, asset-backed commercial paper conduits, commercial mortgage-backed securities, government-sponsored enterprises, open market collateralized loan

(continued)

were published in the Federal Register on December 24, 2014, and compliance with the rules with respect to asset-backed securities (ABS) collateralized by residential mortgages is required by December 24, 2015, and with respect to all other classes of ABS is required by December 24, 2016. See for an update brief: Morgan Lewis, (2018), Guide to the Credit Risk Retention Rules for Securitizations, February 20, via morganlewis.com

312 It is however documented that 5% is too low to provide a meaningful disciplining effect to for banks. Oncelosses reach 5%, the bank has no longer any incentive to care about investors. Some therefore recommend increasing it to 15% and removing the choice of options and require that the retention requirement can only be satisfied by retaining a vertical slice of each tranche, to ensure an alignment of interest all the way between the bank originator and the investor (and thus removing the optionality that exists); Finance Watch, (2015), Ibid. p. 3.

313 See also: Board of Governors of the Federal Reserve System, (2010), Report to the Congress on Risk Retention, October.

314 EBA, (2015), EBA Report on Securitisation Risk Retention, Due Diligence and Disclosure, December 22, London, pp. 17–19. The EBA commented on this matter '[t]he combination of horizontal and vertical risk retention may mitigate some of the costs related to the horizontal only (first-loss option) or vertical only risk retention options. It provides greater flexibility if the retainer

Box 3.2 continued

obligations and qualified tender option bonds (note that the rules apply to both publicly and privately issued 'asset-backed securities', as defined in the Securities Exchange Act of 1934, and that the broad definition encompasses some securities that have not traditionally been considered to be ABS).

In Europe, under there are five different methods of retention, which may not be changed during the term of the transaction: (1) vertical slice, that is, retention of no less than 5% of the nominal value of each of the tranches sold or transferred to the investors; (2) pari passu share; in the case of retention of revolving exposures retention of the originator's interest of no less than 5% of the nominal value of the securitized exposures; (3) on balance sheet, retention of randomly selected exposures, equivalent to no less than 5% of the nominal value of the securitized exposures, provided that the number of potentially securitized exposures is no less than 100 at origination; (4) first-loss tranche, and—if necessary—other tranches that have the same or a more severe risk profile than those transferred or sold to investors and are not maturing any earlier, so that the retention equals in total no less than 5% of the nominal value of the securitized exposures; and (5) retention of a first-loss exposure of no less than 5% of every securitized exposure in the securitization.

The final US rules generally prohibit the transfer or pledging of any interest that the sponsor is required to retain under the rules except to an entity that is a majority-owned affiliate which itself is subject to the same prohibitions, until any applicable sunset date.[315] However, the sponsor or its permitted affiliate may pledge the retained interest as collateral for an obligation that is full recourse to the sponsor or the affiliate.

---

can use any combination of horizontal and vertical slice as long as the 5% requirement is met. Furthermore the 'L-shaped' option as an alternative form of retention has the potential to lower funding costs, which could be beneficial for different types of transactions that do not fit neatly into the traditional model of securitization such as certain managed transactions. However, providing greater choice with an additional form of retention has its drawbacks: by giving originators, original lenders and sponsors the choice of how to retain risk, their chosen 'L-shape' form of retention may not be as effective in aligning interests and mitigating risks for investors. It may also complicate the implementation of risk retention as well as investors' processes for due diligence and the ongoing measurement of compliance due to the wider choices that originators, original lenders and sponsors would enjoy. That is, providing this additional form of retention may create fewer benefits or more costs for investors than other alternatives might. The EBA has considered the 'L-shape' retention method as an additional suitable retention option. However, the features of this additional option would add to the complexity of measuring the net economic interest and the increase of flexibility provided by this option might reduce the overall effectiveness of the retention requirements in terms of alignment of interests (pp. 18–19)'. See also: ESMA & EBA, (2015), Joint Committee Report on Securitization, JC 2015 22, May 12.

[315] Which varies depending on the type of securitized product. For residential mortgage-backed security (RMBS) transactions, the prohibitions on sale or pledging expires no later than seven years after the closing date or later of five years after the closing or the date on which the total unpaid principal balance of the residential mortgages has been reduced to 25% of the original balance. For other ABS transactions, the prohibitions on sale or pledging expire on or after the date that is the latest of (1) the date on which the total unpaid principal balance of the securitized assets has been reduced to 33% of their original balances, (2) the date on which the total unpaid principal obliga-

In the aftermath of the 2008 crisis, regulators have been working on new securitization frameworks, and each one of them are built around five key criteria: (1) the relative prudential treatment of securitization products; (2) accounting issues, especially regarding consolidation and retention; (3) developing guidance on possible measures that could eliminate or reduce the potentially negative effects of differences in securitization regulation and terminology on cross-border transactions; (4) encouraging standardization to increase liquidity in secondary markets; and (5) encouraging sound mortgage underwriting practices (e.g. through implementation of FSB's Principles for sound residential mortgage underwriting practices).[316] In the wake of these framework and regulatory developments, criteria were developed for STS (simple, transparent and comparable securitizations).[317] The BCBS-IOSCO Task Force had three distinct objectives: (1) to identify and assist in the development by the financial industry of simple, transparent and comparable securitizations, (2) to assist investors with their due diligence on securitizations (not a substitute for due diligence) and (3) modular approach: interested parties may complement these criteria with additional and/or more detailed criteria based on specific needs and applications.

Most advancement has been made regarding the STS criteria which have been classified in three ways: (1) asset risk[318]: generic criteria relating to the understanding of the asset pool, (2) structural risk[319]: transparency around the securitization structure, (3) fiduciary risk[320]: governance of key parties to the securitization process.[321] Further work is now being conducted with respect to developing criteria for short-term securitizations and improving the standardization of securitization documentation.

For those banks that comply with STS standards, a lower capital requirement is foreseen for these products.[322] However, as Kolm[323] illustrates,

---

tions of the ABS interests have been reduced to 33% of the total ABS interest on the closing date and (3) two years after the closing date.

[316] See for a very good, but by now somewhat outdated, overview of what has been going on in terms of developing new securitization frameworks: IOSCO, (2012), Global Developments in Securitization Regulation, Final Reports, FR09/12, November 16. A follow through and update however can be found in IOSCO, (2015), Peer Review of Implementation of Incentive Alignment Recommendations for Securitisation: Final Report, FR20/2015, September. The FSB also produces regular implementation report regarding a variety of issues including securitization regulation implementation, via fsb.org.

[317] IOSCO and the BCBS have been working hand in hand on the matter, see BCBS, (2015), Criteria for Identifying Simple, Transparent and Comparable Securitisations, Basel, July.

[318] Falls apart in (1) nature of the assets, (2) asset performance history, (3) payment status, (4) consistency of underwriting, (5) asset selection and transfer and (6) initial and ongoing data.

[319] Falls apart in (1) redemption cash flows, (2) currency and interest rate asset and liability mismatches, (3) payment priorities and observability, (4) voting and enforcement rights, (5) documentation disclosure and legal review and (7) alignment of interests.

[320] Falls apart in (1) fiduciary and contractual responsibilities and (2) transparency to investors.

[321] Ibid.

[322] See EU chapter (Volume II) for a discussion.

[323] J. Kolm, (2014), Securitization, Shadow Banking and Bank Regulation, University of Vienna, Working Paper, August, mimeo, pp. 1 & 25.

> [s]ecuritization allows banks to concentrate risk on their balance sheet, which makes risk taking more profitable. It also allows for financial intermediation by shadow banks that exclusively rely on securitization for external funding. Capital regulation that only covers traditional, deposit taking banks will lead to the emergence of excessively risky shadow banks. When capital regulation is only concerned with the soundness of traditional banks shadow banking may even fully crowd out traditional banking. Unregulated shadow banks can also lead to overinvestment.

He demonstrates that capital regulation can only prevent excessive risk taking when securitization activities and shadow banks are properly taken into account. Capital regulation can prevent excessive risk taking when the amount of equity capital that banks have to raise per unit of investment does not decrease with higher levels of securitization. Such capital requirements must require shadow banks to hold additional capital that exceed their on-balance-sheet investment. Regulating securitization can substitute for capital regulation of shadow banks. Securitization restrictions limit the amount of leverage that shadow banks can take, which has the same effect as capital regulation.

So that is where we might go wrong, still in 2019. The intertwining between banks and shadow banks in the securitization process and the protracted securitization chains do have a profound impact on both originating banks and their shadow banking counterparts or extended part of their business model. Ultimately, asset securitization offers banks the possibility of altering their capital structures and the financial intermediation process. This study shows that the introduction of securitization is associated with fundamental changes in the funding policies of banks. In particular, more intense use of securitization by banks (i) with stronger growth opportunities, (ii) with liquidity constraints, (iii) with costlier alternative sources of funding and (iv) with restricted access to capital markets due to adverse selection. Securitization is also observed to be higher in the pecking order of financing choices of small- and medium-size banks and non-listed banks, which are likely to face more severe adverse selection problems.[324]

That also explains the strong resentment against the EU STS/securitization regulation, that is, the framework fails to address a number of issues (predominantly 'spillovers') related to the screening of systemic risks elicited by certain uses of securitization. The linkages between the banking sector and shadow banks are attributed primarily to some uses of securitization and in particular the way it interplays with the repo market and money market funds, using the best securitized tranches as collateral. The contagion (or correlation as explained in the previous section) is caused by the fact that collateral in repo transactions can be re-used (re-hypothecated) by banks, thereby increasing the correlation between banks' portfolios and the overall systemic risk.[325] That points at a very difficult to resolve coordination problem between the different policy objectives (i.e. four specific areas of concern, viz. the difficulty to define securitization for the purpose of the regula-

[324] A. Almazan, et al., (2015), Securitization and Banks' Capital Structure, Banco de España, Documentos de Trabajo Nr. 1506, March.

[325] S. Claessens, et al., (2012), Shadow Banking: Economics and Policy, IMF Staff Discussion Note, December 4, p. 16; V. Bavoso, (2015), Good Securitisation, Bad Securitisation and the Quest for Sustainable EU Capital Markets, *Butterworths Journal of International Banking and Financial Law* Vol. 30, Nr. 4, pp. 221–225.

tion, the dangers of linkages with the shadow banking system, the unresolved reliance on external ratings and the question of STS supervision). The persistence of these problems in the current design of the securitization proposal leads to questioning whether a revived securitization market would still fuel the shadow banking system and create systemic risks. Basovo[326] further points at the difficulty to regulate complex legal relationships typical of long intermediation chains—such as tranched securitization—and which make the proposed framework still very weak. He asserts that only a tighter approach to transaction standardization could ensure the simplicity and transparency that the Commission is hoping to achieve. Equally so he concludes, a supervisory infrastructure centered on the overseeing power of a pan-European authority is needed to prevent pre-crisis legal problems from recurring and ensure macroeconomic stability.[327] Transactional standardization is resented by the industry as it is seen as intrusion into private ordering, But Basovo correctly asserts '[w]hile standardization is regarded as a non-economic and stifling innovation, it could represent the necessary regulatory strategy to achieve prudential control over the transaction's dynamics'.[328]

But that is only possible when we have developed a decent insight into not only the drivers, but also the dynamics that lead banks to engage in loan securitization. We know very little so far. What we do know is that loan securitization in Europe is a composite decision based on bank-specific as well as market- and country-specific determinants. These determinants remarkably change when separately investigating securitization transactions during the pre-crisis and crisis period. They further depend on the transaction type, the underlying asset portfolio and the regulatory and institutional environment under which banks operate. Farruggio and Uhde comment '[a]s regards bank-specific determinants, we find that larger banks, exhibiting a lower exposure to credit risk along with a higher performance are more prone to enter the securitization market and issue larger transaction volumes during the years before the financial crisis. In contrast, empirical results also indicate that securitization is mainly driven by the banks' need for liquidity during the crisis period. Turning to market- and country-specific determinants, we find that banks operating in European countries with fiercer banking market competition[329] and higher economic growth tend to stronger engage in the securitization business during the crisis period.' That has policy implications '[p]roviding evidence that especially a lower credit risk exposure induces securitization by European banks until the financial crisis, we suggest that only less risky banks with a higher loan portfolio quality are in fact able to transfer risk and are therefore securitizing during this period. Thus, as most banks have to retain the risky first-loss piece of a securitization transaction to serve as a quality signal towards external investors, this may hamper an efficient transfer of credit risk.

[326] V. Bavoso, (2015), High Quality Securitisation and EU Capital Markets Union—Is it Possible?, *Journal of Financial Perspectives*, Vol. 107, pp. 515–536.

[327] R. Meeks, et al., (2014), Shadow Banks and Macroeconomic Instability, Bank of England Working Paper Nr.487, p. ii.

[328] V. Bavoso, (2015), Good Securitisation, Bad Securitisation and the Quest for Sustainable EU Capital Markets, *Butterworths Journal of International Banking and Financial Law* Vol. 30, Nr. 4, pp. 224–225.

[329] See in detail: D.M. Frankel and Y. Jin, (2015), Securitization and Lending Competition, Review of Economic Studies, doi: https://doi.org/10.1093/restud/rdv013, March 30.

Hence, a more transparent securitization design could reduce possible "lemons discounts" and allow even more risky banks to engage in the loan securitization business.'[330]

And then we haven't even discussed the 'diversification' argument. Diversification allows for risk distribution across agents each having their own profile. That in itself is a good thing. But redistribution of risk through structured products also leads (possibly) to concentration of (tail) risks, something our risk management systems can't really deal with very well. And to make things worse, linear diversification[331] increases systemic risk.[332] Literature finds that diversification increases the similarity among institutions. It therefore tends to increase the probability of joint failures or systemic crises, which is the dark side of diversification. Tranching offers nonlinear diversification strategies, which can reduce the failure risk of individual institutions beyond the minimum level attainable by linear diversification, without increasing systemic risk, concluded van Oordt.[333] But, as indicated above, who is going to buy the mezzanine and junior/equity tranches. Are they going to be left behind on the originator's balance sheet against lower capital charges? And maybe more importantly van Oordt indicates '[h]owever, the benefits of securitization do come at a cost'...'structuring claims on loan portfolios into different seniority classes introduces nonlinear effects in the financial system'...'even a small unanticipated confidence shock may strongly increase the risks in the financial system due to those nonlinearities. Such a shock may rise the level of both individual and systemic risks beyond the level without any diversification.'[334] To put differently, even if systemic risk doesn't increase through securitization, it does enhance the aggregate risk profile of the FI market beyond the non-diversification level.

---

[330] C. Farruggio and A. Uhde, (2015), Determinants of Loan Securitization in European Banking, Center for Tax and Accounting Research, Taxation, Accounting and Finance (TAF) Working Paper, Nr. 7, January, pp. 25–27.

[331] Which occurs when financial institutions diversify asset holdings by exchanging shares in their projects. The difficulty with linear diversification is that losses and profits are shared among investors always. Therefore, if two banks share the ownership of two loan portfolios, the losses generated by one portfolio may trigger the insolvency of both banks. This may happen even if the other portfolio performs relatively well; M.R.C. van Oordt, (2012), Securitization and the Dark Side of Diversification, DNB Working Paper Nr. 341, March 21, Amsterdam, pp. 2–3. His conclusions can also be applied to 'syndicated loan' models and are not limited to securitization models only.

[332] Even if it reduces the risk profile if individual financial institutions; W. Wagner, (2010), Diversification at Financial Institutions and Systemic Crises, *Journal of Financial Intermediation*, Vol. 19, Issue 3, pp. 373–386.

[333] M.R.C. van Oordt, (2012), Securitization and the Dark Side of Diversification, DNB Working Paper Nr. 341, March 21, Amsterdam.

[334] M.R.C. van Oordt, (2012), Ibid. p. 3.

4

Securities Lending and Repos

4.1 Introduction

As discussed before, the Financial Stability Board (FSB) has been gearing its efforts toward monitoring and controlling the shadow banking system. It has done so by focusing on five, in their understanding, critical areas. Those areas are specific areas in which policies are needed to mitigate the potential systemic risks associated with shadow banking and aim:

- to mitigate the spillover effect between the regular banking system and the shadow banking system;
- to reduce the susceptibility of money market funds (MMFs) to 'runs';
- to assess and align the incentives associated with securitization;
- to dampen risks and procyclical incentives associated with securities financing transactions such as repos and securities lending that may exacerbate funding strains in times of market stress and
- to assess and mitigate systemic risks posed by other shadow banking entities and activities.

Policy area number four includes the analysis and recommendations related to securities lending and repos. The FSB guidelines set out recommendations for addressing financial stability risks in this area, including enhanced transparency, regulation of securities financing and improvements to market structure. It also included consultative proposals on minimum standards for methodologies to calculate haircuts on non-centrally cleared

For a literature overview, see FSB, (2012), Securities Lending and Repos: Market Overview and Financial Stability Issues Interim Report of the FSB Workstream on Securities Lending and Repos, Annex 3, pp. 36–41.

L. Nijs, *The Handbook of Global Shadow Banking, Volume I*,
https://doi.org/10.1007/978-3-030-34743-7_4

securities financing transactions and a framework of numerical haircut floors. It is on these recommendations that the European Commission proposed EU-specific rules in this area late January 2014 (infra).

The FSB acknowledges itself that the credit intermediation process in itself, when appropriately conducted, provides a valuable alternative to bank funding that supports real economic activity. It also recognizes, helped by the events in 2008 onward, that the shadow banking system has the capacity for some non-bank entities and transactions to operate on a large scale in ways that create bank-like risks to financial stability (longer-term credit extension based on short-term funding and leverage).[1]

Just like traditional banks, a leveraged and maturity-transforming shadow banking system can be vulnerable to 'runs' and generate contagion risk, thereby amplifying systemic risk. Such activity, if unattended, can also heighten procyclicality by accelerating credit supply and asset price increases during surges in confidence, while making precipitate falls in asset prices and credit more likely by creating credit channels vulnerable to sudden loss of confidence (i.e. the dislocation of asset-backed commercial paper [ABCP] in the financial crisis).

One of the key questions often forgotten when it comes to regulating market activities is the focus on proportionality. To what degree is the intended regulation proportionate with the impact it will have in terms of compliance, costs and reduction of market maturity and depth. A lot of the lost pricing power is ultimately pushed forward to the end customer through higher prices. The question is relevant and more refined that some of the political and regulatory responses we all have been witnessing during and after the financial crisis, especially when it comes to the future supervision of the (shadow) banking sector. Nevertheless, there is reason for concern or at least deeper thinking. The global cost of compliance was recently estimated at 1.2 trillion USD[2] and soaring. Against that backdrop the FSB argues that their approach is designed to be proportionate to financial stability risks, focusing on those activities that are material to the system, and includes monitoring of the shadow banking system so that any rapidly growing new activities that pose bank-like risks can be identified early and, where needed, those risks addressed.

Although potentially jumping the gun, I feel that the monitoring models and protocols suggested are like screening the universe in search for intelligent life using human life as we know as the prototype. Logical, but not necessarily successful as the systemic risk transform as activities moving in and out of the paradigm that constitutes the shadow banking sector partly defined by the type and evolution of the regulation imposed on the traditional banking sector.

[1] FSB, (2013), Strengthening Oversight and Regulation of Shadow Banking Policy Framework for Addressing Shadow Banking Risks in Securities Lending and Repos, (29 August), p. ii.

[2] Berwin Leighton Paisner, (2013), Speed of Business. Innovation, Business Growth and the Impact of Regulation.

In November 2012, the FSB published its consultative document[3] 'A Policy Framework for Addressing Shadow Banking Risks in Securities Lending[4] and Repos' which identified the financial stability issues (or shadow banking risks) in securities lending and repo markets and set out 13 policy recommendations to address such risks. These recommendations were based on the discussion documented in the report 'Securities Lending and Repos: Market Overview and Financial Stability Issues'.[5]

These recommendations included improvements in regulatory reporting[6] and market transparency; regulation of securities financing (e.g. minimum standards for methodologies used by market participants in calculating the 'haircuts' [margins] that limit the amount of financing that can be provided against a given security and minimum standards on cash collateral reinvestment), as well as policy recommendations related to structural aspects of the securities financing markets such as central clearing. The FSB also invited at that point in time views on the possible introduction of a framework of numerical haircut floors for certain securities financing transactions which are intended to limit the extent to which financial entities, including non-banks, can use securities financing transactions to obtain leverage.

The FSB had some further concerns: it wanted to ensure that its recommendations minimize the risk of regulatory arbitrage as well as undue distortion of markets and are consistent with other international regulatory initiatives. It therefore ordered a quantitative impact assessment.[7]

The policy recommendations of the FSB on securities lending and repos are categorized in three broad groups in accordance with the nature of the (initial) recommendations:

- improvement in transparency;
- regulation of securities financing and
- structural aspects of the securities financing markets.

---

[3] FSB, (2012), Consultative Document Strengthening Oversight and Regulation of Shadow Banking. A Policy Framework for Addressing Shadow Banking Risks in Securities Lending and Repos, Basel. It translated in the final version released in August 2013. Some thoughts are retaken from the 2012 report before dealing with the 2013 final report.

[4] For a generic introduction to the securities lending market, parties involved and market structure, and status quo: Blackrock, (2015), Securities Lending: the Facts, Viewpoint, May, pp. 1–6; ISLA (International Securities Lending Association), (2014), Securities Lending. A Guide for Policymakers; P.C. Lipson et al., (2012), Securities Lending, Federal Reserve Bank of NY Staff Reports, Nr.555, March (original version August 1989); M.C. Faulkner, (2007), An Introduction to Securities Lending, Spitalfields Advisors, 4th Ed., London.

[5] FSB, (2012), Securities Lending and Repos: Market Overview and Financial Stability Issues Interim Report of the FSB Workstream on Securities Lending and Repos, Basel.

[6] See FSB/BIS, (2018), Securities Financing Transactions, Reporting Guidelines, March 5, via fsb.org on the actual reporting requirements. Also: EC, (2017), Report from the Commission to the European Parliament and the Council under Article 29(3) of Regulation (EU) 2015/2365 of November 25, 2015, on transparency of securities financing transactions and of re-use and amending Regulation (EU) No 648/2012, October 19, Brussels.

[7] To assess the potential impact and unintended consequences associated with its recommendations on minimum haircut methodology standards and numerical haircut floors.

4.2 An Overview of the Securities Lending Market

The securities financing markets can be divided into four main, interlinked segments[8]: (1) a securities lending segment, (2) a leveraged investment fund financing and securities borrowing segment, (3) an inter-dealer repo segment and (4) a repo financing segment.

1. The securities lending segment includes lending of securities by institutional investors (e.g. insurance companies, pension funds, investment funds) or banks to banks and broker-dealers (through their prime brokerage units and/or cash/derivatives trading operations) against the collateral of cash securities. In general, borrowers may borrow specific securities for covering short positions in their own portfolios, for example, arising from market-making activities, or on behalf of their customers. Another option would be for use as collateral in repo financing and other transactions[9] (infra).
2. The leveraged investment fund financing and securities borrowing segment includes financing of leveraged investment funds' long positions by banks and broker-dealers using both reverse repo and margin lending secured against assets held with prime brokers, as well as securities lending to hedge funds by prime brokers to cover short positions.[10] This segment is tightly linked to the securities lending chapter, which is used by prime brokers to borrow securities to on-lend to hedge funds.
3. The inter-dealer repo category includes mainly government bond repo transactions among banks and broker-dealers. These are typically used to finance long positions by using general collateral repos (against T-bonds normally). They can also be used to borrow specific securities via special repos. Banks and certain broker-dealers may borrow specific securities to cover short positions, to hedge trading positions, to support their market-making activities or to take interest rate risk in the case of term repos. This segment of the market is typically cleared by central counterparties (CCPs).[11]
4. The repo financing segment includes repo transactions primarily executed by banks and broker-dealers to borrow cash from 'cash-rich' entities, including central banks, retail banks, money market funds (MMFs), securities lenders and increasingly non-financial corporations. The drivers of this market segment are primarily the short-term financing needs of banks and broker-dealers, as well as the desire of institutional cash managers to hold collateralized, 'money-like' investments. It has become common practice that collateral movements and valuation are outsourced to tri-party agents (the so-called tri-party repo[12]). Collateral often includes government bonds, corporate bonds, structured products, money market instruments and equities. The

---

[8] See for a detailed analysis FSB, (2012), Ibid. Annex 1, pp. 19–31.

[9] FSB, (2012), Securities Lending and Repos. Market Overview and Financial Stability Issues, Interim report of the FSB Workstream on Securities Lending and Repos, p. 2.

[10] FSB, (2012), Ibid. pp. 2–3.

[11] FSB, (2012), Ibid. p. 3.

[12] See on the origins and developments of the US tri-party repo market: A. Martin and S. McLaughlin, (2015), Financial Innovation: The Origins of the Tri-Party Repo Market, Liberty Street Economics,

share of asset-backed securities (ABSs) used as repo collateral has declined sharply since the crisis. Transactions are predominantly short term but there is an emerging longer-term market.[13]

Those four segments interact in the market and are to a large degree integrated often on a global basis.[14] Although this marketplace consists of four segments, there are a number of key drivers that are common to the four segments and help understanding the dynamics of this market as such.

1. Repo as a Near-Substitute for Central Bank and Insured Bank Deposit Money

There is significant demand by certain risk-averse institutions for 'money-like' instruments to support their primary investment objectives of preserving principal and liquidity. This type of investor includes o.a. MMFs, those seeking to reinvest cash collateral from securities lending activities, commercial banks that are required to hold certain liquidity buffers, pension funds, investment funds and insurance companies and securitization vehicles. A key characteristic of repos is that it allows banks, broker-dealers and other intermediaries to create 'collateralized' short-term liabilities provided they can access underlying collateral securities meeting the credit and regulatory requirements of the cash lenders.[15]

2. Securities-Based Financing Needs

This involves the financing needs of leveraged intermediaries. Banks and regulated broker-dealers use these markets both as part of their wider wholesale funding and more particularly for securities dealing. But some unregulated non-bank intermediaries, such as ABCP conduits and CDOs, did make use of repo financing alongside other sources of money market funding such as ABCP issuance before the crisis as part of the shadow banking system.[16]

3. Leveraged Investment Fund Financing and Short-Covering Needs

This segment is built around the facilitation of hedge fund and other investment strategies involving leverage and short selling. A significant amount of hedge funds aren't sufficiently creditworthy in order to borrow securities unsecured or directly from long-term institutional investors. Their prime brokers take care of the financing from them and identify and borrow the securities for them which they intend to short. By bringing together

NY Federal Reserve Bank, May 11 (part 1), May 13 (part 2), via libertystreeteconomics.newyorkfed.org

[13] FSB, (2012), Ibid. p. 4.

[14] See for a visualization, FSB (2012), Ibid. p. 5.

[15] FSB, (2012), Ibid. p. 6.

[16] FSB, (2012), Ibid. p. 6.

the supply of lendable and available securities in the market, prime brokers provide hedge funds with stable securities loans allowing them to maintain short positions while providing securities lenders with the liquidity to recall securities loans if they wish.[17]

4. Banks and Broker-Dealers' Demand for 'Collateral Mining'

This market has been built around the increasing need for banks and broker-dealers to gain access to securities for the purpose of optimizing the collateralization of repos, securities loans and derivatives. 'Collateral mining' refers to the practice whereby banks and broker-dealers obtain and exchange securities in order to collateralize their other activities. Indeed, the creation of money-like repo liabilities requires collateral, and therefore the borrowing capacity of banks and broker-dealers depends on the total amount of non-cash collateral available to them.[18]

5. Securities and Agent Lenders' Demand for Enhanced Returns

Additional returns by institutional investors, such as pension funds, insurance companies and investment funds are another driver behind the repo and securities lending market. Most lend out securities in order to generate additional income on their portfolio holdings at minimal risk, to help offset the cost of maintaining the portfolio or to generate incremental returns. Agent lenders may take a share of their clients' lending income (net of borrower rebates paid out) arising from lending fees or cash collateral reinvestment.[19]

4.3 Positioning of the Repo and Securities Lending Market Within the Shadow Banking Industry

The critical component in the story is the use of the collateral by banks in these transactions. Although not all might require an (immediate) policy response, the FSB identified four main zones of activity within shadow banking for repo and securities transaction[20]:

- Borrowing through repo financing markets, including against securitized collateral, creates 'leverage' and facilitates 'maturity and liquidity transformation'. Repo transactions allow a variety of institutions, including banks, to create short-term collateralized liabilities. Repo financing is typically short term but collateralized with longer-maturity assets, it often has embedded risks associated with 'maturity transformation'. It can also involve liquidity transformation depending on the type of securities used as repo collateral.
- The extent to which leveraged financing leads to maturity transformation and leverage.

[17] FSB, (2012), Ibid. p. 7.
[18] FSB, (2012), Ibid. p. 8.
[19] FSB, (2012), Ibid. p. 8.
[20] FS, (2012), Ibid. pp. 8–9.

- The chain of transactions through which the cash proceeds from short sales are used to collateralize securities borrowing and then reinvested by securities lenders, into longer-term assets, including repo financing. This activity can mutate from conservative reinvestment of cash in 'safe' collateral into more risky reinvestment of cash collateral in search of greater investment returns.
- Collateral swaps (also known as collateral downgrades/upgrades) involving lending of high-quality securities (e.g. government bonds) against the collateral of lower-quality securities (e.g. equities, ABSs), often at longer maturities and with wide collateral haircuts. Banks then use the borrowed securities to obtain repo financing, which can further lengthen transaction chains, or hold them to meet regulatory liquidity requirements.

Given these observations, many countries have enacted specific repo and/or securities lending legislation. By comparison with 'financial market intermediaries' such as banks and broker-dealers, regulations and activity restrictions on lenders such as investment firms, pension funds and insurance companies vary considerably by jurisdiction and type of entity. In general, these regulations are focused more on investor/policyholder protection than financial stability considerations.[21] In most cases, legislation is built around counterparty credit, liquidity and concentration risk and conditions for collateral use.[22]

Already in 2012, the FB concluded that a number of financial stability risks are immanent in the repo and securities lending market, although not equally across all segments distributed. The seven categories identified were[23]:

1. Lack of transparency and the overall lack of data availability/consistency at the macro and micro level as well as corporate and risk disclosures of participants.
2. Procyclicality triggered by system leverage and its interconnectedness (including the valuation of collateralized securities), haircuts and collateral velocity ('or the length of collateral re-use chains, can also be procyclical'). Procyclicality refers to the tendency of financial variables to fluctuate together with the economic cycle. This procyclical behavior of securities financing markets depends, in addition to changes in counterparty credit limits, on three underlying factors: (i) the value of collateral securities available and accepted by market participants. Changes in the market value of lent securities (e.g. equities) feed directly into changes in the value of cash collateral required against securities lending and then reinvested in the money market. This creates a procyclical link between securities market valuations and the availability of funding in the money markets, (ii) the haircuts applied on those collateral securities and (iii) collateral velocity (the rate at which collateral is re-used).

[21] For a full review of the involved legislation, see FSB, (2012), Ibid. pp. 9–14.

[22] See for an overview of securities financing and collateral use: Joachim Keller et al., (2014), Securities Financing Transactions and the (Re)-Use of Collateral in Europe, ESBR Occasional Paper Series Nr. 6, September. Includes analysis regarding to and from banks of collateral flows, collateral re-use, network structures and cross-institutional exposures, collateral and maturity transformation and the reinvestment rate of cash collateral.

[23] See in detail: FSB, (2012), Ibid. pp. 14–19.

3. Increased interconnectedness among firms and for higher leverage with respect to collateral re-use.
4. Risks related to fire sales of collateralized assets in case of defaulting of the counterparty in a transaction. When a defaulting party's collateral assets pool is largely relative to the market and concentrated in less liquid asset classes, this may cause system-wide stress.
5. Agent lender practices' risk (e.g. shortfall of assets held by financial intermediaries in their capacity as custodians. Agent lender offer indemnities for borrowers default but scope, caps and practices vary widely.
6. Cash collateral reinvestment risk. By reinvesting cash collateral received from securities lending transactions, any entity with portfolio holdings can effectively perform 'bank-like' activities, such as credit and maturity transformation, thereby subjecting its portfolio to credit and liquidity risks. Lenders can use securities lending as a means of short-term funding for financing leveraged investment in instruments that, while highly rated when purchased, can become illiquid and risky and lose value quickly.
7. Lack of consistency in collateral valuation and management practices, that is, not mark-to-market their holdings of MBS or based decisions on prices generated by overly optimistic models.

This assessment has been central in the work and ultimately policy suggestions and directions the FSB has been providing ever since 2012. These dynamics will be discussed in the following subsets of this chapter and are based on the final FSB policy recommendations as issued in 2013 regarding securities lending and repos.

4.4 Financial Stability Risk

Securities lending and repo markets play crucial roles in supporting price discovery and secondary market liquidity for a variety of securities[24] issued by both public and private agents. They are central to financial intermediaries' abilities to make markets and facilitate the implementation of various investment, risk management and collateral management strategies.[25] The generic risks that the FSB identified in the shadow banking market are the creation of 'money-like' liabilities, carrying out maturity/liquidity transformation, and obtaining leverage, including short-term financing of longer-term assets, some of which may run the risk of becoming illiquid or losing value. The FSB split those risks in two categories:

[24] See recently N. Foley-Fisher et al., (2019), Over-the-Counter Market Liquidity and Securities Lending, BIS Working Paper Nr. 768, February 19, via bis.org. The shutdown of (AIG's securities) lending program in 2008 caused a reduction in the market liquidity of corporate bonds. Dealers used the inter-dealer market as an imperfect substitute for the securities lending market. They show how over-the-counter market liquidity is affected by securities lending.

[25] FSB, (2013), Strengthening Oversight and Regulation of Shadow banking. Policy Framework for addressing Shadow banking Risks in Securities Lending and Repos, August 29, p. 4.

- 'pure' shadow banking risks—that is, maturity/liquidity transformation and leverage outside the banking sector (1)
- risks that span both banking and shadow banking (2)

1. Pure Shadow Banking Risks

   - Using repos to create short-term, money-like liabilities, facilitating credit growth and maturity/liquidity transformation outside the banking system. The build-up of leverage and maturity transformation outside the scope of the traditional banking regulation regarding liquidity and capital requirements.
   - Securities lending cash collateral reinvestment. This is a very sizeable operation, that is, over 1 trillion USD[26] and is facilitated by custodian banks and agents. The risk is that cash collateral reinvestment can involve maturity and liquidity transformation, which if left unchecked can present risks and negative externalities to firms beyond the beneficial owner or agent lender in a stress event.[27]

2. Risks that Span Banking and Shadow Banking

   - *Tendency of securities financing to increase procyclicality of system leverage.* The wide volatility of asset valuations over time tends to accentuate the procyclicality of any given banking system. A system based on securities lending may be additionally prone to that procyclicality, that is, because of the direct relationship of funding levels to fluctuating assets levels and volatility. A system based on unsecured financing might be equally prone to volatility as counterparty trust erodes.
   - *Risk of a fire sale of collateral securities.* In case of a counterparty default, creditors in the repo and securities lending market tend to have an inclination to sell their collateralized securities also because of regulatory restrictions on portfolio holdings, limited operational or risk management capacity or a need for liquidity. This may lead to sharp price falls that create mark-to-market losses for all holders of those securities.
   - *Re-hypothecation of unencumbered assets.* Re-hypothecation tends to replace ownership of securities with a contractual claim on a financial institution to return equivalent securities, with ownership of the re-hypothecated securities transferring to this institution. Re-hypothecation of client assets can create financial stability risks especially if clients are uncertain about the extent to which their assets have been re-hypothecated. For example, uncertainty may increase the possibility of a run on a prime broker if there are concerns about its credit worthiness. To the extent that the client has no offsetting indebtedness to the financial institution, the contractual obligation to return equivalent securities is akin to an unsecured obligation in some jurisdictions. The financial institution can in turn re-use those securities, for example, as collateral to borrow money in the wholesale markets.[28]

[26] Data from the Quarterly Aggregate Composite survey.

[27] FSB, (2013), Ibid. p. 4.

[28] FSB, (2013), Ibid. p. 5.

- *Interconnectedness arising from chains of transactions involving the re-use of collateral.* Contagion risk might exist due to large exposures among large financial institutions. Securities financing transactions typically involve small direct exposures as the process of daily variation margining largely or entirely offsets the contractual liabilities of the two parties, unless the default of a counterparty coincides with or is quickly followed by a large movement in collateral valuations, or if netting agreements are not legally enforceable.[29]
- *Inadequate collateral valuation practices.* When the prices of sub-prime mortgage-backed securities (MBS) fell during the early stage of the financial crisis, a number of financial institutions failed to mark their positions to true market value (in part due to valuation uncertainty) and later revealed significant losses. Arguably, the decline in MBS prices would have caused a smaller disruption in the market had such price changes been reflected in balance sheets earlier and more gradually through continuous marking-to-market.[30]

4.5 Improving Transparency: More (and Better) Data for Monitoring and Policy Design

It has already been referred to on a number of occasions throughout the book that part of what created the depth of the financial crisis was the lack of understanding and visibility of what were the underlying drivers of the lack of trust in the financial system and to what degree harmless micro-risk exposures could, on aggregate, pose systemic risk(s) to the system. Effective monitoring requires time and the ability to evaluate larger datasets. The (early parts of) financial crisis learned that authorities were hindered by lacking, incomplete or untimely datasets that 'impeded their ability to identify the build-up of vulnerabilities in the lead-up to the crisis and to recognize emerging risks in these markets soon after they emerged, and to get a comprehensive picture of trends and developments across the full range of market participants'…'authorities found themselves repeatedly dealing with relatively late-stage market developments that sparked systemic risk transmission during this period'.[31] The following elements could be considered opaque to authorities at that point in time:

- Vulnerability of some repo market segments to runs and fire sales of underlying collateral
- The flaws in the assumption that securities financing is always durable even in a stressed market
- The degree to which systemically important players were conducting material maturity, liquidity and credit risk transformation in the course of their securities financing and collateral management activities

[29] FSB, (2013), Ibid. p. 6.
[30] FSB, (2013), Ibid. p. 6.
[31] FSB, (2013), Ibid. p. 6.

The fact that in the securities lending and repo markets (large) financial institutions can and do build up large 'direct' exposures vis-à-vis create three categories of 'implicit but significant' risks[32]:

- The failure of a large institution could destabilize one or more of its counterparties and possibly the broader markets in which it is active.
- A systemically important financial institution that is otherwise solvent but highly reliant on short-term wholesale funding could suffer a liquidity shortage during a broad-based run (due, e.g. to concerns about a specific asset class or the stability of a market infrastructure) that threatens its viability and poses risk to its counterparties and broader markets.
- Entities outside the banking system could finance themselves using securities lending and repos in ways that create significant but not necessarily readily apparent system-wide leverage and maturity transformation. For example, the use of securities lending and repos outside the banking system creates liabilities that are thought to be safe, short-term and liquid—in effect cash equivalents. These may be vulnerable to runs in periods of stress as investors realize that their resemblance to cash or insured deposits in normal times has disappeared in the face of uncertainty about their underlying value. The resulting forced sales of assets whose values are already under pressure can accelerate an adverse feedback loop, in which all forms with similar assets suffer mark-to-market losses, which in turn can lead to more fire sales.

Authorities need to augment their data collection so as to capture more granular and timely information on securities lending and repo exposures between financial institutions, including on the composition and evolution of the underlying collateral and this to enhance detection of risk concentrations, such as large exposures to particular institutions and heavy dependence on particular collateral asset classes. The FSB Data Gaps[33] Initiative is one of the recommended tools to leverage on as well, within a European context, the European Systemic Risk Board (ESRB) is currently working to enhance monitoring of securities financing transactions.[34] Regardless of how one compiles those datasets, if the ultimate objective of enhanced data collection is the monitoring of financial stability risks, it is desirable to get a comprehensive (and consistent) view of the securities financing markets. The economic equivalence of, and similarities between, repo and securities lending transactions would easily enable market participants to circumvent transparency requirements targeted at only part of the market by re-characterizing the transactions.[35]

[32] FSB, (2013), Ibid. p. 7.

[33] 'Which currently collects data on securities financing transactions and is developing a framework for pooling and sharing relevant data on the major bilateral linkages between large international financial institutions, and on their common exposures to and funding dependencies on countries, sectors and financial instruments' (FSB, (2013), Ibid. p. 7).

[34] A. Bouveret et al. (2013), Towards a Monitoring Framework for Securities Financing Transactions, ESRB Occasional Paper Series Nr. 2, March 2013.

[35] FSB, (2013), Ibid. p. 8. See also Appendices 5 and 6 for a detailed review of all suggested parameters, pp. 44–46.

One of the challenges is the need for a wide set of different data that are needed to draw meaningful conclusions. A combination of trade flow and position data might be required to provide multiple angles to what might become a systemic problem. Given the fact that national authorities are faced with different types of economies, markets, different levels of financial innovation and more importantly different types of regulation, the FSB doesn't want to be too stringent with respect to what and how datasets should be compiled, including building upon existing datasets, market infrastructure and tools already available. Nevertheless, the FSB acknowledges as well that a national potpourri of different datasets will make global coordination and a global learning curve potentially very difficult when it argues: '[h]owever, national/regional data collection efforts should be designed according to a common set of data standards across borders and financial instruments, to facilitate aggregation at the global level'.[36] The FSB sees itself as the global aggregator of data, at least if they meet a certain standard. Data that would be processed 'would need to be subject to appropriate governance standards, aggregated and would represent a subset of what is collected, regardless of the collection approach used locally'.[37]

The FSB provides an overview of data it might require interesting from a global systemic risk perspective with respect to two categories, that is, repo transactions and securities lending transactions.[38] The regime for data collection is a work in progress and there is a technical data expert group established in order to answer some of the technical, but strategically relevant questions.[39]

The FSB is further looking to enhance the corporate disclosures financial organization make available through their regulatory filings and audited financial statements. The FSB is of the opinion that often such information falls well short of what regulators would ideally seek to be included in order to monitor the build-up of systemic risk in normal times. Also the transmission between firms during a stress event would have to be monitored. That information is not made readily available. In particular the FSB indicates, disclosures are often not only relatively aggregated, they tend to focus more on size than risk and vary significantly across firms and jurisdictions in terms of the level of detail. Disclosure is particularly poor in relation to transactions, such as collateral swaps, that do not involve cash.[40]

The Enhanced Disclosure Task Force (EDTF) was established by the FSB in May 2012 to improve the risk disclosures of banks and other financial institutions. The first report of the Task Force was issued in October 2012 under the title 'Enhancing the Risk Disclosures of Banks'.[41] Then, the primary objectives of the EDTF were to (1) develop fundamental principles for enhanced risk disclosures; (2) recommend improvements to current risk

---

[36] FSB, (2013), Ibid. p. 8.

[37] FSB, (2013), Ibid. pp. 8–9. See FSB, (2015), Standards and Processes for Global Securities Financing Data Collection and Aggregation, November 18, for the most recent and finalized standards and processes for data gathering.

[38] The full list of datasets can be found at FSB, (2013), Ibid. p. 9.

[39] FSB, (2013), Ibid. p. 9 for an overview of the open questions the technical working group is dealing with.

[40] FSB, (2013), Ibid. p. 10.

[41] See Report of the Enhanced Disclosure Group, (2012), Enhancing the Risk Disclosures of Banks, October 29.

disclosures, including ways to enhance their comparability; and (3) identify examples of best or leading practice risk disclosures presented by global financial institutions.[42]

The FSB is also concerned about the use of repos and securities lending transactions by fund managers for 'efficient portfolio management' purposes, that is, either for investment objectives or for enhancing returns. The FSB is particularly concerned about the fact that fund managers, through these transactions, have access to leverage on their client's portfolios. The FSB sees the need for 'appropriate information on such activities needs to be frequently disclosed by fund managers to investors in order to allow those investors to select their investments with due consideration of the risks taken by fund managers'. Often, fund managers rely on information provided by third parties, that is, custodian banks, agents and so on. The FSB would prefer to see a practice emerging whereby fund managers provide proprietary information to end customers directly in a variety of areas.[43]

A number of recent initiatives should help to reduce the data gaps that still exist and fill some remaining gaps. In November 2014, the FSB[44] issued a consultative document 'Standard and Processes for Global Securities Financing', and exactly a year later in November 2015 they released their final outlook on the matter.[45]

It is my personal appreciation that many vulnerabilities continue to exist in both the (third-party) (reverse) repo market and the securities lending market[46] and that despite the regulation implemented in recent years.[47] Most of them relate to leverage and liquidity-related risk, the continued risk of fire sales and the treatment, valuation and indemnification of the collateral position in the pool of transactions possible. Transparency and the creation of more granular datasets will help, but until we can get a better grip on a highly complex environment, I can't feel bad about the fact that volumes in the repo segment, and across the

[42] EDTF Report (2012), Ibid. p. 2.

[43] For an overview, see FSB, (2013), Ibid. pp. 11–12.

[44] FSB, (2014), Standards and Processes for Global Securities Financing Data Collection and Aggregation, November 13.

[45] FSB, (2015), Standards and Processes for Global Securities Financing Data Collection and Aggregation, November 18. This report builds on policy recommendations to address financial stability risks in SFTs published, by the FSB in August 2013, in particular its recommendations to improve transparency of securities financing markets. The report sets out finalized standards and processes to allow the FSB to periodically collect from national and regional authorities aggregated data on SFTs. It also includes recommendations to national and regional authorities for the collection of consistent and comprehensive data from market participants.

[46] For a very good recent and updated overview of the parties, transactions and vulnerabilities in the repo and securities markets, see V. Baklanova et al., (2015), Reference Guide to the U.S. Repo and Securities Lending Market, Federal Reserve Bank of NY, Staff Reports Nr. 740, September (also released as OFR Research Paper 15–17, September 9).

[47] For example, in the EU a proposal was launched regarding transparency and securities financing transactions ('SFTR')—(further discussed in the EU chapter); Proposal for a REGULATION OF THE EUROPEAN PARLIAMENT AND OF THE COUNCIL on reporting and transparency of securities financing transactions, COM(2014) 40 final of January 29, 2014. On October 29, 2015, SFTR was adopted by the European Parliament and on November 16, 2015, the SFTR was adopted by Council of the European Union. The regulation 2015/2365 (OJ L 337, 23.12.2015, pp. 1–34) came into force on January 16, 2016 and applied as of July 17, 2017. Since the regulation came into force, many delegated acts and technical standards have been enacted and implemented. See: ec.europa.eu for further details.

subsegments, have been dropping materially compared to pre-crisis levels.[48] The situation is quite a bit different and where volumes are up throughout the period 2015–2019 and now constitutes a 2+ Tr. USD market. Securities lending was known in the past to relate to hedge funds who used the technique to short certain securities. But in recent years, policy makers have created their own demand for securities lending and which related to the fixed-income segment. Jenkins indicates '[o]n the supply side, you could catalogue it in the bulging file of market distortions caused by ultra-low interest rates. Asset managers have found themselves so desperate for returns that they are getting inventive in their investment strategies and are lending out more of their assets for longer. The fees they get in exchange boost returns but expose investors to the risk that counterparties default'.[49] It is apparent that new rules on bank capital, liquidity and the clearing of derivatives transactions are overhauling the way banks manage their balance sheets—and making the borrowing of ultra-safe bonds a good shortcut to compliance. Also here regulatory arbitrage is a central theme as Jenkins illustrates in a triple fashion: (1) banks are boosting their liquid assets to comply with the new Basel III requirement known as the liquidity coverage ratio; (2) the second trick is that the exchange of assets can be a boon to capital, with equities that tend to attract higher capital weightings swapped for 'risk-free' bonds and (3) with so much derivatives trading moving to central counterparty clearing, there is increasing demand for high-quality assets to be used as collateral. Government bonds—even borrowed ones—avoid punitive haircuts imposed on some equities. This could be seen as moving risk from the banks to the asset managers. The banks reduce their risk, but asset managers assess their additional (counterparty) risk as modest. Somewhere through the backdoor risk moved from the regulated to the unregulated system and even on aggregate reduced, at least as far as the economic agents can oversee at this point in time.

4.6 Future Policy Dynamics

The FSB is convinced that the following areas require further instrumental guidance in terms of policy design and data management: (1) cash collateral reinvestment, (2) requirements in case of re-hypothecation, (3) standards for collateral valuation and management, (4) central clearing in the securities financing market and (5) bankruptcy law treatment of repos and securities lending transactions.

1. Cash Collateral Reinvestment

The minimum standards for cash collateral reinvestment by securities lenders (or their agents) should focus on 'limiting risks arising from cash collateral reinvestment where

[48] However, it is still a multi-trillion dollar/euro market and so therefore still has the potential to destabilize the wider system and economy. The ICMA group (icmagroup.org), the NY Fed (newyorkfed.org), the Eurexpo (eurexpo.com) and the SIFMA (sifma.org) provide details about the volumes of the markets in the different parts of the world.

[49] J. Jenkins, (2015), Regulators' Boost For Securities Lending Has Risky Implications, *Financial Times*, November 30.

securities are lent at call or at short maturities', giving rise to 'liquidity risk'.[50] Given the global nature of securities lending activity, the minimum standards should ideally apply across all jurisdictions and economically equivalent activities in order to limit opportunities for regulatory arbitrage. These minimum standards should apply to all financial entities that are engaged, with or without an agent, in securities lending against cash collateral where the cash collateral is reinvested in a portfolio of assets. Those institutions can include, but are not limited to, pension funds, mutual funds and insurance companies. Financial intermediaries are outside the scope of the minimum standards if they are subject to regulation of capital and liquidity/maturity transformation. In implementing the minimum standards, jurisdictions may need to take into account jurisdiction-specific circumstances while maintaining international consistency to address common risks and to avoid creating cross-border arbitrage opportunities.[51]

The minimum standards suggested by the FSB include a number of principles and a number of specific considerations addressing liquidity risk, maturity transformation and concentration and credit risks. That is beyond the typical implementation and disclosure requirements. In headline terms the following 'principles'[52] were adhered to:

- The securities lender and/or its agent should take into account the possibility that the cash collateral could be recalled at any time by the party that borrowed securities. Does the firm hold sufficient liquid assets to meet potential or foreseeable recalls (liquidity risk).
- Capital preservation should be a primary objective, that is, could an unexpectedly large requests for returning cash collateral be met if the market for the assets in which the cash collateral has been reinvested became illiquid and liquidating the assets would result in a loss.
- Cash collateral reinvestment should be consistent with the securities lender's stated and approved investment policy, so as not to add substantial incremental risk to the firm's risk profile (size of cash collateral reinvestment versus size of total activities of the firm).
- Investment guidelines (and subsequent modifications) for securities lending cash collateral reinvestment should be formally documented.
- Securities lenders should explicitly approve, formally document and regularly review investment guidelines that govern cash collateral reinvestment.
- Assets the securities lender and/or its agent hold to meet cash collateral calls should be highly liquid with transparent pricing so that they can be valued at least on a daily basis and sold, if needed, at a price close to their pre-sale valuation.

[50] See also: F.M. Keane, (2013), Securities Loans Collateralized by Cash: Reinvestment Risk, Run Risk, and Incentive Issues, Federal Reserve Bank of NY, Current Issues in Economics and Finance, Vol. 19, Nr. 3, pp. 1–8.

[51] FSB, (2013), Ibid. p. 12.

[52] See in detail FSB, (2013), Ibid. pp. 12–13.

With respect to the mitigation liquidity, credit and other risks associated with cash collateral reinvestment, the following guidelines were issued[53]:

- The securities lender and/or its agent should reinvest the cash collateral in a way that limits the potential for maturity mismatch and should hold assets that are sufficiently liquid and low risk to meet reasonably foreseeable demands for cash collateral redemption, together with a buffer to guard against stress scenarios. An appropriate risk management structure should be developed.
- Specific requirements for the cash collateral reinvestment portfolio and/or liquidity pool maintained to meet cash collateral recalls should be set by relevant authorities, but adhering to the following guidelines:
- A minimum portion of the cash collateral is to be kept in short-term deposits, held in highly liquid short-term assets (such as high-quality government treasury bills and bonds), or invested in short tenor transactions (such as overnight or open reverse repos backed by highly liquid assets) that can be easily converted to cash over short time horizons (day/week), to meet potential recalls of cash collateral.
- Specific limits for the weighted average maturity (WAM) and/or weighted average life (WAL) of the portfolio in which the cash collateral is reinvested.[54]

  - A maximum remaining term to maturity for any single investment in which the cash collateral is reinvested. The maximum could vary by asset class based on the liquidity of the instruments (optional).
  - Concentration limits for the cash collateral reinvestment portfolio to limit the firm's exposure to individual securities, issuers, guarantors, security types and counterparties. These limits could be lower for less liquid assets (optional).

2. Re-hypothecation Requirements

'Re-hypothecation' (re-use of client assets) and 're-use' (any use of securities delivered in one transaction in order to collateralize another transaction) can be used to facilitate leverage. Therefore a number of safeguards need to be in place[55]:

- Sufficient disclosure should be provided to clients with respect to re-hypothecation of assets so that clients can understand their exposures, particularly in case of stress at the level of the financial intermediary.

---

[53] See in detail FSB, (2013), Ibid. pp. 13–14.

[54] 'In a WAM calculation, the interest rate reset date for variable and floating rate securities can usually be used instead of the stated final maturity date. This provides a view on the interest rate risk but may conceal risks that a fund faces in holding securities to maturity. WAL is a complement measure that allows funds to use the date when a fund may receive payment of principal and interest instead of stated maturity to represent the life of a security. The WAL measure may be more suited to capturing pre-payment, credit or liquidity risks in a portfolio'; FSB, (2013), Ibid. p. 14 footnote 18.

[55] FSB, (2013), Ibid. pp. 15–16.

- Client assets may be re-hypothecated by an intermediary for the purpose of financing client long positions and covering short positions, but they should not be re-hypothecated for the purpose of financing the intermediary's own-account activities.
- Only entities subject to adequate regulation of liquidity risk should be allowed to engage in the re-hypothecation of client assets.

Harmonization of client asset rules with respect to re-hypothecation is preferred from a financial stability perspective in order to limit the potential for regulatory arbitrage across jurisdictions. Such harmonized rules could set a limit on re-hypothecation in relation to client indebtedness. Client asset regimes are technically and legally extremely complex and diffuse systems. IOSCO has been putting some work in recently.[56]

IOSCO identified two particular 'regulatory challenges' related to the protection of clients: (1) where a client unknowingly waives protections to which it might otherwise be entitled and (2) the application of a domestic client asset protection regime where client assets are deposited abroad by an intermediary. IOSCO also had two recommendations for regulators: (1) employ adequate measures to oversee intermediaries' compliance with domestic client asset protection regimes, including receiving appropriate reports directly from intermediaries or self-regulatory organizations that oversee such intermediaries, related to specific requirements of domestic rules, and (2) work with intermediaries under their supervision and foreign regulators to ensure they receive sufficient information regarding the handling of client assets outside their jurisdiction.

In general, client assets are defined as assets for which an intermediary, 'has an obligation (either contractual or regulatory) to safeguard for its securities or derivatives clients, including, to the extent appropriate, client positions, client securities and money (including margin money) held by an intermediary for or on behalf of a client'.

At the end of January 2014,[57] the IOSCO came with its final set of admittedly high level (or minimum standard) recommendations. Among these recommendations are that intermediaries should:

1. Maintain accurate and current records regarding client assets
2. Regularly provide statements to clients regularly regarding client assets held on their behalf
3. 'Maintain appropriate arrangements' to ensure their clients' legal rights to client assets are ensured, and to minimize the possibility of loss and misuse
4. Understand foreign regimes of client protection in order to ensure they comply with domestic requirements when they place client assets abroad
5. Adequately disclose in writing to their clients that there may be material differences between the domestic and foreign protection of client assets and the potential consequences of such differences

[56] See in detail: IOSCO, (2013), Recommendations Regarding the Protection of Client Assets, Consultation Report, February 2013 and IOSCO, (2014), Recommendations Regarding the Protection of Client Assets, Final Report, January 29.

[57] IOSCO, (2014), Recommendations Regarding the Protection of Client Assets, January 2014.

6. Where clients can opt out of regulatory protections, ensure that clients' opt outs are explicitly memorialized (i.e. 'with the client's explicit, recorded consent'), with evidence of consent retained

At the same time, the FSB itself was and is working on developing guidance on the elements that need to be in place to shield client assets from the failure of the firm and, to the extent possible, of any third-party custodian or sub-custodian.[58]

3. Minimum Standards for Collateral Valuation and Management

The following minimum (regulatory) standards were suggested[59]:

- Securities lending and repo market participants (and, where applicable, their agents) should only take collateral types that they are able, in case of a counterparty failure to (i) hold for a period without breaching laws or regulations, (ii) value and (iii) risk manage appropriately.
- Securities lending and repo market participants (and, where applicable, their agents) should have contingency plans for the failure of their largest market counterparties, including in times of market stress. These plans should include how they would manage the collateral following default and the capabilities to liquidate it in an orderly way.
- Collateral and lent securities should be marked to market at least daily and variation margin collected at least daily where amounts exceed a minimum acceptable threshold.

4. Standards for Central Clearing

Across the world many securities and derivatives markets are served by a central counterparty (CCP). In such a centrally cleared market, participants have exposures to a CCP instead of having bilateral exposures to each other, provided they are direct members of the CCP, that is, the CCP clears the counterparty risk in a transaction. Such arrangements reduce the interconnectedness of the financial system through multilateral netting as it reduces counterparty risk and the collateral damage in case of exposure to counterparty risk by any of the market players.

While CCPs can bring advantages to most market segments, such as more robust collateral and default management processes, other benefits and costs of CCPs vary across market segments and jurisdictions, according to the FSB.[60] For example, in the inter-dealer repo market, there is great potential to reduce the size of credit exposures through multilateral netting as dealers often have offsetting trades among themselves. Dealers also have incentives to use CCPs to achieve balance sheet netting and lower capital requirements. In the dealer-to-customer repo market, however, the netting potential is limited as

[58] See in detail FSB, (2013), Application of the Key Attributes of Effective Resolution Regimes to Non-Bank Financial Institutions, Consultative document. The final rules as laid down in FSB, (2014), Key Attributes of Effective Resolution Regimes for Financial Institutions, Basel, October 15 are discussed separately.

[59] FSB, (2013), Ibid. pp. 16–17.

[60] FSB, (2013), Ibid. p. 17.

transactions are more often 'one way', and small institutions are likely to find central clearing costly given the need to pay clearing fees or margins. Potential participants may also not fully take into account the possibility of system-wide risk reduction benefits in times of market stress.[61] The big downside for market players to use a CCP is the fact that in order to clear the transaction for counterparty risk, the contractual terms of the transactions need to be standardized and are therefore to a large degree known by the public. Besides the loss of agility in structuring the contractual term, it might impact the pricing of the products traded through the CCP.

In certain circumstances, for example, in case of repos of less liquid securities, central clearing is practically difficult as CCPs may not be able to properly value and manage the collateral. The use of CCPs can also lead to moral hazard problems since market participants have less incentive to manage collateral risk if the trades are centrally cleared, and this may leave the CCP in a difficult position as the main provider of financing to its selected counterparties when other market participants reduce lines because of credit concerns.[62]

The FSB believes that there may be a case for welcoming the establishment and wider use of CCPs for inter-dealer repos against safe collateral (i.e. government securities) for financial stability purposes. However, existing incentives to use CCPs in these markets seem sufficiently strong (e.g. balance sheet netting) and no further regulatory or other actions appear necessary. In other markets the pros and the cons of using a CCP system needs to be balanced based on the market structure and institutional set-up specific to various jurisdictions. In the CCP chapter, the suggested standards and evolution are discussed.

5. Treatment of Repos and Securities Lending Transactions Under Bankruptcy and Insolvency Laws

Under the bankruptcy law of many of jurisdictions (e.g. US and EU members), repos are exempt from the 'automatic stay'. An automatic stay is simply a legal provision that temporarily prevents creditors from pursuing debtors for amounts owed. An automatic stay goes into effect immediately when a debtor files for bankruptcy or insolvency. Upon the bankruptcy of a financial institution, its repo counterparties are allowed to exercise contractual rights to terminate the contract, set off remaining mutual debts and claims and liquidate and collect against any collateral held, instead of having to wait for the bankruptcy proceedings to conclude. This special treatment, part of the 'safe harbor', was intended to reduce the contagion risk in the repo market.

However, since the financial crisis, a number of academics have argued that the 'safe harbor' status of repos may in fact increase systemic risk, because it can (i) increase the 'money-likeness' of repos and result in a rapid growth in cheap and potentially unstable short-term funding, (ii) facilitate the fire sales of collateral upon default and (iii) reduce creditors' incentives to monitor the credit quality of repo counterparties.[63] A number of proposals have been made with respect to changes in the bankruptcy that could reduce certain systemic or prevent them from occurring. Some of the proposals include:

---

[61] FSB, (2013), Ibid. p. 17.

[62] FSB, (2013), Ibid. p. 17.

[63] FSB, (2013), Ibid. p. 18.

(i) Repos backed by risky or illiquid collateral should not be exempt from automatic stay.[64]
(ii) Repos backed by risky or illiquid collateral should be exempt from automatic stay subject to a tax, which could be varied as a macroprudential tool.[65]
(iii) Repos backed by risky or illiquid collateral should not be exempt from automatic stay. In the event of default, lenders of such repos should instead be able to sell collateral only to a 'Repo Resolution Authority (RRA)' at market prices minus pre-defined haircuts specified by asset class by the RRA. Then the RRA would seek to liquidate the collateral in an orderly manner. The eventual difference between the amount of the liquidity payment and the realized value of the collateral would be paid to the repo lenders or clawed back from them. The pre-defined haircuts set by the RRA should effectively act as a floor on market haircuts.[66]

Common to most of these proposals is that the proposed changes would break into the fundamentals on which bankruptcy laws tend to be built, and so there is a natural resistance to advance with any of the proposals.

4.7 Regulatory Framework for Haircuts on Non-centrally Cleared Securities Financing Transactions[67]

As indicated at the beginning of this chapter, the FSB had engaged in an initial impact study (QIS1 from April to June 2013) to observe and support its (intended) recommendations. In November 2013, a second impact study was initiated ('Quantitative Impact Study (QIS2) on Proposed Regulatory Framework for Haircuts on Securities Financing Transactions').

This proposed regulatory framework for haircuts on non-centrally cleared securities financing transactions is intended to limit the build-up of excessive leverage outside the banking system. It may also reduce procyclicality of that leverage. The initially suggested framework included two mandatory elements[68]:

---

[64] D. Duffie and D. Skeel, (2012), A Dialogue on the Costs and Benefits of Automatic Stays for Derivatives and Repurchase Agreements, Stanford University Working Paper Nr. 108.

[65] E. Perotti, (2010), Systemic liquidity risk and bankruptcy exceptions, CEPR Policy Insight No. 52.

[66] V. Acharya and T. Sabri Öncü, (2013), A Proposal for the Resolution of Systemically Important Assets and Liabilities: The Case of the Repo Market, *International Journal of Central Banking*, Vol. 9, S1, pp. 291–349.

[67] Also: T. Breach and T. King, (2018), Securities Financing and Asset Markets: New Evidence, FRB of Chicago Working Paper Nr. 22, November 27.

[68] FSB, (2013), Ibid. p. 23. See also the finalized framework for haircuts on non-centrally cleared securities financing transactions in FSB, (2015), Transforming Shadow Banking into Resilient Market-based Finance.

(i) Minimum qualitative standards for methodologies used by all market participants to calculate haircuts (including additional guidance for methodologies used by market participants to calculate margins on a portfolio basis).
(ii) A framework of numerical haircut floors that will apply to non-centrally cleared securities financing transactions in which entities not subject to regulation of capital and liquidity/maturity transformation receive financing from regulated financial intermediaries against collateral other than government securities.

The final rules regarding haircuts regarding for OTC (non-centrally cleared) derivatives and securities financing transactions are discussed under the chapter regarding central clearing and CCPs.

4.8 A Lot Has Been Done But...

Since the crisis, regulators have addressed many of the underlying problems of excessive leverage and maturity transformation: (1) securities financing transactions are included in the internationally agreed leverage exposure measure adopted by the Basel Committee, (2) they are also included in the Basel Committee's measures to address liquidity risks, through the Net Stable Funding Ratio, (3) the Financial Stability Board has agreed minimum haircuts in order to limit the leverage that non-banks can obtain through borrowing cash against private sector securities and (4) the US authorities have taken steps to strengthen the tri-party infrastructure.[69] But the reform is not complete. One important missing ingredient is data collection to monitor market trends more closely. That is a reform in the making. Based on the November 2015 FSB suggested standards and the obligations of the already discussed EU securities financing legislation, data gathering and trade repository management are key ingredients for further meaningful development. Data availability is important for a number of factors: (1) to understand the composition of the collateral; (2) to track the terms of transactions, including maturities and haircuts; (3) to identify interconnectedness, leverage and multiple re-uses of securities; (4) identification of regulatory arbitrage is required as incoming regulation will alter the industry structure and agents will consider

Regulatory Framework for Haircuts on Non-Centrally Cleared Securities Financing Transactions, November 12. Their final principles stayed the same: a combination of qualitative standards combined with a framework for numerical haircut floors, which are between 0.5% and 10% and thus higher than those initially proposed, that will apply to non-centrally cleared securities financing transactions in which financing against collateral other than government securities. The qualitative standards imply that '[h]aircuts should be based on the market risks of the assets used as collateral and be calibrated at a high confidence level' and should capture other risks where required. Cash-collateralized securities lending transactions are under certain circumstances exempted (pp. 9–10). Different implementation approaches are discussed (entity-based, product-based and a hybrid approach) (pp. 11 ff.) See the FSB 2015 final report for details.

[69] D. Rule, (2014), Regulatory Reform, Its Possible Market Consequences and the Case of Securities Financing, Speech given by David Rule, Executive Director, Prudential Policy at the Federal Reserve Bank of Chicago Annual International Banking Conference, November 6, 2014, pp. 5–6.

using off-balance-sheet capacity or renting it;[70] (5) to identify concentrated short-selling transactions and (6) to identify vulnerabilities caused by asset managers that make large parts of the portfolio available for securities lending in order to drum up their returns on a low-interest rate environment.[71]

The repo market is a major source of short-term secured funding for financial institutions.[72] Because lending in these markets is collateralized—often by high-quality securities—the stability of the market was, until recently, taken for granted by market participants and regulators. The financial crisis learned that, just like is the case with other forms of secured lending, repo markets can melt down when concern emerges regarding collateral values and aligned issues. It causes panic and contagion through the collateral transmission channel. When observing post-crisis regulation, a minor impact has been realized directly on the functioning of the repo market. In essence, direct reforms of the repo market have been minimal and were limited to heightened transparency requirements in repo contracts, and leverage restrictions placed on certain bilateral repo contracts.[73] Cullen argues and I tend to concur that the repo has been far more constrained by indirect measure which includes capital requirements and liquidity regulation. These requirements were put in place to reduce the reliance of banks on short-term funding of which repo used to be a prime source. The condense bank balance sheets space and force bank asset composition to be more liquid. Through those measures the repo market has experienced post-regulation a contraction of market liquidity.[74]

---

[70] See for a comparative analysis of the legal infrastructure in Europe, Australia and the US: P. Ali et al., (2014), The Legal Structure and Regulation of Securities Lending, Center for International Finance and Regulation (CIFR), Research Working Paper, Law Faculty, University of Melbourne, Nr. 22/2014, May.

[71] M. Miles, (2015), BlackRock Seeks SEC Clearance for Internal Fund Lending, Bloomburg Business, June 27. These moves don't come without market responses: FT Fund Management, (2015), BlackRock Pressured to Reinstate Stock Lending Cap, *Financial Times*, August 18.

[72] See for a good primer on repos: J. Cullen, (2018), The Repo Market, Collateral and Systemic Risk: In Search of Regulatory Coherence, in Research Handbook on Shadow Banking, Legal and Regulatory Aspects (eds. I. H.-Y. Chiu and I.G. MacNeil), Edward Elgar Publishing, Cheltenham, UK, pp. 89 ff. and their role in the financial crisis: G. B. Gorton and A. Metrick, (2009), Securitized Banking and the Run on Repo NBER Working Paper Nr. 15223, August; G. B. Gorton and A. Metrick, (2012), 'Who Ran on Repo?' NBER Working Paper Nr. 18455.

[73] In fact there are three domains the regulators focused on: '(1) minimum haircuts to be applied to various collateral classes; (2) increasing information flow to regulators through mandating heightened disclosure in SFTs; and (3) the centralization of collateral management and repo transactions with the aim of mutualizing risks.' Ibid. Cullen pp. 98ff.

[74] At least that is what J. Cullen concludes after having assessed the post-crisis regulation impacting repo markets. See in detail: J. Cullen, (2018), The Repo Market, Collateral and Systemic Risk: In Search of Regulatory Coherence, in Research Handbook on Shadow Banking, Legal and Regulatory Aspects (eds. I. H.-Y. Chiu and I.G. MacNeil), Edward Elgar Publishing, Cheltenham, UK, pp. 85–116. In line with those conclusions are A. Kotidis and N. van Hooren, (2018), Repo Market Functioning: The Role of Capital Regulation, Bank of England Staff Working Paper Nr. 746, August 3. They find that dealers subject to a more binding leverage ratio reduced liquidity in the repo market. This affected their small but not their large clients. They further document a reduction in frequency of transactions and a worsening of repo pricing, but no adjustment in haircuts or maturities. Evidence of market resilience was also documented. Also: S. Anbil and Z. Senyuz,

Repos further play a material role in bond market intermediation. Repos allow dealers to finance their activities, but they also increase dealers' ability to satisfy levered client demands without having to adjust their holdings of risky assets. Even more, Huh and Infante[75] argue 'the ability to borrow specific assets for delivery allows dealers to source large quantity of assets without taking ownership of them'. Larger asset borrowing demands, increase the borrowing cost for that asset. That higher cost I then passed on through a higher bid-ask spread. As a modus operandi, that seems to work although it increases the dealer's balance sheet materially. Not engaging however will leave dealers ability to engage in market making which also will increase the applied bid-ask spread. An overall reduction of the impact of leverage on the balance sheet in the industry has unknown consequences and will largely depend on nature and intensity of the demand of particularly larger securities lenders.

Nevertheless, certain characteristics of the repo markets continue to pose a threat to financial stability. The prime ones definitely read as 'procyclicality of leverage' leading to systemic shocks or reduced margin spiral following changes in collateral value as well as 'rehypothecation of collateral' used in repo markets. Leverage, liquidity and solvency become intertwined in each of those issues and have a proven ability to lead to systemic issues.[76] Also the combination of (1) low or negative interest rates, (2) large aggregate short positions in bonds and (3) economic or policy surprises may lead to persistent settlement fails.[77]

The repo market is a somewhat strange place. We know it has been prone to a material run during the 2007 crisis. But in fact, that is not completely true or better it is incomplete. The run was a two-way run. Gorton[78] et al. document that lenders that were holding privately produced collateral in the repo market (which often were MBS) ran to get their money back when questions arose about the quality of that collateral. On the other hand, borrowers, who had supplied treasuries as collateral, wanted their collateral back. So when questions are asked about the quality of the collateral or when through regulation a haircut is applied across the board or for a certain type of collateral, what happens is that those specific assets were are taken to the Fed as collateral against emerging funds or facilities. A typical exchange with the Fed would be to exchange that privately produced collateral against Treasuries. Banks that were most exposed to treasury shortage

(2018), The Regulatory and Monetary Policy Nexus in the Repo Market, Finance and Economics Discussion Series 2018-027. Washington: Board of Governors of the Federal Reserve System, https://doi.org/10.17016/FEDS.2018.027

[75] Y. Huh and S. Infante, (2017), Bond Market Intermediation and the Role of Repo, Finance and Economics Discussion Series Nr. 2017-003, December, Washington: Board of Governors of the Federal Reserve System.

[76] See for a particular discussion of these two issues in the repo market: ibid. pp. 93 ff.

[77] J.-S. Fontaine et al., (2017), Repo Market Functioning when the Interest Rate is Low or Negative, Bank of Canada Staff Discussion Paper 2017-3, January. They further conclude that the repo market is unaffected by low or negative overnight rates. Specific repo segments however can be impacted without changes to market convention or institutional structures.

[78] G. Gorton et al., (2018), The Run on Repo and the Fed' Response, NBER Working Paper Nr. 24866, July. Also: N. van Horen and A. Kotidis, (2018), Repo Market Functioning: The Role of Capital Regulation, Bank of England Staff Working Paper Nr. 746, August 3.

pre-crisis now respond the most intensive, as the Fed facility alleviated the scarcity of good collateral. That behavior makes sense I guess. US Treasuries are the best type of collateral because there are never doubts about their value. Under the real condition of limited treasury supply, market agents re-use treasuries in other transactions (re-hypothecation) leading to a high velocity of collateral.[79] What is specific about the velocity of treasury collateral is that the treasury collateral velocity can be in infinite because haircuts are zero. The treasury velocity is therefore in no way linked to the money multiplier (or velocity of money) which is constrained by central bank reserve requirements. The only real constrained in the treasury multiplier market is of an institutional nature.[80]

The treasury velocity is structurally higher than one, which implies that in case all repo borrowers want their collateral back at the same time, there cannot be enough treasury supply. Now that is good to know but there is more. Gorton et al. comment '[i]f the run on repo was driven by repo lenders seeking to obtain cash, banks would be content to borrow cash at an emergency lending facilities because they could repay lenders. On the other hand, if repo borrowers were seeking to regain possession of good collateral, emergency borrowers would be looking to borrow Treasuries, rather than Fed Funds.'[81] When observing all the emerging facilities[82] that were set up during the 2007 crisis, only the TSLF 'was the only one that allowed borrowers to access good collateral, rather than Fed Funds'. Now let it be that the type of collateral brought to the TSLF was especially responsive to the changes in bilateral repo haircuts. Or in other words, when haircuts on privately produced collateral increased, borrowers were very willing to take their collateral and exchange it through the TSLF for treasuries. That in itself provides evidence for the two-way street that a run on the repo market normally constitutes. The run of repo borrowers to regain their high-quality collateral is an important driver of the crisis dynamics in the repo market than the lenders that tried to get their money back. Now we know that the repo market has a bilateral and tri-party segment.[83] They are related but play distinct roles. The tri-party market is about funding and the bilateral market is a market for collateral. Although Gorton et al.'s study focuses on the bilateral market, it doesn't mean that the tri-party market is run-free, although it is very institutional in nature.[84]

---

[79] Collateral re-use can include up to 30% of bank assets. Calculations of re-hypothecation are very difficult as there is no ownership claim and therefore occurs off-balance sheet.

[80] G. Gorton et al., (2018), Ibid. p. 3.

[81] G. Gorton et al., (2018), Ibid. pp. 2–3.

[82] There were three: the Term Auction Facility (TAF), Term Securities Lending Facility (TSLF) and Primary Dealer Credit Facility (PDCF). TSL provided borrowers with Treasury collateral, while the other two—TAF and PDCF—provided Fed Funds. See for a detailed overview: G. Gorton et al., (2018), Ibid. pp. 6–10.

[83] In the tri-party there is a clearing bank positioned between borrowers and lenders.

[84] V. Baklanova et al., (2017), The Use of Collateral in Bilateral Repurchase and Securities Lending Agreements. Federal Reserve Bank of New York Staff Reports, Nr. 758; G. Gorton, (2017), The History and Economics of Safe Assets, Annual Review of Economics, Vol. 9, pp. 547–587.

5

Central Counterparties (CCPs) and Systemic Risk

5.1 Introduction

It was during the G20 in Pittsburgh in 2009 that leaders agreed on a set of reforms that would lead to more stability, transparency and efficiency, with a focus on derivatives. The focus from a regulatory point of view has been since then on the OTC (over-the-counter) markets[1] and the ambition to get them all cleared through a CCP (central clearing party). It has led in Europe to the European Market Infrastructure Regulation (EMIR) (the regulation on OTC derivatives, central counterparties and trade repositories, also known as the European Market Infrastructure Regulation).[2] Two elements that have a large impact on the distribution of risk are the aspect of (1) microprudential requirements for CCPs and (2) the clearing requirement for OTC derivatives contracts.[3] But that also implies that the systemic importance of CCP increases, by concentrating financial system risk at their level. Admitted, the structure of the underlying market (e.g. for certain derivatives co-determines the nature and concentration of that

[1] See for the (global) volumes in the different segments of the OTC market: BIS, (2019), OTC Derivatives Statistics June 4. Updated regularly via bis.org

[2] Regulation (EU) Nr. 648/2012 of the European Parliament and of the Council of July 4, 2012, on OTC derivatives, central counterparties and trade repositories, O.J. of July 27, 2012, L 201, pp. 1–59. Regulatory issues related to derivatives trading in the US are specified in Title VII of the Dodd-Frank Act.

[3] J. Gregory, (2014), Central Counterparties: Mandatory Central Clearing and Initial Margin Requirements for OTC Derivatives, June, Wiley & Sons, Chichester.

L. Nijs, *The Handbook of Global Shadow Banking, Volume I*,
https://doi.org/10.1007/978-3-030-34743-7_5

risk) can be unstable. Therefore, the EMIR raises the macroprudential standards.[4] Also, the elsewhere discussed resolution mechanisms contribute to mitigating that risk.[5]

5.2 The Economics of Central Clearing

The principal risk in the financial system which CCPs seek to address is counterparty credit risk. CCPs intermediate between OTC derivatives counterparties, and thus face substantial counterparty risk. This is partially mitigated as CCPs demand collateral (or 'margin') from their counterparties, through the netting of positions and through other forms of credit enhancement.[6] Due to the size and importance of the risks that they bear, CCPs must have strong risk management practices to ensure that they can correctly value, call for margin on and control the risks of all cleared positions. In order to facilitate this, and since complex or illiquid products can impose substantial risks on a CCP, OTC derivatives clearing should focus on liquid, standardized products.[7] CCPs are important interconnectors in the financial system and thus likely to be systemically important financial institutions. Their operations transform systemic risk. They can both decrease it (for instance, by reducing the impact of clearing member failure) and increase it (for instance, by increasing margin requirements during a period of financial stress). When a CCP cannot meet demands for the return of clearing member collateral and would require CCP access to central bank funding or central bank lending to clearing members. CCPs are a risk-pooling and -sharing mechanism. In particular, clearing members provide funds to the CCP for a default fund which can bear the costs of counterparty non-performance should margin provide inadequate. The use of a default fund results in risk mutualization. Like most such mechanisms, clearing is susceptible to moral hazard and adverse selection

[4] It is an ongoing process and in particular the clearing of OTC derivatives is a constant struggle. Another feature that triggers constant debate is that of margin requirements and haircuts: The key channel for procyclicality of margins and haircuts is through changes in market prices of financial instruments within participants' portfolios and assets posted as collateral. CCP models for setting margins and haircuts may create a positive correlation between price volatility and the level of margins or haircuts, which in turn implies that margins and haircuts might be lowered in periods of low volatility and increased when the latter rises. The lowering of collateral requirements allows CCP clearing members (and their clients) to collateralize a higher level of exposure with the same amount of collateral and may thereby increase leverage, while a sudden and large increase in collateral requirements can create the conditions for a systemic liquidity spiral. The benefits of a procyclical dimension are clear. The EC and the ESRB provide continued guidance to achieve that. See recently: ESRB, (2015), ESRB Report on the Efficiency of Margining Requirements to Limit Pro-Cyclicality and the Need to Define Additional Intervention Capacity in this Area, July 28.

[5] See for a very good introductory document regarding the intricacies of CCPs: DNB, (2013), All the Ins & Outs of CCPs, October, Amsterdam; IMF, (2010), Making Over-the-Counter Safer: The Role of Central Clearing parties, Global Financial Stability Report, April, Chapter 3, pp. 1–27.

[6] See for a good write-up regarding the functioning of CCPs in the wider financial infrastructure: D. Domanski et al., (2015), Central Clearing: Trends and Current Issues, BIS Quarterly Review, December, pp. 60–63.

[7] C. Pirrong, (2011), The Economics of Central Clearing: Theory and Practice, ISDA Discussion Paper, Nr. 1, May, p. 2.

issues. These become more significant if CCP membership is more heterogeneous or if more complex products are cleared. Thus CCPs are best served by relatively high membership criteria which are still consistent with equitable access to clearing.[8]

Central clearing is subject to strong economies of scale and scope arising from netting economies and diversification effects. These scale and scope economies favor the use of a small number of 'utility' CCPs. Fragmentation of clearing on jurisdictional lines will increase the costs and risks of clearing, including systemic risks. The governance of CCPs is an important issue as well. CCPs should be organized so as to align the control of risks with those who bear the consequences of risk management decisions. Failure to align rights with risk bearing will tend to decrease the effectiveness of CCPs in reducing systemic risk.[9]

Pirrong finally argues that some derivatives counterparties will not be CCP clearing members. If they wish to clear, these parties will have to find a clearing member to act for them. Margin will still be required on their portfolio, and thus they could potentially be exposed to the default of that clearing member. He argues in favor of two key mechanisms to reduce the impact of that: (1) CCPs can adopt a variety of rules regarding the segregation of client margin. These rules not only affect the allocation of the risk of clearing member (and client) default, but also the incentive which clients may have to monitor the credit quality of their clearing members, and (2) CCPs may facilitate the ability of clients to port their positions from one clearing member to another. This can reduce client exposure to default losses and discourage customers from engaging in destabilizing runs, but reduces their incentive to monitor the riskiness of their clearing firms.[10] Further a number of legal and jurisdictional risks should be monitored with respect to segregation and netting.

In 2009, the G20 Leaders agreed that standardized over-the-counter (OTC) derivatives contracts should be cleared through central counterparties (CCPs). Since that time, global standard-setting bodies have advanced a number of regulatory reforms that are likely to affect the incentives for central clearing of these contracts. These reforms include requirements to exchange initial and variation margin for non-centrally cleared derivatives exposures, standards relating to the measurement of counterparty credit risk for derivatives contracts and capital requirements for bank exposures to CCPs. The OTC Derivatives Coordination Group commissioned an assessment of the incentives for central clearing of OTC derivatives, recognizing that misaligned incentives in this area—as compared to those for bilateral transactions—could lead market participants to take actions that could undermine the regulatory reforms (e.g. by customizing their derivatives trades to avoid mandatory clearing of standardized OTC derivatives contracts). The results of the quantitative analysis indicate that clearing member banks (i.e. those institutions that clear directly with CCPs) have incentives to clear centrally. Central clearing incentives for market participants that clear indirectly (i.e. that are not directly clearing members of a CCP but clear through an intermediary that is a clearing member of a CCP) are less obvious and could not be comprehensively analyzed on the basis of the data received in the quantitative analysis. These 'indirect clearers' do not constitute a homoge-

[8] C. Pirrong, (2011), Ibid. p. 2.

[9] C. Pirrong, (2011), Ibid. p. 3.

[10] C. Pirrong, (2011), Ibid. p. 3.

neous group. Instead, their trading and clearing patterns vary in a number of ways, such as trading frequency, portfolio composition and regulatory requirements. Some, but not all of them, are banks. This makes it difficult to draw any general conclusions on the effect of the reforms on indirect clearers' incentives for central clearing. After the reforms have been introduced, some indirect clearers may have incentives to clear centrally, while others may not.[11]

5.3 Risk Mitigation and Management

No doubt that CCPs play a critical role in the financial system and they do so by managing and structuring a complex web of counterparty risk. A CCP becomes the buyer to every seller and the seller to every buyer as it interposes between contracting parties. That is quite some risk and therefore membership is 'qualified', that is, 'CCP membership is concentrated as members need to meet minimum criteria, such as in terms of financial soundness, operational capacity and product expertise. The typical member is a large financial institution that engages with CCPs for purposes of trading on their own account or on account of their customers.'[12] CCPs use a variety of techniques to mitigate that overall risk including netting.[13] By reducing counterparty risk on average, CCPs also reduce systemic risk, that is, it avoids that default risk propagates from one counterparty to the other. But having such a large responsibility and being in a concentrated market, the questions have been raised to what degree CCPs have now become 'too big to fail' and that despite the recovery, including loss-allocation rules, and resolution frameworks developed in recent years. Indeed, '[f]rom a microprudential perspective, the most relevant risks faced by a CCP are counterparty risk and liquidity risk. Counterparty credit risk refers to the risk that a counterparty will be unable to fully meet its obligations. Liquidity risk chiefly relates to the risk faced by a CCP when seeking to re-establish a balanced book following default by a member.'[14] But as the 2008 crisis has relearned us, microprudential soundness[15] doesn't mean macroprudential soundness. Hermans et al. highlight '[f]or instance, uncoordinated actions by CCPs, such as sudden changes in collateral requirements in times of crisis, could give rise to macroprudential concerns. The inability of one or more members to meet these could have direct implications for the liquidity or solvency of a CCP, with the potential for severe "knock-on" effects on other members.'[16]

[11] BIS, (2014), Regulatory Reform of Over-The-Counter Derivatives: An Assessment of Incentives to Clear Centrally, A report by the OTC Derivatives Assessment Team, established by the OTC Derivatives Coordination Group, October, pp. 1–2.

[12] L. Hermans et al., (2013), Central Counterparties and Systemic Risk, ESRB Macro-Prudential Commentaries, Issue 6, November, p. 3.

[13] D. Duffie, and H. Zhu, (2011), Does a Central Clearing Counterparty Reduce Counterparty Risk?, Review of Asset Pricing Studies, Vol. 1, pp. 74–95.

[14] L. Hermans et al., (2013), Ibid. p. 4.

[15] See for an overview of the microprudential tools included in the EMIR, L. Hermans et al., (2013), Ibid. p. 6.

[16] L. Hermans et al., (2013), Ibid. p. 5.

That can have procyclical effects on the markets. To avoid that, the EMIR has a number of risk management protocols in place that relate to (1) collateral provision by counterparties, (2) under circumstances additional financial resources to be posted by counterparties and (3) ongoing measurement and monitoring of risk.

The CCP will call in case of a default of a counterparty access the collateral and resources made available by other counterparties and that is done in a pre-described default waterfall system and methodology.[17] As the available resources might not be sufficient to cover the shortfall, the CCP needs a contingency and resolution plan to handle uncovered liquidity shortfalls.[18] The standards laid down in the EMIR are more demanding[19] than those laid down in the CPSS-IOSCO principles for financial market infrastructure. That is not a luxury but a bare necessity. The global market for OTC derivatives is valued at approx. 150 trillion USD and is therefore larger than the value of the global economy. No need to explain the 'collateral damage', not to use the word 'Hiroshima', a default with contagion effect will have on the real economy. Nevertheless its imperfect nature, CCPs are a good step in the right direction, but as most regulation an indirect improvement. The more direct and explicit route would be to effectively limit the size and value of the derivatives market. However, no neoliberal (or other) regulator would go that far. The same arguments can be brought on the table for leverage, liquidity and so on. Hence my strong preference for the use of Pigovian taxes in this respect as a direct alternative to command-and-control regulation, which still seems to be the preferred instrument for most regulators around the world. But CCPs are the next best alternative: they balance counterparty risk, they enhance market efficiency, they monitor risk ongoing and so on. Also the fact that the collateral only needs to cover 'net' exposure makes a large difference.

But being such a large 'node' in the financial system, certain risk will undeniably emerge: (1) growing risk concentration at the level of the CCP, (2) risk concentration with clearing members will enhance, (3) crisis propagation may be driven by interdepen-

---

[17] See for an extensive description of how the waterfall operates: L. Hermans et al., (2013), Ibid. p. 5.

[18] First, the pre-funded default fund contributions of the survivors will be used to cover the losses. Second, the CCP has to deploy recovery tools, such as the replenishment of the default fund, by demanding liquidity from survivors, which can pose problems due to payment delays from members. CCPs calibrate the default fund size based on internal stress tests, but they are under no obligation to disclose details of the methodologies used. Thus, the level of stress that CCPs can withstand cannot be compared. Currently, regulators are considering the introduction of a standardized stress testing framework to enable the comparison of CCP risk profiles; see in detail: A. Armakola and J.P. Laurent, (2015), CCP Resilience and Clearing Membership, Working Paper, June 30, mimeo, p. 2,; J.H. Powell, (2014). A Financial System Perspective on Central Clearing of Derivatives. Speech at the '[t]he new international financial system: analyzing the cumulative impact of regulatory reform'. 17th Annual International Banking Conference. Chicago, Illinois; D. Bailey, (2014), The Bank of England's perspective on CCP risk management, recovery and resolution arrangements'. Speech at the Deutsche Börse Group and Eurex Exchange of ideas conference, London; R. Cont, and T. Kokholm, (2014), Central Clearing of OTC Derivatives: Bilateral vs. Multilateral Netting, Statistics and Risk Modeling, Vol. 31, Issue 1, pp. 3–22.

[19] In case of, for example, confidence intervals, close-out periods, margin and haircut practices, requirements to cover credit and liquidity risk and so on.

dencies of changing complexity and which can exist between CCPs and other financial institutions and (4) collateral rules will increase (high-quality) collateral scarcity.[20]

Other areas of risk management concern regarding CCPs are[21]:

- Procyclicality[22] effect induced by increased margin requirements by CCPs during periods of market distress, which could lead to fire sales and asset price declines and create a loop of haircuts. The EMIR conditions take this into account but do not solve the exposure.[23]
- Wrong-way risk: 'A wrong-way risk is a risk that a credit exposure to a counterparty is likely to increase exactly when the creditworthiness of that counterparty deteriorates.' Also here the EMIR tries to take the effects into account when setting levels for haircuts, collateral and so on.
- Interdependencies: that increases the more CCPs play their roles of 'nodes' in the financial system as they create 'interoperability arrangements' which 'enable firms that are members of different CCPs to trade with each other by allowing each firm to clear a trade through the CCP of which it is a member with the two CCPs engaging in a matching transaction'. Also here the EMIR builds these concerns into the requirement setting. The interdependencies also emerge on an international level and therefore 'regulatory arbitrage is a material risk'.[24] This is important as there is currently no resolution program available in many countries in the world including the EU region[25] and they are now considered one of the most important SIFIs.[26] As Wendt[27] indicates 'CCPs are also highly interconnected with financial institutions and markets and therefore too

---

[20] L. Hermans et al., (2013), Ibid. pp. 8–9. See Collateral Concerns in Financial Markets: a European Perspective, in ESMA, (2013), Report on Trends, Risks, and Vulnerabilities, Nr. 1.

[21] See in detail: L. Hermans et al., (2013), Ibid. pp. 9–12.

[22] See in detail: the role of margin requirements and haircuts in procyclicality, CGFS Papers, Nr. 36, Bank for International Settlements, Basel.

[23] 'The EMIR focuses on the need to maintain margin requirements and haircut policies that avoid strong fluctuations by calling for initial margin requirements and haircuts to be set conservatively': L. Hermans et al., (2013), Ibid. pp. 10–12.

[24] See in detail: BIS, (2011), The Macro-financial Implications of Alternative Configurations for Access to Central Counterparties in OTC Derivatives Markets, CGFS Papers, Nr. 46, Bank for International Settlements, Basel.

[25] See: BIS, (2012), Recovery and Resolution of Financial Market Infrastructures, Consultative Report, July, Basel. See also D. Bailey, (2014), The Bank of England's Perspective on CCP Risk Management, Recovery and Resolution Arrangements, Speech given at the Deutsche Boerse Group and Eurex Exchange of Ideas conference, London, November 24; B. Cœuré, (2014), Central Counterparty Recovery and Resolution, Keynote Speech at 'Exchange of Ideas #2 Central Clearing – Guarantee of Stability or New Moral Hazard?' organized by Eurex Clearing London, November 24; LCH.Clearnet White Paper, (2014), CCP Risk Management, Recovery and Resolution; ISDA, (2013), CCP Loss Allocation at the End of the Waterfall, Working Paper, August.

[26] JP. Morgan Chase & Co., (2014), What is the Resolution Plan for CCPs, Perspectives, September.

[27] F. Wendt, (2015), Central Counterparties: Addressing their Too Important to Fail Nature, IMF Working Paper, Nr. WP/15/21, pp. 1, 14–17, and the nature of the additional measures required, pp. 18–21.

> important to fail. The increased volumes cleared through CCPs and their increasing global scope, in particular in the OTC derivatives market, make it even more important that systemic risks related to CCPs are managed.' Now that Dodd-Frank and the EMIR force many former OTC contracts to be CCP cleared, volumes and therefore interconnectedness[28] are steeply on the rise and current regulation only partly addresses the many different components of systemic risk for CCP. Current regulation focuses on two features: (1) measures aimed at reducing the probability of a CCP's failure by increasing the standards and requirements for CCPs and introducing recovery plans and (2) measures aimed at reducing the impact of a failure of a CCP by introducing resolution frameworks.[29]

Some suggestions were made in recent years. Before looking into those, we need to balance our view with the contemporary situation and the improvements that have been made regarding CCPs in terms of risk management protocols in recent years: they can be summarized as such that: (1) central counterparties (CCPs) are market risk neutral as a normal course of business. CCPs do not engage in trading, lending or any other market risk-creating activities, (2) CCPs serve a crucial market function by ensuring participants do not have 'too big to fail' consequences, (3) monitoring participants to ensure they have sufficient skin in the game to support their activities is a fundamental aspect of a CCP's role, (4) CCPs with a 'systemically important' designation maintain resources at least large enough to cover the default losses of their two largest clearing members[30] and (5) a CCP's most important contribution to managing systemic risk is the management of concentration risk among their largest participants.[31] That leaves the following exposures uncovered: '(1) the composition of the risk waterfall and loss sharing arrangements may be a source of contagion for surviving clearing members, (2) the dependency of CCPs on only a few commercial banks for liquidity, custody, settlement, and other services can put the CCP and surviving clearing members under severe pressure, (3) collateral sales of multiple CCPs may increase market volatility, and (4) diverging interests of authorities in a globally cleared market'.[32] The below mentioned IOSCO principles have tightened conditions for CCPs but 'there are no specific requirements for a CCP that uses a range of services from only a few commercial banks. Also, implementation is subject to interpreta-

---

[28] See on the nature of the interconnectedness of CCPs, Wendt, (2015), Ibid. pp. 5–13. See also: N. Arregui, et al., (2013), Addressing Interconnectedness: Concepts and Prudential Tools, IMF Working Paper Nr. WP/13/199. It didn't go unnoticed with the Bank for International Settlements who issued further recommendations regarding the capital requirements for banking institutions with material exposures to central counterparties: See, BIS, (2014), Capital Requirements for Bank Exposures to Central Counterparties, April, Basel. That interconnectedness also showed up in the FSB annual OTC update report, see FSB, (2014), OTC Derivatives Market Reforms Eighth Progress Report on Implementation, Basel, pp. 16–20.

[29] Wendt, (2015), Ibid. pp. 14–15.

[30] That is for the US situation.

[31] See CME, (2014), Clearing – Balancing CCP and Member Contributions with Exposures, cmegroup.com

[32] Wendt, (2015), Ibid. p. 15.

tion of the CCPs and its authorities. Furthermore, the principles do not address global interconnections, for example, by requesting that a clearing member should hold a diversified set of collateral. The new regulations strengthen supervision and oversight of CCPs, but there is no explicit requirement that authorities analyze interconnections and interdependencies.'[33]

In terms of suggestions for specific resolution plans for CCP (often covered in the term 'non-bank market infrastructure'), the EU made its first effort in 2012.[34] It considered that if 'systemic risk' shows up in the market, CCPs and CSDs (central securities depositories) are particularly prone to its emergence and impact as they are at the heart of the financial markets infrastructure. The systemic risk for CCPs break down into a wide variety of risk components.[35] Capponi et al. demonstrate a build-up of systemic risk, manifested through the increase of market concentration, whose negative size externalities can be internalized via a self-funding systemic risk charge mechanism.[36]

The general trend is that resolution for CCPs is preferred over unwinding, given the material disruptive effects that could bring along for the wider market.[37] To that effect the Bank for International Settlements created a framework with five recovery categories and tools.[38]

---

[33] Wendt, (2015), Ibid. pp. 15–16. See also: D. Russo, (2013), CPSS-IOSCO Principles for Financial Market Infrastructures: Vectors of International Convergence, Banque de France Financial Stability Review Nr. 17.

[34] EC, (2012), Consultation on a Possible Recovery and Resolution Framework for Financial Institutions other than Banks, ec.europe.eu. See also: A. Capponi, (2015), Systemic Risk: The Dynamics under Central Clearing, OFR Working Paper, Nr. 15-08, May 7 and D. Acemoglu et al., (2015), Systemic Risk and Stability in Financial Networks, American Economic Review, Vol. 105, Issue 2, pp. 564–608; A. Capponi, et al., (2014), Centrally Cleared Trading and Concentration Risk, Columbia University and Office of Financial Research Working Paper; F. Cumming, and J. Noss, (2013), Assessing the Adequacy of CCP's Default Resources, Financial Stability Paper Nr. 26, Bank of England; S. Varotto and L. Zhao, (2014), Systemic Risk and Bank Size, Henley Working Paper; M. Elliott, et al., (2014), Financial Networks and Contagion, American Economic Review, Vol. 104, Issue 10, pp. 3115–3153; P. Glasserman, et al., (2014), Hidden Illiquidity with Multiple Central Counterparties, Columbia University Working Paper; and linked with H. Hayakawa, (2014), Does Central Counterparty Reduce Liquidity Requirement, University of Tokyo Working Paper; A.J. Menkveld, (2015), Crowded Trades: An Overlooked Systemic Risk for Central Clearing Counterparties, AFA 2015 Boston Paper.

[35] See in detail for those: joint Report on Principles for Financial Market Infrastructures by the Committee on Payment and Settlement Systems (CPSS) and the International Organisation of Securities Commissions (IOSCO), (2012), Consultative report. The risk classifications to which FMIs are exposed as follows: legal, credit, liquidity, general business, custody/investment, and operational. See also BIS/IOSCO, (2012), Principles for Financial Market Infrastructures: Disclosure framework and Assessment Methodology, Basel. Based on these consultations the ESMA (European Securities and markets Authorities) has issued guidelines and recommendations, see ESMA, (2014), Guidelines and Recommendations regarding the implementation of the CPSS-IOSCO Principles for Financial Market Infrastructures in respect of Central Counterparties, ESMA/2014/1133.

[36] A. Capponi, (2015), Systemic Risk: The Dynamics under Central Clearing, OFR Working Paper, Nr. 15-08, May 7.

[37] See for an analysis: EC, (2012), Consultation on a Possible Recovery and Resolution Framework for Financial Institutions other than Banks, pp. 10–15.

[38] See in detail: BIS, (2014), Recovery of Financial Market Infrastructure, Basel, pp. 17–28.

Those five categories are (1) tools to allocate uncovered losses caused by participant default (e.g. cash calls, haircuts, collateral, etc.), (2) tools to address uncovered liquidity shortfalls (e.g. obtaining liquidity from third-party institutions or participants), (3) tools to replenish financial resources (e.g. cash calls, recapitalization, etc.), (4) tools for a central counterparty (CCP) to re-establish a matched book (e.g. forced allocation of contracts or contract termination) and (5) tools to allocate losses not related to participant default (through capital and recapitalization or insurance and indemnity agreements).

The recovery versus resolution discussed has not ended yet although 'the distinctions between the two is based to a large extent on whether loss allocation is achieved contractually or via a more ad-hoc and externally administered insolvency process that overrides contracts'.[39]

In the wake of the Directive 2014/59/EU (the Bank Recovery and Resolution Directive), discussed in the resolution chapter, on crisis prevention, management and resolution and a set of technical standards issues early 2015, the European banking authority indicated that there will be regulatory initiatives forthcoming for financial institutions other than banks.[40]

Other efforts have been done[41] also by private market agents to come up with a framework for resolution and unwinding of CCP defaults (or at least components for a framework). JP Morgan Chase suggested in 2014[42] the following items and steps as part of CCP recovery plan: (1) a standard, disclosed stress test framework should be mandated by regulators and used to size 'Total Loss Absorbing Resources'; (2) the CCP's entire Total Loss Absorbing Resources should be fully pre-funded; (3) CCPs should be recapitalized rather than liquidated upon failure, to continue systemically important activities; (4) CCPs should have 'Recapitalization Resources' to allow opening on the business day following failure with a fully funded Guarantee Fund; (5) CCPs should contribute to the Guarantee

[39] D. Duffie, (2014), Resolution of Failing Central Counterparties, Working Paper, p. 3. For a further analysis see pp. 3–7. See also: D. Elliott, (2013), Central Counterparty Loss-Allocation Rules, Bank of England, Financial Stability Paper, Nr. 20; ISDA, (2014), Resolution Stay Protocol, isda.org; M. Singh, (2014), Limiting Taxpayer Puts- An Example from CCPs, IMF Working Paper Nr. WP/14/203; R. Steigerwald and D. DeCarlo, (2014), Resolving Central Counterparties after Dodd-Frank: Are CCPs Eligible for 'Orderly Liquidation', Federal Reserve bank of Chicago, Working Paper; M. Gibson, (2013), Recovery and Resolution of Central Counterparties, Bulletin Reserve Bank of Australia, December, pp. 39–48.

[40] It is a slow moving process, ever since the 2012 consultation by the EC and the EBA opinion of the same year on this matter. See in detail: EBA, (2012), Opinion of the European Banking Authority on the European Commission's consultation on a possible framework for the recovery and resolution of financial institutions other than banks.

[41] E.g. by the FSB and this simultaneously with its recommendations regarding recovery and unwinding of financial institutions of financial institutions in October 2014; see: FSB, (2014) Guidance on Resolution of Non-Bank Financial Institutions, Basel.

[42] See: JPMorgan Chase & Co., (2014), What is the Resolution Plan for CCPs?, Perspectives, September, pp. 1–5. See for other proposals: European Association of CCP European Clearing Houses, (2014), An Effective Recovery and Resolution Regime for CCPs, who recommend to build on the EMIR conditions (including their July 2014 paper: EACH paper - Recovery and Resolution of CCPs), eachccp.eu, and AIMA, (2014), Position Paper on CCP recovery and Resolution, aima.org and ISDA, (2015), CCP Default Management, Recovery and Continuity: A Proposed Recovery Framework, isda.org

Fund and Recapitalization Resources requirements the greater of 10% of the Guarantee Fund or the largest single clearing member contribution and (6) beyond this minimum, CCPs should retain flexibility as to how such resources are tranched and allocated.

5.4 Every Battle Has Two Sides: What with Those Derivatives That Aren't Centrally Cleared[43]

The G20 post-crisis created a reform program to reduce the systemic risks coming from OTC derivatives. The four elements of the reform program were and are (1) all standardized OTC derivatives should be traded on exchanges or electronic platforms, where appropriate, (2) all standardized OTC derivatives should be cleared through central counterparties (CCPs), (3) OTC derivatives contracts should be reported to trade repositories and (4) non-centrally cleared derivatives contracts should be subject to higher capital requirements. In early 2015, the final framework was presented related to additional margin requirements on non-centrally cleared derivatives.[44] The margin requirements serve two objectives: (1) reduction of systemic risk as only standardized derivatives are suitable for central clearing. The OTC derivatives market's volume hoovers around 800 trillion USD (2015) and those pose a systemic contagion and spillover risk. The eyed reduction occurs through collateral to offset losses caused by the default of a derivatives counterparty and (2) promotion of central clearing and to avoid regulatory arbitrage between margin requirements for centrally and ORC derivatives. The final proposals are a balance between the risk mitigation factors being capital and margin versus the liquidity impact in the derivatives market. They each serve a different purpose though, that is, 'first, margin is "defaulter-pay". In the event of a counterparty default, margin protects the surviving party by absorbing losses using the collateral provided by the defaulting entity. In contrast, while capital adds loss absorbency to the system, because it is "survivor-pay", using capital to meet such losses consumes the surviving entity's own financial resources.'[45] Capital is put in place to protect all activities collectively the CCP is engaged in whereas 'margin' is more targeted and dynamic within portfolios.

The eight principles laid down by the Bank for International Settlements include[46]:

- Appropriate margining practices should be in place with respect to all derivatives transactions that are not cleared by CCPs.[47]
- All financial firms and systemically important non-financial entities ('covered entities') that engage in non-centrally cleared derivatives must exchange initial and variation margin as appropriate to the counterparty risks posed by such transactions.[48]

---

[43] See J. H. Powell, (2014), A Financial System Perspective on Central Clearing of Derivatives, speech at the 17th Annual International Banking Conference, Chicago, November 6.

[44] That process started already in 2011.

[45] BIS, (2015), Margin Requirements for Non-centrally Cleared Derivatives, Basel, pp. 3–4.

[46] BIS, (2015), Ibid. p. 5.

[47] See in detail: BIS, (2015), Ibid. pp. 7–8.

[48] See in detail: BIS, (2015), Ibid. pp. 8–11.

- The methodologies for calculating initial and variation margin that serve as the baseline for margin collected from a counterparty should (i) be consistent across entities covered by the requirements and reflect the potential future exposure (initial margin) and current exposure (variation margin) associated with the portfolio of non-centrally cleared derivatives in question and (ii) ensure that all counterparty risk exposures are fully covered with a high degree of confidence.[49]
- To ensure that assets collected as collateral for initial and variation margin purposes can be liquidated in a reasonable amount of time to generate proceeds that could sufficiently protect collecting entities covered by the requirements from losses on non-centrally cleared derivatives in the event of a counterparty default, these assets should be highly liquid and should, after accounting for an appropriate haircut, be able to hold their value in a time of financial stress.[50]
- Initial margin should be exchanged by both parties, without netting of amounts collected by each party (i.e. on a gross basis), and held in such a way as to ensure that (i) the margin collected is immediately available to the collecting party in the event of the counterparty's default and (ii) the collected margin must be subject to arrangements that fully protect the posting party to the extent possible under applicable law in the event that the collecting party enters bankruptcy.[51]
- Transactions between a firm and its affiliates should be subject to appropriate regulation in a manner consistent with each jurisdiction's legal and regulatory framework.[52]
- Regulatory regimes should interact so as to result in sufficiently consistent and non-duplicative regulatory margin requirements for non-centrally cleared derivatives across jurisdictions.[53]
- Margin requirements should be phased in over an appropriate period of time to ensure that the transition costs associated with the new framework can be appropriately managed. Regulators should undertake a coordinated review of the margin standards once the requirements are in place and functioning to assess the overall efficacy of the standards and to ensure harmonization across national jurisdictions as well as across related regulatory initiatives.[54]

Within a European context, the ESAs (European Supervisory Authorities) are setting out their goalposts regarding the technicalities in this matter. To be precise: for those over-the-counter (OTC) derivative transactions that will not be subject to central clearing, these draft RTS (regulatory technical standards) prescribe the regulatory amount of initial and variation margin that counterparties should exchange as well as the methodologies for their calculations. This is all based on the EMIR legislation.[55] In addition, these draft RTS out-

[49] See in detail: BIS, (2015), Ibid. pp. 11–16.

[50] See in detail: BIS, (2015), Ibid. pp. 17–19.

[51] See in detail: BIS, (2015), Ibid. pp. 19–22.

[52] See in detail: BIS, (2015), Ibid. p. 22.

[53] See in detail: BIS, (2015), Ibid. p. 23.

[54] See in detail: BIS, (2015), Ibid. pp. 24–25.

[55] EBA, (2015), Second Consultation Paper, Draft Regulatory Technical Standards on risk-mitigation techniques for OTC derivative contracts not cleared by a CCP. The EMIR legislation is, to the

line the criteria for the eligible collateral and establish the criteria to ensure that such collateral is sufficiently diversified and not subject to wrong-way risk. Counterparty risk measurement integrates two sources of risk: market risk, which determines the size of a firm's exposure to a counterparty, and credit risk, which reflects the likelihood that the counterparty will default on its obligations. Wrong-way risk refers to the possibility that a counterparty's default risk increases with the market value of the exposure.[56]

In the US, prudential regulators re-proposed rules regarding margin requirements for uncleared swaps in September 2014. These rules would apply to swap dealers, security-based swap dealers, major swap participants and major security-based swap participants. Initial margin is required to be phased in from September 1, 2016 to September 1, 2020, while variation margin is required to be phased in from September 1, 2016 to March 1, 2017.[57] Most regulation takes into account the risk mitigating protocols as prescribed by IOSCO.[58] When comparing notes on this matter across jurisdictions, three observations can be made according to Yadav and Turing: First, divergences in clearinghouse regulation matter in derivatives markets because these markets are uniquely international in scope. Contracts involve counterparties in different countries. Many transactions comprise cross-border aspects lacking a geographical anchor. Where derivatives traders face uncertainty, they can be disincentivized from observing laws or motivated to seek out lowest-cost compliance options. Second, although both the US and European Union have adopted common ground rules, their approaches to implementation differ in matters of detail. Such divergences prevent regulators from recognizing each other's clearinghouses as sufficiently robust. Third, while acknowledging that mutual recognition is the most appropriate way forward, substantial shortcomings exist with this approach. They point at existing structural divergences like access to emergency funding and bailout and re-iterate the idea that where costs diverge, traders seek out avenues for regulatory arbitrage to lower their costs of compliance.[59]

---

degree necessary given the context of this book, described in the European Chapter. Also other countries, particularly those with a large financial industry relative to their economy are pondering on their options: see, for example, MAS (Monetary Authority of Singapore), (2015), Policy Consultation on Margin Requirement for Non-centrally Cleared OTC Derivatives, P017-2015, October.

[56] See in detail and for measurement options: P. Glasserman and L. Yang, (2015), Bounding Wrong-Way Risk in Measuring Counterparty Risk, OFR Working Paper, Nr. 15-16, August 19.

[57] For a good overview on the OTC treatment in a comparative fashion between the US and Europe, see ISDA, (2014), Overview and U.S. and EU OTC Derivative Regulatory Reform, Working Paper. In a wider context, it can be referred to the FSB Annual Progress reports on the matter; the most recent being FSB, (2015), OTC Derivatives Market Reforms Ninth Progress Report on Implementation, July 24. Overall, it can be stated that most jurisdictions are well underway when it comes to trade reporting and standards (see for a specific review: FSB, (2015), Thematic Review on OTC Derivative Trade Reporting, Peer Review Report, November 4), capital requirements for standardized OTC contracts as well as trade repositories, but only in the initial stage when it comes to margin requirements for OTC derivatives and haircuts.

[58] See in detail: IOSCO, (2015), Risk Mitigating Standards for Non-centrally Cleared OTC Derivatives, FR01/2015, January 28.

[59] Y. Yadav and D. Turing, (2015), The Extra-Territorial Regulation of Clearinghouses, Vanderbilt University Law School, Law & Economics Working Paper Nr. 15-24, mimeo.

5.5 Does a Central Clearing Party Reduce Counterparty or Systemic Risk?

The regulator at least is willing to answer that question in a positive way. The standardized procedures, the collateral, the netting and so on all feed into the idea that CCPs reduce counterparty risk in the market and therefore reduce contagion and spillover effects. However, a deeper analysis reveals that it will all come down to the details. Duffie and Zhu examined different scenarios and concluded that adding a central clearing counterparty (CCP) for a class of derivatives such as credit default swaps reduces netting efficiency, leading to an increase in average exposure to counterparty default. They further concluded that clearing different classes of derivatives in separate CCPs always increases counterparty exposures relative to clearing the combined set of derivatives in a single CCP.[60] They indicate that '[w]hile the central clearing of derivatives can in principle offer substantial reductions in counterparty risk, we provide a foundation for concerns that these benefits may be lost through a fragmentation of clearing services.'

Based on a simple model, they demonstrate the trade-off between two types of netting opportunities 'bilateral netting between pairs of counterparties across different underlying assets, versus multilateral netting among many clearing participants across a single class of derivatives, such as credit default swaps (CDS). The introduction of a CCP for a particular class such as standard credit derivatives is effective only if the opportunity for multilateral netting in that class dominates the resulting loss in bilateral netting opportunities across all uncleared derivatives, such as uncleared CDS and uncleared OTC derivatives of equities, interest rates, commodities, and foreign exchange, among others.'[61] The reduction in counterparty risk emerges 'if and only if' the number of clearing participants is sufficiently large relative to the exposure on derivatives that continue to be bilaterally netted. A single central clearing counterparty that clears both credit derivatives and interest rate swaps is likely to offer significant reductions in expected counterparty exposures, even for a relatively small number of clearing participants.[62] All comes down to the netting ability of the CCP[63] versus the natural netting ability in the OTC market and the different degrees of risk that manifests itself in the different categories of derivatives cleared by the CCP. That is a nightmare from a regulatory point of view, as this objective (reducing counterparty risk and halting spillover effects) is at the heart of the whole wave of regulation that has emerged in recent years. So either the risk profile of the derivatives should be 'compatible' or it is to be preferred to have a single CCP clear all standard positions of a certain derivatives at least for the large global dealers but with the effect that it could reduce netting efficiencies, which will lead to higher expected counterparty exposures and collateral demands.[64] The netting across CCPs through interoperability agree-

[60] D. Duffie and H. Zhu, (2011), Does a Central Clearing Party Reduce Counterparty Risk?, Review of Asset pricing Studies, Vol. 1, Issue 1, pp. 74–95.

[61] D. Duffie and H. Zhu, (2011), Ibid. pp. 75–76.

[62] D. Duffie and H. Zhu, (2011), Ibid. pp. 76–77.

[63] See in detail: D. Duffie and H. Zhu, (2011), Ibid. pp. 77–85.

[64] D. Duffie and H. Zhu, (2011), Ibid. pp. 88–91.

ments is still prone to many legal and financial engineering issues but could help reduce counterparty exposures even when risk profiles of different derivative classes are not 'directly compatible'.[65] However, CCP as a model can still be motivated when taking into account mutualization. However, mutualization fully insures against idiosyncratic risk but cannot provide insurance against aggregate risk.[66]

Garratt and Zimmermann have been looking into the question whether central clearing reduces counterparty risk in financial networks.[67] They have been building further on the discussed work of Duffie and Zhu. What they bring into the equation is the general classes of network structures and the focus on free-scale and core-periphery structures, both which seem to be accurate models to reflect real-world financial networks. Their overall conclusion is that CCPs are unlikely to be beneficial when the link structure of the network relies on just a few key nodes. In large scale-free networks, a CCP is likely to worsen expected netting efficiency. That improved netting efficiency can only occur in case agents have a degree of risk aversion that allows them to trade off the reduced variance against the higher expected netted exposures. That in itself, they conclude, might explain why derivative traders, in the absence of regulation, may not develop a CCP themselves. Introducing a CCP for a single asset class in an OTC environment will impact both the mean and variance of total net exposures between counterparties. In case a small number of agents trade in a relatively large number of asset classes, central clearing increases the mean and variance of net exposures, which may lead to increased counterparty risk and higher margin needs. Their work, in contrast to that of Duffie and Zhu, is based on that of actual exposure networks. Where Duffie and Zhu express the total exposure of one dealer to another of all positions in each asset class by a random variable and specifying the distribution that is assumed to generate these exposures. That implies homogeneity in the distribution across all agents, that is, all agents are ex ante the same in their analysis and position. The benefits of doing so is clear: one can ignore the actual network exposures but the downside is that the implied networks are assumed to be homogeneous, which might conflict with reality. In fact previous research has showed fairly large levels of heterogeneity across financial networks. Realistic financial networks tend to have a number of well-connected counterparties combined with a fairly large pool of poorly connected counterparties.[68] It is the same network model I will be using in the Pigovian chapter for the financial sector to develop a Pigovian instrument. More specifically I will be using the referred Markose's model and its more recent refinements. What

[65] See also J. Mägerle, and T. Nellen, (2011), Interoperability Between Central Counterparties, Swiss National Bank Working Paper, Nr. 2011/12.

[66] B. Biais, et al., (2012), Clearing, Counterparty Risk and Aggregate Risk, IMF Economic Review, Vol. 60, Nr. 2 and B. Biais et al., (2015), Risk-Sharing or Risk-Taking? An Incentive Theory of Counterparty Risk, Clearing and Margins, Working Paper, latest version July 17.

[67] R. Garratt and P. Zimmerman, (2015), Does Central Clearing Reduce Counterparty Risk in Realistic Financial Networks, Federal Reserve Bank of NY Staff Reports Nr. 717.

[68] B. Craig, and G. von Peter, (2014), Interbank Tiering and Money Center Banks, *Journal of Financial Intermediation*, Vol. 23, pp. 322–347 and S. Markose, (2012), 'Systemic Risk from Global Financial Derivatives: a Network Analysis of Contagion and its Mitigation with Super-Spreader Tax', IMF Working Paper, Nr. WP/12/282.

Garratt and Zimmerman add is the network effect and the impact the introduction of a CCP will have on the net exposure of dealers and the effect on the variance of these net exposures.

Their detailed conclusions can be summarized as follows:

- When the number of asset classes is small relative to the number of dealers, introducing a CCP is likely to reduce both the mean and variance of net exposures.
- A CCP is less likely to be beneficial for networks where a high proportion of the links rely on a few key nodes.
- Introducing a CCP may have opposite effects on the mean and variance of netted exposures, leading to a trade-off.
- The optimal policy is likely to depend on the degree of risk aversion among counterparties and, potentially, regulators.[69]

The implications of their analysis and findings are widespread and its implications touch on many issues. For example, the question regarding margin requirements when introducing a CCP.[70]

It is by the way not so that nothing happened in this field between Duffie and Zhu and Garratt and Zimmerman. The 2011 theory of Duffie and Zhu has been used in many varieties between 2011 and 2015 to tackle specific issues. The intermediate analyses include a core-periphery network structure analysis and its quantification[71] and a policy analysis of interoperability between CCPs (but based on a homogeneous linked network).[72] It was in 2014 that Cont and Kokholm started to relax the assumptions used by Duffie and Zhu and demonstrated that Duffie and Zhu's conclusions are potentially sensitive to different distributional assumptions.[73] The difference between Cont/Kokholm's model and the discussed one of Garratt and Zimmerman is the fact that Cont

[69] Garratt and Zimmerman, (2015), Ibid. p. 1.

[70] See in detail on framing the issue and quantification of the impact: (1) S. Anderson et al., (2013), To Link or Not to Link? Netting and Exposures Between Central Counterparties, *Journal of Financial Market Infrastructures*, Vol. 1, Nr. 4, pp. 3–29, (2) D. Duffie, et al., (2014), Central Clearing and Collateral Demand, European Central Bank Working Paper, Nr. 1638, (also published in: *Journal of Financial Economics* Vol. 116, Issue 2, May, pp. 237–256); (3) S. Campbell, (2014), Estimating the Effect of Central Clearing on Credit Derivative Exposures, FEDS Notes, February 26, (4) C. Sidanius, and F. Žikeš, (2012), OTC Derivatives Reform and Collateral Demand Impact, Bank of England Financial Stability Paper, Nr. 18, and (5) S. Borovkova, et al., (2013), Systemic Risk and Centralized Clearing of OTC Derivatives: a Network Approach, Working Paper.

[71] A. Heath, et al., (2013), OTC Derivatives Reform: Netting and Networks, Liquidity and Funding Markets, Conference Proceedings, August 2013, pp. 33–73.

[72] S. Anderson et al., (2013), To Link or Not to Link? Netting and Exposures between Central Counterparties, *Journal of Financial Market Infrastructures*, Vol. 1, Nr. 4, pp. 3–29.

[73] Garratt and Zimmerman, (2015), Ibid. p. 2 and R. Cont, and T. Kokholm, (2014), Central Clearing of OTC Derivatives: Bilateral vs Multilateral Netting, Statistics and Risk Modeling, Vol. 31, Nr. 1, pp. 3–22.

and Kokholm stick with the Duffie and Zhu induced 'homogeneous network assumption' whereas the model that Garratt and Zimmerman developed uses more general and realistic network structures. They examine, as indicated above, 'how the introduction of a CCP affects the variance, as well as the mean, of net exposures. Second, they provide an analytical generalization of the model so that it can be applied to any network.'[74]

Their conclusions have quite some implications, including some welfare effects. When the structure of the network is scale-free, introducing a CCP will undeniably lead to an increase of counterparty exposures, unless that CCP can clear all asset classes. That conclusion holds true for the smaller core-periphery network. The expected increase in net exposures is however offset by a reduction in volatility of these exposures. The larger the network (or a limited number of asset classes), the more that will emerge, which has welfare implications. Garratt and Zimmerman highlight 'net exposures relate to aggregate counterparty risk in the network, and to margin needs. If central clearing reduces both the expectation and variance of exposures, it would appear to be beneficial. If central clearing increase both the expectation and variance, then it would appear to reduce welfare. But in many cases the expectation increases while the variance falls (shown by the gray areas on our charts). In such cases, whether central clearing improves welfare or not here will depend on the risk appetite of the dealers in the network, policymakers and any other relevant agents. In general, if decision-makers are more risk averse, then they are likely to place more value on the effect on variance than the effect on mean, and so are more likely to favor the introduction of a CCP.'[75]

In the Garratt and Zimmerman model, the benefits of central clearing seem to accrue to the dealer-agents. That raises questions about the need and justification of regulatory intervention or as they put it 'what market failure does a regulator address by mandating central clearing, given that the dealer agents have chosen not to set up a CCP themselves?'.[76] The dealers apparently are less risk averse than the social optimum. That could occur 'if high or volatile margin requirements impose externalities on markets for the collateral assets or if agency problems mean that dealers take excessive risks'.[77] Under those circumstances the regulator should have a higher degree of risk aversion (compared to the dealers) and should mandate central clearing as an optimal policy measure. Further implication is that although a CCP may improve netting efficiency on an aggregate market level, it doesn't imply an improvement for each of the agents active in that market. The earlier

---

[74] Garratt & Zimmerman, (2015), Ibid. p. 3. See for other CCP network models (besides the Markose one already indicated): M. Galbiati, and K. Soramäki, (2012), Clearing Networks, *Journal of Economic Behavior & Organization*, Vol. 83, pp. 609–626, R. Song, et al., (2014), The Topology of Central Counterparty Clearing Networks and Network Stability, Stochastic Models, Vol. 30, Nr. 1, pp. 16–47, and S.R. Das, (2014), Matrix Metrics: Network-Based Systemic-Risk Scoring, Santa Clara University Working Paper.

[75] Garratt & Zimmerman, (2015), Ibid. p. 16.

[76] Garratt & Zimmerman, (2015), Ibid. p. 17.

[77] Garratt & Zimmerman, (2015), Ibid. p. 17 and D. Murphy, et al., (2014), An Investigation Into the Procyclicality of Risk-Based Initial Margin Models, Bank of England Financial Stability Paper, Nr. 29, London UK.

indicated research from Heath et al. already signaled that the netting benefits particularly and disproportionately accrue to 'core nodes' in the financial network. So the introduction of a CCP might then be socially but not Pareto-efficient.[78] It therefore might lead to a situation that those benefiting less might prefer to continue to trade bilaterally and as a consequence disrupt netting benefits for those who are inclined to the installed CCP. Another regulatory intervention would then be needed to ensure market efficiency.

Two features that their model ignores, and which might warrant further research, is the fact that there is (1) no correlation between magnitudes of exposures assumed in different asset classes. Multiple asset classes with positively correlated exposures will, when cleared over a CCP, yield limited netting benefits, and a single asset class CCP will improve netting efficiency; and (2) they assume that a link between two agents in one asset class implies a link in all asset classes. Although realistic, it will lead to fewer bilateral netting opportunities and a CCP would deliver greater benefits.[79]

In case of the swap market, the intermediation of a clearing has yielded the following observations: (1) reduced volumes with uncertain net impact on 'systemic risk', (2) increased attempts to avoid clearing leading to less standardized documentation, (3) interposition of clearinghouses will reduce behavior that exacerbates systemic risk during a crisis and (4) clearing is a predicate to reducing systemic risk through disintermediating swaps markets.[80] Material doubt continues to exist whether the clearing mandate effectively reduces systemic risk and 'it becomes difficult to defend the mandate against charges that it represents costly government meddling in private markets'.

5.6 The Need for Additional Collateral: An Issue?

As we have seen, on both counts higher collateral requirements are in place or well underway, that is, when traded OTC or through a CCP. But is all that collateral available and if so is it the quality sought for? As become clear in the introductory chapters of the regional SB analysis chapters, the (re)use of collateral is on the rise, and sometimes in concerning sizes. But there is no escape possible. In all three clearing models available, that is, (1) simple bilateral clearing (where each agent has to secure the trade by giving collateral to his counterparty), (2) segregated collateral clearing through a risk-averse third party (where each agent has to secure the trade by placing collateral in a segregated account managed by a third party) and (3) central counterparty (CCP) clearing (centralized clearing with segregation combined with joint loss sharing), require collateral and thus implies reduced investment income. The more sophisticated CCP model, and preferred by the regulator, is also the one that requires the

[78] Garratt & Zimmerman, (2015), Ibid. p. 17.

[79] Garratt & Zimmerman, (2015), Ibid. pp. 17–18.

[80] I. Beylin, (2015), A Reassessment of the Clearing Mandate: How the Clearing Mandate Affects Swap Trading Behaviour and the Consequences for Systemic Risk, Working Paper, pp. 52–53.

highest levels of collateral.[81] However Monnet and Nellen conclude that most gains will be derived from segregating collateral rather than from mutualization (in terms of welfare gains). Their findings help to explain the absence of CCP clearing in many other markets. They analyze how an optimal waterfall ratio should look like, in particular the relation between composition of defaulter-pays (initial margins) and survivors-pay instruments (total default fund contributions).[82]

Capponi and Cheng in their turn analyzed the collateral requirements in the market and concluded not only that collateral requirements were extreme[83] in many instances and that more specifically very high collateral requirements are imposed when (i) the contract is very risky (on a relative basis; measured by the volatility of the contract value over the depth of the private benefits to be realized), so that participating clients are mostly speculating as opposed to capturing fundamental value, and when (ii) the operational cost of client clearing is high, so that the clearinghouse lowers fee requirements to incentivize the member's participation but increase collateral requirements.[84] In the context of multiple CCPs, the collateral levels may be pushed even higher through hidden illiquidity effects.[85] Prior to Capponi and Cheng, it was assumed that (1) margins are exogenously specified for each contract,[86] (2) margins are set at a portfolio level according to a mixture of the expected shortfall, VaR and maximum shortfall measures[87] or (3) (variation) margin payments on swap transactions are set to track changes in mark-to-market value.[88]

---

[81] C. Monnet and T. Nellen, (2014), The Collateral Cost of Clearing, Swiss National Bank Working Paper, Nr. 2014/4; see also: D. Duffie, et al., (2014), Central Clearing and Collateral Demand, NBER Working Paper Series, Working Paper 19890.

[82] C. Monnet and T. Nellen, (2014), Ibid. pp. 2, 16–18, 34. D. Heller, and N. Vause, (2012), Collateral Requirements for Mandatory Central Clearing of Over-the-Counter Derivatives, BIS Working Papers, Nr. 373, Basel. See also D. Duffie et al., (2014), Central Clearing and Collateral Demand, Rock Center for Corporate Governance at Stanford University Working Paper Nr. 171.

[83] A. Capponi and W.A. Cheng, (2015), Central Clearing: Why Are Collateral Levels So Extreme?, Working Paper, Columbia University Research paper, mimeo, p. 2: On a fee-to-collateral ratio basis. They conclude that given the current regulatory framework, the resulting equilibrium can only involve very low or very high collateral levels, depending on the riskiness of the traded contract and the benefits that clients can capture from trading. Also E. Koechler and A. Simanenka, (2015), Collateral Risk for Fair Valuation and CCR Capital, Working Paper, November, mimeo.

[84] A. Capponi and W.A. Cheng, (2015), Central Clearing: Why Are Collateral Levels So Extreme?, Working Paper, Columbia University Research paper, mimeo.

[85] P. Glasserman, et al., (2014), Hidden Illiquidity with Multiple Central Counterparties, Columbia University Working Paper, mimeo.

[86] N. Garleanu, and L.H. Pedersen, (2011), Margin-Based Asset Pricing and Deviations from the Law of One Price, Review of Financial Studies, Vol. 24, Issue 6, pp. 1980–2022.

[87] D. Duffie, et al., (2015), Central Clearing and Collateral Demand, *Journal of Financial Economics*, Vol. 116, Issue 2, pp. 237–256.

[88] M. Johannes, and S. Sundaresan, (2007), The Impact of Collateralization on Swap Rates, *The Journal of Finance*, Vol. 62, Issue 1, pp. 383–410 and A. Capponi, (2013), Pricing and Mitigation of Counterparty Credit Exposures, In Handbook on Systemic Risk, Cambridge University Press, Cambridge, pp. 485–511.

5.7 Who Benefits from Central Clearing?

The question arises due to the fact that the new regulations that involve collateral is materially on the rise in many segments of the financial fabric. It also implies that new participants will have to enter the collateral and central clearing space. That space for a long time was limited to large dealers as participants. The new entrants will most likely be non-dealers. It is very likely that those large dealers, who are also the most sizeable dealers in that market will, while trying to eliminate counterparty risk and reduce the impact of information asymmetry, transfer their own risk onto the market and in particular on the non-dealers who tend to qualify as 'less risky' as they often don't function as a 'node' in the interconnectedness of the financial system, as dealers do. The new rules could very well have the collateral effect that it will facilitate shifting risk by 'riskier' dealer participants to non-dealer 'new entrants' to the central clearing market.[89]

5.8 Do CCPs Transmit Financial Stress?

It was explained above that the OTC market poses particular systemic risk issues. The uncovered counterparty risk and the concentration of parties engaged in the OTC market make it particularly prone to vulnerabilities resulting from interconnectedness. The links between CCPs and financial institutions take different forms and create several layers of interconnection: (1) at the most basic level, banks are CCP participants, namely, users of central clearing services, (2) banks are key providers of financial resources to CCPs. As direct clearing participants, they supply default fund contributions, (3) banks are key providers of financial services to CCPs and (4) banks may also be the owners of CCPs.[90]

However, it was also indicated that the new regulation might trigger a new and enhanced source of systemic risk. The reforms necessarily concentrate risk in one or a few CCPs and also increase institutions' demand for high-quality assets to meet collateral requirements. Heath et al. as discussed looked into this matter from a liquidity and solvency risk perspective under alternative clearing models. They extended their 2013 model in 2015. There is a two-fold difference between the models. The 2015 model uses actual derivative data and positions of a large pool of global banks active in the OTC markets. The second, and in my understanding, ever bigger improvement is that it 'extends the methodology to consider in greater depth the implications of loss allocation by CCPs to meet obligations once pre-funded financial resources have been exhausted, and in particular the mechanism of 'variation margin gains haircutting'.' The reason why it is so important is because that very same mechanism is preferred by many international supervisors and regulators and already applied in many jurisdictions. Their conclusion however is that designing and operating CCPs in accordance

[89] See S. Mayordomo and P.N. Poch, (2015), Does Central Clearing Benefit Risky Dealers, Working Paper.

[90] D. Domanski et al., (2015), Central Clearing: Trends and Current Issues, BIS Quarterly Review, December, pp. 62–63.

with international standards can limit the potential for stress to propagate through the system, even in very extreme market conditions.[91] Their model and research fits with the different strands of literature that have emerged over time about the role of CCPs, their potential to trigger systemic risk under changing regulatory conditions. Those different strands involve (1) the systemic importance of central counterparties, (2) the aspect of collateral and netting at the level of CCPs, and (3) the position of CCPs is case of recovery, planning and loss allocation.[92] What Heath et al. also add to their model is different triggers in terms of contagion, that is, they apply their model in both a 'pure price shock' environment as well as a scenario where they apply a combination of a 'price and solvency shock' scenario.[93] The different result yield important findings that are relevant from a policy point of view.

They can be summarized as[94]: (i) the trade-off between liquidity and solvency risk as collateral coverage increases, that is, 'the incidence of solvency stress declines sharply as initial margin coverage increases, but at the same time the incidence of liquidity stress steadily rises'; (ii) CCP default fund resources and loss-allocation mechanisms; and (iii) network analysis and also point at the limitations of the model used as it doesn't capture any possible scenario in the matrix using the different variables. It needs to be taken into account here that Heath et al. have been using a series of extreme 'tail-of-tail' scenarios to examine under what circumstances a CCP could be(come) a channel for contagion toward the wider financial system. Their analysis illustrates that 'under circumstances' the CCP, after having consumed its pre-funded resources and equity, a CCP can transmit stress back to its participants by haircutting their variation margin gains. Although the contagion risk is very mild, the analysis and thus also the scope of a potential spillover is dependent on 'a number of factors, including the loss allocation mechanism applied, the distribution and direction of positions among participants, the magnitude of price changes across product classes and their co-movement, and the financial position of participants at the time of the shock'.[95] That is what happens if regulation is model-based. Reality unfolds in frames that might or might not reflect reality during the next crisis.[96]

The good news is that their research underscores the importance of the pre-funded financial resources of the CCP, an element that has shown to be critical for many regulators around the world on this matter in recent years.[97] Understanding how those CCP

---

[91] A. Heath et al., (2015), Central Counterparty Loss Allocation and Transmission of Financial Stress, Reserve bank of Australia Research Discussion paper Nr. 2015-2, March, p. i.

[92] See for an actual review of the literature debate on the different matters: A. Heath, et al., (2015), Ibid. pp. 3–7.

[93] A. Heath, et al., (2015), Ibid. p. 19 and the results for the different scenarios pp. 23–35.

[94] See A. Heath et al., (2015), Ibid. pp. 35–40.

[95] See A. Heath et al., (2015), Ibid. p. 41.

[96] B. Cœuré, (2014), The Known Unknowns of Central Clearing, speech given at the meeting on 'Global Economy and Financial System', Hosted by the University of Chicago Booth School of Business Initiative on Global Markets, Coral Gables, 29 March.

[97] See also: B. Cœuré, (2015), Ensuring An Adequate Loss-Absorbing Capacity of Central Counterparties, special invited lecture by Member of the Executive Board of the ECB, at the Federal Reserve Bank of Chicago 2015 Symposium on Central Clearing, Chicago, April 10, 2015. See also: CPMI-IOSCO, (2014), Recovery of Financial Market Infrastructures, October and FSB, (2014), Key Attributes of Effective Resolution Regimes for Financial Institutions, Basel.

resources respond to different types of shocks and their intrinsic robustness will determine the level of contagion a CCP potentially will end back to the system. Contagion might therefore be caused by extreme price changes, but also the assumed co-movement between products and the closeout periods might have to be analyzed closer. The next step in literature will therefore have to be to gain a better understanding of 'how CCPs could transmit stress under alternative loss allocation mechanisms once pre-funded resources have been depleted'.[98] The same would be true for examining in more depth the 'implications of alternative loss allocation[99] mechanisms for participant incentives', that is, when participants walk away from a stressed CCP 'to avoid future obligations in loss allocation' or those participants that have more directional positions outstanding vis-à-vis the CCP. But the relativity of the model is clear: derivative positions, capital positions and liquidity holdings were given and now there is no doubt that they will 'change endogenously in response to alternative market structures'.[100] Only material disclosure provide a chance to be adequately equipped when tail risk kicks in.[101]

5.9 Non-centrally Cleared Derivatives and Securities Financing Transactions Revisited

Those derivatives do not enjoy the benefits of the counterparty risk mitigation through clearing. The implication is that risk management in an extensive way is the only option left. In an OTC derivatives market with a volume of about 800 Tr. USD, there is a certain volume of OTC derivatives that are not suitable for clearing. After the financial crisis, one of the key components of the reform program was to encourage the central clearing of standardized OTC derivatives. But for those who will not be cleared, standards were developed on margin requirements for non-centrally cleared OTC derivatives. Exchanging margin after all reduces counterparty credit risk and limits contagion by ensuring that collateral is available to offset losses caused by the default of a derivatives counterparty. Both IOSCO and the FSB have been pulling their weight regarding the haircuts applicable for those securities not cleared over a CCP.[102] Beyond the haircuts, extensive risk

[98] A. Heath et al., (2015), Ibid. p. 41.

[99] See also D. Elliott, (2013), Central Counterparty Loss-Allocation Rules, Bank of England, Financial Stability Paper, Nr. 20, April; D. Duffie, (2014), Resolution of Failing Central Counterparties, Graduate School of Business, Stanford University, December 17 and D. Duffie, and D. Skeel, (2012), A Dialogue on the Costs and Benefits of Automatic Stays for Derivatives and Repurchase Agreements, University of Pennsylvania Law School, January.

[100] A. Heath et al., (2015), Ibid. pp. 41–42.

[101] As suggested by IOSCO early 2015, see CPMI-IOSCO (2015), Public Quantitative Disclosure Standards for Central Counterparties, Bank for International Settlements, Basel. Also relevant in the context of resolution planning, see ISDA (2015), CCP Default Management, Recovery and Continuity: A Proposed Recovery Framework, Risk Management Position Paper, January.

[102] FSB, (2014), Regulatory Framework for Haircuts on Non-centrally Cleared Securities Financing Transactions, Strengthening Oversight and Regulation of Shadow Banking, Basel, October 14; IOSCO/BCBS, (2013), Margin Requirements for Non-centrally Cleared Derivatives, Basel, September.

management was advised.[103] Within that risk management framework, other techniques, beyond haircuts, have been suggested. They include 'documentation, confirmation, portfolio reconciliation and compression, valuation, and dispute resolution'.[104] Those all contribute one way or the other to three central benefits regarding non-centrally cleared OTC derivatives: (1) promoting legal certainty and facilitating timely dispute resolution, (2) the facilitation and management of counterparty risk and other risks, (3) increasing overall stability in the market.

But the central risk mitigating technique is and will stay the 'haircut'. In what follows I will provide a short review of the most important aspects and principles of the suggested haircut principles and which have already been introduced in many jurisdictions. Many concerns however remain. Two of the most important are the (1) impact of margin requirements on liquidity and (2) the potential of regulatory arbitrage to circumvent 'haircuts'. It is therefore that the liquidity impact has been carefully considered: '[t]he overall liquidity burden resulting from initial margin requirements, as well as the availability of eligible collateral to satisfy such requirements, has been carefully assessed in designing the margin framework.'[105]

5.9.1 The Philosophies Behind Haircuts

Already in 2012 the FSB,[106] through its workstream five, issued a note regarding the haircuts applied to the collateral used in securities financing transactions (principally repurchase agreements ('repos') and securities lending). It provided 13 recommendations to enhance transparency, strengthen regulation of securities financing transactions and improve market structure. Those recommendations covered areas such as disclosure, reporting, haircut practices, cash collateral reinvestment, re-hypothecation, valuation policies, central clearing and changes to insolvency/bankruptcy law[107] treatment regard-

---

[103] IOSCO, (2015), Risk Mitigation Standards for Non-centrally Cleared OTC Derivatives, FR01/2015, January 28.

[104] Which are all extensively discussed in IOSCO, (2015), Ibid.

[105] IOSCO/BCBS, (2013), Ibid. p. 3.

[106] FSB, (2012), Consultative Document on Strengthening Oversight and Regulation of Shadow Banking: A Policy Framework for Addressing Shadow Banking Risks in Securities Lending and Repos, WS5, Basel, November 18.

[107] A.J. Levitin, (2015), Clearinghouses and the Redundancy of the Bankruptcy Safe Harbors, Prioritization and Mutualization, pp. 1–25. He asks the question: When a firm fails who will bear the losses? Two basic methods of loss allocation appear in a variety of insolvency systems: prioritization and mutualization. Prioritization places creditors in a senior-subordinate priority structure that concentrates losses on a subset of the junior creditors, leaving the senior creditors unimpaired. Mutualization, in contrast, eschews a priority structure and allocates losses on a pro-rata basis. He argues for the repeal of the bankruptcy safe harbors for financial contracts because they are redundant systemic risk safeguards. Clearinghouses are a superior method to the safe harbors for protecting the liquidity of systemically important money substitutes and do not subordinate bankruptcy policy concerns to systemic risk concerns. Clearinghouses are a better guaranty against systemic disruption than the safe harbors because they can absorb the losses

ing repurchase and securities lending transactions. Regarding haircuts these recommendations have led to final recommendations issued in both 2013 and finalized in 2014 (infra). During the interim many assessments and reviews have been performed that detail the specifics of haircuts and measurement issues as well as data availability or the lack of.[108]

Before reviewing the final recommendations regarding haircuts, there are a few general observations and comments regarding the use of haircuts. A haircut is intended to hedge the credit, liquidity and other risks on a security being used as collateral by adjusting its value to reflect the potential loss arising from liquidation during a time of funding need or after a possible default by either a counterparty or the issuer of the asset. However, haircuts create problems. They represent the share of a security which cannot be funded in the repo market and requires a firm to draw on its own funds or unsecured borrowing, which increases the overall cost of funding. They also expose the borrower to the credit risk of the lender. Haircuts therefore can fuel procyclicality as haircuts would narrow in buoyant markets and narrow in depressed markets which would amplify the expansion of credit. Therefore, the FSB ultimately recommended minimum floors in haircuts rather than being very directive toward the markets. But many questions and critical decisions are left to the national regulator and supervisor. Those include to which securities transactions the haircut applies, the data availability to make proper decisions regarding prices and holding periods, the lack of objective criteria to define 'risky' assets, the impact on capital charges and how it relates to the Basel III rules being implemented, exempted transactions and counterparties.

Overall, the implication of haircuts is that they expose the borrower to the credit risk of the lender and increase his overall cost of financing,[109] while limiting his ability to borrow. Haircuts also 'encumber' a portion of the collateral securities, which means they would potentially not be available to recompense unsecured creditors and depositors if the borrower were to become bankrupt.

First, we will review the haircuts for OTC derivatives, where the IOSCO made the necessary recommendations and followed by the FSB recommendations regarding haircuts for securities financing transactions.

---

caused by insolvencies and fire sales due to their deep capital and lack of leverage. Moreover, clearinghouses reduce systemic risk by forcing internalization of systemic externalities on the finance industry through loss mutualization. This reduces the industries' incentive to engage in excessively risky transactions, so he argues.

[108] See, for example, DG for Internal Policies Department A (Economic and Monetary Affairs), (2013), Shadow Banking- Minimum Haircuts on Collateral, Frankfurt, July; H. Zhu, (2015), Margin and Haircut: Transparency, Fire-Sale Risk and Procyclicality, OFR-FSOC Annual Conference 2015, Presentation.

[109] Besides the fact that more collateral is required to service the same transaction and the question has arisen to what the market provides sufficient high quality collateral: see, for example, ECB, (2014), Collateral Eligibility and Availability, ECB, Frankfurt, July. There are also collateral implications. For example, other alternative assets will be used as collateral, for example, commodities. The more intense use will push up those prices. See, for example, K. Tang and H. Zhu, (2015), Commodities as Collateral, Working Paper April 9.

5.9.2 Haircuts for OTC Derivatives

For the OTC derivatives and their haircut, the IOSCO suggests the following principles[110]:

- The development of appropriate margining practices.
- FIs must exchange initial and variation margin as appropriate to the counterparty risks posed by such transactions.
- The methodologies for calculating initial and variation margin that serve as the baseline for margin collected from a counterparty should (i) be consistent across entities covered by the requirements and reflect the potential future exposure (initial margin) and current exposure (variation margin) associated with the portfolio of non-centrally cleared derivatives in question and (ii) ensure that all counterparty risk exposures are fully covered with a high degree of confidence.
- To ensure that assets collected as collateral for initial and variation margin purposes can be liquidated in a reasonable amount of time to generate proceeds that could sufficiently protect collecting entities covered by the requirements from losses on non-centrally cleared derivatives in the event of a counterparty default, these assets should be highly liquid and should, after accounting for an appropriate haircut, be able to hold their value in a time of financial stress.
- Initial margin should be exchanged by both parties, without netting of amounts collected by each party (i.e. on a gross basis), and held in such a way as to ensure that (i) the margin collected is immediately available to the collecting party in the event of the counterparty's default; and (ii) the collected margin must be subject to arrangements that fully protect the posting party to the extent possible under applicable law in the event that the collecting party enters bankruptcy.
- Transactions between a firm and its affiliates should be subject to appropriate regulation in a manner consistent with each jurisdiction's legal and regulatory framework.
- Regulatory regimes should interact so as to result in sufficiently consistent and non-duplicative regulatory margin requirements for non-centrally cleared derivatives across jurisdictions.
- Margin requirements should be phased in over an appropriate period of time to ensure that the transition costs associated with the new framework can be appropriately managed. Regulators should undertake a coordinated review of the margin standards once the requirements are in place and functioning to assess the overall efficacy of the standards and to ensure harmonization across national jurisdictions as well as across related regulatory initiatives.

[110] IOSCO/BCBS, (2013), Ibid. p. 4. They are extensively discussed on pp. 6–24.

5.9.3 Haircuts for Non-centrally Cleared Securities Financing Transactions

For non-centrally cleared securities financing transactions, the FSB set out recommendations late 2014.[111] That occurred after the report on the vulnerabilities and sensitivities characterizing the repo and securities lending markets was issued mid-2013.[112]

To put these measures into perspective, the starting point is that like banks, a leveraged and maturity-transforming shadow banking system can be vulnerable to 'runs' and generate contagion risk, thereby 'amplifying systemic risk'. It can also 'heighten procyclicality by accelerating credit supply and asset price increases' during surges in confidence, while making 'precipitate falls in asset prices and credit more likely by creating credit channels vulnerable to sudden loss of confidence'.[113] One of the workstream (WS5) was dedicated to securities lending and repos.

The FSB has acknowledged that the securities lending and repo markets play a crucial role in international finance and support price discovery and market liquidity for many public and private securities and are central to the ability of many financial intermediaries to make markets in securities and facilitate risk management and are core to the funding needs of many financial institutions. On the other hand, the FSB has also expressed concern at the large number of repo and securities lending transactions entered into by non-banks which it believes can give rise to risks arising from maturity and liquidity transformation. The policy recommendations it produced in 2013, and which are discussed in the relevant chapter (Chap. 4), include (1) requiring non-bank entities engaging in securities lending to be subject to minimum regulatory standards for cash collateral reinvestment, (2) encouraging more central clearing of securities financing transactions, (3) requiring regulatory authorities to adopt principles in respect of the re-hypothecation of securities (particularly requiring sufficient disclosure to clients to enable them to understand their potential exposure in the event of a failure of the financial intermediary) and (4) limiting re-hypothecation to entities subject to adequate regulation of liquidity risks. The recommendations also included a requirement for authorities to adopt minimum regulatory standards for collateral valuation and management. In their 2013 report, they already made suggestions regarding final recommendations in relation to qualitative standards for methodologies used by market participants to calculate haircuts and the introduction of a numerical haircut floor framework. These were finalized in the FSB's 2014

[111] FSB, (2014), Regulatory Framework for Haircuts on Non-centrally Cleared Securities Financing Transactions, Basel, October 16.

[112] That occurred in 2013: FSB, (2013), Policy Framework for Addressing Shadow Banking Risks in Securities Lending and Repos, Basel, August 29. These recommendations regarded financial stability risks in relation to securities financing transactions. The report also included consultative proposals on a regulatory framework for haircuts on certain non-centrally cleared securities financing transactions.

[113] FSB, (2014), Ibid. p. ii. The FSB comments '[t]hese effects were powerfully revealed in 2007–09 in the dislocation of asset-backed commercial paper (ABCP) markets, the failure of an originate-to-distribute model employing structured investment vehicles (SIVs) and conduits, "runs" on MMFs, and a sudden reappraisal of the terms on which securities lending and repos were conducted'.

reporting and added five further recommendations discussed further. In the same 2014 report, the FSB also inserted another consultation regarding the application of numerical haircut floors to cover non-bank to non-bank transactions backed by collateral other than government securities (infra this chapter).

Before examining the final haircut recommendations, I would like to review the less discussed report that accompanied the FSB's 2014 report on haircuts. The FSB issued the report 'Procyclicality of Haircuts: Evidence from the QIS1[114]' setting out the FSB's findings on the procyclicality of haircuts on non-centrally cleared securities financing transactions during the financial crisis. Two questions go hand-in-hand here: (1) are haircuts procyclical? And (2) did the repo market play an important role in securitization and shadow banking in the run-up of the crisis? Those questions already received a fair amount of attention: (1) Gorton and Metrick[115] presented evidence that repo haircuts increased in the US bilateral repo market during the crisis. Both spreads and haircuts respond to collateral risk, and which factors in price volatility and illiquidity/opacity of the collateral as well as mutual counterparty risk of lender and borrower in a bilateral repo. Haircuts rise faster for reasons regarding the latter than the former.[116] However, Copeland et al.[117] found that investors in the US tri-party repo market tended to stop lending completely rather than increasing haircuts[118] during the crisis, and (2) Adrian and Shin[119] showed that repo transactions accounted for most of the procyclical adjustment of the leverage of investment banks in the US. However, Krishnamurthy et al.[120] found that the contraction of repos as an available funding source for financing non-agency MBS/ABS prior to the crisis appeared small for the shadow banking system as a whole. The findings of the FSB 2014 report need to be read in combination with the first stage of the quantitative impact study (QIS1) on the proposed framework for numerical haircut floors on non-centrally cleared securities financing transactions issued in 2013.[121] The 2014 report focuses on the procyclicality of haircuts and its role during the global financial crisis.

---

[114] FSB, (2014), Procyclicality of Haircuts: Evidence from the QIS1, Basel, October 16.

[115] G. Gorton, and A. Metrick, (2011), Securitized Banking and the Run on Repo, *Journal of Financial Economics*, Vol. 104, Issue 3, pp. 425–451.

[116] J.K. Auh and M. Landoni, (2015) The Role of Margin and Spread in Secured Lending. Evidence from the Bilateral Repo Market, Working Paper, August, mimeo.

[117] A. Copeland, et al., (2011), Repo Runs: Evidence from the Tri-Party Repo Market, Federal Reserve Bank of New York Staff Report Nr. 506, NY.

[118] See in detail on the relation between pricing, haircuts, collateral and type of intermediation: Z. Song, (2015), Intermediation and Pricing in Tri-Party Repo Market, Working Paper, July, mimeo. Non-primary dealers that are less active in general tri-party market pay higher borrowing rate than US and foreign primary dealers that are more active. The repo volume of foreign primary dealers decreases sharply at quarter ends because of regulation-induced balance sheet reductions, which may constrain their intermediation capacity.

[119] T. Adrian, and H. S. Shin, (2009), Money, Liquidity and Monetary Policy, American Economic Review, Vol. 99, Issue 2, pp. 600–605.

[120] A. Krishnamurthy, et al., (2014), Sizing up Repo, *Journal of Finance*, Vol. 69, Issue 6, pp. 2381–2417.

[121] See FSB, (2013), Policy Framework for Addressing Shadow Banking Risks in Securities Lending and Repos, Annex 3, pp. 35–39.

The conclusions[122] of the FSB to the two questions poised above were that (1) haircuts increased significantly during the crisis,[123] especially for loans to non-banks where the collateral was non-government securities. However, the evidence is mixed regarding whether haircuts decreased in a procyclical manner after the crisis. Nevertheless, the dataset demonstrates the existence of significant differences in haircut movements across different currencies and market segments,[124] and (2) their estimates[125] show that the reduction in total repo funding was significant in both absolute terms and as a percentage of bank lending to non-banks (relative terms), but the reduction in repo funding against private-label securitization was small as a percentage of total securities outstanding.

5.9.4 The Methodologies for Calculating Haircuts

The FSB recommends that 'regulatory authorities should set qualitative standards for the methodologies that firms use to calculate collateral margins or haircuts, whether on an individual transaction or a portfolio basis'.[126]

When calculating haircuts on an individual basis, the following standards should apply[127]:

- Haircuts should be based on the market risks of the assets used as collateral and be calibrated at a high confidence level, using a long historical time period that includes at least one stress period, in order to cover potential declines in collateral values during liquidation. Haircut methodologies should not be based on a rolling short window.
- Haircuts should capture other risk considerations when necessary. Those include the risk of liquidating large concentrated positions (liquidation risk) and the 'wrong-way risk'[128] between collateral value and counterparty default. Specific characteristics of the

[122] FSB, (2014), Procyclicality of Haircuts: Evidence from the QIS1, Basel, October 16, p. 1. See for similar findings: BIS, (2010), The role of margin requirements and haircuts in procyclicality, Report submitted by a Study Group established by the Committee on the Global Financial System (Chair D. Longworth), CGFS Paper Nr. 36, March, Basel.

[123] 'We can see that haircut levels and dispersion increased dramatically for all collateral types except government securities during the sample (i.e. also during the crisis). After the crisis, haircuts on private label securitisation collateral continued to increase as that market remained illiquid. However, haircuts on equities collateral posted by non-bank counterparties decreased significantly after the crisis' (p. 3)…'The QIS1 data set reflects that haircuts on reverse repos to non-banks were not always greater than those to banks, especially after the crisis. This information was contrary to the general expectation that banks would be considered to be the more creditworthy counterparties' (p. 4).

[124] The FSB asked firms to only report their reverse repos, that is, where they lend cash to banks and non-banks against collateral (the outstanding amount of reverse repos, broken down by counterparty type, collateral type and haircut levels).

[125] FSB, (2014), Ibid. pp. 5–6.

[126] FSB, (2014), Regulatory Framework for Haircuts on Non-centrally Cleared Securities Financing Transactions, Basel, October 16, p. 6.

[127] FSB, (2014), Ibid. pp. 4–5.

[128] 'Wrong-way risk' arises when the exposure to a particular counterparty is positively correlated with the probability of default of the issuer of the collateral due to the nature of the transactions with the counterparty.

collateral, which include asset type, issuer creditworthiness, residual maturity, price sensitivity (such as modified duration), optionality, complexity of structure, expected liquidity in stressed periods and the frequency of collateral valuation and margining, should also be taken into account. Other elements include creditworthiness of counterparties and foreign exchange risk (and its historical volatility).

For measurements on a portfolio basis, similar general principles apply[129]:

- Methodologies for portfolio margin calculation should not be procyclical. They should not lead to an automatic decline in margin requirements as the prices of assets in the portfolio increase or as the (actual or implied) volatility of asset prices in the portfolio decreases.
- When setting margin requirements for different counterparties and portfolios, market participants should consider the following: (1) market risk of the portfolio (as measured by, e.g. the change in the value of the portfolio if market indices rise or fall by defined percentages); (2) portfolio concentration by geographies, economic sectors and individual issuers; (3) illiquidity of the portfolio (e.g. portfolios may be illiquid when positions are concentrated or large relative to either the outstanding amount or the average trading volume) and (4) risks arising from non-correlated price and spread relationships between lent securities and collateral portfolio assets.
- Methodologies should include robust stress testing of margin requirements against a range of historical and hypothetical stress scenarios.

In particular, the FSB believes that regulatory authorities should seek to minimize the extent to which haircut methodologies are procyclical. The FSB indicates as listed above that haircuts should be based on the 'market risks of the assets used as collateral and be calibrated using a long historical time period, including at least one period of stress with a view to reflecting a potential decline in value of the collateral during liquidation'. The FSB further is convinced that 'potential procyclical fluctuations in haircuts can be limited by moderating the extent to which such fluctuations are reduced in benign market conditions (with low volatility and rising prices) to mitigate the magnitude of the potential increase in volatile markets'.

In addition, the assumed timeframe for collateral liquidation should be 'conservative and reflect the expected liquidity or illiquidity of the asset in stressed market conditions and take account of market characteristics of the collateral including trading volumes and market depth'. Haircuts should also take into account other relevant risk considerations including the risk of liquidating large concentrated positions, wrong-way risk (when the exposure to a particular counterparty is positively correlated with the probability of default of the collateral issuer due to the nature of the transactions with the counterparty), specific characteristics of the collateral and any foreign exchange risk. Where margin is calculated on a portfolio basis (where portfolios may include long and short positions in securities and

---

[129] FSB, (2014), Ibid. pp. 5–6.

related derivatives), the FSB states that care should be taken to ensure that the methodologies for the haircut calculation are not procyclical and should consider the market risk of the portfolio, geographic and sectorial concentrations, illiquidity risks and risks arising from non-correlated price and spread relationships between lent securities and collateral portfolio assets.[130] The FSB also recommends that regulators should consider regular testing of the adequacy of margin methodologies used by market participants through regular hypothetical portfolio exercises with a view to identifying any market-wide changes in levels of margin requirements over time and any firms with unusually low margin requirements.

5.9.5 Effective Numerical Floors on Haircuts

5.9.5.1 Floors for OTC Derivatives

For calculating the numerical floors on haircuts, the FSB makes four suggestions[131]:

- For non-centrally cleared securities transactions where banks and broker-dealers provide financing to non-banks against collateral other than government securities, the Basel Committee should review its capital treatment of securities financing transactions and incorporate a framework of numerical haircut floors into the Basel III framework by the end of 2015.
- Following the incorporation of the framework of haircut floors into Basel III as specified above, national authorities should implement such framework by the end of 2017.
- Taking into account the findings on the FSB's consultation on proposed approaches for applying the framework of numerical haircut floors to non-bank to non-bank transactions set out in Annex 4 of the FSB Paper, national authorities should introduce the framework of numerical floors for haircuts applicable to such transactions by the end of 2017.
- The FSB, in coordination with the relevant international standard setting bodies, will monitor the implementation of the framework of numerical haircut floors and will consider reviewing the framework, including its scope and levels as necessary.

The objective of the FSB is that through these haircuts it aims to limit the possible build-up of leverage outside the banking system and reduce the procyclicality of that leverage. It envisages that the haircut floors will act as a backstop in a benign market environment. The FSB stresses, however, that the floors are not intended to dictate market haircuts and participants should conduct their own assessment as to the appropriate level of haircuts. The FSB explains that it is focusing on transactions involving non-banks because applying floors to securities financing received by banks and broker-dealers subject to adequate capital and liquidity regulation on a consolidated basis is likely to duplicate existing regulations. It has also excluded transactions backed by government securities

[130] See above and FSB, (2014), Ibid. pp. 3–6.

[131] FSB, (2014), Ibid. pp. 6–10.

Table 5.1 Haircuts for OTC derivatives and securities financing transactions

	Haircut level	
Residual maturity of collateral	Corporate and other issuers	Securitized products
≤1 year debt securities, and floating rate notes (FRNs)	0.5%	1%
>1 year, ≤5 years debt securities	1.5%	4%
>5 year, ≤10 years debt securities	3%	6%
>10 years debt securities	4%	7%
Main index equities	6%	
Other assets within the scope of the framework	10%	

as it believes that price movements in these securities generally tend not to be procyclical and haircuts on these transactions have been comparatively stable over time at zero or a very low level. The proposed levels for numerical haircut floors in respect of securities against cash transactions based on the FSB's consultation exercise are set out in Table 5.1.

The final haircut levels are also higher than originally envisaged by the FSB. In particular, the haircut for main index equities is set at 6%, increased from 4% as proposed in the August 2013 report.

The FSB notes that the numerical haircut floors are intended to apply both where haircuts are applied at the transaction level and where margin is applied at the portfolio level. The FSB states that special repos (transactions conducted to finance assets in high market demand) are not exempt from the scope of its proposals on haircut floors. The FSB also states that 'collateral upgrade transactions' involving the borrowing of securities against other securities that attract higher haircuts as collateral could potentially be used to circumvent the requirement on numerical haircut floors. It therefore proposes that the floors should apply to such collateral upgrade transactions with the floor being equal to the difference between the floors that would apply to repos of the collateral types on the two legs of the transaction effected separately.

In relation to implementation of numerical haircut floors, the FSB suggests three possible approaches[132]:

(1) Entity-based regulation: numerical haircut floors would be implemented through regulations targeted at each type of entity that engages in securities financing transactions.
(2) Product-based regulation: floors would be implemented through product-based regulation or market regulation targeted at the activity of providing securities financing to non-banks. The providers of the securities financing would be required to conduct transactions above the numerical haircut floor or collect minimum margin amounts consistent with the floor.
(3) Hybrid approach: floors would be implemented through a combination of the above approaches.

---

[132] FSB, (2014), Ibid. pp. 10–12.

5.9.5.2 Floors for Non-centrally Cleared Securities Financing Transactions

In conjunction with its recommendations, the FSB states that, in coordination with relevant international standard setting bodies, it will establish a monitoring framework involving the relevant regulatory authorities seeking to capture the trends and risks in securities financing transactions. The results may be included in the FSB's annual global shadow banking monitoring exercise. It indicates that based on the monitoring results, it could in the future consider reviewing the level of the floors or the counterparty and collateral scope of its requirements.

As part of this 2014 framework discussed above, the FSB recommended that the Basel Committee on Banking Supervision (BCBS) incorporate the haircut floors into the capital requirements for non-centrally cleared SFTs by setting significantly higher capital requirements for transactions with haircuts traded below the haircut floors. To that effect a consultative round was organized that will end early 2016 and aims to create incentives for banks to set their collateral haircuts above the floors rather than hold more capital.

However, there are circumstances under which implementation of the haircut floors could be arbitraged when applied at a netting set (or portfolio) level. That is, banks could implement a strategy using one or more SFT transactions to deliberately avoid the higher capital requirements, while achieving a net position that is economically equivalent to a trade that should be subject to higher capital requirements under the proposal. These situations were considered when developing the proposed higher capital requirements for in-scope transactions under the Basel capital rules. Examples of these arbitrage opportunities include:

(i) Arbitrage between long and short SFT positions using the same security

There is a possible regulatory arbitrage by using two or more offsetting trades with the same underlying securities in a netting agreement that will not be subject to the higher capital requirements at individual level, but would if the net position is considered. The possibility is due to the fact that when the bank lends cash, the SFT is subject to the FSB floors, but if it borrows cash on that same SFT, the transaction will not be subject to the FSB floors.

(ii) Arbitrage using upgrade of collateral with a security not subject to the FSB proposal

At a netting set level, another arbitrage opportunity would consist in 'upgrading' the collateral with a security that is either not subject to a floor (e.g. sovereign debt) or subject to a lower floor. For example, a shadow bank could use an SFT to borrow sovereign debt against corporate debt, and then borrow cash against the sovereign debt. None of these trades would be subject to the FSB floors on an individual basis; however, on a net basis, simply borrowing cash against corporate debt would be penalized under the FSB's proposal.

The higher capital requirements apply at the transaction level and only to the transactions in scope whether or not the transaction is contained in a netting set. To determine whether the higher capital requirements apply to an SFT or a netting set of SFTs, it is necessary to compare the collateral haircut (traded under the SFT transaction or calculated as per the rules) and a haircut floor (from Table above or calculated as per the rules indicated).

5.9.6 Application of Haircut Floors to Non-bank to Non-bank Transactions

Annex 4[133] of the FSB paper sets out, as indicated above, proposed approaches applying numerical haircut floors to non-bank to non-bank transactions backed by collateral other than government securities. The FSB state this is part of its objective of limiting the build-up of excess leverage outside the banking system and to maintain a level playing field between bank and non-bank lenders. It also wishes to reduce the risk of regulatory arbitrage and avoid parties avoiding regulatory requirements by shifting securities financing to non-bank to non-bank transactions.

The FSB outline three general approaches for the application of a framework of numerical haircut floors to non-bank to non-bank transactions, again being entity-based regulation, product-based regulation or a hybrid approach.

Entity-based regulation would involve national authorities modifying existing regulatory requirements for non-bank entities such as insurance companies, pension funds and other funds to implement the floors. The FSB notes this would provide challenges including not being able to capture transactions by entities that are not subject to some type of regulation. In relation to product-based or market regulation, the FSB envisages market regulation being used to prohibit market participants from conducting in-scope transactions below the numerical haircut floors. Unregulated lenders that conduct such transactions could be subject to registration and reporting requirements to enable authorities to monitor compliance. Although the FSB believes this would provide the widest coverage of entities, it notes that there are challenges for this approach including there being no harmonized international standards specifically in relation to securities financing activities and it being possible for market participants to seek to restructure transactions to circumvent the regulations. A hybrid approach would allow a tailoring of existing regulatory rules and provide authorities with flexibility in implementing the haircut floors in the way considered to be most appropriate for the relevant jurisdiction which may involve a mix of entity-based and market regulation. The FSB notes this would be the most complex approach and could result in overlapping requirements. The FSB asks for views on the strengths and weaknesses of these possible approaches or any alternatives.

---

[133] FSB, (2014), Ibid. pp. 14–16, 27–29.

5.9.7 Implementation of These Standards

In the responses to the FSB's consultation on the methodologies for calculating haircuts and the introduction of a haircut floor, concerns were raised that, although the FSB stresses these are minimum requirements and parties should conduct their own assessment as to the appropriate level of haircuts, the FSB minimums will be treated by the market as becoming the de facto norm. Respondents also highlighted the difficulty in calibrating mandatory minimum haircut levels so as to strike an appropriate balance between reducing procyclical risks and the building up of excess leverage as against avoiding compromising market efficiency and liquidity. Although the responses did not suggest the FSB's initially proposed minimum haircuts were likely to cause undue difficulties to the market, the final minimum haircuts are higher in some respects and it remains to be seen what effect these will have on securities financing transactions and the types of collateral used.

These recommendations complete the initial work of the FSB in relation to securities financing transactions with work already well underway by many authorities to implement the recommendations set out in the August 2013 Report. In the EU, the European Commission published a draft regulation in January 2014, which is discussed elsewhere focusing on rules relating to transparency, disclosure and re-hypothecation.[134,135] This regulation does not seek to deal with methodologies for calculating collateral haircuts or the imposition of numerical haircut floors.

The proposed regulation has been subject to a number of modifications which include[136]:

- Securities financing transactions (SFTs): the Regulation should cover repurchase transactions, securities or commodities lending, securities or commodities borrowing, buy-sell back or sell-buy back transactions, liquidity swaps and collateral swap transactions as laid down in Regulation (EU) No 575/2013 or total return swaps as defined in Commission Regulation (EU) Nr. 231/2013.
- Reporting obligation: counterparties to securities financing transactions shall report the details of such transactions to a trade repository registered or recognized in accordance with this regulation. The details shall be reported no later than the third working day following the conclusion, modification or termination of the transaction but as soon as the reporting is possible. The central banks of the European System of Central Banks (ESCB) are exempt from the obligation to report their SFTs to trade

[134] Proposal for a regulation of the European Parliament and of the Council on reporting and transparency of securities financing transactions, 2014/0017 (COD), COM(2014) 40 final, January 19, 2014.

[135] Regulation 2015/2365, OJ L 337 of 23.12.2015, pp. 1–34.

[136] Committee on Economic and Monetary Affairs report on the proposal for a regulation of the European Parliament and of the Council on reporting and transparency of securities financing transactions (COM(2014)0040, April 8, 2015, A8-0120/2015, Plenary Session).

repositories but must cooperate with competent authorities, including by providing them directly with a description of their SFTs, upon request.

- Transparency obligation toward investors: the amended text stipulated that securities financing transactions are also used by other financial counterparties, such as credit institutions, and by non-financial counterparties, thereby creating specific risks for those who hold shares or who are clients of those counterparties. Members proposed that credit institutions should therefore disclose their activities in SFTs. Likewise, listed companies are required to disclose any activities in SFTs to their shareholders, who should be able to make informed choices about the risk profile of the companies in which they invest. Consequently, those credit institutions and listed companies should also inform the public of their activities in SFTs as part of their regular public report.
- Transparency and re-use: this Regulation shall apply to a counterparty engaging in re-use that is established in the Union, including all its branches irrespective of where they are located or in third country, under specific conditions.
- The term 're-use' is defined as the use by a receiving counterparty, in its own name and for its own account or for the account of another counterparty, including any natural person. Members specified the conditions to be met for the counterparties to be able to re-use the financial instruments received as collateral.

An item that has been less discussed in the process of defining these haircuts is the fact that haircuts itself also have an impact on asset prices. The shadow banking system is not a deposit-based system. It is a monetary system that creates money-like claims. Haircuts therefore will have an impact on asset prices.[137] That impact is magnified or mitigated by the level of interest rate in the market.

The genie is out of the bottle and no day goes by or questions are asked if the CCP model as now envisaged and included in regulation (or proposals) doesn't replace one bad by the other. The EU, from its side, was due in May 2015[138] to engage in its review and evaluation of the Regulation (EU) Nr. 648/2012 on OTC derivatives, central counterparties and trade repositories. The idea is to generate feedback regarding the experiences of stakeholders regarding the implementation of the EMIR. The European Commission, only a few weeks later, adopted an implementing act that will extend the transitional period for capital requirements for EU banking groups' exposures to central counterparties (CCPs) under the Capital Requirements Regulation (CRR).

The European Supervisory Authority has been launching consultation rounds for the development draft regulatory technical standards (RTS) outlining the framework of the European Market Infrastructure Regulation (EMIR). For those over-the-counter

[137] J. Hao, (2015), Shadow Banking and Asset Prices, Working Paper, February 8, pp. 24–29.

[138] EC, (2015), Public Consultation on Regulation (EU) Nr. 648/2012 on OTC Derivatives, Central Counterparties and Trade Repositories, Brussels.

(OTC) derivative transactions that will not be subject to central clearing, these draft RTS prescribe the regulatory amount of initial and variation margin that counterparties should exchange as well as the methodologies for their calculations. In addition, these draft RTS outline the criteria for the eligible collateral and establish the criteria to ensure that such collateral is sufficiently diversified and not subject to wrong-way risk.[139] But at the same time, questions are still asked about the nature and methodologies for valuing derivative liabilities,[140] demonstrating the relativity of the different enacted regulation.

5.10 Did We Create New SIFIs Through CCP Regulation?

Through the standardization of OTC contracts and the requirement to clear them over CCPs, those CCPs have become pillars of the new global financial architecture. Its role is to mitigate counterparty risk and contagion, but in order to function properly they have been turned into SIFIs whose failure might have disastrous consequences for financial stability. As discussed capital rules and CCP loss waterfalls have been created to manage that risk or even mitigate it. Also, extensive risk management practices were introduced to monitor and hopefully manage those risks. And stress tests need to account for the interconnectedness of CCPs through common members and cross-margin agreements.

Let's have a closer look at the cash flow waterfall and other loss recovery provisions and see if we can convince ourselves about the SIFI nature of the created CCPs. In any loss-allocation and recovery model, the following principles and incentives should apply[141]:

- Loss-allocation and recovery mechanisms are not only about their effectiveness of absorbing risks but also about risk management incentives.
- Any potential margin requirement for investors using the CCPP (CCP members) should not only be based on the market risk of their portfolios but also include a liquidity charge corresponding to the potential additional cost incurred by the CCP for liquidating the member's portfolio in extreme market conditions.
- Any default fund that should cover default losses (of the CCP or any of its members) should not rely on (unverifiable) assumptions on the default probabilities or default

[139] See in detail: EBA, (2015), Draft Regulatory Technical Standards on risk-mitigation techniques for OTC derivative contracts not cleared by a CCP under Article 11(15) of Regulation (EU) No 648/2012, JC/CP/2015/002, London, June 10. Final version of the RTS published OJ L 340, 15.12.2016, pp. 9–46. Later amendments made were added in 2017.

[140] EBA, (2015), Draft Regulatory Technical Standards, On the Valuation of Derivatives, EBA/CP/2015/10, London, May 13. These technical standards apply to the Bank Recovery and Resolution Directive (BRRD), but the underlying problem has general validity.

[141] See extensively on each of those elements: R. Cont, (2015), The End of the Waterfall: Default Resources of Central Counterparties, Working Paper, April (also released as Norges Bank Working Paper Nr. 2015-16 and published in Risk Management in Financial Institutions, Vol. 8, Issue 4, pp. 365–389).

correlations of members but consider the worst-case scenario loss for the CCP across all possible defaults.

- The contribution of members to the default fund should be based on the exposure of the CCP to the member as other allocation schemes and mechanisms (proportionate to initial margin, open interest or trading volume) might distort risk management and create adverse incentives.
- The capital of a CCP should be exposed to default risk ('skin in the game') before any of the contribution of non-defaulting members are used (in the default fund). The magnitude of the exposure of the CCPs equity should be proportionate to the members' payments in the default fund and should potentially impact a meaningful portion of the CCPs' equity position (non-negligible).
- The resources a CCP has available in case of default ('default resources') should be subject to independent stress testing using a logic and transparent methodology, preferably one that can be used across CCPs clearing the same instruments.
- Assets held in the CCP default fund have the risk profile of the senior tranche of the CCP's exposure to member defaults. The risk weight attached to a CCP default fund should depend on the subordination of this tranche, which in turn depends on the margin pool and the CCP's 'skin-in-the-game'.
- Many members have positions outstanding across multiple CCPs and have interoperating agreements between CCPs outstanding. Stress tests therefore should take into account that interconnectedness (of different CCPs and their clearing members).[142] Ultimately, solvency and liquidity contagion are tail risks.
- Recovery provisions and variation margin haircuts (or even contract tear-ups) may provide relief for the CCP in case of distress and should be captured by the member's contribution in the default fund. An open issue remains to what degree the liquidity shifting from the CCP to its members through recovery provisions will not push other members to the edge of default.
- A conservative stress test should therefore refrain from assuming the availability of unfunded default resources, and priority should be given to funded resources.
- The above-mentioned variation margin haircuts allocate losses in the same way as would happen in a resolution scenario. The benefit is that it will provide for continuity of clearing services and avoids the irreversibility and costs associated with a full resolution. But given its functionality, the variation margin haircut can be efficient when losses arise from large mark-to-market losses in instruments cleared by the CCP, but not when a member defaults due to losses in assets not cleared by the CCP.
- It has been argued that CCPs in case of liquidity shortage should be provided access to central banking liquidity facilities (potentially limited to those members residing in the jurisdiction(s) of the central banks in question). Given the nature and scope of the

[142] The structure of the network through which contagion spreads is critical for propagation of losses and the damage is done; S. Gabrieli et al., (2015), Cross-Border Interbank Contagion in the European Banking Sector, Working Paper Banque de France Nr. 545, March. They indicate 'results show the critical impact of the underlying network structure on the propagation of losses. An econometric analysis of the determinants of contagion shows that the position of a bank in the network and its exposure to the riskiest counterparties are significantly correlated with default outcomes'.

product group cleared and given the wider discussion in this book regarding the functionality and scope of the central bank liquidity window, this view cannot be supported.

- The possibility for the CCP of closing certain unbalanced open positions provides a further backstop against continued losses. However, contract tear-up results in a loss allocation across members which is not transparent ex ante and thus does not provide clear incentives to members.
- It has been suggested to use the initial margin of non-defaulted members as a source of funds for the CCP during recovery. Such 'initial margin haircuts' blur the distinction between margin requirements and default fund contributions, reduce transparency of risk exposures for members and distort members' risk incentives. It would in those situations be better to increase the size of the default fund.
- The objective is to provide stability in the financial markets, not ensure survival of the CCP at all costs. That implies letting CCPs go under extreme circumstances.
- CCPs as well as its members are engaged in what is considered a transnational business (assets, members and structures are international in nature). That requires international guidelines on cross-border resolution.

So the four layers in the waterfall are (1) the margin, (2) defaulter's clearing fund, (3) survivor's clearing fund and (4) other financial resources. Murphy and Nahai-Williamson assess the prudence of the cover II standard[143] for different distributions of risk exposure among CMs (clearing members). They investigate how the distribution of risk exposure among members impacts a CCP's resilience. They find that the cover II charge may not be prudent for uniform exposure distributions. At that point, CCP resilience depends on the CMs' capacity to jointly carry losses beyond the default fund. Especially in a distressed market, a CM's lower payment capability and (possibly) higher default probability may impact his ability to raise (external) funding. Also, if CMs have higher default probabilities, the CCP will rely more on member mutuality to cover losses and possibly undergo more default shocks.[144] Armakola and Laurent investigate the exposures of CMs via risk-sharing mechanisms embedded in the CCP waterfall. They consider pre-funded resources, recovery tools and assessment powers across EU and US CCPs to assess possible CM exposure. As the efficiency of the waterfall, especially the default fund and its replenishment via assessment powers, depends on the soundness of a CCP's surviving member base, we investigate member base quality under normal and stressed scenarios.[145] In case of a CM default, the CCP will use the defaulter's initial margin (IM) and default fund contribution to cover the occurred losses, followed by a designated tranche of CCP capital, the so-called skin-in-the-game (SIG) amount.[146] In case of member defaults with losses exceeding the defaulter's

[143] The regulatory default fund standard (cover II) requires the covering of the default of the two CMs to which a CCP would have the largest unmargined exposure under extreme market conditions in a stressed scenario.

[144] A. Armakola and J.P. Laurent, (2017), CCP Resilience and Clearing Membership, Working Paper, mimeo, p. 2.

[145] Armakola and Laurent, (2017), Ibid. p. 3.

[146] Under EMIR, a CCP is required to contribute a SIG amount equal to 25% of its minimum capital requirement.

IM and default fund contribution, the financial resilience of the CCP depends on two main factors: the CCP's skin-in-the-game and the surviving members' willingness and ability to jointly carry losses.[147] After using the CCP's SIG, losses will be reallocated across survivors via risk-sharing mechanisms (non-defaulting CM guarantee fund contributions or non-defaulting replenish guarantee funds), which are embedded in the default waterfall structure, and possibly as part of either a recovery or a resolution regime (partial or full mutualization). These loss-allocation mechanisms are a possible source of risk for CMs (pre-funded resources plus a contingent liability in case the CCP calls for further liquidity and possibly be further dragged into recovery and resolution regimes).

Two risk-sharing models are common: (1) the default fund, the level of risk exposure of a non-defaulted member depends on the financial resources preceding the default fund. The CMs are interconnected via the default fund and exposed to counterparty credit risk, and (2) the replenishment of the default fund requires CMs to raise liquidity within a short period of time. A third option is the cash calls and margin gain haircutting as suggested in 2014 by the IOSCO in their recovery of financial market infrastructures principles and compliant with EMIR conditions.[148] Armakola and Laurent illustrate that analysis of possible exposures and risks in the context of CCP loss-allocation rules shows that clearing participants are exposed to counterparty credit risk via the default fund,[149] may face liquidity risk (through replenishment)[150] and credit risk via the rights to assessment and finally may not be able to quantify exposure experienced in a recovery or resolution regime (and/or initial margin haircutting which are much higher than default fund contributions by CM).[151]

5.11 Substantive Priorities for the Years Ahead

Many changes have been impacting the CCP market in recent years: higher volumes, more horizontally integrated than pre-crisis, in terms of both products and geographical reach, and indirect participation in CCPs is growing.[152] Recent years and regulatory changes have reduced financial institutions' exposure to counterparty credit risk shocks through netting, margining and collateralization. But central clearing may give rise to other forms of systemic risk. In particular, the concentration of the risk management of

[147] Armakola and Laurent, (2017), Ibid. p. 3.

[148] Armakola and Laurent, (2017), Ibid. pp. 4–5; CPSS-IOSCO, (2014), Recovery of Financial Market Infrastructures, Bank for International Settlements.

[149] Armakola and Laurent, (2017), Ibid. pp. 6–10.

[150] Armakola and Laurent, (2017), Ibid. pp. 10–11.

[151] Armakola and Laurent, (2017), Ibid. pp. 6 & 11–15.

[152] D. Domanski et al., (2015), Central Clearing: Trends and Current Issues, BIS Quarterly Review, December, pp. 63–65; A. Gracie, (2015), CCP resolution and the ending Too Big to Fail agenda, Speech given by Andrew Gracie, Executive Director, Resolution, Bank of England, 21st Annual Risk USA Conference, New York, October 22.

credit and liquidity risk in the CCP may affect system-wide market price and liquidity dynamics in ways that are not yet understood.[153]

Three key areas have been identified that will dominate the agenda for the next couple of years.[154] Those include:

5.11.1 Improving Resilience of CCPs

That would include the evaluation of the adequacy of existing standards with respect to CCP loss-absorption capacity and liquidity, using the (Committee on Payments and Market Infrastructures-International Organization of Securities Commissions) CPMI-IOSCO Principles for Financial Market Infrastructure (PFMI) as a benchmark. It should evaluate the existing stress testing policies and practices of CCPs and consider the need for, and develop as appropriate, a framework for consistent and comparable stress tests of the adequacy of CCPs' financial resources (including capital) and liquidity arrangements, which could involve supervisory stress tests.[155] The above-mentioned Armakola and Laurent[156] assessed the possible exposure of clearing members through pre-funded waterfall resources, recovery tools and assessment powers of major European and US central clearing counterparties. They also investigated loss-allocation rules at the end of the waterfall and the impact of emerging resolution regimes on contingent liquidity. As the resilience of a central clearing counterparty depends on the soundness of the member base, they assessed the payment capacity of a member base under normal and stressed scenarios.[157] They conclude that '[t]he ability of a CCP to withstand member defaults can be improved in various ways, such as better control of membership eligibility, sizing-up IM requirements, especially for clients that do not contribute to the default-fund, increased default fund requirements and limited allowance of unfunded contributions for lower quality clearing members. Each of the above ideas should be considered with moderation, as each has some clear drawbacks in terms of transaction fees for client clearing, limited access to central clearing, freeze of liquid assets and

---

[153] D. Domanski et al., (2015), Ibid. 65–73. It was indicated before that our understanding of networks and how risk propagates through the system is very incomplete and in fact only nascent. Also: V. Albuquerque, et al., (2015), CCPs need thicker skins – Citi analysis, Risk.net, 3 August; B. Cœuré, (2014), Risks in Central Counterparties (CCPs), speech at the conference 'Mapping and monitoring the financial system: liquidity, funding and plumbing', Washington DC, January 23.

[154] See in detail FSB/IOSCO, (2015), Progress Report on the CCP Workplan, September 22; FSB/IOSCO, (2015), 2015 CCP Workplan, April 15. Also: A. Persaud, (2015), The Unintended Consequences and Possible Mitigation of the Clearing Mandate for OTC Derivatives, Intelligence Capital Working Paper, mimeo.

[155] In 2015 assessments have been done that were being processed during late 2015. A CPMI-IOSCO final report on CCP resilience and recovery issues is expected to be published by mid-2016.

[156] See for an excellent review on the topic: A. Armakola and J.P. Laurent, (2017), CCP Resilience and Clearing Membership, Working Paper, mimeo. For the actual analysis of EU and US CMs: pp. 12–25.

[157] Supra.

potentially pro-cyclical requirements.'[158] They show that under a stressed scenario, member base quality erodes and many CCPs may face severe liquidity problems, if CMs cannot provide contingent funding to sustain the CCP's resilience[159] which puts additional focus on membership eligibility, the design of IM requirements and default fund contributions for CMs and their clients.

5.11.2 Recovery Planning for CCPs

This would include further analysis regarding the variety of CCP recovery mechanisms, including loss-allocation tools. CCP default waterfalls typically include the initial margin of the defaulting clearing member, guarantee fund contributions provided by the defaulting clearing member, equity funds provided by the CCP and guarantee fund contributions provided by surviving clearing members. Depending on the CCP, additional losses may be allocated through various recovery tools, such as cash calls on clearing members, variation margin haircutting, forced allocation of contracts, partial or full tear-up of contracts and, where legally permitted, initial margin haircutting. The stock take should be used to compare recovery mechanisms across CCPs. It is very likely that the outcome of such stock taking will drive the need for more granular standards or guidance for CCP recovery planning. Recovery plans should be designed to maximize the probability of successful CCP recoveries, while mitigating the risk that recovery actions undertaken by CCPs could result in contagion to other parts of the financial system.[160]

5.11.3 Resolvability of CCPs

This should mainly focus on the need for and development of appropriate standards or guidance for CCP resolution planning, resolution strategies and resolution tools, including cross-border coordination and recognition of resolution actions. Such standards or guidance would aim to ensure that any CCP can be successfully resolved without resort to a government 'bailout', and without resulting in contagion to other parts of the financial system. The need should also be assessed for additional pre-funded financial resources (including capital) and liquidity arrangements in resolution.

In June 2015 a survey conducted among CCPs indicated that resolution frameworks for CCPs are not well developed. Systematic cross-border resolution planning processes are not yet in place for any of the largest CCPs although efforts are underway to establish such processes. It is well understood that any framework would have to address obstacles that relate to the resolvability of CCPs arising from (i) legal structures, (ii) the arrangement of clearing activities or other services, (iii) relationships and interdependencies between the

---

[158] Armakola and Laurent, (2017), Ibid. p. 25.

[159] Armakola and Laurent, (2017), Ibid. p. 26.

[160] See the recovery and resolution chapter (9).

CCP and participants, (iv) links with other FMIs, (v) CCP rules including default management and recovery procedures and (vi) financial resources including liquidity arrangements.[161]

5.11.4 Interdependency and Contagion Analysis

There is clearly a further need to better understand the interdependencies among CCPs and their direct and indirect members. In many cases, CCP membership is drawn from a common group of large banks, many of which are also important providers of financial services to CCPs as well as to clients (such as liquidity provision, lines of credit, custodianship, settlement and cash management). The interdependencies are very often cross-border. The working group that was established in July 2015 focuses on, for example, the following interdependencies: (1) financial obligations of clearing members, such as default fund contributions, initial and variation margins, assessment rights and so on; (2) financial interdependencies with other financial institutions, which can be clearing members, stakeholders, such as investment counterparties, liquidity providers and deposit banks; and (3) operational interdependencies, such as links with investment counterparties, custodians, settlement agents and so on.[162]

5.11.5 Liquidity Is Key for Central Clearing of Derivatives

Empirical analysis reveals that liquidity is the most important precondition for the effective functioning of central clearing of derivatives and in particular CDSs.[163] By contrast, higher volatility reduces the likelihood of derivatives being centrally cleared. All in all, to protect their own financial viability, CCPs seem to accept primarily liquid and less volatile derivatives for central clearing. Moreover, they also require that the reference entity be in robust financial condition. Considering the fact that after the full implementation of the recent derivatives market reforms, margin requirements for non-centrally cleared products will be prohibitively high, the pricing of some (OTC) derivatives may not be attractive anymore and those will probably vanish from the market.[164]

[161] See the recovery and resolution chapter (13).

[162] See 5.11.6.

[163] Evidence points at the fact that CDS spreads widen with the initiation of central clearing. Kaya documents that the widening in CDS spreads is tantamount among non-financial and financial firms whereas there is heterogeneity in the impact of central clearing with respect to credit rating. Furthermore, he shows that volatility and central clearing widen the CDS spreads jointly whereas CDS liquidity plays little role in determining spreads in the aftermath of central clearing; see O. Kaya, (2015), CDS Spreads in the Aftermath of Central Clearing, Working Paper, mimeo.

[164] See in detail: O. Kaya, (2015), Liquidity is Key for the Central Clearing of Derivatives, Deutsche Bank Research, March 12. Also: P. Glasserman, et al., (2014), Hidden Illiquidity with Multiple Central Counterparties, Columbia University Working Paper, mimeo; J. Slive, et al., (2012), Liquidity and Central Clearing: Evidence from the CDS Market, Bank of Canada Working Paper Nr. 2012-38.

5.11.6 Interoperability of CCPs

An important issue but even more in an environment with an integrated economic zone as the EU,[165] but also more in general due to globalization of capital flows.[166] CCP interoperability is an arrangement that links different CCPs, allowing participants of one CCP to seamlessly deal with participants of another CCP. This can make it cheaper for traders to participate in a wider range of financial markets and can facilitate competition between CCPs by opening up participant networks. However, interoperability also introduces financial stability risks, primarily by creating dependencies between the linked CCPs, and so it may be unsuitable for some markets. Interoperability arrangements are currently in place between some CCPs serving European equity markets,[167] and another type of arrangement is in place linking several US CCPs. In other parts of the world, it by far and large is not the case, for example, Australia.[168] If they are prudently managed and supervised, interoperability arrangements can also be beneficial for the resilience and stability of the financial system. The fact that the same markets are cleared by several CCPs increases the likelihood that these markets can continue to be served in the event that one CCP suffers an operational or financial failure—although it should be pointed out that a CCP failure is an extremely unlikely scenario.[169]

But CCP interoperability and system stability are closely connected. Feng and Hu assess that to control counterparty risk, financial regulations such as the Dodd-Frank Act are increasingly requiring standardized derivatives trades to be cleared by central counterparties (CCPs). It is anticipated that in the near-term future, CCPs across the world will be linked through interoperability agreements that facilitate risk sharing but also serve as a conduit for transmitting shocks. Their paper theoretically studies a networked network with CCPs that are linked through interoperability arrangements. The major finding is that the different configurations of networked network CCPs contribute to the different properties of the cascading failures.[170]

Further, one needs to keep in mind that covering the exposures resulting from interoperability arrangements may create a need for extra collateral. Interoperability agreements

[165] See for a detailed analysis of the EU arrangements in place: ESMA (European Securities and Markets Authority), (2015), Final Report: The Extension and Scope of Interoperability Arrangements, July 1, 2015, ESMA/2015/1067 and an evaluation BOE (Bank of England), (2015), Implementation by the Bank of England of ESMA's Guidelines and Recommendations on CCP interoperability arrangements: summary of feedback received and policy response, July.

[166] N. Garvin, (2012), Central Counterparty Interoperability, Reserve Bank of Australia Bulletin, June Quarter 2012, pp. 59–68.

[167] See for the benefits in an EU context: B. Cœuré, (2015), The International Regulatory Agenda on CCP Links, Speech by Mr. Benoît Cœuré, Member of the Executive Board of the European Central Bank, at the European Systemic Risk Board (ESRB) workshop on CCP interoperability arrangements, Frankfurt am Main, November 2, 2015, pp. 1–2.

[168] N. Garvin, (2012), Ibid.

[169] B. Cœuré, (2015), Ibid. p. 2.

[170] X. Feng and H. Hu, (2015), CCP Interoperability and System Stability, *International Journal of Modern Physics*, C DOI: https://doi.org/10.1142/S012918311650025X.

might have increased liquidity, they also come at a cost.[171] Interoperability however can reduce demand for collateral assets to meet margin requirements, by allowing participants to concentrate all their clearing activity within a single CCP and by increasing netting efficiency across CCPs. One issue that also needs to be further analyzed is whether interoperability arrangements could facilitate the porting of open positions to an alternative CCP, thus preventing a total close-out of transactions and containing any potential knock-on effects to clearing members.[172]

Although netting might lead to contagion, the benefit of netting is expected to outweigh the detriments. Although the regulatory framework surrounding CCPs is carefully designed, the devil will lie in the prudent and consistent application of risk management standards. As Cœuré argues '[t]he task of harmonising risk models and ensuring that interoperating CCPs cannot contaminate each other in the event of a clearing member default is not straightforward.'…'Authorities also have a key role in making sure interoperating CCPs have comprehensively assessed the risks they pose to each other. As an example, CCPs which enter into an interoperability arrangement must collect and exchange margins to cover their reciprocal exposures. Under EU rules, these resources are not part of the CCPs' regular default waterfalls, and are exclusively provided for the purpose of covering losses from one interoperating CCP going into default. In other words, they cannot be used to cover other types of losses, such as a participant default. Authorities must ensure that the resources contributed by one CCP are fully protected from potential defaults or stress events which could occur in the other CCP(s).'[173]

Under the EMIR, there is scope for discretion at the level of the national competent authorities. To ensure prudent application, certain features should deserve more attention. He provides two examples: 'first, the criteria and requirements for harmonising the risk models of interoperable CCPs; and second, the treatment of exposures resulting from interoperability within CCP stress testing frameworks.'[174] He further re-iterates that regulation probably cannot address all issues related to such a complex subject as CCP interoperability and that competent authorities will need to continue playing a role in deciding how best to tackle certain issues not entirely dealt with under the legislation. In that respect they will be helped by the introduction of the CPMI-IOSCO 'Public quantitative disclosure standards for central counterparties' in January 2016. From that point onward, all CCPs with interoperability arrangements will be required to publish data on the volume of activity cleared through these links. They will also have to publish data on the financial resources provided and collected to cover exposures resulting from these links, and on the results of backtesting performed on the level of coverage of these resources.[175]

---

[171] M. Singh, (2013), Making the Over-The-Counter Derivatives Markets Safe: a Fresh Look, *Journal of Financial Market Infrastructures*, Vol. 1, Issue 3, pp. 1 ff. N. Cox, et al., (2013), Central Counterparty Links and Clearing System Exposures, Reserve Bank of Australia Research Discussion Paper, October 2013–12.

[172] CGFS, (2011), The Macrofinancial Implications of Alternative Configurations for Access to Central Counterparties in OTC Derivatives Markets, CGFS Paper Nr. 46, November.

[173] B. Cœuré, (2015), Ibid. p. 3.

[174] B. Cœuré, (2015), Ibid. p. 4.

[175] For limit-setting by regulators, see B. Cœuré, (2015), Ibid. pp. 4–6. See for a general overview of the outstanding issues and overall state of the CCP market in an interdependent world: J. H

The FSB provided in 2018 an analysis on the matter which were largely in line with the findings during earlier reports.[176] Those include (1) pre-funded financial resources are concentrated at a small number of CCPs; (2) exposures to CCPs are concentrated among a small number of entities; (3) the relationships mapped are characterized, to varying degrees, by a core of highly connected CCPs and entities and a periphery of less highly connected CCPs and entities; (4) small number of entities tend to dominate the provision of each of the critical services required by CCPs; and (5) clearing members and clearing member affiliates are also important providers of other critical services required by CCPs and can maintain several types of relationships with multiple CCPs simultaneously.

5.11.7 Consistency Across Jurisdictions

Although the message and options across the different regulators post-2008 crisis were clear, the final black-coded law in this matter works out quite different in the details. Within the EU, the additional complexity is that the EU regulator has left some discretion with the national regulators.[177]

5.11.8 Changing Market Structures and Conditions Due to Incoming Regulation

All the different regulatory initiatives will undeniably have an impact on market structures, contractual terms and the cost of funding for many markets. Also for those transactions that are (now) cleared over CCPs. The EMIR foresees in that and parts are already in force, other like interest rate and credit derivative contracts it will do so shortly or in the course of 2016. Miglietti et al. recently look into the question of how the cost of funding is impacted by all this and focused on the repo markets. The analysis shows that the initial margins, paid by all participants, had a positive and significant effect on the cost of funding.[178] They add '[a]mong the other variables playing a role, we find that

Powell, (2015), Central Clearing in an Interdependent World, Speech by Mr. Jerome H Powell, Member of the Board of Governors of the Federal Reserve System, at the Clearing House Annual Conference, New York City, November 17, 2015.

[176] See FSB, (2018), Analysis of Central Clearing Interdependencies, August 8, via fsb.org; FSB, (2017), Analysis of Central Clearing Interdependencies, July 7, via fsb.org

[177] See for an overview of what needs to be cleared and under what conditions in the US, EU and Japan; A. Rahman, (2015), Over-the-Counter (OTC) Derivatives, Central Clearing and Financial Stability, Bank of England, Quarterly Bulletin 2015, Q3, pp. 287–288 & 294. D. Nixon, and A. Rehlon, (2013), Central Counterparties: what are They, Why Do They Matter, and How Does the Bank Supervise Them?', Bank of England Quarterly Bulletin, Vol. 53, Nr. 2, pages 147–156.

[178] On average, the impact is equal to about three basis points for each one percentage point variation in the margin; A. Miglietti et al., (2015), The Impact of CCPs' Margin Policies on Repo Markets, BIS Working Paper, Nr. 515, October, p. 24.

credit and liquidity risks, as well as variables capturing potential idiosyncratic pressures in liquidity needs, exert a significant and upward impact on the cost of funding.'[179]

5.11.9 Reduction of Large Bank Exposure to CCPs (and Other Counterparties)

The framework, as discussed, has been reframed materially in recent years. The CCP Task Force developed and published in July 2012 its capital requirement standards for (large) exposures to CCPs by banks. Those rules were finalized in 2014.[180] In the final version, derivations were made for exposures to qualifying CCPs (QCCPs),[181] and an explicit cap on regulatory charges for exposures to these QCCPs. Further they clarified the position in case of multi-level client structures.

This initiative should be seen as a wider effort to reduce large (and concentrated) bank exposures to counterparties or to groups of connected counterparties across their books and operations. Large exposures regulation has been developed as a tool for limiting the maximum loss a bank could face in the event of a sudden counterparty failure to a level that does not endanger the bank's solvency. The need for banks to measure and limit the size of large exposures in relation to their capital has long been recognized by the Basel Committee on Banking Supervision and goes back to 1991. The treatment of large exposures could also contribute to the stability of the financial system. The large exposures framework is constructed to serve as a backstop and complement to the risk-based capital standards. A bank must consider exposures to any counterparty. The only counterparties that are exempted from the framework are certain sovereigns. The sum of all exposure values of a bank to a counterparty or to a group of connected counterparties must be defined as a large exposure if it is equal to or above 10% of the bank's eligible capital base.[182] The sum of all the exposure values of a bank to a single counterparty or to a group of connected counterparties must not be higher than 25% of the bank's available eligible capital base at all times. However, this figure is set at 15% for a G-SIB's exposures to another G-SIB. In some cases, a bank may have exposures to a group of counterparties with specific relationships or dependencies such that, were one of the counterparties to fail,

[179] A. Miglietti et al., (2015), Ibid. pp. 24–25. Also: O. Lewandowska, (2015), OTC Clearing Arrangements for Bank Systemic Risk Regulation: a Simulation Approach, *Journal of Money, Credit and Banking*, Vol. 47, Issue 6, pp. 1177–1203, September.

[180] BIS, (2014), Capital Requirements for Bank Exposures to Central Counterparties, April; BIS, (2013), Capital Requirements for Bank Exposures to Central Counterparties, Consultative document.

[181] See for implementation issues in developing countries: A. Kotzé et al., (2014), The Dilemma of a Central Counterparty versus a Qualified Central Counterparty in a Developing Country, Procedia Economics and Finance Vol. 14, pp. 349–358. T. Lane and J.-Ph. Dion and J. Slive, (2013), Access to Central Clearing Parties: Why It Matters and How It Is Changing, Banque de France, Financial Stability Review, Nr. 17, pp. 169–177.

[182] See for measurement guidance: BCBS, (2014), Supervisory Framework for Measuring and Controlling Large Exposures, pp. 3 ff.

all of the counterparties would very likely fail. A group of this sort, referred to in this framework as a group of connected counterparties, must be treated as a single counterparty. In this case, the sum of the bank's exposures to all the individual entities included within a group of connected counterparties is subject to the large exposure limit and to the regulatory reporting requirements as specified above.[183]

In the EU the capital requirements vis-à-vis CPPs by banks are taken care of in the CRR. The phasing in which was initially foreseen to be occurring by June 2015 was extended to December 2015 and now needs to be completed.[184] Although the volumes in terms of exposure of banks to CCPs have dropped in recent years, the regulatory refinement will continue, also beyond 2015. The EBA has put in motion further guidelines, executing the relevant articles of the CRR regulation that deal with limiting exposures to SB entities and large exposures overall.[185]

5.12 The Long Road Traveled and Not Yet There

5.12.1 Introduction

Central clearing[186] 'reduces risk through multilateral netting,[187] collateralization of positions, pricing, and default management practices. However, central clearing also concentrates risk into a CCP, and financial intermediation introduces new risks', argues

---

[183] Further details: BCBS, (2014), Ibid. pp. 4 ff.

[184] EC, (2015), European Commission—Press release—European Commission extends transitional period for capital requirements for banks' exposures to CCPs, 4 June. The transitional period was once again extended in October 2017.

[185] EBA, (2015), Draft EBA Guidelines on limits on exposures to shadow banking entities which carry out banking activities outside a regulated framework under Article 395 para. 2 Regulation (EU) No. 575/2013, EBA/CP/2015/06, 19 March. Final Guidelines EBA, (2016), Guidelines Limits on exposures to shadow banking entities which carry out banking activities outside a regulated framework under Article 395(2) of Regulation (EU) No 575/2013, EBA/GL/2015/20, June 3, via eba.europe.org

[186] For the question of how 'central' clearing is during market turmoil, see A. Ebner et al., (2016), How Central is Central Counterparty Clearing? A Deep Dive into a European Repo Market During the Crisis, Deutsche Bundesbank Discussion Paper Nr. 14, Frankfurt am Main. The effective functioning of a CCP depends on the way counterparty risk is priced and managed by market participants. See, for example, W. Du et al., (2016), Counterparty Risk and Counterparty Choice in the Credit Default Swap Market, Finance and Economics Discussion Series Nr. 2016-087, September, Washington: Board of Governors of the Federal Reserve System. The impact of counterparty risk on pricing of instruments seems limited, but materially more on the choice of the counterparty to engage with. Surprisingly maybe, the evidence seems to point in the same direction for both the cleared as well as OTC market. Also: C. Fei et al., (2018), Managing Counterparty Risk in OTC Markets, Finance and Economics Discussion Series 2017-083. Washington: Board of Governors of the Federal Reserve System, https://doi.org/10.17016/FEDS.2017.083r1

[187] An important aspect of the current regulation is to compress the OTC market and get more trades centrally cleared. That should however be done without impacting market prices and thus individual net positions. That is not without complications; see extensively M. D'Errico and T. Roukny, (2017), Compressing Over-the-Counter Markets, ESRB Working Paper Nr. 44, May. It seems that close-out netting is included in the overall definition of multilateral netting.

Ruffini correctly.[188] The collapse of a CCP occurs rarely, but when it does it seems to impact and destabilize markets materially.[189] The role and protection of customers is in those matters always at the forefront and it should.[190]

The default position, as discussed, is clear. Ruffini reminds us 'OTC bilateral transactions are usually collateralized directly between the counterparties, while central clearing generally involves the use of one or more intermediaries in the clearing and settlement process. Under a bilateral framework,[191] the exposures that participants face can be dispersed across a large number of counterparties, while under the centrally cleared framework these risks are shifted to and concentrated in central counterparties (CCPs) and financial intermediaries, such as clearing members (CMs) and futures commission merchants (FCMs).'[192] Customer losses occur often when customer funds are misused such as was the case with MF global in 2011 and PFG in 2012. A lot of recent legislation both in the US and Europe focus on the protection of customers against CCP defaults.[193] However central clearing does not protect against defaulting FCMs.

Close-out netting occurs when two counterparties agree to combine their various obligations into a single net payment following a default.

[188] I. Ruffini, (2015), Central Clearing: Risks and Customer Protections, Federal Reserve Bank of Chicago, Economic Perspectives, Q. 4, pp. 90–100.

[189] Reminded can be the events in Paris, 1974; Kuala Lumpur, 1984; and Hong Kong, 1987. See in detail on these events: A. Rehlon, and D. Nixon, (2013), Central Counterparties: What are they, why do they Matter and How Does the Bank Supervise them?, Quarterly Bulletin, Bank of England, Q. 2, pp. 1–10.

[190] Since the introduction of the Principles for Financial Market Infrastructures (PFMI) by BCBS/IOSCO in 2012, there is a continuous monitoring system in place, which is consolidated in reports released with regular intervals and often thematically structured (available through bis.org/iosco.org). For example, recent editions are IOSCO/BCBS, (2018), Implementation Monitoring of PFMI: Follow-up Level 3 Assessment of CCPs' Recovery Planning, Coverage of Financial Resources and Liquidity Stress Testing, May 3. See also: B. CŒURÉ, (2017), Central Clearing: Reaping the Benefits, Controlling the Risks, Banque de France Financial Stability Review, Nr. 21, April, pp. 97–110.

[191] For a comparison between central and bilateral clearing, see G. Antinolfi et al., (2018), Transparency and collateral: central versus bilateral clearing, Finance and Economics Discussion Series 2018–17. https://doi.org/10.17016/FEDS.2018.017. Bilateral financial contracts typically require an assessment of counterparty risk. Central clearing of these financial contracts allows market participants to mutualize their counterparty risk, but this insurance may weaken incentives to acquire and to reveal information about such risk. When considering this trade-off, participants would choose central clearing if information acquisition is incentive compatible. If it is not, they may prefer bilateral clearing, when this choice prevents strategic default while economizing on costly collateral. They conclude that central clearing can be socially inefficient under certain circumstances, which is in contrast with earlier studies.

[192] I. Ruffini, (2015), Central Clearing: Risks and Customer Protections, Federal Reserve Bank of Chicago, Economic Perspectives, Q.4, p. 90. She uses the acronym FCM here to mean a financial intermediary for customers that want to transact in centrally cleared markets, although this use is an oversimplification because FCMs are not necessarily direct clearing members (Ibid. footnote 2, p. 98).

[193] See regarding the legal framework for CCP defaults: J. Braithwaite and D. Murphy, (2016), Got to Be Certain: The Legal Framework for CCP Default Management Processes, Bank of England Financial Stability Paper Nr. 37, May. Cohesion and the piecemeal nature of the different pieces of legislation applicable continue to be a concern. See regarding some historical experiences with CCP

Customer protection frameworks are intended to mitigate such exposures. However, the protections offered under the traditional US futures customer segregation are somewhat limited as they only rely on the segregation of customer funds. Bankruptcy codes are often not fine-tuned for these matters as 'individually segregated customer funds are treated as if they were held commingled in a single omnibus account.'[194]

It is in that context that Cui et al. propose their novel central clearing counterparty (CCP) design for a financial network with multilateral clearing, where the participation rate of individual banks depends on the volume-based fee charged by the CCP. They further show that partial participation of banks in the CCP at the optimal fee rate (the one that maximizes the net worth of the CCP) reduces the aggregate shortfall of the financial network and also reduces the overall systemic risk.[195] Alignment of interest and regulation[196] go hand-in-hand.[197]

Regulation has encouraged the use of collateral and central clearing. Such regulation is deemed to promote financial stability.[198] Heider[199] concludes after having reviewed the arguments and initiatives that '[s]ome effects of using collateral and CCPs are already well understood, for example how CCPs and collateral can help avoid losses when default occurs. However, their effects on incentives to avoid default in the first place are less well understood.' But those incentives are key to financial stability.[200] The same problem resur-

---

defaults: V. Bignon and G. Vuillemey, (2017), The Failure of a Clearinghouse: Empirical Evidence, Banque de France Working Paper Nr. 638, August 23. Discusses the case of the failure of the derivatives clearinghouse 'Caisse de Liquidation', which defaulted in Paris in 1974.

[194] Ibid. p. 97.

[195] W. Wenqian and A.J. Menkveld, (2016), Systemic Risk in Real Time, (2016), A Risk Dashboard for Central Clearing Parties, Working Paper, mimeo, December 16.

[196] B. Jopon and J. Rennison, (2017), Trump Administration Calls for Heightened Regulation of Clearing Houses, FT October 6, as they pose systemic risks.

[197] Z. Cui et al., (2016), Systemic Risk and Optimal Fee Structure for Central Clearing Counterparty under Partial Netting, Working Paper, mimeo.

[198] Regarding the aspect of systemic risk in clearing houses, see C. Boissel et al., (2016), Systemic Risk in Clearing Houses: Evidence from the European Repo Market, ESRB Working Paper Series Nr. 10, May. Rather than dive directly in the mechanics of systemic risk, they start from the question: How do crises affect central clearing counterparties (CCPs). CCP stress can be measured through the sensitivity of repo rates to sovereign CDS spreads. Such sensitivity jointly captures three effects: (1) the effectiveness of the haircut policy, (2) CCP member default risk and (3) CCP default risk. Repo rates strongly respond to movements in sovereign risk, their finding shows. For some years now the Federal Reserve Bank of Chicago is holding an annual Central Counterparty (CCP) Risk Management Conference. In 2017, the focus was on CCP risks beyond default risk: that includes liquidity risk, regulatory risk, concentration risk and non-default loss-allocation issues. See for a report on the findings: R. Lewis, (2017), Central Counterparty Risk Management: Beyond Default Risk, The Federal Reserve Bank of Chicago, Chicago Fed Letter, Essays on Issues, Nr. 389.

[199] F. Heider, (2017), Collateral, Central Clearing Counterparties and Regulation, ECB Research Bulletin Nr. 41, December 6.

[200] See also: W. Huang, (2019), Central Counterparty Capitalization and Misaligned Incentives, BIS Working Paper Nr. 767, February 11. She raises the question whether the CCPs' incentives might undermine financial stability. Such CCPs choose how much capital to hold and set the collateral requirement for their clearing members, so as to maximize their own profits. They face a trade-off between fee income and counterparty credit risk. But a CCP's limited liability creates a misalignment between its choices and the socially optimal solution to this trade-off. Optimal capital regulations are

faces over and over again. What one aims to do is 'prevent a fire-sale externality sparking a vicious circle of falling asset prices and the excessive use of variation margins'.[201] In contrast to Heider,[202] I am convinced that the latter can be solved through the regulatory channel. Regarding the former I am, given the discussions throughout these two volumes, a whole lot less convinced that regulation is the answer. In fact, I wonder whether there is a waterproof solution to fire sale externalities, unless you are willing to go as far as prohibiting altogether the structures that bring opacity that allow externalities to emerge to begin with. In the meantime, we need to think hard what the optimal design is and interaction between capital and liquidity regulations particularly during fire sale externalities situations. That is exactly what Kara and Ozsoy did.[203] That concludes that on the one hand can banks insure themselves against potential liquidity shocks by hoarding sufficient precautionary liquid assets. However, it is never optimal (or realistic) to fully insure, so realized liquidity shocks trigger an asset fire sale. Banks who do not internalize the fire sale externality then tend to overinvest in the risky asset class and underinvest in

defined and the significant role of CCP ownership structures in safeguarding financial stability is underscored and detailed. The basic proposition is that a for-profit CCP tends to hold less capital than a welfare optimum would warrant and would require less collateral from its member than is welfare optimizing, thus undermining financial stability and default risk increases through the non-optimal positions. The model developed in this paper implies that better-capitalized CCPs set higher collateral requirements. Optimal capital requirements are derived for different levels of the clearing fees charged by for-profit CCPs. When this fee is low, the capital requirements incentivize CCPs to demand more collateral, thus bolstering financial stability. When fees are high, capital requirements do not change a CCP's incentives but serve to boost its loss-absorbing capacity.

[201] The ESRB, following article 2 of the European Market Infrastructure Regulation (EMIR Regulation (EU) No 648/2012 of the European Parliament and of the Council of July 4, 2012, on OTC derivatives, central counterparties and trade repositories), has been reporting on material risks following interoperability arrangement which are defined as 'an arrangement between two or more CCPs that involves a cross-system execution of transactions' (also known as 'peer-to-peer links') and which are covered by the EMIR. The systemic risk implications are reflected in Chap. 5 (pp. 13 ff). The possible implications are twofold: (1) such arrangements can help to contain systemic risks in a situation where a number of different CCPs clear the same financial instruments, insofar as they allow intermediaries to hold their position with one CCP, instead of 'fragmenting' it across different CCPs. This increases netting possibilities, helps to limit demand for eligible collateral and avoids situations where the default of a clearing member triggers parallel default procedures, and (2) CCP interoperability arrangements can have systemic risk implications, since the establishment of interoperable links introduces a significant element of complexity into the overall risk management system and adds a channel for direct contagion between two or more CCPs. See in detail: ESRB, (2016), ESRB Report to the European Commission on the Systemic Risk Implications of CCP Interoperability Arrangements, January, pp. 2–3. Also: ESMA, (2016), Possible Systemic Risk and Cost Implications of Interoperability Arrangements, Final Report, ESMA/2016/328.

[202] F. Heider, (2017), Collateral, Central Clearing Counterparties and Regulation, ECB Research Bulletin Nr. 41, December 6. Also: B. Biais, (2016), Risk-sharing or Risk-Taking? Counterparty Risk, Incentives and Margins, *Journal of Finance*, Vol. 71, pp. 1669–1698; F. Heider et al., (2017), On collateral: Implications for Financial Stability and Monetary Policy, ECB Working Paper Series, Nr 2107, November.

[203] See G.I. Kara and S.M. Ozsoy, (2016), Bank Regulation under Fire sale Externality, Finance and Economics Discussion Series Nr. 2016-26, March, Divisions of Research and Statistics and Monetary Affairs, Federal Reserve Board, Washington, DC.

the liquid asset. Capital requirements can therefore lead to less severe fire sales[204] by addressing the inefficiency (of not fully insuring) and reducing risky assets. However, they warn banks respond to stricter capital requirements by decreasing their liquidity ratios. Anticipating this response, the regulator pre-emptively sets capital ratios at high levels. Ultimately, this interplay between banks and the regulator leads to inefficiently low levels of risky assets and liquidity. Macroprudential liquidity requirements that complement capital regulations, as in Basel III, are needed to restore constrained efficiency, improve financial stability and allow for a higher level of investment in risky assets.

One of the problems we have, and despite the general validity of the Basel standards, is significant variation exists in the implementation of these standards across countries. Further, a significant number of countries increase or decrease the stringency of capital regulations over time. But what explains those variations? Kara[205] points at the fact that countries with high average returns to investment and a high ratio of government ownership of banks choose less stringent capital regulation standards. Capital regulations may also be less stringent in countries with more concentrated banking sectors.

5.12.2 The Long Road Traveled Regarding CCPs

From a regulatory point of view, many steps have been taken with respect to bringing more OTC transaction under the central clearing model while at the same time trying to take the pain out of the CCP model itself. Many of the items have been discussed before in this chapter, but as a kind of structural approach to this challenge, hereafter I listed the most important regulatory steps taken in the recent decade:

- Central counterparties are part of the financial market infrastructure and are therefore governed by the 2012 IOSCO principles for financial market infrastructure. They are the international standards for financial market infrastructures, that is, payment systems, central securities depositories, securities settlement systems, central counterparties and trade repositories. These principles are part of a wider set of regulation and control to preserve financial stability.

[204] An alternative is to mitigate the risk through contracts. Vuillemey shows that fire sales resulting from coordination failures can be eliminated via private contracting between investors. The contract has two main features: (i) parties pre-commit to buy assets at above-market prices and (ii) free riding is penalized. This contract can be implemented as a central clearing counterparty (CCP) and explains important features of actual CCP design. G. Vuillemey, (2019), Mitigating Fire Sales with Contracts: Theory and Evidence, Working Paper, March 19, mimeo. Also G. Vuillemey, (2018), Completing Markets with Contracts: Evidence from the first Central Clearing Counterparty, CEPR Discussion Paper Nr. 12320, October 22; G. Vuillemey, (2019), The Trade-Creating Effects of a Contracting Innovation: Evidence from the First Central Clearing Counterparty, HEC Paris Research Paper FIN-2018-1307, April 23.

[205] G.I. Kara, (2016), Bank Capital Regulations Around the World: What Explains the Differences, Finance and Economics Discussion Series Nr. 2016-057, July, Washington: Board of Governors of the Federal Reserve System.

- Since 2012, IOSCO have released additional standards. They do not include further standards or regulations but are there to implement the existing standards. They include[206]:

  - Recovery of financial market infrastructures[207]: provides guidance to FMIs such as CCPs on how to develop plans to enable them to recover from threats to their viability and financial strength, along with guidance to relevant authorities in carrying out their responsibilities associated with the development and implementation of recovery plans.
  - Resilience of central counterparties (CCPs)[208]: contains further guidance on the PFMI and aims to improve CCPs' resilience by providing guidance on the principles and key considerations in the PFMI regarding financial risk management for CCPs.[209]
  - Framework for supervisory stress testing of central clearing parties[210]: the supervisory stress testing framework[211] is designed to support tests conducted by one or more authorities that examine the potential macro-level impact of a common stress event affecting multiple CCPs.[212]

---

[206] They can also be tracked, including future updates and additions via https://www.bis.org/cpmi/publ/

[207] See the most recent revised report CPMI/IOSCO, (2017), Recovery of Financial Market Infrastructures - Revised report, CPMI Report Nr. 162, July 5. Compared to the initial 2014 recovery report, the revised guidance provides additional clarifications in four areas: (1) operationalization of the recovery plan; (2) replenishment; (3) non-default related losses; and (4) transparency with respect to recovery tools and how they would be applied.

[208] The most recent reporting in this matter is: IOSCO/CPMI, (2017), Resilience of Central Counterparties (CCPs): Further guidance on the PFMI - Final report, CPMI Report Nr. 163, July 5. The report focuses on five key aspects of a CCP's financial risk management framework: governance, stress testing for both credit and liquidity exposures, coverage, margin, and a CCP's contribution of its financial resources to losses.

[209] S. Maijoor, (2018), Resilience, Recovery and Resolution: Three Essential Rs for CCPs, paper presented at ILF Conference on Resolution in Europe: The Unresolved Questions, Goethe University, Frankfurt am Main, April 23.

[210] IOSCO/CPMI, (2018), Framework for Supervisory Stress Testing of Central Counterparties (CCPs), CPMI Paper Nr. 176, April 10. See also: ESMA, (2018), EU-Wide CCP Stress Test 2017 Report, ESMA70-151-1154, February 2.

[211] Financial systems are typically complex, heterogeneous and rapidly changing, raising questions about the adequacy of conventional tests. Networks that include CCPs involve deep and broad interconnections, making stress testing a challenging task. Berner et al. analyze supplementing both private and supervisory CCP stress tests with a high-frequency indicator constructed from a market-based estimate of the conditional capital shortfall (SRISK) of the CCP's clearing members. Applying their measure to two large CCPs, they analyze how they can transmit and amplify shocks across borders, conditional on the exhaustion of pre-funded resources. Their results highlight how the network created by central clearing can act as an important transmission mechanism for shocks emanating from Europe. See R.B. Berner et al., (2019), Stress Testing Networks: The Case of Central Counterparties, NBER Working Paper Nr. 25686, March.

[212] Central clearing reduced volatility of NYSE returns caused by settlement risk and increased asset values. Results indicate that a clearinghouse can improve market stability and value through a

- Guidance on cyber resilience for financial market infrastructures[213]: provides guidance on the preparations and measures that FMIs should undertake to enhance their cyber resilience capabilities in order to limit the escalating risks that cyber threats pose to financial stability.
- Clearing of deliverable FX instruments[214]: clarifies the expectations of the CPMI and IOSCO with respect to CCP clearing of deliverable FX instruments and the associated models for effecting their settlement.
- Application of the principles for financial market infrastructures to central bank FMIs[215]: provides guidance on how the PFMI apply to financial market infrastructures that are owned and operated by central banks. It further clarifies the interaction between the PFMI and central bank policies.
- Public quantitative disclosure standards for central counterparties[216]: sets out the quantitative data that CCPs should publicly disclose regularly.
- Further reporting has been released regarding the assessment methodology for the oversight expectations applicable to critical service providers and a disclosure framework and assessment methodology that promotes consistent disclosure of information by FMIs and consistent assessments by international financial institutions and national authorities.

By now it has become clear that the regulator sees a cooperative role for recovery and resolution within the CCP area. The FSB's 'Key Attributes of Effective Resolution Regimes for Financial Institutions'[217] set out a framework for CCP resolution which sits

reduction in network contagion and counterparty risk. See in detail: A. Bernstein et al., (2019), Counterparty Risk and the Establishment of the New York Stock Exchange Clearinghouse, *Journal of Political Economy*, Vol. 127, Issue 2, pp. 689–729.

[213] Latest reporting: IOSCO/CPMI, (2016), Guidance on Cyber Resilience for Financial Market Infrastructures, CPMI Paper Nr. 146.

[214] Latest report: IOSCO/CPMI, (2016), Clearing of Deliverable FX Instruments, CPMI Paper Nr. 143, February 5.

[215] Latest Report: IOSCO/CPMI, (2015), Application of the 'Principles for Financial Market Infrastructures' to Central Bank FMIs, CPMI Paper Nr. 130, August 19.

[216] Latest report: IOCO/CPMI, (2015), Public Quantitative Disclosure Standards for Central Counterparties, CPMI Paper Nr. 125, February 25. Major objectives of this report are (1) compare CCP risk controls, including financial resources to withstand potential losses, (2) have a clear and accurate understanding of the risks associated with a CCP, (3) understand and assess a CCP's systemic importance and its impact on systemic risk and (4) understand and assess the risks of participating in a CCP (directly, and, to the extent relevant, indirectly).

[217] Published October 15, 2014 (fsb.org). The EU legislative proposal on CCP recovery and resolution released in 2015 is based on these principles: Proposal for a REGULATION OF THE EUROPEAN PARLIAMENT AND OF THE COUNCIL on a framework for the recovery and resolution of central counterparties and amending Regulations (EU) No 1095/2010, (EU) No 648/2012, and (EU) 2015/2365, COM(2016) 856 final2016/0365 (COD), November 28, 2015. The proposed new EU rules require (i) CCPs to prepare recovery plans envisaging measures to be taken in the event of financial difficulties exceeding the risk management defences under EMIR, (ii) national supervisors to review and approve these plans, (iii) national authorities to lay down resolution plans in the event of a CCP's failure (preparation and prevention tools). The proposal also

alongside the standards on resilience and recovery established in CPMI-IOSCO's principles for financial market infrastructures.[218] To further strengthen the resolution and resolution planning framework, the FSB released their 'Guidance on CCP Resolution and Resolution Planning'.[219] Central objectives are as follows:

- Maintain or restore the continuity of critical CCP functions, return the CCP to a matched book where losses arise from clearing member defaults and address default and non-default losses.
- Potential indicators of circumstances that could lead to a determination to trigger entry into resolution
- The application of the NCWOL ('no creditor worse off than in liquidation') safeguard and determination of the liquidation counterfactual for purposes of determining whether NCWOL compensation is due.[220] In practice that means that clearing members, as creditors of the CCP should be left with the option to liquidate the entity. There is an asymmetric feedback loop in the model: if they are creditors, but due to failing of the CCP, the debt no longer legally exists, they cannot trigger the entity in liquidation. So chances are close to zero that this will happen in practice. Clearing

provides national authorities with powers to step in when a CCP faces financial difficulties and to instruct a CCP to take actions in its recovery plan or other steps (early intervention tools). Finally, it sets out resolution tools to be applied by national authorities to a failing CCP, when it is in the public interest. Such tools include the power to sell a CCP's entire or critical functions, to create a publicly controlled bridge CCP and to allocate losses among owners and participants: see europarl.europa.eu. The ECON Committee adopted its final report on January 24, 2018, after the ESMA report in March 2017 on the matter. The proposed amendments, which delayed the progress materially (S. Wikes, (2018), EU Deadlock Set to Delay CCP Resolution Rules, Risk.net), aim to ensure fair and collective commitment of the private sector to rescue a distressed CCP at the recovery stage, to increased loss absorption capacity and minimize risks to taxpayers. Recovery plan should ensure that that loses should be allocated to involved stakeholders based on their respective levels of responsibility and ability to control risk. Recovery plans should clearly distinguish between losses arising from a clearing member default (default losses) and losses due to other reasons (non-default losses), such as CCP operational failures; the CCP capital would bear first losses in both cases, before any other recovery tools can be activated. Non-defaulting clearing members should be compensated in case recovery was successful when having used the variation margin. As regards resolution, the no-creditor-worse-off (NCWO) principle is amended in order to appropriately reflect the theoretical costs of non-intervention. In addition, the legal protection for the resolution authority is improved when it takes a decision to accelerate the move from recovery to resolution. On March 27, 2019, the EP concluded its first reading and preserved its position for the next term, that is, after the May 2019 European Elections. The New EP will gather for the first time on July 2, 2019, and so finalization of this project will occur after the close of this manuscript. That indeed occurred on 2019, December 4.

[218] BIS, (2017), Chairs' Report on the Implementation of the Joint Workplan for Strengthening the Resilience, Recovery and Resolvability of Central Counterparties, July 5, p. 3. See also M. Lamandini, (2018), Recovery and Resolution of CCPs: Obsessing over Regulatory Symmetry?, CEPS Commentary Nr. 56, August 9, via ceps.eu

[219] Published July 5, 2017 (fsb.org) following the consultative document released February 1, 2017.

[220] Also R. S. Steigerwald and D.W. DeCarlo, (2016), Resolving Central Counterparties after Dodd-Frank: Are they Eligible for 'Orderly Liquidation', Federal Reserve Bank of Chicago Working Paper PDP Nr. 2016-1, September.

members will then prioritize continuing operations and taking haircuts on their outstanding claims on the CCP. This might turn out a bigger legal problem than one would judge on the surface. If the NCWOL means something, it should allow for clearing members to wind down the CCP and retrieve whatever is left. Being forced to continue because otherwise one would destroy more than is needed of its own claims hardly meets the NCWOL criteria. But then again, isn't that what always happens (i.e. a trade-off) when creditors need to decide between restructuring or liquidating the failing debtor (Chaps. 7 and 11 of the US Bankruptcy Code)? But the consequences are clear: if liquidation is not realistic and recapitalization is uneven and blurred between clearing members, the only real option is that the taxpayer steps in. The whole policy design then turns out to be thwarted and a serious rethink is needed.[221]

- Issues to consider in developing resolution plans and conducting resolvability assessments.
- Enhancing cross-border cooperation and information sharing and ensuring the cross-border effectiveness and enforcement of resolution actions.

In February 2016, both the US and Europe agreed to develop a common approach for transatlantic CCPs. The decision was critical in terms of to supporting cross-border trade and investment and maintaining financial stability.[222] Equilibration and condition are required but the regulatory interference in recent years have been introduced in a similar fashion and with mirroring content. But issues remain. Ghamani and Glasserman[223] reported the answer whether all these regulatory interventions have effectively incentivized to centrally clear previously OTC derivatives.[224] That answer is not unanimously positive. The cost comparison, they highlight, does not necessarily favor central clearing and, when it does, the incentive may be driven by questionable differences in CCPs' default waterfall resources. Every transaction that is centrally cleared raises the question about mutualization of losses.[225] A loss distribution model or loss waterfall is critical. The allocation of

[221] M. Singh and D. Turing, (2018), Central Counterparties Resolution—an Unresolved Problem, IMF Working Paper Nr. WP/18/65, March, p. 15.

[222] EC, (2016), European Commission and the United States Commodity Futures Commission: Common approach for Transatlantic CCPs, IP-16-281-EN, February 10.

[223] S. Ghamami and P. Glasserman, (2016), Reform Incentivize Central Clearing, OFR Working Paper Nr. 16-07, July 26. The cost comparison is driven by (1) the netting benefits achieved through bilateral and central clearing, (2) the margin period of risk used to set initial margin and capital requirements and (3) the level of CCP guarantee fund requirements.

[224] M. Hsiao, (2018), Regulating OTC Derivatives: the CCP's Role and the EMIR, in Research Handbook on Shadow Banking, Legal and Regulatory Aspects (eds.) I. H.-Y. Chiu and I.G. MacNeil, Edward Elgar Publishing, Cheltenham, UK, pp. 205–228. The analysis focuses on the reporting obligation to the trade repository (TR) and the clearance obligation of designated OTC derivatives through the central counterparty (CCP).

[225] A. Capponi et al., (2018), Designing Clearinghouse Default Funds, Working Paper, Stern NY University, February 21, mimeo. They highlight that the loss-mutualization default fund works fine to share losses ex post but incentivize excessive risk taking ex ante. Such an arrangement is therefore intrinsically vulnerable. They suggest a model that trades off with ex post risk sharing and ex ante risk sharing. The optimal default fund should be 'designed to cover the default costs of a fixed fraction of the members rather than a fixed number of clearing members' (p. 2). They therefore oppose

losses and residual losses in particular has an impact on welfare. Two models of loss-allocation mechanisms can be identified, that is, variation margin haircutting and cash calls. Each has their own set of private and social optimal levels.[226] Often the discussion about loss allocation is limited to default losses, but that ignores the relevance of the principles required for non-default losses at CCPs. A robust strategy dealing with an appropriate way to allocate non-default losses would answer three distinct questions: (1) who should assume financial responsibility for a non-default loss?, (2) what portion of a non-default loss should each party pay? and (3) how should CCPs and clearing members address catastrophic non-default losses?' Lewis and McPartland[227] attempt to answer those questions and take central stage the idea that 'financial responsibility should be shared among the parties whose decisions contributed to the loss.' Figuring out who contributed to a loss requires an understanding of the type of loss and how it spread over the different players involved. The mathematics behind that question makes them to suggest 'that the CCP and clearing members should establish a loss-sharing formula that takes into account the CCP's ownership structure and the particular needs of the CCP and its clearing members'.[228] The third question requires a different logic. Catastrophic losses are characterized by the fact that the losses are so large that those involved cannot bear them. Looking at the cause of the loss is then not only not relevant but also not meaningful. The CCP and the clearing members should consider whether the implied value in the operations still available is still worth continuing the operations, and whether it justifies covering the losses incurred.

---

the mechanism installed in the Cover II rule (the required contribution by each member is such that the default fund is sufficient to cover the liquidation costs of two defaulting members. In any case, loss mutualization may weaken the incentives to acquire and reveal information about counterparty risk: G. Antinolfi et al., (2018), Transparency and Collateral: Central versus Bilateral Clearing, Finance and Economics Discussion Series Nr. 2018-017, Board of Governors of the Federal Reserve System (US).

[226] See in detail on this matter: R.S. Raykov, (2016), To Share or Not to Share? Uncovered Losses in a Derivatives Clearinghouse, Bank of Canada Working Paper Nr. 4, February. And in a more general sense: C.M. Baker, (2016), Clearinghouses for Over-the-Counter Derivatives, The Volcker Alliance Working Paper, November.

[227] R. Lewis and J. McPortland, (2017), Non-Default Loss Allocation at CCPs, Federal Reserve Bank of Chicago, Discussion Paper Nr. 2017-2, April. The first systematic study of interest rate swaps traded over the counter in the new regulatory regime shows that a client pays a higher price to buy interest rate protection from a dealer (i.e. the client pays a higher fixed rate) if the contract is not cleared via a central counterparty. This OTC premium decreases by posting initial margin and with higher buyer's creditworthiness. Also, OTC premia are absent for dealers suggesting dealers' bargaining power. In detail: G. Cenedese et al., (2018), OTC Premia, Bank of England Staff Working Papers Nr. 751, August 17.

[228] It can get much more complicated than that. A CCP loss can be located in one of the following fields: business or operational, investment or custodial. In case it is business or operational, the CCP is the only one to absorb that risk. If it is custodial in nature, the CCP seems to be the logical first party to pick up that risk combined with the clearing member facilitating the affected custodian. In case it is an investment loss, the question raises whether the CCP invested cash or only advised on possible investment options. If the CCP invested cash both the CCP and the affected clearing members posting cash are due to step in to cover the losses. In case the CCP only advises, the CCP and the clearing members affected by the investment should step in.

But what encourages market parties to clear or not? And an aligned question is how to evaluate the effectiveness of the recently enacted legislation? The latter question could be broadened to include both the question regarding more transactions cleared rather than settled in the private market and the regulation creating more robust CCPs. Structurally? There are four reasons to be identified why parties would consider clearing transactions: (1) the liquidity and riskiness of the reference entity; (2) the credit risk of the counterparty; (3) the clearing member's portfolio net exposure with the Central Counterparty Clearing House (CCP) and (4) post-trade transparency.[229] That is good to know. What is even more interesting to know is the fact that there is a wide variation in clearing behavior between CCP members and non-clearing members but also among clearing members. That seems to be the case even for market parties that are subject to counterparty risk capital requirements. Bellia et al. have been looking into the question why parties decide to clear or not. Unfortunately the study is limited to sovereign CDS contracts but reveals some interesting arguments demonstrating a wide arsenal of reasons argued by market agents. Those arguments include counterparty credit risk exposures, capital and margins costs or the willingness of market agents to reduce their exposures to the CCP and largely clear contracts when at least one of the traders has a high counterparty credit risk.[230] Also noteworthy is the fact that the willingness of non-clearing members to clear indirectly is low. Most likely that decision is driven by the fact that indirect clearing requires the non-member to go through a CCP member. The obstacles are not yet fully understood but cost is likely to be a major factor.[231]

Within the European context, there are two aspects that deserve attention in this context. First, since 2012 the EU's European Market Infrastructure Regulation (EMIR)[232] has required to be more robust. Second, since 2016 certain standardized

[229] M. Bellia et al., (2017), The Demand for Central Clearing: to Clear or Not to Clear, that is the Question, ESRM Working Paper Nr. 62, December, pp. 9–17. See for a parallel study on the same issues: P. Fiedor, (2018), Clearinghouse-Five: Determinants of Voluntary Clearing in European Derivatives Markets, ESRM Working Paper Nr. 72, March 13. He shows that there exist significant economies of scale in central clearing, in terms of both the size of each contract and the scale of total clearing activity. He then continues to demonstrate that maturity of the contract and international frictions affect voluntary clearing of different types of derivative contracts in different ways, linked to the conventional maturity and payout structures of various types of contracts. Significant amount of clearing happens only for credit and interest rate derivatives, while equity, foreign exchange and commodity derivatives are rarely centrally cleared.

[230] Ibid. Bellia et al., (2017), pp. 26–35.

[231] Ibid. Bellia et al., (2017), pp. 24–25 and 37.

[232] Most of the central clearing reform has been established mainly through the European Markets Infrastructure Regulation (EMIR) in Europe and the Dodd-Frank Wall Street Reform and Consumer Protection Act in the US. See for a detailed (comparative) analysis of the reform: Ose Binitie, (2016), Central Counterparty Reform: an Analysis of the Implementation of the CPSS, IOSCO Financial market Infrastructure Principles, August 2 (IOSCO.com).

'over-the-counter' (OTC) derivatives have to be cleared through authorized CCPs.[233][234] There is a third element as well. Since late 2016, there is a proposal in the making addressing the recovery and resolution of CCPs. This proposal[235] deals with four distinct aspects:

(1) Preparation and prevention: each CCP has to draw up a recovery plan (including a risk system) including measures to be taken in case of financial problems; their plans are reviewed and approved by national supervisors. Additionally, these national authorities draw up a resolution plan for each CCP in case of failure of the CCP.
(2) Direct intervention: national authorities have the authority to step in when a CCP fails or gets into trouble. They can further effectively instruct CCPs (preferably with a standardized set of tools) to take certain actions in the context of a recovery plan or otherwise.

---

[233] This has yielded a material increase of OTC derivatives being cleared. About half the (previous) OTC derivatives are now being cleared and that number is expected to rise. B. Cœuré, (2017), Central Clearing: Reaping the Benefit, Controlling the Risks, Banque de France, Financial Stability Review Nr. 21, April, The Impact of Financial Reforms, pp. 97–110; S. Markose et al., (2017), A Systemic Risk Assessment of OTC Derivatives Reforms and Skin-In-the-Game for CCPs, Banque de France, Financial Stability Review Nr. 21, April, The Impact of Financial Reforms, pp. 111–126; R. Cont, (2017), Central Clearing and Risk Transformation, Banque de France, Financial Stability Review Nr. 21, April, The Impact of Financial Reforms, pp. 127–138.

[234] There is a (second) study underway to evaluate the effect of reforms on incentives to centrally clear OTC derivatives: FSB, (2018), Incentives to Centrally Clear Over-the-Counter Derivatives, August 7. The initial FSB study concluded that '(1) the changes observed in OTC derivatives markets are consistent with objective of promoting central clearing as part of mitigating systemic risk and making derivatives markets safer; (2) the relevant post-crisis reforms, in particular the capital, margin and clearing reforms, taken together, appear to create an overall incentive, at least for dealers and larger and more active clients, to centrally clear OTC derivatives; (3) non-regulatory factors, such as market liquidity, counterparty credit risk management and netting efficiencies, are also important and can interact with regulatory factors to affect incentives to centrally clear; (4) some categories of clients have less strong incentives to use central clearing, and may have a lower degree of access to central clearing; and (5) the provision of client clearing services is concentrated in a relatively small number of bank-affiliated clearing firms.'

[235] Proposal for a REGULATION OF THE EUROPEAN PARLIAMENT AND OF THE COUNCIL on a framework for the recovery and resolution of central counterparties and amending Regulations (EU) No 1095/2010, (EU) No 648/2012, and (EU) 2015/2365, COM/2016/0856 final – 2016/0365 (COD). Further relevant aspects to be found in: (1) Opinion of the European Central Bank of September 20, 2017, on a proposal for a regulation of the European Parliament and of the Council on a framework for the recovery and resolution of central counterparties and amending Regulations (EU) No 1095/2010, (EU) No 648/2012 and (EU) 2015/2365 (CON/2017/38), OJ C 372, 1.11.2017, pp. 6–16; (2) Report of the Committee on Economic and Monetary Affairs on the proposal for a regulation of the European Parliament and of the Council on a framework for the recovery and resolution of central counterparties and amending Regulations (EU) No 1095/2010, (EU) No 648/2012 and (EU) 2015/2365 (COM(2016)0856 – C8-0484/2016 – 2016/0365(COD)), A8-0015/2018, January 31, 2018. Throughout 2018–June 2019, various legislative documents and opinions have been issued, but at June 30, 2019, the proposal was not finally approved or enacted.

(3) Effective resolution: the national authorities can put a failing CCP into resolution by national authorities when considered being in national interest; those authorities step in with tools to protect financial stability and the Treasury; part of the toolkit is the power to restructure or sell CCP assets (or the firm as a whole) and distribute losses among owners and participants. In case of going concern later on, the participants should be compensated by the CCP.
(4) Cooperation between supervisors of the different national authorities in order to ensure effective planning and orderly resolution. This includes the set-up of resolution colleges for each CCP containing all the relevant authorities including the European Securities and Markets Authority (ESMA) and the European Banking Authority (EBA).

5.12.3 CCP Interdependency

A feature that continues to cause major concern and which is largely neglected in the aforementioned proposal as well as in the EMIR legislation is the interdependency in the CCP market. Since 2017 the IOSCO in collaboration with the CPMI and the BCBS produce annual reporting demonstrating the interdependencies between central counterparties and their clearing members as well as other financial service providers.[236] The annual frequency is mainly there to provide evidence of the consistency in findings. So far, consistency has been found regarding a number of features. Those include[237]:

- Pre-funded financial resources are concentrated at a small number of CCPs. Or simply put: the market for CCPs is very concentrated.
- Exposures to CCPs are concentrated among a small number of entities.
- The relationships mapped are characterized, to varying degrees, by a core of highly connected CCPs and entities and a periphery of less highly connected CCPs and entities.
- A small number of entities tend to dominate the provision of each of the critical services required by CCPs.
- Clearing members and clearing member affiliates are also important providers of other critical services required by CCPs and can maintain several types of relationships with multiple CCPs simultaneously.

[236] The first report was issued on July 5, 2017. See FSB/IOSCO, (2017), Analysis of Central Clearing Interdependencies. The second report was released on August 9, 2018: FSB/IOSCO, (2018), Analysis of Central Clearing Interdependencies. A variety of interdependencies is examined in both reports: (1) interdependencies between CCPs and their clearing members, (2) interdependencies between CCPs and custodian and settlement banks, (3) interdependencies between CCPs and liquidity and credit providers and (4) interdependencies between CCPs and investment service providers.

[237] FSB, (2018), Analysis of Central Interdependencies, August 9, p. 4.

But not everything turned out to be consistent. For instance, 'the concentration of client clearing activity has decreased'. Compared with the 2016 report, initial margins from clients are now concentrated in two CCPs, compared to only one the year before.

Besides the resolution procedures as discussed, the CCPs themselves have their own closeout procedures that allow CCPs to respond to events that threaten the continuity of their normal ongoing operations. In most cases those events are a default by one of its clearing members. The procedures aim to stabilize normal operations while singling out and closing out the defaulter's portfolio. Reality has demonstrated that formal closeout procedures and real-life events as they unfold tend to be not in line and that all sort of real-life constraints embedded in the management of a default occur for which the formal procedures does not account. And so the question is 'what are the implications of this rift and what does it mean in terms of risks and costs the CCP is exposed to in the process'. Cerezetti et al. have done a brilliant job in shedding some light on those implications. Their findings suggest and evaluate how distinct closeout strategies may expose a CCP to different sets of risk and costs, and consequently could impact the sufficiency of financial resources to cover its risk exposure to a default. In this context that also accounts that CCPs come in different styles and models and therefore respond different to closeout procedures. It is for that reason that that regulation did not engage in 'prescriptive regulatory standard [that define] how CCPs should map default procedures into risk metrics, and a principle-approach [is established] that models, parameters, and assumptions should capture the risk characteristics of products cleared, not limited to market risk.'[238]

And there is more concern about the impact of the new regulations (in particular the CCP mandates and collateral requirements). The whole idea of central clearing was to enhance financial stability and reduce systemic risk. In particular, the idea was to reduce counterparty risk of previous OTC transactions that are now cleared by the CCP. But there is concern that the counterparty has not gone away but simply has transformed into other types of risks and in particular liquidity risk. Or as Cont[239] puts it 'margin calls transform accounting losses into realized losses which affect the liquidity buffers of clearing members.' She advances 'initial margin and default fund[240] calculations should account for this liquidity risk in a realistic manner, especially for large positions.' So rather than focus on CCP solvency, capital and 'skin-in-the-game', the real focus should

---

[238] F. Cerezetti et al., (2017), Market Liquidity, Closeout Procedures and Initial margin for CCPs, Bank of England Working Paper Nr. 643, February, p. 16. Their model analyzes how different hedging strategies may expose a CCP to different sets of risk and costs and consequently could impact the sufficiency of financial resources to cover its risk exposure to a default. The full spectrum ranges from hedging design in a model-free way which is useful for all sorts of different and unexpected states of the world. Other scenarios take into account certain market architectures, which allows to focus on the specific impact of market frictions that affect the portfolio of the defaulter. It would be nice to see further research in this field occurring for other scenarios (i.e. splitting and liquidation). The same is true for expanding the analysis to include different market structures.

[239] R. Cont, (2017), Central Clearing and Risk Transformation, Norges Bank Working Paper Nr. 2017-3, Oslo.

[240] There is a nascent body of literature emerging regarding default fund requirements inter alia.

be on the liquidity of clearing members and the liquidity resources of CCPs.[241] Clearing members should assess their exposure to CCPs no longer in counterparty risk[242] but in terms of liquidity risk and CCPs should frame their exposures along the lines of liquidity stress testing results and the adequacy of their liquidity resources. But determining the resilience of the entire system of CCPs and clearing members requires a combined supervisory stress test across CCPs and their clearing members.[243] Such a system-wide stress test for CCPs would require three changes to the current tests Tompiadis argues: (1) generating a large number of scenarios using a factor analysis technique, (2) using existing stress test results to calculate P/L for a clearing member's portfolio for each scenario and (3) using a structural default model to determine defaults consistent with the stress scenarios.[244]

5.12.4 CCP Stress Tests

The aforementioned stress test developed for CCPs[245] involves six steps: (1) purpose specification, (2) governance arrangements, (3) developing stress scenarios, (4) data collection and protection, (5) aggregating results and developing analytical metrics, use of stress testing results. Clearly step three[246] is the most relevant, although being driven by the choices made in step one and two. Step three consists of eight components:

1. *Identification of risk exposures.* This part describes risk exposures, the role that risk exposures play in a stress test and the factors that are underlying the decision to include certain risks in the analysis. Risk exposures include, but are not limited to, 'the positions, collateral, investments and other financial products or liquidity arrangements'.[247] National authorities can evaluate and direct the inclusion of certain risk factors relative to the purpose of the stress test.

---

[241] Ibid. R. Cont, (2017), pp. 5 ff. See also: to clear or T. Adrian et al., (2016), Market Liquidity after the Financial Crisis, Federal Reserve Bank of New York Staff Report Nr. 796, October.

[242] The multilateral netting can reduce exposures across counterparties. Also: R. Cont, (2015), The End of the Waterfall: Default Resources of Central Counterparties, *Journal of Risk Management in Financial Institutions*, Vol. 8, Nr. 4, pp. 365–389; R. Cont and A. Minca, (2016), Credit Default Swaps and Systemic Risk, Annals of Operations Research, Vol. 247, Nr. 2, pp. 523–547.

[243] See for a suggested model and framework that would use existing stress test results at individual CCPs to create a US system-wide stress test: S. Tompaidis, (2017), Measuring System-wide Resilience of Central Counterparties, OFR Brief Series Nr. 17-03. Tompaidis includes both the analysis of the ESM and CFTC supervisory stress tests in his model (p. 3). European Securities and Markets Authority, Methodological Framework: 2017 EU-wide CCP Stress Test Exercise, Feb. 1 (esma.europe.eu).

[244] Ibid. S. Tompiadis, (2017), p. 7. See also: EACH, (2015), Best Practices for CCP Stress tests, April, Brussels.

[245] IOSCO/CPMI/BIS, (2018), Framework for Supervisory Stress Testing of Central Counterparties (CCPs), CPMI Paper Nr. 176, April 10. CPMI, (2017), Framework for Supervisory Stress Testing of Central Counterparties (CCPs), Consultative Report, June.

[246] Ibid. pp. 16–30.

[247] Ibid. p. 17.

2. *Identification of risk sources.* A risk source is defined as 'anything that may impact the profits and losses or liquidity inflows and outflows incurred by the CCP, or the financial or liquidity resources available to the CCP when managing a response to a stress event (e.g. the close-out of a defaulting clearing participant's portfolio).'[248] The choices made define the design and complexity of the stress-test model. Authorities will have to decide on which factors to include taking into account complexity of implementation, model risk and the level of accuracy needed.
3. *Framing stress-testing scenarios.* This part describes how authorities frame the stress-testing scenarios, that is, they will describe the parameters within which the scenarios have been developed, the selection of core risk factors and the calibration of shocks, as well as the assumptions on the behavioral responses of CCPs on their participants. Further included can/should be the specification of an event-based scenario (a narrative that supports the internal consistency of the shocks used) and the parameters they used (macroeconomic/financial developments, policy regime changes, (geo)political developments, operational shocks [e.g. cyber-attack, pandemic event], large-scale disruptions [e.g. natural disasters]).[249] These event-based scenarios can be developed as an 'exogenous shock that affects multiple markets simultaneously (e.g. flight to quality), or an idiosyncratic shock to one market (e.g. a steep rise in the oil price) that propagates to other markets.'
4. *Identifying core risk factors.* An important element of the development of scenarios for a stress test is 'to select the most relevant risk factors and include a description of (how these risk factors will evolve over the horizon of the test'). This is needed to quantify CCPs' stressed credit or liquidity exposures. It should be noted that there are hundreds of exposures hitting CCPs in their normal operations, but often a most relevant risk and concentrated in a number of specific risks. Calibration is therefore critical during this phase. The guidelines are very thin when it comes to the process or approaches that can or should be used to select those risk factors. They limit the discussion to the reference to 'varying degrees expert judgment or quantitative analysis' with a preference for quantitative analysis as expert judgment might not necessarily lead to the identification of the relevant risk factors.[250] A two-step process beginning with a quantitative analysis followed by judgment.
5. *Calibrating the shocks to core risk factors.* Accordingly, the methodology applied should ensure 'the shock is suitably extreme', and 'scenarios remain plausible and internally consistent and analytical tractability and feasibility will also be important considerations'.[251] These shock scenarios can be based on historic data and/or forward-looking

[248] Ibid. p. 18. See for a suggested overview of risk sources pp. 19–20. Elements include prices moves of cleared positions, price moves of collateral, price moves triggered by entity defaults, transaction costs, wrong-way risk, liquidity outflows following settlements, changes in credit exposures and resources and changes in liquidity exposures and resources.

[249] Ibid. p. 21.

[250] Ibid. pp. 23–24.

[251] Ibid. p. 25.

datasets. It should be noted that the calibration can be parallel for liquidity and credit risk but pending characteristics of both two different calibrating models might be required or recommended each based on a relevant set of criteria.

6. *Extrapolating the shock to other (noncore) risk factors.* Extrapolation is only relevant in case it adds to the credibility of the underlying data and assumptions. A wide variety of model choices are available with on the one hand the option for 'a common methodology for extrapolating shocks to every non-core risk factor covered by the SST, thereby ensuring consistency in non-core risk factor shocks across all in-scope CCPs' and on the other hand a scenario whereby 'the extrapolation task could be assigned to the in-scope CCPs, using their own proprietary models'.[252] The latter might create a situation with all sorts of models which application could be operationally cumbersome and lacking consistency. A default model applied by authorities could and should be available at all times. 'Intermediate options' might involve the authorities 'specifying a principles-based methodology for the calibration of non-core risk factors'.
7. *Specifying defaults or failures.* This step will be driven by the choice to focus on credit or liquidity risk. In case the focus is credit risk, participant or collateral default combined with an adverse market shock is central to the analysis. In case the focus is on liquidity risk, the 'event of a default or the failure to perform of a participant, obligor, liquidity provider, or other relevant service provider' is critical. Outside a default scenario, a simple failing to perform scenario of a participant but also service providers such as a payment bank, a settlement facility, or a custodian might be included in particular as they might cause severe liquidity issues. Market prices or analytical models might be used to model (possibility of) default scenarios.[253]
8. *Specifying the timing of defaults or failures.* Detailing the sequence of events is the most important in this phase. Two models are available for specifying the timeframe over which defaults or failures to perform are assumed to occur[254]: (1) 'simultaneous defaults or failures'. It is assumed in calculating stressed losses and liquidity shortfalls that the participants and service providers selected for default or failure by the authorities 'default and fail simultaneously' and (2) 'sequential defaults or failures'. The authorities would specify 'a path for the default or failure of participants or service providers'. The former model is simpler to design and the latter more realistic to occur but also more complex to design.

We can all agree that CCPs are commitment mechanisms that are ultimately in place to assure the performance of financial contract obligations. How they execute that role sets them apart from other players such as other financial intermediaries or FIs and

---

[252] Ibid. p. 27.

[253] The possibility of a CCP default is likely to be higher than conventional stress tests indicate. See M. Paddrik and H.P. Young, (2017), How Safe are Central Counterparties in Derivative Markets?, OFR Working paper Nr. 6, November 2.

[254] Ibid. p. 30.

banks. Any meaningful risk management protocol to be developed for CCPs will run into trouble quickly when designed through the lens of banks and bank regulation, simply because they are not. In fact, their commitment mechanism bears very little resemblance to the risk-taking function of banks,[255] as well as those of depositories, payment systems, insurance companies or exchanges, although some overlap might exit with the latter. Cox and Steigerwald have been looking into the differences between banks and CCPs—including their business models and risk profiles—taking into account the very specific way that CCPs are subject to the credit and liquidity risk of its clearing members and their potential default. They also observe the specific role capital and collateral play in this context relative to CCP risk management. They conclude as follows: '(1) a CCP's capital cannot be the primary (or a significant) resource for loss absorption without fundamentally altering the incentive structure embedded in the default "waterfall" through which losses are mutualized, if not the business model of the CCP itself; (2) accordingly, capital analysis alone tells us little or nothing about CCP resilience or ability to recover from threats to the viability of the CCP; and (3) stress testing for CCPs must focus on features that are unique to central clearing, principally the possibility and consequences of member default.'[256]

[255] Singh and Turing describe it as follows: '[i]n the case of a bank, the principal tool for resolution is the "lift-out" of a viable business from the mess of failure. The viable business will consist largely of the good-quality loans and assets of the old bank, together with the "priority" liabilities represented chiefly by retail depositors, and the essential service of providing continuing access to payment systems. What is left behind are bad loans and low-priority creditors, and the expectation is that this rump may be liquidated. CCPs are, of course, different: they have no loan book (no "good assets") and no "priority" creditors. They also have only one function, which is to clear. It is thus a priori difficult to describe a "lift-out" in the case of a CCP: what would be left behind?'. See in detail: M. Singh and D. Turing, (2018), Central Counterparties Resolution—An Unresolved Problem, IMF Working Paper Nr. WP/18/65, March, pp. 11–12. CCPs calculate their losses and call for margin or default contributions. Singh and Turing correctly assess that in case of a CCP—in contrast to a bank—there is no good business to be lifted out of the mess, resolution basically 'perpetuates a failed risk model' (p. 12).

[256] In detail and highly recommended: R.T. Cox and R.S. Steigerwald, (2017), A CCP is a CCP is a CCP, Federal Reserve Bank of Chicago, PDP Discussion Paper Nr. 2017-1, April; E. Anderson et al., (2018), Supervisory Stress Testing For CCPs: A Macro-Prudential, Two-Tier Approach, Finance and Economics Discussion Series Nr. 2018-082. Washington: Board of Governors of the Federal Reserve System, https://doi.org/10.17016/FEDS.2018.082. Their key message is that crucial differences in CCPs' role, risk profile and financial structure, when compared to banks, are likely to require significant adaptation in the design of supervisory stress tests (SSTs). They examine how supervisory stress tests may be designed to complement CCPs' own daily stress tests. They propose a two-tier approach that meets the intended policy objectives, while balancing ambition and resource cost. The first tier encompasses more standardized tests that can be conducted frequently to assess the resilience of the clearing network over time. The second tier encompasses less frequent and more complex 'deep dive' assessments. The proposed approach should overcome operational and resource challenges.

5.12.5 Is There an Optimal Structure to a CCP's Waterfall and Default Fund?

To a large degree that question has been answered throughout this chapter. The individual suggested models with its benefits have been discussed and through time refinements were suggested.[257] There are four big components to the CCP default waterfall[258]: (1) each member maintains a margin account with the CCP. That account is replenished through the variation margin (the mark-to-market of the members open positions); (2) the CCP charges each member an initial margin, that aims to cover the risk exposure of the CCP arising from potential future market fluctuations of the member's portfolio over some risk horizon or margin period of risk; (3) each CM contributes to the pre-funded default fund that acts as a form of mutualized loss sharing; (4) the CCP pledges part of its equity (about 20–25%) to be used to cover losses above the initial margin and default fund. The 'skin in the game' for the CCP and (5) the CCP may call for additional capital contribution from the survived clearing members (unfunded default fund).[259]If losses are still not covered, recovery mode kicks in and ultimately resolution.

[257] See in recent years: P. Nahai-Williamson et al., (2013), Central Counterparties and Their Financial Resources—A Numerical Approach, Bank of England Financial Stability Paper Nr. 19, London; R. Cont, (2015), The End of the Waterfall: Default Resources of Central Counterparties, Norges Bank Working Paper Nr. 16/2015; C. Perkins, (2016), Central Counterparties Need Thicker Skins, *Journal of Financial Market Infrastructures*, Vol. 4, Nr. 3, pp. 55–63; D. Murphy, (2017), I've Got You Under My Skin: Large Central Counterparty Financial Resources and the Incentives They Create, *Journal of Financial Market Infrastructures*, Vol. 5, Issue 3, pp. 57–74; W. Huang, (2017), Central Counterparty Capitalization and Misaligned Incentives, Working Paper, January 26, mimeo (also as BIS working Paper Nr. 767); J.P Morgan, (2017), A Balancing Act—Aligning Incentives Through Financial Resources for Effective CCP Resilience, Recovery and Resolution, via jpmorganchase.com; A. Capponi et al., (2018), Designing Clearinghouse Default Funds, NY Stern University Working Paper, February 21, mimeo.

[258] Also: Y. Armenti and S. Crépey, (2017), Central Clearing Valuation Adjustment, SIAM J. Financial Math., Vol. 8, issue 1, pp. 274–313; M. Arnold, (2019), The Impact of Central Clearing on Banks Lending Discipline, *Journal of Financial Markets*, Vol. 36 (C), pp. 91–114; A. Capponi, et al., (2017), Clearinghouse Default Waterfalls: Risk-Sharing, Incentives, and Systemic Risk, Working Paper, mimeo; W. A. Cheng, (2017), Clearinghouse Default Resources: Theory and Empirical Analysis. PhD thesis, Columbia University; Z. Cui, et al., (2017), Failure and Rescue in Central Clearing Counterparty Design, Working Paper, mimeo; B. Deng, (2017), Counterparty Risk, Central Counterparty Clearing and Aggregate Risk, Annals of Finance, Issue 4, S. Ghamani and P. Glassermann, (2017), Does OTC Derivatives Reform Incentivize Central Clearing?, *Journal of Financial Intermediation*, Vol. 32, October, pp. 76–87; M. Paddrick and H.P. Young, (2017), How Safe are Central Counterparties in Derivative Markets, OFR Working Paper Nr. 17-06, November 2, Washington.

[259] T.R. Bielecki et al., (2018), A Dynamic Model of Central Counterparty Risk, Working Paper, February 18, mimeo, pp. 3–4. Also in extenso: J. Gregory, (2014), Central Counterparties: Mandatory Central Clearing and Initial Margin Requirements for OTC Derivatives. Wiley & Sons, Hoboken NJ; D. Murphy, (2013), OTC Derivatives: Bilateral Trading and Central Clearing, Palgrave Macmillan, Basingstoke, UK.

In recent years and in parallel, the attention has shifted to end-of-waterfall situations,[260] that is, what in case the waterfall turns out not be sufficient and the CCP, forced or not, has to take action for restoring its financial health.[261] The reason for that dynamic is clear. Defaults by clearing can become a systemic risk event, when magnified through the interconnectedness facilitated at the level of the CCP. So more OTC transaction now cleared is fine, as long as the infrastructure can tolerate and manage that kind of traffic.[262] Up till today there is still considerable debate over the optimal design of clearinghouse arrangements. Central in this debate is the question regarding the sufficiency of the cover II rule, that is, each clearing member contribution is such that the default fund can cover the liquidation cost of two defaulting members.[263] Even more, there is a conflation of objec-

[260] See also: M. Singh and D. Turing, (2018), Central Counterparties Resolution—An Unresolved Problem, IMF Working Paper Nr. WP/18/65, March, pp. 5–6. They describe a number of end-of-waterfall inadequacies: (1) the CCP calls upon non-defaulting CMs to take over elements of the defaulter's book of positions through an auction process. An auction fails if the lowest price bid exceed the available financial resources of the CCP; (2) meeting ongoing obligations while rebalancing its books; (3) insolvency and illiquidity are in practice often the same, as the CCP has no long-term assets; (4) occurrence of non-default losses.

[261] P. Tucker, (2013), Central Counterparties in Evolving Capital Markets: Safety, Recovery and Resolution, Banque de France Financial Stability Review Nr. 17; D. Duffie, (2014), Resolution of Failing Central Counterparties, in Kenneth E. Scott, Thomas H. Jackson and John B. Taylor, (eds.), Making Failure Feasible—How Bankruptcy Reform Can End 'Too Big to Fail', Hoover Institution Press, pp. 87–109; ISDA, (2017), Safeguarding Clearing: The Need for a Comprehensive CCP Recovery and Resolution Framework, via isda.org; D. Turing, (2016), Clearing and Settlement, 2nd edition, Bloomsbury Professional, West Sussex, UK; M. Paddrik and H. Peyton Young, (2017), How Safe are Central Counterparties in Derivatives Markets?, OFR Working Paper Nr. 17-06; M. Singh en D. Turing, (2018), Central Counterparties Resolution—An Unresolved Problem, IMF Working Paper Nr. WP/18/65. Singh and Turing conclude that the current 'toolkit' insufficient to avoid the costs of resolution being borne by taxpayers. The CCP resolution models are modeled too much according to the resolution mechanism for banks, which provides little chance for success. In most policy models, clearing members one way or the other must bear the end-of-waterfall costs. The policy designs only differ in the way the end-of-waterfall costs must be allocated (often a type of 'variation margin gains haircutting'). And at the end there is the NCWO (no creditor worse off) principle as a kind of backtest for the normative nature of the resolution model. See Table 2 p. 13 at Singh and Turing for an overview of models currently on the table.

[262] M. Bardoscia et al., (2018), Multiplex Network Analysis of the UK OTC Derivatives Market, Bank of England Staff Working Paper Nr. 726; A. Armakolla and J.-P. Laurent, (2017), CCP Resilience and Clearing Membership, Working Paper, May 11, mimeo.

[263] Capponi et al. show that such an arrangement is intrinsically vulnerable: although the default funds allow members to share risk ex post, an inherent externality induces members to take excessive risk ex ante. The default loss of an institution that exceeds its initial margins and its default fund contribution are absorbed by the CCP equity capital and the default fund contributions of the surviving members. Typically, the CCP's equity capital is the first to absorb losses. Residual losses are then allocated to surviving members on a pro-rata basis. They design an alternative that trades off ex post risk-sharing with ex ante risk-shifting. They do so in three steps: (1) they show that the loss-mutualization arrangement by the CCPs is intrinsically vulnerable for the reasons already mentioned; (2) they show that the excessive risk-taking behavior can be mitigated by regulating the amount in the default fund; and (3) they design a default fund level that trades of ex post risk-sharing with ex ante risk-shifting, thus providing regulators an optimal cover rule for default fund collection. In terms of mechanics they demonstrate that 'as the number of clearing members grows large, the

tives ongoing between recovery and resolution,[264] and this besides the fact that the former is the responsibility of the CCP and the latter of the competent authority. That in most cases the best possible scenario is that the CCP continues to exist and operate leaves behind and is distinct from the question about the equitable allocation of losses which in turn obviously leads back—as a kind of feedback loop—to the question about the rebalancing and the best way to organize continuation of operations. By it is a difficult exercise: the governance of the CCP is ultimately with the shareholders of the CCP and the risk exposure through and with the clearing members (despite the fact that CCPs have risk committees).

A straightforward model would be that the CCP equity absorbs all losses, but those are often not sufficient.[265] And so the remaining question boils down to allocation of remaining losses. Many models are floating around[266]: from bridging models where the CCP inherits both the good and bad parts of the failing CCP, a sale of the good parts and a divesture of the failing part, position and loss allocation (this includes all varieties of allocation losses among surviving members), and asking them to cancel their cleared positions, and cash calls. Cash calls however are in essence a recovery technique. Also to the question arises about the realistic nature of the proposition and workability in often short timelines. By the time that the CCP enters resolution territory, the clearing members have reached their liability cap if not before. So nothing all too attractive from a policy point of view and nothing that comes close to tackling the real question: how to deal with a failing risk model at the level of the CCP. Unless you engage in a lift-out of the good part of the CCP business (like it would happen with a bank), the real pain stays in place. Using resolution models without root-cause management creates suboptimal situation and a guaranteed diminished appetite for cash injections and loss sharing by clearing members. That would definitely be the case after the first CCP default under the new regulation will be a fact. The clearing members are getting hit both ways. Forced to contribute to a default fund and when not bear the burden of financial resolution afterward. Higher levels of concentration and interconnectedness following incoming regulation imply that a smaller number of clearing partners should shoulder a greater volume of risk.[267] One can even wonder if it is even realistic that the clearing member community can effectively absorb those systemic

optimal default fund should be designed to cover the default costs of a fixed fraction of the members rather than a fixed number of clearing members (the Cover II rule). See in detail: A. Capponi et al., (2018), Designing Clearinghouse Default Fund, Working Paper, February 21, mimeo.

[264] The real problem in this matter is that the suggestions that are made in terms of resolution in fact also qualify as recovery mechanism. See for an actual overview of the different suggested models: M. Singh and D. Turing, (2018), Central Counterparties Resolution—An Unresolved Problem, IMF Working Paper Nr. WP/18/65, March, pp. 11 ff.

[265] See for the detailed discussion on the matter: M. Singh and D. Turing, (2018), Ibid. pp. 8–13.

[266] See Table two for an overview: M. Singh and D. Turing, (2018), Ibid. pp. 13, 15–16.

[267] On the other hand, fragmented clearing across multiple central counterparties (CCPs) is costly. This is because dealers providing liquidity globally cannot net trades cleared in different CCPs and this increases their collateral costs. These costs are then passed on to their clients through price distortions which take the form of a price differential (basis) when the same products are cleared in different CCPs. In detail: E. Benos et al., (2019), The Cost of Clearing Fragmentation, Bank of England Working Paper Nr. 800, May 31.

losses to begin with. If not, there is an implied taxpayer bailout written into the law.[268] Only recovery is then on the table, which we can call resolution as the distress is deep and wide enough.

The model that is favored the most is the already mentioned 'variation margin gains haircut'. It is often presented as one model but it allows for many variations. The idea of the model is that 'CCPs keep pace at least daily with the movement in market price on the contracts they clear. So, if the value of what the buyer has contracted to buy has risen, the buyer has made a gain which the CCP collects as "variation margin" from the seller and hands on to the buyer. The VMGH occurs when the CCP withholds the on-payment of gains to gainers, while continuing to demand the payment of variation margin (market losses) from losers.'[269]The benefits are clear: the CCP can continue and there is limited risk for the clearing members. The members will obviously incur a loss but ex ante the model is neutral in its functioning. So there seems to be consensus that this is the least troublesome model. However, if the model is repeated, a moral hazard might occur, as well as similar practical objectives that go with 'loss-allocation and re-position models'.[270] Clearing members may at some point be tempted to anticipate the impact and ex ante rebalance their book and portfolios, leaving client positions to shoulder the (future) losses. Continued usage of the model also equals strongly the obligation for clearing members to continue supporting a CCP they in essence no longer trust. It can further trigger price spirals because of the ex ante use of the technique. Then it becomes an ex post 'catch up' to the ex ante shortfalls in the default fund.[271]That sounds far from ideal.

Straightforward (unlimited) haircutting might then be better. Whatever the judgment and opinion on the different models, time and size constraining is needed to make the models realistic and workable. Check and balances are required to mitigate side effects and so far there is no clear issue-free model on the horizon.

A clearing member's default triggering losses beyond the default funds' capacity will be absorbed by the CCP equity capital and the default fund contributions of the surviving members (on a pro-rata basis). However, that rule is more a benchmark than a rule and in practice rules at clearing houses vary quite a bit.[272]

A loss mutualization arrangement by the CCPs is intrinsically vulnerable, argue Capponi et al.[273]: While the default funds allow members to share risk ex post, an inherent externality induces members to take excessive risk ex ante. Based on the abovementioned pro-rata rule, CCPs redistribute counterparty risk through mutualization

---

[268] M. Singh and D. Turing, (2018), Ibid. p. 16; Dodd-Frank Act sections 802–806.

[269] M. Singh and D. Turing, (2018), Ibid. p. 14.

[270] D. Turing, (2016), Clearing and Settlement, 2nd edition, Bloomsbury Professional, West Sussex, UK, Section 10.8/Figure 10.1.

[271] M. Singh and D. Turing, (2018), Central Counterparties Resolution—An Unresolved Problem, IMF Working Paper Nr. WP/18/65, March, pp. 14–15.

[272] See, for example, the default fund rules at Nasdaq: Nasdaq, (2018), Guide to Nasdaq Clearing Default Funds, Revision June 11, 2018; ICE, (2018), Clearing Default Funds and Collateral Management, November.

[273] A. Capponi et al., (2018), Designing Clearinghouse Default Funds, Working Paper, Stern NY University, February 21, mimeo, pp. 2–4.

among all members. This is done ex post. This has a clear downside. A common pool of resources does not only create a dependency among members but a negative externality (can or will) occurs when a member decides to take excessive risk. The size of the contribution is also directly related to the extent of the externality. In case of a lower default fund, the opportunity cost of the members is reduced, but the negative externality among members is larger. Excessive risk taking then reduced total welfare. From a regulatory point of view that leaves the following balanced to be assessed in terms of default fund contributions: on the one hand there is the need to reduce the counterparty risk of members, but on the other hand the default should not allow generating excessive risk taking. Capponi et al.'s contribution is that they have been looking to that optimal relationship and were the first to do so taking into account maximized social welfare as the aggregate value of clearing members and the CCP. Given the level of default fund amount, members of the CCP decide on the riskiness of the projects undertaken (total utility), taking into account the costs the member incurs to absorb losses generated by other member's default. That strategic interaction modeled as a Stackelberg game[274] including the coordination problem is at the core of the trade-off. Setting default fund requirements triggers the implication that due to moral hazard members, the incentive to avoid default reduces. Others would contribute to his default though their contributions. Inefficiency is likely from a systemic risk point of view when designing the optimal position. In a more normative context, the optimal cover number for the default fund rule.

The excessive risk taking can be mitigated by regulating the amount in the default fund (i.e. the size of the contribution by the members in the fund). In such a way, there is a trade-off established between ex post risk sharing with ex ante risk shifting. According to Capponi et al., the optimal level should therefore be designed to cover the default costs of a fixed fraction of the members rather than a fixed number of clearing members as is done in the case of the cover II rule. They clarify 'the optimal default fund level converges to a fixed fraction of the default cost, provided that the opportunity cost of default fund is not too high. In this case, it is socially optimal to mandate a default fund sufficiently high to cover a proportion of the members in the network.'[275] That optimal fund level is, taking into account cost of capital and collateral conditions, higher than prescribed under the cover II rule, in particular in this low interest rate environment. At higher levels of cost of funding for collateral, the cover II levels require suffice. The cover II rules should therefore be viewed in perspective: 'it is optimal when funding illiquidity (associated with marginal opportunity costs of default fund) is so high that it becomes socially preferable to induce a higher number of defaults in the system, than to subject members to the very high costs of raising collateral'.[276]

The policy implication is simple but difficult to execute: the cover rule should guarantee that costs generated by the default of a proportion of clearing members are 'covered'. This way the covering requirement is related to the size of the participating member base. The

[274] See for model set-up, ibid. pp. 7–14.
[275] Ibid. p. 3.
[276] Ibid. pp. 4 and 14–19.

optimal proportion however 'depends on the premium earned by the members who undertakes high-risk projects and the costs incurred at default'...'the proposed rule can also serve as a benchmark against more complex rules based on simulated scenario stress testing.'[277]

So the answer to the question if there is an optimal structure to a CCP's waterfall and default fund is clearly no. A rethink of the policy design is required. At the heart of that necessity is the fact that central clearing is, in contrast to what many regulators believe, not (always) risk reducing.[278] Possible alternatives could include or be a combination of the following elements: (1) suspending the clearing obligation in cases of CCP difficulty at a global basis (something the FSB advocated in 2016) without precluding bilateral clearing or portability models; (2) automatically canceling the clearing mandate for products where a CM default has blown through the default fund layer of the loss waterfall for the product concerned; (3) ensuring that CMs are not thwarted in their own ability to manage losses when a CCP difficulty becomes manifest by inability to register offsetting trades, CCPs' reserves policies should be strengthened and the loss waterfall revised.[279] Some of these elements are at loggerhead with the key incentive to move OTC trades in clearing territory,[280] that is, higher multilateral netting. Now the netting only works across asset classes and not across product groups. Beyond netting there are very few reasons to clear. Ghamani and Glasserman conclude that '[t]he cost comparison does not necessarily favor central clearing, and, when it does, the incentive may be driven by questionable differences in CCPs' default resources'.[281]

[277] Ibid. p. 27. See in detail on this matter also: M. Arnold, (2017), The Impact of Central Clearing on Bank's Lending Discipline, *Journal of Financial Markets*, Vol. 36 (C), pp. 91–114; S. Ghamami, and P. Glasserman, (2017), Does OTC Derivatives Reform Incentivize Central Clearing? *Journal of Financial Intermediation*, Vol. 32, pp. 76–87; C. Pirrong, (2011), The Economics of Central Clearing: Theory and Practice, International Swaps and Derivatives Association, NY; A.J. Menveld, (2017), Crowded Positions: An Overlooked Systemic Risk for Central Clearing Parties, The Review of Asset Pricing Studies, Vol. 7, pp. 209–242; Y.C. Loon and Z.K. Zhong, (2014), The Impact of Central Clearing on Counterparty Risk, Liquidity, and Trading: Evidence from the Credit Default Swap Market, *Journal of Financial Economics*, Vol. 112, pp. 91–115; D. Duffie et al., (2015), Central Clearing and Collateral Demand, *Journal of Financial Economics*, Vol. 116, pp. 237–256; A. Capponi et al., (2017), Clearinghouse Default Waterfalls: Risk Sharing, Incentives, and Systemic Risk, Working Paper, Mimeo; B. Biais et al., (2016), Risk-Sharing or Risk-Taking? Counterparty Risk, Incentives and Margins, *Journal of Finance*, Vol. 71, pp. 1669–1698.

[278] P. Glasserman and H.P. Young, (2016), How Likely is Contagion in Financial Networks?, *Journal of Economic Literature*, Vol. 54, Issue 3, pp. 779–831; C. Pirrong, (2014), A Bill of Goods: CCPs and Systemic Risk, *Journal of Financial Market Infrastructures* Vol. 2. Nr. 4, pp. 55–85; C. Pirrong, (2010), The Inefficiency of Clearing House Mandates, Cato Institute Policy Analysis Nr. 665, July; D. Duffie, and H. Zhu, 2009, Does a Central Clearing Counterparty Reduce Counterparty Risk? Rock Center for Corporate Governance Working Paper Nr. 46; M. Roe, (2013), Clearinghouse Overconfidence, California Law Review Vol. 101. Nr. 6, pp. 1641–1703.

[279] M. Singh and D. Turing, (2018), Central Counterparties Resolution—an Unresolved Problem, IMF Working Paper Nr. WP/18/65, March, pp. 17–18.

[280] See also ISDA, (2018), Clearing Incentives, Systemic Risk and Margin Requirements for Non-cleared Derivatives, ISDA White Paper Series, October 1; ISDA, (2019), CCP Best Practices, January 24; ISDA, (2019), CCP Recovery and Resolution: Incentives Analysis, March 15, all three via isda.org

[281] S. Ghamami, and P. Glasserman, (2017), Does OTC Derivatives Reform Incentivize Central Clearing? *Journal of Financial Intermediation*, Vol. 32, pp. 76–87.

It is very likely a reasonable conclusion that the traditional cash flow waterfall is too easily exhausted and that access to default fund contributions are too easily consumed. It would therefore make perfect sense that CCPs would broaden their capital base and build in reserves that can be tapped into as one works through the cash flow waterfall. That could include default insurance arranged by CCPs. If a CCP is confident in its risk management models, it should be no problem (in fact logical) that the CCP develops own contribution capabilities (beyond its own equity position). That in itself can enhance confidence among clearing members and could be seen as a token of alignment of interest between themselves and the CCP.[282] Failing risk models cannot be dealt with just by a typical cash flow waterfall and then at the bottom a basin of default funding gathered from clearing members. Beyond the CCP equity position and potential dividend stoppers and clawbacks, an enhanced layer of loss-absorbing capital could or should be included.[283] However, the modeling and managing of risk is never fully within control of a particular CCP. And so, any default that might occur has wider implications for the clearing market and other product groups.[284]

So for now the conclusion is that there is no optimal cash flow waterfall and default fund model. The cash flow waterfall is exhausted too hastily, the default fund financed by clearing members consumed too early in the process, moral hazards can occur in multiple scenarios and CCPs only see their equity position at stake. That equity position is often leveled based on activities and normal risk exposures and don't manage to cover extremes. The CCP is seen as responsible for risk management, but reality dictates they can never fully bear that risk as much is beyond its control. The unhealthy default fund model where clearing members need to contribute is not only prone to moral hazards but also raises the question whether that is arithmetically even feasible for them to cover that exposure due to ever increasing levels of transactions, volumes and interconnectivity. The answer is no and so the taxpayer emerges at the horizon as the ultimate bail-out partner. Exactly what we wanted to avoid from a regulatory point of view. The risk-reward model[285] is unbalanced and distortion is likely, as well as the ability to execute some of the models.

---

[282] See also in extenso: C.M. Baker, (2016), Clearinghouses for Over-the-Counter Derivatives, The Volcker Alliance Working Paper, November, pp. 32–52 (risk management) and 52–69 (recovery and resolution).

[283] An add-on question is then if the CCP or its parent (in case so) should be responsible in making that happen through equity contributions or raising extra loss-absorbing debt. Also: L. Carter and M. Garner, (2015), Skin in the Game—Central Counterparty Risk Controls and Incentives, Reserve Bank of Australia Bulletin, June Quarter, pp. 79–88.

[284] M. Singh and D. Turing, (2018), Central Counterparties Resolution—An Unresolved Problem, IMF Working Paper Nr. WP/18/65, March, pp. 18–19.

[285] Attempts are made to restore the equilibrium but most of the times in a marginal way. See, for example, T.R. Bielecki et al., (2018), A Dynamic Model of Central Counterparty Risk, Working Paper, February 18, mimeo, pp. 4 ff. Making the waterfall and initial margin (and their relationship) more risk sensitive in itself sounds like a great plan and improves our understanding up from the current situation but leaves the real question unanswered. Risk sensitivity amounts to accounting for credit migrations of the clearing members and the stochastic dependence between these migrations.

CCPs are not banks and therefore require different treatment also in terms of recovery and resolution. More equity is part of the answer and an operational backstop so that clearing can be halted during a crisis and clearing members can manage their risk exposure individually. For now, the best reality possible is to monitor CCPs in line with a number of indicators such. The European Systemic Risk Board[286] uses in total nine: (1) pre-funded default resources, haircut and margining policies, liquidity policies, collateral practices, market structure and concentration, winding-down ratio, income structure, client clearing and interoperability arrangements.[287]

Also the FSB realized that that story about CCPs and their waterfall, their equity position at risk and more broadly, their possible source of systemic risk is partly or even largely unwritten. But the clearing of a large amount of OTC derivatives was and is a core objective of post-financial crisis regulation with a view toward a safe and sound financial system.[288]

[286] E. Alfranseder et al., (2018), Indicators for the Monitoring of Central Counterparties in the EU, Occasional Paper Series, Nr. 14, March. For the time the CCPs in Europe are regulated and supervised at a national level. The initial EMIR has contributed mainly to providing CCPs a single set of rules. In June 2017 a proposal was introduced to for targeted changes in the EMIR with the aim to enhance the current supervisory arrangement and creating a more pan-European approach to the supervision of CCPs. Two objectives are embedded in the proposal: (1) stabilizing CCPs given their increased importance in capital markets and, (2) with Brexit a reality, although not clear in detail what it exactly means, the impact on the European clearing landscape will and is meaningful. After leaving the EU, the UK-based clearing companies can no longer clear Euro-denominated transactions. The EU proposal: Proposal for a REGULATION OF THE EUROPEAN PARLIAMENT AND OF THE COUNCIL amending Regulation (EU) No 1095/2010 establishing a European Supervisory Authority (European Securities and Markets Authority) and amending Regulation (EU) No 648/2012 as regards the procedures and authorities involved for the authorization of CCPs and requirements for the recognition of third-country CCPs, COM/2017/0331 final – 2017/0136 (COD).

[287] An interoperability arrangement is a link between central counterparties (CCPs) which involves the cross-system execution of transactions. There are currently five such arrangements in Europe. Often those arrangements distinguish between going concern and during resolution/recovery periods. The most ESRB CCP interoperability report highlights that the legislative proposal should provide greater clarity as to how recovery and resolution tools would be applied for interoperable CCPs. An extension of interoperability option beyond cash instruments depends in that input. See the most recent but annual review: ESRB, (2019), CCP Interoperability Arrangements, ESRB Report, January.

[288] Schwarcz raises an interesting question and wonders whether regulators should expand the central clearing requirement to non-derivative financial contracts, such as loan agreements. However, the aggregate monetary exposure on non-derivative financial contracts—and thus the potential systemic risk that could be triggered by that exposure—greatly exceeds that on derivatives contracts. See in detail: S.L. Schwarcz, (2019), Central Clearing of Financing Contracts: Theory and Regulatory Implications, University of Pennsylvania Law Review, Vol. 167, pp. 1327–1373. He concludes that contrary to media portrayal, the systemic riskiness of derivatives contracts turns on the nature of their counterparties, not on their inherent nature. This insight indicates that non-derivative financial contracts with systemically important counterparties could also be systemically risky. In theory, requiring those financial contracts to be centrally cleared could therefore help to reduce systemic costs arising from that counterparty risk. To justify a reasonable cost-benefit balance, he suggests to limit the scope to material standardized non-derivative financial contracts. The deeper question of his conclusion is about the regulatory question whether to control risk and when to mutualize risk.

The FSB realized that more evidence-based guidance is needed and the incorporation of practical experiences in the design and execution of policies, tools and regulation. The discussion above has learned that the evaluation whether the financial resources of a CCP and the allocation of the financial burden among the participants involved is not straightforward and each models triggers as many downsides and the amount of benefits it carries. Also in this case, the FSB[289] stays somewhat unclear about the distinction line between recovery and resolution and most of its focus is on the adequacy of the financial resources available to implement resolution strategies. As we concluded above, the pain often sits in the distribution of losses, and the moral hazards some of the techniques (un)intentionally trigger. The FSB tends to continue the strategy that policy design should by far and large be written from the perspective of the CCP. There is very little room for reflections on the positions of the clearing members who ultimately bear most of the costs in case of recovery or resolution through their variety of contributions.

The FSB[290] offers the following insights into the CCP issue:

A. *Financial resources of the CCP*

The FSB produced a five-step process to evaluate the financial resources and tools for resolution. These five steps include:

- An identification and analysis of hypothetical default and non-default loss scenarios that may lead to resolution.[291]

1. *Default loss scenario*

CCPs should have their loss-allocation arrangements in place in line with FSB/IOSCO guidelines. However this might not always be the case. The following scenarios might occur:

- The CCP has not established resources and tools called for by the relevant guidelines. Often absence or inadequate implementation will lead to uncovered credit losses and/or liquidity shortfalls.
- The CCP loss-allocation arrangement doesn't operate as intended. The consequence is that resources are not available (not legally enforceable or subject to operational and governance mechanisms) or not where needed.

---

[289] The FSB builds its theory design on their earlier FSB, (2014), Key Attributes of Effective Resolution Regimes for Financial Institutions (Key Attributes) and FSB, (2017), Guidance on Central Counterparty Resolution and Resolution Planning. Both have been extensively discussed.

[290] FSB, (2018), Financial Resources to Support CCP Resolution and the Treatment of CCP Equity in Resolution, Discussion paper for public consultation, November 15. I will review the content of this discussion paper somewhat more extensively than it would normally deserve. Reason is that it is unclear and unlikely that the final standards will be released before the deadline of the manuscript. That understanding ultimately turned out to be correct.

[291] FSB, (2018), Ibid., pp. 5–9.

- Multiple clearing members do not meet their obligation under the CCP's recovery actions. That occurs often by not meeting variation margin calls or plain cash calls. The CCP can put non-performing members in default but that in itself poses a financial stability risk. The incentives should not only include letting non-performing members default but also allow the CCP to access the resources of non-performing clearing members to meet obligation. An open situation is when there are many clearing members that turn non-performing and as a consequence the CCP cannot continue operations.
- The CCP's recovery plan is consistent with the relevant guidelines, but the relevant authorities determine that resolution should be initiated before the tools of the CCP's recovery plan are exhausted. The obsolete tools could threaten financial stability and/or the continuity. This could be the case if executing the recovery plan any further could lead to placing additional clearing members into default or haircut positions.

2. *Non-default loss scenario*

In general terms the CCPs should hold financial resources (liquid net assets, with a minimum of six months operating expenses) against (and commensurate with) general business and operational risks. The general guidelines foresee rules regarding loss allocation in case custody and investment losses, but beyond that the CCP should need to absorb any unallocated loss arising from the materialization of general business risk. That risk portfolio can include investment risk, failure of a custodian bank, settlement platform, payment or concentration bank, operational risk exposures, legal risks and non-performing vendors or service providers.[292]

These risks should be managed and mitigated (including insurance) and when exposure occurs handled diligently. However, it is clear that a recovery plan might not be able to cover fully potential non-default losses. Resolution might then be called. Possible scenario might be:

- The CCP does not meet guidelines or does not have sufficient financial resources to cover non-default losses. The loss is larger than the amount of capital and contingent resources (of the CCP and the clearing members).
- The CCP's loss-allocation arrangements, where then available, address (specific) non-default losses in a comprehensive manner but do not operate as intended, so that the resources are unavailable or cannot be replenished or the tools are not able to be used at the time of recovery. This could be due to legal enforceability or subject to operational or governance mechanisms. Incentives to comply and the possible risk of a CCP calling default on a clearing member should keep reality away from such situations.
- The CCP's clearing members and/or shareholders do not meet their obligation or do not support the CCP's recovery actions.
- The CCP's recovery or wind-down arrangements are consistent with the guidelines but the relevant authorities determine that resolution should be initiated before some of the arrangements or plans are applied, because their application could threaten financial stability and/or the continuity of critical functions in the prevailing market conditions.

[292] FSB, (2018), Ibid. pp. 7–8 for details and examples.

- A qualitative and quantitative assessment of existing resources and tools available in light of these scenarios when applied in resolution.[293]

An evaluation of recovery and resolution tools should include possible legal constraints, operational caps, limitations of resolution powers, execution and enforceability risk, possible financial stability risks, meeting certain standards like 'no creditor worse off than in liquidation' (NCWOL), the impact of stakeholder incentives and more overall the feasibility and credibility of achieving the resolution objective. Regarding the latter requirements, a distinction can be made between default and non-default situations.

1. *Default loss scenarios*

   Important features in the assessment include:

- Cash calls: understanding how they work, possible constraints, performance risk and potential financial stability impacts
- Variation margin gains haircutting (VMGH)[294]: how it works and how it can be used, governance processes, possible constraints, calculation methods and how they map out over different settlement cycles, caps and limits and market and financial stability impacts
- *Full tear-up, partial tear-up* or *other position-allocation/matched book tools*[295]: How they work, financial constraints, financial stability impact and so on
- CCP equity: availability of basis and additional loss-absorbing equity, that is, beyond SITG[296] (equity made available as part of a typical default waterfall model including equity provided by the CCP parent). How the equity can be employed to absorb losses and possible constraints. Clear definition to what degree the parent and other parties

[293] FSB, (2018), Ibid. pp. 9–13.

[294] The VMGH is as said being applied at the end of the cash flow waterfall. Under a VMGH methodology, the CCP would impose a haircut on cumulative variation margin gains which have accumulated since the day of the clearing member default. The ISDA favors the model and sees the following benefits: (1) losses fall to those best able to control their loss allocation by flattening or changing their trade positions; (2) clearing members with gains at risk are incentivized to assist in the default management process; and (3) in the event that the CCP runs out of resources, VMGH mimics the economics of insolvency. See in detail: ISDA, (2013), CCP Loss Allocation at the End of the Waterfall, August.

[295] Full or partial tear-up refers to the 'full or partial tear-up of contracts the CCP is engaged in. Full tear-up of contracts is considered a last resort (when the waterfall is exhausted) and would only be applied if the clearing service is not critical and the tear-up will not have systemic consequences, or if no other option will result in a better outcome for financial stability. See in detail: ISDA, (2013), CCP Loss Allocation at the End of the Waterfall, August, pp. 7–8–13, 15 ff. Tear-up can be constructed as mandatory or voluntary modes; Q. Swerts and S. Van Cauwenberghe, (2016), CCP Resilience and Recovery-Impact for CCP Users, NBB Financial Stability Report, pp. 187–202; ESRB, (2017), Opinion on a Central Counterparty Recovery and Resolution Framework, July, pp. 9–10. The latter provides a full overview of mechanisms.

[296] Skin-in-the-game.

have legal, contractual or other commitments (even voluntary) to provide resources that have the ability to cover losses or replenish equity and the size of such commitments

- Replenishment of minimum resources: how would the default fund, SITG and other minimum resources be replenished, authorities required to do so and the effective reliability and viability of such arrangement. Potential constraints with respect to replenishment of minimum resources (caps, limits and frequency)
- Statutory powers of the resolution authority: statutory power and resources of the resolution authority, ability to allocate losses, allocation of resolution costs (and how they are initially funded: most often via additional cash calls and/or new rounds of VMGH). Condition under which powers can be executed, interaction with other authorities and supervising entities as well as possible NCWOL implications

2. *Non-default scenarios*

Important features in this scenario include:

- Availability and effectiveness of insurance coverage and other third party resources in
- Resolution: what types of non-default risks are covered, and the risk of a non-default occurring for reasons outside that coverage. Possible limitation on insurance. Can losses be larger than limits and what is the CCP's own ability to absorb losses. Can legal and operational process create time-lags (i.e. performance risk)
- CCP equity: What amounts are available to cover non-default losses of different types; enforceability of commitments and/or guarantees; excess guarantees (relative to the rulebook) of CCPs shareholders or third parties and the risk or uncertainty surrounding a possible non-payment in case of need be
- Allocation of losses to participants: scope and terms of contractual agreements that govern the allocation of losses; financial caps and legal or operational constraints; members failing to meet cash calls (performance risk) and potential mitigants; and financial stability concerns
- Allocation of losses to creditors in resolution: to what extent can loses be imposed on creditors of the CCP; insolvency hierarchy of the CCP's creditors taking into account different types of creditors and possible ways they can compromise any resolution regime; NCWOL considerations and implications of a non-pari-passu allocation of loses
- Statutory powers of the resolution authority: which statutory powers are available (write-downs/offs, enforced recapitalization, complementary cash calls, collecting insurance proceeds; restitution from shareholders or other stakeholders; and NCWOL implications
- An analysis of potential resolution costs[297]

[297] FSB, (2018), Financial Resources to Support CCP Resolution and the Treatment of CCP Equity in Resolution, Discussion paper for public consultation, November 15, pp. 13–14.

What are the different types of costs, given the scenario at hand? They include at least the amount of losses of the CCP and the costs of replenishing its financial resources and the operational costs that may be incurred by the resolution authority including legal and accounting fees, as well as the costs for continuing the (critical functions of the) CCP's operations as well as residual costs and post-resolution costs. Different scenarios can be defined reflecting different resolution strategies, different timelines involved.

- Comparison of existing tools and resources to full resolution costs and identification of any gaps[298]

The overall ambition is to get a full scope overview of the costs involved as well as whether existing tools and resources are sufficient to cover the type of cost they are intended for; what resources can cover what costs; are there costs not covered by existing tools and resources taking into account the time in the resolution process the resources might be needed.

- A consideration of the availability, costs and benefits of different means of addressing any gaps identified[299]

This would typically include questions such as 'what type of gaps have been identified and how can they be addressed?'; 'do resources and tool need to change accordingly?' or 'are other tools and resources necessary?', taking into different timelines and resolution strategies and blending in unintended consequences. The following questions might also emerge in the process:

- Nature of additional financial resources: nature and size of additional resources needed to fill gaps; possible methodologies to raise additional resources; would additional resources be available also in the recovery phase? and is a change in resolution strategy needed in case the gaps cannot be filled?
- Cash calls: need for transparency when additional calls will be executed; size of call and governance; what purpose of cash call: recapitalization or loss absorption; how can clearing members be prepared for cash calls?; should reasons for (additional) cash calls be exhaustively listed in rulebook or should room be left for discretionary judgment?
- Bail-in/write-down: does the resolution authority possess bail-in power?; does it include loss-absorbing and recapitalization capacity?; can it write down debt or convert liabilities?; how does it impact available collateral?
- Interaction between recovery position and ongoing operations at the CCP: would additional financial requirements impact business continuity?; Would it mean that the cost of central clearing would increase? Is it possible that reserves (or otherwise) are established ex ante that can (legally binding) be used only in case of resolution?; If so,

[298] FSB, (2018), Ibid. p. 14.
[299] FSB, (2018), Ibid. pp. 14–16.

does it have NCWOL implications? Can they be mitigated? Can rulebook changes effectively be implemented during 'targeted events' and do the relevant authorities have the power to do so?

Other factors that might be taken into account are as follows:

- Profile of participants including non-member clients/end users of a CCP. The idea is that loss allocation might work financially destabilizing and that the profile of the clearing members should be taken into account to better anticipate the implications of such events, in particular as the outcome is difficult to predict in case of adverse events.
- Type of CCP (e.g. cash equity CCP, derivatives CCP). The type of products offered by the CCP matters in terms of operations and resolution.[300]
- Multi-service CCPs. Different service lines imply different rules and thus recovery and resolution techniques need to observe spillover effects between the service lines in particular in case common membership of clearing members, concentration or cross-use of collateral or the definition of the cross-margining. Additional stress on CCP and/or clearing members might be caused by these elements.
- CCP services involving physical settlement. Particularly relevant in case of commodities. In case of physical delivery, resolution may be more constrained than for other products due to a limited number of clearing members or the ability to manage positions.
- CCPs with interoperability arrangements. Contagion risk is the central theme. Recovery or resolution of a linked operator might impact operations elsewhere.

B. *Treatment of CCP Capital in Resolution*[301]

An effective resolution regime is there in the first place to provide mechanisms to allow for all stakeholders but in particular shareholders and creditors to assess their positions, and to create visibility about the absorption of losses in a way that respect the cash flow waterfall or other legal hierarchy of claims. Equity structurally absorbs losses right after ex ante created reserves designed with a specific focus to absorb certain losses which can occur in both (non)-default scenarios. The FSB has following the Great Recession developed resolution systems and guidelines for a variety of institutions and scenarios (banks, SIFIs, SI insurance companies, etc.), including the resolution of CCPs, definitely not the least complex of all possible situations to cover. Although there is a tendency to look for similarities between those different resolution models, but doing so would ignore the fact that each of those institutions has distinct legal characteristics and economic positions and function in the marketplace. That is material implications that should be reflected in the different resolution models. For example, the role and position of creditors is different in a bank versus a CCP. That must mean that their different ontology of creditors in the CCP business model versus that of a bank should be properly identified. In particular, it

300 See for some examples FSB, (2018), Ibid. pp. 4–5.

301 FSB, (2018), Ibid. pp. 17–25.

raises questions about the applicability of the NCWOL[302] in the different scenarios and undeniably will lead to different outcomes.

Judging whether—in the context of a CCP—all stakeholders including creditors, equity holders and clearing members. It is clear that when it comes to regular business losses, the CCP's equity bears the risk. When a clearing member defaults, there is the cash flow waterfall and the comprehensive loss-allocation arrangement that should be in place. Both aim to allocate losses in a way that business continuation is possible and liquidation should be avoided. Such arrangement may include as well custody and investment risks and as we've discussed before.[303] Most of the losses realized in these areas are born one way or the other by the clearing members. In such cases only a part of the CCPs equity is at stake. We called it the skin-in-the-game (SITG) part and normally constitutes 20–25% of the total CCPs equity. This SITG part typically sits 'before additional losses are mutualized or otherwise allocated and, with regard to default losses, after the defaulting member's resources'.[304] It is however thinkable that arrangements can foresee in the fact that CCP resources in parallel can be depleted with the default fund (pari passu), or that a complementary portion of the CCPs equity or other resources are made available after using the default fund but before any further resource-raising actions, for example, cash calls. The FSB highlights that the SITG is meant predominantly as a sign of confidence in the CCP's risk protocols rather than brutal force that can absorb any possible fallout at the level of clearing members that default (or otherwise).

The combination and interaction of those full allocation arrangements and the NCWOL safety net yields the effect that it shields the CCPs equity from losses in resolution. These losses will be allocation to other parties. So when a resolution process is initiated and depending on the cause of the loss, equity holders should in principle be able to maintain their equity (besides the part that was ex ante allocated as SITG). If they lose additional equity, they should in principle be compensated based on the NCWOL mechanism (i.e. in case they lose equity in excess of the amount committed under the recovery arrangements.

The tension is clear: a resolution process where shareholders can shield a large part of their equity (legally through the rulebook),[305] knowing that a default of a clearing member of investment or custody risks often is a reflection of the failing risk management practices of the CCP creates a playing field for moral hazard. If, however, the equity portion of the CCP is affected beyond the allocated SITG and thus beyond the portion that would be lost in liquidation. NCWOL claims may arise. The creditor hierarchy in liqui-

[302] The NCWOL ('no creditor worse off than in liquidation') safeguard 'confers on creditors a right to compensation where the hierarchy of claims in liquidation and the principle of equal (pari passu) treatment of creditors of the same class are not respected in resolution and, as a result, they do not receive what they would have received in a liquidation of the firm under the applicable insolvency regime.' See FSB, (2018), Ibid. p. 17.

[303] See NBB, (2018), Securities Clearing, Settlement and Custody, Chapter 2 in Securities clearing, settlement and custody, Brussels, pp. 17–22.

[304] FSB, (2018), Ibid. p. 18.

[305] As said the SITG amounts typically 20–25% of the CCPs equity, leaving about 75–80% shielded from any claims emerging during a resolution phase.

dation is therefore critical to understand when developing CCP protocols as well as the exact cash flow waterfall and where and how losses are allocated.

In the aforementioned 2017 FSB Guidance on Central Counterparty Resolution and Resolution Planning, the FSB already provided indications how to deal with the situation. In short their 2017 pointers were that:

- Existing owners' equity in the CCP should absorb losses in resolution, to the extent not already written down upon enforcement of the CCP's rules and contractual arrangements.
- In resolution, equity should be fully loss absorbing. It should be clear ex ante how any remaining equity would be written down (e.g. no later than at the point at which pre-funded and committed financial resources such as cash calls in recovery available under the CCP's rules and arrangements would have been exhausted).
- In resolution, equity should absorb non-default losses no later than at the point at which any applicable loss-allocation arrangements available under the CCP's rules and arrangements for non-default losses have been exhausted.
- If both default and non-default losses occur concurrently, the losses attributable to each distinct cause should be allocated separately.
- Alternative approaches to allocating losses to existing equity holders and recapitalizing the CCP, such as writing down the equity and selling new equity in the CCP, may be considered by the relevant authority but taking into account conditions and structures in the relevant case.
- CCP participants, equity holders and creditors should have a right to compensation where they do not receive in resolution at a minimum what they would have received if, instead of resolution, the CCP had been liquidated under the applicable insolvency law the NCWOL criterion). To judge that criterion, an assessment should be made of the losses that would have been incurred or the recoveries that would have been made if the CCP had been subject to liquidation (preferably distinguishing between default and non-default positions).

When developing resolution plans, it should be clear how those guidelines are wired into the rulebook and loss-allocation arrangements. With respect to the CCP equity, the FSB considers possible scenarios[306]:

- Possible mechanisms for adjusting the exposure of CCP equity in bearing losses in resolution. Those mechanisms could include:
  - Exposure of some or all of the equity of the CCP via modification of the contractual loss-allocation arrangements. Given the fact that the SITG is typically structured in one or more tranches that are exposed to losses at different point in the cash flow waterfall (often in parallel with the resources provided by the clearing members). In

[306] FSB, (2018), Financial Resources to Support CCP Resolution and the Treatment of CCP Equity in Resolution, Discussion paper for public consultation, November 15, pp. 21–25.

principle this could mean that more than the SITG can be exposed to losses. The situation can even be such that so much equity is depleted that new equity need to be raised, if not for meeting the minimum capital requirements. This situation can effectively occur in both recovery and resolution arrangements.

- Full or partial write-down of equity and cancelation of existing shares. This is by any standard a material instrument. The instrument can be legally derived from or based on an explicit/statutory power, or may be a power derived from the exercise of another resolution tool. In this scenario the capital will most likely be depleted below the minimum regulatory requirements and capital raising to ensure (under circumstances) continuity is most likely needed.
- Transferring critical CCP operations (assets and certain liabilities) to a bridge entity and placing the remnant CCP into liquidation/receivership. Doing so would further increase the equity of the CCP's shareholders to losses.
- Dilution of existing shares as a result of raising new capital through conversion, issuance or transfer of new shares.[307] Clearing members should be compensated for their contribution of financial resources. This could imply that a certain amount of equity or other ownership instruments including convertibles or conversion rights and claims on future profits could be included and provided to clearing members. Equity for additional cash calls or VMGH can also be included. Converting existing claims on the CCP into equity or providing equity to clearing members for their existing or new contribution avoids the potentially difficult scenario of having to raise additional equity under difficult circumstances and low going concern intrinsic value. However, going down this road is not without implications and possible hurdles. Not all clearing members are able to hold equity (either because regulation or their internal procedures restrict them from doing so). Sometimes it is unclear who ultimately bears the losses as, for example, VMGH can be passed on to clients. The next question then is: when is one fully compensated for bearing (additional) losses? That will ultimately depend on what can be recovered from the defaulter. It is, as an alternative route to compensation for members, that the CCP ex ante should commit to repaying the members for VMG haircuts. It would imply that clearing members would receive VMG haircuts over and above those provided in the original recovery arrangements.

- The point in time or in the waterfall for equity bearing losses. Timing and sequencing the imposition of losses in the cash flow waterfall is key. The way the exposure is constructed (beyond SITG) says something about the implicit incentives of the relevant stakeholders to support the recovery and resolution mechanisms. The different times (individually or combined) that the equity position that the CCP can be exposed to are:

[307] To be complete the FSB (p. 23) indicates the range of options: 'a recapitalisation through the issuance of new shares, rights, options or deliverable warrants, the conversion of debt instruments (if any) or other eligible liabilities into equity (bail-in), or the compensation of clearing participants through the issuance of new shares in exchange for bearing losses in excess of their obligations under the CCP's rules and arrangements.'

- At the entry point of the resolution process: that would mean at the moment that the relevant authorities trigger the resolution process.
- A point following entry into resolution that is determined ad hoc and on a case-by-case basis at the discretion of the resolution authority. Allocation of losses would then be at the discretion of the authorities.
- One or more specific, fixed point(s) in the loss-allocation waterfall (including in parallel to the use of other resources in the waterfall). A write-down of equity can occur at any point for non-default losses and for default losses any time within the loss-allocation arrangement (i.e. at multiple times in case there are multiple tranches). The FSB points at a number of logical points in the cash flow waterfall at which such watering down or equity wipe-out could occur: (1) after the pre-funded resources (i.e. defaulter's initial margin and default fund) but before committed resources are used; (2) at a later specified stage, such as once (a certain number of) cash calls are exhausted or after a specified number of cycles of VMGH; or (3) exposing equity to losses at a fixed point but concurrently with the use of other recovery tools such as cash calls. Potential challenges and constraints to CCP equity bearing losses in resolution.[308] Each of these points in time has their pros and cons and more analysis is required, particularly on issues such as (un)intended incentives, the balance between flexibility, predictability and certainty for all parties involved, safeguarding the NCWOL safeguard and so on.

- Potential challenges and constraints to CCP equity bearing losses in resolution. There are many obstacles that can compromise the initial idea of CCP equity absorbing losses beyond SITG. Some of these challenges and constraints include:
  - For some non-default losses but definitely for all default loss scenarios, comprehensive loss-allocation rules should be foreseen and in place. They, one way or the other, limit the losses borne by the CCP to a certain specific amount. Now given a certain allocation of losses (creditor hierarchy) and the local bankruptcy/insolvency laws, shareholders might have or use a NCWOL claim for any loss incurred and imposed on equity before loss allocation. For most non-default losses, the rulebook doesn't limit the extent to which equity is exposed.
  - Lack of powers to impose losses on equity in resolution. The question here is if and to what extent the relevant authorities have the power to write down debt or convert debt into equity. If such powers exist at the level of the relevant authorities, it should be verified whether these powers exist for bank resolution protocols or whether they are also available for CCP resolution protocols (e.g. because the CCP has a bank license or because the law extended the authority to a variety of resolution regimes.
- Any other relevant policy considerations. If and what changes are needed regarding the specific issue of 'the treatment of equity in loss resolution scenarios' in case of CCPs following miscellaneous benchmarks can be assessed:

[308] FSB, (2018), Ibid. p. 23.

- Impact on CCP management incentives to pursue sound risk management. Despite the framework surrounding CCP resolution, the concern continues to exist that the loss of (all) equity by the CCP could be a (direct) cause of moral hazard issues and a source of incentives to act in a way that maximizes return on equity for shareholders. The aim for high return of equity may be accompanied by sluggish risk management practices or by (implicitly or explicitly) limits on exposure to equity to losses. On the other hand, there are those viewpoints that argue that shareholder-owned CCPs have sufficient reasons to have in place strong risk protocols and that in case of losses (whether default caused positioned or not) it is the clearing members that bring risk to the table (by entering into financial transactions) and not the CCP itself. The question itself is valid but one can only point at the clearing members when they are at full liberty to choose a CCP that can facilitate the risk profile of their (netted) transactions. Given the current market structure, netting arrangements, economies of scale, the mandates of clearing parties, it is not necessarily justified to think that those necessary conditions are fulfilled at all times.
- Impact on clearing member incentives to support recovery and avoid resolution. The mechanisms suggested and implemented should be back-tested to meet whether they incentivize adverse impact on the incentives for stakeholders.
- Impact on clients. Nowhere in the CCP resolution protocol clients have a material say. Nevertheless, under circumstances, loses may fall on clients (of clearing members). It should be verified if incentives align the interests of CCP, clearing members and their clients.
- Impact on continuity of critical clearing services following resolution. When equity write-downs are applied means that ownership of the CCP changes, continuity of a variety of services should be observed.
- Impact on different business models and legal structures of CCPs. There are a number of (systemically important) CCPs that generate revenues (i.e. a CCP may clear products traded on an affiliated exchange and/or benefit from a parental guarantee) just by being part of an integrated financial group. In case such situation occurs, it should be observed that when equity is written down (and recapitalized afterward) and ownership changes, it can impact other groups, companies and activities (trading platforms, central securities depositories and other CCPs).

In 2019, more than half of the world's derivatives were cleared.[309] In most countries banks, pension funds and insurers increasingly have their transactions cleared. Not every country has its own CCP infrastructure however. In Europe a large set of transactions is cleared through LCH, ICE Clear Europe and Eurex.[310] For share transactions EuroCCP

---

[309] During late 2018 the ESMA published its first 'Annual Statistics Report' on the European Union's derivative market, which it estimates late 2017 at 660 trillion Euro. See Esma, (2018), ESMA Annual Statistical Report EU Derivatives Markets 2018, October 18, via esma.europe.eu

[310] See for what has been achieved so far: D. Domanski, (2019), CCP Resilience, Recovery and Resolution: Completing the Journey towards Resilient Derivatives Markets, Deutsche Bundesbank, European Central Bank and the Federal Reserve Bank of Chicago Conference on CCP Risk Management, Frankfurt, February 27, 2019, Speech. The thing that remains on the table to be

might be an option. If something has become clear, it is the fact that CCPs are not risk-free as the counterparty risk not sits with the CCP and its clearing members. In Europe the EMIR[311] therefore has put in place quite some conditions for CCPs and its members also in terms of risk management. The above described IOSCO/FSB resolution and recovery instruments and methodology are to a large extent the same. The resolution authority has however a slightly more discretionary authority with respect to the application and sequence of the instruments it intends to use. That is including the initial margin of the clearing members. The controversial nature of this methodology is clear. The purpose of an initial margin is not put in place to cover unexpected losses at the level of the CCP. It affects healthy clearing members and might even impact the continuation of their operations. Whether that is the case or becomes a problem is highly dependent on the moment the supervising authority intervenes. Technically that is the case when 'the CCP is failing or likely to fail'. Or put differently when a(n) insolvency or bankruptcy can no longer be avoided. The scenario analysis that needs to be prepared for such occasion should then limit the financial and operational damage to a minimum and distort market operations as little as possible. Most regulations put in place with respect to CCPs, their clearing mandate, their funding waterfall in case of exposures, their resolution and recovery schemes are all in all 'work in progress'[312] and are continually fine-tuned.[313]

Europe will also at some point introduce specific recovery and resolution regulation. These will very likely be in line with the IOSCO/FSB recommendations.[314] In the US, the market agents are pondering on their position following the November 2018 report. It is clear what the effective pain points are in this matter[315]: (1) initial margin haircutting and forced allocation raise significant market stability concerns, (2) different views exist as to 'variation margin gains haircutting', with some firms believing that it should be used only

solved: Ensuring adequate financial resources and the treatment of CCP equity in resolution (pp. 4–5). However not a word about understanding concentration risk and how it impacts a CCP and its members.

311 See for an in-depth analysis of the EMIR: J.R. Berndsen, (2017), Financial Markets Infrastructures and Payments-A Warehouse Metaphor Textbook, version 2017–2018, draft 0.6. With a view toward Brexit, some changes have been suggested which are discussed in: C. Chamorro-Courtland, (2019), Brexit Scenarios: The Future of Clearing in Europe, *Columbia Journal of European Law*, Vol. 25, pp. 169 ff.

312 See for a recent EMIR update on the CCP matter. The suggested adjustments include exemption for pension funds, small financial intermediaries and enhanced reporting requirements by the CCP. Council of the EU, (2019), Capital Markets Union: Deal on Updated Rules for Financial Derivative Products and Clearing, Press release, February 5, via consilium.europe.eu

313 See for a write-up of the balancing act between confidence in central clearing as a model and the remaining and material concern of creating new systemically relevant nodes in the financial system: Sir J. Cunliffe, (2018), Learning some of the Lessons of Lehmans, speech given at the FIA International Derivatives Expo 2018, London, June 5, via bis.org

314 See for an overview: M. Broos et al., (2018), De CCP als spil in het financieel ysteem, DNB Working Paper, September, Amsterdam.

315 See for the 2019 report 'Recovery and Resolution: Incentives Analysis' issued by the FIA/ISDA and IFF (via isada.org), containing an interesting comparative sheet (pp. 3–14), March. For the write-up of arguments and comment: N.S. Patel, (2019), Trade Groups Respond to FSB on CCP Resolution, April 2, via Mondaq.com

on a limited basis by resolution authorities, and others believing that a CCP should have more flexibility to use the tool in recovery; (3) resolution cash calls are not seen as a suitable CCP recapitalization tool and it is questioned how well aligned interests are when using such a technique; (4) different views also exist as to the 'skin-in-the-game' tranche of CCP funds in a waterfall; also here the alignment issue emerged; (5) not surprisingly strong support exists for compensating clearing members who bear losses beyond their default fund contributions and (capped) assessments, and (6) the appropriateness of a 'no-creditor-worse-off-than-in-liquidation' safeguard for equity holders was questioned. In particular the question was raised that 'it is not at all clear why equity holders should be entitled to anything more than the residual value of a remnant CCP, after payment of creditor claims.' It is clear that many participants of the CCP industry are holding deviant views as to what treatment should be designed for CCP recovery and resolution arrangements given their operations and risks embedded. May I remind in this context the above discussed IMF Paper of Singh and Turing (2018) where they articulate that 'to avoid the costs of resolution being borne by taxpayers, and propose alternative policy suggestions for addressing the problem of a failed CCP…the combination of mandatory clearing and concentration of counterparty risk[316] into a central infrastructure increases the risk of failure of the infrastructure itself. This issue arises for the largest CCPs, which clear OTC derivative products in accordance with the new mandates.' The distinction between recovery and resolution given the instruments available is too small.[317] It is clear that the dust surrounding the understanding of what a meaningful and effective recovery and resolution model encompasses will not settle somewhere very soon, given the fierce opposition of both the CCP and banking community.[318]

A matter that in both Europe and the US has been largely ignored up till this point is the CCP-bank nexus. We have discussed and will discuss the important bank-shadow bank nexus in all its intricacies and for very good reasons. Likewise, when discussing the CCP recovery and resolution regime to be designed, it was often tabled to treat a CCP like a bank and submit them to the same rigid conditions. That would include the capital requirements as they exist under Basel III. Treating them the same however makes no sense from a technical point of view in the sense that a 'CCP doesn't actively seek to take on risk but to independently assess and manage the risks that the banks bring to the system'.[319] Although it took a while, we do now know the capital requirements for banks' exposure to

[316] For example, the Euro-denominated interest derivatives are for 90% cleared by one London-based CCP. See for details: CPB, (2019), Risicorapportage Financiële Markten 2019, The Hague The Netherlands, pp. 25 ff. See in a wider context the Too-Big-To-Fail aspect in CCP markets: L. Országhová, (2018), Central Counterparties: Addressing the Too-Big-To-Fail Problem in Central Clearing, ročník 26, Nr. 4/2018, pp. 22–26.

[317] Also: CEPS Task Force, (2016), How to Deal with the Resolution of Financial Market Infrastructures, Second Interim Report, Implementing financial sector resolution, October, via ceps.eu.

[318] A similar trend is to be observed on the banking side: R. Tunstead, (2019), Banks Bite Back over Resolution Frameworks, April 10, via bobsguide.com

[319] R. Tunstead, (2019), Treating CCPs like Banks is 'not logical and not appropriate', March 4, via bobsguide.com and everybody is dragging their feet on the matter: T. Tunstaed, (2019), Critical CCP Resolution Plans Not Being Prioritized, April 5, via bobsguide.com

central counterparties.[320]At least, that is what we thought as updates are expected that will become effective January 1, 2022.[321] But the bank-CCP nexus as such has always been under highlighted in the sense that either the banks' risk and exposures or alternatively the CCP's risks and exposures were considered. Although justified they paint an accurate but not complete picture.[322]

As Faruqui et al.[323] indicate, one must blend in the 'endogenous interactions between banks and CCPs in periods of stress. As these interactions could potentially lead to destabilizing feedback loops, the risks of banks and CCPs should be considered jointly, rather than in isolation.' They start their analysis by demonstrating that both the universe of CCP parties is small and concentrated both in Europe and the US. On the other hand, SIFIs tend to comprise the main clearing members, and they as a segment are also concentrated. So behavior of banks and CCPs must be closely intertwined. The bank-CCP nexus facilitates the same exposures as in other relations the CCP engages into being market risk, liquidity and counterparty credit risk. When a CCP and a bank engage in a simple clearing transaction (of e.g. a CDS contract), that transaction appears on the CCP's balance sheet as a liability and as an asset on the banks' balance sheet. The transaction in itself has no value yet, but still it leaves markers, that is, the initial margin required by the CCP is a liability for the CCP and an asset for the banks who posted it. CCPs hold liquid assets, banks traditionally less liquid assets. Now going into the transaction, CCPs

[320] BCBS, (2012), Capital Requirements for Bank Exposure to Central Counterparties, July, via bis.org. After a consultation it was replaced by BCBS, (2014), Capital Requirements for bank Exposure to Central Counterparties, April. What was new in that edition was (1) a single approach for calculating capital requirements for a bank's exposure that arises from its contributions to the mutualized default fund of a qualifying CCP (QCCP); (2) employing the Standardized Approach for counterparty credit risk (as opposed to the Current Exposure Method) to measure the hypothetical capital requirement of a CCP; (3) including an explicit cap on the capital charges applicable to a bank's exposures to a QCCP; and (4) specifying how to treat multi-level client structures whereby an institution clears its trades through intermediaries linked to a CCP. Together with the BCBS, (2019), Capital Requirements for Bank Exposures to Central Counterparties, CRE54 (Calculation of RWA for credit risk), effective January 1, 2019, and in March 2014 released BCBS report '[t]he standardised approach for measuring counterparty credit risk exposures' (Nr. 279), it provides comprehensive guidelines for exposures to CCPs.

[321] See bis.org for detail and future updates.

[322] The European position however provides for an interesting counterargument. Lamandini argues that out of the 16 EU-based CCPs, 10 are located in the euro area. Three—and among them LCH—are based in the UK and are therefore bound to become third-country CCPs. Of the remaining three, one is Swedish and is the European leg of Nasdaq OMX clearing. The latter two are Tier 1 CCPs based in Poland and Hungary. Among the ten CCPs located within the euro area, some are licensed as banks and already fall, therefore, within the scope of the BRRD and the Single Resolution Mechanism Regulation (SRMR). Wouldn't it make sense to bring the ten CCPs in the euro system under the umbrella of the SRB as a resolution authority and extend to them, as a last resort, the use of the temporary public sector funding mechanism of the Single Resolution Fund (SRF) and its forthcoming final fiscal backstop, the European Monetary Fund? See in detail: M. Lamandini, (2018), Recovery and Resolution of CCPs: Obsessing over Regulatory Symmetry?, ECMI Commentaries, August 9, via eurocapitalmarkets.org (also as CEPs Commentary Nr. 56).

[323] U. Faraqui et al., (2018), Clearing Risks in OTC Derivative Markets: the CCP-Bank Nexus, BIS Quarterly Review, December 2018, pp. 73–90.

manage counterparty credit risk through the different layers of the default waterfall. They set the initial margins taking into account (i) the likelihood of large fluctuations in the price of the underlying asset, (ii) the expected time needed to close the position at fair price and (iii) the desired confidence level for the loss at default.[324]Also the size of the mutualized default fund is set to cover defaults of even the largest members.

Banks on the other hand take into account CCPs' rules in their risk-taking behavior. The impact works both ways and influences each other. The risk taking by the banks determines the level of initial margin and default fund size required. Contributing to the CCP's default fund is a cost to banks and the size of the initial margin affects the cost of derivative trading and thus affect risk taking by banks. To make things worse, the way that a typical default waterfall structure is designed complicates matters even more as the size of the losses determines which layer(s) is called upon.[325] So the heftier and the intensity of the level of market stress, the deeper the default waterfall structure is impacted and thus the interaction between CCPs and banks become. When there are moderate levels of stress, the initial margin is at stake; when there are medium levels of stress, the committed default fund contribution and possible the funding available by the CCP are called upon. Material stress puts the scenario out that the CCP would call upon unfunded resources at the level of the members. In each of these scenarios, there will be a feedback loop that run through the bank-CCP nexus:

- Low stress level: all good, no issues expected.
- Medium stress level: the CCP consumes the initial margin deposited and requires replenishment by members. Banks have to liquidate (illiquid) assets that could turn into a fire sale if performed across the marketplace. That fire sale could spill over in the derivatives market. The feedback loop will exacerbate the initial stress in particular when assets are sold that were stressed to begin with.

---

[324] U. Faraqui et al., (2018), Ibid. p. 82.

[325] As a gentle reminder of what already has been discussed in terms of the design of default waterfalls for CCPs a quick overview. They tend to be structured as such that in case of counterparty risk materializes and creates permanent losses, the CCP will draw upon funding in the following order: (1) the CCP will draw on the initial margin of the defaulting member(s); (2) in case not sufficient, the CCP will draw upon the default fund contribution of the defaulting member(s); (3) after that, the equity or funding that the CCP has available (the skin-in-the-game) is called upon; (4) then the default fund contributions of the non-defaulting member(s) is called upon and (5) the committed resources by non-defaulting member(s) is being depleted and so the CCP calls on unfunded commitments. They tend to consist of cash calls or VMGH (variation margin gains haircutting whereby the CCP would impose a haircut on cumulative variation margin gains which have accumulated since the day of the member's default). The whole waterfall model isn't without complexities and debate. See, for example, the ISDA, (2013), CCP Loss Allocation at the End of the Waterfall, August, via isda.org; D. Turing and M. Singh, (2018), The Morning after-The Impact of Collateral Supply after a Major Default, IMF Working Paper Nr. WP/18/228, October; R.S. Raykov, (2016), To Share or Not to Share? Uncovering Losses in a Derivatives Clearinghouse, Bank of Canada Staff Working Paper Nr. 2016-4, February. Also the PhD research on the matter: W.-S. A. Cheng, (2017), Clearinghouse Default Resources, Columbia University, via Columbia.edu

- High stress level: One or more members cannot meet the variation margin call due to the stress levels and CCP forbear margin collections. In case the member defaults, the default funds will be called upon, if not the CCP cannot use the default fund's resources. By postponing collection variation margin, the CCP can lose its own equity, reputation and, in case the struggling member doesn't revive, it can destabilize the system. The forbearance by the CCP and the gamble for the struggling bank to revive/resurrect. In case sitting on the wrong side of the fence, steeper losses are ahead as the bank will take larger and riskier positions to survive.
- Extreme stress levels: one or more members' default and losses consume initial margins and the default fund. Remaining members will be called upon to cover remaining losses through cash calls (money they need to secure their own stability in treacherous times or they have to engage in fire sales to meet those calls). The other alternative is to engage in VMGH whereby the CCP would draw upon the VM gains of the non-defaulted clearing members in order to cover losses. It implies that other contracts engaged in by banks are no longer hedged. Non-defaulted banks will end up under stress, which feeds through to the CCP given the concentration of the market on both ends of the relation.[326] Worst case, the CCP will be put in resolution watch. The bank-CCP nexus and the balance sheet interlinkages it creates combined with the way the default waterfall dynamics are structured might and can lead to adverse feedback loops and ultimately systemic risks and system-wide effects. Given the adverse feedback loop under stress, the joint assessment of bank and CCP risks is recommended when assessing counterparty risk.[327]

Member default or CCP default should therefore be avoided at all times. Bignon[328] shed some light on what aspects trigger an enhanced risk of default at the level of a CCP: (1) a weak pool of investors, (2) the inability to contain the growth of a large member position and (3) risk-shifting decisions by the clearinghouse (distortions ex ante, price manipulations or failed private negotiations). Although it was initially understood that central clearing is beneficial for single market participants in the presence of a sufficiently large number of clearing members. Kubitza et al.[329] however show that three elements can render central clearing harmful for a market participant's counterparty risk exposure

[326] See, for example, L. Woodall, (2018), Concentration of Client Positions Rise at LCH, Technical Report, mimeo.

[327] See also on this topic: I. Aldoraso and T. Ehlers, (2018), The Credit Default Swap Market: What a Difference a Decade Makes, BIS Quarterly Review, June, pp. 1–14; J. Cunliffe, (2018): Central Clearing and Resolution – Learning some of the Lessons of Lehman, speech at the FIA International Derivatives Expo 2018, London, via bis.org; H. Holden, et al. (2016): I Want Security: Stylized Facts about Central Counterparty Collateral and its Systemic Context, *Journal of Financial Market Infrastructures*, Vol. 5, Nr. 2, December, pp. 53–75; V. Bignon, and G. Vuillemey, (2020), The Failure of a Clearinghouse: Empirical Evidence, Review of Finance, Vol. 24, Issue 1, pp. 99–128.

[328] V. Bignon, (2017), The Failure of a Clearinghouse: Empirical Evidence, ECMI Working Paper Nr. 6, December 5, via ceps.eu. (also as Banque de France Working Paper Nr. 638, August).

[329] C. Kubitza et al., (2018), The Pitfalls of Central Clearing in the Presence of Systemic Risk, ICIR Working Paper Series Nr. 31/2018, November.

regardless of the number of its counterparties: (1) correlation across and within derivative classes (i.e. systematic risk), (2) collateralization of derivative claims and (3) loss sharing among clearing members.[330]

The BIS has issued recently a position and consultation paper[331] regarding CCP default management auctions. The central part of the discussion contrasts different scenarios of a successful default management protocol and auction and highlights the operational features of each of the options. Since the crisis of 2008, banks have reduced their funding through the bilateral interbank segment and increased their recourse to central counterparties (CCPs). CCPs are third parties that stand between two banks to mitigate credit risk. The results show that both the greater uncertainty on the state of the international economy and the intensified attention to counterparty risk were decisive factors in the growing use of CCPs. The use of CCPs is linked to the loss of long-standing bilateral relationships only for the riskiest banks. These findings support the ongoing effort by national and international regulators to ensure that CCPs continue to have adequate risk control frameworks.[332]

---

[330] See also: V. Acharya and A. Bisin, (2014), Counterparty Risk Externality: Centralized versus over-the-counter Markets, *Journal of Economic Theory*, Vol. 149, pp. 153–182; V. Acharya et al., (2017), Measuring Systemic Risk, Review of Financial Studies, Vol. 30, Issue 1, pp. 2–47; R. Armakolla and J.-P. Laurent, (2017), CCP Resilience and Clearing Membership, Working Paper, May; B. Biais et al., (2016), Risk-Sharing or Risk-Taking? Counterparty Risk, Incentives and Margins, Journal of Finance, Vol. 71, Issue 4, pp. 1669–1698; W. Du et al., (2016), Counterparty Risk and Counterparty Choice in the Credit Default Swap Market, Federal Reserve Board Working Paper Nr. 87; M. Getmansky et al., (2016), Interconnectedness in the CDS Market. *Financial Analysts Journal*, Vol. 72, pp. 62–82; S. Ghamami, and P. Glasserman, (2017), Does OTC Derivatives Reform Incentivize Central Clearing? *Journal of Financial Intermediation*, Vol. 32, pp. 76–87; W. Huang, and A.J. Menkveld, (2016), Systemic Risk in Real Time: A Risk Dashboard for Central Clearing Parties (CCPs), Working Paper, mimeo; A. J. Menkveld, (2017), Crowded Positions: An Overlooked Systemic Risk for Central Clearing Parties, Review of Asset Pricing Studies, Vol. 7, Issue 2, pp. 209–242; O. Arce et al., (2019), The Credit Default Swaps Market: Areas of Vulnerability and Regulatory Responses, CNMV Working Paper Nr. 42, June 19. The latter engage also in a comparative (EU/US) analysis of regulatory changes in recent years to the CDS clearing market.

[331] CPMI/BIS, (2019), A Discussion Paper on Central Counterparty Default Management Auctions, June, via bis.org. See previously: G. Ferrara et al., (2017), Central Counterparty Auction Design, Bank of England Staff Working Paper Nr. 669, August 11.

[332] M. Affinito and M. Piazza, (2018), Always Look on the Bright Side? Central Counterparties and Interbank Markets During the Financial Crisis, Bank of Italy Working Paper Nr. 1181, July 20.

6

Identifying Non-bank, Non-insurer Global Systemically Important Financial Institutions

6.1 Introduction

In the wake of the financial crisis, the international community was eager to put in place guidelines or legislation with respect to those institutions that could become relevant from a systemic risk perspective for the financial industry. Systemically important financial institutions (SIFIs) are institutions whose distress or disorderly failure, because of their size, complexity and systemic interconnectedness, would cause significant disruption to the wider financial system and economic activity. At the Seoul Summit in 2010, the G20 Leaders endorsed the Financial Stability Board (FSB) framework for reducing the systemic and moral hazard risks posed by SIFIs.[1]

The implementation of the SIFI framework requires, as a first step, the assessment of the systemic importance of financial institutions at a global level (or G-SIFIs). The framework recognizes that SIFIs vary in their structures and activities and that systemic importance and impact upon distress or failure can vary significantly across sectors. It requires that the FSB and national authorities, in consultation with the standard-setting bodies, and drawing on relevant indicators, determine which institutions will be designated as G-SIFIs. The assessment methodologies to identify G-SIFIs need to reflect the nature and degree of risks they pose to the global financial system.

[1] For details on the SIFI framework, see FSB, (2010), Reducing the Moral Hazard Posed by Systemically Important Financial Institutions, FSB Recommendations and Time Lines, Basel, October 20 and FSB, (2013), Progress and Next Steps Towards Ending "Too-Big-To-Fail" (TBTF), Report of the Financial Stability Board to the G-20, Basel, September 2.

L. Nijs, *The Handbook of Global Shadow Banking, Volume I*,
https://doi.org/10.1007/978-3-030-34743-7_6

So far, assessment methodologies have been developed for global systemically important banks (G-SIBs)[2] and insurers (G-SIIs).[3]

In January 2014, a consultation document was issued with respect to the proposed assessment methodologies for identifying NBNI G-SIFIs, extending the SIFI framework that currently covers banks and insurers to all other financial institutions. NBNI G-SIFIs in this document also exclude financial market infrastructures (FMIs). Under the CPSS-IOSCO Principles for Financial Market Infrastructures,[4] there is a presumption that all FMIs, as defined in the principles, are systemically important or critical, at least in the jurisdiction where they are located.

This is a challenging task as the high-level framework and specific methodologies have to capture a wide range of business models and risk profiles, while maintaining broad consistency with the methodologies for banks and insurers. Also, and as highlighted throughout the book, unlike banks and insurers, the NBNI financial entities generally face limitations in the data availability.

In developing the methodologies, the FSB based its work on the following principles: (i) the overarching objective in developing the methodologies is to identify NBNI financial entities whose distress or disorderly failure, because of their size, complexity and systemic interconnectedness, would cause significant disruption to the global financial system and economic activity across jurisdictions. (ii) The general framework for the methodologies should be broadly consistent with methodologies for identifying G-SIBs and G-SIIs, that is, an indicator-based measurement approach where multiple indicators are selected to reflect the different aspects of what generates negative externalities and

---

[2] The first findings are also reported that document a first analysis of the experience to date with the global systemically important bank (G-SIB) framework, the methodology for assessing the systemic importance of G-SIBs. Several issues are examined. First, it is investigated whether G-SIBs and non-G-SIBs have behaved differently since the implementation of the G-SIB framework and if observed differences in behavior are in accordance with the framework's aims. Next, the question is asked whether there are regional differences in the behavior of G-SIBs and non-G-SIBs. The analysis reveals that G-SIBs and non-G-SIBs behave differently; however, both groups are heterogeneous, so that the indicator outcomes are often highly influenced by a few banks. Nevertheless, most G-SIBs have reduced their G-SIB scores during the period assessed, changing their balance sheets in ways that are consistent with the G-SIB framework's aims. In contrast, non-G-SIBs have increased their relative G-SIB scores during the same period. Finally, the regional analysis indicates that trends in banks' G-SIB indicators, and the indicators that contribute most to the final G-SIB score, are heterogeneous across countries and regions. While G-SIBs from the euro area, Great Britain (GB) and the United States (US) have reduced their systemic importance for most indicators, Chinese and Japanese G-SIBs have shown relatively positive growth rates for all indicators, and particularly high ones for indicators in the substitutability category. See in detail: BCBS, (2019), An Examination of Initial Experience with the Global Systemically Important Bank Framework, BCBS Working Paper Nr. 34, February, via bis.org

[3] See BIS, (2013), Global Systemically Important Banks: Updated Assessment Methodology and the Higher Loss Absorbency Requirement, Basel and FSB, (2015), Assessment Methodologies for Identifying Non-Bank Non-Insurer Global Systemically Important Financial Institutions, Proposed High-Level Framework and Specific Methodologies Basel, March 4 (Second consultative Document); FSB, (2015), Thematic Review on Supervisory Frameworks and Approaches for SIBs, Peer Review Report, Basel, May 26.

[4] BIS, (2012), Principles for Financial Market Infrastructures, Basel, April 2012.

makes the distress or disorderly failure of a financial entity critical for the stability of the financial system (i.e. 'impact factors' such as size, interconnectedness and complexity).[5]

Before coming up with a framework or technical criteria for identifying NBNI SIFI, the prime question to be answered is how the financial distress or disorderly failure of an NBNI financial entity could be transmitted to other financial entities and markets, and thereby pose a threat to global financial stability.

In considering how financial distress or disorderly failure of an NBNI financial entity could be transmitted to other financial firms and markets and potentially impact global financial stability, it is important to note that these entities have very diverse business models and risk profiles that in many respects are quite different from banks and insurers. This diversity in the business models and risk profiles, combined with the limitations in obtaining appropriate data/information for assessing systemic risks of NBNI financial entities in a global context, makes it difficult to derive a comprehensive view that would capture every foreseeable transmission mechanism for any given NBNI financial entity.[6]

There are three channels identified by the FSB whereby financial distress of an NBNI financial entity is most likely to be transmitted to other financial firms and markets, and thereby pose a threat to global financial stability. These three channels are[7]:

1. the exposures of creditors, counterparties, investors and other market participants to the NBNI financial entity (exposures/counterparty channel). The failure of an NBNI financial entity would affect its creditors, counterparties, investors or other market participants through their exposures to the failing entity. As a result of the failing entity, effects may materialize in a cascading manner, leading to broader financial system instability if their exposures and linkages are significant.
2. the liquidation of assets by the NBNI financial entity, which could trigger a decrease in asset prices and thereby could significantly disrupt trading or funding in key financial markets or cause significant losses or funding problems for other firms with similar holdings (asset liquidation/market channel). This channel describes the indirect impact a failure of an NBNI financial entity could have on other market participants. If an entity has to liquidate its assets quickly, this may impact asset prices and thereby significantly disrupt trading or funding in key markets, potentially provoking losses for other firms with similar holdings. The potential for forced liquidations and market distortions may be amplified by the use of leverage by financial entities.
3. the inability or unwillingness of the NBNI financial entity to provide a critical function or service relied upon by market participants or clients (e.g. borrowers) and for

[5] FSB, (2014), Assessment Methodologies for Identifying Non-Bank Non-Insurer Global Systemically Important Financial Institutions Proposed High-Level Framework and Specific Methodologies, Consultative document, p. 2. They are regularly updated and revised; see lately: BCBS, (2018), Global systemically important banks: revised assessment methodology and the higher loss absorbency requirement, July, via bis.org. Some of these reviews are only implemented in the period 2019–2022 and not enacted yet. They were therefore not included in the review yet.

[6] FSB, (2014), Ibid. p. 3.

[7] FSB, (2014), Ibid. p. 3.

which there are no ready substitutes (critical function or service/substitutability).[8] This channel describes the situation whereby an NBNI financial entity is no longer able or willing to provide a critical function or service that is relied upon by market participants or clients and for which there are no ready substitutes.

6.2 Factors for the Identification of NBNI Financial Entities

The FSB highlights that the NBNI financial entity framework is more complicated and delicate than the work done before. Indeed, in contrast to the methodologies for G-SIBs and G-SIIs, methodologies for identifying NBNI G-SIFIs have to be applicable to a wide range of NBNI financial entities that often have very different legal forms, business models and risk profiles. In reality that implies taking into account different types of risks and different type of externalities while at the same time maintaining a certain level of consistency within the required flexibility. The FSB has attempted to overcome this challenge by establishing detailed indicators by each type/sector as well as introducing a basic set of impact factors to be applied to all NBNI financial entities in general.

The basic set of impact factors include[9]:

- Size: The importance of a single entity for the stability of the financial system generally increases with the scale of financial activity that the entity undertakes.
- Interconnectedness: Systemic risk can arise through direct and indirect interlinkages between entities within the financial system so that individual failure or distress can have repercussions throughout the financial system.
- Substitutability: The systemic importance of a single financial entity increases in cases where it is difficult for other entities in the system to provide the same or similar services in a particular business line or segment in the global market in the event of a failure.
- Complexity: The systemic impact of a financial entity's distress or failure is expected to be positively related to its overall complexity, that is, its business, structural and operational complexity. That is, in principle, the more complex a financial entity, the more difficult, costly and time-consuming it will be to resolve the failing institution.
- Global activities (cross-jurisdictional activities): The global impact from a financial entity's distress or failure should vary in line with its share of cross-border assets and liabilities. The greater the global reach of a financial entity, the more widespread the spillover effects from its failure.

These impact factors are broadly consistent with the impact factors used to identify G-SIBs and G-SIIs. The basic factors will be complemented with criteria that are sector

[8] FSB, (2014), Ibid. p. 3.

[9] FSB, (2014), Ibid. p. 5.

or entity-specific. In that respect, and as already indicated, one of the issues at this stage is the data availability and consistency. Part of that has to do with the fact that NBNI financial entities are primarily and traditionally regulated from a conduct of business (or investor/consumer protection) perspective. While many regulators are increasingly collecting data to facilitate assessments of financial stability risks, data availability varies widely and is likely not to be consistent across jurisdictions.[10] As always in case of data inconsistency or availability, a deeper and more profound of 'supervisory judgment' will be required. Although the collection and ranking of findings will be done by the national authorities, international oversight will be needed to ensure consistent application and to avoid arbitrage across jurisdictions as well as sectors.

The FSB has been developing detailed sector-specific indicators for (i) finance companies, (ii) market intermediaries (securities broker-dealers) and (iii) investment funds (collective investment schemes (CIS) and hedge funds). These are (i) funds, (ii) family of funds, (iii) asset managers on a stand-alone entity basis and (iv) asset managers and their funds collectively. These categories were chosen for their size[11] and relevance.[12] These should be seen as a first step in the further development of a refined and alternative (or more) categories in this space.

In order to be relevant from a systemic criteria point of view, 100 billion USD in balance sheet total assets has been determined. That except for the third category, that is, where the materiality criteria is set at either 100 billion USD in assets under management (AUM) or for hedge funds have a threshold of either the 100 billion USD in AUM or 400–600 billion USD in GNE ('gross national exposure').[13] In addition to 'size', the FSB considered the possibility of setting additional materiality thresholds based on 'global activities' (i.e. cross-jurisdictional activities). This definition is then further refined in the FSB 2015 reports (infra).

6.3 Finance Companies

'Finance companies' are NBNI financial entities that provide finance to individuals and businesses. They mainly fund themselves using wholesale funding sources, including loans from banks, securitization and commercial paper (CP). According to the FSB, finance companies include[14]:

---

[10] FSB, (2014), Ibid. p. 6.

[11] According to the FSB Global Shadow Banking Monitoring Report 2013, (i) finance companies, (ii) market intermediaries (broker-dealers) and (iii) investment funds comprise 70–80% of the total financial assets of all NBNI financial entities (as proxied by other financial Intermediaries) in 25 jurisdictions at the end of 2012. For details, see http://www.financialstabilityboard.org/publications/r_131114.pdf. FSB, (2014), p. 7 footnote 9.

[12] And given historical examples of financial distress or failures in these three sectors that had an impact on the global financial system.

[13] GNE is calculated as the absolute sum of all long and short positions, considering the notional value (delta-adjusted when applicable) for derivatives.

[14] FSB, (2014), Ibid. p. 14.

- Subsidiaries or affiliates of banks—These finance companies are often structured as a separate legal entity of a bank and do not usually take retail deposits.
- Captives owned by manufacturers or distributors that finance sales of their parents' products only—For example, finance companies owned by large car producers to finance sales of their cars.
- Specialist providers, who tend to finance only one particular type of asset—For example, train and aircraft leasing companies or invoice finance providers.
- Independents and captives operating in multiple financing markets—Large finance companies that operate across multiple and diverse finance products and often across multiple jurisdictions as well.

The types of financing provided can be split into four categories:

1. Consumer: Personal loans, credit cards, store credit, mail order and so on
2. Mortgages
3. Motor vehicle: car loans, car leasing
4. Business finance: equipment leasing, factoring

One of the issues with finance companies is that there is quite some variation in the way these organizations are regulated. Some countries treat and regulate them as if they were banks whereas others regulate them from a business perspective which includes the way they fund themselves and the types of financing they provide and to whom. The consequence is that finance companies owned by a bank are treated different than those that are operating on a stand-alone basis.

Besides, the typical funding of a finance company, as mentioned above, in case it is a subsidiary of a bank or industrial corporate, it may also receive funding or benefit from explicit or implicit guarantees from the parent. Finance companies' reliance on wholesale funding could make them susceptible to funding problems in times of market stress, particularly if they are highly leveraged or if their funding is relatively short-dated compared to the maturity of their assets. Further, the failure or severe distress of a large finance company could potentially lead to losses for providers of funding, and even lead to severe disruptions in key wholesale funding markets where finance companies are active (e.g. the securitization and CP markets).[15]

Their systemic importance can occur due to their significance in providing certain types of finance and the potential difficulty of substituting certain types of finance to the real economy that they provide. They may also present risk to the financial system due to their interconnections with other financial institutions and their issuance in key funding markets.

The FSB provides the following indicators related to each of the basic factors highlighted before (Table 6.1):

[15] FSB, (2014), Ibid. p. 15.

Table 6.1 Indicators for the identification of non-bank non-insurance (NBNI) systemically important financial institutions (SIFIs)

Basic factor	Indicator
Size	Total globally consolidated balance sheet assets (including derivatives) Total globally consolidated off-balance sheet exposure
Interconnectedness	1. Intra-financial system assets[a] 2. Intra-financial system liabilities[a] 3. Borrowing split by type (CP, sub-debt, securitization, bank loans, others) 4. Leverage ratio: total shareholder equity divided by the sum of on-balance sheet assets and off-balance sheet exposures
Substitutability	Qualitative assessment of 'substitutability', which takes into account the firm's market share in various financing markets and ease of substitutability by other provider(s) of funding
Complexity	1. Notional amount of over-the-counter (OTC) derivatives. This indicator should capture notional values of all types of non-cleared derivatives (i.e. sum of foreign exchange, interest rate, equity, commodities, credit derivatives) 2. Difficulty in resolving the firm: (i) operational and legal complexity of firm's structure and operations; (ii) degree of internal interconnectedness; (iii) membership of financial market infrastructures (FMIs); and (iv) quality of management information systems (MIS)[b]
Cross-jurisdictional activities	1. Size of cross-jurisdictional claims. Claims include assets such as loans and holdings of securities 2. Size of cross-jurisdictional liabilities 3. Number of jurisdictions in which the finance company 'conducts operations' 4. Assets or revenues in foreign jurisdictions

[a]Consistent with the approach taken in the methodology for identifying global systemically important banks (G-SIBs) by the Basel Committee on Banking Supervision (BCBS), this indicator is calculated on the G-SIBs criteria; for a full list, see FSB, (2014), Ibid. p. 17
[b]Those endogenous firm-specific factors are to be found in FSB, (2011), Key Attributes of Effective Resolution Regimes for Financial Institutions

6.4 Market Intermediaries and Broker-Dealers

'Market intermediaries' generally include NBNI financial entities that are in the business of managing individual portfolios, executing orders and dealing in, or distributing, securities. They may also include NBNI financial entities that engage in any of the following activities:

- Receiving and transmitting orders
- Proprietary trading/dealing on own account
- Providing advice regarding the value of securities or the advisability of investing in, purchasing or selling securities

- Securities underwriting
- Providing funding to clients (e.g. margin loans, reverse repos)
- Placing of financial instruments without a firm commitment basis[16]

Regulation of market intermediaries is generally directed at identifying and mitigating risks to capital, client assets and public confidence. In particular, the insolvency of an intermediary may result in loss of client money, securities or trading opportunities and may reduce confidence in the market in which the intermediary participates. The impact of the financial distress of a market intermediary may also flow through market channels. Market intermediaries are often significant lenders or borrowers in the financial system, and in times of stress, there is a potential for increased margin calls and/or fire sales in the broader market (Table 6.2).[17]

6.5 Investment Funds

This sector-specific category is designed to cover 'collective investment schemes (CIS)', including authorized/registered open-end schemes that redeem their units or shares (whether on a continuous or periodic basis), as well as closed-end ones.[18] The FSB exemplifies: '[t]he methodology would therefore cover disparate fund categories, from common mutual funds (including sub-categories thereof such as money market funds [MMFs] and exchange-traded funds [ETFs]) to private funds (including hedge funds, private equity funds and venture capital). Further, while separately managed accounts (SMAs) are not CIS, these accounts represent a large segment of the asset management industry.'[19] The managed account category will continue to be the focal point of attention and research regarding the optimal way of inclusion and data collection.[20] For the purposes of this category, the demarcation lines for investment funds include both open-end and closed-end funds, regardless of whether their units are traded on regulated or organized markets, and this despite the fact that legal forms and structures might vary significantly across jurisdictions. For those CIS that should be considered as hedge funds, national authorities should clarify which type of NBNI financial entities will fall under the definition of hedge funds for the purpose of identifying NBNI G-SIFIs. IOSCO, in an earlier report,[21] indicated that '[t]he following are the characteristics that in combination may indicate the presence of a hedge fund: (a) use of leverage; (b) performance fees based on unrealized gains; (c) complex strategies, which may include use of derivatives, short selling, high frequency trading and/or the search for absolute returns; and (d) tendency to invest in financial rather than physical assets'.[22]

[16] FSB, (2014), Ibid. p. 21.

[17] FSB, (2014), Ibid. pp. 21–22.

[18] FSB, (2014), Ibid. p. 28.

[19] FSB, (2014), Ibid. p. 28.

[20] One of the problems is the ability to disclose information regarding SMAs, as highlighted in the US Office of Financial Research report on Asset Management and Financial Stability, published in September 2013.

[21] IOSCO (2009) Hedge Funds Oversight.

[22] FSB, (2014), Ibid. p. 28, footnote 35.

Table 6.2 SIFI indicators for broker-dealers

Basic factor	Indicator
Size	1. Total globally consolidated balance sheet assets
	2. Total globally consolidated off-balance sheet exposures
	1. Client assets outstanding: client assets in segregated accounts or pledged by the entity or total client assets under management
Interconnectedness	1. Intra-financial system assets[a]
	2. Intra-financial liabilities[a]
	3. Leverage ratio: total shareholder equity divided by the sum of on-balance sheet assets and off-balance sheet exposures
	4. Short-term debt ratio (<1 year).[b] The short-term debt ratio should be calculated as the ratio of debt with a maturity of less than one year to total consolidated asset. An entity with a short-term debt ratio of 10% or more would indicate that the entity is highly reliant on other financial institutions for its operations and faces liquidity risk
	1. OTC derivatives assets and liabilities[c]
	2. Amount of margin required at clearing houses or central counterparties (if positions are held longer than intra-day, clearing houses or central counterparties [CCPs] will require margin)
Substitutability	1. Qualitative assessment of reliance of the market on the services of the intermediary
	2. Market share, measured by (i) trading as a percentage of daily market volume on domestic exchanges, and (ii) if available, global market transaction volume in securities (including equities, bonds and futures)
Complexity	1. Structural complexity, measured by number of legal entities that are consolidated
	2. Operational complexity, measured by level 3 assets (generally illiquid and complex to evaluate assets)
Cross-jurisdictional activities	1. Number of jurisdictions in which the market intermediary and/or its affiliates 'conduct operations'
	2. Cross-jurisdictional claims and liabilities

[a]Consistent with the approach taken in the methodology for identifying global systemically important banks (G-SIBs) by the BCBS, this indicator is calculated on the G-SIBs criteria; for a full list, see FSB, (2014), p. 24

[b]In analyzing the sources of funding, national authorities should also consider (i) the concentration of counterparties that provide short-term funding to the intermediary and (ii) reliance on funding sources that are from G-SIBs or G-SIIs. FSB, (2014), p. 25

[c]Those should include (1) counterparty concentration, especially concentration with other G-SIBs or G-SIIs, (2) the fair market value of derivative contracts in a negative position ('negative mark to market'), (3) net notional versus gross notional derivative positions (a significant variance would suggest that the intermediary is taking principal risk with its capital) and (4) collateral posted

This category is a bit obscure as it shelters a wide variety of entities and structures, but plays a critical role in channeling resources to securities markets and offering investors means to achieve diversified exposure to investment opportunities. Regulators are concerned with the fact that investors are protected and assets are managed in line with the investment strategy agreed in a stable operational environment. From a systemic perspective, the FSB identified two systemic risk transmission channels[23]:

- Exposures/counterparty channel: Risks through this channel may occur when distress or failure of an investment fund leads to losses or other impairment incurred by banks, brokers and other counterparties (not including equity investors). This may happen in case those counterparties have provided financing to such a fund or in case they have direct trading relations. Losses on investments made by a fund could, in case significant, generate losses to aforementioned counterparties and could lead to destabilized creditors who might be systemically important in their own right.
- Asset liquidation/market channel: This transmission channel involved the indirect impact of distress or a failure of in this category included investment fund on other market participants. Those investment funds can be and are significant investors and/or providers of liquidity in some asset classes. In times of stress (when there tends to be a naturally higher level of correlations between asset classes), forced liquidation of positions by those funds could cause temporary distortions in market liquidity and/or prices that cause indirect distress to other market participants. Those forced liquidations and subsequent market distortions may be magnified by the use of leverage by those investment funds, or by similar events like redemptions or increased margin calls. Investment funds heavily involved in a specific asset class might, as a result of the distress of one particular fund with a similar investment strategy or involvement in the same asset class, experience a 'run' due to an overall reduction of investor's confidence.

The risk indicators identified (below) take into account the very different nature of funds' risk profiles when compared with those of other financial entities. In contrast to banks where capital is set aside to protect depositors and other creditors against the risk of losses, investment management is characterized by the fact that fund investors are knowingly exposed to the potential gains and losses of a fund's invested portfolio.[24] Those investment funds have different 'shock absorbers' that differentiates them from, for example, banks. The investors in such funds take both the upside and the downside, that is, fund investors absorb the negative effects that might be caused by the distress or even the default of a fund, thereby mitigating the eventual contagion effects in the broader financial system.[25]

Despite the many legal structures and vehicles, the investment manager/board acts as an agent on behalf of the underlying investors. Consequently, there are significant differences in risk profile between the investment fund and the investment manager. The FSB, when designing its methodology, has focused only on the fun risk profile (and not that of the fund manager itself). They highlight, besides a number of practical reasons, the following arguments for that choice[26]:

[23] FSB, (2014), Ibid. p. 29.

[24] FSB, (2014), Ibid. p. 29.

[25] Bank depositors, on the other hand, are not in the same position and generally neither benefit from a bank's profits (that goes to bank shareholders) nor do they bear the primary risk of a bank default (FSB, (2014), p. 29).

[26] FSB, (2014), Ibid. p. 30.

- Economic exposures are created at the fund level through the underlying asset portfolio held by the fund. It is therefore the portfolio of assets that creates the respective exposures to the financial system.
- A fund is typically organized as a corporation or business trust under national law, and, as such, is a separate legal entity from its manager. The assets of a fund are separated and distinct from those of the asset manager, and as a result, the assets of a fund are not available to claims by general creditors of the asset manager, as they are often held by third-party custodians in the EU/US.

Asset managers may temporarily implement specific liquidity management tools such as swing pricing, anti-dilution levies, redemption gates, side pockets, redemptions in kind or temporary suspensions. However, the industry is competitive enough to easily absorb the going down of a certain fund. One exception to that is the hedge fund category. The potential global systemic impact of hedge funds in terms of their interconnectedness, size and behavior may be increased by their use of leverage, their lack of transparency and/or information asymmetry (between managers on the one side and markets/regulators/investors on the other).[27] In case of distressed market conditions, a so-called crowded trade may occur in case funds with a similar investment strategy is synchronically exposed to market forces or significant investor redemptions and which might have wider market implications including other parties such as their counterparties and prime brokers, and the wider market.[28]

The FSB already indicated in its consultative document on this matter that there is room to possibly expand the scope of this category and that the methodology is of an organic adaptive nature. The expansion could possibly include:

- Inclusion of a family of funds: families/groups of funds following the same or similar investment strategy that are managed by the same asset manager (consideration of the family of funds on aggregate regarding their systemic relevance).
- Inclusion of asset managers on a stand-alone basis. Under which conditions could asset managers itself become systemically important (e.g. risk management or securities lending and repo transactions).
- Asset managers and their funds collectively.
- A different methodology (or alternative to the one described) focusing on systemic risk that could arise out of certain asset management-related activities. Under this approach, the methodologies would consider how particular activities or group of activities might pose systemic risks.

The following indicators were suggested by the FSB[29] (Table 6.3):

---

[27] FSB, (2014), Ibid. p. 31.

[28] The risks inherent to highly correlated trading strategies by a group of hedge funds operating in turbulent market conditions have been debated, and some believe proven—see footnote 40, p. 31 (FSB 2014).

[29] See in detail FSB, (2014), Ibid. pp. 32–36.

Table 6.3 SIFI indicators for investment funds

Basic factor	Indicator
Size	1. Net assets under management (AUM or NAV) for the fund: the larger the size of a fund, the greater its potential impact on counterparties (counterparty channel) and markets (market channel) 2. For hedge funds,[a] gross notional exposure (GNE) as an alternative indicator: given the different structures used, different investment strategies and different levels of leverage used and since NAV or net AUM do not take into account leverage and additional criteria was required. There is the double threshold: hedge funds with either $100 billion (or more) in net AUM or a value set between $400 and $600 billion (or more) in GNE would be in scope. GNE is calculated as the absolute sum of all long and short positions, considering the notional value (delta-adjusted when applicable) for derivatives[b]
Interconnectedness (with market counterparties including brokerage and trading counterparties)	1. Leverage ratio: Leverage ratio of an investment fund can be measured by 'gross AUM of the fund/NAV of the fund' or, in the case of hedge funds, 'GNE of the fund/NAV of the fund'. The higher the leverage, the higher the potential systemic impact on counterparties and the wider market 2. Counterparty exposure ratio: To be calculated as: total net counterparty credit exposure at the fund/net AUM (NAV) at the fund. Total net counterparty credit exposure is defined as 'the total sum of all residual uncovered exposures that the fund positions represent for its counterparties, after considering valid netting agreements and collateral/margin posted by the fund to its counterparties'. Total net counterparty credit exposure/NAV is a good proxy of the potential losses a fund's failure could immediately cause to its counterparties 3. Intra-financial system liabilities: The larger the exposure of the fund to counterparties, especially with more systemically important financial entities, the greater the impact of its failure
Substitutability	1. Turnover of the fund related to a specific asset/daily volume traded regarding the same asset 2. Total fund turnover vs. total turnover of funds in the same category/classification. The higher the ratio, the higher the potential systemic risk of the fund 3. Investment strategies (or asset classes) with less than ten market players globally. The more substitutable a fund given its investment strategy or the assets it trades, the less of an impact a possible default of that fund would create. Substitutability intends to capture the extent to which a particular fund occupies a specific position in its market that may not be easily and rapidly replaced by other financial entities (particularly relevant for niche markets)

Complexity	1. OTC derivatives trade volumes at the fund/total trade volumes at the fund. Higher levels of OTC derivatives to total trade might imply higher systemic risk 2. Ratio (%) of collateral posted by counterparties that has been re-hypothecated by the fund: a high percentage of collateral that it has re-hypothecated increases exposure risks for counterparties 3. Ratio (%) of NAV managed using high frequency trading strategies. High frequency trading strategies can introduce market risk and erode liquidity 4. Weighted average portfolio liquidity (in days)/weighted average investor liquidity (in days). Or the number of days it takes to liquidate a portfolio of investments divided by the amount of time it takes for an investor to realize their investment. The lower the ratio, the lower the potential risk of the fund as the fund is less exposed to liquidity risk and mismatch with investors' liquidity demands. 5. Ratio of unencumbered cash to gross notional exposure (or gross AUM). The lower the ratio, the higher the potential systemic risk. Consequence is that adverse market conditions or moves can cause the fund to run out of assets to satisfy margin calls or to post collateral. The risks increase, the more complex the strategy and the operations of the fund are
Cross-jurisdictional activities (global activities)	1. Number of jurisdictions in which a fund invests. The more global the fund's reach, the higher the potential impact 2. Number of jurisdictions in which the fund is sold/listed. Same line of reasoning as under 1 3. Counterparties established in different jurisdictions. Having multiple trading and counterparties in many jurisdictions increases the legal (contractual, bankruptcy, etc.) issues the fund is (potentially) exposed to. Indicators 1, 2 and 3 work cumulatively when defining the potential level of systemic risk a fund might pose either because of counterparty or market channel exposure. Further complications might occur of investing in master/feeder structures

[a]'For investment funds other than hedge funds, GNE is deemed to be less relevant as a result of the strict leverage limitations imposed by existing regulations. Furthermore, unlike for hedge funds, use of derivatives is not intended to obtain (synthetic) leverage, but more commonly to hedge exposures and gain exposures to certain asset categories. For these funds, rules on counterparty exposures apply in tandem to limit these funds' recourse to leverage or to any other source of external financing through a counterparty.' FSB, (2014), Ibid. p. 33 footnote 43

[b]'This measure provides a complete appreciation of all the leverage that is employed by a fund to gain market exposure, i.e. financial leverage (repos, prime broker financing, secured and unsecured lending) and synthetic leverage (exposure through derivatives, considering the resulting exposure to the underlying asset or reference). GNE does not directly represent an amount of money (or value) that is at risk of losing. It is a referential figure used to calculate profits and losses. But it still represents a fairer appreciation than NAV of the economic or market exposure (i.e. market footprint) of a fund's positions, looking through to the underlying asset or reference.' FSB, (2014), Ibid. p. 33

Other non-bank and non-insurance entities (those that don't fall in categories 1–3): the following criteria act as a backstop for those entities and structures not falling within those categories discussed. From a definition point of view, this rest category can be defined as 'any corporation, partnership or other legal entity structure that is primarily engaged in financial intermediation or in related auxiliary financial activities, and that is not explicitly assessed by sector-specific methodologies for finance companies, market intermediaries, or investment funds'[30] (i.e. the three previously described categories). Financial intermediation consequently may be defined as 'an activity in which an institution raises funds by incurring liabilities on its own account for the purpose of channeling these funds to other entities by lending or otherwise acquiring financial assets'. These include non-bank deposit-taking institutions as well as finance companies, investment funds and specialized vehicle companies. Financial auxiliaries are closely related to financial intermediation, but these activities are by their very nature separated from the intermediation activities itself. Activities that are auxiliary to intermediation may be performed (on a secondary basis) by traditional financial intermediaries or by separate, specialized financial auxiliaries that do not, as a main business activity, raise funds or extend credit on their own account.[31]

The FSB suggests to use the five basic indicators (supra) for identifying NBNI G-SIFIs (i.e. size, interconnectedness, substitutability, complexity and global activities), to judge the systemic relevance of these institutions. This is clearly a work in progress as more specific indicators will be needed going forward to make the national regulators' exercise effective and meaningful without losing sight on consistency of the dataset to be gathered.

In 2015, IOSCO and the FSB proposed, as a next step, assessment methodologies for Identifying Non-Bank Non-Insurer Global Systemically Important Financial Institutions.[32] This falls however beyond the remit of this volume or book topic. Nevertheless, shadow insurance is a less-documented and researched field and uses techniques that share material characteristics with the shadow banking domain.[33] Asset managers have gotten a much more prominent role in more recent years and will be discussed in Volume II.[34]

[30] FSB, (2014), Ibid. p. 38.

[31] FSB, (2014), Ibid. p. 38.

[32] FSB, (2015), Assessment Methodologies for Identifying Non-Bank Non-Insurer Global Systemically Important Financial Institutions, Basel, March 4; FSB, (2015), Next Steps on the Assessment Methodologies for Non-Bank Non-Insurer Global Systemically Important Financial Institutions (NBNI G-SIFIs), Basel, July.

[33] I spend a few pages, but less than it deserves, on the topic in Chap. 7, Vol. II.

[34] See Vol. II, Sect. 7.7.

7

The Policy Train Chasing Shadow Banking

7.1 Introduction

Ever since the policymakers, bureaucrats and regulators have been recovering somewhat from the first shock after the start of the banking crisis, they have literally been falling over each other to tell the world what was wrong with the current banking regulation and what needed to be done with the shadow banking market, a market that has always been in the shadow of the traditional banking sector. A full review of these events[1] would justify a book on its own and the review of the traditional banking sector regulatory changes is to a large degree out of scope, with the exception of that part of legislation that impacts the nexus between the traditional and the shadow banking market. For the technical review of the new legislation and policy initiatives that have been coming in recent years, it can be referred to the relevant chapter. What we're going to try in this chapter is (try) to define the areas that have raised policy concern, focusing on a number of indirect areas of potential exposure. For the review of the different policy areas, separate chapters have been developed.

As a starting point, we can refer to the Financial Stability Board's (FSB) consolidated statement of areas of concern,[2] where concern is concern that relates to financial stability or systemic risk[3]:

1. To mitigate the spillover effect between the regular banking system and the shadow banking system
2. To reduce the susceptibility of money market funds (MMFs) to 'runs'

---

[1] An excellent summary and schematic overview can be found here: Bankenverband, (2014), Regulation of Shadow Banking. A Guide by the Association of German Banks, January, Berlin.

[2] See in detail: FSB, (2013), Strengthening Oversight and Regulation of Shadow banking. An Overview of Policy Recommendations, 29 August.

[3] See, for example, FSB, (2013), Strengthening Regulation and Oversight of Shadow Banking, Public Framework for Addressing Shadow Banking Risk in Securities Lending and Repos, p. i.

L. Nijs, *The Handbook of Global Shadow Banking, Volume I*,
https://doi.org/10.1007/978-3-030-34743-7_7

3. To assess and align the incentives associated with securitization
4. To dampen risks and procyclical incentives associated with securities financing transactions such as repos and securities lending that may exacerbate funding strains in times of market stress
5. To assess and mitigate systemic risks posed by other shadow banking entities and activities

The FSB, driven by the engagements of the G20 where given a mandate to develop a holistic framework for addressing financial stability concerns associated with shadow banking and shadow banking-related entities and associations, has created a holistic objective. That objective has been fallen apart in two sub-objectives, that is:

- Create a monitoring framework to track financial sector developments outside the banking system
- Develop policies to strengthen oversight and regulation of the shadow banking system.

7.2 Strengthening Regulation and Oversight

Let's start with the latter. We know already its five areas. They are listed at the beginning of the chapter.

7.2.1 Mitigate the Spillover Effect Between the Regular Banking and the Shadow Banking System

Although non-bank financial intermediation provides a valuable alternative to banks in providing credit to support economic activity, the financial crisis revealed that in some cases, the regular banking system was exposed to risks in the shadow banking system. New initiatives were needed to ensure that all banks' activities, including interaction with the shadow banking system, are appropriately captured in prudential regimes. So far, two initiatives have been taken under the leadership of the Bank for International Settlements (BIS).

7.2.2 Introduce Risk-Sensitive Capital Requirements for Banks' Investments in the Equity of Funds

After an initial public consultation in June 2013,[4] the BIS issued its final report in December 2013[5] on this matter. As part of the work by the Financial Stability Board to strengthen the oversight and regulation of shadow banking, the Committee agreed to

---

[4] BIS, (2013), Capital Requirements for Banks' Equity Investments in Funds, June-Consultation document.

[5] BIS, (2013a), Capital Requirements for Banks' Equity Investments in Funds, December. These standards have later on been fully implemented into the consolidated Basel Framework. See bis.org for further details.

review the risk-based capital requirements for banks' exposures to funds. Main objective was to clarify the existing treatment of such exposures in the Basel II capital adequacy framework, and also to achieve a more internationally consistent and risk-sensitive capital treatment for banks' investments in the equity of funds, reflecting both the risk of the fund's underlying investments and its leverage.[6]

The prudential framework agreed by the Committee consists of three approaches, with varying degrees of risk sensitivity: the 'look-through approach' (LTA), the 'mandate-based approach' (MBA) and the 'fallback approach' (FBA). To ensure that banks have appropriate incentives to enhance the risk management of their exposures, the degree of conservatism increases with each successive approach (infra). These standards are mandatory as of January 1, 2017. The framework is applicable to banks' equity investments in all types of funds that are held in their banking book, including off-balance-sheet exposures (e.g. unfunded commitments to subscribe to a fund's future capital calls). One of the things the BIS tried to avoid was a disparate treatment of activities of the bank books and the trading books of the bank. Consequently, the framework applies to all banks, irrespective of whether they apply the Standardized Approach or internal ratings-based (IRB) approaches for credit risk. Further consistency was preferred and is being worked on.[7] Also, the Basel III framework requires banks to deduct certain direct and indirect investments in financial institutions. Those investments should therefore not be risk weighted and excluded from the framework as discussed below.

7.2.2.1 Hierarchy of Approaches

The following approaches were identified:

- The LTA is the most granular approach. Subject to meeting the conditions set out for its use, banks employing the LTA must apply the risk weight of the fund's underlying exposures as if the exposures were held directly by the bank.
- The MBA provides an additional layer of risk sensitivity that can be used when banks do not meet the conditions for applying the LTA. Banks employing the MBA assign risk weights on the basis of the information contained in a fund's mandate or in the relevant national legislation.
- When neither of the above approaches is feasible, the FBA must be utilized. The FBA applies a 1250% risk weight to a bank's equity investment in the fund.

One of the main drivers of risk related to equity investments in funds is their underlying leverage. The adjustment is analogous to proportional consolidation of a fund and would

[6] BIS, (2013a), Ibid. p. 1.

[7] The second consultative document was issued in October 2013: BIS, (2013), Fundamental Review of the Trading Book: A Revised Market Risk Framework, Basel, October. To be read preferably in conjunction with BCBS, (2019), Minimal Capital Requirements for Market Risk, January 14, 2019. These standards have also been fully integrated in the Consolidated Basel Framework. See also BCBS, (2015), Fundamental Review of the Trading Book- Interim Impact Analysis, November.

adjust upward the average risk weight of a fund by its leverage for a given equity investment. These policy changes will be implemented directly in the Basel III capital requirement rules.[8]

First, each of the models will be reviewed,[9] followed by an example for each, including the calculation of leverage.

- **Look-Through Approach**

The LTA requires a bank to risk weight the underlying exposures of a fund as if the exposures were held directly by the bank. This is the most granular and risk-sensitive approach. It must be used when:

(a) there is sufficient and frequent information provided to the bank regarding the underlying exposures of the fund and
(b) such information is verified by an independent third party.

Under the LTA banks must risk weight all underlying exposures of the fund as if those exposures were directly held. This includes, for example, any underlying exposure arising from the fund's derivatives activities and the associated counterparty credit risk (CCR) exposure. Instead of determining a credit valuation adjustment (CVA) charge associated with the fund's derivatives exposures, banks must multiply the CCR exposure by a factor of 1.5 before applying the risk weight associated with the counterparty. Banks may rely on third-party calculations for determining the risk weights associated with their equity investments in funds.

- **The Mandate-Based Approach**

The second approach, the MBA, provides a method for calculating regulatory capital that can be used when the conditions for applying the LTA are not met. Under the MBA banks may use the information contained in a fund's mandate or in the national regulations governing such investment funds. To ensure that all underlying risks are taken into account (including CCR) and that the MBA renders capital requirements no less than the LTA, the risk-weighted assets for the fund's exposures are calculated as the sum of the following three items:

(a) Balance sheet exposures (i.e. the funds' assets) are risk weighted assuming the underlying portfolios are invested to the maximum extent allowed under the fund's mandate in those assets attracting the highest capital requirements, and then progressively in those other assets implying lower capital requirements. If more than one risk weight can be applied to a given exposure, the maximum risk weight applicable must be used.
(b) Whenever the underlying risk of a derivative exposure or an off-balance-sheet item receives a risk-weighting treatment under Pillar 1, the notional amount of the derivative position or of the off-balance sheet exposure is risk weighted accordingly.
(c) The CCR associated with the fund's derivative exposures is calculated using the Current Exposure Method (CEM), which includes a replacement cost and an add-on compo-

---

[8] Included as paragraph 80 in the Basel III rulebook.

[9] See in detail: BIS, (2013a), Ibid. pp. 2–6.

nent. Whenever the replacement cost is unknown, the exposure measure for CCR will be calculated in a conservative manner by using the notional amount as a proxy for the replacement cost. Whenever the add-on factor is unknown, the maximum add-on factor of 15% applies. The risk weight associated with the counterparty is applied to the sum of the replacement cost and add-on components, as in the CEM.

Instead of determining a CVA charge associated with the fund's derivative exposures, banks must multiply the CCR exposure by a factor of 1.5 before applying the risk weight associated with the counterparty.

- **The Fallback Approach**

Where neither the LTA nor the MBA is feasible, banks are required to apply the FBA. The FBA applies a 1250% risk weight to the bank's equity investment in the fund.

Further guidance was provided on the following matters:

- When a bank has an investment in a fund (e.g. Fund A), that itself has an investment in another fund (e.g. Fund B), which the bank identified by using either the LTA or the MBA, the risk weight applied to the investment of the first fund (i.e. Fund A's investment in Fund B) can be determined by using one of the three approaches set out above.
- Equity holdings in entities whose debt obligations qualify for a zero risk weight can be excluded from the LTA, MBA and FBA approaches (approved by the national regulator). To promote specified sectors of the economy, supervisors may exclude from the capital charges equity holdings made under legislated programs that provide significant subsidies or the investment to the bank and involve some form of government oversight and restrictions on the equity investments.

7.2.2.2 Leverage Adjustment

Leverage is defined as the ratio of total assets to total equity. National discretion may be applied to choose a more conservative leverage metric, if deemed appropriate. Leverage is taken into account in the MBA by using the maximum financial leverage permitted in the fund's mandate or in the national regulation governing the fund. When determining the capital requirement related to its equity investment in a fund, a bank must apply a leverage adjustment to the average risk weight of the fund, subject to a cap of 1250%. After calculating the total risk-weighted assets of the fund according to the LTA or the MBA, banks will calculate the average risk weight of the fund (Avg RWfund) by dividing the total risk-weighted assets by the total assets of the fund. Using Avg RWfund and taking into account the leverage of a fund (Lvg), the risk-weighted assets for a bank's equity investment in a fund can be represented as follows:

$$\text{RWA investment} = \text{Avg RWfund} * \text{Lvg} * \text{equity investment}$$

The effect of the leverage adjustments depends on the underlying riskiness of the portfolio (i.e. the average risk weight) as obtained by applying Basel II's Standardized Approach or the IRB approaches for credit risk. The formula can therefore be rewritten as:

$$\text{RWA investment} = \text{RWAfund} * \text{percentage of shares}$$

Risk-weighted assets for equity exposures arising from bank investments in funds that are held in the trading book are subject to the market risk capital rules.[10]

Numerical illustrations are given in Table 7.1.[11]

Table 7.1 Calculation of risk-weighted assets for bank equity investments

A. Calculation of risk-weighted assets using the LTA
Consider a fund that replicates an equity index. Moreover, assume the following:
The bank uses the Standardized Approach for credit risk when calculating its capital requirements
The bank owns 20% of the shares of the fund
The fund holds short-term (less than one year) forward contracts that are cleared through a qualifying central counterparty (with a notional amount of $100)
The fund presents the following balance sheet:
Assets cash $25
Government bonds (AAA rated) $35
Variation margin receivable—forward contracts $40
Liabilities
Notes payable $10
Equity shares $90
Balance sheet exposures of $100 will be risk weighted according to the risk weights applied for cash (RW = 0%), government bonds (RW = 0%) and centrally cleared equity forward positions (RW = 2%). The underlying risk weight for equity exposures (RW = 100%) is applied to the notional amount of the forward contracts, and there is a charge for counterparty credit risk. There is no CVA charge assessed since the forward contracts are cleared through a central counterparty
The leverage of the fund is 100/90 ≈ 1.11
Therefore, the risk-weighted assets for the bank's equity investment in the fund are calculated as follows:
Avg RWfund ∗ Leverage ∗Equity investment = (*RWAcash* + *RWAbonds* + *RWAunderlying* + *RWAforward* + *RWACCR*)/*Total Assetsfund ∗ Leverage ∗Equity investment* =
(($25∗0% + $35∗0% + $100∗100% + $40∗2% + $100∗6%∗2%)/100) ∗ 1.11 ∗ (20%∗90) = $21.60
A. Calculation of risk-weighted assets using the MBA
Consider a fund with assets of $200, where it is stated in the mandate that the fund replicates an equity index. In addition to being permitted to invest its assets in either cash or equities, the mandate allows the fund to take long positions in equity index futures up to a maximum nominal amount equivalent to the size of the fund's balance sheet ($200). This means that the total on balance sheet and off-balance-sheet exposures of the fund can reach $400. Consider also that a maximum financial leverage of 1.2 applies according to the mandate. The bank holds 25% of the shares of the fund, which represents an investment of $21

(*continued*)

[10] See BIS, (2013), Fundamental Review of the Trading Book: A Revised Market Risk Framework, Basel, October, pp. 5–6.

[11] The following examples are adjusted from BIS, (2013a), pp. 8–10.

Table 7.1 (continued)

First, the on-balance sheet exposures of \$200 will be risk weighted according to the risk weights applied for equity exposures (RW = 100%), that is, RWAon-balance = \$200 * 100% = \$200

Second, we assume that the fund has exhausted its limit on derivative positions, that is, \$200 notional amount, which would be weighted with the risk weight associated with the underlying of the derivative position, which in this example is 100% for publicly traded equity holdings. The total risk-weighted assets related to the maximum notional amount underlying the derivative positions are hence RWA underlying = \$200 * 100% = \$200

Third, we would calculate the counterparty credit risk associated with the derivative contract. If we do not know the replacement cost related to the futures contract, we would approximate it by the maximum notional amount, that is, \$200, and also calculate the add-on by applying a 15% conversion factor, resulting in an exposure amount of \$230. Assuming the futures contract is cleared through a qualifying CCP, a risk weight of 2% applies, so that RWACCR = \$230 * 2% = \$4.6. There is no CVA charge assessed since the futures contract is cleared through a central counterparty

The RWA of the fund is hence obtained by adding RWAon-balance, RWAunderlying and RWACCR, that is, \$404.6

When applying the leverage adjustment, the RWA (\$ 404.6) is divided by the total assets of the fund (\$200) resulting in an average risk weight of 202.3%. The average risk weight is then scaled up by a factor of 1.2 to reflect financial leverage = 202.3%*1.2 = 242.76%. Finally, as the bank invested \$21 in the equity of the fund, its total RWAs associated with its equity investment amount to \$21 * 242.76%= \$50.97

B. Calculating the leverage adjustment

Consider a fund with assets of \$200 that invests in corporate debt. Assume that the fund is highly levered with equity of \$10 and debt of \$90. Such a fund would have financial leverage of 100/10 = 10

Consider the following two cases:

Case 1: Fund specializes in low-rated corporate debt

Assets

- Cash \$ 30
- A+ to A– bonds \$ 0
- BBB+ to BB– bonds \$ 90
- Below BB– bonds \$ 80

The average risk weight of the fund is (\$30*0% + \$0*50% + \$90*100% + \$80*150%)/\$200 = 105%. The financial leverage of 10 would result in a risk weight of 1050% for the banks' investment in this highly levered fund; if it were to be higher it would have been capped at a conservative risk weight of 1250%

Case 2: Fund specializes in high-rated corporate debt

Assets

- Cash \$5
- AAA to AA– bonds \$100
- A+ to A– bonds \$95

The average risk weight of the fund is (\$5*0% + \$100*20% + \$95*50%)/\$200 = 33.75%. The financial leverage of 10 results in a risk weight of 337.5%

The above example illustrates that the rate at which the 1250% cap is reached depends on the underlying riskiness of the portfolio (as judged by the average risk weight) as captured by Basel II Standardized Approach risk weights or the IRB methods. Therefore, for a 'risky' portfolio (100% average risk weight), the 1250% limit is reached fairly quickly with a leverage of 12.5×, while for a 'low-risk' portfolio (25% average risk weight), this limit is reached at a leverage of 50×

7.2.3 Framework for Measuring and Controlling Large Exposures[12]

A separate key lesson from the crisis is that material losses in one systemically important financial institution (SIFI) can trigger concerns about the solvency of other SIFIs, with potentially catastrophic consequences for global financial stability. The large exposures framework is a tool that will help to mitigate the risk of contagion between global systemically important banks, thus underpinning financial stability. The BCBS proposals to strengthen the oversight and regulation of the shadow banking system in relation to large exposures were first addressed in 1991[13] albeit in an embryonic way. Large exposures regulation has arisen as a tool for containing the maximum loss a bank could face in the event of a sudden counterparty failure to a level that does not endanger the bank's solvency.

In March 2013 a new consultation[14] was issued and this within the context of the FSB initiatives discussed above. The 2013 proposals include policy measures designed to capture bank-like activities conducted by non-banks that are of concern to supervisors. The new standard aims to ensure greater consistency in the way banks and supervisors measure, aggregate and control exposures to single counterparties. Acting as a backstop to risk-based capital requirements, the standard would supplement the existing risk-based capital framework by protecting banks from substantive losses caused by the sudden default of a counterparty or group of connected counterparties.[15] But neither the 1991 guidance nor the core principles set out how banks should measure and aggregate their exposures to a single counterparty, nor do they explain which factors they should take into account when considering whether separate legal entities form a group of connected counterparties, which has led to significant variation in practices across banks and jurisdictions. A large exposures framework complements the risk-based capital standard because the latter is not designed specifically to protect banks from large losses resulting from the sudden default of a single counterparty. In particular, the minimum capital requirements (Pillar 1) of the Basel capital framework implicitly assume that a bank holds infinitely granular portfolios, that is, no form of concentration risk is considered in calculating capital requirements. Idiosyncratic risk due to large exposures to individual counterparties may therefore be present in banks' portfolios.[16] Although the supervisory process of Pillar II can force further adjustments upon a financial institution, the process and methods are not designed to deal with large concentrated exposures. That framework

---

[12] For a short write-up on the issue, see BIS, (2018), The Treatment of Large Exposures in the Basel Capital Standards, Executive Summary, April 30, via bis.org

[13] The first Basel Committee guidance on this topic, measuring and controlling large credit exposures, was published in January 1991 in an attempt to increase convergence in the supervision of large exposures while recognizing the scope for variation according to local conditions. This best practice for bank supervisors in the monitoring and controlling of large credit exposures was developed in the context of the rules included in Basel I. They related to numerical limits as a percentage of Basel I capital, the definition of which has been subsequently revised in later vintages of the Basel capital framework and more recently and substantively in Basel III; BIS, (2013b), Ibid. p. 1, footnote 2.

[14] BIS, (2013b), Supervisory Framework for Measuring and Controlling Large Exposures, March. Finalized April 2014 and later on included in the consolidated Basel Framework, including the findings of the additional consultation round in December 2017. See for details: bis.org.

[15] BIS, (2013b), Ibid. p. 1.

[16] BIS, (2013b), Ibid. pp. 1–2.

needed to be supplemented with a simple large exposures framework that protects banks from traumatic losses caused by the sudden default of a certain counterparty or group of connected counterparties. To serve as a backstop to risk-based capital requirements, the large exposures framework should be designed so that the maximum possible loss a bank could incur if a single counterparty or group of connected counterparties were to suddenly fail would not endanger the bank's survival as a going concern.[17] Further, material losses in one systemically important financial institution (SIFI) can trigger concerns about the solvency of other SIFIs, with potentially catastrophic consequences for global financial stability. That can happen as investors might fear that certain SIFIs they invested in have exposure (1) either to the failing SIFI (loans, guarantees, etc.) or (2) the same sort of exposure (to certain assets or securitized products) that the failing SIFI has/had.

With respect to strengthen the oversight and regulation of the shadow banking system in relation to large exposures, the guidelines encompass primarily bank-like activities of non-bank institutions. This is done through proposals on large exposures to funds, securitization structures and collective investment undertakings (CIU).[18] The risk from concentrated exposures to single counterparties or groups of connected counterparties is not the only type of concentration risk that could undermine a bank's resilience. Other types include both sectoral and geographical concentrations of asset exposure, as well as reliance on concentrated funding sources.[19] Furthermore, a bank with a net short position in securities may incur losses if the price of these securities increases as well as bank's exposure to sovereigns or sovereign-lined institutions and intra-group exposures. These exposures are not included, as were considered to be preferably dealt with within a broader review of the risk within the regulatory framework. The current rules focus only on the concentration risk associated with the default of single third-party private sector counterparties.

The final BCBS report[20] on this matter included the following measurements and standards. When compared to the large exposure rules proposed in the US under single counterparty credit limit (SCCL) and in EU under Capital Requirements Directive IV (CRD IV), BCBS large exposure framework combines the stricter clauses from both rules. The following directions were provided[21]:

- The Basel Committee definition of large exposures is when the sum of all exposures of a bank to a counterparty, or to a group of connected counterparties, is equal to or above 10% of the bank's eligible capital base (i.e. Tier 1 capital). The 10% threshold is in contrast to the 5% limit proposed earlier and includes exposures which are both on- and off-balance sheet, and in either the banking or trading book.
- Connected counterparties are defined as counterparties with a control relationship or economic interdependence such that one's default can lead to default of the other. They will be treated as a single counterparty when applying the large exposure framework.

[17] BIS, (2013b), Ibid. p. 2.

[18] BIS, (2013b), Ibid. pp. 18–27.

[19] BIS, (2013b), Ibid. p. 3.

[20] BCBS, (2014), Supervisory Framework for Measuring and Controlling Large Exposures, Standards, Basel.

[21] Pierre-Etienne Chabanel, (2014), Supervisory Framework for Measuring and Controlling Large Exposures, Moody's Analytics, August, NY.

- The framework requires that the banks must report: (1) all exposures with values equal to or above 10% of the bank's eligible capital, (2) all other exposures with values measured without the effect of credit risk mitigation being taken into account if they are equal to or above 10% of the bank's eligible capital, (3) all the exempted exposures with values equal to or above 10% of the bank's eligible capital and (4) largest 20 exposures to counterparties included in the scope of application, irrespective of the values of these exposures relative to the bank's eligible capital base.
- The sum of all the exposure values of a bank to a single counterparty or to a group of connected counterparties must never be higher than 25% of the bank's available eligible capital base (i.e. Tier 1 capital). For a G-SIB's exposures to another G-SIB, the cap will be 15%.
- Both on- and off-balance sheet exposures included in either the banking or the trading book and instruments with counterparty credit risk will be constrained by the large exposure limit to manage the concentration risk associated with the default of a single counterparty. The measurement of the exposure value varies by asset type and book.
- Exposures to qualified central counterparties (QCCPs) related to clearing activities, which are currently exempted from the framework, would be under observation until 2016 and then reviewed. The final framework will be applicable as of January 1, 2019. Exposures to non-QCCPs will be sum of both the clearing exposures and the non-clearing exposures, and the general large exposure limit of 25% of the eligible capital base will be applicable.
- There are Credit Risk Mitigating Techniques (CRM) and Netting Conditions provided that will allow the value of the exposure to the counterparty to be reduced.
- Offsetting in the trading book is allowed under the following circumstances: (1) long and short positions in the same issue may be offset, (2) positions in different issues from the same counterparty may be offset only when the short position is junior to the long position, (3) for hedges to be recognized in case of credit derivatives, the underlying hedge and the position hedged should fulfill the condition that the short position is junior or of equivalent seniority to the long position, (4) netting across the banking and trading books is not permitted and (5) net short positions with a single counterparty will not be considered as an exposure for large exposure purposes.
- Sovereign and interbank exposures are exempted.
- Specific rules have been provided for exposures to collective investment undertakings ('CIU'), securitization and other lookalike vehicles.

7.2.4 Reduce the Susceptibility of Money Market Funds (MMFs) to 'Runs'

MMFs provide a deposit-like instrument to investors, especially when they are redeemable at short notice and at par. They are, as such, susceptible to contagious investor runs. Final policy recommendations have been developed by the International Organization of Securities Commissions (IOSCO) that provide the basis for common standards of regulation and management of MMFs across jurisdictions.[22] These recommendations have been used as the basis for regulatory changes, including the European regulation proposed in 2013 as discussed in the regulatory chapter. The starting point of the analysis was that although MMFs did not cause the crisis, their performance during the financial turmoil highlighted their potential to spread or even amplify a crisis. Concerns remain regarding the stability of the money market fund industry and the risks it may pose for the broader financial system. The US and Europe represent around 90% of the global MMF industry and represents around 5 trillion USD[23] and provides a significant source of credit and liquidity. They are key entities in the money and commercial paper markets and are key providers of short-term funding for banks.[24] Money market funds are investment products subject to securities markets regulation. They are considered part of the shadow banking system on the basis that they perform maturity and liquidity transformation and are important sources of short-term funding, particularly for banks. In contrast with bank deposits, MMFs do not have access to official support and backstop facilities, and, whereas they have little ability to absorb losses, they also do not have explicit support from sponsor companies.[25] In the aftermath of the 2008 financial crisis, many regulators in the world sharpened the regulation surrounding MMFs including the US and Europe.[26] The objective of these initiatives was similar across jurisdictions, that is, to make MMFs more resilient to short-term risks and limiting the risks for investors and the financial system that could result from a fund breaking the buck. These limitations intended to limit some risks inherent to MMFs by 'requiring funds to maintain a portion of their portfolios in instruments that can be readily converted to cash, reducing the maximum weighted average maturity of portfolio holdings, and improving the quality of portfolio securities'.[27] Further, the rules included additional reporting requirements and facilitating redemptions under certain conditions or market positions, that is, pricing its securities below par. In Europe one aimed further for a harmonization of the definition of MMFs and created two types of MMFs: 'short-term money market funds' (ST-MMFs) and 'money market funds' (MMFs) and imposed strict standards in terms of portfolio quality and maturity, risk management and disclosure.

[22] IOSCO, (2012), Policy Recommendations for Money Market Funds which was based on the IOSCO consultation report (2012), Money Market Fund Systemic Risk Analysis and Reform Options. The report provided a preliminary analysis of the possible risks that money market funds could pose to financial stability and proposed a broad range of possible policy options to address those risks as well as to address other potential issues identified with regard to money market funds.

[23] See www.ici.org for recent data.

[24] See P. McCabe et al., (2012), The Minimum Balance at Risk: A Proposal to Mitigate the Systemic Risks Posed by Money Market Funds, Staff Report, Federal Reserve Bank of New York, Nr. 564, July 2012.

[25] IOSCO, (2012), Ibid. p. 5.

[26] See US Securities and Exchange Commission (2010), MMF Reform, Final rule, available at http://www.sec.gov/rules/final/2010/ic-29132.pdf. The guidelines were published in May 2010 by the Committee of European Securities Regulators (CESR), ESMA predecessor. The guidelines are available at http://www.esma.europa.eu/system/files/10_049.pdf

[27] IOSCO, (2012), Ibid. p. 5.

Still, the experience was that the 2010 round of legislation didn't solve a number of major problems. In the US, for example, investors still had the incentive to redeem quickly when they fear that the fund will record a loss, which can lead the fund to burn the rest of its liquidity through fire sales and can lead to contagion effects to other funds. In Europe, for example, short-term MMFs are still allowed to use a constant net asset value. Moreover, investment funds are allowed to use amortized cost accounting to value instruments with a residual maturity limit fixed at 397 days, which may create risks and reduce price transparency.[28] In general the following open exposures were identified[29]:

- The stable net asset value (1$/share price): which leaves the impression that the fund is not exposed to risk although it is subject to credit, interest rate and liquidity risk
- The first mover advantage: redemption of investors at stable asset value leaves the risk with the remaining shareholders or they are left with the less liquid assets as the fund managers will liquidate the most liquid asset first when confronted with redemptions
- The discrepancy between the net asset value published and the value of the assets (due to amortized cost accounting)
- The implicit support of sponsors in case of distress[30]
- The importance of ratings (implicitly reducing due diligence by investors)

The additional 2012 IOSCO recommendations were articulated around some key principles of maturity, liquidity and credit risk thereby obeying the difference among jurisdictions and markets. The following recommendations were withheld (Table 7.2)[31]:

In the EU, the second largest MMF market, the European Commission organized in 2012 a public consultation on the asset management regulatory framework including possible ways to strengthen MMFs' resilience to systemic risks (e.g. investor runs). Further, the European Systemic Risk Board (ESRB) also published recommendations on stable NAV MMFs in December 2012 that include mandatory conversion of stable NAV MMFs to floating NAV MMFs in order to reduce the shareholders' incentive to run when the MMF has experienced a loss, additional liquidity requirements, additional public disclosure on important features and more detailed reporting by MMFs. The 2013 (proposed) EU regulation on MMFs is in compliance with the aforementioned standards and recommendations.

7.2.5 Aligning the Incentives Associated with Intermediation

Securitization allows the transfer of risk away from the traditional banking sector and provides a source of funding for banks but the complex structuring of some securitization before the crisis created incentives to weaken lending standards and generated an undetected build-up of leverage.

---

[28] IOSCO, (2012), Ibid. p. 7.

[29] See in detail IOSCO, (2012), Ibid. pp. 7–8.

[30] See in detail S.A. Brady et al., (2012), The Stability of Prime Money Market Mutual Funds: Sponsor Support from 2007 to 2011, Federal Reserve Bank of Boston.

[31] See in detail: IOSCO, (2012), Ibid. pp. 11–18.

Table 7.2 IOSCO 2012 money market fund recommendations

Recommendations	Guidance
General recommendations	
Money market funds should be explicitly defined in CIS ('collective investment schemes') regulation	Money market funds may generally be defined as investment funds that seek to preserve capital and provide daily liquidity, while offering returns in line with money market rates (variations may occur across jurisdictions)
Specific limitations should apply to the types of assets in which MMFs may invest and the risks they may take	Money market funds should invest mainly in high quality money market instruments and other low-duration fixed income instruments No direct or indirect exposures to equities or commodities and the use of derivatives should be in line with the investment strategy of the fund Currency risk and concentration limits should be properly managed Limits should be imposed regarding the remaining maturity until the legal redemption date of the instruments held in the portfolios Limits should be defined on the average weighted term to maturity (WAM) and the weighted average life (WAL) of the portfolio[a] Restrictions should reflect the riskiness of the investment fund's objectives
Regulators should closely monitor the development and use of other vehicles similar to money market funds (collective investment schemes or other types of securities)	To avoid confusion Limit the risk of regulatory arbitrage
Recommendations regarding valuation	These recommendations should be read in conjunction with the IOSCO 2013 recommendation of valuation of collective investment schemes[b]
Money market funds should comply with the general principle of fair value when valuing the securities held in their portfolios. Amortized cost method should only be used in limited circumstances	Current market prices Fair value principle in case current market prices are not available (i.e. models based on current yield curve and issuer spread, or other 'arm's length' valuation method are then acceptable) Sudden movements in interest rates or credit concerns may cause material deviations between the mark-to-market price and the price calculated using the amortization method (risk of mispricing). It can therefore only be applied under tight conditions[c]

(continued)

Table 7.2 (continued)

Recommendations	Guidance
General recommendations	
MMF valuation practices should be reviewed by a third party as part of their periodic reviews of the funds accounts	In particular the sources of pricing
Recommendations regarding liquidity management	Recommendations need to be read in conjunction with the IOSCO 2013 Principles of Liquidity Risk Management for Collective Investment Schemes
Money market funds should establish sound policies and procedures to know their investors	Identify patterns in investors' cash needs, their sophistication, their risk aversion, as well as to assess the concentration of the investor base
	Concentration risk large investors
	Protection through larger lock-in or redemption periods, minimum holding periods and so on
Money market funds should hold a minimum amount of liquid assets to strengthen their ability to face redemptions and prevent fire sales	Daily liquid assets/weekly liquid assets
Money market funds should periodically conduct appropriate stress testing	Based upon certain hypothetical and/or historical events, such as a rise in short-term interest rate, an increase in shareholder redemptions, a downgrade or series of downgrades on portfolio securities or a credit event
Money market funds should have tools in place to deal with exceptional market conditions and substantial redemption pressures	Such as temporary suspensions, gates and/or redemptions-in-kind
Recommendations regarding MMFs that offer a stable net asset value	Aims to reinforce the stability of MMFs in general

MMFs that offer a stable NAV should be subject to measures designed to reduce the specific risks associated with their stable NAV feature and to internalize the costs arising from these risks	IOSCO recommends that stable NAV MMFs convert to floating NAV MMFs (constrains the effects of a credit event impact) Or to develop additional safeguards to reinforce their resilience to losses and their ability to satisfy significant redemption requests (first mover advantage and slow down outflows in the event of significant redemption pressures) To compensate the day-to-day variations in the value of the portfolio's instruments To offset day-to-day deviations between the fixed NAV and the market value of the fund's units/shares Safeguards may take the form of NAV buffers, be constituted by accumulating returns or by any other mechanism which would achieve the same outcome or an explicit commitment from the sponsor Liquidity fees in case of redemptions Hold back a small portion of the shareholder's investments
Recommendations regarding the use of ratings[d]	
MMF regulation should strengthen the obligations of the responsible entities regarding internal credit risk assessment practices and avoid any mechanistic reliance on external ratings	Responsibility for the assessment of credit worthiness lies with the responsible entity
CRA ('credit rating agency') supervisors should seek to ensure credit rating agencies make more explicit their current rating methodologies for money market funds	Methodologies when rating MMFs Information distribution of investors Role of the sponsor supporting the MMF
Recommendations regarding disclosure to investors	
MMF documentation should include a specific disclosure drawing investors' attention to the absence of a capital guarantee and the possibility of principal loss	Absence of deposit insurance The value of the MMF may decrease Possibility of a principal loss Difference between investments in the money market funds and bank deposits

(*continued*)

Table 7.2 (continued)

Recommendations	Guidance
General recommendations	
MMFs' disclosure to investors should include all necessary information regarding the funds' practices in relation to valuation and the applicable procedures in times of stress	Procedures in place regarding the valuation of the instruments held in the portfolios Procedures which may be used by the responsible entities in case of significant market stress or heavy redemption pressures
Recommendations regarding MMFs' practices in relation to repos	
When necessary, regulators should develop guidelines strengthening the framework applicable to the use of repos by money market funds, taking into account the outcome of current work on repo markets	Areas such as settlement, counterparty risks and collateral management, including the nature of the collateral received should be covered Reference to the chapter on securities lending and repos for further details in this matter[e]

[a]'WAM is a measure of the average length of time to maturity of all of the underlying securities in the fund weighted to reflect the relative holdings in each instrument. It is used to measure the sensitivity of a money market fund to changing money market interest rates. WAL is the weighted average of the remaining life (maturity) of each security held in a fund. It is used to measure the credit risk, as well as the liquidity risk'. IOSCO, (2012), Ibid. p. 11 footnote 14

[b]See IOSCO, (2013c), Principles for the Valuation of Collective Investment Schemes, Final Report (May 2013)

[c]See for those conditions IOSCO, (2012), Ibid. p. 13

[d]These principles are in line with the FSB's 2010 Principles for Reducing Reliance on External Ratings Report

[e]The IOSCO team for this subset (on repos and securities lending) has been working with the FSB team, and the input has been presented combined in the report FSB, (2013), Strengthening Oversight and Regulation of Shadow Banking Policy Framework for Addressing Shadow Banking Risks in Securities Lending and Repos (August 2013)

[f]IOSCO, (2013d), Principles of Liquidity Risk Management for Collective Investment Schemes, Final Report (March 2013)

The complex structuring and multistep distribution chains involved in much securitization prevalent in the run-up to the crisis generated misaligned incentives while encouraging a rapid and largely undetected build-up of leverage and maturity mismatches. A number of regulatory reforms have since been introduced to address the information asymmetries and incentive problems associated with these forms of securitization.

IOSCO issued a report in November 2012 that took stock of the implementation of reforms, especially those related to (1) retention requirements, and (2) measures that enhance transparency and standardization of securitization products, and set out further policy recommendations in these areas. These recommendations seek to facilitate convergent implementation across jurisdictions of approaches to align incentives, in particular regarding risk retention requirements.

For further details on this matter, we refer to the separate chapter on securitization and financial intermediation.

7.2.6 Dampen Financial Stability Risks and Procyclical Incentives Associated with Securities Financing Transactions Such as Repos and Securities Lending

Securities financing transactions support markets for a wide variety of securities but they are also used by non-banks to conduct 'bank-like' activities entailing leverage and mismatches between long-term lending and short-term borrowing. During the crisis, these markets shrank dramatically as losses materialized on the securities underpinning these transactions, thereby generating fire sales of assets. The FSB issued a Policy Framework for Addressing Shadow Banking Risks in Securities Lending and Repos.[32] This document sets out final policy recommendations for addressing financial stability risks in this area, including enhanced transparency, regulation of securities financing and improvements to market structure. It also includes consultative proposals on minimum standards for methodologies to calculate haircuts on non-centrally cleared securities financing transactions and a framework of numerical haircut floors for non-centrally cleared securities financing transactions collateralized by non-government securities through which non-banks obtain leverage from regulated financial intermediaries.

The FSB set out in November 2012 proposed policy recommendations for securities financing transactions to reduce the risks associated with the heavy dependence by the shadow banking system on this form of short-term wholesale funding. The FSB in 2013 finalized most of its policy recommendations. These include standards and processes for data collection and aggregation at the global level to enhance transparency of securities financing markets, minimum standards on cash collateral reinvestment, requirements on re-hypothecation, minimum regulatory standards for collateral valuation and management and policy recommendations related to structural aspects of the securities financing markets (central clearing and changes in the bankruptcy law treatment of securities financing transactions).[33]

---

[32] FSB, (2013), Strengthening Oversight and Regulation of Shadow Banking Policy Framework for Addressing Shadow Banking Risks in Securities Lending and Repos.

[33] See the chapter on securities lending and repos for further details.

The FSB published, in August 2013, for consultation specific proposals on (i) minimum standards for methodologies used by market participants in calculating the 'haircuts (margins)' that limit the amount of financing that can be provided against a given security and (ii) a framework of numerical haircut floors intended to prevent the erosion of margins below minimum levels when non-banks obtain leverage through the use of securities financing transactions backed by non-government securities. These measures would help reduce excessive leverage and dampen procyclicality in such financing markets. But given the fact that the impact and potentially adverse or unintended consequences can be material, the FSB has been conducting two quantitative impact studies (or one with two stages if you want) in 2013 and 2014. The QIS has collected historical haircut data from a small pool of large financial intermediaries globally to help calibrate specific haircut proposals issued for public consultation. Their final recommendation on this specific matter was released in 2014.[34]

7.2.7 Assessing and Mitigating Systemic Risks Posed by Other Shadow Banking Entities and Activities

In my understanding, this is one of the most critical aspects, if not the most critical aspect, of the avalanche of policy initiatives taken in recent years. Recognizing that shadow banking entities and activities take a variety of forms and evolve over time, the FSB has developed a forward-looking high-level policy framework for adoption by authorities to detect and assess the sources of financial stability risks from shadow banking in the non-bank financial space and apply appropriate policy measures where necessary to mitigate these risks.

The framework consists of the following three elements[35]:

- Assessment based on economic functions (or activities): Authorities will therefore have to identify the potential sources of shadow banking risks in non-bank financial entities in their jurisdictions from a financial stability perspective by categorizing these with reference to five economic functions, independent of the entities' legal form. They are (1) management of collective investment vehicles with features that make them susceptible to runs, (2) loan provision that is dependent on short-term funding, (3) intermediation of market activities that is dependent on short-term funding or on secured funding of client assets, (4) facilitation of credit creation (e.g. through credit insurance) and (5) securitization-based credit intermediation and funding of financial entities.
- Adoption of policy tools: Authorities will refer to agreed overarching principles for oversight of non-bank financial entities that are identified as posing a threat to financial stability from shadow banking. In addition, where necessary to mitigate financial stability risks, authorities will apply appropriate policy tools from a menu of optional policies (policy toolkit) for each economic function as they think best fits the non-bank financial entities concerned, the structure of the markets in which they operate and the degree of financial stability risks posed by such entities in their jurisdictions.

[34] See the chapter on securities lending and repos for further details.

[35] FSB, (2013), Strengthening Oversight and Regulation of Shadow Banking An Overview of Policy Recommendations, p. 6.

- Information-sharing process: Authorities will share information on (1) which non-bank financial entities are earmarked as being involved in an economic function linked to specific shadow banking risks and (2) which policy tools are being used so the FSB can judge consistency across jurisdictions and assess consistency of data provided.

Essential is the fact that the tools focus on economic functions (rather than legal or accounting constructs) as it that way can capture innovations, mutations and adaptations in the shadow banking industry which will undeniably happen and to judge to what degree they operate (far) beyond the boundaries of traditional banking regulation. It makes perfect sense to look a little deeper into these recommendations.

Non-bank financial entities should be read as all non-banking entities except MMFs as they are, as discussed, caught by separate policy reviews. The objective of the policy framework for other non-banking entities is 'detect and assess the sources of shadow banking risks in the non-bank financial space from a financial stability perspective and apply appropriate policy measures if necessary to mitigate any financial stability risks identified'.[36] The policy framework was developed as a two-step process: first looking at 'size' and 'national experience' (authorities' judgment) to derive a list of entity types ('filtered entities'); then assessing their shadow banking risk factors (e.g. maturity/liquidity transformation and leverage). The filtered institutions retained were (i) credit investment funds, (ii) exchange-traded funds (ETFs), (iii) credit hedge funds, (iv) private equity funds, (v) securities broker-dealers, (vi) securitization entities, (vii) credit insurance providers/financial guarantors, (viii) finance companies and (ix) trust companies.[37] A high degree of heterogeneity and diversity in business models and risk profiles was identified in the retained group not only across the various sectors in the non-bank financial space, but also within the same sector (or entity-type) often fueled by differences legal and regulatory frameworks as well as the constant innovation and immense dynamics in the non-bank financial sector. That (potentially) clouded proper judgment of the economic function of which led the FSB to develop the aforementioned economic function-based (i.e. activities-based) perspective for assessing shadow banking activity in non-bank entities. This approach is forward-looking in that it will be able to capture additional types of entities that conduct these economic functions generating shadow banking risks.

7.3 The Overall Policy Framework

Already in 2011 the FSB tried to identify the shadow banking industry, given the definition it uses (as the system of credit intermediation that involves entities and activities fully or partially outside the regular banking system) by using a two-step process: that is, analyze all non-bank credit intermediation to capture all shadow banking risks that might impact the global financial infrastructure and then 'narrow the focus to the subset of non-bank credit intermediation where there are: (1) developments that increase systemic risk (in particular

---

[36] FSB, (2013a), Strengthening Oversight and Regulation of Shadow Banking Policy Framework for Strengthening Oversight and Regulation of Shadow Banking Entities, p. 1.

[37] FSB, (2013a), Ibid. p. 1.

maturity/liquidity transformation, imperfect credit risk transfer and/or leverage), and/or (2) indications of regulatory arbitrage that is undermining the benefits of financial regulation'.[38]

The final policy framework consists of three elements:

1. **Five key economic activities** to judge whether non-banking FIs are involved in non-bank credit intermediation that may pose systemic risks or in regulatory arbitrage ('financial stability perspective').
   (a) Identify sources of shadow banking risk
   (b) Focus is on credit intermediation activities by non-bank financial entities that are close in nature to traditional banks[39]
   (c) Excluding non-bank financial entities that do not usually involve significant maturity/liquidity transformation and are not typically part of a credit intermediation chain
   (d) Potential to create runs due to procyclicality
   (e) Potential for regulatory arbitrage

The FSB created a full-blown list of criteria that can be used by policymakers and regulators to judge specific entities and its activities.[40]

2. **Policy toolkits:** It presents a menu[41] of optional policies from which authorities can draw, if necessary to mitigate financial stability risks. Policymakers should take into account the size of the market, nature of the (potential) exposure, degree of stability risk, market structure, adequacy and proportionality of tools to be implemented.
3. **Consistent information-sharing among regulators and policymakers:** and also to minimize 'gaps' in regulation or new regulatory arbitrage opportunities.

The order of the policy framework is (1) identification of economic activities and (2) adoption of policy tools per economic activity and (3) info-sharing across jurisdictions.

The five economic activities identified to screen for shadow banking activities that might pose financial systemic and stability risk are as follows:

- Management of collective investment vehicles with features that make then susceptible to runs
- Loan provision that is dependent on short-term funding
- Intermediation of market activities that is dependent on short-term funding or on secured funding of assets

[38] FSB, (2013a), Ibid. p. 2.

[39] That is, credit intermediation that involves maturity/liquidity transformation, leverage and/or credit risk transfer. Such credit intermediation activities by non-bank financial entities often generate benefits for the financial system and real economy, for example, by providing alternative financing/funding to the economy and by creating competition in financial markets that may lead to innovation, efficient credit allocation and cost reduction. Ibid. p. 3.

[40] See for the full list FSB, (2013a), Annex 1, Ibid. pp. 24–28.

[41] See for the full menu FSB, (2013a), Annex 2, Ibid. pp. 29–34.

- Facilitation of credit creation
- Securitization-based credit intermediation and funding of financial entities.

Authorities may classify an entity into more than one type of economic function that gives rise to shadow banking risks if that entity undertakes multiple functions. Authorities will be able to capture new structures or innovations that create shadow banking risks, by looking through to the underlying economic function and risks of these new innovative structures.[42] As these criteria are at the heart of the policy analysis, they require a further analysis.

7.3.1 Management of Collective Investment Vehicles (CIVs) with Features That Make Them Susceptible to Runs[43,44]

As those CIVs often act as a shock absorber in the financial markets by spreading losses due to distress, insolvency or just adverse market conditions impacting the underlying investor group, they require increased attention. Some of them are involved in credit intermediation, leverage and liquidity/maturity transformation and are therefore increasingly prone to 'runs'. The distress often occurs in case the CIV witnesses large redemptions from investors as well as when it has to roll over positions in adverse market conditions. When facing redemptions those vehicles often sell their highest quality assets first leaving the incremental pain for the remaining investors. Fire sale of assets and other 'momentum'-driven initiatives can dislocate the liquidity and pricing of the wider market in which it operates and the other CIVs active in the space (i.e. similar assets, strategies or transactions). When the CIV uses leverage, redemptions by lenders can create similar effects at the level of the CIV or wider market. Understandably, not all CIVs are subject to these phenomena in the same way and to the same degree. Analysis of the market structure, investor base (tolerance for risk absorption), amount of leverage, concentration in certain market segments, correlation between assets in the CIVs portfolio, complexity and liquidity of the CIVs portfolio and the regulation it is subject to will provide guidance in this matter.

The FSB indicates two additional red flags[45] in terms of the sensitivity to runs by CIVs: (1) CIVs with a low investment risk strategy and/or with a rather illiquid asset base (and that are fully redeemable upon demand or within a short timeframe) and (2) CIVs with substantial roll-over risk in their portfolios (where counterparties or, for a leveraged CIV, lenders could suddenly refuse to interact with the CIV). This likelihood increases when it is invested in long-term and/or complex financial instruments (thus, transforming maturity/liquidity).

---

[42] FSB, (2013a), Ibid. p. 6.

[43] For example, redemption risks by investors as well as roll-over risk by counterparties.

[44] See in details FSB, (2013a), Ibid. pp. 6–7.

[45] FSB, (2013a), Ibid. p. 7.

7.3.2 Loan Provision That Is Dependent on Short-Term Funding[46]

This activity includes lending and credit provision activity but arranged outside the banking sector environment and is funded with short-term funding. This can include retail and corporate clients and borrowers for a variety of purposes, that is, consumer finance, car finance, retail mortgages, equipment finance/leasing and so on. These activities, on a secured or unsecured basis, may give rise to maturity/liquidity transformation risks and/or excessive leverage. As the offering institutions are often niche players in certain industries, the risk enhances if those industries are characterized by a certain natural cyclicality (retail, cars, shipping, real estate, etc.). The higher the maturity mismatch, the more intrinsic risks will be magnified under conditions of market distress.

7.3.3 Intermediation of Market Activities That Is Dependent on Short-Term Funding or on Secured Funding of Client Assets[47]

Intermediation typically includes brokerage services (i.e. buying and selling of securities and derivatives on and off exchanges including in a market-making role) and prime brokerage to hedge funds. Activities that are not maturity transforming are naturally excluded from the scope. Considerable (intra-day) liquidity risk might arise depending on the funding model they use. In particular funding that uses clients' assets (often via repos) is economically similar to banks' collection and redeployment of deposits into long-term assets (i.e. bank-like activities). Other examples include (1) market intermediation that is heavily dependent on wholesale funding markets or short-term commitment lines from banks. They are particularly vulnerable in case their funding is heavily dependent on wholesale funding such as CPs, repos or short-term bank commitment lines (securities broker-dealers). Leverage on the books of the non-bank lender will increase vulnerability and (2) market intermediation that is dependent on secured funding of client assets through repos or re-hypothecation (e.g. prime broker), for example, re-hypothecates client assets for the purpose of financing other client's long positions and covering short positions.

7.3.4 Facilitation of Credit Creation[48]

The provision of credit enhancements (e.g. guarantees) is often used to facilitate credit creation. This process is an integrated part of a full credit intermediation chain. In such chains there is the inherent risk of 'imperfect risk transfers' causing excessive leverage in the system leading to the typical boom-bust cycles and systemic instability, through

[46] FSB, (2013a), Ibid. pp. 7–8.

[47] See in detail FSB, (2013a), Ibid. pp. 8–9.

[48] See in detail FSB, (2013a), Ibid. pp. 9–10.

facilitating credit creation that may not be commensurate with the actual risk profile of the borrowers or the perceived risk on the books or a market player. Further examples might include (1) facilitation of credit creation through writing insurance on financial products (e.g. structured finance products) and consequently facilitate potentially excessive risk taking or may lead to inappropriate risk pricing while lowering the cost of funding of the issuer relative to its risk profile. Those companies that ensure or guarantee financial products (e.g. credit default swaps) can lead to excessive leverage. The insurance implicitly lowers the cost of issuance of financial products including asset-backed securities and provide capital relief for bank counterparties through a smaller capital charge for insured structures than for non-insured structures, (2) facilitation of credit creation by non-bank financial entities whose funding is heavily dependent on wholesale funding markets or short-term commitment lines from banks and (3) facilitation of credit creation through providing credit enhancements to mortgages and consequently facilitate potentially excessive risk taking or inappropriate pricing while lowering the cost of funding of the borrowers relative to their risk profiles.

The risk lies in the fact that the enhancement layer potentially compromises the lending decisions of banks and mortgage originators and further may contribute to systemic disruptions if the real risks aren't properly (due to the enhancement layer) reflected in the cost of funding of the bank or the mortgage originator.

7.3.5 Securitization-Based Credit Intermediation and Funding of Financial Entities[49]

Also in the traditional banking sector, providing funding to related banks and/or non-bank financial entities, with or without transfers of assets and risks from banks and/or non-bank financial entities, regularly occurs as part of the credit intermediation chains. Depending on the type of chains, the type of securitization and quality of the balance sheets involved, these transactions may lead to specific shadow banking risks. These activities are described in detail elsewhere in the book.[50] Some forms of securitization discussed are so-called match-funded aka 'term securitization' that is typically backed by self-liquidating asset pools. They (might) involve maturity/liquidity transformation and leverage to a lesser extent than other, more complex, forms of securitization. Some of these transactions will eventually lead to the creation of excessive maturity/liquidity transformation, leverage or regulatory arbitrage in the system, that is, those transactions for funding/warehousing as well as to reduce their capital requirements.

The policy toolkit the FSB suggests includes two layers, one applicable to all types of economic activities in a consistent way and the other specifically for each type of economic activity.[51] Below (Table 7.3), an attempt is made to provide a condensed overview of the activity-specific policy tools suggested by the FSB.

[49] See in detail FSB, (2013a), Ibid. pp. 10–11.

[50] See also: S. Claessens et al. (2012) Shadow Banking: Economics and policy, IMF Staff Discussion Note, and Z. Pozsar et al., (2010), Shadow Banking, Federal Reserve Bank of NY Staff Report Nr. 458, NY.

[51] A full review of the policy toolkit can be found in FSB, (2013a), Ibid. pp. 11–22.

Table 7.3 Linkage between economic activity and FSB suggested policy tools

Management of collective investment vehicles with features that make them susceptible to runs	
Tools for managing redemption pressures in stressed market conditions	1. **Redemption gates.** Allows CIVs to manage redemption requests (max. volume per day). CIVs can in this way manage maturity or liquidity mismatches by prolonging the term of CIVs' liabilities 2. **Suspension of redemptions.** Achieves the same objectives as 1. It places a significant liquidity restriction on CIV investors. Question about impact of cost of funding 3. **Imposition of redemption fees or other redemption restrictions.** Investors bear liquidity costs in times of distress. Unlike 1 and 2, it leaves the choice with investors to redeem or not 1 and 2. Trigger potentially runs on other similar CIVs in sector or with linked transactions or once the CIV is re-opened 4. **Side pockets**, that is, legally separating the impaired or illiquid portions of an investment portfolio to prevent them from impacting a CIV's returns. Used when a portion of the portfolio cannot be properly valued. Consequently, the CIV can continue normal operations. Often applied in adverse market conditions. Once the market stabilizes, the side pockets can be valued and/or needed to be liquidated. Drawback to this technique includes who decides on when to use this technique? Activating side pockets might send negative signals to the market. Not useful as a technique when market distress is generic in nature
Tools to manage liquidity risk	1. **Limits on investments in illiquid assets.** Quantitative limit on the proportion of portfolio assets that could be invested in illiquid assets (with no observable market prices). Makes redemption more difficult. Drawbacks are the likely reduction of investment opportunities, a possible change in the CIV's risk-return profile, and reduced yield 2. **Liquidity buffers.** To meet redemptions, as asset sale in times of distress creates liquidity costs. Appropriate for CIVs with very illiquid portfolios that offer on demand redemptions or for CIVs perceived as very low risk and for CIVs used for cash management, which can have higher redemption levels and volatility 3. **Limits on asset concentration.** Quantitative limit on the proportion of portfolio assets that may be invested in any one issuer/sector. Limits on asset concentration can significantly affect a CIV's investment strategy and risk-return profile
Limits on leverage	Limit the amount of leverage or require them to maintain a sufficient buffer of liquid assets to meet the potential pressures from creditor runs. Limits the number of investment strategies that make economic and financial sense

(*continued*)

Table 7.3 (continued)

Restrictions on maturity of portfolio assets	Helps mitigate the risks arising from maturity and liquidity transformation created by CIVs. Examples of such restrictions are limits on the duration or weighted average maturity of the fund's portfolio and limits on the residual maturity of portfolio securities. Laddering of maturity profile of CIV is impacted
Loan provision that is dependent on short-term funding	
Impose bank prudential regulatory regimes on deposit-taking non-bank loan providers	Since non-bank financial entities that provide loans (non-bank loan providers) raise funds through deposits, the maturity/liquidity transformation and the leverage they create may have exactly the same effect as banks
Capital requirements	Designed and calibrated to be countercyclical. The implementation challenge is in the calibration of the capital level/ratios as well as determination of the eligible capital instruments to suit the sectoral and jurisdictional specificities of these entities
Liquidity buffers	
Leverage limits	To counteract stress from short-term funding and maturity/liquidity transformation. Constraints on leverage should be calibrated to suit the specificities of the entities (market, size, interconnectedness, etc.)
Limits on large exposures	Since risks arising from maturity/liquidity transformation as well as leverage can be exacerbated. Tailored to an entity's specific business model or operations
Restrictions on types of liabilities	Will eliminate or reduce the risks such as run risks, associated with particular liability types such as ABCPs Such restrictions may include prohibiting the use of funding instruments like ABCPs in cases where entities do not have appropriate securitization and risk management processes in place. Also concentration limits should be considered on the particular lender/sector/instrument. They will help mitigate the risks arising from maturity/liquidity transformation
Intermediation of market activities that is dependent on short-term funding or on secured funding of client assets	
Impose prudential regulatory regimes equivalent to those for banks	The maturity/liquidity transformation being carried out, and the leverage used by these non-bank market intermediaries may lead to them having the same risk profile as banks
Liquidity requirements	Impose liquidity requirements on the entities to mitigate risks associated with liquidity transformation. Such liquidity measures should be similar in spirit to the Basel III liquidity requirements. Also limit the entities' reliance on certain types of funding (e.g. repos)

(*continued*)

Table 7.3 (continued)

Capital requirements	Such requirements may take the form of a minimum capital ratio (including risk-adjusted capital ratios) or minimum levels of liquid net capital. Increases broker-dealers' resilience to credit shocks. Minimum requirement may be calibrated to the level of risk
Restrictions on use of client assets	Prime brokers hold client assets. They use client assets to fund their own longer term assets (re-hypothecated for the purpose of financing client long positions and covering short positions), that is, the entities are essentially carrying out maturity/liquidity transformation similar to banks that collect short-term deposits to fund long-term loans
	To mitigate the run risks arising from maturity/liquidity transformation, client monies and unencumbered assets should not be used to finance the entities' own account activities, or sufficiently subject to liquidity rules. Also info disclosure about positions, even on a daily basis
Facilitation of credit creation	
Capital requirements	Credit insurers and guarantors are essentially insurance firms and should be subject to the solvency rules like formal insurance companies. Idea is that they can absorb losses and price their products appropriately to risk. Cross-border arbitrage and cross-border credit intermediation issues?
Restrictions on scale and scope of business	If they aren't able to price and manage the associated risks in an appropriate manner. Implementing appropriate limits for exposure to various types of covered risks relative to the capital/surplus funds
Liquidity buffers	In particular in case of short-term funding. Vulnerable to creditor runs through indirectly taking on risks (no direct maturity/liquidity transformation)
Enhanced risk management practices to capture tail events	Loss modeling including appropriate stress testing. Taking into consideration all relevant risk factors and an appropriate range of adverse circumstances and events. Stress testing may also be used to validate the entities' models and to complement the use of models for risks that are difficult to model
Mandatory risk sharing between the insurer/guarantor and insured/guaranteed (i.e. deductible, co-insurance)	The amount of credit risk transfer, and thus the risk of imperfect credit risk transfer, can be reduced if the insured (or guaranteed) entities retain some of the credit risk. This can be done through (1) a deductible, where the initial loss remains with the insured/guaranteed, or (2) a co-payment, where losses are proportionately shared between the insured/guaranteed and the insurer/guarantor. Leads to better review of risk profile of borrower. But retaining credit risk increases total risk exposure of non-bank FI

(continued)

Table 7.3 (continued)

Securitization-based credit intermediation and funding of financial entities	
Restrictions on maturity/liquidity transformation	Securitization vehicles are used as funding channels via the issuance of short-term liabilities (e.g. ABCP issuance), restrictions on differences in maturity between the securities issued and the underlying asset pool are a direct method to limit the risks arising from the maturity/ liquidity transformation through securitization. Liquidity rules will enhance their resilience and help mitigate the risks arising from the liquidity transformation. It may further reduce the roll-over risk of the asset-backed securities (ABS) issued and excessive reliance on support from sponsors (e.g. banks)
Restrictions on eligible collateral	Non-bank FIs are often used to fund an illiquid portfolio on their balance sheet that cannot otherwise be financed in the wholesale market. Restrictions on the quality of collateral that may be accepted or 'swapped' (i.e. eligible collateral). Tighter collateral requirements are likely to reduce the amount of available eligible collateral and may cause funding pressures
Restrictions on exposures to, or funding from, banks/other financial entities	Avoid excessive leverage build-up and regulatory arbitrage. Restrictions on the exposures of banks or of other financial entities to such funding vehicles. Authorities can impose limits on non-bank entities' overall exposure to banking counterparties (including intra-group), as well as diversification limits to single counterparties, net of collateral requirements

7.4 The Seven Economics of Shadow Banking (and Their Respective Policies)

Common to all the definitions of shadow banking is the fact that they all refer to shadow banking as the system of credit intermediation that involves entities and activities outside the regular banking system, that is, outside the regulated traditional banking system and often without or with minimal supervisory oversight. However, some of the shadow banking activities take place under the umbrella of bank holding companies or insurance companies. That doesn't mean traditional banks are not active in the shadow banking system, in fact they are well represented and increasingly so, as regulatory oversight has pushed more financial activities outside the supervisory bandwidth, for example, banks extend backup lines of credit that allow independent or off-balance sheet entities to issue short-term liabilities. Or has become clear in the earlier part of the chapter: bank holding companies house money market funds, the tri-party repo market and many different types of activities related to securitization. The connection between bank and non-bank credit intermediation activities is often central in the shadow banking activities.

Generally, shadow banking can be defined as maturity transformation, liquidity transformation and credit risk transfer outside of institutions with direct access to government backstops such as depository institutions. One of the arguments is that it is inherently unstable. In fact, the system, as discussed previously, doesn't only live without it backstop, it also cannot live without a backstop (supra).

Adrian[52] identifies seven areas characterizing the economics of shadow banking:

1. Specialization: The credit intermediation process converts risky long-term liabilities into short-term risk-free liabilities (from subprime mortgages to money market-type instruments). This happens as discussed in previous chapters through a chain of wholesale-funded, securities-based lending. The credit intermediation process is sliced into seven or more (or less) steps.[53] These steps are often complemented by the involvement of transactions performed by outside parties, that is, risk repositories of insurance companies, which provide credit risk transfer at various stages of the intermediation chain.[54]
2. Mispriced guarantees from government backstops. Central banks provide credit guarantees through deposit insurance mechanisms liquidity facilities through lending of last resort which incentivizes excessive risk taking, leverage and maturity transformation. Shadow banking can therefore also be defined as 'credit intermediation without explicitly guaranteed liabilities'.[55] Outside the regulated banking circuit, entities have varying degrees of access to public backstops.
3. Regulatory and tax arbitrage: Regulation constrains behavior (less risk taking, taxes, hold more capital, more and more extensive compliance, etc.). The structuring of activities and transactions to avoid these hazards is known as regulatory arbitrage. It doesn't change the risk profile of that activity, but increases the net cash flows to the sponsor by reducing the costs of regulation.[56] The same holds true for taxes and tax avoidance.[57]

---

[52] T. Adrian, (2014), Financial Stability Policies for Shadow Banking, Federal Reserve Bank of New York Staff Reports, Nr. 664 (February). Also in S. Claessens et al. (Eds.), 2015, 'Shadow Banking Within and Across National Borders,' World Scientific Studies in International Economics, 40. These themes have come across in earlier literature: T. Adrian, A.B. Ashcraft, (2012), Shadow Banking: A Review of the Literature. Palgrave Dictionary of Economics; T. Adrian, A.B. Ashcraft, N. Cetorelli, (2013), Shadow Bank Monitoring, Oxford Handbook of Banking, Oxford University Press, Oxford.

[53] These steps have been discussed before. See also Z. Pozsar, et al., (2013), Shadow Banking, Federal Reserve Bank of New York Economic Policy Review Vol. 19, Issue 2, pp. 1–16.

[54] Adrian, (2014), Ibid. p. 2.

[55] Pozsar et al., Ibid. (2013).

[56] See in detail: V. Acharya, et al., (2013), Securitization without Risk Transfer. *Journal of Financial Economics* Vol. 107, Issue 3, pp. 515–536. They documented that the majority of guarantees provided by the government were structured as liquidity-enhancing guarantees aimed at minimizing regulatory capital, instead of credit guarantees, and that the majority of ABCP conduits were supported by commercial banks subject to the most stringent capital requirements.

[57] See for:

- The role of the tax advantages of home ownership, the use of debt in mergers and acquisitions by private equity, the use of hybrid debt instruments as capital by financial institutions and the use of tax havens to structure securitization vehicles: J. Alworth, and G. Arachi, (2012), Taxation and the Financial Crisis, Oxford University Press, Oxford.

4. Neglected aggregate tail risk: The shadow banking system essentially tries to take advantage of mispriced tail risk. To that effect, the accumulate assets are particularly sensitive for tail risk. That tail risk is often mispriced (or neglected) ex ante due to the fact that participants are fundamentally biased against the rational assessment of tail risk. The specific phenomenon was warned for as early as 2005.[58]
5. Agency issues: Or to be precise informational frictions between the following participants in the securitization of (subprime) credit. They include asymmetric information problems between lenders and originators (predatory lending and borrowing), between lenders and investors, between servicers and investors, between servicers and borrowers, between beneficiaries of invested funds and asset managers and between beneficiaries of invested funds and credit rating agencies. In addition, asymmetric information between investors and issuers results in risk-insensitive cost of funding.[59,60] Also over-reliance on external credit ratings can trigger its own agency issue.[61]

- An empirical link between corporate tax rates and the probability of crises: R. de Mooij, et al., (2013), Taxation, Bank Leverage, and Financial Crises. IMF Working Paper Nr. WP/13/48.
- The severity of crises is larger when pre-crisis leverage is higher, suggesting that tax policy could have effects both on incidence and severity of financial stress. E.P. Davis, M. Stone, (2004), Corporate Structure and Financial Stability. IMF Working Paper Nr. WP/04/124.

[58] See R. Rajan, (2005), Has Financial Development Made the World Riskier? Proceedings of the Federal Reserve Bank of Kansas City Economics Symposium: 313–369. This was followed by a string of research, each taking their own angle to the problem: J. Coval, et al., (2009), The Economics of Structured Finance, *Journal of Economic Perspectives* Vol. 23, Issue 1, pp. 3–25; A. Ashcraft et al., (2011), Credit Ratings and Security Prices in the Subprime MBS Market. American Economic Review Vol. 101, Issue 3, pp. 115–119; N. Gennaioli, (2012), Neglected Risks, Financial Innovation, and Financial Fragility, *Journal of Financial Economics* Vol. 104, Issue 3, pp. 452–468; N. Gennaioli, et al. (2013), A Model of Shadow Banking, *Journal of Finance* Vol. 68, Issue 4, pp. 1331–1363. The latter models a world where investors systematically ignore the worst state of the world, generating overinvestment and overpricing during the boom and excessive collapse of real activity and the financial sector during the bust. T.V. Dang, (2009), Opacity and the Optimality of Debt for Liquidity Provision, Yale/MIT Working Paper. Their theory is one of information opacity that can serve as a rationalization of excessive risk taking in the shadow banking system. According to this theory, debt contracts are optimal because they generate opacity. Opacity, in turn, minimizes adverse selection and provides the least possible incentives to collect information. This insight justifies the growth of relatively opaque securitized products in the run-up to the crisis. Relatively little information about the underlying credit quality of these products was known (Adrian, (2014), Ibid. p. 5). They also exacerbate systemic risk once information flows through opaque debt-funded economies.

[59] See in detail: A.B. Ashcraft et al., (2008), Understanding the Securitization of Subprime Mortgage Credit, Foundations and Trends in Finance Vol. 2, Issue 3, pp. 191–209.

[60] B. Keys et al., (2010), Did Securitization Lead to Lax Screening? Evidence from Subprime Loans, Quarterly *Journal of Financial Economics* Vol. 125, Issue 1, pp. 307–362.

[61] A. Cohen (2011), Rating shopping in the CMBS market. Presented at Regulation of Systemic Risk, Washington, DC, Sep. 15–16; J. Mathis et al., (2009), Rating the Raters: are Reputation Concerns Powerful Enough to Discipline Rating Agencies? *Journal of Monetary Economics* Vol. 57, Issue 5, pp. 657–674. The authors' model predicts that a rating agency is likely to issue less accurate ratings in boom times than it would during recessionary periods. H. Xia and G. Strobl, (2012), The Issuer-Pays Rating Model and Ratings Inflation: Evidence from Corporate Credit Ratings, Working Paper.

6. Private money creation: Just like central banks and commercial banks (checking and savings accounts), the shadow banking industry can create additional money supply. That money creation occurs primarily in the commercial paper market and the repo market and is funded by money market funds and short-term investment funds.[62] It has the potential to act as a substitute for central banking money.[63]
7. Short-term funding and the risk of 'runs': Funding sources for shadow banking activities are unsecured and uninsured and therefore fragile in time of stress. Before the government provided backstops to the traditional banking sector they run—ability of liabilities also created often runs on banks with devastating effects.[64] Adrian puts it straight out when indicating that '[s]hadow banks are subject to runs because assets have longer maturities than liabilities and tend to be less liquid as well. While the fundamental reason for commercial bank runs is the sequential servicing constraint, for shadow banks the effective constraint is the presence of fire sale externalities. In a run, shadow banking entities have to sell assets at a discount, which depresses market pricing'…'shadow bank entities do not offer demand deposits, but instead obtain funding in wholesale money markets such as commercial paper or repo'.[65]
8. These activities can either categorize as market-based credit intermediation with specialized financial institutions and/or are regulatory arbitrage responses to particular regulations and/or others are outcomes of market failures.[66] As argued in a number of different chapters, the shadow banking system as such is characterized by a lack of public backstop and the fact that there is always a need for a backstop as the activities always remain exposed to residual tail risk and will be left behind in the system. This, in turn, can create externalities that have the potential to severely impact other areas of the financial infrastructure (systemic distress). Any policy or regulatory response would logically be built around the ambition to correct market failures, government failures and other types of distortions. Adrian reflects[67] on the different policy options vis-à-vis the aforementioned economics characterizing the sector of which a structured summary can be found hereafter.

---

[62] Adrian, (2014), Ibid. p. 6.

[63] A. Sunderam, (2012), Money Creation and the Shadow Banking System, Harvard Business School Working Paper & Review of Financial Studies.

[64] D. Diamond et al., (1983), Bank Runs, Deposit Insurance, and Liquidity. *Journal of Political Economy* Vol. 91, pp. 401–419.

[65] Adrian, (2014), Ibid. p. 6. See in detail: A. Martin et al., (2011), Repo Runs. Federal Reserve Bank of New York Staff Report, Nr. 444 (repo borrowers face constraints due to the scarcity of collateral and the liquidity of collateral). T. Adrian et al., (2013), Repo and Securities Lending, Quantifying Systemic Risk Measurement: NBER Research Conference Report Series, (ed.) J.G. Haubrichet al., University of Chicago Press, Chicago—for a review of the differences between the tri-party repo market and the bilateral repo market.

[66] Adrian, (2014), Ibid. p. 7.

[67] Adrian, (2014), Ibid. pp. 7–11.

Adrian indicates correctly that shadow banking will evolve due to regulatory changes and market conditions, which will require adaptation going forward requiring new policy approaches for new types of shadow banking activities. Adrian illustrates through three case studies the need for highly chirurgical policy design when tackling shadow banking risks. Too broad-brush will destroy market activities and value creation.[68] Policy design has to undeniably start with the question which economic mechanism motivates the particular activity. A highly fragmented regulatory system is and will be playing up going forward. A major step forward is the designation of non-bank financial institutions as systemically important (see designated chapter). That and other rules to come will invariably have to take a macroprudential system-wide view toward what types of oversight and regulation will make most sense given the tight interconnections and potentially powerful spillovers among shadow banking entities, and between shadow banks and core regulated financial institutions.[69]

Adrian[70] illustrates further the dynamics between economics of activities and transaction versus embedded and risks and the policy dynamics which completes the dynamic triangle of elements that constantly interact.

[68] Policies cover areas as diverse as capital regulation, wholesale money market funding, insurance company structure, disclosure policies, underwriting standards, among many others, (Adrian, (2014), Ibid. p. 20.). Run and funding risks emanating from the tri-party repo market and the money market fund sector remain current, while risks from ABCP conduits, SIVs and CDOs have receded, in part due to regulatory and accounting changes.

[69] Adrian, (2014), Ibid. p. 20.

[70] Adrian, (2014), Ibid. pp. 12–20.

8

From Policy to Regulation

8.1 The Different Policy Layers

Although the term shadow banking was coined only in 2007, the different ingredients of the shadow banking sector have been on the radar and reviewed by academia and policy long before. It was an integrated part of their analysis regarding the financialization of the economy prior since the 1990s and the geopolitical dynamics that occurred as a consequence of the globalization of society and the economy and the trade implications, capital flow dynamics and so on that were the consequences of that phenomenon. Three layers can be identified in this context.

The first layer of literature highlighted the changes in the structure and role of banking, the emergence of different banking models and their fragile nodes and interconnections between these banking universes. The conclusion was that the enhanced sensitivity required more granular data, more refined regulatory maps and the necessity for more oversight by regulatory bodies. Or as Nesvetailova argued, that phase '[b]y giving the problem a name and by presenting it as a sum of activities that constitute a system of credit intermediation, researchers argued that the Shadow banking phenomena leads to questioning the orthodox views on banking and finance, and the relationship between finance and banking, and economy and society.'[1]

The second phase asked the question why? Can we explain this and what are the origins of the problem? It was at that stage that the concept of regulatory arbitrage became center stage. Regulatory arbitrage was the result of strategies and tactics that used legal and financial engineering in a context of geographic and judicial relocation. Within that framework it was also considered that existing financial regulation did not serve the purpose for which it was designed and as such contributed to the emergence of the shadow

[1] A. Nesvetailova, (2014), Shadow Banking in Academic and Policy Debate, Presentation Brussels, January 24, p. 12.

L. Nijs, *The Handbook of Global Shadow Banking, Volume I*,
https://doi.org/10.1007/978-3-030-34743-7_8

banking segment. The rest was driven by the innovative drive of the agents active in the financial sector which drove down barriers and rules ('regulatory capture'). The three functionalities that achieve regulatory arbitrage are 'maturity transformation', 'collateral mining' and 'liquidity transformation'. Now even if you can explain a parallel shadow banking sector and explain the fragility of the nodes with the regular banking sector, it doesn't help explain 'why' there is a differentiation between entities and transactions, that although having the same economic substance is treated differently by regulation, most notably financial and tax regulation. Why is the system as large as it is, why has it so many obscure corners and different dynamics?

The third wave of literature looked exactly into those questions and poses the question about the structural limit of finance, and how we are going to deal with a system where the demand for financial assets outstrips the supply of capital. Most reasonably it can be understood as that the financial system has reached its natural limits of growth and is now looking to grow beyond those natural limits. Financial innovation of all sorts is instrumental in achieving that.

It is therefore fair to conclude with Nesvetailova[2] that shadow banking as such deserves attention beyond the 2008 financial crisis. It requires an analysis that involves why there is a need for financial innovation, regulatory arbitrage and the likes where the answer is most likely that profit- and rent-seeking cannot be the only arguments in the mix.

It is therefore all the more surprising that the international regulators, supervisors and more recently the EU within the framework of the development of Capital Markets Union allowed securitization to emerge as a tool to revive capital markets activities and kickstart bank lending. It was discussed elsewhere why that thought is based on the wrong premises and how it ignores reality both pre and post the 2008 financial crisis. It is therefore to be expected that the revival of the securitization market in Europe will do exactly nothing to generate robust and sustainable economic growth in the region. It is all the more surprising as those international regulators and supervisors have moved their positions from 'containing the shadow banking system' post-2008 to creating a resilience market-based financial system.[3]

Solving the implications of a wrongly assessed economic policy dynamic (i.e. austerity) with a questionable model that has all the odds staked against it, it is truly surprising which stories have been manufactured to explain the dismal economic performance of Europe compared to other regions of the world. It is manifestly clear that European banks just like other over time have become materially dependent on their shadow banking activities to regain and maintain profitability. The direct effect of the interventionist measures post-crisis of most governments prevented worse things from happening but also neutralized the electoral pressure for more decisive reforms and actions.[4] The broader

---

[2] A. Nesvetailova, (2014), Shadow Banking in Academic and Policy Debate, Presentation Brussels, January 24, p. 19.

[3] See for a chronological overview of that happening: M.B. Aalbers and E. Engelen, (2015), The Political Economy of the Rise, Fall, and Rise again of Securitization, Environment and Planning, Vol. 47, pp. 1597–1600.

[4] See B. Eichengreen, (2014), Hall of Mirrors: The Great Depression, The Great Recession, and the Uses-and Misuses-of History, Oxford University Press, Oxford.

argumentation seems to be grounded in the effects of mass-financialization. A growing strand of literature explains the inability for real change in this respect to the politics supporting mass-financialization and all the aspects it yielded over time. It has created a situation where financial interests have become self-perpetuating.[5] And there is more: quantitate easing in itself is designed to subsidize the funding costs of governments; however given mass-financialization it has become the ultimate tool to ensure the debt sustainability of investors, banks and mortgages who are mutually linked through the securitization chain.[6]

Walks and Clifford see things in a historical and broader perspective when commenting on the effect of mass-financialization in a situation and environment of uneven financialized capitalist development. They comment: '[n]eoliberalization and financialization have become mutually reinforcing, locking out alternative policy frameworks and creating vested interests opposed to reform of the system. With the federal state and key state institutions as core "bricoleurs" in this system, we understand neoliberalization and financialization in the Canadian context as reflecting a particular, state-centered, form of bricolage.'[7]

Nevertheless, the train seems to have left the station. Even in its most recent communication on the matter, the Financial Stability Board (FSB) is powering along the lines of turning shadow banking into an alternative market-based financial model. Given the fact that also the IOSCO identified risks related to using market-based financing systems, particularly in the field of market liquidity. Also, the previously discussed 'report' involving asset managers was included into the assessment. The overall scoping of the remaining efforts, according to the FSB, should embody addressing the following issues: '(1) mismatch between liquidity of fund investments and redemption terms and conditions for fund units; (2) leverage within investment funds; (3) operational risk and challenges in transferring investment mandates in a stressed condition; (4) securities lending activities of asset managers and funds; and (5) potential vulnerabilities of pension funds and sovereign wealth funds'.[8]

Market liquidity concerns are the keyword here. As Cunliffe indicated recently '[b]ut while we are advanced in the implementation in the UK of a much stronger regulatory framework, and while UK banks already have much greater resilience, we have not abolished the credit cycle. We have I hope, turned off or dampened some of the more damaging amplifying mechanisms in the financial system that drive up risks and create booms and drive the economy down in the resulting bust. We can test how the system is likely

[5] H. Callagha, (2015), Who Cares about Financialization? Self-Reinforcing Feedback, Issue Saliency and Increasing Acquiescence to Market-Enabling Takeover Rules, *Socio-Economic Review*, Vol. 13, pp. 331–350.

[6] Aalbers and Engelen, Ibid. p. 1602 and D. Bryan and M. Rafferty, (2015), Austerity: The New Army of Savers, p. 37, mimeo.

[7] A. Walks and B. Clifford, (2015), The Political Economy of Mortgage Securitization and the Neoliberalization of Housing Policy in Canada, Environment and Planning A, Vol. 47, Issue 8, pp. 1624–1642.

[8] FSB, (2015), To G20 Finance Ministers and Central Bank Governors. Financial Reforms- Progress on the Work Plan for the Antalya Summit, London, p. 4.

to behave under stress.'[9] Following that he comments on the market liquidity[10] issue in market-based financial systems: '[m]arket liquidity is in itself a very good thing. It allows investors to transact at a reasonable size at or close to prices prevailing in the market prior to the trade. It contributes to markets that are "effective" – by which I mean both fair and resilient. Liquid markets play an important role in the financing of investment in the real economy'...'So if market liquidity is a very good thing, can you ever have too much of a good thing? Surely any reduction in market liquidity is unwelcome. This question is very pertinent today as it is clear that market liquidity in the system is more fragile, not just in particular market sectors, but also across the system as a whole. Dealers are holding less inventory'...'How much should we worry about that? If liquidity is always a good thing, how far can we and should we seek to restore liquidity to levels seen before the crisis? This is a question that is increasingly asked of prudential regulators.'[11]

Liquidity will always come at a cost and liquidity will also be a function of the characteristics of the different assets (tail-risk assets, buy-and-hold, opaque structure or term products, information (in)sensitive products, etc.) available in the market. But there are some general rules of thumb Cunliffe argues '[f]irst, funding and monetary liquidity can exacerbate the illusion of market liquidity. The exceptionally accommodative monetary policy seen internationally, which has intentionally increased the amount of cash available for the purchase of risky assets, may have masked the underlying liquidity risk characteristics in a number of markets'...'Second, financial intermediaries and financial engineering can make a very important contribution to liquidity – but they cannot turn lead into gold. The underlying risk characteristics of an asset cannot be changed. They can be separated out, combined with other risks, repackaged. And that is important. Because although the liquidity risks generated by the underlying characteristics of an asset cannot be changed, they can be structured to enable the risk to be held by those most able to bear it. This doesn't change the underlying risks but it does change the impact if they crystallise'...'However, if the effect of financial intermediation and financial engineering to increase liquidity is not to distribute liquidity risk to those most willing and able to bear it but rather to obscure it, then it contributes only to the illusion of liquidity that can evaporate very quickly and painfully.'[12]

In order to avoid illusions, regulatory changes should be coherent and deal with the underpricing of liquidity risk. Changes in market structure and the ability of technology to connect buyers and sellers may increase liquidity. However, Cunliffe comments 'It remains for me, however, an open question whether such liquidity would be resilient in times of

[9] J. Cunliffe, (2015), Market Liquidity and Market-Based Financing, Speech by Sir Jon Cunliffe, Deputy Governor for Financial Stability of the Bank of England, at the British Bankers Association International Banking Conference, London, October 22, 2015, p. 2.

[10] For the sake of accuracy, he details that '[t]here are three concepts of liquidity. Monetary liquidity; funding liquidity; and market or asset liquidity. Monetary liquidity captures the looseness of monetary conditions – it is underpinned by the stance of the monetary policy authority. Funding liquidity is the ease with which banks and other non-bank financial intermediaries can raise funding. And market liquidity refers to the ease with which one asset can be traded for another. All three concepts are tightly related.' J. Cunliffe, (2015), Ibid. p. 3.

[11] J. Cunliffe, (2015), Ibid. pp. 3–4.

[12] J. Cunliffe, (2015), Ibid. pp. 4–5.

stress. Automated markets may have driven down costs, but are possibly less resilient. Dealer-intermediated markets, on the other hand, may have become more costly, but possibly more resilient.'…'It is, however, important to look not only at how to improve the resilience of markets to imbalances between sellers and buyers at times of stress. We need also to look at whether and how the features of financial markets can amplify these imbalances by creating selling pressure.'[13]

This all has particular implications against the background of a continuous struggle to determine the size of the shadow banking system globally and in the respective countries given the diverse nature and setting of individual shadow banking systems. Given the limitations and despite the improvements implemented in measuring shadow banking segments and systems overall, many aspects stay unclear. Also the distribution of assets and asset sizes, which traditionally follows a Pareto distribution, is characterized by a sharp cutoff in the upper tail which we know is characterized by a domination of financial firms. Faschi et al. comment 'Pareto distributions are generally traced back to a mechanism of proportional random growth, based on a regime of constant returns to scale: this makes our evidence of an "interrupted" Pareto distribution all the more puzzling, because we provide evidence that financial firms in our sample operate in such a regime. We claim that the missing mass from the upper tail of the asset size distribution is a consequence of shadow banking activity and that it provides an estimate of the size of the shadow banking system.'[14]

8.2 Economics and Policy of Shadow Banking: Is Puzzling the Pieces Together the Right Macroprudential Approach

It has been observed before. The main regulatory and supervisory responses post-crisis have been dealing with issues in a sectional and fragmented way. That is, it has been breaking down the individual issues that contributed to unleashing the 2008 crisis and then has been dealing with it on an individual basis. The content and quality of those responses have been discussed and one can conclude that the conclusions there are at best 'mixed'. Separate legislation has been put in place for money market funds (often in different layers), securitization, collateral intermediation, repos, OTC derivatives and so on. As a top layer, attention has been given to regulatory arbitrage, tax avoidance and other topics affecting the functioning of the shadow banking market. Although the regulatory work on shadow banking is a 'work in progress', it can be re-iterated here that more policy-oriented research will be needed which will help to focus on macroprudential oversight and supervision.[15]

---

[13] J. Cunliffe, (2015), Ibid. pp. 5–6.

[14] D. Fiaschi et al., (2015), The Interrupted Power Law and the Size of Shadow banking, Working Paper, Mimeo.

[15] S. Claessens et al., (2012), Shadow banking: Economics and Policy, IMF Staff Discussion Note SDN/12/12, December 4, Washington DC, p. 29.

But it should be clear as well that some of the groundwork already in place is questionable in nature. Also the fact that the interwovenness between ex ante and ex post regulation is unclear to say the least. To make the matter worse, it needs to be stated clearly that most regulation enacted post-crisis has some way or the other reduced the propensity or probability of the individual shadow banking sectors to contribute to any future crisis. However, as we all know from statistics, the Darwinian evolutionary theory provides a near-zero likelihood that something like a Platypus exists, still it does, just like Richard Dawkins ranks it highly unrealistic that any sort of Deity exists based on the same probability theory. The problem with low or near-zero probability doesn't matter if nevertheless that small probability becomes reality later on. Just like it doesn't matter than only 10% of men are at risk of been diagnosed with breast cancer, it doesn't really matter, if at some point in time you will.

Therefore we have created a false illusion, and now I'm not even rehashing the analysis that some new pieces of legislation clearly leave room for contagion risk to creep back in through the backdoor of our financial system. Regulation is and will always be imperfect but we have left too many opportunities untapped to make a real difference. That is all the more true realizing how financial services have become stretched over long chains of activities that, although each allocated to individual players, are sheltered under the roof of large financial conglomerates. Lobbying has clearly been worthwhile in this respect.[16] Where it lacks visibility is the analysis of how a system with very troubled (or even non-existing) demarcation lines should be regulated. Many attempts have been made to create some visibility of the flow of funds to and from the individual shadow banking segments[17] to at least create a minimal level of understanding that unisolo segmented regulation will not suffice and that of it will be stillborn in terms of the expected improvements they are expected to generate.[18] Tucker already highlighted in 2012 that (1) shadow banking is not the same as the non-bank financial sector, (2) non-bank intermediation of credit doesn't do any harm in itself and (3) '[s]hadow banking comes in lots of shapes and colours. There are degrees to which any particular instance of shadow banking replicates banking. The liquidity offered by some shadow banks relies pretty well entirely, and more or less openly, on committed lines of credit from commercial banks. In these cases, the liquidity insurance offered by the shadow bank is "derivative"; there is a real bank in the shadows. But for other shadow banks, liquidity services are offered without such back-up lines. In those cases, claims on the shadow bank have, in effect, become a monetary asset.'[19]

[16] See, for example, for the inclusion (or not) of leasing activities in the FSB definition of shadow banking and the response from the leasing industry: LeaseEurope Inside, (2013), Leasing Not a Shadow Banking Activity, Issue Nr. 19, Winter pp. 1–2. I do refrain from the quality of the arguments both ways in this context.

[17] See for an analysis to/from the US shadow banking system: L. Errico et al., (2014), Mapping the Shadow Banking System Through a Global Flow of Funds Analysis, IMF Working Paper, WP/14/10, January, Washington D.C.

[18] See also R. Jovovic and N. Jovovic, (2013), Understanding Shadow banking and its Role in the Recent Financial Crisis, Working Paper, February 24, mimeo.

[19] P. Tucker, (2012), Shadow Banking: Thoughts for a Possible Policy Agenda, Speech given by Paul Tucker, Deputy Governor Financial Stability, Member of the Monetary Policy Committee and Member of the Financial Policy Committee, p. 2.

That links us directly back to a problem already discussed, that is, that of the scope and magnitude of a public safety net for shadow banking entities and activities. Despite the scholarly attention, there have been no instrumental direct or indirect attempts made from a regulatory point of view (leaving the general banking resolution regulation aside) to reduce the reliance on the publicly subsidized safety net. The initial limits of that safety net were that it was available to commercial banks who at the time of the design of that safety net were fueling the real economy. That is no longer the case for commercial banks as a big chunk of their asset is allocated to financial rather than real assets and mortgages. And if that is true for commercial banks then that is all the truer for shadow banking entities. So while the safety net solved the instability issues it has created, it has triggered, besides deficits in public budgets, enormous agency and moral hazard effects. The recommendation should therefore be to limit the safety net—and thus its subsidy—to what the safety net should protect by restricting banking organization activities by business line. Or as Hoenig and Morris indicate '[c]urrent activities conducted by banks that would be prohibited for them, such as trading and market making, are important to the economy. But they should not be subsidized by the safety net because it causes their overproduction, and therefore imposes unnecessary risks and costs on the financial system and economy. In fact, by removing the safety-net's protection for activities such as securities and derivatives market-making, the market for these services should become more competitive and less dominated by the largest investment banks, which currently are all affiliated with commercial banks.'[20]

8.3 The Ongoing Assumption of Safe Assets

Without getting philosophical, Gorton et al. calculated that the amount of safe assets[21] has stayed pretty much stable since the middle of the last century (at around one-third). The stability is remarkable amidst a rapidly evolving financial and economic reality. The ratio of US assets to GDP has increased by a factor of 2.5, and the main supplier of safe financial debt has shifted from commercial banks to the 'shadow banking system'.[22] It is therefore all the more surprising, the authors conclude, that we know so little about the demand and supply of safe debt except for the fact that the demand outstrips the supply for over two decades now.[23]

---

[20] T.M. Hoenig and C.S. Morris, Restructuring the Banking System to Improve Safety and Soundness, Working paper, mimeo, pp. 2, 3–5, 20–29 (also published in 2013 in The Social Value of the Financial Sector, Too Big to fail or Just too Big, Eds. V.V. Acharya, T. Beck, D.D. Evanoff, G.G. Kaufman ad R. Portes, World Scientific Studies in International Economics Vol. 29, pp. 401–425).

[21] 'Safe assets' is a catch-all term to describe such contracts, which may include government debt, bank deposits, AAA-rated corporate debt and asset-backed securities, among others. The International Monetary Fund estimated potential safe assets at more than $114 trillion worldwide in 2011, more than seven times the US economic output that year.

[22] G. Gorton, et al., (2012), The Safe-Asset Share, *American Economic Review: Papers & Proceedings* 2012, Vol. 102, Issue 3, pp. 101–106.

[23] Also the question why the supply of safe assets to GDP has stayed constant stays largely unexplained. We do know however from analysis that the demand for safe assets has been one of the drivers behind the emergence of the shadow banking sector.

Small policy adjustments can drive more activity and thus production of safe assets from the banking to the shadow banking segment.

That requires an even better understanding of the legal infrastructure in which safe assets are produced and the limitations of the 'safe asset' concept, that is, they are only safe because state intervention supplies the essential infrastructure to let people act as if some contracts were risk-free. The law constructs and maintains safe asset fictions and places them at the foundation of institutions and markets. This project is unavoidably distributive, political and fraught with distortions.[24] But we need to keep to continuous awareness that we are using legal fictions here when labeling assets as 'safe'. There is a constant threat of misuse, composition and contagion, or as Gelpern and Gerding indicate '[s]afe assets are especially prone to mismatches among their risk attributes, their regulatory treatment, and the ways in which they are used in the financial markets. Mismatches follow from safe assets' fictional character; they can come about in multiple ways and cause serious damage. First, safe assets breed new risks when market participants adapt them to different uses and combine them in structures far removed from the original purpose for which they had been made safe. Second, making, labeling, and guarantees can become dramatically misaligned. The misalignment, amplified by the credit cycle and exploited by public and private actors, contributes to financial instability. Third, public and private actors use the safety toolkit, especially labeling, to redistribute resources on a large scale in nontransparent and unaccountable ways.'[25]

Any potential response to misalignment must begin with identifying contracts used as if they were risk-free for monitoring throughout the cycle, as the US did, for example, when redesigning the tri-party repo market. That data gathering would include an assessment of who is using them and for what purpose or purposes. Further, the implicit safe asset functions of public intervention tools should be monitored for compatibility with their stated policy functions. But the most important post-crisis feature would be as Gelpern and Gerding indicate 'labels are the most troublesome category of tools supporting safe assets. They can be innocuous enough when aligned with the risk attributes of a contract, or with appropriately priced guarantees; however, in practice, they encourage governments and market participants to take hidden risks and shift the consequences onto others'…'regulators' understandable affinity for simple, discontinuous labels to promote coordination virtually ensures misalignment. Public labels come with the additional cost of muting price signals and pre-empting market-based information discovery. Since they not only describe low risk, but also enable and encourage market participants to buy

[24] See for an excellent review of the 'safe asset' infrastructure, conditionalities and post-crisis reflections: A. Gelpern and E.F. Gerding, (2015), Inside Safe Assets, Georgetown law School Working Paper, draft, September 2. They further highlight sources of instability and distortion in the legal architecture, and the political commitments embedded in it (pp. 38–44). See also R. Portes, (2013), The Safe Asset meme, Presentation, October 8; C. Bertaut et al., (2013), The Replacement of Safe Assets: Evidence from the U.S. Bond Portfolio, Working paper, Mimeo; P.-O. Gourinchas and O. Jeanne, (2012), Global Safe Assets, Paper prepared for the XI BIS Annual Conference held in Lucerne, June 20–21; IMF, (2012), Global Financial Stability Report, Chapter 3: Safe Assets: Financial System Cornerstone, pp. 81–122; G. Gorton and G. Ordoñez, (2013), The Supply and Demand of Safe Assets, Working paper, August, Mimeo.

[25] A. Gelpern and E.F. Gerding, (2015), Ibid. pp. 39–40.

and sell, public labels can introduce distortions and discontinuities on the ground, and with them, potential for instability. Public labels can be justified if market mechanisms fail, but not if the state does no better.'[26] That conclusion becomes all the more problematic realizing and remembering our conclusion that safe assets are in high demand and relatively short supply.

A safe asset's real value is insulated from shocks, but accounting for the aggregate risks the real quantity of safe asset produced is effectively nil.[27] How's that as a conclusion? Safe assets are therefore instrumental for liquidity management in our financial system but only as long as liquidity mismatch doesn't matter.[28] But the absolute shortage of safe assets is problematic as it is the fundament for many other (non-risk-free) transactions to occur. Some are even willing to go that far as to point at a direct correlation between the shortage of safe assets and the sluggish investment recovery and claim that the shortage of safe assets will remain a structural drag on the economy, undermining financial stability and straining monetary policy during contractions.[29]

The role of safe assets[30] for banks is clear. They act as a safety multiplier which also explains why they hold so much safe assets on their books. Weymuller indicates in this respect, 'risk-neutral banks issue debt securities to cater to the safety demand of risk-averse investors. Private safety creation requires banks[31] to hold on their balance sheets government bonds, whose returns are negatively correlated with macroeconomic shocks. When heterogeneity in risk aversion is large enough, there is a safety multiplier in the sense that lowering the supply of public debt induces banks to delever, hurting private debt supply.'[32] The economy lacks long-term securities is the conclusion, as

[26] Ibid. p. 49.

[27] R.J. Barro an A. Mollerus, (2014), Safe Assets, NBER Working Paper Nr. 20652, October.

[28] M. Brunnermeyer and V. Haddad, (2014), Safe Assets, NYFed Research Paper, October 17. The fact that during the last two decades safe US assets have been in high demand by foreign buyers only aggravates the situation, see J. Vavilukis et al., (2014), Foreign Ownership of U.S. Safe Assets,: Good or Bad?, Working Paper, mimeo, September 8.

[29] See R.J. Caballero and E. Farhi, (2015), On the Role of Safe Asset Shortages in Secular Stagnation, in Secular Stagnation: Facts, Causes and Cures (eds. C. Teuings and R. Baldwin), CEPR Press, London, pp. 111–121.

[30] See for a recent overview of literature on the matter: P. Golec and E. Perotti, Safe Asset Demand: A Review, Risk and Macro Finance Working Paper Series Nr. 2015-02, University of Amsterdam.

[31] It also has negative implications for capital structures at banks; see W. Gornall, (2015), Safe Assets and Dangerous Liabilities: How Bank-Level Frictions Explain Bank Seniority, University of British Columbia, Working Paper, Mimeo; see also in this respect: M. Elamin and T. Ahnert, (2014), The Effect of Safe Assets on Financial Fragility in a Bank-Run Model, FRB of Cleveland Working Paper No. 14–37, and D. Bleich and A. Dombret, (2015), Financial System Leverage and the Shortage of Safe Assets: Exploring the Policy Options, *German Economic Review*, Vol. 16, issue 2, pp. 161–180, May.

[32] C.-H. Weymuller, (2013), Banks as Safety Multipliers: A Theory of Safe Asset Creation, Harvard University, Working Paper, mimeo. See also D. Andolfato and S. Williamson, (2015), Scarcity of Safe Assets, Inflation and the Policy Trap, Federal Reserve Bank of St. Louis, Working Paper, January 23 and the reporting: H.M. Ennis, (2015), Discussion on Scarcity of Safe Assets, Inflation and the Policy Trap by Andolfatto and Williamson, Federal Reserve of Richmond, Working Paper Nr. 15/03.

private agents do not internalize the benefits of the negative beta on their own liabilities, which makes them issue to much short-term debt and not sufficient long-term debt. Public debt is non-neutral but there is an interior optimal level of public securities, as their hedging properties deteriorate with their supply, Weymuler concludes.[33] However as a basic proposition it can be argued that public debt is used as an input to private debt issuance (i.e. the multiplier effect). Debt crises can be interpreted as shortages of public safe assets, and the supply of safe assets is welfare improving up till the point that the volume of safe assets would flood the economy to such a degree that its hedging properties would be weakened. But sovereign risk would weaken the hedging properties of public debt and therefore constrains private sector debt. This can be used for QE advocates as an argument that unconventional monetary policies are welfare improving. The spread between public debt and private debt can be used as a financial stability indicator to reveal the extent of the safety multiplier from a macroprudential point of view. However, the pseudo-safe assets created by the (shadow) banking sector perform as a shock multiplier and contagion accelerator during distress and causes recession and deflation.[34] Expanding the central bank's balance sheet, under those circumstances, fills the shortage of safe assets and counteracts the recession. Lowering the interest rate on reserves insulates market interest rates from the liquidity shock and improves risk sharing between borrowers and savers.

But the risk then will become that safe assets are used as commodity money and a medium of exchange for risky assets and therefore disturb liquidity management, lead to continuous overproduction and distort welfare optimization.[35]

8.4 The History of Shadow Banking

Although the recent history starts in 2007 with Paul McCulley[36] defining shadow banking as 'levered-up-financial intermediaries with liabilities perceived akin to bank deposits ('the whole alphabet soup')' and also 'a large segment of financial intermediation that is routed outside the balance sheets of regulated commercial banks and other depositary institutions', the history of shadow banking goes way further back than 2007. The concept of credit intermediation involving lightly regulated entities and activities outside the traditional banking system is not new, especially not in Europe. Many innovations

---

[33] He also concludes 'as for asset pricing, the spread between public debt yield and private debt yield reveals bank leverage and can be used as a macro-prudential tool. In an open economy environment, sovereign risk hurts aggregate private leverage but domestic banks become the natural holders of domestic public debt.'

[34] P. Benigno and S. Nisticò, (2013), Safe Assets, Liquidity and Monetary Policy, Working paper, mimeo.

[35] See, for example, B.S. Kay and M. Eden, (2015), Safe Assets as Commodity Money, Working paper, Mimeo, October 8.

[36] P.A. McCulley, (2007), Teton Reflections, Global Central Bank Focus Series, PIMCO, August/September, pp. 1–4. See also B.J. Noeth, and S. Rajdeep, (2011), Is Shadow Banking Really Banking? The Regional Economist October, pp. 8–13.

developed in the past were adopted by European nations and exported to the rest of the world. And also back then these European innovations unleashed a number of financial crises in which shadowy financial intermediators played a central role. A good example of that is the 'Gebroeders (Brothers) de Neufville Crisis of 1763'[37] who were based in Amsterdam (see Table 8.1). Throughout history European states have faced many innovations through a process of adoption and regulation.

A historical difference is that shadow banking in history did not only relate to the functions of credit intermediation and maturity transformation but also the creation of assets and novel ways to exchange assets or their counter value. A proper understanding and definition of shadow banking is key not only to define what needs to be regulated and supervised and to what degree (and what not), but it is also an ideal position to be in when anticipating which way shadow banking as a segment of market-based finance will go. A lack of consensus regarding the definition will hamper regulatory efforts regarding shadow banking but also issues as (private) money creation and the impact it has on the vulnerability of monetary and economic systems developed in an era in which globalization hardly existed. It has been argued that this was the consequence of the 'European world system', which Wallerstein[38] came to define as 'a social system that has boundaries, structures, member groups, rules of legitimation, and coherence'. It implies conflicting forces held together 'tension and tear' and where each member tries to escape that gravity through what we would call these days 'competitive advantage', that is, specialization and innovation. In the case of European that included 'a power hierarchy between core states and peripheral states that are differentiated on a series of dimensions, such as the complexity of economic activities, strength of the state machinery, cultural integrity, etc.'.[39]

These innovations and chain of specialization can be traced back as being the starting point as what ended in the Lehman Brothers debacle or the system-wide crisis if you want.[40] These innovations all related to the 'private money creating aspect' of our monetary

[37] I. C. Laczano, (2013), The Historical Role of the European Shadow Banking System in the Development and Evolution of our Monetary Institutions, Cityperc Working Paper Series, Nr. 2013/5, pp. 7–8. The other is the Gurney Panic of 1866, see pp. 7–8.

[38] I. Wallerstein, (1976), The Modern World-System. Capitalist Agriculture and the European World-Economy in the Sixteenth Century, Academic Press New York, NY, pp. 229–230.

[39] Laczano, (2013), Ibid. p. 3.

[40] See (1) S. Quinn and W. Roberds, (2012), Responding to a Shadow Banking Crisis: The Lessons of 1763. Federal Reserve Bank of Atlanta. Working Paper Series Nr. 8, and (2) M. Frandreu and S. Ugolini, (2011), Where It All Began: Lending of Last Resort and the Bank of England During the Overend, Gurney Panic of 1866. EHES Working Papers in Economic History Nr. 7. Quinn and Roberds demonstrate that 'the 1763 crisis was manifested in a loss of liquidity of acceptance loans, a form of securitized credit resembling modern asset-backed commercial paper. The crisis began with the failure of a major securitizer ("conduit") in Amsterdam, and quickly spread to neighboring markets. The central bank at the hub of the crisis, the Bank of Amsterdam, responded by broadening the range of acceptable collateral for its repo transactions'. Using archival data on the Bank's operations, they show (1) that the 1763 crisis was proportionately more severe than that experienced in 2008, (2) the Bank's emergency liquidity infusion likely prevented the failure of two other major securitizers and provided indirect benefits to other market participants. While the underlying themes seem to have changed little in 250 years, the modest scope of the 1763 liquidity intervention, together with the lightly regulated nature of the eighteenth-century financial landscape, provided some informative contrasts with events of late 2008.

Table 8.1 The history of shadow banking

The Brother de Neufville Crisis of 1763	The Gurney Panic of 1866[a]
Financial activity was dominated by a group of banking institutions	Crisis started in the British money market
Main role was trading finance/bankers were often also merchants	Instrument of 'acceptance' was used a lot. Acceptances were bills that one merchant or banker had drawn on another merchant or banker
Merchants offered credit to their clients through commercial bills	Bill brokers (through which acceptances were bought) can be seen as a type of 'shadow bankers'
Deposit-taking was seen as risky and scarce	Over time, they expanded activities by investing in acceptances themselves with funding they obtained through call loans (immediately redeemable) from commercial banks
Financial intermediation occurred through securitization (acceptcrediet) which was based on the above-mentioned bill of exchange, that is, the lender was the drawee and the drawer the merchant investor.	The Gurney bank was one of them
These merchant bankers needed to have an account at the Amsterdamsche Wisselbank (solely acting as an exchange bank) and hold proper balance in Dutch Guilder through which the system of debit and direct transfers could be facilitated	During the 1850s the underwriting standards went materially down (due to new management) and expanded in many different activities with different risk profiles, often higher than the traditional intermediation function. It became a nineteenth-century version of a universal bank and converted into a limited liability company
The Seven Years' War led to an economic boom and credit expansion. That could only occur because of the mature legal infrastructure that allowed the ability to lend and commit	The failure of a number of companies which bills it had accepted and it had run for its own account
Gebroeders de Neufville was a lightly regulated banking institution which grew during the war into a large financial powerhouse with a wide set of interests	The stock market collapse of late 1865/early 1966 forced it to declare bankruptcy which caused a cascade of failures among small banks which lost their prime funding source
They engaged into a large and speculative deal buying grain from the Russian army leaving Poland at that time	To avoid further similar events, Walter Bagehot[c] redesigned the bank of England as 'lender of last resort' and allowed, at a cost to lend freely but at a penalty rate, to ailing banking institutions
During that transaction, the Treaty of Hubertusburg[b] was agreed which had large impact on the value of the grain which acted as collateral in this case. To make things worse, Prussia dropped its grain stock on the market leading to an even further decline in grain prices (total of 75%). They all anticipated that the end of the war would lead to a decrease of grain prices.	
The monetary debasement of the 'Reichsthaler' materially reduced the value of the collateral, which led to a flooding of new short-term bills drawn on the market	

It led to the failure of Aron Joseph and Compagnie and which brought down the 'Gebroeders de Neufville' What started as a local failure because a systemic crisis throughout Europe because of the interconnectedness created by the web of 'bill of exchange' between merchants across Europe (but predominantly in Amsterdam and Hamburg) The Amsterdamsche Wisselbank intervened with a liquidity flooding through the repo widow stabilizing the market and backstopping further failures	It was applied first during the Barings crisis of 1890. The principle was adopted in mainland Europe and caused financial market claim for almost half a decade

[a]See in detail: (1) H. Chubb, (1872), The Bank Act and the Crisis of 1866. *Journal of the Statistical Society of London*, Vol. 35, Issue 2, pp. 171–195, (2) N. Ferguson, (2008), The Ascent of Money. A Financial History of the World, The Penguin Press, New York, (3) J.-C. Rochet, (2008), Why Are There So Many Banking Crises? The Politics and Policy of Bank Regulation, Princeton University Press, Princeton, and (4) G. Wetterberg, (2009), Money and Power. From Stockholms Banco 1656 to Sveriges Riksbank todat, Sveriges Riksbank with Atlantis, Stockholm

[b]The Treaty of Hubertusburg (Vrede van Hubertusburg) in 1763 was an agreement between Prussia, the Archduchy of Austria and the Electorate of Saxony and which ended the Seven Years' War

[c]He made quite a name for himself and the 2008 crisis has revived his reputation, see (1) M. King, (2010), Banking – from Bagehot to Basel, and back again, Speech by Mr. M. King, Governor of the Bank of England, at the Second Bagehot Lecture, Buttonwood Gathering, New York, October 25, 2010, (2) R.G. Anderson, (2009), Bagehot on the Financial Crisis of 1825 and 2008, Economic Synopsis, Federal Reserve Bank of St. Louis, Vol. 7, pp. 1–2, (3) P. Mehrling et al., (2012), Bagehot was a Shadow Banker, Shadow Banking, Central Banking, and the Future of Global Finance, working Paper, (4) W.R. Cline and J.E. Gagnon, (2013), Lehman Died, Bagehot Lives: Why Did the Fed and Treasury Let a Major Wall Street Bank Fail?, Peterson Institute for International Economics, Policy Brief, September 2013, pp. 1–13, (5) V. Bignon et al., (2009), Bagehot for Beginners: The Making of Lending of Last Resort Operations in the Mid-nineteenth Century, Working Paper, Nr. 22. See for Bagehot's own thoughts: W. Bagehot, (1873), Lombard Street: A Description of the Money Market, Available at www.gutenberg.org

systems and its use as an easy way to exchange value. These 'mediums of exchange' were initially regulated by the merchants.[41] The bill of exchange was later on created as a way to secure the integrity of the physical coins. The bill of exchange is effectively an 'order to pay' which involved multiple parties of which the contemporary borrower and lender relation is the slimmed down version.[42] Effective monetary value was disconnected from its source and embodied in a simple piece of paper. The implications were enormous and had a large impact on society. Laczano reports '[t]his revolutionary innovation developed by private institutions resulted in the consolidation of the European world-paradigm. The invention of this fiction destroyed feudalism, changed the basis of organization from heredity to money, and it changed the basis of economic power from owning land to owning fictions like stocks, bonds and corporations.'[43] It was the starting point of a non-stop train of financial fictions to be created that led us all the way to 2008. Some scholars[44] are convinced that the following monetary 'train wreck' will derive from the digital monetary revolution, where money takes the role of information flows through computer networks,[45] particularly those that operate in an open nodal network (like Bitcoin, Ripple or Libra).

8.5 The Role of Regulation in the Birth and Emergence of Shadow Banking

8.5.1 Introduction

In literature, most discussions are dealing with the definition and functioning of the shadow banking system. A whole lot less attention has been given to the legal dynamics behind the emergence of the shadow banking system. Regulatory arbitrage is an often heard element in the policy mix but a more broadband analysis of that phenomenon and how it relates to deregulation and legal subsidies is lacking. However, the absence of an analysis of the legal implications and sources explaining the growth of the shadow banking sector will misguide policy actions and their bandwidth.[46]

---

[41] See for the wider historical dimensions of money creation and financial innovation which go as far back as 600 BC, Laczano, (2013), Ibid. pp. 4–5.

[42] See in detail: I. Schnabel and H.S. Shin, (2004), Liquidity Contagion: The Crisis of 1763, Max Planck Institute for Research on Collective Goods, Bonn, p. 8, published in the *Journal of the European Economic Association*, Vol. 2, Issue 6, pp. 929–968.

[43] Laczano, (2013), Ibid. p. 5. It also allowed nimble market players to increase leverage in buoyant financial markets and amass rapid gains at the expense of increased fragility of the system, see Schnabel and Shin, (2004), Ibid. p. 2.

[44] Laczano, (2013), Ibid. pp. 8–10; see also ECB, (2012), Virtual Currency Schemes, ECB Report, Frankfurt.

[45] P. Radovanović, Predrag, (2009), Digital Economy, Digital Money and Digital Banking. Economics and Organization, Vol. 6, Issue 2, pp. 153–160.

[46] See extensively on this topic: E.F. Gerding, (2013), Law, Bubbles and Financial Regulation, Routledge, London and New York, pp. 236–311.

8.5.2 Deregulation and Regulatory Arbitrage

Historically and in the wake of the Great Depression, financial institutions were tightly regulated. They, in general terms, avoided risk taking by banks and focused on customer protection. Until neoliberalism kicked during the late 1970s which triggered deregulation, the abandonment of the Bretton Woods system of fixed exchange rates. The floating exchange rates and volatility in prices led investors and managers to dive into the capital markets and look for investments that helped to make a profit and foremost manage risk.[47] That triggered in many countries the emergence of non-bank FIs which competed with the banks offering credit and investment products. It also fostered more cross-border capital controls and fueled the access of firms to enter foreign new markets. But the heavier movements in terms of inflation and interest rate volatility after the collapse of the Bretton Woods system, combined with higher competition in the banking sector, created a problem for the banks triggering a further deregulation by many regulators.

The new wave of investment products that stated coming in since the 1980s connected borrowers and investors and made them subject to the same market risk within the context of what can be considered still a 'traditional' banking context.[48]

Considering what is called shadow banking today, it is characterized by instruments that provide credit-based products to primarily institutional investors with the characteristics in terms of liquidity and security as bank deposits. It is further a transmission channel for monetary policy as it can create incremental amounts of money supply (private money) and channels monetary policy.[49] Credit and leverage have traditionally been the prime drivers behind the emergence of the shadow banking market.[50] Or to turn it around: the financial sector has created the shadow banking sector primarily to facilitate them borrowing funds, which they in their turn could use to invest (in the market). Leverage ultimately increases the return on equity as long as the return on capital employed is higher than the cost of that leverage. The best example of that is the repo market. The implications are that the incremental provisioning of credit has led to increased leverage through the new innovative products, the collateralization practices create implied leverage in economic terms and the fact that investors now invest in products that were already levered the moment they were bought, which were at that time all novel models of market making. The products and the liquidity of the created new 'credit' market allowed further for risk transfer and channeling to other parties in that market. It injected credit intermediation and maturity transformation in areas such as 'money-like' claims unwitnessed before.

---

[47] Tanya Beder, (2011), The History of Financial Engineering from Inception to Today, in Financial Engineering: the Evolution of a Profession, T. S. Beder & C. M. Marshall (eds.), Wiley & Sons, Hoboken, pp. 3–28.

[48] E. F. Gerding, (2009), Code, Crash, and Open Source: the Outsourcing of Financial Regulation to Risk Models and the Global Financial Crisis, *Washington Law Review*, Vol. 84, Issue 127, pp. 139–164.

[49] E. G. Corrigan, (1982), Are Banks Special?, in FED Reserve Bank of Minneapolis, Annual Report 1982.

[50] E.F. Gerding, (2013), Law, Bubbles and Financial Regulation, Routledge, London and New York, pp. 365–394.

Although all these instruments created have their own functionality and origin, they have over time been used together and have created new credit intermediation chains.[51] These products and channels however anticipated on a certain demand (discussed elsewhere) but also occurred within a certain legal context. To be precise, it can be argued that regulation was a driver behind the emergence and existence of these shadow banking instruments. The shadow banking industry was born out of regulatory arbitrage and thus born out of a need to avoid legal restrictions. In a tighter way 'regulatory arbitrage means when an individual or firm moves from an activity that is regulated to another activity that is functionally equivalent (or an economic substitute) but that is subject to lower regulation and lower legal cost'.[52] It comes down to exploiting legal differences in form while achieving the same economic output or result. It can take the form of 'structuring' or 'investment switching'. The former implies creating legal structures, the latter triggers moving capital to investments subject to other less stringent regulatory regimes. Undeniably, those two components influence each other in their functioning, that is, new structures and products create new capital flows.[53] Given the fact that the benefits in terms of a lower cost of capital easily outpower switching costs in particular when high volumes can be generated through new technologies, the inclination of private market players is high.

It is even higher in circumstances where the regulator allows private agents to move to swiftly and easily and avoid the effects of regulation through a wave of deregulation as experienced since the 1980s. The herding[54] in markets implies that financial institutions have an inclination to copy each other's models. Deregulation includes not only the repeal of laws but also adjustments that pre-empt regulatory action, more permissive interpretations of rules and decisions, a lower intensity of enforcement or new regulation that allows more risk taking on the same capital base and non-adjustments to regulation to adapt to new environments and which makes the current regulation idle.

Part of that regulatory environment are two critical features that explain the rise of the shadow banking market to a large degree[55]: (1) state guarantees and (2) tax deductibility of interest payments (caused by leverage). The latter favors debt over equity holders and creates an asymmetry in the Miller-Modigliani theory that claims that the cost of funding should not matter based on the inputs. It now does. Also implicit bank subsidization by the government have the same effect, that is, debt becomes more attractive than equity. Bailouts and deposit guarantees make debt cheaper in relative terms and foster the inclination to seek regulatory arbitrage to increase and magnify leverage. Deposit guarantee

---

[51] M. K. Brunnermeier, (2009), Deciphering the Liquidity and Credit Crunch 2007–2008, *Journal of Economic Perspectives*, Vol. 23, pp. 77–100.

[52] V. Fleischer, (2010), Regulatory Arbitrage, *Texas Law Review*, Vol. 89, pp. 227–290.

[53] J. F. Houston et al., (2012), Regulatory Arbitrage and International Bank Flows. The Journal of Finance, Vol. 67, Issue 5, pp. 1845–1895.

[54] E.F. Gerding, (2013), Law, Bubbles and Financial Regulation, Routledge, London and New York, pp. 311–336.

[55] See extensively: E.F. Gerding, (2013), Law, Bubbles and Financial Regulation, Routledge, London and New York, pp. 395–470.

regulation and bailout guarantees and also access to liquidity window of the central bank all externalize the cost of risk taking by offloading it on the taxpayer and reduces the cost of doing business by financial institutions.

The regulatory arbitrage as it occurred in the shadow banking markets has been manifesting itself along four distinct lines: (1) shadow banking instruments (ABS, CDS and MMFs) became an alternative to traditional banking instruments; (2) implicit ex ante and ex post subsidization and bailouts and other guarantees of shadow banking institutions and banking conglomerates including their shadow banking activities; (3) the fact that banks can participate in shadow banking activities, which allowed the banks to define the safety net of the central banks and created a contagion line between shadow banking system and deposit-taking banks, and (4) the regulatory arbitrage spilled over and was complemented over time by arbitrage accounting and arbitrage capital regulations.

As elaborated earlier in this volume, the first shadow banking innovation and attempt to arbitrage was the MMF creation to avoid the former regulation Q that placed caps on the interest rates that could be offered to depositors. With the collapse of Bretton Woods, inflation picked up and that created the need for a similar (safe and liquid) model but then without the caps on interest levels. The MMFs were born. In fact the first one was born in 1971, the same year the US unilaterally terminated the convertibility of the US dollar to gold. By 1980 the former regulation Q was eliminated (in phases). The 'net asset value as we still know it today was all put in place to make it look safe regardless of what occurs, within boundaries within the portfolio. Following that we experienced the whole ABS development where the use of SPVs accommodated working around bankruptcy rules so that a possible SPV bankruptcy would not impact the originator (commercial banks) of the loans sold to the SPV. Credit derivatives were developed to 'protect' investors without qualifying as 'insurance' and all the commitments and capital requirements it would bring'.[56]

The wider securitization markets would have been off limits without the shift from originate-to-maturity (or hold to 'originate-to-distribute'). They would have faced the restrictions regarding investing in real estate, the wider 'credit quality' spectrum of bonds and debt markets in general. That caused the gaming of the rating agencies (private actors embedded in regulation) as experienced in the run-up to the financial crisis. The accounting arbitrage was the next step as it allowed banks to move those securitized assets off their balance sheets, although much of the risk off these assets stayed on those books or lingered around somewhere in the financial conglomerate structure all benefiting from the ex post bailout dynamics. The accounting arbitrage had three dimen-

[56] See in detail: L. Schwarcz, (1994), The Alchemy of Asset Securitization, *Stanford Journal of law, Business and Finance*, Vol. 1, pp. 133–154; K. C. Kettering, (2008), Securitization and Its Discontents: the Dynamics of Financial Product Development, 29 *Cardozo Law Review*, Vol. 29, Issue 1, 1553–1728; R. F. Schwartz, (2007), Risk Distribution in the Capital Markets: Credit Default Swaps, Insurance and a Theory of Demarcation, 12 *Fordham Journal of Corporate and Financial Law*, Vol. 29, Issue 167, pp. 181–88; M. T. Henderson, (2009), Credit Derivatives are not "Insurance," *Connecticut Insurance Law Journal*, Vol. 16, Issue 1, pp. 1–60.

sions to it: (1) avoiding the consolidation of securitized vehicles[57] and the assets they hold in case of 'minimal control' (aka variable interest entities) even if they were obliged to provide financial backstops ('liquidity and credit support') for losses incurred by the SPV, (2) the selling commercial bank withheld some of the sold instruments and when sufficiently small did not have to be included in reporting and (3) a timing manipulation which invariably implied that banks reporting those transactions (or the removal of those assets off their balance sheet) just before the end-of-year accounting picture was taken. The books therefore did not reflect the risk on those books for most of the accounting period, which emerged when the securitization market dried up. Most of these asset offloaded were covered by a repo transaction which implied those assets and associated risks would come back on their books in the new accounting period (which was also the technique used by Lehman Brothers aka Repo 105). Accounting arbitrage was and is not limited to securitized products. Also swaps including CDS have been taken off the books using 'window dressing'. Although the FSB historically judged they should be treated as any given asset/liability on the books of FIs, the lobbying machine managed to get the exemption to that rule. They only had to disclose the 'changes in the "fair value" of these contracts over time'.

8.5.3 Capital Arbitrage

The same drivers helped to emerge capital arbitrage. Also here the FIs wanted to hide the leverage for capital adequacy purposes. Although the assets and thus leverage disappeared off the books and thus became irrelevant for capital regulation, the risk continued to stay on the books to a large degree. That risk was now magnified as the FI was able to leverage higher than before.[58] Capital regulation performs as a kind of 'regulatory tax' as it requires more capital to be held by banks than market discipline would require. Regulatory capital arbitrage is then each technique that enables firms to reduce their capital ratios without a proportionate reduction of the economic risk they incur. It reduces the cost of capital relative to the risk exposed when deploying that capital.[59]

As in every ratio, one can compromise the outcome by tampering with the numerator/denominator. That explains the different forms of capital arbitrage. Higher ratios are then the consequence of playing with the numerator (under provisioning, use of hybrid securities, etc.). Tampering with the denominator would include risk tagging which implies the allocation of lower risk to assets on a bundled basis (securitization) leading to higher risk than the risk category tolerates. Also the provisioning of off-balance sheet

[57] F. Partnoy and L. Turner, (2009), Bring Transparency to Off-Balance Sheet Accounting, in Make Markets Be Markets, Robert Johnson & Erica Payne (eds.), Roosevelt Institute, pp. 85–90; S. G. Ryan, (2008), Accounting in and for the Subprime Crisis, *Accounting Review*, Vol, 83, Issue 6, pp. 1605–1638.

[58] V.V. Acharya and M. Richardson, (2009), Causes of the Financial Crisis, *Critical Review*, Vol. 21, pp. 195–210.

[59] See, for example, D. Jones, (2000), Emerging Problems with the Basel Capital Accord: Regulatory Capital Arbitrage and Related Issues, *Journal of Banking and Finance*, Vol. 24, pp. 35–58.

guarantees (to buyers of products) plays a role. The risk exposure is the same but the capital/assets ratio would improve. No capital is held against the guarantee.

The playing around with the numerator and denominator explains the nature of the capital arbitrage strategies: (1) concentrate credit risk (in the senior portions) through securitization to obtain lower right weighting, (2) have the origination done by the ABCP vehicles rather than the sponsoring commercial banks to avoid capital regulation to step in, (3) liquidity and credit enhancement/guarantees (often through CLOs would be indirectly structured to obtain lower risk weighting, (4) use of third-party guarantees via credit derivatives or bond insurance when purchasing ABS, (5) report transactions in or moving assets from to the banking rather than trading book, (6) build accommodating proprietary risk models as a FI. Each of these techniques uses a shadow banking industry or shadow banking entity as a counterparty. The effects of capital regulatory arbitrage are clear: concentration of risk, lower capital available for much more risk and much bigger balance sheets and asymmetric risk build-up in portfolios. That risk was not only offloaded to institutional investors through the well-known SB products but that (un)intentionally much of that incremental risk stayed on the balance sheet of the originating FIs but without being properly hedged.[60]

Also deregulation in general contributed to the rise of the SB market. The cancelation of the Glass-Steagall Act is the most noteworthy event, which allowed investment risks of all sort to come back on the balance sheet of traditional banks which turned into financial conglomerates by expanding functions and offerings.[61] They also were positioned to exploit the implicit public guarantees that were and are available to traditional banks despite the provisions that are available to prevent the leakage of those provisions from banking to non-bank entities and activities.[62] It also facilitated that banks could purchase ABS product and securitize assets on their balance sheets and underwrite and deal in those products or participate in derivative transactions. The derivatives environment became deregulated in 2000 and disclosure exempted[63] as well as received preferential treatment in the bankruptcy process, including exemption from 'automatic stay', which allows them to 'jump to the head of the bankruptcy repayment line'[64] and weakens counterparty monitoring.

---

[60] H. S. Shin, (2009), Securitisation and Financial Stability, *Economic Journal*, Vol. 119, Issue 536, pp. 309–332.

[61] It must be admitted though that commercial banks seem to have a higher default ratio on their underwritten securities than investment banks, see D. Focarelli, (2011), Are Universal banks Better Underwriters. Evidence from the Last days of the Glass-Steagall Act, ECB Working Papers Nr. 1287. This evidence is stronger in the case of ex ante riskier and more competitive issues, and during the first years of bank securities' subsidiaries' entry into the market. Based on their results, it is not possible to reject that the repeal of the Glass-Steagall led to looser credit screening by broad (universal) banking companies trying to gain market share and/or to the lower initial ability of these banks to correctly evaluate default risk.

[62] Section 23A of the Federal Reserve Act. See S. T. Omarova, (2011), From Gramm-Leach-Bliley to Dodd-Frank: the Unfulfilled Promise of Section 23A of the Federal Reserve Act, *North Carolina Law Review*, Vol. 89, Issue 101, pp. 1683–1769.

[63] S. T. Omarova, (2009), The Quiet Metamorphosis: How Derivatives Changed the "Business of Banking", 63 *Miami Law Review*, Vol. 63, pp. 1041–1110.

[64] M. J. Roe, (2011), Bankruptcy's Financial Crisis Accelerator: The Derivatives Players' Priorities in Chapter 11, *Stanford Law Review*, Vol. 63, pp. 539–590.

But also the subsequent Basel accords (and their conversion into national laws) and their facility for banks to create proprietary risk models used for capital adequacy purposes were instrumental in creating a shadow banking market as it allowed to increase leverage (which Basel II and even Basel III don't tightly control) and hold asymmetrically lower levels of capital. Also specific exemptions such as 'Consolidated Supervised Entity' regime facilitated that behavior as it allowed (in particular the largest) banks to set capital under a consolidated approach including their bank holding entity at lower levels relative to their leverage positions. But also other regulatory dynamics contributed to the shadow banking emergence. Notable examples of that are the fact that for a long time, securitization vehicles did not have to register as an investment company under the US Investment Company Act of 1940 as well as the fact that banks that securitized assets and sold asset-backed securities to investors were exempted from the 'dealer' definition in the US Securities Exchange Act 1934. But also the implicit guarantees under which Freddie Mac and Fannie Mae operated until their federal takeover in 2008 (when the implicit guarantee became explicit) is a form of regulatory involvement that fueled the emergence of the shadow banking segment. The benefits[65] (subsidies) they enjoyed ranged from tax breaks, exemptions from securities laws, equalization of their securities to that of government securities (while they in essence are GSE [government-sponsored entities]) and lower capital requirements than other regulated institutions under similar risk conditions facilitating more leverage and therefore more risk.

8.5.4 Shadow Banking as a Regulated Political Economy

Whether it is regulatory arbitrage, subsidies or overall deregulation, once it was in place, it avalanched. MMFs were created to circumvent regulation Q. That fact led to pressure on bank regulation to deregulate which in turn led to the lobby of MMFs to create a stable NAV to create the illusion and direct competition with deposit-taking institutions. Regulatory arbitrage in the securitization field fueled capital adequacy exemptions which triggered Basels II and III which allow(ed) for many risk asymmetries that can be exploited and so on, and so we come full circle. The political framework was assessed by banking institutions to prefer regulatory arbitrage by them as well over trying to create similar regulation for their emerging competition to the one they are exposed to. The wider financial intermediation chains and accompanying financial conglomerates created lumped together financial and political interests.[66]

The deregulated financial sphere overall created a situation where emergence of the shadow and traditional banking sector was not exclusive but symbiotic in nature. Shadow banking became frequent counterparties of traditional banks and vice versa. Given that

[65] See in detail: D. J. Reiss, (2010), Fannie Mae and Freddie Mac and the Future of Federal Housing Finance Policy: A Study of Regulatory Privilege, *Alabama Law Review*, Vol. 61, Issue 5, pp. 907–955.

[66] A. E. Wilmarth, Jr., (2009), The Dark Side of Universal Banking: Financial Conglomerates and the Origins of the Subprime Financial Crisis, *Connecticut Law Review*, Vol. 41, Issue 4, pp. 963–1050; Y. Nersisyan, (2015), The Repeal of the Glass-Steagall Act and the Federal Reserve's Extraordinary Intervention during the Global Financial Crisis, Levy Economics Institute, Working Paper Nr. 829.

historical and contextual emergence, the large levels of regulatory arbitrage and deregulation actually were built upon or at least resulted in the exploitation of government subsidies whether they are implicit (deposit insurance) or explicit (too-big-to-fail).[67] The consequence was an externalization of the costs and an offload on the public system. Post-crisis it turned out that the implicit or explicit subsidy distribution is hard to trace and follow which has led to suboptimal regulation and ex post dealing with the aftermath of the crisis. That besides the fact that the discussion is highly technical and therefore smothered in turbo language which precludes a meaningful public technical debate especially since the expropriation by the financial sector has been occurring through a layering of incremental regulatory changes over time and thus acts as an organic model built out of many different (in)dependent decisions by regulators often around the world. Each time positive economic outlooks lead to boom behavior, another chunk of deregulation and regulatory arbitrage was built into the model and that process started already in the early 1980s.

The features and aspirations that initially fueled the emergence of the SB system were the same that anno 2008 threatened the SB and by extension the entire global financial sector. But when securitized assets needed to be offloaded, and risk turned out to be much more concentrated than the model would predict, maturity transformation seems to have been well embedded in the SB system. That's why it is hard to imagine why anno 2016 some politicians, public policy officials and regulators see a future for SB as a market-based solution for a failed traditional banking-based credit intermediation channel. Few manage to recognize that the involvement of politics and the regulator were part of the DNA that created the SB system as it is. As always after a crisis, the regulator acts in white heat and does not much more than symptom management and built regulation around the previous crisis. Just like we concluded in 2008 that the whole Sarbanes-Oxley circus introduced after Enron and Worldcom anno 2001 has been idle and non-functional. That didn't prevent it to create a whole circus of advisory and consulting services and a huge pile of compliance costs for businesses but it all ended in vain. It is therefore a near certainty that with the regulation as it is now in place within a decade from now, but most likely shorter, we will be facing a non-negotiable same end game. The inability of society as a whole and financial sector in particular to deleverage after a crisis is always short-lived and modest to begin with. A few years after the crisis, higher levels of leverage can be observed compared to before the crisis and so is it also anno 2019 when comparing debt levels with 2007/2008 regardless of whether it is the public sector, private sector or the interbanking market as such. The extraordinary amounts of leverage will continue to create dislocations in a constantly globalizing financial market with no proper exit in the end or when the next market shakeout occurs. And our economic modeling and forecasting efforts will prove to be very unhelpful. Even more, economic modeling is not so much about 'predicting' the future effects on welfare, capital needs or economic growth. It is essentially about 'managing factional expectations'. Engelen, backed by De Ville and Siles-Brügge indicates '[i]n contrast to their putative aim, namely providing reliable

[67] A.E. Wilmarth Jr., (2014), Citigroup's Unfortunate History of Managerial and Regulatory Failures, *Journal of Banking Regulation* Vol. 15, Issue 3/4, pp. 235–265; A.E. Wilmarth Jr., (2011), The Dodd-Frank Act: A Flawed and Inadequate Response to the Too-Big-to-Fail Problem, *Oregon Law Review*, Vol. 89, pp. 951–1057.

guides into an uncertain future, these models help to construct a certain but imaginary future in order to facilitate political consensus on the issue at stake by using a fictional econometric world that due to its technical nature is able to hide its fictional nature from the eyes of non-experts'.[68] De Ville and Siles-Brügge complement (in the context of trade relations and their acclaimed benefits): '[i]n line with the "ideational turn" in political economy, we argue that it is not objective consequences of trade agreements as such (which simply cannot be known for certain a priori), but the management of expectations about their effects which affects the support for and opposition to the launch, conduct and conclusion of free trade negotiations'.[69]

8.5.5 Backtesting Shadow Banking Against the Ex Post Crisis Experience

The areas of intervention of the central banks after the 2008 crisis around the world read as a 'diagnostic test' of the shadow banking sector: money market funds, asset-backed securities and securitized assets in general, repos and so on. By doing so, the central banks converted their deposit insurance mechanism into a 'lender of last resort mechanism' for privately created money, a system that was created to avoid the traditional banking regulation of which deposit insurance and liquidity windows are an integrated part of. I'm not claiming that the shadow banking market would not have existed without deregulation and regulatory arbitrage. But deregulation and regulatory changes in particular allowed the traditional banking sector to feed into the shadow banking market and put public resources at risk. It was the regulatory channel that allowed the transmission of economic and financial contagion from the shadow to the traditional banking sector (and back). Going back to the days before 1971 and the abolishment of Bretton Woods would ignore the fact that the economy to which the financial sector is catering these days has changed and that financial innovation has brought the cost of funding down for many businesses and allowed deals and transactions to occur that otherwise would have never happened. Few recall the days of high interest rates and painfully high levels of cost of funding and related low levels of liquidity. Nobody wants to go back to those days. It would anyway be a matter of time before those regulatory bastions, Chinese walls and so on would become prone again to erosion of all sorts and pressures that would start the cycle over and over again.

8.5.6 Regulation Versus Market Forces

Two items, in my opinion, have not received enough attention and those are (1) robustness of our public system and (2) leverage is and will be the problem.

---

[68] E. Engelen, (2015), TTIP and the Politics of Economic Modeling, blogspot April 26.

[69] F. De Ville & G. Siles-Brügge, (2015), The Transatlantic Trade and Investment Partnership and the Role of Computable General Equilibrium Modelling: An Exercise in 'Managing Fictional Expectations', to be published in New Political Economy, Vol. 20, Issue 5, pp. 653–678.

Let me comment a bit on that. The shadow banking market is a result of market competition that used deregulation as a stepping stone to magnify its volumes. The reason for that makes sense: Deposit banking with all the rules, risk and costs is a very expensive way of credit intermediation. With deregulation and technology kicking in since the 1980s, that expensive channel was less and less needed. Anno 2016 the shadow banking system is at the brink of becoming the principal supplier of credit to the economy. Banks are therefore limited to supplying credit to those that have no other place to go. Those other places are hedge funds, PE firms and the capital markets directly. It also helps explain why most of the bank loans that do make it are collateralized. Commercial and industrial loans are in a continuous declining mode. Banks have become real estate and collateral hubs[70] with limited ambitions to serve the real economy. Regulation surrounding capital requirements to back SME loan are helping that disinterest. It has turned banks into processing businesses minimizing risks rather than credit pools that serve the economy based on actual and hardcore industry knowledge of the industries they serve. That triggered the to-be-discussed fact that credit intermediation chains have become long and organizations that were historically banks became financial conglomerates and hybrid intermediaries. That platform was the best one to dream for when building a shadow banking market. But it created real estate behemoths on the traditional banking side who see their business model reinforced by incoming regulation, that is, as much as possible real estate finance and some minimal risk loans on top. It is therefore not surprising that an analysis post-crisis of the nature and dynamics of those financial institutions generated the following conclusions regarding their relationship with real estate: '[t]he primary driver of commercial bank failures during the Great Recession was exposure to the real estate sector, not aggregate funding strains'.

The main 'toxic' exposure was credit to non-household real estate borrowers, not traditional home mortgages or agency-issued MBS. Private-label MBS contributed to the failure of large banks only. Failed banks skewed their portfolios toward product categories that performed poorly on aggregate and within each category invested in assets of lower quality than survivor banks did. They expanded more rapidly into real estate during the pre-crisis period, but rapid growth alone cannot explain differences in asset performance.[71] The traditional credit intermediation channel is broken and regulation helped a big deal

[70] A. J. Pollock, (2014), Can Banks Resist the Real Estate Temptation?, Housing Finance International, Winter, p. 12.

[71] A. Antoniades, (2015), Commercial Bank Failures during the Great Recession: the Real (Estate) Story, ECB Working Paper Series, Nr. 1779, April, Frankfurt. He works with three types of exposures of banks to real estate (a) illiquid assets, (b) marketable securities and (c) off-balance sheet credit line portfolios. He further concluded that the accumulation of real estate risk was larger the larger the size of the bank analysed. Particularly interesting further is that he has no evidence that holdings of traditional home mortgage loans or of agency-issued MBS contributed more to bank failures than exposures to non-real estate loans and non-MBS securities did. The estimates indicate that the primary drivers of failure were exposure to loans and commitments issued to non-household real estate borrowers. The relationship between the exposure to real estate and the later failure of the FI builds along two lines: (a) failed banks invested more heavily in real estate products that performed uniformly poorly across both failed and survivor banks during the crisis (systematic component) and (b) within each of the potentially toxic product categories failed banks invested in assets of lower quality than survivor banks did (idiosyncratic component).

in achieving that. The second component of that failure is the fact that traditional banks became business models in their own right and went listed and became prone to the short termism that has become the standard in contemporary markets.[72] The surge in dividends and stock-buybacks reveals the kind of financial engineering that is short-lived and for which CEOs and boards are typically not hired.

Taking into account the need for returns in a short-term context and the creeping competition in the financial sector created the need for more leverage to generate those returns. That builds the bridge with the second item listed. Although leverage has been given in a fair amount of attention in regulation and Basel accords, it wasn't necessarily in the way required to make the system safer. There were no real caps and enough escape routes when it comes to the amount of leverage, no real legislation that forced to cut the ties between the traditional and the banking sector and most importantly no 'hardcore unweight capital requirements'. The best medication to stabilize a leveraged patient is (besides deleveraging which takes time) equity (and some more equity). But that has implications. No 15–25% returns on equity any longer. Nobody wants to see the grim and gray face of a commoditized banking sector where returns leverage-free and maturity transformation-free would be around 4–5% in the current market climate and where returns would be effectively a direct function of the central bank set market rate. Traditional banks and even investment banks with their risk-enhanced dealing need staggering amounts of leverage to reach the 5–15% return on equity which has become the new norm post-crisis.

8.5.7 Further Reflection on the Business of Credit Intermediation

It seems impossible for the sector to escape the 'black hole' that is waiting. Competition combined with leverage in a global marketplace that doesn't seem to be able to generate new demand[73]-led growth (and might never do again[74]) sounds like a disaster waiting to happen. And not to forget stagflation, regulatory challenges and a barrage of fines for previous conducts could lead to conclude that banking is in terminal decline. That is more pronounced in Europe[75] than elsewhere, although the basic conditions for a perpetual

[72] See L. Fink, (2015), The Effects of Short-Termism, Letter to all S&P 500 CEOs, April. Repeated by Fink in 2018 with a new letter on how companies must have a social purpose and pursue a strategy for achieving long-term growth.

[73] Over half of the slowdown in advanced-economy export growth since 2011 (relative to the pre-crisis trend) can be explained by weak global demand growth. More specifically, exports in advanced economies have been restrained by the weakness of global investment, a trade-intensive demand component and weak demand out of Europe, a region that accounts for about 40% of the demand for advanced-economy exports. See in detail: L. Morel, (2015), Sluggish Exports in Advanced Economies: How Much Is Due to Demand?, Bank of Canada/Banque de Canada, Working Papers Nr. 2015-3, March.

[74] M. Wolf, (2015), An Economic Future that Might Never Brighten, *Financial Times*, April 15.

[75] 'They are hardly an advertisement for the future of European banking', P. Jenkins, (2015), Stagnation, Fines and Regulation Leave European Banks Struggling, *Financial Times*, April 27.

decline are available everywhere. The artificially extended arm called shadow banking was able to operate without internalizing the true costs of the risk it absorbed and thus created a competitive advantage that still is validated anno 2019 and undermines traditional bank regulation and fuels continuous leveraging. Nevertheless, the regulator is a critical agent on the path to resolution given that '[a]s the source of the most significant competition for the banking industry, the relentlessly growing and efficient capital markets have substantially reduced the role of banks—and hence the importance of bank regulators—in the modern financial system'.[76] With no real private financial backstop to the shadow banking system and an ex ante or ex post public safety net creating moral hazard, the 'equity' route is the only left available. Equity has the benefit of a pricing signal coming from the market, which sounds aligned with the shadow banking as market-based finance. The equity portion will also allow for investors to signal appropriate levels of 'leverage risk' it wants its equity to be subject to. The regulator with all its facilities has made the financial sector numb for external sensations. The saver who got convinced that one can save and reap large rewards on a risk-free basis (enjoying the deposit insurance mechanism) and the financial institutions faced with a return-seeking business model where financial leverage was ignored and where lowering interest rates created an unholy inclination to leverage up. Just like the economy as a market, the shadow banking market is also a market, but markets are no natural phenomenon and the shadow banking market we got has all the regulatory failures encoded in its DNA.

But who goes back to a leverage and maturity transformation-free banking system and focuses on excellent 'capital allocation' as a science and art while generating a +/− 5% return? Credit intermediation is commoditized but 'capital allocation' is still an art that only few really master and requires a lot more than just financial knowledge. It requires deep industry expertise and organizational dynamics capabilities. Some PE firms and hedge funds have entered that space but only on the high-end risk side of the loan spectrum which includes high-yield and leveraged loans. That is necessary to provide the expected returns by their limited partners. But in the normal bandwidth, the vacuum is becoming deeper and more intense and crowdfunding and B2B, C2C and B2C lending platforms are nice contemporary features but will never replace broad-based credit intermediation.

Simply giving the lack of real credit allocation skills or even basic oversight by the platform manager. The regulator, as a direct alternative of a nationalized financial sector, can help to shape a market for institutions that provide credit intermediation leverage and maturity transformation free to savers, potentially with a liquidity window for savers that want to exit early exogenously attached to that private market business model. Not as a deposit insurance as the credit risk would stay with the saver, but where the liquidity risk would be absorbed by the central bank. That would be worth providing a public backstop to. The focus would then be on the quality of 'capital allocation'. Because let's be fair: there is a reason why there is only one 'Berkshire Hathaway' in this world and countless (large) banks. The relentless and committed focus on allocating capital long term in a consistent way is only available to very few in the face of a market

[76] P.J. Wallison, (2015), The Regulators' War on Shadow Banking, AEI Research, January, p. 6.

full of regulatory-induced short-term liquidity, bonus and moral hazard temptations. But even within the banking sector, the dynamics of a non-market-based financing system have been observed. When comparing the private and commercial banking system with the behavior of state investment banks, some interesting features emerged. Mazzucato and Penna indicate '[r]ecent decades witnessed a trend whereby private markets retreated from financing the real economy, while, simultaneously, the real economy itself became increasingly financialized. This trend resulted in public finance becoming more important for investments in capital development, technical change, and innovation.'[77] The role of state-led investment banks have been more than just 'market fixing' but has expanded into market making and this across a series of investment types, that is, countercyclical, developmental, venture capitalist and challenge led. Their role is therefore critical beyond the traditional 'market failure' argument especially in an era of deregulation and accompanying financialization. Sen and DasGupta frame the conundrum as follows: '[f]inancialization creates space for the financial sector in economies, and in doing so helps to raise the share of financial assets in the portfolios held by market participants. Largely driven by deregulation, the process works to make financial assets relatively attractive as compared to other assets, by offering both better returns and potential capital gains. Both the trend toward a more financialized economy and the expected returns on financial investments have provided incentives to corporate managers to invest larger sums in financial assets, resulting in growth of the share of financial assets relative to other assets held in portfolios. Assets held in the financial sector, however, failed to generate asset growth for the corporates. The need to obtain resources by borrowing in order to meet current liabilities reflects a pattern of Ponzi finance.'[78]

That trend seems to have become mainstream as also Duprey, who studied the lending pattern of state-owned banks over the business cycle, argues 'that public bank lending is (i) significantly less cyclical except for low-income countries, (ii) asymmetric along the business cycle, (iii) heterogeneous across stages of economic development, and (iv) related to banks' vulnerability on their funding side. Public banks reduce their lending less during economic downturns, but their ability to absorb negative shocks is marginally decreasing as the size of the shock increases.'[79] The appreciation of risk and the (un)transparency of risk transfers and the matching over- or underestimation of capital levels of counterparties leads to not only wrong appreciation of real risks but also that the lower the level of interest rate exposure, the more risk is underestimated which links it to the unconventional monetary policy spheres of contemporary times. Dubecq et al. highlight '[i]mperfect information about the level of capital per unit of risk, however, introduces uncertainty about the risk exposure of intermediaries. Over-estimation of the

---

[77] M. Mazzucato and C.C.R. Penna, (2015), Beyond Market Failures: The Market Creating and Shaping Roles of State Investment Banks, Levy Economics Institute, Working Paper Nr. 831, January.

[78] S. Sen and Z. DasGupta, (2015), Financialization and Corporate Investments: The Indian Case, Levy Economics Institute Working Paper, Nr, 828, January.

[79] T. Duprey, (2015), Do Publicly Owned Banks Lend Against the Wind?, *International Journal of Central Banking*, March, Vol. 11, Nr. 3, pp. 65–112.

capital held by financial intermediaries, or the extent of regulatory arbitrage, may induce households to wrongly infer from higher asset prices that the fundamentals of risky assets have improved'…'Moreover, the lower the level of the risk-free interest rate, the more risk is under-estimated.'[80]

But what is it we got so far. The incoming regulation on all fronts has led to the fact that European banks relative to their US counterparts are performing badly. Remember, the European continent is much more dependent on banking finance than the US with its capital market-oriented financial infrastructure. The incoming regulation and compliance costs have made many financial behemoths consider shedding their retail arm or at least shrink the branch network that traditionally pressures heavily the performance of retail banking.[81] Those banking groups will do so look in the darker areas of banking or spread out over many segments to regain their competitiveness and ultimately their performance. But that factual situation is much more difficult to manage and monitor from a regulatory point of view. One that is combined with the still somewhat unknown repercussions on the banking sector of protracted periods of ultra-low or negative interest rates and the impact on financial stability and growth. Nothing good can come from investors not being paid for taking risk. Also the impact on economic growth or low or negative monetary rates runs, to a large degree, through the credit channel, by deterring savings and encouraging borrowing, which will drive down the cost of funding either through bank lending or bond market issuance.

Hannoun comments in this respect '[t]his channel is pushed to an extreme by the negative deposit rates introduced by some central banks. Negative nominal deposit rates are presented as a tax imposed by the central bank on commercial banks to encourage them to expand lending, and not as a tax on the savers. But there are two possibilities here: either the banks pass on the tax to their customers, so that negative rates are charged on retail deposits, and banks reduce their lending rates. This will hurt depositors but it could increase bank lending. Or, if this tax is not passed on, the negative deposit rates set by central banks will gain no traction in terms of incentivizing commercial banks to lend more to the real economy.'[82] The other channels through which low interest rates can impact economic growth is through the asset valuation channel, the portfolio risk channel, the reflation channel and the exchange rate channel.[83] Short term that 'can' have its

[80] S. Dubecq et al., (2015), Risk Shifting with Fuzzy Capital Constraints, *International Journal of Central Banking*, January, Vol. 11, Nr. 1, pp. 71–101.

[81] See, for example, J. Ewing, (2015), Deutsche Bank to Shed Postbank Branch Network, NY Times, Dealbook, April 25.

[82] Ultra-low or negative interest rates: what they mean for financial stability and growth. Remarks by H. Hannoun, Deputy General Manager, Bank for International Settlements, at the Eurofi High-Level Seminar, Riga, April 22, 2015, p. 2.

[83] See Hannoun, (2015), Ibid. pp. 2–5. Low interest rates boost asset prices by reducing the discount rate on cash flows from assets and raises expectations of improved economic conditions and consequently higher future revenues from those assets. It will further drive investors out of bonds into riskier assets (portfolio rebalancing) and leads over time to a convergence between the returns of risky assets and those of low-risk assets. That implies some level of interest rate risk which is not covered by any sort of regulation as it has always been hidden in the shadows of monetary policy

distinct benefits although they cannot be overcalled. But longer the outlook is very different. Hannoun[84] highlights five long-term material risks that are not captured by any sort of regulation at this stage:

- Interest rates are the price of leverage and thus low or negative interest rates are effective disincentives for all agents to deleverage.[85] Those low rates flatten the debt service ratio and 'lead to an artificial compression of sovereign spreads, and a weakening of market discipline' and lead to the illusion of a successful 'perpetuation of the debt-driven growth model'.
- It distracts from the real task at hand; raising real economic and productivity growth.
- Central banks that drive pricing of assets in the open market can only lead to distortions and result in the fact that those asset prices fail to reflect the implied risk in those assets. That is particularly true when 'the three major regulatory reforms that could to some extent mitigate the financial stability risks resulting from ultra-low interest rates are still under discussion'. There will be a time that it will create a major and simultaneous loss of 'investor confidence'.
- It will lead to disruptions in the financial industry globally; '[p]rolonged ultra-long interest rates cause disruptions in the business models of financial institutions, implying substantial risks to financial stability'.
- And more overall it creates the illusion that central banks can boost growth and revive the economy and will lead that households, due to financial compression, cannot sufficiently build up retirement reserves which will force them to save more, which is very much the opposite effect than wanted. There is also the element of social welfare implications as Hannoun commented '[f]or all these reasons, the "new monetary orthodoxy" of imposing a tax on savers and providing a subsidy to borrowers is unlikely to result in higher global output or better living standards'. He refers to Masaaki Shirakawa, the former Governor of the Bank of Japan, a country very familiar with unconventional monetary policies who lamented '[m]onetary policy can bring

and macroprudential (and more recently microprudential) oversight. That has led to remarkable situations. Prior to the financial crisis, an investor could make a profit either on bonds or equities, but seldom on both simultaneously. That is due to the traditional negative correlation between equities and bonds. But since a few years, that negative correlation does no longer seem to apply in many parts of the world. For the first time in history, declining bond returns go hand in hand with equity price growth. The conclusion is that 'global monetary policy promotes unbalanced price formation', see DNB, (2015), Monetary Policy Puts Financial Markets on a Different Track, DNBulletin, April 23. The reflation channel (lifting inflation to central bank targets) mainly aim to avoid deflationary spirals and fuel investments. In terms of the exchange rate channel 'a depreciation can boost net exports, and hence growth and employment, while lifting inflation through higher import prices' (p. 5). Problem is often the reciprocity.

[84] Hannoun, (2015), Ibid. pp. 6–9.

[85] See also G. Di Bartolomeo et al., (2015), The Comeback of Inflation as an Optimal Public Finance Tool, *International Journal of Central Banking*, January, Vol. 11, Nr. 1, pp. 43–70. Their results thus provide theoretical support to policy-oriented analyses which call for a reversal of debt accumulated in the aftermath of the 2008 financial crisis.

forward future demand to today by engineering lower real interest rates. But, when tomorrow becomes today, the economy is faced with lower demand, which necessitates bringing forward demand from the day after tomorrow.[86]'

Many of the risks and the likelihood of them occurring goes back to what has been said about monetary policy, macroprudential and microprudential policy. Most of the microprudential policies and their relationship with the other components are 'trial-and-error' based and very limited on solid understanding or economic models. Even for the existing nexus between macroprudential policies and monetary policy, the demarcation line is often unclear. Shin comments 'both policies affect the demand for credit by reallocating spending over time, by either postponing spending (i.e. by inducing consumers and firms to borrow less) or bringing forward spending (i.e. by inducing them to borrow more). Both policies affect the supply of credit by influencing the leverage decision of the intermediary, and both influence the funding cost of the intermediary.'[87] But there are also differences: (1) 'macroprudential policy is aimed at specific sectors' or practices and in contrast 'monetary policy influences risk-taking more broadly, both within the domestic financial system but also across borders, and is harder to circumvent', (2) domestic monetary policy is constrained by global conditions (currencies), (3) they tend to be complementary and not substitutes.[88] But there is more Shin indicates, which brings the discussion home to the regulatory field: '[m]ost macroprudential tools are aimed at the banking sector, especially the regulated banking sector'…'The changing patterns of financial intermediation mean that we need to revise constantly our understanding of the relevant players in the financial system.'[89] What he points at is that macroprudential tools are still very much focused on 'credit growth, leverage, maturity mismatch, complexity and "too big to fail"'. However, future innovations and disruptions might not be centralized around those concepts.

Indeed, many innovations in the past were unforeseen. Innovations in itself are not bad, unless one cannot predict its implications and consequences or in case one cannot prevent the negative collateral implications of those innovations. It refers to what has been coined the 'Achilles Heel' of the global financial infrastructure which Berio[90] type-casted

---

[86] M Shirakawa, (2015), Debate on Deflation and the Role of 'Nominal Anchor', presentation at the Federal Reserve Bank of Minneapolis Inflation Expectations Symposium, March 30.

[87] H.S. Shin, (2015), Macroprudential Tools, their Limits and their Connection with Monetary Policy, Panel remarks at IMF Spring Meeting event: "Rethinking macro policy III: progress or confusion?" April 15, 2015, Washington, DC, p. 1.

[88] V. Bruno, et al., (2015), Comparative Assessment of Macroprudential Policies, BIS Working Papers, BIS Working Papers Nr. 502, June. See also IMF, (2013), The Interaction of Monetary and Macroprudential Policies, Washington. See also E. Cerutti, et al., (2015), Macroprudential Policies: analysing a New Database, paper presented at the DNB-EBC conference on 'Macroprudential regulation: from theory to implementation' on January 29–30, 2015, Amsterdam; K. Kuttner and I. Shim, (2013), Can Non-Interest Rate Policies Stabilise Housing Markets? Evidence From a Panel of 57 Economies, BIS Working Papers, Nr. 433, November 2013; and O. Akinci and J. Olmstead-Rumsey, (2015), How Effective are Macroprudential Policies? An Empirical Investigation, Working paper.

[89] H. S. Shin, (2015), Ibid. p. 3.

[90] See in detail: C. Berio, (2014), The International Monetary and Financial System: Its Achilles Heel and What to Do About It, BIS Working Paper Nr. 456, August, Basel, Switzerland.

as 'excess (financial) elasticity' which refers to the inability of the financial system 'to prevent the build-up of financial imbalances (FIs)'. That inability has led to unsustainable credit and asset price booms that overstretch balance sheets leading to serious financial crises and macroeconomic dislocations, the failure to tame the procyclicality of the financial system and equally so the failure to tame the financial cycle. So the focus should be more on financial institutions in countries than on trade and public financial matrixes. And in particular anchors should be put in place to monitor interactions between jurisdictions with an aim toward '[i]nternalizing the externalities of individual countries' policies'.[91]

8.5.8 Contagion and the International Transmission Channels

That direction seems to relate well to our newest set of understandings regarding 'contagion' and 'contagion effects' through a variety of transmission channels. Ahnert and Bertsch have been examining 'contagion' using novel theories based on coordination games of regime changes in two regions with an initially uncertain correlation of regional fundamentals. A popular theory to explain contagion is the 'wake-up-call hypotheses'. According to this hypothesis, a crisis in region one is a wake-up call to investors in region two that induces reassessment of local fundamentals. Such a reappraisal of risk can lead to a financial crisis in region two, either due to weaker local fundamentals (perhaps because of exposure to region one) or due to greater uncertainty about local fundamentals. Their analysis illustrates that contagion occurs even if investors learn that regional fundamentals are uncorrelated ex post and when common lenders or balance sheet links are absent. Their theory explains how a wake-up call in isolation transmits financial crises. It thereby captures the wake-up-call component of contagion. They conclude that '[c]ontagion after a wake-up call can occur even if investors learn that fundamentals are uncorrelated and common lender effects or balance sheet linkages are absent'.[92] The practical outcome points at a higher need for 'international coordination' among jurisdictions. The understanding of contagion and how it converts 'information-insensitive debt markets' to 'information-sensitive debt markets' (cf. Holstrom) is discussed elsewhere.

8.5.9 Regulation Drives the Design and Capabilities of the Financial Services Industry

The Basel III regulations will drive forward the growth of the shadow banking sector and will deepen the regulatory advantage (and thus the benefit or regulatory arbitrage on the side of the traditional banks) of shadow banking entities as '[t]he current cost advantage of

[91] C. Berio, (2015), The International Monetary and Financial System: Its Achilles Heel and what to do About It, Institute for New Economic Thinking (INET), '2015 Annual Conference: Liberté, Égalité, Fragilité' Paris, April 8–11, 2015, p. 2. See also on the sources of 'excess elasticity' (pp. 3–15).

[92] See in detail: T. Ahnert and C. Bertsch, (2015), A Wake-Up-call Theory of Contagion, Bank of Canada/Banque de France Working Paper Nr. 2015-14, April.

shadow banks is hence seen as rather based on regulatory advantages as on their high level of specialization'.[93] The regulator seems not in a hurry to approach equal activities as traditional banks perform the same way from a regulatory point of view. That will provide asymmetric treatment between traditional and shadow banks and that is already well in the making. It can be envisaged that under the umbrella of performance enhancement, tapping into specialized knowledge and resources, leveraging on the dynamics of the deep international capital markets, traditional banks will access the SB segment without the consolidation requirement. The regulator has, in this case, not yielded a miserable outcome for the first time around. Many examples have been around spanning many decades.[94]

The spreading out and branching out while creating lengthy credit channels and layered credit-related services creates traditional banks that manage the system well but start to lack the real economy knowledge and skills to service it properly. It was already highlighted that the relentless focus on financial assets and real estate has shifted the knowledge curve of financial institutions away from the real economy. According to most theories of financial intermediation, intermediaries diversify risk, transform maturity or liquidity and screen or monitor borrowers. That seems no longer to be the case and turns banks into rent-seeking institutions at the expense of their clients and the wider society and economy[95] and they lost their ability as 'information aggregators' of the economy and businesses they serve (See also Box 8.1).

Box 8.1 The Side Effect of Regulation: Banks Lose Their Abilities as Information Aggregators

Are Banks Losing Their Function as Information Aggregators of the Economy?

According to most theories regarding financial intermediation, intermediaries diversify risk, transform maturity or liquidity and screen or monitor borrowers. That makes sense as FIs are like power strips. Their connectedness with industries and many business provides them with the benefits of aggregate information and information channels based on which they can (better) diversify risk and so on. However, based on recent findings, none of the rationales seem to apply and point at the fact that the role of banks as information aggregators is declining. Yet most end investors place their auction bids through an intermediary rather than submit them directly.

(continued)

[93] B. Bauer and Ph. Wackerbeck, (2013), Into the Shadows: How Regulation Fuels the Growth of the Shadow Banking Sector and how Banks Need to React, *The European Financial Review*, June–July 2013, p. 29.

[94] S. Agarwal et al., (2014), Inconsistent Regulators: Evidence from Banking, *The Quarterly Journal of Economics*, Vol. 129, Issue 2, pp. 889–938.

[95] See, for example, related to US Treasury auctions: N. Boyarchenko et al., (2015), Intermediaries as Information Aggregators: An Application to U.S. Treasury Auctions, Federal Reserve Bank of New York Staff Reports, Nr. 726, April.

Box 8.1 (continued)

In the case examined (which was the US Treasury market), intermediaries submit their customer bids without transforming liquidity or maturity, and they do not screen or monitor borrowers or diversify fiscal policy risk. Boyarchenko et al. comment '[i]n contrast to underwriting theories in which intermediaries, by acting as gatekeepers, extract rents but reduce revenue variance, information aggregators increase expected auction revenue but also make the revenue more sensitive to changes in asset value'. The vast majority of US Treasury auction bids are placed by a small set of primary dealers for either their own or their customers' accounts. The common theme throughout the paper is a reversal of the common wisdom about dealers as underwriters. The researchers contrast their finding with standard theories and conclude that '[t]he prevailing thinking about underwriters is that they lower auction revenue, but also revenue risk. In the information model that we present, we find the exact opposite: when investors bid through dealers, both mean and variance of auction revenue increase. The stark difference in these predictions highlights how policy prescriptions may be heavily dependent on the role of intermediation. While many intermediaries perform roles other than information aggregation, this role is a key one in Treasury auctions and is likely to be present in some form in other markets as well. Thus the unique features of Treasury auctions makes them a useful laboratory to isolate and investigate this new facet of intermediation.'[96] They present a new theory of financial intermediaries who collect information from order flow, use it to advice clients and bid for their in-house account.[97]

8.5.10 Regulation and the Short- and Long-Term Dynamics of Shadow Banking

If the shadow banking market historically has been (to a large degree) driven by regulation, that relationship should become clear both in the short and long run. Duca has been looking into the matter and concluded that shadow banking market rose 'when deposit interest rate ceilings were binding, the economic outlook improved, or risk premia declined, and fell when event risks disrupted financial markets'.[98] The different and already discussed strands of literature[99] illustrate how the shadow banking market historically emerged out of a cascade of financial innovations that often emerged due to regulatory arbitrage. Duca illustrates that the shadow banking share of both short- and long-term financing has increased over the years mainly through commercial paper (held by MMFs) and indirectly through funding from non-bank financial intermediaries. He

[96] N. Boyarchenko et al., (2015), Intermediaries as Information Aggregators: An Application to U.S. Treasury Auctions, Federal Reserve Bank of New York Staff Reports, Nr. 726, April, p. 30.

[97] N. Boyarchenko et al., (2015), Intermediaries as Information Aggregators: An Application to U.S. Treasury Auctions, Federal Reserve Bank of New York Staff Reports, Nr. 726, April, p. 1.

[98] J.V. Duca, (2014a), What Drives the Shadow Banking System in the Short and the Long Run, Reserve Bank of Dallas, Working Paper Nr. 1401, February. See also J.V. Duca, (2014b), How Capital Regulation and Other Factors Drive Shadow banking in the Short and Long Run, Working Paper, April.

[99] See for an overview of the literature Duca, (2014a), Ibid. pp. 2–6.

argues 'the shadow bank share internalizes substitution between commercial paper directly issued by nonfinancial corporations and credit intermediated by nonbank financial intermediaries'.[100] Duca demonstrates that the increasing growth and rise in shadow banking participation was and is directly related to regulatory interventions over the years and further demonstrates, in line with existing literature, that the shadow banking segment is prone to liquidity shocks and intrinsically procyclical in nature. The skin-in-the-game risk exposures now introduced, or at least suggested, level the playing field between traditional and shadow banking segments. It is understood from the discussed works of Schwarcz that many imperfections continue to exist and the regulatory suggestions imply moral hazard and seem to work well in a regulatory framework and not so much isolated in a practical functional context.[101]

8.5.11 Lessons for Those That Claim That 'Market-Based Finance' Is an Adequate Alternative to Banking-Based Finance

We have discussed how, for example, securitized products have been instrumental unleashing the 2008 financial crisis. Securitization was intended to transfer credit to those institutional investors that were better positioned to absorb potential losses. But we ended up with a situation where the system as a whole became more fragile and that situation was exacerbated by leverage, asymmetric maturity mismatches and cross-holdings of securitized assets. As Adrian and Shin comment 'in a market-based financial system, banking and capital market developments are inseparable: Funding conditions are closely tied to fluctuations in the leverage of market-based financial intermediaries. Growth in the balance sheets of these intermediaries provides a sense of the availability of credit, while contractions of their balance sheets have tended to precede the onset of financial crises.'[102] Critical here is the message that in a market-based financial system, the distinction between markets and their natural fluctuations and banking balances becomes inseparable, as funding and capital allocation will occur in a continuous cross-holding fashion. Our current shadow banking regulation is not foreseen for calamities within that remit nor our banking regulation for that matter.

They further indicate that financial regulation that should chain the securitization market can have different dynamics and dimensions '[w]hether the binding regulatory constraints come through leverage bounds, forward-looking provisioning, explicit countercyclical capital rules, or systemic capital rules is a matter of implementation'.[103] What is essential though is that 'the underlying spirit of these different approaches is that

[100] Duca, (2014a), Ibid. p. 6.

[101] See also M.K. Brunnermeier, and Y. Sannikov, (2014), The I Theory of Money, manuscript, Princeton University, April; M.L. Fein, (2013), The Shadow Banking Charade, Working Paper, February 15.

[102] T. Adrian and H.S. Shin, (2009), The Shadow Banking System: Implications for Financial Regulation, Federal Reserve Bank of New York Staff Reports, Nr. 382, July.

[103] Ibid. p. 14.

financial system instability caused by market failures that provide rationales for public policy. Regulation with the aim of mitigating financial system risk must aim at reducing the adverse effects of the market failures that are the root cause of the crisis.'[104]

8.6 Regulating the Shadow Banking Industry

Although the shadow banking industry has been gaining increased attention for its (alleged) role in the 2008 financial crisis, it was only in 2010 and more precisely during the G20 meeting in Seoul that year that the attention by regulators and policymakers has been gaining broadband traction. The G20 together with the Financial Stability Board (FSB) have been coordinating efforts ever since.

Simultaneously with the initiatives undertaken regarding shadow banking, the EU in 2012 issued a report on the restructuring of the EU banking business and reform of the industry.[105]

The council concluded that it is necessary to require legal separation of certain particularly risky financial activities from deposit-taking banks within the banking group. The activities to be separated would include proprietary trading of securities and derivatives, and certain other activities closely linked with securities and derivatives markets. They proposed that proprietary trading and all assets or derivative positions incurred in the process of market making, other than the activities exempted below, must be assigned to a separate legal entity. They suggested that the separation would only be mandatory if the activities to be separated amount to a significant share of a bank's business, or if the volume of these activities can be considered significant from the viewpoint of financial stability. Provision of hedging services to non-banking clients (e.g. using forex and interest rate options and swaps) which fall within narrow position risk limits in relation to own funds, to be defined in regulation, and securities underwriting do not have to be separated. The legally separate deposit bank and trading entity can operate within a bank holding company structure.

To ensure the resilience of the two types of entities, both the deposit bank and the trading entity would each individually be subject to all the regulatory requirements, such as the CRR/CRD IV and consolidated supervision, which pertain to EU financial institutions. Hence they must, for example, be separately capitalized according to the respective capital adequacy rules, including the maintenance of the required capital buffers and possible additional Pillar 2 capital requirements.

The specific objectives of separation are to (1) limit a banking group's incentives and ability to take excessive risks with insured deposits; (2) prevent the coverage of losses incurred in the trading entity by the funds of the deposit bank, and hence limit the liability of taxpayer and the deposit insurance system; (3) avoid the excessive allocation of lending from the deposit bank to other financial activities, thereby to the detriment of the non-financial sectors of the economy; (4) reduce the interconnectedness between banks and the shadow banking system, which has been a source of contagion in a system-wide

---

[104] Ibid. p. 14.

[105] E. Liikannen et al., (2012), High-level expert group on reforming the structure of the EU banking sector, final report, Brussels.

banking crisis; and (5) level the playing field in investment banking activities between banking groups and stand-alone investment banks, as it would improve the risk sensitivity of the funding cost of trading operations by limiting the market expectations of public protection of such activities.[106]

This ultimately didn't happen (yet) as the EU is still bickering over the way forward.[107] In fact they are not separation of retail and investment banks isn't going to happen now or somewhere very soon.

8.6.1 The International Supervisors' Response

The EU, as the poster child when it comes to implementing and supporting G20 initiatives, issued in 2012 a green paper on shadow banking justified by the fact that: 'there is an increasing area of non-bank credit activity, or shadow banking, which has not been the prime focus of prudential regulation and supervision. Shadow banking performs important functions in the financial system. For example, it creates additional sources of funding and offers investors alternatives to bank deposits. But it can also pose potential threats to long-term financial stability'.[108] In line with the FSB, they concluded that the disorderly failure of shadow bank entities can carry systemic risk, both directly and through their interconnectedness with the regular banking system. The FSB has also suggested that as long as such activities and entities remain subject to a lower level of regulation and supervision than the rest of the financial sector, reinforced banking regulation could drive a substantial part of banking activities beyond the boundaries of traditional banking and toward shadow banking.

The October 2012 FSB report,[109] which preceded the EU's green book, represents the first comprehensive international effort to deal with shadow banking. It focuses on (i) the definition of principles for the monitoring and regulation of the shadow banking system; (ii) the initiation of a mapping process to identify and assess systemic risks involved in shadow banking; and (iii) the identification of the scope of possible regulatory measures.

The FSB report, which definition was illustrated in the introduction, breaks down the shadow banking industry into two pillars that are largely intertwined:

First, entities operating outside the regular banking system engaged in one of the following activities:

- accepting funding with deposit-like characteristics;
- performing maturity and/or liquidity transformation;
- undergoing credit risk transfer and
- using direct or indirect financial leverage.

[106] Liikannen et al., (2012), Ibid. p. vi.

[107] J.-A. Verlaine and B. Jennen, (2015), Bank Separation May Face Higher Hurdles in EU Lawmakers' Deal, BloombergBusiness, October 29, via Bloomberg.com

[108] EU (2012), Green Paper on Shadow Banking, COM(2012) 102 final, March 19, 2012, and frequently asked questions March 19, 2012 via ec.europe.eu

[109] FSB, (2011), Shadow Banking: Strengthening Oversight and Regulation Recommendations of the Financial Stability Board, Basel, October 27.

Table 8.2 Linking shadow banking activities to shadow banking entities and their perceived benefits

Entities	Activities
Special-purpose entities which perform liquidity and/or maturity transformation; for example, securitization vehicles such as ABCP conduits, special investment vehicles (SIVs) and other special-purpose vehicles (SPVs);	Securitization
money market funds (MMFs) and other types of investment funds or products with deposit-like characteristics, which make them vulnerable to massive redemptions ('runs');	Securities lending and repo
Investment funds, including exchange traded funds (ETFs), that provide credit or are leveraged;	Credit intermediation
finance companies and securities entities providing credit or credit guarantees, or performing liquidity and/or maturity transformation without being regulated like a bank; and	
insurance and reinsurance undertakings which issue or guarantee credit products	

Second, activities that could act as important sources of funding of non-bank entities. These activities include securitization, securities lending and repurchase transactions ('repo'). Looking at the industry this way, the following 'entities' and 'activities' come on the radar (Table 8.2).

The (perceived) benefits of the shadow banking sector are summarized as being (Table 8.3):

Consequently, the challenges from a regulatory point of view were described as:

- First, the authorities concerned have to identify and monitor the relevant entities and their activities.
- Second, the authorities have to determine the approach to supervising shadow banking entities.
- Third, as shadow banking issues may require extending the scope and nature of prudential regulation, appropriate regulatory responses are needed. The aforementioned FSB report has suggested some general principles which regulators should apply in designing and implementing regulatory measures for shadow banking. It therefore comes down to achieving the right balance between three possible and complementary means: (i) indirect regulation (regulating the links between the banking system and shadow banking entities); (ii) appropriate extension or revision of existing regulation; and (iii) new regulation specifically directed at shadow banking entities and activities.

Along those three lines, the EU has and is spinning its regulatory web around the shadow banking industry. Let's have a look at each of the components and the progress that is being made.

Table 8.3 Perceived benefits and risks of the shadow banking sector

Benefits	Risks
(i) They provide alternatives for investors to bank deposits	(i) Deposit-like funding structures may lead to 'runs': Shadow banking activities are exposed to similar financial risks as banks, without being subject to comparable constraints imposed by banking regulation and supervision. For example, certain shadow banking activities are financed by short-term funding, which is prone to risks of sudden and massive withdrawals of funds by clients
(ii) They channel resources toward specific needs more efficiently due to increased specialization	(ii) Build-up of high, hidden leverage: High leverage can increase the fragility of the financial sector and be a source of systemic risk. Shadow banking activities can be highly leveraged with collateral funding being churned several times, without being subject to the limits imposed by regulation and supervision
(iii) They constitute alternative funding for the real economy, which is particularly useful when traditional banking or market channels become temporarily impaired	(iii) Circumvention of rules and regulatory arbitrage: Shadow banking operations can be used to avoid regulation or supervision applied to regular banks by breaking the traditional credit intermediation process in legally independent structures dealing with each other. This 'regulatory fragmentation' creates the risk of a regulatory 'race to the bottom' for the financial system as a whole, as banks and other financial intermediaries try to mimic shadow banking entities or push certain operations into entities outside the scope of their consolidation. For example, operations circumventing capital and accounting rules and transferring risks outside the scope of banking supervision played an important role in the build-up to the 2007/2008 crisis
(iv) They constitute a possible source of risk diversification away from the banking system	(iv) Disorderly failures affecting the banking system: Shadow banking activities are often closely linked to the regular banking sector. Any failures can lead to important contagion and spill-over effects. Under distress or severe uncertainty conditions, risks taken by shadow banks can easily be transmitted to the banking sector through several channels: (a) direct borrowing from the banking system and banking contingent liabilities (credit enhancements and liquidity lines) and (b) massive sales of assets with repercussions on prices of financial and real assets

8.6.2 Indirect Regulation of Shadow Banking Activities Through the (Traditional) Banking and Insurance Regulation

The EU has taken important steps indirectly to address shadow banking issues raised by securitization structures to deter banks to circumvent existing capital requirements and other legislation:

- The revision of the EU banking capital requirements directive in 2009 (the so-called Capital Requirements Directive, or 'CRD II'),[110] which Member States should have transposed into national law by October 2010, required both originators and sponsors of securitized assets to retain a substantial share of their underwritten risks. The directive also reinforced the treatment of liquidity lines and credit exposure to securitization vehicles. The previous rules had allowed banks to avoid posting capital for the corresponding risks. Also this piece of legislation has been repealed through the implementation of the CRD IV Directive (infra).
- The amendments in the subsequent revision of the directive in 2010 (the so-called CRD III/IV)[111] further strengthened capital requirements. Since December 2011, banks have been required to comply with additional disclosure rules and hold significantly more capital to cover their risks when investing in re-securitizations. This Directive also required competent authorities in all Member States, when carrying out their risk assessment of individual banks under Pillar 2 of the Basel/CRD framework, to take into account reputational risks arising from complex securitization structures or products[112].
- In the so-called CRD IV, the Commission has implemented the introduction of explicit liquidity requirements as of 2015, including liquidity facilities for SPVs and for any other products or services linked to a bank's reputational risk (see infra for coverage).
- The Commission endorsed in November 2011 an amendment to the International Financial Reporting Standards (IFRS) to improve the disclosure requirements relating to the transfer of financial assets (related to IFRS 7).[113] The Commission is also enacted changes to the new standards on consolidation (related to IFRS 10, 11 and 12). The objective of these standards is to improve the consolidation of securitization vehicles and the disclosure requirements relating to unconsolidated participations in 'structured entities' like securitization vehicles or asset-backed financing.
- With regard to the insurance sector, under the rules implementing the Solvency II Framework Directive (Solvency II)[114] for insurance and reinsurance undertakings investing in securitization products, the Commission plans to require originators and

[110] Directive 2009/111/EC of the European Parliament and of the Council of September 16, 2009, amending Directives 2006/48/EC, 2006/49/EC and 2007/64/EC as regards banks affiliated to central institutions, certain own funds items, large exposures, supervisory arrangements and crisis management, O.J. L 302, 17.11.2009, pp. 97–119.

[111] Directive 2010/76/EU of the European Parliament and of the Council of November 24, 2010, amending Directives 2006/48/EC and 2006/49/EC as regards capital requirements for the trading book and for re-securitizations, and the supervisory review of remuneration policies, OJ L 329, 14.12.2010, pp. 3–35.

[112] See Annex V, point 8 of Directive 2006/48/EC as amended by Directive 2009/111/EC.

[113] Commission Regulation (EU) No 1205/2011 of November 22, 2011, amending Regulation (EC) No 1126/2008 adopting certain international accounting standards in accordance with Regulation (EC) No 1606/2002 of the European Parliament and of the Council as regards International Financial Reporting Standard (IFRS) 7 Text with EEA relevance.

[114] Directive 2009/138/EC of the European Parliament and of the Council of November 25, 2009, on the taking-up and pursuit of the business of Insurance and Reinsurance, OJ L335/1 of 17.12.2009. The new Solvency II Directive—a recast of several directives—is applicable from January 1, 2016.

sponsors of such products to meet risk retention requirements similar to those set out in banking legislation. The Framework Directive is principles-based, and the detailed rules of the Solvency II regime will be contained in Implementing Measures adopted by the Commission, and covering about 40 important areas in the Framework Directive. The Commission will propose implementing measures after the Omnibus II directive[115] enters into force.

8.6.3 The Capital Requirements Directive 'CRD' IV Package

8.6.3.1 Introduction

In June 2013, the direct regulation initiatives came together in the CRD IV package[116] which determines capital requirements for credit institutions and investment firms and which aims to put in place a comprehensive and risk-sensitive framework and to foster enhanced risk management among financial institutions. The rules are applicable as of January 1, 2014, with full implementation by January 1, 2019. The CRD IV was put in place to a large degree to implement the upgrade from Basel II to Basel III. The financial crisis has unveiled a number of shortcomings of Basel II and necessitated unprecedented levels of public support in order to restore confidence and stability in the financial system. In particular the following drawbacks of the existing framework were identified: capital that was actually not loss-absorbing, failing liquidity management, inadequate group-wide risk management and insufficient governance. In this regard, the G20 Declaration of April 2, 2009, conveyed the commitment of the global leaders to address the crisis with internationally consistent efforts to, among others, improve the quantity and quality of capital in the banking system, introduce a supplementary non-risk based measure to contain the build-up of leverage, develop a framework for stronger liquidity buffers at financial institutions and implement the recommendations of the Financial Stability

[115] Proposal for a Directive of the European Parliament and of the council amending Directives 2003/71/EC and 2009/138/EC in respect of the powers of the European Insurance and Occupational Pensions Authority and the European Securities and Markets Authority.

[116] Directive 2013/36/EU of the European Parliament and of the Council of June 26, 2013, on access to the activity of credit institutions and the prudential supervision of credit institutions and investment firms, amending Directive 2002/87/EC and repealing Directives 2006/48/EC and 2006/49/EC, O.J. L 176, 27.06.2013, pp. 338–436.Regulation (EU) No 575/2013 of the European Parliament and of the council of June 26, 2013, on prudential requirements for credit institutions and investment firms and amending Regulation (EU) No 648/2012, O.J. L 176, 27.6.2013, pp. 1–337.Corrigendum to Regulation (EU) Nr. 575/2013 of the European Parliament and of the Council of June 26, 2013, on prudential requirements for credit institutions and investment firms and amending Regulation (EU) No 648/2012, O.J. L 208, 2.8.2013, pp. 68–72. Corrigendum to Directive 2013/36/EU of the European Parliament and of the Council of June 26, 2013, on access to the activity of credit institutions and the prudential supervision of credit institutions and investment firms, amending Directive 2002/87/EC and repealing Directives 2006/48/EC and 2006/49/EC, O.J. L 208,2.8.2013, p. 73.

Board (FSB) to mitigate the procyclicality. In December 2010 and then further in 2011 and 2013, the Basel Committee issued its new standards ending in late 2018 with the final package.[117] In short the Basel III rules are built around the following objectives:[118]

Better and More Capital

Several banks appeared to have a capital base on their balance sheet meeting the regulatory standards, which, however, turned out to be not always available when needed for loss absorption. Some contracts restricted the absorption of losses or there were simply no liquid assets mirroring the balance sheet capital figure.

Basel III now prescribes strict criteria that must be met by own funds instruments, in order to ensure that they can effectively absorb banks' losses also in times of stress.

More Balanced Liquidity

A major problem was the lack of liquid assets and liquid funding during the crisis—referred to as 'the market dried up'. Basel III requires bankers to manage their cash flows and liquidity much more intense than before, to predict the liquidity flows resulting from creditors' claims better than before and to be ready for stressed market conditions by having sufficient 'cash' available, both in the short term and in the longer run.

Leverage Backstop

Just in case the calculated risk weights of Basels 2 and 2.5 contain errors, models contain errors or new products are developed and risk weights are not measured precisely yet, a traditional backstop mechanism limits the growth of the total balance sheet as compared to available own funds. A maximum leverage of 12 used to be a rule of thumb in the days that banks were not regulated yet. Today, given the sophistication of risk weight determination, the leverage ratio will be an additional checking tool for supervisors.

As this tool is new for the international framework, it was agreed that data and experience must be gathered before an effective leverage ratio can be introduced as a binding requirement in each jurisdiction.

Capital Requirements for Derivatives (Counterparty Credit Risk)

Basel III also enhances the existing capital requirements for bank derivative transactions and the so-called counterparty credit risk that stems from them. A derivative is an instrument whose value depends on another instrument, underlying it. Derivatives are used for good

---

[117] All documents related to Basel III are available at: http://www.bis.org/bcbs/basel3.htm

[118] See in detail: EU, (2013), Capital Requirements- CRD IV/CRR- Frequently Asked Questions, MEMO, July 16 via ec.europe.eu

reasons in banks' risk management, but the crisis revealed that exposures and losses could be material and that a review of the treatment in the supervisory framework was justified.

The framework also includes the treatment of bank exposures to central counterparties (CCPs). CCP is an entity that interposes itself between the two counterparties to a transaction, becoming the buyer to every seller and the seller to every buyer. A CCP's main purpose is to manage the risk that could arise if one counterparty is not able to make the required payments when they are due—that is, defaults on the deal.

Capital Buffers (See Section Below)

But the European Union went further than the Basel III required. In addition to Basel III implementation, the package introduces a number of important changes to the banking regulatory framework:

- Remuneration. In order to tackle excessive risk taking, the remuneration framework has been further strengthened with regard to the requirements for the relationship between the variable (or bonus) component of remuneration and the fixed component (or salary). For performance from January 1, 2014, onward, the variable component of the total remuneration shall not exceed 100% of the fixed component of the total remuneration of material risk takers. Exceptionally, and under certain conditions, shareholder can increase this maximum ratio to 200%.
- Enhanced governance: CRD IV strengthens the requirements with regard to corporate governance arrangements and processes and introduces new rules aimed at increasing the effectiveness of risk oversight by Boards, improving the status of the risk management function and ensuring effective monitoring by supervisors of risk governance.
- Diversity. Diversity in board composition should contribute to effective risk oversight by boards, providing for a broader range of views and opinion and therefore avoiding the phenomenon of group think. CRD IV therefore introduces a number of requirements, in particular as regards gender balance.
- Enhanced transparency. CRD IV improves transparency regarding the activities of banks and investment funds in different countries, in particular as regards profits, taxes and subsidies in different jurisdictions. This is considered essential for regaining the trust of EU citizens in the financial sector.
- Systemic risk buffer (see section below)
- Other systemic institution buffer (see section below)

Finally, the new rules seek to reduce to the extent possible reliance by credit institutions on external credit ratings by: a) requiring that all banks' investment decisions are based not only on ratings but also on their own internal credit opinion and b) that banks with a material number of exposures in a given portfolio develop internal ratings for that portfolio instead of relying on external ratings for the calculation of their capital requirements.

In the regulation a single rule book is created. For the first time, a single set of harmonized prudential rules is created which banks throughout the EU must respect. EU heads of state and government had called for a 'single rule book' in the wake of the crisis. This will ensure uniform application of Basel III in all Member States, will close regulatory loopholes and will thus contribute to a more effective functioning of the internal market. The new rules remove a large number of national options and discretions from the CRD and allows Member States to apply stricter requirements only where these are justified by national circumstances (e.g. real estate), needed on financial stability grounds or because of a bank's specific risk profile.

8.6.3.2 Structure of the CRD IV

The new framework divides the current CRD into two legislative instruments: a directive governing the access to deposit-taking activities and a regulation establishing the prudential requirements institutions need to respect. While Member States will have to transpose the directive into national law, the regulation is directly applicable, which means that it creates law that takes immediate effect in all Member States in the same way as a national instrument, without any further action on the part of the national authorities. This removes the major sources of national divergences (different interpretations, gold plating). It also makes the regulatory process faster and makes it easier to react to changed market conditions. It increases transparency, as one rule as written in the regulation will apply across the single market. A regulation is subject to the same political decision-making process as a directive at European level, ensuring full democratic control.

8.6.3.3 Widening the Scope of Current Regulations to Shadow Banking Activities

Revision of MiFID

The scope of existing regulations has also been extended to new entities and activities so as to have a broader coverage, address systemic risk concerns and make future regulatory arbitrage more difficult. This is the approach taken as regards investment firms. They are subject to the regime set out in the Markets in Financial Instruments Directive (MiFID).[119] In the review of this framework, the Commission proposed on October 20, 2011, a recast[120]

[119] Directive 2004/39/EC of the European Parliament and of the Council of April 21, 2004, on markets in financial instruments, O.J. L 145, 30.4.2004, pp. 1–44.

[120] Proposal for a directive of the European Parliament and of the Council on markets in financial instruments repealing Directive 2004/39/EC of the European Parliament and of the Council (Recast) COM(2011) 656 final. Proposal for a Regulation of the European Parliament and of the council on markets in financial instruments and amending Regulation [EMIR] on OTC derivatives, central counterparties and trade repositories; COM(2011) 652 final. Directive 2014/65/EU of the European Parliament and of the Council of May 15, 2014, on markets in financial instruments and amending Directive 2002/92/EC and Directive 2011/61/EU.

directive and a regulation in order to broaden the scope of the framework (e.g. to cover all high frequency traders and more commodity investment firms will be brought within the scope of MiFID); increase the transparency of non-equity instruments—which will enhance the ability to identify risks from shadow banking—and entrust competent national authorities and ESMA with enhanced and proactive intervention powers, enabling them to control and mitigate risks from shadow banking. MiFID does not directly impose capital requirements for those firms brought within its scope. However, it cross-refers to the Capital Requirements Directive, thereby imposing bank-like prudential regulation on entities performing shadow banking activities. The final version of the MiFID II was published in June 2014.[120]

Revising MiFID is an essential part of ongoing structural reforms in the aftermath of the financial crisis. These are aimed at establishing a safer, sounder, more transparent and more responsible financial system that works for the economy and society as a whole. The main objectives of the revision are as follows:[122]

(a) A more robust and efficient market structures: MiFID already covered Multilateral Trading Facilities and regulated markets, but the revision will now bring a new type of trading venue into its regulatory framework: the organized trading facility (OTF).
(b) Increased transparency: By introducing the OTF category, the proposals will improve the transparency of trading activities in equity markets, including 'dark pools' (trading volumes or liquidity that are not available on public platforms). Exemptions would only be allowed under prescribed circumstances.
(c) Reinforced supervisory powers and a stricter framework for commodity derivatives markets: The proposals will reinforce the role and powers of regulators. In coordination with the European Securities and Markets Authority (ESMA) and under defined circumstances, supervisors will be able to ban specific products, services or practices in case of threats to investor protection, financial stability or the orderly functioning of markets.
(d) Stronger investor protection: Building on a comprehensive set of rules already in place, the revised MiFID sets stricter requirements for portfolio management, investment advice and the offer of complex financial products such as structured products. In order to prevent potential conflict of interest, independent advisors and portfolio managers will be prohibited from making or receiving third-party payments or other monetary gains. Finally, rules on corporate governance and managers' responsibility are introduced for all investment firms.
(e) Impact on commodity derivatives markets: The review of MiFID will be a key pillar of a comprehensive and ambitious regulatory overhaul on improving commodity market transparency and oversight.

---

[121] Directive 2014/65/EU of the European Parliament and of the Council of May 15, 2014, on markets in financial instruments and amending Directive 2002/92/EC and Directive 2011/61/EU, O.J. L 173, 12.6.2014, pp. 349–496 and Regulation (EU) No 600/2014 of the European Parliament and of the Council of May 15, 2014, on markets in financial instruments and amending Regulation (EU) No 648/2012, O.J. L 173, 12.6.2014, pp. 84–148. The MiFID II regulation has been ondergoing multiple correction and amendments in 2014 and 2016. For details see: ec.europe.eu

[122] See also: EC, (2014), Market in Financial Instruments Directive (NiFID II): FAQs, MEMO 14/305, April 15, via ec.europe.eu

(f) Inclusion of emission allowance: On the emission allowances market, not only are the allowances themselves traded, but allowance derivatives are also traded. It is the latter that forms the largest part of the market. Trading in allowance derivatives already falls under the scope of MiFID and the Market Abuse Directive Status of UCITS: UCITS (Undertakings for Collective Investments in Transferable Securities) are financial instruments and therefore are already fully covered under MiFID. The issue which is touched upon in the MiFID review concerns their classification as complex or non-complex instruments.

The distinction is relevant in order to establish the application of the 'execution-only' regime, under which banks selling certain instruments are subject to less stringent rules for the protection of the retail investors. In particular they are not obliged to assess whether the client has sufficient knowledge to understand the financial instrument—the so-called appropriateness test. The execution-only regime only applies to non-complex financial instruments.

So far, all UCITS have been classified as non-complex instruments. In the meantime, however, certain UCITS have become more complex. In particular 'structured UCITS' are permitted to adopt certain kinds of complex investment strategies which can raise additional challenges for investors to understand how they operate. For this reason—for the mere purpose of the execution-only regime—the MiFID review confirms the general classification of UCITS as non-complex instruments but it introduces the exception of 'structured UCITS' which will now be classified as complex instruments. The consequence is that investment firms will have to apply the appropriateness test when they sell 'structured UCITS'. One of the arguments against this choice was that this can affect the UCITS 'label'. However, the two are different issues. Indeed, the changes in the MiFID only affect the MiFID selling rules of certain funds by banks and not the classification of 'structured UCITS' under the UCITS legislation.

Currently the access of third country firms to the EU markets is not harmonized under the MiFID.[123] Each Member State can introduce its own third country regime, subject to the general principles of the TFEU and provided that national provisions do not result in treatment more favorable than that given to EU firms. In order to overcome the existing fragmentation and to ensure a level playing field in the EU for third country players, the Commission proposes to introduce a harmonized third country equivalence regime in MiFID for the access of third country investment firms and market operators to the EU.

A firm which is authorized in a third country will be able to provide services directly to professional investors on condition that the country where it is based is deemed by the Commission to have equivalent rules and supervision. Equivalence will be granted only if the third country provides access to EU-based firms on a reciprocal basis.

In order to be allowed to provide services to retail investors, the establishment of a branch is required. A third country firm will be able to provide services to investors in other European countries from its branch, provided that it notifies the supervisors of those countries.

---

[123] Anno 2020 that is still the case and no generic third country framework is in place. Consultations are however ongoing at the level of ESMA (Q1/2020).

8.6.4 Intertwining with Other Non-shadow Banking Legislation

The proposed review of the Market Abuse Directive (MAD) and MiFID are published at the same time because together they guarantee the competitiveness, efficiency and integrity of EU financial markets. In order to ensure that they are fully coherent and support each other's objectives and principles, they need to be updated in tandem. Moreover, the pan-EU competition facilitated by MiFID has given rise to new challenges in terms of cross-border supervision, and maximum harmonization of the rules and competent authorities' powers in relation to offenses are a necessary step.

MiFID applies to the provision of investment services or activities by banks and investment firms in relation to financial instruments and to the operation of regulated markets. The objective is to support the development of a more integrated, competitive and efficient EU market in financial instruments with appropriate rules regarding conditions for authorization as investment firms, organizational requirements to ensure they are managed appropriately, market transparency and investor protection.

The EU legislation on OTC derivatives, central counterparties and trade repositories on the one hand, and on short selling and credit default swaps on the other, have different objectives but complement MiFID. The first aims to minimize counterparty credit risk and operational risk, while the second works to increase harmonization and transparency, and mitigate risks associated with short selling and the use of credit default swaps.

PRIPs are common products in the retail investment market, with broadly comparable functions for investors. Although there is no rigid definition of PRIPs ('packaged retail investment products'), they take a variety of legal forms. While offering benefits for investors, PRIPs are often complicated and opaque. The objective of the Commission in the coming months will be to better address the problems identified in the PRIPs market by creating a robust and coherent framework in two key areas:

1. the rules on the form and content of disclosures about the product and
2. the rules governing the sales process for PRIPs, such as the conduct of business and the conflicts of interest requirements for intermediaries distributing the products.

This is achieved by adopting a horizontal approach in the two areas, which builds on the most effective and efficient elements of existing community legislation. In the case of selling practices, MiFID has been identified as the clear benchmark as it contains comprehensive rules covering these aspects.

8.6.5 Direct Regulation with Respect to Shadow Banking Activities

Finally, the EU has also adopted measures to regulate shadow banking entities and activities directly. As far as investment funds are concerned, the Alternative Investment Fund

Managers Directive (AIFMD)[124] already addresses a number of shadow banking issues, provided that the entities concerned are captured as alternative investment funds under that directive. Asset managers are now required to monitor liquidity risks and employ a liquidity management system. Given new methods for calculating the leverage and reporting requirements, activities such as repurchase agreements or securities lending will be easier for the competent authorities to monitor.

As regards MMFs and ETFs ('exchange traded funds'), these funds may be covered by existing legislation on undertakings for collective investment in transferable securities (UCITS).[125] In addition, ESMA has developed guidelines which entered into force on July 1, 2011. These guidelines, which are continuously updated,[126] include recommendations for these funds to restrict the eligible investments, limit the weighted-average maturity and carry out daily net asset value calculations.

Credit rating agencies (CRAs) are not leveraged and they do not directly engage in maturity transformation. Nevertheless, they have an important role in the credit intermediation chain since they assign ratings to products and entities. In the EU, CRAs are subject to stringent regulation and supervision by ESMA.[127] Moreover, the Commission has proposed additional legislative measures to strengthen the credit rating process. That legislation was enacted on June 2013.[128]

Finally, in relation to insurance regulation, Solvency II also addresses a number of shadow banking issues as it provides comprehensive regulation centered on a risk-based and economic approach, along with strong risk management requirements including a 'prudent person' principle for investments. In particular, it explicitly covers credit risks in capital requirements, provides for a total balance sheet approach where all entities and exposures are subject to group supervision and is as stringent in respect of credit risk as CRD IV. Solvency II also requires Member States to authorize the establishment of an insurance SPV.

---

[124] Directive 2011/61/EC of the European Parliament and of the Council of June 8, 2011, on AlternativeInvestment Fund Managers and amending Directives 2003/41/EC and 2009/65/EC and Regulations (EC) No 1060/2009 and (EU) No 1095/2010, OJ L 174, 1.7.2011, p. 1.

[125] Directive 2009/65/EC of the European Parliament and of the Council of July 13, 2009, on the coordination of laws, regulations and administrative provisions relating to undertakings for collective investment in transferable securities.

[126] In July 2011 (2011/273) Q&A on money market funds: http://www.esma.europa.eu/system/files/ESMA_273.pdf and in February 2012 (2012/ 113) Q&A on money market funds http://www.esma.europa.eu/system/files/2012-113.pdf, the ES MA en EBA continue to produce guidelines on MMFs and AIFs on a wide variety of topics (stress testing, competent authority principles, reporting requirements …) all the way into 2020. See: esma.europe.eu and eba.europe.eu.

[127] Regulation (EC) No 1060/2009 of the European Parliament and of the Council of September 16, 2009, on credit rating agencies, O.J. L 302, 17.11.2009, pp. 1–31, and Regulation (EU) No 513/2011 of the European Parliament and of the Council of May 11, 2011, amending Regulation (EC) No 1060/2009 on credit rating agencies, O.J. L 145, 31.5.2011, pp. 30–56.

[128] Regulation (EU) No 462/2013 of the European Parliament and of the council of May 21, 2013, amending Regulation (EC) No 1060/2009 on credit rating agencies. O.J. L 146 of 31.5.2013, pp. 1–33. Directive 2013/14/EU of the European Parliament and of the Council of May 21, 2013, amending Directive 2003/41/EC on the activities and supervision of institutions for occupational retirement provision, Directive 2009/65/EC on the coordination of laws, regulations and administrative provisions relating to undertakings for collective investment in transferable securities (UCITS) and Directive 2011/61/EU on Alternative Investment Funds Managers in respect of over-reliance on credit ratings. O.J. L145 of 31.5.2013, pp. 1–3.

Detailed rules implementing Solvency II includes authorization and ongoing regulatory requirements relating to solvency, governance and reporting as far as insurance SPVs are concerned.

8.7 A Comprehensive Regulatory and Financial Stability Framework for the Shadow Banking Market: Is It Possible?

8.7.1 Introduction

How does one regulate a market-based financial system in a world that embraced capitalism? Either one regulates the system as if it was a traditional banking model. The problem is it isn't and so when doing so many asymmetries and inconsistencies will emerge. If one wants to avoid regulatory arbitrage, a global harmonization will be needed, while is equally unrealistic at it would be complex. The world has therefore engaged into granular data gathering, fragmented regulation to manage particular shadow banking markets and segments. But a market is not a natural phenomenon, it is an artificial construct designed to produce something for the wider society that gave birth to it through regulation, ambitions, policies, lobbying and innovations. But all these variables interact and evolve over time, and the consequence is that regulation doesn't pose the natural agility to ex ante adjust or even better anticipate on future evolution and dynamics. In contrast, legislation that tackles particular issues and products will be more granular in nature and therefore more prone to regulatory arbitrage. It seems that we're running out of options.

The other problem with tackling issues on an ad hoc basis is that if you decide to regulate based on data gathering, massive time will have gone by before market trends show up in data and datasets are consistent enough to design a policy on, that then needs to be converted into regulation which needs to go through the democratic regulatory process, the latter which is not particularly known for its swiftness. But market-based finance provides liquidity and lower cost of funding and many other positive things. Market-based finance as shadow banking is called in contemporaneous terms fits nicely within the wider trend of the financialization of society as a whole.

The French sociologists Boltanski and Thévenot[129] already long time ago indicated that the problem with financialization and market-based models is that they are predatory in nature and their 'value system' gets imposed on all assets in life thereby degenerating other values we typically attach to assets whether it is cultural, religious, social, civil in nature or otherwise. It injects the 'value and efficiency thinking' into all aspects of life, as Habermas predicted already in the 1970s. So we need to ensure that whatever the model now and in the future, the regulatory and policy framework needs to be of such a nature

[129] L. Boltanski and L. Thévenot, (2006), On Justification: Economies of Worth, Princeton University Press, Princeton NJ.

that it will at all times adhere to the prime objective being the 'stability and proper functioning of the public markets'.

But so, for now, we are stuck with the idea that regulating the shadow banking system will be a pool of highly specific projects dedicated to cater to specific activities or shadow banking segments and the risks they bring along. The only thing that all shadow banking activities have in common is the already discussed aspects of 'liquidity, maturity and credit transformation'. In that context it can be referred to the fact that the aggregate literature has deduced seven economic mechanisms that motivate and drive shadow banking activities.[130] They include:

- Specialization through long credit intermediation chains ('vertical slicing') with the involvement of non-bank financial intermediaries involved in a variety of steps.[131] This chain closely intertwines with commercial banks, bank holding companies and security broker-dealer.
- They often involve guarantees provided by the government and are often mispriced. Institutions and system including deposit insurance and liquidity windows 'creates well-known incentives for excessive risk-taking, leverage, and maturity transformation, motivating the need for supervision and prudential regulation'.[132] Whereas in the traditional sector, those facilities come with constraints that is not the case in a market-based financial system. They often gain access to those systems through bank holding companies, the parent companies of a group of companies that include both banking and shadow banking operations.
- The involvement of regulatory and tax arbitrage. The upshot is similar to economic activities with fewer constraints and a lower tax bill attached but with similar risks embedded (also for the system as such). It was discussed elsewhere and it was demonstrated that many of the SB product emerged as an alternative to constraint areas of the banking sector or changing capital rules.[133] The involvement of tax arbitrage has been discussed in the Pigovian chapter, and it became clear that although not causing instabilities and shocks in and to the system, they were severely helpful in directing efforts that led to the crisis.[134] A leveraged environment responds disproportionately large to any shock in the system.

---

[130] See T. Adrian and A.B. Ashcraft, (2012), Shadow Banking: A Review of the Literature. Palgrave Dictionary of Economics; T. Adrian et al., (2013), Shadow Bank Monitoring, Oxford Handbook of Banking, Oxford University, Press, Oxford.

[131] See for a review of those steps: Z. Pozsar et al., (2013), Shadow Banking, Federal Reserve Bank of New York Economic Policy Review Vol. 19, Issue 2, pp. 1–16.

[132] T. Adrian, (2014), Financial Stability Policies for Shadow Banking, Federal Reserve Bank of NY Staff Reports Nr. 664, February, pp. 3 ff.

[133] See, for example, V.V. Acharya et al., (2013), Securitization without Risk Transfer, *Journal of Financial Economics*, Vol. 107, Issue 3, pp. 515–536.

[134] J. Alworth and G. Arachi, (2012), Taxation and the Financial Crisis, Oxford University Press, Oxford; de Mooij R., et al., (2013), Taxation, Bank Leverage, and Financial Crises, IMF Working Paper Nr. WP/13/48; E.P. Davis and M. Stone, (2004), Corporate Structure and Financial Stability, IMF Working Paper Nr. WP/04/124.

- It involves concentration of risk in particular tail risk. Many shadow banking products are designed to take advantage of mispriced tail risk; they tend to be exposed to that risk. When not distributed properly, instabilities occur. That neglected risk is often mispriced on an ex ante basis.[135]
- An 'agency issue' that embody the many informational frictions that exist in many shadow banking products. Adrian indicates '[t]hey include asymmetric information problems between lenders and originators (predatory lending and borrowing), between lenders and investors, between servicers and investors, between servicers and borrowers, between beneficiaries of invested funds and asset managers, and between beneficiaries of invested funds and credit rating agencies. In addition, asymmetric information between investors and issuers results in risk-insensitive cost of funding.'[136]
- The creation of private money which complements traditional forms of money creation.
- The shadow banking system is prone to runs as the traditional system. The difference is that shadow banking assets have longer maturities than their liabilities and tend to be less liquid, causing fire-sale externalities. Adrian comments '[i]n a run, shadow banking entities have to sell assets at a discount, which depresses market pricing. This provides incentives to withdraw funding—before other shadow banking depositors arrive. However, the analogy between bank runs and shadow bank runs goes only so far. The reason is that shadow bank entities do not offer demand deposits, but instead obtain funding in wholesale money markets such as commercial paper or repo.'[137]

Tobias provides a number of case studies where he develops possible policies for certain niche markets of the shadow banking market taking into account these seven dynamics characterizing all shadow banking segments. He first demonstrates the economics behind the segment and nature of the products and how it emerged, followed by the intrinsic or external risks within the segment or product. Following that he makes policy suggestions.[138] All of them as geared toward addressing systemic risk which can include improving the resilience of the repo market, enhancing disclosure requirements and/or indirect regulation

---

[135] See in detail: N. Gennaioli et al., (2012), Neglected Risks, Financial Innovation, and Financial Fragility, *Journal of Financial Economics* Vol. 104, Issue 3, pp. 452–468; N. Gennaioli, et al., (2013), A Model of Shadow Banking, *Journal of Finance* Vol. 68, Issue 4, pp. 1331–1363; A. Ashcraft et al., (2011), Credit Ratings and Security Prices in the Subprime MBS Market, *American Economic Review* Vol. 101, Issue 3, pp. 115–119; J. Coval, et al., (2009), The Economics of Structured Finance, *Journal of Economic Perspectives* Vol. 23, Issue 1, pp. 3–25.

[136] T. Adrian, (2014), Ibid. p. 5.

[137] T. Adrian, (2014), Ibid. p. 6; see also T. Adrian, et al., (2013), Repo and Securities Lending, Quantifying Systemic Risk Measurement, NBER Research Conference Report Series, (ed. J.G. Haubrich, A.W. Lo), University of Chicago Press, Chicago; J. Gallin, (2013), Shadow Banking and the Funding of the Nonfinancial Sector, Federal Reserve Board Finance and Economics Discussion Series Nr. 2013-50; G. Gorton and A. Metrick, (2011), Regulating the Shadow Banking System, Brookings Paper on Economic Activity, pp. 261–312; G. Gorton and A. Metrick, (2012), Securitized Banking and the Run on Repo, *Journal of Financial Economics* Vol. 104, pp. 425–451.

[138] T. Adrian, (2014), Ibid. pp. 12–20. His case studies involve agency mortgage REITs (Agency mortgage REITs (agency REITs) are specialized REITs that invest in mortgage backed securities (MBS) issued by US government-sponsored agencies), leveraged lending and captive reinsurance.

between supervised BHCs. They might also include improving underwriting standards for (leveraged) lending against a macroeconomic background[139] and wrapping together fragmented regulation in the insurance sector might avoid unaccounted risk migration to captives due to limited disclosure rules in the reinsurance sector.[140] Also Adrian concludes that shadow banking activities evolve in response to changing regulations and market conditions. That knowledge implies that policies and regulations need to adapt constantly and might trigger new product design, new forms of regulatory arbitrage and maybe worse of action taking too late as the regulator and policymaker will always be 'behind the curve' in case it will only take action once dynamics have shown up in statistics.

The fragmented nature of financial regulation and the shadow banking regulation in particular is an ongoing concern. Both the European initiatives in terms of 'Oversight Council' and 'European Systemic Risk Board' provide some leeway to supervisors and regulatory to expand their mandate and scope of coverage. Another item that was learned the hard way during and after the 2008 financial crisis was the fact that financial regulation should not only take a micro-view (at the level of the individual FI regulated) but also a system-wide macro-view (at the level of the market as such) if it wants to capture properly the eventuality of 'systemic risk' occurring. That makes sense as a market-based financial system needs to observe the widest monitoring scope possible as the system is now holistic. The discussion of 'systemic risk' and 'contagion effects', 'spillovers' and 'interconnectedness' throughout the book are proof of the fact that our understanding is, albeit growing, still modest and embryonic in many ways. The many different models and outcomes discussed are an illustration which require no further comments.

8.7.2 Can the Shadow Banking Sector Be Stable for Longer Periods of Time?

In any form of equilibrium, a model where banks originate and trade loans, assemble them into diversified portfolios and finance these portfolios externally with riskless debt, outside investor wealth drives the demand for riskless debt and indirectly for securitization. In such a model bank assets and leverage move together, banks become interconnected through markets, and banks increase their exposure to systematic risk as they reduce idiosyncratic risk through diversification. Such a model can be stable and welfare improving under rational expectations. That is what Gennaioli et al. demonstrated.[141] The one aspect

[139] Supervisory rule 13-3, Interagency Guidance on Leveraged Lending, March 21, 2013 (revised November 13, 2014).

[140] See, for example, R.S.J. Koijen and M. Yogo, (2014), Shadow Insurance, Swiss Finance Institute Research Paper Nr. 14–64; The issue was brought to mind first by B. M. Lawsky of the NY Department for Financial Services indicating that the loopholes in the shadow insurance sector might embed material risks for the public markets and the Treasury: see B.J. Lawsky, (2013), Shining a Light on Shadow Insurance, A Little-known Loophole That Puts Insurance Policyholders and Taxpayers at Greater Risk, New York State Department of Financial Services Working Paper, June.

[141] N. Gennaioli et al., (2013), A Model of Shadow Banking, *The Journal of Finance*, Vol. 68, Nr. 4, (August), pp. 1331–1361.

that makes that system become unstable and vulnerable to crisis is the neglect of 'tail risk' which causes liquidity to dry up.

I already indicated before that the 'information-insensitive' debt market become 'information sensitive' under duress or during market shocks. It was framed as such that events always show the dynamics that 'uncertainty about price' becomes 'uncertainty about the quality of the assets that are priced'. The insensitivity at the 'price' level now becomes 'quality' sensitivity, although both obviously might be totally disconnected. But what can we learn from their model and this specific insensitivity aspect? In case FIs need to finance loan portfolios from outside investors, they can only do so properly and at a workable cost if the outside investor is assumed to be infinitely risk averse (i.e. they are only interested in riskless debt). If that outside investor as a group has limited wealth, the FI will have to finance their loan book themselves as there is no demand from external investors. In case wealth is high (i.e. large institutional pools with abundant liquidity), demand will be high and information insensitivity will be high. To meet that demand, sufficient collateral needs to be manufactured (beyond what the market naturally supplies). They can only do so under market constraints by taking on board riskier projects delivering riskier debt than what the outside investor can tolerate.

If we take a step back and reflect on that, we come to the surprising conclusion that, although remarkable, we got accustomed to this way of doing things way too easily. The true risk embedded in a debt security does not matter for (institutional) investors. That leads to a surprising side effect, that is, although debt investors take into account risk when pricing debt securities, they do not take it into account when anticipating a possible capital loss on that investment. Whatever the credit rating, debt investors are expected to receive their principal back. And if they don't, or there might be a likelihood, they respond surprised and do so in a similar way, leading to the well-known contagion and herding effect.[142] So shadow banking products exploit the risk insensitivity of debt investors and 'leave them hanging out to dry when counterparty risk effectively materialized. So this is now becoming a matter of 'bad' and 'evil'.' A well-informed investor might be 'assumed' and if he decides for whatever reason to be 'ignorant' about the material content of the debt products bought, besides 'deceit', it is a decision that was made for their own account. Part of the shadow banking problem is therefore not a shadow banking problem but an 'investor community problem', that is, the fact that under rational expectations debt is always repaid. That debt is considered risk-free regardless of its credit rating.[143] Gennaiola et al. indicate '[t]his is our critical new result: the very diversification that eliminates intermediary-specific risks by pooling loans so as to support the issuance of debt perceived to be riskless actually raises intermediaries' exposure to tail aggregate risks. Still, under rational expectations, riskless debt is always repaid, and the system is very

[142] An exception to that is the junior and distressed investors in the market who 'effectively' anticipate on a possible default by their counterparties.

[143] I ignore the discussion about the credit rating debate and their involvement in providing inadequate ratings to securitized products. It is not part of the shadow banking discussion, although materially important.

stable.'[144] But that is in sharp contrast with the understanding that even the most sophisticated investors didn't have (and don't have) proper models to assess the true dynamics of tail risk, assessing risk in securitized products and overall fail to appreciate bubble formation in markets even under constant monetary terms. The insurance offered by the shadow banking segment covers not only aggregate but also idiosyncratic risk. Most failed to understand that securitization also concentrates the already badly understood tail risk in many fixed-income products. The 'diversification myth', as Brown[145] denominates it, implied that through these channels, the insurance against idiosyncratic risk 'interacts with the neglect of tail aggregate risks in creating extreme financial fragility'.[146] That misunderstood tail risk allowed balance sheets to expand beyond normal rational conditions and created systemic risk. The 'diversification myth' in the information-insensitive markets is a, if not 'the', critical aspect. It also points at the fact that regulating issuers of shadow banking products is only half the battle and that there is a risk embedded in how these markets function. You can take these shadow banking products away, but other will bring them back on the table even if that is in a different format, subject to different regulation and caused by different ambitions.[147]

Although the literature focused initially on the process and design of securitized products and how to overcome adverse selection,[148] in more recent times, more attention has been given to the 'counterparty' dynamics of the issuers, being the fixed-income buyers and the nature of the debt markets. The assumption of 'safe assets' in the information-insensitive debt markets allows market agents to buy and sell without causing ripple effects as all investors in debt markets as symmetrically informed (or ignorant). It creates a liquid debt market. That phenomenon combined with the fact that financial regulation could be stretched, via regulatory arbitrage, to create securitization without risk transfers[149] often by off-balance sheet constructs.[150] That allowed to lower capital charges, benefit tax holidays and still indirectly have access to the liquidity window of the central bank for the privately created money volumes. It allowed risk to be reallocated between risk-averse investors and risk-neutral intermediaries, providing an asymmetry that was well exploited by the intermediaries (FIs).

'Safe debt' is a doubtful concept especially when operational in information-insensitive debt markets. It triggered a relaxation of the discipline of investors at the benefit of liquid deep

---

[144] N. Gennaioli et al., (2013), Ibid. p. 1332.

[145] G. Brown, (2010), Beyond the Crash: Overcoming the First Crisis of Globalization, Free Press, New York.

[146] N. Gennaioli et al., (2013), Ibid. p. 1332.

[147] See, for example, how CDS ('credit default swap') are experiencing their renaissance in recent years and what drives that market; T. Alloway, (2015), Why Would Anyone Want to Restart the Credit Default Swaps Market? Saving Single-Name Credit Default Swaps?, Bloomberg.com, May 11.

[148] See, for example, T. V. Dang, et al., (2009), Ignorance and the Optimality of Debt for Liquidity Provision, Working Paper, Yale University.

[149] V.V. Acharya et al., (2013), Securitization without Risk Transfers, *Journal of Financial Economics*, Vol. 107, pp. 515–536.

[150] See Gennaiola et al., (2013), Ibid. p. 1357; see also V.V. Acharya, et al. (eds.), (2009), Restoring Financial Stability: How to Repair a Failed System, John Wiley & Sons, Inc., Hoboken, NJ.

debt market that come at a cost of funding much lower than would be the case if debt markets would be debt-sensitive. The assumption of safe debt allowed for 'over-issuing debt securities'. It also explains why certain market participants continued to 'on load' those shadow banking securities, even when at a certain point in 2007/2008 the true risk profile of those securities emerged in the market.[151] The uncertainty about private information does then all the rest to cause systemic dimensions in a crisis through the contagion channel.[152] That contagion often finds its origin in the collateral markets. Kuong indicates 'a feedback loop exists between the risk-taking behavior of borrowers (e.g. shadow banks) and the expected price of seized collateral in the secondary market'.[153] What then is left is the reputational fragility of leveraged market players in debt markets.[154] The question then emerges how to balance that information insensitivity with the fact that the knowledge ex ante of potential shock and the likelihood are very small. Not all risks are ignored in the debt markets and not all risk can be weighted forever. It would make debt market dysfunctional and illiquid. But ignoring on aggregate critical risks combined with the typical herding behavior delivered what we got in 2007/2008. The question that needs to be brought back on the table is that of 'herding' in markets, the role of asset managers and the dependence of institutional asset pools on 'third-party analysis' and most likely the 'too thin' knowledge base available (and time constraints) in the teams managing those institutional asset pools. Financial crises are ultimately man-made and lie often in the ignorance or under-appreciation of default risk in the debt markets.[155] In equity markets, the understanding of that risk is more alive as equity will absorb that risk. It also allowed the market to swiftly recover after the technology in 2001.

When it comes to the ignorance of risks by debt investors, the regulator also had and has a role to play. As Gorton and Metrick indicate, 'the evolution of a bankruptcy "safe harbor" for repos[156] has been a crucial feature in the growth and efficiency of shadow banking'.[157] Their suggestion is to create a robust framework and guidelines for the use of collateral (and haircuts[158]) and government guarantees insurance systems regardless whether those risks are on the books or not. Gordon and Metrick comment '[w]hether we

---

[151] M. Kacperczyk, and Ph. Schnabl, (2013), How Safe are Money Market Funds? *Quarterly Journal of Economics*, Vol. 128, Issue 3, pp. 1073–1122.

[152] The fact that informed investors refuse to roll over debt more than uninformed investors exacerbates the probability of a debt crisis; see, for example, T. Ahnert and A. Kakhbod, (2014), Information Choice and Amplification of Financial Crises, Working Paper: 'a slight deterioration in the public information about a debtor's solvency can increase an investor's strategic uncertainty'.

[153] J.C. F. Kuong, (2014), Fragility of Collateralized Short-Term Debt Markets, INSEAD Working Paper, July. He also indicates that lifting an exception on the automatic stay in repo finance and for derivatives can worsen the moral hazard of borrowers and lead to more fire sales.

[154] C.-H. Weymuller, (2013), Leverage and Reputational Fragility in Credit Markets, HBS Working Paper, January.

[155] N. Gennaioli et al., (2013), Ibid. pp. 1359–1360.

[156] G. Gorton and A. Metrick, (2010), Regulating the Shadow Banking System, Yale and NBER Working Paper, October, pp. 12–14.

[157] G. Gorton and A. Metrick, (2010), Ibid. pp. 15–16.

[158] As suggested by the FSB: see FSB, (2014), Regulatory Framework for Haircuts on Non-Centrally Cleared Securities Financing Transactions, Basel, October 14.

keep risks on balance sheet or allow them to go off, there is no escaping the requirement for regulators to evaluate these risks'.[159] The supply of safe collateral is then a concern. A non-AAA collateral or substitute will not and cannot be always information-insensitive. The same is true for the practice of 're-hypothecation'.

8.7.3 Ex Ante Monitoring and Intervention

The Holy Grail would be ex ante monitoring, regulation and/or interventions that would mitigate systemic risk, neutralize externalities and cushion the information insensitivity in the debt markets. Adrian et al.[160] make such a suggestion. They present a forward-looking program that identifies and tracks the sources of systemic risk and facilitate the development of pre-emptive policies to promote financial stability. That distinguishes in their model between 'shocks' which they indicate are difficult to prevent and 'vulnerabilities' that amplify shocks. The key elements in their framework are 'leverage, maturity transformation, interconnectedness, complexity, and the pricing of risk as the primary vulnerabilities in the financial system' and covers four areas (traditional banking, shadow banking, asset markets and the non-financial sector). The tipping point in the model is, as discussed before, that there is a trade-off between reducing systemic risks and the increase in the costs of financial intermediation. So it is 'good' way or 'bad' way: either debt investors appreciate risk for what it really is and price it accordingly or we build a monitoring and framework around non-bank credit intermediation and that will push the cost of funding and credit intermediation up ('policies to address vulnerabilities will likely impose costs in terms of a higher price of risk in "normal" times').[161] The framework suggested by Adrian et al. relates financial shocks, financial vulnerabilities,[162] financial externalities and the overall pricing of risk in the financial system. Vulnerabilities can either be structural or cyclical. The structural ones require monitoring while the structural ones are a material component and determinant of systemic risk.

In most models[163] developed regarding financial stability, the key amplifier is the time variation in the tightness of funding constraints at the level of the intermediary agents. The spectrum between risk-ignorant (in boom times) and risk averse during economic contractions is materially wide. When the pricing of risk is compressed, leverage and liquidity abundance amplify shocks and externalities. Leverage, maturity transformation, interconnectedness and the likes will tend to lower the cost of financial intermediation when shocks in the system are local but crease spillovers when fire sales cannot be contained. So the

[159] G. Gorton and A. Metrick, (2010), Ibid. p. 26.

[160] T. Adrian et al., (2014) Financial Stability Monitoring, Federal Reserve Bank of New York Staff Reports, Nr. 601.

[161] T. Adrian et al., (2014), Ibid. p. 2.

[162] See their empirical analysis regarding cyclical financial vulnerabilities in the shadow banking segment: T. Adrian, et al., (2013), Ibid. pp. 16–21.

[163] See, for example, T. Adrian, and N. Boyarchencko, (2012), Intermediary Leverage Cycles and Financial Stability, FRB of New York Staff Report Nr. 567 and M. Gertler, and N. Kiyotaki, (2012), Banking, Liquidity, and Bank Runs in an Infinite Horizon Economy, Princeton University Working Paper.

wider the system shock, the higher the impact on the pricing of risk. The role of vulnerabilities (leverage, maturity transformation and complexity) in that context is that they will trigger larger externalities and therefore magnify that increase in pricing risk. The difference between a vulnerability and a shock is often difficult to highlight and vulnerabilities can evolve into shocks.[164] That balancing act produces the trade-off already indicated: more vulnerable systems will produce lower pricing of risk and funding in periods of low volatility (no distress) and will generate higher pricing of risk in case of large adverse shocks (under distress). Less vulnerable systems will narrow the bandwidth of pricing risk and will push it higher on the lower bound and somewhat lower on the higher bound.[165] The instability under the vulnerable model points at the inability of FIs to coordinate stable but more expensive funding models in the market (coordination issue).

Reducing systemic risk then equates reducing or mitigating (or neutralizing) vulnerabilities. Macroprudential tools should then 'reduce the sensitivity of the price of risk to adverse shocks, so that increases in the price of risk are more moderate when adverse shocks are larger'.[166] That can occur through higher capital and liquidity charges. The 'equity factor' I already brought into the discussion a number of times. (Much) Higher capital charges would reduce sensitivities in a very material way and reduce contagion to a large degree. But raising equity for financial institutions is costly so is claimed (thereby increasing the cost of credit intermediation), but not everybody agrees (and correctly so).[167] Even a tax on leverage,[168] which in itself will create inefficiency, will make the investor base better off due to the lower amount of systemic risk; that lower incidence of risk benefits the growth trajectory.[169]

---

[164] T. Adrian et al., (2014), Ibid. pp. 2–5.

[165] The latter however is still not empirically tested (to my knowledge).

[166] T. Adrian et al., (2014), Ibid. p. 6.

[167] A. Admati, and Martin Hellwig, (2013), The Bankers' New Clothes: What's Wrong with Banking and what to Do about it, Princeton University Press, Princeton NJ; A. Admati, et al., (2010), Fallacies, Irrelevant Facts, and Myths in the Discussion of Capital Regulation: Why bank Equity is Not Expensive, Stanford University Working Paper. Let's say that in a competitive banking market, higher equity buffers will lead to lower 'return on equity' which is what drives the argument against higher capital buffers. But equity is just another source of funding that can be used to provide credit with into the market.

[168] See the Pigovian chapter and also J. Bianchi, and E. Mendoza, (2011), Over-borrowing, Financial Crises and Macroprudential Policy, IMF Working Paper Nr. WP/11/24.

[169] See, for example, in the housing market: L. Lambertini et al., (2012), Leaning against Boom-Bust Cycles in Credit and Housing Prices, Working Paper. They conclude 'responding to financial variables is socially optimal' and 'responding to credit growth is Pareto improving' and also '[b]orrowers are better off when both the LTV (Loan-to-Value) ratio and the interest rate respond to credit growth, which most effectively Stabilizes credit relative to GDP. Savers are better off under an interest rate response to credit growth coupled with a constant LTV ratio'. See also regarding the impact whether loose monetary policies increase financial stability: A. Cesa-Bianchi and A. Rebucci, (2013), Does Easing Monetary Policy Increase Financial Instability, Inter-American Development Bank Working Paper, Nr. IDB-WP-387, February. They indicate 'when the policy interest rate is the only available instrument, a monetary authority subject to the same constraints as private agents cannot always achieve a (constrained) efficient allocation and faces a trade-off between macroeconomic and financial stability in response to negative shocks'.

Also Adrian et al. point at the repo market as one of the key drivers of vulnerability in the shadow banking segment. That vulnerability runs mainly through the 'broker-dealer' party, why rely heavily on collateralized lending obligations which have a strong inclination to become fragile when values become uncertain. When those broker-dealers are leveraged (and/or their clients) and when the degree of maturity mismatch is greater, systemic vulnerabilities increase.

The vulnerability analysis, with a view to reducing systemic risk in an ex ante fashion, concentrates in a number of areas in the shadow banking segment. Those include[170]:

- Dealer-intermediated financing.
- Wholesale short-term funding markets.
- Securitizations and other new financial products that transform risks.
- Private equity, asset managers and hedge funds should be monitored in case they engage in transformations of maturity, liquidity and credit risk.
- Institutional asset pools (pension funds, insurance firms, etc.) should be monitored when they engage in securities lending and the provision of tail-risk insurance in credit markets.

8.7.4 A Framework Analysis

As indicated, the existing responses across the globe are very partial, very niche and targeting specific segments and instruments. And although, the shadow banking sector has been deeply analyzed since the financial crisis, it still feels that there is no holistic view nor approach to the SB market. That is particularly true now that it is seen as a tool to revive lagging economies globally in times when banks are constraint. Adrian and Ashcraft have focused on 'identifying the gap between the optimal and actual[171] regulation of the shadow banking sector'.[172] They do so by developing a framework, based on existing shadow banking literature,[173] through which the shadow banking segment can be understood ('optimal shadow financial intermediation, characterizing the asset risk, liquidity, and leverage choice of shadow intermediaries in the presence of appropriately risk-sensitive funding'). The framework contrasts 'actual' with 'optimal' and thus asks the question why the market is unable to achieve efficient outcomes on its own.[174] They indicate 'the provision of explicit but underpriced credit and liquidity put options through deposit insurance and discount window access, respectively, create incentives for excessive asset risk,

[170] See in detail: T. Adrian et al., (2014), Ibid. pp. 16–21.

[171] T. Adrian and A.B. Ashcraft, (2012), Shadow Banking Regulation, Federal Reserve Bank of NY, Staff Reports, Nr. 559, April. See for a review: pp. 26–38.

[172] T. Adrian and A.B. Ashcraft, (2012), Shadow Banking Regulation, Federal Reserve Bank of NY, Staff Reports, Nr. 559, April, p. 2.

[173] T. Adrian and A.B. Ashcraft, (2012), Ibid. pp. 3–4.

[174] T. Adrian and A.B. Ashcraft, (2012), Ibid. p. 8.

leverage, and maturity transformation'. Their contribution is to demonstrate that 'the simultaneous impact of mispriced credit and liquidity put options, as well as highlight that implicit put options as well as market-based financial frictions result in similar outcomes' (i.e. creates incentives (ed.)).

The fundamental question is why risk-insensitive funding exists to begin with. There are a number of possibilities[175]:

- the presence of implicit credit and liquidity support
- the presence of asymmetric information between a financial firm and investors
- informational frictions between the beneficiaries of investable funds and their fiduciaries

These frictions occur in a wide variety of shadow banking segments and products:

1. Asset-backed commercial paper (and other types of securitizations).[176] The key frictions in this segment are '[m]ispricing of credit and liquidity put options provided by banks to sponsors through risk-insensitive capital regulation of backup lines of credit and mispricing of credit and liquidity risk by investors created in part by information asymmetries between investors and asset managers that result in overreliance on credit ratings'. With respect to other securitizations, other frictions will include (1) asymmetric information between investors and issuers, resulting in risk-insensitive cost of funding and (2) over-reliance on credit ratings by investors / incentives of issuers to structure long-term opaque risky receivables into AAA liabilities.
2. Tri-Party Repo Market. They key frictions here are: (1) implicit intraday support of term transactions by clearing banks through the daily unwinding of transactions, resulting in risk-insensitive funding by repo investors; (2) over-reliance by repo investors on credit ratings on the securities collateral and counterparty; (3) inability of money market mutual funds to hold securities collateral that secure repos outright over a long enough horizon to facilitate orderly liquidation, combined with the inability of markets to absorb the sudden unwind of a large position without having a significant impact on prices that affects all holders of the asset type (even beyond tri-party repo) and erodes their capital and (4) vulnerability of the tri-party repo market to self-fulfilling run.[177]
3. Money market funds. The key frictions include (1) mispricing of the implicit support by plan sponsors and official sector, (2) over-reliance on ratings by investors/incentives of financial sector to convert long-term opaque risky assets into money market eligible instruments, (3) a lack of capacity for loss absorption in the event of a borrower's failure and (4) the susceptibility of MMFs to runs by their own investors, which create run risk.[178]

---

[175] T. Adrian and A.B. Ashcraft, (2012), Ibid. pp. 8–9.

[176] T. Adrian and A.B. Ashcraft, (2012), Ibid. pp. 10–15 & 23–26.

[177] T. Adrian and A.B. Ashcraft, (2012), Ibid. pp. 15–20.

[178] T. Adrian and A.B. Ashcraft, (2012), Ibid. pp. 20–23.

Although some or even most of the regulation put in place in recent years helps to neutralize, cater to mitigating or reduce overall some of these frictions, most of them do so under a wide variety of assumptions and implied realities.[179] Although questions are asked about the 'effectiveness' despite the robust regulatory effort in many of these new regulations. The reality however is that the regulatory process is prone to lobbying and that creates un-transparent conditions, shaved-off conditions, melted-down capital requirements, unstable risk-weighted models and requisites that might hamper the regulation's effectiveness at moments that it really matters. Some of the legislation is also prone to shifting some of the risk from the institutional to the infrastructural level where it is even more unmanageable. A good example of that is the need to clear previous OTC derivatives over a central clearing facility. Although conceptually good, questions are asked about the concentration and asymmetry of risk (and aligned measurement issues) at the level of the CCP, on top of the question whether the CCP is able to manage these asymmetric counterparty risks in a meaningful way, holds sufficient capital relative to a potential exposure and whether clearing OTC derivatives doesn't create the next 'too-big-to-fail' entity.[180] In particular the issues related to 'interdependencies and interconnections' are a worrisome area in a global marketplace. The OTC derivatives market, which is a market about 8 to 12 times larger than the real global economy,[181] will now be channeled through CCPs who bring asymmetric counterparty risk together (with limited netting opportunities) and under a variety of contracts. These CCPs in itself are also connected through dealings and therefore the question arises how to mitigate the systemic risk created through the requirement to channel OTC derivatives.

Wendt et al. indicate that, although efforts have been made to mitigate some of these risks, there are a material number that still can cause material damage, when emerging at the level of the CCP (which under the new regulation acts as an electricity socket in the OTC system). They identify the following areas of concern: '(i) the composition of the risk waterfall and loss sharing arrangements may be a source of contagion for surviving clearing members; (ii) the dependency of CCPs on only a few, commercial banks for liquidity, custody, settlement, and other services puts additional pressure on CCPs and surviving clearing members during a crisis; (iii) simultaneous collateral sales of multiple CCPs can impact market volatility; and (iv) diverging interests of authorities in a globally cleared market probably hamper effective cross-border solutions to manage systemic risks'.[182] Disclosure requirements for CCPs as issued by BIS-IOSCO will not help

---

[179] T. Adrian and A.B. Ashcraft, (2012), Ibid. pp. 38–53 for an evaluation of actual legislation versus the economic frictions identified.

[180] See, for example, for an evaluation: F. Wendt, (2015), Central Counterparties: Addressing their Too Important to Fail Nature, IMF Working Paper Nr. WP/15/21.

[181] Measurements vary but stand mid 2019 at about approx. 1000 trillion USD.

[182] F. Wendt, (2015), Ibid. pp. 22. See for an evaluation of current legislation that addresses CCPs' systemic risk: pp. 14–18. See also A.J. Menkveld, (2014), Crowded Trades: An Overlooked Systemic Risk for Central Clearing Counterparties, Working Paper. See for an industry perspective: Joint letter to J. Lew, (2015), U.S. Regulatory Oversight of Central Counterparties, March 9. See for a risk assessment overview: FIA, (2015), FIA Global CCP Risk Position Paper, April. Also the CCP dedicated chapter (5).

materially to mitigate any of these risks[183] and nor do the recovery and resolution plans and models CCPs have to develop according to contemporary law.[184]

The real problem of interconnectedness (which was discussed elsewhere specifically for CCPs) is an issue scholars and regulators likewise or only starting to understand. Building giant electricity sockets in the global financial system helps to clean up the OTC market in terms of compliance and understanding the nature and size of that market, but yields another, maybe even bigger problem, instead. The bottom line is often that only sizeable larger equity portions will help reduce vulnerabilities and mitigate contagion (to a certain degree) but it also leaves us behind with the understanding that as long as society (through the regulator) allows that those transactions can occur in parallel with basic public utility functions or worse transactions covered by some sort of public backstop, the problem will not go away sometime soon. The crisis[185] taught us 'the extent to which banks had become the core of the backstop arrangements for the non-bank sector'. The shadow banking sector therefore needs lower levels of many things in order for the system to absorb its implications properly. Adrian and Ashcraft indicate 'a key lesson emerging from the financial crisis is that our non-bank based system of financial intermediation needs less leverage, asset risk and maturity transformation to survive periods of extreme stress'.[186] As long as banks will have to indirectly provide that backstop to shadow banking activities, any level of capital requirements will prove to be insufficient as they are not tailored to secure the 'market as such', because that is what shadow banking or 'market-based finance' effectively is.

The current regulatory framework has done quite the opposite as Basel III has even increased the need for shadow banking activities, 'as the gap between capital and liquidity requirements on traditional institutions and non-regulated institutions has increased'. The proper parameters are (1) a 'limited' and 'transparent' public backstop directly (by the Treasury) or indirectly (through the banking sector), (2) a material reduction of maturity and liquidity transformation risk in the pool of SB products,[187] (3) a proper pricing of intermediation risk which can only be done by reducing systemic risk and creating

[183] See for an overview: BIS-IOSCO, (2015), Public Quantitative Disclosure Standards for Central Counterparties, February, Basel. A good example of how regulators and supervisors know the issues but have a difficulty breaking down into granular concepts that have a chance of being tackled by regulation: Bank of England, (2015), The Bank of England's Supervision of Financial Market Infrastructures—Annual Report, March.

[184] The ISDA suggested a framework for those plans; see ISDA, (2015), CCP Default Management, Recovery and Continuity: A Proposed Recovery Framework, January.

[185] T. Adrian and A.B. Ashcraft, (2012), Ibid. p. 53.

[186] See also for an evaluation of the implications of the Dodd-Frank Act in this context: T. Adrian, (2011), Dodd-Frank One Year On: Implications for Shadow Banking, Federal Reserve Bank of New York Staff Reports, Nr. 533, December.

[187] How that can be achieved is up for discussion: either one forces the system for short-term debt to be fully backed by AAA-securities as Wolf (M. Wolf, (2014), The Shifts and the Shocks: What We've Learned-and Have Still to Learn-from the Financial Crisis, Penguin Books, New York) suggests and/or one considers a Pigovian mechanism as I suggested in the Pigovian chapter that would ex ante neutralize the possible externalities caused by the intermediation process. See for an application of the maturity transformation model in a highly unstable market: A. Krishnamurthy et al., (2014), Seizing Up Repo, *The Journal of Finance*, Vol. 69, Issue 6 (December), pp. 2381–241.

transparent backstops, (4) a true 'Chinese wall' between SB and public backstop protected activities, (5) materially higher capital requirements for those banking groups that have SB and utility banking functions entangled and/or implicitly covered by their deposit insurance mechanism, and (6) the absolute termination of the financial sector's ability to generate 'money and near-money alternatives'.[188]

Two elements will prevent from reaching the optimal solution in this context. We know the answers, but the political channels cannot facilitate such outright solutions. The democratic process is subject to many influences that it literally disallows the 'public and welfare' optimum to be achieved, an objective it was invented to safe harbor. The theoretical 'optimum' and the 'realistic' optimum will never properly converge under a democratic decision-making and regulatory framework as we know it in our neoliberal day-and-age. The other complexity is that it requires to converge not only financial regulation, public backstop facilities, accounting and credit rating regulation and many areas of investor protection and this preferably on a global level. That is not going to happen.[189] 'Opacity[190] might emerge in various ways, from financial innovations and accounting arbitrage to the way supervisors chose to analyze market operations and publish the data', Kalinowski indicates.[191] The problem of economic model-based financial legislation cannot and should be reduced to the 'volatility' and 'fair value' aspects. A third secondary issue will be that of the granularity of data needed to monitor and direct such a global system.[192] Kalinowski once and backed by Paul Volcker's 'thinking more boldly'[193] highlights '[i]n sum, we need a cultural change in the approach to regulation and supervision'…'rather than trying to find out how to save illiquid markets, we should ask what purpose there is in trading assets markets cannot value correctly, in the first place. Who benefits from trading such assets? Is the public good well served by this?'.[194]

---

[188] Keeping Minsky in mind: '[f]inancial crises take place because economic units need or desire more cash than is available from their usual sources and so they resort to unusual ways to raise cash', see H. P. Minsky, (1982), Can "It" Happen Again? Essays on Instability and Finance, M. E. Sharpe Armonk, NY.

[189] The inability of OPEC to coordinate their actions over time is a small-scale example of network inefficiencies and demonstrates larger individual gains than collective detriments in case one of the parties (in this case countries) sidesteps collective agreements or directions agreed upon.

[190] 'The opacity issue should be addressed at its core, i.e. on the level of incentives: when markets are unable to value a security or a structured product, financial intermediaries are in position to take advantage of other market participants'.

[191] W. Kalinowski, (2012), Shadow Banking and the Moral Hazard. Principles for Reducing Model-Based Opacity in Securities Finance, Veblen Institute for Economic Reforms, Paris, p. 2.

[192] See for an example the repo and securities lending market: T. Adrian et al., (2013), Repo and Securities Lending, Federal Reserve Bank of New York Staff Reports, Nr. 529, February (revised). Specifically, they argue that, at a minimum, six shared characteristics of repo and sec lending trades would need to be collected at the firm level: (1) principal amount, (2) interest rate (or lending fee for certain securities loan transactions), (3) collateral type, (4) haircut, (5) tenor and (6) counterparty.

[193] P. Volcker, (2009), Think More Boldly, The Wall Street Journal web edition, December 14.

[194] W. Kalinowski, (2012), Ibid. pp. 3 & 12. He suggests '[t]hese questions lead to three simple principles for an effective regulatory response: radical disclosure beyond what is currently required by international accounting standards (IFRS) and its US equivalent (GAAP), shifted burden of

Given the above it seems like the road to properly regulate the shadow banking segment is a road not yet traveled and it doesn't seem like it is going to happen somewhere soon. Many attempts have been made and different basecamps have been reached. But the road ahead is uncertain and the amount of possible collateral damage as well.[195] The deposit insurance model applied around the world has sedated the public and compromised their understanding as such that it become common ground that one could generate fairly decent returns on a risk-free basis. That one needs highly levered institutions to generate those and that ultimately the backstop became fairly expensive and the system has rebalanced back to the old status quo in no time. Despite the optimum regulatory dynamics, there is no reason why a regulatory framework meeting all the above six criteria would be realistic,[196] however many subtleties will always continue to exist.

There will always be innovators trying to skirt government regulation and issue money-like securities and so continuous directed interventions will be needed. As Rogoff indicates '[t]he bottom line, though, is that as long as the government periodically clamps down before financially disruptive innovations reach systemic proportions, countries should be safe from massive financial crises. True, history suggests that the typical government rarely exhibits backbone in good times when risks are hidden.'[197] And the reality is that the risks embedded in the system also materialize at the point in time that the government lets banking institutions fail. But there is something even strange about a radical change as suggested. In case the government would claim back the monopoly over monetary instruments, 'the government would gain massive funding and revenue potential, since the issuance of money-like instruments is a highly profitable business. Narrow banking would certainly go a long way to ameliorating the long-term public debt problems.'[198]

It would further imply that when a crisis would still occur, the government can bailout the real economic assets rather than that would have to occur indirectly through the banking system. But that line of thinking doesn't serve those parties that control the political apparatus (e.g. in case of the subprime market, a direct government intervention would have save-harbored the lower income groups in the US). So the moral hazard of the shadow banking market is equally so the moral hazard of the political system and the failing discipline of economics.[199]

---

proof as for who is charged to prove how models actually work; and precaution in matter of financial innovation'.

[195] In this case, that collateral damage lies particularly in the impact of a higher cost of funding for the real economy and the liquidity available to flow through to the real economy. The credit intermediation process would also have to be reviewed and right-weighting abolished.

[196] See for parallel evaluations: J. Benes and M. Kumhof, (2012), The Chicago Plan Revisited, IMF Working Paper Nr. WP/12/202 and a twenty-first-century evaluation: L. Kotlikoff, (2010), Jimmy Stewart is Dead, Ending the World's Ongoing Financial Plague with Limited Purpose Banking, Wiley & Sons, Hoboken.

[197] K. Rogoff, (2014), The Shifts and the Shocks: What we've learned – and have yet to learn – from the financial crisis, by Martin Wolf, A Review, by Kenneth Rogoff, Harvard University Prospect Magazine, August 20.

[198] K. Rogoff, (2014), Ibid.

[199] See J.K. Galbraith, (2009), Who Are These Economists, Anyway?, Fall, Though & Action, pp. 85–97.

And even if we could design the perfect regulatory model, it will not prevent crises from happening, shocks tormenting the system and value being destroyed. As Galbraight sums up 'Minsky's analysis showed that capitalist financial instability is not only unavoidable, but intrinsic: instability arises from within, without requiring external disturbances or "shocks". There is no such thing as an equilibrium growth path, indefinitely sustained. Short of changing the system, the public responsibility is to regulate financial behavior, limiting speculation and stretching out for as long as possible the expansionary phase of the cycle.'[200]

Also there the economic models are little helpful in terms of managing reality as is. If we apply, for example, a 10% haircut on the valuation of collateral ex ante that is better than nothing. But it will help very little if later on it will turn out that the initial error margin of the underlying models used turns out to be close to 100%.[201] It triggers 'model-induced opacity' in the markets. Once reality does no longer fit the economic models used underlying the regulation, that regulation becomes a nuisance and magnifies the problem as the regulatory response builds on those models as well. Although the model-based opacity is a giant problem in itself, it gets worse if that opacity can be exploited by certain financial intermediaries and are even incentivized through the 'moral hazard component'. These models 'diffuse temporary illusions of unlimited liquidity' and 'convert rational uncertainty to measurable probabilities'. Kalinowski details 'models create an illusion of functioning market prices where there is no true market price, as there are no true markets. Liquid products presuppose active markets with buyers and sellers: in real economy, the demand for products might fall in distressed market conditions, but it will rarely dry out completely.' That is however exactly what happens in times of market distress. He continues '[t]he more this illusion is diffused among market participants, the less risk-aware they become. One way to maintain the illusion is to rely on stochastic models where the future is deduced from previous time series. Another way is to assume exogenous risk distribution, while financial risks are distributed endogenously. Techniques used in securitization models amount to "statistical mechanics" that treats asset prices as if they were physical particles, each one moving independently from the others. This is obviously not the case of movements of prices in asset portfolios are not comparable events.'[202]

The solution is then not to replace bad models by good (or less bad) ones, as totally eliminating volatility is not the objective of financial regulation as 'this volatility is inherent in portfolio decisions made under conditions of Keynes' radical uncertainty. Rather, it is to radically reduce the "opacity-building" capacity of model-based finance and thus the moral hazard.'[203] It will, in all likelihood, reduce the too large financial sector[204] and free up space for the real economy. The regulatory protection should, in case it has a legitimation to exist, be restricted to the utility banking function. It is there is no proper backstop put in place in defining who has access to the

[200] See J.K. Galbraith, (2009), Ibid. p. 92.
[201] W. Kalinowski, (2012), Ibid. p. 8.
[202] W. Kalinowski, (2012), Ibid. p. 11.
[203] W. Kalinowski, (2012), Ibid. p. 12.
[204] J.-L. Arcand et al., (2012), Too Much Finance?, IMF Working Paper Nr. WP/12/161.

last lender of resort, we might as well ask the government to absorb all entrepreneurial and market-based risk, or at least the definition of that (i.e. what deserves a public backstop and what not) would become highly arbitrary.[205]

Tough financial regulation however doesn't equate financial stability. In fact, financial instability as a function of financial regulation is U-shaped rather than monotonically decreasing as conventional wisdom predicts. That is all the more true for the shadow banking sector in which regulatory arbitrage occurs. Market discipline, in the absence of regulation, in economic downturns forces shadow banking entities to sell assets at fire-sale prices. Huang produced a framework for evaluation and management of regulatory regimes in both the regulated and unregulated banking sector.[206] He argues that stringent financial regulation doesn't secure financial stability in the presence of shadow banking activities. The relative financial stability the regulator can produce in the traditional banking sector is materially compromised as financial activities can always migrate to the unregulated sector and tightening financial regulation could endanger financial stability (see also Box 8.2).

Box 8.2 How Efficient and Effective Is Financial Regulation in the Presence of Shadow Banking Activities?

How Efficient and Effective is Financial Regulation in the Presence of Shadow Banking Activities?

Tighter financial regulation should, under conventional wisdom, also secure financial stability even in the presence of shadow banking activities. But is that effectively so, when shadow banking represents the economic implications of regulatory arbitrage. Huang argues that 'when financial regulation is sufficiently lenient, such financial migration is negligible, and in these circumstances, tightening regulation lowers financial instability and improves social welfare. However, when financial regulation becomes stringent enough, financial migration towards the shadow banking sector is sizable, and further strengthening of regulation heightens financial instability and worsens social welfare.'

The borrowing capacity of shadow banks is a function of market discipline and the level of financial regulation that their traditional counterparties are exposed to, and not some internally defined optimum.[207] Huang concludes 'if the channel connecting the borrowing capacity of shadow banking to financial regulation is turned off, tightening regulation can always lower financial instability because the contraction of the regular banking sector caused by strict regulation dominates the expansion of the shadow banking sector'.[208]

(continued)

[205] B. J. Noeth and R. Sengupta, (2011), Is Shadow Banking Really Banking, The Regional Economist, St. Louis Fed, pp. 8–13.

[206] J. Huang, (2015), Banking and Shadow Banking, Princeton Working Paper, February 2. Later on published in the *Journal for Economic Theory*, Elsevier, Vol. 178(C), pages 124–152. After publication the paper was developed further and therefore 2016/2018 circulate. I used the initial for review.

[207] See also G. Plantin, (2015), Shadow Banking and Bank Capital Regulation, *Review of Financial Studies*, Vol. 28, Issue 1, January, Pages 146–175.

[208] J. Huang, (2015), Ibid. pp. 2–3.

Box 8.2 (continued)

Rephrasing that would lead to the statement that tighter financial regulation causes the larger borrowing capacity of shadow banking, that is, the higher leverage that a regular bank can obtain via shadow banking. Let's flesh that out a bit more. It is very acceptable to assume that more stringent regulation for the traditional banking sector will lead to an enhanced drive for 'regulatory arbitrage' on the side of the traditional banks. More shadow banking implies more unsupervised leverage for the banking group as a whole. Now if a bank defaults on its shadow banking obligations, the creditors to the shadow banking entities of the group will stop lending, which then deprives the traditional to engage in further shadow banking activities. So the cost of default in shadow banking entities for a banking group is larger in financial markets with tighter regulation and the leverage of shadow banking activities is therefore higher, the tighter the level of regulation. Huang sees in all that a feedback loop between the cost of default on shadow banking activities and the leverage in those activities. He argues '[a] lower cost of default leads to a greater incentive to default and a narrower shadow banking channel. A narrower shadow banking channel offers less benefits to regular banks, which implies a lower cost of default. When financial regulation is sufficiently loose, the cost for regular banks to default is small. The feedback loop amplifies the effect of the small cost of default so profoundly as to rule out shadow banking completely.'[209]

Taking into account that shadow banking activities are procyclical in nature, endogenous risk is low in economic boom times. Creditors are consequently willing to lend and shadow banking entities unlikely to end up in distress. The low likelihood (or incentive) to default raises the leverage of the shadow banking segment and the feedback loop does all the rest of the work. Or to be precise 'the feedback loop between the cost of default and the leverage of shadow banking amplifies the expansion of shadow banking in economic booms'.[210] Shadow banking therefore increases financial instability since the leverage in shadow banking entities is high in economic boom times. And since these shadow banking entities are not subject to financial regulation, shadow banks can pile together material amounts of levered assets. When the downturn kicks in, the narrowing shadow banking channel forces these shadow banking entities to engage in fire sales. And since banks are both reluctant to buy these assets and constrained in their ability to buy them, price declines will accelerate and so does the natural instability in the financial system.

The tightness of the traditional banking regulation matters. Huang argues '[w]hen regulation is loose enough, shadow banking is negligible. Tighter regulation of regular banking leads to lower financial instability and higher economic welfare. When regulation is sufficiently tight, considerable amounts of banking activities shift to the shadow banking sector thanks to the ample funding capacity of shadow banking. More stringent regulation causes a larger shadow banking system and higher financial instability.'[211]

(continued)

[209] J. Huang, (2015), Ibid. p. 3.

[210] J. Huang, (2015), Ibid. pp. 4–5.

[211] J. Huang, (2015), Ibid. p. 5.

Box 8.2 (continued)

The body of literature[212] regarding shadow banking typically categorize shadow banking models in terms of their 'motives' and the 'types of externalities' they cause. The motives have been identified throughout the book as being 'demand for money-like claims' and 'regulatory arbitrage'. The externality that SB activities can cause are often driven by the (inferior) quality dimension of the assets produced and traded and/or by the excessive endogenous risk produced (which is not internalized by individual agents) which would not be possible (or heavily constrained) under traditional banking regulation.[213]

But is the presence of shadow banking innocent or not from a risk perspective? One could argue both ways. The answer is positive taking into account all shadow banks hold the same type of physical capital as regular banks. The overall investment quality in the economy does not deteriorate because of the appearance of shadow banking. Huang argues 'if we focus on the asset side of the shadow banking system, no one can blame shadow banking for increasing financial instability'.[214] But even on the liabilities side, a single shadow bank up to the limit can still cause no harm to the system. But when shadow banks in economic downturns expand without taking into account the negative externality of asset fire sales due to a narrowed channel between the shadow banking segment and the traditional banking segment, the answer to that question turns negative.

The more stringent the regulation covering the traditional banking segment, the larger the shadow banking segment. The larger it becomes, the more of a risk to the system as a whole. But now what? Should we relax traditional financial regulation? Relaxing financial regulation doesn't (always) reduce financial stability. It depends, as Huang illustrates, on the relative size of the shadow banking system.[215] More specifically, 'if the regulatory authority lowers the tax rate, both the benefit of shadow banking and the cost of default decline, which, in turn, lowers the maximum leverage of shadow banking and further reduces the cost of default. The feedback loop can be so significant that the shadow banking system simply does not emerge.'[216] In the regime where the level of financial regulation is lenient enough to eliminate the shadow banking system, the conventional wisdom that tightening regulation secures financial stability still holds, which refers back to Huang's monotonic relationship between financial instability and financial regulation in the presence of shadow banking.

(continued)

[212] See for an overview: T. Adrian, and A. B Ashcraft, (2012), Shadow Banking: A Review of the Literature, Technical report, Federal Reserve Bank of New York.

[213] See for literature references of the different strands: J. Huang, (2015), Ibid. pp. 5–6.

[214] J. Huang, (2015), Ibid. p. 29.

[215] J. Huang, (2015), Ibid. p. 30.

[216] J. Huang, (2015), Ibid. pp. 30 ff. See also M.K. Brunnermeier, and Y. Sannikov, (2014), A Macroeconomic Model with a Financial Sector, *The American Economic Review*, Vol. 104, pp. 379–421.

Box 8.2 (continued)

The end conclusion to be derived out of Huang's model is that '[t]he instability-regulation relationship is actually U-shaped: when regulations are relaxed enough, the size of shadow banking is small and financial instability diminishes with decreased regulatory stringency; when regulation is so tight that a large shadow banking system emerges, the reverse is true'.[217] That finding needs to be related to the fact as discussed before that the nature and size of shadow banking responds heavily to monetary policy influences.[218] These influences create or magnify vulnerabilities across asset markets, banking firms, shadow banking and the non-financial sector.[219] Those vulnerabilities affect monetary policy's risk-return trade-off, including (1) pricing of risk, (2) leverage, (3) maturity and liquidity mismatch and (4) interconnectedness and complexity.

Shadow banking and asset volatility are typically negatively correlated but the re-intermediation from assets, during fire sales, back from the shadow banking to the traditional sector is shaped and defined by the nature and intensity of the regulation covering the traditional banking sector.[220]

8.7.5 But Do We Really Know What We're Trying to Tackle?

Vulnerabilities can propagate shocks that lead to crises. Contagion determines[221] the magnitude of such shocks and the vulnerabilities mentioned are a function of the nature, complexity, opacity, asymmetry and magnitude of the interconnectedness[222] in the banking sector as a whole. Who goes first in defining exactly what we need to tackle and how to avoid targeting symptoms rather than causes? Before we can disagree on the solutions, let's try to (dis)agree on what the object of our effort should be. We can disagree about many things when it comes to financial regulation, but if we don't agree what to talk about (or should be talking about), it becomes hard to disagree.

---

[217] J. Huang, (2015), Ibid. p. 31. That has distinct welfare and policy implications; see for a review Huang, (2015), Ibid. pp. 31–38.

[218] See, for example, I. Drechsler, et al., (2014), A Model of Monetary Policy and Risk Premia, Technical report, National Bureau of Economic Research; also: Z. He, and A. Krishnamurthy, (2013), Intermediary Asset Pricing, *American Economic Review*, Vol. 103, pp. 732–770.

[219] See in extenso: T. Adrian and N. Liang, (2014), Monetary Policy, Financial Conditions, and Financial Stability, Federal Reserve Bank of New York Staff Reports, Nr. 690, September. For the shadow banking specifics, see pp. 9–12. See also R. Berner, (2014), Financial Stability: Progress and Challenges, Working Paper.

[220] J. Huang, (2015), Ibid. pp. 50–52. See also J. Huang, (2014), Systemic Run on Shadow Banks: The Minsky Moment, Working Paper, Princeton University. Also: A. Krishnamurthy, (2010), Amplification Mechanisms in Liquidity Crises, *American Economic Journal: Macroeconomics*, Vol. 2, pp. 1–30.

[221] M. Elliott, et al., (2014), Financial Networks and Contagion, *American Economic Review* Vol. 104, Issue 10, pp. 3115–3153.

[222] See in an EU context: EC, (2015), Commission Staff Working Document, European Financial Stability and Integration Review, April 2015, pp. 62–86.

It is more than fair to say that the understanding of many of these concepts is shaky, model-driven and highly uncertain about how these concepts interact. The academic world is working hard to get (somewhat of) an understanding in terms of the nature and behavior of these concepts in different markets, with different products, in different market structures and under duress and different levels of concentration and/or what it means to have imperfect contracts ruling the products and relations involved. Many have attempted to visualize the interlinkages in the banking sector. And they succeeded. But did it teach us anything besides the fact that it is highly complex and a potpourri of different products and relations. (Cross-border) linkages are fairly easy to visualize but what is much harder is to define how they will behave under different scenarios. But the starting point is already 'highly opaque', so the end result must be 'murky'.

And what linkages matter? Those that channel contagion or those that might trigger collateral damage in case of shocks that manifests themselves in other parts of the financial sector and by extension the real economy. Because financial linkages between the financial and non-financial part of the economy also matter (and not just those within the financial sector). Then the question is how central is a bank (or multiple banks) in the business operations of a sector or segment of the economy. We know from experiences with Chaebol and Keiretsu structures that it is not only the bank itself that can be a source of distress and vulnerabilities. Also shocks caused in one of the corporate entities can impact other corporate entities. The bank and its 'centrality' (the intensity and typology of its use) in the structure defines the nature, size and multiplier the bank causes on other group entities. Our experience with these structures can and do learn us a lot about how interconnectedness operates also in wider networks such as the market 'an sich'. Rancan et al. have been looking into this matter and illustrate that a more central position of the banking sector in these so-called macro-networks 'significantly increases the probability of a banking crisis. By analyzing the different types of risk exposures, their evidence shows that credit as well as market risks are important sources of vulnerabilities.'[223] Overall their conclusions are that:

- A more central position of the banking sector in the macro-network increases the probability of a banking crisis.
- A macro-network characterizes the position of a banking sector in a more refined way than if one considers solely the cross-border network of banking sectors.

[223] M. Rancan et al., (2015), Interconnectedness of the Banking Sector as a Vulnerability to Crises, Working Paper, May 13, pp. 12–22. They focus on linkages caused by loans, deposits, securities and shares (p. 3). They also provide an overview of the existing models of assessment of linkages (pp. 1–4). See also J. Caballero, (2015), Banking Crisis and Financial Integration: Insights from Network Science, *Journal of International Financial Markets, Institutions and Money* Vol. 34, pp. 127–146; G. Hale, et al., (2014), Crisis Transmission in the Global Banking Network, Working Paper, December 31; C. M. Buch and L.S. Goldberg, (2014), International Banking and Liquidity Risk Transmission: Lessons from across Countries, Federal Reserve Bank of New York Staff Reports, Nr. 675, May.

- Early warning models[224] augmented with macro-networks outperform traditional models (that only focus on linkages in the banking or financial sector) in terms of predicting recent banking crises.

Although every macro-network is stylized,[225] they can provide a more comprehensive understanding of the linkages between actor in the financial sector or between the financial sector and the real economy.[226]

Obviously, we could make it very easy for ourselves: it could be decided to restrict maturity transformation outside the shadow banking sector altogether. That would however bring along the issue that a lot of the shadow banking activities involving credit intermediation are done off-balance sheet but are covered by a banking license and therewith access to all banking facilities. But let's not forget that every sort and type of legislation comes at a cost. One of the general principles of law is the aspect of 'proportionality'. And there is a reason for that. The problem or issue to be tackled needs to be answered with a proportionate regulatory suggestion that takes into account all direct and indirect expenses and pecuniary and non-pecuniary setbacks of such proposal. If there is an area where that balance should be properly monitored, it is the area of 'financial regulation'. Since the public interest is constantly at stake in the interaction between investors, customers and

[224] See also M. Holopainen, and P. Sarlin, (2015), Toward Robust Early-Warning Models: A Horse Race, Ensembles and Model Uncertainty. Bank of Finland Discussion Paper Nt. 06/2015; J.H. Lang, et al., (2018), A Framework for Early Warning Modelling, ECB Working Paper Nr. 2182, October.

[225] See in detail: F.X. Diebold, and K. Yilmaz, (2014), On the Network Topology of Variance Decompositions: Measuring the Connectedness of Financial Firms, *Journal of Econometrics* Vol. 18, Issue 1, pp. 119–134; P. Sarlin, and T. Peltonen, (2013), Mapping the State of Financial Stability, *Journal of International Financial Markets, Institutions & Money* Vol. 26, pp. 46–76; P. Sarlin, (2014), Macroprudential Oversight, Risk Communication and Visualization, ISE SP Working Paper Nr. 4.

[226] See also (for other models): L. Alessi, and C. Detken, (2011), Quasi Real Time Early Warning Indicators for Costly Asset Price Boom/Bust Cycles: A Role for Global Liquidity. *European Journal of Political Economy*, Vol. 27, Issue 3, pp. 520–533; K. Anand, et al., (2014), Filling in the Blanks: Network Structure and Interbank Contagion, Nr. 02/2014, Discussion Paper, Deutsche Bundesbank. J. Babecky, et al., (2014), Banking, Debt, and Currency Crises: Early Warning Indicators for Developed Countries, *Journal of Financial Stability* Vol. 15, pp. 1–17; F. Betz, et al., (2014), Predicting Distress in European Banks, *Journal of Banking & Finance* Vol. 45, pp. 225–241; M. Billio, et al., (2012), Econometric Measures of Connectedness and systemic risk in the Finance and insurance sectors, *Journal of Financial Economics* Vol. 104, Issue 3, pp. 535–559; O. Castrén, et al., (2014), Macro-networks: An Application to Euro Area Financial accounts, *Journal of Banking & Finance* Vol. 46, pp. 43–58; E. Cerutti, et al. (2014), Global Liquidity and Drivers of Cross-Border Bank Flows, IMF Working Paper Nr. WP/14/69; M. Chinazzi, et al., (2013), Post-Mortem Examination of the International Financial Network, *Journal of Economic Dynamics and Control*, Nr. 37, Issue 8, pp. 1692–1713; M. Lo Duca, et al., (2013), Assessing Systemic Risks and Predicting Systemic Events, *Journal of Banking & Finance*, Vol. 37, Issue 7, pp. 2183–2195; C. Minoiu, et al., (2013), Does Financial Connectedness Predict Crises? International Monetary Fund Working Paper Nr. WP/13/267 and C. Minoiu, et al., (2013), A Network Analysis of Global Banking: 1978–2010, *Journal of Financial Stability*, Vol. 9, Issue 2, pp. 168–184.

the financial sector, the regulator often feels the need to tightly monitor that environment. That is a meaningful reflex. But we have argued before in this and other chapters that financial regulation often has asymmetric and/or collateral implications. That is besides the direct pecuniary impact. The literature that demonstrates a large negative impact of supervisory restrictions on bank loan growth is large, even if that impact is adjusted for 'monetary policy, bank capital and liquidity conditions and any voluntary reduction in lending triggered by weak legacy loan portfolio performance or other bank losses'.[227]

8.7.6 Curbing Moral Hazard Through Legislation

No doubt one can direct and incentivize market agents into a certain direction. But the literature is very silent about what regulatory dynamics and what regulatory mechanics are effective, and under what circumstances, and which ones aren't. And is there a time constraint on that effectiveness? We know very little and therefore command-and-control legislation is often used to block the most harmful practices directly from the market. Our experience as to whether legislation can curb 'moral hazard' is not particularly positive. Recently Bongini et al.[228] examined the response in the financial markets to the regulatory changes implied by the publication of the list of global systemically important insurers (G-SIIs) and the new rules designed to address the systemic risk posed by those institutions. Financial markets seem to answer the question negative in terms of the incoming regulation's ability to curb 'moral hazard in the (shadow) banking and (shadow) insurance industry'.[229] That seems to be in line with, as well as adequately reflecting the economic impact and effectiveness of regulation overall as analyzed by Hartog.[230] It also explains that both types of US bank flows (i.e. cross-border and local financial flows) are significantly lower into host countries with more stringent bank regulations, and US banks are less likely to maintain a local presence in strictly regulated countries as well. Consequently, banks that engage in capital regulatory arbitrage are significantly more profitable in their foreign activities.[231] Arbitrage in the age of globalization is particularly

---

[227] See, for example, recently P. H. Kupiec et al., (2015), Does Bank Supervision Impact Bank Loan Growth, American Enterprise Institute, AEI Economic Policy Working Paper Nr. 2015-07, May 11, with further reference to other literature on the matter.

[228] P. Bongini et al., (2014), Curbing the Moral Hazard of a SIFI: a Mission Impossible?, September.

[229] See for other research pointing in the same direction: Abreu J. F. and M.A. Gulamhussen, (2013), The Stock Market Reaction to the Public Announcement of a Supranational List of Too-Big-to-Fail Banks during the Financial Crisis, *Journal of International Financial Markets, Institutions & Money*, Vol. 25, pp. 49–72; P. Bongini et al., (2014), The Importance Of Being Systemically Important Institutions, *Journal of Banking and Finance*; K. Ueda and B. Weder Di Mauro, (2012), Quantifying Structural Subsidy Values For Systemically Important Financial Institutions, *Journal of Banking and Finance*, Vol. 37, pp. 3830–3842.

[230] J. den Hartog, (2010), Review of Economic Theories, Tjalling C. Koopmans Research Institute, Discussion Paper Series Nr. 10–18. Observed the extended literature list at pp. 47–59.

[231] J. Temesvary, (2015), The Role of Regulatory Arbitrage in US Banks' International Flows: Bank-Level Evidence, Working Paper, May (in 2018 published in Economic Inquiry, Vol. 56, Issue 4, October, pp. 2077–2098).

worrisome since the internationalization of bank activities can significantly increase the amount of risk that banks carry on their portfolio and arbitrage opportunities create 'new risk-taking outlets'.[232] That obviously increases vulnerabilities and stability. That comes on top of the already increasingly vulnerable financial infrastructure.[233] Temesvary examined how differences in the stringency of various types of bank regulations across countries and over time have shaped US banks' cross-border and foreign affiliate flows, as well as their choice to maintain a local presence in certain countries.[234] The role of regulatory differences is examined using bank-level data.[235] The findings are that 'U.S. banks significantly reduce their cross-border flows to host countries with stricter capital standards – an effect that is particularly strong for smaller global banks that may lack the scale benefits in risk management and diversification that larger banks can tap into. Banks are also less likely to maintain a local presence in countries with strict capital rules.'[236] Her second point of attention are the bank-specific drivers of capital arbitrage behavior (e.g. the empirical relationship between individual bank characteristics and the extent of banks' capital regulation avoidance) and their link with profitability of banks. She shows that the intensity of capital arbitrage has a significant positive effect on foreign profitability.[237] The bank-specific drivers that trigger a higher level of regulatory arbitrage are (1) banks with a wider scope, (2) banks with a higher share of foreign (non-US) owners, (3) better capitalized banks and (4) non-commercial banks over commercial banks.[238]

---

[232] See also M. Gulamhussanw, et al., (2014), International Diversification and Risk of Multinational Banks: Evidence From the Pre-Crisis Period, *Journal of Financial Stability* Vol. 13, pp. 30–43; H. Hoque, et al., (2015), Bank Regulation, Risk and Return: Evidence From the Credit and Sovereign Debt Crises, *Journal of Banking & Finance* Vol. 50, pp. 455–474; E. Cubillas, and F. Gonzalez, (2014), Financial Liberalization and Bank Risk-Taking: International Evidence, *Journal of Financial Stability* Vol. 11, pp. 32–48; I. Agur, (2013), Multiple Bank Regulators and Risk Taking, *Journal of Financial Stability* Vol. 9, pp. 259–268.

[233] See, for example, D. Anginer, and A. Demirguc-Kunt, (2014), Has the Global Banking System Become More Fragile Over Time?, *Journal of Financial Stability* Vol. 13, pp. 202–213.

[234] Temesvary, (2015), Ibid. p. 3.

[235] See also S. Ongena et al., (2013), When the Cat's Away The Mice Will Play: Does Regulation at Home Affect Bank Risk-Taking Abroad?, *Journal of Financial Economics* Vol. 108, pp. 727–750.

[236] Temesvary, (2015), Ibid. p. 3.

[237] J.F. Houston et al., (2012), Regulatory Arbitrage and International Bank Flows, *The Journal of Finance* Vol. 67, pp. 1845–1895.

[238] Temesvary, (2015), Ibid. p. 20.

9

What If Things Still Go Wrong: The Quest for Optimal Resolution Regimes and Policies

9.1 Introduction

One of the open ends that still exist is the question what will happen if despite all the regulatory initiatives some of these shadow banking institutions go into distress. For the normal banking system and in particular the systemically important financial institutions, specific rules have been designed that deal with dismantling those kinds of institutions and creating as little collateral as possible. However, that same initiative of creating a dismantling mechanism has not or only partly been developed for shadow banking entities that undergo distress and are failing or are at risk of doing so. What also has been key in designing distress or bankruptcy type of mechanisms is the exposure of taxpayers in those circumstances, who are at risk holding the bag when the music stops. And that will continue to be the case as long as the shadow banking system doesn't have its own proprietary backstop.

The Financial Stability Board (FSB) has been, since 2011, active in developing standards dealing with information sharing and dispute resolution. In October 2014 they issued their final set of recommendations regarding the characteristics and mechanism the regulatory regimes should foresee in order to deal with calamities and defaults in the wider financial sphere, that is, to include systemically important entities, insurance firms and so on.

According to their own assessment the objective of these criteria is that 'their implementation should allow authorities to resolve financial institutions in an orderly manner without taxpayer exposure to loss from solvency support, while maintaining continuity of their vital economic functions'.[1] Indeed, the objective of any resolution system should be to ensure continuity of financial services, payments and so on. But the challenge goes way beyond that. The whole idea is to protect deposit holders and secured creditors and allo-

[1] FSB, (2014), Key Attributes of Effective Resolution Regimes for Financial Institutions, Basel Switzerland, p. 1.

L. Nijs, *The Handbook of Global Shadow Banking, Volume I*,
https://doi.org/10.1007/978-3-030-34743-7_9

cate losses to shareholders and unsecured creditors. Transparency is always a virtue in distress and a good way to avoid further distress than absolutely necessary in a global industry that undeniably will include aligning information and regulatory systems between the different jurisdictions where shareholders, creditors, deposit holders and assets are located. That is easier than it might sound. The EU, as one of the few economic blocks in the world consisting of different regulatory regimes pilled together, is the poster child of the complexity of such an exercise. Out of courtroom workouts are always preferred if possible but there are legal and economic restrictions on how much an intercreditor agreement can tolerate keeping in mind the (information) asymmetry contracts are necessarily prone to. But the absence of cross-border mechanisms to resolve what are in a natural way cross-border issues restricts economic development and integration, hampers economic growth and creates unnecessary concerns especially in times of distress. It also facilitates 'regulatory arbitrage' by financial institutions and other engaged parties.

9.2 The FSB Approach

In 2012, the EU has issued a proposal to facilitate cross-border resolution within the EU in case of distress and bankruptcy.[2] The objective is not only to facilitate cross-border insolvency resolution in the EU, but also 'seeks to shift the focus away from liquidation and develop a new approach of "rescue and recovering" in order to support the restructuring of businesses facing difficulties and create a business-friendly environment'. Their main points of attention in that proposal were (1) to clarify the scope of application (to include pre-insolvency and hybrid proceedings as well as debt discharge and other insolvency proceedings for natural persons), (2) competent jurisdiction for insolvency proceedings, (3) restriction of secondary proceedings (to avoid parallel proceedings in multiple jurisdictions), (4) publicity of proceedings and lodging of claims and (5) insolvency procedures when insolvent company is group member. Although most parties involved seem to evaluate the proposal and its content as positive,[3] not so much progress has been made even though the proposal doesn't harmonize insolvency rules in the EU. In December 2014 the Justice Ministers agreed on the proposal and its content.

---

[2] Proposal for a REGULATION OF THE EUROPEAN PARLIAMENT AND OF THE COUNCIL amending Council Regulation (EC) No 1346/2000 on insolvency proceedings, COM(2012) 744 final, 2012/0360 (COD). This became law in 2015 (with immediate effect): Regulation (EU) 2015/848 of the European Parliament and of the Council of May 20, 2015, on insolvency proceedings O.J. L 141, 5.6.2015, pp. 19–72.

[3] Impact Assessment (of the EU Impact Unit (SWD (2012) 416, SWD (2012) 417 (summary)) for a Commission proposal for a Regulation of the European Parliament and of the Council amending Council Regulation (EC) No 1346/2000 on insolvency proceedings (COM (2012) 744), May 2013 and EP Commission on Legal Affairs: REPORT on the proposal for a regulation of the European Parliament and of the Council amending Council Regulation (EC) No 1346/2000 on insolvency proceedings (COM(2012)0744 – C7-0413/2012 – 2012/0360(COD)), December 2013.

The EU proposal mirrors ex ante some if not most of the key attributes and features as suggested by the FSB in October 2014. Hereafter, I have tried to summarize the key FSB recommended features and their content as well as the necessary updates following the release of the FSBs 'Principles for Cross-Border Effectiveness of Resolution Actions'.[4] I limited the efforts to a short review as it deserves separate writing and does not constitute a key element of this book.[5]

I have brought those features together in Table 9.1.

Nevertheless, and despite all the efforts undertaken in the bankruptcy and insolvency space, it became clear that up till present, the shadow banking space, has not been benefiting from these enhanced rules as often not in scope (unless they are part of an integrated financial group or financial conglomerate). Also the US Dodd-Frank Act did ignore some of the most salient features of some of the larger shadow banking players, for example, MMFs. The US bankruptcy code does not properly account for the unique nature of claims in the money market sphere, as they are more depositor-like as those amounts invested are needed often for short-term operational needs or liabilities. In that sense money market investors make short-term loans for the purpose of cash management rather than investment. Ondersma indicates 'because of this crucial difference between money-claims and ordinary debt obligations, defaults on money-claims are uniquely

[4] FSB (2015), Principles for Cross-Border Effectiveness of Resolution Actions, November 3. And there was more. The FSB at that point in time in November 2015 further released a new standard on the adequacy of Total Loss-absorbing Capacity (TLAC) for global systemically important banks (G-SIBs): FSB (2015), Total Loss-Absorbing Capacity (TLAC) Principles and Term Sheet, November 9 based on BCBS, (2015), TLAC Quantitative Impact Study Report, November. See also FSB (2015), Guidance on Cooperation and Information Sharing with Host Authorities of Jurisdictions where a G-SIFI has a Systemic Presence that is Not Represented on its CMG (Crisis Management Groups), November 3. Further consultations were administered in the following fields: (1) FSB, (2015), Consultative document on Temporary Funding Needed to Support the Orderly Resolution of a G-SIB, November 3; (2) FSB, (2015), Consultative document on Arrangements to Support Operational Continuity in Resolution, November 3 (final report August 18, 2016); (3), FSB, (2015), Consultative document on Developing Effective Resolution Strategies and Plans for Systemically Important Insurers, November 3 (final report June 6, 2016). See for a total coverage on the matter: FSB, (2015), Removing Remaining Obstacles to Resolvability Report to the G20 on progress in resolution, November 9.

[5] Very recommended reading regarding previous crises, their treatment and how they were dealt with and what we can learn from them: A.J. Casey and E.A. Posner, (2015), A Framework for Bailout Regulation, Coase-Sandor Institute for Law and Economics Working Paper Nr. 724, February 11. They conclude '[t]he paradox is that the government wants both to commit not to make bailouts and to be able to make bailouts if they are necessary. The reason for committing not to make bailouts is that if bailouts are not available, then people will be more prudent with their finances, and thus financial crises may never occur. But the reason for making bailouts available is that even if people are prudent with their finances—or, if they are not but are able to exploit loopholes in order to circumvent regulation—then bailouts are necessary to prevent macroeconomic collapse' (p. 63). The discretion of government in what to bailout and what not in itself needs to be contained, if not only at the margins.

Table 9.1 Key features of any resolution mechanism applicable to financial institutions

Scope of mechanism Should include (1) holding companies of a firm, (2) non-regulated operational entities within a financial group or conglomerate insofar significant for the group, (3) branches of foreign firms The resolution regime should require that FIs in its jurisdiction should have a (1) recovery and resolution plan, (2) subject to both resolvability assessments and cross-border cooperation agreements	**Resolution authority** Jurisdictions should have a 'designated administrative authority' responsible for exercising the resolution powers over firms within scope In case multiple authorities within a jurisdiction are parallel or competing in terms of competency, coordination manuals should facilitate proceedings and indicate a 'lead' authority The resolution authority should be competent to contract with foreign authorities The objective of the resolution authority should encompass: (1) pursue financial stability and continuity, (2) protect (deposit) insurance mechanisms, (3) consider the financial stability in other involved jurisdictions
Resolution powers 'Resolution should be initiated when a firm is no longer viable or likely to be no longer viable, and has no reasonable prospect of becoming so'[a] The resolution authority should have a sufficient range of powers (replace management, operate firms, override shareholder rights, impose a moratorium with a suspension of payments to unsecured creditors and customers, etc.…) The resolution authority should have the power to transfer selected assets and liabilities of the failed firm to a third-party institution or to a newly established bridge institution (and have the authority to create such bridge institutions and the conditions under which they operate) The resolution authority should be able to create a bail-in and all the requirements it needs in that respect (write-downs, debt-to-equity swaps, write-down contingent capital, transfer of portfolios, etc.)	**Set-off, netting, collateralization, segregation of client assets** Clear and transparent criteria for set-offs, netting, collateralization and the segregation of client assets (from firm capital) The resolution authority should have the power to stay temporarily such rights where they arise by reason only of entry into resolution or in connection with the exercise of any resolution powers

(*continued*)

Table 9.1 (continued)

Safeguards The resolution powers should be exercised in a way that respects the hierarchy of claims Compensation rights for creditors compared to liquidation scenario Directors and officers of the firm are lawsuit-protected when implementing the decisions of the resolution authority Possibility to allow temporary exemptions from disclosure requirements or a postponement of disclosures required by the firm	**Funding of firms in resolution** Statutory and other policies should be in place so that taxpayer bailout is no longer needed Resolution authority should, when providing bridge financing, be able to recover any losses where needed Jurisdictions should have in place privately financed deposit insurance funds with ex post recovery mechanisms Mechanisms should be in place to avoid moral hazard Should ideally have a system in place that allows to place a firm under temporary public ownership and control to continue critical operations, while seeking for a permanent solution (sale, merger,...)
Legal framework for cross-border resolution The resolution authority should be empowered to act to achieve a cooperative solution with foreign resolution authorities There should be no automatic action provisions in a jurisdiction as a consequence of interventions or the initiation or resolution in another jurisdiction, while reserving the right for discretionary national action to achieve domestic stability (in the absence of effective international cooperation and information sharing) The resolution authority should have powers over local branches in order to (1) assist the foreign home authority executing a resolution and/or (2) to take measures on its own initiative when the foreign authority in its decision-making is not taking into account foreign jurisdictions' financial stability into account National laws should not discriminate against creditors on the basis of nationality, location of their claim and jurisdiction where it is payable Jurisdictions should ensure transparent and expedited processes to facilitate foreign resolution measures, either by way of a mutual recognition process or by taking measures under the domestic resolution regime that support and are consistent with the resolution measures taken by the foreign home resolution authority	**Crisis management groups** Crisis management group's objective is enhancing preparedness for, and facilitating the management and resolution of, a cross-border financial crisis affecting the firm Those groups should report status regarding progress in coordination and information sharing, the recovery and resolution planning and the resolvability of the financial institution

(*continued*)

Table 9.1 (continued)

Cross-border cooperation agreements Those agreements should include: (1) objectives and processes for cooperation, (2) role and responsibilities of authorities pre-crisis, post-crisis and during the intervention, (3) detail the processes of information sharing, (4) set out the procedures for the conduct of resolvability assessments, (5) information and consulting procedures between host and home jurisdictions, (6) procedures in case events tend to have a likely material impact in the other jurisdiction, (6) procedures regarding the implementation of bridge instruments and bail-in powers	**Resolvability assessment** They evaluate the feasibility of resolution strategies and their credibility in light of the likely impact of the firm's failure on the financial system and the overall economy
Recovery and resolution planning Jurisdictions should put in place an ongoing process for recovery and resolution planning, at least for those firms that are 'systemically' relevant They should take into account the specific circumstances of the firm and reflect its nature, complexity, interconnectedness, level of substitutability and size The resolution authority should ensure that systemically important firms maintain a recovery plan that identifies options to restore financial strength and viability when the firm comes under severe stress. Important aspects are how the firm will deal with idiosyncratic stress/market-wide stress, addressing capital shortfalls and liquidity pressures and implementation roadmap for recovery in a variety of stress scenarios Resolution plan should be in place, with the objective to resolve the situation without major disruptions and without exposing taxpayers to losses[b] Recovery and resolution plans in home and host state should be coordinated and integrated	**Access to information and information sharing** No legal, regulatory or policy impediments should exist that hinder the appropriate exchange of information, including firm-specific information, between parties involved Firms should have management information systems in place that facilitate, under any circumstance, recovery and resolution planning, despite legal constraints that might exist regarding the exchange of management information

[a]FSB, (2014), Ibid. p. 6

[b]See for guidance on how to build and assess business reorganization plans under BRRD: EBA, (2015), Final Report: Draft Regulatory Technical Standards and Guidelines on Business Reorganisation Plans under Directive 2014/59/EU (BRRD), EBA/RTS/2015/12 & EBA/GL/2015/21, London, December 17

problematic'.[6] She concurs with Ricks that despite the specific nature of the money-like claims, the regulator 'failed to take this proposition seriously as a regulatory matter'...'we have chosen not to employ the imperative tools dispensed in the wake of the Great Depression—regulating institutions in the maturity transformation business, forbidding risky investments and imposing strict capital requirements, and insuring money-claims in exchange.'[7] Ondersma concludes that institutions are, nonetheless, still able to issue money-claims and to place funds subject to money-claims, and MMFs still remain uninsured. Given the discussion regarding the MMF regulatory changes in this book, that statement holds true to a large degree even after the 2014 changes. Ondersma and Ricks' parallel conclusion is still valid today: '[i]f it is correct that the Great Depression was largely attributable to the lack of insurance of money-claims, we ought to be gravely concerned that shadow banks are not regulated like banks and that the government, in the event of a run on these institutions, now apparently lacks the power to act immediately to stem such a run.'[8] The bottom line is still the same in 2015, that is, MMF investments are still seen as investments (that have investment risk as minimal as it might be) and not as deposit-like claims.

The discussed alternatives to the 2014 MMF regulatory changes included capital provisioning either ex post by MMF investors or ex ante by third parties. We have reviewed the benefits that this could bring. As Fisch indicates 'required sponsor support offers a novel and simple regulatory solution to MMF fragility' by guaranteeing with their capital a $1 share price.[9] That becomes extra problematic in a protracted environment of 'zero lower bound interest rate policies' and their impact on the behavior of MMF, as they are likely to 'invest in riskier asset classes, hold less diversified portfolios, are more likely to exit the market' and 'funds affiliated with large financial institutions are more likely to exit the market while funds managed by independent asset management companies take on relatively more risk — thus inducing a negative selection of risky funds in the market'.[10]

[6] C.D. Ondersma, (2013), Shadow Banking and Financial Distress: The Treatment of "Money-Claims" in Bankruptcy, Columbia Business Law Review, Issue 1, p. 79.

[7] P. Morgan Ricks, (2011), Regulating Money Creation After the Crisis, Harvard Business Law Review, Issue 1, pp. 75–143. See also N. Goralnik, (2012), Bankruptcy-Proof Finance and the Supply of Liquidity, The Yale Law Journal, Vol. 122, pp. 460–506, in particular pp. 96, 122 & 129.

[8] Ondersma, (2013), Ibid. p. 141 and Ricks, (2011), Ibid. p. 132.

[9] J.E. Fisch, (2015), The Broken Buck Stops Here: Embracing Sponsor Support In Money Market Fund Reform, North Carolina Law Review, Vol. 93, pp. 935 ff. See also for an economic validation of the capital reform proposal: C.M. Lewis, (2014), The Economic Implications of Money market Fund Capital Buffers, Vanderbilt Owen Graduate School of Management Research Paper Nr. 2388676. His analysis shows that, after compensating capital buffer investors for absorbing credit risk, the returns available to money market fund shareholders are comparable to default free securities.

[10] M. Di Maggio and M.T. Kacperczyk, (2015), Columbia Business School Research Paper, Nr. 14-25. See also L.D.W. Schmidt et al., (2014), Runs on Money Market Funds, CEPR Discussion Paper Nr. DP9906. See for a relatively similar pattern in the European MMF market: S. Collins and E. Gallagher, (2014), Assessing Credit Risk In Money market Funds during the Eurozone Crisis, Working Paper.

9.3 The EU Approach: The Stabilizing and Winding Up of Banks

It is a challenge to apply normal bankruptcy rules to the insolvency or bankruptcy of a bank. The sheer volume of investors, lenders and deposit holders, combined with the countless counterparties the bank is dealing with through a wide variety of financial products, of which many are subject to different governing laws compared to the location of the head office of the bank, makes not only for unreadable intercreditor agreements but a true challenge to unwind the balance sheet of a bank given the many different stakeholders and their asymmetric relations to the bank.

The EU put it this way. In normal insolvency procedures, the primary objective is to maximize the value of assets of the failed firm in the interest of creditors. However, these may take many years, in particular for complex institutions, leading to uncertainty with a knock-on effect on confidence. In contrast, the primary objective of bank resolution is to respond in a rapid and decisive manner to a bank in financial distress to maintain financial stability and minimize losses for society, in particular in relation to taxpayers, while ensuring similar results to those of normal insolvency proceedings in terms of allocation of losses to shareholders and creditors.[11]

Resolution thus aims to protect certain critical stakeholders and functions of the failing bank (such as depositors and payment systems). Other parts, which are not considered key to financial stability, may be allowed to fail in the normal way. Resolution also ensures that moral hazard is addressed, through minimizing the use of taxpayers' money to support failing banks. Instead, shareholders and debt holders will bear an appropriate share of the losses in the event of a failure and will increase discipline on banks by attributing a suitable price to this risk during normal conditions.[12]

The EU experienced just that once the 2008 crisis came to full effect. However, in an integrated economic zone (or at least the attempt to be one) an unwinding of a complex institution should foresee in a symmetric model regardless of where the lenders or asset owners are located. To achieve that, and based on the experiences within the EU post-crisis, the Bank Recovery and Resolution Directive[13] was designed and came into effect on

[11] J.-H. Binder, (2015), The Position of Creditors under the BRRD, Working Paper, mimeo; G. Psaroudakis, (2018), Proportionality in the BRRD: Planning, Resolvability, Early Intervention, Beiträge zum Transnationalen Wirtschaftsrecht, Heft 159, August; J.H. Binder, (2019), Proportionality at the Resolution Stage: Calibration of Resolution Measures and the Public Interest Test, European Business Organization Law Review pp. 1–22. See for a full and recent list of literature on the matter: EBI, (2019), EBI financial resolution Task Force, List of published academic publications, June 4, via ebi-europe.org

[12] EU Commission, (2014), EU Bank Recovery and Resolution Directive (BRRD): Frequently Asked Questions, April 15.

[13] Directive 2014/59/EU of the European Parliament and of the Council of May 15, 2014, establishing a framework for the recovery and resolution of credit institutions and investment firms and amending Council Directive 82/891/EEC, and Directives 2001/24/EC, 2002/47/EC, 2004/25/EC, 2005/56/EC, 2007/36/EC, 2011/35/EU, 2012/30/EU and 2013/36/EU, and Regulations (EU) No 1093/2010 and (EU) No 648/2012, of the European Parliament and of the Council. The European Banking Authority has since 2014 issued a wide list of technical standards and guidelines for implementation of the directive in national legislations and recommendations for national supervisors.

January 1, 2015. The new rules will harmonize and improve the tools for dealing with bank crises across the EU. Although the rules apply to banks, given the fact that the shadow banking market has become an integrated part of many financial conglomerates, the new rules also impact that part of the market. The idea of the new directive in general is to 'to provide authorities with comprehensive and effective arrangements to deal with failing banks at national level, as well as cooperation arrangements to tackle cross-border banking failures'.

The Directive sets out the rules for the resolution of banks and large investment firms in all EU Member States. Banks will be required to prepare recovery plans to overcome financial distress. Authorities are also granted a set of powers to intervene in the operations of banks to prevent them from failing. If they do face failure, authorities are equipped with comprehensive powers and tools to restructure them, allocating losses to shareholders and creditors following a clearly defined hierarchy. They have the powers to implement plans to resolve failed banks in a way that preserves their most critical functions and avoids taxpayers having to bail them out. Precise arrangements are set out for how home and host authorities of banking groups should cooperate in all stages of cross-border resolution, from resolution planning to resolution itself, with a strong role for the European Banking Authority to coordinate and mediate in case of disagreements. National resolution funds are also being established. In the case of euro area Member States, these funds will be replaced by the Single Resolution Fund as of 2016.[14]

The EU option chosen to deal with the issues of unwinding financial institutions is somewhat different. Indeed, in 2010, the US established a resolution framework for systemic financial institutions under the Dodd-Frank Act. The powers provided under this Act complement those that were already in existence to resolve failing banks, whereby the Federal Deposit Insurance Corporation (FDIC) takes any failing bank into receivership, after which their business is transferred to a new entity or wound down with losses and costs allocated to shareholders and creditors to the necessary degree. In a similar fashion, the Directive will also allow authorities to put banks into an orderly resolution in which their critical functions would be preserved by, for example, a sale to a third party or the creation of a bridge bank, while the non-critical parts of the failed institution would be wound down. In cases where it would be in the public interest to restore an institution back to financial viability, the directive also allows authorities to write down and convert some of the bank's liabilities (bail-in), and through this process and subsequent restructuring, enables the bank to continue in business, albeit as a deeply restructured institution. Such a restructuring process would include dilution of shareholders, changes to management, haircutting of creditors and other structural changes so as to ensure that the surviving entity was viable. All resolution operations would also need to adhere to EU state aid rules.[15]

[14] EU Commission, (2014), A Single Rulebook for the Resolution of failing banks will apply in the EU as of January 1, 2015, Press release, December 31. See for technical advice regarding the contributions to the Single Resolution Fund: EBA, (2015), Technical advice on the delegated acts on the initial period of the single resolution fund under Article 69 of the SRM Regulation, EBA/Op/2015/11, London, June 10.

[15] EU Commission, (2014), EU Bank Recovery and Resolution Directive (BRRD): Frequently Asked Questions, April 15.

I will provide only a condensed and schematic overview (Table 9.2)[16] of the content of the directive,[17] given its non-prime role within the context of this book. Nevertheless, there are some important features that require to be noted within the context of a book on shadow banking and specifically within the context of the future of cross-border resolution techniques within the financial sector. The main aims of a bank resolution are to (1) safeguard the continuity of essential banking operations, (2) protect depositors, client assets and public funds, (3) minimize risks to financial stability and (4) avoid the unnecessary destruction of value.[18]

Article 32(6) of the Directive establishing a framework for the recovery and resolution of credit institutions and investment mandates the EBA to issue guidelines to promote the convergence of supervisory and resolution practices regarding the interpretation of the different circumstances when an institution should be considered as failing or likely to fail. A determination that an institution is failing or likely to fail constitutes one of the three cumulative conditions determining whether resolution authorities should take resolution actions. It is also one of two cumulative conditions determining that an institution is no longer viable and that resolution authorities shall exercise the write down or conversion power indicated above. The most important considerations are the 'capital' and 'liquidity' position of the financial institution.

Article 32(4) of Directive 2014/59/EU provides a general description of the circumstances in which an institution shall be deemed to be failing or likely to fail. In May 2015,[19] the EBA issued guidelines on the objective elements that should guide competent authorities and resolution authorities in determining that:

- an institution infringes, or is likely to infringe in the near future, the requirements for continuing authorization in a way that would justify the withdrawal of its authorization by the competent authority, including but not limited to because it has incurred or is likely to incur losses that will deplete all or a significant amount of its own funds;
- an institution's assets are, or there are objective elements to support a determination that its assets will be, in the near future, less than its liabilities;
- an institution is, or is likely to be in the near future, unable to pay its debts or other liabilities as they fall due.

The identification of a single objective element specified in the guidelines with regard to a particular institution should neither lead to an automatic determination that it is failing or likely to fail, nor automatically trigger resolution actions. On the contrary, in each case, the

---

[16] Content to a certain degree based on: EU Commission, (2014), EU Bank Recovery and Resolution Directive (BRRD): Frequently Asked Questions, April 15.

[17] See for further insights: (1) BoE, (2014), Implementing the bank Recovery and Resolution Directive, Consultation Paper, CP13/14, (2) PWC, (2014), EU Bank Recovery and Resolution Directive 'Triumph or tragedy?', pwc.com, and (3) B. Joosen, (2014), Bail In Mechanisms in the Bank Recovery and Resolution Directive, University of Amsterdam Working Paper.

[18] EU Commission, (2014), EU Bank Recovery and Resolution Directive (BRRD): Frequently Asked Questions, April 15.

[19] EBA, (2015), Guidelines on Failing or Likely to Fail, EBA/GL/2015/07, May 26, pp. 3–4.

Table 9.2 The key points of the recovery and resolution directive

Feature	Content
Scope	The rules will apply to both credit institutions (i.e. banks) and larger investment firms that are subject to the capital requirements directive. That includes subsidiaries of non-EU banking groups, regardless of their home country requirements The rules will further apply to EU-based parent and intermediate financial holding companies and mixed financial holding companies (within the remit of the financial conglomerates directive), and Subsidiary financial institutions of an EU credit institution or an investment firm However, the commission will continue to work on prevention, management and resolution of financial institutions other than banks, such as market infrastructures, the failure of which is capable of having a systemic effect too
Components of the unwinding techniques	
1. Preparation and prevention	Banks and resolution authorities are required to draw up recovery and resolution plans on how to deal with situations that might lead to financial stress or the failure of a bank. If authorities identify obstacles to resolvability during the course of this planning process, they can require a bank to take appropriate measures, including changes to corporate and legal structures, to ensure that it can be resolved with the available tools in a way that does not threaten financial stability and does not involve costs to taxpayers. The directive's annex provides guidance regarding the content of the recovery plan (e.g. isolating essential functions of the financial group, steps to reorganize or restore financial soundness). Different situations will need to be foreseen (e.g. systemic instability, etc.)
2. Early intervention	Bank supervisors are accorded an expanded set of powers to enable them to intervene if an institution faces financial distress (e.g. when a bank is in breach of, or is about to breach, regulatory capital requirements), but before the problems become critical and its financial situation deteriorates irreparably. These powers will include the ability to dismiss the management and appoint a temporary administrator, as well as convening a meeting of shareholders to adopt urgent reforms (e.g. increase capital, reorganization or sell off) and requiring the bank to draw up a plan for the restructuring of debt with its creditors

(*continued*)

Table 9.2 (continued)

Feature	Content
3. Resolution	The objective of resolution is to minimize the extent to which the cost of a bank failure is borne by the state and its taxpayers. To this end, should the bank in distress continue to fail, the directive provides resolution authorities with a credible set of resolution tools. These include the power to sell or merge the business with another bank, to set up a temporary bridge bank to operate critical functions, to separate good assets from bad ones and to convert to shares or write down the debt of failing banks (bail-in). These tools will ensure that any critical functions are preserved without the need to bailout the bank, and that shareholders and creditors of the bank under resolution bear an appropriate part of the losses. They should also prevent the precipitous loss of value in a failing bank associated with bankruptcy, for example by quickly recapitalizing it and allowing it to be restructured
4. Cooperation and coordination	The directive also provides a framework to improve cooperation between national authorities so that, should a cross-border banking group fail, national authorities will be able to coordinate resolution measures to protect financial stability in all affected Member States and achieve the most effective outcome for the group as a whole
Triggers	The authorities may determine that a bank needs to be resolved if: 1. It has reached a point of distress such that there are no realistic prospects of recovery over an appropriate timeframe. This can include objective measures such as breach of the CRD capital requirements, having more liabilities than assets, being unable to pay obligations as they fall due or requiring extraordinary public finance 2. All other private sector or supervisory intervention measures have been proved insufficient to restore the bank to viability 3. Winding up the institution under normal insolvency proceedings would risk prolonged uncertainty or financial instability and therefore resolving the bank would be better from a public interest perspective. There is one caveat in this scenario i.e. the action must achieve and be proportionate to one of the resolution objectives, and only be taken if a winding up or insolvency of the institution or parent undertaking would not meet those objectives to the same extent

(*continued*)

Table 9.2 (continued)

Feature	Content
Execution tools	Authorities may use any of the following tools: 1. Effect private sector acquisitions (parts of the bank can be sold to one or more purchasers without the consent of shareholders) 2. Transfer business to a temporary structure (such as a 'bridge bank') to preserve essential banking functions or facilitate continuous access to deposits 3. Separate clean and toxic assets between 'good' and 'bad' banks through a partial transfer of assets and liabilities; and/or 4. Bail-in creditors (mechanism to cancel or reduce the liabilities of a failing bank, or to convert debt to equity, as a means of restoring the institution's capital position). The scope of liabilities subject to the bail-in is wide and everything is included unless explicitly excluded Excluded liabilities are those with an original maturity of less than one month, secured and other collateralized liabilities (including liabilities arising from repurchase transactions (repos) and other title transfer collateral arrangements), insured deposits, liabilities arising from the holding of client monies or client assets, employee salary and benefit or other fixed remuneration liabilities, tax liabilities and liabilities to commercial or trade creditors for the provision of essential goods and services. Also derivatives liabilities[a] (over one month original maturity) may be excluded if the exclusion is necessary or appropriate to ensure the continuity of critical functions or avoid adverse effects on financial stability. Other tools can be used to the extent that they conform to the principles and objectives of resolution set out under the directive (e.g. public support,...)
Cross-border resolution within the EU	The directive provides for a set of harmonized tools regarding information sharing, cooperation etc. In order to better deal with large and more complex cross-border groups, the consolidating supervisor would play a leading role in overseeing the development of a recovery plan and the group resolution authority (the authority in the Member State in which the consolidating supervisor under EU banking rules is situated) will be responsible for designing a resolution plan for the whole banking group. The resolution plans could allow for intervention both at the level of the parent or holding or of the subsidiaries, depending on the nature of the group. Coordination would be ensured through resolution colleges and binding technical standards by the European Banking Authority ('EBA').[b] The EBA could also carry out binding mediation in case of disagreements. The plans would not dictate how the group operates internally (separated subsidiaries, integrated liquidity and risk management, etc.) but would ensure that the legal structure does not constitute an obstacle to resolvability. The EBA would also help coordinate any joint decisions by national authorities at the stage of early intervention Groups may also enter into arrangements, approved by regulators and shareholders, of financial support between constituent entities for restoring the group's financial health efficiently

(*continued*)

Table 9.2 (continued)

Feature	Content
Impact of directive on bank's counterparties	The resolution trigger leaves a lot of discretion to the resolution authority also in case of bail-ins. That leaves creditors to the bank in the dark It is very likely that from 2018, when the bail-in clause comes into effect, unsecured bank creditors, in case of a bail-in, will see their debt written down or converted into equity with the exception of collateralized creditors and repo counterparties. The writing down might also occur for derivatives liabilities, which is also at the discretion of the resolution authority Creditors might be subject to a temporary moratorium and/or other restrictions regarding enforcing security and other contractual termination rights Financial institutions will be required to hold bail-in capital equal to a percentage of total liabilities of the institution
Financing of resolution	Every Member State will have to set up financing arrangements funded with contributions from banks and investment firms in proportion to their liabilities and risk profile The national financing arrangements would be financed ex ante. To that end contributions will be raised from banks annually in order to reach a target funding level of at least 1% of covered deposits over a 10-year period Each national fund will finance the resolution of the entities established in its own territory. For cross-border groups, the relevant national arrangements will be required to contribute to a financing plan pre-agreed between the competent resolution authorities Recapitalization needs to happen in the first instance by shareholders and creditors. After these stakeholders have borne sufficient losses (i.e. 8% of the liabilities of the bank under resolution) through write down or conversion, in exceptional circumstances the resolution financing arrangement may bear the remaining losses but only up to 5% of the bank's liabilities However, the main use of the resolution funds will be limited to, for example, providing loans to a bridge institution, purchasing specific assets of an institution under resolution, guarantee certain assets or liabilities of the institution under resolution, or in exceptional circumstances contributing to loss absorption by replacing creditors who would have been bailed in No creditor should be worse off under resolution than it would have been had the bank been wound up under applicable insolvency law proceedings
Into effect	January 1, 2015, except for the bail-in tool, which will be applied by a resolution tools authority as of January 1, 2018

[a]See for technical guidance: EBA, (2015), Final Report, Regulatory Technical Standards on the Valuation of Derivatives Pursuant to Article 49(4) of the Bank Recovery and Resolution Directive (BRRD), EBA/RTS/2015/11, London, December 17

[b]A first batch of technical recommendations was issued by the EBA on March 6, 2015: the authority provided a comprehensive set of criteria for testing critical functions of institutions under resolution, as well as core business lines of banks, the exclusion of liabilities from the application of the bail-in tool and on the deferral of ex post contributions.

relevant authorities should decide whether the institution is failing or likely to fail on the basis of a comprehensive assessment of both qualitative and quantitative objective elements, taking into account all other circumstances and information relevant for the institution. The set of elements provided is not exhaustive and does not prevent the relevant authorities from taking into account other considerations signaling that an institution is failing or likely to fail.

In parallel, the EU council reached an agreement at the end of 2014 regarding the implementing determining the contributions to be paid by banks to the EU's Single Resolution Fund (SRF). The fund will be set up under a single resolution mechanism (SRM) that is being established to ensure the orderly resolution of failing banks. The SRF will be built up over a period of eight years to reach a target level of at least 1% of the amount of covered deposits of all credit institutions authorized in all the participating Member States. Banks will have to make annual contributions to the fund. These will be calculated on the basis of their liabilities, excluding own funds and covered deposits, and adjusted for risk.[20]

It can be concluded with Binder that substantial progress has been made and that the new framework certainly reflects a very strong commitment to cooperative rather than 'isolationist' approaches (such as the ring-fencing of foreign-owned branches in insolvency). But it was also concluded that the mere existence of this new framework certainly does not remove residual conflicts in the economic interests of the different jurisdictions involved in cross-border cases and only future practice will show how these conflicts can be balanced out.[21] Some are more careful in their analysis and suggest a global resolution scheme (especially for SIFIs), to avoid regulatory arbitrage. In that context questions are asked whether it wouldn't (have been) be better if such risk taking would be judged by market discipline instead of posing a risk to global financial stability,[22] the main downside of regulatory competition could be restrained and competition would then function and operate as a market-led structure of financial regulation.[23] The balance will always be sensitive. Although our insights enhance and consensus grows on a daily basis with respect to the content of banking laws, from a legal perspective their drafting often leaves something to be desired. Weaknesses are hardly country-specific and often no distinctions are made with respect to the different stages of recovery and resolution.[24] A banks' living will undeniably reflect a framework meeting the following criteria of (i) adequate loss absorption; (ii) distinguishing between weak and sound banks; (iii) little susceptibility to manipulation; (iv) timeliness and (v) scalable from the individual bank to the system.[25]

---

[20] See EU, (2014), Single Resolution Fund: Council Agrees on Bank Contributions, Press Release December 9.

[21] J.-H. Binder, (2015), Cross-Border Coordination of bank Resolution in the EU: All Problems Solved, Working Paper, mimeo, p. 17.

[22] See for a panic-response-based regulatory model design: D. Sabches, Banking Panics and Protracted Recessions, Federal Reserve bank of Philadelphia, Working Paper Nr. 15-39. October 8.

[23] W.-G. Ringe, (2015), Arbitrage and Competition in Global Financial Regulation – The Case for a Special Resolution Regime, Legal Research Paper Series, Nr. 49/2015, September.

[24] See for a full analysis: W. Bossu and D. Chew, (2015), "But we are different!": 12 Common Weaknesses in Banking Laws, and What to Do about Them, IMF Working Paper Nr. WP/15/200.

[25] U.S. Das, (2015), Optimal bank Recovery, IMF Working Paper, Nr. WP/15/217, September. For Islamic banks see E. A. Awadzi et al., (2015), Resolution Frameworks for Islamic Banks, IMF Working Paper, Nr. WP/15/247.

9.4 Will It All Work, and in a Timely Way: The Bank-Sovereign Nexus?

That is a question that should be asked once in a while. Also, in this matter, the methodology seems robust but will it work under duress and with a short timeline? A variety of bank and sovereign (near) collapses in recent years in the EU have taken a strong toll on the policy spectrum. In June 2012 the Banking Union was officially launched. The principal intention was to break the bank-sovereign link and to relieve the euro area's weaker economies from the almost impossible burden of having to finance bank bailouts out of national fiscal resources. Or put in other words the objective of the banking Union was 'mutualization of bailout costs through a common "fiscal backstop"'. Hadjiemmanuil argues that although a good starting point, the policy implementations since 2012 have seen a relaxation if not abandonment of that objective.[26] The Banking Union's Single Resolution Mechanism (SRM), which can be described as the Bank Recovery and Resolution Directive, but then for European sovereigns shares the same burden-sharing norms and cascade.[27] Although that mechanism guarantees the legal consistency of the resolution frameworks in the EU, it stays highly doubtful whether the chosen policy line in this matter can 'insulate national state finances from the costs of bank bailouts and/or ensure the full equalization of the financial conditions for bank resolution everywhere in the euro area'. It would have been better to have a common fiscal backstop at the level of the banking union. The whole point he adds was to 'sever the perverse loop between bank failure and sovereign debt distress by mutualizing the fiscal costs of bank resolution'.[28] The existence of a credible fiscal backstop can and will play a role in assuaging market concern facilitating the exit from the crisis and enabling the reintegration of banking markets in the euro area. That to a large degree hinges on the sufficiency of the resources that can be made available.[29] The direct recapitalization instrument might well work fine in theory, but has never been stress tested[30]

[26] C. Hadjiemmanuil, (2015), Bank Resolution Finance in the Banking Union, LSE Law, Society and Economy Working Paper Nr. 6/2015, London School of Economics and Political Science, law Department, London. Also included in Jens-Hinrich Binder and Dalvinder Singh (eds.), (2015), Bank Resolution: The European Perspective, Oxford University Press, Oxford.

[27] See C. Hadjiemmanuil, (2015), Bank Resolution Finance in the Banking Union, LSE Law, Society and Economy Working Paper Nr. 6/2015, pp. 23–25.

[28] C. Hadjiemmanuil, (2015), Bank Resolution Finance in the Banking Union, LSE Law, Society and Economy Working Paper Nr. 6/2015, pp. 19 ff.

[29] C. Hadjiemmanuil, (2015), Bank Resolution Finance in the Banking Union, LSE Law, Society and Economy Working Paper Nr. 6/2015, p. 35.

[30] That is not completely true as some attempts have been made; see V. V. Acharya and S. Steffen, (2014), Falling Short of Expectations? Stress Testing the Eurozone Banking System, CEPS Policy Brief Nr. 315, January 15. They also laughed off the ECB's capital shortfall tests as 'possibly because systemic risk and feedback effects from the financial sector in the real sector, which are captured in the market data, were completely ignored in regulatory assessment'. Also in C. Hadjiemmanuil, (2015), Ibid. p. 36. See for other concerns regarding the ECB capital shortfall tests: V. V. Acharya and S. Steffen, (2014), Making Sense of the Comprehensive Assessment,

in a systemic risk environment where the EU banking sector accounts (in terms of total assets) for about give or take three times the region's GDP.

Those assets are to a large degree in the hands of large systemically relevant banks 'whose recapitalization could conceivably require huge resources'.[31] That same reasoning I used to advocate that retributions as a bank tax are an oxymoron. As a retribution, the contribution paid by the FI would have to relate to the service received. Since the sovereign is not capable of recapitalizing banks often dozens of times larger than their own GDP a critical condition fails to tolerate retributions.[32] Hadjiemmanuil concludes that the ex ante mechanism and ex post actual needs might be diverse and will act as a regulatory straightjacket and 'builds a significant element of ambiguity and unpredictability into the system and reduces its credibility'. Also the need for a centralized mechanism rather than a country-by-country mechanism will be required '[a]s the legacy assets of the pre-crisis period disappear and the quality of regulation is increasingly seen to depend on the actions of the ECB, rather than of the national authorities, it will become harder and harder to justify the need for national participation in burden sharing. Eventually, the Banking Union will require fully centralized and uniform resolution financing mechanisms'.[33]

The overall process of creating a transparent and operational banking resolution system in Europe seems incomplete. Gordon and Ringe[34] indicate that one of these clear blind spots is the 'structural re-organization of large European financial firms that would make "resolution" of a systemically important financial firm a credible alternative to bailout or some other sort of taxpayer assistance'. They recommend the creation of a 'holding company structure in which the public parent holds unsecured term debt sufficient to cover losses at an operating financial subsidiary would facilitate a "Single Point of Entry" resolution procedure that would minimize knock-on effects from the failure of a systemi-

VoxEU.org, October 29. C. Hadjiemmanuil concludes based on their numbers that '[c]ompared to the highest estimates, the DRI (direct recapitalization instrument, ed.) in its present size pales into insignificance' (p. 36).

[31] C. Hadjiemmanuil, (2015), Bank Resolution Finance in the Banking Union, LSE Law, Society and Economy Working Paper Nr. 6/2015, p. 35.

[32] L. Nijs, (2015), Neoliberalism 2.0: Regulating and Financing Globalizing Markets. A Pigovian Approach for 21st Century Markets, Palgrave Macmillan, London, Chapter 6. C. Hadjiemmanuil, (2015), Ibid. pp. 36–38 did his own, more thorough, analysis and didn't get particularly convinced either. He considered all resources available taking into account the fact that they could suffice for a bailout under 'normal circumstances' or for a single SIFI in Europe under duress assuming this will take place in relative isolation.

[33] C. Hadjiemmanuil, (2015), Bank Resolution Finance in the Banking Union, LSE Law, Society and Economy Working Paper Nr. 6/2015, pp. 38–39. J-H. Binder asks the question: Will the centralization of supervisory powers, over time, also lead to the streamlining of business models, corporate and group structures of banks across the Eurozone?, See J.-H. Binder, (2015), Banking Union and the Governance of Credit Institutions- A Legal Perspective, SAFE Working Paper nr. 96/2015, Frankfurt am Main.

[34] J.N. Gordon and W-G Ringe, (2015), Bank Resolution in Europe: the Unfinished Agenda of Structural Reform, Center for Law and Economic Studies, Columbia School of Law Working Paper Nr. 507, ECGI Working Paper Nr. 282/2015, January 11, published in European Banking Union, (eds.) D. Busch and G. Ferrarini, Oxford University Press, Oxford (2015).

cally important financial institution'. Such a structure would minimize run risk from short-term creditors and minimize destructive ring-fencing by national regulators.

Resolution is a critical element in a project such as the European Banking Union as without a properly functioning 'resolution mechanism', a credible capacity to resolve a large financial firm, a supervisor is deprived of the ultimate disciplinary tool to control moral hazard and to constrain excessive risk taking.[35] They are convinced that the resolution mechanism as discussed above[36] fails two critical tests: (1) first, short-term credit claims will be insufficiently protected, meaning that financial distress could easily lead to an exacerbating spiral of runs, fire sale asset dispositions and credit market freezes,[37] and (2) second, financial distress may have uneven impact along national dimensions, which will lead to national ring-fencing ex ante and ex post. These shortfalls might lead to unacceptable risk of a disorderly resolution and will produce regulatory forbearance and an ultimate bailout by taxpayers.

The holding implementation suggested, which has distinct characteristics in common with the US Single Point of Entry concept in the Dodd-Frank Act,[38] can be done through a variety of methods: (1) through the 'living will' procedure included in the above-discussed bank Recovery and Resolution Direction 'as the supervisor comes to decide that a holding company is essential for "feasibility of resolution" of a particular firm',[39] (2) through capital requirements under the Capital Requirements Regulation and Directive (CRR/CRD IV), (3) through the assessment of extra capital charges for a firm without a holding company structure in the stress tests administered by the European Central Bank or the European Banking Authority, or a structurally sensitive systemic risk assessment on a "G-SIB" (a Global Systemically Important Bank), as contemplated by Basel III.[40]

The mandatory outcome of their solution would entail the creation of a public Holding Company parent for the operating subsidiaries of the banking group 'set up so that the assets of Holding Company consist of shares in its subsidiaries, and that its liabilities are confined to unsecured term debt'.[41] Through the Dodd-Frank Act, this Holding Company would undeniably be the top holding as a 'bank holding company' through which the US

[35] J.N. Gordon and W-G Ringe, (2015), Ibid. p. 2.

[36] And the measures included in the proposal for a Regulation of the European Parliament and of the Council on structural measures improving the resilience of EU credit institutions, COM(2014) 43 final/ 2014/0020 (COD), January 29.

[37] See also M. Ignatowski and J. Korte, (2014), Wishful Thinking or Effective Threat? Tightening Bank Resolution Regimes and Bank Risk-Raking, Journal for Financial Stability, Vol. 15, pp. 264–281.

[38] See Extensively: J.N. Gordon and W-G Ringe, (2015), Ibid. pp. 11–17.

[39] So the regulator forces ex ante such a structure on systemically important banking groups. See in favor of such a model as well: J. H. Binder, (2015), Resolution Planning and Structural Bank Reform within the Banking Union, J. Castaneda et al., (eds.), European Banking Union: Prospects and Challenges, Routledge, London; also G. Franke et al., (2015), Effective Resolution of Banks: Problems and Solutions, SAFE White Paper Series, Nr. 19, Goethe University, Frankfurt am Main.

[40] J.N. Gordon and W-G Ringe, (2015), Ibid. pp. 2–3.

[41] J.N. Gordon and W-G Ringe, (2015), Ibid. p. 3.

banking groups have access to the liquidity window of the central bank and 'Deposit Insurance' facilities.

There seems to be a growing consensus that the Single Point of Entry ('SPE') methodology suggested by Gordon and Ringe (and others) is preferred as opposed to a Multiple Point of Entry ('MPE') approach. The latter requires parent holding of global groups to put up front the equity capital needed to absorb losses possibly emerging in foreign subsidiaries-branches. It was Faia and Weder[42] who recently built a model of optimal design of resolution regimes and compared three regimes: SPE with cooperative authorities, SPE with non-cooperative authorities and MPE (ring-fencing). They find that the costs for bondholders of bail-in able instruments is generally higher under non-cooperative regimes and ring-fencing. They also find that in those cases banks have ex ante incentives to reduce their exposure in foreign assets. That makes sense as banking resolution schemes that take into account the structure of the banks under mandate will 'by definition' be more operational and will make it more credible and reduce the likelihood of a bailout. It also has the potential of facilitating more seamlessly international coordination and cooperation.[43]

9.5 Filling the Gaps: Framework Completion or Contractual Affairs?

The framework for bank resolution is in the making, good way or bad way. But a framework is what it is: a framework and therefore isn't complete and exhaustive in itself. It will require complementary measures. One of the questions that have been asked in recent years is if and to what agree contractual approaches can both fill the gap where no statutory recognition framework is in place and reinforce the legal certainty and predictability of recognition under the statutory frameworks once adopted?

It needs to be concluded in line with Schwarcz et al. that contractual approaches cannot fill that gap. At best, it can to a limited extent help to reinforce legal certainty and predictability in those where a statutory framework is silent or absent. The effectiveness of contractual arrangements will largely depend on how widely and in what way parties will use them in their bilateral or multilateral arrangements. In some areas progress has been made on this front. The ISDA ('International Swap and Derivatives Association') has prepared a master agreement that

[42] E. Faia and B. Weder di Mauro, (2015), Cross-Border Resolution for Banks, SAFE Working Paper Nr. 88, Goethe University, Frankfurt am Main, March.

[43] See also J.-H. Binder, (2015), Resolution Planning and Structural Bank Reform within the Banking Union, in European Banking Union, Prospects and challenges, (J. Castaneda, et al. (eds.)), Routledge, London; also as SAFE Working Paper Nr. 81, Goethe University, Frankfurt am Main. He indicates 'However, in both international standard setting and at the European Union level, issues related to resolution planning (within the context of bank resolution reform) and structural banking reforms to date have been discussed rather separately. This lack of consistency is questionable, given the obvious need to reconcile both approaches in order to facilitate effective implementation and enforcement especially with regard to large, complex banking groups'.

has the potential to create uniformity and fill the gap where the statutory framework is (intentionally) incomplete or silent. It also will support the cross-border enforcement regarding 'early stay or early termination rights'. The 'Resolution Stay Protocol' suggested by the ISDA has become somewhat of a standard, at least judging from the number of banks that have indicated they would adopt the protocol (also in international contracts).

But this example is still an exception. As commented by Schwarcz et al.[44] 'For other types of financial contracts, contractual approaches are much less likely to fill the gap. The holdout problem in sovereign debt restructuring provides a useful precedent. As a solution to this problem, many nations attempted for years to include collective action clauses in their financing agreements, thereby enabling the supermajority (as opposed to unanimous) voting of creditors to change essential payment terms.'[45]

The FSB[46] indicated that a wider implementation is warranted if regulators require financial firms already subject to their prudential regulatory authority to adopt any necessary language in contracts with their counterparties. That in itself is true but assumes that regulators have the authority or competence to do so, which is highly jurisdiction- and detail-dependent.

Even if all that would work out well, the success of contractual affairs would not only depend on a widespread introduction of fairly standardized clauses but also on the legal enforceability of the relevant contractual provisions and the speed and reliability in enforcing such provisions. Many variables play a role (intentions, background, representation, etc.). These variables increase the 'litigation risk and creates less certainty and finality than a statutory approach'.[47] Another item of high uncertainty is the question to what degree contractual provisions and contractual approaches overall have the potential to reinforce the legal certainty and predictability of recognition under the statutory framework once that is in place. The answer to that will very much depend on the size and magnitude of the use of the framework among jurisdiction and can play a critical role in terms of providing transitional statutory certainty and predictability vis-à-vis counterparties in those countries that have not adopted the standardized regulatory framework approach.[48] Schwarcz et al. indicate '[s]uch a contractual approach could combine the inclusion of a resolution provision recognized by the statutory approach with a choice-of-law provision choosing the law of a nation that has already enacted that approach'.[49] But they also acknowledge that such a contractual approach would be much more difficult to reinforce legal certainty or predictability of recognition if 'instead of binding creditors, it purported to bind or impair the rights of an issuer in resolution'.[50]

---

[44] S.L. Schwarcz et al., (2014), Comments on the September 29, 2014, FSB Consultative Document, 'Cross-Border Recognition of Resolution Action', Centre for International Governance Innovation Paper CIGI Paper Nr. 51, p. 2.

[45] S.L. Schwarcz et al., (2014), Ibid. p. 2.

[46] FSB, (2014), Ibid. p. 13.

[47] S.L. Schwarcz et al., (2014), Ibid. p. 3.

[48] See also John C. Coffee, Jr., (2014), Extraterritorial Financial Regulation: Why E.T. Can't Come Home, Cornell Law Review, Vol. 99, Issue 6, pp. 1259–1302.

[49] S.L. Schwarcz et al., (2014), Ibid. p. 3, with example.

[50] S.L. Schwarcz et al., (2014), Ibid. p. 3.

The FSB also threw some questions out of their own with respect to issues that relate to achieving cross-border enforceability of (i) temporary restrictions or stays on early termination rights in financial contracts and (ii) 'bail-in' of debt instruments that are governed by the laws of a jurisdiction other than that of the issuing entity is a critical prerequisite for the effective implementation of resolution strategies for global systemically important financial institutions (G-SIFIs). From an overall perspective it can be stated that restrictions and stays on early termination rights in financial contracts can be important for the effective implementation of resolution strategies. There is a reason why most insolvency laws restrict the early termination of contracts that are favorable to the debtor.[51] The idea is that the debtor should with a certain level of calmness be able to reorganize its business and/or restructure its balance sheet. From a broader market perspective, it can be said that they reduce the likelihood of 'systemic risk' arising, and allow systemically important institutions, subject to insolvency laws, to reduce their counterparty risk and avoid further contagion. Overall, they help to protect markets from disorderly collapses of institutions that have the potential to destabilize the market. Both elements are important in designing a robust resolution mechanism: to enable systemically important financial firms to achieve a successful resolution, and to protect financial markets whose collapse could be systemically risky. Indeed, when judging systemic risk, both market and firm risk are relevant. It therefore can only be concluded that 'although achieving cross-border enforceability of temporary restrictions or stays on early termination rights in financial contracts can facilitate the effective implementation of resolution strategies for G-SIFIs, it sometimes might undermine the integrity of financial markets, with systemic consequences; and therefore the desirability of achieving such cross-border enforceability should be assessed after case-by-case review of the applicable restriction or stay'.[52]

With respect to the second item the answer can be fairly short. Yes, obviously achieving cross-border enforceability of 'bail-in' of debt instruments is a critical prerequisite for the effective implementation of resolution strategies for G-SIFIs.[53] The important feature is the cross-border recognition of debt instruments that are governed by the law of jurisdiction other than the issuer. The problem is clear: if there is risk that the foreign court doesn't recognize the claim or doesn't respects the bail-in, investors might withdraw or prefer other governing laws. Thankfully, there is already an international practice that internationally issued debt securities are either issued under the law of the issuer or governed by Anglo-American law. That concentration helps in practical terms to facilitate bail-ins.[54] Three elements are critical in that process: (1) the terms of the bail-in will be determined by the resolution authority and not by the debt documentation, (2) the enforceability should cover the bail-in provisions the parties agreed upon upfront but also those enacted by the regulator or resolution authority, (3) the cross-border enforceability of the bail-in of equity instruments (converting them into a class subordinate to common equity). It would create

[51] There are exceptions, for example, the derivative exception under US Law; see for that in detail: S. L. Schwarcz and O. Sharon, (2014), The Bankruptcy-Law Safe Harbor for Derivatives: A Path-Dependence Analysis, Washington and Lee Law Review, Vol. 71, pp. 1715–1755.

[52] S.L. Schwarcz et al., (2014), Ibid. p. 5.

[53] FSB, (2014), Ibid. p. 4.

[54] S.L. Schwarcz et al., (2014), Ibid. p. 6.

an asymmetry with the bail-in of debt instruments (converting them into common equity). Schwarcz raises the point that the latter point was not raised by the FSB and brings to mind that '[i]f the latter conversion is not enforceable, then, regardless of the governing law, a court may well refuse to enforce the debt bail-in because the debtholders bargained to have senior, not pari passu (and thus diluted), equity positions after the conversion'.[55]

Other items omitted by the FSB might include a stay on the seizure of a firm's assets and the enforceability outside the firm's jurisdiction and the possibility of concluding a treaty to create consistency in application globally as much as possible.

Another issue, which we already touched upon in terms of the exception to a pari passu treatment is the wide array of 'safe harbors' created by the regulator in favor of financial institutions. They provide a financial institution with a considerably better position as compared to other creditors should one of its counterparties fail or become insolvent. Paech[56] indicates '[t]he common rationale for such safe harbors is that the protection against the fallout of the counterparty's insolvency contributes to systemic stability, as the feared "domino effect" of insolvencies is not triggered from the outset'. But he is swift to add those exceptions are 'also criticized for accelerating contagion in the financial market in times of crisis and making the market more risky'. He argues that the regulator, correctly so, safeguards liquidity in the market this way. Liquidity in the markets is needed as it facilitates exchange and brings the cost of funding down for all market players. Modern financial markets could not properly function without liquidity. Those safe harbor rules allow for the exponentiation of liquidity. Disallowing those safe harbors would reduce liquidity and would accelerate contagion in case of a crisis. He indicates that restrictions on those rules would be counterproductive. Although I agree that those safe harbors can under circumstances facilitate levels of liquidity needed, the issue cannot be judged in isolation. In particular as safe harbors also can engage financial institutions in transactions that they, for a variety of risk-related or other reasons, should not be engaged in. The safe harbor rules might facilitate those institutions taking the extra risk, given the exceptional position they are warranted from a regulatory point of view. A judgment of the safe harbor rules cannot occur in isolation but needs to take into account collateral damage due to moral hazards created by the safe harbor rules, even if they are justified from the perspective of 'liquidity enhancement'.

Even more, although liquidity seems like a good thing to have at all times, it also became clear that liquidity in abundant amounts in itself can be a cause of systemic risk through the fact that large amounts of liquidity seem to contribute to bank failures. Banks create liquidity through a variety of techniques. That liquidity creation effect can increase the probability of default. Fungacova et al.[57] indicate '[w]hen liquidity creation becomes high, the probability of failure for banks in the upper decile of the liquidity spectrum increases significantly more than for other banks'. They produced a 'High Liquidity

---

[55] S.L. Schwarcz et al., (2014), Ibid. p. 6. He indicates that the rationale for this omission would appear to be that the issuer's law always governs equity securities.

[56] Ph. Paech, (2015), The Value of Insolvency Safe harbors, LSE Law, Society and Economy Working Papers 9/2015, April.

[57] Z. Fungacova et al., (2015), High Liquidity Creation and Bank Failures, IMF Working Paper Nr. WP/15/103.

Creation Hypothesis',[58] which demonstrates that liquidity creation by banks can be counterproductive when it becomes high. To be precise '[l]iquidity creation above a certain threshold increases the probability of bank failure, eventually leading to the disappearance of the high liquidity-creating institution and even a reduction in the volume of aggregate liquidity creation in the economy'.[59] This has policy and oversight implications. Liquidity creation might become a parameter for supervision and they might want to include the liquidity element in any sort of early warning or red flag mechanism.[60]

9.6 What About the Others? What About CCPs?

A lot of attention has been going to the recovery and resolution of banks, and rightly so. But on the other hand, we have created other institutions that are now of systemic relevance. A critical one on that list are the central clearing parties. The regulator has created a waterfall along which defaults should be settled. First through margins, then the balance sheet of the CCP and ultimately true mutualization with other CCP members.[61] Although the EC already in 2012 held a public consultation on the matter, it was only in May 2015 that it released a follow-through roadmap for non-bank recovery and resolution providing

[58] Shadow banking liquidity is built traditionally on two hypotheses: (1) the weak fundamentals hypothesis which is built on the idea that bank failure is embedded in its poor financial and economic fundamentals, and (2) which is built around the inability of the bank to meet liquidity commitments. The 'High Liquidity Creation Hypothesis' suggested by Fungacova et al. complements these two strands of literature and research: According to this hypothesis a bank's vulnerability increases when the core output measured by liquidity creation reaches high levels compared to other banks' activities in the system (p. 3). Their model is built on A. Berger, and C. Bouwman, (2009), Bank Liquidity Creation, Review of Financial Studies Vol. 22, pp. 3779–3837; See for an overview of literature and model review: pp. 3–8.

[59] Z. Fungacova et al., (2015), Ibid. p. 16. See also F. Allen, and D. Gale, (2004), Financial Intermediaries and Markets, Econometrica Vol. 72, pp. 1023–1061; A. Berger, and C. Bouwman, (2011), Bank Liquidity Creation, Monetary Policy, and Financial Crises, Working Paper, Wharton Financial Institutions Center: C. Borio, (2014), The Financial Cycle and Macroeconomics: What Have We Learnt? Journal of Banking & Finance Vol. 45, pp. 182–198; C. Brown, and S. Dinç, (2005), The Politics of Bank Failures: Evidence from Emerging Markets, Quarterly Journal of Economics Vol. 120, Issue 4, pp. 1413–1442; R. DeYoung, and G. Torna, (2013), Non-traditional Banking Activities and Bank Failures during the Financial Crisis, Journal of Financial Intermediation Vol. 22, Issue 3, pp. 397–421; D. Diamond, and R. Rajan, (2005), Liquidity Shortages and Banking Crises, Journal of Finance Vol. 20, Issue 2, pp. 615–646; F. Vazquez, and P. Federico, (2012), Bank Funding Structures and Risk: Evidence from the Global Financial Crisis, IMF Working Paper Nr. WP/12/29.

[60] See also M. Dewatripont and X. Freixas, (2011), Bank Resolution: A Framework for the Assessment of Regulatory Intervention, Oxford Review of Economic Policy, Vol. 27, Nr. 3, pp. 411–436.

[61] See in detail the chapter on CCPs as well as: (1) ISDA, (2013), CCP Loss Allocation at the End of the Waterfall, August, (2) R. Cont, (2015), The End of the Waterfall: Default Resources of Central Clearing Parties. Imperial College London WP, (3) B. Cœuré, (2014), Keynote Speech by Benoît Cœuré, Member of the Executive Board of the ECB, At Exchange of Ideas #2 "Central clearing – guarantee of stability or new moral hazard?" organized by Eurex Clearing, London, November 24, 2014, (4) EACH, (2014), An Effective Recovery and Resolution Regime for CCPs, December, (5), JP Morgan Chase, (2014), What is the Resolution Plan for CCPs, Perspectives, September.

a high-level public description of the planned initiative. Since then it has stayed quiet by far and large, despite the enhanced systemic nature CCPs enjoy since OTC trading and so on have now turned them into central nodes of the global and European financial system.

9.7 Effective Resolution Regimes for Financial Institutions

9.7.1 Introduction

The FSB Key Attributes of Effective Resolution Regimes for Financial Institutions (Key Attributes) were adopted in October 2011[62] and endorsed as a new international standard for resolution regimes. They were supplemented in October 2014[63] with new Annexes containing sector-specific guidance that sets out how the key attributes should be applied for insurers, FMIs and the protection of client assets in resolution. These key attributes apply to resolution regimes for any type of financial institution that could be or become systemically significant or critical when it fails. The list includes banks, insurers, investment and securities firms and FMIs as well as holding companies and non-regulated operational entities within a financial group or conglomerate. Because they constitute a boilerplate umbrella model not all attributes are equally relevant for all sectors. They require adaptation, as interpretation is not relevant in certain situations. The FSB has therefore issued a compliance methodology to validate a certain national compliance program with respect to the banking sector.[64]

---

[62] FSB, (2011), Key Attributes of Effective Resolution Regimes for Financial Institutions, October.

[63] FSB, (2014), Key Attributes of Effective Resolution Regimes for Financial Institutions, October. In June 2018, the document was complemented with two supporting documents dealing with (1) Principles on bail-in execution (the operational side of a bail-in), and (2) the funding strategy of a resolution plan. The first document deals with issues such as: disclosures on the instruments and liabilities within the scope of bail-in; valuations to inform and support the application of bail-in; processes to suspend or cancel the listing of securities, to notify creditors, and to deliver new securities or tradeable certificates following entry into resolution; securities law and securities exchange requirements during the bail-in; processes for transferring governance and control rights to a new board and management for the firm emerging from resolution; and communications to creditors and the market at large. The second document provides information on issues such as: firms' capabilities to support monitoring, reporting and estimating funding needs in resolution and executing the funding strategy; the development of resolution funding plans by authorities; the reliance on firm assets and private funding as preferred sources of funding in resolution; access to temporary public sector backstop funding mechanisms and ordinary central bank facilities; and information sharing and coordination between authorities. See FSB, (2018), Principles on bail-In Execution, June 21 and FSB, (2018), Funding Strategy Elements of an Implementable Resolution Plan, June 21, both via fsb.org. The latter should be read in conjunction with and complements their earlier document funding requirements during resolution projects for G-SIBs. See FSB, (2016), Guiding Principles on the Temporary Funding needed to Support the Orderly Resolution of a Global Systemically Important Bank ("G-SIB"), August 18.

[64] FSB, (2016), Key Attributes Assessment Methodology for the Banking Sector Methodology for Assessing the Implementation of the Key Attributes of Effective Resolution Regimes for Financial Institutions in the Banking Sector, October 19. D. Domanski, (2018), Towards Effective Global Resolution Regimes: the Road Ahead, Brussels, June 12, 2018, Remarks.

The methodology is implemented in the single resolution mechanism (SRM)[65] that is in place in the EU since January 1, 2016.[66] But not everybody is convinced that this will solve the issue.[67] Dermine[68] argues that the SRM, in its current format, creates an unin-

[65] The establishment in 2015 of the Single Resolution Board (SRB), a new agency of the European Union, counts as one of the most significant European banking reforms of recent years. The SRB was set up to quickly resolve banks that are failing or likely to fail, as part of a wider effort to break the vicious cycle between banks and sovereigns that nearly destroyed the euro area in 2011–12. The SRB was created following a decision by Europe's leaders in December 2012 to create a Single Resolution Mechanism (SRM), whose legislative basis was enacted in July 2014. It started operations on January 1, 2016, including the possibility of forcing losses on their claimants if need be ("bail-in"); see N. Véron, (2018), Bad News and Good News for the Single Resolution Board, blog Post January 15 (via bruegel.org). Regarding the 'single' dimension, that is, the interaction between the EU and national level in the process, see D. Busch et al., (2019), How Single is the Single Resolution Mechanism? European Banking Institute Working Paper Series 2019, Nr. 30, January; A. Segura and S. Vicente, (2019), Bank Resolution and Public Backstop in an Asymmetric Banking Union, Bank of Italy Working Paper Nr. 1212, March 18 (also as ESRB Working Paper Nr. 83, 2018, August 16).

[66] Regulation (EU) No 806/2014 of the European Parliament and of the Council of July 15, 2014, establishing uniform rules and a uniform procedure for the resolution of credit institutions and certain investment firms in the framework of a Single Resolution Mechanism and a Single Resolution Fund and amending Regulation (EU) No 1093/2010, OJ L 225, 30.7.2014, pp. 1–90. This piece of regulation goes hand-in-hand with the BRRD Directive discussed before: Directive 2014/59/EU of the European Parliament and of the Council of May 15, 2014, establishing a framework for the recovery and resolution of credit institutions and investment firms and amending Council Directive 82/891/EEC, and Directives 2001/24/EC, 2002/47/EC, 2004/25/EC, 2005/56/EC, 2007/36/EC, 2011/35/EU, 2012/30/EU and 2013/36/EU, and Regulations (EU) No 1093/2010 and (EU) No 648/2012, of the European Parliament and of the Council Text with EEA relevance, OJ L 173, 12.6.2014, pp. 190–348.

[67] That besides the fact that the governance structure of the SRM is extremely complex, jeopardizing the effectiveness of the decision-making process. Reaching an agreement on how the structure should look like was a first step toward that complexity. Other issues relate to the complexity of European law and how this mechanism was supposed to fit within the wider regulatory framework. The second element that relates to complexity is the division of tasks between European and national authorities. There are not only exclusive but also parallel responsibilities. It is not always clear how that cooperation should be coordinated. Further there is the division of tasks between the SRB plenary session and the executive session. Tasks are well divided but decision-making is not. The financing of the Fund is an ordeal in itself. That is mainly caused by (1) the calculation of the ex ante contributions, (2) the decision-making behind extraordinary ex post contributions, and (3) it is the participating member states that raise these funds with the institutions covered by the SRM and need to transfer them to the fund. A clear legal foundation for that transferring mandate is still not in place and should ideally be based on Union law. See in detail: D. Busch, (2017), Governance of the Single Resolution Mechanism, Working Paper, mimeo. Based on the earlier quasi-identical chapter in: D. Busch and G. Ferrarini (eds), (2015), European Banking Union, Oxford University Press, Oxford.

[68] J. Dermine, (2017), The Single Resolution Mechanism in the European Union: Good Intentions and Unintended Evil, Monetary Economic Issues Today, Festschrift in Honour of Ernst Baltensperger (ed.), Swiss National Bank, Orell Füssli Verlag, Zurich, pp. 359–372. He comes to that conclusion after considering three objectives that resolution legislation should live up to: '(a) swift decisions, to minimize the impact on the economy, (b) privatization of losses, to stop the linkage between public bailout, budget deficit, and sovereign risk, (c) elimination of moral hazard, with bail-in debt held by private creditors who bear losses.' Also I. Asimakopoulos, (2018), The Veneto Banks Resolution: It Shall Be Called 'Liquidation', European Company Law, Vol. 15, Nr. 5, pp. 156–162.

tended evil: a significant increase in the likelihood of bank runs. Also the first SRB report by the European Court of Auditors wasn't particularly fantastic when it comes to the functioning of the SRB/SRM.[69] Dermine argues so along three major lines of criticism: (1) the current SRM is incomplete and a potential contributor to future panic and disruption of the banking system. He argues so for three reasons. These concern (1) the ability of the private market to bear losses, the implicit cap on losses that would be passed on to creditors and a greatly increased likelihood of a run on fragile banks[70]; (2) the explicit reference that losses could be covered by the single resolution fund after a minimum loss absorption of 8% of total liabilities, including shareholders' funds. Such reference is unanticipated and unnecessary as full exposure to losses would further increase the incentives to monitor a bank; (3) the fact that unsecured deposits with a maturity of more than seven days are potentially exposed creates the risk of a bank run. That will trigger the behavior of not renewing deposits, leading to liquidity risk and a possible run on banks. The directive leaves the door open to exclude certain deposits, but market agents will leave no room for a possible inclusion and will withdraw funding.[71]

[69] ECA, (2017), Single Resolution Board: Work on a Challenging Banking Union Task Started, but Still a Long Way to Go, Special Report, Nr. 23/2017 (via eca.europe.eu). This audit assessed the quality of the SRB's overall rules and guidance, resolution planning for individual banks, and whether the SRB is staffed adequately. The ECA found shortcomings in all of these areas.

[70] Losses on loans do not disappear but are passed on to shareholders. The objective is then not to avoid losses to avoid (a further) loss of confidence in case that happens. It is therefore crucial that designated 'bail in' instruments are known upfront as well as how the bank's own bail-in will be distributed across customers of the bank. See regarding the systemic implications of bail-in: A.-C. Hüser et al., (2017), The Systemic Implications of Bail-In: A Multi-Layered Network Approach, ECB Working Paper Nr. 2010, February including an interesting and extensive literature list (pp. 39–41). They find that there is no direct contagion to creditor banks and also spillover effects are small due to low levels of securities cross-holdings in the interbank network. They also estimate the impact on the different liability holders of a bail-in: shareholders and subordinated creditors are always affected by the bail-in, senior unsecured creditors in 75% of the cases thereby using a multi-layered network model. A bail-in however reshapes significantly interbank linkages within specific seniority layers as '[t]he bank under resolution becomes more central within the equity network layer after the bail-in and less central in the subordinated debt layer' (p. 3). This shows, according to Hüser et al., that resolution authorities will need to carefully consider the level of loss-absorbing capacity—to avoid that certain creditors such as depositors or perhaps even senior unsecured creditors are hit—as well as the composition of loss-absorbing capacity. Also L. Leanza et al., (2019), Bail-In vs Bail-Out: Bank Resolution and Liability Structure, Working Paper, February, mimeo. The latter conclude that a credible bail-in resolution regime endogenously reduces leverage and mitigates default risk. A strict enforcement of the Common Equity Tier 1 (CET1) capital requirement, as introduced by the Basel III regulation, entails a dramatic reduction of the optimal bank leverage.

[71] Solutions to those issues according to Dermine are as follows: (1) exclude short-term debt with a maturity of more than seven days, as it would reduce bank runs; (2) impose rules on seniority for short-term debt. Debt with a maturity of less than one year would rank as senior, with other debt being junior or impose the collateralization of short-term debt. Also this would reduce the risk of a bank run; (3) apply a 'corralito' (the bank is closed and funds cannot be withdrawn); (4) the creation of a private industry fund that would guarantee either short-term deposits or all deposits and (5) ex post penalties. Also E.J. Janger et al., (2015), Implementing Symmetric Treatment or Financial Contracts in Bankruptcy and Bank Resolution, CORP. FIN. &COM. L. 10, Nr. 1, pp. 155–182.

During the period 2016–2018 the EC issued a number of regulatory instruments to amend and revise the BRRD and SRM[72] regulation. These amendments deal with (1) holding a minimum of own funds and eligible liabilities (MREL)[73] to ensure effective and credible application of the bail-in resolution[74] tool[75]; (2) the total loss-absorbing capacity

[72] Proposal for a REGULATION OF THE EUROPEAN PARLIAMENT AND OF THE COUNCIL amending Regulation (EU) No 806/2014 as regards loss-absorbing and recapitalization capacity for credit institutions and investment firms- COM/2016/0851 final – 2016/0361 (COD)- November 23, 2016. The final text was approved April 16, 2019.

[73] The MREL aspects are managed in the EU by the Single Resolution Board (SRB). The SRB started operations on January 1, 2015, and is since January 1, 2016, fully responsible for resolution projects and policy in the EU. The MREL is embedded (in a relatively loose way) in the previously discussed Bank Recovery and Resolution Directive (BRRD) which requires G-SIBs to meet a minimum requirement for own funds and eligible liabilities (MREL) so as to be able to absorb losses and restore their capital position, allowing banks to continuously perform their critical economic functions during and after a crisis. MREL represents one of the key tools in enhancing banks' resolvability. It was in 2017 that the SRB developed its first MREL policies. That process has continued in 2018 and 2019 where it developed policies for more complex scenarios and to facilitate cross-border resolution planning. Interesting is its report on valuation issues in the context of resolution planning (report February 19, 2019), all via srb.europe.eu. See for an evaluation: F. Restoy, (2018), Bail-In in the New Bank Resolution Framework: Is there an Issue with the Middle Class, speech given at the IADI-ERC International Conference: "Resolution and deposit guarantee schemes in Europe: incomplete processes and uncertain outcomes", Naples, Italy, March 23. Restoy highlights that the MREL requirements as set by the SRB are pretty demanding (i.e. close to twice the amount of regulatory capital or to be very precise 'twice the sum of Pillar 1 and Pillar 2 requirements plus the combined buffer requirements plus a market confidence charge'). That triggers a variety of challenges in particular for smaller and mid-tier banks. Also AFME, (2018), Resolution Aspects of the EU Risk Reduction Measures Package, October, via afme.eu, who warn of excessive requirements and urge for simplicity and awareness of the global context in which banks operate. Also B. Berger et al., (2016), Total Assets Versus Risk Weighted Assets: Does it Matter for MREL, Bruegel Policy Contribution Nr. 2016/12, via bruegel.org. Also C. Gortsos, (2019), The Role of Deposit Guarantee Schemes (DGSS) in Resolution Financing European Banking Institute Working Paper Series 2019 – Nr. 37, March 28.

[74] Questions are asked whether a policy of strict bail-in in all cases (bailout only in case of precautionary recapitalization; but this applies only to solvent institutions and cannot cover past losses) of undercapitalization is wise. Even if a financial system has sufficient volumes of junior debt to bail-in, the question is at what cost that will occur. See in detail: C. Hadjiemmanuil, (2017), Limits on State-Funded Bailouts in the EU bank Resolution Regime, EBI Working Paper Nr. 2.

[75] T.H. Troeger, (2018), Why MREL Won't Help Much, European Banking Institute Working Paper Nr. 13, May. Troeger argues '[t]he main problem, echoing the general concerns scholars voiced against the European ü regime, is that the specifications for minimum requirements for own funds and eligible liabilities (MREL) are also highly detailed and discretionary and thus fail to fully alleviate the predicament of investors in bail-in debt…Quite importantly, given the character of typical MREL instruments as non-runnable long-term debt, even if investors are able to correctly gauge the relevant risk of PSI ("Private Sector Involvement") in a bank's failure at the time of purchase, subsequent adjustments of MREL prescriptions by competent or resolution authorities potentially change the risk profile of the pertinent instruments. Therefore, original pricing decisions, and the market discipline that follows from them may prove inadequate and so may.' The TLAC implementation (through the SRM amendments) he considers 'with an exorbitant emphasis on proportionality and technical fine-tuning.' He concludes 'it is barely conceivable that the pricing of MREL instruments reflects an accurate risk assessment of investors because of the many discretionary choices a multitude of agencies are supposed to make and revisit in the administration of the new regime.' He seems little positive about the bail-in mecha-

(TLAC)[76] to deal better with the too-big-to-fail problem.[77] Some are positive on where we are and consider it is now time to focus on implementation[78] rather than the development of the regulatory framework.[79] Overall the sentiment around the BRRD and in particular the SRM is suboptimal or even pretty grim. Part of that has to do with the fact that real-life experience with the models is limited to stylized projections. Another question is to what degree the process is likely to get politicized during what ultimately are acute interventions.[80]Not only the process but also the SRM as a mechanism is complex and

nism: T.H. Troeger, (2017), Too Complex to Work: A Critical Assessment of the Bail-In Tool Under the European Bank Recovery and Resolution Regime, Journal of Financial Regulation, Vol. 4, Issue 4, March, pp. 35–72; C. Hadjiemmanuil, (2017), Limits to State-Funded Bailouts in the EU Bank Resolution Regime, European Banking Institute Working Paper Nr. 2.

[76] FSB, (2015), Principles on Loss-absorbing and Recapitalisation Capacity of G-SIBs in Resolution, Total Loss-absorbing Capacity (TLAC) Term Sheet, November 9; FSB, (2017), Guiding Principles on the Internal Total Loss-absorbing Capacity of G-SIBs ('Internal TLAC'), July 6; BCBS, (2016), TLAC Holding, Standard, October.

[77] See for further details: EC, (2016), Frequently Asked Questions: Capital requirements (CRR/CRD IV) and resolution framework (BRRD/SRM) amendments – Fact Sheet, MEMO/16/3840, November 23. The proposal aims to incorporate international standards on loss-absorbing and recapitalization. In line with the 2015 FSB recommendations on TLAC (total loss-absorbing capacity), the proposal aims to reduce the impact of banking failures on public funds. It applies to all global systemically important institutions (G-SIIs) worldwide as of January 2019. It applies to all G-SIIs, hence to 13 banks within the EU (out of 30). Since TLAC is not binding, it has to be transposed into national or European legislation. As of January 1, 2019, G-SIIs will have to comply with a minimum TLAC requirement of 16% of RWA and 6% of the Basel III leverage ratio denominator (TLAC Leverage Ratio Exposure (LRE) Minimum). See also T.H. Fuertas, (2016), European Banking Resolution: Making it Work! Interim Report of the CEPS Task Force on Implementing Financial Sector Resolution, January.

[78] A. Carstens, (2018), Post-Crisis Bank Resolution: What Are the Main Challenges Now? Concluding Remarks, The 8th FSI-IADI conference on "Bank resolution, crisis management and deposit insurance" February 2, Basel. Also C. Gortsos, (2018), The Role of Deposit Guarantee Schemes (DGSS) in Resolution Financing, European Banking Institute Working Paper Series 2019 Nr. 37, March, about the interaction between the deposit insurance schemes directive and the BRRD.

[79] FSB, (2019), Thematic Peer Review on Bank Resolution Planning, April 29; FSB, (2018), Thematic Peer Review on Bank Resolution Planning: Summary Terms of Reference, June 4; FSB, (2016), Second Thematic Review on Resolution Regimes, March (all via fsb.org).

[80] See for some impressions: M. Feiller, (2017), On the Credibility of Bail-ins. Has the Single Resolution Mechanism become more credible for European Banks after the Banco Popular Bail-in?, StudyLab, December 14; R. Houben, (2017), The Single Resolution Mechanism, Intersentia Ltd., Cambridge; S.M.C. Nuijten et al., (2017), The Bank Recovery and Resolution Directive and the Single Resolution Mechanism: Preadviezen/Reports 2014, Eleven International Publishing, The Hague; M. Henze, (2015), Einheitliche Abwicklung für Europas Banken: Die zentrale Bankenabwicklung in der Eurozone auf dem Prüfstand, Springer Gabler, Wiesbaden; SRB, (2015), The Single Resolution Mechanism. Introduction to Resolution Planning, Brussels; Finance Ministry Germany, (2018), The Single Supervisory Mechanism: Lessons Learned after the First Three Years, Federal Ministry of Finance's Monthly Report, January, pp. 1–5. Also D. Busch and A. Teubner, (2019), Fit and Proper Assessments within the Single Supervisory Mechanism, EBI Working Paper Nr. 34, March.

multi-layered and governance questions are and have been raised.[81] Also the likely impact of those governance issues on the effectiveness of decision-making within the SRM framework. Efficient, impartial, decisive and quick decision-making is obviously crucial in the case of bank resolution.[82]

Resolution funding remains a problematic feature. Any resolution funding arrangement should foremost reflect the broader institutional market and policy context in a particular country. That includes the characteristics of the financial system (size, concentration, structure, etc.) as well as the capacity of the system to contribute to resolution funding and the relationship of traditional banking/shadow banking. It should further include the legal and institutional architecture of the safety net. Considerations are required in terms of the necessity to finance ex ante versus ex post, keeping in mind that the intrinsic arguments for establishing a separate resolution fund aren't strong. Depending on whether there is a deposit-insurance mechanism available the ex ante financing model is preferred to ensure financial firepower for the insurance system.[83] In case it is chosen to go with the separate resolution fund model, they should have clear legal and operational frameworks and safeguards to minimize moral hazard.[84]

The awareness of any possible explicit or implicit damage or cost is relevant in this context. The link between financial institutions and in particular SIFIs implies that recovery and resolution as well as restructuring efforts at SIFIs are materially similar to those undertaken for sovereigns. At that level we know that sovereign debt restructurings are associated with declines in GDP, investment, bank credit and capital flows. Often the

[81] Also J.-H. Binder, (2018), The Relevance of the Resolution Tools Within the SRM, EBI Working Paper, Nr. 29, November; J.-H. Binder, (2019), Resolution Regimes in the Financial Sector: In Need of Cross-Sectoral Regulation? European Banking Institute Working Paper Series Nr. 33, March; J.-H. Binder, (2019), Bank Bail-In and Disputed Claims: Can It Cope? The Case for and against a Vis Attractiva Resolutionis, European Banking Institute Working Paper Series 2019 – Nr. 32, January 30.

[82] See in detail: D. Busch, (2017), Governance of the European Banking Union's Single Resolution Mechanism European Banking Institute Working Paper Series Nr. 9; D. Busch and M.B.J. van Rijn, (2018), Towards Single Resolution and Single Supervision of Systemically Important Financial Institutions in the European Union?, European Business Organization Law Review, Vol. 19, Nr. 2, pp. 301–363. The bottom line in Buschs' story is: 'the increasingly blurred distinction between markets, financial institutions, services and products is not matched in the European Union by an integrated regulatory and supervisory approach. Instead, regulation was and remains largely organized along sectoral lines, with an emphasis on the banking sector.' A coherent supervisory model would '(1) help to eliminate (national) supervisory and regulatory gaps, (2) reduce regulatory arbitrage activities, and (3) contribute to the stability of the financial system and a level playing field.' Also J.-H. Binder, (2019), Resolution Regimes in the Financial Sector: In Need of Cross-Sectoral Regulation?, EBI Working Paper Nr. 33, March.

[83] Managerial overconfidence (in investment performance) is linking insurer shadow banking involvement to government bail-outs (purchasing of distressed assets). S. Chen et al., (2019), CEO Overconfidence and Shadow-Banking Life Insurer Performance Under Government Purchases of Distressed Assets, Risks, Vol. 7, Issue 1, pp. 28 ff. https://doi.org/10.3390/risks7010028, including an interesting literature list for those interested in the shadow insurance (or captive reinsurance) industry.

[84] See in detail on all matters: O. Croituro et al., (2018), Resolution Funding: Who Pays When Financial Institutions Fail?, IMF Technical Notes and Manuals Nr. 18/01, Washington DC.

'transmission channels and associated output and banking sector costs depend on whether the restructuring takes place preemptively, without missing payments to creditors, or whether it takes place after a default has occurred'. Post-default restructurings on the other hand are associated with 'larger declines in bank credit,[85] an increase in lending interest rates, and a higher likelihood of triggering a banking crisis than pre-emptive restructurings'. So not only does it matter what recovery or resolution model one applies but also the timing or timeframe.[86] The bottom line of many studies in this field is that 'the transmission channels and associated output and banking sector costs of debt restructurings differ depending on the restructuring strategy followed'. The most commonly used demarcation line for restructuring techniques is 'based on whether payments were missed (post-default debt restructuring), were missed but only temporarily and with the consent of the foreign creditors (weakly pre-emptive debt restructuring) or whether payments continued to be made in full and on time during the negotiations (strictly pre-emptive debt restructuring)'.[87]Just like a sovereign's decision of how to go about restructuring its debt is influenced by the economic conditions it faces, that seems to be true and valid for (SI)FIs as well. Ultimately, the complex linkages and feedback channels between the real, financial and public sectors shape the response to a debt restructuring. The results of Asonuma et al. demonstrate that 'much of the adverse costs depend on whether a severe sudden stop can be avoided, which is more likely in preemptive restructurings'.[88] Having said that, one must take into account that countries at all times face a

[85] The expectation of a possible bailout has an impact on bank credit growth. Xu engaged in the exercise to identify the patterns that exist in that credit growth. Xu measured each bank holding company's exposure to the systemic bailout factor, which is the sensitivity of each bank's out-of-the-money put option price to the variations of sector-wide put option basket-index spreads. Xu further shows that low market expectations of the banking sector systemic bailouts played a significant role in the weak bank credit recovery after the subprime crisis. Bank holding companies with higher pre-crisis exposure to the systemic bailout factor experienced larger post-crisis deviations from the pre-crisis bank credit growth trend. Such a pattern is persistent even for banks that are less affected by the post-crisis financial regulations and less exposed to borrowers from the deteriorating sectors. Commercial bank subsidiaries within the same bank holding company present the same credit growth patterns even though they have different exposure to financial regulations and deteriorating sectors. Xu also concludes that the securitization market, which connects the two types of banks (shadow and traditional banks), determines how market expectations of systemic bailouts to shadow banks affect the credit origination capacity of the whole banking system. See in detail: Y. Xi, (2018), Shadow Banking and Systemic Bailout Exposure, Working Paper, February 28, mimeo.

[86] T. Asonuma et al., (2019), Costs of Sovereign Defaults: Restructuring Strategies, Bank Distress and the Capital Inflow-Credit Channel, IMF Working Paper Nr. WP/19/69, March, pp. 2–5, 50. Also F. Hett and A. Schmidt, (2017), Bank Rescues and Bailout Expectations: The Erosion of Market Discipline During the Financial Crisis. Journal of Financial Economics, Elsevier, Vol. 126, Issue 3, pp. 635–651.

[87] T. Asonuma et al., (2019), Ibid. p. 4 and their earlier work T. Asonuma, and C. Trebesch, (2016), Sovereign Debt Restructurings: Preemptive or Post-default, Journal of the European Economic Association, Vol. 14, Issue 1, pp. 175–214.

[88] The transmission channels and associated output and banking sector costs depend on whether the 'restructuring takes place preemptively (without missing payments to creditors), or after a default has occurred (and payments are unilaterally missed)', T. Asonuma et al., (2019), Ibid. p. 35.

number of hurdles regarding their choice on how to restructure a SIFI. These are not limited to economic and political choices but the continuous threat that the possibility that a large adverse shock suddenly places the country in a 'bad equilibrium'. That bad equilibrium can traditionally imply that debt service halts as even when payments are missed (post-default), the output costs of a recovery or resolution are or at least can be mitigated by the pace of the resolution or recovery process. In any case, post-default resolution or recovery is more expensive and damaging than pre-emptive interventions. The output cost of a resolution or recovery by far and large will depend, over longer time horizons, on the restructuring or roll-up strategy applied.

An additional layer of complications emerges when a banking and sovereign crisis occurs simultaneously. In line with a pure sovereign crisis, the output cost also depends on the timing and nature of the strategy applied to recover or resolve. It is clear by now that there are good and bad (and even worse) ways of dealing with recovery and resolution. The growing literature in this field in recent years typically identifies two models: (1) 'reprofilings' referring to restructurings that mostly involve an extension of payment terms and (2) those of restructurings that involve deeper haircuts on different measures of borrower and creditor welfare (e.g. growth performance, incidence of future debt crises, return to market access, among others).[89] Asonuma et al. add to the equation that in both cases pre-emptive action reduces output costs thereby blending in an analysis of the linkages that exist between an FI (or the banking sector as such) and the sovereign. Most of it depends on the level of understanding how the (different) transmission channel(s) function and the relationship with the real economy as well as the effect any action will have on the capital inflow-credit channel (i.e. the potential loss in market access by an FI to external financing (domestic or foreign)). The pace at which a conclusion is reached and the process is closed co-determines the outcome.[90] The spillover effects between sovereigns and banks tend to run through two channels. An increase in sovereign's default risk affects financial intermediaries that shows up through (1) banks' funding costs might increase,

---

[89] T. Asonuma et al., (2019), Ibid. pp. 5–7.

[90] Also C. Arellano, et al., (2019), Sovereign Default Risk and Firm Heterogeneity, Federal Reserve Bank of Minneapolis Research Department Staff Report Nr. 547, revised, March; T. Asonuma, (2016), Serial Sovereign Defaults and Debt Restructurings, IMF Working Paper Nr. WP/16/66; T. Asonuma, and H. Joo, (2017), Sovereign Debt Restructurings: Delays in Renegotiations and Risk Averse Creditors, Working Paper, mimeo, February 7; I. Balteanu, and A. Erce, (2018), Linking Bank Crises and Sovereign Defaults: Evidence from Emerging Markets, IMF Economic Review, Vol. 66, Issue 4, pp. 617–664; A. Chari, et al., (2018), The Costs of (sub)Sovereign Default Risk: Evidence from Puerto Rico, Federal Reserve Bank of Richmond WP Nr. 18-03; A. Cesa-Bianchi, et al., (2017), International Credit Supply Shocks, Journal of International Economics, Vol. 112(C), pp. 219–237; G. Cheng et al., (2018), The Macroeconomic Effects of Official Debt Restructuring: Evidence from the Paris Club, Oxford Economic Papers, pp. 1–20; A. Erce, and E. Mallucci, (2018), Selective Sovereign Defaults, International Finance Discussion Paper Nr. 1239, Board of Governors of the Federal Reserve System and European Stability Mechanism, November; N. Gennaioli, et al., (2018), Banks, Government Bonds, and Default: What do the Data Say? Journal of Monetary Economics, Vol. 98, pp. 98–113; G. Gordon, and P. Guerron-Quintana, (2018), Dynamics of Investment, Debt and Default, Review of Economic Dynamics, Vol. 28, pp. 71–85 and C. Sosa-Padilla, (2018), Sovereign Defaults and Banking Crises, Journal of Monetary Economics, Vol. 99, pp. 88–105.

inducing higher interest rates on loans and bonds and a cut back in these assets, and (2) financial regulator's risk-weighted asset framework would assign higher weights to lower quality assets, implying a portfolio rebalancing and more deleveraging.[91]

9.7.2 The Trade-off in Bank Resolutions

We are by now aware of the fact that national authorities had to step in and keep the financial sector floating during the worst periods of the 2008 financial crisis. The post-event bailout is not only prone to moral hazard but leaves expectation as to future public support for distressed financial institutions. Excessive risk taking and lack of market discipline[92] are possible outcomes of that strategy. The legal constraints of bail-ins before distressed scenarios occur and the need to prevent widespread systemic risk in the marketplace created the end-result we all know. The costs of FI failures were and are born by taxpayers, even to the degree that it impacted the creditworthiness and the financial standing of the sovereign was severely and structurally impacted. When the dust settled post-crisis, some deep reflection was needed on how to avoid a situation like this happening again. And in case it would happen again how the burden could be shifted to private investors as well as how to improve the trade-off between bail-ins and bailouts.[93]

Although there is a material consensus that for a variety of reasons (moral hazard, expectations, legal and fiscal rules, etc.) bailouts are not preferred and should be the exception. That way the fiscal link between a systemic event and the sovereign is guaranteed (or at least more or less). Rules have been put in place to formally limit the role of the treasury in the context of resolving a fiscal crisis. The frameworks developed and which we have discussed in this chapter are all largely built around the objective that there are strict conditions on the use of public funds when bailing out banks. The other cornerstone of such a framework typically exists out of large and often discretionary powers to the identified regulatory and supervisory authority to recover or resolve particular cases. Bail-ins are part of the toolbox dragging private investors into FIs into the funding solution. Those would include equity holders, but equally so secured and unsecured creditors. The last would then be faced with liabilities that they hold vis-à-vis the FI either terminated or written down or see those fixed liabilities converted into equity. Those frameworks also force each FI to draft comprehensive and credible plans how to deal with existential exposures and other distressed scenarios while keeping an eye on recovery

---

[91] H.R. Tabarraei et al., (2019), Sovereigns and Financial Intermediaries Spillovers, IMF Working Paper Nr. WP/19/43, February.

[92] Cutura argues that the introduction of the Banking Recovery and Resolution Directive (BRRD) improved market discipline in the European bank market for unsecured debt. His empirical results are consistent with the hypothesis that debt holders actively monitor banks and that the BRRD diminished bailout expectations. J. Cutura, (2018), Debt Holders Monitoring and Impact Guarantees: Did the BRRD Improve Market Discipline, SAFE Working Paper Nr. 232, October 20.

[93] Also P. Poyntner and T. Reiniger, (2018), Bail-In and Legacy Assets: Harmonized Rules for Targeted Partial Compensation to Strengthen the Bail-In Regime, ONB Working Paper Nr. 224, October; A. Segura and J. Suarez, (2019), Optimally Solving Banks' Legacy Problems, ESRB Working Paper Nr. 96, June 17.

where possible but also ensure a maximum of financial stability for the marketplace as a whole while working through the process of cleaning up the mess. That is obviously even more the case for systemically important FIs that are large, complex and have relations throughout the financial system. Making sure there is sufficient loss-absorbing capacity on the balance sheet of the FI is part of the basic toolbox.

Although it was clear when we reviewed the frameworks that there is a trade-off deeply embedded in the choice between a bail-in and a bailout model against the background of strong and discretionary powers by the competent authority, we haven't yet diffused the trade-off between both. It wasn't the right place to do so when we reviewed the comprehensive frameworks but it is a job that needs to happen as concrete and balanced as possible taking into account the spillover effects to be expected when applying a bail-in and the well-documented moral hazard consequences of bailouts. Although the reform in this field continues to deliver better insights as time goes on, it is safe to say at this point that no model designed so far allows to conclude a total and guaranteed isolation of sovereign funds to recovery or resolution programs. But maybe that is not necessary. Maybe it makes sense to allow, or at least factor in the fact that a 'constrained but flexible' usage and availability of sovereign funding in these situations makes sense. That would definitely be the case as systemic exposure to jeopardize the stability of the financial system in a material way and for protracted periods of time. That obviously under the assumption that there was sufficient loss-absorbing capital available at the failing FI and that all stakeholders are on board when it comes to taking a haircut one way or the other.

The starting point in this analysis is the understanding of a policy trade-off between ex ante and ex post interventions in terms of efficiency. We understand the issues surrounding moral hazard and lack of market discipline as well as the potential of excessive risk taking when considering a bailout. All that could lead to more and more intense financial vulnerabilities. It could even fuel a leverage cycle and relaxed lending standards. On the other hand, we know that the sovereign needs to step in to mitigate financial instability in case the private market is no longer able to achieve that objective given fact and circumstances. The one-million-dollar question then is where to exactly position policy-making on the continuum between bail-ins and bailouts. So here we are: bailouts should become the exception and bail-ins are very difficult for a variety of reasons (supra and infra this chapter). Already in 2001 the FSB released their 'key attributes for effective resolution regimes'. The key ingredients of the recipe were 'strong powers for competent authorities, ability to step in at all stages of distress, planning, assessments, capital availability and scenario analysis should do the trick'. Resolving a (SI)FI without disrupting the marketplace and without sovereign money seems like an impossible task. Even when one drags secured and unsecured creditors into the equation. A simple look at most FI balance sheets will lead one to that conclusion. If there is a fighting chance for that to work, it will be ex ante (so bail-in), at the right time, and with material haircuts across all layers of senior and junior debt. And even then I hesitate when writing this if this could possibly work without violating all sorts of intercreditor agreements. The pace at which these mammoth contracts move is not working in favor of a swift and transparent resolution. Knowing the dominance of the senior lenders in most of these contracts, the risk of violating the 'pari passu' principle is extraordinarily large. The chances of being hung up in court for years on end is almost 100%, hopefully without suspensory effect under national law for the resolution scheme. I can't even imagine how that should work when applied in cross-border resolution situations.

No doubt that a timely bail-in, where private stakeholders are exposed to losses, and who in turn will put more discipline on managers, is preferred. That discipline can trigger reduced leverage and risk taking. Having a decent loss-absorbing balance sheet in place for an FI combined with loss-absorbing measures for other stakeholders will reduce systemic spillovers. In case of international stakeholders an ex ante arrangement on distribution of losses across all layers and geographies of creditors is required. The risk of creating a tight and rigid bail-in program is material.[94] And bail-in in its own right can create future expectations, just like bail-in can create rebalancing portfolios by impacted investors, which then triggers spillover effects. All of these externalities are not necessarily priced in correctly at all times (or at all for that matter).

A deeper understanding is needed of the economic intricacies of both bail-ins and bailouts. Thereby it is assumed that in case of bail-ins both shareholders, unsecured and uninsured creditors are impacted. Bailouts invariably refer to the use of public funds to stabilize an FI and the situation post-event. The hardcore question in such an economic analysis is 'when is it necessary for public funds to step in rather than to (further) consume private funding to cover losses'. The trade-off is then between moral hazard costs from bailouts[95] and effective spillover costs from bail-ins (a negative externality on society). But there are aligned issues. For example, the expectation of a bailout reduces the cost of funding and skews risk appreciation.

The IMF has been working through such an exercise[96] and came up with the following conclusions[97]:

- To begin with, the findings re-iterate the discussed benefits of both the bail-in and bailout model and the costs to be expected. An optimal resolution model can occur with and without the occurrence of spillovers. When there are no spillover costs, bail-ins trigger no social welfare costs as the costs of restructuring fall entirely with the private stakeholders. Bailouts in such a scenario always carry a cost due to fixed costs, and moral hazard exposure. In case there are spillover effects bail-ins are costly welfare and social costs since they involve a transfer of losses from the bank to its creditors as well as to society at large. With limited spillovers, the costs of a bail-in seem to be preferable rather than generate moral hazard through a bailout. In case the spillovers are intense or severe, bailouts become more justified. It would then, in the face of a

---

[94] Some fear it will restrict the right and adequate mix of techniques and arrangements used; for instance T. Geithner, (2014), Stress Test: Reflections on Financial Crises, Crown Publishing Group, NY.

[95] See for further details: M. Lucchetta et al., (2018), Systemic Risk, Bank Moral Hazard and Bailouts, CESifo Working Paper, Nr. 6878, Center for Economic Studies and Ifo Institute (CESifo), Munich, January.

[96] G. Dell'Ariccia et al., (2018), Trade-offs in Bank Resolution, IMF Staff Discussion Note SDN/18/02, February, Washington DC. See the details of the model used in appendix 1 (pp. 33–35). The model is based on D. Sandri, (2015), Dealing with Systemic Sovereign Debt Crises: Fiscal Consolidation, Bail-ins or Official Transfers? IMF Working Paper Nr. WP/15/223, International Monetary Fund, Washington, DC and T. Cordella, et al. (2016), Government Guarantees, Transparency, and Bank Risk-Taking, October 19, mimeo.

[97] G. Dell'Ariccia et al., (2018), Ibid. pp. 6–11, 26–28.

system-wide crisis, be more preferable to run the risk of creating moral hazard through a bailout than suffer the potentially uncontrollable impact of a destabilized financial system. That's why it was mentioned earlier that no resolution framework will always be free of consuming public resources.

- Whatever scenario and whatever model used (bail-in or bailout), the social costs intensify as the spillovers are severe. Any resolution program should be connected at the hip with a program to mitigate or reduce the risk of systemic failures and spillovers. The scenario models, liquidity provisions and the loss-absorbing capacity at the FIs should help in this respect. Reducing the cross-holding of bank debt would help as well, but needless to say we haven't made a lot of progress on this matter as the primacy of the free market is preferred in this context.
- One could conclude that recent regulatory reforms have improved the trade-off between bail-ins and bailouts. Effective resolution frameworks are likely to reduce the potential spillovers from bail-ins under the above indicated conditions and constraints. As a consequence, better-defined constraints on the use of public funds have likely reduced the expectation of future bailouts and the associated potential for moral hazard (as often no bailout is required). Greater loss-absorbing capacity has reduced the probability of financial distress and spillovers.
- In case spillovers are weak, and bailouts are not the preferred technique, a time-consistency issue arises. Let's use an example: even if a sovereign limits ex ante the amount of resources it wants to spend on a bailout when necessary (i.e. when spillovers are high), that sovereign will become tempted, in case a bank failure occurs, to step in more forcefully once the fixed-costs threshold is met of a bailout thereby neglecting the moral hazard cost. Staying consistent over time is a challenge in such a scenario. That can only happen in case of robust scenario models being available and are credible. In a worst-case scenario one is confronted with a combination of moral hazard costs as well as spillover effects. Part of such a credible model can also be the use of leverage limits. They reduce moral hazard as such, firm up available capital buffers and as such rebalance the trade-off between a bail-in and bailout.
- So, bailouts should be the exception not the rule—their use justified as a last resort, exclusively when financial stability is gravely threatened, and structured to mitigate the associated costs. They should occur only alongside loss sharing with private stakeholders of the troubled bank and time-bound restructuring plans that address the underlying weaknesses and help restore the bank's long-term viability. But there are four additional considerations that need to be taken into account when deciding between a bail-in and a bailout: (1) the case for a bailout is weaker when the sovereign faces debt sustainability or credit rating issues. A bailout could worsen that situation but so could the risk of a spillover in case it is opted for a bail-in. That would reduce tax revenues through a slowing economy in case of structural financial market issues. Possible fiscal concerns should be balanced against the severity or expected severity of the spillover when deciding to go bail-in or bailout; (2) it was mentioned before that banks that benefit from a bailout outlook benefit from lower funding costs and therefore receive an undue competitive benefit. Inefficient credit allocation and positions of market power could be the consequence. Imposing capital surcharges on those FIs that potentially benefit from a bailout outlook should be considered, although I wonder how

complicated and potentially arbitrary that process can become in practice. Requiring SIFI to contribute more to a resolution fund seems simpler to execute and therefore realistic; (3) the effective pool of challenges as well as of costs for implementing a bail-in program should be accurately and realistically assessed.[98] The bail-in process is full of treacherous waters especially in case of multiple layers of creditors and varying interests, international dimensions and foreign shareholders, legal and tax challenges, liquidity or both domestic credit and equity markets and the potential of state ownership are all material issues against the background of spillovers that need to be managed and preferably not magnified in the process; (4) most models deal with the intricacies that one authority might face when making the trade-off decision. However, in reality most of these scenarios involve multiple sovereigns given the globalized nature of the financial marketplace. Also within a single currency union like the Eurozone, events in one country might impact the public debt situation and conditions of other Eurozone members, including cross-border spillover effects. Asymmetry between those sovereigns, at least in perception, is almost guaranteed and sovereigns will be concerned about what risk and vulnerabilities might explicitly and implicitly be coming their way in case of bank failures in union countries.

- The framework should allow for the use of some public funds, with appropriate safeguards, during systemic crises if and when this is necessary to protect financial stability. Public funds may be needed if imposing extensive losses on private stakeholders would unleash large spillovers. In these exceptional cases, the moral hazard and fiscal costs of bailouts would be preferable to the disruptive effects that spillovers associated with bail-ins could have on financial stability and the economy at large.
- Most resolution frameworks are by and large theoretical constructs and have never been fully tested. Given the different pace of the implementation of resolution models, sufficient loss-absorbing capital is not guaranteed across the board. Close monitoring occurs however in this respect.[99]The FSB often distinguishes its reporting on the matter between SIFI/TBTF institutions and other systematically relevant institutions like CCPs. When it comes to the untested nature of the comprehensive models a number of open questions remain:

  – Do bailouts create moral hazard?: there is sufficient literature demonstrating this phenomenon in a variety of situations. But in this case it can go both ways, that is, do banks take more risk because they are aware they don't have to bear the ultimate risk if something goes wrong while benefiting from the upside or do banks take less

[98] E. Avgouleas, and C. Goodhart, (2015), A Critical Evaluation of Bail-in as a Bank Recapitalization Mechanism. In The New International Financial System: Analyzing the Cumulative Impact of Regulatory Reform, eds. by D. D. Evanoff, A. Haldane, and G. Kaufman, World Scientific Studies in International Economics, Vol. 48, pp. 267–305.

[99] The FSB periodically conducts a review of the resolution regimes. The most recent was the initiated third review FSB, (2018), Thematic Peer Review on Bank Resolution Planning, June, London. The content of the peer review is detailed in the Summary Terms of Reference also released on June 4, 2018, via fsb.org. See the progress report 'Keeping the Pressure Up', FSB 2018 Resolution Report, for an intermediate analysis, November 15. Intermediate reporting also occurs through the annual reports to the G20 (latest report 4th edition, November 28, 2018). The second review conducted dates back to 2016. See fsb.org for all back-up documents.

risk because bailouts increase their franchise- or charter value due to reducing costs of funding triggered by the protective cover of a possible bailout. Therefore, banks take less risks. What phenomenon dominates behavior in reality? The IMF model implies that the former argument dominates (more risk taking as the downside is covered by the sovereign), although there is no real evidence to support that position, besides the more general research regarding the existence of moral hazard and the fact that sovereign risk coverage reduces funding costs.[100]

– Do bail-ins entail systemic spillovers? Although the question is arduous to answer, a proxy can be found in answering the question whether during a crisis and its aftermath the bail-in of a financial institution led to a repricing of (bail-in-able) unsecured debt and equity of other banks. Far from perfect the observed repricing doesn't say anything about the nature of the spillover(s) and whether they are relevant for the purpose of analyzing bail-in/bailout dynamics. Co-movement might ultimately be caused by other factors. Spillovers tend to occur when the outlook economically is generally deteriorating and so separating aggregate shocks and spillovers is an arduous task. Studying past resolution cases might help in understanding the dynamics, but can't be taken as an example of good or bad resolution practice[101] as many cases are characterized by 'a lack of significant prior experience

[100] See also N. Sarin, and L. H. Summers, (2016), Understanding Bank Risk through Market Measures, Brookings Papers on Economic Activity, Fall, pp. 57–127. See G. Dell'Ariccia et al., (2018), Trade-offs in Bank Resolution, IMF Staff Discussion Note SDN/18/02, February, Washington DC pp. 14–17 for a discussion of the broad spectrum of existing research regarding moral hazard in all its dimensions. Those dimensions include: (1) the lower cost of funding (and CDS spreads) for banks that enjoy the outlook of a future bailout (see for a review of the literature on bank costs with and without moral hazard: R. Kroszner, (2016), A Review of Bank Funding Cost Differentials, Journal of Financial Services Research, Vol. 29, pp. 151–174); (2) whether lower funding costs due to bailouts lead to more risk taking: it's not all clear but it has become clear that large banks take on 'larger positions on riskier loan segments, greater reliance on riskier funding, lower buffers against potential loan losses, and greater loan losses after a shock' (see recently: L. Laeven, et al., (2016), Bank Size, Capital, and Systemic Risk: Some International Evidence, Journal of Banking and Finance, Vol. 69, pp. S25–S34). The short answer is thus: yes, large banks increase risk taking while small ones decrease it, but the data are not robust across a variety of scenarios. US literature shows anyway a mixed bag: TARP benefiting banks shifted to riskier segments within the same asset class, leading to increased volatility and default risk, while others suggest that banks with low charter values and high leverage increased risk taking and those with high charter values and low leverage decreased it (see also N.A. Schenk, and J. H. Thornton, (2016), Charter Values, Bailouts, and Moral Hazard in Banking, Journal of Financial Regulation, Vol. 49, pp. 172–202; A.N. Berger, et al., (2016), Do Bank Bailouts Reduce or Increase Systemic Risk? The Effects of TARP on Financial System Stability, Federal Reserve Bank of Kansas City Research Working Paper RWP 16-08, September); (3) results are impacted by the fact that banks that are likely to receive bailouts also suffer from enhanced scrutiny, a factor which was controlled separately.

[101] See G. Dell'Ariccia et al., (2018), Trade-offs in Bank Resolution, IMF Staff Discussion Note SDN/18/02, February, Washington DC, pp. 17–23 for some case study analysis. Some observations include: (1) imposing losses on unsecured creditors may have implications not only for the bailed-in bank but also for other banks; (2) there may be other costs associated with bailing in unsecured creditors, particularly depositors, under an ad hoc regime; (3) US cases that mostly relate to FDIC (Federal Deposit Insurance Corporation) resolutions, find mixed results on the

with bank resolutions[102] that would impose losses on private stakeholders, insufficient clarity ex ante on how losses would be allocated, and lack of explicit loss-absorbing capacity—as enshrined in the recent reforms'.[103]

- To further reduce the recourse to bailouts, policymakers should continue ongoing efforts to enhance resolvability and minimize the risk that bail-ins may result in large spillovers.
- Further clarifying which financial instruments can be subject to bail-in and increasing the loss-absorbing capacity of major financial institutions is key. Regulation should ensure that holders of loss-absorbing capacity in banks are those most capable of understanding and absorbing losses with a low risk of transmitting further shocks to the financial system and the economy. Most reforms so far seem to enhance the 'total loss-absorbing capacity (TLAC) of systemic banks, with clarity on the types of claims that qualify for loss absorption and the amounts and location within a financial group's structure of such claims'. Unsecured and uninsured creditors should be well aware of the risks they face given the position(s) they hold. Regulators should through periodic assessments shed further light on that position and have legal and operational obstacles removed that could hinder an effective bail-in at a time when needed.
- The problem remains and more progress is needed to improve cross-border resolution aspects. Therefore, cross-border banks should have ex ante agreements in place between home and the key host states of operations that detail the resolution strategy and the amount and location of loss-absorbing capacity.
- The frameworks[104] put in place have improved the sketched dynamics between bail-in and bailout, and together with specialty arrangements like 'emergency liquidity assistance'[105] they helped reduce the need for recapitalization, reduce spillovers,

equity prices and CDS spreads of other banks; (4) bailing in some banks may have had spillovers for creditors and equity holders in other banks that were not yet subject to bail-ins; (5) The choice for a bail-in or not might trigger market discipline on other institutions and signaling to investors that supervisors might be less willing or inclined to advanced actions given evolving market conditions (also A. Schafer, et al., (2016), Bail-in Expectations for European Banks; Actions Speak Louder Than Words, ESRB Working Paper Series Nr. 7); It is relevant who holds equity and who holds unsecured debt in the bail-in institution or other players in the field. Experienced and professional might make a difference in terms of behavior at the moment of bail-in and therefore the size and nature of potential spillovers (also A.-C. Huser, (2017), The Systemic Implications of Bail-in: A Multi-layered Network Approach, ECB Working Paper Series Nr. 2010, February).

[102] P. Bolton and M. Oehmke, (2018), Bank Resolution and the Structure of Global Banks, NBER Working Paper Nr. 24737, June.

[103] Also W.-G. Ringe and J. Patel, (2019), The Dark Side of Bank Resolution: Counterparty Risk through Bail-in, EBI Working Paper Nr. 31, March; D. R. Muñoz and J. Solana, (2019), Bank Resolution and Creditor Distribution: The Tension Shaping Global Banking – Part I: 'Individual Bank v. Group' and 'Ex Ante v. Ex Post' Dimensions Part II: The Cross-Border Dimension, mimeo.

[104] See a quantitative assessment of the new EU bank regulatory framework: P. Benczur et al., (2017), Evaluating the Effectiveness of the New EU Bank Regulatory Framework: A Farewell to Bail-Out, Journal of Financial Stability, Vol. 33, pp. 207–223.

[105] Also M. Dobler, et al., (2016), The Lender of Last Resort Function after the Global Financial Crisis, IMF Working Paper Nr. WP/16/10, Washington, DC. In terms of emergency liquidity or

reduce moral hazard, and lend credibility to initiatives that reduce the necessity for the taxpayer to step in. Nevertheless, the IMF also recognizes that although skewed, scenarios where the social cost of a bail-in still exceeds those of a bailout still exist. During a crisis, it is often difficult to make a clear distinction between illiquid and insolvent banks. As a consequence, temporary liquidity assistance easily becomes permanent solvency support (or bailout). Or put differently, there is a residual risk that requires the taxpayer to step in and preserve financial stability.[106]

- Despite the fact that the current scenario of resolution models and regimes isn't perfect and might ultimately require public funding, it has reduced the scope of the situation in which that public funding is needed. Dell'Ariccia et al.[107] summarizes that position such as that public funding might only be needed (1) on a temporary basis and only in systemic cases; (2) after bail-in of shareholders and some creditors[108]; (3) after the use of ex ante resolution funds; and/or (4) subject to ex post recovery of any potential use of public funds through levies imposed on the banking sector. Spillovers in case of a bail-in can be minimized by (1) enhancing loss-absorbing capacity (which includes that all parties understand what equity or credit position they hold and what risk is attached to it); (2) limiting those who can hold claims that qualify as loss-absorbing and (3) improving resolvability which implies regular assessments and removing legal and operational hurdles that would hinder stepping in effectively when needed.
- The EC released a factsheet in April 2019[109] to summarize the adoption and completion of the banking package.

---

liquidity requirements post-resolution but before market confidence is restored see M. Demertzi et al., (2018), How to Provide Liquidity to banks after Resolution in Europe's Banking Union, In-Depth Analysis, November 22, via Bruegel.org

[106] See G. Dell'Ariccia et al., (2018), Trade-offs in Bank Resolution, IMF Staff Discussion Note SDN/18/02, February, Washington DC, pp. 24–26. That residual risk can take many forms: (1) emergency liquidity facilities that remain due because of insolvency; (2) collateral provided that gets consumed due to bigger than expected losses; (3) state guarantees might be needed to ensure market access of failing banks; (4) loss-absorbing capacity might turn out to be insufficient to cover actual losses; (5) the state needs to take temporary bridge ownership or needs to provide 'bridge' financing during the resolution phase. A sufficiently wide mandate and flexible mode of operations for supervisory authorities are needed to minimize the need for public funding. There is however no consensus what the nature and size of the flexibility exactly mean. Being too flexible might 'perpetuate too-big-to-fail premiums, increase contingent fiscal risks, and undermine the credibility of the regime' (see also box 1, p. 28 regarding the fiscal implications of bailouts). Being too strict implies sacrificing future financial stability.

[107] See G. Dell'Ariccia et al., (2018), Trade-offs in Bank Resolution, IMF Staff Discussion Note SDN/18/02, February, Washington DC, pp. 25–26.

[108] E. Martino, (2019), Bail-inable Securities and Financial Contracting: Can Contracts Discipline Bankers? European Journal of Risk Regulation, Vol. 10, Issue 1, pp. 164–179, May 24. doi:https://doi.org/10.1017/err.2019.5. T. Huertas, (2019), Will Bust Banks Be Born Again by Bail-In?, Butterworths Journal of International Banking and Financial Law.

[109] EC, (2019), Adoption of the Banking Package: Revised Rules on Capital Requirements (CRR II/CRD V) and resolution (BRRD/SRM), April 16, via europa.eu.

9.7.3 Rules and Principles Governing a Bail-in[110]

Since 2011 the FSB has been working on recovery and resolution principles and guidelines in particular for G-SIBs.[111] These 'key attributes' set out amongst other things the bail-in powers that authorities should have to achieve or help achieve continuity of critical functions. Under the framework authorities should have the power to carry out a bail-in including writing down claims, convert claims into equity and convert or write down any contingent convertible or contractual bail-in instruments. The absorption of losses (TLAC)[112] by shareholders and unsecured and uninsured creditors is a central theme. However, these principles how good they may sound have never been operationalized. A lot depends however on how these principles are implemented and executed. The range of open questions includes issues such as: (1) identifying the instruments and liabilities within the scope of bail-in; (2) conducting valuations to inform and support the application of bail-in; (3) develop a bail-in process that meets applicable securities laws and exchange requirements; (4) transfer governance and control rights to new owners and obtain the required regulatory approvals and authorizations; and (5) communicate effectively at all stages of the bail-in transaction with affected parties and the market.

The FSB[113] ultimately stringed all these operational questions together and issued guidelines for the operational questions in the bail-in process. They developed 21 principles for administrators and did so focusing on six major areas covering the bail-in process. Those six areas include[114]:

- Scope of the Bail-in[115]: These principles provide guidance on issues like the transparency of the scope of the instruments and liabilities subject to the bail-in powers of resolution authorities; the application of discretionary exclusions from bail-in; information requirements to support the application of bail-in powers; and disclosures on the scope of bail-in to enhance transparency and market confidence.

---

[110] See for some market implications of bail-ins: T. Beck et al., (2018), Sharing the Pain? Credit Supply and Real Effects of Bank Bail-ins, EBA Staff Paper Series Report Nr. 1, June, via eba.europe.org. While banks more exposed to the bail-in significantly reduced credit supply at the intensive margin, affected firms compensated the tightening of overall credit with other sources of funding. Also A. Berger, et al. (2017), Do Borrowers Benefit from Bank Bailouts? The Effects of TARP on Loan Contract Terms, Working Paper, mimeo. A. Bergerand R. Roman, (2017) Did Saving Wall Street Really Save Main Street? The real effects of TARP on local economic conditions. Journal of Financial and Quantitative Analysis, Vol. 52, Issue 5, pp. 1827–1867. B. Bernard et al., (2017), Bail-ins and bail-outs: Incentives, Connectivity, and Systemic Stability. NBER Working Paper Nr. 23747.

[111] The FSB publishes an annual G-SIB list, most recently on November 16, 2018, via fsb.org

[112] FSB, (2015), Principles on Loss-absorbing and Recapitalisation of G-SIBs in Resolution and Total Loss-absorbing Capacity (TLAC) Term Sheet, November. J.-E. Colliard, and D. Gromb, (2017), Financial Restructuring and Resolution of Banks. Working Paper, mimeo. A.-C. Hüser et al., (2018), The Systemic Implications of Bail-in: A Multi-Layered Network Approach, Journal of Financial Stability, Vol. 38, October, pp. 81–97.

[113] FSB, (2018), Principles of Bail-in Execution, June 21, London.

[114] FSB, (2018), Ibid. pp. 2–4.

[115] See in detail: FSB, (2018), Ibid. pp. 7–9.

- Valuation and valuation processes[116]: Decisions by authorities need to be documented and supported by valuations of assets, portfolios and so on. In particular, they provide the basis for certain resolution actions so that those powers can be exercised such that creditors bear losses consistent with their position in the hierarchy of claims, therefore minimizing material risk of successful legal challenges and contributing to public confidence in the resolution process. The principles should assist authorities as they establish a framework for the valuations that are necessary to inform the application of bail-in powers. The principles cover the timing and allocation of responsibilities between authorities in the valuation process; firms' capabilities, including management information systems; information requirements to undertake an effective valuation; and valuation methodologies across a resolution group.[117]
- Exchange mechanics of titles and securities[118]: developing processes for the exchange/conversion of rights/shares is required to deal with issues such as (1) the suspension, cancelation or discontinuation from trading of affected securities on relevant securities exchanges and within central securities depositories (if necessary under the mechanic in question); (2) the notification of creditors; and (3) following entry into resolution, the write down of liabilities and issuance of equity instruments or the interim issuance of tradeable certificates to those unsecured and uninsured creditors subject to bail-in (the latter to allow for trading during resolution with the subsequent issuance of equity instruments once the final conversion rates are determined). The principles provide guidance to address a number of operational issues, including the mechanism by which losses are absorbed; how creditors will document and track their claims; and the method to determine or adjust compensation to creditors.
- Securities law and securities exchange requirements and conditions:[119] a bail-in will need to take into account the jurisdictions' securities law and securities exchange requirements and the extent to which they apply, or continue to apply, during the bail-in period. These requirements may differ in some important aspects across jurisdictions, in particular as regards the required content and timing of disclosures and with respect to the availability of any exemptions or postponements. The principles provide guidance to address the steps that home resolution authorities should take as part of ex ante resolution planning to: identify securities law and securities exchange requirements in connection with the bail-in period; plan for the firms' compliance with applicable disclosure requirements during the bail-in period and the implications of insufficient or incomplete investor information (including a consideration of temporary exemptions from or postponements to applicable disclosure requirements where appropriate); plan for the listing and trading status of a firm's securities during the bail-in period; and plan for the securities law and securities exchange requirements in connection with a bail-in transaction, including issuance, registration and listing requirements.

---

[116] See in detail: FSB, (2019), Ibid. pp. 10–14.

[117] The EBA published a handbook on valuation for purposes of resolution, February 22, 2019, via eba. Europe.eu. It aims at fostering the convergence and consistency of valuation practices as well as the interaction with independent valuers across the EU.

[118] See in detail: FSB, (2018), Ibid. pp. 14–16.

[119] See in detail: FSB, (2018), Ibid. pp. 16–21.

- Governance affairs[120]: during the bail-in period, the powers, rights and privileges of shareholders and creditors of the failed legal entity to vote or give approvals may be terminated or suspended depending on the jurisdiction's approach to bail-in. Following the end of the bail-in period, ownership and control of the firm or newly established financial company is transferred to the new shareholders, including the holders of debt instruments of the failed firm. The change in ownership and control of the firm in resolution is likely to require regulatory approvals and authorizations, including in host jurisdictions. Newly appointed directors and senior managers (including those of subsidiaries and branches) of the firm in resolution may also be required to obtain regulatory approvals, the requirements for which may differ across jurisdictions. The principles in this section seek to provide guidance to home and host authorities on these issues.
- Communication protocols[121]: given the fact that multiple parties and authorities will likely be involved in the bail-in of a firm that has entered resolution, and there may be uncertainty with respect to the impact on creditors and speculation in the market throughout the resolution process. Given the range of stakeholders, ex ante planning and a common understanding of the approach to bail-in communication and the roles and responsibilities of home and host authorities is essential to avoid the risk of delayed or inconsistent communication from authorities that could create creditor confusion and damage market confidence. The principles should assist authorities in the development of a coordinated strategy to manage market and creditor communications during the bail-in period.

[120] See in detail: FSB, (2018), Ibid. pp. 21–23.

[121] See in detail: FSB, (2018), Ibid. pp. 23–26.

10

Money Market Funds Reform

10.1 Money Market Fund Reform in the US

10.1.1 Introduction

The US money market space is the oldest in the world.[1] It emerged in the 1970s when regulation capped the interest that banks were allowed to pay on deposits at a level below money market yields. Money market funds (MMFs) were set up to mimic bank deposits by maintaining a stable value of USD 1 per share while offering money market yields to investors. They became, that way, an alternative to bank deposits but then with better performance.[2] The same evolution was witnessed in France where, like in the US, regulatory restrictions regarding interest on bank deposits led to the emergence of money market funds. But regulatory arbitrage cannot explain the emergence and continued growth of the sector as it continued to do so after interest rate regulation was abolished in 1986, and interstate banking limits were repealed in 1994.

Money market funds offer the benefits of financial intermediation. As such, they perform maturity and size transformation (despite their short-term business model) and offer risk reduction via diversification. In contemporary terms its growth is driven by large institutional cash pools that are in continuous need of safe assets but with a meaningful compensation. Money market funds also invest in banks and therefore have become part

[1] See for an historical overview: T. Cook, et al., (1979), Money Market Mutual Funds: A Reaction to Government Regulation or a Lasting Financial Innovation? Federal Reserve Bank of Richmond. Economic Review, July/August 1979, pp. 15–31.

[2] Another argument of its rapid emergence was that money market funds could gain nationwide scale as they did not fall under the legal restrictions on interstate banking; D. Luttrell, et al., (2012), Understanding the Risks Inherent in Shadow Banking: A Primer and Practical Lessons Learned Federal Reserve Bank of Dallas Staff Papers Nr. 18, November.

L. Nijs, *The Handbook of Global Shadow Banking, Volume I*,
https://doi.org/10.1007/978-3-030-34743-7_10

of the extracted credit intermediation channel.[3] Both European and US money market funds have distinct investors and ways to allocate their resources back into the system.[4]

But as will be explained in this chapter, the specific business models and their 'net asset value' business model make them vulnerable in case of market shocks as under such a model the first redeemer will bear the smallest (or no) loss ('first mover advantage'). Their liquidity shortage impacted all those parties in the system in which they invest and their forced sale (to create liquidity) will send asset price in the market invariably down. The central banks had to step in during 2008/2009. Since then regulators in both the US and Europe have been pondering what to do next and they came up with (staged[5]) regulatory proposals. Both models will be discussed. The US in this chapter, the European proposal in the European chapter. Many questions can still be asked about how resilient the model will be after all the changes.[6] In the US, regulators have thus chosen to treat MMFs as mutual funds instead of a close substitute for bank deposits. Although the regulation is similar it is not identical between Europe and the US. That makes sense partly as the role of MMF is slightly different on both continents. Mai illustrates the difference: 'euro area MMFs seem to be a link in a chain of credit intermediation involving several institutions including banks. Banks are the dominant players in this channel as they use money market funds (mostly CNAV) for short-term cash placement as well as for funding short-term payment obligations which include credit lines to clients in the non-financial sectors'.... 'In contrast US MMFs' direct intermediation of funds between different sectors is more pronounced. On the one hand, not even a quarter of investors in money market funds belong to the financial sector, and there is no noteworthy investment by depository institutions. On the other hand, US money market funds invest only about half of their cash in the financial sector, including banks. Thus, roughly half of the industry's business is direct financial intermediation between non-financial sectors.'[7] It does not only explain the different functionality but also likely the different regulatory approach. In what follows both the 2010 and the 2014 adjustments will be discussed, with focus on the most recent changes adopted and how the build on the 2010 changes.

---

[3] H. Mai, (2015), Money market Funds- an Economic Perspective, Deutsche Bank Research, February 26, pp. 2–3.

[4] H. Mai, (2015), Ibid. pp. 10–16.

[5] The US had MMF incoming regulation both in 2010 and 2014. The European Commission issued its proposal in 2013, which were also based on their experiences with the 2012 eurozone sovereign crisis.

[6] Mai indicates (regarding the European model): '[b]ut in case the industry nevertheless experiences a loss of investor confidence, mitigating the risk of an investor run would probably still be difficult. VNAV funds (with a variable NAV (ed.)) in tight financial conditions might still face accelerated redemption requests, and financial distress might still spread via counterparty or market channels. CNAV funds would be able to draw on a significant 3% capital buffer as a line of defense. However, pairing a CNAV with a capital requirement further blurs the difference between a mutual fund investment and a bank deposit' (p. 17).

[7] H. Mai, (2015), Ibid. pp. 18–19.

10.1.2 The Most Recent 2010/2014 Changes

In July 2014, the US Securities and Exchange Commission issued their final rules regarding the redress of the MMF market[8] (see Box 10.1) for an analysis of the functioning of MMFs in the economy). Under those new rules prime MMFs will be required to transact at a floating NAV and daily share prices float with the market-based portfolio securities. Retail and government MMF will be able to continue using constant NAV pricing. The difference seems to be driven by the fact that the latter is considered less risky, that is, as government bonds MMFs hold either cash or invest in government bonds while prime MMFs invest mainly in corporate debt securities. In particular institutional prime MMFs invest in certificates of deposit, commercial paper and repurchase agreements. In general in times of distress, all MMFs may impose liquidity fees and redemption gates. The amendments are applicable to MMFs that are governed under the Investment Company Act of 1940. The amendments are designed to address money market funds' susceptibility to heavy redemptions in times of stress, improve their ability to manage and mitigate potential contagion from such redemptions and increase the transparency of their risks, while preserving, as much as possible, their benefits. The legislative changes involved 'removing the valuation exemption that permitted institutional non-government money market funds (whose investors historically have made the heaviest redemptions in times of stress) to maintain a stable net asset value per share ("NAV"), and is requiring those funds to sell and redeem shares based on the current market-based value of the securities in their underlying portfolios rounded to the fourth decimal place (e.g., $1.0000), i.e., transact at a "floating" NAV'. The changes also adopt amendments that will 'give the boards of directors of money market funds new tools to stem heavy redemptions by giving them discretion to impose a liquidity fee if a fund's weekly liquidity level falls below the required regulatory threshold, and giving them discretion to suspend redemptions temporarily, i.e., to "gate" funds under the same circumstances'. The changes require that all non-government money market funds impose a liquidity fee 'if the fund's weekly liquidity level falls below a designated threshold, unless the fund's board determines that imposing such a fee is not in the best interests of the fund'. The whole idea is to make 'money market funds more resilient by increasing the diversification of their portfolios, enhancing their stress testing, and improving transparency'.[9,10]

[8] Rule 2a-7 of the Investment Company Act of 1940, which governs the operation of US money market funds ('MMFs').

[9] That transparency includes that money market funds report additional information to the SEC and to investors. It also requires investment advisers to certain large unregistered liquidity funds, which can have many of the same economic features as money market funds, to provide additional information about those funds to the SEC.

[10] See Securities and Exchange Commission, (2014), Money Market Fund Reform, Release No. 33-9616, IA-3879; IC-31166; FR-84; File No. S7-03-13, via sec.gov, pp. 1–2.

Box 10.1 Role and Functioning of MMFs[11]

Role and Functioning of Money Market Funds

1. The Starting Point

Money market funds are a type of mutual funds whose objective is to pay a dividend mirroring the prevailing short-term interest rate and who provide (guarantee) 100% liquidity at all times. Unlike other investment funds they seek to maintain a stable net asset value (NAV), which is normally reflected as $1.00. The characteristics of stability, liquidity and payment of short-term yields have made it attractive with both institutional and retail investors and act as a direct alternative to savings accounts (cash management tool) but with a slightly higher compensation. Given the objective of MMFs, they (but in fact all mutual funds) must price and transact in their shares at the current NAV, calculated by valuing portfolio instruments at market value or, if market quotations are not readily available, at fair value as determined in good faith by the fund's board of directors (i.e. use a floating NAV). That is written into the 1940 Investment Company Act (section 2(a)(41)(B)). This is however an exemption to this, which was enacted in 1983.

That exemption foresees that money market funds can value their portfolio securities using the 'amortized cost' method of valuation and the 'penny rounding' method of pricing. Under the amortized cost method (rule 2a-7(a)(2)), a money market fund's portfolio securities generally are valued at cost plus any amortization of premium or accumulation of discount, rather than at their value based on current market factors. The penny rounding method (rule 2a-7(a)(20)) of pricing permits a money market fund when pricing its shares to round the fund's NAV to the nearest 1% (i.e. the nearest penny).

These valuation and pricing techniques create what they call a 'rounding convention' that allows MMFs to sell and redeem shares at a stable price thereby disregarding small variations in the value of the securities in its portfolio. Other mutual funds don't have these options. These rules would have to make MMFs ideal cash management tools with minimal dilution of assets and returns for shareholders. The SEC was in the understanding that material deviations of a size that would cause material dilution would not (or could) occur given the risk limits that were tight to these rules.

These risk limits (rules 2a-7) embody that 'money market funds seek to maintain a stable share price by limiting their investments to short-term, high-quality debt securities that fluctuate very little in value under normal market conditions'. To put it differently: when you want to use these exemptions, your investments and investment strategy need to be designed in such a way that they also effectively reduced the likelihood that material deviations on value and subsequent dilutions would occur ('to limit deviations between the fund's $1.00 stable share price and the market-based NAV of the fund's portfolio'). In practice, that comes down to the fact that MMFs have to hold significant amounts of liquid assets and invest in securities that meet tight credit quality, maturity (to limit the interest rate and credit spread risk to which a money market fund may be exposed), liquidity (to meet reasonably foreseeable redemptions, generally MMFs must invest at least 10% of their portfolios in assets that can provide daily liquidity, and invest at least 30% of their portfo-

(continued)

[11] See in detail: Securities and Exchange Commission, (2014), Money Market Fund Reform, Release No. 33–9616, IA-3879; IC-31166; FR-84; File No. S7-03-13, via sec.gov, pp. 6–32.

Box 10.1 (continued)

lios in assets that can provide weekly liquidity) and diversification requirements (by generally limiting the funds to investing no more than 5% of their portfolios in any one issuer and no more than 10% of their portfolios in securities issued by, or subject to guarantees or demand features (i.e. puts) from, any one institution).

The MMFs fund management needs to regularly calculate the market-based value of the portfolio ('shadow price') and compare it to the fund's stable share price. In case the deviation between these two values exceeds ½ of 1% (50 basis points), it can be decided by the fund's board to re-price the MMFs securities above or below the fund's $1.00 share price (known as 'breaking the buck').

The rules and the different needs of investors have created different types of MMFs to cater to different needs, which include:

- Prime money market funds: they invest in short-term obligations issued by corporations and banks, repos and ASCP
- Government money market funds: which invest in US sovereign paper including repos collateralized by sovereign paper. A slimmed down version of these funds is called 'treasury money market funds')

The prime funds tend to pay a slightly higher compensation, the government funds higher safety.

2. The Role and Features of MMFs

The attractiveness of the MMF features had made them an important source of short-term finance while providing investors the option to participate in short-term financing market through a portfolio of short-term, high-quality debt securities. However, the same features that make them attractive also make MMFs prone in particular to shareholders who redeem shares heavily during periods of severe market distress. Those reasons can be summarized as follows:

- MMF investors have low or zero risk tolerance: many investors use MMFs for principal preservation and cash management. That makes them highly risk averse often driven by general risk tolerance, legal or investment restrictions and (permanent) short-term cash needs. That leads to a 'flight to quality'[12] under market distress (often from prime MMFs to government MMFs given the perceived lower default risk with the latter).[13]

(*continued*)

[12] And also a flight to liquidity. Gallagher and Collins comment: 'the majority of redemptions reflect a generalized flight-to-liquidity and are, therefore, primarily a function of the liquidity needs of a fund's investor base. Funds holding Treasury securities at greatest risk of default or with market values below their $1 share price experience flows that are insignificantly different from other funds, all else equal. We also find evidence that a significant portion of the outflows stem, not from liquidity concerns, but from an opportunistic yield play on the repo market created by the crises'; E. Gallagher and S. Collins, (2015), Money Market Funds and the Prospect of a U.S. Treasury Default, Working Paper, August 21, mimeo.

[13] See, for example, R. Wermers, et al., (2013) Runs on Money Market Funds, Working Paper; L. Schmit et al., (2016), Runs on Money Market Mutual Funds, Working Paper, mimeo. That implies that the riskier the MMF, the higher the expected outflows will be under distress; see for a confirmation: P. E. McCabe, (2010), The Cross Section of Money Market Fund Risks and Financial Crises, Federal Reserve Board Finance and Economic Discussion Series Paper, Nr. 2010-51.

Box 10.1 (continued)

- MMFs are exposed to permanent liquidity risks: when investors redeem that are guaranteed (near) direct liquidity. A fund can meet those redemptions in three subsequent ways: (1) cash on hand, (2) cash from investors purchasing shares and (3) cash from maturing securities. In case that is not sufficient the MMF sees itself forced to sell portfolio securities, in often not very liquid secondary markets triggering the need to sell at a discount from their amortized cost value, or worse at fire-sale[14] prices.[15] That would trigger further losses. They however tend to avoid that by selling their most liquid assets first, rather than sell a pro-rata slice of all their holdings.[16] That however triggers additional issues. The fund will have to restock its liquid assets (to meet additional redemptions) and as such has to sell less liquid securities, potentially at a discount. That understanding leads to very swift redemptions under distress, leaving the pain with the remaining investors.
- The above-discussed 'amortized cost' and 'penny rounding' valuation method are unique to MMFs. Differences between these valuation techniques and the market value of the portfolio can be caused by changes in market conditions, in particular changes in interest rates, credit risk and liquidity or due to fund-specific events (credit deterioration, asset default). A lot of the changes stemming from interest rates and credit quality are temporary in case those securities are held to maturity (at maturity amortized cost value and market value converge). But in case of asset default or asset sale, potential losses are permanent. That can only be changed in case the MMF will realize a gain elsewhere in the portfolio, which is difficult given the risk-averse profile of MMFs and the fact that they distribute regularly all their earnings. When the shadow price is below $1.00 investors feel the need to redeem, pushing the shadow price even further south, which has a snowballing effect (due to the fact that losses concentrate in a shrinking asset base).
- Lack of proper understanding of actual risk incurred by MMF investors: due to lack of transparency and/or non-disclosure of shadow price. That creates redemptions to avoid 'potential losses' rather than 'actual losses'[17] especially when transparency is low, or fund composition reveals high correlation among securities, or many securities from the same issuer. The lack of understanding

(continued)

[14] 'Fire sales' refer to situations when securities deviate from their information-efficient values typically as a result of sale price pressure. See in detail on the theoretical and empirical research on asset 'fire sales', A. Shleifer & R. Vishny, (2011), Fire Sales in Finance and Macroeconomics, Journal of Economic Perspectives, Vol. 25, pp. 29–48.

[15] It could also lend the cash need from the bank. However, those loans would create liabilities that must be reflected in the fund's shadow price, and thus will contribute to the stresses that may force the fund to 'break the buck.'

[16] See in detail: J. Witmer, (2012), Does the Buck Stop Here? A Comparison of Withdrawals from Money Market Mutual Funds with Floating and Constant Share Prices, Bank of Canada Working Paper, Nr. 2012-25.

[17] See in detail: N. Gennaioli, et al., (2012), Neglected Risks, Financial Innovation, and Financial Fragility, Journal for Financial Economics, Vol. 104, pp. 452–468, in particular p. 453.

Box 10.1 (continued)

of the actual risk involved when investing in MMF is aggravated by the fact that before the 2014 changes there was no requirement for the fund sponsor to disclose financial support provided to the fund (e.g. to avoid having to re-price the MMF shares). That however happens frequently, even outside the realm of market distress. Some MMF investors have even developed an understanding that they expect the fund sponsor to step in, which creates a parallel understanding about who bears the risk in this setting, given the fact that these expectations cannot be enforced. The same holds true for the financial support provided by the government (implicit government guarantee).

3. Behaviors in the MMF and Short-Term Financing Market

When stress at an MMF forces that fund to sell securities at a discount, other MMFs holding the same securities may have to reflect those discounts in their shadow prices.[18] That could lead to a wider 'contagion effect' (through simultaneously decreasing shadow prices) especially now that it has become clear that many MMFs are pretty correlated in terms of their holdings. Since investors tend not to know which MMF owns what securities, they might retreat from funds that don't own the securities and that fund might suffer redemptions and decreasing shadow prices without a cause driven by strategic externalities and information. This can impact all parties involved in the short-term money market, that is, corporations, banks and governments likewise. That phenomenon has type-casted MMFs as a significant contributor to systemic risk. Ultimately, banks rely massively on MMFs for the short-term funding needs. The heavy redemptions, in particular when they are coming from sizeable institutional investors,[19] across the board might drain liquidity from the market. That liquidity strain also creates a situation where MMFs cannot purchase newly issued securities.

Many of these features were displayed during the 2008 financial crisis, with large redemption causing fund managers to retain cash rather than invest in commercial paper, certificates of deposit or other short-term instruments. That led to a freeze in the short-term financing market and locking access to credit. Redemption during the crisis was the heaviest from prime MMFs by institutional investors. It was only when the Treasury Department on September 19, 2008 put in place a 'temporary guarantee program' that redemptions started to slow down.

[18] See in detail: D. W. Diamond & R. G. Rajan, (2011), Fear of Fire Sales, Illiquidity Seeking, and Credit Freezes, Quarterly Journal of Economics, Vol. 126, Issue 2, pp. 557–591.

[19] The abovementioned DERA study reports '[i]nvestor redemptions during the financial crisis, particularly after Lehman's failure, were heaviest in institutional share classes of prime money market funds, which typically hold securities that are illiquid relative to government funds. It is possible that sophisticated investors took advantage of the opportunity to redeem shares to avoid losses, leaving less sophisticated investors (if co-mingled) to bear the losses.' (p. 10).

10.1.2.1 The 2010 Changes

In the remaining part of this subsection, I will try to highlight the most important features of MMFs, their role in the financial infrastructure, the intended objectives of the changes and the likely macroeconomic implications of the legislative changes. For a comprehensive review of the theme I can refer to the excellent write-up provided by the SEC itself.[20] The amendments only apply to US-registered funds and not to UCITS funds. The changes to the rules vary based on the type of fund (i.e. government vs. prime vs. municipal/tax-exempt) as well as the type of investor (i.e. institutional or retail). The legislative changes for the imposition of floating net asset value (NAV) and redemption fees and gates for institutional prime and institutional municipal/tax-exempt funds will only take gradual effect between 2014 and 2016, with the highest-impact changes only taking effect in 2016.[21] The 2014 changes were a follow-up on the 2010 changes to the MMF regime adopted by the SEC that were designed to reduce the interest rate, credit and liquidity risks of money market fund portfolios (Box 10.2).

Box 10.2 The 2010 Changes to the US MMF Regime

The Initial Post-Crisis Changes to the US MMF Regime (2010)

The 2010 amendments 'decreased money market funds' credit risk exposure by further restricting the amount of lower quality securities that funds can hold'. These amendments placed tighter limits on a money market fund's ability to acquire 'second tier' securities by (1) restricting a money market fund from investing more than 3% of its assets in second tier securities (rather than the previous limit of 5%), (2) restricting a money market fund from investing more than ½ of 1% of its assets in second tier securities issued by any single issuer (rather than the previous limit of the greater of 1% or $1 million), and (3) restricting a money market fund from buying second tier securities that mature in more than 45 days (rather than the previous limit of 397 days) .

They also required that 'money market funds maintain liquidity buffers in the form of specified levels of daily and weekly liquid assets. The requirements are that, for all taxable money market funds, at least 10% of assets must be in cash, U.S. Treasury securities, or securities that convert into cash (e.g., mature) within one day and, for all money market funds, at least 30% of assets must be in cash, U.S. Treasury securities, certain other Government securities with remaining maturities of 60 days or less, or securities that convert into cash within one week (rule 2a-7(c)(5)(ii) and (iii)). These liquidity buffers provide a source of internal

(continued)

[20] See Securities and Exchange Commission, (2014), Money Market Fund Reform, Release No. 33-9616, IA-3879; IC-31166; FR-84; File No. S7-03-13, via sec.gov. See also Sec, (2014), SEC Adopts Money Market Fund Reform Rules, Rules Provide Structural and Operational Reform to Address Run Risks in Money Market Funds, 2014–143 via sec.gov.

[21] See Securities and Exchange Commission, (2014), Money Market Fund Reform, Release No. 33-9616, IA-3879; IC-31166; FR-84; File No. S7-03-13, via sec.gov, pp. 713–720 for a breakdown of the individual compliance items.

Box 10.2 (continued)

liquidity and are intended to help funds withstand high levels of redemptions during times of market illiquidity. The amendments also reduced money market funds' exposure to interest rate risk by decreasing the maximum weighted average maturities of fund portfolios from 90 to 60 days'.[22]

The 2010 reforms (which are a mix of bank-like and market-forces based reforms) also increased the amount of information that money market funds are required to report to the SEC. That includes monthly reporting regarding their portfolio holdings (Form N-MFP). The objective is to better understand and monitor the underlying risks of money market fund portfolios. The 2010 amendments also require money market funds to undergo stress tests under the direction of the board of directors on a periodic basis. As the SEC comments, '[u]nder this stress testing requirement, each fund must periodically test its ability to maintain a stable NAV per share based upon certain hypothetical events, including an increase in short-term interest rates, an increase in shareholder redemptions, a downgrade of or default on portfolio securities, and widening or narrowing of spreads between yields on an appropriate benchmark selected by the fund for overnight interest rates and commercial paper and other types of securities held by the fund'.[23]

But not everybody was convinced. Hanson et al.[24] indicate that 'these reforms may not unambiguously promote financial stability for two reasons. First, enhanced MMF liquidity buffers may increase the demand for short-term paper issued by large global financial institutions'. That would reduce the effectiveness of the changes in encouraging banks to not rely too heavily on short-term funding (and associated 'maturity risk') global financial institutions. And secondly, 'optional gating (i.e. redemption restrictions) could exacerbate runs if investors fear that once the gates go down they will not have access to their money in the fund'.[25]

But experiences with events in 2011, including the eurozone debt crisis and an impasse over the US Government's debt ceiling during summer 2011 and once again milder in fall 2013, suggested that additional reforms would assist in addressing potential future situations when credit losses may cause a fund's portfolio to lose value or when the short-term financing markets more generally come under stress. The question however was what was wisdom in terms of potential further improvements. In contrast to the crisis in 2008 MMFs did not suffer capital losses in 2011/2013 and the funds' shadow prices did not deviate significantly from the funds' stable share prices. The MMFs had, also in contrast to 2008, sufficient liquidity to meet the sizeable redemptions that also occurred in 2011/2013. Despite that goods news it appeared to have negatively affected the markets

[22] See Securities and Exchange Commission, (2014), Money Market Fund Reform, Release No. 33-9616, IA-3879; IC-31166; FR-84; File No. S7-03-13, via sec.gov, p. 33.

[23] See Securities and Exchange Commission, (2014), Money Market Fund Reform, Release No. 33-9616, IA-3879; IC-31166; FR-84; File No. S7-03-13, via sec.gov, p. 34.

[24] S.G. Hanson et al., (2014), An Evaluation of Money Market Fund Proposals, HBS Working Paper, p. 14.

[25] See infra this subsection for an evaluation of the alternatives in a post-2014 regulatory environment.

for short-term financing in similar ways. Major concerns were that 'creditworthy issuers may encounter financing difficulties because of risk taking by the funds from which they raise financing' and that 'local branches of foreign banks reduced lending to U.S. entities in 2011'; and further that 'European banks that were more reliant on money funds experienced bigger declines in dollar lending'.[26] Those redemptions didn't cause liquidity issues any longer but tend to have certain contagion effects on the short-term financing markets. However, investor redemptions have a direct effect on short-term funding liquidity in the US commercial paper market[27] (see Box 10.3).

Box 10.3 The Impact of the 2011 Eurozone Debt Crisis on MMFs

The Impact of the 2011 Eurozone Debt Crisis on MMFs

The impact of the 2011 eurozone debt crisis did not have the liquidity constraints impact the 2008 crisis had on MMFs. The 2010 MMF legislation has to be credited for achieving that (at least to a large degree). However, the 2011 crisis demonstrated large outflow for many MMFs (i.e. those that had exposure to European bank debt). Those outflows caused material spillover effects, in particular the fact that non-European issuers relying on MMFs raised no or limited short-term debt following the European events. The MMFs that were not exposed to European bank debt did substitute for that lending but only to pre-event existing clientele, illustrating major frictions in the MMF markets. Understanding those frictions are critical in understanding the impact banks have (or can have) on the broader economy. Banks try to avoid frictions by dealing with individual firms so that information asymmetry cannot be exploited by customers once the bank ends up in some sort of distress.[28] But the implication is that bad decisions at bank level might lead to credit supply shocks also for creditworthy firms. In that sense bank finance, relationship finance and market-based finance are more 'at arm's length'.

But apparently that information asymmetry also exists in 'market-based finance', at least if we consider the evidence of MMF behavior in the 2011 eurozone crisis. The above mentioned study of Chernenko and Sunderam does exactly that. They study the behavior of US MMF intermediaries in the short-term debt market and import material frictions. These frictions have the potential to 'create a channel through which MMFs can transmit distress across firms). In particular in this case, the redemptions MMFs experienced that had been lending to Eurozone banks, reduced the ability of non-European firms to raise short-term financing. The relationship between bank-financing and market-based financing seems, at least "blurred"[29] and further implies that MMFs can transmit distress across firms and that risk taking (due to performance flow incentives) by MMFs can produce negative spillover effects.' The data demonstrate that redemptions among MMFs were concentrated among the 'risky' funds, that is, those that had at that point in time

(*continued*)

[26] SEC, (2012), DERA study, via sec.gov, pp. 34–35.

[27] S. Chernenko & A. Sunderam, (2012), Frictions in Shadow Banking: Evidence from the Lending Behavior of Money Market Funds, Review of Financial Studies, Vol. 27, Nr. 6, pp. 1717–1750.

[28] See most recently: P. Schnabl, (2012), The International Transmission of Bank Liquidity Shocks: Evidence from an Emerging Market, Journal of Finance, Vol. 67, pp. 897–932.

[29] Chernenko & A. Sunderam, (2012), Ibid. pp. 1718–1719.

Box 10.3 (continued)

exposure to eurozone bank debt, which demonstrates an informed investor. Those redemptions caused non-European lenders to raise less total financing from eurozone-exposed MMFs, even when adjusting for riskiness of those lenders.[30] They provide direct evidence that the key friction driving these spillovers is that relationships are important in the money markets. In line with existing research[31] they indicate that 'MMFs with strong relationships with a particular issuer are less likely to cut their lending to that issuer. Moreover, MMMFs actually try to increase their portfolio allocations to issuers whose other lenders are suffering outflows, but only if they have pre-existing relationships with these issuers'. Their conclusions, in a wider perspective, imply that friction in short-term markets can be(come) a source of financing disruptions (even for large highly rated companies), although the magnitude seems fairly mild. However, the 2011 downturn was anyhow mild compared to other periods of distress that have been studied,[32] so that puts perspective in the 2011 findings and requires calibration of those results. Redemptions of investors can create collateral damage, reducing the ability to raise short-term debt. Besides the MMF channel identification through which non-bank financial intermediaries can transmit distress and the fact that fund-issuer relationships matter also in market-based financing, Chernenko and Sunderam illustrate that money market mutual fund risk taking has consequences for issuers and therefore could affect the broader economy. The 2010 MMF regulatory changes (enacting rule 2a-7[33]) in the US did not eliminate the risks of such spillovers occurring. They indicate there are potentially three reasons for that: '(1) incentives for investors to run remain, (2) the required liquidity buffers are fixed over time so funds may not be able to simply draw them down to meet redemptions in periods of turmoil, (3) the tighter restrictions on asset maturity mean that issuers must return to the money markets more often, increasing their vulnerability to short-term disruptions'.

In that context, the 2014 changes to be discussed, and in particular the floating NAV rule, could potentially 'reduce investor incentives to run, but would not affect the funds' ex-ante incentives to take risk' which were underlying the 2011 redemptions. Therefore, the Squam Lake Group[34] advocates for MMFs 'to have capital buffers to insulate their investors from moderate fluctuations in asset values and to reduce the ex-ante incentives to take excessive risks'.

---

[30] 'Our empirical specifications effectively compare the change in lending to the same issuer of two MMMFs, one with high exposure to Eurozone banks and one with low exposure to Eurozone banks. These specifications show that for the same issuer, MMMFs with larger exposures to Eurozone banks are more likely to withdraw financing. Thus, our results cannot be explained by unobservable issuer characteristics, including riskiness or direct or indirect exposure to Europe' (pp. 1721–1722).

[31] P. Bolton, et al., (2013), Relationship and Transaction Lending in a Crisis, BIS Working Paper Nr. 417 and V. Ivashina, and D. Scharfstein, (2010), Bank Lending During the Financial Crisis of 2008, Journal of Financial Economics, Vol. 97, pp. 319–338.

[32] See for an analysis covering the 2008 crisis: H. Almeida, et al., (2012), Corporate Debt Maturity and the Real Effects of the 2007 Credit Crisis, Critical Finance Review, Vol. 1, pp. 3–58; for an analysis covering the Russian sovereign default (1998): P. Schnabl, (2012), The International Transmission of Bank Liquidity Shocks: Evidence from an Emerging Market, Journal of Finance, Vol. 67, pp. 897–932.

[33] Which governs money market funds, requiring funds to invest in higher quality assets of shorter maturities and maintain larger buffers of liquid assets.

[34] Squam Lake Group, (2011), Reforming Money Market Funds, Proposal. Other proposals suggest submitting MMFs (and any other money-like claim issuer) to commercial bank regulation (M. Ricks, (2011), Regulating Money Creation after the Crisis, Harvard Business Law Review,

10.1.2.2 The 2014 Changes

From a conceptual point of view the 2014 changes are to a large degree (that is with the exception of a large list of enhanced disclosure requirements) built around three conceptual features: (1) Floating NAV, (2) liquidity fees, and (3) redemption gates.

(a) Floating Net Asset Value

Under the floating NAV amendments,[35] institutional prime money market funds would be required to transact at a floating NAV, instead of at a $1.00 stable share price. The floating NAV amendments are designed to reduce the first mover advantage inherent in a stable NAV fund, by dis-incentivizing redemption activity that can result from investors attempting to exploit the possibility of redeeming shares at the stable share price even if the portfolio has suffered a loss. They are also intended to reduce the chance of unfair investor dilution and make it more transparent to certain of the impacted investors that they, and not the fund sponsors or the Federal government, bear the risk of loss. The consequence is that institutional prime money market funds would no longer be able to use amortized cost to value their portfolio securities.[36] Daily share prices of these money market funds would fluctuate along with changes in the market-based value of their portfolio securities.

Institutional prime money market funds would be required to price their shares using a more precise method so that investors are more likely to see fluctuations in value. Currently, money market funds 'penny round' their share prices to the nearest 1% (to the nearest penny in the case of a fund with a $1.00 share price). Under the floating NAV amendments, institutional prime money market funds instead would be required to 'basis point round' their share price to the nearest 1/100th of 1% (the fourth decimal place in the case of a fund with a $1.0000 share price).

Government and retail money market funds would be allowed to continue using the amortized cost method and/or penny rounding method of pricing to seek to maintain a stable share price. A government money market fund would be defined as any money market fund that invests 99.5% (formerly 80%) or more of its total assets in cash, government securities and/or repurchase agreements that are collateralized solely by government securities or cash. A retail money market fund would be defined as a money market fund

Issue 1, pp. 75–144 and M. Ricks, (2011), Shadow Banking and Financial Regulation, Columbia Law and Economics Working Paper Nr. 370), insurance to guarantee payment to investors (G. Gorton and A. Metrick, (2010), Regulating the Shadow Banking System, Brookings Papers on Economic Activity 2010, pp. 261–312) or reserve build-up to cover losses in case of a forced liquidation of an MMF (P.E. McCabe et al., (2012), The Minimum Balance at Risk: A Proposal to Mitigate the Systemic Risks posed by Money Market Funds, Federal Reserve Bank of New York Staff Report Nr. 2012-47).

[35] See in detail: See Securities and Exchange Commission, (2014), Money Market Fund Reform, Release No. 33-9616, IA-3879; IC-31166; FR-84; File No. S7-03-13, via sec.gov, pp. 135–202.

[36] See in detail: See Securities and Exchange Commission, (2014), Money Market Fund Reform, Release No. 33-9616, IA-3879; IC-31166; FR-84; File No. S7-03-13, via sec.gov, pp. 277–288.

that has policies and procedures reasonably designed to limit all beneficial owners of the money market fund to natural persons. A municipal (or tax-exempt) fund would be required to transact at a floating NAV unless the fund meets the definition of a retail money market fund, in which case it would be allowed to use the amortized cost method and/or penny rounding method of pricing to seek to maintain a stable share price.

(b) Liquidity Fees[37]

Under the new rules, if a money market fund's level of 'weekly liquid assets' falls below 30% of its total assets (the regulatory minimum), the money market fund's board would be allowed to impose a liquidity fee of up to 2% on all redemptions. Such a fee could be imposed only if the money market fund's board of directors determines that such a fee is in the best interests of the fund. If a money market fund's level of weekly liquid assets falls below 10%, the money market fund would be required to impose a liquidity fee of 1% on all redemptions. However, such a fee would not be imposed if the fund's board of directors determines that such a fee is not in the best interests of the fund or that a lower or higher (up to 2%) liquidity fee is in the best interests of the fund. Weekly liquid assets generally include cash, US Treasury securities, certain other government securities with remaining maturities of 60 days or less, and securities that convert into cash within one week.

(c) Redemption Gates[38]

Under the new 'redemption gate' rules, if a money market fund's level of weekly liquid assets falls below 30%, a money market fund's board could in its discretion temporarily suspend redemptions (gate). To impose a gate, the board of directors would find that imposing a gate is in the money market fund's best interests. A money market fund that imposes a gate would be required to lift that gate within 10 business days, although the board of directors could determine to lift the gate earlier. Money market funds would not be able to impose a gate for more than 10 business days in any 90-day period.

Government money market funds would not be subject to the new fees and gates provisions, unless they would voluntarily opt-in on these rules.

(d) Disclosure Events

The major disclosure events include:

- Money market funds are required to promptly and publicly disclose instances in which the fund's level of weekly liquid assets falls below the 10% threshold and the imposition and removal of any liquidity fee or gate.

---

[37] See in detail: See Securities and Exchange Commission, (2014), Money Market Fund Reform, Release No. 33-9616, IA-3879; IC-31166; FR-84; File No. S7-03-13, via sec.gov, pp. 39–134.

[38] See in detail: See Securities and Exchange Commission, (2014), Money Market Fund Reform, Release No. 33-9616, IA-3879; IC-31166; FR-84; File No. S7-03-13, via sec.gov, pp. 39–134.

- Money market funds are required to disclose on their website, on a daily basis, their levels of daily and weekly liquid assets, net shareholder inflows or outflows, market-based NAVs per share, imposition of fees and gates, and any use of affiliate sponsor support.
- New material event disclosures: these events would include the imposition or removal of fees or gates and the primary considerations or factors taken into account by a board of directors in its decision related to fees and gates; portfolio security defaults; sponsor or fund affiliate support, including the amount of support and a brief description of the reason for support; and–for retail and government funds–a fall in the fund's market-based NAV per share below $0.9975.
- Money market funds are required to provide in their statements-of-additional-information (SAIs) disclosure regarding any occasion during the last 10 years (but not for occasions that occurred before the compliance date) in which the money market fund received sponsor or fund affiliate support.
- Enhanced and timelier reporting of fund portfolio holdings to clarify existing requirements and require reporting of additional information relevant to assessing money market fund risk.
- New 'private liquidity fund reporting' requires a large liquidity fund adviser (a liquidity fund adviser managing at least $1 billion in combined money market fund and liquidity fund assets) to report substantially the same portfolio information as registered money market funds are required to report (Form N-MFP). A liquidity fund is essentially an unregistered money market fund.

(e) Enhanced Stress Testing[39]

The new rules, which build on the 2010 stress-testing rules, require a money market fund to test its ability to maintain weekly liquid assets of at least 10% and to minimize principal volatility in response to certain specified hypothetical stress scenarios.

(f) Diversification Requirements for MMFs[40]

These new rules strengthen the existing diversification requirements for MMF portfolios to include:

- Money market funds are required to treat certain entities that are affiliated with each other as single issuers for purposes of determining whether they are complying with money market funds' 5% issuer diversification limit. Under this limitation, a fund generally could not invest more than 5% of its assets in any one issuer, or group of affiliated issuers.

[39] See in detail: See Securities and Exchange Commission, (2014), Money Market Fund Reform, Release No. 33-9616, IA-3879; IC-31166; FR-84; File No. S7-03-13, via sec.gov, pp. 552–592.

[40] See in detail: See Securities and Exchange Commission, (2014), Money Market Fund Reform, Release No. 33-9616, IA-3879; IC-31166; FR-84; File No. S7-03-13, via sec.gov, pp. 288–373, 488–551.

- For money market funds other than tax-exempt money market funds, the final rules require that all of a money market fund's assets meet the 10% diversification limit for guarantors and demand feature providers, thereby removing the so-called 25% basket that permitted as much as 25% of the value of securities held in a money market fund's portfolio to be subject to guarantees or demand features from a single institution. For tax-exempt money market funds (also referred to as municipal money market funds), the 25% guarantor basket would be reduced to 15% so that no more than 15% of the value of securities held in a tax-exempt money market fund's portfolio could be subject to guarantees or demand features from a single institution.
- Money market funds are required to treat the sponsors of asset-backed securities as guarantors subject to the 10% diversification limit applicable to guarantees and demand features, unless the money market fund's board of directors (or its delegate) determines that the fund is not relying on the sponsor's financial strength or its ability or willingness to provide liquidity, credit or other support to determine the asset-backed security's quality or liquidity.

(g) Reducing the Dependence on Credit Ratings

The Dodd- Frank Act (section 939A) requires the SEC to remove any reference to or requirement of reliance on credit ratings in its regulations and to establish appropriate standards of creditworthiness in place of certain references to credit ratings in SEC rules. Currently, to ensure that these funds are invested in high-quality short-term securities, the rules (i.e. rule 2a-7) require that money market funds invest only in securities that have received one of the two highest short-term ratings (i.e. are rated either 'first tier' or 'second tier') or if they are not rated, are of comparable quality. It also currently requires that a money market fund invest at least 97% of its assets in first tier securities. In addition, it is required that a fund's board of directors (or its delegate) determine that the security presents minimal credit risks. This determination must be based on factors pertaining to credit quality in addition to any rating assigned to the security.

The 2014 changes eliminate the credit ratings requirements for money market funds. Instead, a money market fund can invest in a security only if the fund's board of directors (or its delegate) determines that it presents minimal credit risks, and that determination would require the board of directors to find that the security's issuer has an exceptionally strong capacity to meet its short-term obligations.

10.1.3 Economic Rationale of the New Rules

Obviously, the quality of the new regulation will be in the macroeconomic implications and behaviors it will trigger. In terms of context it is good to remind upfront that about a third of the $3 trillion US MMF market are government funds that are exempted from the new regulation. The other approximate $2 trillion are in funds exposed to the new rules.[41] These funds might be exposed to investors shifting their assets to government funds or other opportunities. During distress however, the new rules will have no or little effect on funds or their investors. Investors will see the gates and fees as a way to avoid costs and be exposed to other investor redemptions. The floating NAV will help funds to manage minimizing shareholder dilution. Overall, it will increase MMFs' resilience and treat investors more equitable,[42] just like the 2010 amendments did. It is also very likely that 'floating NAV money market funds will likely offer higher returns than stable NAV government money market funds'… 'institutional investors are unlikely to reallocate assets from floating NAV institutional prime funds because they will continue to be one of the most conservative and flexible investment alternatives, even with a floating NAV'.[43]

Nevertheless, there will be investors who prefer permanent liquidity and a stable NAV in the trade-off. Those investors will migrate away from institutional prime funds 'because a floating NAV would eliminate the stable value feature that currently makes money market funds attractive to many shareholders'.[44] That would be the case for those who use the MMFs as a cash management tool, and a floating NAV might limit the abilities from that perspective, on top of the fact that they are loss-averse to begin with. Nevertheless, it is expected that the shift to other funds will be moderate with no or little impact on the short-term financing market. Especially now that the IRS has issued a statement that 'an investment in a floating NAV money market fund generally meets the definition of a "cash equivalent."' But those remaining that will re-allocate their assets due to the new regulation will invest 'their cash assets in government money market funds, direct investments, bank deposits, or other investment alternatives'. To be specific, the direct alternatives include: (1) direct investments in money market instruments[45]; (2) money market funds that are not subject to the reforms; (3) bank deposit accounts; (4) bank certificates of deposit; (5) bank collective trust funds; (6) Local Government Investment Pools (LGIPs); (7) US private funds; (8) offshore money

[41] 'Of this approximately $2.1 trillion, we estimate retail prime funds managed approximately 33% of prime fund assets (not including tax-exempt funds) or $593 billion, whereas retail tax-exempt funds managed 71% of tax-exempt fund assets or $197 billion of assets, or $790 billion in total retail fund assets'; See in detail: See Securities and Exchange Commission, (2014), Money Market Fund Reform, Release No. 33-9616, IA-3879; IC-31166; FR-84; File No. S7-03-13, via sec.gov, p. 596. The remaining funds are prime institutional funds subject to a floating NAV requirement.

[42] More equitable in the sense that investors are not exposed to dilution and fire sales and therefore discount prices just because other investors reacted faster or anticipated on potentially lower prices or contagion effect.

[43] Comment Letter of Thrivent Financial for Lutherans (Sept. 17, 2013). They btw argue against the statement that fees and gates improve transparency of risk for investors: '[t]he imposition of a liquidity fee or gate will always be a surprise to the investors that do not redeem quickly enough to avoid it. The need to impose such a fee or gate will not be transparent to the investor unless redemption activity is disclosed in a timely manner providing sufficient time for investors to react.'

[44] See in detail: See Securities and Exchange Commission, (2014), Money Market Fund Reform, Release No. 33-9616, IA-3879; IC-31166; FR-84; File No. S7-03-13, via sec.gov, p. 598.

[45] This will be limited to investors with large cash management requirements and active treasury function given the expertise requirements to self-manage cash and the costs associated with it.

market funds; (9) short-term investment funds ('STIFs'); (10) separately managed accounts; (11) ultra-short bond funds and (12) short-duration exchange-traded funds ('ETFs'). Each of these alternatives have specific features and trade-offs many mirroring the same items included now in the new regulation.[46] Some of these alternatives offer price stability, risk exposure, return, investor protection, disclosure or a combination of any of these features. Those that shift their assets to government funds will trade 'yield' for 'stability and liquidity' of their assets. In fact that shift could also lower the 'yield' of existing government fund investors (and direct buyers) as the demand increase for eligible securities will depress the yield on those securities. How much yield will be deprived is a function of (1) the amount of capital that will shift to those securities and (2) the supply of eligible government securities. Moving those funds back to bank accounts is often no option given the thresholds of the deposit insurance mechanism. Many market fund investors are anyway restricted from investing in many of the aforementioned alternatives, due to (fiduciary or regulatory) restrictions on participation or because they are private offerings (offshore funds). Those restrictions are also a reality when considering European money market funds given the fact that they can take more risk than their US counterparts as they are not subject to similar restrictions regarding 'credit quality, liquidity, maturity, and diversification'.

It is also very likely that the US MMF industry will innovate and cater to clients within the context of the new rules. It is expected that fund managers 'may try to stabilize their funds' NAVs by choosing low principal-risk portfolio investment strategies, whereas other funds may seek to offer higher yields within the current new restrictions'.[47] The new rules will likely trigger more intense competition between government funds, as well as the fact that the option for retail funds to apply gates and fees might deter retail investors away from certain funds that indicate they will consider doing so when conditions dictate.

The new gates and fees rules are enacted to soften redemption (requests) by 'allocating liquidity costs to those shareholders who impose such costs on funds through their redemptions and, in certain cases, stop heavy redemptions in times of market stress by providing fund boards with additional tools to manage heavy redemptions and improve risk transparency'.[48] The enhanced liquidity risk should increase allocation efficiency. Other benefits from the 2014 rules will be that (1) floating NAV should increase allocation efficiency by allocating market-based gain or losses to investor in a proportionate way, (2) some managers, who cater to clients who require price stability, liquidity and higher yields (than government funds), will alter their portfolio and increase exposure to shorter-maturity lower-risk securities. By doing so they reduce NAV fluctuations and reduce the probability of liquid asset levels. That behavior will stimulate competition for

[46] See for a full review of all principal features (valuation, investment risk, redemption restrictions, yield, etc.) of various cash alternatives to MMFs, Securities and Exchange Commission, (2014), Money Market Fund Reform, Release No. 33-9616, IA-3879; IC-31166; FR-84; File No. S7-03-13, via sec.gov, pp. 604–607, Table 1.

[47] See Securities and Exchange Commission, (2014), Money Market Fund Reform, Release No. 33-9616, IA-3879; IC-31166; FR-84; File No. S7-03-13, via sec.gov, pp. 614–615.

[48] See Securities and Exchange Commission, (2014), Money Market Fund Reform, Release No. 33-9616, IA-3879; IC-31166; FR-84; File No. S7-03-13, via sec.gov, pp. 617–618.

a certain type of MMF investor. Interesting is the question whether capital formation is about to change, now that sponsor support needs to be disclosed, that is, will it reduce more risky investments by MMF now that investors are exposed to the understanding they carry the ultimate volatility, credit and liquidity risk of the portfolio?

All the above leads to the following schematic overviews of the 2014 MMF changes (Table 10.1), the changes per type of investor (Table 10.2), and the summary of new US MMF Disclosure Requirements, Diversification Requirements & Enhanced Stress Testing (Table 10.3).

10.1.4 Evaluation of the MMF Legislative Reforms

Given the experiences during the 2008 and 2011 turmoil, it can be confidently stated that, from a macro-perspective, the objective of the MMF regulatory changes was, or should have been, safeguarding global financial stability.[49] Given the above it became clear that spillover effects, contagion risk, runs on MMFs, moral hazard and excessive risk taking by MMFs were all aspects that needed to be tackled. To remind us, MMFs are not only a very large and sizeable player, they are a critical provider of short-term funding to (global) banks. They require up to 35% of such funding. The latter has drawn our attention as it has not been central in any of the regulatory changes implemented. In order to achieve that the regulator should have focused on the bipolar objective of 'reducing the ex-ante incentives for MMFs to take excessive risk and increase the ex-post resilience of MMFs to system-wide runs[50]' in order to capture the full spectrum of issues surrounding MMFs. It was already highlighted in this subsection that some proposals required MMFs to have and build up (subordinated) capital in order to absorb losses and reduce the incentive to take risks (which in the enacted legislation is absorbed by the investor in the MMF).

What regulation for MMF is preferred is determined by the role of MMFs in the global financial fabric. That can be the function of a bank, and therefore they should be regulated as such. Or they are seen as market-based financing. In that way they are part of the shadow banking system. That duality explains the various proposals[51] the Financial Stability Oversight Council came up with in 2012: (1) MMFs are required to report floating NAVs,[52] (2) MMFs are required to have a 1% capital buffer combined with a 'Minimum Balance at Risk' provision and where investors cannot at all times redeem all of their shares (investors are required to leave up to 3% of their funds in the MMF for 30

[49] Regarding the contribution of MMFs to systemic risk see S.G. Hanson et al., (2014), An Evaluation of Money Market Fund Reform Proposals, HBR Working Paper, pp. 8–11. Later on also published in IMF Economic Review 2015, Vol. 63, Issue 4, pp. 984–1023

[50] See S.G. Hanson et al., (2014), An Evaluation of Money Market Fund Reform Proposals, HBR Working Paper (also published as "An Evaluation of Money Market Fund Reform Proposals," IMF Economic Review, Palgrave Macmillan; International Monetary Fund, 2015, Vol. 63, Issue 4, pp. 984–1023, November).

[51] See for the appreciation of the market 'failures' that led to the MMFs regulatory proposals: S.G. Hanson et al., (2014), An Evaluation of Money Market Fund Reform Proposals, HBR Working Paper, pp. 11–16.

[52] Which essentially makes investors in MMFs understand that MMFs also entail a certain level of risk and analysis is required.

Table 10.1 Summary of new US MMF 2014 requirements

	Floating NAV	Liquidity fees and redemption gates	Portfolio diversification/ additional disclosures and stress testing
Content	Market-based valuation methodology (rather than amortized cost accounting methodology or penny rounding) for daily share prices for MMFs, creating a 'floating NAV' (out to the fourth decimal point e.g. $1.0000). The daily share prices of such funds will fluctuate along with the market-based value of the funds securities. Compliance date: October 14, 2016.	In case 'weekly liquid assets[a]' fall below 30% of the fund's total assets, the board could/may (or not in case the board decides that is based on the best interest of the fund): Impose up to 2% liquidity fee on redemptions Impose redemption gates when the board considers it is in the best interest of the fund Suspend redemptions for up to 10 business days (but not more than 10 business days in any 90-day period) In case 'weekly liquid assets' fall below 10% of total fund assets then the fund is required to impose up to 1% liquidity fee on redemptions (can go up to 2%, or as low as zero, at boards' discretion and in fund interest). Money market funds are required to promptly and publicly disclose instances when a fund's level of weekly liquid assets falls below 10% and/or there is an imposition or removal of any liquidity fee or gate. Compliance date: October 14, 2016.	Enhanced diversification, disclosure and stress testing for all MMFs Additional reporting requirements for MMFs and private 'look-alike' funds
Funds 'in scope'	Institutional prime MMFs Institutional municipal & tax-exempt MMFs	Institutional and retail prime and municipal & tax-exempt MMFs	All MMFs
Funds exempted	Institutional and retail government MMFs Retail prime MMFs Retail municipal & tax-exempt MMFs	Institutional and retail government MMFs (but those funds can opt in if disclosed to investors)	Not applicable

That is, US-registered MMFs

[a]Include cash, U.S. Treasury securities, certain other government securities with remaining maturities of 60 days or less, and securities that convert into cash within one week

Table 10.2 Changes per type of investor and type of fund

Institutional Funds[a]	**Government Funds**[b]: Stable NAV No liquidity fee No redemption gates Ability to opt in on these matters in case disclosed in advance **Prime funds (commercial paper)**: Floating NAV(*)[c] Liquidity fees and redemption gates based on the parameters of weekly liquidity levels and board discretion **Municipal (tax-exempt) funds**: Floating NAV(*) Liquidity fees and redemption gates based on the parameters of weekly liquidity levels and board discretion
Retail funds (investors are natural persons through policies and procedures enacted)[d]	**Government funds**: Stable NAV No liquidity fee No redemption gates Ability to opt in on these matters in case disclosed in advance **Prime funds (commercial paper)**: Stable NAV Liquidity fees and redemption gates based on the parameters of weekly liquidity levels and board discretion **Municipal (tax-exempt) funds**: Stable NAV Liquidity fees and redemption gates based on the parameters of weekly liquidity levels and board discretion

[a]An institutional money market fund would be defined as a money market fund that does not meet the definition of a retail fund (i.e. all other fund investor types)
[b]Government funds are defined as those that invest a minimum of 99.5% (previously 80%) or more of their total assets in cash, government securities and/or repurchase agreements that are collateralized solely by government securities or cash
[c](*)*Funds will no longer be permitted to use the amortized cost accounting methodology like stable NAV funds
[d]The full definition of a retail money market fund would be defined as 'a money market fund that has policies and procedures reasonably designed to limit all beneficial owners of the money market fund to natural persons'

days after redeeming the rest. The portion that stays in the fund becomes subordinate and take first loss should the MMF 'break the buck', which makes the remaining portion a 'kind of' junior capital[53]), or (3) MMFs are required to have a 3% subordinated capital buffer. Looking backwards the final rules embody proposal one combined with the redemption gates of proposal two. Table 10.4 provides a condensed[54] overview of the pros

[53] That seems a hard sell, as most MMF investors are risk averse and compromises to a certain degree the risk-sharing of the MMF model.
[54] 'Condensed' as it is a backward looking exercise.

Table 10.3 Summary of new US MMF disclosure requirements, diversification requirements & enhanced stress testing

Enhanced disclosure and reporting requirements	
Objective	Improve the transparency of money market fund operations and risks by, e.g. requiring additional disclosures of holdings
Fund coverage	All funds
Compliance date(s)	For 'new material event disclosure' (form N-CR): July 14, 2015 All other disclosures: April 14, 2016
New material event disclosure	Immediate disclosure (through form N-CR) in case: the imposition or removal of fees or gates and the primary considerations or factors taken into account by a board of directors in its decision related to fees and gates; portfolio security defaults; sponsor or fund affiliate support, including the amount of support and a brief description of the reason for support; and for retail and government funds: a fall in the fund's market-based NAV per share below $0.9975
Website disclosure	On a daily basis the following information requires disclosure: daily and weekly liquid assets net shareholder inflows or outflows market-based NAVs per share imposition of fees and gates, and any use of affiliate sponsor support
Disclosure of sponsor support	Disclosure is required for 'any occasion in the last 10 years (but not for occasions before the compliance date) in which the money market fund received sponsor or fund affiliate support
Additional disclosures	Portfolio holding filing (form N-MFP) publicly available immediately after filing (previously after 60 days) Condition I also applied regarding filing requirements for a large liquidity advisor ((a liquidity fund adviser managing at least $1 billion in combined money market fund and liquidity fund assets)

(continued)

Table 10.3 (continued)

Enhanced disclosure and reporting requirements	
Diversification requirements	Applicable to all funds Compliance date: October 14, 2014 *Aggregation of affiliates*: requires certain entities that are affiliated one way or the other to be treated as a single issuer for purposes of determining whether they comply with the 5% issuer diversification limit *Removal of 25% basket*: It used to be so that as much as 25% of the value of securities held in a MMF's portfolio could be subject to a guarantee or otherwise (demand feature) of a single institution. That rule is now replaced with the following thresholds: (1) Government and prime funds: max. 10% diversification limit for guarantors and demand feature providers, (2) Municipal and Tax-exempt funds: max 15% diversification limit for guarantors and demand feature providers *Asset-backed securities*: requires to treat the sponsors of asset-backed securities as guarantors subject to the 10% diversification limit applicable to guarantees and demand features. Not applicable when board decides that the fund is not relying on the financial capabilities of the sponsor or its ability to provide liquidity, credit or support otherwise.
Enhanced stress testing	Applicable to all funds Compliance date: October 14, 2014 It is required to test the ability of the fund to maintain weekly liquid assets of at least 10% and to minimize principal volatility vis-à-vis a number of pre-determined hypothetical stress scenarios Reporting requirements regarding these stress tests need to be aligned with new rules to enhance the quality of reports.

Table 10.4 Analysis of the different MMF proposals

Junior capital buffer proposal[a]	Minimum balance at risk proposal[b]
Would imply that each $ invested would be backed by more than $1 in assets (over-collateralized) and thus the MMF can absorb credit losses or market price fluctuations. The content of such a buffer can be structured in different ways (subordinate, liquidity facility, stand-by etc.)[c] The subordinated capital absorbs risk and divides the first-loss risk and reward that exist in any MMF portfolio for the benefit of the normal investors holding normal MMF shares. The buffer is estimated at 4–5% of risk-weighted assets lowering the yield for normal MMF investors by about 5 basis points[d]. Benefits are that it reduces risk of system-wide runs and incentives to take excessive risk. It reduces the ex ante probability that investors suffer a (major) loss to begin with and weakens the run incentive[e]. The higher cost of the subordinate capital will also reduce 'ex-ante excessive risk taking' and thus lower the yield to normal investors. The cycle of increasing risk to increase yield will be broken[f] especially when that capital is provided by a parent company.	Implies that a fraction of each MMF investors capital will serve as loss-bearing subordinate capital That subordinate part needs to stay in the fund for 30 days even if the remaining portion is redeemed by investors. Although similar to the junior capital proposal in this scenario the (1) capital is provided by MMF normal investor (and not by the fund sponsor or outside investors) and (2) the capital is provided ex-post (and not ex ante as the junior capital provider model) (1) Both models reduce the ex ante incentives for risk taking because they can force some level of market discipline on fund managers although the evidence of equity for banks' impact on bank executives is a mixed bag[g]. Investors in MMF would no longer chase yield as they would incur losses to a large degree themselves and still doing so would increase operational cost because of the capital that stays behind (for 30 days) The difference with normal capital buffers is that MMF investments become sticky and MMF as a product lose their transactional value to investors (2) ex ante bank capital is provided by sophisticated investors; in this case it is provided ex post by a heterogeneous portfolio of MMF investors who are uniformly risk averse. Ex post loss allocation embeds anyhow the risk of setting off a system-wide run

(*continued*)

Table 10.4 (continued)

Floating NAV Proposal[h]	Transparency[i]
No longer penny rounding, but daily market values of portfolios Analysis can also apply to European NAV MMFs (accumulating MMFs[j]) The benefits of the proposal are: (1) it lowers the probability of runs by taking out strategic motives, (2) it has the potential to reduce panic-based runs investors are more aware of risks in MMFs), (3) it effectively reduces the 'safety' qualification, which reduces future (forced) government interventions The downsides are: (1) floating NAV will be calculated based on models as private money markets are pretty illiquid (like banks do with their loan books) and so no real market prices underlying floating NAV and therefore might not reduce the run risk of investors. Illiquidity and direct-on-demand redemptions cause bank runs, not only the valuations of the MMF portfolio. That illiquidity is caused by the illiquidity of the secondary market the MMF invests in. MMFs are from that perspective more prone to illiquidity-based runs than other mutual funds. The correlation in the MMF portfolios works as a catalyst. The extra sensitivity of MMF is largely to be explained by the fact that: (1) MMFs have risk-averse investors who perform little analysis (information insensitive). The floating NAV mode may reduce information production at the benefit of market-based pricing[k]. (2) the illiquidity of secondary markets as mentioned and associated MMF portfolio correlation (3) MMFs manage short-term funding for the real economy and disruptions impact the economy therefore more directly In 99.9% of the time[l], the floating NAV would hoover only around 10 basis points and so questions can be asked about 'meaningfulness' of market-based pricing in normal times and the persistent 'qualification' of MMFs as risky Rule 2a-7 requirements maintain the rubber stamp of 'safe' MMF funds, in particular as prime MMFs are exempted from the 2014 changes	Would enable more intense monitoring of MMF portfolios Gross yield is already reported and reflects risk taking Investors want MMFs to take risk (to increase yield) because they have a redemption option (e.g. inflows early 2011 in MMFs with material eurozone bank exposure)

(continued)

Table 10.4 (continued)

Liquidity Fees[m]	Redemption Gates[n]
Gating rules take a microprudential view (e.g. position of individual funds). Gates imposed by one fund might trigger system-wide panic and broad-based redemptions (macro-view)	
Linking gates and fees to the amount of liquid assets held by MMFs discourages them to create liquidity themselves in a counter-cyclical way. They would hold ultra-short-term liquid paper (maturing in five days or less) and therefore more prone to runs.	
Rule 2a-7 implemented in 2010 already includes an inefficient gate (suspend redemptions when MMF 'breaks the buck'). This and other gates accelerate the anticipation of investor's behavior in terms of pre-timely redemptions	
Liquidity fees also encourage pre-timely redemptions as the future haircut would be even higher (including the fees)	

[a]See in extenso: S.G. Hanson et al., (2014), An Evaluation of Money Market Fund Reform Proposals, HBR Working Paper, pp. 16–20

[b]See in extenso: S.G. Hanson et al., (2014), An Evaluation of Money Market Fund Reform Proposals, HBR Working Paper, pp. 20–22. See also P. McCabe, et al., (2013), The Minimum Balance at Risk: A Proposal to Mitigate the Systemic Risks Posed by Money Market Funds, Brookings Papers on Economic Activity, pp. 211–278

[c]See appendix A of S.G. Hanson et al., (2014), An Evaluation of Money Market Fund Reform Proposals, HBR Working Paper, pp. 32–34 for more details

[d]So that the capital buffer will lead to a maximum impairment of max. 0.1% per annum for normal MMF investors, see S.G. Hanson et al., (2014), Ibid. pp. 16 & 18. Also O. Vasicek, (2002), Loan Portfolio Value, Risk Vol. 15, pp. 160–162. The relatively high buffer (for not so risky assets when compared to the riskiness for bank assets compared to their capital requirements) is explained by (1) the fact that most issuers in MMF portfolios are global financial firms with a higher 'loan given default' than non-financial issuers than one can find on the books of banks, and (2) correlations are higher in an MMF portfolio as most issuers are financial institutions (p. 18). Reducing concentration risk would therefore not only provide 'true' deposit-like instruments and lower capital requirements. The impact of subordinated capital on the yield for normal MMF investors is somewhat unclear as it will largely depend on the cost of the subordinated portion which can be material. The 5% impact on normal investor yield is based on the comparability of long-term bank debt (see pp. 19–20)

[e]See on a macro-level: S. Morris, and H. S. Shin, (2010), Illiquidity Component of Credit Risk, Princeton University Working Paper

[f]See also M. Kacperczyk, and P. Schnabl (2013), How Safe are Money Market Funds? Quarterly Journal of Economics, Vol. 128, Issue 3, 1073–1122

[g]G. Gorton, and A. Santomero, (1990), Market Discipline and Subordinated Bank Debt, The Journal of Money, Credit, and Banking, Vol. 22, Nr. 1, pp. 119; R. Bliss, & M. Flannery, (2001), Market Discipline in the Governance of U.S. Bank Holding Companies: Monitoring vs. Influencing, in F. S. Mishkin (ed.), Prudential Supervision: What Works and what Doesn't?, pp. 107–143, University of Chicago Press, Chicago; A. Ashcraft, (2006), Does the Market Discipline Banks? New Evidence from the Regulatory Capital Mix, Federal Reserve Bank of New York Staff Report Nr. 244

[h]See in extenso: S.G. Hanson et al., (2014), Ibid. pp. 22–26

[i]See in extenso: S.G. Hanson et al., (2014), Ibid. pp. 26–27

(continued)

Table 10.4 (continued)

[j]See also J.N. Gordon and C.M. Gandia, (2014), Money Market Funds Run Risk: Will Floating Net Asset Value Fix the Problem?, Columbia Business Law Review, Vol. 2014, Nr. 2, pp. 313–332. They show that in the 2008 crisis both European floating and fixed NAV MMFs were exposed to heavy redemptions
[k]See also (1) T.V. Dang, et al., (2010), Opacity and the Optimality of Debt for Liquidity Provision, Working Paper, and (2) S.G. Hanson, and A. Sunderam, (2013), Are There Too Many Safe Securities? Securitization and the Incentives for Information Production, Journal of Financial Economics, Vol. 108, Issue 3, pp. 565–584
[l]See Blackrock (2012), Money Market Funds: A Path Forward, BlackRock Viewpoint, 9/27/2012
[m]See in extenso: S.G. Hanson et al., (2014), Ibid. pp. 27–28
[n]See in extenso: S.G. Hanson et al., (2014), Ibid. pp. 27–28

and cons of the different proposals. These proposals should be judged against the ultimate reason for the reform efforts to begin with, that is, addressing specific 'market failures' that the market and private agents cannot prevent or resolve themselves and that cause externalities that threaten the 'financial stability' of the marketplace. Those market failures are mainly build around the following features: (1) the fact that investors in MMF can withdraw their funds at any given point in time, (2) the fact that, especially after the 2008 interventions of the Treasury, investors in MMFs anticipate on future interventions in case of market turmoil in order to stabilize the markets, (3) the fact that MMF investors are relatively uninformed (as is the case in general in the debt markets), and turmoil will lead to runs (information-insensitive investors become information sensitive). That however ignores the fact that asymmetry between the ex ante private benefits of risk-taking MMFs versus the ex post aggregate cost of ex post intervention and fire sales, and (4) that economic risk taking by MMFs might cause banks (who draw heavily on them for short-term funding) to raise short-term funding below their true economic cost.[55]

Although the main goal of every MMF regulatory change around the world is driven by the objective of safeguarding (global) financial stability, the outcomes have been demonstrated to be quite different. In essence it is fair to assume that the main goal of MMF reform is safeguarding global financial stability. In light of this goal, reforms should reduce the ex ante incentives for MMFs to take excessive risk and increase the ex post resilience of MMFs to system-wide runs.[56] Requiring MMFs to have subordinated capital

[55] See S.G. Hanson et al., (2014), An Evaluation of Money Market Fund Reform Proposals, HBR Working Paper, pp. 11–13. They therefore reduce the objectives of the reform to four key objectives being: '(1) reduce the incentive of MMFs to take on excessive portfolio risk ex ante, (2) reduce the incentive for MMF investors to run ex post, (3) reduce the impact of a MMF run on the global financial system and economy if a MMF run does occur, and (4) reduce the incentive for large financial institutions to rely excessively on unstable, short-term funding from MMFs' (p. 13).

[56] For a comparative analysis of the different proposals that have been floating around: S.G. Hanson, D. Scharfstein and A. Sunderam, (2015), An Evaluation of Money Market Reform Proposal, HBS and NBER Working Paper, July, mimeo (published in IMF Economic Review, 2015, Vol. 63, Issue 4, pp. 984–1023); S. Alnahedh and S. Bhagat, (2017), Shadow Banking Concerns: The Case of Money Market Funds, Working Paper, mimeo.

buffers could generate significant financial stability benefits, conclude Hanson et al., and is in line with their previous analysis. Subordinated capital provides MMFs with loss absorption capacity, lowering the probability that an MMF suffers losses large enough to trigger a run, and reduces incentives to take excessive risks. Other reform alternatives based on market forces, such as converting MMFs to a floating NAV, may be less effective in protecting financial stability, they conclude. It points at fundamental tensions regarding the real options in the MMF regulatory changes and the intrinsic and fundamental tension when it comes to regulating the shadow banking system. MMF regulation should attempt to both reduce the ex ante incentives of MMFs to take excessive risks and increase the ex post ability of MMFs to absorb losses without setting off runs. However, only capital-based solutions reduce ex ante incentives for risk taking. Capital-based solutions also maintain the current fixed NAV structure for ordinary MMF investors and thus preserve any transactional benefits those investors reap from the existing system. The goal of MMF regulation is to address well-defined market failures that private actors are unable to address themselves. Reformulated as objectives Hanson et al. reduce the discussion to four objectives: (1) reduce the incentive of MMFs to take on excessive portfolio risk ex ante, (2) reduce the incentive for MMF investors to run ex post, (3) reduce the impact of an MMF run on the global financial system and economy if a MMF run does occur and (4) reduce the incentive for large financial institutions to rely excessively on unstable, short-term funding from MMFs.

The competing dynamics come down to this: '[i]f the primary objective of regulation is to safeguard the stability of the global financial system, reforms should be designed to curb ex ante incentives for excessive risk taking and to bolster the ex post ability to absorb losses without setting off system-wide runs'...'Alternate reform proposals, including the floating NAV proposal that was adopted by the SEC in July 2014, may be less likely to significantly increase global financial stability'...'reforms based solely on market forces may not be sufficient to address the instabilities associated with MMFs and shadow banking more generally'.

In Table 10.5 the three most dominant lines (and some marginal ones) of thought are reflected and have been analyzed by Hanson et al. along with their summarized thoughts.[57]

In July 2014, the SEC adopted several new rules regarding MMFS. Primary among these was a decision to require institutional prime and municipal funds to adopt a floating NAV structure. These new regulations are set to take effect in the second half of 2016. The analysis of Hanson et al. regarding the floating NAV proposal points to potential limitations of this approach, suggesting that it is unlikely to meaningfully reduce the threat of a widespread run on MMFs.

But here is the thing: relatively small capital buffers are capable of absorbing daily fluctuations between a fund's shadow price and its amortized cost. The ability to absorb large-scale defaults, however, would require a significantly larger and more costly buffer. Second, because a buffer is designed to absorb credit risk, capital providers demand compensation for bearing this risk. After adjusting for this cost, the returns available to prime

[57] Ibid.

Table 10.5 The three trends in MMF regulatory reform

Trends	Analysis
Subject MMFs more fully to market forces by requiring them to report floating net asset values (NAVs)	Can lead to significant financial stability benefits Could reduce the strategic motives for MMF shareholders to run by reducing the benefits with early exits But practice might be very different from theoretical benefits: (1) evidence indicates that floating NAV may not alter investors' incentive to chase risk (and yield); (2) because the paper held by MMFs is illiquid, moving to a floating NAV may not produce significant variation in reported NAVs- turning them into stable NAV products; (3) incentives for investors to run before illiquid MMF assets have to be sold at a loss are likely to remain. Turning it into a floating NAV doesn't reduce the instabilities typically associated with fixed NAV models
Require MMFs to have a 1% capital buffer combined with a "minimum balance at risk" (MBR) provision whereby investors cannot immediately redeem all of their shares	Investors are required to leave up to 3% of their funds in the MMF for 30 days after redeeming the rest "Minimum balance funds" become subordinated and take first loss should the MMF break the buck MBR is junior capital lookalike However, MBR requires the most risk-averse money market investors to provide this capital ex post. This reduces some of the risk-sharing benefits common to MMFs Run is still likely for the 97% of their investment during distress
Require MMFs to have a 3% subordinated capital buffer	Assumed most effective Loss absorption capacity reduced the probability to trigger a run Clear that an investor class bears the cost Best range is 3–4% buffer held against unsecured paper; for concentrated portfolios this should be higher
Increased transparency	For investors to monitor risk taking Problems with approach: (1) existing disclosure is already high and daily; differences in gross yield are due to differences in risk taking, (2) sophisticated institutional investors already monitor fund portfolios carefully and they assume redemption is always possible in a timely way
Liquidation fees and redemption gates	Main concerns exist: (1) gating rules have an inherently microprudential focus; problem in 2008 was on a macro-level (contagion and transmission risk), (2) discourages MMFs from drawing down on their buffers of liquid assets precisely when they should do so from a system-wide perspective, (3) liquidity-based triggers would encourage MMFs to keep their buffers of liquid assets very high to avoid concerns about triggering redemption fees or restrictions, (4) existing gates have proven to be ineffective. Gates can only be effective when being stringent. However, that would amplify the ex ante incentives to withdraw early, before the gating rule is applied.

money market fund shareholders are comparable to default free securities.[58] Remember the above-discussed 2010/2014 adjustments to the MMF regulation and in particular the changes to rule 2a-7. These included: (1) Floating net asset value (FNAV). Institutional prime funds are required to transact at market valuations rather than a stable $1.00. These funds must value their portfolios at market prices and sell and redeem shares using \basis point rounding. This requires funds to price shares to the nearest 1/100th of 1%. The amendment allows government and retail MMFs to retain stable dollar pricing; and (2) Fund boards are permitted to use liquidity fees and redemption gates. Specifically, in the event a fund's weekly liquid assets (WLA) fall below 30%, a board can elect to impose a liquidity fee of no more than 2% or it could impose a temporary redemption gate of no more than 10 days during any 90-day period. If WLA drops below 10%, funds will be required to charge a 1% liquidity fee unless the board decides to opt out. Fees and gates are applicable to all MMFs except government funds.

The FNAV option is designed to ameliorate the first-mover advantage associated with stable dollar funds by mutualizing portfolio losses. This amendment to rule 2a-7 targets only prime institutional funds because they were the only asset class to display run-like behavior following the Lehman Brothers bankruptcy.[59] One of the reasons that the FNAV amendment is not considered a stand-alone policy choice, Lewis argues, is 'even with market pricing there remains an incentive to redeem during periods of market stress. Since most fund assets do not trade in active secondary markets, heavy shareholder redemptions could force funds to sell illiquid assets at re-sale prices. If shareholders pre-emptively redeem shares to avoid taking re-sale losses, it could precipitate a liquidity run as remaining shareholders pay increasingly higher costs to obtain liquidity during periods of market stress'.[60]

In contrast to Hanson et al. discussed above, Lewis provides an alternative perspective that employs an asset pricing framework to help calibrate the size of a capital buffer. He shows that, instead of 2% to 6% (as Hanson et al. suggest), a relatively small capital buffer of 60 basis points is able to absorb gains and losses during normal market conditions. However, a 60 basis point buffer would likely fail if a concentrated position, of say 5%, were to default. If complete loss absorption is the objective, a substantial buffer would be required.[61] For instance, a 3% buffer would accommodate all but extremely large losses. A limitation of a 3% buffer is that the cost of providing this protection would be borne at all times even though it is likely to be depleted only rarely. But what is a defendable cost for

---

[58] C. Lewis, (2015), Money market Fund Capital Buffers, Owen Graduate School of Management, Working Paper, April 6, mimeo.

[59] This interpretation is consistent with the empirical data reported in the relevant RSFI study but other competing explanations exist. One plausible alternative is that retail investors simply were slower to react. The SEC's Division of Risk, Strategy, and Financial Innovation ('RSFI') has since changed its name to the Division of Economic and Risk Analysis; See in detail: Division of Risk, Strategy, and Financial Innovation, U.S. Securities and Exchange Commission, 2012, Response to Questions Posed by Commissioners Aguilar, Paredes, and Gallagher, November 30, 2012.

[60] C. Lewis, (2015), Ibid. p. 5.

[61] C. Lewis, (2015), Ibid. p. 6.

creating resilient MMFs? The capital buffer could be used elsewhere. And if you want someone in the market to provide those buffers they will want to see a return for doing so. Lewis indicates '[m]oreover, because the capital buffer absorbs fluctuations in the value of the portfolio, much of the yield of the fund will be diverted to funding the capital buffer.

Put another way, to the extent that the capital buffer absorbs default risk, those contributing to a capital buffer will demand a rate of return that compensates them for bearing this risk. Since, by construction, a capital buffer absorbs defaults until it is fully depleted, money market funds will allocate that portion of the returns associated with credit risk to capital buffer "investors" and will only be able to offer money market fund shareholders returns that mimic those available for government securities.'[62] This then creates synthetic government funds. The objective of Lewis is to illustrate the economic effects of requiring a money market fund to be supported by a capital buffer. Every choice for a capital buffer needs to go hand in hand with the question of what objective it carries and what it tries to solve. Lewis concludes with the following design options[63]:

- A buffer so that it is able to absorb day-to-day variations in market value relative to the amortized cost of the underlying portfolio assets. A 60 basis point buffer would be sufficient to provide price stability under normal market conditions. Although a 60 basis point buffer is able to withstand most day-to-day price variation, it would most likely fail if a concentrated position, of say 5%, were to default.
- A larger buffer could protect shareholders from losses related to defaults in concentrated positions. If complete loss absorption is the objective, a substantial buffer would be required. For example, a 3% buffer would accommodate all but extremely large losses. A limitation of a large buffer is that the cost of providing this protection would be borne at all times even though it is likely to be significantly depleted only rarely.
- Resilience objectives (more resilient to deviations between the shadow price and amortized cost) do conflict here with the opportunity cost of capital principles. The capital that is used to absorb fluctuations in the value of the portfolio will be looking for a rate of return for bearing that risk.

Lewis's point also makes sense intuitively: investors in MMF see it as an alternative to a savings account but with higher returns. But if you want the MMF to be stable over time and across market conditions, capital buffers are needed to absorb potential shocks and those investors will be seeking a return for doing so. That will eat out of the MMF return to such a degree that it will start to mimic a savings account's return or as Lewis calls it the return of a 'synthetic government fund'. The additional credit risk[64] that justified the higher MMF returns will now be absorbed by the investors in the capital buffer and they will be left with only enhanced returns and not the MMF investor itself. That very likely explains the haggling and shenanigans on both sides of the Atlantic when drafting the necessary adjustments to the MMF legislation.

---

[62] C. Lewis, (2015), Ibid. p. 7.

[63] C. Lewis, (2015), Ibid. pp. 31–32.

[64] See, for example, D. Duffie, and K. Singleton, (2003), Credit Risk: Pricing, Measurement, and Management, Princeton University Press, Princeton NJ.

10.1.5 Can Sponsor Support Be a Source of Fragility?

A floating net asset value model would have to reduce the risk of a fire sale and contagion in the money market fund segment. And so would sponsor support.[65] At least that is the line of the incoming legislation we have witnessed in both the US and Europe in recent times. But questions can be asked and we have tried to capture some of them. A remaining question is to what degree a floating NAV and/or sponsor support itself can be a source of fragility. Parlatore looked into this matter. She analyzed how adopting a floating NAV would affect the liquidity provided by MMFs and their fragility. By doing so their model captures key institutional features of MMFs such as liquidation after "breaking the buck" and voluntary sponsor support. She demonstrates that sponsor support, which is instrumental to attain a stable NAV, may be a source of fragility: it may make the MMF industry prone to runs[66] different from the canonical bank runs.[67] The difference between canonical[68] and non-canonical runs is that these (non-canonical) runs are not runs of investors on the financial intermediaries but runs of financial intermediaries on the asset market.[69] These investors in MMFs are either risk-averse investors or risk-neutral fund managers. The fact that MMFs increasingly access the non-riskless part of the asset market implies that the structure of the relationship between investors and MMF managers is impacted. She explains: '[t]he managers' support decisions determine the demand for the risky asset in the interim period and its liquidation price. At the same time, the liquidation price of the risky asset in the interim period determines the managers' costs and benefits of offering support. This interdependence may give rise to strategic complementarities[70] in the managers' support decisions and may make the model prone to runs.'[71]

[65] See on sponsor support in the MMF industry: S.A. Brady, et al., (2012), The Stability of Prime Money Market Mutual Funds: Sponsor Support from 2007 to 2011, Federal Reserve Bank of Boston, Risk and Policy Analysis Working Papers, RPA 12–3.

[66] L. Schmidt, et al., (2013), Runs on Money Market Mutual Funds, University of Maryland Working Paper, mimeo; also A. Shelifer, and R. Vishny, (2011), Fire Sales in Finances and Macroeconomics, Journal of Economic Perspectives, Vol. 25, Issue 1, pp. 29–48.

[67] C. Parlatore, (2014), Fragility in Money Market Funds: Sponsor Support and Regulation, Wharton Working Paper, January 6 (reprinted as ECB Working Paper Nr. 1772, March 2015). The model she developed takes into account the main characteristics of MMFs: the ability of investors to redeem their shares on demand, the stability of the NAV and the provision of sponsor support, the liquidation of the funds after breaking the buck, and the fluctuation in the value of the funds' assets (p. 25).

[68] The canonical run was first explored by Diamond and Dybvig, see D.W. Diamond, and P. H. Dybvig, (1983), Bank Runs, Deposit Insurance, and Liquidity, Journal of Political Economy, Vol. 91, Issue 3, pp. 401–419.

[69] C. Parlatore, (2014), Ibid. p. 3.

[70] See on strategic complementarities: Q. Chen, et al., (2010), Payoff Complementarities and Financial Fragility: Evidence from Mutual Fund outflows, Journal of Financial Economics, Vol. 97, pp. 239–262.

[71] C. Parlatore, (2014), Ibid. p. 3. The understanding behind the strategic complementarity and the fact that it can lead to runs is that '[i]f an individual manager expects all other managers to offer support to their funds, he expects a high demand for the asset in the interim period and high liquidation prices. These, in turn, imply a low cost of offering support and may increase the individual

Adjusting the MMF model to a floating NAV model[72] will reduce that vulnerability but that 'the regulation would also affect intermediation fees, support decisions, and asset prices. Furthermore, all these could have countervailing effects on the risk and the return of intermediation for investors and MMF managers, and, hence, on the provision of liquidity and on welfare'.[73] When moving from a fixed to a floating NAV model, the investor will lose the insurance provided by sponsor support. All other things held equal that would lead to the fact that the investor will reduce their exposure to MMFs and therefore liquidity will dry up. The new regulation also changes asset prices and fees, and, hence, the risk and the return of investing in an MMF change beyond the loss of insurance, as Parlatore indicates.

The bottom line is that, in the absence of investor-driven runs, the MMF industry might still be fragile. They are prone to sources of fragility different from the typical canonical runs. In this case there might be 'strategic complementarities in the sponsors' support decisions that may give rise to runs of the MMFs on the asset market. These findings are not only relevant for the MMF industry but are applicable in situations in which the absence of recapitalization may lead to the liquidation of assets and, in turn, to fire sales.[74] But in the case of the MMF industry, the implications are widespread. The change of a fixed to a floating NAV will 'affect the risks and returns of intermediation for investors and MMF managers not only directly, but also through the change in equilibrium outcomes such as intermediation fees, the sponsors' support decision, and asset prices'.[75]

While total assets of money market mutual funds contracted from approximately $3.75 trillion at the end of 2008 to about $2.5 trillion in recent years, the focus is still on the 'runnability' of its claims, despite that MMF shares technically do not qualify as debt claims.[76]

---

manager's incentives to offer support. On the other hand, if the manager expects all other managers not to offer support, he expects a low liquidation price for the asset, and high costs of offering support, which may justify him not supporting his fund. The provision of support generates externalities: by providing support to their funds, managers support a high liquidation price of the risky asset and provide liquidity to the economy'.

[72] J. Fisch, and E. Roiter, (2011), A Floating NAV for Money Market Funds: Fix or Fantasy?, Scholarship at Penn Law., Paper Nr. 390.

[73] C. Parlatore, (2014), Ibid. p. 4.

[74] She illustrates: '[a] clear example of this is the banking industry. If there is no recapitalization after a negative shock to the value of banks' assets, banks may be forced to liquidate assets to meet depositor redemptions. This, in turn, would increase the downward pressure on the asset price and, in fact, make recapitalization too costly to be undertaken' (p. 27). The recapitalization plays the role of the sponsor support in the case of the MMF industry.

[75] C. Parlatore, (2014), Ibid. p. 28.

[76] J. Bao, et al., (2015), The Runnables, FEDS Notes, Washington, Board of Governors of the Federal Reserve System, September 3.

10.2 Evolution of the Ongoing MMF Regulation in Europe

It was already discussed that Europe, just like the US and other parts of the world, engaged in enhanced MMF legislation after the crisis, although it took a while. In September 2013 the European Commission issued its initial proposal[77] taking into account the IOSCO 2012 policy recommendations regarding MMFs.[78] The whole idea was to make their position and functioning more resilient.[79]

The Commission proposal for Regulation imposed amongst others the following:

- A requirement on constant net asset value (CNAV) MMFs to have a cash "buffer" equivalent to 3% of their assets
- Binding rules on the types of assets MMFs can invest in
- Limits on how much business MMFs can do with a single counterparty, and restrictions on short selling
- A ban on MMFs to solicit external ratings

The EU Parliament had an impact study[80] done about the impact of those proposed changes and later amendments. That study revealed that the suggested changes would[81]:

- Not imply a substantial take-up of the Retail CNAV or EU Public Debt CNAV. The retail component in European MMF investment is small and likely to remain so. That means that the funds might struggle to be viable, particularly with greater homogeneity in investor behavior (e.g. redemptions at similar times, reflecting similar needs for operational funds). The returns on short-term EU Public Debt are low (the returns on

[77] Proposal for a regulation of the European Parliament and of the Council on Money Market Funds, /* COM/2013/0615 final - 2013/0306 (COD) */ of September 4, 2013.

[78] IOSCO, (2012), Policy Recommendations for Money Market Funds, October 9.

[79] See for the most recent overview of worldwide MMF legislations in place and their evaluation: IOSCO, (2015), Peer Review of Regulation of Money Market Funds; Final Report, FR19/2015, September. The typical evaluation areas are: (1) Scope, (2) Limitations of Assets and Risks accepted, (3) Valuation, (4) Liquidity management, (5) Stable versus floating NAV, (6) Ratings and disclosures and (7) Use of repos and other risk management and hedging tools. See also E.F. Greene and E.L. Broomfields, Promoting Risk Mitigation, not Migration: a Comparative Analysis of Shadow Banking Reforms by the FSB, USA and EU, Capital markets Law Journal, Vol. 8 Nr. 1. They point at a one size fits all kind of trend when tackling the shadow banking market from a regulatory point of view. Schwarcz points at the role of lawyers in this context: S.L. Schwarcz, (2013), Lawyers in the Shadow: The Transactional Lawyer in a World of Shadow Banking, 63 American University Law Review, Nr. 1, Issue 4, pp. 157–172.

[80] See also E. Bengtsson, (2012), Shadow Banking and Financial Stability: European Money Market Funds in the Global Financial Crisis, Working Paper Sveriges Riskbank, Stockholm.

[81] EU Parliament, (2015), Impact Assessment of Substantive EP Amendments, PE 545.547, European Parliamentary Research Service, Research Paper by Europe Economics, March, p. 7.

existing euro-denominated government funds are negative) and, even in the event that rates are higher, there seems to be little appetite for EU Public Debt only funds. The proposed amendments would therefore retain the effect of the Commission's proposals to largely end the use of constant net asset value in the European MMF industry.

- Most of the funds currently invested in European CNAV MMFs would instead be invested in either VNAV MMFs (limited by existing investment policies, tax rules, laws and other restrictions) or bank deposits (limited by the requirements of bank regulation). To some extent, the features that investors value in CNAV MMFs would be replicated in VNAV MMFs. However, that might also mean that any systemic risks associated with CNAV MMFs would also be duplicated in those funds.
- That existing MMF operators have to adjust to managing VNAV MMFs; some corporate issuers see an increase in the cost of short-term debt; and investors may face additional accounting effort in their treasury management operations (this may be severe in some Member States without changes to tax or accounting rules).

The line of thinking is as follows: in order to mitigate the risk of an investor run, the proposal aims at 'improving the liquidity and stability of money market funds'. Liquidity thresholds for 'daily and weekly maturing assets (minimum of 10% and 20% respectively of a fund's portfolio) as well as a requirement to actively monitor the redemption profile of the fund's investors are meant to improve the fund's ability to meet redemption requests'. Moreover, concentration risk in a fund's portfolio is to be contained 'by exposure limits with regard to counterparties and financial instruments'. CNAV funds, which regulators view as particularly prone to runs, will be required to hold 'a cash buffer of at least 3% of total assets in a separate account'. This capital will be 'injected into the fund to maintain the CNAV if the mark-to-market NAV is lower. Beyond this, CNAV funds must not receive any external support in order to prevent contagion via a sponsor'. VNAV funds will only be allowed to receive external (sponsor) support in 'defined exceptional circumstances and with consent of the relevant supervisory authority'. The proposed regulation also calls for less reliance on external credit ratings and obliges funds to clearly state that there is no guarantee investors will always get back in full their invested capital.[82]

Although a step in the good direction toward making MMF portfolios more resilience, the concern is still that instability will spread toward those parties the MMF invests in. Mai explains '[b]ut in case the industry nevertheless experiences a loss of investor confidence, mitigating the risk of an investor run would probably still be difficult. VNAV funds in tight financial conditions might still face accelerated redemption requests, and financial distress might still spread via counterparty or market channels. CNAV funds would be able to draw on a significant 3% capital buffer as a line of defense. However, pairing a CNAV with a capital requirement further blurs the difference between a mutual fund investment and a bank deposit'.[83]

[82] H. Mai, (2015), Money Market Funds – an Economic Perspective, Deutsche Bank Research, February 26, p. 17.

[83] H. Mai, (2015), Ibid. p. 17.

However, the Parliament ECON Committee did not reach a compromise on the initial text. Given the 2014 European elections, works was delayed for a while until the new Parliament was installed and a new ECON Committee was installed.

On February 26, 2015, the new ECON Committee[84] agreed on its position. The main elements of the compromise are as follows:

- CNAV funds would be allowed in two cases only: those with retail investors only (not open for subscription by corporates) and those which invest in EU government debt.
- In addition to this a new category of funds will be created called Low Volatility NAV ('LVNAV') funds, which would also be allowed to show a stable share price. These funds would be allowed to use amortized cost accounting only for assets of maturity up to 90 days.
- For both CNAV funds and LVNAV funds there will be redemption gates and fees.
- External credit ratings would be allowed, contrary to what was originally proposed by the Commission.

During the plenary debate in late April 2015[85] the revised proposal was discussed in the EU Parliament. The following findings and amendments were the result:

- The European Parliament adopted amendments on the proposal for a regulation of the European Parliament and of the Council on Money Market Funds (MMFs). The matter was referred for review to the competent Committee and the vote was postponed to a later meeting.
- Subject matter and scope: money market funds (MMF) provide short-term finance to financial institutions, corporates or governments and thus contribute to the financing of the European economy. For such entities, using their investments in MMFs is an efficient way to spread their credit risk and exposure, rather than relying solely on bank deposits. In the absence of a regulation laying down MMF rules, the Parliament stressed the necessity of adopting a uniform set of rules in order to avoid contagion of the short term funding market and of the sponsors of the MMF, which would put at risk the stability of the Union's financial market. In order to mitigate systemic risk, the amended text provides that the Constant Net Asset Value MMFs (CNAV MMFs) should, from the date of the entry into force of this Regulation, only operate in the Union: as an EU 'public debt CNAV MMF', namely, a CNAV MMF which invests 99.5 % of its assets in public debt instruments and, by 2020, at least 80% of its assets in EU public debt instruments; as Retail CNAV MMFs for small investors, that is, a CNAV MMF that is available for subscription only to charities, non-profit organizations, public authorities and public foundations; or as a 'Low Volatility Net Asset Value Money Market Fund' (LVNAV MMF).

[84] Committee on Economic and Monetary Affairs regarding Proposal 2013/0306(COD): (1) Econ Amendments 472–800 of January 9, 2015, (2) Econ Amendments 224–471 of January 12, 2015, and (3) Econ Amendments 97–223 of January 12, 2015.

[85] Amendments adopted by the European Parliament on April 29, 2015, on the proposal for a regulation of the European Parliament and of the Council on Money Market Funds (COM(2013)0615 – C7-0263/2013–2013/0306(COD)

- Eligible securitizations: the amended test underlines that not all categories of underlying assets have proved to be unstable, including in particular those securitizations where the underlying assets were associated with supporting the working capital of manufacturers and the sales of real economy goods and services. That is why it is proposed that high quality liquid asset-backed securities are deemed to be eligible securitizations. The high-quality liquid asset-backed securities would be deemed eligible if they are liquid in line with Regulation (EU) Nr. 575/2013, and if the underlying exposures have a high credit quality. Within six months following publication of this regulation, the Commission shall adopt delegated acts concerning the specification of the criteria for identifying simple transparent and standardized securitization.
- Specific requirements for Public Debt CNAV MMFs, Retail CNAV MMFs and LVNAV MMFs: the managers of such funds should establish, implement and consistently apply a prudent, rigorous, systematic and continuous internal assessment procedure for determining the weekly liquidity thresholds applicable to the MMFs. In order to be able to mitigate potential client redemptions in times of severe market stress, all the MMFs should have in place provisions for liquidity fees and redemption gates to prevent significant redemptions in times of market stress and to prevent other investors being unfairly exposed to prevailing market conditions: Public Debt CNAV MMFs and Retail CNAV MMFs for small investors should cease to be CNAV MMFs where they cannot meet the minimum amount of weekly liquidity requirements within 30 days of having used the liquidity fees or redemption gates. LVNAV MMFs should only be authorized for a period of five years. The Commission should review the appropriateness of LVNAV MMFs four years after the entry into force of this Regulation. The MMFs should not receive external support on the part of any third party, including the sponsor of the MMF that it is intended for, or would result in, guaranteeing the liquidity of the MMF or stabilizing the NAV per unit or share of the MMF.
- Transparency requirements: in order to develop a transparent and coherent credit assessment procedure, the manager should document the procedures used for the credit assessment. This should ensure that the procedure follows a clear set of rules that can be monitored and that the methodologies employed are communicated upon request to the interested stakeholders, as well as to the competent national authority. Investors should be clearly informed, before they invest in an MMF, if the MMF is of a short-term nature or of a standard nature. In order to avoid misplaced expectations from the investor it must also be clearly stated in any marketing document that MMFs are not a guaranteed investment vehicle. Investors in an MMF should, at least weekly, receive the following information: a) the liquidity profile of the MMF including the cumulative percentage of investments maturing overnight and within one week and how that liquidity is achieved; b) the credit profile and portfolio composition.
- Supervision by the competent authorities: the competent authorities shall supervise compliance with this Regulation on an on-going basis. Authorization of an MMF shall be withdrawn in the event of a breach of the ban on sponsor support.

The implication was that the proposal was sent back to the relevant subcommittee of the EU Parliament. By the end of 2015, not much had moved except for the fact that some details were revealed regarding the reason and nature of the protracted silence in this matter. Luxembourg took over the EU Presidency in July 2015. Luxembourg within the context of the EU is obviously the country that turned the fund industry into an industrialized business model. Luxembourg, Ireland and the UK are home to the largest chunk of constant NAV funds, which would be most prone to intended regulatory changes. Luxembourg is therefore not a particularly neutral party in all this. Claims were made in late 2015 that Luxembourg, with the help of some ally states is looking to water down the reforms intended. The proposal as discussed above and as it stands late 2015 is already a watered-down version compared to the 2013 original.

The proposal intends to create a new category of constant NAV funds. These low-volatility NAV funds face a "sunset clause", which would probably mean they would cease to exist after five years, which is claimed to be unworkable by the industry association. Therefore, Luxembourg is seeking to have the sunset clause removed. It is expected that only in 2016 when the Netherlands takes over the EU Presidency that further progress is expected albeit unsure of what nature, direction and magnitude.[86]

As highlighted further in the European chapter, the MMF proposal was somewhere stuck in limbo as it didn't move since April 2015 any further through the regulatory pipeline. It seems that Luxembourg would like to see some limits applied and some sunset rules removed.[87] It wasn't to be expected with the Dutch Presidency in 2016, that any swift advancement would be realized. See 10.3.2 for the final regulation and discussion.

10.3 Further Regulatory Reforms Related to MMFs

10.3.1 Introduction

The FSB and later on the IOSCO[88] released further recommendations to improve the regulatory model for MMF. In particular the suggestions aimed at enhancing their resilience, in particular to address liquidity/maturity mismatches and improve their ability to cope with large redemptions. The aforementioned IOSCO suggestions became the basis for common standards of regulation and management of MMFs across jurisdictions, including a recommendation that regulators should require, where workable, a conversion of MMFs with stable NAV to floating NAV. Safeguards should further be introduced to reinforce stable NAV MMFs' resilience and ability to face significant redemptions. In 2016 a number of these regulatory proposals came into effect (US and China), later on followed by the EU in 2017.

[86] A. Mooney, (2015), Luxembourg 'Blocking' Money Market Reform, Financial Times, November 29.
[87] A. Mooney, (2015), Luxembourg 'Blocking' Money Market Reform, Financial Times, November 29.
[88] In the period 2011–2012: FSB, (2011), Shadow Banking: Strengthening Oversight and Regulation, October; IOSCO, (2012), Policy Recommendations for Money Market Funds, October

In the US, MMFs qualify as mutual funds. They invest predominantly in corporate debt, government securities and municipal securities. The securities and exchange commission (SEC) adopted amendments to the discussed rule 2a-7[89] (in 2010 and 2014, and later on in 2016). Those amendments forced their prime MMFs to 'float' their NAVs. Institutional prime MMFs are required to value their portfolio securities using market-based factors and to sell and redeem shares based on the floating NAV. Government and retail MMFs are allowed to continue to seek to maintain a stable share price. MMF boards are also allowed to impose liquidity fees or temporarily suspend redemptions. As these rule amendments came into effect, there was a shift of assets from prime MMFs to government MMFs.[90]

Also China regulated their immensely popular MMF market.[91] These measures affected the accounting methods, valuation methods, liquidity management and responsibilities of fund management companies, and required fund managers to adjust the value of constant NAV (CNAV) funds should the fund NAV deviate by more than 0.25% from its stated, stable NAV. Also, the maximum leverage Chinese MMFs are allowed to employ was reduced from 40% to 20%.[92]

Europe introduced their new MMF rules coming into effect July 20, 2017.[93] They introduced uniform prudential, governance and transparency requirements across the region. The rules identify three categories of MMFs: variable NAV (VNAV), public debt CNAV and low volatility NAV (LVNAV) MMFs. Standard MMFs will continue to use variable NAV, while CNAV MMFs will be restricted to holding public debt. The new category of LVNAV MMFs will only be allowed to maintain a constant NAV under strict conditions, notably if the difference with the market NAV does not exceed 20 basis points. CNAV and LVNAV fund managers will have to, when a certain portion of their portfolio falls below a certain threshold, consider or to mandatorily apply liquidity fees or redemption gates, or suspend the fund to address liquidity pressures. Sponsor support of MMFs is prohibited, thus reducing the contagion risk with the rest of the system. Further improvements are strengthening the requirements on eligible

[89] Of the Investment Company Act of 1940. See, for example, O. Akay et al., (2015), Changing Rule 2a-7 and the Risk Profiles of Money Market Mutual Funds, Journal of Applied Finance, Nr. 1, pp. 1–15.

[90] A government MMF is defined as any MMF that invests 99.5% or more of its total assets in cash, government securities and/or repurchase agreements that are collateralized solely by government securities or cash. A retail MMF is defined as an MMF that has policies and procedures reasonably designed to limit all beneficial owners of the MMF to natural persons: see FSB, (2018), Global Shadow banking Monitoring Report 2017, March 5, pp. 21–22, box 2-2.

[91] K. McLoughlin, and J. Meredith, (2017), The Rise of Chinese Money Market Funds, RBA Bulletin, Reserve Bank of Australia, March, pp. 75–84.

[92] People's Bank of China, (2017), China Financial Stability Report 2017, September.

[93] The rules will apply to new funds as of July 21, 2018 and existing funds from January 21, 2019.

assets, liquidity, portfolio diversification, credit assessment and transparency. A common reporting model, standardized stress tests (set by ESMA)[94] and portfolio indicators complete the pack.[95]

Regarding stress tests for investment funds a lot has been said. About the standardization of those tests a lot more. One could state, in general, that stress tests are there to address risks that might adversely impact the collective investment schemes or individual portfolios they manage. A stress test simulates extreme or unfavorable, yet plausible, economic and financial conditions in order to study the consequences on both the performance of a collective investment undertaking or investment mandate and its ability to honor redemption requests, even at a discounted net asset value.[96] Primarily, stress tests are tools that help to analyze the strength of the strategies that have been put in place.[97] The liquidity stress test balances and analyzes redemption shocks and liquidity buffers. If liquidity buffers are not enough to cover the redemption shock, taking into account the liquidation method used by funds' managers, the fund does not 'pass' the stress test and the fund is more likely to trigger fire sales, especially if its portfolio is invested in less liquid securities.[98]

The redemption shock measures the net outflows the fund would be subject to in a severe, but plausible, scenario. The redemption shock is expressed as the net outflows in percentage of Total Net Assets (TNA) of a fund, which can be calibrated using different techniques, the most common being 'the historical approach based on the distribution of net flows and the macroeconomic approach'.[99]

Measuring the liquidity on the asset side of the fund is notoriously more difficult. That is due to data gaps regarding liquidity indicators. Certain assets are not publicly traded (OTC) or in case they are, the bid-ask spread is not necessarily reliable. The methods suggested are the (1) time to liquidation approach (based on aggregated or security-

[94] See ESMA, (2017), Final Report: Technical Advice, Draft Implementing Technical Standards and Guidelines under the MMF Regulation, ESMA34-49-103, November 13. See regarding the practicalities of stress tests for investment funds: A. Bouveret, (2017), Liquidity Stress Tests for Investment Funds: A Practical Guide, IMF Working Paper Series Nr. WP/17/226, October 31. Practical aspects related to the calibration of the redemption shock, the measurement of liquidity buffers and the assessment of the resilience of investment funds are discussed. The integration of liquidity stress tests with banking sector stress tests and possible bank-fund interlinkages are also covered. S. Malik and P. Lindner, (2017), On Swing Pricing and Systemic Risk Mitigation, IMF Working Paper Series Nr. WP/17/159, July.

[95] See FSB, (2018), Global Shadow Banking Monitoring Report 2017, March 5, pp. 22–23.

[96] A quick reminder on the underpinnings of net asset values in the context of MMFs see H.M. Ennis, (2012), Some Theoretical Considerations Regarding Net Asset Values for Money Market Funds, Economic Quarterly, Vol. 98, Nr. 4, Q4, pp. 231–254.

[97] AMF, (2017), The Use of Stress Tests as Part of Risk Management, Guide for asset management companies, Autorité des marchés financiers, February, p. 5. It involves risk mapping, establishing relevant risk factors and design alert mechanisms.

[98] A. Bouveret, (2017), Liquidity Stress Tests for Investment Funds: A Practical Guide, IMF Working Paper Series Nr. WP/17/226, October 31, p. 6.

[99] See for a discussion and case studies: A. Bouveret, (2017), Ibid. pp. 7–12.

by-security data), and (2) grouping securities by liquidity buckets (tiered approach).[100] Once redemption shocks have been calibrated and liquidity buffers estimated, the resilience of investment funds to liquidity shocks can be measured by the Redemption Coverage Ratio (RCR).[101] The RCR measures the ability of funds' liquidity buffers to meet investors' redemptions in the stress scenario.[102] Additionally bank-fund interlinkages should be examined as those linkages can propagate stress in the system.[103]

On numerous occasions throughout the analysis it became clear that money markets funds, although intended as being an alternative to a risk-free investment by far, are not the risk-free instrument as intended. Kacperczyk and Schnabl looked extensively at the risk-taking behavior of MMFs (during the period 2007–2010). They conclude that (1) money market funds experienced an unprecedented expansion in their risk-taking opportunities; (2) funds had strong incentives to take on risk because fund inflows were highly responsive to fund yields; (3) funds sponsored by financial intermediaries with more money fund business took on more risk; and (4) funds suffered runs as a result of their risk taking. This evidence suggests that money market funds 'lack safety because they have strong incentives to take on risk when the opportunity arises and are vulnerable to runs.'[104] Questions can be asked about the MMF regulation and reforms enacted during the last decade. Even with a flexible NAV improper cash management by MMFs can create shareholder (i.e. participant) risks. Cash rebuilding efforts after outflows implies predictable voluntary sales of illiquid assets, thereby generating a decline in NAV. That creates a first-mover advantage, leading to runs even with a flexible NAV.[105] Pro-

[100] The first method uses aggregated data which are not always available or reliable (e.g. dealer inventories or turnover) or rely on security-level data. In this case, sophisticated models are used to estimate the price impact of trades at the individual security level, which can be resource-intensive or expensive, when such a task is outsourced to a third party. Therefore, the emphasis is on the tiered approach, where assets are grouped by liquidity buckets. Within the tiered approach two models are available: (1) the HQLA approach is closely related to the Liquidity Coverage Ratio (LCR) used for banks under Basel III liquidity regulatory requirements, and (2) the cash and short-term debt securities model. Liquidity is measured in the latter by isolating the assets with a residual maturity of less than one year. See for details: A. Bouveret, (2017), Ibid. pp. 12–17.

[101] Liquid Assets/Net Outflows.

[102] A. Bouveret, (2017), Ibid. pp. 17–22.

[103] A. Bouveret, (2017), Ibid. pp. 22 ff. for details, case studies and specifications of channels. Direct channels and indirect channels are envisaged.

[104] M. Kacperczyk and P. Schnabl, (2013), How Safe are Money Market Funds, The Quarterly Journal of Economics, Vol. 128, Issue 3, August 1, pp. 1073–1122. See also regarding the dynamic interactions between investors with differing levels of sophistication within the same money fund and the relationship between observable characteristics and possible tail outcomes (i.e. causing run-like behavior) within intermediated asset pools: L. Schmidt et al., (2016), Runs on Money Market Mutual Funds, American Economic Review, Vol. 106, pp. 2625–2657.

[105] Shareholder runs are essentially driven by a key contractual property of (illiquid) MMFs' NAV: they are flexible but not perfectly forward looking (i.e. they do not take into account the assets sale ex ante a run. See Y. Zeng, (2017), A Dynamic Theory of Mutual Fund Runs and Liquidity Management, ESRB Working Paper Nr. 42, April, pp. 21–30, 35. Also observe the burgeoning literature list on the topic: pp. 36–37.

commitments by the MMF to not rebuild cash buffers[106] after outflows lack credibility in the absence of a 'commitment device'. The conclusion then is that even in the presence of optimal liquidity management, mutual funds are not run-free and (can) lead to high ex ante asset sale losses (or higher in the case of shareholder runs).[107]

When observing both the EU and US legislation enacted in recent years as discussed, we can only observe that this issue remains largely outstanding. After the 2016 changes to the US MMF rules, the MMFs are allowed to use swing prices for their NAV. Those swing prices[108] reflect commissions to asset brokers and dealers, bid-ask spreads, taxes and other trading-related charges. The idea is to reduce the externality from runs imposed by redeeming MMF participants on non-redeeming ones. Unfortunately, swing prices only account for flow-induced price impacts and the NAV reflects that impact. What the NAV however does not reflect is the ex ante future asset sale costs.[109] Rather than swing prices,

---

[106] Mutual funds that internalize more of their price impact hold larger cash buffers and use these buffers more aggressively to accommodate inflows and outflows. As a result, stocks held by these funds have lower volatility, and flows out of these funds have smaller spillover effects on other funds holding the same securities. See S. Chernenko and A. Sunderam, (2020), Do Fire Sales Create Externalities, Journal of Financial Economics, Vol. 135, nr. 4, pp. 602–628.

[107] From a policy point of view that triggers the need to observe the dynamic interdependence of shareholder runs and MMF liquidity management. Ibid. p. 35. Also L. Schmidt et al., (2016), Runs on Money Market Mutual Funds, American Economic Review, Vol. 106, pp. 2625–2657.

[108] See for how swing prices can be best designed to avoid fund failure and increasing redemptions: A. Capponi et al., (2018), Swing Pricing for Mutual Funds: Breaking the Feedback Loop between Fire Sales and Fund Runs, OFR Working Paper Nr. 4, August 28. Properly designed swing pricing transfers liquidation costs from the fund to redeeming investors and, by removing the nonlinearity stemming from the first-mover advantage, it reduces these costs and prevents fund failure. Achieving these objectives requires a larger swing factor at larger levels of outflows. The swing factor for one fund may also depend on policies followed by other funds.

[109] Swing pricing allows a fund to reduce the payout to investors when redemptions are large. This, in principle, discourages investors from selling out at short notice—but little is known about how effective the tool is in practice. Lewrick and Schanz assess the effects of swing pricing by comparing open-end bond funds in Luxembourg, where swing pricing is allowed, with similar funds in the US, where it is not. We find that, during normal times, flows out of Luxembourg funds are less sensitive to bad fund performance than those out of US funds not using swing pricing. This tallies with the expected impact of swing pricing on investor incentives. Yet during periods of market stress, such as the 2013 US taper tantrum, they find no such effect. One possible reason is that funds do not use the tool enough to discourage withdrawals during times of stress. They also show that Luxembourg funds benefited from higher returns during the taper tantrum, as expected, although prices were more volatile. In addition, they find that Luxembourg funds tend to hold less cash than their US counterparts, since swing pricing acts as a substitute for maintaining high reserves. This reduces the stabilizing effect of swing pricing. Swing pricing dampens outflows in reaction to weak fund performance, but has a limited effect during stress episodes. Furthermore, swing pricing supports fund returns, while raising accounting volatility, and may lead to lower cash buffers. See in detail: U. Lewrick and J. Schanz, (2017), Is the Price Right? Swing Pricing and Investor Redemptions, BIS Working Paper Nr. 664, October 11, via bis.org. U. Lewrick and J. Schanz, (2017), Liquidity Risk in markets with Trading Frictions: What Can Swing prices Achieve? BIS Working Paper Nr. 663, October 11, via bis.org. They

forward-looking NAVs reflect that impact.[110] Similar considerations are applicable to the European situation after the 2017 MMF rules were implemented.

The effects of the US regulations (in particular the 2014 changes)[111] regarding MMFs have been documented. Cipriani et al.[112] conclude that:

- In anticipation of the new regulatory framework, investors flowed from prime and muni into government MMFs and especially toward the riskier type of government MMF, agency MMFs, consistent with their likely higher risk appetite profile.
- The flows from prime and muni MMFs into government MMFs mostly occurred within fund families, supporting the hypothesis that the flows were due to the regulatory changes. This contrasts with past outflows from prime and muni MMFs into government MMFs, such as those seen during the 2008 crisis.
- In those situations, investors often left not only their prime and muni fund but also the fund family.
- The outflow from prime and muni MMFs was stronger for institutional investors, consistent with the fact that these investors are more elastic to industry developments and have been subject to a stricter regulation than retail investors.
- As a result of the outflows from prime and muni funds, MMF credit to the private sector has been significantly reduced, whereas credit to government-sponsored enterprises has increased substantially.

---

study how a fund should set the price for investors that want to redeem shares or subscribe to new shares, and how much cash the fund should hold. They find that the best results are achieved if the fund lowers the price when redemptions are large, charging to redeeming investors at least some of the trading costs that the fund incurs. The higher the fund's trading costs, the lower the settlement price. Correspondingly, the fund raises the price if redemptions and trading costs are low or when it experiences inflows. That said, the difference between the optimal settlement price and the market price of the fund's assets remains relatively small. This is to discourage costly arbitrage trades that aim to exploit a large difference between the two prices. The fund should also hold a large enough cash buffer to meet expected redemptions. Reading both their papers together you might conclude that on a theoretical level swing prices can help in easing the risk of runs, but that in practice many obstacles stand between that optimum and realizing it.

[110] Ibid. p. 35. That would however require a change in contract design as MMF participants currently cannot commit to future NAVs. That is currently not possible as MMFs promise to provide daily liquidity to their participants. It would be hard to implement as the rational investor would prefer holding the securities directly in the absence of a daily liquidity promise.

[111] This regulation forces all prime and municipal MMFs to adopt a system of redemption gates and fees and institutional prime and muni MMFs to also operate under a floating NAV. In full, see SEC, (2014), Money Market Fund Reform, Release No. 33-9616, IA-3879; IC-31166; FR-84; File No. S7-03-13 RIN 3235-AK61, October 14, sec.gov.

[112] M. Cipriani et al., (2017), Investors' Appetite for Money-Like Assets: The Money Market Fund Industry after the 2014 Regulatory Reform, Federal Reserve Bank of New York Staff Reports, Nr. 816, June.

10.3.2 The Long-Awaited European MMF Regulation

10.3.2.1 The Difficult Run-Up to the Final Regulation

It took a while (i.e. almost four years after the EC released its first proposal on the matter) but mid-2017 the European MMF regulation saw the daylight. That was a lengthy and painful delivery.

The general changes of the initial proposal relative at that point to the existing MMF situation can be summarized as follows[113]:

- Introducing mandatory conditions on portfolio structure – MMFs would need to hold at least 10% of assets that mature (have to be repaid by the issuer) within a day, and a further 20% that mature within a week.
- Establishing a capital buffer (3% of the assets) for 'constant net asset value' (CNAV) MMFs, which seek to maintain a stable share/unit price (unlike variable NAV MMFs)—this buffer would be used to help ensure stable redemption prices; The 'breaking the buck' originates from MMFs in the US. American MMFs traditionally keep the net asset value at US$1. If the value drops below the $1 NAV level, some of the original investment is depleted and investors will lose money.
- Clear labeling of MMFs, differentiating between short-term and standard kinds; short-term MMFs, which may be either VNAV or CNAV, have residual maturity of less than 397 days.
- Standard MMFs are allowed to invest in longer-term instruments than short-term MMFs. Their residual maturity may not exceed two years. Standard MMFs cannot be CNAV.
- Customer profiling policies to help predict substantial redemptions.
- Internal credit risk assessment by MMF managers, to prevent excessive dependence on external ratings.

Following the initial proposal the EU European Economic and Social Committee adopted its opinion.[114] They recommended (1) that constant net asset value (CNAV) funds are converted into variable net asset value (VNAV) funds and warned that the 3% capital buffer is likely to be insufficient to cope with liquidity demands at a time of stressed market conditions when many investors may seek redemptions simultaneously; (2) recommended introducing robust internal rating measures, reinforcing risk management procedures and safeguards and more stringent oversight.

[113] European Parliament, (2017), Money Market Funds Measures to Improve Stability and Liquidity, Briefing- EU Legislation in Process, July, pp. 3–7.

[114] Opinion of the European Economic and Social Committee on the Proposal for a Regulation of the European Parliament and of the Council on Money Market Funds COM(2013) 615 final—2013/0306 (COD), OJ C 170, 5.6.2014, pp. 50–54.

The legislative process took its time and only in April 2015 the European Parliament voted on its amendments. In short, their amendments included the removal of the obligation to hold a 3% capital buffer for CNAV MMFs and to limit CNAV MMFs to (1) Retail CNAV MMFs, available only for selected investors such as charities, public authorities, and foundations and non-profit organizations; and (2) Public Debt CNAV MMFs (investing 99.5% of their assets in public debt instruments, and, by 2020, at least 80% of their assets in EU public debt instruments)—a new type of Low Volatility Net Asset Value MMFs (LVNAV MMFs may show a constant NAV under strict conditions). Additionally, all MMFs should have in place liquidity fees and redemption gates. Public Debt CNAV MMFs and Retail CNAV MMFs (infra) should cease to be CNAV MMFs if they fail to meet the minimum amount of weekly liquidity requirements within 30 days of having utilized the liquidity fees or redemption gates and should convert to a VNAV MMF or be liquidated. Assets of the MMF need to be valued every day and reported publicly and on a weekly basis to investors based on a pre-defined template model.[115] But the voting didn't go very smoothly and the whole thing was referred to the ECON committee. In June 2016 the ECON Committee agreed on some rules with the EP.[116] The text included negotiated principles with regard to their portfolios and the valuation of their assets, and introduces common standards to boost their liquidity when market conditions are stressed. The new rules introduced a permanent category of LVNAV MMFs, which are to replace most of the existing CNAV MMFs. In December 2016, the negotiations between EC, EP and European Council resulted in an agreement in which it was clarified which liquidity requirements for funds needed to be adhered to: LVNAV and CNAV MMFs will need to invest a minimum 10% portfolio investment in daily maturing assets, and a minimum 30% portfolio investment in weekly maturing assets.[117] Other details were agreed but all will be revisited in the following paragraph as they all made it into the final regulation which was approved by the European Parliament in April 2017.

10.3.2.2 The Final Regulation

The final regulation,[118] which was released on May 16, 2017, will lead to a diversified effect on the industry in terms of its implementation trajectory. It should be noted that the MMF regulation will apply to both the UCITS and the AIF fund models.

---

[115] Commission Implementing Regulation (EU) 2018/708 of April 17, 2018, laying down implementing technical standards with regard to the template to be used by managers of money market funds when reporting to competent authorities as stipulated by Article 37 of Regulation (EU) 2017/1131 of the European Parliament and of the Council, O.J. 119 of May 15, 2018, pp. 5–28.

[116] See EP, (2016), Money Market Funds: Council agrees its Negotiating Stance, Press release, June 15.

[117] See EP, (2016), Money Market Funds: Council Confirms Deal with EP, Press Release, December 7 for further details.

[118] Regulation (EU) 2017/1131 of the European Parliament and of the Council of June 14, 2017, on money market funds, L169/8, O.J. June 30, 2017, pp. 8–45. Further implementing regulations have been taken ever since.

Existing MMFs have until January 21, 2019 to comply whereas newly created MMFs created after July 21, 2018 must comply from inception.[119]

It is fair to say that the incoming regulation doesn't design a totally new MMF framework but only materially adjusts the existing model based on the experiences during the 2007–2009 crisis. The regulation would apply to all MMFs established, managed and/or marketed in the EU and intends to be exhaustive (leaving no room for additional gold-plating at Member State level). Gold-plating can be defined, or better is defined by the EC, as 'transposition of EU legislation, which goes beyond what is required by that legislation, while staying within legality. Member States have large discretion when implementing EU directives. They may increase reporting obligations, add procedural requirements, or apply more rigorous penalty regimes. If not illegal, "gold-plating" is usually presented as a bad practice because it imposes costs that could have been avoided.'[120]

Essentially, the regulation allows for four types of MMFs:

- Public Debt Constant NAV MMFs (Public Debt CNAV MMFs) which invests 99.5% in government securities and maintain a constant NAV.[121] They relate to the former CNAV government short-term MMF. This type of fund will be authorized for a maximum period of five years, but can be re-authorized if the EC confirms continuation of this particular model by then. The technique is known as sunset clause.
- A Low Volatility NAV MMF (LVNAV MMFs) which invests in 'prime' money market fund assets and maintains a constant NAV (within certain boundaries). They replace the CNAV prime previously used.
- Short-term Variable NAV MMF which invests in 'prime' money market fund assets and maintains a variable NAV.
- Standard Variable NAV MMF which invests alongside the short-term variable NAV MMF but invests in assets with long maturities.

The conditions for each category can be found in Table 10.6.

Some further comments should include that[122]:

- For LVNAV MMFs, the 20 basis point threshold (units of an LVNAV MMF are bought and sold at a constant price, unless the constant NAV deviates from the mark to market NAV by more than 20 basis points, in which case units are bought and sold at a price equal to the mark to market NAV) is lower than the existing "break-the-buck" figure of 50 basis points.

[119] See for a full overview of all aspects including post-publication of the main regulation events: Autorité des marches financiers, (2018), Q&A on Money Market Funds. Guide for Asset management Companies, July, Paris.

[120] See in extenso: M. Bocci et al., (2014), 'Gold-Plating' in the EAFRD. To What Extent Do National Rules Unnecessarily Add to Complexity and, as a Result, Increase the Risk of Errors?, European Parliament Policy Department D, Budgetary Affairs, Study, Brussels.

[121] And as of 2020 at least 80% of their assets in EU public debt instruments. That seems largely unrealistic as things stand now.

[122] Matheson, (2018), EU Money Market Fund Reform Finally Published, pp. 4–8; Matheson, (2019), EU Money Market Fund Reform Deadline Set, both via matheson.com

Table 10.6 Overview of new EU MMF categories and conditions

Fund category	Current model	Public Debt CNAV MMF	Low Volatility NAV MMF (LVNAV)	Variable NAV MMF (VNAV)	Standard (VNAV) MMF
Fund type	UCITS short-term CNAV MMF	Short-term MMF	Short-term MMF	Short-term MMF	Standard MMF
NAV dealing	Constant	Constant	Constant NAV, but must use mark-to-market[a] NAV where the constant NAV deviates from mark-to-market NAV by 20 basis points	Variable	Variable
Eligible investment	Money market instruments, overnight deposits, reverse repo, certain securitizations or ABCP, other short-term MMFs	99.5% of portfolio to be invested in public debt securities, reverse repo secured with government securities, and cash currency unrestricted	Money market instruments, securitizations and ABCP, deposits, derivatives, repo, reverse repo, other MMF	Money market instruments, securitizations and ABCP, deposits, derivatives, repo, reverse repo, MMF	Money market instruments, securitizations and ABCP, deposits, derivatives, repo, reverse repo, MMF
WAM/WAL (weighted average maturity/ weighted average life)	60 days/120 days Maturity: 397 days	60 days/120 days Maturity: 397 days	60 days/120 days Maturity: 397 days	60 days/120 days Maturity: 397 days	180 days/365 days Maturity: 397 days
Minimum liquidity	No requirements	30% weekly,[b] includes 10% daily	30% weekly,[c] includes 10% daily	15% weekly, includes 7.5% daily	15% weekly, includes 7.5% daily
Mandatory fees & gates		Apply when weekly liquidity falls below 10%	Apply when weekly liquidity falls below 10%	No	No
Discretionary fees and gates	Technically possible but never used and in most cases not even disclosed	Existing UCITS provisions on fund suspensions apply MMFR extra provisions apply on convergence of 2 events: weekly liquidity drops below 30% and daily net redemptions exceed 10%	Existing UCITS provisions on fund suspensions apply MMFR extra provisions apply on convergence of 2 events: weekly liquidity drops below 30% and daily net redemptions exceed 10%	Existing UCITS provisions on fund suspensions apply	Existing UCITS provisions on fund suspensions apply

Liquid asset restrictions		Minimum 12.5% cash, reverse repo, deposits	Minimum 12.5% cash, reverse repo, deposits	Minimum 7.5% cash, reverse repo, deposits	Minimum 7.5% cash, reverse repo, deposits
		Maximum 17.5% govt. securities to 190 days	Maximum 17.5% govt. securities to 190 days	Maximum 7.5%	Maximum 7.5%
		Other MMF not permitted	Other MMF not permitted	Other MMF	Other MMF
Valuation method	Amortized cost	Amortized cost accounting for all securities	Amortized cost accounting for securities up to 75 days. Securities over 75 days at market/model. Securities more than 10 bp away from market to be valued at market or model	At market or model	At market or model
NAV-rounding		Fund collar – 50 bp rounding (either side)	Fund collar – 20 bp rounding (either side)	N/A	N/A
Fund valuation		To 2 decimal places – €/£/$1.00	To 2 decimal places – €/£/$1.00	To 4 decimal places – €/£/$1.0000	To 4 decimal places – €/£/$1.0000
Shadow NAV calculation		Required: daily "shadow" NAV to be calculated on a per asset M2M basis.	Required: daily "shadow" NAV to be calculated on a per asset M2M basis.	N/A	N/A
Review clause		Regulation reviewed 5 years post implementation	Regulation reviewed 5 years post implementation	Regulation reviewed 5 years post implementation	Regulation reviewed 5 years post implementation
		Review to assess use of alternative product structure and feasibility of establishing 80% EU public debt quota	Review to assess regime for LVNAV product		
Credit rating	Instruments must have one of two highest short-term credit ratings	Internal credit assessment, which can consider but not solely rely on external ratings	Internal credit assessment, which can consider but not solely rely on external ratings	Internal credit assessment, which can consider but not solely rely on external ratings	Internal credit assessment, which can consider but not solely rely on external ratings

(*continued*)

Table 10.6 (continued)

Fund category	Current model	Public Debt CNAV MMF	Low Volatility NAV MMF (LVNAV)	Variable NAV MMF (VNAV)	Standard (VNAV) MMF
Fund type	UCITS short-term CNAV MMF	Short-term MMF	Short-term MMF	Short-term MMF	Standard MMF
In terms of diversification, the following criteria were adopted:					
UCITS short-term CNAV MMF		LVNAV		Public debt NAV	
Money market instruments: UCITS 5/10/40 rules		Money market instruments: 5% per issuer		Money market instruments: N/A	
Government assets: 100%, but at least 6 issues and max 30% per issue		Government assets: 100%, but at least 6 issues and max 30% per issue		Government assets: 100%, but at least 6 issues and max 30% per issue	
Deposits: Max 20% with one institution		Deposits: Max 10% with one institution		Deposits: Max 10% with one institution	
Reverse repo: Max 20% per counterparty		Reverse repo: Max 15% per counterparty		Reverse repo: Max 15% per counterparty	
Reverse repo collateral: Max 20% per issuer (save govt.)		Reverse repo collateral: Max 15% per issuer (save govt.)		Reverse repo collateral: N/A	
Other MMFs: Max 20% in any one		Other MMFs: Max 17.5% total, 5% in any one		Other MMFs: N/A	
Aggregate: Max 20% between money market		Aggregate: Max 15% of money market		Aggregate: N/A	
Instruments, deposits and FDI with a Single body		Instruments, deposits and FDI with a Single body			
Concentration: Max 10% of money market		Concentration: Max 10% of money market		Concentration: N/A	
Instruments of a single issuer		Instruments of a single issuer			

Many charts have been developed following the release of the final regulation. I based mine largely on the one developed by the IMMFA (Institutional Money market Funds Association); see: immfa.org. Also very good is the overview produced by Matheson, (2018), EU Money Market Fund Reform Finally Published, pp. 2–3, which I based Table 10.6 on (adapted)

[a]'Mark-to-Market' and 'Market-to-Model' are used interchangeably in this table both referring to market prices as the prevailing benchmark

[b]Of which 17.5% can be government instruments with residual maturity of <190 days

[c]Of which 17.5% can be government instruments with residual maturity of <190 days

- MMF managers that voluntarily adopt a 30% weekly liquidity requirement often allow themselves to include highly liquid government securities in the calculations, even where their maturities are longer dated.
- The assets in which an MMF can invest have stayed largely unchanged and include money market instruments (high quality and subject to maturity limits); securitizations and ABCPs (subject to liquidity, credit and other limits); deposits (on demand and with a credit institution); repurchase agreements (temporary, only for liquidity management); reverse repurchase agreements (with diversified, high quality, non-correlated collateral); units or shares of other MMFs (pursuant to diversification and concentration limits); and financial derivative instruments (for hedging only, with regulated counterparties, with daily, verifiable valuation and capable of fair value sale at any time). MMFs may not engage in short-selling, securities lending, or may have any direct or indirect exposure to equities or commodities.
- As demonstrated in the table above, the diversification rules are somewhat stricter than under the previous regime.
- The MMF regulation sets out some details regarding the type of information that is used in the internal credit rating assessment. No external credit ratings are allowed; at least that was indicated in the initial proposal. However, the final regulation allows for an external credit rating to be sourced as long as it complies with the Credit Rating Agencies Regulation and the prospectus states that the rating was solicited or financed by the MMF or its manager.
- The MMF manager should provide information on a daily and weekly basis to a variety of stakeholders (maturity breakdown of the portfolio, the MMF's credit profile, the WAM and WAL, the net yield and details of the top ten holdings of the MMF).
- There will be separate regulatory reporting required, which includes details such as the total value of assets, NAV, WAM, WAL, maturity breakdown, liquidity and yield, stress tests results, information on the assets held in the portfolio, information on the liabilities of the MMF and, for LVNAV MMFs, information regarding valuation.
- External support is prohibited. External support refers to step-in risk, that is, an MMF will be prohibited from receiving external support, which is broadly defined to mean direct or indirect support from a third party (including the MMF sponsor) that is intended for or in effect would result in guaranteeing the liquidity of the MMF or stabilizing the NAV per unit or share of the MMF.
- There is a KYC policy to be designed. The idea is not only to understand the investor base but in particular to understand to what extent large redemption can be anticipated. Features looked at are the type of investor, the number of units or shares in the fund owned by a single investor, and the behavior of inflows and outflows, and should look behind nominee accounts or other indirect buyer constructions to reveal the underlying identity of the investors.
- Stress testing is mandatory (see infra in this subchapter), at least twice a year. The tests should seek to identify possible events or future changes in economic conditions that could have unfavorable effects on the MMF and must consider certain required hypothetical factors (such as changes in liquidity levels, credit risk, interest or exchange rates and redemption levels). Guidance is and will be provided by ESMA (infra).

Like any post-crisis MMF regulation its objectives are to ensure that MMFs have a stable structure and improved liquidity, which they invest in diversified assets of a sufficiently high credit quality, and are able to deal with unexpected redemption requests. Before we dive into the details, it can be stated that although the objectives in the US must have been quite the same as in Europe, at the surface the incoming regulation tends to be similar in nature. But when judged at much closer distance the regulation is quite different.[123] As discussed the MMF reform for now ended in the US in October 2016. Since that period over one trillion USD has flown from "prime" funds—that is, funds which invest the majority of their assets in non-government and non-treasury securities—into government-only funds. And there is a reason, in fact reasons, for that: government funds were allowed to retain a stable unit value per share which has been the industry norm for decades. Prime funds moved to a floating unit value per share and therefore are susceptible to price fluctuations. The US introduced rules regarding liquidity fees[124] and redemption gates. The mechanism has been put in place to charge investors for withdrawing money from the fund or even halt temporarily withdrawals altogether in stressed conditions.

Now you could argue that the European regulation could cause similar concerns. However, the European reform foresees a new fund type that is not available in the US. The low volatility net asset value fund (or LVNAV fund) offers investors the combination of 'prime' assets, that is, the ability to buy non-government securities, and an effective stable unit value per share. From an investor point of view that is not all that much different from the existing prime funds in Europe. Judged based on the inflows so far, they evaluate this model as the preferred post-reform model. So, in Europe there is no need to migrate into pure government invested funds unlike the US. The other fact is that Europe has created a much more level-playing field among the different fund models. Fees and gates will also apply to government funds in Europe and that in direct contrast with the US.

Now before providing divine status to these LVNAV funds there are some elements of concern here also:

- LVNAV funds offer a stable unit value per share. These funds however can, under stressed market conditions, convert to a floating or variable unit value per share. To be precise, if the market-to-market price of an LVNAV fund deviates 20 bp away from its stable value, then it is forced to convert to a floating NAV fund. How unlikely it might be, the theoretical option I there. However, it can be assumed that portfolio managers will be even more conservative portfolio practices to avoid a 20 bp disparity.

[123] See in detail: FitchRatings, (2018), European Money Market Fund Handbook, April, pp. 22–23.

[124] Li details that as key lenders in the shadow banking sector, prime money market funds (MMFs) provide funding for banks through various instruments, with maturities up to one year. Post-crisis regulations apply stricter liquidity rules to both MMFs and banks, likely generating contradictory effects, as MMFs are encouraged to do more overnight lending and banks to borrow longer term. She further finds that MMFs and banks seem to resolve this dilemma by developing a 'bundling' strategy across multiple funding markets. In particular, MMFs substantially increase their investments in long-term debt issued by banks that have recently accommodated MMFs' overnight investment needs and charge significantly lower rates on those long-term debts issued by accommodative banks. It has created a strong and reciprocal bond between banks and MMFs. See Y. Li, (2018), Reciprocal Lending Relationships in Shadow Banking, Working Paper, January, mimeo.

- LVNAV funds can also impose gates and fees. European funds, somewhat in contrast to US funds, already pre-reform had a large list of liquidity management tools available. Post-reform it comes down to this: as of a certain threshold the fund's Board of Directors must consider applying fees and/or gates, followed by a second gate after which a fee/gate must be applied. The latter is tied to weekly liquidity. Now weekly liquidity is on average high in European funds relative to European thresholds (almost 40% weekly liquidity)[125] and well above the 10% threshold at which government-only constant net asset value (CNAV) and low volatility net asset value (LVNAV) funds would have to call fees and gates. Also based on historical data it can be concluded that the likelihood of a mandatory imposition of fees or gates is very limited.
- As attractive as they might be, the real appeal will have to come from elsewhere than the fund conditions. The euro-denominated LVNAV fund group and its success will highly depend on the rise in interest rates. In February 2018, the EC released a statement indicating that share cancelation/destruction mechanisms[126] will not be allowed under European money market fund (MMF) reforms.[127] In practical terms that means that these LVNAV funds will not be viable unless short-term Euro interest rates turn positive.[128] To be precise '[g]iven low euro interest rates, euro-denominated constant net asset value (CNAV) MMFs routinely apply share cancelation to maintain a stable net asset value per share, an important feature for many investors. Most providers thought they would convert their CNAV funds to the new LVNAV fund category being introduced by the reforms, and saw LVNAV funds as central to their post-reform product line-up. But the launch of euro LVNAV funds is now in doubt unless short-term rates rise to the extent that such funds could sustainably deliver positive yields and thus avoid need to apply share cancellations.'[129]

[125] FitchRatings, (2018), European Money Market Handbook, April, p. 24.

[126] Many (euro-denominated) MMFs apply share cancellation mechanisms to maintain a stable net asset value per share while passing negative market yields to investors, Ibid. P. 9. The ESMA commented on this specific point already in 2017 following the approval of the new regulation: ESMA, (2017), Final Report Technical Advice, Draft Implementing Technical Standards and Guidelines under the MMF Regulation, November 13, p. 6.

[127] J. Thompson, (2018), Brussels Rules Out Share-Cancellation Mechanism for Money Market Funds, Financial Times FTfm, August 1. See the EC letter: EC, (2018), Implementation of the Money Market Fund Regulation, January 19. The argument is effectively the other way around. Since the reversed distribution is not mentioned in the MMF regulation, the EC argued, in line with the ESMA on the matter, that the reversed distribution mechanism cannot legally comply with the regulation. That is rather strange as it doesn't clarify the position of the MMF regulation, but only concludes that it cannot go hand in hand with the regulation that stays silent on the matter. Seems more a matter of hasty work.

[128] FitchRatings, (2018), European Money Market Handbook, April, p. 8. For MMF funds of this type in other currencies there seems to be no immediate issue.

[129] Ibid. p. 8.

On July 13, 2018, the Commission Delegated Regulation (EU) 2018/990 of April 10, 2018, amending and supplementing Regulation (EU) 2017/1131 of the European Parliament and of the Council with regard to simple transparent and standardized (STS) securitizations and asset-backed commercial papers, requirements for assets received as part of reverse repurchase agreements and credit quality assessment methodologies was published in the Official Journal of the EU (OJ).[130]It basically re-affirms all technical details displayed and reviewed in the aforementioned November 2017 ESMA report.

The next feature to look forward to is the question how the MMFs under the new regulation should conduct their stress tests.[131,132] I will not discuss the proposed stress testing scenarios in detail. I will limit the discussion here to indicating the important items to work with within the context of an MMF stress test: (1) changes in the liquidity of assets held in the portfolio of an MMF; (2) changes in the level of credit risk of the assets held in the portfolio of the MMF; (3) Movement of interest rates and exchange rates; (4) (hypothetical) level of redemptions; (5) (hypothetical) macro-systemic shocks affecting the economy in general; and (6) spread changes of indexes to which interest rates of portfolio securities are tied.

Maybe a final word on the impact of unconventional monetary policy and MMFs. Money market funds are important from a monetary policy perspective because they provide bank-like services and they are active in short-term funding markets. Bua and Dunne document that extreme monetary policy puts money market funds, which do not have access to the ECB's deposit facility, under pressure by depressing the yields available on the assets they typically hold, leaving them at a competitive disadvantage relative to banks. This could cause outflows of investment and unintended intermediation between banks and funds.[133]

---

[130] OJ L 177, 13.7.2018, pp. 1–8.

[131] H. Mai, (2017), New EU Money Market Fund Regulation: Will Growth Continue?, DB research, September 13.

[132] The base document is the ESMA, (2018), Guidelines on Stress Test Scenarios Under Article 28 of the MMF Regulation, which puts out the parameters. The ESMA put the process further in motion with a consultation paper on the matter: ESMA, (2018), Consultation Paper, Draft Guidelines on Stress Test Scenarios under the MMF Regulation, September 28, in which it became more specific on the variables and proposed some adjustments. Also ESMA, (2019), Consultation Paper, Draft Guidance regarding Liquidity Stress Tests of Investment Funds – applicable to alternative investment funds (AIFs) and Undertakings for the Collective Investment in Transferable Securities (UCITS), February 5, via esma.europe.eu. Preferably to be read in conjunction with the final guidelines of IOSCO on the matter: IOSCO, (2018), Recommendations for Liquidity Risk Management for Collective Investment Schemes, Report FR01/2018, February 1, via iosco.org.(see also chapter 7, Vol. 2)

[133] G. Bua and P.G. Dunne, (2019), Monetary Policy and Money Market Funds, via voxeu.org, June 26. Also M. Di Maggio, and M. Kacperczyk, (2017), The Unintended Consequences of the Zero Lower Bound Policy, Journal of Financial Economics, Vol. 123, pp. 59–80.

11

Taxing (Shadow) Banks: A Pigovian Model

11.1 Introduction

In this chapter[1] I will be exploring the application of Pigovian theory to the financial industry that is known for its many particularities. What I have tried to embody is to set off the Pigovian model against the existing corporate income tax covering financial institutions (FIs), pretty much like the rest of the corporate entities. The Pigovian model is just under 100 years old and emerged during the later part and the aftermath of the second industrial revolution. That is not surprising as the second industrial revolution made production processes more efficient and output as a consequence to rise materially. The Pigovian model, embedded in welfare economics, responded to that.[2] Its basic proposition is to charge those activities that create 'negative externalities', that is, those activities that harm a third party[3] (i.e. not one of the parties involved in the transaction that caused the negative externality). A negative externality occurs when the cost structure and framework for measuring the economic cost of a transaction or activity doesn't include all costs associated with that transaction or activity and often only includes the direct economic costs. A typical example is the environmental cost of pollution. Not surprisingly Arthur Pigou, the

[1] The original but condensed version of this chapter appeared in L. Nijs, (2015), Neoliberalism 2.0. Regulating and Financing Globalizing Markets, Palgrave, Basingstoke, pp. 251–324. This chapter constitutes an extended and updated version.

[2] There are those that argue shadow banking provides a channel for banks with efficient investment opportunities to escape regulation such that, even though involving higher risks, it improves welfare. Ordoñez proposes a novel intervention that taxes shadow activities and subsidizes regulated activities to implement an even superior allocation and allow banks to self-select into being regulated or not. See: G. Ordoñez, (2018), Sustainable Shadow Banking, American Economic Journal: Macroeconomics, Vol. 10, Nr. 1, January, pp. 33–56; A. Moreira and A. Savov, (2017), The Macroeconomics of Shadow Banking, The Journal of Finance, Vol. 72, Issue 6, pp. 2381–2432.

[3] It impacts the welfare of that agent.

L. Nijs, *The Handbook of Global Shadow Banking, Volume I*,
https://doi.org/10.1007/978-3-030-34743-7_11

British economist after whom the Pigovian tax model is named, came up with this once the implications of the second industrial revolution became clear.[4] To offset those ignored costs, he introduced the Pigovian surcharge that would lead to a rebalancing of demand and supply for a certain good or service but taking into account those negative externalities. A new Pareto optimum or equilibrium would be generated.[5] Much has been said about the Pigovian model and it had to withstand many harsh reviews and critiques.[6] One of the most persistent critiques is the fact that a Pigovian surcharge neutralizes its own taxable base. Despite all the controversy, the Pigovian model is often used, sometimes in an altered format, in many areas.[7] And that is no surprise given that the number of externalities is on the rise. Also in the financial sector, often caused by deregulation and/or complex and un-transparent financial legislation and regulatory arbitrage.[8]

---

[4] I. Kumekawa, (2017), The First Serious Optimist: A.C. Pigou and the Birth of Welfare Economics, Princeton University Press, Princeton NJ. Pigou is also seen as the birthfather of welfare economics as he believed in the consensus of the great and the good; see the book review by H. James, (2017), The Crusty Professor, IMF Journal 'Finance & Development, June, p. 59. In contrast to that he also seems to be known in a late-Victorian tradition for misogyny and his belief of the inferiority of women; see for a somewhat accommodating review: N. Aslanbeigiu, (1997), Rethinking Pigou's Misogyny, Eastern Economic Journal, Vol. 23, Issue 3, pp. 301–316.

[5] Recently, it has been argued that the Pareto optimum cannot always be achieved through a compensation mechanism. Precise targeting of compensating transfers, however, may not be possible when agents are heterogeneous and the planner faces constraints on the design of transfers. Compensation is a prediction problem. Therefore Sallee derives a necessary condition for an efficiency-enhancing policy to create a Pareto improvement that can be tested directly with data. The condition relates the size of efficiency gains to the degree of predictability between initial burdens and variables used to determine a transfer scheme. He further demonstrates how heterogeneity and predictability more generally impact a planner's ability to control who ultimately loses and by how much and at what cost. Results indicate that it is infeasible to create a Pareto improvement from the taxation of these goods (which refers in his case to gasoline taxes), and moreover that plausible policies are likely to leave a large fraction of households (and other agents) as net losers. It is highlighted here for reasons of completeness, but as the problem doesn't affect the relevance of a Pigovian model in the case of financial services and systemic risk, it will not be discussed further in detail. See in detail: J.M. Sallee, (2019), Pigou Creates Losers: On the Implausibility of Achieving Pareto Improvements from Efficiency-Enhancing Policies, NBER Working paper Nr. 25831, May.

[6] See for an extensive review of the Pigovian model: L. Nijs, (2015), Neoliberalism 2.0. Regulating and Financing Globalizing Markets, Palgrave, Basingstoke, pp. 156–219.

[7] It is easy to understand legitimation of the tax function. Tax simplicity has many benefits; see: Ph. Aghion et al., (2017), Tax Simplicity and Heterogeneous Learning, NBER Working paper Nr. 24049, November.

[8] See, for instance, H. Nabilou, (2017), Regulatory Arbitrage and Hedge Fund Regulation: The Need for a Transnational Response, Fordham Journal of Corporate & Financial Law, Vol. 22, Nr. 4, pp. 557–603; M. Laura and N. Fahad, (2017), Would Hedge Fund Regulation Mitigate Systemic Risk? Direct vs. Indirect Regulation Approach, International Business Research, Vol. 10, Issue 8, pp. 31–43; B. Munyan, (2015), Regulatory Arbitrage in Repo Markets, OFR Working Paper Nr. 15–22, October 29. He tested and concluded that about 170 Billion USD are temporarily removed from the US market for tri-party repurchase agreements (repos) before each quarter-end in order to appear safer and less levered. This occurred particularly in banks with relatively low capital ratios. Also: EBI, (2017), Shadow Banking and Systemic Risk, EBI Working Paper Nr. 1. See regarding

I will apply it in a twenty-first-century context to the financial industry, both the regulated and shadow banking industry. So despite all the critiques, I will demonstrate that the Pigovian model can be used to neutralize the externalities created by the financial sector, but also that the Pigovian model is the preferred model vis-à-vis other options available, that is, command-and-control regulation, normal corporate income tax models that have, as will be demonstrated, fueled the financial crisis of 2008, and quantity regulation which has its intrinsic difficulties when being applied. The Pigovian model is superior from a regulatory efficiency point of view to any other option available and the fact that it is not used abundantly is for a range of political and symbolic reasons.[9]

The financial industry itself has become the poster child for everything that resembles globalization, that is, interconnectedness and the risks that it produces, increased competitiveness and an industry that is constantly fueled by innovations of all sorts.[10] It has also received lots of attention from regulators. In that sense, the financial industry is a typical 'command-and-control'-regulated type of industry. That in itself makes sense. The financial industry is a private industry but to a large degree it exercises a public function: that of managing deposits and subsequently the effective functioning of the credit intermediation process between the demand and supply of capital in the real economy.[11] Not surprisingly, regulators in the different countries, and in more recent decades the EU, have been concerned about the trade-off between the private interest of share- and bondholders in banks on the one hand and the public interest of credit intermediation and deposit management on the other.

A good starting point for this chapter would be a short review of the current regulatory framework that financial institutions (FIs) are subject to, at least to a degree that will facilitate the later discussion about the application of Pigovian taxes in a regional context. That would undeniably have to include the wave of deregulation that the industry has known

the link between foreign investments and regulatory arbitrage: W.S. Frame et al., (2017), Foreign Investment, Regulatory Arbitrage, and the Risk of U.S. Banking Organizations, Federal Reserve Bank of Atlanta Working Paper Nr. 2, March. It was documented that 'U.S. BHCs are more likely to operate subsidiaries in countries with weaker regulation and supervision and that such location decisions are associated with elevated BHC risk and higher contribution to systemic risk.'

[9] Also pointing in that direction: J. Masur and E.A. Posner, (2015), Towards a Pigovian State, University of Chicago Public law and Legal Theory Working Paper, Nr. 503, February. Masur and Pozner indicate that the principal reason regulators do not employ Pigovian taxes is that they do not believe they have the authority to do so under existing law and that Pigovian taxes may lack political support because they do not serve the interests of those with political power (pp. 3–4). They demonstrate in a variety of industries and regulatory fields that a Pigovian model would be feasible or even preferable (pp. 11 ff). But regulators refrain from using them as taxes tend to have a negative connotation and that the divide between regulation and taxes is firmly entrenched in Western public institutional organizations (pp. 31 ff). See for their take on Pigovian taxes and the financial industry (pp. 21 ff).

[10] See, for instance, M. Raddant and D.Y. Knett, (2016), Interconnectedness in the Global Financial Market, OFR Working Paper Nr. 16-09, September 27.

[11] See for a write-up of the process of credit intermediation in the shadow banking system taking explicit account of traditional banks' role as creators of means of payment. See in detail R. Unger, (2016), Traditional Banks, Shadow Banks and the US Credit Boom – Credit Origination Versus Financing, Deutsche Bundesbank Discussion Paper Nr. 11, Frankfurt.

since the 1980s and the neoliberal impact on the industry. Following that we can embark on the exercise of dissecting the true causes of instability for which the industry is known and how a Pigovian model would be applied in such a cross-border environment and with potentially material and devastating spillover effects in other (EU) countries.[12] The potential externalities will be discussed and a Pigovian treatment suggested arriving at a holistic Pigovian instrument for the financial industry. It will be offset against the existing bank-specific type of taxes implemented and/or suggested in the EU and beyond, often and incorrectly under the denominator of Pigovian taxes.

It will also allow us to evaluate the trade-off and opportunity choices to be made between a Pigovian tax model versus a command-and-control type of regulatory framework and a type of quantity regulation if imaginable for the FI sector. One of the general lessons to be learned from the 2008 crisis (and often not sufficiently highlighted) is that risk management in the FI is not and should not be a one-dimensional bottom-up process as the current regulatory framework envisages. It should at least include a top-down macroprudential analysis of the level of systemic risk contained in the FI,[13] which in the FI context is evidently cross-border in nature. Surprisingly enough it was only a number of years after the 2008 crisis that the externalities caused (or that could be caused) by the FI were qualified as such and a Pigovian approach emerged in the scholarly literature. Having said that, the Pigovian approach toward externalities in the financial industry and the body of literature is still very nascent, scattered and even somewhat embryonic on a conceptual basis. This is my attempt to take things for-

[12] See also: J. Ohis et al., (2016), International Banking and Cross-Border Effects of Regulation, Deutsche Bundesbank Discussion Paper Nr. 27, Frankfurt am Main. Their focus is on the responses to the regulatory framework actually implemented including prudential instruments and the quest for regulatory arbitrage and shifting of activities following ex ante directional regulation being implemented. So, the question being asked is how prudential policies implemented in domestic and foreign markets affect (German) banks' local and global lending behavior. They conclude that spillover effects exist but with heterogeneous results depending on the direction of spillovers, the type of banks and prudential instruments, that is, more local loan supply as a response to stricter regulation in countries in which they maintain international activities. In contrast, foreign banks (located in Germany) reduce their loan supply (in Germany) if regulation in their home country tightens. This suggests that no general policy conclusions can be drawn and piecemeal analysis is required. For alternatives: M. Bussière et al., (2016), International Banking and Cross-Border Effects of Regulation: Lessons from France, Banque de France Working Paper Nr. 599, August and O. de Bandt and M. Chahad, (2016), A DSGE Model to Assess the Post-Crisis Regulation of Universal Banks, banque de France Working Paper Nr. 602, September; J. Berrospide et al., (2016), International Banking and Cross-Border Effects of Regulation: Lessons from the United States, Board of Governors of the Federal Reserve System, International Finance Discussion Papers Nr. 1180, September. Domestic prudential regulation can have unintended effects across borders as it shifts capital allocation; H.E. Damar and A. Mordel, (2016), International Banking and Cross-Border Effects of Regulation: Lessons from Canada, Bank of Canada Working Paper Nr. 34, July; J. Frost et al., (2016), International Banking and Cross-Border Effects of Regulation: Lessons from the Netherlands, DNB Working Paper Nr. 520, September; K. Ho et al., (2016), International Banking and Cross-Border Effects of Regulation: Lessons from Hong Kong, HKIMR Working Paper Nr. 12, July.

[13] R. Engle et al., (2015), Global Systemic Risk: What's Driving the Shadow Banking System?, Institute of Global Finance Volume 1. Nr. 1, Research Paper Nr. 1, July.

ward and suggest a holistic Pigovian approach to the financial industry taking into account the many intricacies, many of which remain underexposed.

Throughout the analysis, it has been observed that scholarly involvement in the matter, which is true for the Pigovian area in general, is still largely dominated by the economics and public finance domain. The debate could benefit greatly from the involvement of both the academic and professional law societies in the different (EU) countries, which now unnecessarily restrict themselves to the analysis of and commenting on positive law as it is. It is their contribution that could help tremendously in making a huge leap forward in converting the conceptual economic analysis and application of Pigovian theory to new areas and externalities into effective, meaningful and robust regulation. It would enable the incorporation of real-world industry data into generally applicable legislation and reclaim some of the legal domain that the Pigovian sphere has been lacking and which could account for the limited attention it has received in recent decades.

As highlighted before, the 'too big to fail' adage characterizing the financial industry reveals the actual 'too complex to regulate' adage pointing more harshly to the Mexican stand-off between the financial industry and the command-and-control legislation to which it is increasingly subject to. Until now the regulatory dice have landed in favor of the financial industry[14] and the situation has led to the unsatisfying conclusion that the trade-off I pointed out some years ago[15] has ended on the wrong side of the fence. A reversal of this admission of defeat will however require a new paradigm in which the Pigovian approach can be materially instrumental when building a robust regulatory framework. It can further answer (at least part of) the conundrum I posed some years ago: Is it possible to create a sound, robust and healthy financial industry without it being to the detriment of the real economy and can we create a robust and healthy real economy without systematically massaging the financial sector out of the capitalist economic framework?

11.2 The Financial Sector and Its Regulatory Straitjacket

It was well understood, even in the 1980s, that the financial sector was exposed to a variety of endogenous and exogenous risks. In 1988 the Bank for International Settlements ('BIS'), based on that understanding, developed its first set of Basel rules (Basel I),[16] which then were implemented in national laws despite the fact that the Basel recommendations are only soft law.[17] Soft law is characterized by three distinct elements. First, the concept refers to

---

[14] Ph. Stevens, (2014), Nothing Can Dent the Divine Right of Bankers, Financial Times, January 16.

[15] L. Nijs, (2011), Shaping Tomorrow's Marketplace. Investment Philosophies for Emerging Markets and a Semi-Globalized World, Euromoney, London, pp. 145–159.

[16] See for an evolution of the regulatory capital requirements starting Basel I: M.C. Plossner and J.A.C. Santos, (2018), The Cost of bank Regulatory Capital, FRB of NY Staff Report Nr. 853, June.

[17] Schwarcz indicates that the lack of enforceability creates uncertainty and undermining predictability. He suggests that soft law can be 'chosen' as the governing law between contracting parties. See in detail: S.L. Schwarcz, (2019), Soft Law as Governing Law Duke Law School Public Law & Legal Theory Series Paper Nr. 2019-8, January 29.

'rules of conduct' or 'commitments'. The second element is that these rules or commitments are laid down in instruments which have no legally binding force (they are not directly enforceable) as such. Although soft law lacks the possibility of legal sanctions, it may nevertheless produce indirect legal effects.[18] Third, rules of soft law aim at, and may lead to, some practical effect or impact on behavior.[19] Senden therefore proposes the following definition of soft law: '[r]ules of conduct that are laid down in instruments which have not been attributed legally binding force as such, but nevertheless may have certain indirect legal effects, and that are aimed at and may produce practical effects'.[20]

The Basel I framework was mainly concerned with credit risk and the variation of credit risk among the different types of investment that an FI typically engages in.[21] It therefore modeled the capital requirements of a bank,[22] which was put in place to absorb the risk in the event of default on a loan, in line with the creditworthiness of the assets of the bank (i.e. the loans the bank has outstanding). The rules created five categories with different risk weightings and therefore different capital requirements.[23] Those capital requirements are imposed by the regulator to avoid that banks do not internalize the social cost of

[18] See for an analysis: E. Lee, (2014), The Soft law Nature of Basel III and International Financial Regulations, University of Hong Kong Working Paper, Mimeo.

[19] H. Gribnau, (2007), Soft Law and Taxation: The Case for the Netherlands, Legisprudence, Vol. 1, Issue 3, pp. 296–297. See also H. Gribnau, (2008), Soft Law and Taxation: EU and International Aspects, Legisprudence, Vol. 2, Issue 2, pp. 67–117.

[20] L. Senden, (2005), Soft Law, Self-Regulation and Co-Regulation in European Law: Where Do They Meet? Electronic Journal of Comparative Law, Vol. 9, p. 17. See in detail regarding soft law: U Mörth (ed.), (2004), Soft Law in Governance and Regulation: An Interdisciplinary Analysis, Edward Elgar Publishing, Cheltenham.

[21] Economic uncertainty and risk appetite appear to play a limited role in explaining ex ante credit risk. There is much more evidence of cross-border spillover effects of monetary policy, that is, interest rate policy determines risk-taking in the credit market. See: S.J. Lee et al., (2016), Risk Taking and Interest Rates: Evidence from Decades in the Global Syndicated Loan Market, IMF Working Paper Nr. 17/16, January.

[22] Also D. Corbae and P. D'Erasmo, (2019), Capital Requirements in a Quantitative Model of banking Industry Dynamics, NBER Working Paper Nr. 25424, January. They find that regulatory policies can have an important impact on market structure in the banking industry, which, along with selection effects, can generate changes in allocative efficiency.

[23] They carried weights of 0% (e.g. cash, bullion, home country debt like Treasuries), 20% (securitizations such as mortgage-backed securities [MBS] with the highest AAA) rating 50%, and 100% (e.g. most corporate debt), with some assets given 'No rating'. Banks with an international presence were required to hold capital equal to 8% of their risk-weighted assets (RWA). The 0% capital charge against Treasuries implies that a sudden increase in sovereign default risk may lead to liquidity issues in the banking sector and that capital requirements for government bonds increase the shock-absorbing capacity of the banking sector and thus the financial stability. See in detail: U. Neyer and A. Sterzel, (2017), Capital Requirements for Government Bonds. Implications for Bank Behaviour and Financial Stability, Düsseldorf University Press Working Paper Nr. 275, December. Bank capital charges trigger a different composition of credit on the balance sheet of

default,[24] which in turn would impact their lending decision. The regulator sets a capital requirement to trade off expected output against financial stability. However, the capital requirement that ensures investment efficiency depends on the state of the economy. Because of the general equilibrium effect, the more aggregate banking capital the tighter the optimal requirement. A regulation that fails to take this effect into account exacerbates economic fluctuations and allows for excessive build-up of risk in the financial sector

---

banks. Even increases in capital ratio requirements can locally increase banks' riskiness, due to the complexity of compositional changes, and the relations between prices and regulatory risk weights, and between interest rate pass-through and bank capital scarcity. See in detail: M. Harris et al., (2017), Bank Capital and the Composition of Credit, Working Paper, September 20, mimeo. On the other hand, there is evidence that higher capital requirements can increase bank lending. Government guarantees generate an implicit subsidy for banks. Even though a capital requirement reduces this subsidy, a bank may optimally respond to a higher capital requirement by increasing lending. This requires that the marginal loan generates positive residual cash flows. Since an increase in the capital requirement makes the bank safer, it makes the shareholders internalize such cash flows, known as the 'forced safety effect'. See in detail: S. Bahaj and F. Malherbe, (2018), The Forced Safety Effect: How Higher Capital Requirements Can Increase Bank Lending, Working Paper, July 3, mimeo; higher capital requirements make secured lending more attractive vis-à-vis unsecured lending for the affected banks as secured loans require less regulatory capital. See: H. Degryse et al., (2018), To Ask or Not to Ask? Collateral versus Screening in Lending Relationships, Bank of Portugal Working Paper Nr. 19, Lisbon.

[24] Capital requirements also have a dampening effect on the transmission of risk to the market and the cost of funding. See: A. Galiay and L. Maurin, (2015), Drivers of banks' Cost of debt and Long-Term Benefits of Regulation- An Empirical Analysis Based on EU Banks, ECB Working Paper Series, Nr. 1849, September. See regarding the cyclicality of Capital Requirements: EBA, (2016), Cyclicality of Capital Requirements, EBA-Op-2016-24, December 22. They also have an effect on lending behavior by banks. See for details: H. Fraisse et al., (2017), The Real Effects of Bank Capital Requirements, ESRB Paper Nr. 47, June. Similar results have been observed following the introduction of the Basel III capital and liquidity requirements. See in detail: S.B. Naceur and C. Roulet, (2017), Basel III and Bank-Lending: Evidence from the United States and Europe, IMF Working Paper Nr. WP/17/245, November. Liquidity requirements tend to have a positive effect on lending behavior, but variations exist when comparing US and European effects. Naceur and Roulet further conclude that the ability of a bank to originate credit opportunities determines how they deal with the aforementioned requirements. Under circumstances they become ineffective or even detrimental. See also: R. De Young and K.Y. Yang, (2016), Do Banks Actively Manage their Liquidity, Journal for Banking and Finance, Vol. 66, PP.143–161; P.H. Kupiec et al., (2017), Does Bank Supervision Impact Bank Loan Growth?, Journal of Financial Stability, Vol. 28, pp. 21–48. Shan studied the relationship between credit risk in bank loan portfolios and systemic risk. Shan found that systemically risky banks originate new loans with greater default risk exposure even after controlling for self-selection of lenders by borrowers. See in detail: Y. Shan, (2017), Systemic Risk and Credit Risk in bank Loan Portfolios, Working Paper, November 3. Systemically risky banks take higher (lower) share allocations in loans borrowed by risky (safe) borrowers. This confirms the previous findings and indicates that the positive relationship between systemic risk and credit risk-taking is at least partially driven by supply-side factors. See also: Y. Shan, (2018), Systemic Risk, Credit Risk, and the Effect of managerial Style in Syndicated Bank Loans, Working Paper, January 13.

during booms. Government guarantees[25] amplify this mechanism and, at the peak of a boom, even a small adverse shock can trigger a banking sector collapse.[26]

More than a decade later, when globalization had moved into a higher gear, the next generation Basel rules (Basel II) were implemented (2004). Unlike Basel I, Basel II was intended to create an international standard for banking regulators to control how much capital banks need to put aside to guard against the types of financial and operational risks that they (and the whole economy) face. One focus was to maintain sufficient consistency of regulations so that this does not become a source of competitive inequality amongst

---

[25] See also: F. Allen et al., (2017), Government Guarantees and Financial Stability, ECB Working Paper Nr. 2032, February. Guarantees are welfare improving because they induce banks to improve liquidity provision although in a way that sometimes increases the likelihood of runs or creates distortions in banks' behavior. They further raise questions such as [a]re guarantees effective in preventing banking crises? What are the implications they have for banks' role as liquidity providers and their risk-taking decisions? How do guarantees affect the interaction between liquidity provision and risk-taking? They build their model along the two-risk/crisis model for banks: insolvency risk and liquidity risk. They conclude that 'the probability of both crises is endogenous and depends on the banks' risk choice, as well as on the (type and size of) government guarantees.' They assume two types of guarantees: a minimum repayment for depositors, so that panic-driven bank runs are mitigated and the standard deposit insurance scheme. The effect of the guarantees on the probability of a crisis is twofold: '[o]n the one hand, guarantees have a positive direct effect, since, by increasing depositors' repayments, they reduce their incentive to withdraw early and thus, banks' exposure to liquidity risk. On the other hand, they affect banks' risk-taking decisions and, thus have a negative indirect effect on the probability of a banking crisis.' (pp. 2–3). Also the direction in bank' behaviors (moral hazard) due to the availability of guarantees was discussed. The guarantees avoid the need by banks to internalize externality costs as 'the introduction of guarantees creates a wedge between the deposit rate chosen by banks and the one that the government would like to choose.' However, Allen et al. create a caveat indicating that guarantees do not always lead to excessive risk-taking and therefore increased run sensitivity. Sometimes banks behave the opposite way, that is, in the direction of a social optimum and get exposure to less risk. Whether a bank behaves one way or the other depends on the mechanics of the guarantee. They comment '[t]he important detail is whether the government ends up paying depositors more in the case the bank ends up failing in the longer term for fundamental reasons or in case there is a run and the bank faces a shortage of liquidity. If the former holds, then the cost of a run from the point of view of banks is higher than from the point of the government and the banks choose to limit their exposure to run.' (p. 3)

[26] See in detail: F. Malherbe, (2015), Optimal Capital Requirements over the Business and Financial Cycles, ECB Working Paper, Nr. 1830, July. It requires a bit more context 'On the one hand, more bank capital means that the banking sector can absorb more losses, which suggests that the banking sector could expand. But, on the other hand, there is a general equilibrium effect that dominates the loss absorbing effect. To see the intuition behind the general equilibrium effect, first consider a single (atomistic) bank that doubles its equity base. It should simply be allowed to double the size of its assets. However, if all banks in the economy double their equity base, and if they are allowed to double the size of their assets, this could double aggregate lending in the economy. Given diminishing returns to capital on the real side of the economy and given that banks have incentives to take on too much risk, this will decrease marginal returns to an extent that is far from optimal. In fact, the optimal policy is to let the banking sector expand, but less than proportionally, which corresponds to an increase in capital requirements and resonates with the notion of counter-cyclical capital buffers of Basel' (p. 3). Overlooking this effect will lead to an exacerbation of economic fluctuations and enhanced systemic risk.

internationally active banks. Basel II attempted to accomplish this by setting up risk and capital management requirements designed to ensure that a bank has adequate capital for the risk that the bank exposes itself to through its lending and investment practices. Generally speaking, these rules mean that the greater the risk to which the bank is exposed, the greater the amount of capital the bank needs to hold to safeguard its solvency and overall economic stability.[27]

It did so through three pillars of risk management: (1) Maintenance of (minimum) regulatory capital[28] based on the assessment not only of credit risk (as was the case in Basel I), but also operational risk[29] (caused by people, processes and systems in the financial

[27] The four objectives of Basel II were: (1) ensuring that capital allocation is more risk sensitive, (2) enhanced disclosure requirements which will allow market participants to assess the capital adequacy of an institution, (3) ensure that credit risk, operational risk and market risk are quantified based on data and formal techniques and (4) an attempt to align economic and regulatory capital more closely to reduce the scope for regulatory arbitrage. Regarding the question if bank capital is risk sensitive and in what way, Ahnert et al. documented a model to study the risk sensitivity of capital regulation. With a perfect signal, capital requirements are risk sensitive and achieve the first-best levels of risk and intermediation: safer banks attract cheaper deposit funding and require less capital. With a noisy signal, risk-sensitive capital regulation can implement a separating equilibrium in which low-quality banks do not participate. We show that the degree of risk sensitivity is non-monotone in the precision of the signal and in investment characteristics. Without a signal, a leverage ratio still induces the efficient risk choice but leads to excessive or insufficient intermediation. With perfect and noisy signal they refer to the preciseness and accurateness as well as timeliness of the bank's signal regarding the quality of the bank assets. See in detail: T. Ahnert et al., (2018), Should Bank capital Be Risk Sensitive, Bank of Canada Staff Working Paper Nr. 48, September.

[28] Regulatory capital is the amount of capital that a bank or other financial institution has to hold as required by its financial regulator. This is usually expressed as a capital adequacy ratio of equity that must be held as a percentage of risk-weighted assets. The whole idea is that given the level of risk that the bank holds on its balance sheet, a certain level of capital should be adequate to absorb any potential losses that might occur from risk exposures or sudden devaluations of certain asset prices in order to stabilize the FI and keep it afloat.

[29] Operational risk has always been ignored somewhat. However, these days operational risk accounts for 25% or more of the risk profile of (particularly the largest) banks. Another uncommon relationship is that between operational risk and regulatory arbitrage. Operational risk is broadly defined as the risk of a loss due to the failure of people or processes (i.e. all risks outside of the traditional credit and market risks. That relationship works as follows: '[w]eakness in regulation leads to incentives for banks to increase their overall risk and shift their risk taking to less regulated risk areas, and in particular increase their exposure to operational risk.' (p. 1) So regulatory arbitrage contributed to the increase rise of these less-regulated risk streams such as operational risk. In particular 'operational risk was unregulated prior to the crisis in the sense that banks were not required to hold additional equity capital to cushion against operational losses. This provided banks with an incentive to shift their risk profiles and take on unprecedented levels of operational risk and thus increase their overall risk exposure' (pp. 1–2). See in detail: B. Clark and A. Ebrahim, (2017), Risk Shifting and Regulatory Arbitrage: Evidence from Operational Risk, Working paper, June 23, mimeo. Also: N. Boyson et al., (2016), Why Don't all Banks Practice Regulatory Arbitrage? Evidence from Usage of Trust-Preferred Securities. The Review of Financial Studies Vol. 29, Issue 7, July pp. 1821–1859; A. Chernobai et al., (2016), Business Complexity and Risk Management: Evidence from Operational Risk Events in US Bank Holding Companies, Working paper, mimeo; Y. Demyanyk, and E. Loutskina, (2016), Mortgage Companies and Regulatory Arbitrage, Journal of Financial Economics, Vol. 122, pp. 328–351.

industry) and market risk[30] (the risk of losses due to fluctuations in market prices and interest rates in the market).

FIs were given quite some freedom to develop their own models to assess the aforementioned risks, (2) Supervision: the regulator should be given adequate tools[31] to assess a variety of risks including systemic risk, concentration risk, liquidity risk and so on[32] and (3) Market discipline: a set of disclosure requirements which will allow the market participants to gauge the capital adequacy of an institution.

Still significant room was given to financial institutions, in particular when it concerned the measurement of a variety of risks. Basel II had a difficult start and was politically a difficult sell, causing it to be subjected to modifications pretty much every year after its introduction in 2004 until the start of the 2008 financial crisis. It became manifestly clear that the Basel II norms did miss some of the challenges of the industry in a globalized and interconnected world. It also missed the fact that certain risks have nothing to do with credit, operational or market risk. For example, this was the case for liquidity requirements which were linked to an understanding of how a bank funded itself in the market. Also, and although the capital requirements were clear, financial innovation caused many different products to be used that were cheaper than expensive loss-absorbing capital,[33] while still qualifying for the regulatory capital rules.[34] This caused the capital structure of most

[30] Since 2016 there are minimum capital requirements developed to match market risk. See: BCBS, (2016), Minimum Capital Requirements for Market Risk, Standards, January. They are under revision following a 2018 consultative update: BCBS, (2018), Revisions to the Minimum Capital Requirements for Market Risk, March. Final revisions were implemented through BCBS, (2019), Minimum Capital Requirements for Market Risk, February 25. There is an insurance market for market risk but not without issues: R. Koijen and M. Yogo, (2018), The Fragility of market Risk Insurance, NBER Working Paper Nr. 24182, May (revised).

[31] The Internal Capital Adequacy Assessment Process (ICAAP) is the result of Pillar II of the Basel II accords.

[32] To that effect the ESRB produces (since 2012) a quarterly risk dashboard, which includes de facto analysis of the following items: interlinkages, macro risk, credit risk, funding and liquidity risk, market risk, profitability and solvency risk, structural risk and central counterparty related risks (via www.esrb.europe.eu).

[33] M. Tanaka and J. Vourdas, (2018), Equity, Debt and Moral Hazard: the Optimal Structure of Banks' Loss Absorbing Capacity, Bank of England Staff Working Paper Nr. 745, July 27. Banks in their model are subject to two types of moral hazard: i) ex ante, they have the incentive to shirk on project monitoring, thus increasing the risk of failure, and ii) ex post, poorly capitalized banks have the incentive to engage in asset substitution by 'gambling for resurrection'. Ex ante moral hazard can be eliminated by ensuring that banks have sufficient capital and uninsured 'bail-inable' debt, while ex post moral hazard is mitigated by triggering resolution when the minimum capital requirement is breached. They argue that optimal regulation consists of a high TLAC requirement and high capital buffer. Their analysis also suggests that higher system-wide risk would call for a higher capital buffer. Direct lending by non-banks increases when local banks are poorly capitalized. Non-bank lenders are less likely to monitor by including financial covenants in their loans, but appear to engage in more ex ante screening. Controlling for firm and loan characteristics, non-bank loans carry about 200 basis points higher interest rates. In detail: S. Chernenko et al., (2018), Nonbank Lending, (2018), Fisher College of Business Working Paper Nr. 13, July 25.

[34] See extensively: L. Nijs, (2014), Mezzanine Financing: Tools, Applications and Total Return, Wiley & Sons, London, in general but in particular the chapter on FIs.

banks to be much more vulnerable than intended. The largest and still unsolved sensitivity is that of leverage, that is, the amount of debt financing (short-term and long-term loans excluding deposits, although they technically qualify as debt as well) that the FI uses to fund its assets.[35] The financial industry is known for its material use of leverage compared to other industries[36] and we have been gently reminded of the natural limits to risk modeling in the 2008 crisis.[37]

In the aftermath of the 2008 financial crisis a major revamp of the Basel II rules has been worked on, which has resulted in a new set of Basel III rules. Those were released in the period 2011–2013.

The major themes during the revamp have been[38]:

- Raising the quality, consistency and transparency of the capital base by narrowing down the definition of the criteria for the inclusion of financial products in the different tranches of the bank's balance sheet. The idea is to make it more robust and better able to absorb losses in case of a market shake-out.
- Introducing new liquidity standards. The idea is that banks hold a minimum of products that easily can be liquidated in the event of market turmoil thereby enhancing their ability to self-finance during a protracted period of time when markets are dysfunctional.
- Limiting the use of leverage by FIs by forcing certain limits upon the industry.
- Requiring the procyclical build-up of capital buffers especially when the FI qualifies as systemically relevant (Sect. 11.6.2).
- Introducing wide variety of monitoring tools. This has been complemented in Europe by a variety of institutions to embody the European Banking Union and the processes required to (swiftly) roll-up a bank's operations once it goes into distress.

---

[35] Sir J. Cunliffe, (2016), Credit: Can Trees Grow to the Sky, Speech at the British Property Federation Annual Residential Investment Conference, London, February 9, bis.org. The credit expansion we have witnessed in recent decades did not finance the economic expansion. Rather, the liquidity availability, combined with lowering interest rates, inflated prices.

[36] Average leverage in other industries is around 35–45% of total funding and significantly up from two or three decades ago where it was only on average 20%. In the financial industry the leverage is often as high as 96% and before the crisis 98% of total funding. See in detail: A. Admati and M. Hellwig, (2013), The Bankers New Clothes: What's Wrong with Banking and What to Do About It, Princeton University Press, Princeton, New Jersey, Chapter 1.

[37] J. Danielsson, (2002), The Emperor has No Clothes: Limits to Risk Modeling, Journal of Banking and Finance, Vol. 26, pp. 1273–1296, J. Danielsson et al., (2016), Model Risk of Risk Models, Journal of Financial Stability, Volume 23, pp. 79–91; J. Danielsson et al., (2018), Learning from History: Volatility and Financial Crises, Review of Financial Studies, Vol. 31, Issue 7, July, pp. 2774–2805 and N.N. Taleb, (2010), The Black Swan: The Impact of the Highly Improbable, Random House Trade paperbacks, 2nd Ed., New York.

[38] See in detail: Basel Committee on Banking Supervision (BIS), (2011), Basel III: A Global Regulatory Framework for More Resilient Banks and Banking Systems and Basel Committee on Banking Supervision, (2013), Basel III: The Liquidity Coverage Ratio and Liquidity Risk Monitoring Tools.

There is no need to flesh out the different rules and monitoring procedures at this stage. They ultimately apply to official banking institutions. Being complete is a challenge and the story is still being written and the implementation lasted until 2019 and for some aspects until January 2022.[39] Where needed, I will pick up on the different aspects and details on a need-to-know basis within the context of the different FI-specific externalities analyzed. I will not comment on to what degree these suggested rules have been the correct ones and the degree of effectiveness of these suggested rules. It is clear, however, that enhanced regulatory scrutiny of the banking sector has pushed a lot of capital outside the traditional and regulated banking sector, to an area that we, for now, call the shadow banking sector. These Basel frameworks have been implemented at EU level in a sequencing series of directives known as the Capital Requirements Directives.[40] The first evaluations

[39] See FSB's Basel III – Implementation via fsb.org. Consider also the permanent updates the BIS provides clarifying many technical issues: BIS, (2017), Basel III: Finalizing Post-Crisis Reforms; BIS, (2017), Definition of Capital, Frequently Asked Questions; BIS, (2017), Frequently Asked Questions on Market Risk Capital Requirements; BIS, (2016), TLAC Holding Standard, October, (This document is the final standard on the regulatory capital treatment of banks' investments in instruments that comprise total loss-absorbing capacity (TLAC) for global systemically important banks (G-SIBs). The standard aims to reduce the risk of contagion within the financial system should a G-SIB enter resolution. It applies to both G-SIBs and non-G-SIBs. The main elements of the prudential treatment are as follows: Tier 2 deduction: banks must deduct holdings of TLAC instruments that are not already included in regulatory capital from their own Tier 2 capital. Threshold below which no deduction is required: the deduction is subject to the thresholds that apply to existing holdings of regulatory capital and an additional 5% threshold for non-regulatory-capital TLAC holdings only. Instruments ranking pari passu with subordinated forms of TLAC must also be deducted. The standard also reflects changes to Basel III to specify how G-SIBs must take account of the TLAC requirement when calculating their regulatory capital buffers; BIS, (2016) Minimum Capital Requirements for Market Risk, January; BIS, (2015), Basel III: The Standardized Approach for Measuring Counterparty Credit Risk Exposures: FAQ, August, BIS, (2014), FAQs on Basel III's January Liquidity Coverage Ratio; BIS, (2012), FAQs on Counterparty Credit Risk and Exposures to Central Counterparties and BIS, (2011), FAQs Regarding the Definition of Capital, and BIS, (2011), FAQs Regarding the Framework for Liquidity. S. Kroon and I. van Lelyveld, (2018), Counterparty Credit Risk and the Effectiveness of banking Regulation, DNB Working Paper nr. 599, June 26. The EBA launched recently a consultation on four RTSs with a view toward harmonization of the Standardised Approach for Counterparty Credit Risk (SA-CCR). See EBA, (2019), Consultation Paper on the Standardised Approach for Counterparty Credit Risk (abbr.), EBA consultation document EBA?CP/2018/03, May 2.

[40] The original Capital Requirements Directive (CRD I) comprises Directives 2006/48/EC and 2006/49/EC. Capital Requirements Directive II (CRD II) comprises Directives 2009/27/EC, 2009/83/EC and 2009/111/EC. Capital Requirements Directive III (CRD III) comprises directive 2010/76/EC. CRD II and CRD III amended the Directives that comprise CRD I. The Basel III principles have been implemented through a Directive (Directive 2013/36/EU of the European Parliament and of the Council of June 26, 2013 on access to the activity of credit institutions and the prudential supervision of credit institutions and investment firms, amending Directive 2002/87/EC and repealing Directives 2006/48/EC and 2006/49/EC, OJ L 176, 27/06/2013, p. 338–436), which needed to be transposed in national law by January 1, 2014, and an aligned Regulation (Regulation (EU) No 575/2013 of the European Parliament and of the Council of June 26, 2013 on prudential requirements for credit institutions and investment firms and amending Regulation (EU) No 648/2012 Text with EEA relevance, OJ L 176, 27/06/2013, pp. 1–337). The CRD I, II and III were repealed on December 31, 2013. The Directive and Regulation are known as the CRD IV package.

are coming in and look promising relative to the initial standard set, although it needs to be admitted that the real test is likely yet to come. Focus in the analysis has been on the prevention and mitigation of excessive growth and leverage, addressing misalignments and maturity mismatches/market illiquidity.[41] Capital conservation and countercyclical as well as systemic risk buffers were opted in pretty much across Member States.[42] A little over 2.5 years after the introduction, a review[43] was proposed to further enhance capital requirements within the EU. It is aimed at achieving the following goals: (1) better addressing long-term funding risk; (2) reducing excessive leverage[44]; (3) better addressing market risks by increasing the risk sensitivity of the existing rules and enhancing the proportionality[45] of the prudential framework for institutions; (4) increasing the loss absorption and recapitalization[46] capacity of G-SIIs; (5) increasing legal certainty and enhancing convergence among Member States in the area of insolvency law and restructuring proceedings, particularly in the area of creditor hierarchy. Those last two objectives will be tackled through a

[41] For the international dimension: A. Malkhozov et al., (2017), International Illiquidity, International Finance Discussion Papers Nr. 1201, March.

[42] See for an evaluation at great length: ESRB, (2015), A Review of Macro-Prudential Policy in the EU one year after the Introduction of the CRD/CRR, June, Frankfurt am Main.

[43] This review is known as CRD V/CRR 2: Proposal for a Directive of the European Parliament and of the Council amending Directive 2013/36/EU as regards exempted entities, financial holding companies, mixed financial holding companies, remuneration, supervisory measures and powers and capital conservation measures; Proposal for a Regulation of the European Parliament and of the Council amending Regulation (EU) No 575/2013 as regards the leverage ratio, the net stable funding ratio, requirements for own funds and eligible liabilities, counterparty credit risk, market risk, exposures to central counterparties, exposures to collective investment undertakings, large exposures, reporting and disclosure requirements and amending Regulation (EU) No 648/2012COM(2016)850 & 854, 23.11.2016, 2016/0360,0364(COD). The aim is to implement the most recent international regulatory provisions for banks, set by the Basel Committee on Banking Supervision (BCBS), to address regulatory shortcomings and to contribute to more sustainable bank financing of the economy, especially regarding SMEs. Completion of the CRD V/CRR II package occurred in April 2019; via Europa.eu (MEMO/19/2129).

[44] See regarding the consequences of overleverage on the financial sector and the real economy: M. Gross et al., (2017), Destabilizing Effects of Bank Overleveraging on Real Activity-An Analysis Based on a Threshold MCS-GVAR, ECB Working Paper Nr. 2081, June. They comment 'the reason for why macroeconomic responses to bank capital shocks are likely significantly stronger under an overleveraging regime is that the same percentage point capital ratio shock translates into a stronger asset side reaction than under an initial low-leverage (i.e. high capital ratio) regime.'... 'GDP to credit long-run response ratios are higher under a bank overleveraging regime'...'cross-border spillover effects appear to be more pronounced when capital ratio shocks hit the banking system during a period of overleveraging.' (p. 15).

[45] Also: F. Restoy, (2019), Proportionality in financial regulation: where do we go from here? Speech at the BIS/IMF policy implementation meeting on proportionality in financial regulation and supervision, Basel, Switzerland, 8 May, via bi.org

[46] Material recapitalization is required to have the effect sought after (increase lending, attract deposits and clean up balance sheets). See in detail: T. Homar, (2016), Bank Recapitalizations and Lending: A Little is not Enough, ESRB Working paper Series, Nr. 16, June.

separate new regulation.[47] The CRD-V package therefore contains three groups of provisions, covering capital and liquidity requirements, aspects of proportionality and the EU's resolution framework. It should be noted that although the European legislation is based on the Basel accords, the implementation and execution often differ in details (and sometimes more than details) relative to the founding Basel principles.[48] It became clear that size-dependent capital regulation was a prime choice, at least from an optimal equilibrium model point of view. Goel demonstrates that optimal capital regulation is bank specific and tighter for large banks than for small banks. This is for three reasons he argues: '[f]irst, allowing small banks to take more leverage enables them to potentially grow faster, leading to a growth effect. Second, although more leverage by small banks results in a higher exit rate, these exits are by the less efficient banks, leading to a cleansing effect. Third, failures are more costly among large banks, because these are more efficient in equilibrium and intermediate more capital. Therefore, tighter regulation for large banks renders them less prone to failure, leading to a stabilization effect.'[49]

11.3 Neoliberalism and the Banking Sector

Given the analysis in the previous section, it could be concluded that the banking sector is a regulatory well-encapsulated industry. That shallow assessment looks different once we scratch the surface of the soft law Basel framework. The reality is that since the mid 1980s, the banking sector has seen more compliance but less real supervision and regulation.

[47] See: A. Delivorias, Ranking of unsecured debt instruments in insolvency hierarchy, European Parliamentary Research Service, Briefing, March, 142017.

[48] See a.o.: European Commission, Frequently Asked Questions: Capital requirements (CRR/CRD IV) and resolution framework (BRRD/SRM), amendments, MEMO 16/3840, Brussels, November 26, 2016. Note however already at this stage that the effectiveness of higher capital ratios and lower leverage ratios is continuously being questioned. To a large degree the findings are that rather than reduce bank risk, the risk is sifted because of regulatory intervention outside the 'traditional' banking sector. See, for instance, M. Allahrakha et al., (2016), Do Higher Capital Standards Always Reduce Bank Risk? The Impact of the Basel leverage Ratio on the U.S. Triparty Repo market, OFR Working Paper Nr. 16-11, November 10. Their findings with respect to BHCs (Bank Holding Companies cover all entities (US) that qualify as being a bank themselves or own an entity that does so for 10% or more) point in that direction. They examined the activity of broker-dealers affiliated with bank holding companies (BHCs) and broker-dealers not affiliated with BHCs in the repurchase agreement (repo) market. Their findings are threefold: (1) First, following the 2012 introduction of the supplementary leverage ratio (SLR), broker-dealer affiliates of BHCs decreased their repo borrowing but increased their use of repo backed by more price-volatile collateral; (2) they find that regardless of whether a US BHC-affiliated broker-dealer parent is above or below the SLR requirement, the announcement of the SLR rule has disincentivized those dealers affiliated with BHCs from borrowing in tri-party repo; and (3) they document the increase in the number of active non-bank-affiliated dealers in certain asset classes of tri-party repo since the 2012 introduction of the supplementary leverage ratio.

[49] T. Goel, (2016), Banking Industry Dynamics and Size-Dependent Capital Regulation, BIS Working Paper Nr. 599, December. Bank leverage choices are subject to the risk-return trade-off: high leverage increases expected return on capital, but also increases return variance and bank failure risk.

Within that context one also needs to take into account the increased complexity that the sector has witnessed over the last few decades.

Since the 1980s[50] a significant number of financial hubs (London, New York, Frankfurt, etc.) have seen more liberalization in the financial industry allowing innovative product development, mergers and acquisitions in the industry, technological development and overall a (further) financialization of our societies (Sect. 11.9). In fact, the sector has seen a reversal of historically built-up protective regulation including the gradual repeal of the Glass-Steagall Act in the US which was introduced in 1933 after the previous financial depression occurred. It foresaw, amongst many other things, the separation of traditional savings banks and more risk-focused investment banks. The American Central Bank ('FED') has been instrumental in letting that happen, an institution chaired by Alan Greenspan from 1987 to 2006. During that period, one should take into account that the FED is a privately owned organization in which those who are the targets of financial regulation are also its shareholders (i.e. the major US commercial and investment banks). Greenspan, who is known for his personal encounters with Ayn Rand, has been and is known to the world as a vivid advocate of letting the free market have its way, correcting itself where needed and for his belief that it will produce the best outcome for society as a whole. In his initial understanding this would deepen the financial markets and their liquidity, and produce innovation in the design and implementation of financial products, which will all in some way lower the cost of financing the real economy.[51] The trial-and-error mechanism implicit in the Schumpeterian creative destruction concept, however, implicitly assumes a better outcome over time. As advocated before, creative destruction has the potential to destroy more than it creates[52] and in 2008 it required a government (financial) backstop to prevent the financial sector from doing exactly that.

The regulatory race to the bottom, whereby the different country regulators (of countries worldwide, but in particular in the West) simultaneously engaged in liberalization[53] of the financial sector, was a direct consequence of a neoliberal trend[54] extensively described

---

[50] See in detail also historically: M.A. Centeno and J.N. Cohen, (2012), The Arc of Neoliberalism, Annual Review of Sociology, Vol. 38, pp. 317–340.

[51] See in detail: A. Greenspan, (2008), The Age of Turbulence: Adventures in a New World, Penguin Books, New York. After the 2008 crisis he converted and claimed that he has had to backtrack on his initial belief that (financial) markets can be self-policing and explicitly stepped away from the neoliberal policies he endorsed for decades.

[52] Or to be precise (1) destruction does not always have to be creative and (2) not every creativity is destructive.

[53] See for an excellent analysis of liberalization beyond just being a transition from controlled to competitive markets. Liberalization implies not merely practical processes and legal instruments of economic reorganization and governance, but moreover a higher-level conception of how markets fit within society, and thus how law might be deployed to achieve wider social and economic goals. See in detail: N. Dunne, (2017), Perspectives on Liberalisation, LSE Law, Society and Economy Working Papers Nr. 6/2017, London.

[54] Much has been written about neoliberalism. But the reading of Wilkinson's essay was refreshing; he coins the concept of 'authoritarian liberalism' and applies it to what he sees happening in the EU. Authoritarian liberalism occurs when politically authoritarian forms of governing emerge to

before.[55] The sovereign as state-market is an integrated part of the free market and needs to compete for the attention of capital. As water flows to the lowest point possible, so too does capital flow to the point where it can operate in as unconstrained a fashion as possible, that is, free from the regulatory shackles. Governments have been very cooperative in making that happen while enjoying the benefits of employment, real estate demand and business in general including tax revenues.[56]

Much has been said and written about the causes and remedies of the 2008 financial crisis, none of which I will repeat here as it is a multi-dimensional shifting paradigm that deserves much more attention than I can dignify in this context. But a consistent theme is that governments have consistently grown too close to their financial industry targets in this respect. Even in the aftermath of the 2008 crisis, the entanglement of politics[57] and the financial sector is rampant.

It goes beyond the opportunistic self-dealing of politicians on the boards of FIs and the swift post-political career changes into the FI of many politicians. On a regulatory level too

protect the material order of economic liberalism. This constitutional conjuncture can be grasped by integrating into constitutional enquiry the material dynamic between democracy and capitalism. The post-Maastricht EU construction represents the de-democratization of the economy. The recent assaults on democracy in the Euro crisis appear to be a continuation of, rather than divergence from, the normal path of integration, Wilkinson indicates. See in detail: M.A. Wilkinson, (2018), Authoritarian Liberalism: The Conjuncture behind the Crisis, LSE Law, Society and Economy Working Papers 5/2018 (also published in The Crisis behind the Eurocrisis: The Eurocrisis as a Multidimensional Systemic Crisis of the EU, (eds. E. Nanopoulos and F. Vergis), June 2019, Cambridge University Press, Cambridge). See Epsein and Rhodes who argue in the same direction but with distinct accents. The European Banking Union and Capital Markets Union have emerged as two of the key pillars of European integration since the post-2008 financial crisis. Both imply the same critical shifts in Europe's institutional political economy. The first relocates national oversight and authority to supranational institutions (a political shift), while the second increases the power and responsibility of market actors by reducing national controls (an economic shift). See in detail: R. Epstein and M. Rhodes, (2018), From Governance to Government: Banking Union, Capital Markets Union and the New EU, Competition and Change, Vol. 22 Nr. 2, pp. 205–224. Part of the migration to market-based but state-led finance is the role of public development banks which have become strategic players in the evolution of the European financial system and economic governance. 'Market-based but state-led' seems to be crucial in understanding neoliberalism. See: D. Mertens and M. Thiemann, (2018), Market-Based but State-Led: The Role of Public Development Banks in Shaping Market-Based Finance in the European Union, Competition and Change, Vol. 22, Nr. 2, pp. 184–204.

[55] L. Nijs, (2015), Neoliberalism 2.0. Regulating and Financing Globalizing Markets, Palgrave, Basingstoke, chapter 3.

[56] In the City of London, the financial sector accounted for 40% of all UK corporate income tax revenues in the years running up to the crisis. This has fallen but its corporate tax contributions still account for about 10% of all UK tax revenues (2010) and far beyond that taking into account VAT and so on. For details see: PWC, (2010), The Total Tax Contribution of UK Financial Services, 3rd ed., London. By 2017 that percentage is still at a stable 11% PWC, (2017), Ibid. 10th ed. The study is updated annually.

[57] In fact that is true for the wider sovereign in all its aspects including the DOJ ('Department of Justice'). See in detail: B.L. Garrett, (2014), Too Big to Jail: How Prosecutors Compromise with Corporations, Harvard University Press, Cambridge MA.

that entanglement is still vibrant.[58] Amidst complaints that the banking sector is not engaging in sufficient efforts to make credit available to the real economy, the Basel Committee handsomely included in the Basel III principles the fact that vis-à-vis most investment grade treasury bonds[59] no (or almost no) risk capital needs to be kept in reserve as it is considered risk free. That is relative to lending to the real economy, which is considered risky and therefore requires significant capital requirements. The result of that logic is what we have experienced in the last few years: banks hold more treasury bonds and make less credit available to the real economy (in particular the SME sector)[60,61] as that requires less risk capital.[62] In fact, because of this mechanism, banks hold more treasury bonds and convert other asset classes into government bonds and are incentivized to hold treasury bonds even beyond their own risk appetite. Capital and liquidity regulation[63] leads to a longer-term increase in government bond holdings.[64] It enhances under constant performance the return on equity (ROE) of the FI,[65] while it ensures that the liquidity made

[58] Countless examples can be given regarding the predatory nature of the FI: From the libor manipulation to FIs taking trading positions against their clients, under-highlighting certain risks, to driving SME clients into bankruptcy/insolvency in order to pick up quality assets at bottom prices.

[59] That is the case for most Western nations.

[60] See B. Őztürk and M. Mrkaic, (2014), SME's Access to Finance in the Euro Area: What Helps or Hampers, IMF Working Paper, WP 14/78; R. Bannerjee, (2014), SME's, Financial Constraints and Growth, BIS Working Paper nr. 475. H. Kraemer-Eis, (2017), SME Securitization in Europe-a Short Summary, EIF report and H. Kraemer-Eis et al., (2015), SME Securitizations- At a Crossroads, EIF Working Paper Nr. 2015/31. Kraemer-Eis advocates a securitization market for SME loans that would provide an indirect access to capital markets. He mainly finds support with Altunbas et al. (2007).

[61] Securitization per se is not good or bad—it is a toolbox, it is value-free, claims Kraemer-Eis. Unfortunately, that claim violates reality. Reference can be to the concentration of risk discussion in tranching.

[62] And less capital required means under constant performance a higher return on equity (ROE) for the FI.

[63] See for a recent literature review: A. Mordel, (2018), Prudential Liquidity Regulation in Banking-A Literature Review, Bank of Canada Staff Working Paper Nr. 8, July. His findings suggest that while banks respond to binding requirements by increasing long-term funding and reducing maturity mismatch, there is also evidence that risk in the financial system has gone up. In an environment where both bank liquidity and capital are regulated, it is natural to consider the interactions between them. The main conclusions from this growing literature indicate that while liquidity requirements tend to make capital constraints less binding, capital requirements appear to be more costly to comply with, and that both regulations have a non-trivial effect on financial stability.

[64] See in detail: C. Bonner, (2014), Preferential Regulatory Treatment and Bank's Demand for Government Bonds, DNB Working Papers, Nr. 433. It also creates more stability: M. Bucher et al., (2019), More Stability through Liquidity Regulation, Deutsche Bundesbank Research Brief Nr. 25, May.

[65] For the reason why banks focus more on ROE than, for instance, EPS like other firms, see: G. Pennacchi and J.A.C. Santos, (2018), Why Do Banks Target ROE?, FRB of NY Staff Report Nr. 855, June. Also A. Kovner and P. van Tassel, (2019), Evaluating Regulatory Reform: Banks' Cost of Capital and Lending, FRB of NY Staff Report, 854, May.

available under the wide variety of monetary easing programs[66] by the central banks flows back to the sovereigns, who now can operate at historically low rates.[67]

However, banking sector developments and characteristics influence the propagation of risks from the banking sector to sovereign debt,[68] including how they affect the extent of fiscal costs of banking crises when those occur. Banking sector expansions, especially large ones, can create significant risks for the sovereign. Recessions preceded by a large build-up of banking vulnerabilities—including increasing leverage, expanding balance sheets, and a greater reliance on wholesale external funds—exhibit deeper GDP contractions and longer recovery times, leading to greater deteriorations in the fiscal primary balance and public debt.[69] When banking sector vulnerabilities unravel in banking crises, the risks to the sovereign are further exacerbated by the high fiscal cost[70] of related crisis management policies,

[66] In the EU the LTRO (Long-Term Refinancing Operation) and in the US the scaled quantitative easing (QE) program were the major programs initiated.

[67] Also in the post-2008 world the EMH (efficient market hypothesis), which assumes that markets are constantly rational and therefore price assets (and their embedded risk) appropriately do not stand.

[68] And the other way around. See: T. Jonasson and M. Papaioannou, (2018), Primer on Managing Sovereign Debt-Portfolio Risks, IMF Working Paper Nr. WP/18/74, April.

[69] See for an excellent review of the impact of credit on recessions: J. Bridges et al., (2017), Down in the Slumps: the Role of Credit in Five Decades of Recessions, Bank of England Staff Working Papers Nr. 659, April. They assess whether the growth or level of credit is the better predictor of the severity of a recession. They concluded that 'a period of rapid credit growth in the immediate run-up to a recession predicts a deeper and longer downturn than when credit growth has been subdued, whether associated with a systemic banking crisis or not and whether that credit growth reflects borrowing by households or businesses. Credit growth is a more statistically and economically significant predictor of a recession's severity than the level of indebtedness.' Also: J. Cunliffe, (2016), Credit: Can Trees Grow to the Sky, Speech given by Sir Jon Cunliffe, British Property Federation Annual Residential Investment Conference, London, February 9 (bankofengland.co.uk).

[70] About the predictability (through early warning systems) of fiscal crises see: S. Cerovic et al., (2018), Predicting Fiscal Crises, IMF Working Paper Nr. WP/18/181, August. Both non-fiscal (external and internal imbalances) and fiscal variables help predict crises among advanced and emerging economies. Also: M. Bruns and T. Poghosyan, (2018), Leading Indicators of Fiscal Distress: Evidence from the Extreme Bound Analysis, Applied Economics, Vol. 50, Issue 13, pp. 1454–1478; M. Dawood et al., (2017), Predicting Sovereign Debt Crises: An Early Warning System approach, Journal of Financial Stability, Vol. 28, pp. 16–28; C. Christofides et al., (2016), Did established Early Warning Signals Predict the 2008 Crises?, European Economic review, Vol. 81, pp. 103–114; K. Gerling et al., (2017), Fiscal Crises, IMF Working Paper Nr. WP/17/86, Washington; S. Sumner and K. Berti, (2017), A Complementary Tool to Monitor Fiscal Stress in European Economies, EC Discussion Paper Nr. 49, June. Honda et al. assess the options of waiting for early warning signals to tackle fiscal crises or handle as they emerge. They investigate the interlinkages between early warning signals for fiscal crisis, policy responses and policy outcomes. See: J. Honda et al., (2018), When Do We Repair the Roof? Insights from Responses to Fiscal Crisis Early Warning Signals, IMF Working Paper Nr. WP/18/77, March. The bottom line is that countries with weak institutional environments benefit from acting on early warning signals whereas strong institutional environments are able and willing to introduce fiscal adjustments when needed (at the beginning of a fiscal crisis) and can afford as they tend to have sufficient buffers. Substitutability between fiscal consolidation and institutional quality (in order to prevent a fiscal crisis) points to the importance of capacity (resilience) building. Also: M.G. Attanasi and L. Metelli, (2017), Is Fiscal Consolidation Self-Defeating?

particularly bank bailouts.[71] When a banking crisis occurs,[72] the fiscal costs of dealing with the crisis are influenced by pre-crisis banking sector characteristics, institutional and regulatory frameworks, as well as crisis resolution policies. Direct fiscal costs of banking crises are higher in countries with larger and more leveraged banking sectors that rely more on external funding. Costs tend to be lower in countries that have strong bank supervision[73] and effective safety nets, including broader deposit insurance schemes. Amaglobeli et al. demon-

---

A Panel-VAR Analysis for the Euro Area Countries, Journal of International Money and Finance, Vol. 74(C), pp. 147–164; M. Bruns and T. Poghosyan, (2016), Leading Indicators of Fiscal Distress: Evidence from the Extreme Bound Analysis. IMF Working Paper Nr. WP/16/28; K. Gerling et al., (2017), Fiscal Cries, IMF Working Paper Nr. WP/17/86; S. Cerovic, et al., (2018), Predicting Fiscal Crisis, IMF Working Paper Nr. WP/18/181, August.

[71] Distinction needs to be made between the mentioned bank bailout and other techniques of converting private sector debt into public sector debt. This can be through a crisis or a more orderly deleveraging process. This debt migration 'operates mainly through growth rather than explicit bailouts: private deleveraging weighs on activity, prompting a countercyclical government response to support economic activity. Whenever the private sector is caught in a debt overhang and needs to deleverage, governments systematically come to the rescue through a countercyclical rise in government deficits and debt' (p. 3). It is a form of debt mutualization whereby excess private debt leads to higher public debt. The transmission channel is not debt but growth. 'Private deleveraging weighs on economic activity, thereby prompting both a cyclical deterioration in public finances and a countercyclical rise in public debt. Ultimately, whether this debt substitution results in a net increase or a net decline of overall indebtedness in the economy depends on the extent of the growth slowdown during the deleveraging spell' indicate Mbaye et al. Treating public and private debt in silos should be replaced by assessing the total stock of debt active in the economy. Unchecked private debt is causally related to public sector debt beyond bank bailout programs. See in detail: S. Mbaye et al., (2018), Bailing Out the People? When Private Debt Becomes Public, IMF Working Paper Nr. WP/18?141, June. Also: A. Alter et al., (2018), Understanding the Macro-Financial Effects of Household Debt: A Global Perspective, IMF Working Paper Nr. WP/18/76, International Monetary Fund, Washington, DC.; M. Bernardini and L. Forni, (2017), Private and Public Debt: Are Emerging Markets at Risk, IMF Working Paper Nr. WP/17/61, International Monetary Fund, Washington, DC.; A. Chudik et al., (2017), Is there a Debt-Threshold Effect on Output Growth?, Review of Economics and Statistics, Vol. 99, Issue 1, pp. 135–150; I. Hasan et al., (2016), What Type of Finance Matters for Growth? Bayesian Model Averaging Evidence, Policy Research Working Paper Series Nr. 7645, The World Bank; MS. Mbaye et al., (2018), Global Debt Database: Methodology and Sources, IMF Working Paper Nr. WP/18/111, International Monetary Fund, Washington, DC., May. An interesting read is B. Eichengreen et al., (2019), Public Debt Through the Ages, IMF Working Paper Nr. WP/19/6, January. They observe that the purposes for which governments borrow have evolved over time. Both periods of debt expansion as well as debt consolidation are analyzed, and the economic and political circumstances that made these successful debt consolidation episodes possible are closely examined. Highly recommended including the extensive reference list (pp. 51 ff).

[72] L. Grégory et al., (2019), The Cost of Banking Crises: Does the Policy Framework Matter, Banque de France Working Paper Nr. 712, March 13. They highlight that extremely restrictive policy frameworks are likely to increase the expected cost of banking crises.

[73] Kandrac and Schlusche argue that the 'affected institutions (ed. those subject to reduced or no bank supervision) took on much more risk than their unaffected counterparts elsewhere that were subject to identical regulation.' There seems to be some fading out effect over time of that behavior. See: J. Kandrac and B. Schlusche, (2017), The Effect of Bank Supervision on Risk Taking: Evidence from a Natural Experiment, Board of Governors of the Federal Reserve System Working Paper, May 31, mimeo.

strate that the size of fiscal costs of banking crises depends on pre-crisis banking sector characteristics. Fiscal costs of banking crises[74] are higher in countries where the banking sector is larger, more leveraged or more reliant on external funding. Costs tend, however, to be lower where banking supervision is stronger and deposit insurance coverage is broader. Their findings suggest that recent trends toward more leveraged and internationally integrated banking sectors pose additional risks to public finances, and countries' regulatory and supervisory frameworks can help mitigate these risks.[75]

Other banking sector characteristics further influence risks from banks to the sovereign. Banks' large holdings of domestic sovereign claims amplify the links between banks and the sovereign.[76] While such "home bias" can help reduce borrowing costs and provide fiscal

[74] Cross-border transmission of fiscal shocks is stronger when monetary policy is constrained (i.e. after a banking crisis). See P. Blagrave et al., (2018), Cross-Border Transmission of Fiscal Shocks: The Role of Monetary Conditions, IMF Working Paper Nr. WP/18/103, May. Also: A. Goujard, (2017), Cross-Country Spillovers from Fiscal Consolidations, Fiscal Studies, Vol. 38, Issue 2, pp. 219–267; S.B. Nicar, (2015), International Spillovers from U.S. Fiscal Policy Shocks, Open Economies Review, Vol. 26, Issue 5, pp. 1081–1097; V.A. Ramey et al., (2018), Government Spending Multipliers in Good Times and in Bad: Evidence from U.S. Historical Data, Journal of Political Economy, Vol. 126, Issue 2, pp. 850–901.

[75] D. Amaglobeli et al., (2015), From Systemic Banking Crisis to Fiscal Costs: Risk Factors, IMF Working Paper Nr. WP/15/166, p. 3; 'Most of these are salient for both direct and overall fiscal costs, but policy responses have a differential impact. For example, bank guarantees appear to increase both direct and overall fiscal costs; the correlation is less clear-cut though for other policy measures, such as recapitalizations and asset purchases. Even though these short-term measures have initial direct fiscal costs, they do not necessarily add to the overall fiscal cost of crises. These findings suggest a possible trade-off between costly short-term policy interventions and the overall increase in public debt (p. 3)'.

[76] In fact the link between the sovereign and the economy within that sovereign goes beyond the FI sector. There is a material relationship between the sovereign position and the spillover into corporate credit risk. This is extensively documented using the Greek scenario as a test-case. See in detail: P. Augustin et al., (2016), Sovereign to Corporate Risk Spillovers, ECB Working Paper Series Nr. 1878, January. The sovereign to corporate channels identified are: (10 Corporate income taxation, (2) possible expropriation, (3) the sovereign ceiling concept, (4) downsizing of public investments and consumption and (5) reduced corporate credit of firms that rely on public spending can spread to suppliers. Also Breckenfelder and Schwaab identified spillover effects to that effect: H.-J. Breckenfelder and B. Schwaab, (2015), The Bank-Sovereign Nexus across Borders, Working Paper mimeo and more recently H.-J. Breckenfelder and B. Schwaab, (2017), Bank to Sovereign Risk Spillovers across Borders: Evidence from the ECB's Comprehensive Assessment, Working Paper, November 30, mimeo; G. Dell'Ariccia et al., (2018), Managing the Sovereign-Bank Nexus, ECB Working Papers Nr. 2177, September 24. The latter paper identifies the various channels that give rise to a "sovereign-bank nexus" whereby the financial health of banks and sovereigns is intertwined. They find that banks and sovereigns are linked by three interacting channels: banks hold large amounts of sovereign debt; banks are protected by government guarantees; and the health of banks and governments affect and is affected by economic activity. Evidence suggests that all three channels are relevant. Although there is a certain commitment to break the nexus between banks and the sovereign, there is less consensus how that is about to be made to happen, argue Alogoskoufis and Langfield. In particular the question regarding whether and how to reform the regulatory treatment of banks' sovereign exposures is left open. Simulations highlight a tension in regulatory design between concentration and credit risk. An area-wide low-risk asset—created by pooling and tranching cross-border portfolios of government

breathing space especially during times of stress, it can also lead to increased accumulation of debt and an eventual rise in sovereign risk.[77] Finally, markets appear to reflect concerns regarding bank-sovereign links: the implied probability of sovereign distress conditional on bank stress is markedly higher in countries with more leveraged banking sectors. Markets' perception of government bailout of banks in turn may also contribute to pernicious bank-sovereign links.[78]

The political field is a contaminated party in the relation as it does not shy away from sharpening the regulatory dynamics in favor of its own sovereign operations. That paradigm has broadened, as it now includes the central banks, which have informally broadened their mandates beyond what could be considered healthy.[79] It now includes macroeconomic objectives and indicators, often by pursuing unconventional monetary policies.[80] That occurs to such a degree that the regulator itself could become a source of externalities for the banking sector, as the unconventional policies witnessed in recent years have tended to increase medium term the overall risk exposure of FIs in the medium term.[81] What is still under

debt securities— would resolve this tension by expanding the portfolio opportunity set. Banks could therefore reinvest into an asset that has both low concentration and low credit risk. He thereby apparently refers to the SBBS idea that was proposed in the same period. That discussion will be had in the section of safe assets, where many valid objections are tabled.

[77] C. Arellano et al., (2017), Sovereign Risk Contagion, Federal Reserve Bank of Minneapolis, Staff Report Nr. 559, November (also NBER Working Paper Nr. 24031, November). Also: A. Ari, (2017), Sovereign Risk and Bank-Risk Taking, IMF Working Paper Nr. WP/17/280, December; V.V. Acharya et al., (2016), Caught Between Scylla and Charybdis? Regulating Bank Leverage when there is Rent Seeking and Risk Shifting, The Review of Corporate Finance Studies, Vol. 5, Issue 1, pp. 36–75; L. Boccola, (2016), The Pass-Through of Sovereign Risk, Journal of Political Economy, Vol. 124, Issue 4, pp. 879–926; M.K. Brunnermeyer et al., (2016), The Sovereign-Bank Diabolic Loop and Esbies, American Economic Review, Vol. 106, Issue 5, pp. 508–512; F. de Marco, (2017), Bank Lending and the European Sovereign Debt Crisis, Oesterreichische Nationalbank Working Paper Nr. 213; E. Farhi and J. Tirole, (2018), Deadly Embrace: Sovereign and Financial Balance Sheets Doom Loops, Review of Economic Studies, Vol. 85, Issue 3, July 1, pp. 1781–1823.

[78] See for an extensive coverage on the matter and proposals to mitigate systemic risks: IMF, (2015), From Banking to Sovereign Stress: Implications for Public Debt, March, Washington D.C. Also: A. Pienkowski, (2017), Debt Limits and the Structure of Public Debt, IMF Working Paper Nr. WP/17/117, May. Pienkowski provides a framework for how to assess the structure of debt instruments that can raise the debt limit of a sovereign. Optimal instrument design is not a one-size-fits-all position.

[79] See for an interesting overview of central banking models around the world: A. Khan, (2017), Central Bank legal Frameworks in the Aftermath of the Global Financial Crisis, IMF Working Paper Nr. WP/17/101, May.

[80] See in extenso: R. Mohan and M. Kapur, (2014), Monetary Policy Coordination and the Role of Central Banks, IMF Working Paper, WP 14/70.

[81] See in detail F. Lambert and K. Ueda, (2014), The Effects of Unconventional Monetary Policy on Bank Soundness, IMF Working Paper WP/14/152. Through the mechanism of globalization, this phenomenon has resulted not only in FIs being impacted by those policies, but also the clients they serve, including in emerging economies where the economic infrastructure overall is more susceptible to shocks; see M. Chui, I. Fender and V. Sushko, (2014), Risks Related to EME Corporate Balance Sheets: The Role of Leverage and Currency Mismatch, BIS Quarterly Review (September),

debate is in particular the effectiveness of qualitative easing, a form of unconventional monetary policy[82] that changes the risk composition of the central bank balance sheet with the goal of stabilizing economic activity.[83] A distinction, however, need to be made here between quantitative easing,[84] defined as an increase in the size of the central bank balance sheet, and qualitative easing, defined as a change in its risk composition.[85] A change in the risk composi-

---

pp. 35–47. See also: F. de Graeve and J. Lindé, (2015), Effects of Unconventional Monetary Policy, Sveriges Riskbank Economic Review Nr. 2015/1, pp. 43–74. Unconventional monetary policy and the low interest rate seem to reduce bank profitability in the long run; see: C. Borio et al., (2017), The Influence of Monetary Policy on Bank Profitability, International Finance Vol. 20, Issue 1, pp. 48–63. Bank profitability also impacts financial stability and that is what interests us here. Xu et al. made an attempt to formulate a model for analysis: in short they first developed a theoretical model of the relationship between bank profitability and financial stability by exploring the role of non-interest income and retail-oriented business models. Following that they identified the determinants of bank risks and profitability, and how the level and the source of bank profitability affect risks. Their conclusions can be summarized as being that '[r]esults reveal that profitability is negatively associated with both a bank's contribution to systemic risk and its idiosyncratic risk, and an over-reliance on non-interest income, wholesale funding and leverage is associated with higher risks. Low competition is associated with low idiosyncratic risk but a high contribution to systemic risk. Lastly, the problem loans ratio and the cost-to-income ratio are found to be key factors that influence bank profitability.' That implies that the link between bank profitability and stability risk all depends on the sources of bank profitability, in particular where there is an over-reliance on market-based non-interest income, leverage, and wholesale funding. See: T.T. Xu et al., (2019), Bank Profitability and Financial Stability, IMF Working Paper Nr. WP/19/5, January. Also: P. Abedifar, et al. (2018), Non-Interest Income and Bank Lending, Journal of Banking and Finance Vol. 87 (February), pp. 411–426; V.V. Acharya, et al. (2017), Measuring Systemic Risk, The Review of Financial Studies Vol. 30, Issue 1, pp. 2–47; G. Dell'Ariccia, et al. (2017), Bank Leverage and Monetary Policy's Risk-Taking Channel: Evidence from the United States, Journal of Finance Vol. 72, Issue 2, pp. 613–654; I. Drechsler, et al. (2017), The Deposits Channel of Monetary Policy, Quarterly Journal of Economics Vol. 132, Issue 4, pp. 1819–1876.

[82] If one assumes that the monetary toolkit is supposed to lead one way or the other to a Pareto optimum, one has concluded that (un)conventional monetary policies and prudential tools, capital requirements and the interest rate are not independent instruments, and no choice in itself will lead to that Pareto optimum. Extending the monetary toolkit with additional features (e.g. the payment of interest on bank reserves and QE policies) can in conjunction with the aforementioned instruments restore the Pareto optimum or approach that optimum. See in detail: M. Magill et al., (2016), Unconventional Monetary Policy and the Safety of the Banking System, USC Dornsife Institute for New Economic Thinking, Working Paper, Nr. 17-04, November 11.

[83] Haldane et al. conclude that, besides the fact that only when central bank balance sheet expansions are used as a monetary policy tool they have a significant macroeconomic impact, there is evidence for the US that the effectiveness of QE may vary over time, depending on the state of the economy and liquidity of the financial system. QE can however also have strong spillover effects cross-border, mainly via financial channels. See in detail: A.G. Haldane et al., (2016), QE: The Story so far, Bank of England Working Paper, Nr. 624, October.

[84] Much has been said and written about the optimal level and effectiveness of the QE programs worldwide. The same holds true about a possible QE exit which is proven to be very difficult. A permanent QE model however is never welfare improving, concludes Harrison. See in detail: R. Harrison, (2017), optimal Quantitative Easing, bank of England Staff Working Paper Nr. 678, September 22.

[85] W. Buiter, (2008), Quantitative Easing and Qualitative Easing: A Terminological and Taxonomic Proposal, Financial Times, Willem Buiter's mavercon blog. See more recent: H. Kuroda, (2017),

tion of the central bank's balance sheet (thus qualitative easing) will change equilibrium asset prices. A policy in which a central bank stabilizes non-fundamental fluctuations in the stock market is Pareto improving.[86] In more recent years the question was asked if the new set of tools, commonly labeled as unconventional monetary policies (UMP),[87] should still be used when economic conditions and interest rates normalize.[88] In the Pareto optimum however as

Quantitative and Qualitative Monetary Easing and Economic Theory, Speech by the BoJ Governor at the University of Zurich, November 13. 'Quantitative easing' inflates the Central Bank balance sheet, printing money and adding liquidity to the system while qualitative easing modifies the asset composition. With qualitative easing, Central Banks absorb the risk, flattening the yield curve. Both measures increase inflation and reduce borrowing risk premiums with an impact on company's balance sheet, widening economic and financial margins and decreasing the real value of debt'. See in detail: R.M. Visconti and M.C. Quirici, (2015), Qualitative Easing and Risk Transfer from Corporations to Central banks, Corporate Ownership and Control, Vol. 12, Issue 3, pp. 201–210. Ferrero et al. conclude that large-scale asset purchases by central banks have progressively reduced the slope of the risk-free yield curve, thus lowering banks' net interest margin. This could have induced banks to extend credit to riskier borrowers, increasing concerns about financial stability. A flattening of the yield curve is associated with a reduction in the share of loans with a higher counterparty risk. Monetary policy measures that aim to reduce long-term rates are, therefore, able to stimulate economic activity without increasing banks' credit risk. In detail: G. Ferrero et al., (2019), Credit Risk-Taking and Maturity Mismatch: the Role of the Yield Curve, Bank of Italy Working Paper Nr. 1220, April 29.

[86] See: R.E.A. Farmer and P. Zabczyk, (2016), The Theory of Unconventional Monetary Policy, Bank of England Staff Working Paper Nr. 613, September. Their conclusion is twofold: a central bank that takes risk onto its balance sheet can increase welfare and the optimal intervention restores efficiency and is self-financing.

[87] The follow-up question that emerges after the question about the effectiveness of UMP has been asked is the impact on the global economic fabric of the unwinding of such an UMP position. That unwinding has essentially two dimensions: changes (increases) in short-term policy rates and balance sheet adjustments. That will impact in particular emerging countries whose currency is pegged to the USD and those that have seen massive inflows from advanced economies. Mitigating the spillovers of those unwinding is very difficult, especially as most emerging economies use only short-term rates as a single monetary tool. Capital control and macroprudential policies will be needed to complement the financial stability toolkit. Balance sheet adjustments of central banks tend to impact long-term rates and will indirectly influence short-term rates through what is called 'financial plumbing'. That occurs continuously in financial markets through posting and lifting collateral and which are 'generally received by the collateral desks of the banks not only via reverse-repo but also from securities borrowing, prime brokerage agreements, and over-the-counter (OTC) derivative positions (p. 21)'. Those pledged securities are generally posted mark-to-market. The collateral re-use rate (or collateral velocity) has declined significantly since the crisis (from about 3% to 1.6%), partly due to the incoming legislation on this front. That decline in the re-use rate impacts financial lubrication. Now when the unwinding of central banks' balance sheets (which cause good collateral to be released) goes hand-in-hand with the discussed declining re-use rate, short-term money rate might move away from policy rates. See in detail: M. Singh and H. Wang, (2017), Central bank Balance Sheet Policies and Spillovers to Emerging Markets, IMF Working Paper Nr. WP/17/172, July.

[88] D. Quint and M.S.M. Peria, (2017), Should Unconventional Monetary Policies Become Conventional, IMF Working Paper Nr. WP/17/85, March. They conclude that the benefits of using such UMP in normal times are substantial, but that 'the benefits from using UMP are shock-dependent and mostly arise when the economy is hit by financial shocks. When more traditional

often achieved through inefficient rather than efficient policy instruments, externalities, for example, are typically regulated by quotas or standards, whereas a Pigovian tax could have yielded a Pareto (or near Pareto) optimum more efficiently.[89] The question about effectiveness of monetary policy on bank lending in a low interest rate environment[90] needs to be answered with the suggestion that reductions in short-term interest rates are less effective in stimulating bank lending growth when rates reach a very low level.[91] The impact of low rates on the profitability of banks' traditional intermediation activity explains the subdued evolution of lending during the post-crisis period (2010–2014).[92] The post-crisis environment did also have an impact on the overall banking business model and in particular the funding mix.

business cycle shocks (such as supply and demand shocks) hit the economy, the benefits of using UMP are negligible or zero'.

[89] Often political models and the vested interests obstruct efficient interventions. One could argue that less interventionist policy makers would engage a Pigovian instrument faster as a Pareto dominated instrument and consequently act welfare enhancing. See: D. Austen-Smith et al., (2018), Gridlock and Inefficient Policy Instruments, Working Paper, June 7, mimeo.

[90] To begin with the low interest rate environment presents a significant challenge to banks and is likely to 'entail major changes to their business models over the long-run. Lower returns to maturity transformation in the face of flatter yield curves and an inability to offer deposit rates significantly below zero combine to compress bank earnings in this environment', argue Q. Chen et al. Interestingly enough and in my understanding quite correctly they see a new equilibrium in that situation. Not driven solely by monetary efforts but driven by population aging and slower productivity growth, they see banking drifting toward provision of fee-based, utility services. See in detail: Q. Chen et al., (2018), Banking in a Steady State of Low Growth and Interest Rates, IMF Working Paper Nr. WP/18/192, August. Also: S. Claessens et al., (2017), Low-For-Long Interest Rates and Banks' Interest Margins and Profitability: Cross-Country Evidence, International Finance Discussion Papers Nr. 1197, Board of Governors of the Federal Reserve System, Washington D.C.; G. Dell' Arriccia et al., (2017), Bank Leverage and Monetary Policy's Risk-Taking Channel: Evidence from the United States, Journal of Finance, Vol. 72, Nr. 2, pp. 613–654; I. Dresschler et al., (2017), The Deposits Channel of Monetary Policy, Quarterly Journal of Economics, Vol. 132, Nr. 4, pp. 1819–1876; M. Katagiri, (2018), The Equilibrium Yield Curve, the Phillips Curve and Monetary Policy, IMF Working Paper Nr. WP/18/242, November.

[91] In detail: R. Agarwal and M. Kimball, (2019), Enabling Deep Negative Rates to Fight Recessions: A Guide, IMF Working Paper Nr. WP/19/84, April. The zero lower bound interest rate is not a law of nature, it is a policy choice. But monetary policy remains constrained by the lower bound in many countries, and thus limiting the options to address future deflationary shocks. The existence of cash prevents central banks from cutting interest rates much below zero. Assenmacher and Krogstrup now suggest decoupling cash from electronic money to achieve a negative yield on cash, which would remove the lower bound constraint on monetary policy. See in detail: K. Assenmacher and S. Krogstrup, (2018), Monetary Policy with Negative Interest Rates: Decoupling Cash from Electronic Money, IMF Working Paper Series Nr. WP/18/191, August. Also: G.B. Eggertson et al., (2019), Negative Nominal Interest Rates and the Bank Lending Channel, NBER Working Paper Nr. 25416, January. The latter document that deposit rates stopped responding to policy rates once they went negative and that bank lending rates in some cases increased rather than decreased in response to policy rate cuts. They construct a macro-model with a banking sector that links together policy rates, deposit rates and lending rates. Once the policy rate turns negative, the usual transmission mechanism of monetary policy through the bank sector breaks down. Moreover, because a negative policy rate reduces bank profits, the total effect on aggregate output can be contractionary.

[92] This result holds after controlling for business and financial cycle conditions and different bank-specific characteristics, such as liquidity, capitalization, funding costs, risk and income diversification.

Gambacorta et al. highlight that '[i]n their post-break business model, banks rely less on cross-border liabilities and, instead, tap funds from outside their jurisdictions by making more active use of their subsidiaries and branches, as well as inter-office accounts within the same banking group.'[93]

On a more fundamental level, what can also be considered out of scope are the technical fundamentals on which our banking system is created including the fractional reserve banking model and its implications including the money-creating function of private FIs. Within the context of this work they are a given, despite their many dysfunctional characteristics. The alternative which would translate into a full reserve banking system has always been ignored as it would precipitate a credit crunch or excessive volatile interest rates. There claims have recently been found baseless.[94]

The end result anno 2019 is a FI regulatory infrastructure that is by and large very difficult to operate and not adding to the much-needed transparency. In fact, intense lobbying has contributed to the complexity of the FI regulation. Although a full regulatory review would point to dysfunctionalities across the board, a very problematic aspect is the 'risk weighting' of regulatory capital. The conundrum ahead is that of a choice that needs to be made, either by leaning more heavily on rules, or on regulatory discretion, realizing that we will most likely never succeed in developing a financial regulatory system based purely on market discipline. The complexity of the current financial infrastructure deters rather than facilitates market discipline,[95] in particular the risk weighting rules determining the amount of regulatory capital that a specific FI should hold.[96] Those are invalidated as the correct instrument for determining the level of bank capital required given its risk exposure.[97] In fact, they incentivize (undesired) behaviors by FIs.

See in detail: C. Borio and L. Gambacorta, (2016), Monetary Policy and Bank Lending in a Low Interest Rate Environment: Diminishing Effectiveness?, BIS Working Paper Nr. 612, February. Also: M. Bech, and A. Malkhozov, (2016): How have Central Banks Implemented Negative Policy Rates?, BIS Quarterly Review, March, pp. 31–44.

[93] L. Gambacorta et al., (2017), Changing Business Models in International Bank Funding, BIS Working Paper Nr. 614, March.

[94] See: P. Lainà, (2015), Money Creation under Full Reserve banking: A Stock-flow Consistent Model, Levy Economics Institute, Working Paper Nr. 851, October.

[95] See for the issues with the current regulatory framework and some alternatives suggested: C. Fullenkamp and C. Rochon, (2014), Reconsidering Bank Capital Regulation: A New Combination of Rules, Regulators and Market Discipline, IMF Working Paper, Nr. WP/14/169.

[96] Fullenkamp and Rochon, Ibid. pp. 4–9. Higher capital requirements seem to trigger higher risk taking in particular by large and less profitable banks, ESRB, (2019), E. Dautović, (2019), Has Regulatory Capital Made Banks Safer? Skin in the Game v. Moral Hazard, ESRB Working Paper Nr. Nr. 91.

[97] V. Acharya et al., (2013), Testing Macroprudential Stress Tests: The Risk of Regulatory Risk Weights, NYU Stern, Working Paper. They show that the risk measures used in risk-weighted assets are cross-sectionally uncorrelated with market measures of risk as they do not account for the 'risk that risk will change'. Furthermore, the firms that appeared to be best capitalized relative to risk-weighted assets were no better than the rest when the European economy deteriorated into the sovereign debt crisis in 2011. Also: R. Anderson et al., (2018), Macroprudential Stress Tests and Policies: Searching for Robust and Implementable Frameworks, IMF Working Paper Nr.

It might make sense as a close to this subsection to refer to recent research by the Dutch Bureau for Economic Policy Analysis. They have reviewed the existing pool of research regarding the effectiveness of unconventional monetary policy.[98] They examined the findings of the existing literature on the effects of unconventional monetary policy and conclude that the existing estimates based on vector autoregressions in combination with zero and sign restrictions do not successfully isolate unconventional monetary policy shocks from other shocks impacting the euro area economy. In particular they refer to the schemes used by Burriel and Galesi, Boeckx et al. and Gambacorta et al.[99] The CPB researchers show that 'altering existing published studies by making the incorrect assumption that expansionary monetary shocks shrink the ECB's balance sheet or even ignoring all information about the stance of monetary policy results in the same shocks and, therefore, the same estimated responses of output and prices.' They conclude that 'it is implausible that the shocks previously identified in the literature are true unconventional monetary policy shocks. Since correctly isolating unconventional monetary policy shocks is a prerequisite for subsequently estimating the effects of unconventional monetary policy shocks, the conclusions from previous vector autoregression models are unwarranted.' They show this lack of identification for different specifications of the vector autoregression models and different sample periods.

WP/18/197, September. Other elements play a role, for example the (il)liquidity of the assets held by the bank; see: H. Tomura, (2014), Asset Illiquidity and Dynamic Bank Capital Requirements, International Journal of Central Banking, Vol. 10, Issue 3, pp. 291–317; L. Black et al., (2017), The Systemic Risk of European Banks During the Financial and Sovereign Debt Crises, FRB International Finance Discussion Paper Nr. 1083. Cetine et al. demonstrate the microprudential premise and limited view of systemic risk in supervisory stress tests. They find that indirect effects of a potential default, through the bank' other counterparties, are larger than the direct impact on the bank. Also, taken as a whole, the core banking system has a higher concentration to a single counterparty than does any individual bank holding company (i.e. stress-testing model underestimates exposures). See in detail: J. Cetina et al., (2016), Stressed to the Core: Counterparty Concentrations and Systemic Losses in CDS Markets, OFR Working Paper Nr. 16-01, March 8. Interesting, in an EU context, is the question whether stress testing and its underlying assessment are different at a national versus EU level. How is the contribution of a bank to systemic risk validated and whether the drivers of systemic risk differ at the national and at the euro area level? Buch et al. conclude that '[w]hile the qualitative determinants of systemic risk are similar at the national and euro-area level, the quantitative importance of some determinants differs. For example, banks with a higher loan share contribute less to systemic risk, but this effect is stronger at the national level compared to the euro-area level.' See in detail: C.M. Buch, et al., (2017), Drivers of Systemic Risk: Do National and European Perspectives Differ?, Deutsche Bundesbank Discussion Paper Nr. 9, Frankfurt am Main. Also: E. Jokivuolle et al., (2018), Testing the Systemic Risk Differences in Banks, Bank of Finland Research Discussion Paper Nr. 13, Helsinki.

[98] A. Elbourne and K. Ji, (2019), Do Zero and Sign Restricted SVARs Identify Unconventional Monetary Policy Shocks in the Euro Area? CPB Discussion Paper, February 19, via cpb.nl.

[99] Their models can be found here: P. Burriel, and A. Galesi, (2018), Uncovering the Heterogeneous Effects of ECB Unconventional Monetary Policies across Euro Area Countries, European Economic Review, Vol. 101(C), pp. 210–229; J. Boeckx, et al., (2017), Effectiveness and Transmission of the ECB's Balance Sheet Policies. International Journal of Central Banking, Vol. 13(1), pp. 297–333; L. Gambacorta, (2014), The Effectiveness of Unconventional Monetary Policy at the Zero Lower Bound: A Cross-Country Analysis. Journal of Money, Credit and Banking, Vol. 46(4), pp. 615–642.

As an alternative and to overcome this identification problem their research uses an alternative technique for isolating unexpected changes in monetary policy based on future rate data. Using data on monetary surprises from Jarociński and Karadi[100] and this alternative technique they do not find statistically significant evidence that unconventional monetary policy shocks have affected economic activity and only very weak evidence for an effect on prices. They however had to backtrack on earlier research[101] where they concluded that expansionary unconventional monetary policy shocks had stimulated economic activity in the euro area, although the estimates were only weakly significant. This was based on a vector autoregressive regression with zero and sign restrictions—a well-accepted methodology in the literature. As a conclusion, it can be argued that the 'impulse responses reported by previous studies are not responses to monetary policy shocks and they do not support the conclusion that the ECB's balance sheet policies have been successful at stabilizing the euro area economy.'[102]

11.4 The Financial Sector and Taxation

Despite all its particularities, from a tax perspective the financial sector is not treated very differently. Besides the exemption within the European VAT mechanism, it is subject to the normal corporate income tax systems across Europe and beyond. Admittedly, here and there the tax codes include some specifics that remind us of the intricacies of the financial industry but in general terms the industry is subject to the normal corporate income tax rules that apply to corporations in a specific jurisdiction regardless of their activities. It is therefore taxed on its income as produced by the IFRS standards applicable, adjusted where needed to reflect the specifics of the tax code.[103] It does occur, however, that the regulator imposes additional levies that apply to FIs specifically. In the aftermath of the financial crisis and governments facing large budget deficits, they considered it most appropriate to let the banking sector contribute to those deficits (assumingly caused by the financial sector) largely created by the bailout of FIs and the sharply slowing levels of economic activity in its aftermath. The cost of the financial crisis was and is significant and includes not only the direct costs of the bailouts, but also the indirect costs of the missed tax revenues due to sluggish economic growth for a number of years now in the eurozone. But financial crises evoke the uncomfortable feeling that something should have been done to prevent them. The probability of a crisis has, is and will be debated at length and the

[100] M. Jarocinski, and P. Karadi, (2018), Deconstructing Monetary Policy Surprises: the Role of Information Shocks, Working Paper Series Nr. 2133, European Central Bank, Frankfurt.

[101] A. Elbourne et al., (2018), The Effects of Unconventional Monetary Policy in the Euro Area, CPB Discussion Paper Nr. 371, February 6.

[102] Also: G. Corsetti, et al., (2018), One Money, Many Markets - A Factor Model Approach to Monetary Policy in the Euro Area with High-Frequency Identification, Cambridge Working Papers in Economics Nr. 1816, Faculty of Economics, University of Cambridge.

[103] See for an overview of FS taxation in the EU: European Commission, (2010), Financial Sector Taxation, EC Taxation Papers Series, Working Paper Nr. 25.

variables are somewhat clear. But how they interact is less clear. What we do know is that growth-, fiscal- and financial crises differ from each other[104] and that they occur separately as well as together. Three questions are key: 'which crises to focus on, which estimation method to use, and whether to focus on flagging vulnerabilities to crises or on the timing of crises'.The amount of variables is massive and often external to the underlying discussion. Often these variables include items such as 'reserve coverage, the current account deficit, external debt, and indicators of exchange rate overvaluation'. The best way forward in the analysis is to create a 'history of vulnerabilities', possibly per country.[105]

In the next few sections I will introduce a number of those existing or suggested additional bank levies and judge them on their externality-reducing qualities. Given the wide portfolio of different bank levies that have been introduced in recent years a comprehensive and/or comparative analysis would be unrealistic and to a large degree unnecessary keeping in mind that the backbone theme of this study is that 'neoliberalism (including deregulation) combined with globalization is a source of scalable externalities'.[106] Given the rather disappointing to mildly satisfying nature of the command-and-control legislation, embryonic thinking has been, starting only recently, trying to apply the century-old Pigovian theory to issues in twenty-first-century markets. That undeniably includes the persistent weaknesses of the banking model in a globalizing environment. I have therefore limited the analysis, given the conduct of this analysis, to the Dutch bank tax and the

---

[104] In that triangle variables like the current account, real GDP, the fiscal balance and private sector credit play a role.

[105] See in extenso: S. Basu et al., (2017), A Model to Assess the Probabilities of Growth, Fiscal, and Financial Crises, IMF Working Paper Nr. 17/282, December. Also: J. Abad et al., (2017), Mapping the Interconnectedness between E.U. Banks and Shadow Banking Entities, NBER Working Paper Nr. 23280; L. Alessi and C. Detken, (2017), Identifying Excessive Credit Growth and Leverage, Journal of Financial Stability, Vol. 35, April, pp. 215–225; L. Catão and G.M. Melisi-Ferreti, (2014), External Liabilities and Crises, Journal of International Economics, Vol. 94, Issue 1, pp. 18–32.

[106] Besides the fact that countries are losing control of their domestic financial conditions. See in detail: IMF, (2017), Are Countries Losing Control of Domestic Financial Conditions, Global Financial Stability Report, Getting the Policy Mix Right, April, pp. 83–107. They argue '[g]reater financial integration can complicate the management of domestic financial conditions in several ways. First, policymakers may need to take external factors into greater consideration when pursuing domestic objectives. Second, global financial integration may make it harder for domestic policymakers to control financial conditions at home—for example, it may hamper the transmission of monetary policy' (p. 83). Examplary can be further referred to: L. Catão et al., (2017), International Financial Integration and Funding Risks: Bank-Level Evidence from Latin America Prepared, IMF Working Paper Nr. WP/17/224, October. They draw three main conclusions: (1) international financial liberalization lowers bank capital ratios and increases the shares of short-term funding; (2) large banks substitute interbank borrowing for equity and long-term funding, whereas small banks increase the proportions of retail funding in their liabilities; and (3) riskier bank funding in the aftermath of financial liberalizations is exacerbated by asymmetric information, which rises on geographical distance and the opacity of balance sheets. Also: D. Duffie and A. Krishnamurthy, (2016), Pass-Through Efficiency in the Fed's New Monetary Policy Setting, Stanford University Working Paper. Mimeo; S. Avdjiev et al., (2018), Transmission of Monetary Policy Through Global Banks: Whose Policies Matter, BIS Working Paper Nr. 737, August 20, via bis.org

European Financial Transaction Tax. Their contribution here is limited to demonstrating that none of them, in a meaningful way, is externality-reducing. To that effect, it needs to be pointed out that I will not engage in the analysis of the distortionary effect of the different levies. Such analysis, which is justified in its own right, could complement the externality-inducing analysis, but would become too distant from the main theme as indicated above and would require its own proprietary methodology. It would imply branching out into such areas as the abolition of interest deduction on debt financing, revision of the VAT exemption, and novel alternative models designed for the FI sector such as the financial activities tax (FAT). The same could be said of retributions. They set themselves apart from taxes in the sense that they are a compensation for an individual good or service provided by the (decentralized) state and where the compensation is or needs to be correlated with the price of the service rendered. In such a context a bank levy could be construed as an insurance premium. That would pose tremendous challenges, besides the fact that it would not be externality reducing and the tax incidence sits with the end consumer. An ex ante insurance premium would create moral hazard for future undesired behavior. Also in economic terms, retributions seem to have economic vulnerabilities. It is for example unrealistic to think that a government can 'insure' the balance sheet of (multiple) FIs that are often many times larger than the GDP of a country. Indeed, although trying to protect the 'deposits' of savers, the insurance needs to cover the balance sheet as a whole, as deposits are essentially 'unsecured debt' and would be wiped out in the event of financial distress or insolvency were it not for the deposit insurance mechanism already in place. A retribution would then have to be linked to that existing insurance mechanism. But that mechanism is there to protect savers so that they can save and earn income on a 'risk-free basis' (up to a certain level). The service rendered for which the retribution would be charged would then be vis-à-vis the savers rather than the FIs and the charge would have to sit with them.

11.4.1 The Dutch Bank Tax

In the Netherlands,[107] such a bank-specific levy was introduced.[108] Essentially, it is a levy on all banks active in the Netherlands. Two rates apply: (1) 0.022% on all long-term unsecured debt and (2) 0.044% on all short-term debt, with a minimum threshold of 20 billion Euro (amounts below are exempt). Short-term equals less than one year and long-term everything else. Debt covered by the deposit insurance system is exempt. The amount due cannot be offset against any other tax due by the bank and therefore comes on top of any existing tax liability. The tax was introduced arguing that the banks had been enjoying an implicit state guarantee during the financial crisis, which therefore justifies an enhanced

---

[107] In many other countries that was the case as well. See for an overview: V. Mendoza, P. Carville and B. Larking, (2011), Bank Taxes: Variations on a Theme, Derivatives and Financial Instruments, Vol. 13, Issue 4, pp. 222–230.

[108] Wet Bankenbelasting, Staatsblad (Official Gazette) 2012, p. 325.

contribution.[109] Besides the fact that the answer to what the end-cost of the state guarantee will be is unclear as long as not all state guarantees and bailout amounts are repaid,[110] it also creates a tremendous moral hazard. The introduced tax now institutionalizes the concept of an implicit state guarantee for (systemically important) FIs as a structural insurance for which the premium has been paid up front.[111] Neither the rates nor the ratio between them have been substantiated.[112]

The rationale for the two criteria embedded in the bank tax, (1) the variation in rates between short term versus long term and (2) the levy on unsecured debt, has been justified as an incentive to avoid unbalanced funding on the part of the FI. The differentiation between short-term and long-term unsecured debt and the fact that short-term debt has been considered more risky by the regulator have been criticized.[113] Kavelaars argued '[a] more fundamental issue is whether or not the basic assumption – current debts are riskier than long-term debts – is correct, since current debts can be considered to increase flexibility. They prevent the parties from being stuck with long-term contracts in the event the financial sector faces an economic downturn. As a rule, accelerated redemption of long-term debts can only be effected if penalties are paid. Thus, the conclusion those current debts are riskier than long-term debts is not at all obvious'.[114]

This position seems ill-digested, although I agree that a lack of substance in the explanatory memorandum regarding this aspect does not make this the Dutch regulator's finest intellectual hour.

It is clear that the legal rationale for this law is very weak, but for many other reasons (see Sect. 11.5) than the one mentioned. In the case of the (perceived) riskiness of long- and short-term debt it should be considered that a bank has a natural inclination to finance itself with cheaper short-term debt in the wholesale market, as it will maximize the gross interest rate margin.[115] The natural banking paradigm would therefore be lending-in on a

[109] Kamerstukken (Parliamentary Documents) II 2011–2012, 33121, Nr. 3, p. 2.

[110] In practical terms it means that the regulator was of the opinion that the FIs had an enhanced accountability and that that justified an enhanced contribution toward reducing the government deficit caused by the massive lending needed on the part of the sovereign to materialize the bailout. The bank tax does not mathematically try to equate the exact cost of the bailout mechanism. The taxes raised in this respect will also not be isolated for the purposes of future issues in this sector but will flow to the general means of the sovereign and be used at its discretion.

[111] Although the Dutch government indicated that this was not the idea. See: Kamerstukken (Parliamentary Documents) II 2009/10, 31980, Nr. 9, p. 10; Kamerstukken (Parliamentary Documents) II 2010/11, 21501-07, Nr. 791, p. 15.

[112] The difference in rates is governed by the remaining term of the debts as at the balance sheet date, facilitating redemption and refinancing when long-term debt becomes current debt in its final year.

[113] P. Kavelaars, (2012), Netherlands Bank Tax Introduced, European Taxation (August), paragraph 3.3., pp. 437–442. Van der Geld seems to agree, although not explicitly, see J. Van der Geld, (2013), Bankenbelasting: de foute oplossing voor een echt probleem, Rijkers Bundel, Prisma Print, pp. 115–120.

[114] Kavelaars, (2012), Ibid. p. 441.

[115] Which equals the rate(s) they charge to their customers and the cost of funding for the bank. In general accounting terms the gross interest margin for a bank (at least regarding their lending activities) equals the gross margin for other corporations.

short-term basis and lending-out on a long-term basis.[116] Financing a bank with long-term debt is therefore more expensive in relative terms but provides stability in the event of a shakeout in the market or when the market is temporarily closed for business, as was the case in the early part of the 2008 crisis. It was at that point in time that liquidity in the money market funds (MMFs)[117] dried up overnight and those MMFs finance to a very large degree the short-term debt of banks. The MMFs were in fact a critical component in the cascade of events causing the magnitude of the 2008 crisis.[118] The short-term debt, despite its flexibility, therefore poses much more of a risk to a bank[119] than long-term debt: (1) banks enhanced their gross interest margin when lending-in short and lending-out long, that is, the higher the maturity differential the higher the gross profits for the bank ('maturity risk'), and (2) short-term debt poses large refinancing risk for the bank as it heavily relies on assumed liquidity in the MMFs that finance most of the short-term debt of banks. MMFs themselves provide 100% liquidity to their investors at all times and they will therefore automatically withdraw funding in the event of increased volatility or instability in the market, leading to an inability of banks to refinance their short-term debt in the market. Additionally, the intrinsic risk for the bank will increase as more short-term debt is used. The first incremental euro in short-term debt is therefore less risky relative to a situation where there are already considerable amounts of (short-term) debt on the books of the banks. The problem of short-term versus long-term debt cannot be properly judged in isolation, but should be embedded in the larger risk caused by leverage on a bank's balance sheet.

Any appropriate bank levy that would reflect the riskiness of the bank to the real economy and the sovereign in whose territory it operates would take into account the factors that would lead to the externalities that a bank can cause. The Dutch bank tax definitely does not qualify as a Pigovian tax, as its taxable base and rates are not geared toward

---

[116] With variations based on what is financed. The longer the term of the loans financed in the market the higher the interest rate. This is the direct consequence of the opportunity cost of capital principle, that is, capital that is locked away for a longer period of time will trigger a higher interest rate as that amount of capital cannot be put to work elsewhere for a long period of time, even if better risk-adjusted opportunities would occur in the market. That loss of agility comes at a higher cost.

[117] MMFs are essentially open-ended mutual funds that only invest in short-term risk-free (or near risk-free) debt instruments. They are therefore known for their high level of liquidity. Investors tend to use these vehicles as a quasi-bank account in order to generate a slightly higher return. Access to the full principle amount of their investment at all times is a pre-condition.

[118] And which has triggered new regulation on MMFs in both the US and Europe: see for Europe: Proposal for a Regulation of the European Parliament and of the Council on Money Market Funds, Com (2013) 615 final of September 9, 2013. Given their high level of liquidity these were the first vehicles to be impacted when the market shake-out started, and a fire sale was initiated. A 'fire-sale' can be defined as any sale that investors engage in, under distress, selling assets below their intrinsic value in order to provide liquidity to their customers or to meet proprietary liabilities.

[119] The regulators turn the tables on the issue: The Dutch government stated that research has shown that short-term funding accelerated the spreading of liquidity problems in the banking sector in recent years (Kamerstukken (Parliamentary Documents) II, 2011/12, 33121, Nr. 4, p. 7).

neutralizing or internalizing the externality caused by (systemically relevant) banking institutions.[120] I will therefore suggest an alternative Pigovian model of taxation for FIs which takes into account the risk exposures that lead to a (potential) externality. A variety of risks and their interaction will help in modeling a Pigovian alternative.

Similar bank taxes have been introduced around the world and the first analyses are coming through, e.g. in the case of Germany.[121] Not only did the tax generate very low levels of income and many banks were exempted, it also triggered adverse implications. Most notably banks reduced their loan supply and increased the deposit rates concluding an exogenous policy change.[122] It further led to an increase in wholesale funding costs.

11.4.2 The Financial Transaction Tax

Financial transaction tax, as proposed in a European context, also fails to qualify as a Pigovian tax. On September 28, 2011, the European Commission released a proposal for an EU Directive on a common system of financial transaction tax.[122] Since a Europe-wide introduction has proven to be unrealistic at this stage, a new proposal was issued in 2013[123] under the enhanced cooperation mechanism.[124]

---

[120] It does not really differentiate how a bank is financed relative to others and the cost will most likely be pushed forward to the bank's customers (see also Van der Geld, Ibid. p. 117).

[121] C. M. Buch et al., (2014), Taxing Banks: An Evaluation of the German Bank Levy, Deutsche Bank Discussion Paper, Nr. 38/2014. 'First, they decrease their total stock of loans whereas the provision of new loans remains unaffected. Second, banks try to attract deposits which are not subject to the tax by increasing deposit rates' (Ibid. p. 32).

[122] Com (2011) 594 final of September 28, 2011.

[123] Com (2013)71 of February 2013, Proposal for a Council Directive implementing enhanced cooperation in the area of financial transaction tax.

[124] At the time of closing the manuscript 10 countries (Austria, Belgium, France, Germany, Greece, Italy, Portugal, Slovakia, Slovenia and Spain) are still at the table. Expected implementation was foreseen by 2016 but extended to oversee the implications of Brexit in this matter. The legal basis was article 113 TFEU and Council Decision 2013/52/EU of January 22, 2013 authorizing enhanced cooperation in the area of financial transaction tax authorized the Member States listed in its Article 1 to establish enhanced cooperation in the area of FTT, O.J. L 22, 25.1.2013, p. 11. The EC, in May 2018, played down the initial 57 Billion USD in possible revenues to a meager 23.5Billion USD. It was also acknowledged that collecting could become a problem given the pending Brexit talks. Under the Austrian Presidency in the second half of 2018, the prospects deteriorated again as Austria indicated that the FTT proposal is simply a bad idea and that years of negotiations on the matter has created a situation where 'the scope of the proposed levy has been scaled back so much that it isn't worth the effort anymore'. See: B. Groendahl and A. Weber, (2018), Austria Says EU Financial Transaction Tax is on the Wrong Track, September 5, Bloomberg.com. There is support building for that position from a variety of angles. See, for instance, M. Coelho, (2016), Dynamic and Cross-Platform Optimal Financial Transaction Tax, Working Paper, mimeo; E. Dávila, (2016), Optimal Financial Transaction Taxes, NYU Working Paper mimeo. In May 2019 both France and Germany tried to revive the FTT proposal, this time based on the (already existing) French financial transaction tax model.

The mechanism suggested was embedded in and justified by a proper (non-fragmented) functioning of the EU internal market for capital. It is justified using three arguments[125]: (1) avoiding a fragmentation of the tax treatment in the internal market for financial services, and a possible distortion of competition between products and actors within the EU; (2) ensuring that financial institutions make a fair and substantial contribution to covering the costs of the recent crisis and creating a level playing field with other sectors from a taxation point of view and; (3) creating appropriate disincentives for transactions that do not enhance the efficiency of financial markets thereby complementing regulatory measures to avoid future crises.

The mechanism is a diversified rate on a wide and diverse set of financial transactions.[126] Many countries, including the Netherlands, have opted out. The rationale for the proposal can at least be considered ambiguous. Besides the clear intention to have the financial sector contribute to the budget deficits they created, its true rationale is skewed. That leads back to the basis of the FTT, which is based on the Tobin tax concept. The Tobin tax model was however designed to create a tax on speculative foreign exchange trades that could harm developing nations in their competitive positions. It was not designed to capture all the different types of financial transactions. Furthermore, the 2013 proposal's justification does not claim any correction to adverse market positions or potential market failures[127] as an objective. It would require a diversified rate on potentially harmful transaction (i.e. (naked) short selling of equities, (naked) credit default swap purchases and a variety of derivative positions or portfolio of derivative positions), causing enhanced volatility, an artificial increase in the cost of funding the underlying issuer, or a (temporary) dysfunctionality of the price discovery function in the capital markets on which these traded securities are listed.

11.5 Externalities in the Financial Sector and the Options to Address

11.5.1 Externalities in the Financial Sector

The interwovenness of public and private interests makes the financial sector prone to a large number of potential externalities. Many have always been around, but the 2008 crisis reminded us of their existence. Some have become magnified in scope due to the increased

[125] Com(2013)71 of February 2013, Ibid. pp. 2&4.

[126] See Chapter 1 of the proposal for details.

[127] The Dutch Bureau for Economic Policy Analysis on December 21, 2011 in their note '[e]valuatie van de financiële transactiebelasting' already, based on the 2011 FTT proposal, concluded that there is 'little evidence that the introduction of a financial transaction tax within the EU will be effective in correcting market failures, and finds that other taxes are likely to be more efficient in raising revenues, involving lower deadweight losses' (pp. 6–9). The Dutch Central Bank also finds the introduction of a financial transaction tax within the European Union undesirable. See DNBulletin (February 6, 2012).

interconnectedness of the banking sector worldwide.[128] It has even created new types of externalities. This section will analyze what these externalities entail and how they can be assessed and catalogued. Then, in the next section, we will address the question of what the potential remedies are, taking into account the potential options available. The focus will only be on the financial sector-specific externalities that will not include the more general externalities a bank can cause, for example, due to international tax planning,[129] ex ante risk management protocols,[130] corporate governance[131] or dividend policies.[132]

11.5.1.1 The DNA of a Bank and Its Externality-Causing Activities

An FI performs many different activities, which can be classified in many different ways. From a risk perspective a first classification can distinguish those activities that a bank performs as a service where there is no direct capital risk involved. These can include investment management advice, conducting transactions, credit card management, investment management services on behalf of clients and so on. There are also those that do involve bank capital, that is, lending, trading and other types of capital investments.

Another classification could be to consider the different activities from an exogenous or endogenous perspective. Most of the activities within a bank create endogenous risk[133] whereas the fact that banking institutions are globally interconnected creates an exogenous type[134] of risk, that is, systemic risk.[135] That risk is not intrinsic in any of the FIs involved but merely a consequence of those FIs being part of an integrated economy (i.e. a network

[128] See on the difficulty to measure the interconnectedness between the different players in the financial field and the lengthened financial (intermediation) chains: G. Houton and J.-C. Héan, (2014), How to Measure Interconnectedness between Banks, Insurers and Financial Conglomerates, Banque de France Working Paper, October, Mimeo.

[129] Å. Johansson, et al., (2017). Tax Planning by Multinational Firms, OECD Economics Department Working Paper Nr. 1355, Paris.

[130] D. Hirschleifer and S.H. Teoh, (2009), Systemic Risk, Coordination Failures and Preparedness Externalities, Journal of Financial Economic Policy, Vol. 1, Issue 2, pp. 128–142.

[131] V. Acharya and P. Volpin, (2007), Corporate Governance Externalities, London Business School and Centre for Economic Policy Research (CEPR) Working Paper.

[132] V.V. Acharya, H. Le and H. S. Shin, (2013), Bank Capital and Dividend Externalities, Princeton/NYU Working Paper Series.

[133] Those risks that, when they occur, only impact the party/parties involved in the transaction.

[134] Those risks that when they occur impact not only the engaged party/parties but also third parties.

[135] See for a detailed analysis of systemic risk: O. de Bandt and Ph. Hartmann, (2011), What is Systemic Risk Today, ECB Working Paper, pp. 37–83 (original ECB Paper 2000), in particular pp. 40–48. See in general: O. de Bandt, Ph. Hartmann and J.L Peydró, Systemic Risk in Banking, The Oxford Handbook of Banking, in A. N. Berger, P. Molyneux, and. O. S. Wilson (eds.), Oxford University Press, Oxford; G.G. Kaufman and K.E. Scott, (2003), What is Systemic Risk and Do Bank Regulators Retard or Contribute to it, The Independent Review, Vol. VII, Issue 3, pp. 371–391.

externality). At the heart of systemic risk lies contagion risk.[136,137] This allows us to categorize the different types of systemic risk based on (1) a single systemic event affecting only one institution or market or (2) a system-wide effect affecting many different institutions or markets. Both types, which can occur with varying degrees of intensity, can create narrow shocks (which can be idiosyncratic or limited systemic in nature) or truly system-wide shocks. The causes of these systemic risks can be (1) a lending boom, (2) bank runs,[138] (3) credit rationing[139]

[136] Underlying contagion risk lies coordinated game theory (i.e. behaviors of market participants are (partly) determined by behaviors of other market participants). Or specifically in this case, withdrawals at one bank trigger withdrawals at another bank by increasing players' beliefs that other depositors in their own bank will withdraw, making them more likely to withdraw as well. The level of contagion is higher the higher the FIs are interrelated; see in detail: M. Brown, S. Trautmann and R. Vlahu, (2014), Understanding Bank-Run Contagion, Working Paper Series Nr. 1711. See also for a novel approach to the contagion theory: T. Ahnert and C. Bertsch, (2015), A Wake-Up-Call Theory of Contagion, Bank of Canada/Banque de Canada Working Paper, Nr. 2015-14, April. The most problematic dimension of contagion risk is solvency contagion risk. This includes losses transmitted after banks default, but also losses due to the fact that creditors revalue their exposures when probabilities of default of their counterparties change. Solvency has been on the decline since the financial crisis mainly due to the increase in banks' capital and the decrease in interbank exposures. See in detail: M. Bardoscia et al., (2017), The Decline of Solvency Contagion Risk, Bank of England Staff Working Paper Nr. 662, June.

[137] It is fair to say that much of the literature has focused only on 'direct' contagion arising from firms' contractual obligations. Direct contagion occurs if one firm's default on its contractual obligations triggers distress (such as illiquidity or insolvency) at a counterparty firm. But contractual obligations are not the only means by which financial distress can spread, just as close human contact is not the only way that many infectious diseases are transmitted. Focusing only on direct contagion underestimates the risk of financial crisis given that other important channels exist. More recently attempts have been made to get a more holistic picture in place regarding indirect contagion and the channels which manifest even in the absence of direct contractual links. The first is the market price channel, in which scarce funding liquidity and low market liquidity reinforce each other, generating a vicious spiral. The second is information spillovers, in which bad news can adversely affect a broad range of financial firms and markets. See in detail including interesting literature list: L. Clerc et al., (2016), Indirect Contagion: The Policy Problem, ESBR Occasional Paper Series Nr. 9, January; R.Cont and E. Schaanning, (2017), Fire Sales, Indirect Contagion and Systemic Stress Testing, Norges Bank Working Paper Nr. 2. The latter conclude 'even with optimistic estimates of market depth, moderately large macro-shocks may trigger fire sales which may then lead to substantial losses across bank portfolios, modifying the outcome of bank stress tests.'

[138] After the bank run of 2008, Bernanke organized a monetary injection to fight deflation. When the probability of a bnk run is positive, depositors increase their money demand thereby reducing outstanding deposits. At the macro level that implies that the velocity of money drops and deflation arises. However, in some circumstances, monetary injections have no effect on prices but reduce money velocity and deposits. It has been argued that in case the Fed had not interfered in 2008, the MMF run would have been much smaller. See: R. Robatto, (2017), Flight to Liquidity and Systemic Bank Runs, ESRB Working Paper Nr. 38, March.

[139] Credit rationing occurs different for different borrowers: publicly listed borrowers are rationed more by prices or interest rates (increase in interest rate spread), whereas privately held borrowers are rationed more by the number of loans, but minimal increases in interest rate spreads. Public borrowers are rationed more by price, whereas private borrowers are rationed more by quantities. Private and public firms are statistically not treated different unless one takes into account the granular data on borrower listing status. See in detail: A.N. Berger et al., (2018), Who Pays for

in the interbanking market,[140] and (4) volatility in and structure[141] of (international) financial markets.[142] Systemic risk can be considered a network externality where the structure of the financial industry helps propagate shocks around the system unless this is checked by some form of circuit breaker or 'ring-fence'. Glasserman and Young examined how likely

Financial Crises? Price and Quantity Rationing of Different Borrowers by Domestic and Foreign Banks, IMF Working Paper Nr. WP/18/158, July. They also observe a re-pricing of borrower risk: interest rate spreads become significantly more sensitive to borrower leverage and credit rating during the crisis. A difference was also observed between foreign and domestic banks: foreign banks decreased lending quantities more and, among private borrowers, increased spread less than domestic banks. There are quite some policy implications reviewed (p. 22), not all of them which I agree with however (or at least not the policy design implication recommended implicitly or explicitly). See also: A.N. Berger et al., (2016), Reexamining the Empirical Relation between Loan Risk and Collateral: The Role of the Economic Characteristics of Collateral, Journal of Financial Intermediation, Vol. 26, pp. 28–46; P. Bolton et al., (2016), Relationship and transaction lending in a crisis. Review of Financial Studies, Vol. 29, pp. 2643–2676; S. Carbó-Valverde et al., (2016), Trade credit, the Financial Crisis, and Firm Access to Finance, Journal of Money, Credit, and Banking, Vol. 48, Issue 1, pp. 113–143; D. Weinstein, and M. Amiti, (2018), How Much do Idiosyncratic Bank Shocks Affect Investment? Evidence from Matched Bank-Firm Loan Data, Journal of Political Economy, Vol. 126, pp. 525–558.

[140] See for an analysis of the (German) interbank intermediation market and their determinants: M. Bluhm et al., (2016), Interbank Intermediation, Deutsche Bundesbank Discussion Paper Nr. 16, Frankfurt am Main. Key conclusions are: (1) interbank lending accounts for a significant share of an average bank's balance sheet, (2), the network of interbank loans is both sparse and persistent over time, (3), the average interbank exposure among commercial banks in Germany is longer than one year, and (4) banks hold significant interbank exposures on both sides of their balance sheet simultaneously. Banks use different maturity segments of the interbank market to manage their duration gap, defined as the difference between weighted maturity of a bank's assets and liabilities. Also: N. Bulusu and P. Guérin, (2018), What Drives Interbank Loans? Evidence from Canada, Bank of Canada Staff Working Paper Nr. 5, January. Their results suggest that the key friction-driving behavior in this market is the collateral reallocation cost faced by borrowers. Borrowers therefore adjust unsecured lending in response to changes in short-term cash needs and use repos to finance persistent liquidity demand. They also find that lenders set rates and haircuts taking into account counterparty credit risk and collateral market price volatility. See for a US analysis after the large-scale asset purchases and the new Basel III regulation. It has made the US interbank market basically disappear. They conclude that the new regulations may engender changes in market structure that result in interbank trading being completely replaced by non-bank lending to banks when excess reserves become scarce. In detail: K. Kim et al., (2018), Can the US Interbank Market be Revived?, Finance and Economics Discussion Series Nr. 2018-088. Washington: Board of Governors of the Federal Reserve System, https://doi.org/10.17016/FEDS.2018.088. Also in a broader context: F. de Fiore et al., (2019), Money Markets, Collateral and Monetary Policy, ECB Working Paper Nr. 2239, February 13. The latter paper seeks to understand the implications of these developments (miserable state of the interbank markets) for the broader economy and monetary policy.

[141] S. Titman, (2013), Financial Markets and Investment Externalities, The Journal of Finance, Vol. 68, Issue 4, pp. 1307–1329.

[142] For example caused by a fire sale (financial accelerator) of collateral assets (pecuniary externality) undervaluing liquidity. See M. Miller and L. Zhang, (2011), Whither Capitalism. Financial Externalities and Crisis, Warwick Working Paper on coordination problems (information-based runs, etc.). On the economy-wide effects of the collateral channels see: G. Cerqueiro et al., (2016),

contagion is in financial networks.[143] They conclude that expected losses from network effects are small without substantial heterogeneity in bank sizes and a high degree of reliance on interbank funding. They are also small unless shocks are magnified by some mechanism beyond simple spillover effects; these include bankruptcy costs, fire sales and mark-to-market revaluations of assets.[144] They also concluded that 'it is relatively difficult to generate contagion solely through spillover losses in a network of payment obligations. For contagion to occur, a shock to one node must lead to losses at another set of nodes sufficiently large to wipe out their initial equity (or net worth). This means that either the initial shock must be large (and therefore improbable) relative to the net worth of the infecting node, or that the net worth of the infected nodes must be small. More generally, the probability of contagion[145] depends on the comparative net worths of the various nodes, their level of leverage, and the extent to which the infecting node has obligations to the rest of the financial sector'...'The network structure matters more for the amplification effect, in which losses among defaulting nodes multiply because of their obligations to one another.[146] The degree of amplification is captured by the concept of node depth, which is the expected number of periods it takes to exit from the default set from a given starting point. This clearly depends on the specific structure of the interbank obligations, and is dual to the concept of eigenvector centrality in the networks literature'...'The network structure takes on added importance for both contagion and amplification once we introduce bankruptcy costs and mark-to-market reductions in credit quality. Bankruptcy costs steepen the losses at defaulted nodes, thereby increasing the likelihood that defaults will spread to other nodes. These losses are further amplified by feedback effects, thus increasing the system-wide loss in value. By contrast, reductions in credit quality have the effect of marking down asset values in advance of default.'[147]

Collateral damage? On Collateral, Corporate Financing and Performance, ECB Working Paper Series Nr. 1918, June; G. Cerqueiro et al., (2019), Collateral Damaged? Priority Structure, Credit Supply, and Firm Performance, Norges Bank Working Paper Nr. 9, May 29. The latter analysis is based on a unique legal reform in 2004 in Sweden redistributed collateral rights from banks holding floating liens to unsecured creditors without changing the value of assets on firms' balance sheets.

[143] In a financial network, the concept of financial centrality plays a role. Financial centrality of an agent in a financial network can be defined as the ex ante marginal social value of injecting an infinitesimal amount of liquidity to that agent. See in extenso: A. Chandrasekhar et al., (2018), Financial Centrality and the Value of Key Players, Working paper, mimeo.

[144] P. Glasserman and H.P. Young, (2013), How Likely is Contagion in Financial Networks, Columbia Business School Working Paper, mimeo; reproduced as Office of Financial Research, Working Paper Nr. 9 of June 21 and later on updated in Journal of Economic Literature (2017), Vol. 54, Issue 3, pp. 779–831.

[145] See, for instance, M. Brunnermeier et al., (2013), Assessing Contagion Risks from the CDS Market, ESBR Occasional Paper Series Nr. 4, September.

[146] G. Creamer, (2017), Network Structure and Systemic Risk in the European Equity Market, IEEE Systems Journal, Vol. 99, pp. 1–9; K. Anand et al., (2018), The Missing Links: A global study on uncovering financial network structure from partial data, Journal of Financial Stability. Vol. 35, pp. 107–119.

[147] Glasserman and Young, (2015), Ibid. pp. 27–28. See also: D. Acemoglu, et al., (2013), Systemic Risk and Stability in Financial Networks. Working Paper Nr. 18727, NBER, Cambridge, Massachusetts and R. Bookstaber et al., (2015), Process Systems Engineering as a Modeling Paradigm

Indeed, micro-level risk management and macroprudential risk management are of a different nature. It has been observed that financial market participants in general find it optimal to take on an excessive amount of systemic risk.[148] Individual market participants tend rationally to take the prevailing level of asset prices as given and do not internalize that their fire sales, in aggregate, contribute to the decline in asset prices.[149] As a result of this externality, individual market participants take on (and thus contribute to) excessive systemic risks.[150]

---

for Analyzing Systemic Risk in Financial Networks, Office of Financial Networks, OFR Working Paper Nr. 15-01, February 11. Bookstaber et al. highlight that as financial instability often results from positive feedback loops intrinsic to the operation of the financial system, the challenging task of identifying, modeling and analyzing the causes and effects of such feedback loops requires a proper systems engineering perspective, which is lacking in the remedies proposed in recent literature. They propose a 'signed directed graphs' model that is able to represent and reveal information missed by more traditional network models of financial system. This framework adds crucial information to a network model about the direction of influence and control between nodes, providing a tool for analyzing the potential hazards and instabilities in the system. See also: F. Caccioli et al., (2017), Network Models of Financial Systemic Risk: A Review, Working Pper, mimeo.

[148] Systemic risk is the danger of economy-wide financial feedback effects whereby adverse economic shocks force market participants to sell assets in order to raise liquidity, and the sales in turn push down asset prices and force them to sell even more of their asset holdings. On the productive side of the economy, this is mirrored in declines in output. Regarding the impact of the intrinsic value of macroeconomic news on asset prices see: T. Gilbert et al., (2016), Is the Intrinsic Value of Macro-Economic news announcements Related to their Asset Price Impact, ECB Working paper Series Nr. 1882, February. See for a broader analysis of the relationship between asset prices and monetary policy: L. Alessi and M. Kersenfischer, (2016), The Response of Asset Prices to Monetary Policy Shocks: Stronger then Thought, ECB Working Paper Serie Nr. 1967, September. Key finding is that, using a structural factor model (SFM) (which has material benefits compared to a vector autoregression model [VAR]), particularly in a low interest rate environment the impact is material. They conclude that 'asset prices respond more and more quickly to monetary policy shocks than commonly thought'...and that 'monetary policy is much more important in explaining asset price movements compared to available evidence' (pp. 26 ff).

[149] See for an analysis in the housing sector: J. Bianchi and E. Mendoza, (2011), Overborrowing, Financial Crises and 'Macro-Prudential' Policy, IMF Working Paper Nr. WP/11/24. They conclude that '[a]gents in a decentralized competitive equilibrium do not internalize the negative effects of asset fire-sales on the value of other agents' assets and hence they borrow too much ex ante, compared with a constrained social planner who internalizes these effects. [The] average debt and leverage ratios are slightly larger in the competitive equilibrium, but the incidence and magnitude of financial crises are much larger. Excess asset returns, Sharpe ratios and the market price of risk are also much larger'.

[150] A. Korinek, (2011), Systemic Risk Taking: Amplification Effects, Externalities and Regulatory Responses, ECB Working Paper Series, Nr. 1345. He asserts: '[e]ven though they (individual market participants (ed.)) may have access to a complete market to insure against systemic risk, they insure to a socially inefficient extent because when they trade off the costs and benefits of insurance, they do not internalize the social benefits of insurance in the form of mitigating the economy-wide fire sales. By contrast, a policymaker has the capacity to internalize this externality and make everybody better off by inducing financial market participants to reduce their systemic risk-taking. This in turn will lead to lower fire sales, smaller price declines and greater macroeconomic stability'(p.5). Also: C. Gilbert et al., (2018), Monetary Policy and Long-Run Systemic Risk taking, Banque de France Working Paper Nr. 694, September 14.

The question that remains open for now deals with the relationship between interconnectedness[151] and financial stability.[152] Or to be precise: Do more interbank connections promote stability through risk sharing, or do they lead to greater fragility by creating channels for contagion?[153] That question cannot be answered without bringing in other factors that contribute to contagion, including leverage levels and heterogeneity in size.[154] As I will

[151] The theory development of multilayer networks is still in its infancy, and its further development looks more like meandering than straightforward theory development. Understanding complex systems, including multilayer interconnected financial markets, is a route that involves many choices. Sergueiva et al. argue '[t]he empirical studies have considered the structure as a non-interconnected multiplex rather than as an interconnected multiplex network. No mechanism of multichannel contagion has been modeled and empirically evaluated, and no multichannel stabilisation strategies for preemptive contagion containment have been designed.' A. Sergueiva et al., (2017), Journal of Quantitative Finance, Vol. 17, Issue 12, pp. 1885–1904. They highlight that existing studies that use multilayer networks, in their multiplex form, to analyze the structure of financial systems, have (1) considered the structure as a non-interconnected multiplex network, (2) no mechanism of multichannel contagion has been modeled and empirically evaluated and (3) no multichannel stabilization strategies for pre-emptive contagion containment have been designed. Their model formulates an interconnected multiplex structure, and a contagion mechanism among financial institutions due to bilateral exposures arising from institutions' activity within different interconnected markets that compose the overall financial market. The empirical simulations their analysis produces confirm their capability for containing contagion. The potential for multichannel contagion through the multiplex contributes more to systemic fragility than single-channel contagion; however, multichannel stabilization also contributes more to systemic resilience than single-channel stabilization.

[152] T. A. Peltonen et al., (2015), Interconnectedness of the Banking Sector as a Vulnerability to Crises, ECB Working Paper Nr. 1866; a more central position of the banking sector in the macro-network increases the probability of a banking crisis. Regarding the aspect of uncertainty in the context of financial interconnectedness: C. Bertrand et al., (2018), Global Financial Interconnectedness: A Non-Linear Assessment of the Uncertainty Channel, Banque de France Nr. 661, January 24. Results clearly show that high uncertainty tends to generate more connectedness. From an economic policy point of view, this result suggests that in the presence of high uncertainty, an adverse financial shock in a specific country is likely to propagate more widely and more strongly to the whole financial system.

[153] See in detail: P. Glasserman, (2015), Contagion in Financial Networks, Office for Financial Research Working Paper, 15–21, October 20, in particular pp. 66–67. See also: T. Wag, (2017), Financing through Money Creation, Too Connected to Fail and Systemic Risk, University of Essex Working Paper, mimeo; H. Mao, (2017), Systemic Risk and Cyclical Eco; shadow bank money creation significantly expands during monetary tightening. This 'shadow money channel' offsets the reductions in commercial bank deposits and dampens the impact of monetary policy. Nomic Environment, Shanghai Second Polytechnic University Working Paper, October 24, mimeo. Xiao finds that explains the difference in monetary transmission between commercial and shadow banks. Facing more yield-sensitive clientele, shadow banks pass through more rate hikes to depositors, thereby attracting more deposits when the Fed raises rates. That would imply that monetary tightening unintentionally drives deposits into the uninsured shadow banking sector, amplifying the risk of bank runs. In detail: K. Xiao, (2019), Money Transmission through Shadow Banks, Columbia University Working Paper, April 20, mimeo.

[154] See for a novel approach based on basis swap spreads: J. Lafuente et al., (2016), Dissecting Interbank Risk, Working Paper, mimeo, October 5: they 'analyse interbank risk using the information content of basis swap (BS) spreads, floating-to-floating interest rate swaps whose payments are associated with euro deposit rates for alternative tenors.' They demonstrate that 'changes in systemic

further elaborate on, the interaction between these factors and the network topology is quite complex and not fully understood even at a theoretical level.[155] More theoretical and empirical research needs to be done before we can be confident that these measures are valid predictors of financial contagion in practice.[156] That would invariably include the question how to measure the 'size' of a systemic event.[157] Simply counting the number of bank failures is clearly not sufficient. A more comprehensive measure is the total loss in value of financial and nonfinancial assets. Obviously, from a policy standpoint one would like to be able to quantify the loss in economic welfare associated with a given loss in asset values. But much work remains in order to properly identify the relationship between financial losses, the supply of credit, and their impact on the real economy. Londono[158] had a closer look at what he calls 'bad contagion' which is 'the downside component of contagion' and which is most important given its negative implications for financial stability. Measuring the occurrence and severity of global contagion had led to a variety of models throughout time.

risk are associated with regime shifts. Shocks to aggregate liquidity are also important for describing persistent changes in BS spreads. Sovereign risk and risk aversion are further relevant factors explaining transitory fluctuations.'

[155] The interconnectedness can be mostly explained by investors' search-for-yield behaviour, financial linkages between banks, capital stringency and demand from institutional investors. Interconnectedness doesn't recognize national boundaries. See: T. Fong et al., (2018), Assessing the Interconnectedness between Cross-Border Shadow Banking Systems, HKIMR Working Paper Nr. 5, July.

[156] See also: E, Grant, (2016), Exposure to International Crises: Trade vs. Financial Contagion, Federal Reserve Bank of Dallas, Globalization and Monetary Policy Institute, Working Paper Nr. 280, August; G. Cappelletti and P.E. Mistrulli, (2017), Multiple Lending, Credit Lines and Financial Contagion, ECB Working Paper Nr. 2089, July. The latter examine a long time ignored channel of contagion, for instance, the existence of multiple credit lines. Multiple credit lines exist for a variety of reasons including the diversification of credit risk by lenders, borrowers diversify maturity and premature liquidation risk and of course to avoid or mitigate hold-up problems. They also conclude that during a crisis, multiple lending may be an important channel for contagion. They comment '[w]hen the typical markets for liquidity are impaired, banks may call back credit lines in order to obtain cash from borrowers. However, a reasonable reaction of the latter is that of drawing money from credit lines available at other banks thus propagating the liquidity shocks within the banking system. We find that this channel of contagion might have a significant impact on the stability of the banking system, in particular when that channel interacts with other channels for contagion related to direct interbank exposures' (p. 25). Multiple credit channels propagate and amplify liquidity shocks during a crisis.

[157] During late 2017 the Systemic Risk and Interconnectedness (SyRIN) tool was presented. It allows a comprehensive assessment of systemic risk via quantification of the impact of risk amplification mechanisms, due to interconnectedness structures across banks and other financial intermediaries—insurance, pension fund, hedge fund and investment fund sectors, which cannot be captured when analyzing sectors independently. It produces a variety of outcomes to evaluate systemic risk and this from complementary perspectives: tail risk, cross-entity interconnectedness and the contribution to systemic risk by different entities and sectors. See for details: F. Cortes et al., (2018), A Comprehensive Multi-Sector Tool For Analysis of Systemic Risk and Interconnectedness (SyRIN), IMF Working paper Nr. WP/18/14, December (2017).

[158] J.M. Londono, (2016), Bad Contagion, Board of Governors of the Federal Reserve System, International Finance Discussion Papers Nr. 1178, September.

Common in these models[159] is that 'contagion is measured as the proportion of international stock markets that simultaneously experience unexpected returns beyond a certain threshold. Londono decomposes contagion into its downside or bad component (the co-exceedance of low returns) and its upside or good component (the co-exceedance of high returns) and concludes that episodes of bad contagion are followed by a significant drop in country-level stock index prices and by a deterioration of financial stability indicators,[160] especially for more open economies. An overall problem with contagion is the fact that there is no theory or model that captures the contagion model extensively. That besides the fact that most of the models used imply a certain number of biases. Rigobon[161] therefore argues that there is not a single technique that can deal with all the problems related to contagion and makes some suggestions for a multi-model approach to capture the different angles. Korniyenko et al.[162] studied the interconnectedness of the global financial system and its susceptibility to shocks, thereby linking debt and equity exposures across countries in a multi-layered network. Their main point is that ignoring the heterogeneity of financial exposures, and simply aggregating all claims as is often done in other studies, can underestimate the extent and effects of financial contagion.[163] Despite the fact that the European

[159] See for these models: K.H. Bae, et al., (2003), A New Approach to Measuring Financial Contagion, Review of Financial Studies, Vol. 16, pp. 717–763; G. Bekaert, et al., (2014), The Global Crisis and Equity Market Contagion, Journal of Finance, Vol. 69, pp. 2597–2649; G. Bekaert, (2005), Market Integration and Contagion, Journal of Business, Vol. 78, pp. 39–69; G. Bekaert, (2013), Risk, Uncertainty and Monetary Policy, Journal of Monetary Economics, Vol. 60, pp. 771–788; C.T.Brownlees, and R.F. Engle, (2017), SRISK: A Conditional Capital Shortfall Measure of Systemic Risk, ESRB Working Paper Nr. 37, March. (also published as Review of Financial Studies, Vol.30, Nr.1, pp. 48–79). Also: J. Bian et al., (2017), Leverage Networks and Market Contagion, Working Paper, November, mimeo; E. Gerba and D. Żochowski, (2017), Knightian Uncertainty and Credit Cycles, ECB Working Paper Nr. 2068, May.

[160] R. Heath and E.B. Goksu, (2017), Financial Stability Analysis: What are the Data Needs, IMF Working paper Nr. WP/17/153, July. Weaks spots identified are 'shadow banking, capital flows, corporate borrowing, and granular data'.

[161] R. Rigobon, (2016), Contagion, Spillover and Interdependence, ECB Working Paper Series Nr. 1975, November. He concludes '[i]n consequence, correlations, principal components, OLS regressions, event studies, VAR's, Arch and Garch models, Probit and Logit, are all biased and time dependent. This is not because the structural parameters of the data generating process are unstable but because the models are all misspecified.'… 'The problem is even more complicated because there are no natural experiments nor instruments that could solve the identification problem (p. 19).'

[162] Y. Korniyenko et al., (2019), Evolution of the Global Financial Network and Contagion: A New Approach, IMF Working Paper Nr. WP/19/113, May. Also: E.M. Cerutti and H. Zhou, (2017), The Global Banking Network in the Aftermath of the Crisis: Is there Evidence of De-Globalization? IMF Working Paper, Nr. WP/17/232; P.R. Lane et al., (2017), International Financial Integration in the Aftermath of the Global Financial Crisis, IMF Working Paper Nr. WP/17/115, May.

[163] For the relationship between bank characteristics and financial contagion, see: S. Mazumder and L.R. Piccotti, (2019), Financial Contagion and Bank Characteristics, Working Paper, May 25, mimeo. While tier 1 capital requirements and greater financial constraints reduce a bank's contagion profile, the effect is non-monotonic. Banks with relatively higher total capital ratios tend to contribute more to financial contagion. Geographic distance between banks is negatively related to contagion profiles and they find evidence that institutional ownership increases banks' contagion profiles.

and global financial infrastructure has undergone changes since the great recession,[164] the network is still highly susceptible to shock for countries that are 'central' in the infrastructure or that have large financial systems. Within Europe, the country networks are small(er), but shocks easily emerge from the entire euro area. Similar emerging trends have been observed in Asia as well as in relation to China and Hong Kong SAR.

Institutions establish links with other agents as a way to diversifying risk and facilitate intermediation. But there are other factors: network formation between FIs occurs on different levels (business lines, foreign exchange, trading, repo etc.). The full picture should therefore require a detailed understanding on a granular level and a clear understanding of the incentives faced by those institutions why to create interdependencies. But also contagion has different sources, that is, not only the transmission of defaults through payment shortfalls. A quite different transmission mechanism is the contraction in short-term funding that can occur when institutions pull funding in response to liquidity shocks, which has been little studied, argues Glasserman.[165] And he continues '[o]ther mechanisms for contagion can operate without network linkages while reinforcing network effects. For example, the downward spiral in asset prices that results from the dumping of illiquid assets (fire sales) in response to liquidity shocks can spread losses through markets, amplifying a cascade of defaults. Yet another mechanism is information contagion.[166] This is triggered by changes in market perceptions about the creditworthiness of particular institutions and the value of their assets, which can feed through the system and create a general crisis of confidence'. But the largest weakness so far is the presupposition that complete and full transparent information is available, which doesn't relate well to reality. Network opacity is a first-line concern for both agents, regulators and supervisors. Opacity then in itself becomes a source of contagion risk, he concludes.

Ahnert and Georg[167] examined the effect of ex post information contagion on the ex ante optimal portfolio choices of banks and the welfare losses due to joint default. Their

---

[164] P. Fève et al., (2019), Shadow Banking and the Great Recession: Evidence from an Estimated DSGE Model, Banque Central de Luxembourg Working Paper Nr. 125, March. Also: P. Fève and O. Pierrard, (2017), Financial Regulation and Shadow Banking, Banque Central de Luxembourg Working Paper Nr. 111, July. Shadow banking interferes with macroprudential policies. More precisely, asymmetric regulation causes a leak toward shadow banking, which weakens the expected stabilizing effect, they conclude.

[165] Glasserman, (2015), Ibid. p. 67. To date there has been relatively little research on how institutions actually behave when determining how to ration short-term funding in times of financial stress. See, for instance, K. Fink et al., (2015), The Credit Quality Channel: Modeling Contagion in the Interbank Market, Deutsche Bundesbank Discussion Paper, Nr. 38/2015. Also: M. Pritsker, (2017), Choosing Stress Scenarios for Systemic Risk Through Dimension Reduction FRB Boston Risk and Policy Analysis Unit Paper Nr. RPA 17-4.

[166] D. Wang et al., (2018), Do Information Contagion and Business Model Similarities Explain bank Credit Risk Commonalities, DNB Working Paper Nr. 619, December 20.

[167] T. Ahnert and C.-P. Georg, (2017), Information Contagion and Systemic Risk, Bank of Canada Working Paper Nr. 2017-29. Also: K. Anand et al., (2016), Capturing Information Contagion in a Stress-Testing Framework, Deutsche Bundesbank Discussion Paper Nr. 29, Frankfurt am Main. They define information contagion as 'whereby bad news about one institution precipitates a loss

position is that because of counterparty risk and common exposures, bad news about one bank reveals valuable information about another bank, thereby triggering information contagion.[168] Systemic risk is defined as the ex ante probability of joint bank default ex post.[169] They further find that information contagion increases systemic risk when banks

---

of confidence in the security of holdings across the banking system'. A major problem until today is the quantification of information contagion. Anand et al. developed a model-based stress-testing framework where the solvency risks, funding liquidity risks and market risks of banks are intertwined. The key transmission mechanism is a two-way interaction between the beliefs of secondary market investors and the coordination failure between the creditors of financial institutions. Their findings are material: Not only can information contagion be significant (the probability of one bank entering distress due to contagion alone is nearly 20%, and the extreme tail associated with the system-wide distribution of bank losses is materially larger. A particular interesting feature is the fact that they decompose aggregate losses to the banking system according to their origin, that is, solvency risk, funding liquidity risk and information contagion. See also more recently: T. Ahnert and Co-Pierre Georg, (2017), Information Contagion and Systemic Risk, Bank of Canada Staff Working Paper Nr. 2017-29, July. They examine the effect of ex post information contagion on the ex ante level of systemic risk defined as the probability of joint bank default. They conclude that '[w]hen banks are subject to common exposures, information contagion induces small adjustments to bank portfolios and therefore increases overall systemic risk. When banks are subject to counterparty risk, by contrast, information contagion induces a large shift toward more prudential portfolios, thereby reducing systemic risk.' Further: P. Cerchiello and G. Nicola, (2018), Assessing News Contagion in Finance, Econometrics, Vol. 1, Issue 5, pp. 1–19; T. Ahnert and C. Bertsch, (2018), A Wake-Up Call Theory of Contagion, working Paper, March, mimeo. Key finding here, based on global coordination games, is that contagion can even occur after investors learn that regions are unrelated (zero macro shock); T. Ahnert, and A. Kakhbod, (2017), Information Choice and Amplification of Financial Crises, Review of Financial Studies, Vol. 30, Issue 6, June, pp. 2130–2178; Z. Li and K. Ma, (2017), A Theory of Endogeneous Asset Fire Sales, Bank Runs and Financial Contagion, May, Working Paper, mimeo; J. Idier and T. Piquard, (20170, Pandemic Crises in Financial Systems: A Simulation-Model to Complement Stress-Testing Frameworks, Banque de France Working Paper Nr. 621, January.

[168] 'One bank's investors find information about another bank's solvency valuable for two reasons. First, both banks might have invested into the same asset class like risky sovereign debt or mortgage backed securities. Learning about another bank's profitability helps the investor assess the profitability of its bank. Second, one bank might have lent to the other, for instance as part of a liquidity risk-sharing agreement. Learning about the debtor bank's profitability helps investors assess the counterparty risk of the creditor bank' (p. 24).

[169] See for the ability to predict bank defaults using systemic risk measures: Arndt-Gerrit Kund, (2018), Systemic Risk and Bank Defaults: Assessing the Explanatory Power of Systemic Risk Measures in Forecasting Bank Defaults, University of Cologne Working Paper, January 10, mimeo. Using systemic risk models in the 'probability of default model' might not always improve the initial model; it does entail a substantial improvement of correct predictions. Also: P. Smaga et al., (2016), Can Banks Default Overnight? Modeling Endogenous Contagion on O/N Interbank Market, Working Paper, mimeo. They show how the intrasystem cash fluctuations (the interbanking loan market), 'without any external shocks, may lead to systemic defaults, what may be a symptom of the self-organized criticality of the system'. See regarding predicting financial stress: T. Duprey and B. Klaus, (2017), How to Predict Financial Stress? An Assessment of Markov Switching Models, ECB Working Paper Nr. 2057, May. They conclude that 'the debt service ratio, the property price-to-rent ratio and the annual property price growth significantly affect the prob-

are subject to common exposures since portfolio adjustments are small. In contrast, when banks are subject to counterparty risk,[170] information contagion[171] induces a large shift toward more prudential portfolios and therefore reduces systemic risk.[172] Having said that, unanticipated information contagion will always increase systemic risk and banks are more prudent when they anticipate information spillover.[173]

Regarding the material externalities (i.e. caused by bank activities), a number of externalities have been observed that can be considered the fundamental externalities caused by banking institutions. These, in turn, can cause follow-on externalities (i.e. second-round externalities which on aggregate can cause systemic risk). In the following section those externalities will be systematically reviewed and considered from a Pigovian tax approach. The approach taken will be that of macroprudential behavior given what was said before, that is, that micro-and macro-risk management do not necessarily align in a globally integrated banking sector causing individual market actor to assume too high a level of systemic risk.

Before doing so, however, we will consider more generally what the possible policy responses are with respect to FI externalities, judged on their potential curative impact.

---

ability of entering a high financial stress regime, whereas the credit-to-GDP gap and the economic confidence indicator contribute significantly to the likelihood of exiting a high financial stress episode.' (p. 21). See regarding the role of contagion in the transmission of financial stress: M.C. Herculano, (2018), The Role of Contagion in the Transmission of Financial Stress, ESRN Working Paper Nr. 81, August 2. He identifies that bank default likelihoods depend, to a large extent, on peer effects that account on average for approximately 35% of total distress. Furthermore, he finds evidence of significant heterogeneity amongst banks and some institutions to be systemically more important that others, in terms of the peer effects.

[170] Regarding the mitigation of counterparty risks: Y. Gündüz, (2018), Mitigating Counterparty Risk, Deutsche Bundesbank Discussion Paper Nr. 35, September 14.

[171] See G. Cappelletti and G. Guazzarotti, (2017), The Role of Counterparty Risk and Assymetric Information in the Interbank Market, ECB Working Paper Nr. 2022, February. The rise in counterparty risk substantially decreases the probability of obtaining funds from foreign banks. The effect in the interbank market is meaningful, in particular in the unsecured market, because it is more information insensitive.

[172] See for a very interesting country-specific (i.e. Switzerland) paper regarding systemic risk and contagion analysis: IMF, (2014), TN- Systemic Risk and Contagion Analysis, September. See also: V.V. Acharya and T. Yorulmazer, (2002), Information Contagion and Inter-Bank Correlation in a Theory of Systemic Risk, Working Paper, December 21; V.V. Acharya and T. Yorulmazer, (2006), Information Contagion and Bank Herding, Working Paper, July, mimeo: information contagion induces profit-maximization of bank agents with other bank agents. Herding was also identified across pension funds, that is, they change their strategic allocations in the same direction over time. R. Bauer et al., (2018), Pension Fund Interconnectedness and Hrd Behavior, DNB Working Paper Nr. 612, October 30 and I. Koetsiers and J. Bikker, (2018), Herding Behavior of Dutch Pension Funds in Asset Class Investments, DNB Working Paper Nr. 602, July 24. See regarding the relation between bank herding and systemic risk: Y. Heo, (2019), The Impact of Bank Herding on Systemic Risk, Working Paper, April 4, mimeo.

[173] See also: C.-P. Georg, (2013), Information Contagion and Systemic Risk, Marie Curie ITN Presentation, Konstanz, April 12.

11.5.1.2 Options to Address Externalities in the Financial Sector

The title could equally well have referred to regulating or taxing[174] the financial sector. Indeed, these are the two major options. From a normative viewpoint, taxation is superior in many respects.[175] However, reality shows that financial regulation is adopted more frequently. From a positive, political-economic point of view it can be concluded that when a majority chooses regulation, the level is likely to be too harsh. If it chooses taxation, then the level is likely to be too low.[176]

It can be considered that at a sub-level there are broadly four possibilities to improve stability in the financial sector: (1) Improving capital regulatory requirements[177] through command-and-control legislation, (2) a deposit guarantee scheme levy aligned with a deposit guarantee scheme which has now been institutionalized at a European level,[178] (3) a bank tax as discussed above in the Netherlands, or (4) a financial transaction tax as discussed above at EU level.[179] A fifth could be added as a type of financial activities tax, as proposed by the International Monetary Fund (IMF) in 2010.[180] As already indicated in

---

[174] Although regulating and taxing do not constitute the same dynamics, they do remind us of the stand-off occurring in the FI sector between fiscal instruments and command-and-control legislation all trying to achieve the same objective, but in different ways, the stability of the financial markets and the mitigating of risk exposures.

[175] See in extenso: D. Masciandaro and F. Passarelli, (2013), Financial Systemic Risk: Taxation or Regulation, Journal of Banking and Finance, Vol. 37, Issue 2, pp. 587–596.

[176] Masciandaro and Passarelli, Ibid. pp. 594–596.

[177] The traditional Command-and-Control Legislation as embodied by the CRD packages lately updated in 2014 (CRD IV) and CRD V/CRR II (2019). Although there is initial consensus that capital requirements did improve financial stability, it also became clear that standardized implementation of capital requirements globally took place without taking into account the local dynamics of the financial sector. But to build an effective prudential framework, they may need to adapt international standards taking into account the sophistication and size of their financial institutions, the relevance of different financial operations in their market, the granularity of information available and the capacity of their supervisors. Under a proportionate application of the Basel standards, smaller institutions with less complex business models would be subject to a simpler regulatory framework that enhances the resilience of the financial sector without generating disproportionate compliance costs. Ferreira et al. provide guidance on the matter. See in detail: C. Ferreira et al., (2019), From Basel I to Basel III: Sequencing Implementation in Developing Economies, IMF Working Paper Nr. WP/19/127, June.

[178] Through a thorough revamp (proposal of July 12, 2010, recast, Com/2010/0368 final) of the Deposit Guarantee Scheme Directive: Directive 94/19/EC of the European Parliament and of the Council of May 30, 1994 on deposit-guarantee schemes, O.J. L 135, 31/05/1994, pp. 5–14. The proposal was approved by the European parliament on April 15, 2014 and published in June 2014: Directive 2014/49/EU of the European Parliament and of the Council of April 16, 2014 on deposit guarantee schemes, O.J. L 173, pp. 149–178.

[179] Despite many challenges and adverse implications. See: M. Dell'Era, (2018), Financial Transaction Taxes and Expert Advice, NBS Working paper Nr. 2018/4, October.

[180] In its most extensive form, a financial activities tax is assessed on total profit and wages, and can be viewed as a tax on a proxy for total value added by a financial sector company. The European

the initial part of Sect. 11.4, a wider portfolio of instruments could be construed or identified. These included the Financial Activity Tax, the revision of the VAT exemption of financial services, and retributions. None of them, however, contributes to the externality-inducing behaviors of FIs and are therefore considered outside the scope of this work. A notable exception to that would be the abolition of interest deduction in the corporate tax systems, despite the already existing thin-cap regulation in most countries.[181] This path is also full of major challenges when being applied to the financial industry. Unique to the financial sector is that its debt portfolio covers two different functionalities. There is the short- and long-term debt that is used for the operations of the FI as an organization, and there is the short- and long-term debt (biggest chunk) designated for onward lending to its customers. That part could be considered the inventory of the bank rather than operational debt, despite similar legal characteristics. By any standard, it would be unconvincing to imagine a system that would allow us to separate both components, unless artificially or based on industry averages (which ones?) or that the regulator would be in a position, in an economically justified way, to define the level at which interest deduction would be capped. Ending up with arbitrary levels would be highly probable and these would then have to be applied uniformly across FIs (equality principle). The preference here vis-à-vis externalities, but also in a wider context, would be a Pigovian instrument that allows us to relate the level of interest deductibility to the overall riskiness of the FI, of which leverage is only a component and which interacts with other features (maturities, creditworthiness of loan book, etc.).

Commission views a financial activities tax as a potential solution to the current VAT exemption of financial services, which the commission feels provides (undesired) benefits to the financial sector. See Com(2010)549 final, Communication regarding taxation of the financial sector of October 7, 2010). A proposal for a financial activities tax has not been released, most likely because it has focused on the introduction of the FTT and because it requires an assessment of the interaction with the VAT system if introduced. See also: V. van der Lans, (2012), The Proposed Bank Tax: To Tax or Not To Tax, Derivatives and Financial Instruments, IBFD, pp. 52–62.

[181] Corporate tax systems work in principle according to an origin-based principle. In more recent times however the idea of a destination-based model (like consumption taxes) has risen to prominence. Profits would be taxed where the sales take place. See: S. Hebous and A. Klemm, (2018), A Destination-Based Allowance for Corporate Equity, IMF Working Paper Nr. WP/18/239, November. In the context of shadow banking, corporate tax and interest-based deductions, the concept is interesting as it can facilitate an allowance for corporate equity or corporate capital. The benefit is that it neutralized the different treatment of capital sources as is the case in the current corporate tax model (pp. 8–11). To avoid accounting tricks, not only a destination-based model is suggested but also a shift from corporate taxation on accounting net income to a cash-flow-based tax model has been recommended in recent years. That would boost investments and economic output. See, for instance, B. Carton et al., (2019), Corporate Tax Reform: From Income to Cash Flow Taxes, IMF Working Paper Nr. WP/19/13, January. Although I have serious issues with some of the statements made in the report, this is not the time and place to detail them. My issues relate mainly to the fact that cash-flow-based models on a domestic and thus on a territorial-based frame are very vulnerable to avoidance. Further, the idea that it boosts economic output is very doubtful and the evidence unconvincing even when not taking into account possible avoidance. Spillovers that are positive in the long run are spillovers that often never show up. The authors also implicitly demonstrate the material weakness when indicating that the reform would work best when 'when all countries undertake the reform'. We all appreciate how difficult that is. But there is good news:

So far, capital regulatory requirements have been introduced and (2–4) above create a tax liability but do not solve to any degree the externality aspect discussed. The option to address market failures can be: (1) a Pigovian approach could constitute a meaningful alternative, despite the fact that it is (most likely[182]) politically unpalatable and the externality is sometimes (and not only in the financial sector) difficult to measure. The benefits are that it does not require a lot of government intervention and the taxes that are raised ex ante can be used to reduce taxation on labor and to finance projects with a solid socio-economic dimension or (2) an ex post intervention when the externality materializes. Besides the fact that it is more time consistent with the emergence of the externality and politically more acceptable it raises two major issues. First, the ex post intervention is often unbound with the ex post costs (e.g. government-sponsored bailouts, Fannie Mae and Freddie Mac) and second the fact that an ex post intervention creates its own externalities due to moral hazard and lack of level-playing field (e.g. too big to fail banks).

Recognition and containment of the externality ex ante through (capital) regulation[183] combined with an ex ante tax layer seems to yield the most desired outcome.[184] In a European context, preference has so far been given to command-and control legislation only. The starting point for that was the Laroisière Committee[185] and Liikanen Committee[186] reporting as commissioned by the EC. They focus on command-and-control legislation for both the banking sector as well as the financial markets infrastructure.[187]

---

the main benefit of such a model is that interest payments would no longer be tax deductible. Having said that: taxing free cash flows implies interest deductibility, so a new definition of taxable cash flows would have to be defined. See further regarding the model: A. J. Auerbach, (2017), Destination-Based Cash Flow Taxation, Working Paper Nr. 17/01, Oxford University Centre for Business Taxation, Oxford (also as NBER Working paper Nr. 23881); S. Hebous et al., (2019), Revenue Implications of Destination-Based Cash-Flow Taxation, IMF Working Paper Nr. WP/19/07, January. The latter also point to the fact that large and globally integrated countries would be a material loser of taxable objects when transitioning from profit to cash-flow taxation.

[182] At least technically in its purest form.

[183] À la Capital Requirement Directive (CRD).

[184] A similar conclusion was reached by M. Keen, (2011), The Taxation and Regulation of Banks, IMF Working Paper, WP 11/206. He concludes: '[t]he results suggest a potential role for taxing bank borrowing, perhaps as an adjunct to minimum capital requirements, at marginal rates that rise quite sharply at low capital ratios, reaching levels higher than those of the bank taxes so far adopted or proposed'(p. 30). He observed externalities in two different fashions: those that arise when such institutions are simply allowed to collapse, and those that arise when, to avoid the harm this would cause, their creditors are bailed out. He also asks whether corrective taxation or a regulatory capital requirement is the better way to address these concerns (above); See also M. Keen, (2011), Rethinking the Taxation of the Financial Sector, CESifo Economic Studies, Vol. 57, Issue 1, pp. 1–24.

[185] The High-Level Group on Financial Supervision in the EU, (2009), chaired by J. de Larosière.

[186] High-level Expert Group on Reforming the Structure of the EU Banking Sector, (2012) chaired by E. Liikanen.

[187] See also S. Titman, (2013), Financial markets and Investment Externalities, The Journal of Finance, Vol. 68, Issue 4, pp. 1307–1329.

Once the choice of a tax instrument has become clear as the preferred instrument, the critical point will be to work through the different tax options. Broadly there are two options (1) a revenue-based approach or (2) an externality-based approach, which will lead to the application, one way or another of a Pigovian tax model. However, the idea to apply Pigovian taxes to the financial sector is not totally new,[188] but it has never become a mainstream line of thinking. Nevertheless, some notable economists were instrumental in airing some initial thoughts decades ago[189] in specific fields.

If regulation I is opted for, the focus is (or should be) on (1) loss absorbance via capital buffers and liquidity and debt ratios, and (2) limiting the size, solvability and separation of functions. Many different models have been developed over time including those that focus on capital ratios,[190] liquidity fundamentals,[191] or more general framework models.[192] Despite the fact that taxation is often superior to regulation regarding financial systemic risk,[193] reality tends to go with regulation most of the time.

If the taxation option is chosen, 'revenue'- or 'externality'-optionality emerge as two distinct choices. If a revenue-based tax instrument or model is preferred, a tax instrument would show similarities with a financial activities tax, a financial transaction tax or a financial stability contribution (focusing on systemic risk).[194] As revenue-based taxation models

[188] G.S. Eskeland, (1994), A Presumptive Pigovian Tax Complementing Regulation to Mimic an Emission Fee, World Bank Economic Review, Vol. 8, Issue 3, pp. 373–394.

[189] J.E. Stiglitz, (1989), Using Tax Policy to Curb Speculative Short-term Trading, Journal of Financial Services Research, Vol. 3, pp. 101–115.

[190] A.R. Admati, P.M. DeMarzo, M.F. Hellwig and P. Pfleiderer, (2010), Fallacies, Irrelevant Facts, and Myths in the Discussion of Capital Regulation: Why Bank Equity is Not Expensive, Stanford Graduate School of Business Research Paper Nr. 2065.

[191] V. Acharya, T. Phillippon, M. Richardson and N. Roubini, (2009), Financial Markets, Institutions and Instruments, Vol. 18, Issue 2, pp. 89–137.

[192] K.R. French et al. (2010), The Squam Lake Report: Fixing the Financial System, Princeton University Press, Princeton.

[193] D. Masciandaro and F. Passarelli, (2013), Financial Systemic Risk: Taxation or Regulation, Journal of Banking and Finance, Vol. 37, Issue, 2, pp. 586–596; L. Kaplow and S. Shavell, (2002), On the Superiority of Corrective Taxes to Quantity Regulation, American Law and Economics Review, Vol. 4, Issue 1, pp. 1–17.

[194] The revenue-based models will not be extensively analyzed in the main analysis of this chapter which will focus on externality-neutralizing instruments. Revenue-based models will however be subject to a limited analysis in 11.5.2. regarding alternative models of taxation for FIs. See for extensive coverage of the different models designed and suggested in recent years: M. Keen, (2011), The Taxation and Regulation of Banks, IMF Working paper Series, WP/11/206 and M. Keen and R.A. de Mooij, (2012), Debt, Taxes and Banks, IMF Working Paper Series, WP/12/48; S. Claessens et al. G. Dell' Arriccia, D. Agiz and L. Laeven, (2010), Lessons and Policy Implications from the Global Financial Crisis, IMF Working Paper Series, WP/10/44;R.A. de Mooij and M.P. Devereux, (2011), An Applied Analysis of ACE and CBIT Reforms in the EU, International Tax and Public Finance, Springer, Vol. 18, Issue 1, pp. 93–120; M.P. Devereux, (2012), Issues in the Design of Taxes on Corporate Profit, National Tax Journal, National Tax Association, Vol. 65, Issue 3, pp. 709–730; R.A. de Mooij, (2011), Tax Biases to Debt Finance: Assessing the Problem, Finding Solutions, IMF Staff Discussion Note, SDN11/11 and (2012) in Fiscal Studies, Vol. 33, Issue 4,

are not within the scope of our analysis, and given the fact that they do not seem to yield the desired outcome, these models are not further analyzed in this context. Indeed, it has been demonstrated that the behavioral responses of the banks to the regulation-based policies implemented did reduce leverage but that was offset by overall higher levels of risky assets. The reduction in funding risk clearly dominates for banks with high capital ratios, but is exactly offset by the increase in portfolio risk for banks with low capital ratios. This suggests that while those levies have reduced the total risk of relatively safe banks, they have done nothing to curb the risk of relatively risky banks, which presumably pose the greatest threat to financial stability.[195]

If a Pigovian approach is decided on, one must enter the complex domain of disentangling the externality-causing events in the financial sector. This will be examined in the next few sections, and a Pigovian tax design will be suggested. In most cases, a parallel is initially developed with the environmental sphere and the Pigovian taxes applied in that context.

11.5.2 Evaluation of Bank Taxation Models and Expected Outcome

After the dust of the 2008 financial crisis had settled, policy makers and regulators questioned the way forward regarding the management of the financial sector. In particular there was concern about safeguarding of one of the most precious public goods in a twenty-first-century liberal democratic society, that is, the stability of the (financial) markets. Many things have been said and even more has been written. Many different tax adjustments[196] have been implemented, showing the trial-and-error nature of the current regulatory process.[197] The main objective of these introductions has been the collection of incremental tax revenues to neutralize the gap created by bailout programs[198] and reduced economic activity after the crisis, and the impact that it had on sovereign budgets. What all these bank levies have in common is that they do not reduce systemic risk, do not reduce

pp. 489–512; R.A. de Mooij, M. Keen and M. Orihara, (2013), Taxation, Bank Leverage and Financial Crises, IMF Working Paper Series, WP/13/48;J. Vella, C. Fuest and T. Schmidt-Eisenlohr, (2011), The EU Commission's Proposal for a Financial Transaction Tax British Tax Review, Vol. 6, pp. 607–621; J. English, J. Vella and A. Yevgenyeva, (2013), The Financial Tax Proposal Under the Enhanced Cooperation Procedure: Legal and Practical Considerations, British Tax Review, Vol. 2, pp. 223–259.

[195] See in detail: M.P. Devereux, N. Johannesen and J. Vella, (2013), Can Taxes Tame the Banks? Evidence from European Bank Levies, Working Papers Nr. 1325, Oxford University Centre for Business Taxation.

[196] Taxing bank bonuses, bank levies on bank assets over a certain threshold and so on.

[197] See also: B. Coulter, C. Mayor and J. Vickers, (2012), Taxation and Regulation of Banks to Manage Systemic Risk, Oxford University Presentation.

[198] P. Benczur et al., (2017), Evaluating the effectiveness of the new EU bank regulatory framework: A farewell to bail-out?, Journal of Financial Stability, Vol. 33, December, pp. 207–223.

contagion risk[199] and perform all the same way when systemic risk occurs.[200] Only very gradually, and still very embryonically, has the possibility of using Pigovian taxes been introduced to address the material externalities the sector causes and its dangerous spillover effects.[201] Even the G20 mandated the IMF to explore 'the range of options countries have adopted or are considering as to how the financial sector could make a fair and substantial contribution toward paying for any burden associated with government interventions to repair the banking system'.[202]

Questions have been asked about the role of the contemporary corporate income tax system in triggering the 2008 financial crisis which was mainly caused by a credit boom[203] and a concurrent housing bubble.[204] Although there was near unanimity that income tax systems were not a major proximate cause for the crisis,[205] in many respects, '... the tax system's fingerprints were all over the crime scene'.[206] Income tax rules may have encouraged both excessive corporate leverage and highly leveraged home ownership. Income taxes may also have contributed to pervasive governance problems in publicly traded companies, and to the proliferation of non-transparent financial instruments that played a key role in prompting the crisis. Longstaff and Strebulaev[207]

---

[199] Contagion risk can be broken down in three different 'distance to risk measures': distance to default, distance to capital and distance to inefficiency. See: K. Daly et al., (2017), Contagion Risk in Global Banking Sector, Working Paper, March 23, mimeo. The distance to default is measured by the distance of a theoretical default condition and current condition of a financial institution (p. 5). Other distance criteria are measures alongside this model based on Meeton's option pricing technique.

[200] G. Cannas et al., (2014), Financial Activities Taxes, Bank Levies and Systemic Risk, EC Taxation Papers Series, Working Paper Nr. 43, who review the different levies introduced.

[201] See for the quantification of spillover effects: F. Vitek, (2017), Policy, Risk and Spillover Analysis in the World Economy: A Panel Dynamic Stochastic General Equilibrium Approach, IMF Working Paper Nr. WP/17/89, April. This panel dynamic stochastic general equilibrium model features a range of nominal and real rigidities, extensive macrofinancial linkages, and diverse spillover transmission channels. These macrofinancial linkages encompass bank and capital market based financial intermediation, with financial accelerator mechanisms linked to the values of the housing and physical capital stocks.

[202] Leaders' Statement: The Pittsburgh Summit, 2009, Strengthening the International Financial Regulatory System.

[203] See for more recent credit booms and their dynamic: C. Hansman et al., (2018), Riding the Credit Boom, NBER Working Paper Nr. 24586, May.

[204] Underlying those phenomena was obviously the FED's interest rate policy as an undercurrent determining the course of events.

[205] T. Hemmelgarn and G. Nicodème, (2010), The 2008 Financial Crisis and Taxation Policy, Working Paper Nr. 20-2010. European Commission, Luxembourg; J. Slemrod, (2009), Lessons for Tax Policy in the Great Recession. National Tax Journal, Vol. 62, Issue 3, pp. 387–397.

[206] D.N. Shaviro, (2009), The 2008–09 Financial Crisis: Implications for Income Tax Reform, New York University Law and Economics Working Paper Nr. 09-35. New York University, New York, NY.

[207] F. Longstaff and I. Strabulaev, (2014), Corporate Taxes and Capital Structure: A Long-Term Historical Perspective, NBER Working Paper, Nr. 20372. See regarding the impact of foreign institutional ownership on corporate taxation and avoidance: I. Hasan et al., (2016), The Effect of Foreign Institutional Ownership of Corporate Tax Avoidance: International Evidence, Bank of

demonstrated,[208] (covering the period 1929–2009) that changes in corporate leverage are directly related to changes in corporate tax rates for all but the smallest firms. The adjustment of leverage to changes in corporate tax rates is slower for smaller firms facing financial constraints.

The income tax[209] characteristics causing the above have been around for decades and had not seen a notable expansion in the years prior to the crisis. The belief that income taxation's causal role went beyond pushing in the wrong direction by generally exacerbating biases that existed in any event does not exclude the likelihood that the tax biases served, in effect, as extra gasoline, intensifying the explosion once other causes lit the match.[210] The corporate tax bias,[211] as a strong departure from tax neutrality, is typically criticized for inducing increased bankruptcy costs or distorting firms' responses to asymmetric information problems in the case of firms prone to excessive leverage. Risk externalization may also have been effectively encouraged by an incoherent system of taxing capital income that creates tax arbitrage opportunities, often exacerbated by derivatives.[212] It should, however,

Finland Discussion Paper Nr. 26, Helsinki. See for a good contemporary overview of all corporate tax avoidance models and schemes (including transfer mispricing, international debt shifting, treaty shopping, tax deferral and corporate inversions: S. Beer et al., (2018), International Corporate Tax Avoidance: A Review of the Channels, Effect Sizes, and Blind Spots, IMF Working Paper Nr. WP/18/168, July, including the extensive literature list for reference: pp. 31–40. Specifically, shadow banking instruments and in particular securitization instruments are used to reduce the effective tax rate of the engaging firms. Uhde documents that banks may reduce their tax expenses through securitization via a direct and indirect channel. The results suggest that securitization may be described as an appropriate instrument to pursue tax avoidance, while the tax expense-reducing effect through securitization becomes even stronger under increasing statutory corporate income tax rates. In detail: A. Uhde, (2018), Tax Avoidance Through Securitization, Working Paper, April 3, mimeo.

[208] Taking into account variables for the costs of financial distress, corporate liquidity, and capital market and macroeconomic conditions.

[209] The focus in this section is on income taxation, but note that financial institutions pose challenging problems regarding their exemption in the VAT system as well, such that they invariably receive special treatment that is generally preferential and always non-neutral.

[210] D.A. Schackelford, D.N. Shaviro, and J. Slemrod, (2010), Taxation and the Financial Sector, National Tax Journal, Vol. 63, Issue 4, Part 1, pp. 781–806. They refer to the fact that declining real estate prices would not have created such widespread mortgage default risk had not loan-to-value ratios been so high (p. 784).

[211] See in extenso: S. Fatica, T. Hemmelgarn, and G. Nicodème, (2012), The Debt-Equity Tax Bias: Consequences and Solutions, EC Taxation Papers Series, Working Paper Nr. 33, whoconclude that tax deductibility of interest payments in most corporate income tax systems coupled with no such measure for equity financing creates economic distortions and exacerbates leverage. Leverage increases with the Corporate Income Tax (CIT) rate. The reason is that the statutory CIT rate determines the value of the debt capital structure of banks.

[212] E.D. Kleinbard, (2003), Competitive Convergence in the Financial Services Market. Taxes, Vol. 81, Issue 3, pp. 225–260. See also S. Langedijk et al., (2014), Debt Bias in Corporate Taxation and the Costs of the Banking Crisis in the EU, EC Taxation Paper Series, Nr. 50, who evidence that eliminating the tax bias could lead to a reduction of public finance losses of around 60–90% (given a certain level/bandwidth of bank leverage elasticity) caused by the 2008 financial meltdown. The abolition of the preferential treatment is therefore argued as a tool to complement regulatory reform.

be observed that, given the fact that there are many different motives for the introduction of the many different bank levies, undoing all the wrongdoing that happened in previous years might in itself be a morally justifiable reform effort, but it should not focus unduly on the exotic and new at the expense of the familiar and old. Nevertheless, Hemmelgran and Teichmann demonstrate that there is a direct causality between the corporate income tax rate, with its preference for debt financing, and the balance sheet structure of financial institutions.[213] It has been argued that taking out the debt-equity bias would materially complement the regulatory effort math post-2008-crisis and would effectively strengthen the costs of reducing further crises in particular at the level of banking losses incurred. Langedijk et al. indicate '[e]ven if the tax elasticity of bank leverage is taken at the lower end of the ranges found in recent literature, eliminating the debt bias could lead to reductions of public finance losses in the range of 60 to 90%. The results hold even when considering much smaller effects for banks that are close to the regulatory minimum capital requirement of the Basel III framework. Even when asset portfolio risk is allowed to increase endogenously and considering conservative ranges of the parameter space, they conclude that tax reforms to remove the debt bias can result in very sizable reductions in risks and costs of financial crises.'[214] So, most tax systems create a tax bias toward debt finance. Such debt bias increases leverage and may negatively affect financial stability.[215] This is particularly true for the bank-

[213]T. Hemmelgarn and D. Teichmann, (2013), Tax Reforms and Capital Structure of Banks, EC Taxation Papers Series, Working Paper Nr. 37. They conclude that leverage increases with the CIT rate. The reason is that the statutory CIT rate determines the value of the debt tax shield. A higher tax rate increases incentives to use debt finance when interest payments are deductible from the CIT base. Their results suggest that future tax policies should focus on eliminating the favorable treatment of debt for banks. The reason is that this distortion at least partly undermines the objective of increasing regulatory capital in the financial sector.

[214]S. Langedijk et al., (2014), Debt Bias in Corporate Taxation and the Cost of the Banking Crisis in the EU, EC Taxation Working Papers Nr. 40, October; O. Luca and A. Tieman, (2016), Financial Sector Debt Bias, IMF Working Paper Nr. 16/217, November. Most tax systems create a tax bias toward debt finance. Such debt bias increases leverage and may negatively affect financial stability. The latter find the debt bias to be pervasive, explaining as much as 10% of total leverage for regular banks and 20% for investment banks.

[215]This is true across the board, that is, for financial and non-financial companies, for small and large companies, for domestic and international companies. The strength of this effect (the debt bias contributing to leverage) differs with firm size, the availability of collateral, income and income volatility, cash flow, and capital intensity. See in detail: P. Dallari et al., (2018), Pouring Oil on Fire: Interest Deductibility and Corporate Debt, IMF Working Paper Nr. WP/18/257, December. Also: A. Auerbach et al., (2017), Destination-Based Cash Flow Taxation, Working Paper Nr. 17/01 (Oxford, United Kingdom: Oxford University Centre for Business Taxation); J. Bluedorn, and C. Ebeke, (2016), Investment, Firm Size, and the Corporate Debt Burden: A Firm-Level Analysis of the Euro Area, IMF Working Paper Nr. WP/16/200; M. Faulkender and J. M. Smith, (2016), Taxes and Leverage at Multinational Corporations, Journal of Financial Economics, Vol. 122, Issue 1, pp. 1–20; R.A. De Mooij, and M. Keen, (2016), Debt, Taxes, and Banks, Journal of Money, Credit, and Banking, Vol.48, pp. 5–33; J.H. Heckemeyer, and R. A. de Mooij, (2017), Taxation and Corporate Debt: Are Banks Any Different? National Tax Journal, Vol. 70, Issue 1, pp. 53–76; O. Luca, and A. F. Tieman, (2016), Financial Sector Debt Bias, IMF Working Paper Nr. WP/16/217, Washington, DC.

ing sector. We have seen limited policy reform (outside the (rather limited) efforts undertaken in Basel III) in this matter and that despite its continuous relevance.[216] Indeed, taxes impact the balance sheet structure of financial institutions. When taking into account variables such as bank runs, regulatory closure and endogenous default, and varying tax rates it became clear that 'banks endogenously respond to a reduction in tax rates by reducing nondeposit liabilities more than deposits in addition to lowering leverage'.[217]

Ex post punishment brings with it a lot of complications. The most important in this respect is that using nominally prospective taxes to punish wrongdoing institutions for past acts runs into two distinct types of difficulties under the theory of tax incidence: (1) Bank levies that do not just address market actors' incentives on a forward-looking basis would reduce their profitability, and thus the value of their shares, imposing a transition loss on their shareholders at the time the tax was announced, and these may not be the same shareholders who benefited from the earlier run-up in stock price.[218] (2) Besides this, some or all of the new tax might fall on the banks' transactional counterparties (e.g. customers) after it takes effect.

The situation would not be driven by a retributive rationale and the nature of the tax will affect those who end up bearing its burden. Purely backward-looking taxes are inherently non-distorting[219] with regard to future decisions, other than to the extent that they influence perceptions of future policy.

Two questions deserve attention: (1) what triggers financial institutions (FIs) to engage in certain risky transactions and (2) why are the systemic losses[220] caused so large and wide-

[216] O. Luca and A. Tieman, (2016), Financial Sector Debt Bias, IMF Working Paper Series Nr. WP/16/217, November. Also: J. Bluedorn and C. Ebeke, (2016), Investment, Firm Size, and the Corporate Debt Burden: A Firm-Level Analysis of the Euro Area, in Euro Area Policies Selected Issues Papers, IMF Country Report Nr. 16/220; R. A. De Mooij, and M. Keen, (2016), Debt, Taxes, and Banks, Journal of Money, Credit, and Banking, Vol 48, pp. 5–33; P.B. Sorensen, (2014), Taxation and the Optimal Constraint on Corporate Debt Finance, Working Paper Nr. 5101, CESifo, Munich, Germany.

[217] On the asset side the impact depends on the financial strength of the bank: well-capitalized banks respond to a reduction in tax rates by increasing their assets, but poorly capitalized banks respond by cleaning up their balance sheet. See in detail: L. Gambacorta et al., (2017), The Effects of Tax on Bank Liability Structure, BIS Working Paper Nr. 611, February. Also: G. Schepens, (2016), Taxes and Bank Capital Structure, Journal of Financial Economics, Vol. 120, Issue 3, pp. 585–600.

[218] D. A. Schackelford, D. N. Shaviro, and J. Slemrod, (2010), Taxation and the Financial Sector, National Tax Journal, Vol. 63, Issue 4, Part 1, p. 785.

[219] Backward-looking taxes are, however, not the least distortionary way to raise revenue in comparison to an appropriately designed Pigovian tax.

[220] Both at the level of individual entities as well as at the level of macro-level. See for details: Z. Alla et al., (2018), Macroprudential Stress Tests: A Reduced-Form Approach to Quantifying Systemic Risk Losses, IMF Working Paper Nr. WP/18/49, March. A distinction is made between individual entity losses and losses resulting from systemic risk effects (SE losses). SE losses are measured using a reduced-form model to value financial entity assets, conditional on macroeconomic stress and the distress of other entities in the system. SE losses capture the effects of interconnectedness structures that are consistent with markets' perceptions of risk. SE losses can be decomposed into the likelihood of distress and the magnitude of losses, thereby quantifying the contribution of specific enti-

spread? The first is often referred to as a 'nickels in front of a steamroller' strategy, under which one earns extra-normal returns most of the time but occasionally experiences dramatic losses.[221] Economic incentives (short-term, cash based)[222] and limited liability of the firm caused that the upside are achievable and the downside would lead to a situation where the insurers or investors, facing a systemic decline in market values, would be prevented from making good when the problem materialized.[223]

The second question requires us to focus on the specific role of FIs in today's economy and society. They provide liquidity for non-cash transactions to occur and in that intermediary function they match two distinct groups with mismatched preferences.[224] Without this intermediating function, deposit holders would have to accept the near-zero or negative returns that would otherwise be available and business owners would be strapped for capital, as truly long-term strategic and patient capital would be insufficiently available. The asymmetry between invested funds which are illiquid and the cash needs of depositors created by the fractional reserve banking model underlie any potential run on a bank. The connectedness of the banking system can not only create externalities, but also provide them with the magnitude (contagion) to destabilize the entire banking sector on a global basis. The determinants of such contagion are complex and multifaceted.[225] Relevant factors may include firm liquidity, actual and apparent solvency and riskiness, the complexity or opacity of a given firm's financial positions, its size or market share, its interconnectedness with other firms, and beliefs about its managers. Explicit deposit insurance and too-big-to-fail-typologies provide the willingness for banks to engage in transactions with

ties to systemic contagion (pp. 18–22). Literature regarding systemic risk, quantifying systemic risk and amplification techniques is building up. See, for instance: V.V. Acharya et al., (2017), Measuring Systemic Risk, Review of Financial Studies, Vol. 30, Issue 1, pp. 2–47; R. Anderson et al., (2018), Macroprudential Stress Test and Policies: In Search of an Implementable and Robust Framework, IMF Working Paper Nr. WP/18/197, September; R. Espinoza et al., (2020), Systemic Risk Modeling: How Theory Can Meet Statistics, IMF Working Paper Nr. WP/20/54, International Monetary Fund, Washington, DC., March; M. Segoviano and R. Espinoza, (2017), Consistent Measures of Systemic Risk, LSE Systemic Risk Centre, DP 74, London.

[221] E.D. Domar, and R. A. Musgrave, (1944), Proportional Income Taxation and Risk- Taking, Quarterly Journal of Economics, Vol. 58, Issue 3, pp. 388–422.

[222] See regarding incentive issues in the FI sector Schackelford et al., Ibid. pp. 787–788.

[223] V.V. Acharya and M. Richardson, (2009), Causes of the Financial Crisis. Critical Review, Vol. 21, Issue 2–3, pp. 195–210.

[224] D.J. Elliott, (2010), Tax Policy and Bank Regulation, Manuscript, Brookings Institution, Washington, DC, unpublished. The first consists of investors with savings that they want to invest in a safe and highly liquid manner, permitting them to withdraw cash whenever they like. The second consists of businesses that want to use this pool of savings to fund investment projects that may be riskier and are more long-term, requiring a relatively illiquid commitment of funds.

[225] See in extenso: I. Aldasoro et al., (2016), Bank Networks: Contagion, Systemic Risk and Prudential Policy, BIS Working Paper Nr. 597, December; I. Vodenska et al., (2017), Systemic Risk and Vulnerabilities of Bank Networks, Working Paper, mimeo. They propose a model for systemic risk propagation based on common bank exposures to specific asset classes. They analyzed the

major potential calamities, despite the potential implications. Banks differ from other industries in the sense that they are in the business of 'incurring risk' rather than 'managing risk' caused by real-world transactions as is the case in other industries.

The role of Pigovian taxation and its available tools in combating those externalities with potentially significant social harm is at the center of our interest. The costs that an FI-driven Pigovian tax model would have to neutralize will invariably include: '(1) uninsured counterparties from firm insolvency, (2) taxpayers and beneficiaries of government programs, present and future, who would be worse off to the extent the government offered explicit or implicit insurance coverage, and (3) anyone else directly or indirectly affected by the heightened prospect of runs on the bank (at the same firm or elsewhere) and/or of the negative economic consequences from the associated harm to the liquidity function that banks and other financial firms serve in facilitating transactions that generate surplus'.[226]

The following section will explore and suggest how a Pigovian tax model for the financial industry can be designed. Unfortunately, and in line with our findings for many other externality-causing activities, a simple flat tax cannot be applied given the complexities and interconnectedness of the variables involved. There is no single activity whose aggregate sum equals expected harm. Indeed, many distinct aspects of financial institutions' activities may have negative externalities. Those include externalities that affect liquidity, solvency, systemically relevant characteristics of an FI (interconnectedness), leverage, riskiness of transactions and the size and complexity/opacity of its business model.[227] It is

dynamics of tier 1 capital ratio after stressing the bank network and find that while the system is able to withstand shocks for a wide range of parameters, we identify a critical threshold for asset risk beyond which the system transitions from stable to unstable.

[226] Schackelford et al., Ibid. p. 792.

[227] M. Famè and A. Vouldis, (2017), Business Models of the Banks in the Euro Area, ECB Working Paper Nr. 2070, May. Typically, four types of banking business models are identified, that is, traditional commercial, complex commercial, wholesale funded and securities holding banks are present, alongside with specialized institutions such as state-owned entities aimed at refinancing loans to semi-public and public entities. Performance, efficiency and risk characteristics are materially different across the four business models (p. 39 for details). A. Lucas et al., (2017), Bank Business Models at Zero Interest Rates, ECB Working Paper Nr. 2084 June. Lucas et al. work with six categories in terms of business models: large universal banks, including globally systemically important banks (G-SIBs), international diversified lends, fee-based banks, domestic diversified lenders, domestic retail lenders and small international banks. They also conclude 'as long-term interest rates decrease, banks on average (across all business models) tend to grow larger, hold more assets in trading portfolios to offset declines in loan demand, hold more sizeable derivative books, and, in some cases increase leverage and decrease funding through customer deposits (pp. 2ff.)'. Global systemically important banks (GSIBs) and global systemically important insurers (GSIIs) appear to be main sources of market-based connectedness. Total system connectedness—that is, among all GSIBs and GSIIs—tends to rise during financial stress, which is corroborated by a balance sheet oriented systemic risk measure. See in detail: S. Malik and T. Xu, (2017), Interconnectedness of Global Systemically Important Banks and Insurers, IMF Working Paper Nr. WP/17/210, September.

therefore not only the firm and its activities but also its relationship with other FIs that matter in this context. And even once an activity is identified, the optimal corrective tax is unlikely to be uniform.

There have been some suggestions made that holistically try to bring those elements together and have tried to quantify the marginal damage, but the formulas are too complicated to offer a plausible basis for actual legislation.[228] Ex post bailouts do not fairly reflect the social harm done (nor the interconnectedness, i.e. a firm can cause harm to another firm) for a variety of reasons, and they create the moral hazard of implied insurance. The precise downside risk attributes of a particular financial firm's overall investment position are unlikely to be fully observable by tax authorities. Thus, an actuarially fair risk-adjusted fee structure would not only fall short of giving financial firms the right social incentives at the margin when they make investment choices, but is unlikely to be entirely feasible.[229]

Command-and-control regulation will most likely still be necessary even if the design of a technically perfect Pigovian tax instrument is achieved for the FI sector. The expected social harm is not only multi-dimensional and difficult to measure, but also to a certain degree non-pecuniary in nature. Ex post bailouts do not come close to estimating the full externality cost, that is, the direct cost of the bailouts minus the later returns at exit combined with the indirect costs of years of dismal economic growth and reduced tax revenues.[230] It is argued that capital adequacy regulation[231] will continue to be necessary. I will, however, argue going forward that that might not necessarily be the case as a well-designed Pigovian tax instrument could well cater to the objective of this type of regulation and yield better results.

Schackelford et al. provide some general guidelines on what aspects to take into account when designing a tax instrument for the FI sector (of a Pigovian nature or not), which include taking into account all activities of the broader financial industry, being derivative-proof, and being cross-border proof, and that it should be activity-based and

---

[228] T. Adrian and M. K. Brunnermeier, (2008), CoVaR, Staff Report Nr. 348, Federal Reserve Bank of New York, New York, NY. Later updated as: T. Adrian, and M.K. Brunnermeier, (2016), 'CoVar', American Economic Review, Vol. 106, Nr. 7, July, pp. 1705–1741. See for a variation in Islamic equity markets: S. Braiek et al., (2018), Systemic Risk Contribution in Islamic Equity Markets: CoVaR Based Model, University of Sousse Working Paper, January, mimeo; A. Di Clemente, (2018), Estimating the Marginal Contribution to Systemic Risk by a CoVaR-Model Based on Copula Functions and Extreme Value Theory, Economic Notes, Vol. 47, Issue 1, pp. 69–112. See applied: L. Wang, (2017), Bank Rating Gaps as Proxies for Systemic Risk, University of Alberta Working Paper, mimeo.

[229] Schackelford et al., Ibid. p. 793.

[230] Even if the social harm could be reduced to the fiscal cost of supplying insurance protection, the government would hold a risky position, as the insurer of all financial firms, if their various investment risks (such as from betting against a downturn in real estate prices) were correlated. Thus, even with an actuarially fair fee the insurance fund would have a large positive balance when tail risk was realized less frequently than expected and would leave the government with financial exposure under the opposite scenario, Schackelford et al., Ibid. p. 793.

[231] D.J. Elliott, (2010), A Primer on Bank Capital, The Brookings Institution, Washington, D.C.

[232] See in detail Schackelford et al., Ibid. pp. 794–796. They further analyze the recently introduced

not be institution-based.[232] It should further take into account an FI sector that will be subject to a changing regulatory environment[233] and will mostly rebalance to include more market-based finance.[234]

11.5.3 Inadequacy of the Current Bank Levies

In view of the findings above, we will review the most notable bank levies introduced in recent times before introducing the Pigovian tax model for the financial industry.

11.5.3.1 Financial Transaction Tax

The financial transaction tax was discussed earlier in this chapter in terms of its functioning and technicalities. The analysis here will therefore be limited to an evaluation of its functioning vis-à-vis the intended objectives. The focus is often on its revenue raising potential

---

bank levies given the fundamental objectives they have in common: '(1) a desire for retribution or recompense from parties deemed to have caused, and/or profited from, the recent crisis, (2) a desire to align private incentives with the social cost of activities that demonstrably have potentially catastrophic external contagion effects, so as to reduce the likelihood of future crises, and (3) a desire to raise revenue to offset the government fiscal imbalances exacerbated by the cost of dealing with the financial crisis and subsequent recession' (p. 800).

[233] If the quantity regulation of an activity that generates a negative externality is set optimally, then any tax set at a rate less than or equal to the marginal social damage will raise revenue, but will not alter behavior from the social optimum. Such a tax is attractive because it raises revenue with no distortion rather than because of its Pigovian incentives. A tax set at a rate in excess of the marginal social damage collects further revenue, but at the cost of moving the equilibrium from the social optimum, with too little of the externality-generating activity. If the quantity regulation is set too laxly, a tax at a rate below the implicit marginal social damage implied by the regulation will raise revenue with no marginal effect, while a tax in excess of that amount (but not greater than the actual marginal social damage) will both raise revenue and affect activity in the right direction. If the quantity regulation is set too strictly, a tax raises revenue without affecting behavior; neither would a subsidy offset the suboptimal level of activity, although it would incur a revenue loss, Schackelford et al., Ibid. p. 795)

[234] See F. De Fiore, (2015), Corporate Debt Structure and the Financial Crisis, ECB Working Paper Series Nr. 1759, February, who focus on the amplification of banking distress on non-financial corporate debt and the amplification through the debt structure on balance sheets. US monetary policy and emerging market leverage are associated. See: A. Alter and S. Elekdag, (2016), Emerging Market Corporate Leverage and Global Financial Conditions, IMF Working Paper Nr. 16/243, December. Overall, increasing indebtedness and reducing productivity growth go hand-in-hand. See, for instance, for a case study: G. Anderson and M. Raisi, (2018), Corporate Indebtedness and Low Productivity Growth of Italian Firms, IMF Working Paper Nr. WP/18/33, February. They find significant negative effects of persistent corporate debt build-up on total factor productivity growth, and weak evidence of a threshold level of corporate debt, beyond which productivity growth drops off significantly. The latter most likely implies a gradual reduction of productivity and the fact that the debt accumulation build-up strangles firm productivity throughout the curve and

despite its low tax rate. The economic arguments in support of imposing such a tax center instead of its ability, by increasing the costs of financial asset transactions, to reduce speculative and technical trading that increases financial markets' volatility and susceptibility to bubbles. Despite its claimed benefits, the literature highlights in particular the following effects: (1) raising the costs of capital for entities issuing new securities; (2) through its downward effect on trading volume,[235] reducing liquidity and price discovery, while also potentially increasing short-term price volatility; and (3) displacing securities trades from taxed to untaxed venues.[236] It also does not support the view that an FTT improves market functioning.[237] An FTT is an unlikely candidate as a redistributive tax, given its uncertain incidence and the ability to circumvent its effective functioning.[238]

A critical question with respect to the improving market functioning aspect of the FTT is whether it reduces market failure and consequently reduces systemic risk. An FTT that would live up to its promise would correct market failures by effectively putting a price on negative externalities. Such a tax would be designed to change market participants' behavior to bring market outcomes more in line with the social optimum. There are two hurdles in the way of achieving this; market participants do not fully internalize the systemic risk that is embedded in their actions (leading to

---

not only at high or excessive levels of debt, which makes it a mainstream and across-the-board problem. A different design of the tax system could turn the tide. Also: L. Stépgane et al., (2018), Monetary Policy and Corporate Debt Structure, Banque de France Working Paper Nr. 697, October 17. Conventional and unconventional expansionary monetary policies have similar positive effects on aggregate activity, but their impact on corporate debt structure goes in opposite directions: (i) conventional monetary easing increases loans to non-financial corporations and reduces corporate bond financing; (ii) unconventional monetary easing increases bond finance without affecting the loans.

[235] Colliard and Hofmann however measure no effect and support for the idea that an FTT improves market quality by affecting the composition of trading volume. Instead, their results are in line with the hypothesis that a lower trading volume reduces liquidity, and thereby market quality. See in detail: J.-E. Colliard and P. Hoffmann, (2017), Financial Transaction Taxes, Market Composition, and Liquidity, ECB Working Paper Nr. 2030, February (including literature list to be consulted in case of particular interest in theory design for FTT). They do however observe a shift in terms of securities from short-term to long-term investors. Their reference to the fact that an FTT qualifies as a Pigovian tax (p. 34) cannot be underwritten for the reasons indicated in this chapter. See for other detrimental aspects of a standard FTT pp. 33–35. They analyzed the impact of the French FTT that used to be in place. Also: G. Capelle-Blancard, et al., (2015), The Impact of the French Securities Transaction Tax on Market Liquidity and Volatility, RIETI Discussion Paper Series Nr. 14-E-007, January; P. Gomber, et al., (2016), Securities Transaction Tax and Market Quality - the Case of France, European Financial Management, Vol. 22, pp. 313–337.

[236] T. Matheson, (2010), Taxing Financial Transactions: Issues and Evidence, Working Paper WP/11/54, International Monetary Fund, Washington, DC.

[237] T. Hemmelgarn and G. Nicodème, (2010), The 2008 Financial Crisis and Taxation Policy, Working Paper Nr. 20-2010. European Commission, Luxembourg.

[238] In extenso: P. Honohan and S. Yoder, (2010), Financial Transactions Tax: Panacea, Threat, or Damp Squib?, Policy Research Working Paper Series Nr. 5230. Development Research Group, The World Bank, Washington, DC.

enhanced volatility and bubble creation in asset prices), and certain behaviors are speculation-based rather than creating long-term real economy value for society.[239]

The first aspect under review is systemic risk. Systemic risk[240] refers to the fact that the market can be impacted as a whole (probability) by an endogenous or exogenous shock. This may occur because all banks are exposed to the same risk (a correlated shock), or because a shock hits a subset of banks and then propagates through the financial system (contagion). FIs have an inclination to expose themselves to systemic risk (or just ignore it) due to certain mechanisms that they can rely on, that is, deposit insurance legislation, subsidizing of debt through the tax system, and the implicit ex post bail guarantee.[241] Adding further to this inclination is the existence of interbank externalities from risk taking which arise through fire sales or information spillovers.[242] An FTT does not focus on these sources of externalities. Nevertheless, an FTT might reduce the probability of shocks hitting the financial sector, by reducing volatility or the incidence of asset price bubbles. Studies repeatedly demonstrate that an FTT either has no impact on or enhances volatility in markets.[243]

---

[239] See also: J. Ha, (2015), What Explains Volatility Spillovers in the Financial Systems of Emerging Market Countries: Co-movement, Transmission, or Contagion?, Cornell Working Paper, September version, mimeo. He concludes besides the fact that volatility spillovers between the foreign exchange and stock markets are significant in most EM countries, that such spillovers are found to be contingent on the sample period and market conditions. He also examines the sources of volatility spillovers, namely, co-movement through common information, sequential information transmission, and contagion. Common approaches used to estimate interest rate spillovers tend to understate the degree of monetary autonomy enjoyed by small open economies with flexible exchange rates. See: C. Caceres et al., (2016), Global Financial Conditions and Monetary Policy Autonomy, IMF Working Paper Nr. 16/108, June.

[240] See regarding the analysis of systemic risk: D. Bisias et al., (2012), A Survey of Systemic Risk Analytics, U.S. Department of the Treasury, Office of Financial Research, Working Paper Nr. 1, January 5. They provide a review of 31 quantitative measures of systemic risk that occurred in the financial and economics literature.

[241] Voellmy argues that shadow banks issue only uninsured deposits while commercial banks issue both insured and uninsured deposits. The effect of shadow banking on financial stability is ambiguous and depends on the (exogenous) upper limit on insured deposits. If the upper limit on insured deposits is high, then the presence of a shadow banking sector is detrimental to financial stability. Shadow banking then creates systemic instability that would not be present if all deposits were held in the commercial banking sector. In contrast, if the upper limit on insured deposits is low, then the presence of a shadow banking sector is beneficial from a financial stability perspective. Shadow banks absorb uninsured (and uninsurable) deposits from the commercial banking sector, thereby shielding commercial banks from runs. In detail: L. Voellmy, (2019), Shadow Banking and Financial Stability under Limited Deposit Insurance, Working Paper, March 21, mimeo.

[242] W. Wagner, (2010), In the Quest of Systemic Externalities: A Review of the Literature, CESifo Economic Studies, Vol. 56, pp. 96–111.

[243] M. Bijlsma, M. Lever, J. Anthony and G. Zwart, (2011), An Evaluation of the Financial Transaction Tax, CPB Background Paper, p. 6. For a re-evaluation of the FTT in terms of its impact on informational efficiency, liquidity and volatility, see: M. Cipriani et al., (2019), Financial Transaction Taxes and the Informational Efficiency of Financial Markets: A Structural Estimation, Systemic Risk Centre Discussion Paper Nr. 88, March 1. The introduction of an FTT changes the composition of the market, lowering informational efficiency. Even a small, 5 bps FTT impedes correct price convergence on a sizeable percentage of days.

With respect to the aspect of bubble creation, research has demonstrated that overpaying beyond the expected future value is driven by expectation of other market agents' willingness to pay more for assets in the future. Scheinkman and Xiong[244] conclude: 'theoretical results and numerical exercises suggest that a small trading tax may be effective in reducing speculative trading, but it may not be very effective in reducing price volatility or the size of the bubble', whereas Porter et al.[245] argued that '(...) brokerage fees designed to raise transactions costs significantly reduce the amplitude of bubbles'. Although an FTT might contain bubble creation that does not imply that it reduces systemic risk. Consider the fact that financial crises often come hand-in-hand with collapsing real estate bubbles. Those markets are still (although less so compared to the past) illiquid (with consequently high transaction costs) in nature compared to other asset classes. Consequently, real estate is not widely traded and any mispricing in this market will therefore not likely respond to a transaction tax.[246]

An FTT might reduce the levels of other activities of other socially undesirable market agents such as algorithmic or high-frequency traders, although there is no direct evidence they have contributed to systemic risk or excessive leverage.

Market transactions serve a purpose: they serve the price discovery function that helps investors to understand what positions to hold and which ones to liquidate. They therefore contain information on the assets which fuel efficient decision-making. Excessive trading might not help in understanding the information included in those trades. Two scenarios can occur: (1) Competition may induce firms to invest in activities that are privately beneficial, but socially wasteful. Although certain traders, because of technology, can respond quicker than competitors, the information embedded in those trades is very useful when conducted over nanoseconds. Those trades come at the expense of other market participants, whose research has now become idle forcing an externality on them. Very short-term information acquisition has very little social or even economic value[247] and becomes pure rent seeking.[248]

---

[244] J. Scheinkman and W. Xiong, (2003), Overconfidence and Speculative Bubbles, Journal of Political Economy, Vol. 111, pp. 1183–1219.

[245] D.P. Porter and V. L. Smith, (2003), Stock Market Bubbles in the Laboratory, The Journal of Behavioral Finance, Vol. 4, Issue 1, pp. 7–20.

[246] Reinhart and Rogoff argue that other tools may do better at preventing real estate bubbles. Banking regulators may for example use capital buffers to reduce excessive lending or set minimum collateral requirements for mortgages. K. Rogoff and C. Reinhart, (2009), This Time is Different: Eight Centuries of Financial Folly, Princeton University Press, Princeton.

[247] M. Bijlsma, M. Lever, J. Anthony, and G. Zwart, (2011), An Evaluation of the Financial Transaction Tax, CPB Background Paper, (2011), illustrate: 'when the acquisition concerns information that will anyway be publicly revealed soon, but speculators can earn a profit by getting their hands on the information early'...'But even when such information acquisition is in itself socially beneficial (e.g., long-term fundamental information on the security), duplication of collection efforts need not be efficient. A tax on transactions can then efficiently reduce the incentives to invest in those efforts' (pp. 7–8).

[248] L.H. Summers and V.P. Summers, (1989), When Financial Markets Work Too Well: A Cautious Case for a Securities Transactions Tax, Journal of Financial Services, Vol. 3, pp. 261–286. It convinced Stiglitz already decades ago to suggest a transactions tax, See: J.E. Stiglitz, (1989), Using Tax Policy to Curb Speculative Short-Term Trading, Journal of Financial Services, Vol. 3, Issue 2&3, pp. 101–113.

(2) Financial markets may facilitate free riding on costly information producing activities by others. If markets swiftly process information (obtained at a cost), this essentially reduces the benefits of obtaining that information. Grossman et al.[249] show that in fully efficient markets, prices reveal all available information. In such markets, agents cannot benefit from private information and therefore have no incentive to spend any effort on its acquisition.[250] The question now has become how an FTT affects the willingness to invest in information acquisition and the ability to respond to that event, that is, how do gains from information arise? In a world where it is known that one trader has consistently superior information, other market agents will refuse any trade (known as the 'no trade theorem').[251] Some uninformed traders buy and sell for exogenous reasons, such as liquidity needs; these are called liquidity traders.[252] The liquidity traders provide the cover under which speculators can earn a return on their investment, and for market makers who try to capture some of the informed traders' profits.

If liquidity traders were driven out of the market, the incentives to invest in information would decrease.[253] This has been confirmed independently by Bloomfield et al.[254] It is very likely that the concern is driven by the Lehman Brothers experience, which was a posterchild example of how local contagion can be widespread in the wider interbank market, a market

---

[249] S.J. Grossman and J.E. Stiglitz, (1980), On the Impossibility of Informationally Efficient Markets, American Economic Review, Vol. 70, Issue 3, pp. 393–408.

[250] The reason is that the willingness of one agent to buy at a price p reveals to other traders that this agent has information that the actual value of the good is higher than p. Other traders then prefer to hold on to the good themselves, and the informed agent cannot benefit from the information advantage. Hence, there will be too little investment in information acquisition, Bijlsma et al., Ibid. p. 8.

[251] D. Fudenberg and J. Tirole, (1991), Game Theory, MIT Press, Cambridge, Sect. 14.3.3.

[252] The noise that these traders introduce into the price formation process allows informed traders to make a trading profit under the cover of the liquidity trades. In addition, models may also explicitly describe the price formation process, for example by including market makers or arbitrageurs who do not possess any information themselves, but who try to disentangle the informed trades from the noise and try to capture some of the profits from that information, see in detail: A. Kyle, (1985), Continuous Auctions and Insider Trading, Econometrica, Vol. 53, Issue 6, pp. 1315–1335.

[253] See for an empirical model: J. Dow and R. Rahi, (2000), Should Speculators Be Taxed?, Journal of Business, Vol. 73, Issue 1, pp. 89–107. Results seem to imply that taxation reduces the amount of trade on information, making prices less informative. The latter effect is beneficial for speculators: they get higher revenue on their informed trades. Subramanyam compares long- and short-term investors and concludes that 'that taxes indeed increase the incentives of agents to acquire long-term information over short-term information.' A. Subrahmanyam, (1998), Transaction Taxes and Financial Market Equilibrium, Journal of Business, Vol. 71, Issue 1, pp. 81–117.

[254] They studied the effect of a tax on uninformed arbitrageurs in a laboratory experiment. Arbitrageurs exploit a market inefficiency, that is, they buy identical or very similar assets in different markets (often in different time zones) exploiting the mispricing between those two markets. These uninformed actors trade with informed traders (speculators) and with liquidity traders (who need to trade for exogenous reasons). They find that when only the arbitrageurs' trades are taxed, they trade less, and lose less money on their trades. The information content of prices remains unchanged. However, their experiment does not shed light on the incentives of speculators to acquire information, nor does it take into account the effect of taxes on liquidity traders' presence in the market, R. Bloomfield, M. M. O'Hara and G. Saar, (2009), How Noise Trading Affects Markets: An Experimental Analysis, Review of Financial Studies, Vol. 22, pp. 2275–2302. (Also Bijlsma et al., Ibid. p. 9)

where the bulk of the repo positions occur, and which went into a nuclear lockdown after the Lehman failure. The interbank market is undeniably one of the central networks in the global financial mechanism and thereby extremely prone to systemic freezes.[255] Grigat and Caccioli[256] reverse engineered interbank network stress tests with the aim to identify the potential triggers of systemic events and to remove the contemporary arbitrariness in the selection of shock scenarios in stress testing.[257] A simple policy of capital allocations reduces significantly the vulnerability of the system when constructed in line with the identified scenarios.

The effect of an FTT is not unambiguous. It impacts liquidity traders,[258] arbitrageurs and informed traders, but to what degree it indirectly mitigates externalities (as it definitely does not target them directly) is very much conditional on what assumptions are made. With respect to the application of the FTT to the shadow banking system, it can be high-

[255] See in extenso: S. Gabrieli and C.-P. Georg, (2014), A Network on Interbank Freezes, Deutsche Bank Discussion Paper, Nr. 44/2014. See for a complete review of the literature on interbank networks: A.-C. Hüser, (2015), Too Interconnected to Fail: A Survey of the Interbank Networks Literature, SAFE Working Paper Nr. 91. She presents a systematic overview of our current understanding of the structure of interbank networks, how network characteristics affect contagion in the banking system and how banks form connections when faced with the possibility of contagion and systemic risk. See also: M.R.C. van Ooordt and C. Zhou, (2016), Estimating Systemic Risk under Extremely Adverse Market Conditions, Bank of Canada Working Paper Nr. 22, May. See for some history on the role of interbank networks: C.W. Calomiris and M. Carlson, (2016), Interbank Networks in the National Banking Era: their Purpose and Their Role in the Panic of 1893, BIS Working Paper Nr. 535, January. From the perspective of systemic stability a sparsely connected network is preferred over a more densely connected network, even if the densely connected network is more stable in the absence of intervention. The optimal bail-in plan requires lower taxpayer contributions in more sparsely connected networks. See: B. bernadrd et al., (2017), Bail-Ins and Bail-Outs: Incentives, Connectivity and Systemic Stability, Working paper, April 11, mimeo. Aldaroso and Alves depict the European interbanking sphere. They break the network down by both maturity and instrument type. Interesting as well is the understanding that banks that are well connected in certain networks tend to do so in other networks as well (positively correlated multiplexity). Also the fact that they developed a model to identify systemic importance across multiple layers of different networks simultaneously. See in detail: I. Aldaroso and I. Alves, (2017), Multiplex Interbank Networks and Systemic Importance- an Application to European Data, BIS Working Paper Nr. 603, January. Also: L. Bargigli, et al., (2015), The Multiplex Structure of Interbank Networks. Quantitative Finance, Vol. 15, Issue 4, pp. 673–691; M. Bluhm, et al., (2016), Interbank Intermediation, Deutsche Bundesbank Working Paper Nr. 2016-16; E. Denbee et al., (2018), Network Risk and Key Players: A Structural Analysis of Interbank Liquidity, Working Paper, February 5, mimeo.

[256] See for their findings: D. Grigat and F. Caccioli, (2017), Reverse Stress Testing Interbank Networks, Scientific Reports, Vol. 7, Issue 1, Article number: 15616.

[257] Ramadiah et al. find that the observed credit network significantly displays the highest systemic risk level. They use data on bank-firm credit relationships (in Japan) and conduct a horse race between different network reconstruction methods in terms of their ability to reproduce the actual credit networks. They then compare the different reconstruction methods in terms of their implied systemic risk levels. See in detail: A. Ramadiah et al., (2018), Reconstructing and Stress testing Credit Networks, ESRB Working Papers Nr. 84, September 18.

[258] Also known as noise traders: those traders who are buying or selling securities for a variety of unpredictable reasons rather than reasons based on informed decision-making.

lighted here that its main application would be on the repo book of shadow banking entities and ultimately regulated banks. There is a duality in this as the repo book consists to a large degree of sovereign T-bonds.[259] The regulator is locked in a painful split. Either the FTT will cover repo book (but that might come at the cost of liquidity and volatility in the T-bond market) or it will exempt that segment and narrow the scope of the FTT for the greater good of its own benefit. As far as the eye can see, the latter idea is in pole position,[260] despite the intrinsic vulnerabilities of that position.[261]

11.5.3.2 Bonus Tax and General Bank Levies

If expected to recur, a tax on bonuses is an invitation to avoidance, given the alternative payment options available and the difficulty of ascertaining and monitoring what part of compensation is in fact a bonus.[262] As a one-time ex post measure, it has the economic advantage of being non-distorting. Most bonus taxes introduced are to be remitted by the employer. The burden will therefore be likely to be borne by shareholders rather than by the employees who received the bonuses and thus the penalties are not assigned to individuals according to culpability. That would be the case even if one assumes that receiving a bonus is a good proxy for culpability.[263]

In terms of general bank levies,[264] most introductions foresee a tax on a percentage basis either on the assets of an FI or on its liabilities, often excluding certain items such as deposits. The different bank levies introduced vary on a number of critical features but lack any direct externality-neutralizing element, often also not being one of the core objectives of the introduction of the bank levy.

The different dimensions among the bank levies include: (1) What is the tax base? Is the base uninsured liabilities, or does it also include insured deposits? (2) Is the rate risk-weighted or flat? If it is risk-weighted, what are the risk factors and how are they measured? (3) Is the tax remitted entirely ex ante, or are there also ex post claw-backs within the resolution process? (4) Are the revenues paid into a resolution fund, or do they go into general revenues? If the former, do the revenues effectively constrain the size of future bailouts? (5)

[259] See in detail: D. Gabor, (2016), A Step Too Far? The European Financial Transaction Tax and Shadow Banking, Journal of European Public Policy, Vol. 23, Issue 6, pp. 925–945.

[260] F. Guarascio, (2015), EU Deal on Financial Transaction tax 'Within Reach', Reuters.com, September 12.

[261] See in extenso: T. Adrian et al., (2014), Financial Stability Monitoring, Federal Reserve Bank of NY, Staff Reports, Nr. 601, revised edition June 2014, in particular pp. 16–21.

[262] Function-specific payments, industry-specific payments and more advanced models that are based on derivative 'contract for difference techniques'. See also: R. Albuquerque et al., (2018), Relative Performance, Banker Compensation, and Systemic Risk, European Corporate Governance Institute (ECGI) - Finance Working Paper Nr. 490/2016 (updated), January.

[263] Schackelford et al., Ibid. p. 798.

[264] See for an actual comparative analysis on bank levies: M. Dowell-Jones and R. Buckley, (2015), Bank Levies: An Innovation in Post-Crisis Bank Taxation, Working Paper, mimeo.

How does a liability tax interact with mandated regulatory capital?[265] The answers to these questions provide different (dis)incentives for certain behaviors by FIs, foster countercyclicality (or not) and the ability of the levies to include risk weighting (which most laws do not) to flexibly measure the marginal social damage of the activities of a financial institution.

An IMF report commissioned by the G20 proposed a new tax on financial institutions, called a financial activities tax (FAT), whose basis is profits (in excess of a 'normal' return) plus worker compensation above a per-employee threshold.[266] The report argues that this would approximate taxing rents, and therefore invokes the efficiency arguments for rent taxation. Kleinbard and Edgar[267] proposed a similar tax with a similar justification. They stress that the recent extraordinary profits in the financial sector must have been due to either luck or temporarily successful risk taking, and that either account would suggest the identification of a low-distortion tax base.[268]

Such an excess profits tax would also mitigate risk taking that is socially excessive, because the losses from bad outcomes are often borne by people other than shareholders.[269] An excess profit tax could be rationalized either as primarily reaching rents or as indirectly indicating the presence of tail risk[270] that is an externality from the firms' standpoint. As Schackelford et al. indicate: '[h]owever, the merit and applicability of these arguments remain uncertain, and imposing such a tax would also pose various design challenges, including whether and how to apply it to what are effectively financial firms nestled inside larger firms outside the

[265] Schackelford et al., Ibid. pp. 798–799.

[266] S. Claessens, M. Keen and C. Pazarbasioglu, (2010), Financial Sector Taxation, The IMFs Report to the G20 and Background material, Washington, Washington DC.

[267] E.D. Kleinbard and T. Edgar, (2010), The Financial Sector and the Crisis: Was Tax the Problem? Is It the Solution? Slides presented at a workshop on 'Rethinking the Taxation of the Financial Sector in Light of the Recent Crisis,' February 5.

[268] This argument addresses the fact that a tax on pure profits or rents in any sector has desirable efficiency properties, but in practice it is difficult to separate pure profits or rents from the normal return to capital, and so designing a non-distorting tax is difficult. If one can assert that most of the observed return in a given sector is rent or pure profit, then the potential distorting effect per dollar raised is arguably low, Schackelford et al., Ibid., p. 799, endnote 17.

[269] Such a tax would reduce risk taking given that the tax treatment of losses is punitively asymmetric. Otherwise, a tax on profits might induce decision makers to increase pre-tax risk positions in order to restore the after-tax positions they had in the absence of the tax. Note also that ex post increases in the generosity of the tax treatment of losses are a form of taxpayer bailout, Schackelford et al. Ibid. p. 800, endnote 18.

[270] See, for instance,

S. Ben Hadj, (2014), Financial Institutions Externalities and Systemic Risk: Tales of Tails Symmetry, UCL Working Paper, November. He analyses the contribution of banks to the systemic risk based on the asymmetry of the right and left tails of the loss distribution. The basic idea is that a bank should create as much risk as it undertakes. Any imbalance in the distribution of profit and losses is a sign of the bank's failure to internalize its externalities or the social costs associated to its activities. Tail symmetry and sustainability of the financial system are obviously interwoven.

recognized financial sector'. In fact Huizinga et al. had already demonstrated that in practice, taxes on corporate income in the financial sector are not that ideal, as they distort prices (i.e. interest margins).[271]

More recently a case was made for an industry-specific adoption of unitary taxation with formulary apportionment as a viable alternative to the current regime. Sadiq points at the many hurdles it would face; comfort can be found in the domestic uses as to how the unitary business and business activities of MNFIs should be defined, as well as the factors that should be included in an allocation formula, and the appropriate weighting. She concludes that the method can be validated as a viable industry-specific alternative model for cross-border and global multinational financial institutions.[272]

It will require much more economic analysis to arrive at a proper understanding of which design elements are more likely to achieve which goals. The theory of incidence is relevant for ascertaining whether the burden of new taxes will actually fall on those intended to bear the burden. For forward-looking taxes the scope of the tax matters as well as the alternatives that market participants have to the taxed activity.

Although it has become clear before, the optimum is often difficult to measure and so is the harm. This makes designing a perfect Pigovian instrument difficult. The distribution of the harm, the measurement tools and implementation and monitoring are all complex and multi-dimensional.

Nevertheless, this is exactly what we are going to engage in. Simple versions of the theoretical optima should perhaps be designed to arrive at a workable Pigovian instrument, but they are likely to be imperfect. We will attempt to make the model as simple as possible and as complex as necessary and also agile, so that the model has the ability to evolve as our understanding of harm and measurement of externalities in the FI sector advances. As will be demonstrated, I have opted for a layered Pigovian instrument that is holistic in nature, but the different layers are a technique that facilitates targeting as specifically as possible the different externalities that coincide in the financial industry and their particular characteristics. The aim is to make the model more transparent, more agile, easier to apply, easier to evolve, and easier to document and monitor once implemented. A layered instrument has many advantages over the holistic one-dimensional models that have been suggested so far, which have proven to be academically interesting and correct, but difficult to execute on a regulatory level.

---

[271] Using country differences on double taxation in multinational banks, they show that (1) a large fraction (85%) of such taxes are reflected in prices, and (2) banks adjust their behavior (activities in different countries) to a large extent in response to such tax differences. Huizinga et al. claim that also FAT may suffer from such pass-through rates, and recommend that any such taxes are harmonized across the EU, and across different parts of the financial sector; see H. Huizinga, J. Voget, and W. Wagner, (2011), International Taxation and Cross-Border Banking, European Banking Center, Discussion paper, Nr. 2011-015.

[272] See in extenso: K. Sadiq, (2014), Unitary Taxation of the Finance Sector, International Center for Tax and Development, Working Paper Nr, 25, November.

The optimal coordination of regulation and corrective Pigovian taxation will remain outside of scope here. This will, going forward, be a topic of high importance on the research agenda in order to arrive at a tax model that has all the characteristics of being complementary with regulation in the FI sphere to arrive at a fully holistic approach into this matter.[273]

11.6 A Pigovian Tax Model for the FI Industry

11.6.1 Introduction

It has become clear that the banking sector, given its highly complex nature, requires a multi-dimensional analysis to frame and tackle its externalities in an appropriate way. Some of these externalities are caused by FIs themselves due to the nature of their activities, means of funding, locations in which they operate and so on. The other part of the externality spectrum is caused by the level of interrelatedness of an FI with the rest of the global financial industry worldwide and the nature of those interconnectivities. First, the latter aspect will be covered, that is, the systemic nature of banking operations and the externality-inducing behaviors. We will assess how we can structurally assess the interconnectedness and the level of systemic risk caused by a specific FI.[274]

Afterwards, we will assess what the firm-specific behaviors are that cause externalities to appear and we will suggest a multi-dimensional Pigovian tax instrument to capture the FI sector in an externality-based fashion that could replace the bogus income tax models as

[273] International Monetary Fund, (2010), A Fair and Substantial Contribution by the Financial Sector, Interim Report for the G-20. International Monetary Fund, Washington, DC, p. 26.

[274] The identification and quantification of the systemic component of financial risk require an in-depth understanding of the channels through which shocks can spread and amplify, thereby jeopardizing the stability of a financial system. A holistic view is troublesome as that requires an understanding of the key determinants of the interconnectedness among FIs. Abbassi et al. use CDS prices to measure market-implied interconnectedness (to evaluate how much market information-based measures capture actual balance sheet linkages and risks associated with banks' funding, security investment and credit provision behavior). As a consequence they examine the relationship between market-based measures of credit risk interconnectedness and actual common exposures of banks through their funding and securities holdings. They conclude that the market-based interconnectedness measure strongly reflects the information on banks' exposure to the wholesale funding market and assets associated with securities investments and credit supply. Second, they show that the relation between our market-based interconnectedness measure and the balance sheet positions exhibits asymmetries both over time and cross-sectionally. See in detail: P. Abbassi et al., (2016), Credit Risk Interconnectedness: What Does the Market Really Know, Deutsche Bundesbank Discussion Papers Nr. 9, January (later on published in Journal of Financial Stability, Vol. 29, pp. 1–12). Also P. Giudici, (2017), Sovereign risk in the Euro area: a multivariate stochastic process approach, Journal of Quantitative Finance, Vol. 17, Nr. 12, pp. 1995–2008; C. Brownlees, (2015) Bank Credit Risk Networks: Evidence from the Eurozone Crisis, Working Paper, mimeo;

we know them (or at least the ineffective corporate-income tax-based model currently in vogue as well as the catalogue of measures introduced in recent years and reviewed above). Obviously such an effort would be implicitly embedded in a European supervisory mechanism with respect to FI-induced externalities.[275] The focus will be on the technical aspects that will contribute to the design of such a Pigovian instrument and not on the aligned, and potentially equally relevant, type of regulation needed in the context of monitoring and enforcement.[276]

11.6.2 Taxing Systemic Risk in the FI Industry

It does not require a tremendous amount of analysis to understand that FIs that are connected through a wide portfolio of transactions are at risk of impacting each other when one of the FIs involved in a transaction defaults on that transaction (or on any other transaction in which the FI is involved) one way or the other. It can also easily be imagined that a cascade of contamination occurs because of that, that is, the counterparty of the defaulting FI in its turn will default on a number of transactions, leading to a cascade resembling contagion in the interconnected FI sector. It becomes much more difficult when trying to define systemic risk and the propensity for systemic risk and externality-inducing behavior to impact counterparties in the sector. So before we can evaluate a possible Pigovian tax on systemic risk, we need to engage in defining systemic risk.

BIS, (2016), Annual Report 86th Edition, V. Towards a Financial Stability-Oriented Fical Policy, pp. 93–94. Technology and easy and quick news reduces trend-following behavior: B. Eichengreen et al., (2017), Thick v. Thin-Skinned: Technology, News and Financial market Reaction, IMF Working Paper Nr. WP/17/91, April; F. Diebold, and K. Yilmaz, (2015), Financial and Macroeconomic Connectedness, Oxford University Press, Oxford. Diebold and Yilmaz introduced variance decomposition networks as tools for quantifying and ranking the systemic risk of individual firms. The nature of these networks and their implied rankings depend on the choice decomposition method. There is a standard one known as the 'order invariant generalized forecast error variance decomposition' (H.H. Pesaran and Y. Shin, (1998), Generalized Impulse Response Analysis in Linear Multivariate Models, Economic Letters, Vol. 58, Nr. 1, pp. 17–29). In short, the problem is that the error variation doesn't add to unity and so comparison or ranking become impossible. The model suggested by Lanne-Nyberg (M. Lanne and H. Nyberg, (2016), Generalized Forecast Error Variance Decomposition for Linear and Nonlinear Multivariate Models, Oxford Bulletin of Economics and Statistics, Vol. 78, Nr. 4, pp. 595–603) is known as the order invariance property sharing model. Caution is still warranted when using rakings and risk contributions for guiding financial regulation and economic policy. See in detail: J.A. Chau-Lau, (2017), Variance Decomposition Networks: Potential Pitfalls and a Simple Solution, IMF Working Paper Nr. WP/17/107, May.

[275] See also: D. Schoenmaker and S. Oosterloo, (2005), Financial Supervision in an Integrating Europe: Measuring Cross-Border Externalities, International Finance, Vol. 8, Issue 1, pp. 1–27.

[276] See for example: A.R. Admati, (2000), Forcing Firms to Talk: Financial Disclosure Regulation and Externalities, Review of Financial Studies, Vol. 13, Issue 3, pp. 479–519.

11.6.2.1 Conceptualization of Systemic Risk

The objective of this section is to characterize the phenomenon of systemic risk, although in a condensed format.[277] It is, however, crucial to understand the concept and the complexities surrounding its definition in order to better evaluate a tax instrument that captures the core of the externality-inducing elements. There is no commonly accepted definition of systemic risk at present. One perspective is to describe it as the risk of experiencing a strong systemic event. Such an event adversely affects a number of systemically important intermediaries or markets (including potentially related infrastructures). The trigger for the event could be an exogenous shock (which is either idiosyncratic, i.e. limited in scope, or systematic, i.e. widespread in nature), which means from outside the financial system. Alternatively, the event could emerge endogenously from within the financial system or from within the economy at large.[278] The systemic event is 'strong' when the intermediaries concerned fail or when the markets concerned become dysfunctional (this is often called a non-linearity or a regime change). This includes both a horizontal (impact within the financial industry) as well as a vertical dimension (impact from the financial industry toward the real economy).

A continuing element of concern from a policy point of view is the (lack of) availability of sufficiently long time series and modeled datasets, despite the efforts undertaken by the Financial Stability Board in this respect in recent years.[279] In the context of deeper and broader financial integration within the EU this is problematic. In particular, the effects in

---

[277] For extensive discussions of the concept of systemic risk and comprehensive literature see O. de Bandt and P. Hartmann, (2000), Systemic Risk: A Survey, ECB Working Paper Series, Nr. 35, and O. de Bandt, P. Hartmann and J. Peydró, (2009), Systemic Risk in Banking: An Update, ECB Working Paper Series and in A. Berger, P. Molyneux and J. Wilson (eds.), (2012), Oxford Handbook of Banking, Oxford University Press, Oxford. See further: V. Acharya, et al., (2017), Measuring Systemic Risk, Review of Financial Studies, Vol. 30, Issue 1, pp. 2–47; S. Benoit, et al., (2017), Where the Risks Lie: A Survey on Systemic Risk, Review of Finance, Vol. 21, pp. 1, pp. 109–152.

[278] P. Hartmann, (2009), Systemic Risk, ECB Financial Stability Review, December, pp. 134–142.

[279] See: E. Cerutti, S. Claessens and P. McGuire, (2012), Systemic Risk in Global Banking: What Can Available Data Tell Us and What More Data are Needed, BIS Working Papers, Nr. 376; G. Hale et al., (2016), Crisis Transmission through the Global Banking Network, IMF Working Paper Nr. 16/91 April. Also: E. Cerutti and H. Zhou, (2017), The Global Banking Network in the Aftermath of the Crisis: Is There Evidence of De-globalization?, IMF Working Paper Nr. WP/17/232, November. Post-crisis dynamics show a shrinkage in the overall amount of cross-border bank lending is the traditional conclusion. But not so fast. Cerutti and Zhou claim: while the global banking network has evolved it has not undergone a generalized retrenchment in financial linkages. In fact, some parts of the network are currently more interlinked regionally than before the crisis and less dependent on major global lenders. They confirmed this trend and detailed it later on in E. Cerutti and H. Zhou, (2018), The Global Banking Network: What is Behind the Increasing Regionalization Trend?, IMF Working Paper Nr. WP/18/46, March. They confirm the regionalization trend and conclude that '[d]espite the large decline in aggregate cross-border banking lending volumes, some parts of the global banking network are currently more interlinked regionally than before the Global Financial Crisis'. They developed a simple theoretical model capturing banks' internationalization decisions, and the outcome shows that this regionalization trend is present even after controlling for traditional gravitational variables (e.g. distance, language, legal system, etc.). In fact they argue, 'this regionalization trend was present before the 2008 financial crisis, but it has increased since then, and it seems to be associated with regulatory variables (i.e.

terms of specialization (in lending to certain sectors) and cross-border risk sharing through the interbanking market pose specific contagion challenges going forward[280] within the EU.

The countless market agents and intermediaries act in their self-interest without concern for the aggregate risk in their (concerted) actions. Consequently there is no internalization of the social harm caused by the systemic risk in the system as a whole. The system as such can create a self-containing fallout. This can happen in three distinct ways: the first, as discussed, is contagion.[281] The failure of one financial intermediary can lead to failures of other financial intermediaries, even when the latter have not invested in the same risks and are not subject to the same original shock as the former[282]; second, wide-

the dampening of some barriers to direct cross-border and local affiliate lending) and the opportunities created by the retrenchment of several European lenders' (pp. 6–7, 31–36). See in favor: J. Caruana, (2017), Have We Passed 'Peak Finance'? Lecture, International Center for Monetary and Banking Studies; E. Cerutti and S. Claessens, (2017), The Great Cross-Border Bank Deleveraging: Supply Constraints and Intro-Group Frictions, Review of Finance, Vol. 21, pp. 201–236. Csonto et al. assess the systemic vulnerabilities in the EU banking system using two stress tests: (1) solvency and liquidity shocks to each individual bank and the impact on other banks in the network through their bilateral net asset exposures, (2) country and region-wide tail shocks to GDP affecting capital and liquidity of all banks in the shocked jurisdictions, followed by the rippling effects through the regional network. See in detail: B. Csonto et al., (2018), Bank Network Analysis in the ECCU, IMF Working Paper Nr. WP/18/162, July. The end result is an identification of systemically important institutions, judged by the 'degree of connectivity 'with the rest of the system, and the extent to which they are 'vulnerable to the failure of other banks.' See also: A. Myrovda and J. Reynaud, (2018), Monetary Policy Transmission in the ECCU, IMF Working Paper WP/18/70. Also: J.E. Anderson et al., (2017), Short Run Gravity, NBER Working Paper Nr. 23,458; E. Cerutti and S. Claessens, (2017), The Great Cross-Border Bank Deleveraging: Supply Constraints and Intra-Group Frictions, Review of Finance, Vol. 21, Nr. 1, pp. 201–236.

[280] See F. Fecht, H.P. Grüner and P. Hartmann, (2012), Financial Integration, Specialization and Systemic Risk, ECB Working Paper Series, Nr. 1425. Also: P. R. Lane and G.M. Milesi-Ferretti, (2017), International Financial Integration in the Aftermath of the Global Financial Crisis, IMF Working Paper Nr. WP/17/115, May. The latter finds that the growth in cross-border positions in relation to world GDP has come to a halt (covered period 1970–2015). This reflects much weaker capital flows to and from advanced economies, with diminished cross-border banking activity, and an increase in the weight of emerging economies in global GDP, as these economies have lower external assets and liabilities than advanced economies.

[281] A tough one still is to identify contagion in a network or in particular a banking network. Morrison et al. studied the impact of trading profits and losses on the borrowing costs of the banks' counterparties using derivative data (CDS). They used the network of CDS transactions between banks to identify bank CDS returns attributable to counterparty losses. That makes sense: '[a]ny bank's exposure to corporate default increases whenever counterparties from whom it has purchased default protection themselves experience losses.' In line with that understanding they document an increase in the CDS spread of such a bank. No such effect occurs from losses of non-counterparties. Interesting is that they further observed that the effect on bank CDS returns through this counterparty loss channel is sizeable relative to the direct effect on a bank's CDS returns following on trading losses. See in detail: A. Morrison et al., (2017), Identifying Contagion in a Banking Network, Bank of England Staff Working Paper Nr. 642, January.

[282] F. Allen and D. Gale, (2000), Financial Contagion, Journal of Political Economy, Vol. 108, Issue 1, pp. 1–33; X. Freixas, B. Parigi and J.C. Rochet, (2000), Systemic Risk, Interbank Relations and Liquidity Provision by the Central Bank, Journal of Money, Credit and Banking, Vol. 32, Issue 3, pp. 631–638.

spread financial imbalances can build up over time and then unwind abruptly[283]; and third, negative aggregate shocks can adversely affect intermediaries and markets simultaneously. These shocks are often associated with economic downturns.[284] All three items can reinforce themselves. What ultimately makes the financial system prone to instability[285] is the combination of externalities, the public good character of systemic stability, incomplete markets and information asymmetry,[286] where speed acts as a catalyst that magnifies the impact.[287] On an experimental level the question was raised if news of a crisis in one market may cause a contagion crisis in another market even if there are no links between those markets. Models so far have been lacking empirical evidence, often because the effect of news or events is so difficult to isolate. Two markets that have no linkages are markets where one market can only observe the prices in the other market and vice versa. Any possible model that tries to identify contagion[288] between unrelated markets will do so by simulating a price drop in one of both markets and observe whether prices in the other market drop in a contagious manner. If contagion is identified, trans-

[283] H. Minsky described how in good times consumption and investment increase generates income, which fuels the financing of more consumption and investment but also the neglect of increasing risks. Even small events can then lead to a re-pricing of risk and an endogenous unraveling of the credit boom, which then adversely affects many intermediaries and markets at the same time; see H. Minsky, (1977), A Theory of Systemic Fragility, in E. Altman, and A. Sametz (eds.), Financial Crises: Institutions and Markets in a Fragile Environment, Wiley & Sons, Hoboken, pp. 138–152; C. Kindleberger, (1978), Manias, Crashes and Panics: A History of Financial Crises, Macmillan, Basingstoke.

[284] G. Gorton, (1988), Banking Panics and Business Cycles, Oxford Economic Papers.

[285] The vulnerability of financial markets is caused by (1) the information intensity and inter-temporal nature of financial contracts, (2) the balance sheet structures of financial intermediaries (often exhibiting high leverage and maturity mismatches), and (3) the high degree of interconnectedness of wholesale financial activities; Hartmann, (2009), Ibid. p. 135.

[286] Financial systems allocate funds from agents who have them but possess no specific knowledge about promising investment opportunities, to agents who have knowledge about the opportunities but not the funds to engage in them. This creates an agency problem between the two parties, which may be handled more or less well through the underlying financial contracts. If contracts are incomplete and negative news arrive on some of the investment projects, but information asymmetries do not allow lenders to judge whether this also affects other investment projects, funding may evaporate for all projects alike.

[287] J. Trichet, (2009), Systemic Risk, Clare Distinguished Lecture in Economics and Public Policy, University of Cambridge December 10.

[288] See, for instance, G. Covi et al., (2019), CoMap: Mapping Contagion in the Euro Area Banking Sector, IMF Working Paper Nr. WP/19/102, May. They document the degree of interconnectedness and systemic risk of the euro area banking system based on bilateral linkages. They further developed a contagion mapping model fully calibrated with bank-level data to study the contagion potential of an exogenous shock via credit and funding risks. They observe that tipping points shifting the euro area banking system from a less vulnerable state to a highly vulnerable state are a non-linear function of the combination of network structures and bank-specific characteristics. Also: S. Basu et al. (2017), A System-Wide Approach to Measure Connectivity in the Financial Sector, Working Paper, mimeo; P. Glasserman and H. P. Young, (2016), Contagion in Financial Network, Journal of Economic Literature Vol. 54, Issue 3, pp. 779–831.

mission channels exist.[289] They are often denominated as 'bandwagon channel'[290] and 'strategic risk'[291] channel. These are not the only two options but those are the ones extensively assessed so far. The bandwagon channel 'transfers crisis effects from one market to another when agents in one market think that two markets are similar, and if a crisis happens in one market it is likely to happen in the other market as well. The strategic risk channel transfers crisis effects from one market to another when there is no common knowledge of others' information. When each agent has information that markets are not similar but they do not know if all the agents in their market have the same information, they face strategic risk about the others' information. Each agent may think that others might not have the information about non similarity of markets and that they may create a crisis by trading as if a crisis is likely to happen in their market too.'[292]

Systemic events can be narrow[293] or broad.[294] A systemic event in the narrow sense is 'strong' if the institution(s) affected in the second round or later actually fail as a consequence of the initial shock. That happens although they were fundamentally solvent ex ante and the market(s) affected in later rounds also crash and would not have done so without the initial shock.

Systemic risk (in the narrow and broad senses) can then be defined as the risk of experiencing systemic events in the strong sense.[295] The implication is that the spectrum of systemic risk is wide enough to include the following categories based on the different types of shocks and the implications they have for the financial markets and other FIs.

---

[289] Financial imperfections have macroeconomic implications. They occur mainly through two channels: The first channel, which operates 'through the demand side of finance and is captured by financial accelerator-type mechanisms, describes how changes in borrowers' balance sheets can affect their access to finance and thereby amplify and propagate economic and financial shocks'. The second channel, which is associated with the supply side of finance, 'emphasises the implications of changes in financial intermediaries' balance sheets for the supply of credit, liquidity and asset prices, and, consequently, for macroeconomic outcomes'. See in detail: S. Claessens and M.A. Ayan Kose, (2017), Macroeconomic Implications and Financial Imperfections: a Survey, BIS Working Paper Nr. 677, November. They also determine the link between the real economy and the financial sector.

[290] Initially developed by S. Calvo, and C.M. Reinhart, (1996), Capital Flows to Latin America: Is there Evidence of Contagion Effects?, World Bank Working Paper Nr. 1619.

[291] Initially developed by T. Ahnert, and C. Bertsch, (2013), A Wake-up Call: Information Contagion and Strategic Uncertainty, Sveriges Riksbank Working Paper Series Nr. 282.

[292] S. Vardanyan, (2016), Contagion in Experimental Financial Markets, Charles University CERGE-EI Working Paper Nr. 580, December, p. 2.

[293] 'Bad news' about an FI, or even its failure, or the crash of a financial market leads to considerable adverse effects on one or several other FIs or markets, for instance, their failure or crash. The essential feature is the 'domino effect' from one institution to the other and from one market to the other.

[294] It includes not only the events described above but also severe and widespread ('systemic') shocks which adversely affect a large number of FIs or markets at the same time.

[295] O. de Bandt and P. Hartmann, (2010), What is Systemic Risk Today?, Working Paper, p. 5. See also extensively regarding regulating systemic risk and the fact that systemic shocks are inevitable: S.L. Schwarcz, (2016), Perspectives on Regulating Systemic Risk, in Systemic Risk, Institutional Design and the Regulation of Financial Markets, (ed. Anita Anand), chapter two, Oxford University Press, Oxford. Also: S. L. Schwarcz, (2017), Rethinking Corporate Governance for a Bondholder Financed, Systemically Risky World, William & Mary Law Review, Vol. 58, pp. 1345–1374; S.L. Schwarcz, (2017), Controlling Systemic Risk through Corporate Governance, Center for

The type of shock can be 'narrow', which will propagate either as an 'idiosyncratic shock' (affecting only prices or certain assets), or as a 'limited systemic shock'. When the shock is 'broad' it is termed a system-wide shock. The result (often referred to as second-round effect) will be either a 'single systemic event' (affecting one market or institution) or a 'system-wide event' (impacting multiple institutions and/or markets simultaneously). The events are either 'weak' in both categories, implying that no crash or failure was caused, or 'strong', resulting in a crash or failure. For narrow shocks the catalyst is contagion, which in a wide systemic event will lead to a systemic crisis either 'directly' when the shock is system-wide or 'indirectly' when the shock is narrow.[296] The important distinctions between idiosyncratic or systematic factors, exogenous or endogenous, and sequential or simultaneous impacts illustrate the complexity of this phenomenon.[297]

One way to reduce the dimensions resulting from the combination of these elements is to limit attention to three main 'forms' of systemic risk: (1) the contagion risk, (2) the risk of macro shocks causing simultaneous problems, and (3) the risk of the unraveling of imbalances that have built up over time. These three forms of risk are not mutually exclusive and may materialize independently or in conjunction with each other. Contagion usually refers to a supposedly idiosyncratic problem that becomes more widespread in the cross-sectional dimension, often in a sequential fashion.[298] An illustration of that occurs at the level of the investment strategies of banks. Banks decide about their investment strategy ex ante based on a private belief about the state of the world and a social belief formed from observing the actions of peers. When the social belief is strong and the financial network is fragmented, banks follow their peers and their investment strategies synchronize.[299] This effect is magnified when relations between FIs are bilateral.[300] In a globalized financial industry the largest

---

International Governance Innovation Policy Brief Nr. 99, February. Excessive corporate risk taking and not reducing moral hazard and alignment between managers and investors should be the focus.

[296] See de Bandt et al. (2010), Ibid. p. 5, for a full overview of the different categories.

[297] See for an example analysis in credit markets: N. Boyarchenko et al., (2016), Trends in Credit Market Arbitrage, Federal Reserve Bank of New York Staff Reports, Nr. 784, July.

[298] Hartmann, (2009), Systemic Risk, ECB Financial Stability Review, p. 135.

[299] See also for a number of different hypotheses: C.-P. Georg, (2014), Contagious Herding and Endogenous Network Formation in Financial Networks, ECB Working Paper, Nr. 1700. Financial networks exhibit a core periphery network structure. But a core periphery network cannot be unilaterally stable when agents are homogeneous. A core periphery network structure can form endogenously, however, if allowed for heterogeneity among agents in size; see in detail: D. in 't Veld et al., (2015), The Formation of a Core periphery Structure in Heterogeneous Financial Networks, Risk and Macro Finance Working Paper Series Nr. 2015-1, University of Amsterdam. It is also a valid theory at the level of business cycles and the economy as such. SeeL A. Cesa-Bianchi et al., (2016), Finance and Synchronization, Bank of England Staff Working Paper Nr. 612, August.

[300] K. Anand, B. Craig and G. von Peter, (2014), Filling in the Blanks: Network Structure and Interbank Contagion, BIS Working Paper, Nr. 455. Also: A. Liu et al., (2016), Interbank Contagion: An Agent-based Model Approach to Endogeneously Formed Networks, OFR Working Paper Nr. 16-14, December 20. Extrapolating latent interbank risk exposures is a tough job and many theories exist. Most of the models use highly stylized network models and reconstruction methods with global optimality lending allocation approaches such as maximizing entropy or minimizing costs. In reality however, Liu et al. argue, lending and borrowing decisions are largely suboptimal and performance-driven.

vulnerabilities (in terms of their potential impact) are the credit risk and funding risk of a particular FI. During times of crisis, funding vulnerabilities are associated with negative GDP growth surprises.[301]

The second form of systemic risk refers to a widespread exogenous shock that negatively affects a range of intermediaries and/or markets in a simultaneous fashion. For example, it has been observed that banks are vulnerable to economic downturns. The third form of systemic risk refers to the endogenous build-up of widespread imbalances in financial systems over time, as in the case of a lending boom. Financial institutions with more-diversified business activities can have a lower contribution to systemic risk.[302] It is clear that both the financial as well as operational infrastructure of the FIs and the network environment determine the nature and magnitude of systemic risk. And even organizational design and diversity contribute directly to the size and magnitude of systemic risk.[303] An interesting question that emerges deals with the merits of bank-based versus market-based financing by exploring the relationship between financial structure and systemic risk. Bats and Houben[304] ran a regression model that shows that bank-based financing generates systemic risk while market-based debt and especially market-based stock financing reduce systemic risk. They further conclude that banks no longer contribute to systemic risk when there is little bank-based financing. In the case of relatively market-based financial structures, the influence of banks on systemic risk is low. The findings indicate that countries can increase their resilience to systemic risk by reducing the share of bank-based financing and increasing the share of market-based financing.[305]

---

[301] See in detail: K. Kim and S. Mitra, (2014), Real and Financial Vulnerabilities from Cross-Border Banking Linkages, IMF Working Paper, Nr. WP/14/136.

[302] Insurance holdings with a diversified business mix of traditional life and non-life insurance business contribute less to systemic risk than monoline insurers, argue Kubitza and Regele. Based on a study covering 74 international insurance companies from 2007 to 2015 they conclude that on average insurance holdings with a fraction of slightly more than 50% of premiums written in life insurance exhibit the smallest contribution to systemic risk. This fraction tends to increase with an insurer's investment volatility, leverage ratio and the scope of active reinsurance assumed; see in detail: C. Kubitza and F. Regele, (2018), Diversification of Business Activities and Systemic Risk, ICIR Working Paper Series Nr. 30/17, version January.

[303] O. Butzbach, (2016), Systemic Risk, Macro-Prudential Regulation and Organizational Diversity in Banking, Journal for Policy and Society, Vol. 35, Issue 3: Institutional and Policy Design for the Financial Sector, pp. 239–251.

[304] J. Bats and A. Houben, (2017), Bank-Based Versus Market-Based Financing: Implications for Systemic Risk, De Nederlandse Bank Working Paper, Nr. 577, December. See also: V. Acharya, et al., (2016), The Dark Side of Liquidity Creation: Leverage and Systemic Risk, Journal of Financial Intermediation, Vol. 28, pp. 4–21. Also: S. Von der Becke, (2015), Liquidity Creation and Financial Instability, ETH Zurich PhD thesis, mimeo. The thesis investigates how liquidity creation within the financial system can lead to financial crisis. Also: S. Claessens, (2016), Regulation and Structural Change in Financial Systems, CEPR Discussion Papers, Nr. 11822; S. Langfield, and M. Pagano, (2016), Bank Bias in Europe: Effects on Systemic Risk and Growth, Economic Policy, Vol. 31, pp. 51–106; S. Masciantonio and A. Zaghini, (2017), Systemic Risk and Systemic Importance Measures During the Crisis, Bank of Italy Working Paper, Nr. 1153.

[305] See also: S. Benoit et al., (2017), Where the Risks Lie: A Survey on Systemic Risk, Review of Finance, Vol. 21, Issue 1, March 1, pp. 109–152. A multifactor approach to determining the SIFI nature is required as just focusing on size and assuming that larger banks pose more risks than

Gong and Page[306] asked themselves the following question in the light of the incoming banking regulation witnessed in recent years: Does regulating the banking network increase systemic risk in the entire financial network in the presence of unregulated shadow banks? That requires an analysis of the properties of equilibrium financial networks.[307] Their analysis seems in line with the direction of the empirical evidence in the literature,[308] that is, the systemic importance of 'connections between commercial banks and shadow banks in determining the health of the entire financial network'. An add-on question was what the impact was on systemic risk when different actors in the financial network are exposed to different regulatory policies. They demonstrate (through numerical simulations and assuming different regulatory regimes) that 'imposing bank regulations not faced by shadow banks does indeed increase systemic risk throughout the financial network'.[309]

11.6.2.2 The Definition of a Systemically Important FI (SIFI)

The following issue encountered by policy makers was to define those institutions that could be considered as systemically important, that is, those that were either too big to fail and therefore posed a systemic risk and/or those that were fragile enough to feed contagion into other markets and sectors of the FI labyrinth. Systemically important financial institutions (SIFIs) are institutions whose distress or disorderly failure, because of their size, complexity and systemic interconnectedness, would cause significant disruption to the wider financial

smaller banks. See for a model: OFR, (2017), Size Alone is Not Sufficient to Identify Systemically Important Banks, OFR Viewpoint Nr. 4, October 26. Dávila and Walther show that bank size, purely on strategic grounds, is a key determinant of banks' leverage choices, even when bailout policies treat large and small banks symmetrically. Large banks always take on more leverage than small banks because they internalize that their decisions directly affect the government's optimal bailout policy. Small banks also choose strictly higher borrowing when large banks are present, since banks' leverage choices are strategic complements. Overall, the presence of large banks increases aggregate leverage and the magnitude of bailouts. The optimal ex ante regulation features size-dependent policies that disproportionally restrict the leverage choices of large banks. In detail: E. Dávilla and A. Walther, (2017), Does Size Matter? Bailouts with large and Small Banks, NBER Working Paper Nr. 24132, December.

[306] R. Gong and F. Page, (2016), Shadow Banks and Systemic Risks, SRC Discussion Paper Nr. 55, February. They base systemic risk on 'the equilibrium state dynamics generated by a stochastic game of network formation with banks and shadow banks'.

[307] Ibid. pp. 4–20 for the set-up and pp. 20–26 for the analysis.

[308] See, for instance, D. Acemoglu, et al., (2015), Systemic Risk and Stability in Financial Networks, American Economic Review, Vol. 105, Nr. 2, pp. 564–608; L. Eisenberg, et al., (2001), Systemic Risk in Financial Systems, Management Science, Vol. 47, Nr. 2, pp. 236–249; M. Elliot et al., (2014), Financial Networks and Contagion, American Economic Review, Vol. 104, Nr. 10, pp. 3115–3153; R. Gong, et al., (2015), Endogenous Correlated Network Dynamics, SRC Working Paper Nr. 39, June; R. Gong and F. Page, (2016), Systemic Risk and the Dynamics of Temporary Financial Networks, SRC Working Paper Nr. 62, July.

[309] Ibid. pp. 33–42 for the policy analysis.

system and economic activity. The G20 has been a strong proponent of the development of a SIFI framework to identify, assess and monitor similar institutions. Any such framework would require the ability to recognize that SIFIs vary in their structures and activities, and that systemic importance and impact upon distress or failure can vary significantly across sectors. The assessment methodologies to identify global SIFIs (G-SIFIs) further need to reflect the nature and degree of risks that they pose to the global financial system. So far, frameworks have been developed for G-SIFI,[310] domestic SIFI (D-SIFI),[311] global systemically important insurers (G-SII)[312] and non-bank G-SIFI.[313] The distinction drawn is key in understanding how systemic risk emerges in FIs, with different characteristics and different indicators helping to identify ex ante or nascent systemic risk.[314]

[310] The most recent version: Bank for International Settlements (BIS), (2013), Global Systemically Important Banks. Updated Assessment Methodology and the Higher Loss Absorbency Requirements. See for a scorecard analysis for the year 2013: BIS, (2014), The G-SIB Assessment Methodology- Score Calculation, (November 2014) and FSB, (2015), Thematic Review on Supervisory Frameworks and Approaches for SIBs. Peer Review Report, May 26. Fique analyzed the 'additional loss absorbency requirement' for G-SIBs from the perspective of a microfounded design of capital surcharges that target the interconnectedness component of systemic risk. These costs increase the cost of establishing interbank connections, which has a welfare effect. Two conclusions were drawn: (1) [w]hile reduced interconnectedness decreases welfare by restricting the ability of banks to insure against liquidity shocks, it also increases it by reducing contagion when an interconnected bank fails. The regulator faces a trade-off between efficiency and financial stability; and (2) capital requirements are more effective than default fund contributions when tail-risk exposure is the private information of banks. See in detail: J. Fique, (2016), A Microfounded Design of Interconnectedness-Based Macroprudential Policy, Bank of Canada Working Paper Nr. 6, February.

[311] BIS, (2012), A Framework for Dealing with Domestically Important Banks.

[312] International Association of Insurers, (2013), Global Systemically Important Insurers: Initial Assessment Methodology. For an overview of the challenges in the insurance sector see: J. Adams, (2014), Global Systemically Important Insurers: Issues, Policies and Challenges After Designation, Speech Bank of England, March 24, 2014. Also: H. Chen and T. Sun, (2017), Tail Risk Networks of Insurers Around the Globe: An Empirical Examination of Systemic Risk for G-SIIs v.s. Non G-SIIs, Fox School of Business Research Paper Nr. 17-038; S. Harrington, (2016), Systemic Risk and Regulation: The Misguided Case of Insurance SIFIs, Wharton School Working Paper, October. Also here a framework was developed for the effective resolution of SIIs: FSB, (2016), Developing Effective Resolution Strategies and Plans for Systemically Important Insurers, June 6.

[313] FSB, (2014), Assessment Methodologies for Identifying Non-Bank Non-Insurer Global Systemically Important Financial Institutions, consultation document; 2nd Consultative Document by FSB on March 4, 2015. Following feedback on earlier released proposals, the new paper includes near-final methodologies for finance companies and market intermediaries (broker-dealers), a revised methodology for investment funds (including hedge funds), and a new proposed methodology for asset managers. The methodologies are expected to be finalized by the end of 2015, after which the FSB and IOSCO will begin work to develop any policy measures needed to address the risks posed by NBNI G-SIFIs, which are expected in the course of 2016. See also: FSB, (2015), Next Steps on the Assessment Methodologies for Non-Bank Non-Insurer Global Systemically Important Financial Institutions (NBNI G-SIFIs), press release, July 30. See also: BIS, (2017), Global systemically important banks - revised assessment framework - consultative document, March 30.

[314] See M. Billio et al., (2015), An Entropy-Based Early Warning Indicator for Systemic Risk, University of Venice, Department of Economics Working Paper Nr. 09/WP/2015, May 7. The analysis is based on the cross-sectional distribution of marginal systemic risk measures such as Marginal Expected Shortfall, Delta CoVaR and network connectedness. Entropy indicators show

The indicators selected for the G-SIFIs (equal weighted) reflect the size of banks, their interconnectedness, the lack of readily available substitutes or financial institution infrastructure for the services they provide, their global (cross-jurisdictional) activity and their complexity. They are further broken down into individual categories. For the other SIFI categories these components have been adjusted to reflect the specifics of the type of organizations assessed, although size and interconnectedness are standardized criteria. Complexity, opaqueness and substitutability are given different interpretations when comparing the different frameworks. Each year the Financial Stability Board produces a list of the relevant institutions per category.[315]

Many attempts have been made to quantify and estimate the 'Too Big to Fail' problem. A summary can be found in Box 11.1.

Although most discussions about systemic risk have focused on the private sector, the US Federal Government is the world's largest and most interconnected financial institution,

Box 11.1 Estimating the Too Big to Fail Problem

How big is the 'too big to fail' (TBTF) problem? Different approaches have been developed[316] to estimate the impact being perceived as TBTF might have on banks' costs of funding. One approach is to look at how the values of banks' equity and debt change in response to events that may have altered expectations that banks are TBTF. Another is to estimate whether debt costs vary across banks according to features that make them more or less likely to be considered TBTF. A third approach is to estimate a model of the expected value of government support to banks in distress. Certain communalities have been found between the different approaches. Many of the studies try to estimate any implicit subsidies received by TBTF banks. But these subsidies are not straightforward to define if one takes into account how TBTF status might change a bank's behavior. Most existing have used potentially noisy proxies to assess a potential TBTF status. That leads to a variety of issues and new challenges. For instance, it would be interesting to explore the links between TBTF status, the behavior of banks and the structure of the banking system, and the aggregate supply of financial services.

---

promising forecast abilities to predict financial and banking crisis. The proposed early warning signals reveal to be effective in forecasting financial distress conditions. In line herewith see: S. Markose et al., (2017), Early Warning and Systemic Risk in Core Global banking: Balance Sheet Financial Network and Market Price-Based Methods, SSRN E-Journal, January. They conclude, and in line with Markose's earlier work discussed, that '[t]he network based eigen-pair method simultaneously gives early warning of instability of the global banking system in terms of tipping points identified by regulatory capital thresholds and also the centrality measures for both systemically important and vulnerable banking systems.' Also: I. Aldoraso et al., (2018), Early Warning Indicators of banking Crises: Expanding the Family, BIS Quarterly Report, April, pp. 29–45.

[315] Most recent lists were published on their website in 2018 (www.financialstabilityboard.org)

[316] See in detail: C. Siegert and M. Willison, (2015), Estimating the Extent of the 'Too Big To Fail Problem- A Review of Existing Approaches, Bank of England, Financial Stability Paper Nr. 32, February; O. Couwenberg and S.J. Lubben, (2019), Not a Bank, Not a SIFI; Still Too Big to Fail, Emory Bankr. Dev. Journal Vol. 35, pp. 53 ff.

and through its activities—as a banker, rule-maker and regulator—represents a major source of systemic risk.[317] Several factors contribute to the fact that the government is a significant source of systemic risk. Lucas highlights this and most importantly: (1) its sheer size as a financial institution,[318] (2) the government's direct effect on the allocation and riskiness of credit is its influence on the incentives facing private individuals and institutions through its regulatory, tax and other policies. The government is as an institution guided by an invisible hand. The consequence is that its decisions often reflect a variety of sometimes competing political objectives.

11.6.2.3 Taxing Systemically Important FIs

Once we have managed to identify and assess SIFIs the next challenge is to define a taxation mechanism that reflects the contribution of a single SIFI to systemic risk and preferably the magnitude of it. Although there have been different models suggested, the model developed by Markose[319] has matured the most since the start of the financial crisis and has in my understanding the best technical fundamentals. Markose has been developing, starting in 2009, a multi-agent financial network (MAFN) allowing macroprudential policies to be built using visualization and modeling techniques.[320] Initially, she applied it to network model segments of the FI sphere, for example over-the-counter ('OTC') derivatives (i.e. those not cleared by an exchange),[321] of which only 5% is used for hedg-

[317] See: D. Lucas, (2014), Evaluating the Government as a Source of Systemic Risk, Journal of Financial Perspectives, Vol. 2, No. 3.

[318] Or to be more precise a collection of loosely affiliated financial institutions including Fannie Mae, Freddie Mac, the Federal Home Loan Banks, deposit insurance, and the Pension Benefit Guarantee Corporation (PBOC).

[319] That is based on Markose's historical work on markets. Markose looks at markets as Complex Adaptive Systems (CAS); See: S.M. Markose, (2003), Computability and Evolutionary Complexity: Markets as Complex Adaptive Systems, Working Paper, September, mimeo.

[320] See for the most recent version: S. M. Markose, (2013), Systemic Risk Analytics: A Data-Driven Multi-Agent Financial Network Approach, Journal of Banking Regulation, Vol.14, Issue 3/4, pp. 285–305, Special Issue on Regulatory Data and Systemic Risk Analytics.

[321] S.M. Markose, (2012), Systemic Risk from Global Financial Derivatives: A Network Analysis of Contagion and its Mitigation with Super-Spreader Tax, IMF Working Paper, WP/12/282. Based on 2009 FDIC and individually collected firm-level data covering gross notional, gross positive (negative) fair value, and the netted derivatives assets and liabilities for 202 financial firms, which includes 20 SIFIs, the bilateral flows are empirically calibrated to reflect data-based constraints. This produces a tiered network with a distinct highly clustered central core of 12 SIFIs that account for 78% of all bilateral exposures and a large number of financial intermediaries on the periphery. The topology of the network results in the 'Too-Interconnected-to-Fail' (TITF) phenomenon in that the failure of any member of the central tier will bring down other members with the contagion coming to an abrupt end with the demise of the 'super-spreaders'. Besides the fact that the OTC derivatives are not cleared and therefore prone to counterparty risk, there seems to be asymmetries in a lot of the OTC market in terms of discriminatory pricing. See in extenso: H. Hau et al., (2019), Discriminatory pricing of Over-the-Counter Derivatives, IMF Working Paper Nr. WP/19/100, May 7.

ing purposes,[322] credit default swaps,[323] and collateralized debt obligations.[324] Although her initial focus was on the development of the network model and the anticipation of changes over time, in recent years her focus has been on the prevention of systemic instability through the use of a Pigovian instrument. Macroprudential policy is concerned with mitigating system-wide risks arising from negative externalities from monetary and financial activities, with the total cost of the 2008 crisis estimated at 14 billion USD. Holistic visualization has become mainstream in the understanding and management of systemic risk and therefore Markose rejects the notion of a fixed list of SIFIs and advocates Pigovian-like surcharges.[325] That only happened after Markose[326] released her

---

[322] In the wake of Markose, Arsov et al. have developed a systemic financial stress index measuring the tail risk in the financial industry; see: I. Arsov, E. Canetti, L. Kodres and S. Mitra, (2013), 'Near-Coincident' Indicators of Systemic Stress, IMF Working Paper Series, WP/13/115. See also for an alternative stress index: R. Vermeulen et al., (2015), Financial Stress Indices and Financial Crises, DNB Working Paper Nr. 469, March. See for an alternative financial stress index: B. Vasicek et al., (2015), Leading Indicators of Financial Stress: New Evidence, DNB Working Paper Nr. 476, June.

[323] S. Markose, S. Giansante, M. Gatkowski and A.R. Shanghaghi, (2010), Too Interconnected To Fail: Financial Contagion and Systemic Risk in Network Model of CDS and Other Credit Enhancement Obligations of US Banks, Original Essex University Working Paper Series, Nr. 683, which was later on updated; see: S. Markose, S. Giansante, and A. Shaghaghi (2012), Too Interconnected To Fail Financial Network of U.S. CDS Market: Topological Fragility and Systemic Risk, Journal of Economic Behavior and Organization, Vol. 83, Issue 3, August 2012, pp. 627–646. Regarding the relationship between CDS and systemic financial risk see: S. Giglio, (2016), Credit Default Swap Risk and Systemic Financial Risk, ESRB, Working Paper Series Nr. 15, June and M. D'Errico et al., (2016), How Does Risk Flow in the Credit Default Swap market?, ESRB Working Paper Series Nr. 33, December. Paddrik et al. analyzed counterparty exposure in the CDS market. In particular they looked at the impact of severe credit shocks on the demand for variation margin, which are the payments that counterparties make to offset price changes. Large and sudden demands for variation margin may exceed a firm's ability to pay, leading some firms to delay or forego payments. These shortfalls can become amplified through the network of exposures. Also they refer to the role of CCPs in this matter. Typically seen as transmitting risk less than individual firms (firms that are large net sellers of CDS protection), they are positioned so that in case of large shortfalls it could lead to further shortfalls for their counterparties, amplifying the initial shock. See in detail: M. Paddrik et al., (2016), Contagion in the CDS Market, OFR Working Paper Nr. 16-12, December 1.

[324] S. Markose, B. Oluwasegun and S. Giansante, (2012), Multi-Agent Financial Network (MAFN) Model of US Collateralized Debt Obligations (CDO): Regulatory Capital Arbitrage, Negative CDS Carry Trade and Systemic Risk Analysis, Chapter in Simulation in Computational Finance and Economics: Tools and Emerging Applications, Alexandrova-Kabadjova B., S. Martinez-Jaramillo, A. L. Garcia-Almanza, and E. Tsang, (eds.) IGI Global, August 2012. E. Gerding, (2016), The Dialectics of bank Capital: Regulation and Regulatory Capital Arbitrage, Washburn Law Journal, Vol. 55, pp. 357–384.

[325] The FSB developed such a list in 2010: See FSB, (2010), Reducing the Moral Hazard by Systemically Important Financial Institutions. FSB Recommendations and Time Lines.

[326] S. Markose, (2012), Systemic Risk from Global Financial Derivatives: A Network Analysis of Contagion and Its Mitigation with Super-Spreader Tax, International Monetary Fund Working Paper Nr. 12/282.

eigen-pair[327] approach in 2012, which prices the cost of failure of an FI in an interconnected system of financial obligations. The financial network is identified as being unstable when its maximum eigenvalue is greater than a common threshold of Tier 1 capital. The corresponding eigenvector centrality (i.e. the centrality of an FI vis-à-vis other FIs and the global FI system as a whole), EVC, gives the rank order of the FIs contributing to the instability. A scaling Pigovian surcharge is recommended based on the outcome of the EVC analysis.

It is now widely acknowledged[328] that the exclusive focus in Basel I and II on managing risk and stress tests relating to how a bank's activities affect its individual chances of failure, with no consideration as to how these individual-level choices affect system-wide tail risks,[329] underlay the failure of the system and more macroprudential oriented mechanisms are needed that take into account firm-specific measures. Indeed, what may appear rational from the point of the individual FI, if adopted by all could lead to system instability and/or failure.

The model Markose developed functions as an equilibrating mechanism which manifests a misalignment of interests at the level of individual FIs, when pursuing short-term profits and market share, and identifies when system-wide instability occurs. The system-wide instability does not get transmitted back to the individual FIs signaling the need to adjust.[330] The lack of

---

[327] An eigen-pair is the mathematical pair of an eigenvector and its associated eigenvalue. The eigenvalue is a special set of scalars associated with a linear system of equations (i.e. a matrix equation), which in math is often used as a technique to measure the stability of a certain proposition. The eigenvector centrality (EVC) measures the nature and intensity of the relatedness of nodes in a network. It is applied in math or physics but also in social science. In this context it measures the nature and magnitude (what transactions, what volumes, what type of risks, how often these transactions change or expire) of the relationship of an FI with other FIs in the interconnected financial industry. Eigenvector centrality is one of the methods for computing the 'centrality', or approximate importance, of each node in a graph. The assumption is that each node's centrality is the sum of the centrality values of the nodes that it is connected to. The nodes are drawn with a radius proportional to their centrality.

[328] A. Haldane, (2009), Why Banks Failed the Stress Test, In Speech given at the Marcus-Evans Conference on Stress Testing, Bank of England (February). See regarding the decomposition of the effect of changing economic conditions, interest rates and balance sheet compositions on stress testing models: R. Busch et al., (2017), Deutsche Bundesbank Working Paper Nr. 7, Frankfurt am Main.

[329] These tail risks seem to be very good indicators of bank distress. Early warning models including estimated tail dependencies consistently outperform bank-specific benchmark models without networks to predict systemic risk. See T.A. Peltonen et al., (2015), Network Linkages to Predict banking Distress, ECB Working Paper Nr. 1828, July. They use a multivariate extreme value theory to estimate equity-based tail-dependence networks, whose links proxy for the markets' view of bank interconnectedness in case of elevated financial stress. See also: J. So and T.U, (2017), VAR and Stress Tests: The Impact of Fat-Tail Risk and Systemic Risk on Commercial Banks in Hong Kong and China, HKIMR Working Paper Nr. 14/2017; T. Breuer and M. Summer, (2018), Systematic Systemic Stres Tests, ONB Working Paper Nr. 225, December.

[330] The parallel with the Pigovian application in environmental situations is clear. Also in that context an indicator signaling externalities with system-wide ecological ramifications is absent.

modeling reflecting the interconnectedness and the build-up of stress in the system has lead post-crisis to a variety of suggestions regarding the development of models to identify and monitor the systemic risk from financial contagion[331] through the interconnectedness of balance sheets.[332] Most macroeconomic models have fallen behind the technology curve, and therefore they are as such not directly applicable.

The FSB, as indicated, created a list of the most important SIFIs and suggested imposing capital surcharges on a sliding scale from 1% to 2.5% depending on factors such as large size, prominence in markets or functions (non-substitutability), complexity, global activity and interconnectedness.[333] In line with that suggestion, the US in 2014 introduced such legislation.[334] It was suggested that the tax would address the significant implicit subsidy bestowed on big Wall Street banks and other financial institutions and should help recapture a portion of that implicit subsidy.[335] Implicit subsidies refer to the gains that banks implicitly obtain due to the expectation that governments will act as guarantor of last resort during a financial crisis.

These implicit guarantees bring substantial gains to banks in the form of an implicit subsidy, as creditors in financial markets factor in these guarantees and therefore those that benefit from them can borrow at lower funding rates. They are called implicit—as opposed to explicit—because there is no contractual agreement specifying the amounts or conditions

[331] S. Choi et al., (2017), Financial Contagion in Networks: A Market Experiment, Working Paper, June 27, mimeo. They investigate how the network structure of financial linkages and uncertainty about the location of a shock affect the likelihood of contagion and the formation of prices. They conclude that 'core-periphery' networks (highly connected at the core and poorly connected at the periphery) are highly susceptible to contagion and generate fire sales of assets that exacerbate financial contagion beyond the mechanical role of network structure. In contrast, contagion is minimal on circle networks (in circle networks each participant is the sole creditor of one participant and the sole debtor of another participant) and market prices remain stable.

[332] A. Haldane, (2009) Rethinking the Financial Network, Speech Delivered at the Financial Student Association, Amsterdam; J.D. Hamilton, (1989), A New Approach to the Economic Analysis of Non Stationary Time Series and Business Cycle, Econometrica, Vol. 57, Issue 2, pp. 357–384. See also regarding the relationship between financial contagion and spillover effects through both (in)direct channels: G. Peralta and R. Crisóstomos, (2016), Financial Contagion with Spillover Effects: A Multiplex Network Approach, ESRB Working Paper Series Nr. 32, December.

[333] More recent analysis demonstrates that surcharges of 3.00 to 8.25% would be justified and that they would have to be even higher for GSI-Bs that rely on short-term funding. See in detail: W. Passmore and A.H. von Haffen, (2019), Are Basel's Capital Surcharges for Global Systemically Important Banks Too Small?, International Journal of Central Banking, March, pp. 107–156.

[334] Section 7004 of the 'Tax Reform Act of 2014' would impose a quarterly excise tax of 0.035% on systemically important financial institutions (SIFIs). The excise tax would be applied to a SIFI's total consolidated assets in excess of $500 billion. For the purposes of the legislation, a SIFI would be any bank holding company with at least $50 billion in total consolidated assets, or any non-bank financial institution designated for SIFI treatment by the Financial Stability Oversight Council and subject to oversight by the Federal Reserve Board. The $500 billion threshold would be indexed for increases in the gross domestic product (GDP) after calendar year 2015.

[335] See: Committee on Ways and Means, (2014), Tax Reform Act 2014, Chairman Dave Camp, Section-by-Section Summary, pp. 180–181.

of government support[336] and are considered distortive in terms of financial stability, the size of FIs relative to the real economy, competition with those market players that do not benefit from such implicit subsidies, shifting resources from the real economy to the financial economy and so on.[337]

Given the public availability of stock market and other market price data for FIs, the most popular method for systemic risk analysis is statistically based on market price data with interconnections relying on correlation measures.[338] However, the real problem is that market-price-based systemic risk measures suffer from what has been called the volatility paradox. This is similar to the Minsky[339] paradox of instability associated with the procyclicality of leverage with asset price booms when the threats to the macroeconomy and financial stability are masked.[340] Likewise, during boom market conditions, risk and volatility are subdued and the volatility index registers its lowest level just before an extreme market collapse. Hence, market-price-based systemic risk measures may be misleading in

---

[336] The Greens, (2014), Implicit Subsidies in the EU Banking Sector, Intermediate Reporting (January). Credit Subsidies do however seem to function well as an alternative macroprudential tool. See: I. Correia et al., (2016), Credit Subsidies, ECB Working Paper Series Nr. 1877, January. Gudmundsson uses a jump diffusion option-pricing approach to provide estimates of implicit subsidies gained by these banks due to the expectation of protection to creditors provided by governments. He concludes that '[w]hile these subsidies have declined in the post-crisis era as volatility has declined and capital levels have increased, they remain non-trivial. Even conservative parameterizations of default and loss probabilities lead to macroeconomically significant figures.' See: T. Gudmundsson et al., (2016), Whose Credit Line is it Anyway: An Update on Banks' Implicit Subsidies, IMF Working Paper Nr. 16/224, November.

[337] See also: S. Schich and S. Lindh, (2012), Implicit Guarantees for Bank Debt: Where Do We Stand?, OECD Journal, Financial Market Trends, Vol. 2012, Issue 1, pp. 1–22.

[338] See for a full overview of all models: S. Markose and S. Giansante, (2014), Pigou Tax of Systemically Important Financial Intermediaries (SIFIs) In Financial Networks: An Empirical Application of Systemic Risk Monitoring and Governance, Working Paper. See also: G. Demange, (2015), Contagion in Financial Networks: A Threat Index, CESifo Working Paper Nr. 5307, April. This paper introduces 'a measure of the spill-over effects that a bank generates when it defaults. The measure is based on an explicit criterion, the aggregate debt repayments, and is bank's specific, affected by the bank's characteristics and links to other banks. Such measure can be useful to a regulator to determine in which banks cash should be injected during a default episode or to evaluate the impact of raising capital before the occurrence of default. The approach applies more generally to a system of entities that are linked through financial claims. Interbank claims are a concern to regulators as they might facilitate the dissemination of defaults and generate spill-over effects'.

[339] H. Minski, (1982), The Financial-Instability Hypothesis: Capitalist Processes and the Behavior of the Economy, in Ch. P. Kindleberger and J-P. Laffargue (eds.), Financial Crises: Theory, History and Policy, Cambridge University Press, Cambridge, pp. 13–38. See for a very good overview of Minsky's work and thinking on financialization: C.A. Whalen, (2017), Understanding Financialization: Standing on the Shoulders of Minsky, Levy Economics Institute of Bard College, Working Paper Nr. 892, June.

[340] See for a comprehensive analysis of financial stability risk in shadow banking systems: K. van der Veer et al., (2015), Shedding a Clearer Light on Financial Stability Risks in the Shadow Banking System, DNB Occasional Studies Vol. 13–7.

the build up to a crisis as they underprice risk during market booms.[341] Also, analysis based on aggregate data from countless financial statements has proved not to be robust.[342]

Any system to monitor systemic risk[343] would have to include at a minimum a metric that can identify if financial intermediation[344] is growing more unstable relative to Tier 1 capital (the core of a bank's balance sheet) in the system. Which FIs contribute more to systemic risk than others and how can a Pigovian instrument mitigate the negative externality are valid questions. The eigen-pair approach proposed by Markose prices the negative externality of an FI from being too interconnected and its capacity to propagate financial contagion.[345]

341 Markose et al., (2014), Ibid. p. 5.

342 See also: G. Leyngar et al., (2017), Towards a Financial Statement Based Approach to Modeling Systemic Risk in Insurance and Banking, Columbia Business School Research Paper Nr. 17-77. They highlight that one of the important limitations of the SRISK measure of systemic risk is its reliance on stock market data without much validation against the institutions' fundamentals based on its financial statements. They therefore propose a financial-statement-based approach to estimating the vulnerability of an institution to a systemic event (labeled CRISK). Applying their model to three different businesses, they conclude that under circumstances SRISK is likely to overstate (misstate) capital requirements and overstate capital requirements for banks heavily reliant on FDIC insured deposits. They suggested methodology could be used as a first-line filter to identify systemically important institutions.

343 Recently Battiston et al. produced a 'novel, very interesting three-level monitoring framework for systemic risk. The modular structure of the framework allows to accommodate for a variety of shock scenarios, methods to estimate interbank exposures and mechanisms of distress propagation. The main features are as follows. First, the framework allows to estimate and disentangle not only first-round effects (i.e. shock on external assets) and second-round effects (i.e. distress induced in the interbank network), but also third-round effects induced by possible fire sales. Second, it allows to monitor at the same time the impact of shocks on individual or groups of financial institutions as well as their vulnerability to shocks on counterparties or certain asset classes. Third, it includes estimates for loss distributions, thus combining network effects with familiar risk measures such as VaR and CVaR. Fourth, in order to perform robustness analyses and cope with incomplete data, the framework features a module for the generation of sets of networks of inter- bank exposures that are coherent with the total lending and borrowing of each bank. They find that second-round and third-round effects dominate first-round effects, therefore suggesting that most current stress-test frameworks might lead to a severe underestimation of systemic risk'; see: S. Battiston et al., (2015), Leveraging the Network: A Stress-Test Framework based on DebtRank, Working Paper, March 3, Mimeo; M. Paddrik et al., (2016), Bank Networks and Systemic Risk: Evidence from the National Banking Acts, OFR Working Paper Nr. 16-13, December 6; E. Frohm and V. Gunnella, (2017), Sectoral Interlinkages in Global Value Chains, ECB Working Paper Nr. 2064, May. Sectoral spill-overs are both statistically significant and of economic importance.

344 Financial Intermediation in a 'global' context might be added. The interbanking market is by definition global and the propagation shocks are material running through that channel. International transmission of a crisis through the balance sheet of global banks is directly connected to the international asset market and its pricing mechanism. See in detail: V. Nuguer, (2016), Financial Intermediation in a Global Environment, IJCB, Vol. 12, Nr. 3, pp. 291–343.

345 'How, and to what extent, does an interconnected financial system endogenously amplify external shocks' is the question that Visentin asked themselves. They conclude that regardless of the shock distribution and the network topology, precise ordering relationships on the level of aggregate systemic losses hold among models. They argue that 'the extent of contagion crucially depends on the amount of information that each model assumes to be available to market players.' Under no uncertainty about the network structure and values of external assets, the lowest level of contagion is delivered. That phenomenon is known as 'loss conservation' which implies that 'aggregate

The instability of the financial network is measured in terms of the maximum eigenvalue of the financial network and there is cause for concern for the regulator if it is greater than the common threshold of Tier 1 capital. The corresponding eigenvector centrality of the FIs in the network determines the rank order of the FIs contributing to the instability of the network. Markose et al. in 2014 developed the methodology for making an assessment of the Pigovian tax that can price in an FI's systemic risk to a network of current financial obligations.[346] Empirically documented they demonstrate that in some cases 98% or more correlation exists in the rank order of EVC-dominant FIs and the rank order of their capacity to produce domino-type losses.[347]

This shows how the EVC metric is a very good proxy for actual losses of capital that could follow if a high EVC FI is to fail. The MAFN earlier developed is used as the blueprint network for analysis.[348]

The intrinsic strength of the Markose model is not only documented; the benefits of her model over a market-based mechanism have also been highlighted. The same is true for command-and-control regulation under the Basel rules, where the capital ratios are not only modest but did not mitigate risk when needed.[349] It is also superior to other suggested models including the Acharya et al. model which suggests a 'tax' based on the expected loss conditional on the occurrence of a systemic crisis. They suggest two models for estimating the tax: (1) pricing of contingent capital insurance for systemic risk, that is, an insurance for each firm against itself becoming undercapitalized[350] when the financial sector as a whole becomes undercapitalized[351]; and, (2) market-based discovery of the price of such risk insurance which

losses after contagion are equal to the losses incurred by those institutions initially hit by a shock. This property implies that many contagion analyses rule out by construction any loss amplification, treating de facto an interconnected system as a single aggregate entity, where losses are simply mutualised.' On the other hand 'non -conservative losses' get compounded through the network. The endgame in terms of policy implication is that by reducing the levels of uncertainty in times of distress, we would be able to move toward lower levels of contagion; see in detail also for the set of models analyzed: G. Visentin et al., (2016), Rethinking Financial Contagion, University of Zurich Working Paper, mimeo, August 28. Also: D.F. Ahelegbey et al., (2019), Tree Networks to Assess Financial Contagion, MPRA Paper Nr. 92632, March 29.

346 See Markose et al., (2014), Section 3, pp. 20–23.

347 C.H. Furfine, (2003), Interbank Exposures: Quantifying the Risk of Contagion, Journal of Money, Credit and Banking, Vol. 35, Issue 1, pp. 111–28. Furfine developed the framework for quantifying contagion risk and the domino effect it creates. See Markose et al., (2014), pp. 24–27. Also interesting in a wider context: M. Carlson and D.C. Wheelock, (2016), Did the Founding of the Federal Reserve Affect the Vulnerability of the Interbank System to Contagion, BIS Working Paper Nr. 598, December. They find that the interbank system became more resilient to solvency shocks, but less resilient to liquidity shocks, as banks sharply reduced their liquidity after the Fed's founding.

348 Supra 11.6.2.3.

349 Lehman Brothers capital ratios did meet all the Basel criteria on the last working days before it failed on Sunday, given the lack of government support or backstop.

350 L. Blattner et al., (2019), When Losses Turn into Loans: the Cost of Undercapitalized Banks, ECB Working Paper Nr. 2228, January 28.

351 See for an extensive analysis of systemic risk in the insurance sector: EIOPA, (2017), Systemic Risk and Macroprudential Policy in Insurance, European Insurance and Occupational Pension Authority Report.

financial institutions must purchase partly from the private sector but mostly from the government or the central bank. In their preferred approach, individual firms would be required to purchase contingent capital insurance, that is, insurance against the losses that they would incur during systemic crises. The cost of this insurance determines the firm's systemic risk tax.[352]

Besides the moral hazard that comes with denominating the tax as an insurance, the main problem with this suggestion is that it assumes that the loss of an FI equals the damage that the FI burdens the system with. The centerpiece of their scheme is to measure the firm's share of expected losses conditional on the occurrence of a systemic crisis. Their analysis is solely built on the 'systemic expected shortfall' (SES), that is, the measurement of systemic risk as the amount by which a bank is undercapitalized in a systemic event in which the entire financial system is undercapitalized (using market data).[353] SES increases

[352] V.V. Acharya, L. H. Pedersen, T. Philippon and M. Richardson, (2009), Measuring Systemic Risk, Working Paper, New York University Stern School of Business; V.V. Acharya, L. H. Pedersen, T. Philippon and M. Richardson (2009) Regulating Systemic Risk, Chapter 13 in Restoring Financial Stability: How to Repair a Failed System, V. V. Acharya and M. Richardson (eds.), New York University Stern School of Business, John Wiley and Sons, Hoboken; V.V. Acharya, L.H. Pederson, T. Philippon and M. Richardson, (2010), A Tax on Systemic Risk, Working Paper. V.V. Acharya, (2009), A Theory of Systemic Risk and Design of Prudential Bank Regulation, Journal of Financial Stability Elsevier, Vol. 5, Issue 3, pp. 224–255. And more recently: S. Benoit et al., (2015), Where the Risks Lie: A Survey on Systemic Risk, University of Orléons Working Paper, Mimeo; J.H. Dalhuizen, (2015), The management of Systemic Risk from a Legal Perspective, Working Paper, January, Mimeo; Z. Feinstein et al., (2015), Measuring of Systemic Risk, Working Paper, March, Mimeo. G. Löffler and P. Raupach, (2014), Pitfalls in the Use of Systemic Risk Measures, Working Paper, October 2. They identified several cases in which a change in a bank's systematic risk, idiosyncratic risk, size or contagiousness increases the risk of the system but lowers the measured systemic risk contribution of the bank. In such cases, assessments based on estimated systemic risk contributions could produce false interpretations and incentives. See also: V. de Bruyckere, (2015), Systemic Risk Rankings and Network Centrality in the European Banking Sector, ECB Working Paper Nr. 1848, September and C. Siebenbrunner, (2017), Clearing Algorithms and Network Centrality, Working Paper, April 28, mimeo. Regarding the informational value of systemic risk rankings see: F. Nucera et al., (2016), The Information in Systemic Risk Rankings, ECB Working Paper Series Nr. 1875, January. Das proposes a novel framework for network-based systemic risk measurement and management. A new systemic risk score is defined that depends on the level of individual risk at each financial institution and the interconnectedness across institutions, and is generally applicable irrespective of how interconnectedness is defined. This risk metric is decomposable into risk contributions from each entity, forming a basis for taxing each entity appropriately. The paper further develops other risk measures such as system fragility and entity criticality. An assessment using a measure of spillover risk is obtained to determine the scale of externalities that one bank might impose on the system; the metric is robust to this cross risk and does not induce predatory spillovers. The analysis shows that splitting up too-big-to-fail banks from the system does not lower systemic risk; see: S.R. Das, (2015), Matrix Metrics: Network-Based Systemic Risk Scoring, Leavy School of Business Working Paper, Santa Clara University, November 15.

[353] V.V. Acharya, C. Brownelees, R. Engle, F. Farazmand and M. Richardson, (2010), Measuring Systemic Risk, Chapter 4 in Regulating Wall Street: The Dodd-Frank Act and the New Architecture of Global Finance, V.V. Acharya, T. Cooley, M. Richardson and I. Walter (eds.), John Wiley & Sons, Hoboken, pp. 199–232. In a European context regarding this model see: V.V. Acharya and S. Steffen, (2012), Analyzing Systemic Risk in the Banking Sector, Working Paper. See also: B. Weder di Mauro,

with the institution's leverage and its marginal expected shortfall (MES), that is, its losses in the tail of the system's loss distribution. Institutions internalize their externality if they are 'taxed' based on their SES.[354]

Having said that, the model, like some of the other suggested models,[355] can have useful predictive power with respect to the behaviors of SIFIs prior to and during a

(2010), Taxing Systemic Risk: Proposal for a Systemic Risk Levy and a Systemic Risk Fund, University of Mainz Working Paper. See for a ranking of European financial institution based on the MES: A. Derbali, (2017), Systemic Risk of European Financial Institutions: Estimation and Ranking by the Marginal Expected Shortfall, University of Sousse Working Paper, mimeo, November 28. He concludes that the systemic risk supported by European banks is very high. Moreover, the contribution of financial institutions in the risk of their system is very important as a result of the high correlation between institution returns and market returns. He further produced a measurement based on the MES for Chinese, Greek and US financial institutions. Avikran did the same for Japanese banks: N.K. Avkiran, (2017), Measuring the Systemic Risk of Regional Banks in Japan, University of Queensland Business School Working Paper, November 20, mimeo. For Russian banks see: A. Karminsky and M. Stolbov, (2016), Assessing the Link between Financial Soundness and Systemic Risk for Key Russian Banks, Journal of Corporate Finance Research, Vol. 10, Nr. 1, pp. 77–87; C. Buch et al., (2017), Drivers of Systemic Risk: Do National and European Perspectives Differ?, Bundesbank Discussion Paper Nr. 09/2017; T. Beck et al., (2017), Bank Sectoral Concentration and (Systemic) Risk: Evidence from a Worldwide Sample of Banks, CEPR Discussion Paper Nr. DP12009, June. Li and Saiz measure systemic risk in the network of financial market infrastructures (FMIs) as the probability that two or more FMIs have a large credit risk exposure to the same FMI participant. They not only observe large differences between the contributions to systemic risk across participants, they also find that when participants are in financial distress, they tend to create large credit exposures in two or more FMIs. In detail: F. Li and H.P. Saiz, (2016), Measuring Systemic Risk across Financial market Infrastructures, Bank of Canada Working Paper Nr. 10, March.

354 C. Brownlees and R. Engle, (2011), Volatility, Correlation and Tails for Systemic Risk Measurement, Working Paper Series, Department of Finance, NYU advanced the model. Idier et al. however conclude that standard balance-sheet metrics like the tier one solvency ratio are better able than the MES to predict equity losses conditionally to a true crisis (using the 2008 datasets); See: J. Idier, G. Lamé, and J.-S. Méssonier, (2013), How Useful is the Marginal Expected Shortfall for the Measurement of Systemic Exposure, A Practical Assessment, ECB Working Paper Series, Nr. 1546.

355 I will limit myself to referring to other models developed insofar as they are not mentioned in the main text. They have contributed one way or the other to the understanding of the occurrence of systemic risk but have, as insight has progressed, become known for adding particular features or a specific understanding rather than a continued validation of their overall model. They include:

- Conditional VaR (CoVaR): T. Adrian and M.K. Brunnermeier, (2011), CoVaR, Federal Reserve Bank of New York Staff Reports, No. 348, original [2009]. The Value at Risk (VaR) of financial institutions conditional on other institutions being in distress (using six risk factors). The increase of CoVaR relative to VaR measures spillover risk among institutions. They also created a network CoVaR which makes the model resemble Markose's model, but still based on market data. The model was extended years later and they coined multidimensional value at risk (MVAR) . It generalizes VaR in a natural way as the intersection of univariate VARs. Building on new insights regarding volatility, tail events are modeled into long-term trend and short-term cycle components. See in detail: A. Polanski and E. Stoja, (2017), Forecasting Multidimensional Tail Risk at Short and Long Horizons, Bank of England Staff Working Paper Nr. 660, June.
- Distance to Distress (DD): O. Castren and I.K. Kavonius, (2009), Balance Sheet Interlinkages and Macro-Financial Risk Analysis in the Euro Area, ECB Working Paper, Nr. 1124.

systemic crisis.[356] Markose's model focuses explicitly on the question of whether the capital held by FIs in the system is sufficient to maintain stability of the network of financial obligations from threats of contagion in the intra-financial system. As Solorzano-Margain et al.[357] have demonstrated in a Mexican context, bilateral data are essential to gauge systemic risk and calibrating the network of financial obligations often underestimates these threats.

- Distress Insurance Premium (DIP): X. Huang, H. Zhou, and H. Zhu, (2010), Systemic Risk Contribution, BIS Working Paper, Nr. 60-3.
- POD (Probability that at least one bank becomes distressed): M. Segoviano and C. Goodhart, (2009), Banking Stability Measures, IMF Working Paper Series, Nr. WP/09/04.
- For an extensive combined review of these models see: D. Bisias, M. Flood, A. Lo, and S. Valavanis, (2012), A Survey of Systemic Risk Analytics, Office of Financial Research Working Paper, Nr. 0001; and for backtesting of these models against previous crises: C. Brownlees et al., (2015), Backtesting Systemic Risk Measures During Historical bank Runs, Reserve Bank of Chicago Working Paper Nr. WP 2015-09, July. And more recently: C.T. Browlees and R. Engle, (2017), SRISK: a Conditional Capital Shortfall Index for Systemic Risk Measurement, Review of Financial Studies, Vol.30, Nr.1, pp. 48–79; C. Brownlees et al., (2017), Back to the Future: Backtesting Systemic Risk Measures During Historical Bank Runs and the Great Depression, CEPR Discussion Paper Nr. DP12178. See for a variation to the integrated shortfall model: I. Torchiani et al., (2017), An Integrated Shortfall Measure for Basel III, Deutsche Bundesbank Working Paper Nr. 26, Frankfurt am Main. They propose measuring a bank's non-compliance with regulatory requirements as a portfolio that the bank has to add to its balance sheet in order to comply with the requirements. The portfolio measure allows incorporating the interdependencies of all requirements in a natural way.
- A more recent model developed to identify and measure systemic risk is the SenSR: Sentiment-based Systemic Risk Indicator. This measure is constructed by dynamically aggregating the sentiment in news about systemically important financial institutions (SIFIs). Its performance to other well-known systemic risk indicators as well as with macroeconomic fundamentals has been analyzed. It was found that SenSR anticipates other systemic risk measures such as SRISK or VIX in signaling stressed times. See in detail: S. Borovkova, (2017), SenSR: A Sentiment-Based Systemic Risk Indicator, DNB Working Paper Nr. 533, April, Amsterdam.
- Another model also recently added to the list is the M-Press-CreditRisk model: N. Tente et al., (2017), M-Press-CreditRisk: A Holistic Micro- and Macroprudential Approach to Capital Requirements, Deutsche Bundesbank Discussion Paper Nr. 15/2017. This model combines macroprudential capital buffers and stress testing. That should create two benefits: it provides an advanced portfolio model for credit risk, which captures extreme losses in the banking system that may materialize during crisis-lie systemic events (tail risk). It further brings together different prudential instruments that address credit risk either at the bank level or system level, creating a coherent approach to their calibration. As such, the model combines the portfolio model with a macroeconomic model which generates multi-rik factor, multi-country stress scenarios. The M-PRESS-CreditRisk model provides estimates for the banks' own funds required to cover credit risk, forward-looking loan provisioning, minimum capital requirements and capital buffers in place to cover systemic risk. Also: S. Masciantonio and A. Zaghini, (2017), Systemic Risk and Systemic Importance Measures During the Crisis, Bank of Italy Working Paper Nr. 1153.
- See for a comprehensive overview of systemic risk indicators: A. Di Cesare and A.R. Picco, (2018), A Survey of Systemic Risk Indicators, Working Paper, October, mimeo.

[356] See for a comparison of the different models suggested: John Sedunov III, (2013), What is the Systemic Risk Exposure of FIs?, Midwest Finance Association 2013 Annual Meeting Paper. See also J.-P. Fouque and J.A. Angsam, (2013), Handbook on Systemic Risk, Cambridge University Press, Cambridge; and S. Giglio et al. (2016), Systemic Risk and the Macroeconomy: An Empirical Evaluation, Journal of Financial Economics, Vol. 119, Nr.1, pp. 457–471.

[357] J.P. Solorzano-Margain, S. Martinez-Jaramillo and F. Lopez-Gallo, (2013), Financial Contagion: Extending the Exposures Network of the Mexican Financial System, Computational Management Science, Vol. 10, Issue 2–3, pp. 125–155.

Previously trivial banks have turned out be to systemically relevant and therefore Markose argues against an a priori list of SIFIs. The systemic risk of an FI must be analyzed from the perspective of its dominance in the network representing financial obligations, for which Markose uses the EVC.[358]

It should be noted that despite the strong arguments in favor of Markose's model, key challenges remain. To complete the toolbox for macroprudential policy and systemic risk monitoring developed by Markose,[359] answers are needed in a variety of areas. Markose herself indicates: 'it involves addressing issues of dealing with multi-layer network consequences of activities of FIs in multiple financial products and markets, including central clearing platforms, integrating the digital model of the financial sector with the macroeconomic sectoral uses and flow of funds[360] and assessing adequacy of liquidity in the face of extant financial liabilities of the FIs'.[361]

The expanding body of research in the area of systemic risk is welcome, but also complicates the view, as most research focuses on a single or consolidated source of risk rather than a broader focus on an integrated or holistic analysis of systemic risk.[362] As the granularity of the dataset is refined, and given the fact that it is not an exact science, policy making and regulating based on those countless datasets will become near-impossible. The Pigovian models suggested in the FI sector suffer from the same risk as the underlying systemic risk research, that is, the focus on a single aspect of systemic risk or risk exposure overall in the FI sector.

It is therefore instrumental to organize my analysis in systemic and firm-specific risk separately first, and then later on detail the different subcategories and suggest a holistic Pigovian instrument with different layers that correspond immediately to the externality as given at that level of activity of a specific FI. The end result of this exercise will therefore be a proprietary multi-layered Pigovian instrument, of which I have just created the first layer, that is, compensation for systemic risk based on the eigenvector centrality model as suggested by Markose. The model demonstrates the exposure and ranking and allows for the development of a scaled Pigovian instrument based on the ranking (e.g. bi-annualized) it yields. In Table 11.1 the structure and content of the Pigovian instrument are reflected as they will plausibly facilitate further reading of the firm-specific risk analysis from an externality point of view, which is what follows in this chapter.

---

358 A similar non-EVC model was recently used to visualize the Dutch Overnight Money Market; See: R. Heijmans, R. Heuver, C. Levallois and I. van Lelyveld, (2014), Dynamic Visualisation of Large Transaction Networks: The Daily Dutch Overnight Money Market, DNB Working Paper Series, Nr. 418.

359 S. Markose, (2013), Systemic Risk Analytics: A Data Driven Multi-Agent Financial Network (MAFN) Approach, Submitted Special Issue Journal of Banking Regulation: Future of Regulatory Data and Systemic Risk Analytics, Bank of England Workshop January 17–18, 2013.

360 See, for instance, for a regional study: N. Zhang and X. Zhao, (2018), Measuring Global Flow of Funds: A Case Study on China, Japan and the United States, Paper prepared for the 35th IARIW General Conference Copenhagen, Denmark, August 20–25, mimeo.

361 Markose et al., (2014), Ibid. p. 29.

362 See for an attempt of an integrated approach in this matter: A. Serguaiva, (2013), Systemic Risk Identification, Modelling, Analysis, and Monitoring: An Integrated Approach, University College London, Working Paper.

Table 11.1 Build-up of a proprietary Pigovian instrument for the FI Sector

Risk layer	Targeted externalities	Suggested pigovian capture
Systemic risk		
SIFI and contagion risk	Externalities related to strategic complementaries,[a] externalities related to fire sales and externalities related to interconnectedness[b] including spillover effects[c] or interaction of various bank regulations[d]	A scaled Pigovian surcharge based on Markose's eigenvector centrality demonstrating the contribution of a specific FI to systemic risk in the FI system. This is essentially a modified (Heckscher-Ohlin) H-O model adapted to reflect the dynamics of a globalized financial industry
Firm-specific risk		
Credit risk	Fire sale,[e] run on banks[f]	A scaled Pigovian surcharge based on credit exposure relative to the loss absorption levels of the FIs funding structure[g,h]
Maturity risk	Fire Sale, run on banks, liquidity exposure,[i] hoarding- and network externality	A scaled Pigovian tax taking into account the maturity mismatch[j] between the average funding maturity and the average maturity of the wider loan book (with a number of cyclical adjustments)
Risk transformation	Network externality, bubble creation, fire sale, pecuniary externality	A Pigovian surcharge capturing the externality of the shadow banking product (or product categories) i.e. the loss in asset quality, collateral value often caused by fire sales
Liquidity risk[k]	Fire sale,[l] bank run, hoarding externality,[m] pecuniary externality[n]	A scaled Pigovian surcharge based on short-term debt of an FI corrected for the degree of maturity mismatch and accounting for the economic cycle
Leverage-related risk[o]	Fire sale,[p] network externality, bubble creation, pecuniary externality	A scaled Pigovian tax based on the amount of noncore liabilities taking into account the amount of short-term unsecured debt and the total volume of noncore debt
Volatility-related risk	Fire sale, hoarding-, network externality	A Pigovian surcharge based on the type of volatility-inducing products and volumes running through those categories

[a]For the role of international taxation in this matter see: H. Huizinga, J. Voget, and W. Wagner, (2014), International Taxation and Cross-Border Banking, American Economic Journal, Economic Policy, Vol. 6, Issue 2, pp. 94–125; B. Steil, (2010), Debt and Systemic Risk: The Contribution of Fiscal and Monetary Policy, Cato Journal, Vol. 30, Nr. 2, pp. 391–396.

[b]See in detail: G. de Niccolò, G. Favara and L. Ratnosvki, (2012), Externalities and Macro-Prudential Policy, IMF Staff Discussion Note, SDN/12/05; A.M. Buffa, (2011), Strategic Banks and Systemic Externalities, LBS Working Paper; M. Bluhm and E. Faia, (2013), Endogenous' Banks' Networks, Cascades and Systemic Risk, University Frankfurt Working Paper.

[c]See in detail: S. Claessens et al., (2014), The Impact of the Global Financial Crisis on Banking Globalization, IMF Working Paper Nr. WP/14/197; Y. Shinagawa, (2014), Determinants of Financial Markets Spillovers: The Role of Diversification, Trade, Home Bias and Concentration, IMF Working Paper Nr. WP/14/187; This paper defines financial market spillovers as the comovement between two countries' financial markets and analyzes financial market spillovers over the period 2001–2012 through four channels: bilateral portfolio investment, bilateral trade, home bias and country concentration. See for cross-border spillover effects of monetary policy: J. Chen et al., (2014) Spillovers from United States Monetary Policy on Emerging Markets: Different This Time, IMF Working Paper Series, Nr. WP/14/240 and S. Bernhard and T. Ebner, (2016), Cross-Border Spillover Effects of Unconventional Monetary Policies and Swiss Asset Prices, SNB Working Papers, Nr. 9, August.

[d]D. Kirti and V. Narasiman, (2017), How is the Likelihood of Fire Sales in a Crisis Affected by the Interaction of Various Bank Regulations, IMF Working Paper Nr. WP/17/68, March. They conclude that regulation affects the likelihood of fire sales by giving banks, subject to capital regulation, the incentive to sell certain assets and retain others (concentration and minimal diversification). In their model risk shifting motives drive how banks recapitalize (asset sale and equity issuance) following a negative shock, leading banks to concentrate their portfolios. They introduce the aspect of 'time-varying risk weights' to prevent such a fire sale and highlight that those might be more effective than 'time-varying capital requirements' or 'time-varying liquidity requirements'. That indirectly adds to my basic premises of preferring a Pigovian model over a command-and-control model. They comment 'we show that the assignment of risk weights can affect whether banks engage in fire sales when recapitalizing. If the risk weight on a particular asset is sufficiently high, banks will choose to sell it because retaining it forces them to be underleveraged, limiting the amount of risk that can be shifted on to creditors. Since high risk-weight assets are likely to be illiquid, fire sales can result. However, fire sales may be prevented if the risk weights on all assets are the same because banks will retain the asset that has the greatest underlying risk and sell assets that are safer and probably more liquid.' (p. 27). The same is true for liquidity requirements: banks will choose to concentrate their portfolios into one asset but instead of selling the other assets, they will only be sold to the degree the liquidity requirements allow. The consequence is that banks have an incentive to build up holdings of a desired asset so that in case it is needed the undesired asset(s) can be maximally offloaded within the parameters of the liquidity requirement. However, the appeal to retain a risky illiquid asset is diminished because banks are forced to hold a certain amount of safe, liquid assets, creating (unwanted) diversification. To avoid that, banks might build up holdings in a different asset and sell the illiquid asset in a fire sale. Also, mandatory equity issuance can potentially mitigate the severity of fire sales when it is binding because it forces banks to do less net selling of potentially illiquid assets. However, if the circumstances are such that banks are issuing sufficient amounts of equity on their own, fire sales may still occur. This issue can potentially be addressed by setting mandatory equity issuance amounts aggressively.

[e]F. Duarte and T.M. Eisenbach, (2014), Fire-Sale Spillovers and Systemic Risk, Staff Reports Nr. 645, Federal Reserve bank of NY and in general see: A. Schleifer and R. Vishny, (2011), Fire Sales in Finance and Macro-Economics, Journal of Economic Perspectives, Vol. 25, Number 1, Winter 2011, pp. 29–48.

[f]M. Brunnermeyer, (2009), G20 London Summit, Pre-Meeting HM Treasury, January 31.

(continued)

Table 11.1 (continued)

[g]See how FinTech can help in scaling a Pigouvian charge: M. Bazarbash, (2019), FinTech in Financial Inclusion Machine Learning Applications in Assessing Credit Risk, IMF Working Paper Nr. WP/19/109, May. Four channels were identified: (1) leveraging nontraditional data sources to improve the assessment of the borrower's track record; (2) appraising collateral value; (3) forecasting income prospects; and (4) predicting changes in general conditions.

[h]Designing the model is critical. See the findings of Grundke et al. who developed a credit risk stress test model: P. Grundke et al., (2019), Model and Estimation Risk in Credit Stress Tests, Deutsche Bundesbank Discussion Paper Nr. 9, March 8. They comment: 'our findings show that stress forecasts of default probabilities highly depend on the modelling assumptions and that seemingly only minor variations can affect the results of stress tests considerably'. Also: T. Siemsen and J. Vilsmeier, (2018), On a Quest for Robustness: About Model Risk, Randomness and Discretion in Credit Risk Stress Tests, Deutsche Bundesbank Discussion Paper Nr. 31, August 28. They argue in the same line as Grundke et al. '[t]his leaves stress test results subject to significant model uncertainty'; P. Van Roy et al., (2018), Sensitivity of Credit Risk Stress Test Results: Modelling Issues with an Application to Belgium, NBB Working Paper Nr. 338, March. They find that the impact of a stress test on banks' Tier 1 ratios can differ substantially depending on the credit risk variable and the level of data aggregation considered. In case solvency stress tests are going to be used as a supervisory tool or to set regulatory capital requirements, there is a need to further harmonize their execution across institutions and supervisors in order to enhance comparability, in particular within an EU context.

[i]See (also for a full literature overview) T. Yorulmazer, (2014), Literature Review of the Stability of Funding Models, Federal Reserve bank of NY Economic Policy Review, February, pp. 3–16. See also the interesting literature list pp. 31 ff.

[j]Maturity transformation is a material driver of the net interest margin (together with higher short-term rates and a steeper yield curve). Higher maturity transformation is typically associated with higher net interest margin. But there is more: the more the maturity transformation raises the net interest margin the more steeper is the yield curve. However, there is a tipping point as 'excessive' maturity transformation—even without leading to systemic vulnerabilities—increases banks' interest rate risk exposure and lowers their net interest margin. Using maturity transformation is directly related to regulatory boundaries or its changes. Loosening the regulatory limit on maturity transformation almost consistently equals expansion of maturity transformation. Most banks do so by carrying out 'a significant rebalancing of their balance sheet, in terms of maturity, interest rate, and lending type, resulting in an increased exposure to interest rate risk and in a lower net interest margin'. (p. 25) See in detail: P. Bologna, (2018), Banks' Maturity Transformation: Risk, Reward, and Policy, IMF Working Paper Nr. WP/18/45, February. The implications of their findings are critical: in a low interest rate environment as we know it, banks' net interest margin could benefit from a higher maturity transformation, particularly if it comes in conjunction with a steeper yield curve. The net interest margin is the component most sensitive to interest rates and maturity transformation. Also: A. Segura, and J. Suarez, (2017), How Excessive Is Banks' Maturity Transformation?, Review of Financial Studies, Vol. 30, Issue 10, pp. 3502–3537.

[k]See in detail: E. Banks, (2013), Liquidity Risk. Managing Funding and Asset Risk, 2nd Ed., Palgrave Macmillan, Basingstoke. See also: A. Abbate and D. Thaler, (2015), Monetary Policy and the Asset Risk-Taking Channel, Deutsche Bundesbank Discussion Paper Nr. 48. The basic dynamic of Abbate and Thaler is that monetary policy might influence financial sector risk through the so-called risk-taking channel, i.e. the mechanism by which low levels of the risk-free interest rate induce financial institutions to make riskier investments. Setting interest rates impacts therefore bank asset risk and so the question emerges whether monetary authorities should observe that relationship. The short answer is yes and points at the policy relevance that 'if the risk-taking channel is active, monetary policy should stabilize the real interest rate, in order to reduce the welfare detrimental volatility of the banks' risk choice'. Also: L. Pastor and R.F. Stambaugh, (2019), Liquidity Risks after 20 Years, NBER Working Paper Nr. 25774, April; S. Imhof et al., (2018), The Risk-Taking Channel of Liquidity Regulations and Monetary Policy, SNB Working paper Nr. 13, August.

[l]D. Li, (2013), How Does Liquidity Risk Disturb Asset Prices? A General Equilibrium Approach, Working Paper.

[m]P. Gai and S. Kapadia, (2009), Liquidity Hoarding, Network Externalities and Interbank Market Collapse, Working Paper; V.V. Acharya and D. Skeie, (2011), A Model of Liquidity Hoarding and Term-Premia in Inter-bank Markets, Journal of Monetary Economics, Elsevier, Vol. 58, Vol. 5, pp. 436–447.

[n]For the relationship with macroprudential regulation in the absence of perfect international coordination see: J. Bengui, (2013), Macro-Prudential Policy Coordination, University of Montreal Working Paper.

[o]See extensively X. Freixas and K. Ma, (2014), Banking Competition and Stability: The Role of Leverage, CEPR Working Paper, who show that the effect of competition on financial stability depends crucially on banks' liability structure, on whether banks are financed by insured retail deposits or by uninsured wholesale investors, whether indebtedness is exogenous or endogenous and on the degree of competition in the banking industry. In particular they show that, while in a classical originate-to-hold banking industry competition might increase financial stability, the opposite might be true for an originate-to-distribute banking structure characterized by a larger fraction of market short-term funding.

[p]See: A. Arquié, (2014), Fires Sales, Pecuniary Externality and Inefficient Banking: Going Beyond Liquidity Ratios, Paris School of Economics Working Paper.

It can be judged against the typical regulatory approach regarding systemic risk, the efforts of which are often categorized as: (1) incentive regulation: to foster ex ante internalization of externalities, (2) structural or quantity regulation: often putting restrictions on certain activities or minimal thresholds, and (3) ex post crisis intervention: dampening the mechanisms causing the systemic risk spreading.[363] To facilitate the reading of the remaining part of this section and keep an overview on the different layers embedded in the suggested Pigovian instrument, I have developed the following chart indicating the risk layer, the targeted externality in that risk layer and the suggested 'legal' Pigovian mechanism to capture the externality-inducing behavior.

11.6.3 Taxing Firm-Specific Risk in the FI Industry

Within the context of systemic risk, it should be observed that the vulnerability of FIs and their contribution to the emergence of externalities is (partly) linked to their private position as an FI. Further it requires attention that many of the vulnerabilities an FI exposes itself to are linked to each other and impact each other.[364] Table 11.2 provides an overview of those vulnerabilities and how command-and-control regulation has responded during the Basel III introduction cycle.

Another way to frame the macroprudential framework that was built around the financial sector post-crisis can be built around three thematic measures[365]:

[363] See in detail: M. Bijlsma, J. Klomp and S. Duineveld (CPB), (2010), Systemic Risk in the Financial Sector: A Review and Synthesis, CBP Documents Nr. 210, pp. 53–70. For the impact on the most adequate form of supervision see: T. Beck and W. Wagner, (2013), Supranational Regulation: How Much and From Whom?, CEPR Discussion Paper Nr. DP9546.

[364] See S.G. Cechetti, (2014), Systemic Risk and the Solvency-Liquidity Nexus of Banks, Brandeis International Business School Presentation, April 25 and T. Adrian, (2015), Discussion of 'Systemic Risk and the Solvency-Liquidity Nexus of Banks', Federal Reserve bank of NY Staff Reports, Nr. 722, April.

[365] NBB, (2015), Financial Stability Review, June, p. 12. Ari et al., (2016), conclude that 'the shadow banking sector has a tendency to expand to a size where it ferments systemic risk. When the shadow banking sector is relatively small, secondary market purchases by traditional banks cushion the liquidation value of shadow banks and help keep their borrowing costs low. In periods of stability, this culminates in the expansion of the shadow banking sector until it reaches a size where purchases by traditional banks cannot prevent a re-sale in the event of a fundamental run. The liquidation of shadow banks then leaves traditional banks susceptible to liquidity runs. This increases the borrowing costs of traditional banks and weakens market discipline on them, engendering greater risk-taking and a rise in insolvency risk' (pp. 28–29). See in detail: A. Anil et al., (2016), When Shadows Grow Longer: Shadow banking with Endogeneous Entry, ECB Working Paper Series Nr. 1943, August. Particular is the natural flow of events and the destabilizing consequences. They propose a tax on shadow banks with the purpose of reducing the size of the shadow banking sector to a level compatible with financial stability. They refer to their proposal as a Pigouvian tax since the adoption of a shadow banking strategy imposes a negative externality on the remainder of the financial sector through its contribution to re-sales.

Table 11.2 Externalities and their treatment under Basel III

Risk exposures	Externality-inducing position	Regulatory response[a]
Credit transformation	Too much risk	Weighted minimum capital requirements with additional buffers (conservation, systemic and countercyclical)[b]
Liquidity transformation	Too little liquidity	Liquidity coverage ratio (LCR)[c]: The LCR promotes short-term resilience by ensuring that banks have an adequate stock of unencumbered high-quality liquid assets (HQLA) to meet their liquidity needs for a 30 calendar day liquidity stress scenario.[d] It limits liquidity transformation activities and requires banks to hold more liquidity relative to its assets base so it can meet liquidity needs without causing a fire sale or reliance on central banks.[e]
Maturity transformation[f]	Too big a duration mismatch	Net stable funding ratio (NSFR)[g]: The NSFR requires banks to maintain a stable funding profile in relation to the composition of their assets and off-balance-sheet activities. The NSFR limits overreliance on short-term wholesale funding, encourages better assessment of funding risk across all on- and off-balance-sheet items, and promotes funding stability. It limits maturity transformation requiring banks with long-term assets to hold long-term funding. Large banks seem to be more vulnerable to the NSFR impact.[h]
Exposure to leverage	Too much leverage, duration mismatch	Leverage ratio[i]: (1) constrain the build-up of leverage in the banking sector, helping avoid destabilizing deleveraging processes, which can damage the broader financial system and the economy; and (2) reinforce the risk-based requirements with a simple, non-risk-based 'backstop' measure. Although leverage ratios are essentially there to increase the resilience of banks, their nature also becomes macroprudential in a contemporary environment known for its excessive liquidity, very low interest rates and quantitative easing[j]

[a]Annual evaluations can be found in the BCBS annual Basel III monitoring reports. Most recent: March 20, 2019, via bis.org/

[b]See BIS, (2011), Basel III: A Global Regulatory Framework for More Resilient Banks and Banking Systems, pp. 12–65. BCBS, (2015), FAQ on the Basel III Countercyclical Capital Buffer, October. The question is asked and being asked if and to what degree macroprudential regulation on residential lending influences commercial lending behavior. Overall, the question is what spillover one can expect in a targeted regulation in a model of relationship lending. The answer seems largely positive i.e. there is spillover from regulation applicable to segments of the lending spectrum. See in detail: R. Auer and S. Ongena, (2016), The Countercyclical Buffer and the Composition of Bank Lending, BIS Working Paper Nr. 593, December, in particular pp. 11–19 and 28–33; BCBS, (2017), Range of Practices in Implementing the Countercyclical Capital Buffer Policy, June.

(*continued*)

Table 11.2 (continued)

[c]BIS, (2013), Basel III: The Liquidity Coverage Ratio and Liquidity Risk Monitoring Tools and BIS, (2010), Basel III: International Framework for Liquidity Risk Measurement, Standards and Monitoring. See for a first evaluation: R. Banerjee and H. Mio, (2014), The Impact of Liquidity Regulation on Banks, Working Paper Nr. 470 (October). And for disclosure standards: BCBS, (2014), Liquidity Coverage Ratio Disclosure Standards – final document, Basel, January 12. Further updates, clarifications and updates occurred later, see: BIS, (2017), Basel III – The Liquidity Coverage Ratio: frequently asked questions, June 8. See regarding the relation between liquidity policies and systemic risk: T. Adrian and N. Boyarchenko, (2017), Liquidity Policies and Systemic Risk CEPR Discussion Paper No. DP12247. Liquidity requirements are preferable to capital requirements, as tightening liquidity requirements lower the likelihood of systemic distress without impairing consumption growth, they conclude.

[d]See for liquidity stress testing for SIFS: A. Jobst et al., (2017), Macroprudential Liquidity Stress Testing in FSAPs for Systemically Important Financial Systems, IMF Working Paper Nr. WP/17/102, May. Liquidity stress testing tends to be more complex and therefore also underdeveloped relative to other stress testing models e.g. solvency, because of data limitations but also because of the interactions among multiple factors.

[e]It is highly disputed how effective the implementation of the LCR is: A.W. Hartlage, (2013), The Basel III Liquidity Coverage Ratio and Financial Stability, Michigan Law Review, Vol. 111, Nr. 3, (December), pp. 453–484. The first-line effects on banking behavior have been analyzed: R.N. Banerjee and H. Mio, (2015), The Impact of Liquidity Regulation on Banks, Bank of England Staff Paper Nr. 536, July. They find that banks adjusted the composition of both assets and liabilities, increasing the share of high-quality liquid assets and non-financial deposits while reducing intra-financial loans and short-term wholesale funding. They do not find evidence that the tightening of liquidity regulation caused banks to shrink their balance sheets, nor reduce the amount of lending to the non-financial sector. The LCR was introduced to promote short-term resilience. Duijm and Wierts observe however a cointegration of liquid assets and liabilities, to maintain a minimum short-term liquidity buffer and that adjustment in the liquidity ratio is skewed toward the liability side. This finding contrasts with established wisdom that compliance with the LCR is mainly driven by changes in liquid assets. They further conclude that microprudential regulation has not prevented a procyclical liquidity cycle in secured financing that is strongly correlated with leverage. See: P. Duijm and P. Wierts, (2016), The Effects of Liquidity Regulation on bank Assets and Liabilities, International Journal of Central Banking, Vol. 12 Nr. 2 (June), pp. 385–411; M. Macchiavelli and L. Petit, (2018), Liquidity Regulation and Financial Intermediaries, Finance and Economics Discussion Series 2018-084. Washington: Board of Governors of the Federal Reserve System, https://doi.org/10.17016/FEDS.2018.084

[f]P. Bologna, (2018), Banks' Maturity Transformation: Risk, Reward and Policy, ESRB Working Paper Nr. 63, January. The results show that maturity transformation (or maturity mismatch, both referring to this mismatch in maturity between asset and liabilities) is an important driver of the net interest margin, as higher maturity transformation is typically associated with higher net interest margin. However, there is a limit to this positive relationship as 'excessive' maturity transformation—even without leading to systemic vulnerabilities—has some undesirable implications in terms of higher exposure to interest rate risk and lower net interest margin.

[g]See BCBS, (2014), Basel III: Net Stable Funding Ratio, Basel, October 31; BCBS, (2014), Basel III: Net Stable Funding Ratio, consultative document, Basel, January 12. For the first EU impact assessment: EBA, (2015), On Net Stable Funding Requirements under Article 510 of the CRR, EBA/Op/2015/22, London, December 15. The EBA did not find strong statistical evidence of significant negative impacts of the NSFR on bank lending, financial assets markets or trading book positions. See BCBS, (2015), Net Stable Funding Ratio Disclosure Standards, Basel, June 22. The Basel Committee has provided further updates after the initial release in 2014. See: BIS, (2018), Basel III: Treatment of extraordinary monetary policy operations in the Net Stable Funding Ratio, (June 29); BIS, (2017), Implementation of net stable funding ratio and treatment of derivative liabilities, October 6; BIS, (2017), Basel III – The Net Stable Funding Ratio: frequently asked questions, February 24 (which updated the initial document of July 13, 2016); BIS, (2015), Net Stable Funding Ratio Disclosure Standards, June 22.

[h]J. Gobat, M. Yanase, and J. Maloney, (2014), The Net Stable Funding Ratio: Impact and Issues for Consideration, IMF Working Paper, WP/14/106. See for practices and experiences outside the EU: HK Monetary Authority, (2016), Net Stable Funding Ratio, Consultation Paper, CP 16.02, November; Apra, (2016), Basel III liquidity – the net stable funding ratio and the liquid assets requirement for foreign ADIs (Australia), September 29; Monetary Authority of Singapore, (2016), Consultation Paper on Local Implementation of Basel III: Liquidity Rules – Net Stable Funding Ratio ("NSFR") and NSFR Disclosure, CP013-2016, November 16; M. Martin Windl, (2016), Net Stable Funding Ratio and Liquidity Hoarding, working paper, University of Augsburg, mimeo; Bank Negara Malaysia, (2017), Net Stable Funding Ratio, September 27; FED, (2016), Net Stable Funding Ratio: Liquidity Risk Measurement Standards and Disclosure Requirements (USA), August 4; OSFI, (2017), OSFI's Implementation timeline for the Net Stable Funding Ratio, Canada, March 6. Lallour and Mio are in favor of the ratio as it has predictive power. Its predictive power seems to come from the liability side and in particular from the fact that they count retail deposits as a highly stable funding source. Indeed, a deposits-to-assets ratio would outperform the other structural metrics we investigated as failure predictors for this crisis. See in detail: A. Lallour and H. Mio, (2016), Do We Need a Stable Funding Ratio? Banks' Funding in the Global Financial Crisis, Bank of England Staff Working Paper Nr. 602, May.

[i]See BIS, (2011), Basel III: A Global Regulatory Framework for More Resilient Banks and Banking Systems, pp. 62–65. For an evaluation of the leverage ratio over the economic cycle: M. Brei and L. Gambacorta, (2014), The Leverage Ratio over the Cycle, BIS Working Papers, Nr. 471 and BCBS, (2015), FAQ on the Basel III Leverage Ratio Framework, July (initial publication October 2014). Further updates: BCBS, (2016), Revisions to the Basel III Leverage Ratio Framework – consultative document, April 6; BIS, (2016), Frequently asked Questions on the Basel III Leverage Ratio Framework, April 6. D. Schoenmaker and P. Wierts, (2015), Regulating the Financial Cycle: An Integrated Approach with a Leverage Ratio, Duisenberg School of Finance –Tinbergen Institute Discussion Paper TI15-057/IV/DSF 93. They advocate much higher capital ratios than the traditional leverage ratio approach based on endogenous feedback mechanism and resource allocation dynamics. J. Acosta Smith, M. Grill and J. H. Lang, (2017), The Leverage Ratio, Risk-Taking and Bank Stability, ECB Working Paper Series, Nr. 2079. They address the trade-off between additional loss-absorbing capacity and potentially higher bank risk taking

(*continued*)

Table 11.2 (continued)

associated with the introduction of the Basel III Leverage Ratio. They conclude that a leverage ratio requirement can incentivize banks that are bound by it to increase their risk taking. This increase in risk taking, however, should be more than outweighed by the benefits of higher capital and therefore increased loss-absorbing capacity, thereby leading to more stable banks. The empirical tests conducted (on a large sample of US banks) demonstrate that a leverage ratio requirement would lead to a significant decline in the distress probability of highly leveraged banks. See also: EBA, (2016), Preliminary investigation into the potential impact of a leverage ratio requirement on market liquidity, October. The leverage ratio seems to act as a backstop to the risk-sensitive capital requirement: it is a tight constraint during a boom and a soft constraint in a bust. See in detail: L. Gambacorta and S. Karmakar, (2016), Leverage and Risk Weighted Capital Requirements, BIS Working Paper Nr. 586, September (also in IJCB, December 2018, pp. 153–191).

[j]E. Avgouleas, (2015), Bank Leverage Ratios and Financial Stability: A Micro- and Macroprudential Perspective, Levy Economics Institute Working Paper Nr. 849, October. The FED, more recently, has suggested to integrate stress testing and the leverage ratio by introducing a 'stress capital buffer'. See in detail: H.C. Conroy Jr. and L. Gilbert, (2018), Federal Reserve Proposes "Stress Capital Buffer" and Scales Back Enhanced Supplementary Leverage Ratio An Effort to "Simplify", Nevertheless Adds Complexity, April 16, Alert Memorandum Cleary Gottlieb. Also: J. Acosta-Smith et al., (2018), The Leverage Ratio, Risk-Taking and Bank Stability, Bank of England Staff Working Paper Nr. 766, November 9. A leverage ratio requirement can incentivize banks that are bound by it to increase their risk taking. This increase in risk taking, however, should be more than outweighed by the benefits of higher capital, thereby leading to more stable banks. There is also an impact on client clearing in some parts of the derivative market. See: J. Acosta-Smith et al., (2018), The Impact of the Leverage Ratio on Client Clearing, Bank of England Staff Working Paper Nr. 735, June 15. As part of the post-crisis regulatory reform, many interest-rate derivative transactions are required to be centrally cleared. Nevertheless, the treatment of this type of transaction under the leverage ratio (LR) requirement does not allow for the use of initial margin to reduce the exposure, thereby increasing capital costs. As a result, LR-affected clearing member banks may be more reluctant to provide central clearing services to clients given this additional cost. This in turn can prevent some real economy firms from hedging their risks. Their results suggest that the LR had a disincentivizing effect on client clearing, both in terms of daily transactions as well as the number of clients, but this impact seems to be driven by a reduced willingness to take on new clients.

1. Capital-based measures[366]: The objective is to enhance resilience[367] and increase loss-absorption capacity. Instruments implemented are (1) countercyclical capital buffer,[368](2) sector-specific buffers (e.g. real estate), (3) global and other systemically important institution buffers, (4) systemic risk buffers and (5) leverage ratio.[369]

---

[366] An interesting question is whether higher capital banks really decrease systemic risk. Bostandzic et al. Looked into this. Their results are sobering as they find an individual bank's contribution to systemic fragility to decrease only marginally after the introduction of higher capital requirements. Moreover, this decrease in systemic risk is transitory and vanishes two years after the EBA capital exercise: see in detail: D. Bostandzic et al., (2017), Do Higher Bank Capital Requirements Really Decrease Systemic Risk?, Leeds University Business School Working Paper Nr. 18-02, mimeo.

[367] T. Gehrig et al., (2018), Did the Basel Process of capital Regulation Enhance the Resilience of European Banks, Bank of Finland Research Discussion Paper Nr. 16, Helsinki. To reach some interesting conclusions: they find that the exposure to systemic risk as measured by SRISK has been steeply rising for the highest quintile, moderately rising for the second quintile and remaining roughly stationary for the remaining three quintiles of listed European banks. This observation suggests that the Basel process has succeeded in containing systemic risk for the majority of European banks but not for the largest and most risky institutions. They find compelling evidence that the increase in exposure to systemic risk (SRISK) is intimately tied to the implementation of internal models for determining credit risk as well as market risk. Based on this evidence, the subprime crisis found especially the largest and more systemic banks ill-prepared and lacking resiliency. They also point out that the EU banking union has not restored aggregate resiliency to pre-crises levels.

[368] See for an optimal macroprudential policy, similar to a countercyclical capital requirement that can eliminate systemic risk: S. Laséen et al., (2017), Systemic Risk: A New Trade-Off for Monetary Policy?, Sveriges Riksbank Working Paper Series Nr. 341, August. See for an application of countercyclical capital buffers: V. Flamini et al., (2019), Credit Cycle and Capital Buffers in Central America, Panama, and the Dominican Republic, IMF Working Paper Nr. WP/19/39, February. What makes the case study interesting is the fact that emerging countries are more exposed to sudden external shocks and reversal in capital flows. Monitoring the credit cycle therefore is crucial to avoid excess aggregate credit growth and the build-up of imbalances in the system that could turn systemic in nature. The 'credit gap' which they use as an early warning feature refers to the credit-to-GDP gap (i.e., the difference between private sector credit-to-GDP ratio and its estimated trend). One ultimate needs a model to assess whether an observed surge in credit is excessive (or not) and/or requires a response. Although the credit-to-GDP gap can be used as an anchor to assess imbalance and systemic risk ahead, a more comprehensive assessment is often required. Under those circumstances the countercyclical capital buffers introduced by Basel III tend to work their magic. For an EU application see: A. Samarina et al., (2017), Credit Cycle Coherence in the Eurozone: Was There a Euro Effect?, Journal of International Money and Finance, Vol. 77, pp. 77–98. There are however some conceptual issues in the calibration of the countercyclical capital buffer. Under Basel III, the main indicator for buffer decisions is the credit-to-GDP gap. It however doesn't work best in terms of covering bank loan losses that go beyond what could be expected from economic downturns. Instead, in the case of countries with short financial cycles and/or low financial deepening such as transition and developing economies, the Basel gap is shown to work best when computed with a low, smoothing factor and adjusted for the degree of financial deepening. Also finding an appropriate trade-off between stability of the buffer size and cost efficiency seems problematic. See in detail: T. Wezel, (2019), Conceptual Issues in Calibrating the Basel III Countercyclical Capital Buffer, IMF Working Paper Nr. WP/19/86, May. Also BCBS, (2019), Towards a Sectoral Application of the Countercyclical Capital Buffer, BCBS Working

2. Liquidity-based measures: The objective is to increase the stability of the funding base, and increase the liquid asset holdings to cover outflows. Instruments implemented are (1) net stable funding ratio (NSFR), (2) other stable funding requirements, (3) liquidity coverage ratio (LCR) and (4) other liquidity asset buffers.
3. Lending limits: leading to direct restrictions on credit supply. Instruments implemented: (1) caps on loan-to-value (LTV),[370] loan-to-income (LTI) and debt service to income (DSTI),[371] and (2) large exposure restrictions.

Paper Nr. 36, April. To be read in conjunction with: BCBS, (2018), Towards a Sectoral Application of the Countercyclical Capital Buffer: A Literature Review, BCBS Working Paper Nr. 32, March, via bis.org. Yet, countercyclical capital buffers, both broad-based and sectoral, remain largely untested and more work is needed to assess their ability to achieve the different objectives attributed to them. Furthermore, a sectoral application of the CCyB entails several challenges with respect to the design of the instrument and its interactions with the Basel III CCyB and other (targeted) instruments. Also: S. Ferrari and P. R. Kaltwasser, (2018), Sectoral Credit Cycles and Systemic Risk in the United States, Working Paper, February 28, mimeo; C. Couaillier et al., (2019), Activation of Countercyclical Capital Buffers in Europe: Initial Experiences, Banque de France Bulletin Nr. 222, May 17. Also F.M. e Castro, (2019), A Quantitative Analysis of Countercyclical Capital Buffers, FRB of St. Louis Nr. 8C, June. First, he shows that raising capital buffers during leverage expansions can reduce the frequency of crises by more than half. Second, he shows that lowering capital buffers during a panic can moderate the intensity of the resulting crisis.

[369] There is a trade-off between additional loss-absorbing capacity and potentially higher bank risk-taking associated with the introduction of the Basel III Leverage Ratio. Smith et al. document that banks can feel incentivized especially those that are bound by the leverage ratio to increase their risk-taking. This increase in risk-taking, however, should be more than outweighed by the benefits of higher capital and therefore increased loss-absorbing capacity, thereby leading to more stable banks. See in detail: J.A. Smith et al., (2017), The Leverage Ratio, Risk-Taking and Bank Stability, ECB Working Paper Nr. 2079 June. See for a recent revision to the ratio: BIS, (2019), Leverage Ratio Treatment of Client Cleared Derivatives, June 26, via bis.org

[370] Changes in maximum LTV ratios have modest and imprecisely estimated effects on output and inflation. The output effect is more pronounced in emerging market economies than in advanced economies, and mainly driven by tightening LTV limits. Tightening LTV limits reduces housing credit and house prices. Our results indicate that for central banks, macroprudential measures may serve as a complementary policy tool. See in detail: B. Richter et al., (2018), The Macroeconomic Effects of Macroprudential Policy, BIS Working Paper Nr. 740, August 27, via bis.org. J. Kelly et al., (2019), Pockets of Risk in European Housing Markets: Then and Now, ESRB Working Paper Nr. 7, February. Kelly et al. documented higher LTV/LTI ratios prior to the crisis, but despite the long period of historically low interest rates and substantial house price increases in some countries, they do not find similar credit easing as before the crisis. In times of high LTV ratios, effects of monetary policy on real mortgage credit, real house prices, real consumption of durables and non-durables, and, ultimately, on real GDP are more pronounced. In detail: T. Franz, (2019), Monetary Policy, Housing, and Collateral Constraints, Deutsche Bundesbank Discussion Paper Nr. 2, January 29; H. Balfoussia et al., (2018), Loan-to-Value Ratio Limits: An Exploration for Greece, Bank of Greece Working Paper Nr. 248, July; G. Cokayne, (2019), The Effect of Macro-Prudential Policies on House Price Cycles in an Agent-Based Model of the Danish Housing Market, DNB Working Paper Nr. 138, May 24.

[371] A simple cap on the LTV ratio is effective in smoothing the credit cycles against the background of systemic crises, which are rare and non-linear events. See in detail: E. Gerba and D. Żochowski, (2017), Knightian Uncertainty and Credit Cycles, ECB Working Paper Nr. 2068, May, p. 47; S. Pool, (2018), Mortgage Debt and Shadow Banks, DNB Working Paper Nr. 588, March, 6–7.

It has been shown earlier in this chapter that command-and-control regulation often fails to deliver the intended results and that tax instruments are in most cases superior in their ability to deliver a certain result. A combined use of Pigovian instruments and command-and-control legislation seems to be preferred when taking into account the compliance aspects required for monitoring purposes. In what follows I will provide an adequate Pigovian alternative for the different externality layers identified for FIs and provide a fully adequate mechanism to capture the externality-inducing behavior respecting the interconnectedness between those layers.[372] Those will complement the initial Pigovian layer reflecting the systemic risk component of the Pigovian instrument as reflected in Table 11.1.

11.6.3.1 Credit (Risk) Transformation

Financial institutions have a critical role in the functioning of our economy. Although there are private agents, their function is to secure a public good, that is, safeguarding public deposits. Those deposits are reinvested and liquidity toward deposit holders is guaranteed through a central banking liquidity window. The deposit holders are (up to a certain level) guaranteed a risk-free environment (through a deposit insurance mechanism) where the government acts as a backstop or lender of last resort.

Playing around with the LTV ratio as is often done by regulators and supervisors has less effect that often thought. In that sense the initial LTV level appears to matter more than the adjustments made later on. When LTV limits are already tight, the effects of additional tightening on credit is dampened. See for more numerical analysis on LTV-ratio tampering and its effect on other economic factors: Z. Alam et al., (2019), Digging Deeper—Evidence on the Effects of Macroprudential Policies from a New Database, IMF Working Paper Nr. WP/19/66, March, pp. 3–4. For an interesting way of constructing the LTV limit see appendix 2 (p. 27). See also more in general: O. Akinci, and J. Olmstead-Rumsey, (2018), How Effective are Macroprudential Policies? An Empirical Investigation, Journal of Financial Intermediation, Vol. 33, pp. 33–57; A. Alter, et al., (2018), Understanding the Macro-Financial Effects of Household Debt: A Global Perspective, IMF Working Paper, WP/18/76; L. Brandao, et al., (2019), Toward a Cost-Benefit Analysis of Macroprudential and Monetary Policies, forthcoming; G. Galati, and R. Moessner, (2018), What Do We Know About the Effects of Macroprudential Policy? Economica, Vol. 85: pp. 735–770; T. Poghosyan, (2019), How Effective is Macroprudential Policy? Evidence from Lending Restriction Measures in EU Countries, IMF Working Paper Nr. WP/19/45, March.

[372] It is not only the linkages within the banking sector but also between the banking sector and the shadow banking sector that create the interconnectedness which fuels that contagion channel during runs and market distress. An add-on complicating factor (e.g. in the EU) is when shadow banking entities are located in different jurisdictions (within the EU and outside, e.g. the EU where the exposure of EU banks during the Great Recession was 27% of total exposures). The expected diversification at the single bank level has been observed in terms of exposure (which in itself is rather low) to shadow banking entities but creates in an EU block a high overlap across different types of shadow banking entities. See for further analysis: J. Abad et al., (2017), Mapping the Interconnectedness between EU Banks and Shadow Banking Entities, ESRB Working Paper Nr. 40, March, pp. 9 ff.

In order to provide deposit holders and other lenders with a guarantee, the bank invests those amounts in the real or financial economy. The returns generated minus the compensation provided yields the gross interest margin for the bank. The yield will typically be higher the more risky the investment the FI engaged in, although the risk-return curve is not linear in nature. Given the fact that the bank guarantees a risk-free investment (at least to deposit holders) and needs to ensure that it can pay other (senior or unsecured) lenders back, the FI ultimately absorbs the credit risk neutralization that occurs at the level of the FI.

The minimum capital requirements (which have increased under Basel III in recent years) and the uniformization of the capital structure that are required under Basel III are put in place to provide a cushion that can absorb risk exposures when they occur in the risk neutralization process.[373]

Reality (not least in the Lehman Brothers scenario) has taught us that capital ratios have clear limitations in terms of their effectiveness. Part of the issue relates to the fact that the capital requirements are calibrated based on the risk exposure as classified by the regulator and suggested by BIS. Besides the clear political footprint in the risk rankings which makes the FI sector fragile by design,[374] they omit the understanding of a wider un-weighted capital ratio that can absorb losses (and stabilize the FI) in case of distress.[375]

---

[373] To be precise it is both Basel III and IV that contributed to that end result. Since Basel III was rolled out (one can see in the December 2017 publication by the BCBS of the final regulatory standards in its post-crisis Basel III reforms a kind of culmination point of the Basel III maturity process; see bis.org), the Basel Committee on Banking Supervision (BCBS) has been reviewing risk-measurement approaches internationally and among banks. One outcome of this review was the new standardized measurement approach (SMA) for operational risk, which was proposed in 2016. The committee also began a discussion on aggregated internal-rating model floors, concerned about the wide variation in the levels of risk-weighted assets (RWA) issuing from banks' internal models. The committee finalized standards for minimum capital requirements for market risk—the fundamental review of the trading book (FRTB)—in January 2016. All post-Basel III recommendations and changes are collectively referred to as Basel IV. In the period 2017–2019 many of the technical revisions have been processed, but (country-specific) implementation is somewhat opaque and sketchy in terms of timeline. The idea of Basel IV is not to 'increase the total regulatory capital requirements' although the impact can be material for individual banks. McKinsey did some digging and concluded that the impact of Basel IV goes further and that the impact of Basel IV will be significant throughout the banking industry. See: S. Koch et al. (2017), "Basel 'IV': What's next for banks?", McKinsey.com and S. Koch et al., (2018), Bringing Basel IV into Focus, April, McKinsey.com

[374] C.W. Calomiris and S.H. Haber, (2013), Fragile By Design. The Political Origin of Banking Crisis and Scarce Credit, Princeton University Press, Princeton.

[375] See also: R. Nyman et al., (2018), News and Narratives in Financial Systems: Exploiting Big Data for Systemic Risk Assessment, Bank of England Working Paper, Nr. 704, January; S.R. Baker, (2016), Measuring Economic Policy Uncertainty, Quarterly Journal of Economics, Vol. 131, Issue 4, pp. 1593–1636; S.A. Sharpe, et al., (2017), What's the Story? A New Perspective on the Value of Economic Forecasts. Finance and Economics Discussion Series, Nr. 2017-107. Board of Governors of the Federal Reserve System, Washington. On multiple occasions it was argued that the reflection on forecasts has not been sufficiently profound to trigger meaningful changes to the models, despite the fact that continuous proof is delivered that even the sophisticated (growth) forecasting models hardly do a better job than the models simply based on historical global sample average (constant) growth rate. There is too much weight placed on observable predictors and underestimating the forces of mean

Furthermore, the uniformization of the capital structure under Basel III[376] was put in place due to the wide variety of structures and (hybrid) financial products invented, which made the capital often less robust than anticipated on paper. Even after Basel III, and although the regulatory straitjacket is tighter, financial products are used to reduce the cost of funding for the bank often at the cost of the loss-absorbing capacity[377] of the capital structure.[378]

reversion. There are many large noise components, especially in long-term forecasts. It raises the question about 'the usefulness of judgment-based medium and long-run forecasts for policy analysis (due to poor predictive performance, poor predictor of future developments, and underestimating the uncertainty in the forecasts), including for debt sustainability assessments'. See in detail: K.-P. Hellwig, (2018), Overfitting in Judgment-based Economic Forecasts: The Case of IMF Growth Projections, IMF Working Paper Nr. WP/18/260, November. He blames 'overfitting' for the lack of accuracy in the forecasting models. Hellwig explains: '[o]verfitting occurs when forecasters attempt to construct stories about the future based on past experience, not taking into account that this experience is limited. Whenever this occurs, forecasters behave like statistical models that are estimated on small non-representative samples. They pay too much attention to details that explain the data well in a limited sample but turn out to be less informative in a larger sample. As a result, overfitted models (and human forecasters) respond to noise rather than relevant information. (p. 2)' Also: P. Beaudry and T. Willems, (2018), On the Macroeconomic Consequences of Over-Optimism, IMF Working Paper Nr. WP/18/122; P. Bordalo et al., (2018), Overreaction in Macro-Economic Expectations, Working Paper, March, mimeo; T. S Eicher, et al., (2018), Forecasts in Times of Crises, IMF Working Paper Nr. WP/18/48; P. Chatterjee and S. Nowak, (2016), Forecast Errors and Uncertainty Shocks, IMF Working Paper Nr. WP/16/228. Can Machine learning help in this context? See: J.-K. Jung, et al., (2018), An Algorithmic Crystal Ball: Forecasts Based on Machine Learning, IMF Working Paper Nr. WP/18/230, November and S. Mullainathan and J. Spiess, (2017), Machine Learning: an Applied Econometric Approach, Journal of Economic Perspectives, Vol. 31, Issue 2, pp. 87–106.

[376] See BIS, (2011), Basel III: A Global Regulatory Framework for More Resilient Banks and Banking Systems.

[377] Contingent Convertible (CoCo) bonds and other products with refined covenants are put in place to serve that purpose. See, for instance, S. Advjiev et al., (2017), CoCo Issuance and bank Fragility, BIS Working Paper Nr. 67, November 22, via bis.org. Contingent convertible capital securities (CoCos) are hybrid capital securities that absorb losses when the capital of the issuing bank falls below a certain level. CoCos can absorb losses either by converting into common equity or by suffering a principal write-down. They have a 'trigger' which can be either mechanical (i.e. defined numerically in terms of a specific capital ratio) or discretionary (i.e. subject to supervisory judgment). CoCos have become an important part of the post-crisis regulatory framework. However, up until now there has been little evidence on how they work in practice. Advjiev et al. draw four major conclusions: First, larger and better-capitalized banks are more likely to issue CoCos. Second, issuing CoCos causes the issuers' CDS spreads to decline. This indicates that CoCos reduce banks' credit risk and lower their funding costs. This is especially true for CoCos that convert into equity or have mechanical triggers. Third, CoCos with only discretionary triggers do not have a significant impact on CDS spreads. Fourth, CoCo issues do not affect stock prices, except for principal write-down CoCos with a high trigger level, which have a positive effect. Also: N. Martynova and E. Perotti, (2018), Convertible Bonds and Bank Risk-Taking, Deutsche Bundesbank Discussion Paper Nr. 27, July 31; P. Bologna et al., (2018), Contagion in the CoCo Market? A Case Study of Two Stress Events, Bank of Italy Working Paper Nr. 1201, November 6.

[378] In October 2016 the BCBS produced the final TLAC (Total Loss-Absorbing Capacity) Standards. See: BCBS, (2016), TLAC Holdings, October. These standards were introduced as an amendment to the Basel III standards. The document predominantly describes the criteria instruments need to fulfill in order to qualify as TLAC. In general, TLAC-eligible instruments must be subordinated to

Therefore it is recommended to replace the minimum capital requirements with a scaled Pigovian surcharge, reflecting the magnitude of the risk-neutralizing operation versus the robustness of the balance sheet. Admittedly, the measurement of risk exposure and categorization will continue to be a challenge.[379] Leaving that econometric challenge aside, the advantage of using a Pigovian instrument is not centered on the improved chirurgical measurement of risk, but the natural inclination that a Pigovian tax produces for FIs to mitigate the credit exposure adjusted for the robustness of its balance sheet (and the ability to absorb losses) without causing moral hazard relative to an ex post intervention. It also allows direct interference in the construction of the gross interest margin, potentially narrowing it down to levels at which the FI would no longer be willing to engage in certain activities. The Pigovian tax would erode the gross interest margin to such a degree that the margin left could no longer justify accepting the risk of certain transactions from a market perspective. The robustness of the FI could be measured using a methodology based on the existing uniform capital base definitions as agreed under Basel III.[380] The market risk that an FI incurs is undeniably linked to the outstanding position it holds and is therefore captured in the analysis above. The operational and business risk of an FI is of a nature than can be sufficiently captured with existing demand-and-control regulation as exists under Basel III.

Obviously, we have been focused here only on those activities of an FI that create potential negative externalities toward the public good of 'market stability'. Many transactions that a bank engages in are activities that yield no risk exposure for the bank (all fee-based activities) and can therefore be ignored within the context of an externality-based Pigovian system for the FI sector.

The type of risk exposure discussed in this section should not be mixed with the risk transformation discussed in Sect. 11.6.3.3 below. The risk transformation in this section is the natural consequence of exposures between the portfolio exposure of the bank and its funding structure. That discussed under 'risk transformation' deals with explicit exposures engaged in by FIs when constructing financial transactions using repos, guarantees and priorities, which tends to happen outside the traditional banking sector in the shadow banking market.[381]

---

a list of excluded liabilities (e.g. insured deposits). Subordination may be embedded in contractual terms, prescribed in statute or achieved by being issued by a resolution entity that does not have any excluded liabilities that rank pari passu or junior to TLAC-eligible instruments (structural subordination). There are limited exemptions to the subordination requirements (p. 2).

[379] See for a recent update of the different models currently in vogue: A. Lucas, B. Schwaab and X. Zhang, (2013), Measuring Credit Risk in a Large Banking System: Econometric Modeling and Empirics, Presentation Cleveland FED, May 30–31 also as paper: Tinbergen Institute Discussion Paper 13-063/IV/DSF56.

[380] See BIS, (2011), Ibid. supra.

[381] See: S. Krieger, (2011), Shadow Maturity Transformation and Systemic Risk, FED of New York Presentation, March 6.

11.6.3.2 Maturity Risk Transformation

The next category of firm-specific exposure is known as maturity exposure. Maturity exposure occurs when a bank finances itself on aggregate with shorter duration debt relative to the aggregate maturity of the loans or investments that the bank has outstanding in the market. The intrinsic logic of this is based on the 'opportunity cost of capital' principle, which implies that since each euro can only be invested once, a lock-in for a longer period will drive up the expected compensation as for longer periods no other investments can be accepted for that amount. Therefore a bank (on aggregate) prefers longer duration loans outstanding and finances those loans with cheaper shorter-duration wholesale funding. That way the FI maximizes its gross interest margin and boosts its profitability.[382] The problem occurs when the short-term funding market dries up, which tends to occur each time the market is experiencing an endogenous or exogenous shock. Money market funds (MMFs)[383] provide the biggest chunk of liquidity to the short-term wholesale market (together with other banks through the interbanking liquidity window). The fact that the short-term funding market is particularly vulnerable to shocks is linked to the reality that investors in MMFs are seeking slightly higher compensation than that on saving accounts, but require preservation of the principal amount and liquidity at all times. The moment that this is endangered they will withdraw funding from the market, so this is normally the first sphere of the wider financial market that responds to shocks.[384] The other large part of funding in the short-term wholesale market comes from other FIs, so the risk of potential contagion is immense. Therefore it is my suggestion to create a scaled Pigovian surcharge based on the size of the maturity mismatch between funding and invested amounts. It will

[382] At least that is the conventional wisdom. This holds that banks benefit from a steep yield curve because they intermediate funds across maturities by borrowing 'short' and lending 'long'. However, a steepening of the yield curve caused by rising long-term interest rates will also result in immediate capital losses on longer-term assets, which may offset part of any benefits of higher net interest margins. The share prices of banks that engage more heavily in maturity transformation have a significantly less negative reaction to an unanticipated steepening of the yield curve, a result that partially confirms the conventional wisdom that banks benefit from a steeper yield curve due to their role as maturity transformers. More recently, it was also demonstrated that bank stocks respond significantly to exogenous fluctuations in interest rates induced by monetary policy announcements. Bank stock prices decline substantially following an unanticipated increase in the level of interest rates or a steepening of the yield curve. A large maturity gap, however, significantly attenuates the negative reaction of returns to a slope surprise, a result consistent with the role of banks as maturity transformers. The share prices of banks that rely heavily on core deposits decline more in response to policy-induced interest rate surprises, a reaction that primarily reflects ensuing deposit disintermediation; See: W.B. English, S.J. Van den Heuvel and E. Zakrajšek, (2014), Interest Rate Risk and Bank Equity Valuations, University of Pennsylvania (Wharton), Working Paper.

[383] Together with the interbanking market, the asset-backed commercial paper market (ABCP) and the tri-party repo market. The latter two categories are part of the shadow banking market (Sect. 11.7).

[384] It also explains most of the suggested changes regarding MMFs, Proposal for a Regulation of the European Parliament and of the Council on Money Market Funds (Com/2013/0615 final - 2013/0306 (COD) of September 3, 2013.

naturally incline to reduce the maturity gap by dis-encouraging severe maturity mismatches. In the creation of the scales and level of the surcharge, a benchmark can be used in terms of the market interest rate that would (on aggregate) be charged if there were no longer any maturity mismatch at the level of the FI, and the surcharge would be scaled based on that starting point (the further away from that point on the scale, the larger the surcharge). In case of no minimal maturity mismatch, no surcharge would be due. Besides maturity exposure through which the bank is exposed to refinancing risk, which becomes larger the larger the maturity gap is, the bank is equally exposed to interest rate risk as a consequence of the changing market conditions occurring between different rounds of refinancing.

This so-called 'maturity transformation' discussed above has the potential to affect the propagation of stochastic shocks (i.e. those caused by a random variable). Nevertheless, funding in the wholesale market as such cannot be avoided. In economically prosperous times, the demand for long-term funding will accelerate faster than the rate of deposit growth (the demand for long-term credit arises because firms borrow in order to finance their capital stock which they only adjust at infrequent intervals). The delta will have to be financed with other sources of funding. The normal economic business cycle will therefore have an impact on the level of maturity exposure, which can therefore be adjusted on an annual basis[385] on a Pigovian scale. Although the volatility creates a potential externality affecting many in the market, the downside of maturity transformation is priced into the gross margin toward end customers.[386] A further refinement of the Pigovian scale should be built on the type (idiosyncratic or aggregate) and nature of the potential shock impacting an FI to which its response will depend on its size, distribution of loans, size of fixed-loan rates and so on.[387]

The benefits of managing the funding-to-loan book maturity of an FI are not limited to managing potential exposures including the contagion effect. FIs that enhance their

[385] See M.M. Andreasen, M. Ferman and P. Zabczyk, (2012), The Business Cycle Implications of Bank's Maturity Transformation, ECB Working Paper Series, Nr. 1489.

[386] See in detail: O. Entrop, C. Memmel, B. Ruprecht and M. Wilkens, (2012), Determinants of Bank Interest Margins: Impact of Maturity Transformation, Deutsche Bundesbank Discussion Paper Nr. 17/2012; C. Memmel, (2010), Bank's Exposure to Interest Rate Risk, Their Earnings from Term Transformation, and the Dynamics of the Term Structure, Deutsche Bundesbank, Banking and Financial Studies Series, Nr. 7/2010; C. Meppel, (2017), Why Do Banks Bear Interest Rate Risk, Deutsche Bundesbank Discussion Paper Nr. 35, Frankfurt am Main. Credit and interest rate risk cannot be fully separated when granting loans. But also long optimization horizons are a part of the banks and the hedging of earning risks arising from a decline of the interest rate level are reasons for bearing interest rate risk by FIs. Also: R. Busch, and C. Memmel, (2017), Banks' Net Interest Margin and the Level of Interest Rates. Credit and Capital Markets, Vol. 50, Issue 3, pp. 363–392; S. Claessens, et al., (2017), Low-for-Long Interest Rates and Banks' Interest Margins and Profitability: Cross-Country Evidence, International Finance Discussion Papers Nr. 1197, Board of Governors of the Federal Reserve System (U.S.).

[387] See: A. Penalver, (2013), Managing Maturity Transformation Under Aggregate Uncertainty, Work in Progress, Paris School of Economics Working Paper.

short-term funding size not only pass on the cost of that to the end consumer, but also reduce the maturity of the outstanding loan-book to the real economy, which is problematic as it not only creates higher yields but implicitly transfers refinancing- and interest-rate risk to the real economy.[388] Segura et al. considered the fact that unregulated debt maturities are inefficiently short due to pecuniary externalities in the market for funds during crises and their interaction with banks' refinancing constraints. They therefore suggest a similar Pigovian tax complemented with a command-and-control regulation that effectively limits debt maturity.[389] It is unclear, however, what the added value would be of such incremental 'command-and-control' regulation assuming the proper construction of a Pigovian instrument unless it would qualify as a minimal threshold, although initial findings under the new Basel III rules are promising.[390] Credit maturity ultimately

[388] Which is then often offset by interest-rate derivatives offered by those same banks. See: T. Paligorova and J.A.C. Santos, (2014), Rollover Risk and the Maturity Transformation Function of Banks, Bank of Canada Working Paper Series, Nr. 2014-8. See also recently: S. Chen, (2015), Uncertainty and Investment: The Financial Intermediary Balance Sheet Channel, IMF Working Paper, Nr. WP/15/65. Rollover risk imposes market discipline on banks' risk-taking behavior but it can be socially costly. Chen presents a two-sided model in which a bank simultaneously lends to a firm and borrows from the short-term funding market. When the bank is capital constrained, uncertainty in asset quality and rollover risk create a negative externality that spills over to the real economy by ex ante credit contraction. Macroprudential and monetary policies can be used to reduce the social cost of market discipline and improve efficiency, she concludes. Also: C. Borio, (2016), Seven Don'ts and One Hope: The Nexus between Prudential and Monetary Policies, SUERF-Deutsche Bundesbank-IMFS Conference "SSM at 1", Frankfurt, February 3–4. Li and Su on the other hand investigate the effects of financial globalization on bank risk by highlighting the role of rollover risk. Their conclusion is threefold: '(1) [i]n the short term, financial globalization will induce those banks with more short-term funding to be more risk-taking; (2) the mid-tier banks are more sensitive to the effects of financial globalization and will become more risk-taking than the rest; and (3) in the long term, financial globalization tends to affect the systemic risk in the financial system, but the precise effects depend on the country's economic fundamentals and institutional quality.' See: X. Li and D. Su, (2017), Effect of Financial Globalization on bank Risk: Role of Rollover Risk, Working Paper, June 28, mimeo.

[389] A. Segura and J. Suarez, (2012), Dynamic Maturity Transformation, CEMFI Working Paper Nr. 1105 and (2013), Recursive Maturity Transformation, CEMFI Working Paper. For a quantification of the issue see: A. Segura et al., (2014), How Excessive is Bank's Maturity Transformation, CEMFI Working Paper. See for a model design regarding optimal debt maturity: R.M. Darst and E. Refayet, (2017), A Collateral Theory of Endogenous Debt Maturity, Finance and Economics Discussion Series Nr. 57, Washington: Board of Governors of the Federal Reserve System, May.Obviously that assumes an optimal between long- and short-term debt. Issuing both long- and short-term debt balances financing costs because different debt maturities allow firms to cater to risky promises across time to investors most willing to hold risk. Collateral explains why different types of debt are issued simultaneously but also that secured loan covenants become redundant when collateral is or becomes scarce as they act as perfect substitutes for short-term debt.

[390] L. de Haan, and J.W. van den End, (2012), Bank Liquidity, the Maturity Ladder, and Regulation, Presentation DNB.

matters for economic growth and is further supported by strong institutions, low inflation,[391] large financial markets and transparency of information about FIs and borrowers.[392]

Financial intermediaries transform assets with certain risk characteristics into assets with other risk characteristics, yielding a certain net asset transformation from liabilities to assets in terms of the pricing characteristics of contingent claims. Maturity transformation can be defined as a special case, across the whole balance sheet or locally to one contract type of asset,[393] and is one of the key risks in a globalizing industry. It has been proven that the central banking liquidity window was not insufficient during the 2008 downturn,[394] and more precise regulation is required beyond the interest-rate risk analysis as required under Basel II/III.[395] Given the reality that banks, while constructing their maturity mismatch, act as rent-seeking self-centered optimizing agents they do not internalize the externalities they create.[396] While the banks are supported by the legal safety nets created, financial crises tend to occur also in their absence,[397] justifying a Pigovian tax not only from an externality point of view but also from a macroprudential standpoint. Despite the fact that there is a nexus between interest-rate exposure and

[391] Y. Abdih et al., (2018), Understanding Euro Area Inflation Dynamics: Why So Low for So Long?, IMF Working Paper Nr. WP/18/188, August; Y. Abdih, et al., (2016), What is Keeping U.S. Core Inflation Low: Insights from a Bottom-up Approach, IMF Working Paper Nr. 16/124; R. Auer et al., (2017), The Globalisation of Inflation: The Growing Importance of Global Value Chains, Bank for International Settlements Working Papers, Nr. 602; F. Busetti et al., (2017), Trust, but Verify. Deanchoring of Inflation Expectations under Learning and Heterogeneity, ECB Working Paper Nr. 1994, Frankfurt; M. Ciccarelli and C. Osbat, (2018), Low Inflation in the Euro Area: Causes and Consequences, ECB Occasional Paper Nr. 181; ECB, (2017), Domestic and Global Drivers of Inflation in the Euro Area, Economic Bulletin, Issue 4, pp. 72–96.

[392] N. Tasić and N. Valev, (2009), The Maturity Structure of Bank Credit: Determinants ad Effects on Economic Growth, Working Paper.

[393] Within the context of the EU observations are in line with the theory highlighted: these banks transform short-term customer deposits and one- to five-year hybrid and subordinated debt liabilities into loan assets with greater than five years' maturity. The value-weighted average maturity of the assets of these banks exceeds their liabilities by 2.07 years, with a standard deviation of 1.44 years; see in detail: G. Sher and G. Loiacono, (2013), Maturity Transformation and Interest Rate Risk in Large European Bank Loan Portfolios, Working Paper.

[394] In fact it was demonstrated that through facilitating maturity transformation, the lender of last resort gives banks an incentive to lever, diversify and lower their lending standards. Bank leverage increases shareholder value because maturity transformation effectively allows banks to borrow against lower interest rates than their shareholders.When the gains from maturity transformation are passed on to bank customers, lending standards deteriorate. This risk-taking intensifies when the term spread is steeper and is thus procyclically related to the stance of the macroeconomy; See: M. Mink, (2011), Procyclical Bank Risk-Taking and the Lender of Last Resort, DNB Working Paper Series, Nr. 301.

[395] B. Winters, (2012), Review of the Bank of England's Framework for Providing Liquidity to the Banking Sector, Bank of England Reporting, pp. 79–83.

[396] R.S. Rajan and G. Bird, (2001), Banks, Maturity Mismatches and Liquidity Crises: A Simple Model, CIES Working Paper, Nr. 0132.

[397] Just like asset bubbles can also occur under constant monetary supply.

maturity transformation, the relationship has been studied very little,[398] despite its special role in a monetary area with converging interest rates.[399] Avoiding market shocks, protracted periods of economic dislocation and bank runs,[400] while keeping the fractional reserve banking system[401] in place, puts the emphasis on managing both at an individual FI and macroprudential level as a holistic approach toward managing FI-induced externalities and maturity transformation in particular.[402] A Pigovian approach seems the better option relative to the avoidance of interest rate risk through the use of swap arrangements where the risk ends up on other FI balance sheets.[403]

It further allows us to use a dynamic model where command-and-control regulation, macroeconomic policies and taxation can be jointly assessed.[404] The holistic approach will however, require a macroprudential assessment that includes many other variables[405] in particular as certain intrinsic risks are inherent to the interbanking market.[406]

---

[398] For an exception to that: H. Scholz, S.K.H. Simon and M. Wilkens, (2007), Maturity Transformation Strategies and Interest Rate Risk of Financial Institutions: Evidence from the German Market, Working Paper.

[399] I.J.M. Arnold and S.E. van Ewijk, (2014), The Impact of Sovereign and Credit Risk on Interest Rate Convergence in the Euro Area, DNB Working Paper Series, Nr. 425; See also: C. Roulet, (2011), Empirical Essays on Bank Liquidity Creation and Maturity Transformation Risk, Dissertation, Université de Limoge, Economics Department, in particular pp. 21–49.

[400] Also: M. Bucher et al., (2018), Coordination Failures, Bank Run and Asset Prices, Deutsche Bundesbank Discussion Paper Nr. 39, September 26.

[401] In which the FI has to hold in cash only a fraction of the deposits submitted at the bank. Central liquidity can close the gap except in the event of a run, during which the liquidity lines are not sufficient. However, requiring the banks to hold equal amounts of cash relative to deposits would starve the real economy of credit and would make credit yield spike and materially increase the cost of funding.

[402] A.D. Smith, (2009), How To Make a Run-Proof Bank, Achieving Maturity Transformation Without Fractional Reserves, Griffith University Working Paper; C. Rossi, (2012), Is Maturity Transformation the Devil's Work or just Bedeviled, Presentation, Atlanta FED, April 12.

[403] B. Ruprecht, O. Entrop, T. Kick and M. Wilkens, (2013), Market Timing, Maturity Mismatch and Risk Management: Evidence from the Banking Industry, Working Paper.

[404] G. de Niccolò, A. Gamba ad M. Lucchetta, (2012), Capital Regulation, Liquidity Requirements and Taxation in a Dynamic Model of Banking, Presentation, Cleveland FED, April 13.

[405] M.K. Brunnermeier and M. Oehmke, (2013), Predatory Short Selling, Princeton University Working Paper, who demonstrate that financial institutions may be vulnerable to predatory short selling. When the stock of a financial institution is shorted aggressively, leverage constraints imposed by short-term creditors can force the institution to liquidate long-term investments at fire-sale prices.

[406] M.K. Brunnermeier and M. Oehmke, (2010), The Maturity Rat Race, Journal of Finance, American Finance Association, Vol. 68, Issue 2, pp. 483–521. Individual creditors can have an incentive to shorten the maturity of their own loans to the institution, allowing them to adjust their financing terms or pull out before other creditors can. This, in turn, causes all other lenders to shorten their maturity as well, leading to excessively short-term financing. This rat race occurs when interim information is mostly about the probability of default rather than the recovery in default and is most pronounced during volatile periods and crises.

11.6.3.3 Risk Transformation

The third source of FI-specific risk relates to the concept of risk transformation and as highlighted earlier needs to be separated from the concept of credit transformation risk. Banks manage this type of risk by diversifying their investment funds, pooling risks, screening and monitoring borrowers, and holding capital and reserves to be able to make up for unexpected losses without affecting the savers badly. Risk transformation however relates specifically to transactions and products designed by or engaged in by FIs and where the critical component is that the aggregate risk going into the product or transaction does not equal the risk observed at the end of the transaction or of the new product designed or constructed which is often a derivative product. A specific area of concern is that of securitization, especially in those situations where multiple parties are involved and the distribution of aggregate risk is spread over multiple balance sheets of which some are typically offshore and require no consolidation on the books of the FI. As it is part of the shadow banking scene, the content will be discussed in that Sect. 11.6.[407]

Other transactions involved do relate to situations where certain financial products are used by the FI in order to raise more (or cheaper) debt financing in the market. This can occur through (tri-party) repo transactions or by providing collateral[408] that the FI has received from customers or instruments that they financed themselves. A typical example of that is re-hypothecation,[409] where the FI can use the collateral provided by their clients and use it themselves to obtain more or cheaper funding for their activities.[410] If the collateral is weaker than initially expected or after witnessing a drop in market value (e.g. drop in housing prices), re-hypothecation leads to exposure on behalf of both the lender and borrower in the secondary transaction (both often being FIs). Risk transformation is a complex and product-specific process. This is often made more complicated[411] due to the

---

[407] D. Luttrell, H. Rosenblum and J. Thies, (2012), Understanding the Risks Inherent in Shadow Banking, A Primer and Practical Lessons Learned, Staff Paper, Dallas FED.

[408] J. C.-F. Kuong, (2013), Self-Fulfilling Fire-Sales. Fragility of Collateralized Short-Term Debt Markets, London School of Economic Working Paper. This paper shows that collateralized lending, although optimal to reduce borrower moral hazard, can lead to multiple equilibria and endogenous aggregate risk. This is because of a feedback loop between the risk-taking behavior of borrowers and the expected price of seized collateral in the secondary market. When the fire-sale price of collateral is expected to be low, lenders demand more collateral and higher debt yields, making it more attractive for borrowers to engage in risk-taking ex ante (due to limited liability). The riskier pool of projects will lead to more liquidation ex post and hence more seized collateral to be sold off, justifying the expectation of low fire-sale prices.

[409] M. Singh and J. Aitkin, (2010), The (Sizeable) Role of Rehypothecation in the Shadow Banking System, IMF Working Paper, WP/10/172.

[410] Re-hypothecation can in general be described as the practice by banks and brokers of using, for their own purposes, assets that have been posted as collateral by their clients. Often the client will be compensated through a lower borrowing fee or rebate of costs incurred. There are many technical variations in re-hypothecation; see in detail Sect. 11.7.

[411] See L.M. Sweet, (2010), Central Counterparties: Understanding Risks and Risk Transformation, Presentation, NY FED, October 21.

fact that most of these transactions do not run over a Central Clearing party (CCP) and the exposure is often reported on a net basis (after netting of the different position counterparties that have outstanding with each other). It was claimed that regulation enacted after the 2008 crisis would constrain financial markets by reducing collateral volatility, a claim that was recently debunked.[412]

It is suggested to apply a Pigovian surcharge to mitigate the exposure of possible externalities created by risk transformation. These can include a fire sales[413] of assets combined with a synthetic decrease of overall asset prices, excessive fueling of asset prices[414] in the market (bubble creation, e.g. real estate) and the excessive impact on the impairment levels of capital available for the real economy. Mitigation of the shadow banking sector will be done primarily through 'command-and-control' regulation.

That does not seem to be the right way to go about this for a number of reasons: (1) Shadow banking activities evolve constantly due to the evolving needs of the sector, the impact of regulation on the traditional banking sector and the carousel of innovation in the FI sector, which is always open for business and is therefore very difficult to capture especially since the moment it becomes verifiable and measurable the inherent risk has

[412] V. Maurin, (2014), Re-Using the Collateral of Others. A General Equilibrium Model of Rehypothecation, European University Institute Working Paper; M. Katagiri, R. Kato and T. Tsuruga, (2013), Prudential Capital Controls or Bailouts: The Impact of Different Collateral Constraints Assumptions, Kobe University Working Paper.

[413] Pecuniary externalities such as fire sales lead to overinvestment in illiquid assets or underprovision of liquidity. Internalizing the externality should be welfare enhancing. However, under imperfect (Cournot) competition this is far from guaranteed. In a standard model of liquidity shocks, when liquidity is sufficiently scarce, Cournot competition leads to even less liquidity and overinvestment, because price-taking agents do not internalize how their portfolio choices will affect prices after adverse shocks. The Cournot equilibrium overcorrects for the fire-sale externality and holds less capital than socially efficient. Implications for welfare and regulation therefore depend highly on the nature (i.e. sources) of the shocks and the competitiveness (i.e. the degree of price-taking behavior) of the industry considered. See in detail: T.M. Eisenbach and G. Phelan, (2018), Cournot Fire Sales, Federal Reserve Bank of New York Staff Reports, Nr. 837, February. Cournot competition is imperfect as it essentially is a duopoly, in which two firms with identical cost functions compete with homogeneous products in a static setting. Cournot buyers decide separately how their decision impacts prices when they are a buyer or seller, and those decisions are never weighted or averaged. They do not care about aggregate price impact but the price when they 'buy or sell'. Cournot competition can therefore mitigate or exacerbate the externality. The value of liquid assets is not affected by whether or not an agent receives a liquidity shock. Hence, what matters for price impacts of buying and selling is initial liquidity holdings, which are primarily determined by the aggregate risk of agents receiving liquidity shocks. The theory of Eisenbach and Phelan can be identified in practice. More markets and segment of industries are dominated by one or a few large firms. Simultaneously, these segments experience underinvestment by some matrixes. Their theory explains that phenomenon as 'firms with market power will tend to under-invest when the primary shocks they face are productivity (asset-side) shocks' (p. 3). The same holds true for financial markets which are increasingly concentrated and as a consequence liquidity holdings are inefficiently low, making effects of a moderate or severe financial crisis more damaging than would occur otherwise.

[414] See for an ex ante identification/quantification model: B. Jones, (2014), Identifying Speculative Bubbles: A Two-Pillar Surveillance Framework, IMF Working Paper Series, Nr. WP/14/208.

already been in the system for quite a while,[415] (2) Command-and-control legislation does not focus on the externalities the shadow banking might trigger, (3) The gradual movement from a banking- to a market-based financial sector in Europe and many emerging markets (as is the case in the US) as a credit constraint seems to persist. The explicit consequence is an additional level of vulnerability due to the enhanced reliance on the market-based pricing. (4) The implicit risk of regulatory arbitrage in the absence of global standards, (5) The continued reliance on (external) credit ratings, (6) The continued absence of risk retention on behalf of the FI designing the instruments, (7) The shadow banking system is not regulated in the same way as the traditional banking sector including capital requirements. The consequence is that the shadow banking system is inherently stable as it does not have a backstop like the regulated banking sector, which will make it continuously and inherently unstable and prone to shocks which command-and-control does not solve.

My suggestion for an additional Pigovian surcharge will keep the focus on the externality-causing dynamics of shadow banking activities regardless of how they evolve in terms of activities and products. The core of the issue here is that the shadow banking industry has a clear incentive to misprice risk. Indeed, producing synthetic products with a good credit rating allows the global regulated banking sector to buy and invest with perceived decent returns but with minimal capital requirements.[416] It requires implicit acknowledgment by the regulator that these shadow banking activities, although instrumental under certain circumstances, have a hard time justifying themselves vis-à-vis the real economy and the fact that they are needed to free up balance sheet capacity to ramp up lending to the real economy is bogus.[417] The instrument could (should) be constructed in such a way that it captures the externality potential included in the instrument, which invariably translates into the loss of asset quality or a total evaporation of the asset value involved. The alternative would be a (too) broad-brush ex ante measure that would discourage the use of certain instruments but would undeniably lead to unnecessary interference with macroeconomic policies.

The alternative of a Pigovian surcharge caters to all these side effects of command-and-control regulation and has already been suggested once (although in a broader context) by the Commission Issing in 2011.[418] A Pigovian tax also has the ability for the system to control itself despite the lack of a natural backstop. That is a critical component when considering that large parts of the shadow banking sector, although unregulated, are linked to the traditional banking sector (either through transactions or

---

[415] The FSB acknowledges that by pointing consistently in their shadow banking reporting to the need for better and more consistent measurement tools and the complexities it brings for international cooperation as shadow banking systems in different countries have very different characteristics.

[416] See on the justice aspect: B. de Bruin, (2017), Information as a Condition of Justice in Financial Markets: The Regulation of Credit-rating Agencies, in Just Financial Markets?: Finance in a Just Society, (ed. Lisa Hertog), Oxford University Press, Oxford.

[417] A. Admati and M. Hellwig, (2013), The Bankers New Clothes, Princeton University Press, Princeton, pp. 81–100 and pp. 148–167.

[418] O. Issing, J.P. Krahnen, K. Regling and W. White, (2012), White Paper, Recommendations By the Issing-Commission, Goethe University Frankfurt, p. 10.

because these operations are owned by the bank holding[419] (in)directly) and can materially burden FIs' balance sheets without proper and permanent supervision. Market stability as a public good benefits from a Pigovian instrument while avoiding the distortionary effect of regular taxes and enhances the willingness to pay for public goods.[420] Due to regulatory changes in the repo and OTC derivatives markets[421] in recent years combined with the Basel III liquidity rules as discussed, it is expected that the demand for high-quality liquid collateral will outstrip its supply, having the potential for lower underwriting standards in the interbanking market,[422] which enhances the need for ex ante macroprudential tools. Contrasting the Pigovian model with its direct counterpart 'benefit-costs' or 'command-and-control' regulation leads more often than not to the conclusion that these traditional methods of regulation are too lax when the externality impacts public goods or public interest. Pigou and Samuelson[423] have always advocated that taxes should be set equal to marginal damages whereby it was Samuelson's contribution to lay the conditions for optimal pure public good provisions and warned that free-riding that impacts public goods has the potential to massively distort which and how much public goods and services will be provided. Both therefore concluded that government intervention was needed to achieve an optimal outcome. Coase[424] on the

[419] R. Adams and J. Driscoll, (2018), How the Largest Bank Holding Companies Grew: Organic Growth or Acquisitions?

FEDS Notes, December 21, https://doi.org/10.17016/2380-7172.2282; L. Fan and M.D. Flood, (2018), An Ontology of Ownership and Control Relations of Bank Holding Companies, OFR Staff Discussion Papers Nr. 1, June 27.

[420] M. King, (1985), A Pigouvian Rule for the Optimal Provision of Public Goods, NBER Working Paper, Nr. 1681; A. Tsuneki, (2002), Shadow-Pricing Interpretation of the Pigovian Rule for the Optimal Provision of Public Goods: A Note, International Tax and Public Finance, Vol. 9, Issue 1, pp. 93–104.

[421] See for an initial analysis of the changes in the OTC market after the regulatory interventions post-financial crisis: J. Abad et al., (2016), Shedding Light on Dark markets: First Insights from the New EU-Wide OTC Derivatives Dataset, ESBR Report Nr. 11, September. Considers both interest rate derivatives, Credit Default Swaps (few are centrally cleared yet), and foreign exchange derivatives (mostly forwards, highly decentralized, limited central clearing). Alo: R. Ali et al., (2016), Systemic Risk in Derivative markets: A Pilot Study Using CDS Data, Bank of England Financial Stability Paper Nr. 38, July; M. Bardoscia et al., (2018), Multiplex Network Analysis of the UK OTC Derivatives Market, bank of England Staff Working Paper Nr. 726, May 18. A key finding of the paper is that, in extreme theoretical scenarios where liquidity buffers are small, a handful of institutions may experience significant spillover effects due to the directionality of their portfolios. S. Schreft and S. Zhang, (2018), Network Analysis: Defending Financial Stability by Design, OFR Brief Nr. 2, August 1.

[422] A. Levels and J. Capel, (2012), Is Collateral Becoming Scarce: Evidence from the Eurozone, DNB Occasional Studies, Vol. 10, Issue 1, pp. 1–74.

[423] Largely based on: A.C. Pigou, (1920), The Economics of Welfare, Macmillan and Co., London (4th edition, 1932) and P.A. Samuelson, (1954), The Pure Theory of Public Expenditure, Review of Economics and Statistics, Vol. 36, pp. 387–389.

[424] R.H. Coase, (1960), The Problem of Social Cost, Journal of Law and Economics, Vol. 3 (October), pp. 1–44; R.H. Coase, (1974), The Lighthouse in Economics, Journal of Law and Economics, Vol. 17 (October), pp. 357–376.

contrary believed that as long as transaction costs are low and the legal system functions well government intervention is unnecessary, as externalities would be self-internalizing. The question is of course about the stringency of the conditions underlying the Coase theorem.[425] That discussion has been ongoing until today. Graves[426] recently added an up till now unexplored relationship in the discussion. That is the relationship between externalities, public goods and property rights. Hi highlights that non-excludable goods are positioned in markets that prevail to provide optimal quantities (which can be clean air or water, etc.) and are undervalued by contemporary economic models. Command-and-control is generally too lax in this respect. That is caused by the benefit-cost framework underlying the tax. Graves argues 'benefit-cost analysis will be biased against environmental (and perhaps some other) projects because households have no incentive to work to purchase goods that cannot be individually purchased—and those unseen demands will not be picked up by the analyst.'[427] Therefore the Pigovian tax should be higher to compensate for that market dysfunctionality. Remarkable enough economic scholars never come to the same conclusion when it comes to features characteristic of the financial industry: excess liquidity leading to (housing) and other asset bubbles, liquidity shortage leading to shocks and contagion effects, excess and uncontrolled capital flows jumping in and out of asset classes and countries' economies and investments in (green) technologies that simply re-orient the focus to other asset uses and depletion of public resources. Benefit-cost models that lead to command-and-control are not only too lax, they are very poor in identifying market failures to begin with.

[425] More recently Martin Wolf (M. Wolf, (2018), We Must Rethink the Purpose of the Corporation, Financial Times, December 11) lamented on the urgent need to rethink the purpose of the corporation and its use in the economic infrastructure in the twenty-first century. This after decades of pure focus on shareholder wealth and profits as the main purpose for corporations. Exclusive shareholder focus triggers three dire outcomes that are human (profit is not an objective but the result of a purpose; substituting money with purpose triggers massive issues) economic (limited liability for corporations was to ensure they could focus on optimal capital allocation and long-term innovation) and social in nature (Coase argued that the market could be a less efficient way of organizing production due to transaction costs thereby favoring hierarchical organizations. Markets are incomplete and often inefficient). Beyond the broader conclusion that capitalism is materially broken (J. Tepper, (2018), The Myth of Capitalism, John Wiley & Sons, Hoboken), the exclusive magic of pure shareholder focus has had its best days. See also recently Larry Fink's Letter to Shareholders 2019 (via blackrock.com) on Purpose and Profit on the matter. As we will see later, the relationship between corporate governance and shadow banking is full of complications. Regarding the financing of innovation and the many issues that traditional lending experiences financing innovation in business models and the implication of a shift from asset-based financing to cash-flow-based financing see: H. Toxopeus et al., (2018), Financing Business Model Innovation: Bank Lending for Firms Shifting Towards a Circular Economy, Sustainable Finance Lab Working Paper, January 30.

[426] Ph. E. Graves, (2017), Externalities, Public Goods, and Property Rights Revisited: Regulations Based on Traditional B-C Analyses Are Too Lax, Working Paper, mimeo.

[427] Ibid. p. 11.

11.6.3.4 Liquidity Exposure in the FI Sector

One of the most visible shortcomings of the financial infrastructure and accompanying regulation before the 2008 financial crisis was the enormous liquidity trap[428] that emerged and the swiftness with which liquidity dried up in the financial markets, in particular the short-term money market.[429] Asymmetric information in the quality of capital endogenously determines the amount of liquidity available. Liquidity is determined by balancing the costs of obtaining liquidity under asymmetric information against the benefit of relaxing financial constraints.[430] The regulatory response was the introduction of the liquidity coverage ratio (LCR) as part of the Basel III package. That was more recently complemented with the LCR requirements, which intend to improve the transparency of regulatory liquidity requirements and enhance market discipline and the guidance for supervisors on market-based indicators of liquidity. To assist supervisors in their evaluation of the liquidity profile of assets held by banks and, for the purposes of Basel III's LCR, to help promote greater consistency, high-quality liquid assets (HQLA) classifications across jurisdictions[431] were developed.[432] As was pointed out before in this chapter, serious concerns

[428] Liquidity shocks can have many different sources and its magnitude is dependent on many exogenous and indigenous factors from an FI's point of view; see in detail: P.D. Karam et al., (2014), The Transmission of Liquidity Shocks: The Role of Internal Capital Markets and Bank Funding Strategies, IMF Working Paper, Nr. WP/14/207. See for a UK-based analysis of the impact on liquidity Shocks: Hills et al., (2015), International Banking and Liquidity Risk Transmission: Lessons from the United Kingdom, Bank of England, Staff Working Paper Nr. 562. They examined the impact of changes in funding conditions on UK-resident banks' domestic and external lending. Their results suggest that, following a rise in the liquidity shock measure, UK-resident banks that grew their balance sheets quicker relative to their peers pre-crisis, decreased their external lending more, relative to other banks, and increased their domestic lending. When they accounted for country of ownership, they found that the same pattern was true for both UK-owned and foreign-owned banks, but more pronounced for UK-owned banks' domestic and foreign-owned banks' external lending. Also: B. Philippe et al., (2018), Money and Capital in a Persistent Liquidity Trap, Banque de France Working Paper Nr. 703, December 17.

[429] See for the different types of liquidity exposure and liquidity concepts: K. Nikolau, (2009), Liquidity (Risk) Concepts. Definitions and Interactions, ECB Working Paper Series, Nr. 1008.

[430] See in detail: S. Bigio, (2013), Endogenous Liquidity and the Business Cycle, Working Paper, December 18.

[431] BIS, (2014), Liquidity Coverage Ratio Disclosure Standards and BIS, (2014), Guidance for Supervisors on Market-Based Indicators of Liquidity.

[432] D. Roberts et al., (2018), Bank Liquidity Provision and Basel Liquidity Regulations, FRB of NY Staff Reports Nr. 852, June. There has been reduced liquidity creation by LCR banks compared to non-LCR banks, occurring mostly through greater holdings of liquid assets and lower holdings of illiquid assets. The asset-side liquidity categories and weights are calculated using two dominant models: (1) Berger-Bouwman measure (BB) and the Liquidity Mismatch Index (LMI). See N. Berger, and C. H. S. Bouwman, (2009), Bank Liquidity Creation, Review of Financial Studies, Vol. 22, Issue 9, pp. 3779–3837 and J. Bai, et al. (2018), Measuring Liquidity Mismatch in the Banking Sector, Journal of Finance, Vol. 73, Issue 1, pp. 51–93. Also C.H.S. Bouwman, (2018), Creation and Regulation of Bank Liquidity, Texas A&M University Working Paper, October 7, mimeo. It latter covers a full literature overview on bank liquidity creation. The focus is on the

remain with respect to market-based indicators as a tool for macroprudential supervision.[433] Some intrinsic flaws can also be highlighted with respect to the new LCR which is a synthetic model to ensure liquidity under duress. We still know little about the actual magnitudes and mechanisms for transmission of liquidity shocks[434] through international banks,[435] including the reasons for heterogeneity in transmission across banks.[436]

A notable example of such flaws is the inclusion in the asset base, which is supposed to guarantee the liquidity of the FI at all times, of securitization products (of a certain standard). Given the experiences regarding liquidity in those products under duress and the

---

economics of bank liquidity creation, both in the traditional relationship banking context and in the shadow banking context. Related prudential regulation issues – pertaining mainly to capital requirements and liquidity requirements – are also discussed.

[433] See for a technical analysis: J.W. van den End and M. Kruidhof, (2012), Modelling the Liquidity Ratio as Macroprudential Instrument, DNB Working Paper Series, Nr. 342; D.C. Hardy and Ph. Hochreiter, (2014), A Simple Macroprudential Liquidity Buffer, IMF Working Paper, Nr. WP/14/235.

[434] See also: W.G. Choi et al., (2017), Global Liquidity Transmission to Emerging Market Economies, and Their Policy Responses, IMF Working Paper Series, Nr. WP/17/222, October. Bernales and di Filippo studied the information dynamics contained in the interaction between unsecured and collateralized money markets thereby capturing the probabilities of migration between lending segments, and probabilities of liquidity shocks. Useful information seems extractable from those interactions. See in detail: A. Bernales and M. di Filippo, (2016), The Information Contained in Money Market Interactions: Unsecured vs. Collateralized Lending, Banque de France Working Paper Nr. 598, July, Paris; P.A. Guerron-Quintana and R. Ginnai, (2019), On Liquidity Shock and Asset Prices, Bank of japan Working Paper Nr. 19-E-4, March 13. H. Degryse et al. study the impact of higher capital requirements on banks' decisions to grant collateralized rather than uncollateralized loans. Secured lending becomes more attractive vis-à-vis unsecured lending for the affected banks as secured loans require less regulatory capital. After a shock banks required more collateralization, but less for relationship borrowers. In Detail: H. Degryse et al., (2019), To Ask or Not to Ask: Bank Capital Requirements and Loan Collateralization, Bank of England Staff Working Paper Nr. 778, February 1.

[435] Buch et al. show that global banks transmit liquidity shocks via their network of foreign affiliates. In their case German affiliates of global US banks. They conclude threefold: during the TAF period (Federal Reserve's Term Auction Facility), the German affiliates with US parents with higher US funding expanded their foreign assets; the overall effect is driven by affiliates in financial centers; US-dollar-denominated lending particularly increased in response to the TAF program. Global banks spread liquidity through their systems. See: C. Buch et al., (2018), Crisis and Rescues: Liquidity Transmission through Global Banks, International Journal for Central Banking, September, pp. 187–228.

[436] Buch and Goldberg summarized the common methodology and results of empirical studies conducted in 11 countries to explore liquidity risk transmission. Among the main results are, first, that the explanatory power of the empirical model is higher for domestic lending than for international lending. Second, how liquidity risk affects bank lending depends on whether the banks are drawing on official-sector liquidity facilities. Third, liquidity management across global banks can be important for liquidity risk transmission into lending. Fourth, there is substantial heterogeneity in the balance sheet characteristics that affect banks' responses to liquidity risk; See: C.M. Buch and L.S. Goldberg, (2014), International Banking and Liquidity Risk Transmission: Lessons from Across Countries, Federal Reserve Bank of NY, Staff Reports, Nr. 675. Also: C. Gauthier, (2015), Emergency Liquidity Facilities, Signalling and Funding Costs, Bank of Canada Staff Working Paper Nr. 44, December.

limited ability to define the credit quality of the underlying assets[437] it seems less prudent to include those with only a small haircut.[438] Beyond situations of duress, the liquidity transformation that creates externalities is triggered by the fact that FIs on an ongoing basis engage in investing in illiquid assets (or less liquid assets) with liquid assets that they receive from lenders and deposit holders. So liquidity is not only a concern under duress, but a part of the ongoing management of any FI.[439] Given the tremendous contagion effect that the lack of liquidity can cause, and which is considered a major factor behind the emergence of systemic risk[440] in the FI sector, alternative solutions to the fragile (quantity) command-and-control regulatory mechanisms that LCR embodies have been sought. They take the form of larger liquidity buffers[441] and fixed limits on the size of unstable funding. But tight fixed ratios are seen by industry as very expensive and they have been significantly watered down from their original proposals.

Indeed, liquidity is the most central cause of externality in the FI sector and is closely linked to the different transformation processes discussed in this chapter. It is therefore also closely linked to refinancing risk and the risk transformation process. It was argued before that there are clear benefits to be derived from disentangling the different drivers of externalities rather than lumping them together. The latter makes understanding the dynamics of these drivers more difficult but also triggers a tremendous challenge for regulators when designing a Pigovian instrument for the FI sector.

---

[437] Deterioration of collateral quality is typically associated with higher interbank rates both in the unsecured and report segments. Reducing interbank market volatility restores confidence and is welfare enhancing. See in detail: M. Wolski and M. van de Leur, (2016), Interbank Loans, Collateral and Modern Monetary Policy, ECB Working Paper Series Nr. 1959, September.

[438] Haircut, which can have different meanings, can be defined here as the percentage by which an asset's market value is reduced for the purpose of calculating capital requirement, margin and collateral levels; see BIS, (2013), Basel III: The Liquidity Coverage Ratio and Liquidity Risk Monitoring Tools, bis.org, pp. 13–15.

[439] BIS, (2008), Principles for Sound Liquidity Risk Management and Supervision, bis.org

[440] See for an extensive conceptual analysis: P. Smaga, (2014), The Concept of Systemic Risk, LSE/SRC Special Paper Nr. 5, August. He defines systemic risk as 'the risk that a shock will result in such a significant materialization of (e.g. macrofinancial) imbalances that it will spread on the scale impairing the functioning of financial system and to the extent that it adversely affects the real economy (e.g. economic growth). The blueprint intends to break down and clearly categorize the processes of accumulation, materialization and spreading of systemic risk'.

[441] Butnik and Bochmann wonder how do capital and liquidity buffers affect the evolution of bank loans in periods of financial and economic distress? They find that banks with high capital and liquidity buffers show a more muted response in their lending to adverse real economy shocks. Capital and liquidity buffers also affect bank responses to monetary policy shocks. High bank capitalization reduces the degree to which banks increase the average duration of loans to the non-financial corporate sector, while high bank liquidity strengthens the positive response to policy easing of both long- and short-term loans to the non-financial corporate sector. In detail: K. Budnik and P. Bochmann, (2019), Capital and Liquidity Buffers and the Resilience of the Banking System in the Euro Area, ECB Working Paper Nr. 2120, 22 December.

Short-term funding has advantages, as it can support rapid expansion of credit over GDP (e.g. because insured deposit supply expands slowly), or because short-term lenders do not need to become informed about bank credit risk. Sudden withdrawals may lead to disruptive liquidity runs,[442] causing fire sales, which spread losses or trigger counterparty risk externalities for exposed intermediaries.[443] Each bank's funding decision has an impact on the vulnerability of asset prices to liquidity runs. So even if an individual bank takes into account its own exposure, it will not internalize its contribution to system-wide cost, which constitutes a classic externality.[444] The differential between the net private value and the social cost of short-term funding allows (or better triggers) banks to rely excessively on short-term funding, Perotti and Suarez argue, when building the framework for the hereafter discussed liquidity surcharge.

Perotti and Suarez[445] evaluate the performance of Pigovian taxes (aimed at equating private and social liquidity costs) and quantity-based regulations in containing this systemic externality. They do so within the context of externality regulation as initiated by Weitzman,[446] who pointed to the fact that the optimal regulatory tool depends on the response elasticity of banks. He thereby recognized that the regulator is information-constrained in targeting individual bank characteristics.[447]

[442] D. Diamond and P. Dybvig, (1983), Bank Runs, Deposit Insurance, and Liquidity, Journal of Political Economy, Vol. 91, pp. 401–419.

[443] M. Brunnermeier, (2009), Deciphering the Liquidity and Credit Crunch 2007–2008, Journal of Economic Perspectives, Vol. 23, pp. 77–100. F. Allen, A. Babus, and E. Carletti, (2010), Financial Connections and Systemic Risk, NBER Working Paper, Vr. 16177.

[444] E. Perotti, J. Suarez, (2009), Liquidity Insurance for Systemic Crises, CEPR Policy Insight 31, February. Overnight (repo) secured credit feeding the final stage of the securitization wave grew explosively during 2002–2007 to a volume over $10 trillion. Rapid withdrawals forced an unprecedented liquidity support by central banks, undermining their control over the money supply. The need to contain the future accumulation of liquidity is thus a core challenge for macroprudential policy; see G. Gorton, (2009), Slapped in the Face by the Invisible Hand: Banking and the Panic of 2007, paper prepared for the Federal Reserve Bank of Atlanta's 2009 Financial Markets Conference, May.

[445] E. Perotti, and J. Suarez, (2011), A Pigovian Approach to Liquidity Regulation, CEPR Discussion Paper, Nr. 8271, March. The paper has been re-issued and updated on a number of occasions; see E. Perotti, and J. Suarez, (2011), A Pigouvian Approach to Liquidity Regulation, IMF, Paper presented at the 12th Jacques Polak Annual Research Conference, November 10–11; E. Perotti and J. Suarez, (2011), A Pigovian Approach to Liquidity Regulation, DNB Working Papers nr. 291, Netherlands Central Bank, Research Department; E. Perotti and J. Suarez, (2011), A Pigovian Approach to Liquidity Regulation, Tinbergen Institute Discussion Papers 11-040/2/DSF15, Tinbergen Institute and ultimately published: E. Perotti, and J. Suarez, (2011), A Pigovian Approach to Liquidity Regulation, International Journal of Central Banking, Vol. 7, Issue 4, pp. 3–41. See for earlier work: E. Perotti and J. Suarez, (2010), Liquidity Risk Charges as a Macro-Prudential Tool, DSF Policy Paper Series, Nr. 1.

[446] M.L. Weitzman, (1974), Prices vs. Quantities, Review of Economic Studies, Vol. 41, pp. 477–491. The method used is linked to the discussion started by Poole (1970): that methodology concerned the optimality of price or quantity of monetary policy instruments when the system is exposed to a variety of negative or idiosyncratic risks; see W. Poole, (1970), Optimal Choice of Monetary Policy Instruments in a Simple Stochastic Macro Model, Quarterly Journal of Economics, Vol. 84, pp. 197–216.

[447] E. Perotti and J. Suarez, (2002), Last Bank Standing: What Do I Gain if You Fail, CEMFI Working Paper.

The results of Perotti and Suarez show, in line with Weitzman, how the industry's responses to regulation depend on the composition of bank characteristics as banks differ in their credit ability and their incentives to take risk. High-quality banks are inclined to lend more and do so by expanding credit. In contrast, shareholders of less capitalized banks gain from investing in risky investments, since they retain the upside and shift downside risk to the public budget, in the absence of a large enough pool of credit allocation opportunities.[448] They conclude that, 'depending on the dominant source of heterogeneity, the socially efficient outcome may be generated with Pigovian taxes, quantity regulations, or a combination of both'.[449]

When banks differ only in their capacity to lend profitably (reflecting credit assessment capability or access to credit opportunities), a simple flat-rate Pigovian tax on short-term funding (possibly scaled up by the systemic importance of each bank, e.g. to capture contribution to counterparty risk) implements efficient allocation.

It can be considered that liquidity risk charges allow better banks to lend more, without the requirement of the regulators to ex ante identify them through a burdensome set of command-and-control legislation. In this context, a quantity approach such as a net

[448] Loose monetary conditions in recent years have raised concerns regarding the allocation of credit to risky investors and the potential long-term effect on financial stability. There is actual evidence that periods of low interest rates and easy financial conditions may lead to a decline in lending standards and increased risk taking. See for an interesting analysis of corporate credit allocation: IMF, (2018), The Riskiness of Credit Allocation: A Source of Financial Vulnerability, in Global Financial Stability Report 2018: A Bumpy Road Ahead, Chapter 2, pp. 57–92. The analysis looks at the evolution of the riskiness of corporate credit allocation—that is, the extent to which riskier firms receive credit relative to less risky ones, its relationship to the strength of credit expansions, and its relevance to financial stability analysis. So, not only the volume of credit growth but the distribution of credit across lenders with a variety of profiles. They find the riskiness of credit allocation rises during periods of fast credit expansion, especially when loose lending standards or easy financial conditions occur concurrently. The riskiness of credit allocation increased in the years preceding the global financial crisis and peaked shortly before its onset. It declined sharply after the crisis and rebounded after the crisis to land well above historical averages in 2019. An increase in the riskiness of credit allocation signals heightened downside risks to GDP growth and a higher probability of banking crises and banking sector stress; it constitutes an autonomous source of financial vulnerability. Also on the latter: D. Kirty, (2018), Lending Standards and Output Growth. IMF Working Paper Nr. WP/18/23, International Monetary Fund, Washington, DC; T. Adrian and N. Liang, (2018), Monetary Policy, Financial Conditions, and Financial Stability. International Journal of Central Banking, Vol. 14, Issue 1, pp. 73–131. On lending standards and default rates: J. Gaudêncio, et al. (2019), The Impact of Lending Standards on Default Rates of Residential Real Estate Loans, ECB Occasional Paper Nr. 220, March 19. The first study to use EU-wide data, they conclude, confirms the key influence of lending standards—in particular, loan-to-value and loan-to-income ratios at origination, original loan maturity and borrower employment status—on loan default rates. The impact of other variables, such as interest rate fixation and payment type, varies depending on the country of loan origination.

[449] See Nabilou and Pacces who prefer quantity regulation over a Pigovian model: H. Nabilou and A.M. Pacces, (2017), The Law and Economics of Shadow Banking, in I. H. Chiu & I. MacNeil (eds.), Research Handbook on Shadow Banking: Legal and Regulatory Aspects, Edward Elgar Publishing, Cheltenham, pp. 7–46.

stable funding ratio or a liquidity coverage ratio (as part of the Basel III package) is considered to be highly distortionary, reallocating credit away from banks with good lending opportunities.[450]

Liquidity coverage ratios that force banks to hold fractional reserves of liquid assets against short-term funding work as an implicit tax, but with poor and adverse incentive effects, Perotti and Suarez conclude.[451] In boom times, the yield on liquid assets equals the cost of short-term liabilities,[452] as was the case prior to the crisis. At this stage, buffers impose no cost on carrying liquidity. So banks will simply increase their gross short-term funding, so that their net short-term funding is as high as in the unregulated equilibrium. Perotti and Suarez therefore conclude that 'the only effect is an artificial demand from banks for liquid assets, traditionally kept in money market mutual funds rather than banks. When the spread between liquid asset yields and bank borrowing costs is positive, a liquidity requirement operates as a tax on short-term funding. The effective tax rate will be market determined and the tax rate will equal the product of the buffer requirement per unit of short-term funding times the interest spread. The 2008 crisis demonstrated that interbank spreads over safe assets have been minimal just as aggregate liquidity risk was building up,[453] while it escalated once the crisis started'.[454] Unless buffers are adjusted frequently, they will contribute to procyclical effects, relaxing the opportunity cost of unstable funding in good times and increasing it after a shock. Buffers as currently in place are either ineffective or procyclical.

Banks do not vary only on credit quality, but also on solvency incentives. These reflect capitalization and charter value[455] (or a behavioral determinant of risk taking,

---

[450] Net stable funding ratios (also part of the Basel III package) impose an upper threshold on short-term debt that reduces overall liquidity risk, but 'redistributes liquidity risk inefficiently across banks'. Banks with better credit opportunities will be constrained by this, 'while the reduced systemic risk actually encourages banks with low credit ability to expand their loan book': see: E. Perotti, and J. Suarez, (2011), A Pigovian Approach to Liquidity Regulation, CEPR Discussion Paper, Nr. 8271, March, p. 3.

[451] See for an alternative analysis and the value of the HQLA stamp and the impact on asset prices: L.M. Fuhrer et al., (2016), The Liquidity Coverage Ratio and Security Prices, SNB Working Paper Nr. 11. August.

[452] See also: G. Lopez-Espinosa, A. Moreno, A. Rubia, and L. Valderrama, (2012), Short-Term Wholesale Funding and Systemic Risk, A Global CoVaR Approach, IMF Working Paper, WP/12/46; G. Lopez-Espinosa, A. Moreno, A. Rubia, and L. Valderrama, (2012), Systemic Risk and Asymmetric Responses in the Financial Industry, IMF Working Paper Series, WP/12/152, later on published in: (2015), Journal of Banking and Finance, Vol. 58, pp. 471–485.

[453] See regarding the relationship between aggregate liquidity and banking sector fragility: M. Mink, (2016), Aggregate Liquidity and Banking Sector Fragility, DNB Working Paper Nr. 534, November. As compared to non-banks, banks adopt relatively fragile balance sheet structures characterized by leverage, maturity mismatch and asset diversification. He builds his model around the understanding that liquidity (funding) risk for banks is on aggregate lower than for non-banks and explains the banks' regulatory equity and liquidity requirements' resistance.

[454] E. Perotti, and J. Suarez, (2011), A Pigovian Approach to Liquidity Regulation, CEPR Discussion Paper, Nr. 8271, March, p.4.

[455] The going-concern value of an FI as reflected in the share price.

such as overconfidence). This case qualifies the Perotti and Suarez results quite radically. Low charter value banks (or banks with a higher risk appetite) have incentives to shift risk to deposit insurance mechanism and other forms of (public safety) support.[456]

Perotti and Suarez illustrate that 'when bank decisions are to a large degree driven by risk-taking incentives, banks are not properly deterred by levies'. In contrast, 'quantity constraints appear to be more effective. Short-term funding limits (e.g. a net stable funding ratio) as well as capital requirements can contain risk shifting[457] by "limiting the scale of lending". Levies will not be very effective because the most risk-inclined banks will also be the most inclined to pay the tax and expand their risky lending. In this situation, they conclude, quantity instruments such as net funding or capital ratios are best to contain (or constrain) excessive credit expansion.'

Their price versus quantity instruments suggest that combining them may be adequate for the simultaneous control of risk-taking incentives and systemic risk externalities.[458] If strengthening capital requirements is an effective strategy for the control of gambling incentives,[459] the case for regulating liquidity risk with levies on short-term funding is considerably reinforced. In the stand-off between (Pigovian) charges and ratios, charges have the potential to be less costly to adjust than ratios, Perotti and Suarez indicate. They might be easier to change, as in the likely case that regulatory ratios are embedded in an international agreement while charges are under the control of a macroprudential authority. It is important to note that these charges would impose lower adjustment costs than changing funding volumes on short notice.[460] Changes in levies are 'less likely to induce procyclicality than buffers', since the effect of a Pigovian charge is more directly controlled by the regulator 'rather than being set by the interaction of a (controlled) quantitative

---

456 M.C. Keeley, (1980), Deposit Insurance, Risk, and market Power in Banking, American Economic Review, Vol. 80, Issue 5, pp. 1183–1200; D. Gale, (2010), Capital Regulation and Risk-Taking, International Journal for Central Banking, pp. 187–204.

457 Acharya et al. argue that dividend payouts can constitute a form of risk shifting ('dividend payouts can shift the relative value of stakeholders' claims across firms') in case FIs have contingent claims outstanding against each other. Dividend payments then contain negative externalities and bank capital takes the attribute of a public good. See in detail: V.V. Acharya et al., (2016), Bank Capital and Dividend Externalities, BIS Working Papers Nr. 580, September.

458 A. Wischnewsky and M. Neuenkirch, (2019), Shadow Banks and the Risk-Taking Channel of Monetary Policy Transmission in the Euro Area, University of Trier, Research Paper in Economics, Nr. 3, June 6, mimeo.

459 T. Hellmann, K. Murdock and J. Stiglitz, (2000), Liberalisation, Moral Hazard in Banking, and Prudential Regulation: Are Capital Requirements Enough?, American Economic Review, Vol. 90, pp. 147–165. Capital requirements and other regulation imposed on traditional banks also lead to higher shadow bank lending. See: S. Gebauer and F. Mazelis, (2018), The Role of Shadow Banking for Financial Regulation, Beiträge zur Jahrestagung des Vereins für Socialpolitik 2018: Digitale Wirtschaft - Session: Macrofinance I, No. E11-V2, version May 22. Many macromodels have been developed (pp. 4–7 for overview) to depict the relationship between traditional and shadow banks from a regulatory point of view. In particular the question seems to be what role shadow banking plays for financial regulation and the effectiveness of financial regulation.

460 E. Perotti, and J. Suarez, (2011), A Pigovian Approach to Liquidity Regulation, CEPR Discussion Paper, Nr. 8271, March.

requirement and the (freely fluctuating) market price of the rationed quantity'. From an ex ante perspective, controlling 'time-varying liquidity risk' may be best achieved 'by a combination of some (variable) levies aimed at controlling the generation of risk externality by normal banks, while ratios may be aimed at containing the risk-appetite of gambling banks. Price versus quantity rules target ultimately different incentives for risk creation'.[461]

For SIFIs in particular, a liquidity risk index was developed that could help to estimate a Pigovian tax on large banks for the externality on the international banking system due to their risk exposure.[462] The novelty of the Pigovian surcharge in this area meant that it was not accepted overnight and has led to a barrage of questioning on the basis that there has been very little research in finance supporting the implementation of such instruments.[463]

Perotti and Suarez suggest 'a flat-rate Pigovian (possibly scaled up by the systemic importance[464] of each bank) surcharge on short-term funding to implement the efficiency allocation'. This would make most sense if it were not only scaled on SIFI relevance but were also to take into account the maturity mismatch and the uninsured dimension of the funding that exists at the level of individual banks. As Perotti asserts: '[s]ystemic risk is propagation risk. In a systemic crisis, an initial shock spreads beyond its own market, start a vicious spiral of price shocks and disrupt the real economy. We have learned that liquidity runs are a

[461] E. Perotti, and J. Suarez, (2011), A Pigovian Approach to Liquidity Regulation, CEPR Discussion Paper, Nr. 8271, March.

[462] G. Gianfelice, G. Marotta and C. Torricelli, (2013), A Liquidity Risk Index as a Regulatory Tool for Systemically Important Banks, An Empirical Assessment across Two Financial Crisis, Working Paper, mimeo.

[463] The difficulties of formulating a theory of the systemic role of bank balance sheets are indeed considerable, ranging from the question of the transmission of idiosyncratic shocks in interbank markets to the questions of the costs and benefits of maturity transformation and the inefficiency of markets with cash-in-the-market pricing; see E.-L. von Thadden, (2011), Discussion of a 'Pigovian Tax' to Liquidity Regulation, International Journal of Central Banking, Vol. 7, pp. 43–48. The simplicity of the model is its strength and weakness at the same time: 'it makes it difficult to evaluate how other aspects of banking and financial markets interfere with banking liquidity and why the regulation of banking liquidity may, after all, be such a complicated and controversial problem' (p. 44).

[464] Systemic risk and systemic importance are two different concepts that emerged from the crisis and are now widely employed to assess the potential impact of shocks that hit a specific bank or the banking system as a whole. However, these two measures are often improperly used and misunderstandings arise. Empirically, the two measures provide different information. The measurement of systemic importance deals with the assessment of the consequences on the global financial system of the failure of a bank, whereas systemic risk contributions (often measured by MES and ΔCoVaR) try to capture the joint probability of distress of financial institutions in the presence of a systemic event (p. 31). See for a full analysis: S. Masciantonio and A. Zanghini, (2017), Systemic Risk and Systemic Importance Measures During the Crisis, Bank of Italy Working Paper Nr. 1153, December. The information they provide is almost orthogonal and does not present significant overlaps, suggesting that it is inherently different. This should not be surprising since the measurement of systemic importance is almost entirely based on balance sheet data while the measurement of systemic risk contribution mainly relies on market data (p. 32).

primary cause of propagation. Banks that suffer rapid withdrawals of short- wholesale funding cause rapid fire sales in a panic,[465] forcing others in fire sales, and propagating the shock.[466] Accordingly, we propose to introduce liquidity risk charges as a macro prudential policy tool. Taxing short uninsured term funding is aimed at making banks internalize the negative systemic effects of fragile funding strategies. A macro prudential authority can manage the charges to prevent excess build up of liquidity risk during good times'.[467] Short-term funding the liquidity risk is central in their understanding of propagation risk, as it did not occur in previous financial crises: '[r]apid capital withdrawals was the primary source of propagation in the last crisis. This occurred in combination with opaque assets.[468] Yet other episodes of opaque asset overvaluation, such as the internet bubbles, produced huge losses

[465] Interesting is the question about the chronological order between panic, bank distress and credit contraction and so on. M. Baron et al. provide some insight as they highlight in their quest to develop an informative and objective measure of the occurrence and severity of banking crises that 'large bank equity declines predict persistent credit contractions and output gaps, after controlling for non-financial equities, even outside of banking crises defined by narrative approaches. In particular, severe bank distress without panic is associated with adverse future outcomes. Large bank equity declines tend to precede other crisis indicators, suggesting that substantial bank losses are already present at the early stages of the crisis. Finally, large bank equity declines allow us to refine existing narrative chronologies of banking crises'. See: M. Baron et al., (2018), Bank Equity and Banking Crises, Working Paper, November, mimeo, later on re-issued and modified as M. Baron et al., (2019), Salient Crises, Quiet Crises, Working Paper, April 7, mimeo. Quiet crises are defined by large bank equity declines without panics. They refine the narrative chronology of banking crisis using information from bank equity returns, rather than the old methodologies based on narrative and policy models and whose findings contradicted each other. For the interest specifically regarding the chronology of banking crises, see section VII (pp. 29 ff) of their report. Also: B. Matthew and W. Xiong, (2017), Credit Expansion and Neglected Crash Risk, Quarterly Journal of Economics Vol. 132, Issue 2, pp. 713–764 and C. Romer and D. Romer, (2017), New Evidence on the Impact of Financial Crises in Advanced Countries, American Economic Review, Vol. 107, pp. 3072–3118; A. Grodecka et al., (2018), Predictors of Bank Distress: The 1907 Crisis in Sweden, Sveriges Riksbank Working Paper Series Nr. 358, October.

[466] Informational frictions often are the root cause of (liquidity) panics which convert into outright distress. See in detail: D. Garcia-Massia and A. Villacorta, (2016), Macroprudential Policy with Liquidity Panics, ESRB Working Paper Series Nr. 24, September.

[467] E. Perotti and J. Suarez, (2009), Approach to Liquidity Regulation, CEPR Discussion Paper, Nr. 8271, March, pp. 3–5.

[468] Logic would tell us that the more opaque the assets are on the balance sheet of an intermediary, the higher the rollover risk in wholesale funding markets. And indeed, greater opacity means investors form more dispersed beliefs about an intermediary's profitability. The endogenous benefit of opacity is lower fragility when profitability is expected to be high. However, the endogenous cost of opacity is a 'partial run', whereby some investors receive bad private signals about profitability and run, even though the intermediary is solvent. Intermediaries choose to be transparent when expected profitability is low and opaque when expected profitability is high. Intermediaries with less volatile profitability are also more likely to choose to be opaque conclude Ahnert and Nelson. See in detail: T. Ahnert and B. Nelson, (2016), Opaque Assets and Rollover Risk, Bank of Canada Working Paper Nr. 17, April.

but basically no propagation across markets. The explanation is simply that these investments were funded with equity. Once losses materialized, investors could not escape, and took their losses without spreading them'.[469]

The different liquidity and transformation layers creating inherent liquidity shortfalls have not only many complexities in terms of understanding liquidity risk,[470] but also in how liquidity risk translates into systemic risk,[471] how liquidity responds to regulatory interventions and ex post capital support (bailouts),[472] how liquidity differs on an intra-day versus over longer periods of time,[473] how banks behave under duress with different levels of liquidity,[474] the relationship between liquidity distress and bank failure,[475] and the relationship between liquidity risk and systemic risk.[476]

Our understanding of liquidity regulation is still at a very early stage.[477] There is no clear analysis of whether liquidity should be thought of as corresponding to short-term

---

[469] E. Perotti, (2010), The Governance of Macro-Prudential Taxation. See also: B. Weder di Mauro, (2010), Taxing Systemic Risk, University of Mainz, Working Paper.

[470] C.H.S. Bouwman, (2013), Liquidity: How banks create it and How It Should Be Regulated, Wharton Financial Institutions Center Working Paper.

[471] D. Bonfim and M. Kim, (2012), Liquidity Risk in Banking: Is there Herding?, Working Paper.

[472] A. N. Berger, C.H.S. Bouwman, T.K. Kick and K. Schaeck, (2014), Bank Risk Taking and Liquidity Creation Following Regulatory Interventions and Capital Support, Wharton Financial Institutions Center Working Paper.

[473] A. Ball, E. Denbee, M.J. Manning and A. Wheterilt, (2011), Intraday Liquidity: Risk and Regulation, Bank of England Financial Stability Paper, Nr. 11.

[474] A.N. Berger, C.H.S Bouwman, T. Kick and K. Schaeck, (2010), Bank Liquidity Creation and Risk Taking During Distress, Deutsche Bundesbank Discussion Paper Series, Working Paper Nr. 2: Banking and Financial Studies, Nr. 5; J. Cao and G. Illing, (2010), Regulation of Systemic Liquidity Risk, Munich University Discussion Paper Nr. 2010-2011; E. Farhi, M. Golosov and A. Tsyvinski, (2009), A Theory of Liquidity and Regulation of Financial Intermediation, Review of Economic Studies, Vol. 76, pp. 973–992.

[475] D. Wu and H. Hong, (2013), Liquidity Risk, Market Valuation and Bank Failures, Working Paper.

[476] F. Allen and E. Carletti, (2011), Systemic Risk and Macro-Prudential Regulation, University of Pennsylvania Working Paper. They identify six types of systemic risk, namely: (i) common exposure to asset price bubbles, particularly real estate bubbles; (ii) liquidity provision and mispricing of assets; (iii) multiple equilibria and panics; (iv) contagion; (v) sovereign default and (vi) currency mismatches in the banking system.

[477] Most of the literature emerged only after the 2008 financial crisis with a few notable exceptions: see J.-C. Rochet, (2004), Macroeconomic Shocks and Banking Supervision, Journal of Financial Stability, Vol. 1, Issue 1, pp. 93–110; J.-C. Rochet, (2008), Liquidity Regulation and the Lender of Last Resort, Financial Stability Review, Vol. 11, pp. 45–52. He focuses on a number of market failures that can justify liquidity regulation. These include potential problems in payment systems, moral hazard problems at the individual bank level due to opaqueness of assets, and moral hazard at the aggregate level due to expectations of a generalized bailout if there are macro shocks. While the first two can be managed by ratios the latter requires more complex intervention. More recent: M. Hoerova et al., (2018), Benefits and Costs of Liquidity Regulation, ECB Working Paper Nr.n 2169, July 13. They find that liquidity tools are beneficial but cannot completely remove the need for Lender of Last Resort (LOLR) interventions by the central bank. Full compliance with current

real assets or to monetary instruments.[478] There are still a number of open questions: (1) Why is the provision of liquidity that the market provides insufficient?; (2) What is (are) the market failure(s) these regulations are designed to correct? and (3) Are the regulations proposed the best way of correcting the market failures? And as time went by the controversial fog didn't lift on the issue and some claim that liquidity regulation is a double-edged sword.[479] That is because under conditions, liquidity regulation may hamper, rather than strengthen, a bank's resilience to financial stress. The reason is the existence of two opposing effects of liquidity regulation, a liquidity effect and a solvency effect. The liquidity effect arises because a bank mitigates its risk of illiquidity when it increases its liquidity buffer.[480] The solvency effect arises because a larger liquidity buffer reduces the bank's returns and may therefore raise its insolvency risk. Liquidity regulation is effective in reducing a bank's overall default risk[481] only if the former effect dominates the latter,

Liquidity Coverage Ratio (LCR) and Net Stable Funding Ratio (NSFR) rules would have reduced banks' reliance on publicly provided liquidity during the global financial crisis without removing such assistance altogether. Costs of liquidity regulation are modest.

[478] V. Bruno and H. Shin, (2014), Cross-Border Banking and Global Liquidity, BIS Working Papers, Nr. 458. See also on the effectiveness of capital flow measures in the Asean Region: V. Bruno, I. Shin and H.S. Shin, (2015), Effectiveness of Macroprudential and Capital Flow Measures in Asia and The Pacific, Working Paper in BCBS, (2015), Cross-Border Financial Linkages: Challenges for Monetary Policy and Financial Stability, BIS Paper Nr. 82, pp. 183–196; P. Lindner et al., (2018), International Monetary Policy Spillover Through the bank Funding Channel, Deutsche Bundesbank Discussion Paper Nr. 13, May 22.

[479] Regarding the Impact on Collateral: K. Schmidt, (2019), Does Liquidity Regulation Impede the Liquidity Profile of Collateral, ECB Working Paper Nr. 2256, March 27.

[480] See also: C. Hu et al., (2016), Leverage Illiquidity Contagion, Working Paper, version June 2016, mimeo. Interesting about their findings are the distinction between illiquidity spillovers and information asymmetry, which drive their results considering how 'variations in stock-level leverage lead to dynamic intraday trading behavior and illiquidity transmission'. Their insights contribute to the understanding regarding funding liquidity and the overall flight for quality effect during the deleveraging process in financial market turmoil. Also: G. Ferrara et al., (2016), Systemic Illiquidity in the Interbank Network, Bank of England Staff Working Paper Nr. 586, April. Failure to roll-over short-term funding or repay obligations when they fall due generates an externality in the form of systemic illiquidity. Also on the matter: S. Langfeld et al. (2018), Systemic Illiquidity in the Interbank Network, ESRB Working Paper Nr. 86, November 15. Failure to roll-over short-term funding or repay obligations when they fall due generates an externality in the form of systemic illiquidity, they conclude. Systemic illiquidity is minimized by a macroprudential policy that skews the distribution of liquid assets toward banks that are important in the network.

[481] There is a 'significant and robust positive correlation between parent banks' and foreign subsidiaries' default risk.' This correlation is lower for subsidiaries that have a higher share of retail deposit funding and that are more independently managed from their parents. Host country bank regulations also influence the extent to which shocks to the parents affect the subsidiaries' default risk. In particular, the correlation between the default risk of subsidiaries and their parents is lower for subsidiaries operating in countries that impose higher capital, reserve, provisioning, and disclosure requirements, and tougher restrictions on bank activities. See in detail: D. Anginer et al., (2016), Foreign Bank Subsidiaries' Default Risk during the Global Crisis: What Factors Help Insulate Affiliates from their Parents?, IMF Working Paper Nr. 16/109, June.

concludes König[482] recently and derived the conditions under which this is the case and argues the resulting relationship between capital and liquidity regulation.[483]

Within the context of the existing ambiguity it can only be concluded with Allen, that'[w]ith capital regulation there is a huge literature but little agreement on the optimal level of requirements, but with liquidity regulation we do not even know what to argue about'.[484] Perotti and Suarez have contributed to our understanding that 'market failure is that even though each individual bank takes into account its own exposure to refinancing risk, it does not internalize the system-wide effect of its decision. When banks differ in credit opportunities, Pigovian taxes are best, when they differ in their risk taking incentives, net funding liquidity ratios are best but if capital controls can be used as well as liquidity ratios, then taxes can again be optimal. Since the release of their model many variations of a liquidity capture have emerged'.[485]

[482] Ph. J. König, (2015), Kiquidity Requirements: A Double-Edged Sword, International Journal of Central Banking, Vol. 11, Nr. 4, pp. 129–168.

[483] Also the relationship between liquidity and solvency aspects and systemic risk is to a large degree still to be discovered (as well as how to reflect it all properly in stress tests): see BCBS, (2015), Making Supervisory Stress Tests More Macroprudential: Considering Liquidity and Solvency Interactions and Systemic Risk, Working Paper Nr. 29, November; H. Asgharian et al., (2017), Systemic Risk and Centrality Revisited: The Role of Interactions, Lund University Working Paper, mimeo.

[484] F. Allen, (2014), How Should Bank Liquidity be Regulated?, Wharton School, University of Pennsylvania Working Paper.

[485] As they are not Pigovian related they will not be discussed in detail in this context. Refer A. Milne, (2013), Register, Cap and Trade: A Proposal for Containing Systemic Liquidity Risk, Loughborough University Working Paper, who proposed a Cap and Trade model for liquidity; S. Nicoletti -Altimari and C. Salleo, (2010), Contingent Liquidity, Banca D'Italia, Occasional Papers, Nr. 70, who suggest a new category of securities to satisfy bank's liquidity needs. These would include a Roll-Over Option Facility (ROOF) that allows the issuer, for a price, to keep the funds if at maturity a readily observable variable correlated with systemic liquidity risk (e.g. the LIBOR-OIS spread) is above a trigger threshold. At rollover the yield would reflect the current price of liquidity and credit risk, making ROOFs attractive to investors. The instrument could attenuate a liquidity crisis by reducing banks' need to roll debt over or sell off assets, and diminish the probability of runs, if markets are convinced that banks can secure sufficient liquidity when needed thanks to the widespread use of this contingent claim. Other suggestions were made by: (1) J. Stein, (2013), Liquidity Regulation and Central Banking, Remarks made at 'Finding the Right Balance', 2013 Credit Markets Symposium, Federal Reserve Bank of Richmond, Charlotte, NC; he develops a framework where the market failure is that banks do not take into account all the social benefits of increased liquidity reserves in terms of enhanced financial stability and lower costs to taxpayers. The central bank acting as LOLR is one way to solve this problem. However, Stein argues that it is socially costly to use LOLR capacity because it is difficult to distinguish between illiquidity and insolvency. As a result, it may be better to have liquidity regulation. In addition, it may, in cases where high-quality collateral is in short supply, be optimal to price access to the LOLR as well; (2) M. Bech and T. Keister, (2013), Liquidity Regulation and the Implementation of Monetary Policy', BIS Working Paper Nr. 432: They consider the effect of liquidity regulation on the implementation of monetary policy. Since monetary policy is typically implemented by central banks targeting the rate in the market for central bank reserves, liquidity regulation may change the relationship between market conditions and the interest rate. That happens in their model because banks are worried about violating the liquidity regulation and are therefore more likely to seek term funding

Recently, it was argued[486] that liquidity regulation and the 'lender of last resort' (LOLR)[487] concept are complementary tools and serve different purposes. That is argued because liquidity shortfalls can arise for two very different reasons: First, sound institutions can face runs or a deterioration in the liquidity of markets they depend on for funding. Second, solvency concerns can cause creditors to pull away from troubled institutions. Central bank lending is the best response in the former situation, while orderly resolution (by the institution as it gets through the problem on its own or via a controlled failure) is the best response in the second situation. They also contend that liquidity regulations are a necessary tool in both situations: They help ensure that the authorities will have time to assess the nature of the shortfall and arrange the appropriate response, and they provide an incentive for banks to internalize the externalities associated with any liquidity risks.

But also sovereign bonds know distress every now and then. And in e.g. repo transactions, banks borrow against their sovereign creditworthiness rather than their own creditworthiness. However, Basel III's current LCR does not protect banks against sovereign bond distress. In accordance, currently compliant banks can be exposed to a neglected

in the market. This results in a steeper yield curve at short maturities; and (3) C. Bouwman, (2014), Liquidity: How Banks Create It and How It Should Be Regulated, A.N. Berger, P. Molyneux, and J.O.S. Wilson (eds.), The Oxford Handbook of Banking (2nd ed.), which also includes an extensive literature review: In her view, the need for regulation arises because of moral hazard associated with deposit insurance and the discount window. One of the points she stresses is the importance of the interaction between capital and liquidity regulation and the need for both to be done in concert. See also J.R. Mason, (2014), Pigouvian Principles of Externalities and Cap and Trade, Remarks Delivered before 2014 A&WMA Conference, October 29, mimeo; Economics Brief, (2017), Pigouvian Taxes, What To Do When The Interest of Individuals and Society Do Not Coincide?, The Economist, August 19.

[486] See extensively: M. Carlson et al., (2015), Why Do We Need Both Liquidity Regulations and a Lender of Last Resort? A Perspective from Federal Reserve lending during the 2007–2009 US Financial Crisis, Finance and Economics Discussion Series, Divisions of Research & Statistics and Monetary Affairs Federal Reserve Board, Washington DC, Working Paper Nr. 2015-11 (was also released as BIS Working Paper Nr. 493 in February 2015).

[487] The idea that banks in difficulty just wait for the central bank to step in is structurally besides the truth however. In contrast to the widespread belief that distressed banks gamble for resurrection, we document that distressed banks take actions to reduce leverage and risk, such as reducing asset and loan growth, issuing equity, decreasing dividends and lowering deposit rates, document Ben-David et al. See in detail: I. Ben-David et al., (2019), Do Distressed Banks Really Gamble for Resurrection, NBER Working Paper Nr. 25794, May. The same works for the insurance industry. Kirti documents that rather than taking on more risk, US insurers hit hard by the crisis pulled back from risk taking, relative to insurers hit less hard by the crisis. Capital requirements alone do not explain this risk reduction: insurers hit hard reduced risk within assets with identical regulatory treatment. State-level US insurance regulation makes it unlikely this risk reduction was driven by moral suasion. Other financial institutions also reduce risk after large shocks: the same approach applied to banks yields similar results. My results suggest that, at least in some circumstances, franchise value can dominate, making gambling for resurrection too risky. In detail: D. Kirti, (2018), When Gambling for Resurrection is Too Risky, ESBR Working Paper Nr. 69, February 19.

liquidity risk stemming from distressed sovereign debt moving through the collateral channel.[488] This unaccounted risk can translate into a system-wide liquidity shock. To gauge the potential damage caused by such a shock, Buschmann and Schmaltz[489] developed a model in which sovereign distress triggers bank distress. Their model shows how deteriorating sovereign collateral can lead to an overall liquidity squeeze and non-compliance with Basel III's liquidity standards. Since this risk is highly material, they conclude that LCR should address this event. To that effect they suggest an altered version of the LCR model, which takes into account the liquidity impact of sovereign distress ('LCR+').

The hatchets will not be buried anytime soon over this topic, as liquidity is a 'public good'.[490] Before the financial crisis capital regulation was mostly used,[491] and liquidity regulation made its entrance only after the crisis. The LCR and NSFR have been introduced recently and it is widely anticipated that they will change over time.[492]

The account of the literature on liquidity regulation indicates that it is still at an early stage. In particular, the models the analysis is based on are quite simple and capture only a small part of the market failures that have been identified in the literature

---

[488] Regarding the dynamics of the collateral channel in relation to central bank haircut policies. Higher haircuts lead to magnified (relative to increased % in haircut) reduced use of that type of collateral (mostly low rated), and higher funding spreads commensurate with haircut rate increases. See in detail: N. Cassola and F. Koulischer, (2016), The Collateral Channel of Open market Operations, Banque de France Working Paper Nr. 593 May, Paris.

[489] C. Buschmann and C. Schmaltz, (2015), Sovereign Collateral as a Trojan Horse: Why Do We Need an LCR+, Working Paper, August 19, mimeo.

[490] W. Buiter, (2007), Lessons from the 2007 Financial Crisis, CEPR Discussion Paper, Nr. DP6596: 'Liquidity is a public good. It can be managed privately (by hoarding inherently liquid assets), but it would be socially inefficient for private banks and other financial institutions to hold liquid assets on their balance sheets in amounts sufficient to tide them over when markets become disorderly. They are meant to intermediate short maturity liabilities into long maturity assets and (normally) liquid liabilities into illiquid assets. Since central banks can create unquestioned liquidity at the drop of a hat, in any amount and at zero cost, they should be the liquidity providers of last resort both as lender of last resort and as market maker of last resort…'; also cited in Allen, (2014), How Should Bank Liquidity be Regulated?, Wharton School, University of Pennsylvania Working Paper, p. 3. See regarding the moral dimension of systemic risk: A. James, (2017), The Distinctive Significance of Systemic Risk, Ratio Juris, Vol. 30, Issue 3, pp. 239–258. He argues that the systematic imposition of risk can be wrongful or unjust in and of itself, even if harm never ensues. There may be no one in particular to blame. We can explain both ideas in terms of what he calls responsibilities of "Collective Due Care." Collective Due Care arguably precludes purely aggregative cost-benefit decision-making and requires one kind of 'precautionary' attitude in public choice.

[491] See on a (possible) optimal relationship between capital and liquidity regulation: A. Walther, (2013), Jointly Optimal Regulation of Bank Capital and Liquidity, Cambridge University Working Paper. Also: S. Di Tella, (2017), Optimal Regulation of Financial Intermediaries, NBER Working Paper Nr. 23586, July. Di Tella argues that financial intermediaries don't internalize that high asset prices force everyone to bear more risk. The socially optimal allocation can be implemented with a tax on asset holdings, he argues.

[492] D. Elliott, S. Salloy and A Santos, (2012), Assessing the Cost of Financial Regulation, IMF Working Paper, Nr. 12/233, p. 43.

on liquidity provisions.[493] There is no clear analysis of whether liquidity should correspond to short-term real assets or to monetary instruments. Real models of banking focus on the former, while monetary ones focus on the latter. Distorting the allocation of real assets through regulation may be socially costly. In contrast, if the central bank creates liquidity that is held by commercial banks then that is potentially costless.[494]

11.6.3.5 Leverage-Induced Externalities

Earlier in this chapter it was already indicated that leverage has become commonplace in the corporate sector compared to one or two decades ago. What is true for the corporate sector in general, where leverage has gone up to mirror an average of 60–40% debt-to-equity (and beyond), is even more true for the financial sector, where leverage has shot up to an average 95–98% equity.[495] Admittedly, credit-driven growth is what has kept the economy growing ever since productivity rates started to curb down starting in the early 1980s. There is undeniably a correlation between credit creation, a process that is largely in the hands of private FIs (in Europe) and economic growth in an economy.[496] It partly makes up for the chronic lack of patient long-term capital in most economies (with the normal variations), an effect that neoliberalism has only fueled (infra Sect. 11.9).

But leverage also extends the 'fixed cost to total cost ratio' of an organization. Every industry is characterized by a natural bandwidth regarding the fixed-to-total-cost ratio, known as operating leverage.[497] Funding an organization with large amounts of leverage

---

[493] See in detail: N. Anderson, et al., (2015), The Resilience of Financial Market Liquidity, Bank of England Financial Stability Paper, 30 October; J. Cunliffe, (2015), Market Liquidity and Market-Based Financing, Speech to the British Bankers Association International Banking Conference; W. Dudley, (2015), Regulation and Liquidity Provision, Remarks at the SIFMA Liquidity Forum, New York City. See also regarding market liquidity, stability risk and market-making after the new regulations came in place in recent years: ESRB, (2016), Market Liquidity and Market-Making, October. Market-makers' ability to absorb temporary order imbalances by warehousing risk for short periods of time is key for markets to function properly. Market-makers themselves may finance these positions through repo markets, providing a connection between market liquidity and funding liquidity. There have been some signs of a decrease in the availability of repo market financing. The liquidity illusion remains a constant risk to financial stability.(p. 24). Also: C. Bonner et al., (2018), Drivers of Market Liquidity-Regulation, Monetary Policy or New Players, DNB Working Paper Nr. 605, September 17.

[494] F. Allen, (2014), Ibid. p. 24 and W. Buiter, (2007), Ibid. and J.E. Stiglitz, (2014), Tapping the Brakes: Are Less Active Markets Safer and Better for the Economy?, Presented at the Federal Reserve Bank of Atlanta 2014 Financial Markets Conference, April 15.

[495] See for further details: European Banking Federation, (2014), Bank Leverage and its Economic Implications, Working Paper.

[496] In the US that is more balanced between FIs and market-based lending. It is very likely that Europe will evolve in that direction, given the content of the Basel III rules.

[497] The airline industry is a notable example of having a very high fixed-to-total cost ratio (around 85–90% depending on efficiency) requiring a load factor of around 85–86% just to break even.

extends that natural fixed-to-total-cost ratio artificially with financial leverage, as most leverage comes with fixed obligations in terms of interest due and repayment of the principal amount.[498]

The higher levels of leverage can partly be explained by ever decreasing interest rates since the mid 1980s. However, this also has adverse effects now that the cost of leverage is at record lows. It is not only used to fund operations, but also to pay dividends, to finance leveraged acquisitions and to perform share buy-backs, increasing the financial performance but not the operational performance of institutions. Within the financial sector, which benefits from the deposit insurance mechanism, it can lead not only to moral hazard but also to performance targets vis-à-vis shareholders that do not match the economic reality of the industry. Indeed, more leverage enhances the return on equity (ROE) as long as the cost of debt[499] is smaller than the return on capital employed (ROCE) than the FI generates.

However, it also comes at a cost to shareholders when the ROCE is smaller than the cost of debt. The FI sector is highly dependent on leverage to generate the ROE it had become used to before and after the 2008 financial crisis.

As leveraged institutions are a threat to the economic fabric of an economy, that is all the more true for an FI whose performance is closely related to the real economy which it finances. Under Basel III, a non-risk-weighted leverage ratio[500] has been introduced, a type of quantity regulation that forces banks to keep leverage in check. Besides the qualifications needed when calculating the leverage, it was demonstrated that the nominal leverage ratio is too low to have a meaningful effect on a bank's long-term stability.[501]

---

[498] There is hybrid capital with profit-dependent interest rates and floating interest rates. This category of mezzanine debt is still a minor player relative to fixed senior debt. See in detail on the category: L. Nijs, (2014), Mezzanine Financing: Tools, Applications and Total Return, Wiley & Sons, Surrey. Rebalancing leverage creates asymmetric forces, that is, when reducing leverage shareholders are biased toward selling assets relative to potentially more efficient alternatives such as pure recapitalizations. See in detail: A. Admati et al., (2018), The Leverage Ratchet Effect, Journal of Finance, Vol. 73, Issue 1, pp. 145–198; R. Gropp et al., (2019), Banks Response to Higher Capital Requirements: Evidence from a Quasi-Natural Experiment, The Review of Financial Studies, Vol. 32, pp. 266–299.

[499] A question regularly asked is whether the higher liquidity regulations for banks would trigger higher cost of debt levels. Often the answer was affirmative. See a contrario: S. Miller and R. Sowerbutts, (2018), bank Liquidity and the Cost of Debt, Bank of England Staff Working Paper Nr. 707, January 19. They endogenize banks' funding costs as a function of their liquidity and show how they are negatively related, therefore offsetting some of the costs from higher liquidity requirements. They find evidence for this relationship using post-crisis data for US banks, implying that liquidity requirements may be less costly than previously thought.

[500] See for a novel approach toward the measurement of the leverage ratio: J. Villar Burke, (2015), Marginal Leverage ratio as a Monitoring Tool of Systemic Risk, Working Paper, May. He proposes an innovative approach to assessing leverage based on flows using the concept of a marginal leverage ratio, 'which reveals the leverage related to new activities, as a valuable supplement to the traditional absolute leverage ratio. The marginal leverage ratio can be used as an early warning tool to signal potential episodes of excessive leverage and to understand if, and how, banks deleverage. Besides capturing the leveraging-deleveraging cycles better than the absolute leverage ratio, the marginal leverage ratio provides an indication of risks that a stable absolute leverage ratio can conceal'.

[501] I. Kienna and E. Jokivuolle, (2014), Does a Leverage Ratio Requirement Increase Bank Stability?, ECB Working Paper Series, Nr. 1676. The leverage ratio induces FIs with low-risk lending strategies to

There are several different ways one could eliminate the debt/equity distortion, including (1) eliminating the deduction for interest paid[502] which seems to have a profound impact on the capital structure of multinational organizations once introduced, (2) allowing a deduction for corporate equity[503] or (3) moving to a corporate cash-flow or consumption tax.

It has also been advocated to introduce a Pigovian tax based on the leverage that an FI holds on its balance sheet. It might be noted upfront that such a surcharge would be most meaningful when scaled based on the absolute amounts of leverage, and with a higher surcharge for short-term lending, given its highly volatile nature. A Pigovian tax naturally conflicts with the debt-preferred tax code as we know it. That is not without consequences however.[504] Fleischer does not advocate a Pigovian tax in this matter as he considers: '[w]hile I am not averse to tax policy solutions to social problems, there are times when the taxing authorities are not the ideal regulatory agency'.[505] When properly introduced, a Pigovian instrument will yield better results. 'Properly introduced' in this scenario means a fairly simple measurement base. A solution for that can be found with Hahm et al., who developed a model of credit supply as the flip side of a credit risk model where a large stock of noncore liabilities serves as an indicator of the erosion of risk premiums and hence of vulnerability to a crisis.[506] They suggest a tax base equal to the noncore liabilities of the bank:

---

diversify into high-risk investments until the leverage ratio no longer constitutes a binding capital constraint on them. More recently, it was argued, based on stress testing models, that a 4–5% Leverage ratio would constrain banks' risk-taking earlier during financial booms, providing a consistent and more effective backstop to the RWRs (Risk-Weighted Capital Requirements): I. Fender and U. Lewrick, (2015), Calibrating the Leverage Ratio, BIS Quarterly Review, December 2015, pp. 43–58.

[502] See for an overview of the rules regarding deduction of interest deduction ('thin capitalization rules'): J. Blouin et al., (2014), Thin Capitalization Rules and the Multinational Firm Capital Structure, EC Taxation Papers Series, Working Paper Nr. 42. Tax deductibility in a multijurisdictional world can lead to potential distortions in the patterns of asset ownership; see for an analysis and some alternatives: M.A. Desai and D. Dharmapala, (2015), Interest Deductions in a Multijurisdictional World, Coase-Sandor Institute for Law and Economics Working Paper Nr. 725, Chicago.

[503] Which is an option the Belgian government took through its 'notional interest deduction program' introduced in 2006. In recent years the program has been scaled back materially to avoid abuse and dampen the impact on the state budget. See for an update on the matter: R. de Mooij et al., (2018), Growth-Enhancing Corporate Tax Reform in Belgium, Nordic Tax Journal, Vol. 1, pp. 1–17.

[504] See for an overview: V. Fleischer, (2011), Tax Reform and the Tax Treatment of Debt and Equity, Joint Hearing, U.S. House of Representatives, Committee on Ways and Means, U.S. Senate Committee on Finance, pp. 2–4, who suggests a thin-cap like tax on debt to remove the tax incentive to increase leverage beyond the ratio that would arise in a world without taxes and avoid regulatory arbitrage.

[505] Fleischer, (2011), Ibid. p. 11.

[506] J.-H. Hahm, H.S. Shin and K. Shin, (2013), Non-Core bank Liabilities and Financial Vulnerability, Journal of Money, Credit and Banking, Vol. 45, Issue 1, pp. 3–36. Their position is in line with other literature to this effect, that is, credit demand is larger than deposit growth ('sticky') in economic boom times. In this way, a higher incidence of noncore funding will be associated with above-trend growth in credit and compressed risk premiums.

the core liabilities being the deposits. The ratio of the non-core to core liabilities will reflect the underlying pace of credit growth[507] relative to trend and may be expected to give a window on the risk premiums ruling in the economy'[508] They find evidence that various measures of noncore liabilities and especially the liabilities to the foreign sector serve as a good indicator of vulnerability to a crisis. Their remarkably consistent measure of the noncore bank liability ratio has significant predictive power for currency crises and credit crises.[509]

The noncore bank liability ratio has independent predictive power over the much better-known and debated credit to GDP ratio. The empirical evidence strongly suggests that noncore liability measures contain considerable information value on financial vulnerability.[510] The countercyclical buffer, as implemented under Basel III will make use of the credit to GDP ratio as the indicator of procyclicality that triggers increased capital requirements on banks.[511] The concern is that the simple 'credit to GDP' aggregate may

---

[507] Macroprudential policies in general tend to have and are structurally associated with lower credit growth (also with lower investment and sales growth). These effects are especially significant for small and medium enterprises (MSMEs) and young firms that are more financially constrained and bank dependent. Among MSMEs and young firms, those with weaker balance sheets exhibit lower credit growth in conjunction with the adoption of macroprudential policies, suggesting that these policies can enhance financial stability. See in detail: M. Ayyagari et al., (2018), The Micro Impact of Macroprudential Policies: Firm-Level Evidence, IMF Working Paper Nr. WP/18/267, December, including an interesting literature list (pp. 26–28). Rapid domestic credit growth and house price growth positively influence the chances of a banking crisis. As well, a crisis in other countries with high trade and financial linkages raises the crisis probability. The coordinated use of macroprudential policies can help lessen the incidence of banking crises. It was largely untested whether coordinated implementation of macroprudential policies can reduce crisis probabilities. A prudent yes seems to be the answer. See: S.M. Choi et al., (2018), Friend or Foe? Cross-Border Linkages, Contagious Banking Crises, and "Coordinated" Macroprudential Policies, IMF Working Paper Nr. WP/18/09, January. Pure information sharing, which is the contemporary way of internationalizing macroprudential policies, therefore seems inadequate.

[508] Hahm et al., (2012), Ibid. p. 2.

[509] But less predictive in the event of a stock market crash.

[510] Hahm et al., (2012), Ibid. p. 47. The concept of financial vulnerability has been framed by D. Aikman et al., (2015), Mapping Heat in the U.S. Financial System, Finance and Economics Discussion Series Nr. 59, Board of Governors of the Federal Reserve System. Later on the framework has been expanded and geographically diversified: S.J. Lee et al., (2017), The Anatomy of Financial Vulnerabilities and Crises, International Finance Discussion Papers Nr. 1191, Board of Governors of the Federal Reserve System, February. The typical anatomy of the evolution of vulnerabilities before and after a financial crisis is and evolves as follows: pressures in asset valuations materialize, and a build-up of imbalances in the external, financial and non-financial sectors follows. A financial crisis is typically followed by a build-up of sovereign debt imbalances as the government tries to deal with the consequences of the crisis. Also: P. Giordani and S. Kwan, (2019), Tracking Financial Fragility, FRB of San Francisco Working Paper Nr. 6, February. Available at https://doi.org/10.24148/wp2019-06

[511] Concern has risen about the effectiveness of the Basel III capital buffers implemented. Occhino analyzes and proposes adopting a rule-based countercyclical buffer, that is, a buffer that is automatically lowered during recessions according to a rule. See: F. Occhino, (2018), Federal Reserve Bank of Cleveland, Economic Commentary, Nr. 2018-3, full issue. Also: R. Aliaga-Díaz, et al. (2018), Monetary Policy and Anti-Cyclical Bank Capital Regulation, Economic Inquiry, Vol. 56, Issue 2

be too noisy in capturing finer institutional details that are relevant when considering harmonized international standards for bank capital regulation.[512] Although not suggesting a Pigovian tax,[513] under the umbrella of macroprudential instruments they refer to the case of South Korea, which is the only country in the world so far to have implemented (in 2010) a macroprudential[514] tax on noncore liabilities of FIs.[515] The first indications are that the measures are promising, as they find that the sensitivity of capital flows into South Korea to global conditions decreased in the period following the introduction of macroprudential policies.[516] Their measurements are based on an earlier developed framework[517] on global liquidity[518] where global financial conditions drive banking sector capital flows through the funding and lending operations of international banks.[519] Their findings suggest that the driving force behind banking sector capital flows is the leverage cycle of the banking sector, through the interaction of the supply and demand of whole-

---

pp. 837–858; S. Eickmeier et al., (2018), Macro-Economic Effects of Bank Capital Regulation, Deutsche Bundesbank Discussion Paper Nr. 44, December 4. Also: J. Poeschl and X. Zhang, (2018), Bank Capital Regulation and Endogeneous Shadow Banking Crisis, MPRA Working Paper Nr. 92529, December 20.

[512] Hahm et al., (2012), Ibid. p. 28.

[513] One of the authors had already done so in 2010; see: H.S. Shin, (2010), Non-Core Liabilities Tax as a Tool for Prudential Regulation, Policy Memo.

[514] Measures aimed at building resilience against external financial shocks, especially against its well-known vulnerability to capital flow reversals in the banking sector and the associated disruptions to domestic financial conditions. South Korea is particularly sensitive to external capital shock in their banking system and economy. Regarding the international dimensions of financial shocks see: M. Isoré, (2016), International Propagation of Financial Shocks in a Search and Matching Environment, Bank of Finland Discussion Paper Nr. 28, November 4, Helsinki. Financial shock occurs despite flexible exchange rate regimes and substitutable financial assets. Interestingly, she distinguishes, contrary to most literature, between two types of financial shocks: (1) pure liquidity contractions and (2) shocks to banks' capitalization costs in one country do generate international financial contagion. At this stage, the economic discipline is still figuring out what vulnerabilities to financial shocks are out there. They tell us something about country-specific fragility. See in detail: J. Fisher and L. Rachel, (2016) Assessing Vulnerabilities to Financial Shocks in some Key Global Economies, Bank of England Working Paper Nr. 636, December.

[515] V. Bruno and H.S. Shin, (2013), Assessing Macro-Prudential Policies: Case of Korea, Scandinavian Journal of Economics, Vol. 116, Issue 1, pp. 128–157.

[516] The macroprudential measures introduced from 2010 were aimed at moderating the procyclicality of the banking sector by dampening the fluctuations in the growth of so-called noncore bank liabilities, especially cross-border banking sector liabilities (p. 32).

[517] V. Bruno, and H. S. Shin, (2011), Capital Flows, Cross-Border Banking and Global Liquidity, Princeton Working Paper.

[518] Ph. Hartmann, (2017), International Liquidity, LSE Financial Markets Group Paper Series, Special Paper Nr. 247, August. He identifies five dimensions of international liquidity (p. 4). In fact there are six: (1) International financial market liquidity, (2) International funding liquidity, (3) Private monetary liquidity, (4) Central bank liquidity, (5) International payments liquidity, and (6) International public liquidity support. The particular role for regulators is to preserve money-making in international assets and channeling cash to real investments.

[519] Bruno and Shin, (2013), Ibid. p. 2.

sale bank funding.[520] The post-crisis period has seen a considerable shift in the composition and drivers of both bank lending and international bond issuance. They are considered to be the two main components of global liquidity.[521] The sensitivity of both types depended heavily on the immediate post-crisis period (2009–2013) and then partially reverted since 2014. The responsiveness of international bank lending to global risk conditions declined considerably post-crisis and became similar to that of international debt securities.[522] The reversal starting 2014 is very likely the consequence of the (expected) 'divergence of the monetary policy of the US and other advanced economies, highlighting the sensitivity of capital flows to the degree of commonality of cycles and the

[520] They confirm the earlier findings on the importance of gross capital flows between countries in determining financial conditions, especially the gross flows intermediated by the banking sector; see: C. Borio, and P. Disyatat, (2011), Global Imbalances and the Financial Crisis: Link or no Link?, BIS Working Papers, Nr. 346 and P.-O. Gourinchas, and M. Obstfeld, (2012), Stories of the Twentieth Century for the Twenty-First, American Economic Journal, Macroeconomics, Vol. 4, Issue 1, pp. 226–265; M. Obstfeld, (2012), Financial Flows, Financial Crises, and Global Imbalances, Journal of International Money and Finance, Vol. 31, pp. 469–480. Bank capital flows have also been pivotal in the European financial crisis. The credit booms in countries such as Ireland and Spain were financed primarily by capital flows through the banking sector; see: P. Lane, and B. Pels, (2011), Current Account Balances in Europe, Working Paper, Trinity College Dublin. Cross-border financial flows arise when (otherwise identical) countries differ in their abilities to use assets as collateral to back financial contracts. Financially integrated countries have access to the same set of financial instruments, and yet there is no price convergence of assets with identical payoffs, due to a gap in collateral values. Home (financially advanced) runs a current account deficit. Financial flows amplify asset price volatility in both countries, and gross flows driven by collateral differences collapse following bad news about fundamentals, document Fostel et al. Their model can explain financial flows among rich, similarly developed countries, and why these flows increase volatility. See in detail: A. Fostel et al., (2019), Global Collateral and Capital Flows, NBER Working Paper Nr. 25583, February.

[521] E. Cerutti et al., (2017), Global Liquidity and Drivers of Cross-Border Bank Flows, Economic Policy, Vol. 32, pp. 81–125.

[522] Two comments: (1) a bank's capitalization influences the conditions on its corporate loans, including the volume and spread (S. Claessens et al., (2018), How do Credit Ratings Affect Bank Lending under Capital Constraints, BIS Working Paper Nr. 747, September 28, via bis.org). Rating adjustments trigger changes in loan terms that are asymmetrical: downward adjustments increase spreads by some 40 bps and reduce committed loan sizes and maturities. By contrast, upward adjustments lead to much weaker (yet opposite) effects. Importantly, we find these effects to be stronger for smaller, riskier, and banks with less capital strength, as well as for borrowers with poorer credit quality and for non-guaranteed loans; (2) Cross-border versus local lending of global banks: the distinction between the two types of lending is important for two reasons. First, local lending is much more stable, growing more slowly during expansions and shrinking less sharply during bad times. Second, local lending has grown much more important over the past two decades. S. Avdjiev et al., (2018), What Drives Local Lending by Global Banks, BIS Working Paper Nr. 746, September 26, via bis.org. They find that host-specific factors tend to influence local lending by global banks more strongly than owner-specific factors do. Specifically, the state of the host country's economy and the financial health of local subsidiaries are more important than the macroeconomic conditions in parent countries and the financial condition of a bank's parent company.

stance of policy.'[523] Further observations were that global liquidity fluctuations have largely been driven by policy initiatives in creditor countries and that policies and prudential instruments that reinforced lending banks' capitalization and stable funding levels reduced the volatility of international lending flows.[524]

Macroprudential tools foster financial stability[525] in a globalizing world with globalizing capital flows.[526] The globalization of capital flows[527] has put the focus on how

---

[523] S. Avdjiev et al., (2017), The Shifting Drivers of Global Liquidity, BIS Working Paper Nr. 644, June. Also: E. Cerutti et al., (2017), Global Liquidity and Cross-Border Bank Flows, Economic Policy, Vol. 32, Issue 89, pp. 81–125; D. Puy, (2016), Mutual Fund Flows and the Geography of Contagion, Journal of International Money and Finance Vol. 60, pp. 73–93.

[524] Ibid. S. Avdjiev et al., (2017), pp. 15 ff. Also: S. Avdjiev, et al., (2017), International Prudential Policy Spillovers: A Global Perspective, International Journal of Central Banking, Vol. 13, Issue 2, pp. 5–33; E. Cerutti and S. Claessens, (2017), The Great Cross-Border Bank Deleveraging: Supply Constraints and Intra-Group Frictions, Review of Finance, Vol. 21, Issue 1, pp. 201–236; K.J. Forbes, et al., (2017), The Spillovers, Interactions, and (Un)Intended Consequences of Monetary and Regulatory Policies, Journal of Monetary Economics, Vol. 85, pp. 1–136, January; H. Kang et al., (2017), Macroprudential Policy Spillovers: A Quantitative Analysis, IMF Working Paper Nr. WP/17/170, July.

[525] Excessive credit growth often leads to the build-up of systemic risk to financial stability. See for a review of the instruments and an early warning framework (decision-tree): L. Alessi and C. Detken, (2014) Identifying Excessive Credit Growth and Leverage, ECB working Paper Series Nr. 1723, August. See also extensively: J. Henry and C. Kolk (eds.), (2013), A Macro-Stress Testing Framework for Assessing Systemic Risk in the Banking Sector, ECB Occasional Paper Series Nr 152, October. Also: S. Albanesi et al., (2017), Credit Growth and the Financial Crisis: A New Narrative, NBER Working Paper Nr. 23740, August. A broadly accepted view contends that the 2007–09 financial crisis in the US was caused by an expansion in the supply of credit to subprime borrowers during the 2001–2006 credit boom, leading to the spike in defaults and foreclosures that sparked the crisis. Albanesi et al. show that credit growth between 2001 and 2007 was concentrated in the prime segment, and debt to high-risk borrowers was virtually constant for all debt categories during this period. The rise in mortgage defaults during the crisis was concentrated in the middle of the credit score distribution and mostly attributable to real estate investors.

[526] See for a review of capital flows and controls around the world in recent years: IFC Bulletin, (2017), Assessing International Capital Flows after the Crisis, IFC Bulletin Nr. 42, February. For the impact of macroprudential policies on the (increasing) resilience of countries to large and volatile capital flows see the IMF case study document: IMF, (2017), Increasing Resilience to large and Volatile Capital Flows: the Role of Macroprudential Policies- Case Studies, June 21; I. Aldasoro and T. Ehlers, (2017), Highlights of Global Financial Flows, BIS Quarterly Review March, pp. 15–23. A new measure of capital flow pressures in the form of a recast Exchange Market Pressure index was developed. The measure captures pressures that materialize in actual international capital flows as well as pressures that result in exchange rate adjustments. From that index the Global Risk Response Index was developed, which reflects the country-specific sensitivity of capital flow pressures to measures of global risk aversion. See in detail: L. Goldberg and S. Krogstrup, (2018), IMF Working Paper Nr. WP/18/30, January.

[527] Traditionally globalizing capital flows are seen as a two-way street: from advanced to emerging economies (i.e. downhill capital flows) and from emerging economies to advanced economies (uphill capital flows). The latter is more recent in nature and its magnitude is material these days. Both include reserve accumulation and private capital flows and qualify as foreign official purchases; most of that liquidity is looking for 'safe assets' overseas. Both these have the potential to act as a transmission channel and distort monetary stability (excessive buildup of financial risks, spillovers from poli-

global financial conditions induce greater synchronization of risk taking across regions and sectors,[528] thereby magnifying the potential for systemic shocks or meltdowns. The post-crisis years have exposed substantial strains in the workings of the international financial system. Excessive volatility in international capital flows[529] have raised questions about the efficacy of self-oriented monetary policies and the benefits of flexible exchange rates under conditions of inflation targeting. There is clear evidence of international transmission shock.[530] Capital flow volatility is thus a concern for macroeconomic and financial stability. That has two dimensions: which measure of volatility to use and understanding the determinants of volatility.[531] In this context the importance

cies in advanced economies, inadequate global financial safety net). See for a quantification and examination: B. Csonto and C.E. Tovar, (2017), Uphill Capital Flows and the International Monetary System, IMF Working Paper Nr. WP/17/174, June. Interesting is as well their observation that the findings contradict somewhat standard economic theory indicating that 'capital should flow from slow-growing developed countries to fast-growing developing countries' (p. 4).

528 See comprehensively: V. Bruno and H.S. Shin, (2014), Globalization of Corporate Risk Taking, Princeton Working Paper, mimeo.

529 S. Avdjiev et al., (2018), Gross capital Flows by Banks, Corporates and Sovereigns, BIS Working Paper Nr. 760, December 4, via bis.org. They draw some novel conclusions: First, banks in advanced economies are responsible for the high correlation between capital inflows and outflows. Second, the private sector is the main driver of the procyclicality of capital inflows. By contrast, inflows to emerging market sovereigns move countercyclically. Third, advanced economy banks and emerging market sovereigns drive the procyclicality of capital outflows. Fourth, when global risk aversion is high, private sector flows decline, while sovereign flows show no significant response; I. Shim and K. Shin, (2018), Financial Stress in lender Countries and Capital Outflows from Emerging Market Economies, BIS Working Paper Nr. 745, September 19, via bis.org. As proxies for financial stress in lender countries, they use bank CDS spread, sovereign CDS spread and corporate bond spread. They find that when financial stress of lender countries increases, international banks decrease their lending to EMEs, which acts as a major driver of capital outflows from EMEs. In particular, financial stress in lender countries is a more important driver than the local financial conditions and macroeconomic fundamentals of EMEs. Cross-border lending to EMEs is more susceptible to financial stress in lender countries than is local lending in foreign currency. Also: M. Hoffmann et al., (2019), International Capital Flows, External Assets and Output Volatility, Journal of International Economics, Vol. 117, pp. 242–255.

530 R. Bannerjee et al., (2016), Self-Oriented Monetary Policy, Global Financial Markets and Excess Volatility of International Capital Flows, BIS Working Paper Nr. 540, January. However an optimal monetary policy can substantially improve the workings of the international system, even in the absence of direct intervention in capital markets through macroprudential policies or capital controls. Also: O. Jeanne and D. Sandri, (2017), Global Financial Cycle and Liquidity Management, Working paper, October, mimeo.

531 Typically they are classified as being either push factors like the US monetary policy stance, US economic performance, international reserves and global risk aversion or pull factors such as real GDP growth and growth differential relative to other countries. Push versus pull is often replaced by global versus domestic. See: M. Fratzscher, (2012), Capital Flows, Push versus Pull Factors and the Global Financial Crisis, Journal of International Economics, Vol. 88, Issue 2, pp. 341–356. Pagliari an Hannan observed that push factors can be more important than pull factors in explaining volatility, illustrating that the characteristics (or determinants) of volatility can be different from those of the flows levels. For instance, risk aversion can be more important than domestic macro-

of a global financial cycle (GFCy) for capital flows cannot be underestimated. The GFCy is an unobservable concept and so indirect methods need to be used to represent it. Traditionally there are two methods: direct observable variables such as the VIX[532]/push-and-pull factors[533] or indirect manifestations where actual capital flows are identified through proxies called 'common dynamic factors' such as credit creation, interest rate movements and domestic asset prices. The research into the phenomenon of a global financial cycle for capital flows has yielded limited results insofar that both methods fail to explain the variation in global capital flows[534] for more than a quarter and that the variation in capital flows doesn't seem to behave as being the result of common shocks nor can they be attached to observables linked to a certain central country (e.g. the US).[535] The interest in global financial cycles stems from the fact that global risk (which includes both risk aversion and economic uncertainty) tends to be well associated with extreme capital flows and can be traced back as a solid predictor of capital flow movements. Domestic factors have proven to show only limited correlation with capital flow volatility.

---

economic variables like GDP growth. See: M.S. Pagliari and S.A. Hannan, (2017), The Volatility of Capital Flows in Emerging Markets: Measures and Determinants, IMF Working Paper Nr. WP/17/41, February. They also lament (correctly) about the limited amount of research available regarding the topic of capital flow volatility, but did bring together nicely everything that is around at this stage on the topic (pp. 43 ff). They also demonstrate that portfolio and bank debt flows are more volatile than FDI flows. See for an updated review including literature: S.A. Hannan, (2018), Revisiting the Determinants of Capital Flows to Emerging Markets—A Survey of the Evolving Literature, IMF Working paper Nr. WP/18/214, September. The capital flow landscape is still determined by global- and country-specific factors but the relative importance of these factors has varied over time and depends on the type of capital flow. In that context both source and host country measures have proven relevant. Also: A.R. Ghosh et al., (2016), When Do Capital Inflow Surges End in Tears?', American Economic Review, Vol. 106, Issue 5, pp. 581–585. Also: A.R. Ghosh et al., (2017), Managing the Tide: How Do Emerging Markets Respond to Capital Flows, IMF Working Paper Nr. WP/17/69.

[532] A measure of uncertainty and risk aversion of the markets.

[533] Sensitivities to global factors can vary between inflows and outflows, between gross and net flows, and by flow type.

[534] Post-crisis the focus has been on gross capital flows (prior to the crisis that was net capital flows (current account). Davis et al. find evidence of two global factors, which we call the GFCy (global financial cycle) factor and commodity price factor. These factors together account for half the variance of gross flows in advanced countries and 40% of the variance of gross flows in emerging markets. See for details: J.S. Davis, (2019), Global Capital Flows Cycle: Impact on Gross and Net Flows, NBER Working Paper Nr. 25721, April; J.S. Davis et al., (2019), Global Drivers of Gross and Net Capital Flows, FRB of Dalles, Globalization Institute Working Paper Nr. 357, March 27; M.M. Habib and F. Venditti, (2019), The Global Capital Flows Cycle: Structural Drivers and Transmission Channel, ECB Working Paper Nr. 2280, May 15; P. McQuade and M. Schmitz, (2019), America First? A US-Centric View on Global Capita Flows, ECB Working Paper Nr. 2238, February 13.

[535] E. Cerutti et al., (2017), How Important is the Global Financial Cycle? Evidence from Capital Flows, IMF Working Paper Nr. WP/17/193, September, including an interesting literature list (pp. 25 ff). The lack of visibility is disappointing in terms of the usefulness for emerging market policy design. In case the GFCy would explain much of the variation in capital flows it would be difficult for emerging market policy design to manage their economies as the GFCy would be

It has further become clear that the recent financial crisis was of a systemic nature, which was caused and fed by a liquidity shortage.[536] In fact, we have come to realize (or relearn) that the amount of liquidity (through credit) that is available determines to a large degree the valuation of asset prices and as such can singlehandedly cause asset bubbles.[537] Credit-induced bubbles seem to cause way more economic damage than other bubbles.[538] When fueled by credit booms, asset price bubbles[539] increase financial crisis risks; upon collapse they tend to be followed by deeper recessions and slower recoveries.[540] Nevertheless, current regulation guarantees run-prone bank liabilities and instead tries to regulate bank assets and their values. The liability-based taxation model as discussed above has also found its way to replace the 'command-and-control' legislation enacted after the crisis. It would constitute a much simpler model to avoid runs on banks and ensure the public good that can be described as stability of the financial market.

Cochrane[541] suggests a Pigovian tax to replace the capital ratios. Runs are a pathology of specific contracts, such as deposits and overnight debt, issued by specific kinds of intermediaries. In an equity situation where liquidity dries up, investors absorb their losses and move on, as the late 1990s tech bubble demonstrated, causing only a mild recession. There

driven by common shocks including factors that would have emanated from the center (a larger country like the US, e.g.) and would lead to large capital flow fluctuations. Capital controls could then insulate them from the variations at the expense of international financial integration. Would the GFCy not explain most of the variation in capital flows, which it didn't, small and emerging countries have greater degrees of freedom to manage their economies, at least in terms of the impact of the GFCy on capital flow fluctuations.

[536] See for a break-down of the liquidity shortage during the financial crisis: F. Dong et al., (2017), Flight to What? Dissecting Liquidity Shortages in the Financial Crisis, Federal Reserve Bank of St. Louis Working Paper Nr. 25B, October. Their model reveals that 'a sharp reduction in the quality, instead of the liquidity, of private assets was the culprit of the recent financial crisis'. They also comment on the fact that the provision of public liquidity endogenously affects the provision of private liquidity and the policy implications.

[537] J. Dow and J. Han, (2014), Contractual Incompleteness, Limited liability and Bubbles, Swedish House of Finance Research Paper, Nr. 14/03.

[538] And it raises systemic risk in the market and for banks in particular: M. Brunnermeier et al., (2017), Asset Price Bubbles and Sytemic Risk, CEPR Discussion Paper Nr. DP12362. They analyze the effects of asset price bubbles on systemic risk and show that asset price bubbles in stock and real estate markets raise systemic risk at the bank level. The strength of the effect depends strongly on bank characteristics (bank size, loan growth, leverage and maturity mismatch) as well as bubble characteristics (length and size). In a median real estate bust, systemic risk increases by almost 70% of the median for banks with unfavorable characteristics. These results emphasize the importance of bank-level factors for the buildup of financial fragility during bubble episodes, document Brunnermeier et al. See in detail: M.K. Brunnermeier, (2019), Asset Price Bubbles and Systemic Risk, NBER Working Paper Nr. 25775, April.

[539] There is a relationship between asset price bubbles and systemic risk. Systemic risk of banks rises already during a bubble's buildup phase, and even more so during its bust. The increase differs strongly across banks and bubble episodes. It depends on bank characteristics (especially bank size) and bubble characteristics.

[540] See for an extensive analysis of the different types of bubbles and their economic impact after deflation: Ò. Jordà et al., (2015), Leveraged Bubbles, CESifo Working Paper Nr. 5489, August.

[541] J. Cochrane, (2014), Towards a Run-Free Financial System, Chicago Booth School of Business Working Paper, mimeo.

was no run in the tech stock bust because tech companies were funded by stock, and stock does not have these run-prone features.

In the tradition started by Kocherlakota,[542] Cochrane suggests that '[f]or every dollar of short-term debt that a bank or other intermediary issues, it has to pay, say, five cents tax per year. That tax could, in principle, decline smoothly with maturity, be larger depending on capital ratios and other measures of how run-prone the institution is (providing a nudge rather than a brick wall at a specific ratio), could be larger for "systemically important" institutions, and could be varied over time as macro-prudential policymakers sniff trouble'.[543] He explicitly leaves the equilibrium aspirations behind as he prefers Pigovian taxes over capital regulation when he asserts: '[p]igouvian taxes are better than quantity controls in many areas of regulation, from import tariffs versus quotas to pollution taxes versus direct emission regulation, especially when, as in this case, precise costs and benefits are hard to measure'.[544]

Capital regulation leaves banks with awful incentives.[545] It is easy to construct assets whose value is low but whose risks (betas) are large. Risk-weighting individual assets sound better, but then we argue about risk weights. The riskiness of a pool of assets does not just depend on the riskiness of the individual assets but equally so on the correlation between those assets included in the pool, a feature that capital regulation ignores.

---

[542] N. Kocherlakota, (2010), Taxing Risk and the Optimal Regulation of Financial Institutions, Economic Policy Paper Nr. 10-3, Federal Reserve Bank of Minneapolis. Perotti and Suarez Ibid. follow in that tradition. It has also created alternative movements, for example those who suggest a cap-and-trade model: See in detail: J. Stein, (2012), Monetary Policy as Financial Stability Regulation, Quarterly Journal of Economics, Vol. 127, pp. 57–95 and J. Stein, (2014), Incorporating Financial Stability Considerations into a Monetary Policy Framework, Speech, March 21.

[543] J. Cochrane, Ibid. p. 19.

[544] J. Cochrane, Ibid. p. 19. However there seem to be limits to this argument. Recent behavioral literature suggests that explicit financial penalties/rewards may undermine willingness to behave pro-socially. See: B. Lanz et al., (2017), The Behavioral Effect of Pigouvian Regulation: Evidence from a Field Experiment, Research Brief MIT Center for Energy and Environmental Policy Research, online via ceepr.mit.edu (also as extended research paper in the Research Paper Series nr. 32 of the Graduate Institute Geneva). They conclude that 'experimental results show that a monetary incentive explicitly motivated by the regulation of carbon emissions is less effective as compared to a neutrally framed price change of the same magnitude. This is evidence of negative behavioral effects associated with price-based regulation of externalities. We further observe that the extent of behavioral effects varies with substitutability: for products with close substitutes (cola and milk in our setting), we observe very substantial negative behavioral effects, while for products where substitution requires more effort (spreads and meat) behavioral effects are small and statistically indistinguishable from zero.' The implication is that a Pigovian tax would need to be set above its socially efficient level (i.e. the cost of the damages produced) in order to compensate for the discussed behavioral effect. See also: D. Nerudová and M. Dobranschi, (2016), Procedia- Social and Behavioral Sciences, Vol. 220, May 31, pp. 302–311. See somewhat in line: P. Fitzgerald et al., (2016), Will I Pay for Your Pleasure? Perceptions of Negative Externalities and Responses to Pigovian Taxes, Working Paper, mimeo.

[545] Quantitative capital ratio regulations quickly lead to arguments and games. Should the denominator be 'risk-weighted' assets or total assets, or should the capital requirement be based on a full-Value-at-Risk model? The total-assets approach has a satisfying simplicity. See in detail: D. Duffie, (2014), Is Keeping It Simple for Banks Stupid?, Bloomberg View, January 7 and D. Duffie, (2010), How Big Banks Fail and What to Do about It, Princeton University Press, Princeton, NJ.

Capital regulation is flawed as it does not allow rewards on a scaling basis. Cochrane states that the top of a hill is flat, that is, more capital is always better, but capital buffers do not include an incentive to do better than the minimum standards. 'A Pigovian tax allows rewarding those FIs that perform better than a minimum threshold as set by regulation. Those critics who advocate the need for a (a lot of) short-term funding will be satisfied to understand that the position will withstand a run-prone externality tax. Pigovian taxes set a price, and maybe the wrong price,[546] but at least then we know the shadow value of the constraint'. A quantity constraint may actually have a small shadow value, especially to society or to an industry as a whole if not to an individual bank. Cochrane therefore concludes: '[a] quantity constraint may have a very large shadow value that nobody knows about and do far more damage than its advocates realize. With a Pigouvian tax we will at least learn something about the necessity of run-prone contracts. With quantity constraints, we don't learn'.[547] The Pigovian instrument not only provides material benefits vis-à-vis other regulatory alternatives, but also facilitates the combination of a tax instrument, meeting the three criteria discussed before, with the functionality to operate as a tool for macroprudential management and in that way keep the focus on something I mentioned before, that is, that risk management in this respect is different depending on the angle from which it is observed. What constitutes excessive risk on behalf of an FI does not necessarily match the concerns of the financial marketplace as such and the requirement to manage the public good of 'stability' of the financial markets. Its nexus will be further analyzed in 11.8.

11.6.3.6 Volatility-Inducing Externalities

The last layer in my suggested Pigovian tax model for the FI sector is the layer responding to those instruments used or managed by financial institutions that create (enhanced) levels of volatility in the market. That has the ability to distort the (temporary valuation) of asset prices to such a degree that it can lead, through herding in the market, to material losses for investors which were unexpected when considering the intrinsic value of the assets priced. It is common knowledge that there is a natural amount of volatility in markets, particularly in equity markets. It is also common knowledge that certain types of market-making activities engaged in by FIs enhance (or have the potential to enhance)

---

[546] See also: N. Tideman and F. Plassmann, (2016), Efficient Bilateral Taxation of Externalities, Working Paper, version August 15, mimeo. See regarding the administrative cost of applying Pigovian taxes, in particular in the case of multiple externalities: D. Jaqua and D. Schaffa, (2016), Pigouvian Taxation with Costly Administration and Multiple Externalities, Working Paper, version: August 27, mimeo. Their two main conclusions are '[i]f administrative cost varies only with the pollution generating activity, the optimal tax is equal to the externality added to the marginal administrative cost, and the private market fully internalizes the externality and administrative cost. If, due to the nature of enforcement, administrative cost varies with tax rates, then optimal policy leaves some portion of externalities uncorrected. As a result, using taxes to modify complement and substitute activities will be welfare increasing.'

[547] Cochrane, Ibid. p. 20.

the levels of volatility in a variety of markets and/or distort the effective price discovery function of financial markets. That enhanced volatility can lead to instability as investors act upon those enhanced levels of volatility, a process potentially magnified by herding behavior.

It is my suggestion to include a Pigovian-based levy calibrated on a per unit-amount charge, for example per 100.000 Euro or USD. The tax charged to individual FIs (which can be broader than only banking institutions but also asset managers and a wider variety of investment funds) would be related to the total amount of certain products that they have outstanding and the volumes embedded in those earmarked net of volatility-enhancing products. The product group should include, amongst others: (1) exchange traded funds[548] (ETFs[549]),

[548] I. Ben-David, F. Franzoni and R. Mousawai, (2014), Do ETFs increase Volatility, NBER Working Paper, Nr. 20071 (later on published in updated form as I. Ben-David, F. Franzoni and R. Mousawai, (2018), Do ETFs increase Volatility, The Journal of Finance, Wiley library online). They study whether exchange traded funds—an asset of increasing importance—impact the volatility of their underlying stocks. Using identification strategies based on the mechanical variation in ETF ownership, they present evidence that stocks owned by ETFs exhibit significantly higher intraday and daily volatility. They estimate that an increase of one standard deviation in ETF ownership is associated with an increase of 16% in daily stock volatility. The driving channel appears to be arbitrage activity between ETFs and the underlying stocks. Consistent with this view, the effects are stronger for stocks with lower bid-ask spread and lending fees. The evidence further suggests that ETF ownership increases stock turnover, which in turn suggests that ETF arbitrage adds a new layer of trading to the underlying securities. Also: K. Pan and Y. Zeng, (2017), ETF Arbitrage under Liquidity Mismatch, ESRB Working paper Series Nr. 59, December. They conclude that '[a] natural liquidity mismatch emerges when liquid exchange traded funds (ETFs) hold relatively illiquid assets' and that 'that this liquidity mismatch can reduce market efficiency and increase the fragility of these ETFs'. Regarding the relation between volatility and systemic risk: S. Malik and Peter Lindner, (2017), On Swing Pricing and Systemic Risk Mitigation, IMF Working Paper Nr. WP/17/159. It has become clear that the FSB definition (both large and narrow) will only take us so far in terms of defining what is included or not. The EC has structurally included investments funds including ETFs. See also: P.F. Hanrahan, (2018), Exchange Traded Funds in the Shadow Banking System, in Research Handbook on Shadow Banking, Legal and Regulatory Aspects (eds. I. H.-Y. Chiu and I.G. MacNeil), Edward Elgar Publishing, Cheltenham, UK, pp. 363–396.

[549] And related categories ETNs (Exchange Traded Notes) and the wider category of Exchange traded Products (ETPs). In the background plays the marketplace where the passive investment thesis has now become dominant. Large swings in investor sentiment can have a profound effect on the stability of the marketplace when being dominated by passive ETF and other products. The media impact in equity prices and volatility has now been properly documented. See: S.P. Fraiberger et al., (2018), Media Sentiment and International Asset Prices, IMF Working Paper Nr. WP/18/274, December. In particular changes in global news sentiment have a large(r) impact on equity returns around the world, which does not reverse in the short run. Positive news creates short-term equity inflows, negative news creates long-term (i.e. permanent) equity outflows. Also: A. Ghosh and G.M. Constantinides, (2017), What Information Drives Asset Prices, NBER Working Paper Nr. 23689, August. Regarding the systemic risk nature of ETFs see: M. Pagano et al., (2019), Can ETFs Contribute to Systemic Risk? Reports of the Advisory Scientific Committee, Nr. 9, June 17. The short answer: yes, and it is further linked to increased price volatility, used as an arbitrage mechanism and associated with greater co-movement of asset prices.

which are essentially listed mutual funds,[550] (2) high-frequency[551] and/or algorithmic trading,[552] (3) margin-based investing,[553] (4) dark pools[554] and (5) short-sellers.[555]

[550] Long-term investors on the other hand work countercyclical and thereby improve financial stability and reduce volatility. See: T. Fong et al. (2018), Do Long-Term Institutional Investors Contribute to Financial Stability? – Evidence from Equity Investment in Hong Kong and International Markets, HK Institute for Monetary Research Working Paper Nr. 22, September.

[551] F. Zhang, (2010), High Frequency Trading, Stock Volatility and Price Discovery, Yale School of Management Working Paper. It contrasts however with a more recently but commercially commissioned study by the Futures Industry Association: N.P.B. Bollen and R.E. Whaley, (2013), Futures Market Volatility, Vanderbilt University, Owen Graduate School of Management Working Paper. The latter found that there is 'no evidence to suggest that realized return volatility in electronically-traded futures markets has changed through time.'… '[w]e now have empirical evidence that volatility in the futures markets has neither increased nor decreased once the effects of macro-economic shocks are removed.' Also: FCA, (2016), Are High-Frequency Traders Anticipating the Order Flow? Cross-Venue Evidence from the UK Market, Occasional Paper Nr. 16, September. Illiquidity brings more illiquidity, contrary to the dynamic that in normal market conditions illiquidity, by moderating the demand for immediacy, produces a self-stabilizing effect, highlight Cespa and Vives. In a crash, they indicate 'an increase in illiquidity fosters a disorderly "run for the exit," accentuating the price movement'… 'this source of fragility (can be traced back, ed.) to the fact that modern markets' pervasive presence of automated trading hampers market participants' access to (i) trade, and (ii) quote information. That is, two frictions shape trading activity nowadays: a participation friction (not all liquidity suppliers are continuously present in the market), and an informational friction (not all traders have access to timely market information).' See in detail: G. Cespa and X. Vives, (2017), High Frequency Trading and Fragility, ECB Working Paper Nr. 2020, February.

[552] See B. Biais, T. Foucault and S. Moinas, (2014), Equilibrium Fast Trading, Working Paper. They argue that high-speed market connections and information processing improve the ability to seize trading opportunities, raising gains from trade. They also enable fast traders to process information before slow traders, generating adverse selection, and thus negative externalities. When investing in fast-trading technologies, institutions do not internalize these externalities. Besides banning them altogether, a Pigovian tax is suggested on the technology that enables high-speed trading.

[553] Margin-based investing is essentially investing with someone else's capital (often that of your bank or broker, who provides the capital as a debt facility) while depositing only a limited amount of collateral yourself, in case your trade goes wrong but you still have to repay your debt to your broker. It has been proven that pure command-and-control regulation seems to have little effect on volatility. A countercyclical Pigovian instrument seems to dampen volatility better caused by the collateral constraint through margin lending. See in detail: J. Brumm et al., (2014), Margin Regulation and Volatility, ECB Working Paper Series, Nr. 1698; M. Bakoush et al., (2017), Margin Requirements and Systemic Liquidity Risk, University of Southampton Working Paper, November, mimeo. They find that 'distress due to margin procyclicality in the derivatives market can spillover to the interbank market leading to systemic liquidity risk. Interconnectedness further amplifies the effects of systemic risk within the interbank market. The model shows that central clearing might increase the possibility of systemic liquidity risk due to tight margin requirements and the timing of cash flows required from banks.' See in detail on the aspect of central clearing chapter 5 (Volume 1). Also: O. Brossard, and S. Saroyan, (2016), Hoarding and Short-Squeezing in Times of Crisis: Evidence From the Euro Overnight Money Market, Journal of International Financial Markets, Institutions and Money, Nr. 40 (Supplement C), pp. 163–185. A. Eross, et al.,

11.7 Pigovian Taxes and the Shadow Banking Industry

11.7.1 Introduction

It has already been highlighted that the financial industry consists of much more than the traditional regulated banking sector. The regulated banking sector and the shadow banking sector correspond to each other as communicating vessels. The implication is that the shape of the shadow banking sector is partly defined by the regulation that the traditional banking sector is confronted with, its activities and its (new) products. The shadow banking sector is therefore constantly in flux and will evolve over time, based not just on demand but also based on its nexus with the traditional banking sector.[556] That is ultimately what interests us here, that is, the impact that the shadow banking sector might have on the real economy through its facilitator, the traditional banking sector.

(2016), Liquidity Risk Contagion in the Interbank Market, Journal of International Financial Markets, Institutions and Money, Nr. 45 (Supplement C), pp. 142–155; D. Murphy, et al., (2016), A Comparative Analysis of Tools to Limit the Procyclicality of Initial Margin Requirements, Bank of England Staff Working Paper Nr. 597, London; P. Tasca, and S. Battiston, (2016), Market Procyclicality and Systemic Risk, Quantitative Finance, Vol. 16, Issue 8, pp. 1219–1235; M. Bakoush et al., (2017), Margin Procyclicality and Systemic Risk, University of Southampton Working Paper, mimeo.

[554] H. Zhu, (2014), Do Dark Pools Harm Price Discovery, Review of Financial Studies, Vol. 27, Issue 3, pp. 747–789. Dark pools are equity trading systems that do not publicly display orders. They offer potential price improvements but do not guarantee execution. Zhu concludes that the existence of dark pools tends to improve the price discovery function on the official exchanges (though it also leads to reduced exchange liquidity), but draws uninformed investors into the dark pools. He further concludes that the effect of the dark pool on price discovery can become weaker the longer the information horizon, and that although the dark pool can improve price discovery on average, it can harm price discovery in some rare realizations of uninformed order imbalance. See in general S. Patterson, (2013), Dark Pools: The Rise of the Machine Trader and the Rigging of the U.S. Stock Market, Crown Business, New York and M. Lewis, (2014), Flash Boys: A Wall Street Revolt, W.W. Norton & Company, New York; FCA, (2016), Asymmetries in Dark Pool Reference Prices, Occasional Paper 21, September; L. Ye, (2016), Understanding the Impact of Dark Pools on Price Discovery, Working Paper, December 27; M. Petrescu and M. Wedow, (2017), Dark Pools in European Equity Markets: Emergence, Competition and Implications, Occasional Paper Series, Working Paper nr. 193, July; B. P. Baxter, (2017), The Securities Black Market: Dark Pool Trading and the Need for a More Expansive Regulation ATS-N, Vanderbilt Law Review, Vol. 70, pp. 311–337.

[555] See a contrario: A. Beber et al., (2018), Short-Selling Bans and Bank Stability, ESRB Working Paper Series Nr. 64, January. They conclude that financial institutions whose stocks were banned experienced greater increases in the probability of default and volatility than unbanned ones, and these increases were larger for more vulnerable financial institutions.

[556] Z. Pozsar and M. Singh, (2011), The Nonbank-Bank Nexus and the Shadow Banking System, IMF Working Paper, WP/11/289.

One of the key characteristics of the shadow banking industry, particularly before the 2008 crisis, was that it was largely unregulated and operated literally in the shadow of the traditional banking sector. That has changed materially since then, although many aspects remain similar.[557]

The shape and form of the shadow banking market evolve over time, and therefore so also does its definition.[558] The constituent elements of the shadow banking sector include the fact that it is largely unregulated, and that it engages financial intermediaries that conduct maturity, credit and liquidity transformation without access to central bank liquidity[559] or public sector credit guarantees which invariably involves regulatory arbitrage.[560] Examples of shadow banking entities include finance companies, asset-backed commercial paper conduits, limited-purpose finance companies, structured investment vehicles, credit hedge funds, money market mutual funds, securities lenders and government-sponsored enterprises. A parallel universe also exists in the insurance sector, where externalities occur between the insurance and captive insurance or re-insurance sector[561]

[557] The objective here is not to provide a full analysis of shadow banking but only to focus on the externality-inducing activities embedded in the shadow banking sector.

[558] See supra regarding the different methodologies and schemes to assess the size of the shadow banking sector.

[559] See regarding the (stabilizing) role of central banks in matching bank liquidity: L. Vincent et al., (2018), Stabilising Virtues of Central Banks: (Re) Matching Bank Liquidity, Banque de France Working Paper Nr. 666, March 7.

[560] R. Ayadi et al., (2016), Regulatory Arbitrage in EU Banking: Do Business Models Matter, IRCCF Working Paper, July. Different business models lead to different levels of bank risk (measured by distance to default). The choice between business models is driven by regulatory arbitrage and once the choice is made, the choice of business model drives the intensity of future regulatory arbitrage engaged into. Also: R. Ayadi, et al., (2016), Bank Business Models Monitor, 2015, Europe, IRCCF, HEC Montreal; R. Ayadi, (2016), Bank Business Models in Europe: Why Does it Matter for the Future of Regulation and Resolution, IRCCF Working paper, July. See regarding the impact of extreme monetary policies on business models A. Lucas et al., (2017), Bank Business Models at Zero Interest Rates, ECB Working Paper Nr. 2084 June. Another reminder of the legal dimensions of regulatory arbitrage and the reasons behind the failure of global financial regulation: A. Rise, (2014), Managing Regulatory Arbitrage: A Conflict of laws Approach, Cornell International Law Journal, Vol. 47, pp. 63–119. Her position is to treat conflicts in law as arbitrage in finance. Rather than focusing on the gap created by differences in national legislation, they are seen as conflicts and can be resolved as such, closing the opportunity gap.

[561] Also here the question arises to what degree counterparty arrangement poses a threat to financial stability. First it sould be observed that interconnectedness is not very well understood in the (re) insurance sector. Models of the complex interactions among reinsurers and with other participants in the financial system and the real economy are at a very early stage of development. The market remains opaque including the counterparty arrangements among (re)insurers known as retrocession agreements. Retrocession agreements involve risk sharing among reinsurers and are an important source of off-balance-sheet capital. These agreements create a complicated network of institutions exchanging their risk exposures in order for each institution to achieve a desired risk profile. An important feature of the retrocession market is its opacity. Davison et al. have been looking into this and conclude that '[r]einsurers generally have detailed information on their direct counterparty but not necessarily on their counterparty's retrocession arrangements. This exchange of risk has the potential to result in a transfer of exposures to the same set of players. A reinsurance spiral can occur when reinsurers extensively underwrite each other's risk exposures, possibly resulting in the circulation of exposures among the same set of players.' They make an attempt to model the arrangements

often based on regulatory arbitrage.[562] Only after years of rehashing the potential systemic risk that comes with existing (re)insurance models, it was acknowledged that the insurance sector—particularly of life insurers—to systemic risk has increased, although not yet to the level of the banking sector.[563] An attempt to define the shadow banking sector requires an open structured paradigm to capture the ever changing nature of the sector.

The Financial Stability Board, which had been mandated by the G20 to provide and develop a framework for regulating and managing the shadow banking sector, therefore suggested an open framework for the assessment of sector and the drawing of the demarcation lines. Rather than define its activities or the type of entities involved, it provided five criteria based on which non-regulated entities can be assessed.

---

consistent with the financial statement data of the reinsurers involved and is then stress-tested. They then apply a banking-based network model approach to the insurance industry. They then assess the interconnectedness among reinsurers based on potential claims (rather than premiums). They conclude that contagion is very likely but that reinsurance spirals are rare, and that further research is needed. They were able to conclude however that 'the size of the potential market disruption is sensitive to (1) the distribution of risk among counterparties, (2) the trigger for financial distress, (3) the time horizon for claims resolution and (4) the degree of loss netting'. See in detail: M. Davison et al., (2016), Are Counterparty Arrangements in Reinsurance a Threat to Financial Stability, Bank of Canada Working Paper Nr. 39, August.

[562] See in detail: B.M. Lawsky, (2013), Shining a Light on Shadow Insurance: A Little-known Loophole That Puts Insurance Policyholders and Taxpayers at Greater Risk, New York State Department of Financial Services Report; R.S.J. Kooijen and M. Yogo, (2013), Shadow Insurance, NBER Working Paper, Nr. 19568. See further: E. Berdin, and M. Sottocornola, (2015), Insurance Activities and Systemic Risk, Goethe-University, Frankfurt, ICIR Working Paper Nr. 19/15; C. Bierth, et al., (2015), Systemic risk of insurers around the globe. Journal of Banking & Finance, Vol. 55, pp. 232–245; C. Kaserer, and C. Klein, (2017), Systemic Risk in Financial Markets: How Systemically Important are Insurers? TU Munich, Working Paper, mimeo; D. Kessler, (2013), Why (Re)Insurance is Not Systemic, Journal of Risk and Insurance, Vol. 81, Issue 3, pp. 477–487; R.S.J. Koijen, and M. Yogo, (2016), Shadow Insurance, Econometrica, Vol. 84, Issue 3, pp. 1265–1287; and F. Irresberger and Y. Peng, (2016), Why Do Life Insurers use Shadow Insurance, Working Paper, November 19, mimeo. Shadow insurance (i.e., reinsure their risks using affiliated, unauthorized and unrated off-balance sheet entities rather than traditional reinsurers) leads to greater market shares, reduced leverage, and improved risk-based capital ratios. Hepfer et al. document that shadow insurance arrangements are concentrated in tax haven subsidiaries and are associated with significant tax savings. Since shadow insurance is also associated with larger cash payouts to shareholders, shadow insurance can be seen as 'tax motivated'. The model operates as such that reserves that are held to pay out future policy claims can now be freed up for other purposes (shareholder payouts, investment and compensation). See: B.F. Hepfer et al., (2016), Taking Shadow Insurance Out of the Shadows: Regulatory Arbitrage, Taxes and Capital, Working Paper, September, mimeo; D. Zafeiris, (2018), The Role of Regulation and Supervision in Shadow Banking: An Insurance Sector Perspective, in Shadow Banking: Financial Intermediation beyond Banks (Ed. Esa Jokivuolle), SUERF Conference Proceedings 2018/1, Larcier, pp. 60–65.

[563] IMF, (2016), Global Financial Stability Report. Potent Policies for a Successful Normalization, Chapter 3: The Insurance Sector-Trends and Systemic Risk Implications, pp. 87–118. Some of the conclusions include that '[l]ife insurers' contribution to the aggregate capital shortfall and Value at Risk of the financial sector has returned to historically high levels and may remain elevated if interest rates continue to be low for long' and that 'together with banks, insurers are important transmitters of volatility spillovers across financial sectors and across regions, and they have become more

Those five economic activities are: (1) management of collective investment vehicles with features that make them susceptible to runs, (2) providing loans that depend on short-term funding, (3) intermediation of market activities that is dependent on short-term funding or on secured funding of assets, (4) facilitation of credit creation, and (5) securitization-based credit intermediation and the funding of these entities.[564] Within these five parameters, the shadow banking sector will be defined in terms of its activities and entities involved.[565] Securitization has been found to have a material effect on banks' balance sheets and the financial intermediation process. The introduction of securitization is associated with fundamental changes in the funding policies of banks. In particular, Almazan et al. present evidence of more intense use of securitization by banks (i) with stronger growth opportunities, (ii) with liquidity constraints, (iii) with costlier alternative sources of funding, and (iv) with restricted access to capital markets due to adverse selection. Securitization is also observed to be higher in the pecking order of financing choices of small and medium-size banks and non-listed banks, which are likely to face more severe adverse selection problems.[566]

But what makes the shadow banking sector so important in this respect is the fact that it creates a material ability, given its activities, to enhance systemic risk in the (regulated) FI sector, whereby the non-bank-bank nexus acts as a catalyst and facilitates contagion risk. This can occur because traditional banks either have dealings with shadow banking intermediaries or because the traditional banking sector owns the credit intermediaries that shape the shadow banking sector. Although the definition remains blurred, some aspects have become very clear. As Claessens et al. point out, a critical element in the analysis is to understand that given the externality-inducing activities that the shadow banking sector is involved in (credit, maturity and liquidity transformation), and given the absence of capital regulation in the sector, the shadow banking sector can from that perspective be defined as 'all financial activities, except traditional banking, which require a private or public backstop to operate'.[567] Backstops can come in the form of the franchise value of a bank or

central to the financial systems of North America and advanced Asia'. The exposure to aggregate risk as a result of maturity mismatches has risen for the sector (pp. 107–108).

[564] See in detail: FSB, (2013), Strengthening Oversight and Regulation of Shadow Banking Policy Framework for Strengthening Oversight and Regulation of Shadow Banking Entities, pp. 6–11.

[565] A tremendous problem still is the data availability of the sector and the consistency in reporting terms on a per-country basis. That is particularly relevant as shadow banking markets differ significantly in nature and content between countries. One can study them one by one, country by country or one can look for patterns and comparative analysis. See for the latter: S. Wei, (2018), Demystifying Shadow Banking in a Bank-Centric Paradigm: A Comparative Approach, Banking & Finance Law Review, Vol. 33, Issue 1, pp. 1–39. The comparative study helps pierce the veil of shadow banking by looking into the foundational contrasts as well as the dynamic interconnections between the shadow and regular banking sectors, which further deepen the understanding of the potential regulatory logic of shadow banking. Including a specific sub-segment on China shadow banking markets.

[566] A. Almazan et al., (2015), Securitization and Banks' Capital Structure, Working Paper, March, Mimeo.

[567] S. Claessens and L. Ratnovski, (2014), What is Shadow Banking?, IMF Working Paper, WP/14/25.

insurance company, or in the form of a government guarantee. The need for a backstop is in their view a crucial feature of shadow banking, which distinguishes it from the 'usual' intermediated capital market activities, such as custodians, hedge funds and leasing companies. Contagion risk is directly correlated with information flows. The theory and experiences are closely aligned: 'although in both markets private information is only imperfectly aggregated, subjects are able to make correct inferences based on the public information coming from the market that opens first. The correlation between asset prices is very close to that predicted by the theory. Finally, there is no contagion when asset fundamentals are independent: That is, subjects only react to the history of prices and trades in the first market when it is rational to do so because they convey information'.[568]

The purpose of risk transformation is to strip assets of risk unwanted by (certain) investors who do not want to, or cannot, bear them for reasons of regulation, competition or otherwise. Traditional banking transforms risks on a single balance sheet, that is, that from the bank and transforms risky loans into safe deposits. Shadow banking transforms risks using different mechanisms, many more akin to those used in capital markets. It aims to distribute the undesirable risks across the financial system. Further in this section, a number of the most dominant techniques in shadow banking are discussed.

While shadow banking uses many capital market instruments, it also differs from traditional capital markets activities—such as trading stocks and bonds—in that it needs a backstop. This is because, while most undesirable risks can be distributed and diversified away, some residual risks, often rare and systemic ones ('tail risks'),[569] can remain. Examples of such residual risks include systemic liquidity risk in securitization, risks associated with large borrowers' bankruptcy in repos and securities lending, and the systematic component of credit risk in non-bank lending (e.g. for leveraged buyouts). Two problems exist with respect to tail risk: the identification and the probability/measurement. Both remain problematic up till today and constantly new constructs are introduced to improve the measurement of systemic tail risk often using a combination of models or approaches more often than not adding to the complexity.[570]

Entities involved in shadow banking need to show that they can absorb these risks so as to minimize the potential exposure of the ultimate claimholders who do not wish to bear them. The problem, however, is that shadow banking entities cannot absorb that risk

---

[568] M. Cipriani et al., (2015), Informational Contagion in the Laboratory, Federal Reserve Bank of NY Staff Papers Nr. 715 (March).

[569] Claessens et al., (2014), Ibid. p. 5.

[570] See, for instance, the model introduced recently by Harris et al.: They propose new systematic tail risk measures constructed using two different approaches. The first extends the canonical downside beta and co-moment measures, while the second is based on the sensitivity of stock returns to innovations in market crash risk. The first follow naturally from existing downside beta and co-moment measures, respectively, while the second is based on the demand of investors to hedge against extreme downside risk (p. 15). They show that tail risk is more relevant for longer horizons. See R.D.F. Harris et al., (2016), Systemic Tail Risk, Bank of England Working Paper Nr. 637, December.

internally by themselves. That is due to the fact that shadow banking activities have margins that are too low to provide that backstop themselves internally.[571]

To be able to distribute risks across the financial system easily, shadow banking focuses on 'hard information' risks that are easy to measure, price and communicate. That occurs for example through credit scores and verifiable information. This means that these services are contestable, with margins too low to generate sufficient internal capital to buffer residual risks. Therefore, shadow banking needs access to a backstop, that is, a risk absorption capacity external to the shadow banking activity.[572] That backstop needs to be significant because (1) shadow banking activities operate on a large scale to absorb significant start-up costs and its low margins, and (2) residual tail risks in shadow banking are systemic in nature and therefore tend to occur en masse.

That backstop can be either: (1) private, produced by the franchise value of the bank, that is, shadow banking activities occurring within a traditional banking group, or (2) public, in the form of implicit or explicit government guarantees.[573] Besides the many policy implications of this phenomenon, it raises some concerns with respect to the potentially sizable externalities it can create.

In contrast to typical market-based finance activities, which do not need external risk absorption capacity, shadow banking activities need—because they combine risk transformation, low margins and high scale with residual 'tail' risks—an external backstop and is therefore considered systemically important. Indeed, even when the tail risk is absorbed by a traditional banking group (variant (1) above),[574] they also use the government backstop

[571] Buchak et al. studied which types of activities migrate to the shadow banking sector and why migration occurs in some sectors, and not others. Focus is on the US residential mortgage market, where shadow banking accounts for half the lending volume. Banks and shadow banks compete for borrowers in this segment. Banks face regulatory constraints, but benefit from the ability to engage in balance sheet lending. Like shadow banks, banks can choose to access the securitization market. They conclude that disruptions in securitization markets rather than capital requirements have the largest quantitative impact on aggregate lending volume and pricing. In detail: G. Buchak et al., (2018), The Limits of Shadow Banks, NBER Working Paper Nr. 25149.

[572] Claessens et al., (2014), Ibid. p. 5.

[573] Claessens et al. provide some examples: '[e]xamples include, besides the general implicit guarantee provided to the "too-big-to-fail," large banks active in shadow banking, the Federal Reserve Term Securities Lending Facility (TSLF) that backstops the collateral intermediation processes, the implicit too-big-to-fail guarantees for tri-party repo clearing banks and other dealer banks, the bankruptcy stay exemptions for repos which in effect guarantee the exposure of lenders, or the implicit, reputational and other guarantees on bank-affiliated products or on liabilities of non-bank finance companies' (pp. 5–6).

[574] See f.e. M.A. Rivera-Castro et al., (2016), Tail Systemic Risk and Banking Network Contagion: Evidence from the Brazilian Banking System, ICMA Centre Discussion Paper Nr. ICM-2016-05, September. Larger banks in the country like Bradesco and Itaú are the origin of the larger systemic shocks from the banking system to the financial system network. See also: T.C. Silva, et al., (2016), Network Structure Analysis of the Brazilian Interbank Market. Emerging Markets Review, Vol. 26, pp. 130–152. For a US analysis: F. Duarte and C. Jones, (2017), Empirical Network Contagion for U.S. Financial Institutions, Federal Reserve Bank of New York Staff Reports, Nr. 826, November. Network spillovers arise through default cascades. Duarte and Jones highlight that '[d]efault spillovers can be large when nodes inside the network are more exposed to losses outside the network or when the topology of the network implies a higher degree of connectivity among nodes'(p. 38). K. James et al., (2019), Network Contagion and Interbank Amplification during the Great Depresion, Journal of political Economy, Vol. 127, Nr.2, pp. 465–507.

if it is needed. Whatever the situation, the taxpayer seems the only material backstop for those activities.

Three of the most important shadow banking activities will be reviewed with a focus on the externality-causing activities.[575] Needless to say, because of its nature shadow banking activities require significant macroprudential and regulatory attention owing to the large amounts of risk they can accumulate and the fact that risk transformation happens imperfectly, that is, there is tail risk left behind in the shadow banking entities that has the potential to cause significant externalities. That is derived from what is called 'tail interdependence'[576] which can be defined as the situation where extreme outcomes for some variables are informative about such outcomes for other variables. Polanski and Stoja extend the concept of multi-information to quantify tail interdependence at different levels of extremity, decompose it into systemic and residual part and measure the contribution of a constituent to the interdependence of a system.[577]

An extra complication is that shadow banking risk is distributed over a cascade of (offshore) entities and therefore multiple balance sheets, in contrast to a traditional banking entity where risk transformation occurs on a single balance sheet.[578]

11.7.2 Securitization

Securitization[579] as a technique dates back to the late 1970s when there was insufficient bank capital to provide mortgages for all the baby boomers. Trying to offload existing mortgages to institutional investors in order to free up capital was only possible when those securities were tradable and (near) risk-free. The securitization process does exactly that: it redistributes packages of loans (which can be mortgages or student, car, medical, infrastructure or personal loans), through a cascade of entities to arrive at a special-purpose vehicle (SPV) that securitizes the pool of assets into certificates that can be bought by individual investors. They now carry a proportion of the intrinsic risk that is in the

---

[575] It is impossible to provide a full review of the techniques, and therefore the focus will be on the externality-inducing elements of the shadow banking activities as that is what links to a Pigovian application in the shadow banking sector.

[576] See also: A. Polanski and E. Stoja, (2016), Extreme Risk Interdependence, ESRB Working Paper Series Nr. 12, June. They decompose tail risk interdependence into systemic and residual interdependence and measure the contribution of a constituent to the interdependence of a system. Also interesting is their analysis of the symmetry of the interdependence structure in the tails (pp. 8 ff). Rigibon complements with his analysis regarding the relationship between contagion, spillover and interdependence. See in detail: R. Rigobon, (2016), Contagion, Spillover and Interdependence, Bank of England Staff Working Paper nr. 607, August. It contains a full review of the empirical literature on international spillovers and contagion. Also: R.D.F. Harri et al., (2016), Systematic Tail Risk, Bank of England Staff Working Paper Nr. 637, December.

[577] A. Polanski and E. Stoja, (2015), Extreme Risk Interdependence, Bank of England Staff Working Paper, Nr,. 563, November. They further assess: a) tail independence; b) whether an empirical interdependence structure is generated by a theoretical model; and c) symmetry of the interdependence structure in the tails.

[578] E. Perotti, (2013), The Roots of Shadow Banking, CEPR Paper, Nr. 69.

[579] A. Jobst, (2008), What is Securitization, Finance and Development, September, pp. 48–49.

[580] The drivers behind the rise in investor demand for securitized products in the run-up to the crisis

underlying pool of assets. Over time, however, securitization became mainly a demand-driven product,[580] where investors could indicate their preference for how much risk they were willing to tolerate (tranching).[581]

A critical component in understanding the securitization system is that tranching allows a pool of assets of a certain quality or assets of different qualities to arrive with a securitized product. Alternatively, a pool of assets with different qualities may result in a securitized asset with a quality different (and often better) from the aggregate asset qualities that underlie the securitized product.[582] The material chance of tail risk remaining in the shadow banking entity has two principal drivers: (1) The risk transformation process occurred imperfectly leaving tail risk behind in the shadow banking entity. Tail risk[583] emerges when the risk distribution in an asset (or in this case a pool of assets) is skewed or abnormal, leaving more risk at the tail ends of the distribution curve. Econometric models do not perform well when quantifying these risks,[584] (2) When credit risk is not passed on to the other parties in the credit intermediation chain leaving manufactured tail risk in the shadow banking entity.

This occurred in the newer securitization models where the securitization SPV and/or its parent bank provided constant liquidity or even buy-back facilities to the buyers of the certificates. The implication was that potential exposures would land on the balance sheet of the SPV and ultimately the parent bank. However, on the books of the shadow banking entities or banks one could only observe the highest quality securities (the lower tranches were sold off, but as noted the risk often (partially) remained).[585]

The direct consequence is that those FIs that engaged in securitization activities enhanced their profitability and magnified the scope for leverage, enhancing their

have long been ignored. More recently it was identified that both agency problems and neglected risks played an important role in driving investor demand for non-traditional securitizations prior to the crisis; see S. Chernenko, S. Hanson and A. Sunderam, (2014), The Rise and Fall of Securitization, NBER Working Paper Nr. 20777.

581 See in detail: S. Claessens et al. (2012), Shadow Banking: Economics and Policy, IMF Staff Discussion Note, SDN 12/12, December, pp. 6–10.

582 See for a detailed analysis of the securitization process: Z. Poszar, (2008), The Rise and Fall of the Shadow Banking System, Regional Financial Review, July, pp. 13–25. For a detailed analysis of the intermediation process see: Z. Poszar, T. Adrian, A. Ashcraft and H. Boesky, (2013), Shadow Banking, Federal Reserve Bank of New York Economic Policy Review, December, pp. 1–16.

583 M. Knaup, and W. Wagner, (2010), Measuring the Tail Risks of Banks, Working Paper; W.S. Frame, L. Wall and L.J. White, (2012), The Devil is in the Tail: Residential Mortgage Finance and the U.S. Treasury, Working Paper Federal Reserve Bank of Atlanta 2012, Financial Markets Conference; M.R.C. van Oordt and C. Zhou, (2013), Systematic Tail Risk, DNB Working Paper, Nr. 400.

584 F. Battaglia and A. Gallo, (2012), The Impact of Securitization on Tail and Systemic Risk: Evidence From the Financial Crisis, Working Paper.

585 V.V. Acharya, T.F. Cooley, M.P. Richardson and I. Walter, (2010), Regulating Wall Street: The Dodd Frank Act and the New Architecture of Global Finance, Wiley and Sons, Hoboken, Chapter 4.

profitability even further[586] and leading to a cascade of derivative products that had no real portfolio of assets underlying them.[587] The argument that securitization allowed FIs to free up balance sheet capacity for more lending toward the real economy needs to be nullified as lending can occur out of the different components of an FI's funding structure. Unfortunately it must be observed that even monetary policy makers are seduced by that invalid argument as the ECB, starting in mid-2014, aspires to free up capital at European banks by buying asset-backed securities that they have in portfolio, supported by regulators.[588] Remarkably enough, the securitization market rebounded vividly after the dust of the financial crisis settled, particularly in the US.[589]

Credit creation following the freeing up of the banks' balance sheets should also bring inflation at target levels.[590] The unnecessary monetary intervention reveals not only a misunderstanding of some basic economic principles, but encourages using monetary tools to facilitate continued neoliberal intervention. That intervention now targets the central democratic decision-making system,[591] as monetary policy runs ahead of democratic decision-making on what essentially are societal challenges, the answers to which require democratic legitimation and re-affirm Rajan's contemplation that finance adds riskiness to this world rather than reducing it, on aggregate.[592]

Loan modification in the case of securitized loans also unbalances the relationship between lender and borrower.[593] Empirical evidence provides some support to the proposition that securitization leads to lower levels of win-win (benefiting both the borrower and

---

[586] W. Jiangli and M. Pritsker, (2008), The Impact of Securitization on bank Holding Companies, FDIC/FRB Working Paper; W. Jiangli, M. Pritsker and P. Raupach, (2007), Banking and Securitization, FDIC Working Paper.

[587] That happened because the demand for those products was higher than the supply despite the fact that in the years before the crisis the industry produced over 1 Trillion USD in securitized assets.

[588] J. Brunsden et al. (2014), Draghi's ABS-Market Revival Set for Boost from Regulators, Bloomberg.com, September 16. Remarkably enough, there seems to be no relationship whatsoever between the size of the program suggested by the ECB and the actual securitization market in Europe (see: C. Altomonte and P. Bussoli, (2014), Asset-Backed Securities: They Key to Unlocking Europe's Credit markets, Bruegel Policy Contribution, Nr. 2014/7) hinting at a shadow agenda on behalf of the ECB.

[589] T. Alloway, (2014), Sliced and Diced Debt Deals Make Roaring Comeback, Financial Times, June 4.

[590] Low or no inflation is, however, caused by the deleveraging that is ongoing at the level of households, corporations and governments alike and reflects the decrease in purchasing power in large parts of society due to unemployment and a variety of austerity measures. Low inflation is therefore totally acceptable and perfectly explainable and cannot warrant monetary intervention.

[591] See: S. Fleming and C. Giles, (2014), Bank of England: Crashing the Party, Financial Times, June 24.

[592] R.G. Rajan, (2005), Has Financial Development Made the World Riskier?, NBER Working paper, Nr. 11728.

[593] Also: G. Anderson et al., (2018), Lending Relationship and the Collateral Channel, Bank of England Staff Working Paper Nr. 768, November 16. Collateral and private information are substitutes in mitigating credit frictions.

the lender) loan modification, in that securitized loans are more likely to be foreclosed upon when they go into default than non-securitized loans.[594] Solomon demonstrates that the legal structure of the securitization process and the type of entities involved facilitate the shifting of the default risk to non-adjusting creditors. He further demonstrates how the potential gain from externalizing default risk creates distorted incentives for asset securitization. That leads in turn to its excessive use, even when economically inefficient.[595] Beyond the reduced clarity of the mortgage title[596] and the asymmetric information

[594] T. Piskorski, A. Seru and V. Vig, (2010), Securitization and Distressed Loan Renegotiation: Evidence from the Subprime Mortgage Crisis, Chicago Booth School of Business Research Paper, Nr. 09-02; J.P. Hunt, (2010), What Do Sub-Prime Securitization Contracts Actually Say About Loan Modification? Preliminary Results and Implications, Berkeley Center for law, Business and the Economy Working Paper. The current monetary policies also add to inequality as they favor investors in certain securities over others. See, for instance, regarding the inclusiveness of Abenomics in Japan: C. Aoyagi et al., (2015), How Inclusive is Abenomics?, IMF Working Paper Series Nr. WP/15/54, Washington D.C. They observe a 'positive effect on average income growth, but an adverse effect on income equality'. The package of structural reforms planned under Abenomics is found to be effective in increasing both average income growth and income equality. The main policy implication of their analysis is that 'full implementation of structural reforms– especially labor market reforms–is necessary to both foster growth and increase equality'. Also: D. Furceri et al., (2016), The Effects of Monetary Policy Shocks on Equality, IMF Working Paper Series Nr. WP/16/245, December. They focus on the effect of monetary policy shocks on income inequality. They conclude that 'contractionary (expansionary) monetary actions increase (reduce) income inequality. The effect, however, varies over time, depending on the type of the shocks (tightening versus expansionary monetary policy) and the state of the business cycle, and across countries depending on the share of labor income and redistribution policies.' They also evidence that 'the effect is larger for positive monetary policy shocks, especially during expansions'... and that 'the effect is larger in countries with higher labor share of income and smaller redistribution policies'. Please observe their literature references (pp. 22–24), which include some interesting items. More straightforward are the conclusions of D. Domanski et al., (2016), Wealth Inequality and Monetary Policy, BIS quarterly Review, March, pp. 45–64. Their simulation suggests that wealth inequality has risen since the Great Financial Crisis. While low interest rates and rising bond prices have had a negligible impact on wealth inequality, rising equity prices have been a key driver of inequality. A recovery in house prices has only partly offset this effect. Their conclusion that monetary policy 'may' have added to inequality can be seen I guess as professional courtesy. See a contrario: A. Samarina and A. Nguyen, (2019), Does Monetary Policy Affect Income Inequality in the Euro Area, DNB Working Paper Nr. 626, March 8. The latter find that expansionary monetary policy in the euro area reduces income inequality, especially in the periphery countries. J. Frost and R. van Stralen, (2018), Macroprudential Policy and Income Inequality, DNB Working Paper Nr. 598, June 1; A. Colciago et al., (2018), Central bank Policies and Income and Wealth Inequality: A Survey, DNB Working Paper Nr. 594, May 22.

[595] D. Solomon, (2012), The Rise of a Giant: Securitization and the Global Financial Crisis, American Business Law Journal, Vol. 49, Issue 4, pp. 859 ff.

[596] A.J. Levitin, (2013), The Paper Chase: Securitization, Foreclosure and the Uncertainty of the Mortgage Title, Duke Law Journal, Vol. 63, pp. 637–734. Further: securitization leads to excessive (insufficient) foreclosures in a bad state if the mortgage pool is of low (high) quality; see: J. Kuong and J. Zeng, (2015), Servicing Securitization through Inefficient Foreclosure, Working Paper, September, mimeo and S. Krueger, (2014), The Effect of Mortgage Securitization on Foreclosure and Modification, Working Paper, mimeo.

distribution across the parties involved in the securitization process,[597] the securitization process facilitates bubble creation,[598] ambiguity[599] and fire sales.[600]

In the Netherlands the real estate sector[601] has been particularly prone to price inflation[602] due to excessive debt liquidity availability,[603] where asset pricing was no longer supported by and disconnected from economic fundamentals.[604] The imperfect tranching and subsequent information asymmetry[605] magnified that effect, and more liquidity

[597] M. Pagano and P. Volpin, (2012), Securitization, Transparency and Liquidity, London Business School Working Paper.

[598] X. Dou and J. Wang, (2014), Asset Securitization and Bubbles: An Illustration of Subprime Mortgage Default Crisis, Advances in Economics and Business, Vol. 2, Issue 2, pp. 112–119.

[599] A.G. Anderson, (2013), Ambiguity in Securitization Markets, Cornell University Johnson School Research Paper Series, Nr. 5-2013.

[600] A. Schleifer and R.W. Vishny, (2010), Asset Fire Sales and Credit Easing, American Economic Review: Papers & Proceedings, Vol. 100, Issue 2, pp. 46–50. Credit easing has often been used to successfully reduce stress in financial markets, thus avoiding larger output losses. The question that emerged was whether credit easing is also a viable policy tool to cope with banking crises. Jácome et al. conclude that credit easing leads to a sharp increase in domestic currency depreciation, high inflation and a substantial reduction in economic growth in a large panel of emerging and developing economies. For advanced economies, they find the effects to be benign. Credit easing with a view toward reducing systemic stress during a banking crisis doesn't seem to be a walk in the park and may fuel adverse macroeconomic repercussions. See in detail: L.I. Jácome et al., (2018), Is Credit Easing Viable in Emerging and Developing Economies? An Empirical Approach, IMF Working Paper Nr. WP/18/43. Also: R. Barnichon et al., (2016), Theory Ahead of Measurement? Assessing the Nonlinear Effects of Credit Market Shocks, CEPR Discussion Papers Nr. 11410.

[601] Also in the US as generally understood: A.J. Levitin, A.D. Pavlov and S.M. Wachter, (2009), Securitization: Cause or Remedy of the Financial Crisis? Georgetown Law and Economics Research Paper, Nr. 1462895.

[602] There is, EU wide, a material subsidization of home ownership that should not be underestimated in terms of its impact on housing prices. Fatica and Prammer conclude that tax benefits to homeowners reduce the user cost of housing capital by almost 40% compared to the efficient level under neutral taxation. The bulk of the subsidies stems from under-taxation of the return to home equity, while the average contribution of the tax rebate for mortgage interest payments is driven down by relatively low loan-to-value ratios applied. In detail: S. Fatica and D. Prammer, (2017), Housing and the tax Sytem: How large are the Distortions in the Euro Area? ECB Working Paper Nr. 2087, July 12.

[603] Besides the typical demand-supply relationship, the liquidity availability (and the innovative product design it triggered) was considered the major driver behind the housing bubble in The Netherlands. See the official reporting: Tweede kamer der Staten-Generaal, Parlementair onderzoek 'Huizenprijzen', Eindrapport van de tijdelijke commisie huizenprijzen, En reconstructive van twintig jaar stijgende huizenprijzen, Tweede Kamer, vergaderjaar 2012–2013, 33194, nr. 3, pp. 7–8.

[604] In the period 2017–2019 a similar phenomenon occurred in that market. The Dutch Central Bank reported in their most Recent Financial Stability Report that materially elevated housing prices and global debt levels are the two dominant themes in terms of financial stability issues; see DNB, (2019), Overzicht Financiële stabiliteit (Financial Stability Report), Spring edition, June 5, via dnb.nl.

[605] See in detail: D.O. Beltran and C.P. Thomas, (2010), Could Asymmetric Information Alone Have Caused the Collapse of Private-Label Securitization?, International Finance Discussion Papers, FED US.

became available for an asset class than a fully informed free market would engage in.[606] That enhanced liquidity resulted in a deterioration of underwriting conditions creating a vicious cycle.[607]

What still seems to be very often misunderstood is the fact that (besides demand and supply but only to a (very) minor extent) asset pricing[608] is a function of the liquidity availability in the market.[609] Let's look quickly at some details: In the early 1980s, business

[606] A. Fostel and J. Geneakoplos, (2011), Tranching, CDS and Asset Prices: Bubbles and Crashes, Princeton Working Paper; J.C. Stein, (2010), Securitization, Shadow Banking and Financial Fragility, Harvard University Working Paper; S. Liu et al., (2017), What Drives Systemic Credit Risk? Evidence from the US State CDS Market, Working Paper, mimeo.

[607] A.J. Levitin and S.M. Wachter (2012), Explaining the Housing Bubble, Georgetown Law Journal, Vol. 100, Issue 4, pp. 1177–1258; M.N. Baily, R.E. Litan, and M.S. Johnson, (2008), The Origins of the Crisis, Fixing Finance Series, Nr. 3, Brookings Institute; M. Aalbers, (2017), The Financialization of Housing: A Political Economy Approach, Abingdon. In recent years similar events are repeating themselves. See in detail: T. Blackwell, and S. Kohl, (2017), Varieties of Housing Finance in Historical Perspective: The Impact of Mortgage Finance Systems on Urban Structures and Homeownership. MPIfG Discussion Paper Nr. 17/2, Köln, Max-Planck-Institut für Gesellschaftsforschung; S. Kohl, (2018), More Mortgages, More Homes? The Effect of Housing Financialization on Homeownership in Historical Perspective, Politics & Society, published online January 27; H. Joebges et al., (2015), What Causes Housing Bubbles? A Theoretical and Empirical Inquiry, Berlin Working Paper on Money, Finance, Trade and Development Nr. 1, November. As was discussed previously the housing market has recovered and the Trump administration announced it considers privatizing the two GSEs (Fannie Mae and Freddie Mac) as a good idea. So housing markets have recovered but there is equal consensus that risks remain (see: Housing and Mortgage Markets May Have Recovered, but Risks Remain, 2018, September 11, Knowledge@Wharton via wharton.upenn.edu). The problem is not the reform of the GSEs (insofar as they really took place already), but that 'broader changes need to be made across the entire mortgage landscape to stabilize the system, even before the final state of the GSEs is fully determined'. See in detail: R. Koss, (2017), Stabilizing the System of Mortgage Finance in the United States, IMF Working Paper Nr. WP/17/186, August. See footnote 48 p. 27 and reference list (pp. 30 ff) for proposals released so far to reform the GSE model and housing finance market. Koss however indicates that it is not clear if any of the systematic proposals offer an appropriate path forward (p. 27) as '[m]any of them are based on the idea of multiple entities for which the government would provide catastrophic insurance for securities, but not the debt of the entities themselves. The fatal flaw of these proposals is that there are increasing returns to scale in underwriting and securitization, so it is quite likely that the result would be rapid consolidation…'. He concludes in sadness when pointing out that 'it may be that "GSE reform" is so buried in ancient culture wars that a new approach is needed altogether.' One of the lessons to be learned but often forgotten is that complexity and lack of transparency create an environment for opportunistic behavior by private agents that can have serious spillover effects.

[608] A. Buraschi and C. Tebaldi, (2017), Asset Pricing in Network Economies with Systemic Risk, Working Paper, version November 10. See also: D. Acemoglu, et al., (2017), Microeconomic Origins of Macroeconomic Tail Risks, American Economic Review, Vol. 107, Issue 1, pp. 54–108; S. Azizpour, et al., (2018), Exploring the Sources of Default Clustering, Stanford Working Paper, November 15; Journal of financial economics, Vol. 129, Issue 1, pp. 154–183; A. Barattieri, (2016), Banks Interconnectivity and Leverage, CEPR Discussion Papers 11502; B. Herskovic, (2018), Networks in Production: Asset Pricing Implications, Journal of Finance, online edition, April 16.

[609] How that relationship works mathematically is still largely undefined. Nevertheless, the causality has been repeatedly proven. See in detail regarding the relationship between liquidity and real estate prices: A. Cesa-Biachi et al., (2015), Global Liquidity, House Prices, and the Macroeconomy: Evidence from Advanced and Emerging Economies, IMF Working Paper, Nr. WP/15/23. What has also been proven is that capital flows when being synchronized tend to create co-moving real

lending equated to around 40% of GDP on average in advanced economies, while mortgage lending was around 25%. By the time of the financial crisis, mortgage lending had grown to 75% of GDP while business lending had only grown slightly, to 45%.[610] I have lamented elsewhere throughout the two volumes that the change in business model for bank was underlying the real estate dynamics we have witnessed in recent decades. And the regulator helped: for asymmetric risks, which is the case more for real estate than business loans, lower capital requirements were foreseen, and the mortgage loan book is easier and more profitable to securitize.[611] The real estate markets we live with are not the unchangeable consequence of divine law or the consequence of demand and supply but the product of 'financialization', just like neoliberalism is as well. It's the consequence of an unwritten script meticulously executed by policy makers around the world. The monetary easing by central banks has allowed, at almost no expense for banks, to raise capital and earn still a decent risk-adjusted return on mortgage loan books. It is regulatory-facilitated market failure of unprecedented scope and scale rather than the often proclaimed demand-supply imbalance. Banks will ultimately always be able to develop or create credit faster than homes can be built.[612] Demand and supply side policies need a decent rethink and so do fiscal and financial policy regarding real estate.

---

estate prices. A good case study has been the financial integration of the US banking sector in the 80/90's. They resulted in synchronized housing prices and co-movements across the different US states. It implicitly also proves that free or freeing capital flows has material contagion (due to idiosyncratic risks) effects across regions and between capital market movements and the emergence of contagion. In more recent times, synchronization of housing prices has been fueled by another capital market movement, that is, securitization. Demand or price shocks on the securitization market affect directly the lending ability of agents. Mortgage lending then becomes dependent on the conditions in the securitization market. See in detail: A. Landier et al., (2017), Banking Integration and House Price Comovement, ESRB Working Paper Nr. 48, June.

[610] K. Allen, (2018), No, the Housing Crisis Will Not Be Solved By Building More Homes, Financial Times Alphaville, October 15.

[611] The fact that we have witnessed an avalanche of (new) real estate brokers in recent decades, up till today, helps as well. If you put a barber at every corner of the street, we'll all end up bald.

[612] It is therefore very unconvincing that the ECB chair Draghi felt the need to reply with the statement that QE is also good for normal people as the family home makes up a large part of family wealth. Due to QE house prices have risen throughout Europe in recent years. The problem is, it is a latent equity that only matters once liquidated. Very few people feel the need to liquidate their homes just to get their hands on the capital gain. As they need to buy anew the capital gain is lot and handed for free to the new seller of the home they are buying. Banks who allow to re-up the mortgage loan to consume the equity built up just keep the circus going. See also on the various elements: J. Ryan-Collins, (2018), Blame the Bank: How Finance Caused Today's Housing Crisis, October 18, via cityam.com. The stricter mortgage regulation post-crisis was offset by QE, which did not only create additional liquidity but also drove down rates. Because of the latter not only banks but also non-FI players entered the field. Other studies analyzed the existence of 'wealth effects' derived from net equity (in the form of housing, financial assets and total net worth) on consumption. In general terms, wealth effects are found to be relatively large and significant for housing wealth, but less so for other types of wealth, including stocks. Also, the analysis shows how these estimated marginal propensities to consume (MPC) from wealth are closely linked to household characteristics, including income and demographic factors. See in detail: C. Caceres, (2019), Analyzing the Effects of Financial and Housing Wealth on Consumption using Micro Data, IMF Working Paper Nr. WP/19/115,

Liquidity shocks are therefore crucial to be managed by an adequate set of monetary policy and housing market tools.[613] For real estate in particular, elements such as real estate culture can be added, that is, how often do individuals and families move home in their lives and how many own their homes rather than rent, a characteristic that differs significantly per country. Household debt levels relative to GDP have risen rapidly in many countries over the past decade.[614] What is the (macroeconomic) impact of that happening? Well, besides the fact that it reduces purchasing power immediately for items beyond loan and interest repayment,[615] it reduces materially the long-term growth potential of an economy.[616] Lombardi et al. figured out that that effect, that is, real

May; also: K. Ji et al. (2019), Disentangling the Effect of Household Debt on Consumption, CPB Discussion Paper, April, The Hague. The latter estimate the contemporaneous relationship between household debt and consumption (the Netherlands). They observe that the average consumption of households with high debt has decreased much more during the crisis than that of other households. They disentangle this into an effect through the availability of credit for direct consumption and an effect through household debt overhang. On the micro level, the consumption drop is the sharpest for the households who are less able or willing to finance one-off high consumption with new debts after the crisis. On the macro level, however, the drop in consumption of households who have negative home equity for a longer period had a much bigger impact on macro consumption, because their number sharply increased during the crisis. Precautionary savings motives among the highly indebted households contributed most to the consumption decline during the crisis.

[613] See for an analysis how different choices and policies yield different results in both advanced and emerging economies: C. banti and K. Phylaktis, (2017), Global Liquidity, House Prices and Policy Responses, Working Paper, February 14, mimeo.

[614] A. Zabai, (2017), Household Debt: Recent Development and Challenges, in BIS Quarterly Review, Q$, December, pp. 39–54.

[615] Even though that can mean that household debt can boost consumption in the short run given the real estate-related payments that need to be made.

[616] Also: A. Alter et al., (2018), Understanding the Macro-Financial Effects of Household Debt: A Global Perspective, IMF Working Paper Nr. WP/18/76, April. They also confirm the negative relationship between household debt and future GDP growth. Three mutually reinforcing mechanisms explain this relationship: (1) debt overhang impairs household consumption when negative shocks hit (also for the inverse relationship: L. Zhang, (2019), Do House Prices Matter for Household Consumption, CPB Discussion Paper, April); (2) increases in household debt heighten the probability of future banking crises, which significantly disrupts financial intermediation; (3) crash risk may be systematically neglected due to investors' overoptimistic expectations associated with household debt booms. Flexible exchange rates, higher financial development and inclusion are found to mitigate the described impact. Further and concluding in the same direction: A. Mian and E. Verner, (2017), Household Debt and Business Cycles Worldwide, Quarterly Journal of Economics, pp. 1–63; S. Albanesi et al., (2017), Credit Growth and the Financial Crisis: A New Narrative, NBER Working Paper Nr. 23740, National Bureau of Economic Research, Cambridge, MA; J.L. Arcand, (2015), Too Much Finance? Journal of

estate-related debt reducing economic growth accelerates as household debt[617] levels rise. Coibion et al. stayed short of confirming the hypothesis that the greater the inequality, the higher the aggregate household debt.[618] Lombardi et al.[619] further demonstrated that 'the negative long-run effects on consumption tend to intensify as the household debt-to-GDP ratio exceeds 60%.[620] For GDP growth, that intensification seems to occur when the ratio exceeds 80%'.[621] What has also become clear however is that mortgage lending compromised corporate (or business) lending.[622] There seems to be a crowding out of business loans favoring mortgage loans. That works pre-crisis or systemic event but also ex post. During the latter phase, once again the business loan

Economic Growth, Vol. 20, Issue 2, pp. 105–148; M. Baron and W. Xiong, (2017), Credit Expansion and Neglected Crash Risk, Quarterly Journal of Economics, pp. 713–764; M. Drehmann et al., (2017), Accounting for Debt Service: The Painful Legacy of Credit Booms, BIS Working Paper Nr. 645.

617 Household debt is on the rise globally. See for a US analysis: A. Haughwout et al., (2019), Trends in Household Debt and Credit, FRB of NY Staff Report Nr. 882, April.

618 O. Coibion et al., (2017), Does Greater Inequality Lead to More Household Borrowing? New Evidence from Household Data, Federal Reserve Bank of Minneapolis Working Paper Nr. 17-04, Minneapolis, MN. The hypothesis behind the analysis is that low-income households increased their demand for credit to finance higher consumption expenditures in order to 'keep up' with higher-income households. They concluded that 'low-income households in high-inequality regions accumulated less debt relative to income than their counterparts in lower-inequality regions'.

619 M. Lombardi et al., (2017), The Real Effects of Household Debt in the Short and the Long Run, BIS Working Papers Nr. 607, January. Cross-country differences can often be explained away by referring to the different degree of legal protection (full recourse vs. non-recourse) of creditors as a variable in the analysis (pp. 19 ff). They conclude on that specific matter that 'household borrowers' actual debt service burden is higher for countries with stronger creditor protection than those with weaker creditor protection to the extent that lower loan spreads due to stronger creditor protection do not fully offset higher debt service burden, and thus household consumption and GDP growth is more likely to be lower for these countries' (p. 23). See also footnote 19 for an overview of supporting literature.

620 Also: J. Nakajima, (2018), The Role of Household Debt Heterogeneity on Consumption: Evidence from Japanese Household Data, BIS Working Paper Nr. 736, July 24, via bis.org. Japanese households tend to save more when they have a higher level of debt. In particular, they are sensitive to unexpected declines in income. These results are consistent with findings for other countries. Savings are driven by anticipated unemployment and later stages of life. Reducing sensitivity is possible through a funded pension model and health insurance system.

621 See also: A. Chudik, et al., (2017), Is There a Debt-Threshold Effect on Output Growth?, Review of Economics and Statistics, Vol. 99, Issue 1, pp. 135–150.

622 V. Meursault, (2017), Bank Credit Supply and Shadow Mortgage Growth, Working Paper, October 15, mimeo.

segment is hit as lending behavior during that period will be very sensitive to the riskiness of banks' mortgage portfolios.[623] Even more, more mortgages have a strong potential to lead to lower growth.[624]

Lian[625] from his side has added to our understanding by shedding light on the fundamental versus speculative demand nature of housing. Although since the financial crisis it

---

[623] L. Zhang et al., (2017), Did Pre-Crisis Mortgage Lending Limit Post-Crisis Corporate Lending? Evidence from UK Bank Balance Sheets, Bank of England Working Paper Nr. 651, March. They conclude '[b]anks having more mortgages to borrowers with impaired credit history, or more mortgages to the self-employed, or mortgages with higher loan to value ratios prior to the crisis reduced their lending to non-financial businesses more' (pp. 23–25). That seems to be very much in line with the findings of D. Bezemer et al., (2017), The Shift in Bank Credit Allocation: New Data and New Findings, DNB Working Paper Nr. 559, June. In their international study covering 78 jurisdictions they categorize bank lending in four categories: home mortgages, consumer credit, bank loans to non-bank financials and loans to non-financial business. They document key trends including the shift in bank credit allocation away from traditional business lending particularly in advanced economies. They suggest substantial consequences of this 'debt shift' for growth, income distribution and macroeconomic resilience. They point at financial deregulation as (one of) the main culprit(s) for this debt shift. The shift was ubiquitous across jurisdictions and can therefore not be traced back to micro-level bank features. The shift away from business loans was also identified here toward mortgages. That seems a general conclusion; see also: D. Bezemer et al., (2016), More Mortgages, Lower Growth? Economic Inquiry, Vol. 54, Issue 1, pp. 652–674; O. Jorda et al., (2016), The Great Mortgaging: Housing Finance, Crises, and Business Cycles, Economic Policy. Vol. 31, Issue 85, pp. 107–152; A. Samarina, and D. Bezemer, (2016), Do Capital Flows Change Domestic Credit Allocation?, Journal of International Money and Finance, Vol. 62(C), pp. 98–121. The shift away from business loans toward real estate is also driven by the effects of the corporate sector transition toward a greater use of intangible assets (with lower collateral values). The amount of C&I (commercial and industrial) loans thereby drops proportionately in the portfolio of business loans. Dell'Ariccia et al. argue that banks do not shrink their balance sheets but rather reallocate their lending capacity away from commercial loans and primarily toward real estate and liquid assets. That seems to be in line with A. Caggese and A. Perez, (2017), Capital Misallocation and Secular Stagnation, Finance and Economics Discussion Series Nr. 2017-009, Board of Governors of the Federal Reserve System (U.S.).Also: G. Beningo and L. Fornaro, (2017), Stagnation Traps, ECB Working Paper 2038, March. See regarding the dynamics of resource misallocations during and after the great recession: T. Libert, (2017), Misallocation Before, during and After the Great Recession, Banque de France Working Paper Nr. 658, December 29. Thibault provides an exact decomposition of allocational inefficiency into three components: labor misallocation, capital misallocation and a third term representing the interplay between both. Misallocation increased substantially between 1997 and 2007. The main feature behind the rise in misallocation during the crisis is the predominance of the interplay component. It suggests that one should pay special attention to mechanisms disrupting both labor and capital markets in the wake of financial crises. Finally, allocational efficiency remains rather constant after 2010. Also: F. Schivardi et al., (2017), Credit Misallocation during the European Financial Crisis, Bank of Italy Working Paper Nr. 1139, September 27. They find that during the Eurozone financial crisis (i) undercapitalized banks were less likely to cut credit to non-viable firms; (ii) credit misallocation increased the failure rate of healthy firms and reduced the failure rate of non-viable firms; and (iii) nevertheless, the adverse effects of credit misallocation on the growth rate of healthier firms were negligible.

[624] D. Bezemer, et al., (2016), More Mortgages, Lower Growth? Economic Inquiry, Vol. 54, Issue 1, pp. 652–674. Also: S. Bahaj, et al., (2016), The Residential Collateral Channel, Centre for Macroeconomics Discussion Paper, Nr. 2016-07; O. Jordà, et al., (2016), The Great Mortgaging: Housing Finance, Crises, and Business Cycles. Economic Policy, pp. 107–152.

[625] W. Lian, (2019), Fundamental and Speculative Demands for Housing, IMF Working Paper Nr. WP/19/63, March.

has often been lamented that there has been and is a housing bubble in a variety of countries in the world (and in particular a number of concentrated cities), it remained and remains challenging to quantify the phenomenon and the size of such a bubble. It seems fairly straightforward in theory.[626] One sets apart demand for real estate from the belief (or shift in belief) about future house prices. If that price change gets disconnected from the fundamentals one could argue there is some sort of a bubble in the making.[627] A lot of the bickering that is still going on has to do with the 'relative' inability of 'existing approaches to separate the roles of belief about future house prices disconnected[628] from today's fundamentals and demand for housing services in a house price cycle'.[629] An economic cycle is demand driven, a bubble belief-driven one could say. Whatever the case, the impact of housing speculation[630] and the role of credit policy have been well documented by now.[631]

---

[626] R. Dieci and F. Westerhoff, (2009), A Simple Model of a Speculative Housing Market, Working Paper Nr. 62 uni. Bamberg, February, mimeo via uni-bamberg.de.

[627] G. Kaplan et al., (2017), The Housing Boom and Bust: Model Meets Evidence, National Bureau of Economic Research, Working Paper Nr. 23694. Also as Kreisman Working Paper Series in Housing Law and Policy 2017/51, University of Chicago. Also: N. Barberis, et al. (2018), Extrapolation and Bubbles, Journal of Financial Economics, Vol. 129, Issue 2, pp. 203–227. See also for the moral hazard with mortgage insurers in the run up to the great recession (expanded insurance on high-risk mortgages at the tail-end of the housing boom, contradicting the industry's own research regarding house price risk). In detail: N. Bhutta and B.J. Keys, (2018), Eye Wide Shut? The Moral Hazard of Mortgage Insurers during the Housing Boom, NBER Working Paper Nr. 24844, July.

[628] G. Sutton et al., (2017), Interest Rates and House Prices in the United States and Around the World, BISWorking Paper Nr. 665, October 13, via bis.org. They find a surprisingly important role for short-term interest rates as drivers of house prices, especially outside the US. In addition, they find a strong link between US interest rates and changes in house prices in other countries. Studies that treat housing as a form of investment whose alternative is renting property predict much higher interest rate sensitivity of house prices than those we obtain.

[629] W. Lian, (2019), Fundamental and Speculative Demands for Housing, IMF Working Paper Nr. WP/19/63, March, p. 1.

[630] A. Mian and A. Sufi, (2019), Credit Supply and Housing Speculation, NBER Working Paper Nr. 24823, April (revised edition). They conclude '[s]peculation is a critical channel through which credit supply expansion affects the housing cycle. The surge in private label mortgage securitization in 2003 fueled a large expansion in mortgage credit supply by lenders financed with noncore deposits. Areas more exposed to these lenders experienced a large relative rise in transaction volume driven by a small group of speculators, and these areas simultaneously witnessed an amplified housing boom and bust'. Cox and Lugvigson discuss the two driving forces of house price fluctuations: credit conditions and beliefs. Changes in credit conditions are positively related to the fraction of riskier non-conforming debt in total mortgage lending. Credit conditions explain quantitatively large magnitudes of the variation in quarterly house price growth and also predict future house price growth. Beliefs bear some relation to contemporaneous house price growth but have little predictive power. In detail: J. Cox and S.C. Lugvigson et al., (2019), Drivers of the Great Housing Boom-Bust: Credit Conditions, Beliefs, or Both? NBER Working Paper Nr. 25285, January, Revised.

[631] Recently: Z. Gao et al., (2018), Economic Consequences of Housing Speculation, Working paper, mimeo, December, including a massive literature list with supporting documentation (pp. 28–31). Regarding the role of credit policy, see: M. Pidkuyko, (2019), Heterogeneous Spillovers of Housing Credit Policy, University of Manchester Working Paper, mimeo, February.

Lian has recently separated demand from belief dynamics using a 'user-cost-of-housing' feature. Demand versus belief will have a different impact on the feature that makes them better identifiable. The housing price at this stage is a 'given and a positive belief shift in the form of higher expected future prices reduce user-cost-of-housing today, whereas a positive demand shift drives it up'. User-cost-of-housing is sensitive to demand only and therefore both can be measured accurately.[632] Lian develops an interesting model based on four types of shocks which the housing market undergoes as it evolves in any given market cycle: (1) housing demand shocks (which shift housing preferences of both current and future generations equally and permanently), (2) belief shocks (which shift housing preference of future generations permanently), (3) total factor productivity (TFP) shocks (which shift the productivity of producing non-housing goods)[633] and (4) shocks to structure prices.[634]

What stays somewhat of a mystery however is the valuation of the baseline scenario. Rather than use prices,[635] one could turn to an intrinsic valuation approach (modeled based on adjusted net rental income) or to what is known as the borrowing capacity approach to housing valuation.[636] The borrowing capacity of households, together with

---

[632] There is still no consensus however on how to determine the user-cost-of-housing at an aggregate level. Suggestions are CPI rent, but that has its own challenges. Lian suggests as an alternative model 'to construct user-cost-of-housing as the difference between house price today and the discounted value of expected house price in the next period' (p. 2). He immediately admits that the challenge here is that there is no reliable measurement of house price expectations at a national level. He circumvents that problem by using the supply in the market for housing services as a proxy. He argues '[u]nder the assumption that the market for housing services is under perfect competition, the price of housing services (user-cost-of-housing) is the same as the cost of producing housing services, which further depends on housing services production function and input costs' (p. 2, also for further details on how he constructs the (de)nominator).

[633] By including this factor he avoids capturing conventional business cycle shocks.

[634] W. Lian, (2019), Fundamental and Speculative Demands for Housing, IMF Working Paper Nr. WP/19/63, March, pp. 3–4 for his findings. Also: C. Burnside, et al., (2016), Understanding Booms and Busts in Housing Markets, Journal of Political Economy, Vol. 124, Issue 4, pp. 1088–1147; E. Glaeser, et al., (2018), The Economic Implications of Housing Supply, Journal of Economic Perspectives, Vol. 32, Issue 1, pp. 3–30; R. Greenwood et al., (2018), Bubbles for Fama, Journal of Financial Economics, https://doi.org/10.1016/j.jfineco.2018.09.002. Davis and Haltiwanger highlight that housing markets, credit conditions and boom-bust cycles impact young firm survival and performance. See in detail: S.J. Davis and J. C. Haltiwanger, (2019), Dynamism Diminished: The Role of Housing markets and Credit Conditions, NBER Working Paper Nr. 25466, January. Alo: B. Őzturk et al., (2018), The Relation between Supply Constraints and House Price Dynamics in The Netherlands, DNB Working Paper Nr. 601, July 18. In particular, the latter look at whether income shocks lead to stronger house price increases in regions characterized with higher supply constraints. Their results suggest that income shocks lead to significantly larger increases in house prices in municipalities that are relatively more supply constrained.

[635] Prices are often driven by the dynamics of appraisals by realtors. There is a systemic dimension to appraiser valuation and pricing in real estate markets. See, for instance, in the Netherlands where the central bank concluded that the quality, reliability and independence of appraiser reporting are poor: R. van der Molen and R. Nijskens, (2019), De kwaliteit en onafhankelijkheid van woningtaxaties, DNB Occasional Studies, Amsterdam.

[636] See M. Andrle and M. Plašil, (2019), Assessing House Prices with Prudential and Valuation Measures, IMF Working Paper Nr. WP/19/59, March. See Chap. 2 for the borrowing capacity approach (pp. 6–13) and the more familiar intrinsic value approach in chapter three (pp. 14–19).

their down payment, implies how much housing they can attain. That would allow to the degree of market over-and undervaluation.

Securitization as a technique removes assets (mortgage loans in this case) from an FI's balance sheet. That frees up capital for the bank to issue more mortgage loans than would be the case if that securitization process had not occurred and the loans were held by the bank until maturity. Such excess[637] liquidity created through the securitization process flows to the market as additional credit liquidity. That excess liquidity,[638] enhanced under circumstances by elevated levels of economic growth, leads to asset bubbles.[639]

Securitization has caused banks to be able to free up more liquidity for more mortgages, thereby enhancing their return. By the same token, the excess liquidity, which lowers the net margin on mortgages compared to a situation without securitization but on a much large capital base, leads to asset inflation,[640] concentration of risk[641] and ultimately bubble creation, besides the moral hazard created by the disentanglement of the value chain in

They applied both methods to value real estate in the Czech Republic and the level of over- or undervaluation. See also: N. Geng, (2018), Fundamental Drivers of House Prices in Advanced Economies, Working Paper Nr. WP/18/164, International Monetary Fund, Washington DC and N. Philiponnet, and A. Turrini, (2017), Assessing House Price Developments in the EU, Discussion Paper Nr. 048/2017, European Commission, Brussels.

[637] 'Excess' refers here to levels elevated above those normally warranted given the level of economic activity and interest rates in the market at any given point in time.

[638] Y. Amihud et al., (2005), Liquidity and Asset Prices, Foundations in Trends and Finance, Vol. 1, Nr. 4, pp. 269–364. Also: J. Tripathy, (2017), Bubble Equilibria with Credit Misallocation, Bank of England Working Paper Nr. 649, February. It was concluded that asset bubbles raise interest rates and lower investment productivity by directing financial resources to the sector with lower financial constraints. Such states are coined 'bubbly growth traps'. In such a state, 'asset bubbles not only crowd-out investments, but also absorb valuable financial resources that (if used in real economic activity) provide the wealth essential to initiate financially constrained, productive projects in the future'... '[t]The loss of financial resources to asset bubbles can rule out the transition to the high investment productivity phase when the economy never acquires the wealth necessary to make the said transition.' Also: A. Martin and J. Ventura, (2016), Managing Credit Bubbles. Journal of the European Economic Association, Vol. 14, Issue 3, pp. 753–789, June.

[639] A. Bruggeman, (2007), Can Excess Liquidity Signal an Asset Price Boom?, NBB Working Paper, Nr. 117; B. Bierut, (2013), Global Liquidity as an Early Indicator of Asset Price Booms, DNB Working Paper, Nr. 377. It also leads to excessive private debt, see: M. Jarmuzek and R. Rozenov, (2017), Excessive Private Sector Leverage and Its Drivers: Evidence from Advanced Economies, IMF Working Paper Nr. WP/17/72, March, in particular pp. 14–17. Excessive private debt also triggers collateral implications. It was observed that monetary policy is more effective as private household debt increases. Although the responsiveness of household consumption has diminished since the crisis, household balance sheets are not the culprit. The factor that can explain reduced responsiveness to monetary policy is overall economic uncertainty (since the financial crisis of 2008). See in detail: G. Gelos et al., (2019), Has Higher Household Indebtedness Weakened Monetary Policy Transmission?, IMF Working Paper Nr. WP/19/11, January.

[640] P. Hörhdahl and F. Packer, (2006), Understanding Asset Prices An Overview, BIS Working Papers Nr. 34.

[641] Through tranching; see in detail: A. Antoniades and A. Tarashev, (2014), Securitizations: Tranching Concentrates Uncertainty, BIS Quarterly Review December, pp. 37–53. The new December 2014 issued securitization standards contribute very little to solving this problem; see in extenso: BIS, (2014), Revisions to the Securitizations Framework, Basel III Document.

the credit intermediation business. That happens through securitization where the initial issuer of debt seems to be less concerned about the long-term creditworthiness of the debtor. That is reflected in lower underwriting standards, which are or should always be relative to the price levels of the assets financed. Those price levels also function often as collateral to the loan and determine the interest rate charged, reflecting the intrinsic riskiness of the loan.[642] The financialization here leads to a distancing and non-accountability of the capital-providing parties involved in the transaction.[643] So when endorsing securitization,[644] the regulator is required to understand that the stability of the financial market in terms of asset pricing stability, for real estate in this particular case, takes a backseat. The current post-crisis interventions, which do not enhance credit supply to the real economy, but lead only (through direct liquidity injections) to a lowering of the cost of supplying liquidity, have material welfare consequences.[645] That is a concerning step back by the regulator from viewing 'stability of the public markets which include the real estate market as a public good' as a leading principle in public policy. That is all the more true since the value of the family home is often a very large part of a family's wealth in the eurozone[646]

---

[642] Banks tend to extract informational rents through collateral use. The rent extraction declines post-IPO and for lower-risk firms. See: B. Xu et al., (2016), Do Banks Extract Informational Rents through Collateral, Hong Kong Institute for Monetary Research Working Paper Nr. 1, January. The rent extraction of shadow banks follows the fact that banks reduced lending to risky lenders. The leveraged lending guidance of banks, which encouraged banks to reduce lending to leveraged borrowers, had an adverse effect on the profitability and investment levels of the affected firms, that is, the lenders of last resort, non-banks extract rents from borrowers with limited access to external finance. In detail: S. Biswas et al., (2019), Non-Bank Loans, Corporate Investment, and Firm Performance, Working Paper February 1, mimeo.

[643] S. Kohl, (2018), More Mortgages, More Homes? The Effect of Housing Financialization on Homeownership in Historical Perspective, Politics and Society, Vol. 46, Nr. 2, pp. 177–203.

[644] J. Hessel and J. Peeters, (2011), Housing Bubbles, the Leveraging Cycle and Role of Central Banking, DNB Occasional Studies, Vol. 9, Nr. 5; A. Nocera and M. Roma, (2017), House Prices and Monetary Policy in the Euro Area: Evidence from Structural VARs, ECB Working Paper Nr. 2073, June; A. Martin et al., (2018), The Financial Transmission of Housing Bubbles: Evidence from Spain, bank of Spain Working Paper Nr. 23. They show that if firms and banks face collateral constraints, a housing bubble initially raises credit demand by housing firms while leaving credit supply unaffected. It therefore crowds out credit to non-housing firms. If time passes and the bubble lasts, however, housing firms eventually pay back their higher loans. This leads to an increase in banks' net worth and thus to an expansion in their supply of credit to all firms: crowding-out gives way to crowding-in.

[645] J. Huang and J. Wang, (2010), Market Liquidity, Asset Prices and Welfare, Journal of Financial Economics, Vol. 95, Issue 1, pp. 107–127, previously released as MIT Working Paper (2008) and NBER Working Paper, Nr. 14058 (2008).

[646] L. Arrondel et al., (2014), Wealth and Income in the Euro Area. Heterogeneity in Households' Behaviours, ECB Working Paper Series, Nr. 1709. Mortgage debt is a key contributor to high household indebtedness, which tends to be a key vulnerability to the financial sector. Higher LTV ratios tend to occur in places with strong house price growth. In technical terms, these mortgages have a higher LTI-ratio than on average as well as longer maturities. Mutatis mutandis households with mortgages that have these two characteristics are more vulnerable in the event of a major adverse shock to household income. These trends are more pronounced among younger households. They are also concentrated in regions with imbalances in the housing market. See, for instance, for a Canadian study on the matter: O. Bilyk et al., (2017), Analysis of Household vulnerabilities Using Loan-Level Mortgage Data, Bank of Canada, Financial System Review, November, pp. 21–33.

and instability can cause material economic hardship given the debt financing nature of most purchases.[647]

Housing bubbles, ripping apart the wealth creation process, particularly of the middle class——as the family home is the central asset in their wealth build-up—is a matter of public interest and the market should not be left on its own in this matter.[648] It can only be agreed with Wolf that a more material reform of housing and real estate finance in general is needed in order to validate the experiences of the recent past.[649] Different and novel insights should be warranted a place in this future discussion. Justiniano et al. recently

[647] One would think that the financial crisis provided sufficient insights into the matter for it not to happen again. However, a decade after the financial crisis we are drawing the same conclusions all over again. See, for instance, D. Olick, (2018), Run-Up in Home Prices is 'Not Sustainable': Realtors' Chief Economist, cnbc.com, May 30, update.

[648] To put it differently: Asset bubbles in assets that have a widespread utility function have regressive welfare effects. By raising the housing price, the bubble benefits high-income savers but negatively affects low-income borrowers, claim Graczyck and Phan. By creating a bubble in the market price, 'savers' demand for the housing asset for investment purposes imposes a negative externality on borrowers, who only demand the housing asset for utility purposes'. There is also a feedback loop: 'high income inequality depresses the interest rates, facilitating the existence of housing bubbles, which in turn have regressive welfare effects'. The key aspect here is that 'by creating a bubble in the market price of housing, savers' demand for the housing asset for investment purposes imposes a negative pecuniary externality on borrowers, who only demand the housing asset for utility purposes' (p. 3). See in detail: A. Graczyck and T. Phan, (2018), Regressive Welfare Effects of Housing Bubbles, Federal Reserve Bank of Richmond Working Paper Nr. WP18-10, April 13. What is particularly interesting in this study is the fact that they distinguish between buyers with savings and those that need to borrow to acquire a home (that has a satisfiable utility function to both). Those buyers with liquidity will acquire housing in excess of the satiation level, because they would like to use the housing asset as an investment vehicle to save for old age (pp. 10 ff). By extension this category also includes buyers who buy-to-let as thus as a 100% investment vehicle. Housing bubbles have opposite effects on borrowers and savers. They highlight: '[t]he housing bubble increases the return from real estate investment for high-income savers, who demand storage of value, and hence increases their welfare (relative to the bubbleless benchmark). In contrast, the housing bubble reduces the welfare of borrowers, because it raises the price of housing and the speculative demand of savers for the housing asset crowds out the allocation of housing to borrowers, who in equilibrium have a relatively higher marginal utility from housing' (pp. 2–3). By positively affecting high-income savers and negatively affecting low-income borrowers, the housing bubble thus has regressive welfare effects. The crowding effect on housing that was prevalent in the housing bubble case is absent in the presence of a pure bubble (p. 4). The logic behind it is simple. In a pure bubble, the price of an asset without a fundamental value inflates and constitutes an investment opportunity for savers. In such a pure bubble, an endogenous segmentation exists, because only savers purchase a bubble asset for investment purposes (although one can imagine non-savers could borrow to do so as well). Credit-constrained borrowers have no demand for the asset (besides the aforementioned consideration) and thus no crowding out occurs. No negative externality is put on borrowers in such cases and this is in contrast to the housing market. Also: E. Farhi, and J. Tirole, (2012), Bubbly liquidity. The Review of Economic Studies, Vol, 79, Issue 2, pp. 678–706; S. Giglio, et al., (2016), No-Bubble Condition: Model-Free Tests in Housing Markets, Econometrica, Vol. 84, Issue 3, pp. 1047–1091; T. Hirano, and N. Yanagawa, (2017), Asset Bubbles, Endogenous Growth, and Financial Frictions, Review of Economic Studies, Vol. 84, pp. 406–443; D. Ikeda, and T. Phan, (2016), Toxic Asset Bubbles, Economic Theory, Vol. 61, Issue 2, pp. 241–271; B. Zhao, (2015), Rational Housing Bubble, Economic Theory, Vol. 60, Issue 1, pp. 141–201.

[649] M. Wolf, (2014), Deeper Reform of Housing Finance is Vital for Stability, Financial Times, September 18.

raised the point that although the housing boom[650] is explained by credit expansion combined with lending constraints in the collateral market, however, when analyzing the housing dataset pre- and post-crisis they observe four aspects the unprecedented rise in home prices, the surge in household debt, the stability of debt relative to home values and the fall in mortgage rates. They conclude it is difficult to reconcile with the idea that attributes the housing boom to looser borrowing constraints associated with lower collateral requirements.[651] In fact, a slackening of collateral constraints at the peak of the lending cycle should trigger a fall in home prices. Their argument is that post-crisis our focus should migrate from a loosening of constraints on lending to obstacles to lending in order to understand the boom phase of the cycle.[652]

Cerutti et al.[653] analyzed the conflict between the objective of increasing access to housing finance[654] and the dangers associated with fast-growing housing credit.[655] Their findings can be summarized as follows:

---

[650] Between 2003 and 2006, the Federal Reserve raised rates by 4.25%. Yet it was precisely during this period that the housing boom accelerated, fueled by rapid growth in mortgage lending. There is deep disagreement about how, or even if, monetary policy impacted the boom. Using heterogeneity in banks' exposures to the deposits channel of monetary policy, Drechsler et al. show that Fed tightening induced a large reduction in banks' deposit funding, leading them to contract new on-balance-sheet lending for home purchases by 26%. However, an unprecedented expansion in privately securitized loans, led by non-banks, largely offset this contraction. Since privately securitized loans are neither GSE-insured nor deposit-funded, they are run-prone, which made the mortgage market fragile. See in detail: I. Drechsler et al., (2019), How Monetary Policy Shaped the Housing Boom, NBER Working Paper 25649, March. The more recent re-emergence of privately securitized mortgages has closely tracked the recent increase in rates. When the share of mortgage lending during the great recession slowed at larger banks, shadow banks and fintech lenders stepped in. However, that did not prevent the more relevant role that small banks started to play in this field. Small banks were twice as responsive as shadow banks to fill the gap left by the big banks' retreat, and more than four times more responsive than fintech lenders. Small banks are key in the economy despite the rise in shadow banking and the ascent of fintech business models. In detail: T.A. Begley and K. Srinivasan, (2019), Northeaster U. D'Amore-McKim School of Business Research Paper Nr. 3317672, May 21.

[651] Benes et al. evidence how household demand for housing, house prices and bank mortgages are intertwined in what we call a deadly embrace. Without macroprudential policies, this deadly embrace naturally leads to housing boom and bust cycles, which can be very costly for the economy. See in detail: J. Benes et al., (2016), Mitigating the Deadly Embrace in Financial Cycles: Countercyclical Buffers and Loan-to-Value Limits, IMF Working Paper Nr. 16/87, April.

[652] See in detail: A. Justiniano et al., (2015), Credit Supply and the Housing Cycle, Federal Reserve Bank of NY, Staff Nr. 709, February. Also observe the attractive reading list on pp. 37–42 on the matter of credit supply and (housing) booms.

[653] E. Cerutti et al., (2015), Housing Finance and Real-Estate Booms: A Cross-Country Perspective, IMF Staff Discussion Note, June, SDN/15/12.

[654] See for a historical perspective on housing finance: T. Blackwell and S. Kohl, (2017), Varieties of Housing Finance in Historical Perspective. The Impact of Mortgage Finance Systems on Urban Structures and Homeownership, MPIfG Discussion Paper 17/2, Max-Planck-Institut für Gesellschaftsforschung, Köln, February.

[655] Many studies highlight the strong link that exists between housing prices and credit. Often there is a full synchronization between the credit cycle and housing prices. See, for instance, I. Ioannou,

- Housing finance characteristics vary widely across countries, and several characteristics are correlated with the relative depth of mortgage markets. Larger loan-to-value ratios (LTVs),[656] larger reliance on wholesale funding and, to some extent, longer loan maturities are positively correlated, together with institutional quality and macro stability, with the depth of a country's mortgage markets and homeownership rates (with the associated benefits of higher school attainment, higher social capital, lower crime).
- Some of the housing finance characteristics associated with deeper mortgage markets are also associated with increased risks of crisis. For example, higher LTVs are associated with excessively rapid house-price and credit growth during booms, and wholesale funding is associated with worse outcomes in the aftermath of housing booms.[657]
- Both advanced and emerging markets should avoid relaxing house financing standards in order to achieve deeper mortgage markets, and focus first on doing so through improving institutions (e.g. legal rights) and the macroeconomic environment.
- Macroprudential policies,[658] and in particular housing finance regulation, should be the first line of defense for handling mortgage market booms, as their narrow focus gives them an advantage over monetary policy. However, their effectiveness beyond the short run has yet to be proven.
- The role of monetary policy in addressing house-related credit booms should not always be downplayed. Despite the absence of important inflation[659] pressures, about 60% of the identified past real-estate booms occurred as a result of, or at the same time as, rapid

(2018), Housing Price, Credit, and Output Cycles: How Domestic and External Shocks Impact Lithuania's Credit, IMF Working Paper Nr. WP/18/160, July; E. Dermani et al., (2016), Is a Bubble Forming in Swedish Housing Prices? Sveriges Riksbank Economic Review pp. 2 ff; N. Geng, (2017), Are House Prices Overvalued in Norway?—A Cross-Country Analysis, Norway 2017 Selected Issues, IMF Country Report Nr. WP/17/181; Z. Smidova, (2016), Betting the House in Denmark, OECD Economics Department Working Paper Nr. 1337.

[656] Ungerer documents that expansionary monetary policy leads to increased household leverage and housing sales rates. Both the housing sales rate and loan-to-value ratios increase after expansionary monetary policy. The interaction between credit frictions and housing market search frictions generates endogenous movements in the loan-to-value ratio, which amplify the economy's response to monetary policy; see: C. Ungerer, (2015), Monetary Policy, Hot Housing Markets and Leverage, Finance and Economics Discussion Series Divisions of Research & Statistics and Monetary Affairs Federal Reserve Board, Washington, D.C., Working Paper Nr. 2015-048, May 22.

[657] D.K.G. de Araujo et al., (2018), Loan-to-Value Policy and Housing Finance: Effects on Constrained Borrowers, BIS Working Paper Nr. 673, November 17, via bis.org. The objective of LTV limits for housing loans is to increase borrower resilience and to lower bank losses during downturns. Imposing LTV limits shifts several characteristics of the loan contract and influences borrowers' behavior. In all segments of housing finance, constrained borrowers end up meeting the new LTV limit. However, the impact on middle-income borrowers is greater. In this segment, borrowers affected by the new regulation purchase more affordable houses.

[658] See for a write-up of the FED's framework for implementing monetary policy prior to the expansion of its balance sheet during the financial crisis: A. Kroeger et al., (2017), The Pre-Crisis Monetary Policy Implementation Framework, Federal Reserve Bank of New York Staff Reports, Nr. 809, March.

[659] See about the globalizing nature of inflation (and its limits): R. Bems et al., (2018), Is Inflation Domestic or Global. Evidence from Emerging Markets, IMF Working Paper Nr. WP/18/241, November.

economic growth and broad high credit growth in the economy. Monetary policy would be a necessary complement of macroprudential measures in those cases.

- Dealing effectively with real-estate booms requires a broad mix of policies. Macroprudential and monetary policies are key ingredients, but fiscal incentives and house supply considerations are structural country-specific elements that may bear heavily on the probability of booms occurring and the potential costs of a bust.

Bubb and Krishnamurthy[660] trash the Dodd-Franck Act[661] in terms of protection of the housing and mortgage market. The specific provisions on mortgage lending and securitization are not designed to protect the economy from a housing bubble. Instead, these reforms 'tinker with the incentives of securitizers and lenders to prevent their exploitation of naïve investors and borrowers. In particular, they require securitizers to retain credit risk and lenders to assess borrowers' ability to repay. This approach misses the mark'. Indirect incentive-based regulation is ineffective in a bubble. It relies on 'rational behavior by supposedly sophisticated parties, will do little to protect the economy from a bubble. They might even increase systemic risk by concentrating mortgage risk in large financial institutions'. They suggest a wide array of 'direct regulations' to limit mortgage leverage, debt-to-income levels and other contractual features that enable or induce borrowers to take out larger loans. They further show how such limits can curb bubbles, lower defaults and reduce household exposure to housing risk.[662] Elul[663] demonstrates that private-securitized

[660] Turk argues that 'given the rollback of Dodd-Frank that is currently being contemplated within Congress and the Trump administration will further marginalize the post-crisis rulemakings and reinforce the centrality of regulation by settlement' in particular in areas such as securitization; see: M.C. Turk, (2018), Securitization Reform After the Crisis: Regulation by Rulemaking or Regulation by Settlement?, Review of Banking and Financial Law, Vol. 37, pp. 870–874.

[661] D. Schwarcz and D. Zaring, (2017), Regulation by Threat: Dodd-Frank and the Nonbank Problem, The University of Chicago Law Review, Vol. 84, pp. 1813–1881. About the relationship between 'too big to fail', moral hazard, bailouts and corporate responsibility: S.L. Schwarcz, (2017), Too Big to Fool: Moral Hazard, Bailouts, and Corporate Responsibility, Minnesota Law Review, Vol. 102, pp. 761–801. Schwarcz argues that the too-big-to-fail problem is exaggerated, but that moral hazard 'causes systemically important firms to engage in excessive risk-taking. Such risk-taking is more likely to be caused by other factors, including a legally embedded conflict between corporate governance and the public interest that allows managers of those firms to ignore systemic externalities'. This is a pure legal problem that can and should be addressed by making managers account for systemic externalities.

[662] R. Bubb and P. Krishnamurthy, (2015), Regulating Against Bubbles: How Mortgage Regulation Can Keep Main Street and Wall Street Safe- From Themselves, University of Pennsylvania Law Review, Vol. 163, Nr. 6 (May), pp. 1539–1630.

[663] R. Elul, (2015), Securitization and Mortgage Default, Federal Reserve Bank of Philadelphia Working Paper Nr. 51-15. The global crisis narrative has suggested that an expansion of subprime credit was the reason for rising mortgage defaults, leading to the large-scale recession in 2007–2009. Taking a closer look at the characteristics of subprime credit holders over the period, it is argued that the growth in mortgage defaults did not occur predominantly amongst subprime credit holders. Instead, it was real estate investors that played a critical role in the rise in mortgage debt, specifically among the middle and the top of the credit score distribution. See in detail: S. Albanesi et al., (2017), Mortgage Default during the Great Recession Came from Real Estate Investors, not Subprime Credit Holders, October 3, via voxeu.org

loans perform worse than observably similar, non-securitized loans, which provides evidence for adverse selection. The effect of securitization is strongest for prime mortgages, he shows, which have not been studied widely in the previous literature and particular prime adjustable-rate mortgages (ARMs): These become delinquent at a 30% higher rate when privately securitized. However, early defaulting loans account for this: those that were so risky that they defaulted before they could be securitized. For subprime mortgages, this default effect is concentrated in loans with low or no documentation of income and assets, although prime private-securitized mortgages are riskier overall (although the effect is stronger for low-/no-documentation loans).[664]

Cesa-Bianchi et al. analyzed housing price data in emerging economies and concluded that housing prices grow faster, are more volatile, less persistent and less synchronized across emerging countries than in advanced economies.[665] We also find that they correlate with capital flows more closely than in advanced economies. Changing capital flows and in extremis a liquidity shock have a much stronger impact on house prices and consumption in emerging markets than in advanced economies.[666] In terms of the synchronization of housing prices across countries and the extent to which it arises in developed economies the question remained about what drives the synchronization. Katagiri[667] assessed the conditions surrounding international housing price synchronization and concluded that (1) the degree of synchronization has been rising since the 1970s,[668] and (2) a large heterogeneity in the degree of synchronization exists across countries and (international-oriented) cities. The heterogeneity itself is partly accounted for by the progress in financial and trade openness. An analysis at intercity level then demonstrates that there is a certain level of international synchronization mainly driven by the city-level connectivity between large and international cities. House price dynamics are connected with macroeconomic performance, and this through a variety of channels for which open cities provide a good incubator. Concerning the question how housing prices are synchronized through various channels the following observations were made: (1) house price synchronization reflects synchronization of real economic activity and economic variables like consumption, input, output and so on. It determines the real demand for real estate by households. International price synchronization can occur through import and export relations; (2) prices are synchronized due to simultaneous changes in financial factors. Global financial conditions or

---

[664] That is economically and policy-wise materially important, as the largest chunk of the mortgage market were prime instruments.

[665] See, for instance, in the case of China: R.N. Lai and R. Van Order, (2016), Shadow Banking and the Property Market in China, Working Paper, March, mimeo. They found that house prices grew 'more rapidly with availability of shadow banking funds', which have grown rapidly.

[666] A. Cesa-Bianchi et al., (2015), Global Liquidity, House Prices, and the macro-economy: Evidence from Advanced and Emerging Economies, IMF Working Paper Series, Nr. WP/15/23.

[667] M. Katagiri, (2018), House Price Synchronization and Financial Openness: A Dynamic Factor Model Approach, IMF Working Paper Nr. WP/18/208, September.

[668] The variance explained by the global common factor rose from 10 to 40% during 1970–2016. That in itself is concerning as 'a risk to macro-financial stability through the housing cycle in one country could be amplified and transmitted to another country, thus possibly causing macro-financial instability on a global scale' (Ibid., p. 4).

expectations regarding future economic performance of a region could and does lead to synchronization of house prices across the countries involved. Also synchronization of capital flows as global cash pools access (housing) markets simultaneously will lead to synchronization of housing prices.[669] Financial openness can thus lead to synchronization in an independent way meaning separate from the synchronization induced by real economic activity through trade linkages.[670] Geng[671] made a comprehensive attempt to bring together the fundamental drivers of house prices (both institutional and structural factors). He identified the following dynamics. On the demand side: (1) household disposable income, (2) household net financial wealth, (3) declining interest rates, and (4) demographic trends.[672] On the supply side: undersupply conditions (i.e. below demographic needs). Regarding the structural and institutional factors he highlights: (1) differences in price elasticity of housing supply (given a certain long-run demand). The more inelastic the supply curve the higher the supply gap, the higher the price will evolve; (2) tax incentives for mortgage financing and home ownership, which reduce the user cost of housing (that can include absence of capital gains tax, tax relief on mortgage interest payments, etc.); (3) rent controls, by reducing incentives to use housing efficiently (renters stay in real estate exceeding their needs, creating queues and reducing effective housing supply). Geng argues that policy, institutional and structural factors are found to be important determinants of long-run equilibrium house prices and that assessing the sustainability of house price developments has become an integral part of macro-financial surveillance. Structural reforms in the housing market should be considered alongside macroprudential instruments.[673] Also Alter et al.[674] observed an increasing synchronization of housing prices across countries and

[669] As global portfolio volumes get bigger, so does the tendency to spread capital across countries and regions as a dynamic of diversification. But as the research demonstrates, this behavior leads to synchronization across different housing markets.

[670] Ibid. pp. 4–5.

[671] N. Geng, (2018), Fundamental Drivers of House Prices in Advanced Economies, IMF Working Paper Nr. WP/18/164, July, in particular pp. 7–13.

[672] See regarding the relationship between demography and inflation: M. Juselius and E. Takáts, (2018), The Enduring Link Between Demography and Inflation, BIS Working Paper Nr. 722, May 7. Inflationary pressure rises when the share of dependants increases and, conversely, subsides when the share of working age population increases. This relationship accounts for the bulk of trend inflation. It predicts rising inflation over the coming decades.

[673] Geng claims, and I fully concur, that structural reforms can over time improve housing affordability, thereby reducing debt accumulation and enhancing financial stability. These structural reforms include, but are not limited to, 'reforms to raise the long-run elasticity of housing supply, phasing out rent control, and reducing tax incentives for home ownership and debt financing. Such instruments may complement and support the more commonly used macroprudential tools such as limits on loan-to-value ratios, as the impact of reforms on supply and demand fundamentals may shape longer-term expectations in the housing market (p. 21)'. See also: A.K. Anundsen and C. Heebøll, (2016), Supply Restrictions, Subprime Lending and Regional US House Prices, Journal of Housing Economics, Vol. 31, pp. 54–72; S. Hviid and A. Kuchler, (2017), Consumption and Savings in A Low Interest-Rate Environment, Working Paper Nr. 116, Danmarks National bank.

[674] A. Alter et al., (2018), House Price Synchronicity, Banking Integration, and Global Financial Conditions, IMF Working Paper Nr. WP/18/250. Also: O. Akinci, and J. Olmstead-Rumsey. 2017. How Effective Are Macroprudential Policies? An Empirical Investigation." Journal of

regions fuelled by the 'abundance of liquidity owing to accommodative financial conditions'. Synchronicity across major cities may differ from that of their respective countries', perhaps due to the influence of global investors on local house price dynamics. Looser global financial conditions are associated with greater house price synchronicity but can also be associated with a stronger transmission of external shocks. It comes, in such a context, as no surprise that 'house price growth in countries that experience lower house price synchronicity with the rest of the world, on average, are more sensitive to macroprudential policies that are aimed at reducing domestic vulnerabilities, compared to high synchronicity countries'.[675] Liquidity plays a much more central role in the real estate industry and (residential) housing prices that are typically assessed. The most vocal author so far on the issue is Josh Ryan-Collins. He makes it clear that we are at risk of pushing a whole generation out of the housing market by allowing the relentless feedback loop between liquidity and housing prices to continue. He laments '[u]nlimited credit and money flows into an inherently finite supply of property, which causes rising house prices, declining home ownership, rising inequality and debt, stagnant growth and financial instability'.[676] Any material solution will have to break the housing-finance feedback cycle.

Financial Intermediation, Vol. 33 (January), pp. 33–57; C. Badarinza, and T. Ramadorai, (2018), Home away from Home? Foreign Demand and London House Prices, Journal of Financial Economics, Vol. 26, pp. 21–34; E. Cerutti et al., (2017), Housing Finance and Real-Estate Booms: A Cross-Country Perspective, Journal of Housing Economics, Vol. 38 (C), pp. 1–13; M. Demirer et al., (2018), Estimating Global Bank Network Connectedness, Journal of Applied Econometrics, Vol. 33, Issue 1, pp. 1–15; IMF, (2018), House Price Synchronization: What Role for Financial Factors? Global Financial Stability Report, April, Washington, DC.

[675] A. Alter et al., (2018), Ibid. p. 26. Also: M. Katagiri, (2018), House Price Synchronization and Financial Openness: A Dynamic Factor Model Approach, IMF Working Paper Nr. WP/18/209, International Monetary Fund, Washington, DC.; Ò Jordà et al., (2017), The Rate of Return on Everything, 1870–2015, NBER Working Paper Nr. 24,112, National Bureau of Economic Research, Cambridge, MA; K.N. Kuttner, and I. Shim, (2016), Can Non-Interest Rate Policies Stabilize Housing Markets? Evidence from a Panel of 57 Economies, Journal of Financial Stability, Vol. 26 (October), pp. 31–44; A. Landin et al., (2017), Banking Integration and House Price Co-movement, Journal of Financial Economics, Vol. 125, Issue 1, pp. 1–25.

[676] J. Ryan-Collins, (2018), Why Can't You Afford a Home, 1st edition, Polity, Cambridge, UK and K. Allen, (2018), No, the Housing Crisis will not be Solved by Building more homes, FT Alphaville, October 15. See also the documentation for the conference on the same topic at Sustainable Finance Lab Amsterdam, January 15, 2019 as well as K. Haegens, (2019), Econoom Josh Ryan-Collins: 'Stijgende huurprijzen zijn een sociale én economische ramp', De Volkskrant, January 16; J. Ryan-Collins et al., (2017), Rethinking the Economics of Land and Housing, Zed Books, London, UK. The demand-supply relationship is less dominant in the price formation than traditionally thought, and credit liquidity a whole lot more. Ryan-Collins refers to markets where supply of real estate grew much faster than the economy and prices still grew disproportionately. But prices did follow tune with credit availability in those markets. You can expand mortgage credit faster in any situation than the effective supply of real estate. Rising real estate prices are a social and economic demon for a number of reasons: real estate is a low value-add industry, it drains liquidity away from industries and activities where the liquidity would be badly needed, expanding mortgage lending by banks is matched with reduced corporate and business lending, and it reduces purchasing power as households and businesses spend more on real estate year-on-year. It was only two days later that the Dutch scientific council for government policy brought

Not surprisingly, the IMF devoted a whole chapter in its 2019 Global Financial Stability Report on housing prices under the meaningful title 'Downside Risk to House Prices'.[677] Interestingly enough it justified the effort by indicating that large and sudden house price declines can adversely impact macroeconomic performance and financial stability, thereby referring to the 2008 financial crisis episode. Indeed, the many macro-financial linkages that exist between housing and firms, financial intermediaries, consumption, investments, wealth accumulation and its role as collateral all play a role in this context.[678] The IMF researchers (and that makes it interesting) qualify and quantify what they call 'house prices

---

out an extensive report demonstrating pretty much the same as well pointing at the overall issues that money creation in effect is out of control and pointing to the largely uncontrolled ability of banks to increase the money/credit supply. See: WRR, (2019), Geld en schuld. De publieke rol van banken, The Hague, January 17. The liberalization of credit markets and removal of credit guidance are significantly associated with a lower share of lending to non-financial firms also, conclude Bezemer et al. See: D. Bezemer et al., (2018), Credit where it's Due: A Historical, Theoretical and Empirical Review of Credit Guidance Policies in the 20th Century, UCL Institute for Innovation and Public Purpose (IIPP) Working Paper Nr. 2018-11, December, London. Ee also: J. Arcand, et al. (2015), Too Much Finance? Journal of Economic Growth, Vol. 20, Issue 2, pp. 105–148; D. Bezemer, et al. (2016), More Mortgages, Lower Growth? Economic Inquiry, Vol. 54, Issue 1, pp. 652–674; D. Bezemer, et al. (2017), The Shift in Bank Credit Allocation: New Data and New Findings, De Nederlandsche Bank Working Paper Nr. 559, Amsterdam D. Bezemer and L. Zhang, (2019), Credit Composition and the Severity of Post-Crisis Recessions, Journal of Financial Stability, Vol. 42, pp. 52–66; G. Epstein, (2018), On the Social Efficiency of Finance, Development and Change, Vol. 49, Issue 2, pp. 330–352; S. Storm, (2018), Financialization and Economic Development: A Debate on the Social Efficiency of Modern Finance, Development and Change, Vol. 49, Issue 2, pp. 302–329; L. Zhang, (2017), Did Pre-Crisis Mortgage Lending Limit Post-Crisis Corporate Lending? Evidence from UK Bank Balance Sheets, Bank of England Staff Working Paper Nr. 651, London; F. Brever et al. (2018), Scheitern der sozialen Wohnungspolitik: Wie bezahlbaren Wohnraum schaffen? Ifo Schnelldienst Vol. 17, Issue 21, pp. 3–30, Ifo-Institut für Wirtschaftsforschung, via cesinfo-group.de. Anenberg and Kung conclude that the rent elasticity is low, and thus marginal reductions in supply constraints alone are unlikely to meaningfully reduce rent burdens, all pointing at underwriting Ryan-Collins's argument. See: E. Ananberg and E. Kung, (2018), Can More Housing Supply Solve the Affordability Crisis? Evidence from a Neighborhood Choice Model, Finance and Economics Discussion Series 2018-035. Washington: Board of Governors of the Federal Reserve System, https://doi.org/10.17016/FEDS.2018.035

[677] IMF, (2019), Global Financial Stability Report, Chapter two: Downside Risk to House Prices, April 4, Washington D.C. Also: B. Algieri, (2013), House Price Determinants: Fundamentals and Underlying Factors, Comparative Economic Studies Nr. 55, pp. 315–341; G. Kaplan et al., (2017), The Housing Boom and Bust: Model Meets Evidence, NBER Working Paper 23694, National Bureau of Economic Research, Cambridge, MA.

[678] Also: J. Favilukis et al., (2017), The Macroeconomic Effects of Housing Wealth, Housing Finance, and Limited Risk Sharing in General Equilibrium, Journal of Political Economy, Vol. 125, Issue 1, pp. 140–223. On the matter of the relation between household debt and house prices see: A. Mian and A. Sufi, (2016), Who Bears the Cost of Recessions? The Role of House Prices and Household Debt, Chapter 5 in Handbook of Macroeconomics, edited by John B. Taylor and Harald Uhlig, Elsevier, Amsterdam. Also on the same matter: J. Cloyne et al., (2017), The Effect of House Prices on Household Borrowing: A New Approach, NBER Working Paper Nr. 23861, September. The latter conclude twofold: First, there is a clear and robust effect of house prices on

at risk', a measure of downside risks to future house price growth and this across a set of emerging and advanced economies and cities. They indicate four items or conditions if you want to predict heightened downside risks to house prices: (1) lower house price momentum, (2) overvaluation (house price misalignment) measured as house prices-to-GDP-per capita, (3) excessive credit growth,[679] and (4) tighter financial conditions (such as restrictions on loan-to-value and debt-service-to-income ratios).[680] In particular, overvaluation and credit growth tend to have severe effects on downside house price risk and therefore seem in line with the above-mentioned findings of Josh Ryan-Collins.

Not only does it predict downside risk to house prices but also downside risk to GDP[681] growth, which then in turn helps predicting financial crises. The IMF also explores the relationship between policies and house prices at risk. While house price levels for them 'should not be considered a direct target for monetary or macroprudential policies or for capital flow management measures', they indicate that 'the link between policy actions and downside risks to house prices can shed light on how these actions map into housing sector vulnerabilities and financial stability'.[682] As expected, tightening of macroprudential

borrowing, but the responsiveness is smaller than recent US estimates. Second, the effect of house prices on borrowing can be explained largely by collateral effects.

679 IMF, (2018), Ibid. p. 70, footnote 19: Credit booms are defined as periods during which the credit-to-GDP ratio is above the long-term trend. Credit booms tend to have a direct effect on house price risk is the consequence that the rapid credit expansion correlates with overstretched household balance sheets. Also: G. Favara and J. Imbs, (2015), Credit Supply and the Price of Housing, American Economic Review, Vol. 105, pp. 958–992; B. Bianchi, (2018), Structural Credit Ratios, ESRB Working Paper Nr. 85, October 15. The macroeconomic variables that correlate most with the credit-to-GDP ratio are economic development, the investment share in GDP and inflation.

680 The model developed builds upon the Growth-at-Risk Model developed by the IMF in their 2017 Global Financial Stability Report. The growth-at-risk approach is a measure for financial stability and links current financial conditions to the distribution of future growth outcomes. See also: T. Adrian et al., (2018), The Term Structure of Growth-at-Risk, IMF Working Paper Nr. WP/18/180, August. They produce a forward-looking analysis, based on historical data.

681 Also: T. Adrian et al., (2019), Vulnerable Growth, American Economic Review, Vol. 109, Issue 4, pp. 1263–1289. L. Agnello and L. Schuknecht, (2011), Booms and Busts in Housing Markets: Determinants and Implications, Journal of Housing Economics, Vol. 20, Issue 3, pp. 171–190.

682 See for the role of shadow banks in the housing sector and its implications: H. Desgagnés, (2017), The Rise of Non-Regulated Financial Intermediaries in the Housing Sector and its Macroeconomic Implications, Bank of Canada Staff working Paper Nr. 36, September. Her results suggest that the non-regulated sector contributes to stabilize the economy by providing an alternative source of capital when the regulated sector is unable to fulfill the demand for credit. As a result, an economy with a large non-regulated sector experiences a smaller downturn after an adverse financial shock. Culp and Neves from their part highlight that the economic purpose of shadow banking is to enable commercial banks to raise funds from and transfer risks to non-bank institutions. In that sense, the shadow banking system is a shock absorber for risks that arise within the commercial banking system and are transferred to a more diverse pool of non-bank capital instead of remaining concentrated among commercial banks. Also, they hint at the fact that most recent and incoming regulations could result in a less stable financial system to the extent that higher regulatory costs on shadow banks like insurance companies and asset managers could discourage them from participating in shadow banking. And the net effect of this regulation, by limiting the amount of market-based capital available for non-bank risk transfer, may well be to increase the concentrations of risk in the banking and overall financial

policies is associated with a reduction in downside risks to house prices. Policies aimed at strengthening the resilience of borrowers, such as limits to the maximum loan-to-value or debt-service-to-income ratios are envisaged. Poghosyan assessed the effectiveness of lending restriction measures, such as loan-to-value and debt-service-to-income ratios. The overall conclusion is that they are effective in curbing house prices and credit. Having said that, their impact is delayed (on average three years) relative to the situations they want to avoid. The impact of the measures is often also asymmetric, that is, tightening and weakening efforts respond differently relative to the target outcome.[683]

Just to be on the safe side, a quick reminder of where shadow banking fits into the picture. Since the '80s, the banking sector has been undergoing three mainstream trends: (i) a secular decline in interest rates, (ii) a reallocation of bank investments from corporate loans toward mortgages and (iii) the rise of shadow banking relative to regulated banking.[684] The downward pressure on real interest rates increases the share of mortgage investments and as a consequence the interbank market for mortgage securities became more liquid. The consequence was that funding liquidity became more liquid. In such a situation shadow banks identified the opportunity to gain competitive advantage over traditional banks with respect to the supply of mortgage loans. The more the economy grew, the more shadow banks issued uninsured deposits. Shadow banks tend not to participate in the deposit insurance mechanism.[685] The inflows experienced since the '80s in the mortgage market are correlated with growth of shadow banking liabilities during that same period. Demonstrating that causality became an absolute necessity when a reallocation of lending toward housing investment rather than physical capital formation impacted productivity as well as financial stability (through fire sales and bank runs). The order is

system. See: C.L. Culp and A.M.P. Neves, (2017), Shadow Banking, Risk Transfer, and Financial Stability, Journal of Applied Corporate Finance, Vol. 29, Issue 4, pp. 45–64.

[683] T. Poghosyan, (2019), How Effective is Macroprudential Policy? Evidence from Lending Restrictions Measures in EU Countries, IMF Working Paper Nr. WP/19/45, February. Also: K. Kuttner, and I. Shim, (2016), Can Non-Interest Rate Policies Stabilize Housing Markets? Evidence from a Panel of 57 Economies, Journal of Financial Stability, Vol. 26, pp. 31–44; L. Jacome, and S. Mitra, (2015), LTV and DTI Limits—Going Granular, IMF Working Paper Nr. WP/15/154, International Monetary Fund: Washington, D.C; E. Cerutti et al., (2017), Housing Finance and Real-Estate Booms: A Cross–Country Perspective, Journal of Housing Economics, Vol. 38, pp. 1–13.

[684] Used as a baseline for identifying the role of shadow banks in the mortgage industry in: S. Pool, (2018), Mortgage Debt and Shadow Banks, DNB Working Paper Nr. 588, March, Amsterdam. The inflow of deposits leads to more mortgage lending and less corporate lending. As housing stock is fixed (or cannot grow as fast as deposits and thus mortgage lending), the value of the collateral rises rather than the volume of collateral. Increasing levels of mortgage loans only supported by higher collateral values dampens productivity and price boom-bust cycles. In order to reduce the involvement of shadow banks in the mortgage industry he suggests restrictions on admissible loan-to-value ratios for mortgage loans to reduce house price and mortgage supply fluctuation as well as the introduction of interest-paying central bank deposits for households to raise the costs for banks to finance themselves with uninsured deposits. See for model development (pp. 12–28) and findings (pp. 29–35).

[685] S. Hanson, et al., (2015), Banks as Patient Fixed-Income Investors, Journal of Financial Economics, Vol. 117, Issue 3, pp. 449–469.

important: deposit inflows coming from the shadow banking market reduce interest rates and increase the share of mortgages on bank balance sheets.[686] That fosters growth in the shadow banking sphere, increasing the financial stability risk. To mimic deposit insurance,[687] shadow banks offer early liquidation options to investors. As such, through regulatory arbitrage they create lower funding costs, while holding liquidity risk on their books. More liquidity at the level of the banks implies more liquid interbank liquidity and trading. Banks can then anticipate paying close to fundamental value for assets. More mortgage loans equals over time a deeper interbank market for mortgage loans. The value of those mortgage assets then increases and fuels further funding liquidity. Shadow banks in this model face less liquidity risk and exploit the regulatory arbitrage model further.

The shadow banking market continues to grow larger and faster than the traditional banking market as long as the mortgage loans segment outgrows the traditional corporate loan market. That dynamic increases overall stability risk, particularly in the light of securitization models that allow banks to take large mortgage loan bundles off their balance sheet. Shadow banks have no need to internalize the cost of fire sales. Why would they? More liquidity in the shadow banking sector triggers the risk that traditional banks must liquidate their assets, thereby reducing liquidity in the interbanking market. In such a scenario, shadow banks that create a lot of uninsured deposits increase the need for traditional banks to rely on central banking liquidity support.[688] However, as that support is not linked to the size of the shadow banking market, it can not only grow disproportionately but also doesn't have to internalize the cost of such scenario, and therefore the increase in liquidity risk isn't properly reflected in the liquidation price of the shadow banking assets,[689]

---

[686] For those who wonder how that last step works: lower interest rates in the market reduce your net interest margin (for a bank). As you only manage that up to a certain point, you need to go with the market dynamics as a bank. At lower interest rates you will prefer loans with decent collateral. Residential houses for mortgages and physical capital for corporate loans both constitute collateral but not of the same quality. More supply of bank funding triggers more demand for both types of loans. But housing supply is more inelastic than business loan demand. The consequence is rising housing prices, thereby increasing the collateral value received by the banks (larger than the collateral of business loans). The reallocation by banks of funding from business loans to mortgage loans makes sense. Collateral with a low supply elasticity demonstrate more price and credit supply fluctuations than collateral with a high(er) supply elasticity.

[687] Regarding the relation between shadow banking, financial stability and deposit insurance: L. Voellmy, (2018), Shadow Banking and Financial Stability under Limit Deposit Insurance, in Shadow Banking: Financial Intermediation beyond Banks (Ed. Esa Jokivuolle), SUERF Conference Proceedings 2018/1, Larcier, pp. 107–111.

[688] S.T. Omarova, (2018), Central banks, Systemic Risk and Financial Sector Structural Reform, in R. Lastra and P. Conti-Browen (eds.), Research Handbook on Central Banking, Edward Elgar Publishing, London. Also: S.R. Das et al., (2018), Systemic Risk and the Great Depression, NBER Working Paper Nr. 25405, December. Their systemic risk measure captures both the credit risk of an individual bank as well as a bank's position in the network. They also find that the pyramid structure of the commercial banking system (i.e. the network's topology) created more inherent fragility. They conclude that network measures such as the discussed eigenvector centrality combined with balance sheet insights provide good prediction regarding survivorship of banks during a crisis.

[689] Liquid interbank markets tend to always lead to excessive liquidity creation (and bank leverage): M. Mink, (2016). Aggregate Liquidity and Banking Sector Fragility, De Nederlandsche Bank Working Paper Nr. 534, Amsterdam; H. DeAngelo, and R.M. Stulz, (2015), Liquid-Claim

simply as they overissue uninsured deposits. It gets worse. Dissatisfied with the idea that classic models of fire sales that emphasize liquidity-constrained natural buyers cannot fully account for the asset fire sales during the financial crisis of 2008, Ebrahimy documented that fire sales may happen even when there is a sizable pool of natural buyers and in the absence of asymmetric information, due to a coordination failure among buyers. When trade is decentralized and participation is endogenous, constrained asset demand and liquidity needs that are expected to increase over time create complementarity among buyers' decisions to wait.[690] This complementarity makes competitive markets prone to coordination failures and fire sales which may be inefficient.[691] Conditions under which markets are fragile: liquidity shocks that are increasing in magnitude over time, a medium degree of liquidity as well as imbalance between sellers and buyers in the market. These fire sales may be inefficient in that they lead to a suboptimally low aggregate trade surplus relative to the equilibrium with the higher asset price.[692] Although holding liquid assets can buffer against liquidity shocks in the market, the question whether and under what conditions holding more liquid assets can make markets less fragile is still an open one. Part of the problem is that investors typically hold a portfolio of assets with different liquidity. Holding liquid assets might function as a buffer but at the same time it might also crowd out buyers and reduce the effective demand for the less liquid assets in the market.[693]

The securitization industry had changed dramatically in the years[694] prior to the crisis and many impediments remain post-crisis[695] to the creation of a level playing field free of

---

Production, Risk Management, and Bank Capital Structure: Why High Leverage is Optimal for Banks, Journal of Financial Economics, Vol. 116, Issue 2, pp. 219–236.

690 Banks constrained by the leverage ratio prefer to first sell assets that are liquid and held in small amounts, while banks constrained by the risk-weighted capital ratio and the liquidity coverage ratio need to trade off assets' liquidity with their regulatory weights. Banks' optimal liquidation strategies translate into moderate fire-sale losses even for extremely large solvency shocks. By contrast, severe funding shocks can generate significant losses. Thus models focusing exclusively on solvency risk may significantly underestimate the extent of contagion via fire sales. Moreover, when studying combined funding and solvency shocks, we find complementarities between the two shocks' effects that cannot be reproduced by focusing on either shock in isolation. In detail: J. Coen, (2019), Taking Regulation Seriously: Fire Sales under Solvency and Liquidity Constraints, Bank of England Working Paper Nr. 793, April 26.

691 E. Ebrahimy, (2019), Inefficient Fire-Sales in Decentralized Asset Markets, IMF Working Paper Nr. WP/19/92, May, pp. 1–4. Let it now be the case that shadow banking entities are largely active in markets and segments with such intrinsic characteristics.

692 E. Ebrahimy, (2019), Ibid. pp. 24–25.

693 Also: B. Chang, (2018), Adverse Selection and Liquidity Distortion. The Review of Economic Studies, Vol. 85, Issue 1, pp. 275–306; J. Dow, and J. Han, (2018). The Paradox of Financial Fire Sales: The Role of Arbitrage Capital in Determining Liquidity, Journal of Finance, Vol. 73, Issue 1, pp. 229–274.

694 However, the regulatory framework has always been quite unstable, see: E.J. Janger, (2002), Muddy rules for Securitization, Fordham Journal of Corporate and Financial Law, Vol. 7, Issue 2, pp. 300–320.

695 M. Segoviano, B. Jones, P. Lindner and J. Blankenheim, (2013), Securitization: Lessons Learned and the Road Ahead, IMF Working Paper, WP/13/255.

regulatory arbitrage[696] and according to globally accepted securitization[697] and loan underwriting standards. But what has become apparent as well is that the volume of securitization, although traditionally associated with credit markets, influences the outcomes of other asset markets. Aksoy and Basso[698] investigated the link between securitization and asset prices and show that increases in the growth rate of the volume of ABS issuance lead to a decline in both the bond and equity premia (and thus overall higher asset values). A Pigovian instrument as outlined is the most adequate ex ante instrument taking into account the fact that securitization enhances bank competition[699] and that intrinsic bank

---

[696] There is an international regulatory market for regulatory arbitrage with material competition in which a large part of the (shadow) banking market participates, however, with some notable exceptions; see: N. Boyson et al., (2016), Why Don't All Bank Practice Regulatory Arbitrage? Evidence from Usage of Trust-Preferred Securities, The Review of Financial Studies, Volume 29, Issue 7, July 1, pp. 1821–1859.

[697] Those standards have been awaited and were under development by the Bank for International Settlements. A consultative document was released in 2013, see: BIS, (2013), Revisions to the Securitization Framework, December. The final securitization framework has been released; see BIS, (2014), Revisions to the Securitization Framework, Basel III Document, Basel Committee on Banking Supervision, Basel. Major changes include the drivers behind risk exposures and the regulatory capital that banks should hold when engaging in various types of securitizations. Ever since the release of those finals standards in 2014 further refinements and updates have been implemented (see also the chapter on securitizations). See: BIS, (2015), Capital Treatment for 'Simple, Transparent and Comparable' Securitizations, November 10 (Consultative Document); BIS, (2016), Revision to the Securitization Framework, July 11; BIS, (2017), Capital Treatment for Simple, Transparent and Comparable Short-Term Securitizations, July 6 (Consultative Document); Some of these documents have then later on been rewired with(in) the existing policy, see: BIS, (2017), Basel III: Finalizing Post-Crisis Reforms, December 7.

[698] Y. Aksoy and H.S. Basso, (2015), Securitization and Asset Prices, CESifo Working Paper Nr. 5213, February. They demonstrate further that the creation of synthetic securities (the pooling and tranching of credit assets) relaxes both the funding and the risk constraints financial entities face, allowing them to increase balance sheet holdings. This increase in asset demand depresses the compensation for undertaking risk in the economy, confirming our empirical results. Crucially, we show that declines in the compensation for risk taking in equity and bonds due to securitization may not be related to a decline in actual risk.

[699] Bank competition in its turn can induce excessive risk taking (through the credit supply channel) due to risk shifting (e.g. by lowering lending standards in the mortgage market) leading to real economic outcomes. See A.X. Feng, (2018), Bank Competition, Risk Taking and their Consequences: Evidence from the U.S. Mortgage and Labor Markets, IMF Working Paper Nr. WP/18/157, June. Also: C. Palmer, (2015), Why Did so Many Subprime Borrowers Default During the Crisis: Loose Credit or Plummeting Prices?, Working Paper, mimeo; J. Dagher and N. Fu, (2017), What Fuels the Boom Drives the Bust: Regulation and the Mortgage Crisis, The Economic Journal, Vol. 127 (June), pp. 996–1024; G. Haoyu et al., (2019), Rise of Bank Competition: Evidence from Banking Regulation in China, NBER Working Paper Nr. 25795, May. The latter document that performance of private banks rises under deregulation. Such deregulation leads to higher screening standards, lower interest rates and lower delinquency rates for corporate loans from entrant banks. In contrast, the performance of state-owned enterprises (SOEs) does not improve following deregulation. Deregulation also amplifies bank credit from productive private firms to inefficient SOEs due mainly to SOEs' soft budget constraints.

risk cannot be mitigated through capital adequacy regulation or other 'command-and-control regulation'.[700] In general it can be confirmed that macroprudential policies are directly related to bank risk. Beyond that general observation it was observed that the way that banks respond to changes in macroprudential tools differs among banks depending on their specific balance sheet structure and characteristics. Those banks that are small, under-capitalized and that have a high stake in wholesale funding react more strongly.[701]

As a final note, it might be pointed out that it was observed by Turk[702] that little of the reform in this field post-crisis 'has been imposed by the statutory rulemaking process established under the Dodd-Frank Act. Instead, the bulk of actual policymaking has occurred much more informally, through enforcement actions against large financial institutions that have resulted in a series of multi-billion dollar settlements. By pursuing a strategy of "regulation by settlement," regulators have implicitly promulgated a novel legal prohibition on misconduct in securitization markets, roughly equivalent to a negligence standard.'

11.7.3 The Repo Market and Securities Lending

The repo- and securities lending market traditionally consists of four segments, as reported by the Financial Stability Board,[703] but with fairly similar characteristics. It consists of (1) a securities lending segment, (2) a leveraged investment fund financing and securities borrowing segment, (3) an inter-dealer repo segment, and (4) a repo financing segment.

The first comprises lending of securities by institutional investors to banks and broker-dealers against the collateral of cash or securities. The second category comprises financing of leveraged investment funds' long positions by banks and broker-dealers using both reverse repo and margin lending secured against assets held with prime brokers, as well as

[700] M. Marques-Ibanez, Y. Altunbas and M. van Leuvensteijn, (2014), Competition and Bank Risk. The Effect of Securitization and Bank Capital, ECB Working Paper Series Nr. 1678.

[701] See Y. Altunbas et al., (2017), Macroprudential Policy and Bank Risk, BIS Working Paper Nr. 646, June.

[702] M.C. Turk, (2018), Securitization Reform after the Crisis: Regulation by Rulemaking or Regulation by Settlement, Review of Banking and Financial Law, Vol. 37, pp. 870–874. He raises three questions: Why did the Dodd-Frank regulations prove so ineffectual? Can regulation by settlement be justified as an adequate substitute for shortcomings in the conventional rulemaking process? And, what lies ahead for the future of securitization regulation? While answering the second questions he concludes that 'when the entire set of agency-bank settlements are considered as a whole, they can been seen as imposing a Pigouvian tax on the specific market externality associated with securitization, and therefore come surprisingly close to a first-best policy intervention'. The broader conclusion of his article is that the securitization field is a policy space which remains poorly understood and is still in flux. See also: P. de Gioia Carabellese, (2017), Securitization and Structured Finance: from Shadow Banking to Legal Harmonization? in Iris H. Chiu & Iain MacNeil (eds.), Research Handbook on Shadow Banking: Legal and Regulatory Aspects, Edward Elgar; Steven L. Schwarcz, (2018), Securitization: Ten Years After the Financial Crisis: An Overview, Review of Banking and Financial Law, Vol. 37, pp. 757–769.

[703] See in detail: FSB, (2012), Securities Lending and Repos: Market Overview and Financial Stability Issues, Interim Report of the FSB Workstream on Securities Lending and Repos, pp. 1–5.

securities lending to hedge funds by prime brokers to cover short positions. The third category comprises primarily government bond repo transactions amongst banks and broker-dealers. These may be used to finance long positions via general collateral (GC) repos (primarily against government securities), or to borrow specific securities via special repos. The last category comprises repo transactions made primarily by banks and broker-dealers to borrow cash from 'cash-rich' entities, including central banks, retail banks, money market funds (MMFs), securities lenders and increasingly non-financial corporations. The drivers of this last market segment are primarily the short-term financing needs of banks and broker-dealers, as well as the desire of institutional cash managers to hold collateralized, 'money-like' investments. Collateral movements and valuation are increasingly outsourced to tri-party agents, often custodian banks ('tri-party repo'). Collateral typically includes government bonds, corporate bonds, structured products, money market instruments, equities and (before the crisis) a share of asset-backed securities (ABSs).

Repos include a seller who sells the securities to a lender and agrees to repurchase them at an agreed future date at an agreed price. They are usually very short-term, from overnight to 30 days or more. In the case of a reverse repo a dealer buys government securities from an investor and then sells them back at a later date for a higher price. The drivers,[704] according to the FSB, of this segment of the financial market include the need for a substitute for insured bank deposits. A key attribute of repo is that it allows banks, broker-dealers and other intermediaries to create 'collateralized' short-term liabilities provided they can access underlying collateral securities meeting the credit and regulatory requirements of the cash lenders. Another source of demand comes from the leveraged intermediaries who use this market as a replacement for the uninsured lending market. Increasingly there is a need for banks and broker-dealers to gain access to securities for the purpose of optimizing the collateralization of repos, securities loans and derivatives. The creation of money-like repo liabilities requires collateral, and therefore the borrowing capacity of banks and broker-dealers depends on the total amount of non-cash collateral available to them. 'Collateral mining' refers to the practice whereby banks and broker-dealers obtain and exchange securities in order to collateralize their other activities (centralized collateral management). The repo and securities lending market is often seen as a return enhancer for institutional investors. The FSB later on inventoried the risks embedded in the repo and securities lending market,[705] which led to their policy proposals.[706]

The repo and securities lending market is particularly prone to fire sales. Fire sales have already been described and represent 'a forced sale of an asset at a dislocated price. The asset sale is forced in the sense that the seller cannot pay creditors without selling assets….Assets sold in fire sales can trade at prices far below their value in best use, causing severe losses to sellers'.[707] They (the 'FSB') go on to discuss the roles of investor specialization and limited

---

[704] FSB, (2012), pp. 6–10.

[705] FSB, (2012a), Strengthening Oversight and Regulation of Shadow Banking. A Policy Framework for Addressing Shadow Banking Risks in Securities Lending and Repos.

[706] FSB, (2013), Strengthening Oversight and Regulation of Shadow Banking. A Policy Framework for Addressing Shadow Banking Risks in Securities Lending and Repos.

[707] A. Shleifer and R. Vishny, (2011), Fire Sales in Finance and Macroeconomics, Journal of Economic Perspectives, Vol. 25 (Winter), pp. 30 ff.

arbitrage as factors that drive the magnitude of observed price discounts in fire sales. There is by now a large body of empirical research that supports the importance of these factors. The existence of substantial price discounts in distressed sales speaks only to the positive economics of fire sales, not the normative economics, and hence is not sufficient to make a case for regulatory intervention. For a fire sale to have the sort of welfare effects that create a role for regulation, the reduced price in the fire sale has to hurt somebody other than the original party making the leverage decision. This adverse impact of price has to run through something like a collateral constraint, whereby a lowered price actually reduces, rather than increases, the third party's demand for the asset. The repo market is one where a large number of borrowers finance the same securities on a short-term collateralized basis, with very high leverage, often in the range of 20:1, 50:1, or even higher.

Hence there is a strong potential for any one borrower's distress, and the associated downward pressure on prices, to cause a tightening of collateral or regulatory constraints on other borrowers. One source of risk would be an initial shock either to the expected value of the underlying collateral or to its volatility that leads to an increase in required repo-market haircuts (e.g. the default probability of the corporate bond going up). Another source of risk would be concerns about the creditworthiness of the broker-dealer firm that causes lenders in the tri-party market to step away from it.[708] This macroeconomic risk is aggravated by a number of regulatory interventions. The most noteworthy is the risk of fire sales related to exemptions from bankruptcy's automatic stay provision enjoyed by a number of financial contracts, such as repos. An 'automatic stay' prohibits collection actions by creditors against bankrupt debtors or their property. It prevents a creditor from liquidating the collateral of a defaulting debtor, since collateral is a lien on the debtor's property.[709]

In either case, if the associated externalities are deemed to create significant social costs, the goal of regulatory policy should be to get private actors to internalize these costs. The same is valid for the tri-party repo market. This has become a large and important market in recent years,[710] where securities dealers find short-term funding for a substantial portion of their own and their clients' assets. Begalle et al. distinguish between (1) fire sales of assets by a dealer who, facing a run that could lead to default, sells securities to generate liquidity, and (2) fire sales of assets by repo investors after a dealer's default has occurred. While fire sales do cause damage no matter how they arise, the tools available to lessen the harm from the two types of fire sales are different. They find that limited tools are available to mitigate the risk of pre-default fire sales and that no established tools currently exist to mitigate the

[708] See J.C. Stein, (2013), The Fire-Sales Problem and Securities Financing Transactions, Speech October 3, At the Federal Reserve Bank of New York Workshop on Fire Sales as a Driver of Systemic Risk in Tri-party Repo and other Secured Funding Markets, New York, NY.

[709] G. Antinolfi, F. Carapella, C. Kahn, A. Martin, D. Mills and E. Nosal, (2013), Repos, Fire Sales and Bankruptcy Policy, Federal Reserve Bank of Chicago Working Paper Nr. 2012-15.

[710] See for the historical context: A. Copeland, A. Martin, and M. Walker, (2010), The Tri-Party Repo Market before the 2010 Reforms, Federal Reserve Bank of NY Staff Report Nr. 477 and A. Copeland, D. Duffie, A. Martin, and J. McLaughlin, (2012), Key Mechanics of the U.S. Tri-Party Repo Market, Federal Reserve Bank of New York Economic Policy Review, Vol. 18, Issue 3, pp. 17–28.

[711] B. Begalle, A. Martin, J. McAndrews, and S. McLaughlin, (2013), The Risk of Fire-Sales in the Tri-Party Repo Market, Federal Reserve Bank of New York Staff Reports, Nr. 616.

risk of post-default sales.[711] Broker-dealers, by reducing the amount of maturity transformation they perform, can mitigate the risk of pre-default fire sales by a dealer that loses access to tri-party repo funding. Central bank emergency lending can be used to mitigate this risk by facilitating an orderly deleveraging process.[712] In contrast, there are currently no established tools in place that mitigate ex ante the risk of post-default fire sales. In today's tri-party repo market, dealers can default for a variety of reasons, and the default of a large dealer could lead to fire sales no matter how the default arises. Hence an effective regime for risk mitigation must feature a mechanism or process to ensure ex ante that the incentives faced by tri-party lenders will not result in fire sales in the aftermath of a dealer default. That will require cooperation and contractual arrangements among all the parties involved.

Given these findings[713] it can be concluded that the repo market is a market in which parties finance themselves short-term at relatively low cost. Given the interconnectedness and the fact that securities can be used multiple times between different market agents the risk of a fire sale is very material.[714] Additional capital and liquidity regulation as suggested[715] conflicts with the short-term funding aspect of the repo market. A Pigovian instrument would focus on the critical aspects leading to fire sales as discussed in the layered Pigovian instrument suggested: (1) leverage, (2) maturity mismatch, and (3) liquidity exposure.[716]

---

[712] In more recent years central banks have also provided support to securities markets, see: D. King et al., (2017), Central Bank Emergency Support to Securities Markets, IMF Working Paper Nr. WP/17/152, July. King et al. tend to agree with the idea that, within the context of the central banks' mandate with respect to financial stability, emergency support to securities markets is an important part of the crisis management response. But it needs to come with a serious amount of scrutiny. It should focus on '(1) ensuring that credit flow is not unduly disrupted resulting in a detrimental impact on the real economy; and (2) mitigating the risk that financial asset fire sales could threaten solvency in important parts of the economy'. (p. 38) And it should only come as part of a comprehensive policy package and as a stepwise process (p. 39). That package should take into account questions such as 'what types of securities markets may be important for financial stability, what market conditions could trigger emergency support measures, and how programs can be designed to restore market functioning while minimizing moral hazard'.

[713] See also: G. Gorton, and A. Metrick, (2012), Securitized Banking and the Run on Repo, Journal of Financial Economics, Vol. 104, Issue 3, pp. 425–451; A. Krishnamurthy, S. Nagel, and D. Orlov, (2012), Sizing Up Repo, NBER Working Paper, Nr. 17768; A. Martin, D. Skeie, and E.-L. von Thadden, (2010), Repo Runs, Federal Reserve Bank of New York Staff Report, Nr. 444; A. Martin, D. Skeie, and E.-L. von Thadden, (2012), The Fragility of Short-Term Funding Markets, Working Paper; C. Merrill, T. D. Nadauld, R. M. Stulz, and S. M. Sherlund, (2012), Why Did Financial Institutions Sell RMBS at Fire Sales Prices During the Financial Crisis? Manuscript, unpublished.

[714] A fire sale in this scenario is caused by a flight from maturity ('shortening maturities'); see in detail: G.B. Gorton et al., (2014), The Flight from Maturity, NBER Working Paper, Nr. 20027.

[715] V.V. Acharya, and S. Öncü, (2013), A Proposal for the Resolution of Systemically Important Assets and Liabilities: The Case of the Repo Market, International Journal of Central Banking, Vol. 9, Issue 1, pp. 291–350.

[716] T. Adrian, and H. S. Shin, (2010), Liquidity and Leverage, Journal of Financial Intermediation, Vol. 19, pp. 418–437.

[717] A. Shleifer and R. Vishny, (1992), Liquidation Values and Debt Capacity: A Market Equilibrium Approach, Journal of Finance, Vol. 47, Issue 4, pp. 1343–1366.

It is the only instrument that would focus directly on the issue of liquidation value (fire-sales prices)[717] and re-establish the equilibrium under leverage duress on an ex ante basis.[718] The challenge going forward will be to create a consistent ex ante measurement model of how fire-sale spillovers and systematic risk relate, as that will be instrumental in determining the social harm exposure and the correct understanding of which technique magnifies the social harm based on Markose's eigenvector network assessment (systemic risk, supra).[719] A volatile variable in this respect is and will be the strategic behavior and positions taken by the parties involved in the (tri-party) transactions characterizing this market.[720] The recently suggested[721] haircut on the valuation of collateral used in repo transactions is nothing but a good start. History will be the judge of its quantifiable effect under duress, but given the discussion regarding systemic risk a standardized haircut, based on qualitative criteria, will have minimal effect on the behavior of economic agents. The valuation protocol suggested, based on long historical time series, tends to imply a fully rational marketplace and synchronous emergence of systemic risk. That seems to contradict reality as we know it.

11.7.4 Re-hypothecation and Collateral Lending

Re-hypothecation,[722] as elaborated on before refers to the practice of financial intermediaries who use the collateral provided by customers and use it as collateral to obtain more (or cheaper) funding than they would normally be granted access to given their balance sheet structure. If the customer initially provided the collateral benefits through a reduced cost of

[718] R. Greenwood, A. Landier, and D. Thesmar, (2012), Vulnerable Banks, NBER Working Paper, Nr. 18537.

[719] A first attempt is made. See: F. Duarte and T.M. Eisenbach, (2015), Fire-Sale Spillovers and Systemic Risk, Federal Reserve Bank of NY Working Paper, Nr. 645, revised edition (initial edition October 2013); A. Falato, (2016), Fire-Sale Spillovers in Debt Markets, Working Paper, August 24, Mimeo.

[720] H.M. Ennis, (2011), Strategic Behavior in the Tri-Party Repo Market, Economic Quarterly, Vol. 97, Nr. 4, pp. 389–413.

[721] FSB, (2014), Strengthening Oversight and Regulation of Shadow Banking, Regulatory Framework for Haircuts on Centrally-Cleared Securities Financing Transactions, October 14.

[722] There are more specifically two notions of re-hypothecation. The first (narrow) notion of re-hypothecation relates to how broker-dealers (and no other market participants) should handle the securities of their customers: If they can use their customers' securities as they see fit, we say that broker-dealers enjoy a re-hypothecation right. The second notion, as proposed by the International Swaps and Derivatives Association (ISDA), applies to any secured lender, not only to broker-dealers: The right of re-hypothecation refers to the right of a secured party to sell, pledge, re-hypothecate (in its narrow definition above), assign, invest, use, commingle or otherwise dispose of posted collateral. In what follows, I will use the broader definition of re-hypothecation, which, simply put, says that a lender with collateral can use it as if it was his or her own asset; see: C. Monnet, (2011), Rehypothecation, Philadelphia FED Business Review, quarter 4, pp. 18–25.

lending (or lower fees),[723] the intermediary can enhance leverage and increase return (to shareholders). It is common practice that lenders who receive such collateral advance it by using it for proprietary funding purposes as well. The same collateral is thereby used multiple times to finance transactions with the different parties involved. The magnitude of re-use of (the same) collateral is called the velocity of collateral. Re-hypothecation is considered one of the major drivers behind the 2008 financial crisis.[724] It is well understood that counterparty risk increases as collateral velocity[725] increases and that a sudden drop in the market value of (certain types) of collateral will undeniably lead to fire sales in the collateral lending market. Re-hypothecation has identifiable benefits[726] as it reduces the lending costs and liquidity[727] needs of traders in particular when collateral is scarce, but it also amplifies market constraints under duress and introduces material counterparty risk.[728] It improves welfare by permitting liquidity to flow where it is needed most. However, there can be too much of it and regulatory constraints might then be appropriate which will enhance the demand for real cash balances.[729] An interesting question that has been studied only to a limited degree is the question how changes in supply and demand affect the specialness of a

---

[723] There are some countries in which there are limitations on how much (of their total collateral portfolio) an intermediary can put to work this way; however, in most countries it is uncapped.

[724] M. Singh and J. Aitken, (2010), The (Sizable) Role of Rehypothecation in the Shadow Banking Sector, IMF Working Paper, WP/10/172.

[725] Collateral velocity is anno 2019 back on the rise. See: M. Singh, (2019), Collateral Velocity is Rebounding, FT Alphaville, May 22.

[726] Among the greatest benefits of re-hypothecation is capital efficiency in funding intermediation. Because collateral is repledged, less capital is needed to fund new debt or yield-seeking activities. Re-hypothecation reduces the cost of pledging collateral, leveraging a greater amount of funding on a relatively smaller capital base. However, there are significant risks when leverage and financial layering become too complex and opaque to discern whether a reasonable capital cushion exists to cover potential asset price declines (infra); see: D. Luttrel, H. Rosenblum and J. Thies, (2012), Understanding the Risks Inherent in Shadow Banking. A Primer and Practical Lessons Learned, Dallas FED Staff papers, Nr. 18, pp. 35–40. Kahn and Park highlight that 'rehypothecation has trade-off effects; it enhances provision of funding liquidity to the economy so that additional productive investments can be undertaken, but incurs deadweight cost by misallocating the asset among the agents when it fails'. It is clear that the re-hypothecation model rarely delivers a socially optimal outcome. See in detail: C.M. Kahn and H.J. Park, (2019), Collateral, Rehypothecation and Efficiency, Journal of Financial Intermediation, Elsevier, vol. 39(C), pages 34–46. Also: J.R. Donaldson and E. Micheler, (2018), Resalable debt and Systemic Risk, Journal of Financial Economics, Vol. 127, pp. 485–504. Their point of focus is the heterogeneous nature of the resalability of debt claims. Higher market frictions lead to an increase in borrowing via non-resalable debt, but that comes with a problem, that is, it causes credit chains to form. A bank that needs liquidity cannot sell a non-resalable instrument and has to engage in a new contract. The credit chains are a source of systemic risk. A default of a bank harms its creditor and their creditors.

[727] M. Brunnermeier, and L. Pedersen, (2008), Market Liquidity and Funding Liquidity, Review of Financial Studies, Vol. 22, Issue 6, pp. 2201–2238.

[728] C. Johnson, (1997), Derivatives and Rehypothecation Failure. It's3:00 pm. Do You Know Where Your Collateral Is? Arizona Law Review, Vol. 30, pp. 949 ff.

[729] D. Andolfatto et al., (2015), Rehypothecation and Liquidity, Federal Reserve Bank of St. Louis, Working Paper Nr. 2015-003B, May.

security. And how are shocks to that demand and supply transmitted from cash markets to repo markets[730] where these assets are used as collateral? And what are the implications for the functioning of the market?[731]

The regulation[732] introduced post-crisis, requiring more collateral, particularly[733] for derivative contracts (in the OTC market[734]), seems not to constrain the collateral market[735] but also does not solve the problem of material externality due to fire sales under duress.[736]

---

[730] CGFS, (2017), Repo Market Functioning, CGFS Working Paper Nr. 59, April.

[731] Based on the security market program (SMP) it could be concluded that 'specialness is affected by the amount of a security that is effectively available for trading on the market. This results from the combined effect of the auction cycle, the amount of securities that resides in the portfolio of buy-to-hold investors and security-specific demand, e.g. arising from shortellers. Specialiness drops after a new issuance takes place and securities are less available for trading tend to be more special. Bonds bought by the central bank through the SMP tended to have higher specialness and purchases likely affected also the distribution of specialness, inducing a larger right-hand tail'. See in detail: S. Corradin and A. Maddalino, (2017), The Importance Being Special: Repo Markets during the Crisis, ECB Working Paper Nr. 2065, May.

[732] BIS, (2013), Asset Encumbrance, Financial Reform and the Demand for Collateral Assets, Report submitted by a Working Group established by the Committee on the Global Financial System, CGFS Papers, Nr. 49; J.C. Lopez, R. Mendes and H. Vickstedt, (2013), The Market for Collateral: The Potential Impact of Financial Regulation, Bank of Canada, Financial System Review (June), pp. 45–53. See also: T. Ahnert et al., (2016), Asset Encumbrance, Bank Funding and Financial Fragility, Deutsche Bundesbank Discussion Paper, Nr. 17, Frankfurt am Main (also as LSE Systemic Risk Centre Discussion Paper Nr. 83, September). Ahnert et al. focus on covered bonds. They have been used extensively particularly in Europe and are considered the cornerstone of bank funding. Theoretical analysis however is lacking and this against the background of increasing concerns regarding the financial stability implications of the collateralization of bank balance sheets. From a legal perspective, asset encumbrance is a claim against a property by another party. From a financial perspective, such claims have traditionally taken the form of security interests, such as pledges, given on assets by a borrower to a lender. Asset encumbrance affects bank fragility. Certain (discussed) features make covered bonds safe assets and a cheap source of funding. At the same time, they argue, these features asymmetrically shift risks onto unsecured creditors, which can heighten bank fragility and increase the cost of unsecured funding. They show that a bank's usage of covered bonds balances this trade-off between profitability and fragility. The EBA releases an annual Report on asset encumbrance; latest edition: September 2019.

[733] The other part of regulation focuses on more transactions being cleared over a central clearing party (CCP); see: D. Duffie, M. Scheicher and G. Vuillemey, (2014), Central Clearing and Collateral Demand, ECB Working Paper Series Nr. 1638.

[734] M. Singh, (2010), Undercollateralisation and Rehypothecation in the OTC Derivative Markets, Financial Stability Review (July), pp. 113–119.

[735] Short-term market rates are effectively determined in the pledged collateral market, where banks and other financial institutions exchange collateral (such as bonds and equities) for money. Singh and Goel document and develop a methodology to show that transactions using long dated collateral also affect short-term market rates. The implication is that the (future) unwinding of central bank balance sheets will likely strengthen the monetary policy transmission, as dealer balance-sheet space is now relatively less constrained, with a rebound in collateral reuse. See in detail: M. Singh and R. Goel, (2019), Pledged Collateral Market's Role in Transmission to Short-Term Market Rates, IMF Working Paper Nr. WP/19/106, May.

[736] V. Maurin, (2014), Re-Using the Collateral of Others: A General Equilibrium Model of Rehypothecation, European University Institute Working Paper.

It also does not solve the legal distortion that the re-hypothecation practice implicitly introduced and in particular the violation of a certain legal principle.[737]

That legal principle is nemo dat quod non habet (nemo dat)—one cannot give what one does not have. The central normative issue is when to allow or tolerate these types of distortions, given their potential costs.

The post-Lehman effect whereby about 4–5 trillion USD was withdrawn from the collateral market did not fail to affect the lubrication of the financial intermediation process.[738] The fire-sale externality is similar to the fire-sale phenomenon discussed above regarding the repo market.[739] A sudden drop in the market value of collateral will provide not only a systemic shock, but also a magnified exposure to contagion due to the cascade of collateral that the re-hypothecation process created. Hypothecation in capital markets occurs mainly through the use of margin accounts. Investors borrow funds from a broker to acquire assets, most commonly stocks. Assets purchased by an investor on margin are hypothetically held by the brokerage as collateral.

If the securities' value drops, the broker will satisfy credit repayment with a margin call (compelling the investor to deposit more money to cover the original loan amount) or through sale of the securities. While the investor has legal ownership of the securities, since they were bought with the investor's money and partially borrowed funds from the broker, both the original deposit and the securities become collateral. Re-hypothecation, also referred to as repledging, occurs when a broker-dealer reuses the collateral posted by a client to back the broker's own trades and borrowing. The process may be repeated several times, with the same collateral repledged simultaneously in a number of transactions. This is known as 'churn' and effectively increases

---

[737] See in detail: S.L. Schwarcz, (2010), Distorting Legal Principles, The Journal of Corporate Law, Vol. 35, Issue 4, pp. 697–727. However, its distortion of 'nemo dat' creates uncertainty (in the case of re-hypothecation) when customer securities become subject to claims of an intermediary's creditors, to whom the securities have been re-hypothecated. If customer securities were to become subject to those claims, customers could lose their securities if the intermediary fails. Although re-hypothecation is a long-standing practice (one may always grant a security interest in property to the extent of one's rights therein), its operational execution has changed and become flawed. Lehman Brothers Inc. (e.g.), like many other prime-brokerage intermediaries, insisted that customers contractually consent to allow the intermediary to directly re-hypothecate the customers' securities as collateral for financing obtained by the intermediary. The practice is conceptually flawed in that the intermediary does not own those securities but merely holds those securities on behalf of its customers, who at most give the intermediary a security interest in those securities. Lacking ownership of the customers' securities, the intermediary should not be able, under the principle of 'nemo dat', to grant a security interest that enables its creditors to obtain ownership of those securities through foreclosure. Conceptually, therefore, Lehman and other prime-brokerage intermediaries ignored *nemo dat* when engaging in this form of re-hypothecation (pp. 702–703); For an evaluation of the net benefit or harm of the technique see pp. 705–711); see also M. Singh and J. Aitkin, (2009), Deleveraging after Lehman - Evidence from Reduced Rehypothecation, IMF Working Paper, WP/09/42.

[738] See in detail: M. Singh, (2011), Velocity of Pledge Collateral: Analysis and Implications, IMF Working Paper, WP/11/256.

[739] A. Copeland, D. Duffie, A. Martin and S. McLaughlin, (2012), Key Mechanics of the U.S. Tri-Party Repo market, FRBNY, Working Paper.

financial institution leverage in an opaque way. The assessment of a negative externality is often complicated due to the off-balance-sheet nature of the transactions.[740] The FSB in more recent years has analyzed re-hypothecation extensively and concluded that there is no immediate need for harmonizing regulatory approaches to re-hypothecation of client assets but does encourage monitoring of volumes in a national and international level.[741]

11.7.5 Shadow Banking as Market-Based Financing

It has been shown that shadow banking activities, given the nature of their transactions and the context in which they engage in liquidity, maturity and credit risk transformation, (potentially) produce material negative externalities. The barrage of regulation that the sector has been exposed to in the years after the crisis was warranted. The more recent trend[742] to position shadow banking as market-based finance, now that the shadow banking system is tending to go mainstream, depicts the system as a democratization of finance and needs to be approached with the utmost care. The currently dysfunctional credit-creation intermediation process through the traditional banking sector cannot justify the emergence or continued existence of shadow banking activities as a market-based financing model, especially not insofar as the ultimate backstop, 'moral hazard', has not been resolved. A market-based funding system works wonderfully well when there is a private actor at the end of the line, who is part of the transaction and absorbs the risk left in the transaction which is the case with equity-type instruments[743] but not, for now, with debt-type instruments.

Financial innovation[744] has enabled credit intermediaries to spread risk through the financial system, slicing risk exposure into segments and distributing the pieces to those supposedly willing to bear it. Globally connected financial markets provide an incredible

[740] A most notable example is that of MF Global, which went bankrupt in 2011. MF Global's demise is often attributed to its use of off-balance-sheet repurchase agreements called 'repo-to-maturity'. The repo-to-maturity transactions involved borrowing billions of dollars backed by European sovereign debt due to expire at the same time. Because the loan collateral and the loan itself were set to mature simultaneously, MF Global was allowed to treat the transaction as a 'sale' under generally accepted accounting principles.

[741] FSB, (2017), Transforming Shadow Banking into Resilient Market-based Finance. Re-hypothecation and Collateral Re-Use: Potential Financial Stability Issues, Market Evolution and Regulatory Approaches, January 25, London.

[742] J. Authors, (2014), Democratization of Finance, Financial Times, June 23; P. Jenkins, (2014), Into the Shadows: Taking Another Path, Financial Times, June 16 and P. McCulley, (2014), Make Shadow Banks Safe and Private Money Sound, Financial Times, June 16.

[743] The technology stock bubble of the late 90s had very few lasting economic effects on the economy due to this once it deflated.

[744] The relationship between financial innovators and regulators has been historically tense, with financial innovators taking advantage of loopholes and regulators desperately trying to keep pace with innovations while dealing with limited resources and long bureaucratic processes. Nonetheless, in recent years, FinTechs—unregulated start-ups applying technology to finance—have exponen-

opportunity to decrease the cost of funding and increase capital efficiency, serving the consumption and investment needs of businesses and households worldwide. However, no matter how risk is distributed and transferred outside regulation and safety nets, it cannot be eliminated from the financial system.[745]

Capital regulation goes a long way in terms of symptom treatment, but consistently fails to neutralize ex ante the possible externalities, nor does it contribute to a swift socio-economic recovery once the harm is incurred.[746] Pigovian taxes, despite the imperfections characterizing the instrument, is the instrument that by and large allow the neutralization of externalities on a regional or global basis and avoid the moral hazard embedded in many other regulatory approaches. Globalization[747] has the potential to create tremendously scalable externalities.[748] A neoliberal free market requires a balancing act to turn

tially accelerated such race, making new regulatory approaches and perspectives necessary. See in detail: E. Macchiavello, (2017), Financial-Return Crowdfunding and Regulatory Approaches in the Shadow Banking, Fintech and Collaborative Finance Era, European Company and Financial law Review, Vol. 14, Issue 4, pp. 662–722, December.

[745] D. Luttrel, H. Rosenblum and J. Thies, (2012), Understanding the Risks Inherent in Shadow Banking: A Primer and Practical Lessons Learned, Dallas FED Staff papers, Nr. 18, p. 38.

[746] Regarding the evaluation after the 1930 crisis see in detail: K.J. Mitchener and K. Wandschneider, (2014), Did Capital Controls Help Countries Recover from the Great Depression of the 1930s, NBER Working paper, Nr. 20,220, June 26. Similar results have been yielded regarding the aftermath of the 2008 crisis; V.N. Landi and A. Schiavone, (2018), The Effectiveness of Capital Controls, Bank of Italy Working Paper Nr. 1200, November 6. They conclude: controls reduce the volume of capital flows, even if the effects vary across investment types and between emerging and advanced economies. Controls tend to reduce the volatility of capital flows and foreign exchange borrowing. The effects on domestic credit are driven by advanced economies. Finally, capital controls are associated with a depreciation of the exchange rate in relation to the equilibrium level. Also: V.N. Landi, (2018), Capital Control Spillovers, Bank of Italy Working Paper Nr. 1184, July 20. The results show that the tightening of capital controls in an emerging economy induces the advanced economy to move a considerable share of foreign investments to the other emerging country, whose business cycle becomes more volatile. Moreover, the results show that coordination between the two emerging countries produces some benefits for both those economies, though only slightly greater compared with the scenario without coordination.

[747] See for a current state of affairs: BIS, (2018), Globalization and Deglobalization, BIS Papers Nr. 100, December with a compilation of articles on the topic. Also: R.N. McCauley et al., (2017), Financial Deglobalization in Banking, BIS Working Paper Nr. 650, June 29, via bis.org

[748] They can come in many different natures; to start with the difference in gains from globalization. Lang and Tavares examined globalizations and observe differential gains from globalization both across and within countries: Income gains are substantial for countries at early and medium stages of the globalization process, but the marginal returns diminish as globalization rises, eventually becoming insignificant. Within countries, these gains are concentrated at the top of national income distributions, resulting in rising inequality. See in detail: V.F. Lang and M.M. Tavares, (2018), The Distribution of Gains from Globalization, IMF Working Paper Nr. WP/18/54, March. The gains from globalization are unequally both across and within countries. To be precise 'global inequality of incomes between individuals is increasingly driven by within-country inequality and decreasingly by between-country inequality' (p. 39). See also: D. Acemoglu, et al., (2019), Democracy Does Cause Growth, Journal of Political Economy, Vol. 127, Issue 1, pp. 47–100; F. Alvaredo, (2017), Global Inequality Dynamics: New Findings from WID. World, American Economic Review, Vol. 107, Issue 5, pp. 404–409; P. Antràs, et al., (2017), Globalization, Inequality and Welfare, Journal of

rough capitalism into careful capitalism that allows us to engage our limited resources toward a long-term optimization of our economic output, wealth creation and hopefully well-being.[749]

11.8 Pigovian Taxes as a Macroprudential Tool

11.8.1 Introduction

Every economy, and also the global economy, is prone to waves, that is, cycles of economic activity. Those cycles have in recent times not been as identifiable, partly due to the interference of heterogeneous shocks to the system. In fact, they have never been as identifiable as the economic model predicts, something they have in common with most if not all economic models ever developed. The understanding, or at least my understanding, is that the functionality of these models is not expected to be centered on their predictive value, but (merely) on the understanding the implications once a model-suggested situation occurs in reality.

The (global) economy is supposed to be more than the Homo economicus, who always acts rational and is in constant pursuit of self-enrichment and where prices evolve constantly based on demand and supply dynamics. The multi-variable equation to which an economy can be reduced is difficult to solve without a tremendous backlog of assumptions of which statistically a number will not align with reality.

That, however, does not imply that it is not possible to steer certain trends, especially those that are policy induced and characteristics of certain economic environments. The credit creation function, which in the current economic model operates as a system allocated to the private banking sector, has distinct implications in the field of inflation management, but also in the field of asset valuation and the management of credit volumes throughout the economic boom and bust cycles. Debt accumulation and lower interest rates in the market will lead to higher asset prices, including higher prices for real estate, equity and commodities. The lower market interest rate as set by central banks is the start of the credit and pricing chain. As such, the pricing and return on assets feed off the market interest rate. The lower market interest rate signals a lower opportunity cost of capital for

International Economics, Vol. 108, pp. 387–412; T. Cordella, and A. Ospino, (2017), Financial Globalization and Market Volatility, World Bank Policy Research Working Paper Nr.8091; F. Dorn, et al., (2018), Globalization and Income Inequality Revisited, CESifo Working Paper Nr. 6859; D. Furceri, and P. Loungani, (2018), The Distributional Effects of Capital Account Liberalization, Journal of Development Economics, Vol. 130, pp. 127–144; D. Rodrik, (2017), Populism and the Economics of Globalization, NBER Working Paper Nr. 23559; M. El Hamiani Khatat and R. Veyrune, (2019), Liquidity Management under Fixed Exchange Rate with Open Capital Account, IMF Working Paper Nr. WP/19/58, February.

[749] Freedom without restrictions has never yielded an optimal long-term optimum (short-term seems unsatisfying as well, as it cannot be sustained). Optimization requires balancing resources and capabilities over longer periods of time and carefully monitoring the net benefits of efforts undertaken so as to ensure the accumulation of wealth across generations.

savings and unlocks (or is expected to do so) capital flows that will have to find their way to higher yielding territories.

Although there is a natural dynamic in this (equilibrium) model, the starting point is artificial, that is, the market interest rate as set by the central bank. It could help explain the credit cycle and the pricing cycle that aligns with it. Embedded in macroprudential supervision and policy is the need to manage those cycles, especially when they are caused by heterogeneous factors. The most recent financial crisis has triggered an understanding that the Pigovian tax instrument is not only more instrumental and superior to manage externalities at the level of individual FIs and the financial markets in general; it also urged to understand that they have the potential to help manage the economic cycles in general and the capital flows (or reversal of) that it causes. The Pigovian tax instrument on this front also tends to perform in a superior way relative to command-and-control regulation.

11.8.2 Managing Credit Booms and Busts

The interaction between debt accumulation (at the level of FIs, households, corporations and the sovereign alike) and asset prices contributes to magnifying the impact of booms and busts. Increases in borrowing and in collateral prices feed each other during booms. In busts, the feedback turns negative, with credit constraints leading to fire sales of assets and further tightening of credit. It is meaningful to assume that prudential policies could be used to mitigate the buildup in systemic vulnerability during the boom. Debt accumulation and aligned asset pricing can lead to material distortions when bubbles deflate, causing more damage[750] than the potential aggregate value derived from temporary higher asset prices.[751] Remarkably enough, there were few welfare models before the 2008 crisis and those that existed were based on a command-and-control style to arrive at an optimal set of policies to deal with booms and busts in credit and asset prices. Jeanne and Korinek[752] made a significant step forward on two fronts in 2010 by suggesting not only a Pigovian approach in this respect but also to do so in the context of a created dynamic optimizing model of (collateral-

---

[750] Insofar one can identify credit booms and busts with unlimited capitalism, the understanding is emerging that unconstrained capitalism is actively damaging society and that the libertarian views on free markets do not correspond with the historical evidence of how free markets were designed and operated. See recently, for instance, N. Shaxson, (2018), The Finance Curse. How Global Finance is Making is Al Poorer, October, Bodley Head, London, UK; O. Bullough, (2018), Moneyland. Why Thieves & Crooks Now Rule the World & How to Take it Back, Profile Books Ltd., London, UK.

[751] Regarding the linkages between asset prices and macroeconomic output there is a lot of literature (see e.g. S. Claessens and M.A. Kose, (2017), Asset Prices and Macroeconomic Outcomes: a Survey, BIS Working Paper Nr. 676, November for a literature overview), but the last word has not been said on many questions. Both at the level of the theoretical linkages as well as empirical evidence supporting these linkages many questions remain unanswered and many answered questions are still somewhat nebulous and this across all major asset classes.

[752] O. Jeanne and A. Korinek, (2010), Managing Credit Booms and Busts: A Pigovian Tax Approach, NBER Working Paper Series, Nr. 16377. Also: O. Jeanne, (2012), Capital Flow Management, American Economic Review, Vol. 102, Issue 3, pp. 203–206.

ized) borrowing.[753] The model attempts to capture, in a stylized way, a number of economic settings in which the systemic interaction between credit and asset prices may be important. The use of a common framework has a benefit in that it brings out the commonality of the problems and of the required policy responses. Jeanne and Korinek were successful in doing so as they comment: '[o]ne of our main results is that the asset-debt loop entails systemic externalities that lead borrowers to undervalue the benefits of conserving liquidity as a precaution against busts. A borrower who has one more dollar of liquid net worth when the economy experiences a bust relaxes not only his private borrowing constraint but also the borrowing constraints of all other insiders. Not internalizing this spillover effect, the insider takes on too much debt during good times.'[754]

They suggest a cyclical (Pigovian) tax on borrowing by leveraged insiders to prevent them from taking on socially excessive debt. The level of the tax on a given sector should be adjusted to its vulnerability to credit and asset price busts. Even when the model is extended the model preserves its essential properties.[755] Their work is related to analysis of the ongoing worldwide credit crisis that emphasizes the amplifying mechanisms involving asset price deflation and deleveraging in the financial sector, as discussed earlier in this chapter.[756] Their bottom line contribution is that (1) they found that decentralized agents do not internalize that their borrowing choices in boom times render the economy more vulnerable to credit and asset price busts involving debt deflation in bust times. Therefore their borrowing imposes an externality on the economy, (2) In terms of a Pigovian tax they produce a baseline scenario in which the regulator would impose on average an ex ante tax of half a percent per dollar on borrowing, so as to reduce the debt burden and mitigate the

[753] They do so by using a specific starting point: 'consider a group of individuals (the insiders) who enjoy a comparative advantage in holding an asset and who can use this asset as collateral on their borrowing from outsiders. The borrowing capacity of insiders is therefore increasing in the price of the asset. The price of the asset, in turn, is driven by the insiders' consumption and borrowing capacity. This introduces a mutual feedback loop between asset prices and credit flows: small financial shocks to insiders can lead to large simultaneous booms or busts in asset prices and credit flows' (p. 2). The same occurs on the level between countries: see M. Gelman et al., (2016), Transmission of Global Financial Shocks to EMU Member States: the Role of Monetary Policy and National Factors, Deutsche Bundesbank Discussion Paper Nr. 23, Frankfurt am Main. Financial shocks and the credit contraction it causes obviously also have an impact on the real economy and markets as 'unemployment'. See in detail: F. Berton et al., (2017), Banks, Firms and Jobs, Working Paper Nr. 17/38, February.

[754] Jeanne et al., Ibid. p. 2.

[755] (1) They change the nature of the shock by assuming that it affects the availability of credit rather than the income of insiders. Then they look at the case where insiders can issue (2) long-term debt or (3) equity. All three of these extensions change some features of the boom-bust cycle equilibrium, but it remains true that the constrained optimum can be achieved by a countercyclical tax on debt, and this tax is of the same order of magnitude as in the benchmark model. Finally, they compare ex ante prudential taxation to ex post interventions that provide funds to constrained borrowers in a bust. They find that a bailout insurance fund that accumulates resources in good times and transfers them to debtors in a bust does not increase welfare (unless the resources are levied through the optimal Pigovian tax) (p. 3).

[756] See among others G. Lorenzoni, (2008), Inefficient Credit Booms, Review of Economic Studies Vol. 75, Issue 3, pp. 809–833.

decline in consumption in case of crisis, (3) They indicate, although more modeling work is required, that the level of Pigovian tax will need to be higher the more the FI is leveraged.[757] It needs to be observed that their model involves all economic agents, and not only FIs, although they naturally hold a specific position in this context. In their model they ignore the impact of credit booms and busts on production and income, which are considered as exogenous, although in reality busts in credit and asset prices are likely to affect investment and other productive expenditures.

Although investments under those conditions will not necessarily fall below an optimal level, the investment channel might magnify the welfare cost of the fire-sale externality in busts and justify more aggressive prudential taxation in booms. That can be justified by reality, which demonstrates that the long-term negative impact on economic activity (long-run output) generally does not catch up with pre-financial crisis levels.[758] This is particularly the case when collateral constraint reduces the productivity-enhancing expenditures. The open question for now is how monetary policy should respond to credit cycles assuming a non-independently operating and implemented Pigovian tax system[759] without compromising on any of its other objectives.

11.8.3 Managing (Cross-Border) Capital Flows

Balanced and non-disruptive capital flows are a crucial component of a well-functioning global economic and financial infrastructure.[760] It has often been observed that under certain circumstances those capital flows get concentrated due to herding or move with enhanced agility out of countries in the event of exogenous shocks or during times of deleveraging of the system. Although each economy perceives the need to manage those capital flows, the overall openness of an economy determines the vulnerability of these capital flow reversals. Developing economies tend to demonstrate enhanced sensitivity in this respect when being exposed to the global economic and credit cycles.[761] Both banks and

[757] The case where the sensitivity of the credit constraint to the collateral price is large enough to produce multiple equilibria and self-fulfilling asset price busts (p. 33).

[758] See in extenso: IMF, (2009), What's the Damage? Medium-Term Output Dynamics after Financial Crises, Chapter 4, World Economic Outlook, pp. 121–151.

[759] If there is nominal stickiness, a monetary restriction that raises the real interest rate in the boom should have the same macroprudential effect as the Pigovian tax discussed (Jeanne et al., Ibid. p. 34)

[760] See, for instance, the determinants of the probability of withdrawals of capital inflows in (Asian) emerging economies: C.-s. Tam and Ip-wing Yu (2017), Determinants of the Probability of Abrupt Contraction in Gross Capital Inflows to Emerging market Economies, HKMA Research Memorandum 08/2017, June 15. Examples are: countries with higher levels of debt denominated in foreign currencies, a weaker equity market, weaker global growth, a decrease in foreign reserves, a narrowing growth differential between emerging countries and the West, … Also: O. Merrouche et al., (2017), Capital Inflows, Monetary Policy, and Financial Imbalances, Journal of International Monetary and Finance, Vol. 77, pp. 117–142.

[761] See in detail: E. Nier and T. Sadi Sedik, (2014), Gross Private Capital Flows to Emerging Markets: Can the Global Financial Cycle be Tamed, IMF Working Paper Nr. WP/14/196. Cross-border bank

shadow banking entities play a critical role in this matter.[762] It has been assessed what role bank and non-bank financial institutions' balance sheet foreign exposures and risk management practices in driving capital flow responses to global risk have played. Hashimoto and Krogstrup[763] document that the response of overall capital flows to global risk shocks is associated with the on-balance-sheet foreign exposures of non-banks, but not with that of banks. The literature is scarce on the role of non-bank FIs driving capital flows in response to global risk, but a possible interpretation is that risk-averse and dynamically optimizing non-banks reduce their foreign risk exposure when global risk perceptions increase, leading to capital flows, while banks tend to be hedged against these risks off balance sheet. In advanced countries, the findings suggest that non-bank portfolio adjustment to changing risk conditions may take place through derivatives transactions with banks, the hedging practices of which trigger bank-related capital flows rather than portfolio flows.

Hashimoto and Krogstrup conclude that '[b]anks tend to be relatively well hedged against foreign risks, while this is less the case for nonbanks such as real institutional investors. To the extent that nonbanks hedge risks dynamically, they may respond to changes in global risk conditions by increasing their hedging of risks. They can do this directly by buying and selling foreign assets, or by entering into derivatives contracts. When nonbanks offload risk to resident banks using derivatives contracts, the banks in turn may offload this risk in the interbank markets, giving rise to bank capital flows that are ultimately driven by

flows are greater between source countries with more and target countries with less de iure bank regulation, which indirectly provides evidence of regulatory arbitrage in international bank flows. See in detail: G.A. Karolyi et al., (2017), Cross-Border Bank Flows and Systemic Risk, Working Paper, March 13, mimeo. Regarding the drivers of capital flows to emerging markets see in extenso: S.A. Hannan, (2017), The Drivers of Capital Flows in Emerging Markets Post Global Financial Crisis, IMF Working Paper Nr. WP/17/52, February, later on published in Journal of International Commerce, Economics and Policy, Vol. 8, Nr. 2, pp. 1–28. To be precise: 'the capital flow slowdown witnessed in recent years is due to a combination of lower growth prospects of recipient countries and worse global risk sentiment. However, the determinants of flows can be considerably different across instruments and across the type of flows considered'. More erratic are drivers such as the gap between the US long- and short-term maturity bond yields, trade openness and interest rate differentials can play a role during high episodes but not so much during normal times.

[762] See regarding the bank vs. non-bank credit cycles: C. Bora Durdu and M. Zhong, (2019), Understanding Bank and Nonbank Credit Cycles: A Structural Exploration, Finance and Economics Discussion Series Nr. 2019-031. Washington: Board of Governors of the Federal Reserve System, https://doi.org/10.17016/FEDS.2019.031; E. Kemp et al., (2018), 'The Non-Bank Credit Cycle, Finance and Economics Discussion Series' Nr. 2018-076. Washington: Board of Governors of the Federal Reserve System, https://doi.org/10.17016/FEDS.2018.076. The cyclical properties of non-bank credit cycles differ from those of bank credit. Non-bank credit cycles are highly correlated with bank credit cycles in some countries but not in others. Moreover, non-bank credit cycles are less synchronized than bank credit cycles across countries. Finally, non-bank credit cycles could act as a leading indicator for currency, but not for systemic banking crises. The opposite is true for bank credit cycles.

[763] Y. Hashimoto and S. Krogstrup, (2019), Capital Flows: The Role of Bank and Nonbank Balance Sheets, IMF Working Paper Nr. WP/19/85, April, pp. 4–5, 24–25. See also: L.S. Goldberg, and S. Krogstrup, (2018), International Capital Flow Pressures, NBER Working Paper Nr. 24286, February; N.-J. Hansen, and S. Krogstrup, (2019), Capital Flows and Global Factors in Korea: An Investor Base Perspective, mimeo, International Monetary Fund.

nonbank risk management behavior. If the counterparties are nonbanks or foreign banks, the flows can look different.'[764] The findings suggest that changes in the mix of financial institutional structure over time can contribute to shifting capital flow volatility and sensitivity to global risk conditions.

Capital controls were long seen as the preferred approach[765] to manage those possible sensitivities and prevent instability.[766] It would also mitigate the asset price volatility that it would normally trigger, reducing credit availability as well.[767] In particular developing economies with a history of operating a predominantly closed economy and a not yet fully mature financial infrastructure have chosen that option.[768] Jeanne and Korinek[769] propose, however, a Pigovian tax approach with a view toward control-

764 Y. Hashimoto and S. Krogstrup, (2019), Ibid. p. 24. Also: S. Krogstrup, and C. Tille, (2018), Foreign Current Funding and Global Factors, Working Paper The Graduate Institute of Geneva, mimeo; N. Magud, (2018), Discussion of Capital Flows: The Role of Bank and Nonbank Balance Sheet, presentation at the Research Department workshop on Too Many Objectives or Too Few Instruments? Economic Policy Challenges Ten Years After the Crisis. March 22; S. Avdjiev, et al. (2017), The Shifting Drivers of Global Liquidity, CEPR Working Paper Nr. 12127.

765 In a way they still are, although it is acknowledged that policy design is still 'incomplete'. See for guidance: G. Pasricha, (2017), Policy Rules for Capital Controls, Bank of Canada Staff Working Paper Nr. 42, October.

766 See for support: M. Saeed Qureshi et al., (2014), Regulating Capital Flows at Both Ends. Does it Work, IMF Working Paper Nr. WP/14/188. They focus on the coordination between source and recipient countries as a policy tool to manage cross-border capital flows and the spillover effects they might create. Cross-border capital flows may destabilize economic activity in particular if the domestic financial system is underdeveloped and institutions are weak: C. Buch, (2017), Macroprudential Measures and Capital Controls: Towards a Framework for Policy Evaluation, Banque de France Financial Stability Review, April, Nr. 21, pp. 157–166. Also: A.R. Ghosh, et al. (2016), When Do Capital Inflow Surges End in Tears? American Economic Review, Vol. 106, Issue 5, pp. 581–585; D.J. Scott and I. Presno, (2017), Capital Controls and Monetary Policy Autonomy in a Small Open Economy, International Finance Discussion Papers Nr. 1190, February. The former conclude that shocks to capital flows into a small open economy lead to volatility in asset prices and credit supply. Typically, that process is managed by the central bank using the domestic interest rate to manage the capital account. The use of capital controls allows to work more on domestic variables rather than the foreign interest rate.

767 S.L. Schwarcz, (2017), The Financial Crisis and Credit Unavailability: Cause or Effect, CIGI Policy Brief Nr. 98, February.

768 Experiences with capital controls in small economies are consistently positive. However, in large open economies where domestic financial constraints may bind following a large negative shock, Scott Davis et al. consider both ex ante capital controls (prudential) and ex post controls (crisis management). In a large open economy, there is a tension between the desire to tax capital inflows to manipulate the terms-of-trade and tax capital outflows for either prudential or crisis management purposes. When capital controls are chosen non-cooperatively, they show that ex post capital controls are unsuccessful in alleviating financial constraints in a crisis, and ex ante capital controls are unsuccessful at reducing financial instability before the crisis. Non-cooperative capital controls leave the crisis-hit country even worse off than in an environment with unrestricted capital flows. See for details: J. Scott Davis and M.B. Devereux, (2019), Capital Controls as Macro-Prudential Policy in a Large Open Economy, NBER Working Paper Nr. 25710, March.

769 O. Jeanne and A. Korinek, (2010), Excessive Volatility in Capital Flows: A Pigovian Taxation Approach, NBER Working Paper Series, Nr. 15927. Later on A. Korinek, (2018), Regulating Capital Flows to Emerging Markets: An Externality View, Journal of International Economics, Vol. 111, pp. 61–80.

ling capital flows.[770] They analyze prudential controls on capital flows to emerging markets from the perspective of a Pigovian tax that addresses externalities associated with the deleveraging cycle. They present a model in which restricting capital inflows during boom times reduces the potential outflows during busts.[771] This reduces the feedback effects of deleveraging episodes, when tightening financial constraints on borrowers and collapsing prices for collateral assets have mutually reinforcing effects. Their model[772] envisages collateralized international borrowing, in which the value of collateral assets endogenously depends on the state of the economy. When financial constraints[773] are binding in such a set-up, financial amplification effects (sudden stops) arise as declining collateral values, tightening financial constraints and falling consumption mutually reinforce each other.[774] Such amplification effects are not internalized by individual borrowers and constitute a negative externality that provides a natural rationale for Pigovian taxation of international borrowing. Their findings

[770] Mainly to and from emerging markets in their case. See in more recent times about the correlation between capital inflows and outflows: J.S. Davis and E. van Wincoop, (2017), Globalization and the Increasing Correlation between Capital Inflows and Outflows, Federal Reserve Bank of Dallas, Globalization and Monetary Policy Institute, Working Paper Nr. 323, August. The correlation between capital inflows and outflows has increased substantially over time due to financial globalization, both in advanced as well as emerging economies. They conclude '[t]rade globalization has the exact opposite effect, but has been significantly dominated by financial globalization in the last several decades. Even if trade and financial globalization had grown proportionally, we find that the higher correlation between inflows and outflows due to financial globalization would still have dominated.' (Ibid. p. 31). Also: E. Cerutti et al., (2017), How Important is the Global Financial Cycle? Evidence from Capital Flows, IMF Working Paper Nr. WP/17/193, September; F. Gourio, et al., (2016), Uncertainty and International Capital Flows, Stanford Working Paper, mimeo; F. Broner, and J. Ventura, (2016), Rethinking the Effects of Financial Globalization, The Quarterly Journal of Economics, Vol. 131, Issue 3, pp. 1497–1542; R. Correa et al., (2017), Cross-Border Bank Flows and Monetary Policy, Bank of Canada Working Paper Nr. 17-34, August; B. J. Eichengreen and P. Gupta, (2016), managing Sudden Stops, Policy Research Working Paper Nr. 7639.

[771] Igan et al. draw some conclusion studying the real effect of capital flows: (1) the higher the volumes of capital inflows, the more external finance dependent industries emerge, (2) a reduction of output volatility occurs in case of equity inflows, (3) the nexus of capital flows and growth is more pronounced in countries with well-functioning banks. See in detail: D. Igan et al., (2016), Real Effects of Capital Inflows in Emerging Markets, IMF Working Paper Nr. 16/235, December. See for the effect of capital inflow in combination with financial deregulation within the context of the financial crisis: M. Hoffmann and I. Stewen, (2016), Holes in the Dike: the Global Savings Glut, U.S. House Prices and the Long Shadow of Banking Deregulation, CAMA Working Paper Nr. 6, February. Interesting in this paper is the fact that they break down in terms of the effect between states that opened up for out-of-state banks and those that did not. In those that did, house prices were more sensitive to capital inflows. Capital inflows relaxed the Value at Risk of integrated and regionally diversified US banks (more than local banks).

[772] See also A. Korinek, (2010), Regulating Capital Flows to Emerging Markets; An Externality View, John Hopkins University Working Paper, updated as A. Korinek, (2017), Regulating Capital Flows to Emerging Markets: An Externality View, NBER Working Paper Nr. 24152, December.

[773] M. Linn and D. Weagley, (2017), Systemic Risk and Firm Financial Constraints, Georgia Tech Scheller College of Business Research Paper Nr. 17-36.

[774] Jeanne et al., (2010), p. 10.

point to a calibrated 1.3% Pigovian tax per foreign USD of capital borrowed for an economy that experiences sudden stops.[775]

Although Jeanne et al. have helped to simplify our understanding of taxation-related capital controls, the real-world experiences have been mixed.[776] In recent times, during the 2008 crisis, a number of countries (Brazil, Taiwan, etc.) all implemented a similar measure of foreign investments in certain domestic asset classes (which normally include at least equity and fixed-income products). They have helped to stabilize or at least mitigate the volatility of capital flows into those countries to some degree, while other examples have proven unsuccessful.[777] In other scenarios they caused international (investors) to decrease portfolio holdings (i.e. externalities caused by capital controls) in that country for the benefit of non-control countries.[778] Part of the opacity in the application of such a welfare model is built on the correlation and level of herding embedded in the targeted cross-border capital flows.[779] A recent and broader study (139 countries) assesses the effectiveness and associated externalities that arise when macroprudential policies (MPPs) are used to manage international capital flows. They take into account the structure of the banking system as well as the presence of potential cross-country and cross-asset class spillover effects. Their results indicate that the structure of the domestic banking system matters for the effectiveness of MPPs. We specifi-

[775] With a 10% probability.

[776] Capital controls have a bad reputation regardless of whether they are used as a tax instrument or not. Advanced economies use capital controls to tame speculative inflows. However several factors undermine their use as a prudential tool: (1) it appears that inflow controls became inextricably linked with outflow controls. The latter have typically been more pervasive, more stringent and more linked to autocratic regimes, failed macroeconomic policies and financial crisis—inflow controls are thus damned by this 'guilt by association'; (2) capital account restrictions often tend to be associated with current account restrictions. As countries aspired to achieve greater trade integration, capital controls came to be viewed as incompatible with free trade; and (3) as policy activism of the 1970s gave way to the free market ideology of the 1980s and 1990s, the use of capital controls, even on inflows and for prudential purposes, fell into disrepute. See in detail for a great analysis on the matter: A.R. Ghosch et al., (2016), What's In a Name? That Which We Call Capital Controls, MF Working Paper Nr. 16/25, February.

[777] Chile had a similar measure in place during the period 1991–1998, See in extenso: F. Gallego, L. Hernandez and K. Schmidt-Hebbel, (2002), Capital Controls in Chile: Were They Effective?, Banking, Financial Integration, and Crises, L. Hernandez and K. Schmidt-Hebbel (ed.), Central Bank of Chile, Santiago, pp. 361 ff. See broader: G. Pasricha, et al., (2015), Domestic and Multilateral Effects of Capital Controls in Emerging Markets, ECB Working Paper Nr. 1844, August.

[778] Interesting is that the decrease followed the signaling of the introduction of control rather than the introduction itself. See in detail: K. Forbes et al., (2012), Bubble Thy Neighbor: Portfolio Effects and Externalities from Capital Controls, Working Paper, Mimeo, April 27. Their focus is on the introduction of capital controls in Brazil.

[779] See E. Takáts and J. Temesvary, (2019), How Does the Interaction of macroprudential and Monetary Policies Affect Cross-Border Bank Lending, BIS Working Paper Nr. 82, May 15, via bis.org. Also: BCBS, (2019/2018), Survey on the Interaction of Regulatory Instruments: Results and Analysis, Working Paper Nr. 35 (March 2019), Working Paper Nr. 33, (July 2018). BCBS, (2016), Literature Review on Integration of Regulatory Capital and Liquidity Instruments, BCBS Working Paper Nr. 30, March.

cally find that a high share of non-resident bank loans in the MPP-implementing country reduces the domestic effectiveness of most MPPs, while a high return on assets in the domestic banking system has the opposite effect. They further find that a high return on assets in the banking system of countries other than the MPP-implementing one leads to a reduction, and a greater degree of trade integration leads to an increase in spillovers across countries. However, the economic significance of the results suggests that only a limited number of countries will tend to experience substantial geographical spillover effects. Second, they also find some evidence of spillover effects across asset classes within countries.[780]

A meaningful introduction and modeling of the instrument, at least from a Pigovian point of view, would necessitate a better understanding of the directional causality of capital flows during a regional or global deleveraging process. The case for an ex ante[781] intervention has become pronounced,[782] but for the simple observation that financial (de)regulation, although often viewed from an efficiency point of view, also has ongoing distributive effects. There is a trade-off, when implementing financial regulation (or not).[783] The financial sector benefits from risk taking by earning greater expected returns. However, risk-taking also increases the incidence of large losses that lead to

[780] See J. Beirne and C. Friedrich, (2015), Capital Flows and Macro-Prudential Policies- A Multilateral Assessment of Effectiveness and Externalities, Bank of Canada/Banque de Canada Working Paper Nr. 2014/31. Cerutti et al. assess five types of prudential instruments on the nature and type of effect: capital buffers (subcategories: general capital requirements, real state credit-specific capital buffers, consumer credit-specific capital buffers and other specific capital buffers), interbank exposure limits, concentration limits, loan to value (LTV) ratio limits and reserve requirements (subcategories: domestic currency capital requirements and foreign currency capital requirements). See: E. Cerutti et al., (2016), Changes in Prudential Policy Instruments–A New Cross-Country Database, IMF Working Paper Nr. 16/110, June.

[781] The optimal policy mix in such models involves a combination of both types (i.e. ex ante and ex post) of measures since they offer alternative ways of mitigating binding financial constraints. Comparing their relative merits, ex post policy interventions are only taken once a crisis has materialized and are therefore better targeted, whereas ex ante measures are blunter since they depend on crisis expectations. However, ex post interventions distort incentives and create moral hazard. This introduces a time consistency problem, which can in turn be solved by ex ante policy measures. See for the very examined area of whether autonomous changes in expectations (i.e. changes in expectations that are not due to changes in fundamentals) cause cycle fluctuations: Z. Enders et al., (2017), Growth Expectations, Undue Optimism and Short-Run Fluctuations, Deutsche Bundesbank Discussion Papers Nr. 11/2017. Business sentiment seems to not only correspond to changes in current or future fundamentals, but is in itself a 'genuine, psychological cause of (inefficient) business cycles aka undue optimism.

[782] O. Jeanne and A. Korinek, (2013), Macro-prudential Regulation versus Mopping Up after the Crash, NBER Working Paper Series, Nr. 18675.

[783] Financial regulation has adopted processes that are inconsistent with adherence to the rule of law. Calomiris refers to 'flawed regulatory processes especially those related to the use of "guidance," which avoids transparency, accountability and predictability, and thereby increases regulatory risk – has resulted in poor execution of regulatory responsibilities, unnecessary regulatory costs and opportunities for politicized mischief.' See: C.W. Calomiris, (2017), Restoring the Rule of Law in Financial Regulation, CATO Working Paper Nr. 48, September. His baseline: regulatory practice should be grounded in formal rule making rather than the reliance on guidance.

credit crunches and impose negative externalities on the real economy. Korinek and Kreamer in this context highlight: '[a] regulator has to trade-off efficiency in the financial sector, which is aided by deregulation, against efficiency in the real economy, which is aided by tighter regulation and a more stable supply of credit. We also show that financial innovation, asymmetric compensation schemes, concentration in the banking system, and bailout expectations enable or encourage greater risk-taking[784] and allocate greater surplus to the financial sector at the expense of the rest of the economy'.[785]

International capital flows[786] can create significant financial instability[787] in emerging economies because of pecuniary externalities associated with exchange rate move-

[784] Traditionally the focus has been on inefficiently high bank risk-taking in the run-up to financial crises. In contrast, Schroth focuses on inefficiently low bank risk-taking during financial crises. The reason for the latter inefficiency is that a regulator can mitigate the risk of binding bank funding conditions by increasing a bank's future profits to offset decreases in bank equity. The first main policy implication is that banks should build up capital buffers during normal times. The second main policy implication is that banks should be given ample time to rebuild capital buffers following a financial crisis and that regulation should increase bank profitability in that process. The idea is to raise the prospect of future profitability during the financial crisis with a view to increasing a bank's access to outside funding and reducing ex post the severity of a financial crisis. Schroth studies optimal bank capital requirements in a model of endogenous bank funding conditions and finds that requirements should be higher during good times such that a macroprudential 'buffer' is provided. However, whether banks can use buffers to maintain lending during a financial crisis depends on the capital requirement during the subsequent recovery. The reason is that a high requirement during the recovery lowers bank shareholder value during the crisis and thus creates funding-market pressure to use buffers for deleveraging rather than for maintaining lending. Therefore, buffers are useful if banks are not required to rebuild them quickly. See in detail: J. Schroth, (2019), Macroprudential Policy with capital Buffers, BIS Working Paper Nr. 771, February 22, via bis.org

[785] See A. Korinek and J. Kreamer, (2013), The Redistributive Effects of Financial Deregulation, NBER Working Paper Series, Nr. 19572.

[786] You could call it international capital market pressures that occur. To visualize and understand a new measure of capital flow pressures in the form of a recast exchange market pressure index has been developed. The measure captures pressures that materialize in actual international capital flows as well as pressures that result in exchange rate adjustments. The input for the analysis is the balance of payments equilibrium conditions and international asset portfolio considerations. It therefore combines price and quantity information. Also global risk response index, which reflects the country-specific sensitivity of capital flow pressures to measures of global risk aversion. See in detail: L. Goldberg and S. Krogstrup, (2018), International Capital Flow Pressures, Federal Reserve Bank of New York Staff Reports, Nr. 834, February. They comment '[c]apital flows respond differently to global risk factors depending on whether a country's monetary authorities intervene in foreign exchange markets to influence the local currency exchange rate, or whether capital flow pressures result in changes in the exchange rate or interest rate sufficient to discourage capital flow pressures from being realized in actual flows. In fully floating exchange rate regimes, capital flow pressures would materialize in exchange rate adjustments while in fixed exchange rate regimes, the price adjustment is prevented, and a capital flow is fully realized in response to the same pressure' (p. 1). A closer look at the interesting literature list might be justified for those interested in the supporting literature that led to the design of the model.

[787] See for if and how monetary easing increases financial instability: A. Cesa-Bianchi and A. Rebucci, (2015), Does Easing Monetary Policy Increase Financial Instability, IMF Working Paper, Nr.

ments.[788] Should that be captured by capital controls or macroprudential regulation? Korinek and Sandri present a tractable model to show that it is desirable to employ both types of instruments[789]: reduces overborrowing, while capital controls increase the aggregate net worth of the economy as a whole by also stimulating savings. The two policy measures should be set higher the greater an economy's debt burden and the higher domestic inequality. They find optimal capital controls and macroprudential regulation in the magnitude of 2% for the emerging market sphere. In advanced countries where the risk of sharp exchange rate depreciations is more limited, the role for capital controls subsides, without making the role of macroprudential regulation abundant when mitigating booms and busts in asset prices.[790]

Welfare can be improved by ex ante macroprudential policies such as debt limits and mandatory insurance requirements,[791] but this necessitates global coordination as domestic

---

WP/15/139. An implication of their analysis is that the weak link in the US policy framework in the run-up to the Global Recession was not the excessively lax monetary policy after 2002, but rather the absence of an effective regulatory framework aimed at preserving financial stability. That is somewhat contradicting with the traditional view that a different interest rate policy would have reduced both the likelihood and severity of the Great Recession (p. 36). When a pallet of different instruments is available (besides interest rate policy), expansive monetary policy doesn't have to increase financial instability. Also: A. Zdzienicka et al., (2015), Effects of Macroprudential Policies on Financial Conditions: Evidence from the U.S., Working paper Nr. 15/288, December. Monetary policy shocks have significant and persistent effects on financial conditions and can attenuate long-term financial instability. Cecchetti et al. observed that the leverage ratio, as well as other measures of firm-level vulnerability, increases for banks and non-banks as domestic monetary policy easing persists and therefore increases financial vulnerability. See in detail: S. Cecchetti et al., (2017), Does Prolonged Monetary Policy Easing Increase Financial Vulnerability, IMF Working Paper Nr. WP/17/65, February.

[788] G. Plantin and H.S. Shin, (2016), Exchange Rates and Monetary Spillovers, BIS Working Paper Nr. 537, January; J. Kearns et al., (2019), Explaining Monetary Spillovers: The Matrix Reloaded, BIS Working Paper Nr. 757, November 20. Also here regulatory arbitrage plays a role, see: J. Temesvary, (2018), The Role of Regulatory Arbitrage in U.S. Banks' International Flows: Bank-Level Evidence, Economic Inquiry, Vol. 56, Issue 4, pp. 2077–2098.

[789] See regarding the most important sustainability dimension in macroprudential regulation: K.N. Johnson, (2013), Macroprudential Regulation: A Sustainable Approach To Regulating Financial Markets, University of Illinois Law Review, pp. 882–918; L.A. Górnicka, (2015), Regulating Financial Markets: Costs and Trade-Offs, Tinbergen Institute Research Series Nr. 621, Amsterdam; M. Rubio, (2018), Shadow Banking, Macroprudential Regulation and Financial Stability, Nottingham University Working Paper, September, mimeo.

[790] See in detail: A. Korinek and D. Sandri, (2015), Capital Controls or Macroprudential Regulation?, IMF Working Paper Nr. WP/15/218. Also: G. Benigno et al., (2016), Optimal Capital Controls and Real Exchange Rate Policies: A Pecuniary Externality Perspective, Journal of Monetary Economics, Vol. 84, 147–165; in the context of a wider imperfect financial union (i.e. Europe): F. Balestrieri and S. Basu, (2018), An Imperfect Financial Union With Heterogeneous Regions IMF Working Paper Nr. WP/18/205, September.

[791] A. Korinek and A. Simsek, (2016), Liquidity Trap and Excessive Leverage, American Economic Review, Vol. 106, Issue 3, pp. 699–738. Also: J. Lukkezen et al., (2016), Macro-Economics of Balance-Sheet Problems and the Liquidity Trap, CPB Background Document, August; T. Akram, (2016), Japan's Liquidity Trap, Levy Economics Institute Working Paper Nr. 862, March. The latter concludes that generating effective demand might be a more appropriate remedy for the country's liquidity trap.

macroprudential policies and prudential capital controls[792] have international spillovers through their impact on capital flows, potentially leading to capital wars, which tend to trigger depression of global interest rates.[793] It was learned in recent times that a simple leaning-against-the-wind policy can reduce systemic risk and improve welfare. It was also assessed that an unexpected increase in policy rates reduces output, inflation, and asset prices without fundamentally mitigating financial risks. Laseen et al.[794] also find that while a systematic monetary policy reaction can improve welfare, it is too simplistic: (1) it is highly sensitive to parameters of the model and (2) is detrimental in the presence of falling asset prices. Macroprudential policy, similar to a countercyclical capital requirement, is more robust and leads to higher welfare gains.[795]

Macroprudential policy[796] has largely been viewed and implemented as a form of banking regulation in recent practice.[797] However, the externalities to be addressed by

[792] I. Alonso Ávarez, (2015), Institutional Drivers of Capital Flows, Bank of Spain, Working Paper Nr. 1531.

[793] As we have experienced in most parts of the Western world in recent years. A number of countries have stepped out of that rate race (Australia, Brazil, Russia, …) for a variety of reasons. See also in detail the proposition of international coordination in the context of a Pareto optimum through international coordination of policies: O. Jeanne, (2014), Macro-prudential Policies in a Global Perspective, NBER Working Paper Series, Nr. 19967.

[794] S. Laseen et al., (2015), Systemic Risk: A New Trade-Off for Monetary Policy, IMF Working Paper, Nr. WP/15/142. Their study captures the non-linear behavior of financial variables and their interaction with the real economy. 'These frictions (financial intermediaries try to maximize the return on intermediaries' equity and fundraising is difficult during periods of financial distress) and their interaction with the real economy generate systemic risk. That can then be described as 'a fall in asset prices that induces a sufficiently large decline in the return on financial intermediaries' equity renders them unable to raise equity. As a result, their portfolio becomes riskier, prompting risk averse managers to require higher risk-adjusted returns in the future (the Sharpe ratio increases). To deliver the higher expected returns the price of capital must decline. Lower asset prices propagate the financial stress to the real economy by reducing the volume of investment in physical capital which results in a further deterioration in the macroeconomic environment, raising the possibility of a vicious cycle' (p. 3).

[795] See for the role of macroprudential policy in safeguarding financial stability: R. Vergara, (2015), The Role of Macroprudential Policy and Monetary Policy in Safeguarding Financial Stability, Speech given at the First Conference "Banking Development, Stability and Sustainability", organized by the Chilean Superintendency of Banks and Financial Institutions and the Diego Portales University, Santiago, November 5. Cizel warns for the substitution effects (of macroprudential policy) toward non-bank credit, especially in advanced economies, reducing the policies' effect on total credit. Quantity restrictions are particularly potent in constraining bank credit but also cause the strongest substitution effects. See: J. Cizel et al., (2016), Effective Macroprudential Policy: Cross-Sector Substitution from Prize and Quantity Measures, IMF Working Paper Nr. 16/94. Also: A. Prasad et al., (2016), Macroprudential Policy and financial Stability in the Arab Region, IMF Working paper Nr. 16/98, May. See also the annual review of macroprudential policy in the EU: ESRB, A Review of Macroprudential Policy in the EU, from 2016 onwards.

[796] See for an overview of the effectiveness of macroprudential policies: E. Cerutti et al., (2017), The Use and Effectiveness of Macroprudential Policies: New Evidence, Journal of Financial Stability, Elsevier, Vol. 28(C), pp. 203–224.

[797] For the operational dimensions see: ESRB, (2014), The ESRB Handbook on Operationalising Macro-Prudential Policy in the Banking Sector, March, Frankfurt am Main. The framework is built

macroprudential policy stretch beyond the banking sector and also play a prominent role in the household and corporate sectors.[798] Trying to address these externalities with banking regulation alone leads to various forms of leakage as they encourage lending to move to non-banking financial intermediaries and foreign banks—a problem that has affected the implementation of macroprudential policies in recent times. Jeanne and Korinek therefore advocate a focus on borrowers rather than lenders when designing macroprudential policies and aligned tools,[799] including their Pigovian tax model as a macroprudential tool.

But things evolve and by 2019 Pigovian levies have been granted their justified position within the macroprudential toolbox. During late 2014 already, the IMF released its 'macroprudential toolbox' report,[800] reviewing the different macroprudential policies and tools, that is, those policies aiming to reduce systemic risks arising from 'excessive' financial procyclicality and from interconnections and other 'cross-sectional' factors. In an ideal setting macroprudential policies should be driven by externalities and market failures arising from various financial frictions[801] and market imperfections that exist. However, very few of these macroprudential theories have been tested or analyzed, and therefore many of

around four objectives: addressing (1) excessive credit growth and leverage, (2) excessive maturity mismatch and market illiquidity, (3) direct and indirect exposure concentration, and (4) misaligned incentives and moral hazard. See, for instance, the impact of macroprudential policies focused on leveraged lending: S. Kim et al., (2017), Macroprudential Policy and the Revolving Door of Risk: Lessons from Leveraged Lending Guidance, Federal Reserve Bank of New York Staff Reports, Nr. 815, May. They conclude that '[w]hile we do not find that nonbanks had more lax lending policies than banks, we unveil important evidence that nonbanks increased bank borrowing following the issuance of guidance, possibly to finance their growing leveraged lending. The guidance was effective at reducing banks' leveraged lending activity, but it is less clear whether it accomplished its broader goal of reducing the risk that these loans pose for the stability of the financial system'.

[798] Changes in macroprudential policy via loan-to-value limits and local currency reserve requirements have a significant impact on international bank lending. Balance sheet characteristics tend to play an important role in determining the strength of these effects, with better capitalized banking systems and those with more liquid assets and less core deposits reacting more. The tightening of macroprudential measures can be associated with international spillovers. See in detail: S. Avdjiev et al., (2016), International Prudential Policy Spillovers: A Global Perspective, BIS Working Paper Nr. 589, October.

[799] O. Jeanne and A. Korinek, (2014), Macro-Prudential Policy Beyond Banking Regulation, Banque de France, Financial Stability Review, Nr. 18, April 2014, pp. 163–171.

[800] S. Claessens, (2014), An Overview of Macro-Prudential Policy Tools, IMF Working Paper Series, Nr. WP/14/214.

[801] Financial frictions are central to understanding the non-linearities observed during financial crises. Financial frictions lead to an amplification of cross-border shocks, but most empirical studies on macro-financial linkages resort to linear models that fail to account for the non-linear amplification mechanisms implied by the theoretical literature; See: N. Metiu et al. et al., (2015), Financial Frictions and Global Spillovers, Deutsche Bundesbank Discussion Paper, Nr. 04/2015. Also: M; Pietrunti, (2017), Financial Frictions and the Real Economy, ESRB Working Paper Nr. 41, April; R. Duval et al., (2017), Financial Frictions and the Great Productivity Slowdown, IMF Working Paper Nr. WP/17/129, May. Duval et al. demonstrate that the productivity slowdown post-crisis can be linked to the combination of pre-existing firm-level financial fragilities and tightening credit conditions. Or to be more precise: '(i) firms that entered the crisis with weaker balance sheets experienced decline in total factor productivity growth relative to their less vulnerable counterparts after the crisis; (ii) this decline was larger for firms located in countries where credit conditions tightened

these policies so far have been designed out of 'generic concern'.[802] The result has been that we have not only produced lots of them through command-and-control legislation but also that they have been implemented without proper and effective calibration to circumstances and with very little understanding of which tool to use in order to capture what type of risk. After all, procyclicality[803] and systemic risks can have many sources, including aggregate shocks and policy deficiencies, and not all of them require macroprudential attention.[804] Equally little is known about the cost of those policies and how they interact with other policy domains (monetary policy, micro-economic policy, etc.) as well as how they impact resource allocation in markets.[805] The upshot is that such blind introductions can make things worse. Claessens concludes that '[i]dentifying precisely the source of externalities operating through the financial system thus help determine the corresponding, specific macroprudential policies'.[806] Externalities have in common that they either induce procyclicality or are caused by interconnectedness and can interact. The rapid

more; (iii) financially fragile firms cut back on intangible capital investment compared to more resilient firms, which is one plausible way through which financial frictions undermined productivity'.

[802] Claessens, Ibid. p. 3

[803] H. Huizinga and L. Laeven, (2019), The Procyclicality of Banking, ECB Working Paper Nr. 2288, June 7. Loan loss provisions in the euro area are negatively related to GDP growth, that is, they are procyclical they conclude. Loan loss provisions tend to be more procyclical at larger and better capitalized banks.

[804] M. Houdala, (2018), Off the Radar: Exploring the Rise of Shadow Banking in the EU, Czech National Working Paper Nr. 16. The EU shadow banking system is found to be highly procyclical and positively related to increasing demand of long-term institutional investors, more stringent capital regulation and faster financial development. He further documents that the relationship between monetary policy and shadow banking growth is level-dependent and may be determined by the relative magnitude of interest rates in the economy. In this respect, two main motives driving the relationship are identified: the 'funding cost' motive and the 'search-for-yield' motive (pp. 15 ff.). Second, the driving forces of shadow banking differ between the old and new EU countries, largely due to the missing legal framework for securitization (which lowers the funding costs) in the new members. The funding cost motive dominates when interest rates are high, while the search for yield motive matters when interest rates are low (p. 16).

[805] Regarding monetary policy for financial stability see: J. Caruana, (2016), Monetary Policy for Financial Stability, Speech at the 52nd SEACEN Governors' Conference Naypyidaw, Myanmar, November 26, bis.org

[806] Claessens, Ibid. p. 5. He uses a more reduced number/categories of externalities than was done in our chapter. He limits himself to (1) externalities related to strategic complementarities, that arise from the strategic interactions of banks and other financial institutions and agents, and which cause the build-up of vulnerabilities during the expansionary phase of a financial cycle; (2) externalities related to fire sales and credit crunches, that arise from a generalized sell-off of assets causing a decline in asset prices, a deterioration of balance sheets of intermediaries and investors, and a drying up of financing, especially during the contractionary phase of a financial (and business) cycle; and (3) externalities related to interconnectedness, caused by the propagation of shocks from systemic institutions or through financial markets or networks ('contagion'). The anticipation of bailouts perversely affects the (risk-taking) incentives for SIFIs and other market participants. It introduces a race among institutions to become systemically important, as this lowers the cost of funding, and reduces market discipline for creditors of SIFIs, especially the riskiest ones. See in detail: Claessens, Ibid. pp. 6–8.

growth of large financial institutions during a boom means that procyclicality gets reinforced by contagion risks. Conversely there can be complementarities in the tools to be used to mitigate either source of externalities. Financial booms were often amplified by 'political regulatory stimuli, credit subsidies, and an increasing light-touch approach to financial supervision'. The regulatory backlash following a crisis therefore often focuses on solving the previous crisis and as a consequence that type of regulation often does not survive the following crisis. Political ramifications are an important part of understanding the financial sector and its regulatory positioning. There is an interplay between politics and financial policy across the cycles. Some are willing to go as far as stating that politics is the undoing of macroprudential regulation.[807]

The joint impact of macroprudential and capital control measures against a background of cross-border banking and cross-border banking flows is however prone to regulatory arbitrage. While lender countries' macroprudential policies reduce direct cross-border banking outflows, they are associated with larger outflows through local affiliates. Direct cross-border inflows are higher in borrower countries with more usage of macroprudential policies and are linked to circumvention motives, assess Cerutti and Zhou.[808] They studied the impact of macroprudential (MPM) and capital control measures (CCM) on cross-border banking flows.[809] They start from the understanding that 'although most CCM do not specifically target cross-border banking flows, but it is likely that they could directly or indirectly affect cross-border banking flows as they are designed to impact cross-border

[807] J. Dagher, (2018), Regulatory Cycles: Revisiting the Political Economy of Financial Crises, IMF Working Paper Nr. WP/18/08, January. Dagher reviews ten previous financial crises and analyzes them from the perspective of a political economy and the regulatory implications. As Dagher indicates '[i]t shows that episodes of financial boom went hand in hand with a period of significant deregulation. These episodes were generally accompanied, and sometimes triggered, by procyclical policies by governments that actively amplified credit booms, weakened existing financial regulations and supervision, and engaged in regulatory forbearance. While in most cases the incumbent governments championed laissez-faire policies, they nevertheless engaged in subsidization of credit and intensification of symbiotic relations with bankers and large companies' (p.3). After a crisis, policies were often reversed. Dagher is the first to closely examine the pattern of financial regulatory policies, their political economy and political consequences across different episodes, over time and across countries. Patterns of financial regulation are documented. It shows that in most cases 'regulation has been pro-cyclical, effectively weakening during the boom and strengthening during the bust. Regulators do not operate in a vacuum, and [the] paper shows how, in most cases, political interventions have helped fuel the boom in similar ways across time and countries. The political repercussions of crises, partly due to changes in the public's perception about the role of the government, are usually very significant' (p. 61). Relevant in a time and age where the Volcker rule and the Dodd-Franck Act are prone to renewed deregulation efforts: B. Jopson and R. Wigglesworth, (2018), US Regulators Begin to Ease Volcker Rule, Financial Times, May 30.

[808] E. Cerutti and H. Zhou, (2018), Cross-Border Banking and the Circumvention of Macroprudential and Capital Control Measures, IMF Working Paper Nr. WP/18/217, September.

[809] Others have studied the impact of country-specific uncertainty as a key (pull and push) factor of international capital flows. See S. Choi and D. Furceri, (2018), Uncertainty and Cross-Border Banking Flows, IMF Working Paper Nr. WP/18/4, January. The findings, and this despite the challenges of observing uncertainty as it is often difficult to separate between credit demand and credit supply factors, can be summarized as being that '(i) uncertainty is both a push and pull factor that robustly predicts a decrease in both outflows (retrenchment) and inflows (stops); (ii) global banks

capital flows in general. Similarly, while authorities often employ MPM to target local bank lending, the resulting changes in the incentives of lenders and/or borrowers may generate spillover effects on cross-border banking flows.'[810] It needs to be observed in that context that there are other variables that affect cross-border banking.[811] The analysis asks the question about effectiveness of such measures and the nature of optimal international coordination. They, however, in the first instance determine that substantial policy spillovers exist. Market agents tend to react pretty aggressively to both CCM and MPM directly or indirectly adjusting their international lending/borrowing decisions. CCM seems to have a difficult time avoiding this circumvention of macroprudential policies by market agents. Interesting is their philosophical conclusion that further analysis of the impact of post-crisis financial regulatory reform is still highly relevant and still poorly understood as well as documented.[812]

The aforementioned IMF report suggests that although command-and-control regulation is still dominant in the macroprudential domain, experiences are mixed to disappointing. Claessens does reiterate though that Pigovian instruments play a critical role in all phases of the economic cycle (expansionary, contractionary and contagion- or shock propagation phase),[813] a role that can be either on a stand-alone basis or back-to-back with command and control. Either way, the promising initial results in some countries around the globe confirm that the 'pricing signal' characterizing Pigovian levies to which economic agents respond delivers better results than pure ex ante directive measures and uses the market mechanism to discipline economic agents in the FI sector.

---

rebalance their lending towards safer foreign borrowers from local borrowers when facing higher uncertainty; (iii) this rebalancing occurs only towards advanced economies (flight to quality), but not emerging market economies'. See also: E. Cerutti, et al., (2017), Global Liquidity and Cross-Border Bank Flows, Economic Policy Vol. 32.89, pp. 81–125; S. Choi, (2018), The Impact of US Financial Uncertainty Shocks on Emerging Market Economies: An International Credit Channel, Open Economies Review, Springer, Vol. 29, Issue 1, pp. 89–118, February; S. Choi, et al., (2018), Aggregate Uncertainty and Sectoral Productivity Growth: The Role of Credit Constraints, Journal of International Money and Finance, Vol. 88, pp. 314–330.

[810] E. Cerutti and H. Zhou, (2018), Ibid. p. 4.

[811] E. Cerutti and H. Zhou, (2018), Ibid. pp. 8–12.

[812] E. Cerutti and H. Zhou, (2018), Ibid. pp. 18–19. See also on this matter: P.-R. Agenor and L.P. da Silva, (2018), Financial Spillovers, Spillbacks, and the Scope for International Macroprudential Policy Coordination, BIS Working Papers Nr. 97; A. Avdjiev et al., (2017), International Prudential Policy Spillovers: A Global Perspective, International Journal of Central Banking, Vol. 13, pp. 5–32; V. Bruno et al., (2017), Comparative Assessment of Macroprudential Policies, Journal of Financial Stability, Vol. 28, pp. 183–202; E. Cerutti et al., (2017), The Use and Effectiveness of Macroprudential Policies: New Evidence, Journal of Financial Stability, Vol. 28, pp. 203–224; K. Forbes et al., (2017), The Spillovers, Interactions, and (Un)intended Consequences of Monetary and Regulatory Policies, Journal of Monetary Economics, Vol. 85, pp. 1–22; J. Temesvary et al., (2018), A Global Lending Channel Unplugged? Does U.S. Monetary Policy Affect Cross-Border and Affiliate Lending by Global U.S. Banks? Finance and Economics Discussion Series Nr. 2018-008, Washington: Board of Governors of the Federal Reserve System.

[813] See also regarding that analysis: S. Claessens et al., (2013), Macro-Prudential Policies to Mitigate Financial System Vulnerabilities, Journal of International Money and Finance, Vol. 39, pp. 153–185; M. Giannetti and F. Saidi, (2017), Shock Propagation and Banking Structure, Sveriges Riskbank Working Paper Series Nr. 348, December.

11.9 Financialization as the Neoliberal Tool to Penetrate Non-economic Spheres of Life

In a previous work,[814] I extensively described neoliberalism and its historical emergence. In that context, I commented on the fact that neoliberalism does not include the idea that more public functions should shift from the sovereign to the private market.[815] It was detailed how neoliberalism essentially changes the dynamics of the state itself and turns it into a state market whose functioning follows the dynamics of the private market. It explains why the state has not become smaller in recent years, but is effectively larger. It leverages the magnitude of the private market by mirroring its dynamics. The political elite is only there to assist in the administration of such conversion and reshaping of its essential components. Despite the fact that this phenomenon has been displayed with varying degrees of intensity when comparing countries, the ideological margin between the left and right of the political scene has substantially narrowed during the last two decades. Both wings of the spectrum have embraced the fundamental elements of neoliberalism. The different appearance in the garden variety of ideological paradigms is marginal. That has created opportunities for political coalitions which were never possible in previous times and reduces fundamental social and economic problems to managerial dimensions that require attention in terms of percentages, categories and the like.

Since the private and free market fundamentals have become the standard in a variety of non-economic spheres, the colonization of those non-economic spheres has happened somewhat unnoticed and without notable objections from the side of civil or political society.

The instrument that neoliberalism has used to accomplish that without a material outcry is defined as 'financialization'.[816] Referring to the concept of financialization triggers a myriad of conceptual issues. The term 'financialization' has been defined by many scholars

[814] L. Nijs, (2015), Neoliberalism 2.0. Regulating and Financing Globalizing Markets, Palgrave, Basingstoke, chapters 2 and 3. See also more recently: T. Biebricher, (2019), The Political Theory of Neoliberalism, Stanford University Press, Palo Alto, CA; C. Barthold, (2018), Resisting Financialization with Deleuze and Guattari, Routledge, Abingdon; D. Cahill and M. Cooper, (2018), The SAGE Handbook of Neoliberalism, SAGE Publications, Thousand Oaks, CA; M. Eagleton-Pierce, (2016), Neoliberalism, Routledge, Abingdon; W. Davies, (2016), The Limits of Neoliberalism, Sage Publications, Thousand Oaks, CA; H. Cleaver, (2017), Rupturing the Dialectic: The Struggle Against Work, Money, and Financialization, AK Press, London.

[815] Regulation is instrumental in that transition and codifying this economic ideology into law is central to the existence of the neoliberal discourse; see also: B. Farrand and Marco Rizzi, (2018), There Is No (Legal) Alternative: Codifying Economic Ideology into Law, in E. Nanopoulos & F. Vergis (eds.), The Euro-Crisis as a Multi-Dimensional Systemic Failure of the EU, Cambridge University Press, Cambridge; N. Perrone, (2017), Neoliberalism and Economic Sovereignty: Property, Contracts, and Foreign Investment Relations, in H. Brabazon (Ed.), Neoliberal Legality: Understanding the Role of Law in the Neoliberal Project, Routledge, Abingdon; V. Tarko, (2017), Neoliberalism and Regulatory Capitalism: Understanding The 'Freer Markets More Rules' Puzzle, Dickinson College Working Paper, mimeo.

[816] See: T.I. Palley, (2008), Financialization: Why It Is and Why It Matters?, Levy Economics Institute Working Paper Nr. 525. Palley documents that its principal impacts are to (1) elevate the significance of the financial sector relative to the real sector, (2) transfer income from the real sector

in a variety of contextual and factual frameworks.[817] The most commonly accepted definition is Epstein's, who describes it as 'societal changes which result in an increasing role of financial motives, financial markets, financial actors and financial institutions in the operation of the domestic and international economies'.[818] It captures both the hard and material side of financialization (accumulation and innovation) as well as the softer and culturalist accounts.[819] Despite the many definitions that have been produced over time, its fundamental components have stayed similar, if not the same, that is, financialization is a term that describes an economic system or process that attempts to reduce all value that is exchanged (tangible, intangible, future or present promises, etc.) into a financial (tradable) instrument. It implicitly requires that the object of financialization be broken down in its smallest unit, which can be referred to as a process of commoditization. The effect of commoditization is that it is stripped of all other social or cultural value. What is left and only relevant is the economic and financial value of the object.[820]

In its most general dynamics financialization refers to a pattern of accumulation in which profit making occurs increasingly through financial channels rather than through trade and commodity production.[821] That is observable. During the last two decades the proportion of a nation's GDP contributed by the financial sector has risen substantially to reflect a mean-

to the financial sector, and (3) increase income inequality and contribute to wage stagnation. Additionally, there are reasons to believe that financialization may put the economy at risk of debt deflation and prolonged recession. Brei et al. however document that the relationship between financial development and income inequality is not linear. Up to a point, more finance reduces income inequality. Beyond that point, inequality rises if finance is expanded through market-based financing, but not when finance grows via bank lending. See in detail: M. Brei et al., (2018), Financial Structure and Income Inequality, BIS Working Paper, Nr. 756, November 15, via bis.org

[817] A lot of the differences in definition can be traced back to issues and contestation that relate to the demarcation lines and in particular between financialization and commoditization on the one hand and marketability on the other. How does it relate to globalization and neoliberalization? See in detail E. Engelen, M. Konings and R. Fernandez, (2010), Geographies of Financialization in Disarray: The Dutch Case in Comparative Perspective, Economic Geography, 86(1), pp. 53–73.

[818] G.A. Epstein (ed.), (2005), Financialization and the World Economy, Edward Elgar, Cheltenham, p. 3.

[819] See for a literature review in this respect: I. Ertürk, J. Froud, S. Johal, A. Leaver and K. Williams (eds.), (2008), Financialization at Work, Routledge, Abingdon.

[820] Or in fact subject. Under neoliberalism humans can be ranked on their ability to produce and consume and are appreciated in social terms based on the accumulated wealth they have so far produced (Forbes ranking) in their life. Even if it is inherited wealth, the commoditization process does not recognize the difference as the process is disconnected from every possible judgmental ability. In fact, the accumulated wealth indicator is often used as a proxy for (unproven) qualities in other fields (entrepreneurs becoming politicians. Whose opinion matters more: those who represent capital or who possess the better quality argument? It facilitates categorization and the ability to ignore subjects that do not preach free market dynamics, disqualifying them as populists or as marginal in nature ('deplorables').

[821] In the case of shadow banking the argumentation can be as follows: the accumulation of leverage in the shadow banking system and the creation of credit money by the traditional banking sector are symbiotic processes. As such those processes operate a perverse form in which household debt is stored on the balance sheets of shadow banks, allowing the banking system to break the historical connection between money creation and productive activity. See in detail: J. Michell, (2016), Do

ingful 9%[822] at the higher end of the spectrum, but embodies about 300–5400% in assets relative to the GDP of the country[823] in which the FIs are headquartered. 'Too big to fail' can be complemented with 'too big for the economy'. Although that in itself might not be a preferable trend it is not the core of our focus in this context.

Financialization has penetrated many spheres of life and has always used a different Trojan horse to penetrate uncharted territory. That can be a specific financial technique, a changing environment or a particular asset. In the broader sense, real estate has proven to be the ultimate tool to increase the dependency of citizens upon financial markets, hence increasing their vulnerability to financial market volatility.[824] This process is often accompanied by interprofessional contestation as these financial metrics and models are adopted, institutionalized and legitimized by distinct professions.[825] It has been widely demonstrated in the literature which areas have been penetrated: they include, besides real estate as already mentioned: universities,[826] care,[827] commodity markets,[828] agriculture[829] and food,[830] art[831] and industry as a whole,[832] despite sound bites that claim that the end of the

---

Shadow banks Create Money? 'Financialisation' and the Money Circuit, PKSG Working Paper Nr. 1605 March. Aligned with Michell see: A. Botta et al., (2016), The Macro-economics of Shadow Banking, PKSG Working Paper Nr. 1611, June.

[822] In the US. See also: R. Greenwood and. Scharfstein, (2012), The Growth of Modern Finance, HBS Working Paper.

[823] Source: Haver analytics, Central Banking datasets (2013 numbers).

[824] See: C.M. Reinhart and K. Rogoff, (2011), This Time is Different: Eight Centuries of Financial Folly, Princeton University Press, Princeton; H. Schwartze and L. Seabrooke, (2008), Varieties of Residential Capitalism in the International Political Theory: Old Welfare States and the New Politics of Housing, Comparative European Politics, Vol. 6, pp. 237–261.

[825] See: D. MacKenzie, (2006), An Engine, Not a Camera: How Financial Models Shape Markets, MIT Press, Cambridge.

[826] E. Engelen, R. Fernandez and R. Hendrikse, (2014), How Finance Penetrates its Other: A Cautionary Tale on the Financialization of a Dutch University, Antipode, March, pp. 1–20. That is quite remarkable given the long-standing tradition of self-managed guild-oriented public funded universities in continental Europe.

[827] J. Tronto, (2017), There is an Alternative: Homines Curans and the Limits of Neoliberalism, International Journal of Care and Caring, Vol. 1, Issue 1, pp. 27–43.

[828] I-H. Cheng and W. Xiong, (2013), The Financialization of Commodity Markets, NBER Working Paper Series, Nr. 19642.

[829] L. Nijs, (2014), Global Agricultural Markets: The Handbook of Land, Water and Soft Commodities, chapter 16 on Speculation in soft commodity markets, Palgrave Macmillan, London, including a material literature review of the matter.

[830] S. R. Isakson, (2013), The Financialization of Food: A Political Economy of the Transformation of Agro-Food Supply Chains, ICAS Review Paper Series Nr. 5; J. Clapp, (2012), The Financialization of Food: Who is Being Fed?, Waterloo University Working Paper, and also J. Clapp, (2013), Financialization, Distance and Global Food Politics, Conference Paper Nr. 5, Food Sovereignty: A Critical Dialogue, September 14–15.

[831] M.C. Taylor, (2011), Financialization of Art, Capitalism and Society, Vol. 6, Issue 2, Article 3, updated in 2013. As well: N. Horowith, (2014), Art of the Deal: Contemporary Art in a Global Financial market, Princeton University Press, Princeton NJ, in particular pp. 143–187.

[832] M. Hudson, (2010), The Transition of Industrial Capitalism to a Financialized Bubble Economy, Levy Economics Institute, Working Paper, Nr. 627; G.A. Epstein, (2005), Financialization of the World Economy, Edward Elgar, Cheltenham.

financialization process is nearing.[833] Although for a long time it was asserted that the growth of the financial sector and financialization as a process contributes to economic growth, recent research sheds a more refined light on the matter. It claims that although this is correct in the first stages of the economic development of a country (developing countries), it is no longer the case when those emerging economies mature. For mature economies, the growth of the financial sector and financialization is a drag on overall aggregate growth.[834] It has been shown that this is primarily caused by the fact that investments in the real sector of the economy falls when financialization rises. Moreover, rising fees paid by nonfinancial corporations to financial markets have reduced the internal funds available for investment, shortened their planning horizon and increased uncertainty.[835] From a financial point of view, the interesting question has risen whether global and country-specific uncertainty can be measured, preferably within the context of the traditional capital asset pricing model (CAPM). Ozturk and Sheng[836] decompose the uncertainty of a typical forecaster into common and idiosyncratic uncertainty.[837] They developed monthly measures of macroeconomic uncertainty covering 45 countries and construct a measure of global uncertainty as the weighted average of country-specific uncertainties. They conclude that common uncertainty shocks produce the large and persistent negative response in real economic activity,[838] whereas the contributions of idiosyncratic uncertainty shocks

[833] A. Sheng, (2013), The End of Financialization, Institute for New Economic Thinking, blog article.

[834] S.G. Cecchetti and E. Kharroubi, (2012), Reassessing the Impact of Finance on Growth, BIS Working Papers Series, Nr. 381; C. Lapavitsas, (2014), Profiting Without Producing: How Finance Exploits Us All, Verso, NY and K. Polanyi-Hewitt, (2013), From the Great Transformation to the Great Financialization: On Karl Polanyi and Other Essays, Zed Books, London.

[835] Ő.Orhangazi, (2008), Financialisation and Capital Accumulation in the Non-Financial Corporate Sector: A Theoretical and Empirical Investigation on the US Economy: 1973–2003, Cambridge Journal of Economics, Vol. 32, pp. 863–886.

[836] They developed monthly measures of macroeconomic uncertainty covering 45 countries and constructed a measure of global uncertainty as the weighted average of country-specific uncertainties. Measure captures perceived uncertainty of market participants and derives from two components that are shown to exhibit strikingly different behavior; see in extenso: E. O. Ozturk and X.S. Sheng, (2017), Measuring Global and Country-specific Uncertainty, IMF Working Paper Series, nr. WP/17/219, October. Also: R. Rich and J. Tracy, (2017), The Behavior of Uncertainty and Disagreement and Their Roles in Economic Prediction: A Panel Analysis, Federal Reserve Bank of New York Staff Reports, Nr. 808, February. Rich and Tracy point at the difference between uncertainty and disagreement. Both are subjective magnitudes and therefore difficult to manage. Also: A. Haberis et al., (2017), Uncertain Forward Guidance, Bank of England Working Paper Nr. 654, March. S. Morris and H.S. Shin, (2018), Central Bank Forward Guidance and the Signal Value of Market Prices, BIS Working Paper Nr. 692, January. The relationship works based on circularity: monetary policy relies on market prices, and yet monetary policy influences market prices.

[837] See also: K. Forbes, (2016), Uncertainty about Uncertainty, Speech given at the J.P. Morgan Cazenove "Best of British" Conference, November 23. See more in detail: S. Bahaj and A. Foulis, (2016), Macroprudential Policy under Uncertainty, Bank of England Staff Working Paper Nr. 584, January. One of the elements in their mix is 'presence of unquantifiable sources of risk' and how to deal with it in the face of uncertainty designing macroprudential policies.

[838] Both in the short-run as known for a while but also long term. It leads to a short-term fall in demand because of precautionary savings and rising markups, as well as creating a fall in productivity. But long term it causes a decline in the main macroeconomic aggregate. Households become

are negligible.[839] Richter and Throckmorton on the other hand developed a new method to quantify the effects of uncertainty. The model is characterized by enhanced flexibility compared to existing models and can be used to examine the causal effects of any type of uncertainty in a broad class of models.[840] Uncertainty shocks can potentially be a major source of business cycle fluctuations.[841] Although findings so far are somewhat ambiguous, it can be concluded that although surprise increases in micro-uncertainty have a larger impact on output than macro uncertainty,[842] these surprise increases account for a small

averse to these long-term risks affecting their consumption process (long-run risk channel), which strongly exacerbates the precautionary savings motive and the overall negative effects of uncertainty shocks. See in detail: D. Bonciani and J.J. Oh, (2019), The Long run Effects of Uncertainty Shocks, Bank of England Working Paper Nr. 802, June 7.

[839] Macroeconomic forecasts are persistently too optimistic. Forecast errors tend to drive uncertainty shocks; see: P. Chatterjee and S. Nowak, (2016), Forecast Errors and Uncertainty Shocks, IMF Working Paper Series Nr. WP/16/228, November. Also: P. Chatterjee, (2017), Uncertainty Shocks, Financial Frictions and Business Cycle Asymmetries Across Countries, UC Irvine Working Paper, mimeo; N. Bloom, (2014), Fluctuations in Uncertainty, Journal of Economic Perspectives, Vol. 28, Nr. 2, pp. 153–175; K. Jurado, et al., (2015), Measuring Uncertainty, American Economic Review, Vol. 105, Nr. 3, pp. 1177–1216; M. Weale, (2016), What's Going On? Uncertain Data and Uncertain Outcomes, Speech given at Liverpool University, Bank of England, May 13; H. Armelius et al., (2016), The Timing of Uncertainty Shocks in a Small Open Economy, Sveriges Riksbank Working Paper Series Nr. 334, December. For a country example, see M. Shin et al., (2017), Measuring International Uncertainty: the Case of Korea, Finance and Economics Discussion Series Nr. 66, Washington: Board of Governors of the Federal Reserve System, April; J. Bluedorn and D. Leigh, (2018), Is the Cycle the Trend? Evidence from the Views of International Forecasters, IMF Working Paper Nr. WP/18/163, June. Forecasting in times of crisis is possibly even more difficult but also more relevant. Eicher et al. demonstrate that—based on an examination of 29 macroeconomic variables in terms of bias, efficiency and information content—two-thirds of the key macroeconomic variables that they examine are forecast inefficiently and 6 variables (growth of nominal GDP, public investment, private investment, the current account, net transfers and government expenditures) exhibit significant forecast bias. When they decompose the forecast errors into their sources, they find that forecast errors for private consumption growth are the key contributor to GDP growth forecast errors. Similarly, forecast errors for non-interest expenditure growth and tax revenue growth are crucial determinants of the forecast errors in the growth of fiscal budgets. Forecast errors for balance of payments growth are significantly influenced by forecast errors in goods import growth. See in detail: T.S. Eicher et al., (2018), Forecasts in Times of Crises, IMF Working Paper Nr. WP/18/48.

[840] A.W. Richter and N.A. Throckmorton, (2017), A New Way to Quantify the Effect of Uncertainty, Federal Reserve Bank of Dallas Working Paper Nr. 1705, May 4.

[841] It also pushes out risk-taking to shadow banks. See in detail: X. Tian, (2019), Uncertainty and the Shadow Banking Crisis: Estimates from a Dynamic Model, University of Toronto Working Paper, January, mimeo.

[842] As in general uncertainty can be defined as 'changes in the variance of the exogenous processes driving the model economy', macro-uncertainty can be defined as 'uncertainty about aggregate shocks, such as the time-varying variance of the economy-wide total factor productivity' and micro-uncertainty as 'uncertainty about idiosyncratic shocks, such as the cross-sectional dispersion of firm-level productivity in models with heterogeneous firms'. See in detail: A. Cesa-Bianchi and E. Fernandez-Corugedo, (2017), Uncertainty, Financial Frictions and Nominal Rigidities: A Quantitative Investigation, IMF Working Paper Nr. WP/17/211, September, p. 4. See also footnote 3 p. 4 for a full overview of uncertainty literature.

(or non-trivial) share of overall output volatility. That would imply that uncertainty shocks have a limited impact on and unlikely are a major driver behind business cycle fluctuations.[843]

The financial industry extracts economic rents from the real economy rather than the return of greater economic value. It triggered a brain drain from the real sector to the financial sector and caused the effect that the share of capital in total is increasing to the detriment of the share of labor income, a phenomenon that has been in effect since the early 1970s. It has also affected many policy areas, notably the climate change area,[844] as financialization can be denominated as financial neoliberalism.[845] Neoliberalism is the driver of financialization as it embodies both a political (the deregulated market economy is the best way to promote individual freedom) and economic (a laissez-faire economy is the best way to promote economic efficiency and economic well-being) philosophy. Financial markets are given a special elevated standing under neoliberalism as they are portrayed as ideal markets, that is, they are cleaned continuously via rapid price adjustments as prices embody all economically relevant information. As financial markets operate through (large) FIs, they have gone hand in hand with enhanced corporate control (corpocracy).

Neoliberalism can be understood as the latest institutional form of capitalism. The social structure of the accumulation theory offers an analysis of the periodic changes in the capitalist institutional structure.[846] A social structure of accumulation (SSA)[847] is interpreted here as a coherent, long-lasting capitalist institutional structure that promotes profit-making and forms a framework for capital accumulation. While the post Second World War SSA was characterized by a strong regulatory dynamic built around the function of the sovereign, the SSA that has developed since the 1980s is quite different.

The neoliberal SSA has entailed a major restructuring of the global capitalist system as well as a transformation of domestic institutions. The change in the role of the financial sector in the neoliberal era has not just involved a quantitative expansion of its activities and profits. In this era financial institutions, particularly the larger global FIs, broke out of their role as servants of non-financial capital accumulation to pursue their own profits

843 See also: N. Balke et al., (2017), Understanding the Aggregate Effects of Credit Frictions and Uncertainty, Globalization and Monetary Policy Institute Working Paper Nr. 317, Federal Reserve Bank of Dallas; S. Basu and B. Bundick, (2017), Uncertainty Shocks in a Model of Effective Demand, Econometrica, Vol. 85, Issue 3, pp. 937–958.

844 L. Lohman, (2013), Financialization, Commodification and Carbon: The Contradictions of Neoliberal Climate Change, Working Paper.

845 T.I. Palley, (2013), Financialization: The Economics of Finance Capital Domination, Palgrave Macmillan, Basingstoke, pp. 31–43, passim.

846 D.M. Kotz, T. McDonough, and M. Reich (Eds), (1994), Social Structures of Accumulation: The Political Economy of Growth and Crisis, Cambridge University Press, Cambridge, pp. 45–47. See also why the 'double movement' Polanyi predicted is not emerging: H. Callaghan, (2015), Who cares About Financialization? Explaining the Decline in Political Salience of Active markets for Corporate Control, MPIfG Discussion paper Nr. 13/4 Max-Planck-Institut for Gesellschaftsordnung, Köln.

847 D.M. Kotz, (2017), Social Structure of Accumulation Theory, Marxist Theory, and System Transformation, Review of Radical Political Economies, September 14, https://doi.org/10.1177/0486613417699050

through financial activity. They increasingly did so through financial market-based activities, rather than just making loans to non-financial sector institutions.[848] This has created an invisible struggle between financial and non-financial segments of capital-invisible because small capital has always supported a liberal view. Financial deregulation then allowed the process of financialization to start. Neoliberal restructuring led to financialization, rather than the alternative view that the growing power of the financial sector led to neoliberal restructuring. Corporate capitalism as a stage in capitalism acted as a catalyst for financialization. Corporate capitalism is a way for capitalism to shelter from the effective functioning of the market and its intrinsic risk, that is, competition, new technologies and so on, and the implications in terms of eroding profits. Kotz argues: '[s]hifting ownership of capital from real capital to financial capital is the best way to insulate against the inherent risks of the capitalist marketplace'. The ideal is to hold wealth whose form can be changed instantaneously when any threat appears. In that way, capital remains safe, with only workers bearing the risks of new products and new processes.[849] Neoliberalism was ultimately the response of the elite 'to re-establish the conditions for capital accumulation and to restore the power of economic elites'[850] after the macroeconomically tumultuous decade of the 1970s had led to declining profits.

---

[848] D.M. Kotz, (2008), Neoliberalism and Financialization, University of Massachusetts Amherst Working Paper.

[849] Kotz, (2008), Ibid. p. 10. He further illustrates: '[t]his is likely the reason why the Rockefellers' huge fortune, born in oil, was soon shifted to finance and real estate. Chase Manhattan Bank, the Rockefeller bank, was not tied to any particular company or industry'. Regarding workers left assuming the risk, Lin et al. provide compelling evidence to show rising income inequality as a consequence. They argue that the increasing reliance by firms on earnings realized through financial channels decoupled the generation of surplus from production, strengthening owners' and elite workers' negotiating power relative to other workers (see in line Piketty (2014), T. Piketty (2014), Capital in the 21st Century, Harvard University Press, Cambridge MA regarding the enhanced bargaining power of corporate managers leading to higher salaries rather than higher levels of productivity). Moreover, the financial conception of the firm reduced capital and management commitment to production, further marginalizing labor's role in US corporations. The result was an incremental exclusion of the general workforce from revenue generating and compensation setting processes. They (Lin et al.) further suggest that financialization accounts for more than half of the decline in labor's share of income during the period 1070–2008; see K.-H. Lin and D. Tomaskovic-Devey, (2011), Financialization and U.S. Income Inequality, 1970–2008, University of Massachusetts at Amherst Working Paper and K.-H. Lin and D. Tomaskovic-Devey, (2011), Income Dynamics, Economic Rents and the Financialization of the U.S. Economy, University of Massachusetts at Amherst Working Paper. Similar results for the OECD region were found by: B. Kus, (2013), Financialization and Income Equality in the OECD Region: 1995–2007, University of Massachusetts at Amherst Working Paper.

[850] G. Dumenil and D. Levy, (2005), Costs and Benefits of Neoliberalism, in G. Epstein, (ed.), Financialization and the World Economy, Edward Elgar, Cheltenham and Northampton, p. 19; D. Kotz, and T. McDonough, (2008), Global Neoliberalism and the Contemporary Social Structure of Accumulation, in T. McDonough, M. Reich, and D. Kotz (eds.), Understanding Contemporary Capitalism: Social Structure of Accumulation Theory for the Twenty First Century, Cambridge University Press, Cambridge, pp. 73–83; D. Kotz, (2012), Social Structures of Accumulation, the Rate of Profit, and Economic Crisis, University of Amherst Working Paper and D. Kotz, (2014), The Rise and fall of Neoliberal Capitalism, Harvard University Press, Cambridge MA, in particular Chapter 4.

Although financialization refers to finance penetrating different spheres of life, it also points to a contradictory movement, that is, a growing separation of finance from non-financial activity, and financialization involves the separation of finance from productive activity. This contradiction led and will lead to systemic crises[851] and enhanced economic and social instability,[852] while the possibilities for continued real (non-debt induced) economic growth within the neoliberal model appear highly uncertain. It also has material and policy-relevant implications for the non-financial industry, which has shifted its behavior due to financialization, that is, a shift in behavior of non-finance firms away from production and non-financial services and toward financial investments and services. This shift has had both strategic and normative components and has reduced the bargaining power of labor and the centrality of production.[853]

Financialization has not been the sole playground of the 'Barbarians at the gate'[854] but has become the mainstream practice of pension funds and other public fund administrators. It has affected corporate structure, and thereby economic and social structures, and importantly from an unemployment point of view it has crowded out manufacturing.[855]

The argument can even be taken a step further. A consistent neoliberal approach toward market functioning will lead over time to a smaller state and lower economic growth, pointing to a critical paradox in neoliberal ideology. Any given economy needs to be financed often through a combination of banking intermediation or market-based intermediation. The optimal relationship of that financial structure evolves alongside the changing profile of the economy. Demirgüç-Kunt et al. observe that as economies grow, economic output tends to become less sensitive to changes in bank development but more so to changes in financial market development.[856]

The next element is then the link between financial structure and economic growth. Recent findings[857] suggest that banks and markets foster economic growth in a comple-

[851] Financialization also leads to enhanced levels of correlations between different asset classes directly contributing to systemic exposures; See: A. Zaremba, (2013), Implications of Financialization for Strategic Asset Allocation: the Case of Correlations, Poznan University Working Paper.

[852] E. Caverzasi, (2014), Minsky and the Sub-Prime Mortgage Crisis: The Financial Instability Hypothesis in the Era of Financialization, Levy Economics Institute, Working Paper Nr. 796.

[853] K.-H. Lin and D. Tomaskovic-Devey, (2014), Financialization: Causes, Inequality Consequences, and Policy Implications, University of Amherst Working Paper.

[854] Referring to the book written about the Leveraged Buy-Out (LBO) of RJR Nabisco, which has become iconic for predatory capitalism and avarice; See:, J. Heylar and B. Burrough, (1989), HarperCollins, New York.

[855] When it comes to the reduction of manufacturing in the West the most frequent explanations for this decline are productivity gains and increased trade with low-wage economies. Pressures came from the financial markets to offload activities that sustain manufacturing and depleted the manufacturing ecosystem. See in detail the MIT Project 'Production in the Innovative Economy' and S. Berger, (2014), How Finance Gutted Manufacturing, Boston Review April 1.

[856] A. Demirgüç-Kunt, E. Feyen, and R. Levine, (2011), The Evolving Importance of Banks and Securities Markets, World Bank, Policy Research Working Paper, Nr. 5805.

[857] L. Gambacorta, J. Yang, and K. Tsatsaronis, (2014), Financial Structure and Growth, BIS Quarterly Review, March 2014, pp. 21–35.

mentary way. There also comes a point of negative returns beyond which additional banking intermediation or larger markets produce lower growth. Cecchetti and Kharroubi[858] examined how the size of the financial system affects productivity growth. They conclude that, at low levels, a larger financial system goes hand in hand with higher productivity growth. But there comes a point where greater financial activity is associated with lower growth. Law and Singh[859] find a similar effect in the relationship between GDP growth and the size of the financial sector.

11.10 Wrapping It Together

In this chapter a layered Pigovian tax instrument has been suggested based on the different externality-inducing activities engaged in by financial institutions. The traditional distinction between non-firm-specific risk (systemic risk) and firm-specific risk has been obeyed. It has been demonstrated that a layered Pigovian instrument allows us to focus much better on each of the different externality-inducing organizational and transactional behaviors that an FI typically engages in, that is, at least compared to some of the integrated Pigovian levies that have been suggested in previous years. Admittedly, most of these layers are interconnected or even influence each other while engaging in certain activities. From a regulatory design point of view, however, it is necessary to build a Pigovian instrument around individual externality-inducing behaviors rather than a holistic concept.

Using a holistic concept it becomes problematic to justify the Pigovian model from an externality-and-harm-inducing point of view. It would either create an instrument that qualifies as 'too broad-brush' realizing an 'over-inclusiveness' for the instrument to be effective or the regulator would be constantly at risk of failing to arrive at a workable instrument that has a fighting chance of making it through the political grinder. Notwithstanding that, it will take more than five minutes of political courage to introduce a Pigovian model for the financial industry. That is despite the evidence that a Pigovian instrument is better validated and more efficient than the command-and-control/quantity regulation[860] enacted after the 2008 crisis. However, it cannot be ruled out that an optimal regulation will take the form of a combination of both forms of regulation to arrive at an optimal management of the global FI sector on both domestic and global/regional levels.

A sector that is instrumental to well-being both economically as well as socially requires continual updating in terms of what infrastructure is adequate in a globalization context. It has become evident that banks that fund themselves domestically

[858] S. Cecchetti and E. Kharroubi, (2012), Reassessing the Impact of Finance on Growth, BIS Working Papers, Nr. 381.

[859] S. Law and N. Singh, (2014), Does Too Much Finance Harm Economic Growth?, Journal of Banking and Finance, Vol. 41, pp. 36–44.

[860] See, for instance, on capital controls: C. Saborowski, S. Sanya, H. Weisfeld, and J. Yepez, (2014), Effectiveness of Capital Outflow Restrictions, IMF Working Paper, WP/14/8; Juan Pablo Medina and Jorge Roldós, (2014), Monetary and Macroprudential Policies to Manage Capital Flows, IMF Working Paper, WP/14/30.

(multinational funding model) in those countries or regions they are active in have been much more stable than those that use a more global funding model (i.e. raising capital in hard currencies in one of a few locations and redistributing it across the globe: an international funding model).[861] A pure and consistent thin capitalization instrument could be instrumental in avoiding certain externalities emerging or intensifying.[862]

Reforms need to start from three tenets: (1) adopting a system-wide perspective explicitly aimed at addressing market failures; (2) understanding and incorporating into regulations agents' incentives so as to align them better with society's goals; and (3) acknowledging that risks of crises will always remain, in part due to (unknown) unknowns—be they tipping points, fault lines or spillovers.[863] Part of countercyclical regulation includes an understanding that the government can be a cause of market failure and/or excessive risk taking. This is, for example, the case in the current environment, with protracted periods of extremely low interest rates,[864] and induces a need for monetary policy coordination regionally and globally.[865]

The interconnectedness[866] of the financial system and the size of some of the global banks will continue to be a specific point of contention as it is not just the size of the

---

[861] R. McCauley, P. McGuire and G. von Peter, (2010), The Architecture of Global Banking: from International to Multinational, BIS Quarterly Review, March 2010, pp. 25–37; R. De Haas and I. van Lelyveld, (2010), Internal Capital Markets and Lending by Multinational Bank Subsidiaries, Journal of Financial Intermediation, Vol. 19, pp. 1–25. Internal capital markets in business groups can propagate corporate shareholders' credit supply shocks to their subsidiaries. Equity exchanges are one channel through which corporate shareholders transmit bank credit supply shocks to the subsidiaries. For example, one study documents that an average of 16.7% local bank credit growth where corporate shareholders are located would increase subsidiaries investment by 1% of their tangible fixed asset value. See in detail: Y. Shi et al., (2019), Internal Capital Markets in Business Groups and the Propagation of Credit Supply Shocks, IMF Working Paper nr. WP/19/111, May. Also: L. Alfaro et al., (2019), On the Direct and Indirect Real Effects of Credit Supply Shocks, NBER Working Paper Nr. 25458, January. Credit supply shocks have sizable direct and downstream propagation effects on investment and output throughout the period, the latter conclude. Also: L. Alfaro et al., (2018), On the Direct and Indirect Effects of Credit Supply Shocks, Bank of Spain Working Paper Nr. 9; A. Cesa-Bianchi et al., (2017), International Credit Supply Shocks, Bank of England Staff Working Paper Nr. 680, October 4. House prices and exchange rates can potentially amplify the expansionary effect of capital inflows by inflating the value of collateral.

[862] J. Blouin, H. Huizinga, L. Laeven and G. Nicodème, (2014), Thin Capitalization Rules and Multinational Firm Capital Structure, IMF Working Paper, WP/14/12.

[863] S. Claessens and L. Kodres, (2014), The Regulatory Responses to the Global Financial Crisis: Some Uncomfortable Questions, IMF Working Paper, WP/14/46.

[864] T. Tressel and T. Verdier, (2014), Optimal Prudential Regulation of Banks and the Political Economy of Supervision, IMF Working Paper, WP/14/90. Low interest rates lead to enhanced inequality as the affluent hold more equity positions relative to the non-affluent part of society and therefore benefit disproportionately more, see: McKinsey, (2013), QE and Low Interest Rates: Distributional Effects and Risks, Working Paper.

[865] R. Mohan and M. Kapur, (2014), Monetary Policy Coordination and the Role of Central banks, IMF Working Paper, WP/14/70.

[866] C. Minoiu, C. Kang, V.S. Subrahmanian, and A. Berea, (2013), Does Financial Connectedness Predict Crisis, IMF Working Paper, WP/13/267.

banks that creates or magnifies systemic risk.[867] It has become apparent that 'command-and-control' regulation will not suffice under those circumstances.

Behavioral changes at FIs are equally needed as well as a better understanding that more leverage arithmetically means more profits, but that bank funding is materially impacted by creditworthiness, the return on its market value, and importantly, the level and quality of capital.[868] The regulator, on its part, needs a better understanding that inadequate regulation creates compliance costs that are then left with a financial system that can hardly be called safer.[869] It calls upon the need for sound financial indicators[870] to develop counter-cyclical regulation[871] while fostering non-debt-induced[872] growth and access for those that

---

[867] L. Laeven, L. Ratnovski and H. Tong, (2014), Bank Size and Systemic Risk, IMF Staff Discussion Note, SDN/14/04. For a full and updated review of systemic banking crises including information on crisis dates, policy responses to resolve banking crises, and the fiscal and output costs of crises see L. Laeven and F. Valencia, (2018), Systemic Banking Crises Revisited, IMF Working Paper Nr. WP/18/206, September, in particular pp. 12–23. The authors conclude that crises in high-income countries tend to last longer and be associated with higher output losses, lower fiscal costs, and more extensive use of bank guarantees and expansionary macro policies than crises in low- and middle-income countries. Also: M. Baron, (2018), Identifying Banking Crises, Princeton University Working Paper, Mimeo; D. Romer and C. Romer, (2017), New Evidence on the Aftermath of Financial Crises in Advanced Countries, American Economic Review, Vol. 107, Issue 10, pp. 3072–3118. Lorenc and Zhang conclude that stress experienced by banks in the top 1% of the size distribution leads to a statistically significant and negative impact on the real economy. This impact increases with the size of the bank. The negative impact on quarterly real GDP growth caused by stress at banks in the top 0.15% of the size distribution is more than twice as large as the impact caused by stress at banks in the top 0.75%, and more than three times as large as the impact caused by stress at banks in the top 1%. These results are broadly informative as to how the stringency of regulatory standards should vary with bank size, and support the idea that the largest banks should be subject to the most stringent requirements while smaller banks should be subject to successively less stringent requirements. In detail: A.G. Lorenc and J.Y. Zhang, (2018), The Differential Impact of Bank Size on Systemic Risk, Finance and Economics Discussion Series 2018-066. Washington: Board of Governors of the Federal Reserve System, https://doi.org/10.17016/FEDS.2018.066

[868] R. Babihuga and M. Spaltro, (2014), Bank Funding Costs for International Banks, IMF Working Paper, WP/14/71. Regarding the impact of Monetary Policy and Funding Costs see: M. Girotti, (2016), How Monetary Policy Changes Bank Liability Structure and Funding Cost, Banque de France Working Paper Nr. 590, April, Paris; S. Schmitz et al., (2017), Bank Solvency and Funding Cost: New Data and New Results, IMF Working Paper Nr. WP/17/116, May.

[869] See the findings of an analysis in this matter: J. Viñals, C. Pazarbasioglu, J. Surti, A. Narain, M. Erbenova, and J. Chow, (2013), Creating a Safer Financial System: Will the Volcker, Vickers, and Liikanen Structural Measures Help?, IMF Staff Discussion Note, SDN/13/4. See for an evaluation of the Volcker rule from a systemic risk point of view: J.A.D. Manasfi, (2013), Systemic Risk and Dodd-Frank's Volcker Rule, William and Mary Business Law Review, Vol. 4, Issue 1, pp. 181–212, February. Also: M. Bitar et al., (2017), Basel Compliance and Financial Stability: Evidence from Islamic Banks, IMF Working Paper Nr. WP/17/161, July. Bitar et al. demonstrate that compliance with Basel standards reduces the Z-score (which forecasts bankruptcy) of conventional banks as well as Islamic banks (but to a leser degree).

[870] N. Xingyuan Che and Y. Shinagawa, (2014), Financial Soundness Indicators and the Characteristics of Financial Cycles, IMF Working Paper, Nr. WP/14/14.

[871] Ph. Aghion and E. Kharroubbi, (2013), Cyclical Macroeconomic Policy, Financial Regulation and Economic Growth, BIS Working Paper Nr. 434.

[872] A. Pescatori, D. Sandri, and J. Simon, Debt and Growth: Is There a Magic Threshold, IMF Working Paper, Nr. WP/14/34. Also: B. Jiang and T.S. Sedik, (2019), The Turning Tide: How

often are a critical part of economic cohesion in many countries.[873] This is all the more valid when macroeconomic variables are often a strong driver behind the discretionary fiscal policy choices made by governments.[874]

A last element of consideration relates to the size of the financial sector required for optimal functioning of the real economy. It has become clear that beyond a certain point the growth of the financial sector does not contribute to the growth of the real economy, and in fact crowds out the real sector in both growth and productivity terms.[875] To be precise, in the Postwar-period the financial system grew rapidly relative to the nonfinancial sector, rising from about 10% of value added and a 10% share of corporate profits to 20% of value added and 40% of corporate profits in the US. To a large degree, this was because finance, instead of financing the capital development of the economy, was financing itself.

Vulnerable are Asian Corporates?, IMF Working Paper Nr. WP/19/93, May. Higher global interest rates and exchange rate depreciation increase the probability of default of Asian firms. See also their literature list pp. 16–17 for further analysis and additional dimensions.

[873] B. Öztürk and M. Mrkaic, (2014), SMEs' Access to Finance in the Euro Area: What Helps or Hampers?, IMF Working Paper, Nr. WP/14/78 and N. Klein, (2014), Small and Medium Size Enterprises, Credit Supply Shocks, and Economic Recovery in Europe, IMF Working Paper, Nr. WP/14/98. Credit supply shocks have sizable direct and downstream propagation effects on investment and output also, conclude Alfaro et al. in L. Alfaro et al., (2018), On the Direct and Indirect Real Effects of Credit Supply Shocks, Working Paper, July 24, mimeo. Wider confirmation can be found in: M. Bottero et al., (2017), Sovereign Debt Exposure and the Bank Lending Channel: Impact on Credit Supply and the Real Economy, Working paper, mimeo, December and F. Manaresi and Nicola Pierri, (2018), Credit Supply and Productivity Growth, BIS Working Paper Nr. 711, Monetary and Economic Department, March.

[874] S. Cevik and K. Teksoz, (2014), Deep Roots of Fiscal Behavior, IMF Working Paper, Nr. WP/14/45.

[875] S.G. Cecchetti and E. Kharroubi, (2012), Re-assessing the Impact of Finance on Growth, BIS Working Paper, Nr. 381 and S.G. Cecchetti and E. Kharroubi, (2013), Why Does Financial Sector Growth Crowd Out Real Economic Growth?, BIS Working Paper; S.H. Law and N. Singh, (2013), Does Too Much Finance Harm Economic Growth, Working Paper. They demonstrate similar findings. Cecchetti et al. draw two important conclusions: '[f]irst, the growth of a country's financial system is a drag on productivity growth. That is, higher growth in the financial sector reduces real growth. In other words, financial booms are not, in general, growth enhancing, probably because the financial sector competes with the rest of the economy for resources. Second, they examined the distributional nature of this effect and find that credit booms harm what we normally think of as the engines for growth: those that are more R&D-intensive.' Their findings point to a pressing need to reassess the relationship of finance and real growth in modern economic systems. Cecchetti and Kharroubi expanded their study in 2015: (2015), Why Does Financial Sector Growth Crowd out Real Economic Growth, BIS Working Paper Nr. 490, February. They identify which parts of the real economy are hurt most by financial outcrowding (R&D intensive, high asset/low productivity sectors), that after they concluded that financial growth in the West reduced real growth overall and financial booms don't trickle down and generate real economic growth. The financial sector often competes with the other real sectors for resources. This also has a globalization dimension. See: S. Chen and E. Dauchy, (2018), International Technology Sourcing and Knowledge Spillovers; Evidence from OECD Countries, IMF Working Paper Nr. WP/18/51, March and J.L. Eugster et al., (2018), International Knowledge Spillovers, IMF Working Paper nr. WP/18/269, December. The authors highlight: '[f]or all countries, and especially for emerging economies, inflows of foreign knowledge have a growing and quantitatively important impact on domestic innovation.'

At the same time, the capital development of the economy suffered perceptibly.[876] The crowding out will lead to confidentiality shocks[877] in the industry, and therefore regional and global (coordinated) macroprudential and countercyclical policy making[878] and regulation are required. That is required to balance both in an equilibrium where they no longer drain each other's resources and restore the liquidity balance whenever needed.[879] Also the increase in financial investments by non-financial firms lead consistently to lower and reduced total value added. That reduced value add produced by financialization was born strikingly by labor and the state.[880]

The suggestion for a possible standardization of the risk-weighted asset (RWA) methodology (rather than bank-specific proprietary models) could constitute a humble first start,[881] as measuring risk only makes sense when done in a consistent way and with sufficient granularity. In fact, any risk-weighting methodology will continue to be prone to defects and vulnerabilities when including the assessments of spillover risks.

---

[876] See for an excellent analysis including the policy actions taken post-2008 crisis: M. Mazzucato and L.R. Wray, (2015), Financing the Capital Development of the Economy. A Keynes-Schumpeter-Minsky Synthesis, Levy Economics Institute Working Paper Nr. 837, May. They do not only conclude that most of the financial innovation was direct outside the sphere of production, but also the real economy itself has retreated from funding investment opportunities and is instead either hoarding cash or using corporate profits for speculative investments such as share buybacks. It is therefore not just a matter of runaway finance and an investment-starved real economy. The real economy is part of that momentum.

[877] S. Dées and J. Güntner, (2014), The International Dimensions of Confidentiality Shocks, ECB Working Paper Series, Nr. 1669.

[878] C. O'Neill and N. Vause, (2018), Macroprudential margins: A New Countercyclical Too? Bank of England Staff Working Paper Nr. 765, November 9. Macroprudential margins to eliminate fire-sale externalities can work but not in all sorts of market conditions and only when introduced ex ante.

[879] T. Ahnert, (2014), Rollover Risk, Liquidity and Macro-Prudential Regulation, ECB Working Paper Series, Nr. 1667; V.V. Acharya and H. Naqvi, (2012), The Seeds of a Crisis: A Theory of Bank Liquidity and Risk-Taking over the Business Cycle, CEPR Discussion Papers Nr. 8851.

[880] D. Tomaskovic-Devey et al., (2015), Did Financialization Reduce Economic Growth, Amherst Working Paper, University of Massachusetts, Mimeo. The impact of financialization goes way beyond reduced value add, but impact economies and entrepreneurship and entrepreneurial intent at its core; see: P. Kedrosky and D. Stangler, (2011), Financialization and Its Entrepreneurial Consequences, Kauffman Foundation Research Series: Firm Formation and Economic Growth, March, Mimeo: an orientation toward shareholder value has led to substantial changes in corporate strategies and structures that have encouraged outsourcing and corporate disaggregation while increasing compensation at the top. Second, financialization has shaped patterns of inequality, culture and social change in the broader society. Underlying these changes is a broad shift in how capital is intermediated, from financial institutions to financial markets, through mechanisms such as securitization (turning debts into marketable securities). Enabled by a combination of theory, technology and ideology, financialization is a potent force for changing social institutions; see: G.F. Davis and S. Kim, (2015), Financialization of the Economy Annual Review of Sociology, Vol. 41, pp. 203–221.

[881] BCBS, (2014), Review of the Pillar 3 Disclosure Requirements- Consultative Document, June 24. Final version: January 28, 2015 via bis.org

Pigovian taxes can play a role in a variety of existing and not yet so visible externalities.[882] The reduction of corporate taxes has, for example, led to a proportionately higher amount of people pursuing careers in accounting or banking (versus research for example). That talent has been lost, as it now contributes to banking externalities versus the net positive externalities of, for example, research.[883] As time progresses Pigovian instruments[884] will be tested in a wider set of contexts and factual settings, providing for the trial-and-error environment[885] required to refine the instrument. That would be the case based on the setting the instrument is used in and adjusting for a changing economic, social and cultural framework[886] when neoliberal-induced globalization advances.[887] Indeed, neoliberalism is still the dominant model in the state-market nexus. Although an initial observation could leave the observer with the impression that the sovereign is claiming back territory from the market after the 2008 near melt-down, I would argue quite the opposite in line with McCarthy's distinction.[888] He argued there are two neoliberal paradigms that interact: (1) the weak state intervention thesis, which argues that neoliberal policy change is driven by state retreat and deregulation, and (2) state-managed transition thesis, which argues that neoliberal policies are both enacted and managed through new regulations.

---

[882] (Capital) Income taxes become problematic the more the economies they cover become open economies, which is the case in terms of globalization as the elasticity of capital income taxes becomes larger as economies become open structured, see: E. Mendoza, L. Tesar and J. Zhang, (2014), Saving Europe: The Unpleasant Arithmetic of Fiscal Austerity in Integrated Economies, NBER Working Paper, Nr. 20200.

[883] See in detail also for the quantification of the externalities involved: B. Lockwood, C. Nathanson, and E.G. Weyl, (2014), Taxation and the Allocation of Talent, Harvard University Working Paper. Similar dynamics can be identified with respect to marketing and the negative externalities it causes in terms of overconsumption, pollution and debt, see: S. Steed and H. Kersley, (2014), A Bit Rich: Calculating the Real Value to Society of Different Professions, NEF Working Paper, mimeo.

[884] See for example the application of Pigovian taxes in tourism: C. Piga, (2003), Pigouvian Taxation in Tourism, Environmental and Resource Economics, Vol. 26, pp. 343–359.

[885] See: C. Todd, S. Kallbekken and S. Kroll, (2011), The Impact of Trial Runs on the Acceptability of Pigouvian Taxes: Experimental Evidence, Cicero Working Paper, Nr. 2011/01.

[886] See how shadow banking is co-defined by culture and cultural differences: A. Wolter, (2016), Shadow Banking a Cultural Phenomenon? Cultural Dimensions as by Hofstede and others, Master Thesis, Radboud Universiteit Nijmegen, October, mimeo. She uses the six dimensions of culture as developed by Hofstede (chapter four). There is more financial behavior defined by culture. See B. Guin, (2017), Culture and Household Saving, (2017), ECB Working Paper Nr. 2069, May. The German-speaking parts of Switzerland save materially more than the French-speaking part adjusted for all variables.

[887] Even domestic applications of Pigovian instruments, despite their natural limitations, have the potential to spur regional or even global applications, given the spillover effects that exist in international taxation; see: IMF Policy Paper, (2014), Spillovers in International Corporate Taxation, May 9.

[888] M. McCarthy, (2014), Neoliberals without the Neoliberals, Evidence from the Rise of 401(k) Retirement Plans, MPIfG Discussion Paper 14/12, Max Planck Institute for the Study of Societies, Cologne.

Although pre-crisis the focus was on the former, the crisis has shifted the momentum to the second.[889] A critical observer will most likely have noticed that the austerity measures tabled, driven by financial market arguments, are often implemented in a one-sided welfare-dismantling mode ripping apart the socio-economic fabric built up in Europe since the end of the second World War. That is combined with the skewed budgetary autonomy at the level of the EU Member States and monetary policy tools used as market instruments by technocratic institutions, behind the curtain of democratic legitimacy and accountability. That sounds very much as a 'von Mises-Hayek-Buchanan' triangular work-out of their neoliberal program.[890]

[889] Although the first is still the dominant line of thinking across the political spectrum and at the level of international institutions (EU, IMF, etc.) when judged based on the conditions they imposed on countries receiving emergency funding.

[890] See chapter two of L. Nijs, (2015), Ibid. for details on their individual contributions to the neoliberal program.

12

An Interim Conclusion: Shadow Banking as Market-Based Financing

It was illustrated throughout this first volume that shadow banking has known a remarkable turn from being the scapegoat after the 2008 crisis (hence the somewhat murky name shadow banking) to being an alternative form of financing (next to the traditional banking channel). It is true that the banking channels, with quite some variation across jurisdictions, have not really recovered in their ability to provide credit to all economic domains in a way that fuels sustainable long-term growth. The credit intermediation process is still on the mend. And yes, our new avalanche of financial legislation has played a role in creating that disability to provide credit full-fledged. But that in itself is not a justification for creating an alternative channel (hence the synonym parallel banking). That would mean you would structurally doubt the ability of the banking sector to re-create a sustainable credit intermediation process despite all the income legislation.

Ultimately, there are ample ramifications to that choice. The largest of them all is that in a shadow banking world much of the banking is not conducted in a firm but facilitated by markets. And we have come to realize (I hope) when working through the book that structurally balancing and developing a structurally stable financial market is next to impossible. It would also highly disregard the imperfect nature of regulation and contractual terms, a given that every decent lawyer should be brought up with. It is therefore all the more surprising that the Financial Stability Board (FSB) changed its tone on shadow banking but also, almost as a kind of trophy, was willing to list all the achievements (which have all been untested by reality obviously) that would make shadow banking safer and a perfect alternative financing channel and is even earmarked to solve some of the problems the banking sector couldn't so far. What I found always explicitly lacking is support for the argumentations given. For example, for this one '[n]on-bank financing provides a valuable alternative to bank funding and helps support real economic activity. It is also a welcome source of diversification of credit supply from the banking system,

L. Nijs, *The Handbook of Global Shadow Banking, Volume I*,
https://doi.org/10.1007/978-3-030-34743-7_12

and it provides healthy competition for banks.'[1] The uncomfortable reality is that no argumentation or proof is given, simply because no such evidence exists.

Indeed, despite the macro-economic and econometric modeling madhouse[2] we have available these days for every segment of the (shadow) banking market, none comes close to supporting that view. Obviously, the incoming regulation has made MMFs less susceptible to run, creates more transparent and aligned securitization schemes, reduces the interconnectedness between banks and shadow banks,[3] creates countercyclical behavior and transparency in securities financing business and the repo-segment as well as reduces overall systemic risk in the system. But so did Sarbanes-Oxley introduced after the Enron and WorldCom affairs, until it did no longer. What is going to be the story that we're going to hear months or years from now, when the markets materially destabilize again? That creative destruction[4] is an intrinsic part of every capitalist system, and that regulation can do only so much? That no root-cause analysis was made that would truly redesign the credit intermediation system in a sustainable way, and that regulation was too much driven by banking lobby and other characters and the fact that we depend too much on model-based financial regulation. Within the context of all the macro-economic and econometric modeling madhouse just mentioned, we have forgotten the power of verbal logic needed to make regulation work effectively over longer periods of time. The nexus between the models and regulation is very brittle and prone to many translation error and misconceptions.

Starting in 2015 with the name change to market-based finance[5] and given the road traveled already,[6] we see that the FSB and Basel Committee (BCBS) feel their efforts are

[1] FSB, (2015), Transforming Shadow Banking into Resilient Market-based Finance. An Overview of Progress, November 12, p. 1.

[2] A contrario L.A. P. da Silva, (2018), In Defence of Central Bank DSGE Modelling, Speech of Luiz Awazu Pereira da Silva, Deputy General Manager, Bank for International Settlements at the Seventh BIS Research Network meeting on "Pushing the frontier of central banks' macro-modelling" Basel, March 8, via bis.org

[3] See also T.J. Carter, (2017), Optimal Interbank Regulation, Bank of Canada Staff Working Paper Nr. 48, November. Two interesting observations Carter makes are that the literature has tended to make ad hoc assumptions about the interbank contract space, which makes it difficult to generate convincing policy prescriptions; second, the literature has tended to focus on ex-post interventions that kick in only after an interbank disruption has come underway. He also concludes that optimal policy requires careful coordination between ex-post and ex-ante interventions, with the ex-ante component surprisingly doing most of the heavy lifting. It was however concluded that ex ante is necessary albeit insufficient.

[4] Known through the works of Schumpeter, but with a history going back to Hinduism and the Tandava dance. With application to contemporary monetary policy: J. Rambarran, (2015), Shiva's Wrath – Divali, Creative Destruction and Central Banking, Speech by Mr. Jwala Rambarran, Governor of the Central Bank of Trinidad and Tobago, at the Central Bank of Trinidad and Tobago's annual Divali celebrations, Port-of-Spain, October 25, 2015.

[5] FSB, (2015), Ibid. pp. 2–3 & 13–14. The process was reinforced up till and when at the end of 2018, the Basel III was fully finalized.

[6] FSB, (2015), Ibid. pp. 4–12 & BCBS, (2015), Finalizing Post-Crisis Reform: an Update. A Report to G20 Leaders, November.

coming to a close.[7] It is also demonstrated that there is no real holistic approach to this regulation, not in a material, not in a geographical way.[8] We needed a new context, in which we could redesign the future of our financial system and we let the opportunity go to waste. Future generations will lambast us for that. Because not every destruction is creative and creates value as we have witnessed ourselves in recent times. Because we got lost in the perpetual macro-economic theorizing and econometric madhouse we created for ourselves, thereby failing to blend in the existing understanding that the global financial interconnectivity leads to vulnerabilities.[9] We only start to understand that the financial universe is an object that, just like a moving paradigm cannot be fully captured, because by the time that you do, the puck has moved on. It takes time for trends to drill down into numbers, data-sets and ultimately theory. That time we don't have. Regulation needs a different dimension that capture and orchestrate such environment.[10] So the real question unanswered is 'are we done now?'.[11]

Although the economic functionality approach of the FSB deserves to be approached with respect, we all (even intuitively) know that, when the next crisis arrives,[12] most of it will not matter and will not be instrumental in mitigating the impact of the next crisis. Chan comments in this respect 'the main cause of the market failure and near meltdown of the market was the collective failure of the various "safety valves" that maintain the orderly operation of the market'.[13] Some even go as far as questioning what it means if the financial system would be truly re-engineered and reshaped, as if it is a theoretical and rhetorical or hypothetical question.[14]

We can't just pile credit, liquidity and maturity risk together, blend it with leverage, regulatory arbitrage and liquidity requirements and think that something meaningful will come out of the blender. There is also the demand side,[15] where institutional cash pools

---

[7] The annual updates and working progress updates can be consulted through fsb.org

[8] See for an overview of what has been achieved so far: FSB, (2015), Ibid. pp. 3–12.

[9] See T.A. Peltonen et al., (2015), Interconnectedness of the Banking Sector as a Vulnerability of Crises, ECB Working Paper Nr. 1866, November.

[10] Also: T. Adrian, (2017), Shadow Banking and Market-Based Finance, IMF Speech, September 14, via imf.org

[11] S. Ingves, (2018), Basel III: Are We Done Now?, Keynote speech by Mr. Stefan Ingves, Chairman of the Basel Committee on Banking Supervision, at the Institute for Law and Finance conference on "Basel III: Are we done now?", Goethe University, Frankfurt am Main, January 29, 2018, via. org

[12] See for good write-up regarding the constituents of a financial crisis: J. McAndrews, (2015), Modern Recipes for Financial Crises, Remarks by Mr. James McAndrews, Executive Vice President and Director of Research of the Federal Reserve Bank of New York, at the University of Iowa, Iowa City, December 4, 2015, pp. 2–3.

[13] N. T. L. Chan, (2015), When Markets Fail, Speech by Mr. Norman T L Chan, Chief Executive of the Hong Kong Monetary Authority, at the 6th Caixin Summit 2015, Hong Kong, November 6, 2015, p. 1.

[14] MnKinsey, (2018), Banks in the Changing World of Financial Intermediation, Report McKinsey Classics, Financial Services, November 2018.

[15] See, for example, M. Carlson, et al., (2014), The Demand for Short-Term, Safe Assets and Financial Stability: Some Evidence and Implications for Central Bank Policies. Board of Governors

are looking for more safe assets than the world can produce. And with QE still in force we have created more capital chasing the same amount of risk.[16] And the icing on the cake has been the interplay between monetary, fiscal and macroprudential policies. A fair chunk of that, in particular on the macroprudential side, has been largely undocumented and theory-less. Other parts of that spectrum ignore economic history.[17] The different and interacting layers that need to be wired through legislation and policy become less pronounced, and for the attentive observer it could well be so that it has become totally unclear what the real long-term objectives of all this are or have become. Boosting economic growth in a sustainable way makes sense, but how do growth and sustainability (from an environmental point of view) go together?

Technology cannot be the only factor in that mix as some claim. Or is it, partly, safeguarding financial stability? But that is never an objective in itself but merely the result of something else. For instance, by avoiding asset bubbles, controlling (or not) capital flows, creating low rate environments,[18] creating regulatory arbitrage,[19] and yes control private money and private credit creation through the system. Or is it price

of the Federal Reserve System Finance and Economics Discussion Series, November; A. Krishnamurthy, and A. Vissing-Jorgensen, (2015), The Impact of Treasury Supply on Financial Sector Lending and Stability, Journal of Financial Economics Vol. 118, Nr. 3 (December), pp. 571–600; R. Greenwood, (2015), A Comparative- Advantage Approach to Government Debt Maturity, The Journal of Finance, Vol. 40, Nr. 4 (August), pp. 1683–1772.

[16] Or too little risk, for example, in the insurance sector: J. Loh, (2015), Managing Risks in an Uncertain World, Keynote address by Ms. Jacqueline Loh, Deputy Managing Director of the Monetary Authority of Singapore, at the 13th Singapore International Reinsurance Conference, Singapore, November 3, 2015, p. 1.

[17] For example, the fact that there is no clear negative relationship between deflation and economic growth across countries. Furthermore, in the postwar period, bouts of deflation have been milder and less persistent than before, with average growth during deflation years exceeding that of inflation years; see: C. Borio. et al., (2015), The Costs of Deflation: A Historical Perspective, BIS Quarterly Review, March, pp. 31–54; and P. Ryska, (2014), Deflation and Economic Growth in Long-Term Perspective, Charles University in Prague, Institute of Economic Studies Working Paper Nr. 18/2014; as well: M. Sánchez, (2015), The Powers and Limits of Monetary Policy, Remarks by Mr. Manuel Sánchez, Deputy Governor of the Bank of Mexico, at the Cato Institute's 33rd Annual Monetary Conference "Rethinking Monetary Policy", Washington DC, November 12, 2015, p. 2.

[18] It causes MMF to delve into riskier assets than their strategy can tolerate: G. La Spada, (2015), Competition, Reach for Yield, and Money Market Funds, Federal Reserve Bank of New York Staff Reports, Nr. 753, December.

[19] S. Kleimeier, et al., (2015), Deposit Insurance in Times of Crises: safe Haven or Regulatory Arbitrage?, University of Maastricht Working Paper Nr. RM/15/026 and the case of sovereign debt regulation under Basel III: A. Dombret, (2015), Firm as a Rock – is Bank Capital an All-Purpose Tool? The Example of Sovereign Debt Regulation, Public speech by Dr. Andreas Dombret, Member of the Executive Board of the Deutsche Bundesbank, at Columbia University, New York City, December 4, 2015, pp. 3–4. See for a critical review: European Systemic Risk Board (ESRB), (2015), ESRB Report on the Treatment of Sovereign Exposures, March.

stability? But given the long-term neutrality of money, any attempt to use it to boost growth is by nature limited.[20]

What makes us believe that the regulator or supervisor is much better at achieving that than someone else? In fact it is often contributing to asset bubbles, systemic risk[21] and so on.[22] Milton Friedman commented on that almost fifty years ago: 'the biggest risk with additional goals is that monetary policy[23] may end up not accomplishing what it is most suited to do in the pursuit of what it is less suited to do'.[24] What adds to that tragedy is the lack of time consistency in all these measures and policies. If there is one thing we know it is that longer-term consistency and guidance goes historically hand-in-hand with good economic performance.[25] Overburdening monetary policy (or other areas in play) with possibly incompatible objectives has diminished credibility. Especially since nothing is what it seems to be, especially in the banking sphere, making regulatory efficiency a top priority.[26] I did my fair share of work in the Pigovian chapter, demonstrating their regulatory superiority vis-à-vis command-and-control regulation, also or especially in the financial sector.

Whether market- or bank-based systems are better have been debated at length and for ages now and there is no need for rehashing.[27] What we do know is that market-based systems react more procyclically than bank-based economies because of more pronounced asset price booms and busts. However, bank-based systems are also beset by procyclicality (bank-based systems are more effective at smoothing the impact of business cycle fluctuations; market-based economies recover more quickly after crises).[28] Dombret's middle of

[20] M. Sánchez, (2015), Ibid. p. 6.

[21] E. Jondeau and A. Khalilzadeh, (2015), Collateralization, Leverage and Systemic Risk, University of Lausanne, Working Paper, June 3, mimeo.

[22] M. Sánchez, (2015), The Powers and Limits of Monetary Policy, Remarks by Mr. Manuel Sánchez, Deputy Governor of the Bank of Mexico, at the Cato Institute's 33rd Annual Monetary Conference "Rethinking Monetary Policy", Washington DC, November 12, 2015, p. 4.

[23] See for an evolution of US monetary policy: R.L. Hetzel, (2018), The Evolution of U.S. Monetary Policy, FRB of Richmond Working Paper Nr. 1.

[24] M. Friedman, (1968), The Role of Monetary Policy, American Economic Review, Vol. LVIII, Nr. 1, pp. 1–17. To be read preferably in conjunction with R.L. Hetzel, (2017), What Remains of Milton Friedman's Monetarism?, FRB of Richmond Working paper Nr. 9, July 13.

[25] A. Nikolsko-Rzhevskyy, et al., (2014), Deviations from Rules-Based Policy and Their Effects, Journal of Economic Dynamics and Control, Vol. 49, and J.B. Taylor, (2015), A Rules-Based International Monetary System for the Future, October, Working Paper, mimeo.

[26] For example, P. Behr et al., (2015), Cyclicality of SME Lending and Government Involvement in Banks, Deutsche Bundesbank Discussion Paper Nr. 39/2015.

[27] For example, R. Levine, (2002), Bank-Based or Market-Based Financial Systems: which is better? Journal of Financial, Intermediation, Vol. 11, Issue 4, pp. 398–428.

[28] See: A. Dombret, (2015), Firm as a Rock – is Bank Capital an All-Purpose Tool? The Example of Sovereign Debt Regulation, Public speech by Dr. A. Dombret, Member of the Executive Board of the Deutsche Bundesbank, at Columbia University, New York City, December 4, 2015, pp. 1–2; T. Adrian and H.S. Shin, (2010), Liquidity and Leverage, Journal of Financial Intermediation, Vol. 19, Issue 3, pp. 418–437; L. Gambacorta, J. Yang, and K. Tsatsaronis, (2014), Financial Structure and Growth, BIS Quarterly Review, March 2014, pp. 21–35.

the road approach that we need both (and/or) rather than either/or and his claim that SMEs prefer bank financing ('are convicted to' seems to be the better and preferred choice of wording) are both unconvincing and untested.[29] In that context it is unjustified to reflect the actual by referring to Roosevelt's statement: '[i]n any moment of decision, the best thing you can do is the right thing, the next best thing is the wrong thing, and the worst thing you can do is nothing'.[30]

A modern day crisis is one where multiple recipes are mixed and which include, besides the 'old run on the bank model': (1) the procyclicality of financial intermediary leverage and its impact on asset pricing[31] and the fact that it is tied to systemic risk, and (2) the role played by the private sector in creating money-like assets, such as repos, asset backed commercial paper (ABCP), and other short-term and ostensibly safe assets (MMF shares and auction-rate securities). McAndrews comments '[w]hen able to issue such assets, private issuers pay a very low interest rate, as others in the economy demand the apparent safety that those assets provide. That situation gives the private financial sector strong incentives to issue money-like claims.'[32] But there are systemic risks involved when the private sector creates money-like assets. If private intermediaries run into difficulty issuing those assets or in rolling over their short-term debt, then they must deleverage abruptly, creating runs. When others cannot buy at that time, fire sales occur, while buyers and sellers try to keep or create liquidity of their money-like liabilities such as deposits, repos and other short-term debt.

The financial crisis of 2008 therefore manifested another type (not a classical bank run) of run on banks as well as non-banks, a run on the short-term, non-deposit debt issued by the intermediaries. The underlying mechanisms are 'excessive leverage or the scarcity of loss-bearing capacity that builds up in an expanding economy and the other is about the excessive provision of liquidity in the private sector, or excess private money creation'.[33] The former has been dealt with but only marginally and the latter not at all. McAndrews suggests that 'official sector efforts should aim at forward-looking monitoring of financial vulnerability that take both leverage and maturity transformation into

[29] Untested whether the CMU will improve access to finance for SMEs. There is to my knowledge no evidence for that available. Nor is there evidence that securitization leads to more and better SME finance coming through the bank channel. At best, these are stylized, hypothetical models with no direct relationship with reality as is. It seems to be a problem for policymakers these days: we make statement, the media magnifies it and then it becomes reality; see, for example, Draghi claiming that QE works without providing proof that it is so and in what way: '[s]o let me say this very clearly: we are doing more because it works, not because it fails. We want to consolidate something that's been a success': Mario Draghi, President of the ECB Introductory statement to the press conference (with Q&A), Frankfurt am Main, December 3, 2015.

[30] A. Dombret, (2015), Ibid. op. cit. p. 4.

[31] See: T. Adrian, et al., (2014), Dynamic Leverage Asset Pricing, Federal Reserve Bank of New York Staff Report, Nr. 625, December.

[32] J. McAndrews, (2015), Modern Recipes for Financial Crises, Remarks by Mr. James McAndrews, Executive Vice President and Director of Research of the Federal Reserve Bank of New York, at the University of Iowa, Iowa City, December 4, 2015, pp. 4–7.

[33] J. McAndrews, (2015), Ibid. p. 8.

account'.[34] However, once observable, the genie is out of the bottle. Haircuts and somewhat higher capital buffers for regulated banks will not cut it (nor the opposite of making SB subject to full-blown banking regulation).[35] Or the change from a constant net asset value (CNAV) to a variable net asset value (VNAV). Nor the blind reliance on rules and total bureaucracy and the illusion that they all are applied equally and consistently.[36] There is a reason why even the BCBS in its third progress report for effective risk data aggregation and risk reporting in December 2015 indicates that 'supervisors should conduct more in-depth/specialized examinations on data aggregation requirements to evaluate weaknesses'.[37]

Indeed, all the efforts that have been done and rules implemented since the dust settled on the 2008 crisis have contributed to making the system marginally safer, better and more robust. But each of them is also prone to the same issue, that is, of not being able to jump beyond their own shadow and treat the root cause rather than the symptoms.

Let's have a quick look:

- **MMFs**: changing from CNAV to VNAV/FNAV helps just like redemption gates and so on. But the illusion of risk-free earnings above risk-free market levels of return is kept intact. It hasn't solved the issue of runs that made MMFs problematic and has kept the moral hazard of running for the exit first fully intact. Building a real backstop through capital buffers is an opportunity left used. That is because it would erode the business model and reduce the real return of MMF investing to the actual market interest rate as excess returns would be absorbed by the providers of those additional capital buffers.
- **Securitization**: The capital buffer rules have been revised upwards (on Basel level), but then again revised downwards for STS securitizations. STS is an artificial construct that even on a theoretical level is still very opaque, and the pace at which Europe wants to push it through the regulatory channel reveals accuracy and considered decision-making is not its main concern. It is only a matter of time before financial innovation has found its way around the concept without losing access to the lower capital requirements. Disclosure, skin-in-the-game ('retention') rules are fine and contribute to a balanced relationship between originators, facilitator and ultimate investors, but some of the most painful moral hazards in that relationship have stayed untouched. Some leave room for regulatory arbitrage and some like the skin-in-the-game facilitate multiple techniques which not all yield a true skin-in-the-game end result.
- Many topics however have been fully ignored. The fact that securitization, no matter how safe, increases risk levels above the levels where no securitization techniques are

---

[34] Ibid. also for examples.

[35] See for an investor-based review: CFA, (2015), Shadow Banking. Policy Frameworks and Investor Perspectives on markets-Based Finance, pp. 44–67.

[36] See for an enjoyable review of that idea: D. Graeber, (2015), The Utopia of Rules, Melville House, Brooklyn, NY.

[37] BCBS, (2015), Progress in Adopting the Principles for Effective Risk Data Aggregation and Risk Reporting, December 16, pp. 9 ff.

used and that concentration of risks rises materially even when securitization techniques are STS compliant. Adverse selection, moral hazard and the fact that even prime securitizations have a higher default rate than the average banking loan book are fully and intentionally ignored. And yes, sometimes the truth is even harshly brutalized. The fact that securitization would contribute to freeing up capital for SMEs is truly fabricated and violates pretty much every evidence that is out there: (1) Banking channels, due to enhanced information asymmetry, have always been the preferred credit channel for SMEs; (2) also before the crisis there was hardly an SMS market due to reasons of information asymmetry, but also the fact that asymmetric risk exposure in the underlying SME loan book makes the intermediation margin for banks lower if you want to provide the ultimate investor with a real risk-adjusted return. If risk retention does not occur across the different tranches, moral hazard does not only persist, but would also leave the bank with more junior/mezzanine or even equity tranches, which doesn't relate well to the lower capital requirements now attached to any STS securitization; (3) the opportunity wasn't used to engage in a transactional analysis for securitized products;[38] (4) the root cause that debt markets are information insensitive and that this leads to shocks and runs in case, due to stress or market panic, that pattern changes and the debt markets turn information sensitive if fully ignored.

- The tax side, with its idolatry for debt, persistently favors debt over equity and therefore consistently fuels the excessive use of leverage. Nothing has been done from that end. The choices for Pigovian instruments to control the financial system have been far and few in between, and preference was continued to be given to command-and-control legislation despite its regulatory inferior status.
- Haircuts in the repo and securities financing are good but have proven to be non-instrumental in case of severe and/or market-wide shocks. The haircuts are very mild to begin with and by any standard. The repo is a typical market, despite its relevance, that has been hit with multi-layered regulation initiatives, with limited coordination. Unnecessary regulation with suboptimal effects and high costs is the endgame.
- There has been only modest interest in the position of collateral, hypothecation use and re-use, since supply was able so far to meet demand. Demand supply market issues for safe collateral and multiple re-uses of collateral creating a cascade or contagion chain in case the valuation of collateral is severely impacted by market shocks are only researched from 30,000 feet (i.e. 'we see no direct constraints') and those in-depth analyses available don't show a lot of positive dynamics and comforting outcomes. Asking for more collateral in many cases is a good thing, but little attention has been given to the impact of that on the macro level. The fact that central banks were the first to adjust and enhance their collateral requirements vis-à-vis market parties means little collateral available between market agents.

[38] See for a number of these issues: V. Bavoso, (2016), High Quality Securitisation and EU Capital Markets Union- Is it Possible?, Accounting, Economics and the Law, pp. 73 ff.; S.L. Schwarcz, (2016), Securitization and Post-Crisis Financial Regulation, Cornell Law Review Online, Vol. 101, pp. 115–139.

- Data gathering has improved and swings wildly across jurisdictions, but is still very opaque for those segments of the SB market that are of real concern and that pose a material threat to the stability in the market.
- Very little thought has been going into the fact that complexity and opacity in the financial sector means that instability from time to time is inevitable and that ex post regulation is as important as ex ante legislation in the field. Although there is now resolution and recovery legislation in place for regulated banks, there is none yet (although suggested) for other systemically important players like CCPs and dealer-brokers. However, it is full of open questions regarding waterfall structure, default funding and systemic risk issues.
- Only very recently the macro-demand side for safe assets has been given attention. The fact that a lot of it is driven by welfare-induced institutional cash pools is concerning and might lead to the conclusion that the system can only survive through more risk taking and by lowering expectation regarding the potential outcome. Or it might impact the systemic nature of the business models like the case with (re)insurance.
- Maturity and liquidity transformation, benchmarking implications, shock-inducing (block) trades and volatility-enhancing trading strategies by asset managers were only recently given attention and regulation seems a long way down the road.
- Due diligence and disclosure rules were enacted but often without a direct link to quality-enhanced decision-making and transparency objectives leaving a lot of arbitrary decision-making in this respect with the industry.
- Tail risk and the use of proven flawed financial models persist and are almost completely ignored.[39]
- Credit rating dependence is reduced within the regulated banking sector but still widespread elsewhere, including the typical investors in shadow banking products.[40]
- The implications of new features like stablecoin 'libra', or the equivalent of that issued by central banks themselves only in its early stages.[41]

---

[39] A. Richards, (2015), Financial Services Place Too Much Faith in Flawed Risk Models, Financial Times, September 20.

[40] N. Roubini, (2015), Rating Agencies Still Matter and That Is Inexcusable, Financial Times, August 10.

[41] M. Kumhof and C. Noone, (2018), Central Bank Digital Currencies- Design Principles and Balance Sheet Implications, Bank of England Staff Working Paper Nr. 725, May. They find that if the introduction of (central bank digital currency) CBDC follows a set of core principles, bank funding is not necessarily reduced, credit and liquidity provision to the private sector need not contract, and the risk of a system-wide run from bank deposits to CBDC is addressed. These core principles are: (i) CBDC pays an adjustable interest rate. (ii) CBDC and reserves are distinct, and not convertible into each other. (iii) No guaranteed, on-demand convertibility of bank deposits into CBDC at commercial banks (and therefore by implication at the central bank). (iv) The central bank issues CBDC only against eligible securities (principally government securities). Also: K. Löber et al., (2018), CPMI Markets Committee Report Central bank Digital Currencies, March, via bis.org; T. Mancini-Griffoli et al., (2018), Casting Light on Central bank Digital Currency, IMF Staff Discussion Note, Nr. SDN/18/08, November; B. Cœuré, (2018), The Future of Central Bank Money, Speech by Benoît Cœuré, Member of the Executive Board of the ECB, at the International Center for Monetary and Banking Studies, Geneva, May 14; J. Fernández-Villaverde and D. Saches, (2018), On the Economics of Digital Currencies, FRB of Philadelphia

- Market fragmentation, extra-jurisdictional issues and the role of regulation are recently being looked at, and consultations started.[42] The same can be indicated for emerging and not so emerging (but actual risk) issues like cybersecurity in the financial sector.[43]
- Overall, mental fatigue is kicking in and consensus seems to emerge that the conversation about optimal financial regulation is broken.[44]
- The intertwining between government and the banking system is still ongoing. Sovereign (domestic) debt still triggers no capital requirements, even though there is clear risk of default on these bonds.[45] Financial uncertainty is almost always endogenous, especially if the sovereign is involved.[46]
- Even the concept of market and thus of financial market(s) is subject to change, both in real terms and semantically. It has created a 'market universalism' referring to the 'non-metaphorical tendency to use the term market to describe a wide variety of arrangements or processes in the real world'. However, some of these particular arrangements are not markets. And so 'market solutions' are then leading to second-best solutions documenting that markets aren't necessarily the answer to every economic or financial problem. Although this issue can be applied to many spheres it definitely works for the shadow banking markets and their issues.[47]

Working Paper Nr. 7, February. They see major issues for private digital currencies like Libra as private arrangement fails to implement an efficient allocation, even though it can deliver price stability under certain technological conditions; T. Keister and D. Sanchez, (2019), Should Central Banks Issue Digital Currency?, FRB of Philadelphia Working Paper Nr. 26, June.

[42] F. Restoy, (2019), Market Integration: the Role of Regulation, Speech by Mr. Fernando Restoy, Chairman, Financial Stability Institute, Bank for International Settlements, at the IIF Market fragmentation roundtable, Washington DC, United States, April 10, via bis.org

[43] For a framework regarding cyber risk in the financial space see: A. Bouveret, (2017), Cyber Risk for the Financial Sector: A Framework for Quantitative Assessment, IMF Working Paper Nr. WP/17/143, June.

[44] T. Hale, (2018), The Broken Conversation about Financial Regulation, FT September 19.

[45] The failure to recognize the riskiness of government debt allows (and induces) domestic banks to 'gamble'

with depositors' funds by purchasing risky government bonds (and assets closely correlated with them). A sovereign default in this environment then results in a banking crisis. Critically, we show that permitting banks to gamble this way lowers the cost of borrowing for the government document D'Erasmo et al. See in detail: P. D'Erasmo et al., (2019), Banking Regulation with Risk of Sovereign Default, FRB of Philadelphia Working Paper Nr. 15, February. They also go back for proof to the 1998 Russia crisis as well as the more recent Euro crisis. Also about the implicit juniority of sovereign debt versus private claims: M. Schlegl et al., (2019), The Seniority Structure of Sovereign Debt, FRB of Minneapolis Working Paper Nr. 759, May.

[46] A. Carriero et al., (2018), Endogenous Uncertainty, FRB of Cleveland Working Paper Nr. 5, March.

[47] G.F. Hodgson, (2019), How Mythical Markets Mislead Analysis: An Institutionalist Critique of Market Universalism, Socio-Economic Review, January 9, online: https://doi.org/10.1093/ser/mwy049. Market universalism compromises the distinctive non-market nature of the political and legal sphere, and corrodes the conceptual separation of civil society from the state, Hodgson adds.

It is therefore fair to say the glass is 'half-empty' rather than 'half full' when it comes to the quality of the efforts taken so far. The regulatory is still in a mindset that throwing some liquidity, macroprudential disclosure legislation in the blender will do the trick. Financial stability and investors' protection are not equal to f(liquidity, price stability, contagion controls, SIFI controls, capital requirements,[48] macroprudential and monetary policy,[49] interconnectedness mapping, disclosure and due diligence compliance). But that is the way we have been going. It has turned the financial regulatory field even more in a muckheap than it already was. Although the regulators around the world have been talking to Team Sky about the 'aggregation of marginal gains' theory which made them successful beyond belief, transposing that into the financial regulatory field has no potential for success and will end in vain. And the regulatory dunghill created leaves all the more room for the techniques that we don't seem to be able to capture properly not in the financial sector and not elsewhere in the regulatory field, that is, the many faces of regulatory arbitrage. The financial sector is known for its widespread use of the technique and more evidence keeps pilling on with respect to the shadow banking sphere.[50] Avoiding that will require a holistic regulatory framework within which there is no room for segmentation and regulation follows the economic function of an activity and associated risk(s) to create a capital backstop.[51] We are unfortunately further away from that than ever.[52] It would create stability more than any other methodology and would avoid issues like step-in risks.[53]

[48] Admati has been arguing for years that there is no reason why banks cannot raise 'normal' equity levels and still earn returns, just like any other industry. Gimber and Rajan documented recently that when banks have more equity and less subordinated debt they have lower risk premia on both. When banks have more subordinated and less senior unsecured debt, senior unsecured risk premia are lower. So normal balance sheet behavior, also for banks. See in detail: A.R. Gimber and A. Rajan, (2019), Bank Funding Costs and Capital Structure, Bank of England Staff Working Paper Nr. 805, June 21.

[49] I. Agur and M. Demertzis, (2015), Will Macro-prudential Policy Counteract Monetary Policy's Effects on Financial Stability?, IMF Working Paper Nr. 283.

[50] See regarding regulatory arbitrage on the Basel securitization framework: M. Efing, (2015), Arbitraging the Basel Securitization Framework: Evidence from German ABS investing, Deutsche Bundesbank Discussion paper Nr. 40/2015.

[51] Has the world changed since the last crisis and has turned monetary policy into voodoo economics? The question is not so much if it has changed but what it tells us is how and to what extent regulation and policy should reflect those changing dynamics and increased complexity. See, for example, F. Luna, (2019), Mr. Taylor and the Central Bank: Two Inference Exercises, IMF Working Paper Nr. WP/19/33.

[52] Schnyder et al. wrap it together with 'how does law matter?', providing an account of the disappointing state of the law and finance scene approximately 20 years after its emergence. See: G. Schnyder et al., (2018), Twenty Years 'Law and Finance': Time to Take Law Seriously, Socio-Economic Review, November 2, Oxford University Press, online: https://doi.org/10.1093/ser/mwy041

[53] Step-in risk is the risk that a bank may provide financial support to a(n) ((shadow) banking) entity beyond or in the absence of any contractual obligations, should the entity experience financial stress. Basel just woke up to the issue and is looking to scratch together initial insights that

I'm therefore less inclined to participate in the carnival of self-congratulating supervisors and regulators have been engaging in every time a small step was taken along the way. I'm also not prepared to smother the analysis and observations in qualifiers as 'it is empirically difficult to single out the effects of reforms from other (particularly conjunctural) factors and post-crisis economic developments' or 'since most reforms are still in the process[54] of implementation, longer-term effects (in terms of the reduced frequency and severity of financial crises) may not yet be fully apparent' leading to 'given these factors, the analysis of effects remains tentative…'.[55] The ultimate statements that 'shadow banking has now been tamed' or '[t]oxic parts of 'shadow banking' no longer pose systemic risk'[56] are statements I'm not prepared to underwrite. I can only hope that the next (financial) crisis will prove me wrong.[57] It will be announced abundantly but will emerge in silence overnight.[58]

would help to identify and measure them: BCBS, (2015), Identification and Measurement of Step-in Risk, Consultative Document, December, Basel.

[54] See for extensive reporting of the financial reforms and their (alleged) impact: Banque de France, (2017), The Impact of Financial Reforms, Financial Stability Review Nr. 21, April. The FSB publishes regularly their own updates of where they feel things stand: FSB, (2017), Implementation of G20/FSB Financial Reforms in Other Areas, Summary of key findings based on the 2017 FSB Implementation Monitoring Network (IMN) survey, November 8, via fsb.org. Most recent: FSB, (2019), Implementation of G20/FSB Financial Reforms in Other Areas, Summary of key findings based on the 2018 FSB Implementation Monitoring Network (IMN) survey, May 3, via fsb.org

[55] FSB, (2015), Implementation and Effects of the G20 Financial Regulatory Reforms, Report of the Financial Stability Board to G20 Leaders, Basel, November 9, p. 15.

[56] Philip Stafford, (2017), Global Regulators say 'Shadow Banking' Market has Been Tamed, FT, July 3. See for a good recent compilation of how they feel about what has been achieved and how future risks are perceived: L.F. Signorini, (2019), Non-Bank Finance: Opportunities and Risks Speech by the Deputy Governor of the Bank of Italy Luigi Federico Signorini, Euromed Workshop "Non-Bank Finance and Financial Intermediation", Naples, June 18, via bis.org

[57] What I'm prepared to underwrite is the position Carsten is taking in terms of where we're in terms of a regulatory cycle that started after the financial crisis. Such a regulatory cycle is known by typical steps, which starts with design of regulation to address areas of regulatory and supervisory deficiency, followed by implementation (full, timely and consistent) to ensure that societies can reap the financial stability benefits. The third phase is the phase of testing and reflection, during a period when the experiences and memories of the last crisis start to fade. It is characterized by a weakening in the will to persevere with the ambition and implementation of the reforms. The third one however is key as the choices made in that phase determine the financial regulatory framework and its effectiveness in mitigating the impact of future crises. See in detail: A. Carstens, (2019), Keynote address by Mr. Agustín Carstens, General Manager of the BIS, at the Bank of Spain and CEMFI Second Conference on Financial Stability, Madrid, June 3, via bis.org

[58] N. Roubini, (2018), Is the Next Crisis already Brewing?, Ft Opinion Markets Insight, December 9.

List of Abbreviations[1] and Glossary

Asset-Backed Commercial Paper (ABCP)

An asset-backed commercial paper (ABCP) is a short-term investment product that typically has a maturity between 90 and 270 days. It is therefore considered a money market instrument. In most cases, the security is issued by a bank or non-bank financial institution. The instrument is backed by physical or other financial assets. The instrument is used for short-term financing purposes. Given its short-term maturity, it can be considered a promissory note backed by the credit rating of the issuer. The instrument is bought at a discount to fair value and is repaid at maturity at face value. Occasionally, the security is not backed by collateral and its risk then solely depends on the creditworthiness of the issuer. During the 2007–2009 financial crisis it played a crucial role as the creditworthiness of these ABCPs was not in line with combined creditworthiness of the underlying assets, which created an imploded ABCP market and subsequent loss of liquidity.

Asset-Backed Commercial Paper Conduits (ABCPC)

These conduits (or structured investment vehicle (SIV)) are typically set up by a sponsoring financial institution. This happens in case the bank or non-bank financial institution plans on rolling out a comprehensive asset-backed commercial paper program. The sole purpose of such a conduit is to purchase and hold (financial) assets. The conduit raises funds to finance these assets by selling asset-backed commercial paper

[1] See for an excellent and very extensive and global abbreviation and glossary overview regarding the post-2008 crisis (shadow) banking (regulatory) environment: Morrison and Foerster, (2014), A Regulatory Reform Glossary, NY.

L. Nijs, *The Handbook of Global Shadow Banking, Volume I*,
https://doi.org/10.1007/978-3-030-34743-7

(ABCP) to investors such as insurance firms, pension funds and money market funds. The asset pool that serves as collateral is often diversified (but fixed-income generating) and typically consists of asset-backed securities (ABS), residential mortgages (RMBS), commercial loans and collateralized debt obligations (CDOs). In most cases, these assets hold an AAA-rating, although some assets might not have an independent rating attached.

Asset-Backed Securities (ABS)

An asset-backed security is a security whose value and income payments depend on the underlying pool of assets, which also serve as collateral. Often a pool of assets contain assets such as loans, leases, credit card debt, home equity loans, royalties, car or student loans, receivables and/or corporate debt. In case mortgage loans are included, the product is often referred to as mortgage-backed security. The individual assets held are often illiquid and cannot be sold individually. By securitizing ('bundling') the pool of assets, the instrument becomes marketable and tradable. The pool of assets can be diversified or put together based on a certain risk profile. Concerns related to the product include the understanding that the credit rating or risk profile of the instrument is not in line with the aggregate risk profile of the underlying asset pool and therefore it can be riskier than anticipated. In understanding the risk profile it is critical to observe the quality and characteristics of the asset pool although an open question will always be how the assets respond in case of a systemic market shock and how concentration of certain risks in the portfolio behaves during periods of enhanced market distress.

Alternative Investment Fund Management Directive (AIFMD)

The Alternative Investment Fund Management Directive (AIFMD) (2011/61/EU with amendments in 2013 (2013/14/EU) and 2014 (2014/64/EU)) is a European Directive that governs and applies to hedge funds, private equity funds and real estate funds. The AIFMD was developed following the crisis to capture all financial operators and vehicles that were not covered yet by European financial regulation including the MiFID legislation (Market in Financial Instruments Directive I and II) that has been in place since 2007 and the UCITS (Undertakings for Collective Investment in Transferable Investment Schemes, 2009/65/EC) regulation in place since 2009, which is Europe's collective investment scheme regulation. The AIFMD has as its principal objective the protection of investors and the monitoring of potential systemic risks that could arise in these funds that could destabilize the marketplace.

Auction Rate Security (ARS)

An auction rate security (ARS) refers to a debt instrument with a typically long-term nominal maturity (often 20–30 years) for which the interest rate is reset regularly. In principle the technique can be applied to all sorts of fixed-income instruments but is mainly used for corporate and municipal bonds. The resetting of the interest rate occurs based on the principle of a Dutch auction (i.e. whereby the auction starts from a high rate and drops until demand and supply meet for the instrument; then the interest rate is locked in for the next period). The auction rate security is therefore sold at an interest rate that will clear the market at the lowest yield possible. The technique is used as it traditionally offers lower funding costs for the issuers of the debt instrument, at least compared to the cost of fixed rate instruments or variable rate demand obligations or notes. For buyers it provides a (somewhat) higher yield than alternative money market instruments. Most instruments for which the technique is used have an AAA credit rating.

Asymptotic Single Risk Factor (ASRF)

This refers to an asset value factor of credit risk. The asymptotic single risk factor (ASRF) model is a simplified credit portfolio risk model that documents the Basel II capital requirements (the internal ratings-based (IRB) approach to capital adequacy for credit risk). It uses as input the risk characteristics of a portfolio of credit (sensitive) instruments and calculates the necessary capital using an asymptotic single risk factor model. The model implies that for each instrument, the capital is defined as the loss in excess of the expected loss (EL) at a high confidence level. It uses a number of assumptions and limitations: it uses a one-year risk horizon, a single factor model (risk revolves around one factor), a normal distribution pattern (of the variables involved) and a homogeneous and large pool of exposures (assuming a large but homogeneous pool of credit instruments). The asset pool is often also internationally diversified, but that is not a necessity.

Assets Under Management (AUM)

The assets under management (AUM) measures the total market value of all financial assets that a fund, investment firm, bank or brokerage manages on behalf of its clients and/or themselves. It includes both the capital of outside investors and the capital of the firm and/or its managers that they have left in the investment vehicle. The managers of the vehicle have a fiduciary responsibility vis-à-vis the outside investors to invest the allocated capital as ex ante agreed upon, and act as a good steward during the investment period. AUM needs to be set apart from assets under administration (AUA), which refers to the assets owned and managed by outside clients but for which the firm or fund provides administrative services, which typically include fund accounting, tax reporting, trade reporting, custodian services and so on. It also needs to be set apart from the net asset value (NAV), which refers to the value (and in most cases price) of each unit in the fund or vehicle. The NAV can be calculated by dividing the AUM by the total number of units in the fund or vehicle.

Basel Committee on Banking Supervision (BCBS)

The Basel Committee on Banking Supervision (BCBS) is a committee of banking supervisory authorities, which was established by the central bank governors of the Group of Ten Countries in 1974 and which expanded over time to become a group of 45 members (2019) from 28 jurisdictions. The BCBS is the primary global standard setter for the prudential regulation of banks and provides a forum for regular cooperation on banking supervisory matters.

Bank for International Settlements (BIS)

The Bank for International Settlements (BIS), established in 1930, is an international financial institution owned by central banks (60 (2019)) representing 95% of global gross domestic product (GDP), whose mandate is to foster international monetary and financial cooperation and which serves as a bank for central banks. The BIS's mission is to serve central banks in their pursuit of monetary and financial stability, to foster international cooperation in those areas.

Bank Holding Company (BHC)

A bank holding company (BHC) is a company that controls one or more banks, although it doesn't necessarily. The holding doesn't have to engage in banking activities itself. According to the US Bank Holding Act of 1956, a bank holding company is defined as 'any company that has control over a bank'.[2] The benefits of being a bank holding company lie in the flexibility. In case multiple banks are held by the holding, the holding can buy problem assets from the banks so that they don't have to be sold to the open market under distressed terms, the holding can create a market for the stock of the bank(s), something the bank itself cannot engage in, and a variety of regulatory simplifications, which smaller banks might consider as excessively burdensome in case they have to meet those requirements on a standalone basis. In turn, the BHC is subject to a whole set of regulatory, reporting and balance sheet requirements including financial buffers. Becoming a bank holding also provides access to the discount and liquidity window of the central bank, which a standalone investment bank cannot. That was the main reason why most

[2] See for an analysis D. Avraham et al., (2012), A Structural View of U.S. Bank Holding Companies, Federal Reserve Bank of NY Economy Policy Review, July, pp. 65–81 and R. Chami et al., (2017), What's Different about Bank Holding Companies, IMF Working Paper Nr. WP/17/26, February.

Wall Street banks during the 2007 financial crisis converted into being a BHC. Investment holdings have to register as a bank holding the moment they acquire or exceed 5% of the outstanding shares of any class of voting securities in a bank or bank holding company. Particularly most small- and mid-tier banks in the US are held by a BHC.

Bank Recovery and Resolution Directive (BRRD)

The Bank Recovery and Resolution Directive (BRRD) was adopted in 2014 to provide authorities with (1) comprehensive and effective arrangements to deal with failing banks at national-level cooperation arrangements to tackle cross-border banking failures; (2) the directive requires banks to prepare recovery plans to overcome financial distress. It also grants national authorities powers to ensure an orderly resolution of failing banks with minimal costs for taxpayers. The directive includes rules to set up a national resolution fund that must be established by each European Union (EU) country. All financial institutions have to contribute to these funds. Contributions are calculated on the basis of the institution's size and risk profile. The EU's bank resolution rules ensure that the banks' shareholders and creditors pay their share of the costs through a 'bail-in' mechanism. If that is still not sufficient, the national resolution funds set up under the BRRD can provide the resources needed to ensure that a bank can continue operating while it is being restructured.

Contractual Bail-In (CBI)

A contractual bail-in (CBI) is, next to a statutory bail-in (SBI), a tool to impose losses on private stakeholders to recapitalize a bank in resolution. In case a jurisdiction does not recognize mandatory bail-ins, a CBI might not be feasible absent sufficient provisions in the debt contracts of banks that allow a resolution authority to bail-in claims under such contracts. The International Swaps and Derivatives Association (ISDA) members are required to include such clauses in their debt contracts such that a later bail-in is feasible when needed. Conditions can still be attached.

Central Clearing Party (CCP)

A central counterparty (CCP) is a financial institution that takes on counterparty credit risk between parties to a transaction and provides clearing and settlement services for trades in foreign exchange, securities, options and derivative contracts. Most CCPs are owned by a conglomerate of banks. CCPs bear the largest share of the buyers' and sellers' credit risk when clearing and settling market transactions. A CCP concentrates therefore a large portion of market- and client-specific risk. CCPs avoid the non-cleared contracts that float in the market carrying risks that stay undocumented and unaccounted for. But having many contracts cleared also implies that large volumes of (a)symmetric risks are concentrated and could create issues when adverse market conditions occur. A large chunk of the remaining discussion deals with how CCP losses should be allocated (and in what order) between the CCP, its shareholders and its members.

Collateralized Debt Obligation (CDO)

A collateralized debt obligation (CDO) is a structured financial product that pools cash flow-generating debt instruments and repackages this asset pool into tranches (often with different risk profiles) that are sold to investors. The name refers to the fact that the pooled assets (often mortgages, bonds and loans) are all debt obligations and serve as collateral for the CDO. The more senior the tranche, the safer it is assumed to be. That is because they have first priority on payback from the collateral in the event of default. They often have a higher credit rating.

Credit Default Swap (CDS)

A credit default swap (CDS) is a financial contract whereby a buyer of often corporate or sovereign debt attempts to eliminate possible loss arising from default by the issuer of the bonds. The buyer buys insurance against possible future losses on the instrument. The underwriter (of the CDS) therefore absorbs (or better swaps) potential losses on the underlying instrument in line with contractual terms. A future loss can be offset with the benefits of the CDS. To swap the risk of default, the lender buys a CDS from another investor who agrees to reimburse the lender in case the borrower defaults. The insurance premium tends to reflect the anticipated risks. In a CDS, the buyer of the swap makes payments to the swap's seller until the maturity date of a contract. The seller from his side agrees that in case of a default of the issuer of the debt instrument he will pay the buyer the security's value as well as all interest payments that would have been paid between that time and the security's maturity date.

Commercial Mortgage-Backed Securities (CMBS)

Commercial mortgage-backed securities (CMBS) are a type of mortgage-backed security backed by commercial mortgages rather than residential real estate. CMBS tend to be more complex and volatile than residential mortgage-backed securities due to the unique nature of the underlying property assets and the fact that the product group isn't standardized as some others, which also makes valuation often problematic. A CMBS can provide liquidity to real estate investors and commercial lenders alike. Commercial mortgage loans act as the collateral, with principal and interest passed on to investors. The loans are typically contained within a trust, and they are highly diversified in terms of term, property type and amount. Different tranches with different risk profiles are created, thereby appealing to different types of investors with different risk appetites.

Collateralized Mortgage Obligation (CMO)

A collateralized mortgage obligation (CMO) is a fixed-income security that has mortgage-backed securities as collateral. CMOs are typically subdivided into different risk classes, called tranches. Structured by maturity and level of risk, CMOs receive cash flows as borrowers repay the mortgages that act as collateral on these securities. CMOs distribute principal and interest payments to their investors based on the predetermined CMO rules and agreements. CMOs are sensitive to a number of market conditions such as interest rate changes, foreclosure rates, refinance rates and the rates at which properties are sold.

Capital Markets Union (CMU)

The Capital Markets Union (CMU) is a plan of the European Commission being rolled out to mobilize capital in Europe. It will channel it to all companies, including small- and medium-sized enterprises (SMEs), and infrastructure projects that need it to expand and create jobs. Deeper and more integrated capital markets will (1) provide businesses with a greater choice of funding at lower costs offering new opportunities for savers and investors and (2) make the financial system more resilient. The creation of a true single market for capital in the EU by 2019 as was originally planned hasn't been fully achieved. Part of the reason is that it involves many areas of law and conflicting views exist. Also the EU Parliamentary elections of May 2019 have delayed progress. The CMU program was launched in 2014 by the European Commission and carries the following objectives: (1) develop a more diversified financial system complementing bank financing with deep and developed capital markets; (2) unlock the capital around Europe which is currently frozen and put it to work for the economy, giving savers more investment choices and offering businesses a greater choice of funding at lower costs; (3) establish a genuine single capital market in the EU where investors are able to invest their funds without hindrance across borders and businesses can raise the required funds from a diverse range of sources, irrespective of their location.

Constant Net Asset Value (CNAV)

Constant net asset value (CNAV) refers to funds (money market funds or MMFs) which use amortized cost accounting to value all of their assets. They aim to maintain a net asset value (NAV), or value of a share of the fund, at €1 or US$1 and calculate their price to two decimal places known as 'penny rounding'. Because it is rare for the NAV of an MMF to move by as much as 50 bps, the share price of a CNAV fund tends to remain constant, hence the description of the fund as tending to have a 'constant' NAV. CNAV funds that fail to maintain a constant price are described as having 'broken the buck'. CNAV funds are inherently prone to large redemptions because they provide investors with a 'first redeemer advantage'.

Contingent Convertible Bonds (CoCos)

Contingent convertible bonds (CoCos) are a hybrid type of security that absorbs losses when the capital of the issuer falls below a certain preset threshold. They pose two characteristic features[3]: they include (1) a mechanism that specifies how losses will be absorbed (conversion into common equity or principal write-down) and (2) a trigger that activates this mechanism (often a given level of the common equity Tier 1 (CET1) ratio and sometimes a 'point of nonviability trigger' (PONV) left at the discretion of the supervisor). An important benefit of CoCos—especially relative to equity—is their lower after-tax cost. Regulatory capital eligibility considerations determine the other CoCo features, including maturity. CoCos are supposed to be a first line of defense and to be triggered/depleted by the time a resolution authority decides to use its bail-in powers. These instruments play a crucial role in the context of resolution frameworks but also and maybe more importantly in the context of the Basel III to make bank balance sheets more robust and loss absorbing.

Commercial Paper (CP)

Commercial paper (CP) is an unsecured, short-term debt instrument issued by a corporation. It is typically used for the financing of accounts payable and inventories (working capital) and meeting other short-term liabilities. Maturities on commercial paper hardly range longer than 270 days, but can go up to one year. Issuers need to be investment-grade firms or vehicles (given the unsecured nature of the instrument). CP is raised directly from the market, without involvement of an investment bank, and comes often at significantly lower costs than bonds for the issuing party.

Commercial Paper Funding Facility (CPFF)

The Commercial Paper Funding Facility (CPFF) was a system created by the US Federal Reserve Board during the global financial crisis of 2008 to improve liquidity in the short-term funding markets. The CPFF funded a special-purpose vehicle (SPV) that purchased three-month unsecured and asset-backed commercial paper from eligible issuers. This resulted in greater availability of credit for firms doing business. The facility expired February 1, 2010.

[3] See G. Dell'Ariccia et al., (2018), Trade-offs in Bank Resolution, IMF Staff Discussion Note SDN/18/02, February, p. 29.

Credit Rating Agency (CRA)

A credit rating agency (CRA) is a company that assigns credit ratings, which rate a debtor's ability to pay back debt by making timely principal and interest payments in the likelihood of default. A credit rating facilitates the trading of securities in the secondary market. Most traded instruments (debt or equity, vehicles, securitized products, etc.) require a credit rating by law. The most visible CRAs are Moody's, Standard & Poor's (S&P) and Fitch. China has its own agency (Dagong).

Capital Requirements Directive (CRD)

A capital requirement (also known as regulatory capital or capital adequacy) is the amount of capital a bank or other financial institution has to hold as required by its financial regulator. This is usually expressed as a capital adequacy ratio of equity that must be held as a percentage of risk-weighted assets. There are different models available through which the capital requirement is calculated. In the European Union, there are a set of five directives that cover the issue, the first edition being implemented in 1993. See also *Capital Requirements Regulation (CRR).*

Commercial Real Estate (CRE)

The term 'commercial real estate' (CRE) refers to buildings or land intended to generate a profit, from either capital gain or rental income. Commercial real estate includes office buildings, retail/resto buildings, apartment complexes, land and self-storage, hospitals and hospitality infrastructure. The term is often used to contrast with residential real estate, which is typically owner occupied, although that trend is changing as well.

Credit Risk Mitigating (CRM) Techniques

Credit risk mitigating (CRM) techniques refer to the pool of techniques that allow reducing the credit risk (including default risk) of an instrument, firm or vehicle. The methods can include: (1) risk-based pricing, or adjusting the cost of credit according to the credit strength of the borrower; (2) credit tightening, or reducing the amount of credit available to higher risk applicants; (3) diversification, or increasing the portfolio mix of borrowers and purchasing credit insurance. Particular instruments include netting (offsetting a variety of risk profiles of the same issuer), hedging, using off-balance-sheet credit and volatility-reducing instruments.

Capital Requirements Regulation (CRR)

Capital requirements are set to ensure that banks and depository institutions are not holding investments that increase the risk of default. They also ensure that banks and depository institutions have enough capital to sustain operating losses while still honoring withdrawals. Implemented through Capital Requirements Regulation (EU) Nr. 575/2013. See also *Capital Requirements Directive (CRD).*

Capital Relief Transaction (CRT)

Regulatory capital relief is an investment strategy whereby non-bank investors underwrite losses on portfolios of bank loans. The transactions that they structure transfer the risk of a portion of losses away from the bank, without removing the assets from their balance sheets. The banks themselves then have to hold less capital, while keeping the loan portfolio on their books. In that sense, one can see it as a parallel instrument for securitization, with the difference that under securitization the assets leave the securitizers' balance sheet.

Central Securities Depositories (CSD)

A central securities depository (CSD) is a specialist financial organization holding securities such as shares in either certificated or uncertificated (dematerialized) form so that ownership can be easily transferred through a book entry rather than the transfer of physical certificates. A CSD can be national or international in nature, and may be for a specific type of security, such as government bonds. There exist domestic and international CSD models. The functions include: (1) safekeeping of securities; (2) deposit and withdrawal of securities; (3) dividend, interest and principal processing, as well as corporate actions including proxy voting; (4) securities lending and borrowing, matching and repo settlement, or international securities identification number (ISIN) assistance; and (5) pledging of shares and securities. CSD is often regulated separately by law and in the EU by Regulation. Annually a list, in both Europe and the US, of certified CSD is published.

Diversified Broker-Dealer (DBD)

A broker-dealer is typically a firm that buys and sells securities for its own account or on behalf of its customers. The term 'broker-dealer' is used in securities regulation to describe stock brokerages because most of them act as both agents and principals. A brokerage acts as a broker (or agent) when it executes orders on behalf of its clients, whereas it acts as a dealer, or principal, when it trades for its own account. Broker-dealers can perform different functions: they provide investment advice to customers, supply liquidity through market-making activities, facilitate trading activities, publish investment research and raise capital for companies.

Dodd-Frank Act (DFA)

The Dodd-Frank Wall Street Reform and Consumer Protection Act is a law enacted in 2010 that regulates the financial markets and protects consumers. Its components help prevent (or at least that is the idea) a repeat of the 2008 financial crisis. The act pools a wide variety of topics including financial stability, liquidity, supervision and oversight, oversight of alternative investment managers, transparency and accountability, investor protection, clearing and settlement, mortgage and mortgage-reform, securitization and consumer finance. Because of the wide scope, individual chapters of the law are continuously under review and subject to amendments.

Development Finance Institutions (DFIs)

Development finance institutions (DFIs) provide directly or indirectly equity, loans and guarantees to companies operating in the world's most challenging markets. They are often categorized based on the development index categories by the United Nations (UN). These institutions are often fully or partially funded by development aid budgets. Historically, their mandate was closely linked to development objectives. Gradually that is changing as they often receive a wider mandate to attract non-public office capital and manage their balance sheet independent from the Treasury. Also in terms of investment strategy there is a gradual shift occurring whereby the DFIs weigh commercial motives and bankability of a project or proposal with the pure development objectives.

Department of Energy (US) (DoE)

The US Department of Energy is a cabinet-level department of the US government concerned with the US policies regarding energy and safety in handling nuclear material.

Debt-Service-to-Income (DSTI)

The debt-to-income (DTI) ratio is the percentage of your gross monthly/annual income that goes to paying monthly/annual debt payments on, for example, a mortgage loan. The DTI ratio is one of the metrics that (mortgage) lenders, use to measure an individual's ability to manage monthly payments and repay debts. To calculate the debt service coverage ratio, simply divide the net operating or spendable income by the annual debt. The ratio is also used for macroprudential oversight as in periods of credit expansion the ratio reduces, which might indicate stability risk, overvaluation of real estate and/or bubble scenarios.

Deposit-Taking Institutions (DTIs)

A deposit-taking institution (DTI) is one of the three main chapters in the financial system, encompassing those which accept deposits and make loans. This category includes banks, trust companies, credit unions and mortgage loan companies. DTIs are specifically licensed and are subject to capital requirements and intense oversight taking into account their deposit-taking nature. They benefit from the deposit insurance mechanism in place in many countries, assuming compliance with all regulations.

European Commission (EC)

The executive branch of the European Union's institutional framework. The European Commission is an institution of the European Union, responsible for proposing legislation, implementing decisions, upholding the EU treaties and managing the day-to-day business of the EU. The Commission operates as a cabinet government, with 28 members.

European Union (EU)

The European Union is a political and economic union of 28 member states. Historically it emerged out of the European Coal and Steel Community and later on the economically centered European Economic Community (EEC).

European Banking Authority (EBA)

The European Banking Authority (EBA) is a Paris-based regulatory agency of the European Union. Its activities include conducting stress-tests on European banks to increase transparency in the European financial system and identifying weaknesses in banks' capital structures. The EBA is thus an independent EU Authority that works to ensure effective and consistent prudential regulation and supervision across the European banking sector. Its overall objectives are to maintain financial stability in the EU and to safeguard the integrity, efficiency and orderly functioning of the banking sector. The Authority also plays an important role in promoting convergence of supervisory practices and is mandated to assess risks and vulnerabilities in the EU banking sector. The EBA was established on 1 January 2011.

Regulation on OTC Derivatives, Central Counterparties and Trade Repositories (EMIR)

In 2012 the EU adopted the European Market Infrastructure Regulation (EMIR). The aims were to increase transparency in the over-the-counter (OTC) derivatives markets, mitigate credit risk and reduce operational risk. It further established common rules for central counterparties and trade repositories. The overall objective of the legislation is to reduce systemic counterparty and operational risk, and help prevent future financial system collapses.

European Supervisory Authorities (ESAs)

The European System of Financial Supervision (ESFS) is the framework for financial supervision in the European Union in operation since 2011. The system consists of the European Supervisory Authorities (ESAs), the European Systemic Risk Board, the Joint Committee of the European Supervisory Authorities and the national supervisory authorities of EU member states. There are three European Supervisory Authorities (ESAs). They are responsible for microprudential oversight at the European Union level: (1) the European Banking Authority (EBA), (2) the European Securities and Markets Authority (ESMA) and (3) the European Insurance and Occupational Pensions Authority (EIOPA).

European Systemic Risk Board (ESRB)

The European Systemic Risk Board (ESRB) was established in 2010 to oversee the financial system of the EU and prevent and mitigate systemic risk. The ESRB is responsible for the macroprudential oversight of the EU financial system and the prevention and mitigation of systemic risk. The ESRB therefore has a broad remit, covering banks, insurers, asset managers, shadow banks, financial market infrastructures and other financial institutions and markets. In pursuit of its macroprudential mandate, the ESRB monitors and assesses systemic risks and, where appropriate, issues warnings and recommendations. Its operations are organized through Regulation (EU) No 1092/2010.

European System of Central Banks (ESCB)

The European System of Central Banks (ESCB) consists of the European Central Bank (ECB) and the national central banks (NCBs) of all 28 member states of the EU. The ESCB is not the monetary authority of the eurozone, as not all EU member states use the euro as their currency. The European System of Central Banks (ESCB) consists of the European Central Bank (ECB) and the national central banks (NCBs) of all 28 member states of the European Union (EU).

European Securities and Markets Authority (ESMA)

ESMA is an independent EU Authority that contributes to safeguarding the stability of the European Union's financial system by enhancing the protection of investors and promoting stable and orderly financial markets. It achieves this by assessing risks to investors, markets and financial stability; completing a single rulebook for EU financial markets; promoting supervisory convergence and directly supervising credit rating agencies and trade repositories. It works closely with the other European Supervisory Authorities competent in the field of banking (EBA), and insurance and occupational pensions (EIOPA). The three main objectives are: investor protection, orderly markets and financial stability.

Employee Retirement Income Security Act (ERISA)

The Employee Retirement Income Security Act of 1974 (ERISA) is a US federal law that sets minimum standards for most voluntarily established retirement and health plans in private industry to provide protection for individuals in these plans. The main purpose of ERISA is to protect the interests of employees (and their beneficiaries) who are enrolled in employee benefit plans, and to ensure that employees receive the pensions and group-sponsored welfare benefits that have been promised by their employers.

Exchange-Traded Fund (ETF)

An exchange-traded fund (ETF) is an investment fund traded on a stock exchange, much like individual stocks. An ETF holds assets such as stocks, commodities or bonds (or a mixture) and generally operates with an arbitrage mechanism designed to keep its trading close to its net asset value, although deviations can occasionally occur. Historically, most ETFs were index-tracking funds and were positioned as low-cost passive products. Over time, that has changed in the sense that while continuing to compete on costs, the product group became more strategic for investors and the investment strategies they used being more complex, and focused on more than just capturing the beta in the market. Enhanced strategies combined with low costs are now the focal point of the product group. The ETF group in a way became a more 'active product' or at least a passive product in an active strategy-denominated portfolio.

Eigenvector Centrality (EVC)

Eigenvector centrality (EVC) is a measure of the influence of a node in a network. Relative scores are assigned to all nodes in the network based on the concept that connections to high-scoring nodes contribute more to the score of the node in question than equal connections to low-scoring nodes. In finance, and particularly the literature on systemic risk and systemically important institutions, the concept refers to the element to assess the systemic importance of a node (e.g. a financial player) by reference to the importance of the nodes it is connected to. In the case of systemic risk, it is possible to become systemically important either by having links to a large number of nodes or by having a smaller number of links to nodes which themselves are systemically important.

Financial Activities Tax (FAT)

A financial activities tax (FAT) is a tax on the sum of bank profits and bankers' remuneration packages, with the proceeds going into general government revenues. Not to be confused with a financial transaction tax or a financial stability contribution. See *Financial Transaction Tax.*

Fallback Approach (FBA)

This refers to one of the methods used to determine the capital standard for funds investment or more in general for credit risk by institutions subject to capital requirements. It is typically the last option in row as the name reveals that it is a kind of contingency option as all the other options for whatever reason don't work or aren't preferred.

Federal Deposit Insurance Corporation (FDIC)

The Federal Deposit Insurance Corporation (FDIC) is a US government corporation providing deposit insurance to depositors holding deposits with US commercial banks and savings institutions. The standard deposit insurance coverage limit is 250,000 USD per depositor, per FDIC-insured bank and per ownership category, even in case they are held at the same bank. The FDIC thus provides separate coverage for deposits held in different account ownership categories. The FDIC covers all the traditional consumer banking products such as checking, savings and money market deposit accounts and certificates of deposit (CDs). 401(k) plans are considered investment products or plans and are therefore not covered. Also excluded are stocks, bonds, mutual funds, life insurance policies, annuities or securities. The FDIC is funded by member banks (which all must meet certain criteria in terms of liquidity and capitalization) and the government acts as a backstop in case the FDIC runs out of cash.

Federal Reserve Bank (US) (Fed)

The Federal Reserve Bank is the central bank of the US. It was created in December 1913, after a series of financial panics led to the desire for central control of the monetary system in order to alleviate financial crises. Its mandate includes the following: (1) conducting the nation's monetary policy by influencing money and credit conditions in the economy in pursuit of full employment and stable prices; (2) supervising and regulating banks and other important financial institutions to ensure the safety and soundness of the nation's banking and financial system and to protect the credit rights of consumers; (3) maintaining the stability of the financial system and containing systemic risk that may arise in financial markets and (4) providing certain financial services to the US government, US financial institutions and foreign official institutions, and playing a major role in operating and overseeing the nation's payments systems.

Federal Housing Administration (FHA)

A US government agency established in 1934, it provides mortgage insurance and sets standards for constructing and underwriting and insures loans made by banks while others provide lending for home building. The overall objective is to improve housing standards and conditions and also build and maintain an adequate financing system through the insurance of mortgage loans. Stabilizing and maintaining a stable mortgage market is also included in its mandate.

Federal Housing Financing Agency (FHFA)

An independent US federal agency with its legal and regulatory authority inherited from the Federal Housing Finance Board (FHFB). Its authority includes the ability to place government-sponsored enterprises (GSEs) into receivership and conservatorship. It regulates Fannie Mae and Freddie Mac and another 11 Federal Home Loan Banks. It operates separate from the Federal Housing Administration (FHA), which provides mortgage insurance.

Federal Home Loan Banks (FHLB)

The Federal Home Loan Banks (FHLB) are 11 US government-sponsored banks that provide reliable liquidity to member financial institutions. Collectively, the FHLB represent the largest collective source of home mortgage and community credit in the US. The system was established in 1932. The prime mission is to provide member financial institutions with financial products and services that assist and enhance the financing of housing and community lending. The banks are each structured as owned and governed by their member financial institutions, which today include savings and loan associations, commercial banks, credit unions and insurance companies. A primary benefit of FHLB membership is access to reliable liquidity through secured loans.

Financial Institution (FI)

FI refers typically, as an umbrella term, to the collectivity of institutions that are active in the (private and/or public) financial markets. A financial institution typically provides a wide variety of deposit, lending and investment products to individuals, businesses or both. As the term covers a wide spectrum of activities, it is classified for regulatory, oversight and other purposes. A possible classification would be: central banks, retail and commercial banks, internet banks, credit unions, savings and loan associations, investment banks, investment companies, brokerage firms, insurance companies and mortgage companies.

Financial Market Infrastructure (FMI)

Financial market infrastructure (FMI) refers to critically important institutions responsible for providing clearing, settlement and recording of monetary and other financial transactions. A payment system is a set of instruments, procedures and rules for the transfer of funds between or among participants. On a global scale the FMIs are governed by a set of principles developed by CPMI/IOSCO. The principles for financial market infrastructures are the international standards for financial market infrastructures, that is, payment systems, central securities depositories, securities settlement systems, central counterparties and trade repositories.

Floating Net Asset Value (FNAV)

A floating NAV (FNAV) money market funds prices and transacts at a net asset value per share that can change or fluctuate based on pricing of the underlying fund holdings. FNAV funds are priced using basis point rounding, to four decimal places. Floating NAVs are calculated at pricing intervals throughout the day. This differs from a stable NAV fund, which calculates NAV once a day. The same factors that can have the biggest impact on a stable money market fund's NAV—changes in credit, interest rates and investor flows—are the most significant drivers of a money market fund's FNAV.

Financial Stability Board (FSB)

The Financial Stability Board (FSB) is an international body that monitors and makes recommendations about the global financial system. It was established after the G20 London summit in April 2009 as a successor to the Financial Stability Forum. The FSB monitors and assesses vulnerabilities affecting the global financial system and proposes actions needed to address them. In addition, it monitors and advises on market and systemic developments, and their implications for regulatory policy.

Financial Transaction Tax (FTT)

A financial transaction tax (FTT) is a levy introduced on a specific type of financial transaction and often for a particular purpose. The FTT has been most commonly associated with the financial sector, but the levy is attached to the transaction and not the transaction-engaging institution. So it doesn't fall within the category of bank taxes, stability contributions or financial activities taxes (FAT). The philosophy is to selectively discourage excessive speculation without discouraging broader economic activities and development. The financial transaction can carry securities, derivatives or currencies.

Financial Vehicle Corporations (FVC)

See *Special-Purpose Entity (SPE)*

Gross Domestic Product (GDP)

Gross domestic product (GDP) is a monetary measure of the market value of all the final goods and services produced in a period of time, often quarterly or annually (for a particular country, region or the world). Different definitions exist, although they essentially capture the same phenomenon. The Organisation for Economic Co-operation and Development (OECD) frames it as 'an aggregate measure of production equal to the sum of the gross values added of all resident and institutional units engaged in production (plus any taxes, and minus any subsidies, on products not included in the value of their outputs)'. The International Monetary Fund (IMF) states: 'GDP measures the monetary value of final goods and services—that are bought by the final user—produced in a country in a given period of time (say a quarter or a year).'

Guaranteed Investment Contract (GIC)

A guaranteed investment contract (GIC) is an agreement between the purchaser (of a contract) and an insurance company whereby the insurance company provides a guaranteed rate of return in exchange for keeping a deposit for a fixed period of time. A guaranteed investment contract therefore is a contract that guarantees repayment of principal and a fixed or floating interest rate for a predetermined period of time. Guaranteed investment contracts are typically issued by life insurance companies. A GIC is used primarily as a vehicle that yields a higher return than a savings account or US Treasury securities.

Global Flow of Funds (GFF)

The global flow of funds (GFF) concept is an extension of the domestic flow of funds. It connects domestic economies with the rest of the world. GFF data could provide valuable information for analyzing interconnectedness across borders and global financial interdependencies. Flow of funds (FOF) accounts is used to track the flow of money to and from various sectors of a national economy. Flow of funds accounts are collected and analyzed by a country's central bank. The FSB also uses the data sets to formulate analysis and policy recommendations.

Government-Sponsored Entity (GSE)

Government-sponsored enterprises, or GSEs, are quasi-governmental, privately held entities established to improve or enable the flow of credit to specific sectors of the economy or to otherwise provide essential services to the public. GSEs do not lend money to the public directly. Instead, they guarantee third-party loans and purchase loans in the secondary market, thereby providing money to lenders and financial institutions. GSE bonds carry the implicit backing of the US government, but they do not qualify as direct obligations by the US government unlike Treasury bonds.

High-Quality Liquid Assets (HQLA)

A concept to be situated as part of the 'liquidity coverage ratio', which is part of the Basel III standards for deposit-taking regulated banking institutions. The aim of the requirement is to have sufficient liquidity at all times to meet short-term obligations and deposits withdrawals. The high-quality liquid assets (HQLA) include only those with a high potential to be converted easily and quickly into cash (in times of distress). HQLA are cash or assets that can be converted into cash quickly through sales (or by being pledged as collateral) with no significant loss of value. A liquid asset can be included in the stock of HQLA if it is unencumbered, meets minimum liquidity criteria and its operational factors demonstrate that it can be disposed off to generate liquidity when needed. The HQLA group includes Level 1 assets, which can be included without limit, and Level 2 assets, which cannot exceed 40% of the liquidity reserve. Level 2 assets are themselves subdivided into Level 2A assets, whose value is subject to a 15% haircut, and Level 2B assets, which are subject to higher haircuts but cannot exceed 15% of the stock of HQLA.

Internal Assessment Approach (IAA)

The internal assessment approach allows banks to map their internal credit assessment of a securitization exposure to an equivalent (i.e. to mirror) external credit rating from a recognized statistical rating organization. It results in a risk-weighted amount of capital to be held against a certain portfolio of securitized products. As the methodology used is 'internally generated' it needs to be approved by the designated supervisory body in terms of the robustness of the methodology, the quality of the data used and policies, procedures and controls used to mitigate risks and ex post interventions.

Insurance Corporation and Pension Fund (ICPF)

Insurance Corporation and Pension Fund is used as a reporting group by the ECB for statistical purposes. Insurance corporations comprise both insurance (life and non-life) and reinsurance types of business. Pension funds consist only of those pension funds that are institutional units separate from the units that create them.

Investment Fund (IF)

An investment fund is a way of investing money (through a vehicle) alongside other investors in order to benefit from the inherent advantages of working as part of a group. These advantages include, among others, an ability to engage professional managers, benefit from lower transaction costs and economies of scale, and reduce idiosyncratic risk through enhanced asset diversification. It is an umbrella term that includes a wide variety of funds with a variety of strategies and governed by different regulations and oversight. Terminology therefore varies with country but investment funds are often referred to as investment pools, collective investment vehicles, collective investment schemes, managed funds or simply funds. An investment fund can be held by the public, such as a mutual fund, exchange-traded fund, special purpose acquisition company or closed-end fund, or it may be sold only in a private placement, such as a hedge fund or private equity fund. They therefore can be listed or private.

International Financial Reporting Standards (IFRS)

International Financial Reporting Standards (IFRS) is a set of accounting standards developed by an independent, not-for-profit organization called the International Accounting Standards Board (IASB). The goal of IFRS is to provide a global framework for how public companies prepare and disclose their financial statements. IFRS provides general guidance for the preparation of financial statements, rather than setting rules for industry-specific reporting. Currently, well over 100 countries permit or require IFRS for public companies. IFRS is sometimes confused with International Accounting Standards (IAS), which are older standards that IFRS has replaced.

Insurance-Linked Securities (ILS)

Insurance-linked securities are financial instruments whose value is affected by an insured loss event. The term 'insurance-linked security' includes catastrophe bonds and other forms of risk-linked securitization. Insurance-linked securities are generally thought to have little to no correlation with the wider financial markets as their value is linked to non-financial risks such as natural disasters, longevity risk or life insurance mortality. As securities, insurance-linked securities can be and are traded among investors and on the secondary market. They allow insurers to offload risk and raise capital.

Internal Ratings-Based Approach (IRBA)

The internal ratings-based approach (IRBA) is one of the methodologies under the Basel II guidelines to be used by banks to calculate the level of regulatory capital required to compensate for credit risk. Only banks meeting certain minimum conditions, disclosure requirements and approval from their national supervisor are allowed to use this approach in estimating capital for various exposures. Each of the exposures by banks (corporate, sovereign, bank, retail and equity) has its own classification and subclassification. To effectively calculate the required capital, the methodology uses certain risk parameters, a weighting system for the different exposures while the bank must fulfill certain minimum standards.

International Organization of Securities Commissions (IOSCO)

The International Organization of Securities Commissions (IOSCO) is the international body that brings together the world's securities regulators and is recognized as the global standard setter for the securities sector. IOSCO develops, implements and promotes adherence to internationally recognized standards for securities regulation. It works intensively with the G20 and the Financial Stability Board on the global regulatory reform agenda.

(Total) Loss-Absorbing Capacity ((T)LAC)

Loss-absorbing capacity (LAC) refers to the question to what extent, in the case a bank is facing failure, a systemic crisis or other displacement scenarios that might put the bank's survival at risk, the bank's balance sheet is composed of financial instruments that can effectively and under such circumstances absorb risk in such a way that depositors with the bank stay unaffected and/or public funding is required to stabilize the firm and ensure continued operations. Even in case a bank goes into receivership or resolution, the LAC allows for an orderly unwinding of the bank's business operations. Under Basel III, the systemically important banks are required to have TLAC in accord with their risk-weighted assets and leverage ratios. The EU version, known as 'minimum requirement of own funds and eligible liabilities (MREL)', applies to all EU banks, regardless of size, at both the individual and group consolidated levels.

Leveraged Buyouts (LBOs)

A leveraged buyout (LBO) is the technique used for buying a company thereby using a significant amount of debt. The assets and operations of the company are often used as a collateral for the loans. This is in addition to the assets of the acquiring company in case the buyer is an operational or strategic buyer. In case the buyer is a financial sponsor (private equity firm or venture capital firm) such assets are typically not available. The LBO scheme works with an equity portion of between 5% and 15% complemented with additional layers of debt from senior secured to junior and subordinated and with a maturity scale to avoid too much debt becoming due at the same time or during a short period of time. Typically the acquired company is sold in a five- to seven-year period and remaining acquisition debt is then fully repaid. The LBO scheme also uses bridge financing to cover the initial period after acquisition (normally 12–24 months), during which potential re-organizations, sell-offs and other restructuring efforts are completed to ensure that continued operations afterward can meet the debt service that follows from the acquisition debt.

Liquidity Coverage Ratio (LCR)

The liquidity coverage ratio (LCR) refers to the proportion of highly liquid assets that need to be held by a financial institution subject to the Basel III framework. It ensures that under a wide set of market conditions the firm can meet its short-term obligations. Essential in the Basel III arrangements regarding the LCR is the definition of what constitutes a highly liquid asset. The LCR ratio essentially is a stress test (typically measured over a 30-day period) that aims to anticipate on a variety of market- and system-wide shocks and the necessity for banks to maintain sufficient liquidity to meet short-term obligations.

Legal Entity Identifier (LEI)

The Legal Entity Identifier (LEI) is a unique and global identifier for individuals, funds, firms or public entities that participate in financial transactions. The LEI is used in a variety of reporting standards to financial regulators. It consists of 20 characters. The objective is to connect the LEI to key reference information that enables clear and unique identification of legal entities engaged in financial transactions. In short, it can be seen as a global directory of 'who is who' in global financial markets. The Global Legal Entity

Identifier Foundation (GLEIF) accredits those parties that can issue LEIs. Those parties typically are financial exchanges or financial data vendors as they are best suited to act as primary interfaces to such a database and maintain its operational and up-to-date status.

Loss Given Default (LGD)

Loss given default (LGD) is that part of an asset that is lost in case a borrower defaults. It is a common element in risk models and further a parameter used in the calculation of economic capital, expected loss or regulatory capital under Basel II(I) for a banking institution. The most frequently used method to calculate this loss compares actual total losses to the total amount of potential exposure sustained at the time that a loan goes into default. In most cases, LGD is determined after a review of a bank's entire portfolio, using cumulative losses and exposure for the calculation. Banks and other financial institutions determine credit losses by analyzing actual loan defaults.

Local Government Financing Vehicles (LGFVs)

Local government financing vehicle (LGFV) is a financing company which is typically owned by a local government in China. They often sell local land's bond to the China Development Bank, which is in turn used to finance real estate development. There is structural concern about the indebtedness of these entities, the subprime nature of many securities they hold and the real estate or portfolio they own or have financed. Lianhe Ratings Global, a local Chinese credit rating agency, developed a rating model for this specific type of institution (2018). The problem is that they operate in relative obscurity and provide very little guidance or transparency. Nevertheless, under adverse market conditions they can pose a systemic risk and impact the public debt record of the Chinese government. In recent years the pace of issuing new debt has decreased but concerns continue to emerge given the massive historic build-up of their portfolio and the political, rather than bankable, nature of their investment decisions.

Local Government Investment Pool (LGIP)

A government investment pool (GIP), or local government investment pool (LGIP), is a state or local government pool (the US) offered to public entities for the investment of public funds. These pools offer safety with a competitive yield. Many GIPs are managed by the government, but there are also GIPs that are managed by outside investment firms. Participants in a government investment pool may include state or local municipalities, counties, school districts, utility districts and local government units. Investments may include, but are not restricted to, certificates of deposit (CDs), US Treasuries, US agencies, repurchase agreements, and commercial paper. LGIPs aren't Securities and Exchange Commission (SEC) regulated.

Lender of Last Resort (LOLR)

A lender of last resort (LOLR) is the institution in the financial system that is the provider of liquidity to a financial institution in case it finds itself unable to obtain sufficient liquidity in the interbank lending market and when other facilities or sources have been exhausted. The concept became more mainstream after the 2008 financial crisis when the central banks in countries around the world had to step in and provide a liquidity window to avoid solvency issues or outright defaults of banks and other financial intermediaries. It refers more broadly to the fact that when markets go sideways, there is no intrinsic mechanism to correct the situation and an external (public) body is required to avoid further defaults in the market.

Long-Term Note (LTN)

A long-term note is a(n) (often secured) debt security with a maturity beyond one year.

Limited Purpose Finance Company (LPFC)

Under limited purpose banking, all financial corporations engaged in financial intermediation, including all banks and insurance companies, would function exclusively as middlemen who sell safe as well as risky collections of securities (mutual funds) to the public. They would never, themselves, own financial assets. A limited purpose finance company is a company engaged in such activities. Limited purpose banking can also be structured as a trust and is then referred to as a 'limited purpose trust company'.

Look-Through Approach (LTA)

The look-through approach (LTA) is one of the (preferred) methodologies to determine the capital requirements for banks to hold against equity investment in other funds. The LTA embodies the most granular approach. The look-through methodology essentially looks through the equity investment and analyzes the assets held by the fund invested in. What is important is that the institution knows with sufficient certainty the underlying assets contained in the fund. If the risk weight of the underlying asset is known, the use of the look-through approach will provide the most accurate measure of the fund's overall risk and ensure capital requirements are commensurate with the risk. Where an institution does not have sufficient information about the underlying individual exposures to use the look-through approach, it may calculate the risk-weighted exposure amount of those exposures in accordance with the limits set in the fund's mandate and relevant legislation.

Loan-to-Income (LTI) Ratio

The loan-to-income ratio is used in real estate finance and indicates the relationship between the mortgage loan taken out and the annual income of the lender. It says something about the ability of the lender to repay the loan. In some countries there are caps on the ratio that banks have to apply (e.g. 3.5 times), and others only provide guidance on the matter but do not effectively interfere. The concern is with the amount of credit flowing into real estate, the prime or subprime nature of the loan and lender, and the macroeconomic risks that might be attached to the volume of credit floating in real estate markets. Often, distinction is made between 'principal-dwelling' and 'secondary real estate' markets in setting potential limits or caps.

Loan-to-Value (LTV) Ratio

The 'loan-to-value' (LTV) ratio means the ratio of the amount of a housing loan to the (market) value of the real estate pledged as loan collateral. In case the ratio is 100%, the loan covers the market value (or any other ex ante determined value) of the collateral (i.e. the property). In case transaction-related expenses are also debt-financed the ratio will even be higher than 100%. On aggregate it says something about how much credit is flowing into a real estate market, which in itself influences the valuation in that market. As real estate bubbles are almost always credit-induced, and a steep fall in real estate prices always tends to adversely impact confidence and therefore fosters panic in markets, supervisors tend to carefully monitor the amount of credit in the real estate market through a number of these ratios and some even set (mandatory) limits to the ratios. The ESRB regularly advises on limits in respective European real-estate-sensitive markets.

Market Abuse Directive (MAD)

The Market Abuse Directive (MAD) is a European Directive which contains a comprehensive framework that addresses situations whereby investors have been unreasonably disadvantaged. The objective is to address abusive behavior often enabled by (new) technology and to protect the financial market integrity and to strengthen investor confidence. The initial MAD I which was adopted in 2003 operated its objective by requiring the market participants to commit to transparency, closer cooperation and equal enforcement of the framework. However, as the financial infrastructure has changed materially during the last decade allowing for new forms of market manipulation, the MAD I was replaced by MAD II/MAR (Market Abuse Regulation) in 2015 (effective July 2016). The most important changes are related to both capturing new technologies and their abusive applications, but predominantly by expanding the scope of the directive. For example, MAR doesn't apply only to financial instruments traded on a regulated market, but also to those traded or admitted to trading on a multilateral trading facility or on an organized trading facility, as well as to instruments traded over the counter, which might influence the price or rate of the financial instruments and commodities covered by the MAR definition. Moreover, manipulation of financial instruments might also take place outside of trading venues or just by having the intention to trade, that is, placing orders without executing them.

Multi-Agent Financial Network (MAFN)

The term is used in the context of understanding, identifying and analyzing systemic risk in financial markets and to build a model to reflect the complexity and nature of financial markets. There is still both a data and a skills gap in implementing large-scale data-driven multi-agent financial network models that can operationalize macroprudential policy. The idea is to provide a quantitative integrative financial framework using multi-agent modeling, which can monitor and analyze systemic risk from activities of financial intermediaries within the context of the regulatory incentives and prevailing market conditions.

Mandate-Based Approach (MBA)

The mandate-based approach (MBA) is one of the (three) methodologies supported by the Basel Committee on Banking Supervision to calculate the capital requirements banks must hold for equity investments in other funds. The approach should be used when the look-through approach cannot be used or when the conditions for use aren't met. Under the MBA banks may use the information contained in a fund's mandate or in the national regulations governing such investment funds.

Mortgage-Backed Securities (MBS)

A mortgage-backed security is a type of asset-backed security, secured by a pool of mortgages. It usually pays periodic payments that are similar to coupon payments and the mortgages typically originate from a regulated and authorized financial institution. It is issued by a federal government agency, government-sponsored enterprise (GSE) or private financial company. Secondary trading of those securities occurs through regulated brokers. There are two common types of MBS: pass-throughs and collateralized mortgage obligations. Both are differently structured and have different maturities, but both can have fixed rates or adjustable mortgage rates. They both have tranches that have their own credit rating, and the rates of return depend on the tranche held by the investor.

Marginal Expected Shortfall (MES)

Marginal expected shortfall (MES) is the prime statistical methodology used to measure systemic risk. It was first coined by V. Acharya et al. (2010). The MES of an institution can be defined as its expected equity loss when the market itself is in its left tail. Or more technically the MES of a financial firm can be defined as its short-run expected equity loss conditional on the market taking a loss greater than its Value at Risk at α %. The expected shortfall of the market (ES) equals the expected loss in the index conditional on this loss being greater than the tail risk in the market.

Micro-finance Institutions (MFI)

Micro-finance is a type of financial services targeting predominantly individuals and small businesses who often lack access to conventional banking. Micro-finance includes the provision of microcredit, the provision of small loans to poor clients, savings and checking accounts, micro-insurance and payment systems. They tend to be regulated either as banks or under a different but similar regulatory model. In terms of its usefulness to society and underserviced customers elsewhere, the views are mixed. Concerns exist with respect to its contribution to higher indebtedness in society, loan pricing and the depth of impact.

Markets in Financial Instruments Directive (MiFID)

The Markets in Financial Instruments Directive (MiFID) 2004/39/EC (implemented November 1, 2007) is a European Union law that provides harmonized regulation for investment services across the 31 member states of the European Economic Area. There are currently two MiFID Directives in place. The latter is accompanied by a regulation (Markets in Financial Instruments (MiFIR)— Regulation (EU) No 600/2014). MiFID 1 governs provisions of investment services in financial instruments by banks and investment firms and operation of traditional stock exchanges and alternative trading venues. MiFID 2 was enacted after flaws were detected after the 2008 financial crisis. The second directive (applicable as of January 3, 2018) reinforces the rules on securities markets by (1) ensuring that organized trading takes place on regulated platforms introducing rules on algorithmic and high-frequency trading; (2) improving the transparency and oversight of financial markets, including derivatives markets; and (3) addressing some shortcomings in commodity derivatives markets, enhancing investor protection and improving conduct of business rules as well as conditions for competition in the trading and clearing of financial instruments.

Microprudential Instruments (MIPI)

Microprudential instruments consist of measures concerned with the stability of individual entities and the protection of clients of the institutions. Although micro- and macroprudential instruments show a certain overlap, the focus of microprudential instruments is different, that is, the main focus of microprudential supervision is to safeguard individual financial institutions from idiosyncratic risks and prevent them from taking too much risk. The macro-view is, however, needed as individual actor stability isn't sufficient to guarantee market stability. The focus of microprudential policy therefore is the stability of individual financial institutions. By contrast, the focus of macroprudential policy is the stability of the financial system as a whole.

Money Market Funds (MMFs)

A money market fund is a type of mutual fund that typically invests only in highly liquid instruments, that is, cash and cash equivalent securities, as well as high credit rating debt-based securities with a short-term maturity (often less than 13 months). Different types of MMFs exist (e.g. those with a constant net asset value and those with a floating net asset value). These funds offer high liquidity with a very low level of risk. The fund typically invests in instruments such as bankers' acceptances, certificates of deposits, commercial paper, repurchase agreements and US treasuries. During the 2008 financial crisis, they were part of the problem as liquidity dried up in this segment of the market quite materially, which was caused by investors withdrawing hoping to benefit from a first-mover advantage. Multiple regulatory interventions occurred in recent years. In Europe, the common denominator for these kinds of funds is UCITS.

Money Market Mutual Funds (MMMFs)

See *Money Market Funds (MMFs)*

Monoline Insurance (Company) (MI(C))

A monoline insurance company is an insurance company that provides coverage for a variety of insurable risks. The term 'monoline' refers to the practice of insurers specializing in a single domain or discipline of the financial services industry. As such, it often refers to company providing its services in only one industry or segment, product or service (e.g. life insurance, credit card issuance and mortgages). Historically, they commenced providing their services for municipal bonds issues, but have broadened their scope of operations ever since. The objective is to enhance the credit of the issuer (maintain or improve credit rating). Although the instrument used can vary, the coverage is often provided in the form of credit swaps. These insurers were and are also active in the shadow banking segment enhancing the credit profile of mortgage-backed securities and collateralized debt obligations. Some of them participated as counterparties in credit default swaps and sold assurance of payment to the buyer of swaps if the credit quality of the securitized product deteriorated.

Macroprudential Instruments (MPIs)

The focus of macroprudential policy is the stability of the financial system as a whole. However, macroprudential instruments (MPIs) go hand in hand with microprudential instruments. The latter is concerned with stability at the level of the individual actor in the financial space. The former, however, focuses on the market as a whole. Macroprudential supervision takes into account the interactions among individual financial institutions, as well as the feedback loops of the financial sector with the real economy, including the costs that systemic risk entails in terms of output losses.

Minimum Requirements for Own Funds and Eligible Liabilities (MREL)

The minimum requirement for own funds and eligible liabilities (MREL) is the European equivalent of the internationally used concept of TLAC (total loss-absorbing capital). The Bank Recovery and Resolution Directive, which has been transposed in all participating Member States' legislation, requires banks to meet a minimum requirement for own funds and eligible liabilities so as to be able to absorb losses and restore their capital position, allowing banks to continuously perform their critical economic functions during and after a crisis. It is a key tool in enhancing the resolvability of banks. In 2017, the European Single Resolution Board (the overarching resolution authority in Europe) developed its MREL-specific policy. That process is still ongoing whereby the Single Resolution Board makes explicit its position and policies for a variety of scenarios.

Modified Supervisory Formula Approach (MSFA)

The Modified Supervisory Formula Approach (MSFA) is the new Basel methodology for calculating capital requirements to be held against securitized products. The methodology replaces the former supervisory formula approach (SFA), which assumes a one-year maturity for the underlying pool of securitized loans ('pool') and is based on the Value-at-Risk approach, with adjustments to reflect the securitized products held. The MSFA, on the contrary is based on an underlying expected shortfall. Expected shortfall refers to the tail risk and the unknown nature of some of these exposures. The regulatory model is assumed to be an unbiased, but nevertheless imprecise. Concentration risk is still neglected in the model. Improvements, however, were made in the methodology regarding how a system of equations is designed for approximating a tranche's capital charge.

Medium-Term Note (MTN)

A medium-term note (MTN) is a debt instrument with a maturity of five to ten years, but may be (considerably) more. They can carry a fixed or floating coupon. MTNs are most commonly issued as senior, unsecured debt of investment-grade credit rated entities, which have fixed rates.

Net Asset Value (NAV)

Net asset value (NAV) is the value of an entity's assets minus the value of its liabilities. It is a term often used in relation to open-ended or mutual funds, in particular since shares of such funds registered with the US Securities and Exchange Commission are redeemed at their net asset value. The term is also applicable to ETFs, in which case the NAV represents the per share/unit price of the fund on a specific date or time. In the context of companies and business entities, the difference between the assets and the liabilities is known as the net assets or the net worth or the capital of the company.

Non-bank Financial Intermediary (NBFI)

Non-bank financial intermediaries (NBFIs) are a large and mixed bag of institutions ranging from leasing, factoring and venture capital companies to various types of contractual savings and institutional investors (pension funds, insurance companies and mutual funds). The common denominator is that none of these institutions hold a banking license and should comply with banking capital requirements. Also supervision is absent and/or differently organized. These are material parts of the shadow banking segment of the market and concerns existed and persist to what degree these institutions engage in activities that involve credit-, maturity-, and liquidity transformation without being sheltered by the capital buffers like banks.

Non-bank Non-insurance (NBNI)

Non-bank non-insurance (NBNI) institutions are those institutions that don't qualify as banks, nor as insurance firms. NBNI financial entities often have very different legal forms, business models and risk profiles. This makes the task of supervisory bodies particularly challenging in that the methodologies have to allow sufficient flexibility to capture different risks (or externalities) posed by entities in each type/sector appropriately while maintaining a certain degree of consistency across the entire NBNI financial space. Also the systemic nature of such entities is difficult to establish. The FSB therefore provided, in their 2015 methodology for NBNIs, not a definition, but a set of criteria that can help in identifying those entities. Those criteria include (1) the size of a single entity, (2) the level of interconnectedness of such an entity, (3) the substitutability of those entities, (4) the business, structural and operational complexity of entities and (5) the global nature or remit of the entities' activities.

Notice of Proposed Rulemaking (NPRM)

A notice of proposed rulemaking (NPRM) is a US public notice issued by law when one of the independent agencies of the US government wishes to add, remove or change a rule or regulation as part of the rulemaking process. It typically starts a process of public comments on the raised matter. NPRM procedure is required and defined by the Administrative Procedure Act, but is not a constitutional requirement.

Net Stable Funding Ratio (NSFR)

The net stable funding ratio (NSFR) is defined as the amount of available stable funding (ASF) relative to the amount of required stable funding (RSF). This ratio should be equal to at least 100% on an ongoing basis. The requirement is a minimum requirement that is applicable to all internationally active banks since January 1, 2018. In terms of the definition, the ASF of a bank refers to the portion of its capital and liabilities that will remain with the institution for more than one year. The broad characteristics of an institution's funding sources and their assumed degree of stability are the basis for determining ASF.

Other Depository Corporation (ODC)

The other depository corporation (ODC) is a subsector of the financial institutions sector. It consists of all financial corporations, excluding the financial bank, whose principal activities consist of intermediation and which have liabilities in the form of deposits or financial instruments such as short-term certificates of deposit, which are close substitutes for deposits in mobilizing financial resources and which are included in the broadly defined concept of 'measures of money'. The institutional coverage of the ODC sector varies per country, but at the broadest level may include commercial banks, credit unions, savings institutions and money market mutual funds.

Other Financial Corporation (OFC)

Other financial corporations consist of non-money market investment funds, other financial intermediaries, financial auxiliaries and captive financial institutions and moneylenders. The term is used by supervisor and policy bodies to indicate a subsector of the shadow banking segment in their jurisdiction as consisting of other financial intermediaries (excluding insurance corporations and pension funds), financial auxiliaries and captive financial institutions and moneylenders.

See also *Other Financial Intermediary (OFI)*.

Other Financial Intermediary (OFI)

See *Other Financial Corporation (OFC)*.

Over the Counter (OTC)

Over the counter (OTC) refers to the process of how securities are traded that are not listed on a formal exchange. It can involve debt instruments, equities, derivatives or any other assets class. The benefits are that parties can agree on pretty much whatever they want. The downside is that parties are directly exposed to counterparty risk without clearing. From a macro-point of view the concern is that there is no comprehensive view of whether systemic risk is building up in the financial system as contracts and their contents are largely unknown to authorities. Given the highly concentrated nature of some parts of the financial sector, clearing of, for example, OTC derivatives has been mandated in recent years.

Originate-to-Distribute (OTD)

'Originate-to-distribute' refers to the business model whereby lenders intend to securitize part of their (or their entire) loan book. It implies that the loans are not kept on the balance sheet of the lender but sold off at some point before maturity of the loans. The income for the lenders in this model originates predominantly from the fees and gains realized when selling off the loan bundles, both paid for by the buyers of the loan bundles (securitization certificates). It has been documented that lenders tend to be less strict in applying their lending standards when they intend to sell off the loans as the risk ultimately doesn't sit on their balance sheet until maturity. Particular discretion is required as some securitized product contracts refer default risk back to the securitizer (in this case the initial lender). The originate-to-distribute business model is part of the shadow banking segment although it involves traditional banks.

Organized Trading Facility (OTF)

An organized trading facility (OTF) is any facility or system designed to bring together buying and selling interests or orders related to financial instruments. OTFs were introduced by the European Commission as part of MiFID II and are focused on non-equities such as derivatives and cash bond markets. The original MiFID covered only multilateral trading facilities. OTFs are intended to be similar in scope to a swap execution facility (SEF), a type of entity created by the Dodd-Frank Act in the US. The goal of SEFs and OTFs is to bring transparency and structure to OTC derivatives trading.

Originate-to-Hold (OTH)

'Originate-to-hold' refers to a business model where the lenders intend to hold the loans they (intend to) sell and keep them on their balance sheet until they mature. The income in this model predominantly comes from the borrowers who pay interest and at maturity the principal amount. Front-loaded and back-end expenses are also incurred by the borrowers. In this model the intrinsic credit quality and quality of the borrowers matter. The risk ultimately sits with the lender throughout the entire lending period and default risk eats directly into the equity position of the lender.

Probability of Default (PD)

Probability of default (PD) describes the methodology to assess the likelihood of a default over a particular time horizon of a debtor/debt obligation. It provides an estimate of the likelihood that a borrower will be unable to meet its debt obligations. PD is used in a variety of credit analyses and risk management frameworks, including Basel II. The 'expected loss' on an instrument is the product of PD, the loss given default and the exposure at default.

Private Equity (PE)

Private equity is an alternative investment class and consists of investment vehicles that raise and/or invest equity in private (non-listed) companies. Some strategies, however, use material volumes of senior, junior and/or mezzanine debt to acquire the company. Investments can be in non-listed young or start-ups (venture), more mature companies (LBO), firms facing a restructuring and across a variety of industries and assets (infrastructure, real estate, etc.). Independent financial investors are often organized as a partnership, whereas listed private equity firms are often corporate. Within larger conglomerates and multinationals private equity activities tend to take place in corporate structures as well.

Principles for Financial Market Infrastructure (PFMI)

Issued by the CPMI and the International Organization of Securities Commissions (IOSCO), the principles for financial market infrastructure are part of a set of 12 key standards that the international community considers essential to strengthening and preserving financial stability. They are based on the 2012 report issued by IOSCO called 'Principles for Financial Market Infrastructures' and which establishes new international standards for payment systems that are systemically important, central securities depositories, securities settlement systems, central counterparties and trade repositories. There is a second 2012 report by IOSCO that deals with the disclosure framework preferred to support the objectives and principles.

Packaged Retail Investment and Insurance-Based Products (PRIIPs)

Packaged retail investment and insurance-based products (PRIIPs) are a broad category of financial instruments that are provided to consumers in the European Union, often through banks or other financial institutions and developed as an alternative to savings accounts. It intends to cover all packaged, publicly marketed financial products that have exposure to underlying assets (stocks, bonds, etc.), provide a return over time and have an element of risk. The group covers all packaged retail investment products marketed in the European Union, including insurance policies. Relevant PRIIP regulation is in place since January 1, 2018.

Qualifying Central Counterparties (QCCPs)

A qualifying central counterparty (QCCP) is an entity that is licensed to operate as a CCP and is permitted by the appropriate regulator to operate as such with respect to the products offered. Their role is to essentially clear transactions between market participants and thereby reduce counterparty risk. The implication is that contracts cleared are (more) standardized than often is the case in private non-cleared markets.

Revised Ratings-Based Approach (RRBA)

Under Basel II a bank must determine the risk-weighted asset amount for a securitization exposure that is eligible for the ratings-based approach (RBA) by multiplying the amount of the exposure by the appropriate risk weight. Under Basel III, that rule was 'revised'. Under the new rules (2013), a securitization exposure is eligible for the RBA depending on whether the bank holding the securitization exposure is an originating bank or an investing bank. An originating bank is eligible to use the RBA for a securitization exposure if (1) the exposure has two or more external ratings or (2) the exposure has two or more inferred ratings.

Research and Development (R&D)

Research and development refers to all sorts of activities built around the objective of improvement and/or innovation. Activities can be undertaken by corporations or governments in developing new services or products, or improving existing services or products. It can be directed toward application (i.e. improvements to existing products or services, or the development of new products or services) or it can be fundamental in nature (i.e. develop new insights and knowledge that can at a later stage be used in an applied setting). Fundamental research remains largely the activity of public bodies, as most firms don't have the risk appetite to conduct such research or don't prioritize it over applied research.

Real Estate Investment Trust (REIT)

A real estate investment trust (REIT) is a company that owns and/or operates real estate. It generates income through rental, buy/sell activities and auxiliary services. An REIT can focus on a certain type of real estate or can hold a mix of real estate classes. Greenfields and/or developments are often excluded. REITs can be public or privately held. They can specialize in terms of the asset classes to access real estate (e.g. equity or mortgages). In some countries (like the US) they are obliged to pass on at least 90% of their annualized net income to investors in the form of dividends.

Repurchase Agreement (Repo)

A repurchase agreement (repo) is a short-term loan where both parties agree to the sale and future repurchase of assets (or pool of assets) that act as collateral within a specified (usually short) contract period. The seller sells, for example, a Treasury bill or other government security with a promise to buy it back at a specific date (often after the closing date of the current accounting period) and at a price that includes an interest payment. The sector got a bad name during the 2008 crisis, as Lehman Brothers used the technique to deleverage its balance sheet prior to closing the accounting quarter or year, leaving investors with a skewed view regarding the actual leverage on the company's balance sheet. In order for the technique to work accounting rules and contract rules should go hand in hand, which was the case with Lehman Brothers International. Nevertheless, they fulfill a genuine financing need for large financial institutions, banks and some businesses as they provide temporary lending opportunities to fund ongoing operations. They come in a variety of models, that is, reverse repos (buying securities with the intention of returning—reselling—those same assets back in the future at a profit), or tri-party repo (an agent in the middle intermediates the deal between the two parties to the repo to facilitate services like collateral selection, payment and settlement, custody and management during the life of the transaction). Also the Fed uses the repo instrument to facilitate liquidity in the markets.

Residential Mortgage-Backed Securities (RMBS)

Belongs to the securitized product group. They are debt instruments backed by a pool of residential mortgages. The pool acts as a collateral and ensures payment of interest and repayment of the principal. Pooling can occur based on different real estate criteria, or based on the credit quality of the mortgages (prime or subprime). The benefits include diversification and a slightly higher rate for any given level of risk included in the pool. Risk profiling can be a challenge, however, especially in mixed pools of mortgages. The ultimate investor carries the investment and credit/default risk, although contractual stipulations might deviate.

Return on Capital (ROC)

Return on capital employed is an accounting ratio. It measures the profitability of projects or companies and provides for a percentage outcome which makes comparisons possible across firms, sectors and projects with many different characteristics. The difference with the return on equity (ROE), is the fact that in this ratio all funding sources are included (including debt instruments). The ratio should be set apart from return on investment (ROI) and return on invested capital (ROIC). The ROIC focuses on the actual invested capital and compares it with the operating profits generated. The ROI measures the return assessing all income (thus also non-operating income).

Return on Capital Employed (ROCE)

An accounting ratio that measures the return generated by a firm or project (net operating profits or EBIT) by investing the actual capital invested. Most often capital employed refers to the total assets of a company less all current liabilities. Return on capital employed (ROCE) includes all capital available in the firm or project; ROIC considers only the capital actively used in the business. ROCE is a pre-tax measure, whereas ROIC is an after-tax measure.

Return on Equity (ROE)

An accounting ratio that measures the net income (thus in principle after tax, unless stated otherwise) generated by investing the equity portion available to the project or firm, often averaged out over the maturity of the project or averaged across the accounting cycle of the firm, to ensure correspondence with the net income measurement used in the ratio.

Recovery and Resolution Planning (RRP)

Recovery and resolution planning (RRP)[4] is a joint task of national authorities and the supervised institutions and deals with scenarios whereby a bank or banks cannot continue operations due to either intrinsic reasons or market instability (or both). These resolution protocols tend to end in a bailout or bail-in. The national authorities are responsible for 'ensuring that resolution frameworks are put in place and that banks are subject to periodic resolvability assessments as part of resolution planning exercises'. Recovery plans are required to be 'prepared by the governing boards of banks to help their recovery from financial distress, with a minimum disruption of critical services'. These plans typically include 'scenario analysis' to cover different firm and market conditions. Resolution authorities are further required to 'prepare resolution plans for each bank reflecting concrete strategies for resolving them while safeguarding financial stability'. Supervisory and resolution authorities are also required to undertake 'annual resolvability assessments for banks, and to require changes in the legal and operational structures of a firm if that is necessary to ensure continuity of critical functions in resolution. RRPs must reflect cross-border issues, including ex ante agreement on operational resolution strategies to be used for resolving such firms.' In case there are banks in a specific jurisdiction that operate cross-border operations, a crisis management group should be established with members of each of the relevant jurisdictions to prepare for and facilitate resolution of cross-border banks as well as to enter into institution-specific cooperation agreements for each bank that is active cross-border. The agreements negotiated facilitate execution of any agreed resolution strategy. In such a case typically two strategies are used: (1) the single point of entry (SPE) whereby the home resolution authority resolves the holding company in their country; shareholders and designated creditors of the holding absorb losses of the entire group and capital freed up is passed down to subsidiaries; and (2) multiple points of entry (MPE). In this case the relevant authorities resolve their own part of the group structure under separate proceedings, but which was formalized in an ex ante agreement between all authorities involved.

Reverse Repo Program (RRP)

See *Repurchase Agreement (Repo).* Often a matter of perspective, as it resembles the opposite view of a 'normal' repo. In this transaction, banks purchase government securities from the central bank and lend money to the banking regulator.

---

[4] See G. Dell'Ariccia et al., (2018), Trade-offs in banks Resolution, IMF Staff Discussion Note SDN/18/02, February, p. 31.

Regulatory Technical Standards (RTS)

Regulatory Technical Standards are standards published regularly by the EBA or other European supervisory bodies. The standards clarify legislative positions or substantiate items that were intentionally left blank by the regulator to be documented by the EBA. By definition, a regulatory technical standard 'is a delegated act, technical, prepared by a European Supervisory Authority'. Accordingly, an implementing technical standard is a technical implementing act providing for the uniform application of certain provisions in the basic legislative act.

Risk-Weighted Assets (RWA)

Risk-weighted assets are a bank's assets or off-balance-sheet exposures, weighted according to risk. The Basel guidelines provide guidance on classification and categorization. This sort of asset calculation is used in determining the capital requirement or capital adequacy ratio for a financial institution. The underlying principle: the riskier the assets, the most capital should be held against those assets.

Shadow Banking (SB)

In the most general terms the shadow banking sphere contains all entities and activities that engage in financial activities, including those that involve credit-, maturity- and liquidity transformation but are unregulated or regulated differently from banks who engage in those activities but are regulated and hold capital against the risk profile of the assets held on their balance sheet. The real nature of the activities and entities involved changes materially per country as the design and make-up of the sector are the consequences of the outlook of the traditional banking sector in that respective jurisdiction.

Small Business Administration (SBA)

The Small Business Administration (SBA) is a US government agency that provides support to entrepreneurs and small businesses. The SBA also provides loans, although the actual lending takes place through normal banks, credit unions and other lenders partnering with the agency. The SBA provides a government-backed guarantee on part of the loan.

Statutory Bail-in (SBI)

The statutory bail-in (SBI) is a resolution tool that enables the recapitalization of a failed financial firm through cancelation, conversion, transfer or write-down of claims of equity holders and unsecured and uninsured creditors, to the extent necessary to absorb losses on its balance sheet. Bail-in-able claims must be clearly specified in legislation or contracts. They can exclude certain claims of being bailed-in or leave that authority to the resolution authority to judge on a case-by-case basis. Typically a bail-in framework must respect the order of priorities of claims established in a given jurisdiction for bank liquidation. That typically implies that equity must bear losses first, followed by subordinated debt, with deposits being the last to absorb losses in jurisdictions that provide for depositor preference. In case certain claims are excluded from bail-in that order changes and will deviate from the standard liquidation schedule.[5]

Shadow Banking System (SBS)

This refers to the segment of the financial markets where transactions take place and entities engage in activities not covered by traditional banking supervision and not buffered by capital regulations and adequate balance sheets.

Single Counterparty Credit Limit (SCCL)

The credit limits of the single counterparty credit limit (SCCL) rule apply to aggregate net credit exposure, which means the sum of all net credit exposures of a covered company and all of its subsidiaries to a single counterparty, including all of its affiliates. On June 14, 2018, the Federal Reserve Board passed a final rule to establish single counterparty credit limits for covered large US bank holding companies, foreign banking organizations and intermediate holding companies.

Securities and Exchange Commission (SEC)

An agency within the US federal government. The Securities and Exchange Commission holds primary responsibility for enforcing the federal securities laws, proposing securities rules and regulating the securities industry, the nation's stock and options exchanges and other activities and organizations, including the electronic securities markets in the US.

Securitization Internal Ratings-Based Approach (SEC-IRBA)

See *IRBA*.

[5] See G. Dell'Ariccia et al., (2018), Trade-offs in banks Resolution, IMF Staff Discussion Note SDN/18/02, February, p. 30.

Securitization External Ratings-Based Approach (SEC-ERBA)

See *ERBA*.

Securitization Standardized Approach (SEC-SA)

The securitization standardized approach (SEC-SA) is the Standardized Approach for measuring credit risk/capital requirement when analyzing securitized products. The SEC-SA is used when the SEC-IRBA cannot be used. It will define the capital requirements based on the pool capital requirement calculated under the Standardized Approach for credit risk (known as 'K_{SA}'). The capital surcharge for the SEC-SA is typically higher than the capital surcharge under the SEC-IRBA methodology.

Systemic Expected Shortfall (SES)

A bank's contribution, denoted as systemic expected shortfall (SES), is its propensity to be undercapitalized when the system as a whole is undercapitalized, which increases its leverage, volatility, correlation and tail-dependence. SES, the systemic risk component, is equal to the expected amount a bank is undercapitalized in a future systemic event in which the overall financial system is undercapitalized.

Supervisory Formula Approach (SFA)

A bank using the SFA determines the risk-weighted asset amount for a securitization exposure by multiplying the SFA risk-based capital requirement for the exposure as provided. The seven criteria relevant for such measurement are as follows: (1) the amount of the underlying exposures; (2) the securitization exposure's proportion of the tranche that contains the securitization exposure; (3) the sum of the risk-based capital requirement and Expected Credit Loss (ECL) for the underlying exposures; (4) the tranche's credit enhancement level; (5) the tranche's thickness (the volume of a tranche within the total pool of assets distributed); (6) the securitization's effective number of underlying exposures; and (7) the securitization's exposure-weighted average loss given default. A bank may only use the SFA to determine its risk-based capital requirement for a securitization exposure if the bank can calculate each of these seven inputs on an ongoing basis. The bank may not use the SFA in case it cannot compute the risk-based capital requirement for all underlying exposures (K_{IRB}).

Securities Financing Transactions (SFTs)

Securities financing transactions (SFTs) are broadly defined as any transaction where securities are used as a collateral to borrow cash or vice versa. Practically, this mostly includes repurchase agreements (repos), securities lending activities and sell/buy-back transactions.

Structured Finance Vehicles (SFVs)

A structured finance vehicle (SFV) or investment vehicle (SIV) is a pool of investment assets that tries to profit from the difference in credit spreads between short-term debt (lower) and long-term structured finance products (higher). These entities can be involved in a variety of activities but often borrow for the short term by issuing commercial paper in order to invest in long-term assets with credit ratings of BBB or higher (e.g. mortgage-backed securities, asset-backed securities and the less risky tranches of collateralized debt obligations). They are often also referred to as structured investment vehicles or special-purpose funds (SPFs) as well as special-purpose entities (SPEs). Funding for SIVs comes from the issuance of commercial paper that is continuously renewed or rolled over. The credit differential is banked as profit.

Systemically Important Financial Institution (SIFI)

A systemically important financial institution (SIFI) or systemically important bank (SIB) is a bank, insurance company or other financial institution whose failure might trigger a financial crisis because of its size, interconnectedness and/or assets held. The FSB has laid out criteria which institutions qualify as SIFIs, based on certain categories (banks, non-banks, insurance companies, non-insurance companies, non-bank non-insurance companies), and for each category the domestic or global relevance. Each year the FSB issues a list with all the SIFIs per category.

Structured Investment Vehicle (SIV)

See *Structured Finance Vehicle (SIV)*.

Small- and Medium-Sized Entity (SME)

Small- and medium-sized entities (SMEs) are privately held organizations whose asset levels, staff numbers, turnover or other criteria don't meet certain thresholds. Standardized criteria exist (International Chamber of Commerce), but thresholds differ per country.

State-Owned Enterprises (SOEs)

A state-owned enterprise (SOE) is a legal entity that is created by a government in order to engage in commercial activities on the government's behalf. It can be either wholly or partially owned (or even a minority stake with a golden share) by a government and is typically earmarked to participate in specific commercial activities. Although each country and government has SOEs, the concept often refers to a wide body of entities that engage in a wide set of economic activities in countries where the government holds tight control over (large parts of) the economy. Poster child example is China, where small and large SOEs engage economy-wide in transactions and even dominate segments of the economy. They are often also used to acquire foreign strategic activities or firms.

Special-Purpose Entity (SPE)

An SPE is an entity created by another entity (e.g. parent company of a group) to engage in certain predefined activities, but whose assets, risks and leverage it doesn't want to see emerge on its own balance sheet. In that sense, the SPE is 'bankruptcy remote' as it cannot impact the balance sheet of the creating parent company. Its operations are limited to the acquisition and financing of specific assets as a method of isolating risk. SPEs are often also used to load-on leverage without further burdening the balance sheet of the parent company. The Enron bankruptcy reminds us of the possible consequences.

Special-Purpose Vehicle (SPV)

See *Special-Purpose Entity (SPE).*

Single Resolution Board (SRB)

The Single Resolution Board (SRB) is the European Banking Union's resolution authority. It is a key element of the Banking Union and its Single Resolution Mechanism. The SRB is the central resolution authority within the Banking Union. Together with the National Resolution Authorities (NRAs) of participating Member States (MS), it forms the Single Resolution Mechanism. Its mission is to ensure an orderly resolution of failing banks with minimum impact on the real economy, the financial system and the public finances of the participating MS and beyond.

Social Structure of Accumulation (SSA)

The Social Structure of Accumulation (SSA) approach provides a new way to analyze the structure and development of capitalist economies and societies. The term SSA refers to the complex of institutions which support the process of capital accumulation.

Simplified Supervisory Formula Approach (SSFA)

Simplified Supervisory Formula Approach (SSFA) is a Basel III formulated approach for measuring risk embedded in (a pool of) assets. The SSFA is based on the prior supervisory formula approach (SFA/Basel II). SSFA is a formula-based approach which takes into account the risk weighting of the underlying assets, the exposure's subordination level, the performance of the underlying assets and whether or not the exposure is a re-securitization in order to define capital adequacy.

Short-Term Note (STN)

Short-term notes are financial debt instruments that typically have original maturities of less than nine months. Short-term paper is typically issued at a discount and provides a low-risk investment alternative. They can be either unsecured or backed by assets such as loans issued by a corporation. Examples of short-term paper include US T-bills, commercial paper, promissory notes, bills of exchange and certificates of deposit.

Simple, Transparent and Standardized (Securitization) (STS)

Securitization products in the EU issued after December 2018 need to meet the simple, transparent and standardized (STS) criteria in order for the securitizer-originator to benefit from reduced capital requirement for the pool of assets securitized. The EU's securitization regulation leaves the definition of the STS criteria largely open. The EBA was mandated to document and substantiate the criteria. It took until December 2018 before final guidelines were released. By creating simple, transparent and standardized products the EU, under the umbrella of the Capital Markets Union project, tries to revive the securitization market in Europe, which, in contrast to the US securitization market, has largely been in the doghouse since the 2008 financial crisis.

Term Asset-Backed Loan Facility (TALF)

The Term Asset-Backed Loan Facility (TALF) was a funding facility that helped market participants meet the credit needs of households and small businesses by supporting the issuance of asset-backed securities collateralized by loans of various types to consumers and businesses of all sizes. The program was administered by the Federal Reserve Board and financed with both public and private funding. The TALF began operation in March 2009 and was closed for new loan extensions on June 30, 2010.

To Be Announced (Market Facility) (TBA)

The TBA market allows for the sale of securities before they have been finalized—as in before the mortgages that back the securities have been identified. 'To be announced' (TBA) is a term describing forward-settling mortgage-backed securities trades. The term TBA is derived from the fact that the actual mortgage-backed security that will be delivered to fulfill a TBA trade is not designated at the time the trade is made. The securities are announced 48 hours prior to the established trade settlement date.

Tender Option Bond (TOB)

Tender option bonds are special-purpose trust investments that create leverage by borrowing from money market funds to invest in high-quality municipal bonds. A tender option bond therefore is the common phrase for a security issued by a special-purpose trust (a tender option bond trust) into which bonds are deposited, and which then issues two types of securities. One of the securities—the floating rate security—is typically sold to a money market fund that is only permitted to buy investments of high quality and short maturity. The other security—the inverse floating rate security—is retained by the fund/trust. The product is often used by MMFs to generate higher yields (difference between yields on long-term bonds and the borrowing rate paid on short-term floating securities).

Tri-Party Repo (TPR)

See *Repurchasing Agreement (Repo)*.

Tri-party repos are typical repo instruments with the difference that a tri-party agent acts as an intermediary between the two parties to the repo to facilitate services like collateral selection, payment and settlement, custody and management during the life of the transaction. It is considered a market of systemic importance, and policy design issues to neutralize possible exposures remain until today despite numerous but more elusive regulatory interventions ever since the 2008 crisis. During the 2008 financial crisis three weaknesses were exposed in the tri-party repo market: (1) markets' reliance on intraday credit from the clearing banks; (2) the procyclical risk management practices or procyclicality of risk management practices and (3) the lack of effective plans to support the orderly liquidation of the defaulted dealer's collateral. Interventions since then include: moving the daily unwind of some tri-party repo transactions, which shortens the period of intraday exposure, and the implementation of a mandatory three-way trade confirmation between dealers, cash investors and the clearing banks. Less progress has been made on issues like creating an alliance with this market on intra-day credits or improving risk management and collateral practices to avoid fire sales in the event of a large dealer fault.

Total Return Swap (TRS)

Total return swap (TRS) is a financial contract that transfers both the credit risk and market risk of an underlying asset. They are typically classified as credit derivatives. Total return swaps allow the party receiving the total return to gain exposure and benefit from a reference asset without actually having to own it. The instrument is attractive for financial sponsors who want to get exposure to certain risks without having to own the asset and suffer the associated cash outlay.

Trust Preferred Securities (TruPS)

Trust preferred securities (TruPS) are securities issued by (often) large banks and bank holding companies. The bank opens a trust account which is funded with debt. The bank then sells shares in the trust to investors. The resulting share is called a trust preferred security, or TruPS. It has as a security the characteristics of both debt and equity. The security is a hybrid security with characteristics of both subordinated debt and preferred stock (paying dividend) in that it is generally very long term (30 years or more), allows early redemption by the issuer, makes periodic fixed or variable interest payments, and matures at face value. In addition, trust preferred securities issued by bank holding companies will usually allow the deferral of interest payments for up to five years.

Undertakings for Collective Investments in Transferable Securities (UCITS)

UCITS are investment funds regulated by the European Union. The UCITS regulation was put in place to provide transparency and liquidity to investors but also to ensure that products could be sold in other EU member countries (EU-wide distribution) regardless of where the sponsor or issuer was located. The EU therefore standardized the rules and regulations across Europe regarding open-ended funds and transferable securities. The UCITS regulation is in place since 2003 and has been amended on a number of occasions. The UCITS group is the main European framework and product group covering collective investment schemes. This category of investment funds accounts for around 75% of all collective investments by small investors in Europe. All funds that do not meet the UCITS criteria fall within the scope of other European fund legislation (real estate, money market funds, venture funds, long-term investment funds or alternative investment fund regulation). UCITS is the European retail investment fund brand.

Value at Risk (VaR)

Value at Risk (VaR) is a measure of the risk of loss embedded in an investment. It estimates how much an investment (or pool of investments) might lose (with a given probability) in value, given normal market conditions, in a set time period, often a day (24 hours). One measures VaR by assessing the amount of potential loss, the probability of occurrence of the amount of loss and the time frame. Despite the hiccups in its performance over time, it is still a central metric in the investment fund industry.

Variable Net Asset Value (VNAV)

A concept of the money management fund industry. Next to fixed or constant net asset value funds, the market offers variable net asset funds. VNAV, or variable net asset value, refers to funds which use mark-to-market accounting to value some of their assets. The NAV of these funds will therefore vary by a slight amount, due to the changing value of the assets and, in the case of an accumulating fund, by the amount of income received. This results in a degree of variability in the investment values calculated and reported, as the market values of the underlying investments change. This method of accounting is contrasted by using an amortized cost basis of accounting for all of the investments, which is what constant net asset value (CNAV) funds do.

Variable Rate Demand Obligation/Note (VRDO/VRDN)

A variable rate demand note (VRDN) is a debt instrument (offered to investors through money market funds) that embodies borrowed funds and which accrue interest based on a prevailing money market rate (prime rate). The interest rate applicable to the borrowed funds is set upfront (mostly the specified money market rate plus margin). The notes allow a municipal government to borrow money for long periods of time while paying short-term interest rates to investors. Typically, the interest rate on VRDN is adjusted periodically, that is, daily, weekly or monthly to reflect the current interest rate environment. The instrument is payable on demand, that is, the investor or lender of the funds can request repayment of the entire debt amount at his or her discretion. It has the dynamics of an embedded put option. VRDN issuers often use credit enhancement techniques through letters of credit (LOCs) from highly rated financial institutions.

Weighted Average Maturity (WAM)

Weighted average maturity (WAM) is the weighted average amount of time on mortgages in a mortgage-backed security until they mature. The term is used more broadly to describe average maturity in a portfolio of debt securities, including corporate debt and municipal bonds.

Weighted Average Life (WAL)

The weighted average life (WAL) of an amortizing loan or amortizing bond, also called average life, is the weighted average of the times of the principal repayments: it's the average time until a dollar of principal is repaid.

Wealth Management Product (WMP)

A wealth management product is an uninsured financial product sold in China by banks and other financial institutions. Typically they offer a high rate of interest (i.e. higher than savings accounts), and, sometimes, guaranteed return. Given their uninsured nature, they tend to pose a financial stability risk. Therefore the PBOC (Central Bank China) and the China Banking and Insurance Regulatory Commission (CBIRC) for a couple of years now have been trying, through a variety of measures, to curtail the volume and the growth of the product group and more importantly to de-risk the product group. Given the fact that the investment options for Chinese residents are limited, capital supply is abundant and cash pools continue to look for enhanced yields. Wealth management products and funds are, for example, allowed to directly invest in stocks since October 2018.

Index[1]

[1] Note: Page numbers followed by 'n' refer to notes.

L. Nijs, *The Handbook of Global Shadow Banking, Volume I*,
https://doi.org/10.1007/978-3-030-34743-7

Bankruptcy costs, 535, 549

E

Q

R

S

T

The manufacturer's authorised representative in the EU is Springer Nature Customer Service Centre GmbH, Europaplatz 3, 69115 Heidelberg, Germany. If you have any concerns regarding our products, please contact ProductSafety@springernature.com

Printed and bound by CPI Group (UK) Ltd, Croydon, CR0 4YY
30/09/2026
02225649-0020